A NEW DICTIONARY OF
CHRISTIAN THEOLOGY

A NEW DICTIONARY OF CHRISTIAN THEOLOGY

EDITED BY
ALAN RICHARDSON
AND
JOHN BOWDEN

SCM PRESS

0 334 02208 8

First published 1983
by SCM Press Ltd
9–17 St Albans Place, London N1 0NX

Fifth impression (paperback) 1989
Ninth impression 1996

Printed and bound in Great Britain by
Mackays of Chatham PLC, Chatham, Kent

PREFACE

The first edition of *A Dictionary of Christian Theology* was published, after a long period of gestation, in 1969. Since then it proved its usefulness by being reprinted regularly, and has become a familiar reference book to a wide international audience. However, a decade and more is a long time, even in theology, and with the very different climate of the 1980s it seemed time for a thorough revision of its contents. *A New Dictionary of Christian Theology* has therefore been reworked from beginning to end, and while its relationship and indebtedness to its predecessor will be obvious, it is in fact a completely new – and rather different – work, which marks one further step forward in what at best can be the most fascinating of all disciplines.

All readers owe a great debt of gratitude to the Editor of the original *Dictionary*, Alan Richardson. Without his unsparing effort it would never have seen the light of day, and he made an enormous personal contribution to its contents. While there always were, and always will be, those with very different views from his own, no one can question his great gift of seeing the important questions of the time and attempting to answer them in terms which were never those of introverted theological jargon. The *Dictionary* was very much his child: he gathered together a relatively small group of faithful contributors to bring it to birth, and when others who had been asked for articles on particular subjects failed him, as many did, he sat down and produced the relevant entry himself.

The words with which he introduced the work still bear repeating:

Theology is a subject of immensely wide range. It is bound up with the long history of ideas, especially those of Western civilization, upon which it has exercised a powerful influence. In this new age of rapid world-wide communication these ideas are disseminated to every part of the globe, and they have not remained unaffected in the process. The roots of Christian theology lie deep in the civilizations of the ancient world, particularly those of Israel and Greece. Since the days of the early church the Christian proclamation has engaged in dialogue with non-Christian ways of thinking, and Christian theologians have constantly been driven to define their standpoint either in terms of or in opposition to the philosophical presuppositions of their environment. Especially is this true since the days of the Enlightenment (*c.* 1650–1780), when new forms of secular and non-religious thinking about man and the universe were developed. Today it is patently true that theology is being done in dialogue with or sometimes in reaction from the various modes of philosophical and scientific thinking which prevail in our time. It is with the theological issues of today that this Dictionary is primarily concerned.

A Dictionary of Christian Theology, though, was inevitably a product of its time, and looking back we can now see how some of its concerns were retrospective and obsolescent: the aftermath of a biblical theological movement whose weakness had already become evident; the last stages of the domination of a German theology represented by Barth, Bultmann and others which has since proved to have less and less to offer; and a preoccupation with the notion of a 'secular Christianity' all too parasitic on a brief period of unparalleled prosperity and irresponsibility in the Western world. If these characteristics dated it, so too did the lack of coverage in areas where more recent readers would expect entries. Far-sighted though he was, Alan Richardson could not transcend his time and its concerns. As the passage from his introduction shows, he understood 'non-Christian ways of thinking' in terms of post-Enlightenment philosophies rather than other religious traditions; pluralism in a multi-cultural society was barely touched on; political theology had yet to become a significant theme; doctrinal criticism, the application to Christian doctrine of the kind of historical criticism which had long been directed towards the Bible, was virtually unknown; and there were some strange blind spots: there was not even a cross-reference, for example, to 'Incarnation'! Minimal attention was paid to the psychology and sociology of religion, and although an attempt was made to produce as ecumenical a work as possible, Roman Catholic and Orthodox contributions were almost completely absent. Lastly, and sadly not least, there were places were articles tended to turn into sermons, thus giving the entries a rather odd parochial air.

Alan Richardson would certainly have disapproved of a good deal of what has gone into *A New Dictionary of Christian Theology*, but were he still alive I hope that he would recognize the spirit behind the revision. It is a tribute to his judgment that few of the original entries have been abandoned altogether, and that many of the new ones are simply the result of circumstances he could not have foreseen. Positively, the main difference in the new work is the greatly extended coverage of virtually all the subject matter in the light of the growth in our knowledge and concerns; above all the focus is on theological thinking against a historical back-ground rather than on historical events or figures. For the revision, this has had one negative consequence: biographical entries have been dropped altogether (though the *Dictionary* has an index of names of important theological figures). Whom to include and whom to omit is always a problem, and to be generous all round while adding the new theological treatment called for would have made the new volume impossibly large and expensive; as it is, it is almost half as long again as its predecessor. Readers are therefore referred in this respect either to other reference works or to a companion volume, *Who's Who in Theology*, currently in preparation, which provides concentrated information about individuals who have contributed to the development of theology and the main works by and about them.

For the production of what now in fact amounts to virtually a new work (even those articles from the original which have been retained have been worked over and updated), we have drawn on a very much wider range of contributors, not only from England and the United States, but from Europe and the British Common-wealth. Given the many different perspectives of those whose articles have been brought together here, it is remarkable that taken as a whole the *New Dictionary* presents, in its own way, quite a coherent picture. At a time when interest is reviving strongly in the theological content of religious belief and the polarization between over-traditional and over-radical views, so characteristic of the 1960s, has given way to a concern for new patterns of Christian belief which do not abandon the wealth of past tradition but express it in a way which takes more account of the modern world, readers will find here a guide book, a map which they can use for their explorations, a collection of wise judgments by which they can test new proposals.

And then a personal note. I worked closely with Alan Richardson on the original *Dictionary*, and as a labour of love and token of admiration very much wanted to be closely associated with the new version. As I write these words I can still hear Alan's voice in my ears and recall his characteristic comments. However, I have neither the ability or knowledge, nor the time, to tackle the task as he once did, so I have relied heavily on the help and advice of others. Nicholas Lash and Dennis Nineham gave invaluable support in the preparation of the new list of entries and contributors, and James Heaney of Westminster, along with his advisers (not least Stanley Harakas in the Orthodox field) ensured that a proper transatlantic balance was maintained. John Macquarrie and Frances Young took on the laborious task of revising and checking articles from the original *Dictionary* when the authors were no longer in a position to undertake the work themselves. Rosamund Bacon kept track of the complicated business of sending out invitations, dealing with replies and welcoming the contributions with her customary efficiency and inimitable style. And above all, the contributors made the whole task a quite unexpectedly pleasant one. Composite volumes are never easy and require much boring and pedestrian work, but at every turn I was cheered by the kindness, courtesy and good wishes of people who agreed to write, produced what they had been asked for, and wished the *New Dictionary* well. As they see it in its finished form, I hope they will not be too unhappy with the result.

The time spent working on this revision has brought with it two further delights: this would seem a particularly appropriate place to thank King's College, London, and the University of Edinburgh, for including me among the theologians.

JOHN BOWDEN

CONTRIBUTORS

Larry J. Alderink, *Associate Professor of Religion, Concordia College.*
Cosmogony; Cosmology

H. T. Allen, Jr, *Assistant Professor of Worship, Boston University School of Theology.*
Liturgical Calendar

A. H. Armstrong, *Emeritus Professor of Greek, University of Liverpool.*
Emanation; The One

Richard Stoll Armstrong, *Professor of Evangelism, Princeton Theological Seminary.*
Evangelism

James Atkinson, *Emeritus Professor of Biblical Studies, University of Sheffield.*
Benefits; Blood of Christ; Deus pro nobis; Exemplarism; Passion; Precious Blood; Recapitulation; Reparation

Paul Badham, *Senior Lecturer in Theology, Saint David's University College, Lampeter.* **Death; Soul**

Michael Barnes, SJ, *Lecturer in Religious Studies, Heythrop College, University of London.* **Cultural Relativism**

James Barr, *Professor of Hebrew Bible, Vanderbilt Divinity School.*
Allegory and Typology; Semantics

Simon Barrington-Ward, *Bishop of Coventry.* **Theology of Mission; Proselytism**

Harold J. Berman, *Professor of Law, University of Harvard.* **Law and Theology**

J. E. Biechler, *Professor of Religion, La Salle College.* **Coincidentia oppositorum**

Roberta C. Bondi, *Associate Professor of Church History, Candler School of Theology, Emory University.* **Apophatic Theology; Immutability**

Jack S. Boozer, *Professor of Religion, Emory University.* **The Holy**

John Bowden, *Editor and Managing Director, SCM Press.*
Biblical Criticism; Death of God Theology; Jesus; Kerygmatic Theology; Literary Criticism; Narrative Theology; Word of God

James Bradley, *St Edmund's House, Cambridge.* **Hegelianism; Idealism**

Marcus Braybrooke, *Vicar of Christ Church, Bath.* **Christianity and Other Religions; Universalism**

Raymond E. Brown, *Auburn Distinguished Professor of Biblical Studies, Union Theological Seminary.* **Virginal Conception of Jesus**

T. P. Burke, *Department of Religion, Temple University, Philadelphia.*
Ontologism; Ontology

John E. Burkhart, *Professor of Theology, McCormick Theological Seminary.*
Deacon

David B. Burrell, CSC, *Professor of Philosophy and Theology, University of Notre Dame.* **Analogy; Divine Attributes; Scholasticism; Transcendentals**

James T. Burtchaell, CSC, *Professor of Theology, University of Notre Dame.*
Inspiration

Robert P. Carroll, *Professor, Department of Biblical Studies, University of Glasgow.* **Cognitive Dissonance**

James F. Childress, *Commonwealth Professor of Religious Studies and Professor of Medical Education, University of Virginia.* **Agape**

Stephen R. L. Clark, *Lecturer in Moral Philosophy, University of Glasgow.* **Nature and Theology**

J. P. Clayton, *Lecturer in Religious Studies, University of Lancaster.* **Projection Theory**

Keith W. Clements, *Co-ordinating Secretary for International Affairs, Council of Churches for Britain and Ireland.* **Baptist Theology; Faith; Sola fide; Sola gratia; Sola scriptura**

R. E. Clements, *Samuel Davidson Professor of Old Testament, King's College, London.* **Covenant; Henotheism; Monotheism; Old Testament Theology**

John B. Cobb, Jr, *Ingraham Professor, School of Theology at Claremont.* **Concrescence; Creationism; Panentheism**

Raymond F. Collins, *Professor of New Testament Studies, Katholieke Universiteit, Leuven.* **Exegesis; Fundamentalism; Structuralism**

James H. Cone, *Charles A. Briggs Professor of Systematic Theology, Union Theological Seminary.* **Black Theology**

Richard F. Costigan, SJ, *Associate Professor of Theology, Loyola University of Chicago.* **Bishop; Episcopacy**

William J. Courtenay, *Professor of History, University of Wisconsin.* **Consubstantiality; Consubstantiation; Neoscholasticism; Nominalism; Occasionalism; Voluntarism**

J. D. Crichton, *formerly Editor of* Liturgy/Life and Worship. **Sacramentals**

Adrian Cunningham, *Senior Lecturer, Department of Religious Studies, University of Lancaster.* **Jungian Psychology; Psychology of Religion**

Gabriel Daly, OSA, *Lecturer in Systematic and Historical Theology, Milltown Institute, Dublin.* **Modernism; Traditionalism**

Brian Davies, OP, *monk of Blackfriars, Oxford.* **Impassibility; Infinity; Ubiquity**

J. G. Davies, *late Professor of Theology, University of Birmingham.* **Character; Deaconess; Elder; Insufflation; Religious Orders; Schism; Validity**

Rupert Davies, *formerly Principal of Wesley College, Bristol.* **Adoption; Assurance; Calling; Election; Methodist Theology; Vocation**

Charles Davis, *Professor of Religion, Concordia University.* **Critical Theory**

F. W. Dillistone, *Fellow Emeritus of Oriel College, University of Oxford.* **Atonement; Redemption; Religious Experience**

John W. Dixon, Jr, *Professor of Religion and Art, University of North Carolina at Chapel Hill.* **Aesthetics and Theology**

Peter Donovan, *Senior Lecturer in Religious Studies, Massey University, New Zealand.* **Religious Language**

Eamon Duffy, *Lecturer in Divinity and Fellow of Magdalene College, University of Cambridge.* **Depravity; Pietism**

A. O. Dyson, *Samuel Ferguson Professor of Social and Pastoral Theology, University of Manchester.* **Anthropology; Autonomy; Dependence**

James P. Etzwiler, *Lecturer in Philosophy, St Joseph College, West Hertford, USA.*
  Act; Averroism; Method of Distinction; Habit
C. F. Evans, *Emeritus Professor of New Testament, King's College, London.*
  Kerygma; Resurrection
G. R. Evans, *Lecturer in History and Fellow of Sidney Sussex College, University of
  Cambridge.* **Ontological Argument; Senses of Scripture; Sensus Plenior; Summa;
  Supernatural**
Gabriel Fackre, *Abbot Professor of Christian Theology, Andover Newton Theo-
  logical School.* **Antinomianism; Blasphemy; Evangelical, Evangelicals; Imputation;
  Merit**
Robert Faricy, SJ, *Professor of Spiritual Theology, Gregorian University, Rome.*
  Charismatic; Spiritual Gifts; Witness of the Spirit
M. Jamie Ferreira, *Assistant Professor, Department of Religious Studies, University
  of Virginia.* **Certainty; Doubt**
J. C. Fenton, *formerly Canon of Christ Church, Oxford.* **Salvation**
Peter E. Fink, SJ, *Associate Professor of Liturgical Theology, Weston School of
  Theology.* **Consecration; Ordination; Priesthood**
Raymond Firth, *Emeritus Professor of Anthropology, University of London.*
  Animism
J. Massyngberde Ford, *Associate Professor of New Testament, University of Notre
  Dame.* **Celibacy; Chastity; Virginity**
Duncan B. Forrester, *Professor of Christian Ethics and Practical Theology, University
  of Edinburgh.* **Orthodoxy; Orthopraxis; Practical Theology; Praxis; Work**
W. H. C. Frend, *Emeritus Professor of Ecclesiastical History, University of
  Glasgow.* **Augustinianism; Martyrs, Martyrdom, Martyrologies**
Sean V. Freyne, *Professor of Theology, Trinity College, Dublin.* **Apostle, Apostolicity**
Brian A. Gerrish, *Professor of Historical Theology, University of Chicago.*
  Justification; Theological Curriculum; Theological Encyclopaedia
Mark Gibbs, *late Director of the Audenshaw Foundation.* **Laity**
Jerry H. Gill, *Professor of Philosophy, Barrington College, Barrington, Rhode Island.*
  **Analytic Philosophy; Modes of Cognition; Philosophy of Religion; Rationalism;
  Reason**
Robin M. Gill, *William Leech Research Professor, University of Newcastle-Upon-
  Tyne.* **Sociology of Religion**
Kenneth Grayston, *Emeritus Professor of Theology, University of Bristol.*
  Apocryphal Gospels; Benediction, Blessing; Finality; Gospel
Garrett Green, *Professor of Religious Studies, Connecticut College, New London,
  Connecticut.* **Loci theologici**
Robert C. Gregg, *Associate Professor, The Divinity School, Duke University.* **Arianism**
Lucas Grollenberg, OP, *Monk of Albertinum, Nijmegen.* **Basic Communities**
Shirley C. Guthrie, Jr, *Professor of Systematic Theology, Columbia Theological
  Seminary, Georgia.* **Doctrine**
John S. Habgood, *Archbishop of York.*
  Creation; Evolution; God of the Gaps; Model; Paradigm; Science and Religion
Robert T. Handy, *Henry Sloane Coffin Professor of Church History, Union Theo-
  logical Seminary.* **Empirical Theology; Mercersburg Theology; New England
  Theology; Pragmatism; Revivalism**

A. T. Hanson, *late Professor of Theology, University of Hull.* **Communion of Saints; Descent into Hell; Eschatology; Parousia; Pre-existence; The Risen Christ; Schism**

R. P. C. Hanson, *late Professor of Historical and Contemporary Theology, University of Manchester.* **Apostasy; Authority; Canon; Disciplina arcani; Iconoclasm; Papacy; Patrology; Reserve; Tradition; Una santa**

Stephen Happel, *Associate Professor of Systematic Theology, St Meinrad School of Theology, Indiana.* **Romanticism**

Stanley S. Harakas, *Professor of Orthodox Christian Ethics, Holy Cross Greek Orthodox School of Theology, Brookline.* **Arche; Eastern Orthodox Theology; Meon; Monoenergism; Mystical Theology; Transfiguration**

Richard Harries, *Bishop of Oxford.* **Contemplation**

James J. Heaney, *Publisher, The Pilgrim Press.* **Divine Ideas; Middle Platonism; Monism**

Brian L. Hebblethwaite, *Dean of Chapel, Queen's College, Cambridge.* **Anthropomorphism; Apologetics; Epistemology; Incarnation; Mediator; Omnipotence**

R. W. Hepburn, *Professor of Moral Philosophy, University of Edinburgh.* **Absolute; Contingency; Induction; Logic**

John H. Hick, *formerly Danforth Professor, Department of Religion, Claremont Graduate School.* **Arguments for the Existence of God; Life after Death; Reincarnation; Theocentricity**

Walter Hollenweger, *formerly Professor of Mission, University of Birmingham.* **Glossolalia**

William Hordern, *President, Lutheran Theological Seminary, Saskatoon, Canada.* **Donum superadditum; Guilt; Mortal Sin; Natural Law; Original Righteousness; Similitudo dei**

Rodney J. Hunter, *Associate Professor of Pastoral Theology, Candler School of Theology, Emory University.* **Pastoral Theology**

J. L. Houlden, *Professor in the Faculty of Theology, King's College, London.* **Biblical Theology; Ecumenism; Mercy**

Grace M. Jantzen, *Lecturer in the History and Philosophy of Religion, King's College, London.* **Time and Timelessness**

R. C. D. Jasper, *formerly Dean of York.* **Liturgical Movement**

Daniel T. Jenkins, *Minister of Regent Square United Reformed Church, London.* **Congregational Theology; Culture**

Walter Kasper, *Bishop of Rottenburg, West Germany.* **Roman Catholic Theology**

Aidan Kavanagh, OSB, *Professor of Liturgics, The Divinity School, Yale University.* **Anamnesis; Anaphora; Christian Initiation; Epiclesis**

Alistair Kee, *Professor in Religious Studies, University of Edinburgh.* **Liberation Theology; Marxist Theology; Political Theology; Utopianism**

David H. Kelsey, *Professor of Theology, Yale Divinity School.* **Doctrine of Scripture; Theological Method**

E. W. Kemp, *Bishop of Chichester.* **Canon Law**

John Kent, *Emeritus Professor of Theology, University of Bristol.* **Freethinking; History; Oxford Movement; Positivism; Reductionism; Scepticism; Subjectivism; Unitarianism**

Edward J. Kilmartin, *Professor of Liturgical Theology, University of Notre Dame.*
Ministry
David Konstant, *Bishop of Leeds.* **Catechesis**
Kosuke Koyama, *Professor of Ecumenics and World Christianity, Union Theo-
logical Seminary.* **Indigenous Theology**
Alban J. Krailsheimer, *Student of Christ Church, Oxford.* **Jansenism**
Michael J. Langford, *Professor of Philosophy, The Memorial University of New-
foundland.* **Determinism; Foreknowledge; Free Will; Predestination; Providence**
Nicholas Lash, *Norris-Hulse Professor of Divinity, University of Cambridge.*
Doctrinal Development; Ideology; Marxism; Materialism
Symeon Lash, *Lecturer in Biblical and Patristic Studies, University of Newcastle
upon Tyne.* **Conciliarity; Deification; Economy; Icon; Theology of Relics**
Daniel E. Lee, *Associate Professor of Religion, Augustana College, Rock Island,
Illinois.* **Categorical Imperative**
John H. Leith, *Pemberton Professor of Theology, Union Theological Seminary in
Virginia.* **Creeds**
Barnabas Lindars, SSF, *late Rylands Professor of Biblical Criticism and Exegesis,
University of Manchester.* **Miracle**
David Little, *Professor of Religious Studies, University of Virginia.*
Freedom; Religious Liberty
Timothy Lull, *Professor of Systematic Theology, Lutheran Theological Seminary,
Philadelphia.* **Anonymous Christianity; Indulgences; Symbolics**
Richard P. McBrien, *Crowley-O'Brien-Walter Professor of Theology and Chairman
of the Department of Theology, University of Notre Dame.* **Church**
Herbert McCabe, OP, *monk of Blackfriars, Oxford.* **Thomism**
Enda McDonagh, *Professor of Moral Theology, Pontifical University of Maynooth,
Ireland.* **Forgiveness; Love**
Sallie McFague, *Professor of Theology, Divinity School, Vanderbilt University.*
Metaphor; Parable
John McIntyre, *Emeritus Professor of Divinity, University of Edinburgh.*
Imagination; Transcendence
Henry McKeating, *Principal, Wesley College, Bristol.*
Aetiology; Apocrypha; Circumcision; Form Criticism; Idolatry
James Mackey, *Thomas Chalmers Professor of Theology, University of Edinburgh.*
Binitarianism; Essential Trinity; Trinity; Vestigia trinitatis
J. T. McNeill, *formerly Professor of Church History, Union Theological Seminary.*
**Calvinism; Council of Trent; Counter-Reformation; Lutheranism; Protestantism;
Puritanism; Reformation; Socinianism**
John Macquarrie, *Emeritus Professor of Divinity and Canon of Christ Church.
University of Oxford.* **Being, Becoming; Demythologizing; Deus absconditus; En-
hypostasia; Epiphany; Hagiography; Humanism; Identity; Immanentism; Limit
Situation; Natural Theology; Protestant Principle; Secular Christianity**
Daniel C. Maguire, *Professor of Moral Theology, Marquette University, Wisconsin.*
Moral Theology; Religious Values
Joseph Martos, *Lecturer in Theology, Xavier University, Cincinnati.*
Anointing; Eucharistic Theology; Holy Orders; Penance; Sacrament; Unction
Anthony Meredith, SJ, *Campion Hall, Oxford.* **Aristotelianism**

Hugo A. Meynell, *Professor, Department of Religious Studies, University of Calgary.*
Functional Specialization; Metaphysics; Universals
Margaret R. Miles, *Associate Professor of Historical Theology, Harvard University.*
Body; Body Theology; Matter
Donald E. Miller, *Associate Professor of Religion, University of Southern California.*
Liberalism
Jürgen Moltmann, *Professor of Systematic Theology, University of Tübingen.*
Hope; Perseverance; Theodicy; Theology of Cross
Lewis S. Mudge, *Dean and Professor of Theology, McCormick Theological Seminary,*
Chicago. **Hermeneutical Circle; Hermeneutics; Heuristics**
Robert Murray, SJ, *formerly Lecturer in Theology, Heythrop College, University of*
London. **Promise and Fulfilment; Prophecy**
George M. Newlands, *Professor of Divinity, University of Glasgow.* **Christology;**
Doctrinal Criticism; Hypostatic Union; Kenosis; Monophysitism; Monothelitism;
Nestorianism; Soteriology
Dennis Nineham, *Emeritus Professor of Theology, University of Bristol.*
Continuity; Historical Criticism
R. A. Norris, *Professor of Church History, Union Theological Seminary.*
Anhypostasia; Aseity; Homoousios; Person
Gerald O'Collins, SJ, *Professor of Fundamental Theology, Gregorian University,*
Rome. **Anathema; Articles of Faith; Assent; Decretals; Deposit of Faith; Dogma;**
Dogmatic Theology; Fundamental Theology; Magisterium; Prolepsis; Venial Sin
Edward O'Connor CSC, *Associate Professor of Systematic Theology, University of*
Notre Dame. **Pentecostalism**
Schubert M. Ogden, *Professor of Theology and Director of the Graduate Program*
in Religious Studies, Southern Methodist University, Dallas. **Myth; Pluralism**
J. C. O'Neill, *Dunn Professor of New Testament Language, Literature, & Theology,*
Westminster College, Cambridge. **Absolution; Arminianism; Concupiscence; Dis-**
pensationalism; Federal Theology; Final Perseverance; Heilsgeschichte; Invincible
Ignorance; Presbyterian Theology; Regeneration; Satisfaction; Simul justus et pec-
cator; Sin; Temptation; Works; Wrath of God
Helen Oppenheimer, *member of the Inter-Anglican Doctrinal and Theological Com-*
mission. **The Good; Good Works; Theology of Marriage; Virtue**
David A. Pailin, *Senior Lecturer in Philosophy of Religion, University of Manchester.*
Antinomy; Deism; Enlightenment; Process Theology; Religious a priori; Revelation
Norman W. Porteous, *formerly Professor of Old Testament, University of Edin-*
burgh. **Old Testament Theology**
Gerald Priestland, *late Journalist.* **Inner Light; Society of Friends**
Michael Pye, *Professor of Religious Studies in the University of Marburg.*
Syncretism
Lewis R. Rambo, *Associate Professor of Religion and the Personality Sciences, San*
Francisco Theological Seminary and the Graduate Theological Union, Berkeley,
California. **Conscience; Conversion; Cult; Repentance; Ritual**
A. Michael Ramsey, *late Archbishop of Canterbury.* **Catholicism**
Alan Richardson, *late Dean of York.* **A priori; Adiaphora; Beatific Vision;**
Bibliolatry; Chiliasm; Chrism; Christendom; Christening; Christian; Confession,
Confessionalism; Death of God Theology; Demiurge; Dispensation; Dys-

teleology; Enhypostasia; Epicureanism; Epiphany; Eudaimonism; Euhemerism; Fideism; Hagiography; Hermetic Literature; Heterodox; Kairos; Koinonia; Limbo; Manichaeism; Marcionism; Millenarianism; Mithraism; Montanism; Natural Theology; Naturalism; Non-being; Palingenesis; Paraclete; Pneumatology; Problem of Evil; Theology of Prayer; Protestant Principle; Satan; Self-Understanding; Stoicism; Synergism; Worship

James Richmond, *Professor of Religious Studies, University of Lancaster.*
Angst; Crisis Theology; Dialectical Theology; Existentialism; Liberal Protestantism; Neo-Orthodoxy; Nihilism; Personalism; Religionsgeschichtliche Schule

N. G. H. Robinson, *formerly Professor of Divinity, University of St Andrews.*
Accident; God; Theocracy; Theonomy

Philip J. Rosato, SJ, *Gregorian University, Rome.* Holy Spirit

Leroy S. Rouner, *Professor of Philosophical Theology, Boston University.* Dualism

Christopher Rowland, *Dean Ireland's Professor of Holy Scripture, University of Oxford.* Angel; Apocalypse; Apocalyptic; Messiah

Rosemary Radford Ruether, *Georgia Harkness Professor of Theology, Garrett-Evangelical Theological Seminary and Northwestern University.*
Assumption of Blessed Virgin Mary; Corredemptrix; Feminist Theology; Immaculate Conception; Mariology; Mediatrix

E. Gordon Rupp, *late Dixie Professor of Ecclesiastical History, University of Cambridge.* Perfection

Jeffrey Burton Russell, *Professor of History, University of California.*
Demonology, Demons; Devil

Don Saliers, *Professor of Theology and Worship, Candler School of Theology, Emory University.* Liturgical Theology

Eric J. Sharpe, *Professor of Religious Studies, University of Sydney.*
Kingdom of God; Social Gospel

D. W. D. Shaw, *Professor of Divinity, University of St Andrews.*
Accident; God; Pantheism; Theonomy

Aylward Shorter, WF, *missionary priest of the Society of Missionaries of Africa.*
Polytheism

Ninian Smart, *J. F. Rowny Professor of Comparative Religions, University of California at Santa Barbara.* Perennial Philosophy; Phenomenology; Religion

Dorothee Sölle, *Visiting Professor of Systematic Theology, Union Theological Seminary.* Representative

Placid Spearritt, OSB, *monk of Ampleforth.* Neoplatonism

John Stacey, *formerly Editor, Epworth Press.* Homiletics; Preaching

Christopher Stead, *formerly Professor of Divinity, University of Cambridge, and Emeritus Canon of Ely.* Essence; Logos; Platonism; Substance; Theandric Acts

Stewart R. Sutherland, *Vice-Chancellor, University of London.*
Absurd; Agnosticism; Atheism; Damnation; Fanaticism

Richard Swinburne, *Nolloth Professor of the Philosophy of the Christian Religion, University of Oxford.* Causality; Theism

Stephen Sykes, *Bishop of Ely.* Absolute Dependence; Heresy; Systematic Theology; Theology; Thirty-Nine Articles

J. Heywood Thomas, *Professor of Christian Theology, University of Nottingham.* **Correlation; Heteronomy; Ultimate Concern**

John Tinsley, *formerly Bishop of Bristol.* **Ascetical Theology; Asceticism; Casuistry; Discipline; Imitation of Christ; Mystery; Mystery Religions; Mysticism; Numinous; Rigorism; Via negativa; Via positiva; Vision of God**

Thomas F. Tracy, *Assistant Professor of Religion, Department of Philosophy and Religion, Bates College.* **Action Theory**

Denys Turner, *Lecturer in the Philosophy of Religion, University of Bristol.* **Alienation; Dialectic; Objectification**

H. E. W. Turner, *formerly Professor of Divinity, University of Durham.* **Appropriation; Coinherence; Communicatio essentiae; Communicatio idiomatum; Communicatio operationum; Double Procession; Filioque; Homoeans; Homoeousians; Ingeneracy; Modalism; Modes of Being; Monarchianism; Novatianism; Opera ad extra; Patripassianism; Procession; Prosopon; Sabellianism; Social Analogy; Spiration**

Bruce Vawter, *Professor, Department of Religious Studies, De Paul University, Chicago.* **The Fall; Original Sin**

Alec R. Vidler, *late Honorary Fellow of King's College, Cambridge.* **Anglo-Catholicism**

Victor de Waal, *former Dean of Canterbury.* **Apostolic Succession; Hierarchy**

Geoffrey Wainwright, *Professor of Systematic Theology, The Divinity School, Duke University, Durham, North Carolina.* **Adoration; Pentecost; Proclamation; Rapture; Sanctification**

Gordon S. Wakefield, *formerly Principal of the Queen's College, Birmingham.* **Cambridge Platonists; Ecstasy; Spirituality**

Benedicta Ward, SLG, *Member of the Community of the Sisters of the Love of God, Fairacres, Oxford.* **Cult of the Saints; Monastic Theology**

Herold Weiss, *Professor, Saint Mary's College, Notre Dame.* **Christ Event; Restoration of All Things**

John Whale, *Editor,* Church Times. **Papacy**

E. C. Whitaker, *Emeritus Canon of Carlisle.* **Confirmation**

Rowan S. Williams, *Lady Margaret Professor of Divinity, University of Oxford.* **Ascension of Christ; Christocentrism; Freudian Psychology; Religious Imagery; Interiority**

B. R. Wilson, *Fellow of All Souls' College, University of Oxford.* **Sect; Secularism; Secularization**

R. McL. Wilson, *Professor of Biblical Criticism, St Mary's College, University of St Andrews.* **Gnosticism**

E. J. Yarnold, SJ, *Tutor in Theology, Campion Hall, Oxford.* **Concomitance; Efficacy; Ex opere operato; Grace; Immolation; Infallibility; Pelagianism; Psychological Analogy; Sacramental Theology; Semi-pelagian; Transsubstantiation**

Frances M. Young, *Edward Cadbury Professor of Theology, University of Birmingham.* **Adoptionism; Alexandrian Theology; Antiochene Theology; Cappodocian Fathers; Communicatio essentiae; Docetism; Donatists; Double Procession; Generation; Hypostasis; Nature; Patristics; Prosopon; Sacrifice; Subordinationism; Suffering**

J. A. Ziesler, *formerly Lecturer in Theology, University of Bristol.* **NT Theology; Righteousness**

ABBREVIATIONS

AV	Authorized Version of the Bible
CBQ	*Catholic Biblical Quarterly*
CD	Karl Barth, *Church Dogmatics*
DTC	*Dictionnaire de Théologie Catholique*
EB	*Encyclopaedia Britannica*
ET	English Translation
ETR	*Etudes Théologiques et Religieuses*
HTR	*Harvard Theological Review*
IDB	*Interpreter's Dictionary of the Bible*
JEH	*Journal of Ecclesiastical History*
JQR	*Jewish Quarterly Review*
JRT	*Journal of Religious Thought*
JSOT	*Journal for the Study of the Old Testament*
KJV	King James Version of the Bible
LCC	Library of Christian Classics
LCL	Loeb Classical Library
NT	New Testament
NTS	*New Testament Studies*
OED	The Oxford English Dictionary
OT	Old Testament
RC	Roman Catholic
RGG	*Die Religion in Geschichte und Gegenwart*
SEDOS	Servizio di Documentazione e Studi
SJT	*Scottish Journal of Theology*
ST	Thomas Aquinas, *Summa Theologiae*
TDNT	G. Kittel(ed), *Theological Dictionary of the New Testament*
TRE	*Theologische Real-Encyclopaedie*
TS	Theologische Studien
VuF	*Verkündigung und Forschung*
WA	Weimarer Ausgabe (standard edition of Luther's works)
WCC	World Council of Churches

* An asterisk denotes a reference to another article in the *Dictionary*.

The Index of Names of important theologians and philosophers referred to often in the text will be found on pp. 609f.

A Priori, A Posteriori

A priori (Latin, meaning 'something prior' or 'going before') is used in philosophy of that which precedes or is independent of sense-experience, as opposed to *a posteriori*, that which follows upon or is known from sense-experience.

See **Religious** *A Priori.*

ALAN RICHARDSON

Absolute

As an adjective, 'absolute' in philosophy has meant 'unconditioned', 'independent', 'free from contingency*', 'necessary'. As a substantive, 'the Absolute' has played important, if obscure, roles in speculative metaphysics, particularly in post-Kantian idealism*. To Hegel the Absolute is not a transcendent deity, existing independently of the world, but it is reality considered as a whole and as aware of itself. It is in individual finite minds that reality reaches self-awareness, in art, religion, and most notably in the systematic activity of the philosopher as he seeks to understand the cosmic process as a whole. Nature, from this viewpoint, becomes the necessary objective condition for the appearance and life of spirit, and thus for the goal of self-awareness. Aristotle had spoken of God as self-aware, self-contemplating: but Aristotle's God, unlike Hegel's Absolute, had a centre of consciousness distinct from the consciousness of finite minds such as our own. Hegel was not content to define the Absolute as 'infinite substance' (compare Spinoza); it is also Subject and Spirit.

Idealists have differed considerably in their conceptions of the Absolute. To Bradley, for instance, the Absolute was the totality of things, in which is reconciled or harmonized whatever in the world of appearance is contradictory and incoherent. In itself, the Absolute is inaccessible to our understanding, though we may have hints and clues in our experience. (Contrast Hegel, to whom the 'contradictory' phases in the world's processes are *retained* in the life of the Absolute, as phases necessary to its development.)

The Absolute is a prime example of a concept that can be elucidated only within the context of a metaphysical system as a whole: the existence or non-existence of an Absolute cannot be verified or falsified like that of a material object by observation or experiment, and the accusations of logical positivism that *therefore* the Absolute is a meaningless notion were unjustified. Real logical difficulties do, however, arise in theories that speak of the Absolute as Mind – but not this or that particular mind, or as containing or including particular finite minds, or seeing how an Absolute could be both perfect in some sense and yet contain the minds of very imperfect beings within it. At the root of many doctrines of the Absolute are *epistemological* arguments, claiming that all reality is in a sense mental or mind-dependent. But although to conceive an entity as existent is necessarily to conceive it as it would be apprehended by a subject, it is a hazardous inference to conclude that therefore to exist is to be the object of a knowing mind. Lastly, the onus falls heavily on the proponent of a theory of the Absolute to justify his claim that the world is more rational and less fragmentary than it appears to ordinary experience – indeed, that it is rational and complete in the highest degree.

For an example of a writer making central use of the idea of the Absolute, in recent years, see the writings of J. N. Findlay listed below.

F. C. Copleston, *A History of Philosophy*, VII, 1963; A. C. Ewing, *Idealism: A Critical Survey*, 1934; J. N. Findlay, *Ascent to the Absolute*, 1970; *The Transcendence of the Cave*, 1967.

R. W. HEPBURN

Absolute Dependence

The 'consciousness of being absolutely dependent' is a phrase employed by the

German Protestant theologian, Friedrich Schleiermacher (1768–1834). By it he meant the sense which human beings have of being in a relationship to God. Schleiermacher, who had reacted sharply against the excessive rationalism of the preceding (Leibniz-Wolffian) school of theology, placed the strongest emphasis on 'sense' or 'feeling' as providing the key to the interpretation of religion. By 'feeling' he meant, not a state of transient emotion, but the fundamental consciousness a person has of their own existence, the irreducible core of personal selfhood.

This interior sense of the self is always combined with an awareness of its interactions with society and the world, in the usual activities of thinking and doing. But of the three (feeling, knowing and doing), Schleiermacher wished to insist that it was the first by which the essence of all religion was to be interpreted. Knowing and doing also belong to the religious state, that is, feeling *must* express itself as both knowledge and action; but they do not constitute its inner essence.

Schleiermacher's philosophical psychology identified two elements in the self's consciousness of itself, a capacity for origination (a feeling of freedom) and a sense of being determined by outside factors (a feeling of dependence). These two 'feelings' (again, they are not to be thought of as emotions), are present in each experience in variable quantity. But while there is no such thing as a feeling of absolute freedom, there exists, as an accompaniment of the feelings of relative freedom and dependence, a sense of absolute dependence, 'the consciousness that the whole of our spontaneous activity comes from a source outside of us'. God, according to Schleiermacher, is the whence of this feeling. Thus to know oneself to be absolutely dependent and to be conscious of God is one and the same thing. This is the original revelation of God to humanity, the basic element which differentiates human beings from animals.

Schleiermacher believed that all human beings had this sense of God, but he did not regard it as possible to provide an argument for God's existence or for the immortality of the soul * based upon it. He interpreted the Christian faith as the transmission of the impression of Jesus' unimpeded consciousness of God, in and through the Christian church, in such a way as to bring about a liberation or redemption of the clouded human God-consciousness. His major and revolutionary interpretation of theology, *The Christian Faith* (1821, ET 1928), rests upon this fundamental understanding of religion and has proved to be of lasting interest. Two major objections have been made to it. The first, which is based on a misunderstanding, is that the 'feeling' to which Schleiermacher referred is a merely subjective emotion. The second concerns the alleged tendency to place human consciousness, rather than divine revelation, at the centre of the theological system. But Karl Barth, who repeatedly expressed this criticism in the course of his life, came in the end to regard it as an open question whether Schleiermacher's method actually entailed this shift of emphasis.

R. R. Niebuhr, *Schleiermacher on Christ and Religion*, 1965; M. Redeker, *Schleiermacher: Life and Thought*, 1973; S. W. Sykes, *Friedrich Schleiermacher*, 1971.

S. W. SYKES

Absolution

The NT statements about the power of binding and loosing show the existence of some officers in the church who had judicial authority either to pardon sins or to declare that sins were not yet absolved (Matt. 16.19; 18.18, 19, 20; John 20.23; II Cor. 2.10). Similar authority was exercised by the priests and other leaders among the Essenes (Josephus, *Jewish War* 2.143–5; 1QS vi.24–vii.25; viii.16–ix.2, 7; 1QSb iv.26), and by the scribes (Matt. 23.13; Luke 11.52).

Absolution was originally a public declaration that the sins of a specific penitent sinner were absolved. This practice never died out, but two developments became more important: the private confession and absolution of individual sinners, who were required to confess mortal * sins and advised to confess venial * sins, and obliged to go to confession once a year; and the general absolution pronounced on all penitent sinners before the eucharist. The precatory form, 'May Jesus Christ absolve you from your sins', was generally used up to the twelfth century in the West. Aquinas ruled that the absolute form, 'I absolve you from your sins in the name of the Father and of the Son and of the Holy Spirit', was necessary in private absolution. The precatory form was the form which survived in the East and was used in all parts of the church in the context of the eucharist.

J. C. O'NEILL

Absurd, The

This expression is used by a variety of thinkers and writers in an equal variety of senses and meanings. Its most influential uses this century have been in the writings of two French philosophers and novelists, Albert Camus and Jean-Paul Sartre. Yet even there, one finds significant differences.

In the case of Sartre, the notion of the absurd plays an important part in the exposition of his philosophy in *Being and Nothingness*. Thus man's existence is absurd, because no explanation of or justification for it can be given. There is no meaning or significance laid down in the order of things to which human beings can appeal as justification for what they do, or in which they might find what is significant in life. Only in the *angst** and despair which recognizes that life is absurd lies the possibility of the freedom which can affirm value and meaning in life. Human projects which point towards unattainable goals will fracture in encounter with the absurd.

Camus makes rather a different use of the term; the idea of absurdity is a constant theme throughout his works, but is stated in a particularly powerful fashion in his philosophical discussion of reasons for rejecting the path of suicide, *The Myth of Sisyphus*, and the novel which is a counterpoint to it, *The Outsider*. In *The Myth*, he asks the question, 'Who is *l'homme absurde*?' and answers: 'the man for whom the eternal doesn't matter.' Referring to Ivan Karamazov as an example, he notes that *l'homme absurde* makes no attempt to appeal to moral rules or beliefs to justify what he does, 'for there is nothing to justify'. In *The Outsider*, Meursault is the picture of the embodiment or incarnation of such views.

It is perhaps no accident that both of these writers were influenced by Kierkegaard, for whom religious belief was to be grasped at the limits of the attempts of the intellect to grasp the nature of God, and man's relation to him. Kierkegaard more than any other theologian came close to re-affirming Tertullian's provocative *'Credo quia absurdum'*. The reaction of both Sartre and Camus to Christian belief are secular responses to a shared conception of the limits of the intellect in the ascription of meaning and significance to human life and the world in which it occurs. They are deeply serious responses in that, as with Kierkegaard, they eschew the trivializing of this notion by those who mistake walking on thin intellectual ice for courageous faith.

Albert Camus, *The Myth of Sisyphus*, ET 1955; Jean Paul Sartre, *Being and Nothingness*, ET 1966.

STEWART SUTHERLAND

Accident(s)

For Aristotle, whose thought was so influential in the formation of the classical Christian doctrine of God (*see* **Aristotelianism**), an accident is a characteristic which may belong to a substance (or particular type of enduring subject) but which need not do so. Thus a man may be fair-haired but need not be, but he must be male. Here, fair-hairedness is an accident, maleness is not. In the Christian conception of God, there are thus said to be no accidents in the divine nature, there being nothing in God which is not God himself. The distinction between substance and accidents has been extensively used in Roman Catholic teaching concerning the Mass, in particular in the doctrine of transubstantiation*. Here it is not the accidents, perceptible to the eye, of the elements of bread and wine which are transformed by God's power into the substance of the body and blood of Jesus Christ: rather it is the substance or inner reality, imperceptible to the senses, which is so transformed.

N. H. G. ROBINSON / D. W. D. SHAW

Act, Actuality

Act or actuality in mediaeval theory derives ultimately from Aristotle's concept of *energeia*, a word he coined to denote the completely realized dimension of a reality. He opposed it to *dynamis* (potency, capability), which points to that aspect of a reality by which it is capable of changing, of reaching the fullness of being it can become. Thus the seed has in it the potency to become the mature plant. When it achieves that state, its capacity has been actualized, 'energized' one might say. Aristotle seems to have wanted a word that would characterize a being not as something static and inert, but as vibrant and active. Of course, no physical reality is ever fully act; it always retains a capacity to change in some way. Only the unmoved mover is pure act; it alone has no potentiality to any further modification in any way. When Aristotle's works became known to theologians in Europe in the thirteenth century, his notion of act became a standard fixture of mediaeval thought. In the theology of Thomas Aquinas it plays a particularly important role. He uses it to explain that, at root, beings are 'composed' of an essence which is actualized by the act of existing (*esse*). In God, of course, the essence *is* the act of existing so that God is pure act. But whereas for Aristotle the unmoved mover is pure act as substance with no accidental modifications, for Aquinas God is pure act as pure existence, as Subsistent Being. In the Neo-Scholastic revival in modern times act receives special attention in the philosophies of Jacques Maritain and Joseph Maréchal.

Jacques Maritain, *Existence and the Existent*, ET 1948; Joseph Owens, *The Doctrine of Being in the Aristotelian Metaphysics*, 1957.

JAMES P. ETZWILER

Action Theory

A branch of philosophy of mind that seeks to understand the nature and possibility of purposive behaviour. Philosophers of action are centrally concerned with concepts like motive, intention, will, choice, freedom and responsibility. The fundamental task of action theory is to give an account of the difference between action (what an agent does) and happening (what an agent undergoes), and to explain what it means to say that an action was performed on purpose, or intentionally. One traditional proposal is that an intentional action is distinguished from an unintentional bodily motion by having an act of will as its cause. The notion of inner mental acts of will (or 'volitions') has been subjected to sustained criticism in contemporary philosophy (e.g. Gilbert Ryle, *The Concept of Mind*, 1949). A number of philosophers have argued that intentional actions are distinguished by the kind of ex-

planation we give of them, viz., in terms of reasons rather than causes (e.g. G. E. M. Anscombe, *Intention*, 1957). Others have responded that the distinction between reasons and causes cannot be sustained, and that actions are best understood as caused by distinctive mental events of desiring or wanting (e.g. Alvin Goldman, *A Theory of Human Action*, 1970). Since this leads to a thorough causal determinism, anti-determinists have maintained that intentional actions are not caused by particular mental events but rather by the agent as an integrated centre of choice (e.g. Richard Taylor, *Action and Purpose*, 1966).

These philosophical discussions bear directly upon a number of central topics in Christian theology. Christian self-expression is deeply indebted to images of man and God interacting as agents whose identities are formed (on the human side) and revealed (on the divine side) in their actions towards each other. Long-standing puzzles arise here about the relation of human and divine action both in the lives of individuals (e.g. questions about human freedom and divine grace) and in the providential unfolding of God's purposes for human history. In addition, Christian theology must wrestle with questions about how to conceive of God as an agent and how to explicate the notion of an act of God. The language available to theology in speaking of God as one who acts is the language we use in speaking of one another as agents. A theologian's understanding of human agency, whether explicitly formulated or not, will provide the central analogies which structure his account of God's active relation to our world. This correlation of action theory and doctrine of God is particularly clear in recent efforts to explain what it means to say that God acts in history (e.g. Schubert Ogden, *The Reality of God*, 1963; Gordon Kaufman, *God the Problem*, 1972). Theological discussions of divine action need to be alert to the philosophical credibility of their claims about human agency, and they need to be sensitive to the questions of intelligibility which arise when ordinary patterns of speech about human action are dramatically modified for theological purposes.

K. Barth, *Church Dogmatics*, II/1, ch. VI, 1957; C. A. Campbell, *On Selfhood and Godhood*, 1957; A. Farrer, *Faith and Spe-*

culation, 1967; L. Gilkey, *Reaping the Whirlwind*, 1976.

THOMAS F. TRACY

Activism see Quietism

Actus purus see Act, Actuality

Adiaphora

A Greek word meaning 'things indifferent'; it refers to matters not regarded as essential to faith which might therefore be allowed, if the 'weaker brother' found them helpful. In particular the Adiaphorists were those Protestants who with Melanchthon held certain Catholic practices (e.g. confirmation, veneration of saints) to be tolerable for the sake of unity; controversy continued over what were adiaphora until the Formula of Concord (1577). Generally speaking the more rigid forms of Protestantism, including the English Puritans, tended to hold that everything not explicitly allowed in the scriptures was forbidden; while others (e.g. Anglicans) regarded many traditional practices, though without scriptural warrant, as adiaphora.

ALAN RICHARDSON

Adoption

There was no legal procedure for adoption in ancient Israel. But there are cases in the OT of what may be called 'virtual adoption'. Jacob accepts the two sons of Joseph as his own (Gen. 48.5). Naomi says of Ruth's newborn child: 'a son is born to Naomi' (Ruth 4.16–17). A 'custom of adoption' seems to be described when the new parent takes the child 'between the knees' (Gen. 48.12; 50.23). But all these are adoptions within the family, and seem to have no legal consequences.

The prophet Nathan announces God's intention of saying about David's successor: 'I will be his father and he shall be my son' (II Sam. 7.14). In Psalm 2.7 God says to his anointed king: 'You are my son; this day I become your father.'

In the Roman Empire adoption was legally controlled. There were different processes for the adoption of minors and of adults; in both cases those adopted had full rights of inheritance. Adoptions of adults were common in the imperial family.

There are five NT passages, all in the Pauline writings, in which the setting up of the new relationship to God of those redeemed

through Christ is called adoption. Both Jewish and Roman customs are no doubt in mind, though the juridical aspect is certainly subordinate to the personal. The believer, freed from sin and fear by Christ, is no longer a slave but, by adoption, a child of God, who cries: 'Abba, father' (Rom. 8.15). Stress is laid not so much on the believer's need for a change of status if he is to be a child of God – though indeed this need exists, since only Christ is son of God by natural right – as on the benefits which he receives from adoption, by which he becomes an heir of God and a joint heir with Christ (Rom. 8.17).

But his adoption is not yet complete. He still awaits its fullness in the final deliverance, when his whole body will be set free (Rom. 8.24). So adoption is part of the theology of hope.

M. Bernoulli, 'Adoption', in J.-J. von Allmen, *Vocabulary of the Bible*, 1958; R. de Vaux, *Ancient Israel*, ET 1961, part I, ch. 4.

RUPERT DAVIES

Adoptionism

Adoptionism is a term that has come to be used with a very wide application for any christology* which implies that the man Jesus was 'adopted' as son by God. It is often treated as the earliest form of christological belief to be traced in the most primitive strata of the NT (see e.g. Rom. 1.4; Acts 2.22–24), only gradually superseded by a doctrine of preexistence and incarnation. The term is also used for the christology of sects like the Ebionites who appear to have been survivals of primitive Jewish Christian groups. The christology of the Dynamic Monarchians (see **Monarchianism**) and of Paul of Samosata is often said to be adoptionist, and those who wish to criticize the christology of the Antiochenes (see **Antiochene Theology**), or modern revisionist theologies which stress the genuine manhood of Christ, are apt to use the term as a condemnatory weapon. This is often less than justified, but those who object to adoptionism have generally been motivated by the need to uphold: 1. the priority of God's intention and action in the Christ-event – God did not have to wait around for a perfect man to appear so that he could adopt him; rather God's coming in Christ was his predetermined purpose and deed;

and 2. the distinction between Christ's true Sonship and the adoptive sonship of believers incorporated into him. The term Adoptianism is properly restricted to an eighth-century Spanish heresy which taught that in his manhood, Christ was not true Son of God but adopted, a view revived later by Abelard and others; its aim was to prevent a blurring of the distinction between the eternal Son and the incarnate Christ.

FRANCES YOUNG

Adoration

Adoration appears to be the strongest English word for worship*; it is thus equivalent to *latria* in ecclesiastical Latin (already used by Augustine for the worship of God in himself) and *latreia* in Greek (where the supreme usage has been established since John of Damascus). The pejorative intent always attaching to such formations as idolatry, bibliolatry or mariolatry confirms that the highest reverence is properly reserved for God alone. This accords with the First Commandment (Ex. 20.1–4).

Christians very early included Jesus Christ in their worship of God: e.g. Phil. 2.9–11, which makes a remarkable application of the strictly monotheistic Isa. 45.22f. Bowing and prostration before Jesus in the gospel stories (*proskyneo*) is to be seen stereoscopically as both homage to the man and, by later light, reverence towards the Lord. The worship addressed to Christ contributed powerfully to the victory of Nicene orthodoxy over Arianism*: Athanasius argued that the church's existing practice either recognized Christ's full divinity or else (unthinkably) fell into creature-worship (e.g. *Ad Adelphium*, 3).

The Holy Spirit* is rarely singled out as an object of Christian worship, but triadic doxologies are the liturgical counterpart to doctrinal trinitarianism: 'with the Father and the Son together he is worshipped and glorified' (Nicene–Constantinopolitan creed). While doxology to the Father *through* the Son *in* the Holy Spirit is suitable for thanksgiving (since God's benefits in the economy of salvation reach us from the Father through the Son in the Holy Spirit), Basil the Great defends doxology to the Father *with* the Son *with* the Holy Spirit as appropriate when God is contemplated in himself (*On the Holy Spirit*). Finally, the dominant form in both East and West left the equality of adoration in no doubt, though the order in which the divine persons are usually mentioned remains significant: 'Glory to the Father and to the Son and to the Holy Spirit.'

The 'content' of our adoration is self-giving love, made possible by God's having first so loved us (I John). Like love among humans, our adoration of God expresses itself in gestures, words and silence. The 'sacrifice of praise' (Heb. 13.15) is not meant to flatter God but to enact our responsive self-surrender to him.

In Catholic practice liturgical adoration is shown towards Christ present in the eucharistic species. The *adoratio crucis* is intended for the 'crucified God'. Created persons and objects may receive a lesser veneration (in later usage: *dulia*; though Augustine had used that term for the worship of God as creator).

E. J. Lengeling, 'Kult', *Handbuch Theologischer Grundbegriffe*, ed. H. Fries, 1962, pp. 865–80; N. Smart, *The Concept of Worship*, 1972; G. Wainwright, *Doxology*, 1980.

GEOFFREY WAINWRIGHT

Aesthetics and Theology

The dominant modern use of the word aesthetic to designate the philosophy of beauty in nature and the arts dates only from the eighteenth century. Etymologically, the word derives from a Greek word meaning 'of or pertaining to things perceptible by the senses, things material (as opposed to things thinkable or immaterial)' (OED).

Thus, the problem of theology and aesthetics is threefold: the understanding of the role of matter, the role of art and the role of beauty. The problem has been identified with its propositional treatment, but it is insufficiently understood if the decisive thinking of the artists is not considered. They had their own treatment of the problem and, until modern times, there was a symbiotic relation between art and theology, between visual theology and verbal theology. Only major themes can be identified here, not the infinitely varied and complex historical development.

This problem is a particular mode of the paradox of Christianity conceived as a conflicting fusion of Hebraism and Hellenism: Hebrew iconoclasm and Platonic mistrust of matter and material images; Hebrew particularity and the Greek use of images. The negative Christian contribution was made in the moralist denial of the flesh. The positive contribution began with the catacomb paintings and the earliest churches. The modest paintings defined a new role of the image which, as visual prayer, led to the distinctively Christian sense of the symbol as a true participation in the symbolized. The propositional debate was carried on in terms of the ancient idea of imitation (in all its varied meanings). On the one hand, imitation creates the substitute or the representation, which leads to idolatry. On the other hand, the symbol was not understood in the modern sense as a sign or an ornament to thought but as giving the only true access to a reality which is on the other side of the symbol. Thus the church building was an image of the heavenly Jerusalem and entering the church was truly entering the City of God. Through the double influence of Augustine and Pseudo-Dionysius the Areopagite, this idea became fused with Neoplatonist aesthetics, which no longer saw the image as two or three stages removed from the Real, the ideal essence, but as a representation of the eternal Idea directly. When this ultimate reality was identified with God the most enduring theme of visual theology was determined.

Initially, the image was a theophany, a manifestation of the divine, and beauty was understood as the splendour of the divine. Further, the image served a vital didactic function: the image does not contain the sacred and is not entitled to adoration but it instructs the faithful what they should adore. The image became the occasion for the devotional act. In the East, the debate set forth the two extremes. On the one hand, the incarnation did not sanctify matter but was a voluntary humiliation of God which man should not intensify by further linking God to corruptible matter in the image. On the other hand, because of the incarnation, the image was an indispensable means for the manifestation of the divine. Gradually this modulated into the idea of the icon*, the image that does not contain the sacred but is an indispensable means for communicating with the sacred. The Jewish idea of man as the image of God was essential to this development.

Beauty became 'the radiance of truth'. This gave it moral legitimacy, but the idea of radiance gathered up the multiple strands of light imagery in Neoplatonism* and the gospel: light became one of the major symbols (or icons) in both East and West. In the East, the church as the heavenly Jerusalem was defined by mosaic surfaces that had been transmuted into light; the mass of the walls was concealed, the building became a shimmering vision, unearthly. To go into an Orthodox church was to go apart from the earth into sacred space.

Initially, the technologically less advanced West could not so elaborate the light imagery beyond the gold and jewels of ornament. With the development of the great windows, light became of the substance of the church which was still the embodiment of the City of God. It was a transfiguration of the natural light which, in Flemish painting, could be linked to the representation of objects as the radiance of God's creation. Visual theology became rooted in the earth, not detached from it.

At the same time, Augustine's emphasis on the harmony and proportion was taken up in the West, a neo-Pythagorean interpretation of mathematics in the East; number, proportion, became a prime symbol of God. This profoundly influenced the development of music in the Western church and was basic to the idea of much architecture throughout Christendom. It came to its purest statement in the aniconic churches of the Italian Renaissance which confined images to altar paintings, reduced ornament to a minimum, no longer treated light as either splendour or radiance but as clarity and lucidity, and concentrated on the harmonic proportions as truly iconic: experiencing the geometric harmonies of the building was receiving or experiencing the creative act of God.

Northern Christianity, rooted in the art of the pre-Christian Celts, took a wholly different path. There are no engendering or corroborating verbal texts; the thinking was done solely in forms. The north rejected substantial form and representation, thus rejected the image, nature and the body and reduced matter to its least substantial elements, colour and the infinitely moving line. The interlace became a true symbol of the infinite beyond the sensuous and the organic, and an expressive form, glorifying the Word. Fused with the weight of the Romanesque and, later, with the organicity of Mediterranean Christianity, it became a prime instrument in the exploration of power and energy.

The harmonic space became the setting for a new development of the image. Jewish particularity and specificity of personality had been slow in making its way into the mind of the church. Mediaeval statues are highly individualized, but most have no personality; they manifest one or another state of grace as a part of the complex abstract linear whole of the building. The achievement of the Renaissance was the realization of personality in matter and the presentation and detailed examination of the moral issues emerging from the interaction of personalities. Images did not totally lose their iconic quality, but the iconic became more fully vested in the form than in the image. In the late Renaissance (the so-called 'Baroque'), all the ancient themes are harmonically fused in many combinations and modalities from the splendour of light and the flesh (Rubens) to the humbling of the Word in the ordinary (Rembrandt). For a time the ancient dualisms were harmonized, body and soul were seen as fused. This fusion of the body-soul with God was seen in Reformation art as the presence of the divine downward into the human, in the Counter-Reformation as the taking up of the earth, including this body-soul, into the divine in an ecstatic mystical union.

With the gradual modulation of the Word from Logos into proposition, the symbiotic relation between theology and art was broken. Theology became prescriptive, either driving the artist into privatism or reducing art to instrument. The image became illustration, beauty became ornament and sensuous pleasure, matter was considered no more than the occasion for moral commands, nature an object. In any creative sense, theological aesthetics died. Divorced from the image and from matter, the liturgy became simple magic, or a device for the manipulation of emotion.

Without the iconic image, art was pure symbol of mystical union. With the weakening of the principle of the symbol, the union became inner experience which, combined with the disembodied thought of Descartes, produced the solipsistic energies of Romanticism. In the church, this merely reinforced the recoil into law and propositions away from the aesthetic, generating a new denial of matter and the earth. After this interregnum, the existentialist* attempt to recreate a theological aesthetic revived the imageless experience in a neo-Gnostic union with a postulated Being* or Ground of Being.

Despite the efforts of a few, theology today has not recovered its proper aesthetic. The materials are present. The physicists have undertaken their explorations of 'the architecture of matter', essential to any adequate theological account. Many artists continue that exploration of spiritual states that is fundamental to the definition of art. All true artists are continuing the exploration of the possibilities of the matter of art. The historians (and the book publishers) have opened up the formal possibilities within other traditions. None of this has yet penetrated very far into the mind of the church nor has it been much informed by the thought of the church.

The objectivity of the old symbolism, which began in the catacombs (or in the Burning Bush) is no longer accessible and no new sense of the reality of symbols has replaced it. There is no theory of matter and image that is adequate to the characteristically modern sense of the creative fusion between subject and object. It is quite possible that no further progress will be made until theologians, visual and verbal, have absorbed the lessons of such artists as Paul Klee.

Titus Burckhardt, *Sacred Art in East and West*, 1957; John W. Dixon, Jr, *Art and the Theological Imagination*, 1978; Paul Klee, *The Thinking Eye*, ET 1961; Gervase Matthews, *Byzantine Aesthetics*, 1971; Rudolph Schwarz, *The Church Incarnate*, ET 1958; Otto von Simson, *The Gothic Cathedral*, 1962; Rudolph Wittkower, *Architectural Principles in the Age of Humanism*, 1952; Wilhelm Worringer, *Forms in Gothic*, ET 1957.

JOHN W. DIXON, JR

Aetiology

An aetiological story is one which offers an ostensible *explanation* of some phenomenon. E.g. the story of the Flood is aetiological in that it purports to account for the origin of the rainbow.

The term 'aetiology' was first made prominent in biblical study by H. Gunkel, who divided the narrative traditions of Genesis into three main categories: myth, historical saga and aetiological saga. The 'aetiological sagas' Gunkel further subdivided. There are aetiologies explaining the origins of nations, and/or the relations between them (e.g. Jacob/Esau relations mirror Israel/Edom relations); aetiologies explaining the meanings of particular *words* (e.g. Gen. 11 explains the word 'Babel' – the Hebrew name for Babylon); aetiologies of sanctuaries or particular religious rites or customs (Gen. 28 concerns the alleged origin of the Bethel sanctuary and Gen. 32.22–32 that of a food taboo), and aetiologies accounting for some feature of the landscape (e.g. Gen. 19 explains the devastated area south of the Dead Sea).

A distinction must be made between stories whose sole or main purpose seems to be aetiological and the very many which have quite other purposes but which offer an aetiology as it were in passing. It should also be observed that a story whose original purpose may have been primarily aetiological may be re-employed for some other purpose. E.g. Gen. 28.10ff, which may have begun life as a sanctuary foundation legend, fulfils a wider and profounder function in the context of the Jacob cycle. Correspondingly, a story not primarily aetiological may acquire secondary aetiological motifs. Gen. 1 explains the origin of the sabbath, but few would consider this to be its primary purpose. One consequence of these observations is that the presence of aetiological motifs can count neither for nor against the historicity of a particular narrative.

J. Bright, *Early Israel in Recent Historical Writing*, 1956, pp. 91–100; O. Eissfeldt, *The Old Testament, an Introduction*, ET 1965, pp. 38–45; O. Kaiser, *Introduction to the Old Testament*, ET 1975, pp. 48–52; B. O. Long, *The Problem of Etiological Narrative in the Old Testament*, 1968.

                                H. MCKEATING

Agape

Agape (love) is commonly viewed as the primary requirement and guide for conduct and character in Christian ethics. Its biblical basis appears in Jesus' summary of the law and the prophets by the double commandment: 'Love the Lord your God with all your heart, with all your soul, with all your mind', and 'Love your neighbour as yourself'. (Matt. 22.37ff. and parallels; cf. Deut. 6.5; Lev. 19.18). Determination of the weight and meaning of *agape* is a major task of Christian ethics. It is generally agreed that *agape* requires seeking the neighbour's (even the enemy neighbour's) welfare, but there are sharp disagreements about whether *agape* excludes self-love, mandates self-sacrifice, or pursues mutuality. These disputes involve the distinctions and relations of *agape*, *philia* and *eros*. Recent Christian theology has also debated whether *agape* can be expressed in rules of action or can only be determined in the situation (the so-called 'situation ethics' debate). A related but distinct issue is how agape, as a guide for Christian action, relates to justice, conceived as a standard for society and the state. This issue emerges particularly when agapistic agents cannot meet the needs of all the neighbours in question (e.g. the distribution of welfare) or cannot meet the needs of one neighbour without harming another (e.g. lethal force in protection of the innocent). Several proposals have emerged in recent Christian ethics for relating love and justice, including love as a motive for justice (Emil Brunner), love and justice in dialectical relation (Reinhold Niebuhr), love transforming justice (Paul Ramsey), justice as the form of love (Paul Tillich) and the identity of love and justice (Joseph Fletcher).

Anders Nygren, *Agape and Eros*, 1957; Gene Outka, *Agape: An Ethical Analysis*, 1972.

                        JAMES F. CHILDRESS

Agnosticism

Agnosticism stems from the recognition that there are some things which we do not know. This recognition is compatible with an understanding of human beings as finite and limited, but its elaboration in the context of religious belief has several different forms.

The first recorded use of the term 'agnostic' is attributed to T. H. Huxley, apparently stimulated by St Paul's reference to the altar 'to the unknown God' (1869). Such a use was tolerant of the possibility of some form of – albeit limited – 'religious' belief, but the term soon came to be used also of those who 'neither denied nor affirmed God, but simply put him on one side'. This ambivalence towards religion has continued to show itself through the variety of forms which agnosticism can take.

Agnosticism may simply be the personal confession of uncertainty about whether or not there is a God to whom we can be related. As such it is clearly an interim statement from which an individual may one day depart towards the greater certainties of either atheism or belief.

More strongly, however, it may be allied, as in Philo of Hume's *Dialogues Concerning Natural Religion* (1779), to the affirmation based on argument and reflection that there is no adequate evidence or justification for almost all of the claims that theistic belief makes about God. Philosophically this form of agnosticism is the inevitable outcome of scepticism, and it may even be claimed not only that there *is* no adequate justification for belief in God but that there *can be* no adequate evidence for belief in God. This radical form of agnosticism may then develop in one of two different directions.

On the one hand it can stress the negative element and thus ally agnosticism with the various other forms of unbelief; for it would be argued that surely it would be wrong to give assent where there can be no adequate basis for it. On the other hand there are those who have insisted that the impossibility of giving sufficient evidence or rational support for belief in God is to be expected; for surely God is infinite, transcending the limitations of human reason. Indeed, it could be argued that meditation on the limits of human reason is a necessary prolegomenon to true faith. A classic statement of this view is to be found in H. L. Mansel's Bampton Lectures, *The Limits of Religious Thought* (1858).

Thus just as agnosticism in the late Victorian period came increasingly to be associated with and attacked as the denial of belief, so too, as Mansel attempted to show, it can be compatible with that strand in Christian thought recognized in an earlier age through stress on the *via negativa* *, or throughout the history of theism * in recognition of the transcendence and mystery of God. However, even where the tendency towards agnosticism takes a form which is compatible with religious belief, it is not generally tolerant of the aspirations of theologians to make affirmations about God.

R. W. Hepburn, *Christianity and Paradox*,

1958; D. Hume, *Dialogues Concerning Natural Religion*, ed. N. Kemp Smith, 1947.
STEWART SUTHERLAND

Alexandrian Theology

Alexandria was a centre of theological thinking over many centuries, beginning with the influential work of Clement and Origen; but it is misleading to imagine a continuous and homogeneous theological tradition. The term 'Alexandrian theology' is most commonly used in contrast to Antiochene theology *; both are modern categorizations and refer to different christological and exegetical approaches which developed in response to Arianism * and were associated with the two ancient patriarchates of the East. In the Nestorian controversy they came into conflict, though both appealed to the authority of Athanasius, and the differences were exacerbated by terminological confusion. The principal representative of Alexandrian theology was Cyril of Alexandria, who later became the foremost authority for the anti-Chalcedonian Monophysites even though certain of his dogmatic epistles had been canonized at Chalcedon. The principal characteristic of Alexandrian theology was its stress upon the unity of the person of Christ: the 'Godhead' and 'Manhood' of Christ were regarded as indistinguishable after the union which was to be described as 'hypostatic'. There was one nature of the Logos * enfleshed, not two natures. Some of the classic slogans used to encapsulate this position were actually drawn from pseudonymous Apollinarian writings, which gives some substance to the charge of Apollinarianism levelled by Antiochene opponents of this view. However, Cyril's own position was not Apollinarian: he denied 'mixture' of the natures and accepted the human soul of Christ. His primary concern seems to have been to defend the coherence of the Nicene creed by insisting that it was improper to ascribe some of the credal statements to the Logos and others to 'his Man'; all its statements were made of the one divine subject who existed in a pre-incarnate and an incarnate state yet without change.

See also **Christology**.
FRANCES YOUNG

Alienation

A term in widespread use today in the fields

of psychology, theology, political and social theory, as well as in everyday language. In general the term denotes the processes, or results of the processes, whereby a person or thing expresses itself in the form of something foreign or even opposed to itself. Probably the oldest major sources for our contemporary uses of the term are Christian, where it designates that brokenness of relationship between God and man and between man and man which is sin.

St Paul makes much of the connection between sin and alienation on the one hand and reconciliation/salvation in Christ on the other. As he says, 'and you who once were estranged and hostile in mind, doing evil deeds, he has now reconciled in his body of flesh by his death' (Col. 1.21).

In some contemporary readings of the OT (as in much liberation theology*) the two dimensions of estrangement of man from God and of man from man are said to be intimately linked, if not identified, so that the restoration of man's relationship with God becomes no more than notionally distinct from the overcoming of social alienation and injustice. As José Miguez Bonino puts it, 'knowing God is doing justice'.

Less obvious, but just as important for the later philosophical history of the term, is the Pauline notion of the Father's redemptive *kenosis** (self-emptying) in Jesus. For this cycle of the alienation of the Godhead in man overcoming the alienation of man from the Godhead finds a philosophical expression in Hegel, for whom a parallel cycle of alienation and its overcoming is the very mechanism of human history itself.

For Hegel, Absolute Spirit (God) is dynamic, a process the law of whose development is dialectical* (*see also* **Hegelianism**). In its self-affirmation, Spirit negates itself by giving birth to its opposite in a series of progressions through nature and man. In man Spirit finds the point of its return to itself, since man is the highest expression of Spirit. This progression of the alienation and return to itself of Spirit finds its highest symbolic and pictorial form in the Christian doctrines of incarnation* and redemption*.

Feuerbach and Marx reverse the Hegelian process. For both, God is the self-alienation of man. For Feuerbach, in so far as man affirms God he negates himself, for in theism man affirms himself in the form of an alien, external object 'over-against' himself. Man can therefore recover himself only in the negation of the religious form of his self-alienation.

Marx in turn accepted Feuerbach's criticism of Christianity, but went much further, asserting that religious alienation is rooted in man's social alienation, which reaches its highest point in capitalist society and has a four-fold form. Man in capitalist society is alienated from nature, from others in society, from the products of his labour, but above all from his own productive activity itself. For Marx, then, religious alienation can be abolished only by the abolition of religion itself. But religion can be abolished only in and through the abolition of the social and economic conditions (capitalism) which require it. Such a state of affairs can be achieved only by the abolition of private property itself in communist society.

See also **Marxism, Marxist Theology.**

DENYS TURNER

Allegory and Typology

Many modern scholars have distinguished typology from allegory by saying that typology is a comparison of events or persons along a scale of time (Adam and Christ, or the Exodus and the deliverance of Cross and Resurrection) and is thus 'historical', while allegory is anti-historical and makes the text into an indicator of eternal, often philosophical, truths. According to this view, typology is basic to the internal structure of the Bible, while allegory, though not completely absent, is marginal; typology is Jewish, but allegory is Greek; typology can be fitted in with modern critical understanding, while allegory cannot.

Though a useful distinction, this oversimplifies the situation. Within scripture, and still more in post-biblical times, typology and allegory naturally interpenetrate. Moreover, there are other phenomena which do not easily fall into the simple dichotomy allegory/typology and make the distinction still more blurred. Allegory is deeply founded on Jewish as well as on Greek soil.

The following are the chief factors which encouraged the rise of typology and allegory:

1. The Qumran community and early Christians considered that ancient scripture had spoken of themselves, their sects and their situation. Once this key was known,

obscure references and figurative allusions would be unlocked and the persons or events identified. Where the text of Nahum says 'he rebukes the sea', it is explained that 'the sea is the Kittim', i.e. the Greek rulers of Syria. Any biblical expression may have a hidden sense which is thus revealed.

2. Persons conscious of standing within the biblical tradition might deliberately cast their actions and sayings in the patterns of earlier biblical materials, or might be so depicted: thus John the Baptist cast himself as Elijah, Jesus on the mountain is perhaps the new Moses. Such typologies were sometimes intended by the men of the Bible themselves, sometimes read into their thoughts and actions by the later writers.

3. For Christianity in particular the idea of the fulfilment of prophecy was immensely important. The prophets had known in advance about the coming of Christ and had foretold elements, sometimes major features and sometimes quite small details, which were fulfilled when he came. But the NT, though claiming steadfastly that this was so, in fact used only a small selection of OT passages in this way. Yet it had shown that the smallest details of the OT could find correspondence in details of Christianity; moreover, not only the strictly prophetic books, but any part of the OT, could act predictively. Thus Christian expositors soon after NT times began to explore the entire OT text and interpret it in a Christian sense.

4. Within Christianity this enterprise was immensely reinforced by the prominence of the *parable** within the teaching of Jesus. A parable was not an interpretation of scripture but a tale drawn from images and similes of ordinary life; yet it invites the hearer to discern a secret inner meaning which has some analogy with the story as told but stands on a quite other level than its obvious surface meaning. A few parables have an explanation attached; the majority do not.

The parable has a significant connection with allegory. This is not to say that they are identical. Some scholars have made the distinction that the parable has as a whole only one single point. In a parable nothing is directly 'meant' by the hole in the ground in which a man buried a large sum of money, nor by the garden in which the hole was dug: only the story as a whole has a meaning relatable to reality. In an allegory, on the other hand, each element would have its own relation to reality. This view of parables is helpful; nevertheless it cannot be taken as universally correct. In some parables of Jesus, at least in their present form, more than one element in the story seems to be identifiable as an external reality. But, however we evaluate the parables of Jesus themselves, our main point is their effect in guiding Christian readers to the conclusion that the Bible contains much material that does not mean exactly what it says. The surface expressions are a coded representation of a hidden and more spiritual meaning.

5. Very important in the same way was the common Christian attitude to Judaism. The OT, though it was the Word of God for Christians, contained many legal and ceremonial commands which Christianity no longer maintained, or maintained only in greatly modified form; similarly, it had many references to the land of Israel and the Hebrew possession of it. Christians thought that the reference must be to more than *merely* this place, more than *simply* the performance of this or that act. Thus the law of circumcision was understood by Jews as requiring this physical act – even if along with all its spiritual consequences – while for Christians there was no such act and the passages had to mean something inward, symbolic or spiritual or an act like baptism which was physically quite different. They could point to OT passages which themselves insisted on a 'circumcision of the heart' or the like; while the NT said that the Jews had a 'veil' over their faces in the reading of the scriptures, a veil which could be removed only in Christ.

This does not mean that Jewish interpretation itself was always 'literal': it was often as allegorical as Christian interpretation was. But even allegorical interpretation in Judaism was tied to actual ceremonies and legal requirements which were at least supposed to be close to the actualization of the Mosaic law. Thus the command 'thou shalt not seethe a kid in its mother's milk' has long served as the basis for the custom by which meat and milk are not served in the same meal. This is allegorical in itself, and yet it is 'literal' in a sense in which a Christian understanding would not be literal: in effect, in the sense that it makes the passage refer to a custom factually observed in Judaism.

6. The Jewish technique of *midrash* also has a relation to allegory. Basically, it worked by a massive decontextualization. A linguistic element might have several meanings, and when found in one place it could be understood with the sense it bears in any other. There was no redundancy in biblical language: any element, however small, any unusual writing or variant spelling, must be there for a purpose. The end result of such interpretation conforms, however, to the total network of perceptions within Judaism, enriching them by re-applying them to an ever-increasing number of biblical phenomena. There is no sense of anachronism, and the (often quite recent) institutions of rabbinic Judaism are read back into the most ancient times.

7. Christianity affirmed the revelation* of God to ancient Israel; and yet it had peculiar doctrines, which Judaism did not share, in particular the Trinity* and Incarnation*. On the other hand, it did not continue, as a matter of direct practice, many moral and ceremonial features commanded in the OT. Thus it sought, on the one hand, to discern signs of its own peculiar doctrines within ancient scripture; and, conversely, where scripture concerned practices which Christianity no longer followed, it was natural to seek to show that these passages had another meaning, superior and more spiritual.

This can be expressed again, for both Judaism and Christianity, as the removal of anachronism and historical distance. A true and universal religion has been achieved. A book like Genesis refers to a state of religion that for rabbinic Judaism as for early Christianity was long past. But these were universal religions, the principles of which were eternal. Therefore the institutions of rabbinic Judaism and its way of seeing the world had already existed in the time of Adam or of Noah; while in Christianity the incarnate Jesus – not just the pre-existent Son of God – had been present and active already in OT times.

8. There were also moral and philosophical elements. God was a moral being and must have acted morally by the standards of the great religions. The same was true of the great men of biblical times. Abraham could not possibly have commanded his wife to tell a lie. God could surely not have simply forbidden man to eat a particular fruit; and

so the fruit of the story must have been a symbol for something more important. This argument was already current in older Hellenistic allegory. The gods could not really be quarrelsome, deceitful, gluttonous and adulterous, and the passages which say so must be speaking symbolically of something else.

Paraenesis, the provision of warning and advice, worked in the same way. Sarah was an example to Christian women; yet one could not be in exactly the position of Sarah. Allegorization was a process of universalization: it stripped away the elements in Sarah's position which were temporary and contingent, and extracted an element which was morally lasting.

The great religions required a certain degree of consistency and rationality in the picture of God and his works. Things told about God must be indicators of great principles, and could not be concerned with minor and rationally inexplicable factors. If God 'saw that it was good' at the end of other days of the creation process, but not at the end of the second, this must have a reason, perhaps connected with the universal significance of the number 'two'. In Philo's version of Judaism, and in much Greek Christianity, the coinherence of the religion with the greater Greek philosophies, especially Platonism, was important.

9. Etymology also has a relation to allegorical interpretation. Many Hebrew names were semantically transparent, e.g. Ezekiel meant 'Let God strengthen'. A name was not just a conventional label, it had a message to convey, and within the OT itself some names had been given etymological explanations – mostly, paradoxically, where the meanings of the names were in fact unknown. Name explanation made meaningful that which in itself was unmeaningful. In the Bible itself only a very limited number of names were thus explained, mostly persons of high importance: Abraham, Moses, Jesus. Later interpreters did not leave it at this. The Bible contained long lists of names: the places where the Israelites had stopped in the desert, the lists of generations. It was not possible that these should be mere names: they must mean something, they must have a message, otherwise why would God have revealed all this material? Etymological explanation of names was another form of allegory. The Bible itself offered

only a few; in patristic times *onomastica*, methodical collections of names, explained every name in the Bible, sometimes giving three or four meanings for a name. The finest of these, like 'vision of peace' for Jerusalem, became part of the Christian poetic heritage.

The basis for allegory and all the associated forms of understanding, then, is the fact of change in religion. Religion developed new forms, but the scriptures which it revered had grown up under older forms of religion and older understandings of literature. The rise of these understandings did not take place immediately after the production of scripture. On the whole, one might say, after the basic biblical books had been produced, the first impulse was not to interpret these allegorically, or in any other way, but to write more biblical books, or more books in the same style and pattern as the Bible – hence the sort of literature we find in the so-called Apocrypha *. The completion and canonization of scripture, and the realization that there are to be no more biblical books, accentuates the difference of religion and of literary type and promotes the rise of these newer understandings. Moreover, the newer religious movements, like Christianity, began not by appropriating equally everything that was in ancient scripture, but by building upon a certain limited area that was specially useful to their needs. This is the reason why allegorical explanation is limited in extent within the N T. As soon as the attempt was made to expound the *entire* O T in the same way, allegorization flowered. The peak of the allegorical approach is reached with Origen in Alexandria, about A D 200.

It is normal to contrast allegorical interpretation with the 'literal' sense, but the 'literal' is even more difficult to define than the typological or the allegorical. If the allegorical in one respect sought to depart from the literal sense, in another sense allegory depends upon literality and works in harmony with the literal details: every detail of scripture as it stands comes from God and has a meaning, and so the literal form provides the hints and indications which enable us to know what the allegorical meaning is. Acceptance of an allegorical meaning does not necessarily imply that the literal sense is evaded. Philo's allegorical interpretations of the Mosaic law were not intended to

assist Jews in ignoring compliance with the commandments; rather, they provided a 'spiritual' reason why the commandments should be literally fulfilled. Interpreters are often both allegorical and literal at the same time, or in different aspects of the same subject matter. Moreover, when an allegorical interpretation comes to be authoritative, or to be accepted with sufficient conviction, people often come to consider it to be actually literal. The linguistic features which mark the sense as allegorical come to be psychologically perceived as normal and thereby as indicating a literal sense.

One of the supreme areas for allegorical interpretation, both in Judaism and in Christianity, was the Song of Songs. Some suppose that it could not have been accepted within the canon but for the allegorical interpretation, but this is not certain. Its use in this way is still not clearly evidenced in N T times: Ephesians develops the analogy of marriage for the relation between Christ and the church without quoting the Song.

In due course systematic accounts of the relation between various senses came to be offered (*see* **Senses of Scripture**). Attempts were made to systematize these as a fourfold sense or the like, both in Judaism and in Christianity, but there are complicated questions in ascertaining what exactly the various senses are and whether the distinctions are commonly maintained. Theoretically it was maintained that the 'plain' or 'literal' sense was authoritative for doctrine and religious practice, but what was deemed to be 'plain' or 'literal' seems often to be closer to what we would call allegorical. The purpose and effect of allegorization and of more complex systems such as the fourfold sense is to create a harmonious coinherence of the ancient scripture and the present religion. If the scripture provided the nodal points upon which developments of the religion were built, the religion then returned into the scripture to mould its meanings into conformity with itself.

Allegorization therefore means that the existing religious pattern always has scriptural authorization. In rejecting the existing religious pattern, the Protestant Reformation rejected, or at least discouraged, allegory. It maintained, however, aspects of the doctrine of the early church which could not have been established but for the assistance of allegory. In any case Protestantism produced its own allegory, in which the methods were not clearly distinguishable from those of mediaeval allegory, but the content was provided by established Protestant doctrine.

It is sometimes thought that modern critical biblical scholarship has abandoned all interest in allegory and restricted itself to the literal sense. This, however, seems doubtful. It seems more probable that critical scholarship has divided up the sense of scripture in an entirely different way, interesting itself in what we might call the linguistic/literary sense on the one hand and the religious/theological sense on the other. Neither of these coincide with any element in the ancient distinction of senses.

In modern times an interest in matters of allegory and typology continues to be maintained also through the work of literary critics * and literary theorists. The relevance of their thinking for biblical studies is being widely appreciated at the present time.

J. Barr, *Old and New in Interpretation*, 1966; B. S. Childs, 'The Sensus Literalis of Scripture: an Ancient and Modern Problem', in H. Donner, R. Hanhart and R. Smend, *Beiträge zur alttestamentlichen Theologie* (Zimmerli Festschrift), 1977, pp. 80–93; N. Frye, *The Great Code*, 1982; R. P. C. Hanson, *Allegory and Event*, 1959; G. W. H. Lampe and K. J. Woollcombe, *Essays in Typology*, 1957; A. Louth, 'Return to Allegory', in *Discerning the Mystery*, 1983.

JAMES BARR

Analogy

Analogies are proportional similarities which also acknowledge dissimilar features, hence Aristotle linked good metaphors to apt analogies (*Poetics*, 1459a5). In theological use, however, two features of analogy have been underscored: 1. properly analogous expressions as distinguished from metaphorical ones; 2. analogous terms as 'between' univocal (synonymous) and equivocal (homonynous) terms, and so susceptible of use in argument. So while nearly every expression may be used analogously – as in 'grasping the point', some are more apt to be so used, others can only be used analogously, and many expressions embody 'dead metaphors', like 'comprehending'.

Plato's dialogues often trace the vagaries of properly analogous terms, such as 'love' in the *Symposium* and 'good' in the *Republic*, elaborating certain strategies for using them to help gain some understanding of what lies beyond our ken yet powerfully influences our human arrangements. Aristotle was more directly concerned with the ways analogous expressions might be employed in argument, though he was aware of their general utility in assisting human understanding (*Rhetoric*, 1410b12). He often employs the scheme of mathematical proportion (a:b::c:d) to display the proportional similarities involved (since Greek *analogia* = Latin *proportio*), yet also recognizes another yet more general pattern of 'reference to one' (*pros hen*), whereby many senses of a term bear on a single paradigmatic use. His tracing of all uses of 'to be' to that of *substance* (what exists in itself and not in another – *Metaphysics*, 1016b6–10) offers the best illustration of this pattern, and laid the groundwork for the celebrated mediaeval 'analogy of being' (*analogia entis*).

The Arab philosophers – Alfarabi (870?–950), Avicenna (980–1037), Algazali (1058–1111) and Averroes (1126–1198) – employed the second pattern, referring to it by the then conventional 'prior/posterior' predication, and generally classifying such expressions by the alternate Greek term *amphibolous*. Maimonides (1135–1204) was acquainted with the strategy through this literature, but was unpersuaded that such expressions could be used to gain a 'positive' understanding of divinity (*Guide for the Perplexed*, 1.56).

Aquinas (1225–1274) had abundant recourse to this peculiar feature of predication, employing it primarily in those regions where creatures sought to speak to or of their creator. The century preceding him had scrutinized the modes of expression found in scripture, and developed ways of attending to diverse uses of language. Their distinctions were of special use to Aquinas, allowing him to elaborate analogous expression *in divinis* to a fine art. Later scholastics would try to codify Aquinas' observations into a *theory* of analogy, laying great stress on his major distinction (based on the two uses of Aristotle) between 'analogy of proper proportionality' and 'analogy of attribution'. Yet Aquinas himself used one or the other as befitted the occasion, and one extracts a *doctrine* from his writings at the expense of attending to the skilfulness with which he teaches one to discern among analogous uses. Such has been the verdict on the efforts of Cajetan (1469–1534).

It was this 'doctrine', however, which later came under fire as an overly-subtle *theory* purporting to make human language reveal something of divinity. The attacks came from philosophers and theologians alike, the first insisting that no set of strategies could so extend human meanings to a transcendent level; the latter insisting that none should, for God's transcendence must be sustained. Karl Barth represents the strongest voice against what he understood to be the use of *analogia entis* in theology, although subsequent discussion has attenuated this polemic considerably. For once one distinguishes the history of the discussion up to and culminating in Aquinas from later scholastic codifications, the issue is clearly that posed by Aristotle and the mediaevals: how may discourse about what transcends our customary categories proceed by way of arguments, and so lead to a form of knowledge?

Analogy stands for the series of proposals made to answer that question. Hence its concerns are primarily semantic, not ontological, although the prime example of the various irreducible senses of 'to be' led one to identify 'analogy' with 'being', as in *analogia entis*. The expressions most susceptible of analogous use are evaluative in character: 'wise', 'powerful', 'living', 'good', reminding us of Socrates' discovery that the wise man is one who realizes he is not wise. Thus the use of such terms – among us but especially and of God – will involve an affirmative and a negative component, which combine to what Aquinas called the *via eminentiae*. Such 'eminent' use can be monitored, if not justified, by a discussion of human language, and its propensities to analogous use.

J. F. Anderson, *Bond of Being*, 1949; D. Burrell, *Analogy and Philosophical Language*, 1973; R. McInerny, *Logic of Analogy*, 1961; G. E. L. Owen, 'Logic and Metaphysics in Some Earlier Works of Aristotle', in During and Owen (eds), *Aristotle and Plato in mid-Fourth Century*, 1960; J. Owens, *Doctrine of Being in the Aristotelian Metaphysics*, 1963; H. A. Wolfson, 'Amphibolous Terms in Aristotle, Arabic Philosophy and Maimonides', in *Studies in History and Philosophy of Religion* I, 1973.

D. BURRELL

Analytic Philosophy

This term is generally used to designate a philosophical movement which began in the early years of the twentieth century in England. Although the movement has certain historical ties with British empiricism and the epistemology* of Kant, its primary impetus came from a fresh and in many ways original concern with the nature of language and meaning.

There are two 'tap-roots' out of which analytic philosophy grew, one indigenous to Britain and the other imported. The former consists of the work of Bertrand Russell, especially his 'logical atomism', and that of G. E. Moore. Both Russell and Moore were trained as Cambridge Platonists or British Idealists, following F. H. Bradley's adaptation of Hegel's philosophy (*see* **Hegelianism, Idealism**). However, both began to have serious doubts about the meaningfulness of metaphysical abstractions, each in his own way asking for an *analysis* of the syntactic and semantic *meaning* of all linguistic utterances.

Russell sought to show, through his 'theory of descriptions' and his 'theory of types', that the logic of ordinary language is frequently misleading with respect to what there is in the world and what can be said to be meaningful. He proposed to clean up the ambiguities and vagaries of ordinary talk. More specifically, Russell's logical atomism was designed as an account of the relation between language and reality which clarifies the one-to-one correspondence between the basic 'atomic facts' which make up the world and the simple propositions affirming them.

Moore, on the other hand, struck a less grandiose and less metaphysical posture, one which reflected a great concern for the certainty of common-sense and the reality of the external world. At the same time, while he was adamant about the *truth* of such consideration, he nonetheless maintained that the *meaning* of these truths remained to be properly analysed. Surprisingly enough, Moore sought to carry out this analysis in terms of the rather uncommonsensical notion of sense-data. Here again, in his view, ordinary usage stood in need of correction.

The second tap-root of analytic philosophy, the imported one, came to Britain through Ludwig Wittgenstein and A. J. Ayer. The young Wittgenstein, who came from Vienna, was a student of Russell's and put together, in his *Tractatus Logical-Philosophicus* (1922), a powerful if enigmatic presentation of logical atomism. After concluding that the business of describing the world in propositions which 'mirror' its various facts belonged to the scientist and not the philosopher, and that metaphysical (including theological), ethical and aesthetic utterances are without sense in the strict sense, Wittgenstein 'retired' from philosophy, returning to Austria to teach in a school and work as a gardener.

During this fifteen-year retirement he had occasional interaction with a group of philosophically inclined scientists who were gathering around Moritz Schliek at the University of Vienna, a group referred to as 'The Vienna Circle'. In their efforts to render philosophy scientific, and thus respectable, these thinkers made considerable use of Wittgenstein's *Tractatus*, even though the latter rightfully contended that they had little in common. A. J. Ayer studied in Vienna and was responsible for introducing its 'positivism' into England. The rise of Nazism dispersed the Vienna Circle, with most of its members settling and working in America.

Ayer's now infamous book, *Language, Truth and Logic* (1936, rev. ed. 1946), sought to encapsulate the main themes of this new brand of empiricism. Focussing on the 'verifiability criterion of meaning', which defines meaningful utterances as those which are in principal testable by empirical observation, Ayer argued that metaphysical, theological, ethical and aesthetic discourse must be eliminated from philosophy because they are by definition untestable. Some years later, in response to various criticisms of his position (the most troublesome being that which asked if the verifiability criterion is itself verifiable), Ayer published a new and lengthy 'Introduction' to his book in which he softened its dogmatic tone and reformulated the criterion of meaningfulness in the form of a 'proposal' rather than a dogma. But the essential and vastly influential thrust of Ayer's work remained essentially the same.

As there are two sources of analytic philosophy, so there are two main branches in its development. The one, drawing most heavily on Russell and the early Wittgenstein (as well as from G. Frege), together with the transplanted Vienna Circle, became increasingly interested in the philosophy of science and logic, focusing especially on the construction of 'ideal' languages within which to carry on the work of philosophy with absolute precision. Herbert Feigl and Rudolph Carnap are particular noteworthy examples of this tendency. Although W. V. O. Quine comes out of this tradition, he, along with Wilfrid Sellers, can also be read as a strong critic of it, from what might be termed a 'pragmatist' perspective.

The other main branch of analytic philosophy draws most heavily on the later work of Wittgenstein, work done between 1930 and 1950, after his return to Cambridge, and presented in his *Philosophical Investigations* (ET 1953). Following up on Moore's 'common sense philosophy', Wittgenstein came to the conclusion that ordinary language does not need to be made more precise, that it is all right as it is (ambiguities, vagaries and all). He maintained that philosophical problems arise only when theorists of one sort or another (especially logicians and psychologists) try to force ordinary speech into abstract moulds, rather than acknowledging that language and thought follow patterns which have arisen non-systematically in concrete, task-oriented contexts. For Wittgenstein, the meaning of an utterance is mediated through its use in context.

A number of important thinkers have followed Wittgenstein's return to ordinary speech as the guide which will lead us out of philosophical muddles. Gilbert Ryle (*The Concept of Mind*, 1949) employed this method in seeking to overcome the inherent dualism of our thinking about the relationship between mind and body. J. L. Austin (*Sense and Sensibilia*, 1962; *Philosophical Papers*, 1961; and *How To Do Things With Words*, 1962) sought to sort out the intricacies of language about sense perception, knowledge claims, and moral and legal responsibility. John Wisdom (*Philosophy and Psychoanalysis*, 1952; *Paradox and Discovery*, 1966) focussed mainly on the nature of philosophical activity itself, stressing its therapeutic value and the complexities of rational justification. P. F. Strawson (*Indivi-

duals, 1964), S. Hampshire (*Thought and Action*, 1959) and A. I. Melden (*Free Action*, 1961) have all sought to follow Wittgenstein's lead with respect to our understanding of persons, intentions and decision making.

As a specific movement, analytic philosophy is no longer with us. As a pervasive influence, however, upon the way current philosophers carry on their work, it is very present indeed.

JERRY H. GILL

Anamnesis

A Greek word meaning 'memorial' or 'commemoration', referring to two distinct aspects of an anaphora *. The first is the commemorative content of an anaphora, embracing mention of all God's past benevolence throughout salvation history with particular stress on the acts of Christ. Some anaphoras are very detailed about this, beginning with creation (Byzantine Basil). Others have less creational content (Rome), and some focus almost exclusively on the works of Christ (Hippolytus). Structurally, the account of the institution of the eucharist by Christ figures as the last and principal act of divine benevolence in the commemorative cursus, especially in the West Syrian type of anaphora still employed by churches of Byzantine usage (the anaphoras of John Chrysostom and Basil). It is the institution account, ending with the words 'Do this for my *anamnesis*', which gives rise to the second anaphoral aspect of commemoration: an overt textual statement that the eucharistic liturgy is now obeying that dominical command as it remembers the Lord's saving acts – his passion, death, resurrection, seating in glory, and coming again. To this statement is often joined a specification of how the assembly understands its response in obedience to the whole sweep of anaphoral commemoration culminating in Christ's command, an understanding usually if not always couched in terms of oblation. This then leads into petition for God to continue his beneficence for the church in the future by sending the Holy Spirit on the gifts and the people (Eastern) or by accepting the gifts and those who participate in them (Western). This petition is the epiclesis *, and it often opens out into specific petitions for all classes of Christians and worldly needs. Anamnesis thus has both subjective and objective senses: the liturgical assembly is called by the anaphora prayer to remember, and then acts objectively in obedience to that remembrance, appropriating what is remembered by word and sacrament.

AIDAN KAVANAGH

Anaphora

A Greek word, 'offering', designating the Eucharistic Prayer, called in the west 'Canon of the Mass' or 'Prayer of Consecration'. The prayer almost certainly developed out of Jewish euchological forms used by Christ at the Last Supper, on which recent research has thrown much light. The stages in the prayer's development may be seen first in *Didache* 9 and 10, in the East Syrian Anaphora of the Apostles Addai and Mari, in the Maronite Anaphora of St Peter the Apostle, and in the *Apostolic Tradition* of Hippolytus. In these texts, as in subsequent tradition East and West, there is 1. a notable move from Jewish euchology's stress on blessing of God for favours received (*berakah*) to thanksgiving (*yadah, eucharistia*); 2. a varying mixture of the twofold pattern of thanksgiving and petition; and 3. a central focus on the acts of Christ as summing up God's benevolence towards man and the world throughout salvation history both past and future. In the several Christian traditions the role of the anaphora has been to anchor the church's faith in eucharistic terms rather as the classic creeds anchor that faith in trinitarian terms arising from the threefold questions asked in baptism. Anaphoras and creeds thus function as complementary 'canons' of belief and prayer, along with the canon of scripture, in a church's life of faith and worship. The great historical variety of anaphoras makes it difficult to discern an unvarying common structure: some were wholly variable (Hispano-gallican), some invariable (Eastern), and one combined both features (Roman). Some had no institution account (*Didache*), some may originally have had none (*Addai and Mari*), the rest seem always to have had one. All have an epiclesis * of one kind or another, but some have no pneumatic epiclesis (*Didache*, Rome). All commemorate at least the works of Christ (Hippolytus), but not all have an anamnesis * stated clearly (*Didache*) or in the same way (*Serapion*).

L. Bouyer, *Eucharist*, ET [2] 1968; G. Dix, *The*

Shape of the Liturgy, 1945; J. Heinemann, *Prayer in the Talmud: Forms and Patterns*, 1977; L. Ligier, 'The Origins of the Eucharistic Prayer: From the Last Supper to the Eucharist', *Studia Liturgica* 9, 1973, pp. 176–85.

AIDAN KAVANAGH

Anathema

This is a Greek term (literally meaning 'suspended') used in the early church of Christians who for serious sin were excluded from the community and so understood to be exposed to God's anger, 'accursed' or under the ban (Hebrew, *ḥerem*). The word itself appears in such passages as Rom. 9.3; I Cor. 16.22 and (of those who would preach a false gospel) Gal. 1.9. We find some anathematizing practice at work in the case of an incestuous man (I Cor. 5.1–5) and false teachers (I Tim. 1.18–20; Titus 3.9–11; see also Matt. 18.15–18).

Originally anathematization did not differ from excommunication. But from the sixth century they gradually began to be distinguished, in that excommunication merely prevented reception of the sacraments and full participation in public worship, whereas anathematization (eventually identified as *excommunicatio major*) meant the severest form of excommunication which formally excluded heretics from the church. When *excommunicatio minor* was removed in 1869 from RC canon law, anathematization and excommunication became essentially the same – except for the solemn ceremony used for anathematization.

At the end of 'canons' issued by councils (for example, the Council of Trent*), anathemas were normally added against heretics. However, prior to Vatican I (1869–1870), 'heresy' was not so closely defined. It could cover not only wilful separation from church faith and unity, but also broader kinds of opposition to ecclesial authority and practice. In the terminology of Vatican I, an anathematized doctrine is understood to be heretical and its contradictory is to be defined as revealed truth. Vatican II (1962–1965), under the leadership of Pope John XXIII, decided to teach in a consistently positive and pastoral fashion and not to introduce any 'canons' anathematizing errors.

See also **Heresy.**

GERALD O'COLLINS

Angel, angelology

The word 'angel' comes from the Greek word *angelos*, messenger, a function apparent in NT descriptions of angels (Matt. 1.20; Luke 2.9ff.). In the OT the Hebrew word *mal'āk* is applied to both human (Gen. 32.3; Isa. 42.19; Mal. 2.7) and divine (Gen. 28.12; Zech. 1.9) messengers. A special category of references in the early strands of the Pentateuch is that which mentions the angel of the Lord, a being who embodies the glory of God himself (Gen. 16.7ff.; Ex. 23.20f.; Num. 22.22ff.; Judg. 6.11ff.; 13.6ff.). Reference is made in several OT passages to the celestial court of God, a belief probably derived from Canaanite mythology (Gen. 1.26; Isa. 6.1ff.; Ps. 82.1 and probably also Isa. 42.1).

In post-biblical literature there is evidence of an extensive development of angelology, in which good and bad angels make their appearance (e.g. I Enoch 6ff. and 9.1ff.). Some have suggested that this development may have been the result of foreign influence, but there can be little doubt that the raw material for such speculation is deeply rooted in the Jewish traditions. Angelic beings were believed to represent the nations of the world in heaven (Dan. 10.13; 10.21) as well as individuals (Matt. 18.10; Acts 12.15) and churches (Rev. 1–3). The archangel Michael was thought to have had a special responsibility as the guardian angel of Israel (Dan. 12.1; 1QM 17.5). In the apocalyptic and later mystical literature of Judaism angelic speculations reached extravagant proportions (III Enoch).

Early Christianity inherited Jewish beliefs about angels. In the NT there is evidence that the saving work of Christ is interpreted as a triumph over the angelic powers ('principalities and powers'), e.g. Eph. 1.20f.; Phil. 2.10f.; Col. 2.14f.; 1 Peter 3.20; Rev. 5.6. The supremacy of Christ over the angels is never in doubt (Col. 1.16; Rev. 5.9f.), though there were clearly problems in differentiating between Christ and the angels (Heb. 1–3). Angelomorphic categories contributed to the earliest beliefs about Jesus. Such a christology had a long history within primitive Christianity and may have contributed to the outlook which was later anathematized as Arianism*.

In later Christian thought there continued to be speculation about the nature and order of higher intelligences, but this contributed little to the mainstream of theological and christological development.

J. Barbel, *Christos Angelos*, 1964; H. Bietenhard, *Die himmlische Welt im Urchristentum und Spätjudentum*, 1951; A. W. Carr, *Angels and Principalities*, 1981; J. Daniélou, *A History of Early Christian Doctrine. Vol. 1: The Theology of Jewish Christianity*, ET 1964; H. Odeberg, *III Enoch*, reprinted 1973; E. E. Urbach, *The Sages: Their Concepts and Beliefs*, 1975.

CHRISTOPHER ROWLAND

Anglo-Catholicism

The epithet 'Anglo-Catholic' has been applied to the Church of England as a whole because of its claim to be the English branch of the Catholic Church, but it usually refers only to a party within the Anglican Communion which, though it had plenty of antecedents, became self-conscious and more or less identifiable from the time of the Oxford Movement* of the 1830s. This so-called Catholic revival within Anglicanism has passed through a number of phases. To begin with, it was mainly academic and centred in Oxford where Keble, Newman, Pusey and other contributors to the *Tracts for the Times* sought to affirm their church's apostolic character and its independence of the state in opposition to whiggish Erastianism. After Newman's secession in 1845 the Movement spread out into the parishes, where it laid emphasis on the sacraments and introduced unaccustomed or forgotten ritual and ceremonial into public worship. This led to Anglo-Catholics' being called 'ritualists'. Priests were prosecuted and even sent to prison for alleged lawlessness, but their cause seemed to thrive on persecution. Some Anglo-Catholics, especially in slum parishes, became Christian Socialists. Another outcome of the revival was the foundation of religious communities for both men and women. Originally and during its early phases the Movement was conservative and backward-looking both politically and theologically. A new phase opened when the authors of *Lux Mundi* (1889), led by Charles Gore, accepted and assimilated the critical study of the Bible and other liberal or modernizing developments. This process was carried further in the twentieth century with the publication of *Essays Catholic and Critical* (1926), though there continued to be a very conservative wing of the party which opposed all forms of Liberal Catholicism and Catholic Modernism*. Anglo-Catholicism was probably most popular, influential and flamboyant during the 1920s, when large and enthusiastic Anglo-Catholic Congresses were held in London and elsewhere, patronized now by many ecclesiastical dignitaries. But thereafter as an organized party it was weakened not only by theological differences but by disagreements with regard to Prayer Book revision and liturgical niceties. Meanwhile many of the ideas which the party represented had been spreading far and wide and were being disseminated throughout the Anglican Communion, raising its standards of worship everywhere and, in particular, popularizing the eucharist as the principal Sunday service. Anglo-Catholics have always had a concern for church unity even if their activities have often been divisive in effect: it has been reunion with Rome that they have chiefly desired, and few of them have been noted for a positive appreciation of the Protestant tradition. Although there are still Anglo-Catholic organizations and pressure groups, such as the Church Union, they now have more the appearance of a survival than of a revival.

Owen Chadwick, *The Mind of the Oxford Movement*, 1960; W. L. Knox and A. R. Vidler, *The Development of Modern Catholicism*, 1933; W. J. Sparrow Simpson, *The History of the Anglo-Catholic Revival from 1845*, 1932; Dieter Voll, *Catholic Evangelicalism*, 1963; N. P. Williams and C. Harris (eds), *Northern Catholicism*, 1933.

A. R. VIDLER

Angst

This term is best translated by the English 'dread'. In existentialist thought, it is the most fundamental affective state of human existents, disclosing human beings' precarious position between possibility and freedom, between what they are (facticity) and what they are obliged to become.

See **Existentialism; Phenomenology.**

JAMES RICHMOND

Anhomoeans

The term applied to the extreme Arians* (Aetius, Eunomius) who held that the Son was 'utterly unlike the Father'. The view was carried in some cases to the point at which the Son could not even know the Father. Since they lacked a common *ousia* (substance*), the sole relationship between them lay in the divine will.

See also **Homoeans; Homoeousians.**

H. E. W. TURNER

Anhypostasia

This abstract noun (never employed theologically in the patristic* era) is used to signify the idea that the human nature of Christ has no subject or concrete subsistence of its own. In the sixth-century debates over the Council of Chalcedon, defenders of the two-natures doctrine stressed the distinction between nature* and hypostasis* ('subject', 'subsistence'). They contended that Christ is one as being the one hypostasis which is the second 'person' of the Trinity*. This hypostasis, however, was the subject of two complete and distinct natures, divine and human. This did not mean, though, that the humanity of Christ was 'without hypostasis' – especially since, in the language of the time, *anhypostatos* meant either 'non-existent' or 'accidental'. 'We do not seek,' wrote Leontius of Jerusalem (*Adv. Nest.* 2.10), 'to show that the human being which the Lord is has no hypostasis . . . but that it does not have its own hypostasis . . . in separation from the Logos.' Leontius, followed by John of Damascus, taught that Christ's humanity is concrete and 'hypostatic' because it subsists in the divine Son. The term used to express this idea was *enhypostatos* (John of Damascus, *Dialectica* 44).

See also **Christology.**

R. A. NORRIS

Animism

The word (from Latin *anima*, soul or spirit) has been used in the history of religious thought in two senses: to refer generally to a belief in spiritual beings; and as a label for the religious systems of people not belonging to any of the great faiths. It was introduced into English by the Oxford anthropologist Edward Burnett Tylor, in an article on 'the religion of savages' in the *Fortnightly Review* of 15 August 1866. 'The theory which endows the phenomena of nature with personal life might perhaps be conveniently called Animism,' wrote Tylor, arguing that this represented an elementary religious phase of human society. In developing these ideas later Tylor made it clear that he had adopted and generalized a classic concept of vital principle (*anima humana*) held by the eighteenth-century physician Georg Ernst Stahl of Halle to be the central energizing and organizing force of the human body. Stahl's great work on medical theory was essentially designed as refutation of views interpreting human physiology in mechanistic and chemical terms, but he argued strongly that a reasoning spirit, a 'soul which thinks', controlled the operations of the body. It was perhaps this reasoning element in Stahl's theory, especially as interpreted by Lemoine in a controversy between French medical schools, which attracted Tylor, who held that in studying the early history of man we should always look for practical and intelligible motives for the habits and opinions of different peoples.

Looking for a common denominator in all religious systems, Tylor thought he had found it in animism; the belief in spiritual beings could be taken as a 'minimum definition of religion'. He divided the theory of animism into two main sections: ideas of the human soul, an animating, separable, surviving entity, the vehicle of individual personal existence; ideas of other spirits, non-human, from spirits of nature to the most powerful deities, affecting the life and prosperity of men and often involving active worship. Tylor tried to deal with religious phenomena in an ethnographic scheme and to avoid dogmatic emotional treatment from a fixed ethical standpoint. His analysis gave an important stimulus to the study of comparative religion, since he argued that animistic beliefs, though most prolific among the less developed cultures, could be identified in every form of human society. His approach was basically evolutionary. He argued, for example, that ideas of divinity were essentially developed from basic concepts of the soul, and that animism as a theory of personal causes developed into a philosophy of man and nature.

The notion of animism had its limitations. Tylor did not, as some of his critics alleged, deny that concepts of divinity in the form of a supreme or 'high' god existed in some societies otherwise set low in the cultural scale. But he made insufficient allowance in religious systems for belief in immaterial mystical forces or powers not specifically conceptualized in any personal way as spiritual beings. (This led R. R. Marett to apply to notions such as *mana* and taboo the term animatism, and to speak of preanimistic religion.) More sophisticated anthropological enquiry in the field has shown the concept of animism to be oversimplified, and too vague to serve as a distinguishing term for any particular religious category or system. For anthropologists it has now no more than historical interest. Animism has been replaced in anthropology by a range of more directly phenomenological descriptions of statements and actions relating to ideas of the human soul, nonhuman spirits, mystic powers, as expressed in varying social and ritual contexts.

Albert (J. A. F.) Lemoine, *Le Vitalisme et L'Animisme de Stahl*, 1864; R. R. Marett, *The Threshold of Religion*, 1909, [4]1929; E. G. Parrinder, 'Religions of Illiterate People', *Historia Religionum: Handbook for the History of Religions*, ed. C. Jonco Bleeker and Geo. Widengren, Vol. 2, 1971, pp. 551, 632ff.; Edward B. Tylor, *Primitive Culture*, two vols., 1871.

RAYMOND FIRTH

Anointing

The practice of pouring or smearing oil on the body or some parts of it is both ancient and common to many cultures. In the Middle East, oil was used from pre-Israelite times as a medicine and as a cosmetic (in which case it was often perfumed). Its association with health and beauty made anointing connote strength and glory when it was performed in a religious setting. Such ceremonial anointing was a ritual means of making persons sacred and investing them with spiritual power. Oil could even be used to consecrate objects, making them holy (cf. Ex. 30.22–32).

The OT speaks of the anointing of kings, priests and prophets. Kings received God's power to rule over Israel, and this divine selection as well as the reception of authority was reflected in the anointing of Saul (I Sam. 10.1), David (I Sam. 16.1–13) and Solomon (I Kings 1.34–39). Cultic priests were likewise literally anointed, for they were selected by God and given the authority to offer prayer and sacrifice on behalf of others (Ex. 28.41; Lev. 6.13ff.). The Bible speaks once of the literal anointing of prophets (I Kings 19.16), but more often anointing is used

metaphorically to signify selection and empowerment by God (Isa. 61.1; I Chron. 16.22).

In exilic and post-exilic times, there was a hope that God would restore a David-like king to a united and strengthened Israel (Isa. 9–11; Ezek. 37.24), or that God would send another 'anointed one' (Hebrew *mashiah*, Greek *christos*) to redeem his people (Isa. 40–55; Hos. 2). That person was sometimes identified with particular individuals (e.g. Cyrus in Isa. 45.1; Zerubbabel in Zech. 4.6–14), but their failure to inaugurate the kingdom of God * as a political entity gave the messianic hope eschatological * overtones and prepared the way for perceiving Jesus as the Christ (*see also* **Messiah**).

In Christian times, anointing became a sacrament of physical healing and spiritual strengthening (*see* **Unction**). An anointing with oil which signified the reception of the Holy Spirit very early became part of the rite of baptism *, and later became the separate sacrament of confirmation *. In the Middle Ages, a ceremony of anointing was added to the more ancient imposition of hands in the ordination * rite, and bishops likewise were consecrated with oil. Anointing in one form or another also became integral to the installation of royalty in many parts of mediaeval Europe, and is still retained as part of the coronation ceremony in England (*see also* **Chrism**).

C. Bouman, *Sacring and Crowning*, 1957; E. Kutsch, *Salbung als Rechtsakt im Alten Testament und im Alten Orient*, 1963; D. Lys, 'L'Onction dans la Bible', *ETR* 29, 1954, pp. 3–54; P. Murray, 'The Liturgical History of Extreme Unction', *Furrow* 11, 1960, pp. 572–93.

J. MARTOS

Anonymous Christianity

This term has been popularized by Karl Rahner to describe the situation of those who are justified by grace even while they remain outside the Christian community. His preferred term is 'anonymous Christians', since a number of his critics have agreed that anonymous Christians may well exist, but that anonymous Christianity is impossible.

The Second Vatican Council took a more optimistic view of the potential for salvation among those outside the church than had been common in many parts of the tradition. The most important of these comments is found in *Lumen Gentium* 16: 'Those can also attain to everlasting salvation who through no fault of their own do not know the gospel of Christ or his Church, yet sincerely seek God and, moved by his grace, strive by their deeds to do his will as it is known to them through the dictates of conscience. Nor does divine Providence deny the help necessary for salvation to those who, without blame on their part, have not yet arrived at an explicit knowledge of God, but strive to live a good life, thanks to his grace.'

This hopeful view of the salvation of those who are not church members, have not been baptized, do not confess Christ and even do not believe explicitly in God stands in contrast to the tradition from Cyprian that there is no salvation outside the church and also to the Augustinian pessimism which considers the mass of humanity damned for lack of baptism and faith. Rahner has worked to show how the new and the more traditional view of salvation can be reconciled.

The key to this understanding is found in Rahner's theology of grace. The universal salvific will of God is known not only in explicit faith, but already in a preconscious openness to the mystery of Being*, which can already be considered justifying and sanctifying grace, even if it still needs to come to full expression in the church. In one sense all humanity is confronted by the mystery of God's being, but Rahner reserves the term 'anonymous Christian' for that person who 'lives in a state of Christ's grace through faith, hope and love, yet who has no explicit knowledge of the fact that his life is oriented in grace-given salvation to Jesus Christ'.

Critics have complained that Rahner's concept of anonymous Christianity destroys the motivation for missionary work. But he argues that Christian mission * is possible only because the gospel confronts some reality already present in the life of the person. Other critics have accused Rahner of trying to rescue a declining Christendom or to impose religious belief on people against their will. But it is clear that Rahner's primary concerns are to expand on the suggestions made by Vatican II and to consider positively the religious life of the vast majority of humanity which does not embrace the gospel in any direct or explicit

way. The concept affirms that one cannot set limits to God's salvific activity, but even more positively that grace can be found widely in the world, and that such grace can be justifying and can lead to salvation even for those who do not possess all that the church has usually required.

Karl Rahner, 'Anonymous Christians', *Theological Investigations* VI, 1976, pp. 390–8; 'Anonymous Christianity and the Missionary Task of the Church', *Theological Investigations* XII, 1974, pp. 161–78; 'Observations on the Problem of the "Anonymous Christian"', *Theological Investigations* XIV, 1976, pp. 280–94; Anita Roper, *The Anonymous Christian*, 1976.

TIMOTHY F. LULL

Anthropology, Christian

Today this proves an expansive, untidy and constantly shifting doctrinal theme because: Christian anthropology has always partly reflected its own secular and ecclesiastical age, and the contemporary families of Christian piety and the types of national and ethnic culture are many; anthropology is now seen closely to intertwine with other major Christian doctrines; the theological enquiry into human existence abuts on to the ever mutable debates and findings about human life in the empirical sciences; the enquiry proceeds, rarely by deductive logic, but by a variety of methods which must somehow, and circumspectly, be correlated; historically and today, Christian anthropology derives from a wide and complex range of sources (e.g. OT, Stoicism, existential philosophy); the theological use of critically sifted material from OT and NT is a far from straightforward matter; and, of all the theological themes, anthropology involves the precarious and enigmatic aspect that *we* are both subject and object of our enquiry.

Until the eighteenth century most of the great, and tenaciously persisting, doctrinal systems took for granted dogmas about human beings based jointly on scriptural propositions and Graeco-Roman philosophical categories. But then new vistas and new challenges in European society prompted changes in assumptions, methods and substance, and Christian anthropology edged nervously towards a *self-critical* outlook. Seismic shifts began to take place:

from anthropological categories drawn from the Bible treated as an infallible encyclopaedia of the arts and sciences towards a handling of texts on literary, historical and theological criteria (e.g. J. Semler); from an anthropocentric philosophy towards a geo- and then cosmo-centric Christian framework; from a picture of reality as given, static and complete towards dynamic, evolutionary (and often naively progressivist) conceptions; from 'Christendom*' and theistic heteronomy as the controlling assumptions for human ideals and behaviour in law, education, etc., towards hopes and experiments in respect of the autonomy* of human beings; from androcentrism pointing to the consistent and continuing subordination of women in church and society towards, more recently, fugitive intimations of a post-sexist society and doctrine.

Thus the ethos of most, but not all, endeavours in theological anthropology has markedly changed. Instead of rehearsing a comprehensive and rounded theological anthropology already supplied from a revealed and authoritative source, it is now more a case of setting what we know about humankind from many sources in a theological perspective which seeks to provide it with final depth and meaning. But because of course this kind of openness to the sources of knowledge about human beings runs the risk of a 'progressive etching away of belief by enquiry', a Christian anthropology must hold fast to several primordial convictions, even if it does not always know how best (or at all) to articulate and defend them. Some modern writers have used a single category (e.g. christology*) by which to develop an anthropology, but this tends to pre-empt the appeal to rich and various empirical evidence. The theme must rather be attacked from different theological directions:

1. Human nature as *created*. Although human life is finite (expressed in weakness, ignorance and mortality), it is not the product of inscrutable fate or chance. Creation* is not the corrupted or emanated form of an ideal world, but the object of God's purposive and communicative love – and is good by nature. Thus the human being is not ultimately a tragic figure. However, human existence, as finite, is dependent on God as absolute being and is also subject

to all manner of causal determinants in the world.

2. Human nature as *social and political*. Much post-Reformation Christian thought has been too individualistic. For many earlier Christian thinkers, human life was social and corporate, exemplified as much in the public sphere as in private religion. Thus the communal worshipping church reflects the communality of God-as-Trinity; the zeal for the unity of the church is an anticipation of the unity of humankind. Responsibility for the political realm is therefore a *cantus firmus* in human existence, not a decorative postlude (*see* **Political Theology**, **Liberation Theology**).

3. Human nature as *sexual*. In some parts of the Christian tradition sexuality *per se* seems to be treated as evil. Does *agape* (self-sacrificial love) stand in final contrast to *eros* as self-affirmation? But selfless love and self-love can both be proper responses to God as creator of human life. The self-destructive spirit of modern romanticism is certainly alien to Christian ideas of the purposes of God. Labouring under the weight of a profoundly negative tradition, Christian thought has to forge new meanings in sexuality and, in overcoming androcentrism, understand afresh male and female.

4. Human nature as *culture-creating*. Philosophical idealism* in its many forms has imaged a human self that is ahistorical, spiritualized and introjected. This is also a danger if mysticism in Christian tradition is not contained in social and personalist bounds. Such views have little hope for history. 'As a whole there is no progress in history towards the Kingdom of God' (Althaus). At the opposite extreme, others have identified the coming of the kingdom* with mundane progress. But the creation of culture* can be affirmed as a distinctively human enterprise congruous with God's fulfilment of his creative and redemptive purposes in and for history (cf. Teilhard de Chardin's 'formation of the noosphere').

5. Human nature as *equal among persons*. On the basis of living in a common history and for a common destiny before God, ethnocentrism and other discriminations are transcended. Such an emergent view in the OT is developed in the NT, in terms of Christ's acceptance of all as less-than-human sinners *and* potential heirs of God. These provide starting-points for contem-

porary theological grounding of human rights.

6. Human nature as *part of nature*. Christian tradition has often tended to sever human beings from the natural order. This has given to human beings too great a sense of their own importance over nature and has assumed that God values them at the expense of microscopic and macroscopic wonder. But the world is a structural whole by virtue of being the realm of God's creativity. Ecological awareness has helped to restore this more unified picture of humankind-in-and-of-nature (*see also* **Nature and Theology**).

7. Human nature as *religious*. Some writers (e.g. Kraemer) sharply contrast religion and Christianity. Others (e.g. Cantwell Smith) seem to envisage 'faith' as the constant and different religious systems as variables. Although phenomenological discussion of 'religion' is complicated by the variety of definitions given to the term, it is often used to express a unique type of awareness of the holy, utterly distinct from theoretical understanding, and common to all people.

8. Human nature as *moral*. By general or by special revelation*, or as a natural capacity, human beings receive from God the capacity to appreciate his moral attributes (love, justice, holiness, etc.), and to live, make decisions and develop a moral sense (conscience*), in the power of the Spirit. This moral capacity is part of human life's real but limited freedom. Christian existentialists emphasize the ever-renewed decisions of faith and love as the quintessential pre-condition for authentic life.

9. Human nature as *unfulfilled*. As human beings are, both to their advantage and disadvantage, biologically incomplete, 'not a fixed form of animal' (Nietzsche), so this paradox is experienced at all levels of human existence. In different ways Christian thinkers have seen the gift of immortality and/or resurrection as the reversal or transformation of incomplete human life into a fulfilment in the nearer presence of God. 'We'll swim in milk and honey till we drown' (Elinor Wylie). Whether a few, some, many or all shall be admitted to such a destiny has traditionally been a matter of tense dispute. Though Christians share similar hopes with e.g., Jews and Moslems, the Christian hope* is often theologically focussed on the resur-

rection* of Christ (*see also* **Life after Death**).

So far the focus has been on themes in theological anthropology which mix all-too-human finitude with higher potential and promise. But a note of deeper pessimism is introduced by reference to human nature as *fallen*, a condition which affects all aspects of human existence. The Fall*, whether a pre-mundane catastrophe or a historical event at the dawn of collective or individual human moral consciousness, or interpreted figuratively, refers to profound disorder in the self, and in society and beyond, arising from a prideful assertion of sovereignty by human beings. According to the doctrine of original sin*, everyone participates in this fallen world, though whether each is also 'guilty' has been a moot point among theologians. If theologians have also disagreed about the cause, locus and degree of this disorder, if they have disagreed about the effect of sin upon that 'image of God' which characterizes human beings as created by God, all agree that the central theme of Christian theology is the fact of, and the remedy for, this disordered reality and broken image.

It is, all in all, appropriate to describe human existence, in its contradictions and ambiguities, as irreducibly mysterious, as at once dignified and miserable, as human but less than human. To refer to 'mystery' is not to plead for theological silence; it *is* to warn of the dangers of excessive confidence and precision in theological anthropology. Nonetheless the notion of 'mystery' suggests that human life does transcend the temporal system.

Christian thought has often turned to the historical Jesus as the exemplar of true humanity (*see also* **Imitation of Christ**). Where piety may move freely, theology must exercise caution. Is an imitable Jesus historically recoverable or psychologically desirable? Is it wiser to pursue themes of having the 'mind of Christ' and being 'in union with Christ' as these are explicated and imaged in countless ways in Christian tradition and life? In the fullest theological sense, Christ is said to be the 'proper man' because he, as Lord, possesses the dignity that is recoverable for human beings.

Those who regard the human situation before God as serious but not parlous will see humans in need of moral correction and education. The more serious the human condition, the greater and deeper is the divine response of grace and forgiveness required. In this case the cross becomes more than a symbol of divine goodwill. It is seen as an actual acceptance by God of humanity in its lack of humanness, and then a renewed creation of human freedom to share in altering the course and content of history seen as a divine-human history of salvation. For this approach, suffering* is the key both to the present human condition and to its overcoming.

At times, theological anthropology has been so dominated by the doctrine of God* as to lose its own proper content and qualities (cf. K. Barth's account of divine providence). The giving of rich human content to theological anthropology (as in K. Rahner; and cf. borderlands between theology and literature, psychology, etc.) has been an indisputable gain. This was, in motive, a merit of theological existentialism, though it was too individualistic and introverted. If theological anthropology is to engage with the arts and sciences about the nature of humanity, it must openly meet philosophical issues of determinism and reductionism in the natural and social sciences, and the implications of e.g. the new genetics for the control and alteration of human beings. It is not enough to rely on a *post mortem* justification for Christian claims; those claims refer as much, in principle, to historical existence where human beings are already seen, in Christian tradition, not as full of wisdom, but as loved for their worth in God's sight. Collisions, practical and theoretical, between human and scientific-pragmatic horizons of life will become more common and more severe if a functional and manipulative ethos continues to dominate a technical culture.

R. Alves, *A Theology of Human Hope*, 1969; E. Brunner, *Man in Revolt*, ET 1939; R. Bultmann, *Existence and Faith*, ET 1961; D. S. Cairns, *The Image of God in Man*, 1973; M. d'Arcy, *Humanism and Christianity*, 1969; R. W. Hepburn, 'Optimism, Finitude and the Meaning of Life', in B. Hebblethwaite and S. Sutherland (eds), *The Philosophical Frontiers of Christian Theology*, 1982; P. J. Jewett, *Man as Male and Female*, 1975; G. Kaufman, *Systematic Theology*, 1968, Part 3; E. W. Kemp (ed), *Man Fallen and Free*, 1969; K. Rahner, *Theological Investigations*, Vol. 13, ET 1975; Pierre Teilhard de Chardin, *The Future of Man*, ET 1964; H. Thielicke, *Theologische Ethik*, II/I, 1955, pp. 328–58.

A. O. DYSON

Anthropomorphism

The representation of something other than man – e.g. the sea, an animal, a computer, or God – as possessing quasi-human characteristics. In its wider use, this is a matter of attributing not only something like human form or shape, but also something like human attitudes, feelings, characteristics, actions and intentions to non-human entities. In the case of talk about God, many such uses are clearly metaphorical, as indeed is the use of inanimate or animal imagery such as 'rock' or 'lion'. To speak of the 'hand' or 'eye' of God or of God 'walking in the garden in the cool of the day' is metaphorical talk. Aquinas held that not all anthropomorphic talk of God is metaphorical. Such talk *is* metaphorical when the words used contain 'imperfections' (e.g. corporeality) in their very meaning, as do those mentioned above. But anthropomorphism is not wholly metaphorical, when perfections such as love, wisdom, mind, or actions such as creating, reconciling, transforming are ascribed to God. These are analogies that may literally be ascribed to God, since their human exemplification, from which admittedly we learn their meaning initially, is only one mode in which they may be exercised. Imperfection is not of their essence. Indeed, in reality, they are applied most properly to God and only derivatively to man. Analogical anthropomorphism in talk of God is justified, on this view, by the doctrine that man is made in the image of God. Notwithstanding all the qualifications that have to be made in transferring the sense of words first used of man to the transcendent, infinite and 'incomprehensible' God, there nevertheless exists a resemblance between God and man made in his image that legitimates those personal analogies that are not, as metaphors are, inextricably bound up with imperfection. The propriety of such anthropomorphism is enhanced in Christian theism by the doctrine of the Incarnation*, according to which God anthropomorphizes himself in becoming man.

G. B. Caird, *The Language and Imagery of the Bible*, 1980, ch. 10; G. F. Woods, *Theological Explanation*, 1958, Parts III and IV.

BRIAN HEBBLETHWAITE

Antinomianism

A term (*anti*, against, *nomos*, the law) introduced by Luther in a sharp disagreement with a younger colleague, Johannes Agricola, but describing a theory and practice recurrent in Christian history. Antinomianism rejects the moral law in general and the Decalogue in particular as regulative for Christian behaviour. The reasons vary in its multifarious expressions: a rigorist interpretation of justification * by faith holds that the teaching of the law is not necessary in evoking repentance or guiding the believer in moral choices; a reliance on the power of the Holy Spirit * to direct the actions of the believer declares moral norms to be unnecessary; a stress upon personal election concludes that those so chosen are not bound by moral law, nor is their deviance from it held against them; some pantheist * and mystical perspectives asserting the unity of God with creation or with souls rightly sensitized to that fusion hold moral injunctions to be spiritual detours; gnostic * beliefs that deny the significance of the physical and historical infer that moral mandates touching these areas are not binding (the same gnostic presuppositions can take the alternative direction of radical asceticism); a confidence that a benevolent will can bring together love and the facts in each decision-making moment precludes the intrusion of moral laws. Some antinomians, while rejecting the use of law for believers, acknowledge its validity for the wider community (natural law), especially as it is necessary for civil order.

Antinomian tendencies appeared in some NT communities and were addressed accordingly (I Cor. 5.1–6; Eph. 5.5–6; II Tim. 3.1–13; Titus 1.10–16f.; II Peter 3.16; Rev. 2.2, 14–15, 20), and Paul struggled with critics who seemed to have suggested that antinomianism followed from his views on justification (Rom. 3.8, 31; Rom. 6.12–23). In the early centuries of Christianity marginal groups like the Adamites, the Satanists and the Cainites held to recognizably antinomian views. In the Middle Ages the Brethren of the Free Spirit espoused these opinions.

During the Reformation the views of Agricola called forth Luther's vigorous defence of the Ten Commandments and his denial that the proclamation of the sufferings of Christ and justification by faith were sufficient to bring repentance and give adequate direction to Christian conduct. The seventeenth century in England produced a variety of sects that espoused antinomian views, the most vocal being the Ranters, who acquired a reputation for the rhetoric and practice of licentiousness. At the same time in North America Anne Hutchinson became the centre of 'the antinomian controversy' by her juxtaposition of the 'covenant of grace' and the 'covenant of works.' The term is used currently as a charge against situation ethics, and is in a wider sense applied to movements in culture that are critical of received moral norms or structures.

Antinomianism has been resisted in classical Christian traditions on the grounds that: 1. its naïveté about human nature removes mandates and controls needed also in the life of faith and love (the believer as *simul justus et peccator* *); 2. sole attention to the indicatives (from election and justification to the presence of the Spirit) eliminates the imperatives integral to the biblical dialectic and responsible human conduct; 3. the exclusive emphasis on grace and the gospel in theoretical antinomianism neglects the call to obedience that cannot be separated from the invitation to trust; 4. while good works do not save, unrepented and self-congratulating bad works do condemn; 5. the excision of moral law from Christian preaching and pedagogy weakens the general state of social responsibility.

C. F. Adams, *The Antinomian Controversy*, 1892, 1976; G. Huehns, *Antinomianism in English History*, 1951; M. Luther, *Against the Antinomians*, 1539.

GABRIEL FACKRE

Antinomy

An 'antinomy' occurs in philosophical thought when each of a pair of apparently contradictory propositions seems to be conclusively proved to be true. Since they cannot coherently be conjointly maintained, the antinomy demands solution. Attempts may be made to show that the assumptions and reasoning used in the proofs are unsatisfactory or that the alleged contradiction is not a genuine one. If no such solution appears possible, then the conclusion to be drawn is that in this case reason is attempting to deal with matters which lie beyond its competence. It is in this latter respect that Immanuel Kant (1724–1804) puts forward four antinomies in *The Critique of Pure Reason* (1781). These are 1. that the world is limited both spatially and temporally *and* that it is infinite; 2. that everything is either simple or is composed of parts which are simple *and* that there are no simple substances; 3. that causality according to the laws of nature in not sufficient to explain all that happens *and* that everything occurs solely according to the laws of nature; 4. that an absolutely necessary being exists either as a part of the world or as its cause *and* that no such being exists. Presenting in each case what he claims (and critics have disputed) to be conclusive proofs for both the thesis and its antithesis, Kant considers that the antinomies indicate some of the proper limits of human reason and in particular the impossibility of a metaphysical grasp of the nature of reality as it is in itself and as a whole and of God as its ground.

S. J. Al-Azm, *The Origins of Kant's Argument in the Antinomies*, 1972; C. D. Broad, *Kant, An Introduction*, ed. C. Lewy, 1978; P. F. Strawson, *The Bounds of Sense*, 1966.

DAVID A. PAILIN

Antiochene Theology

'Antiochene theology' is a modern categorization, referring to a particular christological and exegetical approach which was associated with the ancient patriarchate of Antioch and seems to have developed in response to Arianism* and Apollinarianism*. Whether it had roots in older Antiochene tendencies (e.g. Paul of Samosata) is a matter of dispute; even a direct connection with Eustathius is difficult to substantiate in view of the complicated political situation in the Antiochene church in the fourth century. The principal representatives of Antiochene theology were Diodore of Tarsus, the teacher of John Chrysostom, Theodore of Mopsuestia and Theodoret of Cyrrhus, the friend and defender of Nestorius. The reputation of all three has suffered through association with Nestorianism*, but there has been a reassessment in modern times, not least of

the theology of Nestorius himself. This reassessment has pronounced favourably upon two features of Antiochene theology: 1. its stress on the genuine and complete humanity of Christ, who had to advance in moral goodness and achieve a moral victory for mankind as man, and 2. its stress upon literal and historical interpretation of scripture in reaction against allegorism. In fact a primary concern of Antiochene theologians was defence of the *homoousion**, and stress on Christ's complete humanity was a device to protect his full, changeless and passionless divinity. The proper character of each of the two natures had to be preserved. The 'hypostatic union' taught by Cyril of Alexandria was treated with suspicion because it seemed to introduce change and mixture into the divine and to resurrect Apollinarianism (*see* **Alexandrian Theology**). In their turn the Antiochenes were accused of reducing the saviour to a 'mere man' or preaching 'two sons' by dividing the natures.

See also **Christology**.

FRANCES YOUNG

Anxiety *see* **Angst**

Apocalypse

A literary composition found in Jewish, early Christian and Gnostic* literature. The apocalypse purports to offer revelations of divine mysteries (cf. Rev. 1.1). These revelations are given by a variety of means; the result of a heavenly ascent, angelic communications, dream-visions etc. The Jewish (and many of the Christian) apocalypses are pseudonymous (Rev. is a notable exception) and are attributed to biblical heroes (e.g. Enoch, Abraham, Isaiah and the Apostles).

See also **Apocalyptic**.

John J. Collins (ed), *Apocalypse: Morphology of a Genre* (Semeia 14), 1979.

CHRISTOPHER ROWLAND

Apocalyptic

Apocalyptic or apocalypticism is a word used in two senses: 1. as an adjective to describe works or ideas; 2. as a noun. In this latter usage it refers to a pattern of thought in religion exhibiting particular characteristics. In both cases the opening words of the book of Revelation in the NT (Revelation or Apocalypse of Jesus Christ) are determinative. Comparison with the form, claims and ideas of Revelation have led to the use of the term 'apocalyptic' in a wide range of contexts to speak of similar phenomena in other writings. Among the Jewish literature written round about the beginning of the Christian era there is a group of writings which resembles, at least in general terms, the book of Revelation in both form (i.e. the claim to be a revelation of divine secrets) and content. As far as content is concerned, two major approaches to this problem may be found in contemporary discussion.

1. There are those (e.g. Vielhauer, Hanson) who consider that apocalyptic or apocalypticism is best understood as a strand of thought within Jewish eschatology* emerging from a particular sociopolitical matrix. It represents the views of those who have despaired of seeing the Jewish hope for a reign of God on earth being manifested in this world. Instead they look for a realm of a transcendent kind which could only be established as a result of a divine irruption into the present order to overthrow it and its evils. It is said to be a type of Jewish hope which differs from the materialist/nationalist eschatology prevalent in other Jewish writings, particularly the rabbinic corpus. The main features of this religious outlook can be summarized in the following way: a doctrine of the two ages (II Esd. 7.50); a pessimistic attitude towards the present age; the other-worldly character of the new age; universalism; a deterministic attitude towards history, and an imminent expectation of the kingdom* of God (Syriac Bar. 85.10).

2. By contrast, it is suggested that an understanding of apocalyptic which speaks of it as a type of eschatological belief with fairly clear characteristics does not do justice to the religious outlook of both Jewish and Christian apocalypses. What is more, the eschatological material in these works does not by any means conform to the outline given above. This view takes more account of the claim made in these works to offer disclosures of divine mysteries and attaches less importance to the disparate material said to be revealed in them. An essential mark of the apocalyptic outlook is said to be its quest for 'higher wisdom through revelation' (Hengel), so that it forms part of the emerging irrational element in the religion of the Hellenistic age. Such an approach to apocalyptic recognizes the variety of material contained in the apocalypses (e.g. information about the heavenly world, angels*, the stars, theodicy*, as well as eschatology), while stressing that the writers of the apocalypses believed that this information was divulged by means of divine revelation*. Thus the claim to revelation and the knowledge of divine mysteries is the distinctive mark of apocalyptic, and the presence of this outlook in the apocalypses marks them off from other Jewish works of this period.

P. D. Hanson, *The Dawn of Apocalyptic*, [2]1979; M. Hengel, *Judaism and Hellenism*, ET 1974; C. C. Rowland, *The Open Heaven*, 1982; D. S. Russell, *The Method and Message of Jewish Apocalyptic*, 1964; M. E. Stone, *Scriptures, Sects and Visions*, 1980; P. Vielhauer, 'Apocalypses and Related Subjects', *New Testament Apocrypha*, ET ed. E. Hennecke, W. Schneemelcher and R. McL. Wilson, Vol. II, 1965, pp. 581–607.

CHRISTOPHER ROWLAND

Apocatastasis
see **Restoration of All Things**

Apocrypha

A division of the canon* of scripture, printed in Protestant Bibles, if it is printed at all, between the OT and NT. It generally includes the following: I and II Esdras, Tobit, Judith, Additions to Esther, Wisdom, Ecclesiasticus, Baruch and the Epistle of Jeremiah, Additions to Daniel, viz. The Song of the Three, Susanna, Bel and the Dragon; then the Prayer of Manasseh and finally I and II Maccabees. The Common Bible, which effects a compromise between Catholic and Protestant usage, includes all the foregoing (though not in that order) plus Psalm 151 and III and IV Maccabees.

At the beginning of the Christian era the canon of scripture was not firmly defined by the Jews. The Jews of Palestine read as authoritative a selection of books entirely written in Hebrew (with some small Aramaic sections). Jews of the Dispersion mostly read the Bible in Greek and were accustomed to use a wider selection of books, some of which had no Semitic original. Furthermore, the Greek version of Daniel and Esther was substantially longer than the Semitic equivalent. The Christians also for the most part read the Bible in Greek and it was this wider selection which they also acknowledged.

Judaism, allegedly at the Council of Jamnia in AD 90, eventually defined the canon rather narrowly, not only confining it to books originally written in Hebrew/Aramaic but rejecting all works, of whatever language, which did not appear to have been written in the period of inspiration*, held to end with Ezra. By following these principles the Jews excluded a number of works to which Christians had found it congenial to appeal. The church never formally defined its canon of the OT but continued in practice to use the larger body of literature previously current in Hellenistic Judaism.

This position remained unquestioned until Jerome in the fourth century was asked to prepare a new Latin translation of the Bible. This obliged him to decide which text, and from what language he was to translate; i.e. was he to translate from the LXX, itself a translation, or from the Hebrew? After a false start on a translation from the Greek he eventually took the Hebrew as his exemplar, but that raised a further question: what of the books which had no Hebrew exemplar, and those which the Jews did not regard as canonical?

Jerome's answer was to suggest keeping the books of the Jewish canon together, as 'Old Testament', and placing the rest in a separate division of the canon, to be called the Apocrypha (and implicitly treating the latter as of lesser authority). This suggestion did not at the time meet with favour but it was revived at the Reformation*. Luther had the Apocrypha printed in a separate section. Calvin went further and declared the apocryphal books to be of no authority at all; a position restated in the Westminster Confession. The Thirty-nine Articles* (Article 6) declare the Apocrypha worthy to be read but not to be used to establish doctrine. The Council of Trent* reacted by reasserting the full canonicity of all the books of the Vulgate, which included nearly all the ones called 'apocryphal' by Protestants. (They did not include I and II Esdras or the Prayer of Manasseh, though these were added to the Vulgate as an appendix.)

The British and Foreign Bible Society in 1827 decided not to include the Apocrypha in their printed Bibles. Since they were and are a major Bible publisher this decision has greatly affected the use of the Apocrypha among Protestants.

The Apocrypha is effectively a collection of books emanating from the inter-testamental period. Whatever may be said of their status as scripture, their usefulness as historical source materials is beyond dispute.

———

L. H. Brockington, *A Critical Introduction to the Apocrypha*, 1961; O. Eissfeldt, *The Old Testament, an Introduction*, ET 1965, pp. 571ff.

H. MCKEATING

Apocryphal Gospels, Acts, etc

This refers to a varied body of partly popular, partly sectarian writings from the first three centuries which claim a formal relation to the canonical NT and purport to supplement, interpret and revise understanding of the Christian tradition. (The word apocryphal is unhelpful, especially if it implies an analogy with OT apocrypha*.) Such movements of thought are already evident within the NT itself: the Fourth Gospel as a variation on the synoptic type, the deutero-Pauline letters as a revision of the Pauline teaching, and Revelation as an attempt to change Christian awareness. Statements in the early Fathers, and fragmentary quotations, indicate their knowledge of an extensive variant literature on the life and teaching of Jesus, on the supposed teaching and actions of the several apostles, and on the apocalyptic visions of persons as various as Isaiah and Peter. Recent manuscript discoveries have produced ample evidence for the early existence of material ranging from fragmentary Gospels and sayings of Jesus to elaborate religious treatises. Some of this was composed of prodigies and romance (like the Infancy Gospels and the Acts of Paul and Thecla) to satisfy popular taste. More seriously, the elaborate apocalypses served the needs of Christian minority groups within a hostile community, and put them in possession of an inexhaustible mystery which guaranteed their part in a great design. Those sections of the material which tell of Jesus and his teaching may possibly preserve some historical memories, though it has been the custom to reject them as historically worthless and heretical. But since it is no longer possible to speak with simple confidence about the historical status of the canonical Gospels, it is irrelevant to assess the apocryphal Gospels as historical sources. Nor does it say much to describe them as heretical when we hesitate to affirm that primitive Christian thought began with a coherent (though undeveloped) orthodoxy and grew by repelling perversions of it. These Gospels are often modestly or strongly Gnostic (*see* **Gnosticism**). Some rely on an elaborate cosmogony*, with heavenly journeys and semi-magical key-words; but others attempt to work out with the help of fashionable Hellenistic religious language the consequences for self-awareness of the Christian offer of knowledge of God in Christ. The Gospel of Thomas does so by means of genuine, adapted or invented sayings of Jesus. The Gospel of Truth (possibly Valentinian) is a sustained meditation somewhat in the Johannine manner on the human predicament, caught between truth and error. The Gospel of Philip is mystical devotion with moments of particular beauty. These Gospels can therefore now be studied in their own right. They can even be read (though not with universal approval) as a powerful alternative to the 'orthodox' tradition, asserting the superiority of Gnostic secret traditions over those of the priests and bishops, and finding the way of salvation* through self-knowledge rather than through ecclesial obedience. These Gospels may have been wrong-headed but they posed serious questions to orthodox theologians.

Texts with introductions in E. Hennecke – W. Schneemelcher, *New Testament Apocrypha* (two vols), ET ed. R. McL. Wilson, 1963, 1965; *The Nag Hammadi Library*, ed. J. M. Robinson, 1977; see also E. Pagels, *The Gnostic Gospels*, 1979.

KENNETH GRAYSTON

Apollinarianism *see* **Christology**

Apologetics

In the history of Christian theology, this means the defence, by argument, of Christian belief against external criticism or against other world views. Such argument usually takes the critics' questions or the problems posed by the philosophy and culture of the age as its starting point, and looks for some common ground or shared criteria of rationality or morality, in terms of which

to build up the case for Christianity against objections.

There are many kinds of apologetic. The Christian may argue philosophically in defence of the greater reasonableness of belief in the existence of God. He may argue religiously in defence of the greater spiritual power of a religion of redemption. He may argue morally in defence of the greater moral force of incarnational belief. He may argue historically in defence of the historicity of the Gospel narratives. He may attempt to argue for the compatibility of Christianity and modern science, or indeed for the greater intelligibility of the cosmos in terms of creationist belief.

The dangers of apologetics are obvious: the blurring of differences, the subjection of Christian truth to alien standards of judgment, the more or less surreptitious control of theological interpretation by some particular philosophy. In twentieth-century theology, Karl Barth has maintained the most uncompromising hostility to all apologetics. For Barth, there is no common ground, no point of connection outside Christian revelation for the apologist to appeal to. Preacher and theologian alike must think and speak purely on the basis of divine revelation, which creates its own conditions of intelligibility in the response of faith.

It is hard to see how such a position can get off the ground, let alone remain a viable option. The Christian gospel itself presupposes the capacity in man to recognize not only the reality of God but the moral and religious power of the Christ event. Factors inhibiting such recognition include beliefs and attitudes open to rational and moral criticism, and it is incumbent upon Christian theologians both to make a case against alternative world-views and to answer criticism. Only so is the humanity of the critic of Christianity taken seriously.

Examples of apologetics include Paul's sermon on the Areopagus (Acts 17.22–31); Justin Martyr's *Disputation with Trypho* the Jew; Athenagoras' *Supplication* to the Roman Emperor, Marcus Aurelius; Augustine's *City of God*, written in reply to pagans who attributed the fall of Rome in 410 to the abandonment of their religion; Thomas Aquinas' *Summa Contra Gentiles*, written for Christian missionaries in dispute with Muslim theology; Joseph Butler's *The An-*

alogy of Religion (1736), written in refutation of deism*; F. D. E. Schleiermacher's *Religion: Speeches to its Cultured Despisers* (1793); and J. H. Newman's *An Essay in Aid of a Grammer of Assent* (1870). Among twentieth-century exponents of apologetics may be mentioned P. Tillich, who developed the method of correlation*, by which Christian doctrine may be shown to answer man's existential questions, and W. Pannenberg, who has insisted, against Barth, that it is the duty of Christian theology to argue with modern atheism and 'to let theology be discussed without reservations in the context of critical rationality'. Fine examples of modern R C apologetics are to be found in Hans Küng's *On Being a Christian* and *Does God Exist?*

A. Richardson, *Christian Apologetics*, 1947; B. Mitchell, *The Justification of Religious Belief*, 1973; W. Pannenberg, *Basic Questions in Theology, Vol III*, ET 1973, ch. 3.

BRIAN HEBBLETHWAITE

Apophatic Theology

Both a way of talking about God and a method of approaching God by looking beyond all created categories of sensation and thought to the God who can in no way be conceptualized. Apophatic theology is characteristic of Eastern Christian thought, going back to Clement of Alexandria and Origen.

Though the early church had affirmed the basic unknowability of God the Father even in scripture ('No one knows the Father, save the Son,' Matt. 11.27), it was not until the conflict with late Arianism* that this unknowability became an issue. Eunomius and his followers seem to have found God as comprehensible to human minds as he is to himself. Over against this, first Basil the Great and then Gregory of Nyssa argued that not only is the essence of God even in theory unknowable, but the essence of even such a tiny creature as the ant is unknowable as well. Indeed, central to the theology of Gregory of Nyssa is his view of the Christian life as a progression through the stages of purification (the defeat of the passions and the restoration of the image of God) and illumination (in which one sees God in the cleansed mirror of the soul) in order to reach the highest stage, in which the soul, longing more and more for God, realizes God's unutterable otherness and transcendence with respect to all created things. Using the symbol of the divine darkness which Moses entered on Sinai when he went to meet God, Gregory makes it clear that only within this darkness, after intellectual and sense impressions have been stripped away, does the soul come as close to God as it can, by faith. Evagrius Ponticus, a follower of both Origen and the Cappadocians, and one of the fourth century's most influential writers on the spiritual life, speaks of this highest union with God as 'pure prayer'. Pure prayer is communion with God without words or images of any kind, in which a person is rendered unconscious of anything except the God who lies beyond all that is created.

Pseudo-Dionysius, writing most likely in the first part of the sixth century, distinguishes between cataphatic theology, which has as its object the intelligible names of God revealed in scripture, and apophatic theology. Cataphatic theology involves contemplation of God as he is in relation to the world, beginning with the most universal names, such as 'the Good', 'Being', and 'Life'. But Dionysius insists that while these names provide us with real knowledge of God, they are themselves only provisional, for though all that is has its existence in him and his nameable characteristics, he himself lies beyond them. Thus, he is 'Life', but yet more truly beyond life. Where cataphatic theology involves an ever increasing movement of the mind towards a positive understanding of God in relation to creation, it is only an introduction to apophatic theology. Apophatic theology moves towards God by asserting that he is not, in fact, any of the things he is called. This movement is from the physical creation through the intelligible to a union with God in the divine darkness which lies beyond concept.

Vladimir Lossky, 'The Divine Darkness', *The Mystical Theology of the Eastern Church*, 1957.

ROBERTA C. BONDI

Apostasy

The deliberate disavowal of belief in Christ made by a formerly believing Christian. The most famous apostate was probably the Emperor Julian (332–363).

R. P. C. HANSON

Apostle, Apostolicity

The fact that some later polemics concerning apostolic succession * have been waged around the NT concept of apostle has not aided the clarification of certain historical questions associated with this term in the earliest church. It occurs eighty times in the NT writings and only very infrequently outside that corpus in the whole of extant Greek literature. To trace the history of the term is, therefore, to follow one particular thread of early Christian self-understanding through various stages of its development. In particular, the relation of the term to the Jewish *shaliah* institution has definite implications for the nuances that came to be attached to it in later Christian reflection.

1. *Linguistic Considerations*. Though the word originally had nautical associations in early Greek usage, it occurs in Herodotus (I, 21; IV, 38) in the sense of messenger, and in some Egyptian papyri as late as the eighth century AD it has a similar meaning. This suggests that it may well have been an accepted secular term at the period of the NT, even though we do not have any literary or epigraphic evidence to support such a view. Certainly the NT writings give it great currency, and even though the preponderance of the occurrences are in Paul and Luke, the fact that it appears at least once in eight other NT writings strongly suggests that it was a common term in early Christian parlance of quite different backgrounds. Though, as we shall see, the word is not used exclusively for the leaders of the church, statistical evidence alone would seem to support Cerfaux's conclusion that the early church's strong sense of mission together with its desire to have an appropriate designation for the first leaders of the new movement, caused an obscure Greek word, with very little prior history, to emerge as a technical term.

2. *Apostolos and the Jewish Shaliah institution*. While earlier scholars, going back to John Lightfoot in 1675, had suggested association between the Christian apostle and the *shaliah* institution of Judaism, the idea has recently received widespread acceptance (mainly through the writing of K. H. Rengstorf, *TDNT* I, pp. 407–46). There are, nevertheless, a number of difficulties about such an easy identification, however appealing it might appear for dogmatic reasons with its emphasis on authoritative and legal commissioning. The evidence for such an institution in the NT period is lacking both in Jewish and Christian sources, and the idea of mission, so central to the NT, is not at all characteristic of the Jewish usage, where instead the notion of legal administrator for a particular task is predominant. This does not exclude the possibility that both emphases are only different aspects of a common institution of first-century Jews and Christians (Barrett). However, to build any elaborate theory on such a suggestion – or equally on the suggestion of a Gnostic * origin – would call for much clearer evidence from the first century than would seem likely to become available. One is, therefore, on more solid grounds in examining the NT writings on their own terms in order to decipher various nuances and suggest possible internal lines of development.

3. *Paul, an Apostle of Jesus Christ*. Paul knows of groups existing in the early Jerusalem church prior to his own call who could be designated apostles (I Cor. 15.7; Gal. 1.17). Nevertheless, when all due allowance is made for these references, the one coming to him in the tradition, the other occurring in a polemical passage, it is as a self-designation that the term has special importance for him, often with the qualifier 'of Jesus Christ', a possessive genitive denoting a special relationship of intimacy, which Paul elsewhere describes as having seen the risen Christ (I Cor. 9.1; 15.8). The context is both eschatological and christological, since Paul the apostle understands his function to be that of making present by a gift or call from God the activity and person of Christ through his own ministry of preaching the good news of salvation (Rom. 1.1; II Cor. 5.16–20; Gal. 2.19f.). Apostle is, then, the term that Paul chooses to express most appropriately his own role in the divine mystery or plan for mankind, as this had been revealed in Christ. It has been suggested that by focussing on Paul's apostolate, as both the starting point and criterion for understanding the term's origin and history, one is in danger of adopting an over-rigid line of development that cannot be historically substantiated. In speaking of those 'who were apostles *before* me' (Gal. 1.17), Paul included some members of the Twelve as well as James and Barnabas (Gal. 1.19; 2.7–

9). He thereby implicitly recognizes that the term was current as a designation for others whose apostolate could not be identical with his own, either in terms of its origin or scope. Besides, Paul's usage elsewhere allows for such flexibility, for he speaks of the 'apostles of the churches' (II Cor. 8.23) for what appears to be a limited mission in relation to a particular task. It would seem likely, therefore, that we are dealing with an older, pre-Pauline term, which Paul with characteristic enthusiasm has brought into prominence because of his own unique and assured awareness of his mission. But this raises the question of where the term first became current for various prominent people in the early church, if Paul had found it already to hand.

4. *The Twelve Apostles*. One answer to that question that is often repeated, following Rengstorf's article, is that the term originated with the historical Jesus' temporary mission of the Twelve in Galilee, a mission that was subsequently confirmed after Easter. In this view, there is both continuity and discontinuity between the two sendings, in that both imply a mission, but the later sending is of a different order since it is universal in scope and has the risen Christ as its authoritative warrant. As has been suggested already, there are difficulties about the *shaliah* hypothesis in relation to the Gospel usage, and more recent studies of the Gospels from a redaction-critical point of view stress the distinctive presentation of the individual Synoptists in their usage of the term. In general the tendency is to see all uses of the term as belonging to the final, redactional strata of the Gospels, and this would mean that the term does not have its origins in the actual ministry of Jesus. Mark has one, almost casual usage at 6.30, where it could reflect an understanding of the Twelve as apostles – especially in view of his use of the verb *apostellein* at 3.15 in relation to the group – though it could also have the non-technical meaning of 'those sent'. Matthew's only use is in the expression 'the twelve apostles' at 10.2 in relation to the list of names of the Twelve, and has a much more sharply defined ring about it, even though the Evangelist does not appear to be particularly interested in developing this aspect of the group's identity elsewhere. Luke, it has been claimed, is the originator of the twelve-apostle idea (cf. 6.13), with the positive intention of excluding Paul from its range (cf. Acts 1.21) for polemical reasons in the post-Pauline church. There seems to be little question that the twelve apostle-witnesses are extremely important for Luke as one of the links that bind the church to Jesus in his two-volume account of Christian origins, but to say that Luke plays down Paul's role seems exaggerated, especially since he twice slips in the term apostle for him (Acts 14.4, 14). To suggest that Luke is the originator of the idea of the twelve apostles is to ignore the usage of the other two Synoptists, as well as the internal dynamic, based on the early Christian sense of mission, that attracted together these two terms, twelve and apostles, despite their quite separate backgrounds and horizons of reference. Whether or not that development took place during the actual ministry of Jesus it is impossible to say, but already by Paul's time it would seem that it was well under way, and it is in relation to this development that he sought to define his own call and mission.

5. *Apostolicity*. One of the marks of the church mentioned in the Nicene Creed is that it is apostolic, that is, founded on the apostles and in continuity with them (Eph. 2.19f.). It was used in this sense by a number of early Christian writers, e.g. Tertullian and Augustine, as a criterion against various heretical trends, but it was the sixteenth-century Reformation* that gave it particular prominence, focussing on apostolic succession of the episocopacy among Roman Catholics and on the primitive, and therefore pure, form of Christianity by the Reformed churches. In such a polemical atmosphere there were inevitable distortions and exaggerations. In the light of the discussion of the notion of apostle in the earliest period it is necessary that in contemporary discussion the concept be kept flexible without at the same time making it devoid of meaning. Apostolicity, in the sense of faithfulness to the witness of the apostles, is a mark of the whole church, and it must be expressed in the whole life of the church, not just in its organizational structure. The apostolic witness as preserved in the Scriptures is one vital criterion of apostolicity for the later church, since it was under the pressures of defining its true identity in the faith with the primitive community that the church of the second century drew up a

canon or list of authoritative and apostolic books. Yet, as we have seen, those books allow for a greater degree of diversity within unity than later discussions about the apostolicity of the church would seem to tolerate.

———

F. Agnew, 'On the Origin of the Term *Apostolos*', *CBQ* 38, 1976, pp. 49–53; C. K. Barrett, *The Signs of an Apostle*, 1970; S. Freyne, *The Twelve Disciples and Apostles. A Study in the Theology of the First Three Gospels*, 1968; G. Klein, *Die Zwölf Apostel. Ursprung und Gehalt einer Idee*, 1961.

SEAN FREYNE

Apostolic Succession

The doctrine refers to the formal connection between the episcopate of today and the apostles of the first age of the church. It first appears in the second century in response to the perennial concern, already evident in the NT (Luke 1.1–4; I John 1.1–4), of Christian communities to be assured that their belief and practice are identical and continuous with the faith of the first disciples of Jesus Christ. In the face of Gnostic* claims to secret traditions, Christian apologists pointed to the universal tradition being crystallized at this time in the canon* of the NT and the baptismal rule of faith and openly taught and handed down in the churches by a duly appointed ministry. Tertullian speaks of churches coming from the apostles as the apostles had come from Christ and Christ from God (*De Praescrip. Haer.* xxi, 4), and earlier Clement of Rome had already written of the apostles making provision for men to succeed them in their ministry, to be succeeded by others in their turn 'with the approval of the whole church' ((I) *Cor.* XLII–XLIV). In order to demonstrate the continuity of the apostolic tradition in the principal churches Irenaeus is the first to draw up succession lists of bishops, notably for Rome, where the earlier names, though undoubtedly of leaders in the churches, are anachronistically so described and ordered (*Adv. Haer.* III, ii–iii; IV, xxxiii, 8). The emphasis in the succession in his case is on the historical *continuity* of teaching. Complementary to this is the emphasis in the earliest ordination prayers on the *identity* through the outpouring of the Spirit of the ministries being ordained today, in response to prayer and the laying-on of hands, with the work of Christ and of his apostles (Hippolytus, *Apostolic Tradition*, ii–ix).

Implicit in the function of teaching is the necessity to *interpret* the received tradition in changing circumstances, and it is this function of interpretation that lends to the apostolic ministry an authority distinct in kind from that of the other elements of the Christian heritage. It is thus that the church of Rome, the church of the apostles Peter and Paul, and to a lesser extent the other patriarchal sees assume an increasing importance in the determination of the faith; and in the course of the christological* controversies of the next centuries the concern for authentic teaching results in apostolic succession becoming associated with the bishops* acting collectively in council on the model of the apostolic college in Acts 15, a view renewed in the doctrine of the collegiality of the episcopate of Vatican II. It is from this authority to interpret the tradition that RC theology derives the power of the *magisterium* * of the Pope and the bishops.

To this is added the power given in ordination*. From the belief that God empowers the bishop at his ordination to fulfil the spiritual functions of his office, and from the rule that came early to prevail to ensure good order within each community and between the churches that only those themselves so ordained might ordain others, it was a short step to the belief that it is he who passes on the charism of which he is possessed when he ordains in his turn. At the beginning of the fifth century Augustine in defending the validity of schismatical baptism extends the notion of indelible sacramental character* to ordination, though he denies the efficacy of the sacraments to those outside the charitable communion of the church. This allows for the development of a doctrine of apostolic succession which concentrates on the lineal descent, person to person, of spiritual powers. As a curious consequence this has resulted in the phenomena of titular bishoprics and of the *episcopi vagantes* unrelated to any real Christian community. More seriously, any break in the 'pipeline' of succession inescapably invalidates all subsequent offices, whether it be the authority of bishops or their and other ministers' sacramental acts, irrespective of whether the actual substance of the Christian tradition has been faithfully preserved, including indeed an ordered ministry of the Word and sacraments. It underlies much controversy among the churches of the West since the Reformation* and remains a principal obstacle to the mutual recognition of ministries in the divided churches.

More recently in the course of the ecumenical movement theologians have been returning to the recognition that apostolic succession is primarily manifested in the apostolic tradition of the church as a whole, which the apostolic succession of the ministry exists to serve and of which it is itself a sign.

Edward Schillebeeckx, *Ministry*, 1981; C. H. Turner, 'Apostolic Succession', *Essays in the Early History of the Church and Ministry*, ed. H. B. Swete, 1918; 'Apostolic by Succession', *Concilium*, Vol. 4 No. 4, April 1968; *Baptism, Eucharist and Ministry*, WCC Faith and Order Paper No. 111, 1982.

VICTOR DE WAAL

Appropriation

Appropriation is a linguistic procedure in patristic* and later theology whereby an attribute which properly belongs to the whole Godhead is assigned pre-eminently to one Person*, not because it is his exclusive property but because it has a greater resemblance to his properties in particular. This resemblance must be clear and not arbitrary and is the better if it is based upon scripture. Thus Augustine appropriated unity to the Father, equality to the Son and connection (as the bond of love between the Father and the Son) to the Spirit. Other examples are power, wisdom and goodness (Aquinas); unity, truth and loving-kindness (Bonaventura); origin (*principium*), wisdom and virtue (Calvin). Another form of appropriation (based upon Rom. 11.36) distinguishes the prepositions which can be properly applied to the activity of the three Persons, from whom (*ex quo*) of the Father, through whom (*per quem*) of the Son, and in whom (*in quo*) of the Spirit. The same technique can be applied to the external operations of the Trinity*. Creation may be appropriated to the Father, redemption to the Son and sanctification to the Spirit, provided that it is remembered that the whole Trinity is involved in the work of each Person.

See **Opera ad extra.**

H. E. W. TURNER

Arche

A Greek word meaning the beginning, a principle, an authority, a source. It is used in the Septuagint, the NT and the Greek Fathers in the above senses. *Archē* denotes the beginning of time as in Gen. 1.1, or the beginning of any action. Used as a word for a principle or foundational reality it has philosophical connotations, as implied in the title of Origen's foundational theological work *De Principiis* (*Peri Archōn*). *Archē* is also used to indicate civil authority. Christ is described as seated 'far above every rule (*archē*) and authority (*exousia*)' (Eph. 1.21). Used in all the above senses by the Greek Fathers, the word has found special application in Eastern Christian trinitarian theology. The Father is described as the *archē*, or cause, of the divinity of the Son and the divinity of the Holy Spirit by the Greek Fathers. 'The Trinity is to be referred back to the one ... unity ... and one source (*archē*) who is God and Father' (Epiphanius, *Expositio Fidei* 14). Thus, the Father is the source of divinity within the Trinity and as such without cause (*anarchos*). The Son is for ever born of the Father. 'The Father is the source (*archē*) of the Son and his begetter' (Athanasius, *Orationes Adversus Arianos* 1.14). 'Divine generation is spiritual ... time does not come into the begetting of the Son from the Father ... for what he is now; that has he been timelessly begotten from the beginning' (Cyril of Jerusalem, *Catecheses Illuminandorum* XI, 7). In like manner the Holy Spirit proceeds eternally from the Father (John 16.26). The Father is thus the *archē* of the Holy Spirit. Both Son and Holy Spirit are perceived by the Greek Fathers as co-eternal with the Father and uncreated; however, the generation of the Son is not the same as the procession of the Holy Spirit. This Eastern doctrine was challenged by the addition of the *Filioque* * clause in the Nicene-Constantinopolitan creed by the Latin church. The *Filioque* remains a source of conflicting theological positions between Eastern and Western Christianity.

See also **Trinity, Doctrine of the.**

S. HARAKAS

Arguments for the Existence of God

Philosophical arguments for the existence of God have been propounded in the West since the time of Plato, and have been central to the 'natural theology' * which has, in large parts of the Christian world, provided the accepted preamble to 'revealed theology'.

In Catholic thought the most prevalent philosophical argument for the existence of God has been the *cosmological argument*, moving from the contingent, caused or dependent character of the world to God as its non-contingent source. In one form (Aquinas' First Way) this is an inference from the fact of change to an original initiator of change. The illustration has been used of a line of railway trucks in motion. The immediate explanation of the movement of a given truck is that it is being pulled by the truck in front; and that by the one in front of it, and so on. But even if we multiply the number of trucks to infinity, in a beginningless and endless series, we shall still not have found the ultimate explanation of the movement of any of them. In order to do this we have to postulate something – namely the engine – which is not merely one more truck but which has within itself the power to move without requiring something else to act upon it. Likewise a changing universe, even if it should be beginningless and endless, is ultimately explicable only by reference to an unchanged originator of change.

Aquinas' Third Way hinges upon the task of rendering intelligible the existence of contingent things. Everything to which we can point is dependent for its existence and its character upon factors beyond itself. It could not exist but for various prior conditions, and its presence can only be explained by reference to those preconditions. For example, the pen that I am now holding is contingent upon the past activity of its manufacturer and the existence of the necessary raw materials. But these prior factors are also themselves contingent entities or circumstances, and likewise point beyond themselves for their explanation. Thus the search for an ultimate explanation has launched upon a regress. And either this regress is endless or it must terminate in a non-contingent, i.e. self-explanatory or necessary, reality, which is God.

But could a self-existent creator provide an ultimate explanation of contingent things? Might not the universe itself, as a beginningless and endless changing network of contingent events, be regarded as ultimate? The answer is that the idea of God is the idea of a more ultimate reality than the universe; for God is defined as the uncreated creator of everything that exists other than himself. Thus the universe is, in principle, susceptible of explanation by reference to God, but not vice versa.

It would seem, then, that if the universe is ultimately to be explained, rather than just accepted as 'brute fact', that explanation will have to be in terms of a self-existent creator. Thus the cosmological argument presents the dilemma: either the universe is divinely created or it is an ultimately inexplicable given fact. But the argument does not compel us to choose one of these alternatives rather than the other.

Among Protestants the most favoured of the theistic arguments has been the *design or teleological argument*, which moves from the orderly and apparently designed character of the world to a divine designer.

The physical universe is not a chaos of random events but a system functioning in accordance with universal regularities or 'laws'. It is in fact an efficiently functioning mechanism, in this respect comparable with a complex human artefact – such as a clock, which was the most obvious example available in the eighteenth century, when the design argument was at the height of its popularity. William Paley (*Natural Theology*, 1802) pointed out that if we find a watch on waste ground we are not tempted to think that it was formed by the random effects of natural causes. Its complex internal organization and its precise aptness for indicating the time require us to infer an intelligent maker. And this would be true even if we had never encountered a watch before and knew nothing of its manufacture. Consider then, for example, the eye. With its lens focussing light onto a photo-sensitive area, is it not as manifestly designed for seeing as is a telescope? Or again, consider the ozone gas layer in the upper atmosphere which surrounds our planet, filtering the radiations which fall upon the earth's surface. If it was appreciably thicker than it is, it would absorb radiations that are necessary to life; and if appreciably thinner it would let through radiations fatal to life. Thus it is just the right thickness to sustain earthly life. Is not this an evidence of deliberate arrangement?

This eighteenth-century form of the argument was powerfully criticized by David Hume (*Dialogues concerning Natural Religion*, 1779). Amongst other things, he pointed out that any order of nature, in order to persist, must involve living creatures being adequately adapted to their environments. The important question is how this order and adaptedness have come about. Hume propounded a basic naturalistic hypothesis in which the universe consists of a vast number of particles moving about at random. If there is any possible arrangement of them which will constitute a self-sustaining order, sooner or later, in unlimited time, they will fall into that order. Perhaps we are now in such a (permanent or temporary) phase of order, in which the universe has an appearance of design but which has nevertheless come about without the intervention of any designer.

The general theory that apparent design has been produced by the operation of natural forces was strikingly confirmed in the nineteenth century by Darwin's theory of the evolution of the forms of life. The innumerable instances of the efficient adaptation of organisms to their environment are results of a process of natural selection whereby, given small random mutations in the genetic process, features which have positive value to the species tend to be preserved and built into the genetic stream, whilst those with negative value tend to be eliminated in the struggle to survive. Thus species develop over long periods of time towards more perfect adaptation to their environment, and also in response to changes in that environment. Again, applying this general principle to the ozone gas layer, the situation is not that humanity and the other forms of life were in place first, and God then added this layer for their protection, but the other way round: the ozone gas layer was there first and only those forms of life have developed that can emerge and survive within the kinds and levels of radiation that it lets through.

Various attempts have been made in the twentieth century to reformulate the design argument. Some stress the remarkable fact that the universe exhibits a character which is amenable to investigation and comprehension by the human mind. Does not the structure of the universe, then, reflect an Intelligence analogous to our own? It is replied that the human brain has been formed as part of the evolving universe, and is therefore naturally adapted to analyse and understand its environment. Other recent forms of design argument seek to demonstrate the improbability that life could have come about on the earth's surface purely by chance. Thus protein, for example, is an essential constituent of living organisms. An astronomically high improbability has been calculated for the formation of a single protein molecule by the chance coming together of its constituents in the right proportions and pattern. Given the volume of substance available on the earth one can further calculate the order of time that would be required for such a chance event to occur, and this turns out to be many times greater than the age of the earth. Therefore, it is argued, some anti-chance factor (namely God) must be at work. Against this it is argued that whilst the improbability of a protein molecule being instantaneously formed out of a random distribution of atoms is indeed immense, this immensity is dissipated when we see the complex protein molecule as the end-product of a long evolutionary process in which later stages of chemical synthesis have built upon earlier ones.

In one of its forms the *moral argument* can be seen as a component within a comprehensive design argument. The universe has produced ethical animals. Must there not then be a transcendent moral Source or Ground of our moral nature? In another form of the argument it is claimed that the existence of God is a necessary presupposition of the absolute claim upon us which we find moral obligations to have. When I *ought* to do something this 'ought' is unconditional and does not depend upon my own desires or preferences. But its absolute and unconditional character cannot arise from any merely human or natural source. It must derive from an absolute source of value, which we may equate with God.

Against this position, however, it has been argued that morality can be seen as a human device, required by the exigencies of communal life. The human animal is gregarious, and communal living is impossible without the development of rules, implying general principles and supported by sanctions. These rules are taught in the socialization of each new individual and become internalized as conscience; and the idea of God is used to support this moral consensus. But all this may happen, it is claimed, without there having to be a transcendent divine being.

The most philosophically subtle and interesting of the theistic arguments is the *ontological* argument*, first clearly formulated by St Anselm.

Anselm defines God as 'that than which no greater (or more perfect) can be conceived'. The fact that we can conceive of such an unsurpassably perfect being means that it at least exists as a thought in our minds. The question is whether it also exists as a reality outside our minds. Anselm argues that it must. If it exists only in the mind, it is not that than which no more perfect can be conceived; for we could then conceive of something more perfect, namely that same being existing in reality. So long as we think of the unsurpassably perfect being as existing only in the mind, we are not yet thinking of the unsurpassably perfect being. In order to be unsurpassably perfect, such a being must exist not only in the mind but also in reality. Thus when we understand what God uniquely is, we find it impossible to think of him as not existing.

Anselm adds that, as the unsurpassably perfect being, God not only exists but exists necessarily – i.e. exists in such a way that he cannot be thought not to exist. This mode of existence is self-existence or *aseity*. That which is defined as existing eternally, and without dependence upon anything other than itself, cannot be thought of as not existing. As Anselm says, 'that alone cannot be conceived not to be in which conceiving discovers neither beginning nor end nor combination of parts, and which it finds existing always and everywhere in its totality' (*Responsio*, 4). But it is more perfect to exist necessarily than to exist contingently; so that the unsurpassably perfect being must exist necessarily – and therefore undoubtedly exists. This is the 'second' form of the argument, identified and defended by a number of recent writers.

The ontological argument has been the subject of an immense and still continuing discussion since its revival by Descartes in the sixteenth century. A central criticism, formulated by Immanuel Kant, is that the argument presupposes an understanding of 'existence' as a predicate which something may have or fail to have and possession of which makes it more perfect than it would be without it. Hence the most perfect conceivable being must have this attribute of existence. But it is claimed by the critics that the function of 'exists' is not to add another element to the concept of a kind of thing, but to assert that that concept is instantiated. Thus, for example, 'horses exist' does not mean that as well as having such attributes as four-footedness, horses also have the attribute of existence. It means that the concept 'horse' has instances. And whether a concept has instances cannot be settled by the content of the concept, but only by some kind of observation of the universe. This empiricist analysis means that having defined God as omnipotent, omniscient, eternal, etc., to say that God exists is to say that this concept or definition is instantiated – that there is a reality corresponding to it. And even if we put existence, or even necessary existence, into the definition – defining God as an eternally existing omnipotent, omniscient, etc. being – this does not settle the further question whether this enlarged concept answers to any reality. We can never guarantee God's existence by defining him as existing. Thus despite its subtlety and perennial fascination the argument seems finally to fail.

If, as seems to be the case, God's existence cannot be philosophically proved, it does not necessarily follow that there is no God. It may be that, in W. H. Auden's words,

All proofs or disproofs that we tender
of His existence are returned
Unopened to the sender.

William Craig, *The Cosmological Argument from Plato to Leibniz*, 1980; Charles Hartshorne, *Anselm's Discovery*, 1965; John Hick, *Arguments for the Existence of God*, 1970; John Hick and Arthur McGill (eds), *The Many-Faced Argument*, 1968; Thomas McPherson, *The Argument from Design*, 1972; Wallace I. Matson, *The Existence of God*, 1965; H. P. Owen, *The Moral Argument for Christian Theism*, 1965; William Rowe, *The Cosmological Argument*, 1975; Richard Swinburne, *The Existence of God*,

1979; Richard Taylor, *Metaphysics*, 1963, ch. 7.

JOHN HICK

Arianism

Both a set of beliefs and a church within a divided Christianity, Arianism originated with Arius (d. 336), an Alexandrian priest. The movement asserted itself in late Roman society (i) as a prominent Christian party of the fourth century in the eastern Empire, where it enjoyed imperial support (e.g. Constantius II and Valens), and (ii) as the religion of the Goths and Vandals who settled in the West in the fifth–sixth centuries.

Denounced as heresy in councils at Nicaea (325) and Constantinople (381), Arian teaching underwent shifts of emphasis in the course of the century. The fundamental Arian assertion of the creaturehood of God's Son led the creed of Nicaea to speak of the Son as 'one-in-essence' (*homoousios* *) with the Father. Subsequent groups of Christians resistant to that definition of relationship were branded, often unfairly, as 'Arian' – e.g. followers of Basil of Ancyra, who favoured the term 'similar-in-essence' (*homoiousios* *). Embroiled in the debate by the end of the century were the 'radical-' or 'Neo-Arians' and a group labelled 'Pneumatomachians' for their denial of the plenary deity of the Holy Spirit *.

Most important for Christian theology are the related but distinct doctrines of the early Arians (Arius and his allies, Eusebius of Nicomedia and Asterius 'the Sophist') active in the second quarter of the fourth century, and the Neo-Arians (notably, Aetius and Eunomius) whose ideas were influential in the succeeding fifty years. Historians of doctrine have generally treated the Arians as uncompromising monotheists of a philosophical, rather than biblical, orientation. Their insistence on calling the Son 'creature' and 'work', like Arius' catch-phrase, 'There was when he [the Son] was not,' are thus interpreted as strategies of subordination necessary for confession of one God, alone uncreated and without beginning. On this view of Arianism's chief objective, Arius' reasons for declaring a 'Triad not in equal glories', and a Son who 'does not know the Father perfectly or accurately' are manifest: the Son is demoted in order to protect the singularity and sov-

ereignty of God. Nicaea's *homoousion* is a counter-assertion of the Son's co-equality and co-eternality with the Father and, as articulated by Athanasius (328–373), is a doctrinal guarantee that the Son, because he shares the Father's essence (*ousia*), is a powerful saviour.

Another scholarly perspective on Arianism has emerged, concentrating on Arian christology and soteriology. Clearly the Arians conceived the Trinity hierarchically, thinking of the Son as a secondary being dependent upon his creator for his existence and powers. Thus they denied that the Son was generated from the Father's essence; he was, rather, called into being by an act of the Father's 'will and pleasure' and was related to his Father by will, not essence. Arian Christians viewed the Son as 'full God', honouring him as 'first among creatures' through whom God created all else. Simultaneously they pointed to his creaturely attributes: his finite knowledge, his ethical freedom as a 'changeable' (*treptos*) being capable of moral advance (*prokopē*). Early Arians apparently put forward a positive christology: a Son created and elected before all worlds by the Father who foreknew his faithfulness performed as incarnate Christ the paternal will, meriting his adoption and exaltation as Son and becoming finally 'unchangeable' (*atreptos*) in virtue and fidelity. This portrait is informed by biblical texts – notably, Ps. 44.7 (LXX); Isa. 1.2; Luke 2.52; John 10.30; 17.11, 22; Phil. 2.5–11; I Tim. 6.15–16; Heb. 1.9; 3.2; 4.5; 5.8. The Son's performance is exemplary, a model for the salvation and sanctification of believers. An opponent reports the Arians' claim: 'Certainly we also are able to become sons of God, just like that one [Christ]. For it is written, "I begot and raised up sons" (Isa. 1.2).' Viewed in this way, early Arian understanding of a God related to his Son and the Son's fellow creatures by will is fundamental to a scheme of redemption intentionally opposed to the Nicene doctrinal programme built upon the consubstantiality of the Father and Son.

By contrasting Father and Son as 'ungenerated' (*agennētos*) and 'generated' (*gennētos*) beings, and thus 'unlike' (*anomoios*), the later Arians denied commonality of essence in the Trinity and proceeded to depict the Son as God's servant, as the Holy Spirit, in turn, was his. The chief neo-Arian spokesmen, Aetius (d. 367) and Eunomius (d. c. 394) argued, unlike the earlier Arians, that the Son's divine status was due to his being uniquely generated or begotten (while other creatures were made through the agency of the Son), not bestowed as a reward for his obedience. The Cappadocian* Fathers' response, which informed proceedings at Constantinople in 381, promoted a view of the God of Christian worship as three co-eternal and co-equal persons, one divine essence.

See also **Christology, Trinity.**

É. Boularand, *L'Hérésie d'Arius et la 'foi' de Nicée*, 1972; R. Gregg and D. Groh, *Early Arianism*, 1981; A. Grillmeier, *Christ in Christian Tradition* Vol. I (rev. ed), 1975; T. A. Kopecek, *A History of Neo-Arianism*, 1979; R. Lorenz, *Arius Judaizans?*, 1979; M. Simonetti, *La crisi ariana nel IV secolo*, 1975.

ROBERT C. GREGG

Aristotelianism

Aristotle (384–322 BC), though a pupil of Plato, reacted critically against the teaching of his master. Plato had taught that there existed a world of changeless perfection, which he called Forms, the object of the mind, not of sense, and at the same time the patterns of sensory reality (*see* **Platonism**). Aristotle denied their existence and defined the supreme being, or God, as the unmoved mover, moving the world as the object of its love and desire (*Metaphysics* XII.7). Further Plato had argued, especially in the *Phaedo* and *Meno*, for the immortality of the soul. This, too, Aristotle denied (*De Anima* 430a 22; *Eth. Nic.* 1111b 20), making the soul instead the active principle of the body.

After his death the leadership of the Lyceum, which he had founded in 335, passed to his pupil Theophrastus, who kept alive his master's interest in empirical observation. After this the school was eclipsed by the rise of the Stoics and Epicureans. In the first century BC and thereafter certain teachings of Aristotle were absorbed into Middle Platonism* by Albinus and into Neo-platonism* by Plotinus (cf. *Vita Plotini* 14). In the latter's system the Aristotelian conception of God as 'self thinking thought' became fused with the Platonic world of Forms and together they formed the second hypostasis in his scheme. By far the most utilized part of Aristotle was his logic, and commentaries on it were produced by the last distinguished representative of the school, Alexander of Aphrodisias, at the beginning of the third century AD. Neoplatonists like Porphyry in the third, Themistius in the fourth and Olympiodorus and Simplicius in the sixth century also produced commentaries on the logical works of Aristotle.

Interest in the logical works was not restricted to pagans. Not only do Origen (cf. *De Principiis* i.2) and Gregory of Nyssa (*Contra Eunomium* i.181) use Aristotelian logic to establish doctrinal points. The Christian, John Philoponus, in the sixth century commented on the logic of Aristotle, and in Italy Boethius (c. 480–524/5) translated into Latin and wrote commentaries on the *Categories*, *De Interpretatione*, *Topics*, *Analytics* and *Sophistical Arguments*. But otherwise, with the exceptions of Basil (330–379) in his *In Hexaemeron* and John Damascene (c. 675–c. 749) in his *De Fide Orthodoxa* iv.13, the Fathers had little liking for Aristotle, whom they regarded as an atheist because of his supposed restriction of providence to the superlunary sphere (cf. Tatian, *Adv. Graecos* 2; Athenagoras, *Leg.* 25.2; Origen, *Contra Celsum* i.21; Gregory of Nazianzus, *Or.* 27.10), and as an immoralist because he denied the immortality of the soul (cf. Tatian, *Or.* 25; Origen, *Contra Celsum* ii.12). That Aristotle was a sort of patriarch of all heretics was suggested by Gregory of Nyssa (*Contra Eunomium* i.46; ii.411).

Knowledge of Aristotle in the West during the Middle Ages came primarily from three sources. (i) Knowledge of his *Organon* came through the work of Boethius, already mentioned. (ii) Already by the ninth century the Arabic philosophers, who had become acquainted with Aristotle through Syriac translations, were making use of his writings. Al Farabi (d. 930), Avicenna (d. 1037), Averroes* (*fl.* 1190) and Al Gazali (*fl.* 1111) translated all of Aristotle except his *Politics* together with several other writings, supposed to be by him, as for example, *Theologia Aristotelis* (= Plotinus, *Ennead* iv.6) and the *Liber de Causis*, in fact the work of Proclus, as Thomas Aquinas later proved. These Arabic writings were themselves translated into Latin in the twelfth century, above all in Spain by

Johannes Hispanus, but also in Italy by Dominicus Gundesalvus and Gerhard of Cremona. Through these Latin versions, partly at any rate, the non-logical works of Aristotle became available to the West. (iii) At roughly the same time, but not necessarily in competition with these translations from the Arabic, there appeared the translations made straight from the Greek by William of Moerbeck, Archbishop of Corinth between *c*. 1260 and his death in 1286. This he seems to have done at the request of Thomas Aquinas and he was the first to translate the *Politics*. With the help of these translations the latter was able to acquire a picture of Aristotle's thought stripped of its Averroist dress. Three truths in particular were claimed as Aristotelian, which could not be accepted by a Christian: (i) the doctrine of the eternity and necessity of the world – against the Christian doctrine of a free creation in time; (ii) the unity of the separate intellect of all men – implying a denial of the doctrine of personal immortality; (iii) a theory of double truth, implying the independence of and superiority to revelation of reason. It was part of the aim of Aquinas to show both that Averroes' version of 'the Philosopher' was inadequate and that the true Aristotle could be harnessed to the cause of revelation.

Aquinas' modification of his inherited Neoplatonism with the help of Aristotle is evident in his empiricism. He regarded individual material objects as the first source of knowledge, from which he inferred the existence of spiritual reality. Again the proofs for God's existence at the beginning of the *Summa Theologiae* owe much to Aristotle. This is particularly true of the first proof from motion, which stems from *Metaphysics* XII.7; 8 and *Physics* VIII.6 and concludes to an original unmoved mover, and the second proof from causality, which leads to an uncaused first cause and owes much to *Met*. II.3. Finally, Aquinas takes over from Aristotle a hylomorphic vision of the universe, in which all beings, with the solitary exception of God himself, derive their present state from the coincidence of two elements, matter and form. A human being on these principles is a composite of two interdependent realities, soul and body, the former being the form of the latter. In asserting this, Aquinas rejects the Platonic picture of the soul as a prisoner in the body,

waiting to escape. He does not go quite as far as Aristotle, however, in denying to the soul personal immortality, though Aquinas himself would have maintained, probably falsely, that Averroes had misinterpreted Aristotle in his contention that the latter denied personal immortality. It is obvious, both from his modification of the Philosopher in this last matter and in his assertion that the Unmoved Mover of *Met*. XII.7 was the same as the personal God of the Bible, that Aquinas was not an uncritical Aristotelian.

Mention should also be made of the influence of Aristotle upon Jewish mediaeval thought, and especially of Moses Maimonides (born Cordoba 1135, died Cairo 1204), whose *Guide to the Perplexed* purported, with the help of Aristotle, to establish reason as the basis and criterion of the OT. In so doing he was following in the footsteps of Avicebron in the previous century and of Philo in the first century AD.

Despite Aquinas' critical but positive attitude towards Aristotle, neither then nor immediately afterwards did the teaching of Aristotle receive approval in the universities of Europe. Thomism was condemned at Paris in 1277 by Stephen Tempier, bishop of Paris, and shortly afterwards in the same year at Oxford by Robert Kilwardby, OP, archbishop of Canterbury. Gradually, however, Aristotle came to be accepted as philosophically orthodox and he held this position unchallenged until the resurgence of Platonism in the Renaissance and the challenge to his whole system and approach presented by Martin Luther, the determined enemy of scholastic Aristotelianism. The two main objections to his views were then as always his exaltation of the importance of reason and his materialistic account of the nature of the human soul.

J. A. Smith and W. D. Ross (eds), *The Works of Aristotle Translated into English*, 12 volumes, 1912–1952; J. L. Ackrill, *Aristotle the Philosopher*, 1981; Jonathan Barnes, *Aristotle*, 1982; W. W. Jaeger, *Aristotle*, 1948; G. E. R. Lloyd, *Aristotle*, 1968; W. D. Ross, *Aristotle*, 1923.

ANTHONY MEREDITH

Arminianism

The theological system proposed by James Arminius (1560–1609), professor of divinity in the University of Leiden. Arminius' father died while he was an infant. He was educated by a former priest and then at Marburg by a professor who was a fellow townsman. His mother, brother and sister were slaughtered by Spanish troops and the town destroyed in 1575. He studied at the new University of Leiden, and at Geneva (under Theodore Beza), Basle and Padua. He was influenced by the theology of Peter Ramus (1515–1572), a Huguenot convert, who attacked Aristotelianism* and based his teaching on the Bible. Arminius was a minister in Amsterdam from 1588 and came to reject the doctrine of predestination*. The plague of 1602, in which he showed himself a devoted pastor, carried off two of the Leiden theological professors, leaving only Francis Gomarus (later the opponent of Arminius), and Arminius was appointed in the place of one of them (1603). His Calvinist* orthodoxy was fiercely attacked and he defended himself by denying the doctrine of predestination in any of its forms, while still maintaining the necessity of grace* for salvation. 'That teacher obtains my highest approbation who ascribes as much as possible to Divine Grace; provided he so pleads the cause of Grace, as not to inflict an injury on the justice of God, and not to take away the free will to that which is evil.'

After his death in 1609, his sympathizers, who called themselves Arminians, produced the *Remonstrance to the States-General*, asking for a revision of the catechism and the Belgic Confession. The five points of Arminianism were: 1. God in Christ decreed to elect from fallen humanity those who through grace believed and persevered, and to reject unbelievers; 2. Christ died for everyone; 3. no one could believe without the help of God's grace; 4. all good works must be ascribed to grace, but this grace was not irresistible (Acts 7.51); 5. that true believers might fall away from faith was discussable (and, soon they said, possible). The Remonstrants were condemned at the international Synod of Dort (1618–1619), and they were expelled from the church. The Remonstrant Brotherhood was formed in 1619, which still exists as a small separate denomination with a seminary in Leiden. The most famous Remonstrant was Hugo Grotius (1583–1645), jurist and author of *The Truth of the Christian Religion* (1622).

Arminianism was enthusiastically adop-ted by Archbishop Laud (1573–1645), and deeply influenced John Milton (1608–1674, who pictured some of the fallen angels deadening the pain of their loss by arguing 'Of Providence, Foreknowledge, Will, and Fate – Fixed fate, free will, foreknowledge absolute, And found no end, in wandering mazes lost'), and John Wesley (1703–1791), so that all streams of English theology are imbued with Arminianism. Arminianism developed a theory of toleration in religious matters, but thought the state should be superior to the church when disputes arose.

The Works of James Arminius, 1825–1828, 1875; A. W. Harrison, *The Beginnings of Arminianism to the Synod of Dort*, 1926; *Arminianism*, 1937.

J. C. O'NEILL

Art and Theology *see* Aesthetics

Articles of Faith

Aquinas took up the term 'article of faith' and specified its meaning as a revealed doctrine which contains salvific truth and is to be found in the official creeds of the church. On the basis of Heb. 11.6 ('whoever would draw near to God must believe that he exists and that he rewards those who seek him'), he argued that:

> All the articles of faith are implicit in certain primary ones, namely that God exists and that he has providence over man's salvation. For the truth that God is includes everything that we believe to exist eternally in God and that will comprise our beatitude. Faith in God's providence comprises all those things that God arranges in history for man's salvation and that make up our way towards beatitude. As to the remaining articles, some are implicit in others, e.g. faith in the Redemption implies Christ's Incarnation and Passion and all related matters (*ST*, 2a2ae 1.7).

A concern for the scientific status of theology (in the Aristotelian* sense of 'science') lay behind Aquinas' appeal to the articles of faith. Theology could rank as a science (in the broader sense), as it drew deductively on basic principles, the articles provided by faith. Theology could move from these articles of faith to establish its conclusions in a scientific manner (*ST*, 1a 1).

With the Reformation * came a desire to list fundamental 'articles of faith' which could serve as a basis for union between groups of separated Christians or at least could form an agreed profession of faith to secure a proper unity within a given body of Christians. Thus the Forty-Two Articles (1553) brought together Anglican doctrinal formulations which constituted the basis for the Thirty-Nine Articles that received the force of law in 1571.

Vatican II did not adopt the expression 'article of faith', but in its Decree on Ecumenism (*Unitatis Redintegratio*) it endorsed the principle of the 'hierarchy of truths':

> In ecumenical dialogue, Catholic theologians . . . when comparing doctrines with one another . . . should remember that . . . there exists an order or 'hierarchy' of truths, since they vary in their relation to the foundations of the Christian faith (n. 11).

These foundational truths or basic articles of faith were named as the doctrines of the Trinity *, the Incarnation * and human redemption * (ibid., n. 12; see also the treatment of the 'basic dogmas' of Christian faith in ibid., n. 14).

See **Creed, Dogma, Thirty-Nine Articles.**

Wolfhart Pannenberg, *Theology and the Philosophy of Science*, ET 1976, pp. 229ff.

GERALD O'COLLINS

Ascension of Christ

Although the exaltation of Jesus to the right hand of the Father is a fundamental element in the NT preaching, it is Luke alone who presents this clearly in narrative form, both at the end of his Gospel (apparently on Easter Day itself) and at the beginning of Acts, with far more theological and typological detail. In both accounts, the connection is made with the apostles' approaching reception of the Spirit: Jesus' departure is not so much the conclusion of a sequence of resurrection appearances as the first movement in the creation of a worldwide mission and witness by the church in the power of the promised Spirit. Jesus is 'received' in heaven, and given his authority (which is not the bestowal of any merely contingent sovereignty in or of Israel – Acts 1.6); and the universal nature of that authority is now

to be realized in the world as the church's mission spreads out, enacting in history the lordship already realized in Jesus' heavenly life, the life which makes him free to pour out God's Spirit (Luke 24.49).

The pattern is similar in John 20, though there is no *moment* of parting. The risen Jesus has not yet finished 'ascending' to the Father, but his risen existence *is* precisely this process of ascension, exaltation, growth into the universal dimension of divine power. So what his risen manifestation gives the church is, again, Holy Spirit *, the power of binding, loosing, i.e. of re-creating, redrawing the boundaries of the holy community. The emphasis here is – typically – less on the *universality* of mission than on the inner integrity of the church, though John clearly links the mission of the community with the mission of Jesus himself through the action of the Spirit.

Phil. 2.9–11 describes Christ's exaltation in terms of the universality of his authority, but it is Ephesians which develops this a little further, seeing the heavenly enthronement as involving the *present* exaltation of all who are in Christ (2.6): this is what it means for the church to be filled with Christ's fullness (1.23; 3.19; 4.7–13). The content of the gift of the Spirit, the eschatological seal (1.13–14; 4.30), is this present participation in the glory and liberty of the exalted Christ.

Thus in Luke, Christ's exaltation involves the universal mission of the church; in John and Ephesians it involves his being empowered to penetrate and transform the lives of Christians in every aspect; and inner transformation and outward mission are alike the work of the Spirit and are eschatological * signs, manifesting the still 'hidden', the non-worldly authority of Christ crucified and raised. And for the writer of Hebrews, Christ's being received in heaven means the acceptance of his atonement * offering of his blood, by which we are all given the priestly privilege of entering the sanctuary (10.19): our transformation is (cf. Eph. 3.12) freedom to be in the Father's presence, purified to worship him in all we are and all we do – to be where Jesus is, do what he does, pray as he prays. The receiving of Jesus in heaven fulfils the promise expressed in John's Farewell Discourses: a place to stand before God is laid open to us through the death of Jesus. And to receive the Spirit in our baptismal entry into his humiliation and death is to enter this 'place' of trust and love between creature and Creator, and, more significantly, between Son and Father.

Variations on the descent-ascent scheme reflected in Philippians and Ephesians appear in Jewish–Christian and Gnostic literature: the *Ascension of Isaiah* employs this imagery extensively, with an important visionary account of Son and Spirit worshipped by the lesser angels and other creatures, but themselves worshipping the Father. Apocalyptic* mysticism, drawing on its roots in Ezekiel and Daniel, shows an abiding interest in the theme of entry into the heavenly places and sharing in the heavenly liturgy – following Jesus' way to the Father. But on the whole, patristic* and mediaeval treatment of the subject concentrates not on any visionary *experience* of sharing the life of heaven, but on the Ascension as sealing and perfecting the renewal of human nature by Christ. His glorification is the firstfruits of deified humanity (Chrysostom); we are glorified as members of the ascended head of the Body, and are presented by him to his Father (Augustine). Also, very importantly, the Ascension is the pledge of the glorification of the whole person, body and soul – a point underlined in the fine office hymn (from perhaps the fifth century) for Matins on Ascension Day (*Aeterne Rex*): *Peccat caro, mundat caro, Regnat Deus Dei caro* ('flesh hath purged what flesh had stained, And God, the Flesh of God, hath reigned').

Doctrinally, then, the Ascension (whatever its historical and narrative uncertainties) marks the culmination of the resurrection gospel – the universalizing of Jesus' relevance to all aspects of human life, individual and global; the present possibility of a share in Jesus' loving union with his Father, i.e. a life of both trustfulness and authority; the crowning of the purpose of Jesus' life and death in the restoration of fellowship between heaven and earth. It represents both the call to witness (and to recognize Christ in the world of which he is declared Lord) and the promise of transformed – 'deified' – life, as the ground and source of that witness.

J. G. Davies, *He Ascended into Heaven*, 1958; Joseph Ratzinger, 'Ascension of Christ', *Sacramentum Mundi*, Vol. I, 1968.
ROWAN WILLIAMS

Ascetical theology

This is concerned with the Christian life from the beginnings up to the lower reaches of contemplation*. It is a systematic analysis of the life of grace under the Spirit in terms of the discipline and endeavours required of the ordinary believer to purify oneself of self-reference. This discipline has been analysed in a threefold way. 1. The way of purgation, a basic stripping of the self from excessive attachment to personal wants; 2. the way of illumination, during which the believer is conformed to the image of Christ by the practice of the virtues; 3. the unitive way, in which the believer has a profound awareness of union with God. At the latter point ascetical theology merges into mystical* theology.

F. P. Harton, *The Elements of the Spiritual Life*, 1932; K. E. Kirk, *The Vision of God*, 1931; M. Villier, SJ (ed), *Dictionnaire de spiritualité ascetique et mystique*, 1932–.
E. J. TINSLEY

Asceticism

This is a term used to cover all those exercises and forms of discipline which are believed to be necessary to the Christian *in via*. Negatively it concerns forms of renouncing things which in themselves are good in the interests of greater order, control and simplicity. Positively, asceticism is regarded as a necessary preparation for the higher reaches of the spiritual life, particularly the dimension of contemplation (*see* **Mystical Theology**). Theologically, asceticism is regarded as a necessary feature of the Christian life as an imitation* of Christ.

Ascetical practices in the OT are the exception rather than the rule, a close grip on the doctrine of creation* preventing the Hebrews from accepting a thorough-going world-renouncing asceticism such as became a characteristic of some Hellenistic religions.

In post-biblical Judaism this feature of the OT became still more prominent, the rabbis insisting that human beings were to enjoy created existence and that not to do so constituted blasphemy*. This essentially non-ascetical attitude of the Hebrew tradition is prominent in regard to sex and marriage (*see also* **Celibacy**).

There are both 'world-renouncing' and 'world-affirming' elements in the practice and teaching of Jesus. His attitude seemed ambivalent and he was himself aware of the irony of it (Matt. 11.17–19; cf. Luke 7.31–34). The ascetical note in the teaching of Jesus does not spring from any metaphysically dualistic * or gnostic * view of the material or of the sexual (cf. Mark 7.15f.). He believed that people must be alert to recognize the signs of the kingdom, and ready to act on them, and this, he indicated, would often involve painful renunciation. The asceticism of Jesus was empirical and practical, not metaphysical or dualistic, and was orientated towards the eschatological * character of the kingdom *.

In the NT, as a whole, the 'flesh' is something that can be defiled (and it is all too likely that it will be!), but it is not in itself defilement. It is redeemable, and while Paul may use terms which are capable of thorough-going dualistic interpretations, he does not himself use them dualistically. Nevertheless, there are features of the NT which can be detached from the whole and used in a one-sided way. The history of Christian ascetical teaching shows only too clearly how this happened. A NT tension which is eschatologically based was changed into a dualism which is metaphysically based.

In the patristic * period, Christian asceticism centres upon the ideals of martyrdom and celibacy, which were regarded as the high peaks of the Christian ascetic endeavour. The primary motivation behind patristic notions of asceticism was the imitation of Christ. This ideal underlay both forms of monasticism*, whether solitary or communal. The eremite particularly was seen as an imitator of the lonely Christ, travelling along the path which led mankind back to the lost paradise.

The Middle Ages saw further development of the ascetical ideal and its full articulation in terms of monasticism. There was a marked development of ascetical discipline: the use of the hair shirt, iron girdles, flagellation and so on, and the ideal of the imitation of Christ was actualized in the practice of pilgrimage. More and more Christian ascetical devotional practice was centred on the humanity of Christ, particularly the

sufferings of Christ, and there are some curious examples of attempts literally to mimic the sufferings of the historical Jesus, as for instance in Henry Suso.

The Reformation * and the Renaissance saw a marked reaction against the Christian ascetical ideal. A strong polemic against monasticism is to be found in the works of Martin Luther, mainly on the ground that it produces a doctrine of justification * by works, and similar reservations are to be found in John Calvin.

This suspicion of the monastic ideal and of the asceticism associated with it remained a feature of Puritan * thought. A reaction in favour of the mediaeval type of asceticism is to be found in counter-Reformation writers.

The problems which arise for the modern Christian concerning asceticism can be tabulated as follows:

1. What is the meaning of asceticism, mortification and so on in modern, technological and 'consumer' societies? Here it is important to remember that the Christian ideal of poverty is not to be confused with destitution. Traditional Christian ascetical teaching has a good deal to say, which is still relevant, on the necessity for simplicity and austerity in the midst of wealth and plenty. Greater demands are made on inner austerity in modern society, and traditional ascetical teaching is relevant also in the stress which it puts on the need for meditation and contemplation. It is just these features of Indian religions which attract many in the West.

2. There is the problem of the relationship between Christian ascetical attitudes and aesthetics *. This can best be focussed in the attitude of Christians to the arts. What is the place of the enjoyment of creation in the Christian ideal? The voice of a writer like Thomas Traherne, writing in exultation of created life, is not common in Christian history, and yet even the most austere mystics, like St John of the Cross, will inculcate detachment from what he calls creatures and created existence, not in order to despise creation, but in order to have a keener eye for its grateful enjoyment.

3. This raises the question whether Christian asceticism is conditioned by a metaphysic of dualism or by an eschatology. There can be no dispute that an asceticism which is based upon a dualistic conception of the inherently evil character

of matter is incompatible with the Christian religion. On the other hand, Christian eschatology prevents the believer committing himself entirely to time and creation.

Dom Anselme Stolz, *L'Ascèse Chrétienne*, 1948; Blackfriars, *Christian Asceticism and Modern Man*, 1955; E. F. Schumacher, *Small is Beautiful*, 1974; A. Tanquerey, *The Spiritual Life*, 1923; John V. Taylor, *Enough is Enough*, 1975.

E. J. TINSLEY

Aseity

As applied to God, the term connotes his being 'from himself' (Latin *a se*, whence *aseitas*) and not 'from another'. In scholastic* and especially Thomistic* thought, aseity entails the identity in God of existence and essence*, since he is the ground of his own being, and thus marks him out as 'pure act'*, the fullness of being. More recently Karl Barth has reinterpreted the divine aseity to refer to God's freedom, his possession of absolute initiative as ultimate subject.

See also **Arguments for the Existence of God.**

R. A. NORRIS

Assent

In this century many Christian theologians have radically revised their ways of describing and explaining the assent of faith*. Generally their aim has been to enrich matters, not to reject authentic themes of earlier church teaching and theology.

In nineteenth-century versions of faith's assent, varied though they are, key themes are reason, authority, freedom, grace and certainty. Even though the assent of faith is not as such simply grounded on intrinsic evidence provided by the light of reason, it is, nevertheless, responsibly motivated. Signs like the story of Jesus' ministry and the fruits of holiness in the life of the church make the path towards faith credible, while the assent itself is formally based on the trustworthy authority of God's infallible self-testimony. Assent to revelation* occurs when through the prompting of divine grace* the will freely moves the intellect to make such an assent. The word of revelation demands (and the inward light of grace effects) an unqualified assent. The absolute claim of God calls for such an utter certitude.

At their worst, exponents of this approach turned faith into a mere intellectual assent to a set of revealed doctrines proposed as such on divine authority. They forgot that faith is more than a matter of the intellect alone. It is a fundamental decision of the *whole* human being (*a*) – negatively – to renounce efforts to secure independently one's own existence, and (*b*) – positively – to enter a personal relationship of confession, obedience and trust with the self-revealing God.

Seen in these integral terms the assent of faith has a triple dimension: a confession which recalls God's saving self-revelation in the past (Rom. 10.9), an obedient commitment here and now to Christ as Lord (Rom. 1.5; I Cor. 12.3), and a hopeful confidence that the truth of faith will be validated through future resurrection (Rom. 6.8). Further, to believe is to enter a community of faith, appropriating as one's own its history and tradition. Thus the assent of faith is essentially a social, historical and traditional act.

What then of human reason and will and their interaction in the making of faith? First, Michael Polanyi, various existentialist philosophers and others (including John Henry Newman) in their different ways have helped to show that knowledge, and in particular knowledge in the religious sphere, comes about through personal participation. Hence the truth of faith will prove luminously intelligible for those who accept it within a commitment of their whole existence, but not for those who continue to consider it merely 'objectively'. Second, through the figure of the beloved disciple, the Fourth Gospel suggests how knowing and loving mutually condition each other in the act and life of faith (John 20.8; 21.7). Likewise a high sense of the dynamic unity between the human intellect and will leads such contemporary theologians as Karl Rahner to stress that the commitment of love both depends upon *and makes possible* the confession of faith. Negatively, this means that without some repentance and conversion of life one will not be able to see, assent to and personally align oneself with the truth of faith.

A full discussion of assent would also cover such themes as: the role of the Holy Spirit* in the making of faith; the place of historical knowledge; the special nature of faith's certitude; the self-acceptance or self-assent entailed in accepting God as the basis for one's life through faith in Jesus Christ; and the method of correlation* (between human questioning and divine response) variously developed by Rudolf Bultmann, Rahner, Paul Tillich and others.

Rudolf Bultmann, *Theology of the New Testament*, ET, I, 1952, pp. 314–30; II, 1955, pp. 70–92; Gerhard Ebeling, *The Nature of Faith*, ET 1966; Walter Kasper, *An Introduction to Christian Faith*, ET 1980; Jean Mouroux, *I Believe: The Personal Structure of Faith*, 1959; John Henry Newman, *An Essay in Aid of a Grammar of Assent*, 1870; Gerald O'Collins, *Fundamental Theology*, 1981, pp. 130–60; Michael Polanyi, *Personal Knowledge*, 1962.

GERALD O'COLLINS

Assumption of the Blessed Virgin Mary

Legends of Mary's miraculous preservation from death began to appear in the fifth century, probably originating from Egypt. Two primary versions of Mary's *Dormition* became current. In one version, 'The Falling Asleep of the Holy Mother of God', by Pseudo-John the Evangelist, Mary's body is carried away by angels to be preserved incorrupt until the final resurrection. Her soul is carried directly to heaven. In another version, the *Transitus Mariae*, by Pseudo-Melito, Mary's body is resurrected three days after her death and carried by angels to heaven. When these apocryphal texts appeared in the West in the fifth century, they were sufficiently foreign to tradition to be condemned by Pope Gelasius (AD 492–496). Popular accounts of the heavenly translation of Moses and Elijah influenced these legends (R. L. P. Milburn, *Early Christian Interpretations of History*, 1954, 161ff.). Influential theologically was the belief that the corruptibility of the body was the consequence of sin. Mary, preserved from sin to be the pure vessel of the Incorruptible One, must have been preserved from bodily death and decay.

Apocryphal accounts of Mary's death in the seventh to ninth centuries remained divided between the two different traditions. Some, such as Gregory of Tours (d. 594), boldly declared her bodily translation to heaven. John of Damascus (d. 749) ques-

tioned the biblical and historical foundations of the Assumption and limited the doctrine to bodily incorruption. The same uncertainty persists in ninth-century writings, with the 'Epistle of Pseudo-Jerome to Paula and Eustochium' taking the view that Mary's body was kept from corruption and her soul taken to heaven, while Pseudo-Augustine's 'On the Assumption of the Virgin' accepts the bodily assumption of Mary.

The celebration of the Feast of the *Dormition* on 15 August passed from East to West, and by AD 813 it was accepted as an official festival for Western Christendom under the title *Assumptio sanctae Mariae*. Only in the thirteenth century did earlier caution about the doctrine disappear and the opinion of Pseudo-Augustine prevail. Through the seventeenth and eighteenth centuries, theologians continued to regard it as an article of piety, but not an article of faith, especially since the writings upon which the story was based were shown to be apocryphal. Popular Marian piety built up pressure for the formal declaration of the doctrine, with more than eight million signatures gathered in Italy, Spain and Latin America in its favour in 1940. The Assumption was formally declared an article of faith in 1950 by Pope Pius XII in the bull *Munificentissimus Deus*.

M. Jugie, *La Mort et l'Assomption de la Sainte Vierge: Etude historico-doctrinale*, 1944; G. Miegge, *The Virgin Mary*, ET 1955, pp. 83ff.

R. R. RUETHER

Assurance

The placing of the doctrine of assurance in the forefront of Christian teaching was characteristic of the 'experimental' (i.e. experiential) emphasis of the Evangelical Revival. Assurance of salvation had indeed been claimed by many Christians throughout the history of the church, and renounced by others. Calvin* taught that membership of the elect, manifested by the evidence of a good life, gave an objective and inalienable assurance of God's eternal favour. The Calvinistic wing of the Revival accepted this teaching.

But its basis in the doctrine of predestination* was unacceptable to John Wesley, the principal exponent of assurance in the eighteenth century. Guided in the early stages by the Moravian teachers who greatly influenced him at a critical period of his life, he reformulated the doctrine as an exegesis of Rom. 8.16: 'The Spirit himself beareth witness with our spirit that we are children of God.' He distinguished between the witness of the Holy Spirit and the witness of our own spirit. 'The Spirit of God directly witnesses to my spirit that I am a child of God; that Jesus Christ hath loved me and given himself for me; and that all my sins are blotted out, and I, even I, am reconciled to God' (*Standard Sermons* I, 208). The claim to this testimony has to be tested by various scriptural 'marks', such as awareness of a change from death to life, and 'the fruits of the Spirit'; and these tests must be rigorously applied, in view of the danger of relying on feelings and sinking into 'enthusiasm'. Later comes the testimony of our own spirit which chimes in with that of the Spirit of God. These testimonies are the privilege of believers, but not granted to all of them.

It cannot be said that the doctrine has the same prominence in modern Methodist theology as it had in Wesley's.

W. R. Cannon, *The Theology of John Wesley*, ch. 9, 1946; C. W. Williams, *John Wesley's Theology Today*, ch. 7, 1960.

RUPERT DAVIES

Atheism

There are as many forms of atheism as there are forms of belief. 'Atheism' is to be literally translated as 'the belief that there is no God', but this simple definition masks a variety of forms each corresponding to the rejection of a central element of theistic belief and some to forms of belief that, even if they were prevalent, now no longer exist in our society. For example, the triumphant claim of the Russian astronaut that he had been 'up there' and had seen no God can hardly be treated as a serious form of atheism. There are, however, some very influential and sometimes profound forms of atheism which can be exemplified set alongside the types of belief which they deny.

The most easily recognizable form is the belief that although it might be true that God exists, there are good grounds for denying that this is so, e.g. that on balance the evidence of our flawed world and the random play of forces in our universe suggests that there is no benevolent purposive creator at work.

A rather different type of atheism which received a sophisticated exposition in this century by the Logical Positivists (*see* **Analytical Philosophy**) consists in asserting that since 'it is impossible to define God in intelligible terms, then one is allowing that it is impossible for a sentence to be both significant and to be about God' (A. J. Ayer). In fact Ayer would want to confine atheism to the insistence that there is no God, but it is a legitimate extension of the term 'atheism' to include the view that claims about God are unintelligible. This version of atheism depends upon the acceptance of a theory of meaning which is unacceptable to many philosophers.

A third type of atheism is best defined as the rejection of God. Its most powerful statement is to be found in the figure of Ivan in Dostoyevsky's *The Brothers Karamazov*. Ivan strikes a theme often re-echoed since in his insistence that if the price of the eternal harmony is the suffering of children, then 'too high a price is asked for harmony; it's beyond our means to pay so much to enter on it. And so I hasten to give back my ticket ... It's not God that I don't accept, only I most respectfully return Him the ticket.' But of course he is rejecting belief in God, and in so doing gives paradoxical expression to one of the most profound statements of atheism in all literature.

A closely related account of atheism is to be found in Camus' classic work *The Rebel*. He shows how unwittingly certain forms of belief can be eliminated by the judgments one makes: 'When man submits God to moral judgment, he kills Him in his own heart.' Camus' point, which is an elaboration of the account of Abraham in Kierkegaard's *Fear and Trembling*, is that there is a type of belief in God which is denied by the question 'Was it right that God should do this?'

Throughout the nineteenth and into the twentieth century there were developed a series of theories about or explanations of the nature of religious belief which were essentially atheistic. The most significant of these include Feuerbach's account of *The Essence of Christianity*, in which he insists, for example, that 'the personality of God is nothing else than the projected personality of man'. Marx drew heavily on Feuerbach and argued for atheism from the premiss that 'Man makes religion'. This led to the famous definition of religion as 'the opiate of the masses', implying that what was true of religion in general was true of belief in God. A third example of what we might call 'atheism by explanation' is the account offered by Freud (*see* **Freudian Psychology**) of religion as based on illusion or wish-fulfilment, in which he argued that belief in God can be explained as a projection of wishes, and in some case projections on to an imaginary external being (*see also* **Projection Theory**). He did concede, tongue-in-cheek, that occasionally dreams come true, but along with those of Marx and Feuerbach his theory is atheistic in character. However, in each case the atheism is dependent upon an elaborate and unproven theory about human nature and human society. Interestingly the theories of Marx, Freud and Feuerbach are not compatible with one another, so they cannot all be correct.

Atheism is generally and correctly taken to be antipathetic to all forms of religious belief, but this is not universally so. Two classic statements to this effect are to be found respectively in the writings of Paul Tillich and Simone Weil. Tillich gives para-doxical statement to an important implica-tion of his philosophical theology when he writes 'It is as atheistic to affirm the exist-ence of God, as it is to deny it.' His point here is that there is a danger that any state-ment about God, even the bare affirmation of his existence, can carry atheistic implica-tions. The reason for this is his belief that even a term such as 'existence' is a limiting term only properly used of limited finite beings. Consequently, to use it of God is to deny his transcendence.

A rather different, but spiritually deep and related point made by Simone Weil, is that intellectual acceptance of certain forms of atheism may become a type of religious purification which is, for some, the only way to reach a more profound form of belief than the view which defines the difference between atheism and belief as a difference in attitude to the proposition that God exists.

Lastly, there is a type of atheism which has many manifestations and which could be the product of any one of the above ver-sions of atheism, but is more commonly quite innocent of any such theorizing – namely the atheism of indifference. How-ever, an unreflective atheism can be combined with forms of superstition and even theism, perhaps even justifying the claim of Alasdair MacIntyre that 'The creed of the English is that there is no God and that it is wise to pray to him from time to time.'

A. J. Ayer, *Language, Truth and Logic*, 1936, rev. ed. 1946; A. Camus, *The Rebel*, ET 1953; A. MacIntyre and P. Ricoeur, *The Religious Significance of Atheism*, 1969; S. R. Suth-erland, *Atheism and the Rejection of God*, 1977.

STEWART SUTHERLAND

Atonement

1. *Meaning.* The English word 'atonement' originally signified the condition of being 'at-one' after two parties had been estranged from one another. Soon a secondary mean-ing emerged: 'atonement' denoted the means, an act or a payment, through which harmony was restored. It occurs only once in the AV/KJV of the NT (Rom. 5.11), where it translates the Greek word *katallage* (liter-ally: 'downing the otherness') elsewhere rendered 'reconciliation' (e.g. II Cor. 5.18f.).

In the OT (AV/KJV) the phrase 'to make atonement' frequently occurs in a cere-monial context. It denoted an action or series of actions by means of which guilt could be removed. At some time in Israel's history an annual Day of Atonement (Lev. 23.26ff.) began to be observed. Elaborate ceremonies were performed and these were designed to expiate the sins of the whole nation. In a striking way the author of the Epistle to the Hebrews (9.6ff.) contrasts the once-for-all character of Christ's atoning act with that of the Jewish high priest which had to be constantly repeated.

2. *The death of Jesus: the framework of interpretation.* The consentient testimony of NT writers is that Jesus died on a cross: the Gospels give details of his betrayal, trial, and final committal by Pontius Pilate to crucifixion. But how could God allow his chosen Messiah to be so treated? Paul gives the shortest answer in his summary of apos-tolic preaching (I Cor. 15.3): 'Messiah died for our sins according to the scriptures.' But the phrase 'for our sins' has proved capable of many interpretations and these have in

time been expanded into what have come to be called 'theories' of atonement. A 'theory' (lit: 'viewing') tries to see the particular event of the death of the Messiah within the wider context of what is believed to be true of the relations between God and man. The meaning of 'according to the scriptures' is not to be found by accumulating proof-texts, but rather by learning from the stories and testimonies contained in the OT the ways in which God has made known his judgments and his saving grace on behalf of mankind.

3. *Biblical frameworks.* (*a*) The most prominent was that of the release from the bondage of Egypt and the safe passage through the Red Sea. Moses had identified himself with his people at great cost and had led them out into freedom. One greater than Moses had been 'made like unto his brethren' (Heb. 2.17) in every respect and as 'captain of their salvation' (Heb. 2.10) had led them out to victory over death, sin and the devil. Passover and Red Sea imagery provided one framework within which the passion, death and resurrection of Messiah took on meaning.

(*b*) After the deliverance from Egypt came another critical event in Israel's history: the establishment of God's covenant * with his people at Sinai. A covenant normally involved both verbal promises and dramatic actions. At Sinai demands were made which the people promised to obey: sacrificial actions were performed in which the sprinkling of blood occupied the central place (Ex. 24.7f.). In the NT the records of the inauguration of the Lord's Supper refer to the establishment of a covenant and to the blood symbol. Further, the Epistle to the Hebrews celebrates the 'better covenant' made through Jesus the Messiah, its mediator. Through his death the new covenant was made. Those who by faith entered into the new relationship could be assured that their sins and iniquities would be remembered no more (Heb. 8.12).

(*c*) Disasters and reverses, individual and social, were attributed to unfaithfulness to the covenant and failure to keep divine laws. How could the transgressor be relieved of guilt? The oft-repeated call of prophet and psalmist was for *repentance*, a new commitment to the covenant. Concurrently, priests called for the performance of sacrificial rites by which guilt could be covered

or removed. Yet there also emerged the conception of a great day of judgment when God would bring all peoples to account for their disobedience and unfaithfulness; further, on the annual day of atonement, the high priest acted to cleanse away the sins of the whole people. Both these conceptions are regarded in the NT as having found a critical fulfilment in and through the death of Christ.

It is Paul's clarion proclamation in the Epistle to the Romans that God's righteous judgment has been openly revealed in the cross of Christ. At Calvary he was set forth openly as the one bearing the judgment on the world's sin: 'He was delivered for our offences and was raised for our justification' (Rom. 4.25). God's righteousness was vindicated: 'being justified by faith' sinners could become 'at-one' with God through Christ (Rom. 5.1–10). Similarly it was the central proclamation of the writer to the Hebrews that Christ, the great high priest, had performed the necessary rites of ablution so that it became possible for sinners to enter the very presence of God 'by the blood of Jesus' (Heb. 10.19) and thereby to enjoy the at-one-ment which he had procured.

(*d*) It might have been expected that in the NT frequent reference would have been made to the framework of vicarious *sacrifice* * so vividly depicted in Isa. 53. There are indeed echoes of phrases used in that chapter, but the only major appeals to the career of the suffering servant are to be found in Acts 8.27ff., where the emphasis is on the innocence of the sufferer, and in I Peter 2.21–25, where the result of vicarious suffering is clearly defined: 'He bare our sins in his own body on the tree; by his stripes we are healed.' As in John 1.29, there is a simple affirmation that through the self-offering of Christ the sin of the world is taken away. It is doubtful whether many would have accepted this even as a possibility. But it was the Christian claim that Christ was indeed God's righteous servant who fulfilled his will and thereby opened the kingdom of heaven to all believers.

4. *Later interpretations.* (*a*) *The Hellenistic world.* In the early centuries of the Christian era, teachers and pastors tried to express the new faith in terms of the cultural forms of Hellenism. In this culture there was a deep sense of the division between the heavenly

world of purity, truth and immortality and the earthly world of natural ills, delusion and mortality. How could humans be saved from darkness and death into light and immortality?

Christian missionaries proclaimed that the Son of God had come down to earth and assumed a human body within a sinful world just as a seed is sown in the ground and thereby enters a realm of darkness. By so doing he shared human nature and then proceeded to reverse the whole process through which Adam had condemned his successors to toil, pain, weakness and death. Jesus had resisted all temptation, had lived a life of perfect obedience and had submitted to the ravages of man's ultimate enemies – death and the devil. Out of it all he emerged victorious and thereby enabled his followers to share in the fruits of his victory and to become partakers of the divine nature. So at-one-ment was achieved. Preachers loved to dwell on details of the great *recapitulatio* through which human dereliction had been reversed and transformed by the incarnation, death and resurrection of Christ.

(b) *The Middle Ages.* The dominant power was Rome, the language of the educated was Latin, the major concern was to establish *order* in the empire, in the church, in structures of belief and practice. To ask questions about general assumptions, to initiate rational enquiries and to attempt to give resolutions concerning the ways of God with nature and mankind became leading exercises in new centres of learning.

In relation to the death of Christ, the most famous enquiry was that of Anselm (c. 1033–1109). He entitled his relatively short book *Cur Deus Homo* (Why a God-man?). At the centre of his argument he asserted that it was impossible for God to leave his world in a state of *disorder*. Yet man had disobeyed and dishonoured his creator, and it was impossible for him to make adequate amends. Only God could achieve what man was incapable of doing. The supreme wonder was that the Son of God had not only lived a life of perfect obedience as man but had also offered himself to endure death, an act which won for mankind the means of completely satisfying the righteous demands and rightful honour of God. Within the hierarchical structure of mediaeval society and the growing concern for order in the tradition of Roman law, Anselm's exposition of *satisfaction** as the necessary way to at-one-ment seemed a convincing rational explanation.

(c) *The Reformation.* Two leaders of thought and action stand out pre-eminently in the history of the Reformation*. Luther* was the apostle of *freedom* in relation to God and so to his fellow-men. He had been deeply conscious of formidable constraints: sin, the devil, death and, in particular, the holy law of God. How could he escape from the righteous judgments of God and gain the victory over his adversaries? Through a new apprehension of Paul's testimonies in Galatians and Romans Luther gained his own freedom: the knowledge of the forgiveness of sins and of access to God through the atoning work of Christ. This did not mean the nullification of divine law. The dialectic between law and grace continued for the believer. But Luther made the leap of faith to believe that Christ had touched bottom on his behalf – the sense of the uttermost reaction of divine righteousness to human sinfulness – and in so doing had brought about at-one-ment between man and God such as no agencies, human or demonic, could destroy.

Calvin* in his early career attained outstanding proficiency in the study of law, logic and language: later he never ceased to be conscious of the majesty of divine law as revealed in Holy Scripture. Moreover he had no doubt that all were guilty of complete failure to keep the injunctions of this law. It followed inexorably that all stood condemned to bear the penalty they deserved. Yet the incarnate Son of God lived a life of perfect obedience and then 'on this righteous person was inflicted the punishment which belonged to us'. In all his actions, Calvin declared, Christ acted as our *substitute* suffering on our behalf the penalty, condemnation, even the curse which, apart from him, would have been our lot. This view of at-one-ment seemed entirely conformable to the great system of Roman law which had gained enormous respect in European society. It was logical and, at the same time, it appealed to human feelings when the victim was seen suffering and dying as a substitute for guilty mankind.

(d) *The nineteenth century.* The most important new factor influencing views of the nature of atonement was the increasing sense of the autonomy of the individual and of the significance of inter-personal relationships. Philosophers had already directed attention to the individual: thinking and feeling and constrained by moral demands. Now the question began to arise: How could atonement be viewed in the context of familiar human feelings and relationships? In the middle of the century McLeod Campbell wrote a notable book exploring the relationship between father and son. Almost at the same time Horace Bushnell concentrated attention on the nature of vicarious sacrifice, while late in the century R. C. Moberly, in *Atonement and Personality*, drew upon experiences of family relationships between parents and children to expand understanding of what at-one-ment meant within the divine economy.

During the past hundred years there has been a vast increase in the number of attempts that have been made to set forth aspects and interpretations of the atoning work of Christ, not only through theological treatises but also through hymns, sermons, passion-music, oratorios, novels. There has been little diminution in the sense that the cross and its significance occupies a central place in the NT and must therefore retain that centrality in Christian thought and experience. At the same time, there has been a growing recognition that no single interpretation of atonement can be regarded as definitive or all-embracing. There are many facets to cultural experience, and if at-one-ment is designed to affect the total life of mankind, all must be in some way open to inclusion.

5. *Conclusion*. In seeking today to understand the meaning of a doctrine of atonement we draw upon:

(*a*) The witness of NT writers and the evidence provided by the early traditions of baptism* and the eucharist*. These are necessarily viewed within the context of OT law and prophecy and in the light of the Jewish culture of the first century AD.

(*b*) The writings of leading Christian theologians at successive periods of Christian history. These are necessarily viewed within the context of the cultural assumptions and interests of their own time and need to be supplemented by reference to the forms of worship and of popular preaching belonging to each period.

(*c*) The testimony of the literature of any particular period to the nature of alienation and estrangement which seems to have been uppermost at the time. At-one-ment only becomes meaningful when there is some sense of brokenness, of disruption, of things being 'out of joint', of falling short, of estrangement from the ideal self, from social well-being, from God. It is those who have penetrated most deeply into the nature of the variations of the human predicament as manifested at particular times under particular conditions who can speak most effectively about at-one-ment, achieved through the once for all self-offering of the Christ on the cross and continually re-enacted and re-experienced as its significance is recognized and accepted for every contingency of human living.

See also **Redemption, Salvation.**

Gustav Aulén, *Christus Victor*, ET 1931; Karl Barth, *Church Dogmatics, IV. The Doctrine of Reconciliation*, 1, 2, 3.1–2, ET 1956; Emil Brunner, *The Mediator*, ET 1934; J. McLeod Campbell, *The Nature of the Atonement*, 1856; James Denney, *The Christian Doctrine of Reconciliation*, 1917; F. W. Dillistone, *The Christian Understanding of Atonement*, 1968; P. T. Forsyth, *The Work of Christ*, 1910; R. S. Franks, *The History of the Doctrine of the Work of Christ*, two vols, 1918; Martin Hengel, *The Atonement*, ET 1981; Leonard Hodgson, *The Doctrine of the Atonement*, 1951; H. R. Mackintosh, *The Christian Experience of Forgiveness*, 1954; R. C. Moberly, *Atonement and Personality*, 1901; J. Moltmann, *The Crucified God*, 1974; Hastings Rashdall, *The Idea of the Atonement in Christian Theology*, 1919; Vincent Taylor, *The Atonement in New Testament Teaching*, 1940; L. S. Thornton, *The Atonement*, 1937; Paul Tillich, *Systematic Theology*, Vol. 2, 1957; Frances Young, *Sacrifice and the Death of Christ*, 1975.

F. W. DILLISTONE

Attributes, Divine

The Bible and the Qur'an say many things about God. While Jews and Christians, along with Muslims, adhere to the truth of what their respective books teach about divinity, they also recognize that some things are said less properly than others. The 'Lord sits on his holy throne' will be distinguished from 'his mercy endures from age to age'. And one may also want to distinguish scriptural quotations from philosophers' assertions like 'God is immutable', although these can also overlap, as in 'God is one'. Theological discussion of divine attributes begins, then, with these specific attributions to God, and the discussion itself has been considerably shaped by the relative capacity of current philosophical treatments of attribution. The fact is that believers speak of and to God in ways that attribute features – existence, life, power, wisdom, and will (to use Maimonides' list) – to divinity; the question asks what they can mean by this.

The issue was joined early, in Plato's dismissing the poets from the Republic for saying ungodly things about the gods (383c). The rational route to monotheism* lay largely in philosophers' identifying those features alone consistent with divinity, which also demanded that there be but one God. This intellectual pressure was intensified in those religious traditions which further identified this god with the 'creator of heaven and earth'. The twin insistence, then, that this God alone *exists* (while all else *has* existence), and be supremely *one*, represents the specific contribution of Judaism and of Islam to the discussion.

The key figure linking East with West was Moses Maimonides (1135–1204), whose own position on the question proved idiosyncratic, yet whose *Guide for the Perplexed* apprised the Christian West of the considerable debate among Islamic philosophers and theologians. That debate raged over the *reality* of divine attributes, for it proceeded on the assumption that predicating something of another introduces plurality into the subject: to speak *about* something is to presuppose its being *composed* of those aspects. For this reason the Muslim *falasifa* (philosophers) preferred consistency with the root affirmation of Islam, 'Allah is one', and tended to deny the reality of attribution *in divinis*; whereas the 'theologians' (or *mutakallamin*: those upholding what *was said*), less concerned with consistency and more concerned lest the truth of all the Qur'an says of God be undermined, insisted they be really identified with God. Such a division among intellectuals, coupled with the inherent instability in the 'theologians'' position, prompted Maimonides to use the

Torah to settle the confusion. He accepted the presumption that predication inevitably introduced composition into the subject of the proposition, and so restricted attribution *in divinis* to the biblical 'God is one'.

Since *unity* (or *simpleness*) cannot be thought to introduce plurality, it becomes the only acceptable attribute for God. All the other things said of God in the scriptures will either be recognized to be improper yet useful imagery, according to the rabbi's dictum: 'the Bible speaks in the language of men'; or when acknowledged to 'speak essentially' – as in existence, life, power, wisdom, and will (1.56) – must be understood negatively. It was this teaching which Aquinas (1225–1274) would counter directly (*ST*, 1.13.2), as would the Jewish philosopher-theologian, Gersonides (1288–1344), using an analogous predication scheme like that of Aquinas to show how 'essential terms' could properly be said of God 'priorly and posteriorily' (*Wars of the Lord* 3.3).

Aquinas' motivation for opposing Maimonides' clever resolution was that 'this is not what people want to say when they talk about God'. His attentiveness to analogous uses of language, sharpened by distinctions from twelfth-century 'speculative grammar' between 'the thing signified' and 'the mode of signifying' (*ST*, 1.13.3), allowed him to show that 'when we use ['wise'] about God we do not intend to signify something distinct from his essence, power or existence' (1.13.5), thus eliminating the earlier presumption. This capacity to 'intend to signify' as well as 'imperfectly signify' (1.13.4), turns on Aquinas' skilful elaboration of analogous usage in theology (*see* **Analogy**). A further useful distinction could be made between those primarily philosophical attributions: simple, good, unchangeable, limitless, and the more religious qualities from scripture: faithful, merciful, everlasting. In the measure that the former are taken as supplying the *grammar* for the latter, much-touted opposition between 'classical philosophical' and 'biblical' attributes of divinity can be attenuated.

A. Badawi, *Histoire de la philosophie en Islam*, 2 vols., 1972; D. Burrell, *Aquinas: God and Action*, 1979; *Gersonides on God's Knowledge*, ed. Norbert Samuelson, 1977; C. Hartshorne, *Divine Relativity*, 1948; Maimonides, *Guide for the Perplexed*, 1956;

H. A. Wolfson, 'Avicenna, Algazali and Averroes on Divine Attributes', *Studies in the History and Philosophy of Religion* I, 1973; id., 'Maimonides on Negative Attributes' and 'Maimonides and Gersonides on Divine Attributes as Ambiguous Terms', ibid. II, 1973.

DAVID BURRELL

Augustinianism

Augustine of Hippo (354–430) was born at Thagaste in Roman North Africa, son of a city councillor Patritius, who was a pagan, and Monnica, a Catholic Christian. His thought was to reflect his many varied experiences throughout a life of great activity and achievement. His influence on the theology and ethics of Western Christianity is comparable to that of Origen on that of the East. In the Middle Ages, Anselm of Canterbury and Francis of Assisi's disciple, Bonaventura, were both deeply indebted to his thought. Aquinas himself regarded Augustine as his teacher. The Reformers, as is well known, turned to him for instruction and inspiration. While in the present century Augustine's influence has waned and his moral and ethical teaching have been largely repudiated, his conception of the relation of faith to reason has left its traces on the ideas of theologians such as John Baillie and H. R. Niebuhr. As an observer of human behaviour (see his *Confessions*), Augustine may be considered a pioneer in the field of psychological science.

Many strands converged to form Augustine's ideas. From his father (whose influence Augustine always tended to play down) Augustine derived his love of the Latin classics, his sense of civic and provincial and, in less guarded moments, Roman patriotism. From his mother, he derived his basic allegiance to a universalist ideal of Christianity from which he never wavered, a strong moral sense that he retained throughout his life despite his assertions to the contrary, and after his baptism in 387 acceptance of the church as an authoritative institution.

By that time he was nearly thirty-three, and many of the distinctive features of his mature thought had already taken shape. As a student at Carthage from 372–375 his intense intellectual curiosity had been quickened by his reading of Cicero's (now lost) *Hortensius*. Cicero's debate on the question 'What is happiness?' and his con-

clusion, that this was not only possession of truth but questing after it, guided him throughout his life. As a student, the primary object of his search had been the problem of evil. This had attracted him to the Manichees*, whose mystical but dualist* interpretation of Christianity seemed a more convincing explanation of the universe than that provided by his Catholic teachers. He was to spend nearly ten years (373–382) as a Manichaean 'hearer' (second grade of membership), an immensely important formative decade, but regarding most of which he preferred to be silent. Only when he reached Milan in 384 and held the posts of professor of rhetoric and public orator did he find a satisfactory answer to Manichaeism.

He tells how chance introduction to Neoplatonic* writings, probably in 385 (these would have been Latin translations of the third-century Platonists, Plotinus and Porphyry) changed his outlook and removed his last lingering Manichaean sympathies.

Rational knowledge, he now believed, was possible only if one accepted the prior existence of God, but if access to God through divine illumination was available to all, how was it to be achieved? At Milan (384–387) two other factors pushed him steadily towards finding his answer by returning to Catholic Christianity: 1. the arrival of his mother, who exerted an ever-stronger moral influence on her son in that direction; 2. Augustine's realization through an increasingly close contact with Bishop Ambrose that the Bible could be interpreted allegorically* and in a way compatible with Platonic concepts. More than thirty years later, while writing the middle books of the *City of God* (*c.* 420), he describes how he had learnt about God and the Divine Word (Logos) from the philosophers, but one thing he had not found among them was 'that the Word became flesh and dwelt among us' (10.29). Nor had he been able to learn from the Platonists the virtue of humility and of complete submission of the will to God. It needed the examples of Marius Victorinus, a North African Platonist who openly declared himself a Christian in Rome (*c.* 360), and young civil servants, like Augustine himself, who threw up their appointments to embrace an ascetic life dedicated to Christ, to move him finally towards the religion of his upbringing. The scene in the garden in Milan, his baptism at Milan on Easter Eve 387, and his journey to Ostia where Monnica died (autumn 387), are among the best-known events in early Christian history.

Another four years elapsed before Augustine developed his ideas in the service of the church. His early works were aimed at refuting the Manichees and bringing back to Catholicism the friends he had earlier converted to the sect. He argues against them more as a Neoplatonic philosopher than as a Christian, stressing the uniqueness and omnipotence of God, that creation was his handiwork and was good, and asserting the sovereign freedom of the human will. Christ hardly figures in these early extant philosophical debates, and though the Manichees had been proscribed by edict with savage penalties, Augustine made no attempt to invoke the law against them. His appeal was to reason alone.

His unexpected ordination as presbyter in the flourishing Numidian seaport town of Hippo Regius in 391 brought him face to face with the church as an institution and its controversies. In December 393 he addressed a major Catholic Church Council in Hippo though still a presbyter. In 395 he became co-adjutor to Bishop Valerius, Bishop of Hippo, and next year, on the latter's death, succeeded him. He remained Bishop of Hippo until his death in August 430.

Augustine now becomes a servant and representative theologian of the Catholic Church in North Africa, as he had once been the representative and spokesman of the imperial court at Milan. Augustinianism develops from the controversies in which he was involved in defence of the church during the period 395–430, though the background of his previous intellectual evolution was always present.

The first major strand in Augustine's theological system concerns the nature of the church and its relations to the secular power. Between 393 and 412 he was involved in a ceaseless controversy with the Donatists*, who claimed to be the true Catholic Church in Africa. Augustine countered by claiming that Catholicism entailed universality, the heritage of God's promises to Abraham (Gen. 22.18; 26.4), its members being bound together through the sacra-

ments whose purity was guaranteed through their sole origin, Christ himself. Sacraments, however, though always valid even if dispensed by a schismatic or heretic, remained without effect unless administered within the church. There was no salvation outside the Catholic Church.

How were individuals to be saved? What were the pastor's responsibilities for the salvation of his flock? Augustine did not doubt that he would be accountable for the latter at the Last Day, and hence that the church had the right of paternal correction (correptio) against sinners, heretics and schismatics. The means lay to hand in the emperor Theodosius' comprehensive edict against heretics of 15 June 392. To Augustine, the Donatists were 'heretics', and c. 400 he argued in his tract against them, the Contra Epistolam Parmeniani, that if kings could legislate against pagans and poisoners they could legislate against Donatists (1.10.16). Not every persecution, he claimed, was unjust. Those outside the church could be coerced into submission. In 408, Augustine admitted that he accepted coercion by the state among the means at the church's disposal to enforce unity. His forced interpretation of Luke 14.23, 'Compel them to come in', with the state as the church's executor, was to have grave effects on the history of religious persecution in the Middle Ages and in Reformation times. So did his later justification of coercion, on the grounds that it was preferable for a heretic to be coerced in this life than to be allowed to perish, body and soul, hereafter. The uniqueness and unity of the Catholic Church, with resultant attitudes towards dissenters, played a fundamental part in his theology and its legacy to the West.

The relations between the ecclesiastical and secular, however, transcended those of church and Roman Empire. On 24 August 410, Alaric the Visigoth took and sacked Rome. The disaster roused the pagans in Rome and Africa to one last effort to discredit Christianity, by pointing to the calamities that now befell the empire following the triumph of the new religion. Augustine responded. The City of God took him fifteen years to complete (411–426). Less emotionally patriotic than Jerome, he applied the lessons of biblical teaching on secular events. He based himself, as had the Donatist theologian Tyconius (c. 370), whom he admired, on the traditional analogy of the two cities, Jerusalem and Babylon. These represented the earthly and heavenly cities. For the Platonist philosopher in Augustine, however, they were not states but ideal societies composed of individuals, and their membership was determined by the wills or loves of these individuals according to whether they were directed towards Christ or towards the Devil. The Roman empire was indeed a representative of the *civitas terrena*; its pagan rulers had been inspired by love of conquest. *Roma aeterna* was a myth. Only the City of God was eternal. Even so, the earthly city had a role to play under providence. It provided the necessary disciplines for humanity under the servitude of original sin *, and its rulers, if Christians, could share with the church in furthering God's purposes. The fall of Rome must be seen in the perspective of God's intentions that were hidden from man.

Here was a new theology of history, ultimately optimistic, though offering little solace to the immediate sufferer from disaster. Augustine had never ceased to ponder the problem of evil. The *City of God* was written while he was engaged actively in defending the intellectual position he had arrived at. In the decade that had followed his baptism, Augustine had immersed himself in the Bible and, in particular, had sifted carefully through the Pauline epistles. If the antitheses of 'flesh' and 'spirit', 'old man' and 'new man', worked out by the Manichees to justify their dualist interpretation of Christianity, were false, what was Paul's message? By 396, he seems to have made up his mind. Replying to a series of questions sent to him by his old friend Simplicianus, soon to be Bishop of Milan, Augustine said that he had wrestled with the problem of human freewill and divine grace, but the grace of God gained the upper hand. Without grace, it was impossible to resist concupiscence, and yet the choice of God as to who would be saved and who was destined for damnation, was hidden from us. His own experience of the influence of habit made him doubt the reality of human freedom, while the Donatists' claim on freedom of religion as a right, brought the answer that such liberty was simply 'liberty to err'.

Without the spur of Pelagius' views (*see* **Pelagianism**), Augustine's ideas on grace * and predestination * would have formed an integral part of his theology. The fall of Rome, however, brought crowds of refugees to North Africa, including Pelagius and his disciple Celestius. The statements particularly of the latter, drew Augustine into a controversy that in one form or another lasted until his death. Against the Pelagian assertion of the possibility of man achieving perfection, Augustine urged man's imperfection, his perpetual need for the work of the Spirit given by God. 'The Spirit gives life', and was to be contrasted with the letter of the Mosaic Law that killed; this was the theme of the *De Spiritu et Littera* (c. 415). Freedom lay not merely in freedom of choice, but in freedom to understand and devote oneself more effectively to searching for God and the perfected life. Grace was not like the Law and the prophets, external aids, but God's supernatural and uncovenanted gift for human salvation. Baptism was necessary for salvation, and the church's custom in favour of infant baptism was justified. Infants that died unbaptized would not inherit eternal life.

Up to this point, Augustine was only voicing the beliefs of most Christian North Africans, whether Catholic or Donatist. Pelagius' views, however, were shared by a considerable number of south Italian bishops, and when Pope Zosimus (417–418) reluctantly condemned the Pelagians (summer 418), resentment against Augustine and the triumphant irruption of North African theology into the remainder of the West came into the open.

Under the unrelenting pressure of twelve years of debate with an old pupil, Julian of Eclanum, Augustine elaborated and refined the theology of grace and predestination that posterity associated with his name. There is little doubt that he reverted to some of the ideas he had held as a Manichee forty years before. Humanity was now seen as 'a mass of sin, waited upon by death'. The abiding guilt of some catastrophic but long-forgotten sin became the directing power in mankind's history. Man's present life was the product of the Fall * and intelligible through its consequences. By persistent mistranslation of Rom. 5.12 ('in whom' all sinned, instead of 'on account of whom' . . .) from the time Augustine wrote his *Confessions*, sin was shown as transmitted literally to the human race and exaggerated beyond recognition. Creation could thus be interpreted in terms acceptable to Manichees, who regarded it as the result of the successful irruption of evil into the hitherto harmonious and good. In addition, the 'great sin' that lay behind existing human misery was identified in Augustine's mind with sex and sexual intercourse. When Adam and Eve ate the forbidden fruit, they covered their genitals. They were ashamed. That was the place whence the first sin was passed on. Fifty years had passed since the adolescent had become conscious of his new potentialities. Augustine ended his intellectual quest as he had begun, with the problem of evil*.

The long quest involved a close-knit synthesis between the Bible and philosophy in the service of the church. However great his debt to the Platonists, Augustine's thought remained biblical. For him the scriptures constituted a special revelation* which availed where the philosophers and reason failed. Faith in Christ alone enabled man to understand the world and his own position within it on a rational and secure basis. 'Understanding is the reward of faith. Therefore do not seek to understand in order to believe, but believe in order that you may understand.' The *Commentary on John*, where he says this (29.6), was written during the Pelagian controversy, but it sums up the mystic in Augustine, and his complete trust in the grace of God.

Augustine's theology, however, was not without the weaknesses of its author. These lay in the direction of pressing arguments too far, in love of debate and controversy, failure to see justice in an opponent's case, and in a legalism that deprived a logical theology of the requisite element of mercy. Against this, Augustine had a lifelong passion for truth and certainty, a dedication to the cause of the universal church, and to those members directly committed to him. He was a man of complete integrity and uprightness in an age when those qualities were not easily found. His theology combined many currents of North African teaching with others resulting from its author's genius of intellect and powers of synthesis and organization. Not surprisingly, Augustinianism formed a major part of the theology of the West, and its legacy has lasted down to the present century.

There is a vast literature on every aspect of Augustine's life and work. Literature published up to 1960 is catalogued in C. Andresen, *Bibliographia augustiniana*. Selections of Augustine's writings are: E. Przywara, *An Augustine Synthesis*, 1945; LCC, Vols. 6, 7, 8; there are several editions of the *Confessions, The City of God* and the *Letters*; for the last see especially *Select Letters*, LCL. For the controversial writings see *The Works of St Augustine*, ET 1870–1872.

Other useful introductions in English are: G. Bonner, *St Augustine of Hippo: Life and Controversies*, 1963; P. Brown, *Augustine of Hippo: A Biography*, 1967; J. Burnaby, *Amor Dei: A Study of the Religion of St Augustine*, 1938; R. F. Evans, *Pelagius: Inquiries and Reappraisals*, 1968; W. H. C. Frend, *The Donatist Church*, 1952, 1971; R. A. Markus, *Saeculum: History and Society in the Theology of St Augustine*, 1970; J. O'Meara, *The Young Augustine*, 1954; F. van der Meer, *Augustine the Bishop*, 1961; G. G. Willis, *St Augustine and the Donatist Controversy*, 1950.

W. H. C. FREND

Authority

It is useful to divide authority into external and internal authority. External authority is that attaching to a person as an official or to an office as an office. When someone obeys a policeman who asks him not to park his car in a certain place it is not the intrinsic conviction of the policeman's words that counts but his holding office as a guardian of the law. Internal authority is the authority residing in convincing argument or weighty moral or spiritual example or experience. If a woman buys a product advertised on television, for instance, it is the authority of the words and actions of the advertiser which has moved her. The authority of a bishop is an example of external, and the authority of a writer or a saint is that of internal, authority.

In the NT almost all authority is internal. The ultimate authority (which is the word of God) is expressed through preaching or through miraculous occurrences, or found in meditation or prayer or inspired vision and dream or in reading the (OT) scripture. Even the twelve apostles do not hold authority because they have been invested with an office, but because they are in a position to witness to what Christ did in the days of his flesh and to his appearances as risen Lord. But as the church gradually became a fixed and relatively uniform institution, official, external, authority inevitably came to play a greater and greater part. By the fourth century Christian writers are appealing to earlier authors as 'the tradition of the Fathers' – having regard rather to who they were than to what they said. This century also sees the advent of decisions of councils, which, once made, naturally have external authority attaching to them as expressing the judgment of the whole church or of a large part of it. As the centuries passed, more and more external authorities came into being. Fathers, doctors, councils, popes, and the origin and extensive growth of a codified Canon Law* assisted this development. By the end of the Middle Ages the church was supported by a vast system of external authority.

But the advent of the Reformation* with its emphasis upon the response of the individual in faith to the demand of the word of God, and the divisions of the church which resulted from it, assisted by the many impulses created by the Renaissance towards individualism and the rejection of established authority in metaphysics and theology, gradually brought about an entire change of attitude towards authority in the minds of Christians. Today the pendulum of opinion has swung to the other extreme. Internal authority is now widely regarded as the only authority in matters religious. The pronouncements of Fathers, councils and popes are regarded as purely historical (i.e. as witnessing to the state of opinion in their own periods) or are simply judged on their own merits according to contemporary criteria. In this sense it could be said that reason is the only authority recognized now, but this would be to use the word 'authority' in a quite different sense. *Reason* is the means whereby we reach religious convictions, not the matter which affords the material for making our judgments. All Christian traditions (certainly including the Roman Catholic) have in theory recognized this, at least as far as allowing that a man must always follow the authority of his own conscience in making moral decisions. In fact the question of reason or conscience as authority parallel with scripture, tradition, etc. can only be raised in a situation where external authority is regarded as the norm.

Judged by modern conceptions of authority, then, the authority of scripture will not be that of an inerrant oracle delivering equal truth in all its parts nor the authority of the church that of an autonomous institution under no responsibility to refer to the sources of its doctrine, but the Bible will be considered as the unique witness to the acts of God in history by which he makes himself known to all men and demands their response, and the church as the organ chosen by God to point to the Bible, to preach it, teach it, and to order its life by the light of the Bible. The authority of the Bible does not lie in the book itself but in the subject to which it witnesses, and the authority of the church lies ultimately in the Word of God whom it obeys and whose witness it finds in the Bible. The old maxim 'the church to teach and the Bible to prove' is no less true today than it ever was. In the barest terms, the church, and the church alone, had authority to offer to everybody the opportunity of being convinced by the authority of the Bible. But once this position is understood, it must be pointed out that it is impossible and indeed disastrous to attempt to exclude external authority altogether. Every organization claiming to be the church, or to have any association with the church, or to represent the church, even partially and locally, must wield administrative and executive authority in some form and must claim in some sense to wield it in the name of Christ. Again, the collective experience of the church, either in forming and holding to fundamental dogmas of the Christian faith tested by centuries of discussion and worship, or in learning moral and spiritual wisdom through a continuous history of prayer, worship and practice, still forms a very impressive argument not easily overthrown when rightly understood and handled.

Two more forms of authority must be mentioned. One is the authority of scholarship. To this, fluctuating and subjective though it be, the church and its theologians must pay full and respectful attention, without elevating it to a position of ultimate authority. The development of historical, literary and linguistic studies in the last two centuries has made this essential. The other is the authority of religious experience*. In one sense this must be decisive for every individual, because the personal, existential nature of Christian belief in God implies prayer and worship. And properly handled (e.g. by P. T. Forsyth or F. von Hügel), this aspect of Christian truth can become a strong argument. But it never can stand alone because of its subjective nature. If religious experience is our sole authority then the experience of a Joseph Smith, a Bernadette Soubirous or a Mrs Eddy is as authoritative as that of an Augustine or of a John of the Cross. The authority of religious experience must be supported and balanced by that of scripture and tradition. Authority for the Christian is a combination or harmony of several forms of authority, all fused in faith.

N. Lash, *Voices of Authority*, 1976; J. H. Newman, *An Essay in Aid of a Grammar of Assent*, 1870; J. Oman, *Vision and Authority*, 1902; J. G. Rogers and D. C. McKim, *The Authority and Interpretation of the Bible. An Historical Approach*, 1979; J. Yarnold and H. Chadwick, *Truth and Authority* (commentary on the Anglican/Roman Catholic Commission's Report on Authority), 1977.

R. P. C. HANSON

Autonomy

The right and freedom of self-determination as contrasted with determination by somebody or something else (heteronomy). Thus in ethics, for example, it has been widely claimed since Kant that the moral sphere of life is autonomous, i.e. is independent of religion or indeed of any other authority. Again, some assert that all knowledge derives from human reason and experience. They apply this principle to religious knowledge, saying therefore that religious knowledge is autonomous rather than being based on an externally given revelation * of God communicated in a sacred book or through a holy community.

Recent religious discussion of autonomy has explored two seemingly different, but in fact related, themes:

1. Autonomy can refer to a proud human self-reliance totally at odds with a proper dependence upon, and obedience to, God. In this sense autonomy is a primary manifestation of sin, which can be overcome only by God's transforming action in Christ. Some writers find the modern origins of this view of autonomy in the eighteenth-century Enlightenment *, with its radical shift from a sense of the helplessness of human beings to that of the progressive alteration of history by human powers. Certain subsequent theological movements, e.g. liberal * Protestantism, have (it is argued) absorbed this anthropocentric attitude, grievously undermining classical affirmations of divine sovereignty and grace.

2. However, other theologians have spoken of the rise of autonomy in a more neutral sense, as 'the discovery of the laws by which the world lives and deals with itself in science, social and political matters, art, ethics and religion' (Bonhoeffer). This outlook supercedes a world-view in which scientific laws could supposedly be deduced from theological axioms, in which human and natural regularities were open to constant divine invasion. Instead, acting autonomously, human reason could now quite properly proceed by a hypothetical method, and thus 'as if God did not exist'. In this sense autonomy is closely related to the notion of secularization *, understood not as a deliberate rejection of God, but as a legitimate realization of human freedom and knowledge. While it can be argued that this autonomy is God-intended and God-given, nonetheless the actual (if unintended) effect of this autonomy may in fact be to relegate God to a sphere beyond experience where he may be believed in against the appearances, but where he easily becomes irrelevant and is even experienced as dead.

If autonomy is to be seriously treated, Christian theology has to reconceive its doctrines of God * and the person (*see* **Anthropology**), so that God can be affirmed as significantly present, but not as a totally determining power, and human beings allowed a positive autonomy in sharing with God some responsibility for the outcome of historical and natural life. Process theology * provides one instance of such a reconception of theism *; political * and liberation * theology proposes a spirited account of the autonomous self-in-community. But these and other types of reconception can easily fall back into, respectively, generality and utopianism *. The perception of human autonomy as involving *both* bondage *and* liberation summons theology to unprecedented but disciplined integrations of Christian claims with the natural and human sciences and with the modern experience of action and contemplation.

Gerhard Ebeling, *Word and Faith*, 1963, ch.

4; Gordon D. Kaufman, *Systematic Theology*, 1968, Part 3.

A. O. DYSON

Averroism

A movement that sprang up in thirteenth-century European intellectual history and continued as a force of varying strength even in the Renaissance, at least in Italy. Averroes (1126–1198), an Arab commentator on Aristotle from Cordoba, was renowned as 'the commentator' for the acuity of his understanding of Aristotelian* philosophy. The widespread Latin Averroist movement of the thirteenth and fourteenth centuries was characterized by a general tendency to pursue philosophy independently of theology. Often its conclusions conflicted with Christian doctrine; the teachings of one of its chief proponents, Siger of Brabant, were condemned by church authorities in 1270 and 1277. Specifically Averroists taught, following Aristotle, that the world is eternal and that God acts only indirectly in the world through intermediaries. Thus miraculous events are precluded. Further, Averroists maintained that God knows only necessary and not contingent facts.

Consequently God has no direct knowledge of events on earth. But the tenet most closely associated with Averroism is that all humans share one and the same intellect and have one intellectual soul. Thus, properly speaking, only the one intellect knows; individual humans only participate in the act of knowing. Because we only share in the one universal soul, there can be no personal immortality for the individual. Our highest good, therefore, must be found in this life. Although condemned, Averroism spread in the fourteenth century, as evidenced by the frequent attacks on it. It came to be seen as a general assault on religion, or at least as promoting religious scepticism. It remained a force in philosophy in Italy in the fifteenth and sixteenth centuries, but died out subsequently as philosophical interest turned away from scholasticism*.

E. Renan, *Averroès et l'averroisme*, 1925; E. Gilson, *History of Christian Philosophy in the Middle Ages*, ET 1955.

JAMES P. ETZWILER

Baptism, Theology of
see **Initiation, Christian**

Baptist Theology

Baptists are distinguished among Protestants by two chief emphases in church order: 1. Congregational polity, i.e., the visible church manifest as the local gathered community of believers which is competent under Christ to interpret and administer his laws, without higher human authority; 2. Believers' baptism, i.e. baptism of those who on their own behalf profess repentance and faith in Christ, thus precluding infant baptism (but inaccurately described as 'adult baptism').

Apart from these emphases, there is no single scheme of doctrine which exactly typifies all branches of this, one of the most numerous and widespread denominations in the world. While Baptists have always been ready to identify with orthodox belief as expressed in the ecumenical creeds*, they have generally been more concerned about the possible misuse of verbal confessions of faith, either in coercing belief, or in obscuring true faith as a free, personal response to God in Christ. Some theological pluralism has marked Baptists almost from their very beginnings in seventeenth-century English separatism. The earliest 'General' Baptists, led by Thomas Helwys who founded the first Baptist church on English soil in 1612, were Arminian* in theology, while the 'Particular' Baptist stream which arose by the mid-century was strongly Calvinist*. Among the latter, there were lively debates in the late eighteenth century on the compatibility of a strict doctrine of election* with the obligation to preach the gospel to the heathen. It was the moderate or evangelical form of Calvinism which inspired the pioneering missionary enterprise led by William Carey. Ever since, Baptist theology may be said to reflect an evangelicalism in which missionary activism takes precedence over theological definition for its own sake. There are even diverse theologies of believers' baptism, from the view that it is primarily an outward demonstration of faith, to a more genuinely sacramental understanding of it as a means of grace and incorporation into the body of Christ.

However, certain theological presuppositions underlie the range of Baptist beliefs. Most important is the authority of scripture as the guide to faith and practice.

The rejection of infant baptism as not conforming to the NT involves Baptists, more rigorously than most other Protestants, in setting scripture against tradition *, however venerable. But again, this biblical emphasis can take varying expression. Thus while much Baptist preaching leans towards a conservative and sometimes even fundamentalist interpretation of scripture, a major Baptist contribution to modern theology has been through biblical-critical scholarship, especially in OT studies. Baptists contain a wide spectrum of conservative and liberal thought under a common sense of personal accountability to Christ. As the Declaration of Principle of the Baptist Union of Great Britain and Ireland states carefully: 'Our Lord and Saviour Jesus Christ, God manifest in the flesh, is the sole and absolute authority in all matters relating to faith and practice, as revealed in the Holy Scriptures', i.e. the authority of scripture derives from *the* supreme authority and head of the church, who is directly accessible to believer and congregation, and to whom alone the conscience is ultimately responsible.

This belief in the immediacy of Christ with his people has vital bearings on both the ecclesiological and social views of Baptists. Classic Baptist thought has a high concept of the ministry of word and sacrament, but not an authoritarian one. The minister is both set apart and called by the congregation which, under Christ, has competence to decide on such matters. Any form of episcopacy * or synodical government which would place the congregation under external authority is therefore hard to accept. Equally, while Baptists (unlike many of the earlier Anabaptists) have taken a typically Protestant, positive attitude towards social and civic responsibilities, they have from the first been adamant in calling for full religious liberty * for all citizens, and for the independence of church from state.

Baptists have continually had to face the theological issues posed by their own position. For instance, given the emphasis on the local congregation, what of wider manifestations of the visible church? In practice, Baptist polity has been connectional as well as local, i.e. churches forming associations, unions and conventions for mutual support, mission, ministerial education, etc. They are associated internationally in the Baptist World Alliance. Baptists have also yet to arrive at an agreed theology of children in the church.

A. Gilmorc (ed), *The Pattern of the Church: A Baptist View*, 1963; W. L. Lumpkin, *Baptist Confessions of Faith*, 1969; E. A. Payne, *The Baptist Union: A Short History*, 1959; R. G. Torbet, *A History of the Baptists*, 1963.

KEITH CLEMENTS

Basic Communities

This term is used for a recent phenomenon in Christianity. It is derived from the model of human society as a pyramid: ordinary people are governed by those belonging to upper strata in a hierarchical order. In modern industrialized countries the structure of these strata has become so complicated and weighs so heavily that they make human social life very difficult for people at the lowest level. 'Ordinary' people feel manipulated, powerless and isolated. That has led to all kinds of initiatives towards alternative forms of community in small social groupings. The great institutions of the church have a similar pyramidic structure. 'Ordinary' members of the church express their faith passively and individualistically. Their gatherings too are regulated from above, even down to points of detail. Recently, on a larger scale than ever before in the history of Christianity the feeling has been aroused that believing is not so much a question of true doctrine and obeying laws, but first and foremost the practice of love and service which can only be experienced in direct contact with others and therefore both demands and creates community.

Every member is equipped for this community by his or her baptism and contributes distinctive personal gifts, 'charismata', even though from the standpoint of the world he or she may belong among the poorest and least developed. In the RC church this awareness was expressed, and as a result also stimulated, at the Second Vatican Council, which in its dogmatic constitution on the church (*Lumen Gentium*, 1964) gave priority to the concept of the 'people of God'. This new awareness was expressed throughout the Christian world by the formation of tens of thousands of small Christian communities, basic communities, the members of which live out their faith in close relationships with each other.

Their position over against the 'official' church is extremely varied, depending on the circumstances in which they came into being. Where the initiative came from the clergy, as in Latin America, this position differs from that where laity began communities in opposition to the institutional church. Recruiting also differs widely. In Latin America basic communities have been formed among the poor and illiterate peasant population, sometimes as a result of the work of catechists and even of radio courses which have made people aware of new possibilities. In many Western countries basic communities have grown up among the middle classes, as the Christian form of an alternative life-style over against the dominant consumer society. There are also considerable differences in size and form. Sometimes members live close together, in a commune or in the same neighbourhood; sometimes their contacts are mainly at the meetings.

The sense that the church of Christ must be leaven in this world always also makes the basic communities the source of activities in the social and political spheres. These too are extremely varied, depending on the local situation and the possibilities open to the members. For all these reasons it is extremely difficult to describe the phenomenon under one heading. As general characteristics one might mention a maximum of living out faith and a mimimum of structures; room for everyone's 'charisma'; collective rather than individual leadership; stress on liturgical celebrations and shared listening to the Bible, the stories of which are related to the situation of the community; social involvement; ecumenical openness because different denominations are involved. There is a conviction that here, at the grass roots, the real life of the church is being lived, that here the church is 'happening'.

This new phenomenon presents an enormous challenge to the leaders of the great institutional churches. Sometimes it is vigorously repudiated, and sometimes thankfully welcomed as a work of God's spirit, as the way to a renewal through which Christianity will be able to make a better contribution to human salvation.

There is an enormous bibliography in the form of articles in many languages, but not many books. For an extensive listing see A. Müller and N. Greinacher, *Basisgemeinden/Les communautés de base, Concilium* 104, 1975 (not in English); Sergio Torres (ed), *The Challenge of Basic Christian Communities, 1981.*

LUCAS GROLLENBERG

Beatific Vision

The name used traditionally for the vision of God as he is, which will be the joy of the redeemed in heaven: man's *summum bonum* or ultimate fulfilment for which he was created. It will be enjoyed *in patria* (i.e. in heaven), but cannot be attained *in via* (i.e. during man's earthly pilgrimage), although it was held by some later mediaeval theologians that the beatific vision had been vouchsafed to certain favoured mortals in this life, especially Moses, Paul and Thomas Aquinas.

See also **Vision of God.**

ALAN RICHARDSON

Becoming *see* Being

Being, Becoming

The language of being developed in ancient Greek philosophy, and passed at an early stage into Christian theology. 'Being' denotes that which is real or has existence; its opposite is non-being or nothing. For Plato*, reality belonged to the eternal unchanging Forms or Ideas, while the realm of becoming was held to be intermediate between being and non-being. The Jewish philosopher Philo of Alexandria applied this Platonist teaching to the OT. The obvious link was the name of God as revealed to Moses: 'I am who I am' (Ex. 3.14). While this expression had originally, in all probability, a very active sense, it came to be interpreted as static immutable being. Philo's name for God is *ho ōn*, 'the Being' or 'He who is'. This combination of Platonist and OT thinking about God passed into patristic theology, and profoundly influenced Clement of Alexandria, Origen, Augustine and many others. There is still controversy about the so-called 'Hellenizing' of Christian theology. On the one side it is argued that it was necessary to find philosophical categories that would be free from the anthropomorphic* and sometimes naive ways of talking about God, derived from the OT; on the other side, it is claimed that the particular categories used spring from a concept of being as timeless, immutable, impassible and, in general, very hard to reconcile with the biblical conception of a God who is active in history and deeply involved with his people. It is true that there was an alternative tradition in Greek philosophy. Heraclitus had taught that everything is in flux, and Aristotle * had claimed that it is individual things that have being, and that the forms or ideas are abstractions, existing only in thought and having no independent being of their own. But in spite of the rediscovery of Aristotle in the Middle Ages, the Platonist understanding of being continued to be dominant. Thus Thomas Aquinas is echoing the tradition that goes back to Philo when he tells us that the most appropriate name for God is *Qui est*, 'He who is'. Classical Christian theism has followed Thomas in thinking of God as transcendent of the world of time and space (*see also* **Time and Timelessness**). He gives being to the world, and many theologians have recognized an analogy of being (*analogia entis*) which serves as a foundation for natural * theology and permits us to use the creature as a clue to the Creator. On the other hand, classical theists have denied that God is affected by the world. The question of being has been raised anew in twentieth-century philosophy and theology. Tillich is the best known theologian who has made extensive use of the concept of being in his teaching about God. He has two typical ways of speaking: God is being itself, and God is the ground of being. It has to be asked whether these two ways are consistent with one another. In the first case, God is identified with being, and at least in one stage of his thinking, Tillich believed that this is the only literal statement that can be made about God. But when it is said that God is the ground of being, he seems to have been removed to a distance from the world. In fact, this expression 'ground of being' comes from the Protestant mystic, Jakob Boehme. German mysticism can be traced back through such figures as Nicholas of Cusa and John Eckhart to Dionysius the Pseudo-Areopagite, who taught that God is 'above being' (*hyperousia*). Tillich in fact acknowledged that his own talk about 'God above God' was derived unconsciously from Dionysius.

Much of the twentieth-century theological talk about being has been influenced by the philosophy of Martin Heidegger. That philosophy has been concentrated on the question of the meaning of being. In the West, Heidegger believes, there has been increasingly a forgetting of being in a preoccupation with the beings, and this has culminated in the age of technological exploitation. Being has withdrawn itself, and this is possible, because being is 'wholly other' than the beings, though it is known only in and through the beings; at this point one can see Heidegger's relation to the German mystical tradition. There are many levels of being. The being of a stone, for instance, is very different from the active being of a human person. But the greatest difference of all, the 'ontological difference', is the difference between being as such and the beings. In his early philosophy, Heidegger tried to find a path from the being of man (*Dasein*) to being itself, but in the later works the order is reversed: one tries to be open to being in a meditative way and then to understand one's own being-in-the-world in the light of being. The word which Heidegger seems to find most appropriate in speaking of this ultimate or wholly other is 'giving'. Being is like an act of giving. Heidegger has departed from the notion of being as timeless. Being includes becoming, and has its own history in which it sometimes manifests itself and sometimes hides itself. Heidegger always speaks of being in impersonal language, and says it is not God. Certainly, being could not be God, if God is *a* being, as he has often been regarded. However, Heidegger's being seems close to the mystics' 'God beyond God', and it may well be that theology will have to find a concept of God that will allow for both personal and non-personal attributes (*see also* **Existentialism**).

Finally, we may note that process * philosophers and theologians, drawing upon the philosophies of Whitehead and Hartshorne, have declared that becoming has precedence over being. They have claimed that this leads to a much more dynamic conception of God, closer to the biblical God; and that it allows us to suppose that God is affected by the world and participates in the world's suffering. This may well be a valid criticism of some traditional ways of conceiving God as being, but it would not affect those theories which acknowledge that being includes becoming or that being has a history. It would seem that any adequate account of God or of reality in general would have to admit both being and becoming.

M. Heidegger, *Being and Time*, 1927, ET 1962; *Introduction to Metaphysics*, 1953, ET 1959; J. Macquarrie, *God-Talk*, 1967; E. L. Mascall, *He Who Is*, 1943; P. Tillich, *Systematic Theology*, I, 1951.

JOHN MACQUARRIE

Benediction, Blessing

In common use, a blessing is something one is fortunate to possess. The word reflects an ancient way of regarding life as subject to good or bad fortune, as being under a blessing or a curse. In biblical tradition God is the source of both, that is of a satisfactory or a self-destructive life (Deut. 30) according as his instruction is followed or not. They are blessed who trust God and keep his commandments; in turn they bless him (i.e. thank him) for all his benefits (Ps. 103.1–5). Upon his faithful people the priesthood is instructed to invoke the divine blessing (Num. 6.22–26). In the NT 'blessed' is attached to the divine name (following Jewish practice), to him who comes in the divine name, to his mother, and once (Matt. 25.34) to those approved by God. The following uses of verb and noun are notable: 1. Jesus blessed God (i.e. said the appropriate thanksgiving) before distributing food and drink at the Last Supper and the feeding miracle, so following Jewish custom which was continued in the old Christian practice of saying grace before and after meals. 2. Christians are urged to bless those who curse them (Luke 6.28; Rom. 12.14; I Cor. 4.12; I Peter 3.9). 3. In Paul's teaching, the blessing bestowed on Abraham is extended to Gentile Christians (Gen. 12.3; Gal. 3.8), though in Heb. 7.1–7 Abraham takes second place as a fount of blessing to the priest-king Melchizedek. 4. In Eph. 1.3 the reference to 'every spiritual blessing in the heavenly places' is a semi-gnostic development which later gave rise to speculation about the blessedness of heavenly life after death. Subsequent use added the belief that consecrated persons can bless objects and in some way transform them, no doubt helped on when the Latin 'benediction' was translated by the English root 'bless', which originally meant to mark by blood, and so to consecrate.

H. W. Beyer, *TDNT* II, 754–65, for biblical information; E. Mangenot, *DTC* II, 1, 629–39, for ecclesiastical usage.

KENNETH GRAYSTON

Benefits

In the OT the word connotes the gifts and favours and spiritual blessings of God to man (II Chron. 32.25; Pss. 68.19; 103.2). It was a natural transition for the word to pass over into the NT as the summing up of Christ's atoning work (I Tim. 6.2) in the sense of reconciliation as the end of creation (*see* **Recapitulation**), the final proof of the mercy of God. It has come to be in liturgical and theological language a synonym for Christ's redemptive work. Melanchthon's statement is typical of the thought of the Reformation *: *hoc est Christum cognoscere, beneficia eius cognoscere* ('to know Christ is to know his benefits'), which for him, and all the Reformers, meant an experiential knowledge of the benefits of Christ's work for man's redemption *, rather than an intellectual or doctrinal knowledge.

JAMES ATKINSON

Bible *see* **Scripture, Doctrine of**

Biblical Criticism

A loose term used to describe a complex field of study within which in modern times a variety of principles and techniques have developed, all aimed at a clearer understanding of the Bible. During the nineteenth and early twentieth century a distinction was drawn between 'lower criticism', concerned with the text of the Bible, and 'higher criticism', concerned with literary and historical matters, but this has proved too simplistic and is no longer in current usage.

Ideally, biblical criticism would be a neutral approach, no more than the process by which discerning (Greek *krinein*) judgments on the Bible are made (cf. literary criticism or music criticism). However, from the start it has been associated with controversy, and there seems little possibility of ridding the term completely of negative and polemical connotations (which are not present in near-synonyms like 'exegesis' or 'biblical interpretation'). This is a consequence of the settings in which biblical criticism originated and developed, the course it took from the Renaissance onwards, and many of the conclusions it has reached. It also has to be noted that the presuppositions and findings of modern biblical criticism have been little understood and accepted outside specialist academic circles and are in fact virtually unknown to the majority of Christians, who in practice adhere to mild forms of fundamentalism *. Moreover, because of its always inevitably provisional character, biblical criticism has proved notoriously difficult to relate to systematic theology.

Christian preoccupation with the Bible in the earliest period included two major controversial critical issues: the interpretation of what hitherto had been solely the Jewish Bible, now to be called the Old Testament, and the formation of a second collection of writings, to be given the same status and called the New Testament.

1. Arguments with Judaism often involved rival interpretations of O T passages, and on both sides this led to a critical concern to establish the most reliable text possible; a prime example of this concern is Origen's Hexapla (c. 231–45), which contained in six parallel columns – hence its name – the Hebrew text, the Hebrew text transliterated into Greek characters, and four different Greek translations. This was used by the great biblical scholar Jerome in his translation of the Bible into Latin, the Vulgate (from 382), aimed at ending the differences between texts of the previous Latin translation circulating in his time.

2. In Christianity, as in Judaism, the formation of a canon of scripture was a long-drawn out matter, never brought to a fully agreed conclusion in the case of the O T, where Protestants and Catholics, reflecting long-standing differences, have variant lists of canonical books (see **Apocrypha**). Arguments over which books belonged in the N T were still vigorous in the third century: Hebrews and Revelation are among the doubtful books which were eventually included; the Epistle of Barnabas and the Shepherd of Hermas among those which were not. That theological criticism played a major part in the discussion is highlighted in the case of Marcion, second-century founder of a church whose Bible was limited to a bowdlerized version of the Gospel of Luke and ten Pauline epistles.

Origen's critical concern with the Bible was, of course, only a part of his work. In interpreting it for his fellow Christians he worked on the basis that scripture had three senses: literal, moral and allegorical. In developed form this approach was to play a major role through the Middle Ages and beyond (see **Allegory and Typology, Senses of Scripture**). While enriching the devotional life of Christianity and contributing to moral and doctrinal formation, such a multi-level interpretation tended to disguise the actual content of the Bible and to discourage sustained critical questioning. This would accumulate problems for the future when the Bible was read in a different context. So too would the way in which, from even before Augustine, the Bible had also come to be regarded as an encyclopaedia containing authoritative information on every branch of knowledge. Furthermore, given that its precepts, interpreted along the lines indicated above, were part of the fabric of the ordering of Christian society (see **Christendom**), any form of criticism was bound to have social and political, as well as devotional and doctrinal consequences. This is evident from developments up to and including the Reformation * (not least the translation of the Bible into the vernacular) and the controversy following the findings of Copernicus and Galileo (the old Ptolemaic system was taken to have biblical support). The harsh treatment of critics proposing new interpretations or changes in the established position clearly shows them to have been seen as enemies of society.

There is, however, a fundamental difference between the conflict represented by the Reformation and that sparked off by Copernicus and Galileo. In the end, both sides in the Reformation controversy accepted the authority and the truth of scripture; the question was the nature of that authority and how it was to be exercised. Luther's critical principle was a scriptural principle (Scholder). Copernicus and Galileo, on the other hand, represented the beginnings of another challenge to Christian thought, that of scientific investigation, which appealed to an alternative source of authority for its findings: human reason and experimental investigation. When allied, most notably from the Enlightenment *onwards, with a profound moral concern, ultimately traceable back to the spiritualist movements of the twelfth and thirteenth centuries and continued through the 'left wing' of the Reformation and Puritanism (Reventlow), this approach was to question not only the accuracy of what had been thought to be factual statements in the Bible but also the moral values of much of its content.

New discoveries round about the time of Copernicus and Galileo were to bring changes to people's ideas not only of the heavens but also of the earth. This was the period of the great voyages, when for the first time the basic geography of the world was established. Discovery of new lands raised revolutionary new questions about human history which inevitably clashed with the biblical record. An important pioneering work in this respect was Isaac de La Peyrère's work *The Pre-Adamites* (1655), as a result of which he suffered a fate reminiscent of Galileo's. In his book he showed how the new findings relating to chronology and geography conflicted with the picture presented by the Bible: the only way he could find of reconciling the two was by arguing that Adam was not the first man, but only the ancestor of Israel.

Other, better-known figures to be included among the precursors of modern biblical criticism are Hugo Grotius (de Groot, 1583–1645), who wrote notes (*Annotationes*) on the books of the Bible, quietly commenting on their content as though the Bible were any other book; Thomas Hobbes (1588–1679), systematically criticizing the Bible in his concern with authority; Richard Simon (1638–1712), an Oratorian until he was expelled, and generally regarded as the founder of OT criticism because of his recognition of sources in the Pentateuch; and Simon's opponent Baruch Spinoza (1632–1677), who commented on the books of the Old Testament in seeking to reconcile the light of nature with the light of revelation.

The Deists*, though, were the ones who determined how later biblical criticism would develop. It is interesting, in view of the later dominance of Germany in biblical scholarship, that until the middle of the eighteenth century England led the questioning. The Deists gave nineteenth-century biblical criticism from Reimarus onwards (*see* **Jesus**) much of its ethos and determined the concerns by which it was motivated: for example, from them come the notion that a pure natural original religion was distorted by ritualism; the prominence assigned to the prophets and their alleged 'ethical monotheism'; and the central role accorded to the preaching of Jesus. Deistic views, too, still dominate popular critical discussion of the

Bible, which continues to view it rationalistically, without that sense of the nature of history* and cultural relativity* which are so much a mark of the best of contemporary criticism.

Two new factors were increasingly to bring a different tone to biblical criticism and lead to the enormous increase in activity from the nineteenth century onwards.

1. In varying degrees, depending on the scholar and setting, there developed the historical consciousness just referred to; i.e. it was realized that people from other times are not just modern men and women dressed up in other clothes; they look at the world and ask questions about it quite differently from us, so that understanding the Bible involves becoming acclimatized to a quite different world whose mind-sets, customs and assumptions all need carefully to be rediscovered (*see also* **Historical Criticism**).

2. Light was shed on the ancient world by archaeological exploration, through the reconstruction of the history of sites by stratigraphic analysis and the extensive new material, from artefacts to texts, which was discovered and could be dated accurately. For the first time, it was possible to begin to recreate a past age, in this case the world of the Ancient Near East and the Graeco-Roman world, and to locate the biblical texts in it.

These texts themselves were subjected to rigorous scrutiny and analysis, and during the nineteenth century major hypotheses were established, many of which, though still questioned in detail, have yet to be superseded. For example, Moses is no longer accepted as the author of the first five books of the Bible, the Pentateuch, which contains at least four major strands of tradition dating from different periods of Israelite history; the prophetic books grew organically from at most a nucleus containing sayings of the prophets whose names they bear; the psalms are a collection from many different stages in Israelite worship; there is a special relationship between the first three Gospels (known as the Synoptic Gospels: *see* **Jesus**); some of the letters attributed to Paul (the so-called Pastoral Epistles, to Timothy and Titus) are pseudonymous and come from a later period. Names of scholars involved in this research can be found in the books listed below.

The new approach to interpreting the

Bible was not achieved without many false moves and much opposition. Scholars like David Friedrich Strauss (1808–1874) in Tübingen and William Robertson Smith (1846–1894) in Aberdeen were dismissed from their professorial chairs for the views they held; the great German OT scholar Julius Wellhausen chose to resign his chair to become a lecturer in Semitics because he could not see how his work was helping the students in his charge who were training for the ministry. The publication of *Essays and Reviews* (1860) was a *cause célèbre* in mid-Victorian England. Arguing, among other things, that the Bible should be read like any other book, it was attacked in a petition from 11,000 clergymen and condemned in the Church of England's Convocation. Biblical criticism was rightly seen to be challenging the traditional authority of the Bible and this challenge was countered by a bitter rearguard action.

That such conflict is not evident in the latter half of this century does not mean that the issues which gave rise to it have been resolved. Quiet has been achieved largely by the disengagement of forces. On the one hand, biblical criticism is now largely carried on within the academic setting of universities, and the major areas of study relating to it are similar to those in other like disciplines. (Indeed, biblical criticism contributed substantially to the interpretation of Graeco-Roman classical literature in the nineteenth century, *see also* **Literary Criticism.**) Its sub-divisions (textual criticism, historical criticism, grammatical criticism, literary criticism, form criticism, tradition criticism and redaction criticism, to mention the main ones) could equally well be applied to other bodies of literature. Contributions to biblical criticism from e.g. cognitive dissonance *, structuralism * and cultural anthropology show how more recently the pioneering work has been done in other fields and only subsequently applied to the Bible. On the other hand, the churches have far less influence and, as indicated above, have largely ignored or shelved the problem of biblical authority, affirming it but not substantiating their claim.

Viewed as an academic discipline, biblical criticism has a great deal to its credit: we can gain a deepened understanding of the Bible and its cultural setting, and particularly in the case of the OT the amount of

territory still unexplored promises that there will be further significant discoveries in the future. But the relationship of all this activity to understanding the role of the Bible in the theology, ethics and worship of the Christian church is a problem which cries out for a better solution.

Because in modern scholarship, research into the Bible and its setting is like research into any other text and its historical background, the reader is taken back into an increasingly realistic reconstruction of another world, literary and historical. But this does not help relieve the tension between an understanding of the Bible as a document from a culturally conditioned past and an understanding of the Bible as the authority for today's church. The problems run parallel to those arising over the person of Jesus *, and the difficulties they present can be seen from the conspicuous failures to solve fundamental issues. Thus OT study seems to have lost any focal point and rapidly turns into Near Eastern archaeology or comparative religion; neither OT theology* nor NT theology * have convincingly established themselves as disciplines (*see also* **Biblical Theology**), bearing witness more to the personal idiosyncrasies of their practitioners than to a coherent subject-matter; and grave doubts attach to attempts to ground ethics or doctrine in the authority of the Bible. Attempts to establish an adequate hermeneutical * approach even to the NT (as chronicled by A. C. Thiselton, *The Two Horizons*, 1980) would seem to end in hypersophistication or chaos. There is no disguising the fact that the problems associated with biblical criticism are one of the major factors in the contemporary theological malaise.

H. F. von Campenhausen, *The Formation of the Christian Bible*, ET 1972; R. E. Clements, *A Century of Old Testament Study*, 1976; G. Ebeling, 'The Significance of the Critical Historical Method for Church and Theology in Protestantism', in *Word and Faith*, ET 1963, pp. 17–61; P. Henry, *New Directions in New Testament Study*, 1979; D. H. Kelsey, *The Uses of Scripture in Recent Theology*, 1975; H. J. Kraus, *Geschichte der Historisch-kritischen Erforschung des Alten Testaments*, 1956; W. G. Kümmel, *The New Testament: The History of the Interpretation of its Problems*, ET 1972; Bruce J. Malina, *The New*

Testament World: Insights from Cultural Anthropology, 1983; S. Neill, *The Interpretation of the New Testament. 1861–1961*, 1964; D. E. Nineham, *The Use and Abuse of the Bible*, 1976; H. G. Reventlow, *Bibelautorität und Geist der Moderne*, 1980; K. Scholder, *Ursprünge und Probleme der Bibelkritik im 17. Jahrhundert*, 1966; B. Smalley, *The Study of the Bible in the Middle Ages*, rev. ed., 1964. Convenient accounts of the various sub-disciplines of biblical criticism may be found in the Guides to Biblical Scholarship published by Fortress Press, 1969ff.

JOHN BOWDEN

Biblical Theology

The expression is used in a number of senses, ranging from the very general to the specific. It may describe any theology which seeks to base itself largely or wholly on scripture, whether out of simplicity or because of elaborated doctrinal principles. But in particular, it refers to a movement which was in its heyday in the 1940s and 1950s, though its roots lay further back, and which, while possessing certain common features, was not wholly homogeneous. The reaction to liberal theology *, led by Karl Barth in the years immediately following the First World War, was the major impulse behind it, though it involved chiefly biblical scholars of various kinds rather than dogmaticians. This often gave it an appearance of 'scientific' scholarship whose concealed presuppositions the critics of the movement were in due course only too ready to expose. By contrast with the older liberal theologians, those involved in the new movement emphasized the distinctive nature of biblical concepts as opposed to their connections with the cultures surrounding ancient Israel and the early church. They stressed too, over against the secular philosophical bases of much liberal theology, the sufficiency of the Bible itself as the source for all necessary theological material. Added to that was a conviction of the essential coherence of the Bible, seen in terms of overarching and pervasive themes and concepts. Undoubtedly, the positive concern which marked the biblical theologians gave welcome refreshment to many who had come to see biblical scholarship as interested chiefly in questions of language and literary analysis and the assimilation of the biblical writings to the surrounding cultures of the Near East and the Hellenistic world.

The movement was, however, marked by variations of emphasis and of usefulness. In the RC church, it served in effect as the route whereby the new freedom accorded to biblical scholarship in the 1940s could win its way, free from charges of theological irrelevance or risky liberalism. Many Protestants, on the other hand, were glad to unite the fruits of good critical scholarship with renewed attention to the scriptural roots of their doctrinal tradition. In the work of the Albright school in the USA (notably in G. E. Wright, *God Who Acts*, 1954, and, implicitly, John Bright's popular *History of Israel*, 1959), the theological stress fell on the idea of God's action in history as the medium of revelation *, and a sense of solidity was conveyed as Judaeo-Christian faith was seen to be grounded in events as opposed to mere ideas. There was, too, a moderately conservative (and perhaps unsophisticated) attitude to the historical value of the biblical writings themselves.

German biblical theology was more strongly conceptual in its orientation, though Oscar Cullmann developed the highly influential idea of salvation history (notably in his *Christ and Time*, 1946), which again stressed the 'event' aspect of the Bible, but now linked it to the notion of a seemingly insulated stream of biblical history, moving onwards under the saving intentions of God, within the flow of secular history. But this way of seeing unity in the Bible was one of many. Others saw key themes in 'covenant', 'proclamation', or 'confession' (cf. G. von Rad's profound and influential *OT Theology*, 1957). The very variety of alleged key themes cast some doubt on the adequacy of the enterprise itself, as did the fact that no attempt to synthesize the Bible's theology seemed able to do justice to the whole of the material. Always some part tended to be left aside. In the case of the OT, the historical material often received the lion's share of attention, at the expense of the wisdom writings; or, in a book like C. H. Dodd, *The Authority of the Bible* (1928), the centre of gravity was placed in the prophets at the expense of the law. Cullmann's key concept of salvation history seemed, when it came to the NT, to square more with Luke–Acts than the Fourth Gospel. In other words, biblical theology, in the hands of some of its leading exponents, was less free from presuppositions, less simply 'read off' the text itself, than it seemed to claim.

Similarly, on the linguistic side, many of the contributors to G. Kittel's *Theological Dictionary of the NT* (1933 onwards), as indeed the structure of the work as a whole, conveyed the message that words used in the Bible often acquired new and special senses when written by the canonical writers. This was reinforced (in works like T. Boman, *Hebrew Thought Compared with Greek*, 1954) by the claim that there were clear and sharp contrasts between Hebrew and Greek thought, which were presented as disadvantageous to the latter when it came to the expression of Christian faith.

One of the first substantial challenges to biblical theology (James Barr, *The Semantics of Biblical Language*, 1961) concentrated on this aspect. He saw much of the work in this area as making exaggerated and mistaken claims as well as following misleading methods. It placed the distinctiveness of the biblical writers at the wrong points and viewed it in a false perspective, largely determined by doctrinal considerations. Cool enquiry indicated that much work produced from the general standpoint of biblical theology had made scholarship the servant of insufficiently subtle or untenable theological ideas.

It is chiefly in relation to these ideas that more recent scholarship has made much biblical theology look oversimplified; though on the historical side a number of major works (e.g. M. Hengel, *Judaism and Hellenism*, ET 1974) have demonstrated the complexity of the interpenetration of Jewish and Greek thought and culture in the period of the origins of Christianity. Complexity has also come to the fore in new emphasis on the diversity within the Bible, not only over the wide range of the OT but also within the relatively narrow compass of the early church as witnessed in the NT (cf. J. D. G. Dunn, *Unity and Diversity in the NT*, 1977; J. L. Houlden, *Ethics and the NT*, 1973). The greater awareness of pluralism of thought (and especially a heightened perception of the implications of the differences between the Gospels) has caused a revolution in the theological approach to the Bible, whose coherence now seems less easy to define. The revolution has been strengthened by a new sense in some quarters of the cultural distance between the Bible and the present day, rendering otiose and even naive the ease and directness with which the advocates of biblical theology made use of biblical ideas and language (cf. D. E. Nineham, *The Use and Abuse of the Bible*, 1976).

In other ways, too, greater subtlety has supervened; for example, in the removal of the blur which marked the distinction between the events behind the biblical narrative and the narrative itself. There is a new perception of the theological value of the Bible as a literary entity (or collection of entities), as containing 'story', whose message is of value apart from events which may lie behind it (*see also* **Narrative Theology**). There is also a new clarity in seeing that the biblical writings are secondary – the expression of a faith which was located in the communities of Israel and then the church; and that the theological understanding of the documents must depend upon a grasp of the realities of life as experienced by those communities. The hermeneutical* task (how to interpret the documents now in a different world, related by the tradition of faith) follows. Some have gone so far as to see biblical theology as an almost wilful refusal to face the profound theological difficulties of our times, in effect a retreat into a citadel which has proved all too vulnerable (D. Cupitt, *The World to Come*, 1982, p. 22).

For those who are impressed by these criticisms of biblical theology and by the developments in theology which have given rise to them, there can be no doubt that the role of the Bible in the pattern of Christian thought is a question demanding urgent reappraisal.

All the same, biblical theology itself continues to bear fruit. It was highly influential in the theological achievement of the reformists at the Second Vatican Council and contributed much to the provision of an alternative and more flexible theological framework over against the heritage of scholasticism. It has impressed itself upon the arrangements for thematic scripture readings in the revised lectionaries of the RC, Anglican and other churches; so that its diffused effect will be felt for many years by preachers and congregations. And it has provided a hopeful background for ecumenical negotiations, notably between Roman Catholics and Anglicans, hitherto locked in an inability to bring their theological traditions into fruitful relationship but somewhat released by common attention to biblical ideas and themes (cf. *ARCIC Final Report*, 1982).

See also **Old Testament Theology; New Testament Theology.**

James Barr, *The Bible in the Modern World*, 1973; W. J. Harrington, *The Path of Biblical Theology*, 1973; J. D. Smart, *The Past, Present and Future of Biblical Theology*, 1979.

J. L. HOULDEN

Bibliolatry

A term used pejoratively for theories of biblical inspiration which assert the inerrancy of the Bible and demand the submission of the human reason to the literalist interpretation of it ('a paper pope'). Derived from the Greek, the word means 'bookworship' (cf. idolatry, Mariolatry, etc.).

ALAN RICHARDSON

Binitarianism

The term refers to a two-fold (rather than a three-fold) expression of that mysterious self-differentiation which is believed to occur in God because of God's creative and salvific outreach to the world. Binitarianism is accidental when it results from complete, or almost complete, lack of attention to the theological needs of a second distinction in the deity. As such it is fairly common. It is much more than accidental, though not necessarily as yet explicit, when uses of the terms Word and Spirit (or their equivalent) for the divine dimension which constitutes God's outreach towards the world coincide to such an extent as inevitably to give impressions of twofoldness rather than threefoldness. As such it can obviously claim strong scriptural support; it was quite common in those Christian centuries which coincided with the Middle-Platonic* period (itself predominantly binitarian), and its quiet possession of the early theological scene was no more disturbed by triadic baptismal formulae and confessions than by the many alternative terms which could be used for its expression (Wisdom, Son and so on). In the Neoplatonic* period, particularly in the fourth century, trinitarianism became the norm in Christian theology. This coincided with, and may partly have resulted

from, two quite different movements, both of which were judged heretical. The first was an Arian* trinitarian theology which as resolutely subordinated Spirit to Son as it subordinated Son to Father: it was rejected in Basil's *On the Holy Spirit*. The second was a form of Nicene orthodoxy which confessed the *homoousios** of the Son but refused a *third* co-equal one in the Trinity and called Spirit a superior angel: it was rejected by Athanasius in his *Letters to Serapion*. Elements of binitarianism continued to emerge in orthodox authors as evidence of its intact orthodox possibilities.

See **Trinity, Doctrine of the.**

J. P. MACKEY

Bishop

A ministry in the Christian church, the term stemming from the Greek *episkopos*, 'overseer'. In the NT *episkopos*, as a term for persons exercising some leadership in the Christian community, is used expressly in Phil. 1.1; I Tim. 3.1–7; Titus 1.7–9, but is not really distinguished from *presbyteros*, 'elder'. For example, both terms are used to refer to the leaders of the church of Ephesus in Acts 20.17, 28. Thus, there is not a clarified single use of the term in the NT. Moreover, the use of the plural in Phil. 1.1; Acts 20.28 indicates that there was not one official called *episkopos* in these communities.

In the second century, *episkopos* came to be the accepted term for the single chief leader of the Christian community in a given place, Ignatius of Antioch being the most striking early witness to this 'monarchical episcopate'. This became the settled historical use of the term in RC and Orthodox church order: the bishop is the supreme governing, teaching and liturgical authority in a territory known as a diocese. Theologically and ideally speaking, the bishop should be the living symbol and effective principle of unity in the community of faith. Sacramentally, ordination* to the episcopate is considered the conferral of the fullness of the priesthood. In this ecclesiology, the bishops collectively are believed to be successors of the apostles* and thus empowered, especially when assembled in council, to state Christian doctrine authoritatively for the whole church and to apply it in pastoral and liturgical legislation (*see also* **Conciliarity**).

In early centuries, bishops were chosen

by the clergy and people of the place in a process presided over by the metropolitan (archbishop) of the area. This practice was confirmed by councils and periodically reaffirmed in the West by popes, who had no other involvement in the process. From the fourth century on, emperors and kings intervened covertly or overtly in the choice. This intervention, induced both by a caesaropapistic concept of the role of the temporal ruler and by the large amounts of property pertaining to the bishoprics, was at times resisted (as in the Gregorian Reform of the eleventh century) and at times accepted (as in a system like that of Gallican France) by the church. By the thirteenth century, popes began asserting a major role in choosing bishops in the R C Church, but this did not become the prevalent practice until recent times when direct papal appointment of bishops became the established norm. The Second Vatican Council, in its doctrine of collegiality, stresses ways in which the whole body of bishops shares in authority and responsibility in the church.

Most churches issuing from the Reformation * of the sixteenth century rejected the office of bishop, but several, notably the Church of England and the Lutheran Church in certain countries, retained it together with the doctrine of apostolic succession *.

See also **Episcopacy.**

R. Brown, *Priest and Bishop*, 1970; B. Cooke, *Ministry to Word and Sacraments*, 1976; W. Telfer, *The Office of a Bishop*, 1962.

R. F. COSTIGAN

Black Theology

The concept refers to a theological movement that emerged among North American black people during the second half of the 1960s. During the early part of the 1970s, the North American idea of black theology began to make an impact in South Africa. This article is limited to the origin and meaning of North American black theology.

1. *The Origin of Black Theology.* This has three contexts: 1. the civil rights movement of the 1950s and 1960s, largely associated with Martin Luther King, Jr; 2. the publica-

tion of Joseph Washington's *Black Religion* (1964); 3. the rise of the black power movement, strongly influenced by Malcolm X's philosophy of black nationalism.

(*a*) *The civil rights movement.* All persons involved in the rise of black theology were also deeply involved in the civil rights movement, and they participated in the protest demonstrations led by Martin King. Unlike most contemporary theological movements in Europe and North America, black theology's origin did not take place in the seminary or the university. In fact, most of its early interpreters did not even hold advanced academic degrees. Black theology came into being in the context of black people's struggle for racial justice, which was initiated in the black churches, but chiefly identified with such protest organizations as the Southern Christian Leadership Conference (S C L C), National Conference of Black Churchmen (N C B C), Interreligious Foundation for Community Organization (I F C O), and many black caucuses in white churches.

From the beginning, black theology was understood by its creators as a Christian theological reflection upon the black struggle for justice and liberation, largely defined in the life and thought of Martin Luther King, Jr. When Martin King and other black churchpeople began to relate the Christian gospel to the struggle for justice in American society, the great majority of white churches and their theologians denied that such a relationship existed. Conservative white Christians claimed that religion and politics did not mix. Liberal white Christians, with a few exceptions during the 1950s and early 1960s, remained silent on the theme or advocated a form of gradualism that denounced boycotts, sit-ins and freedom-rides.

Contrary to popular opinion, Martin King was not well-received by the white American church establishment when he inaugurated the civil rights movement with the Montgomery bus boycott in 1955. Because black people received no theological support from white churches and their theologians (who were too occupied with Barth, Bultmann and the death of God controversy!), black people themselves had to look deeply into their own history in order to find a theological basis for their prior political commitment to set free the black

poor. They found support in Richard Allen
(the founder of the African Methodist Episcopal Church [AME] in 1816), Henry
Highland Garnet (a nineteenth-century
Presbyterian preacher who urged slaves to
resist slavery), Nat Turner (a slave Baptist
preacher who led an insurrection that killed
sixty whites), Henry McNeal Turner (an
AME bishop who claimed in 1898 that 'God
is a Negro'), and many others. When blacks
investigated their religious history, they were
reminded that their struggle for political
freedom did not begin in the 1950s and 1960s
but had roots stretching back many years. It
was also encouraging to find out that the
black people's struggle for political justice
in North America has always been located
in their churches. Whether we speak of the
independent Northern churches (AME,
AMEZ, Baptists, etc.), the so-called 'invisible institution' among slaves in the South
(which merged with the independent black
churches after the Civil War), or blacks in
white denominations, black Christians have
always known that the God of Moses and
of Jesus did not create them to be slaves or
second-class citizens in North America. In
order to make a theological witness of this
religious knowledge, black preachers and
civil right activists of the 1960s developed a
black theology that rejected racism and
affirmed the black struggle for liberation as
consistent with the gospel of Jesus.

(b) *Joseph Washington's black religion.*
When black preachers and lay activist
Christians began to search for the radical
side of their black church history, they also
began to ask about the distinctive religious
and theological contributions of black
people. It was assumed by most whites, and
many blacks as well, that black people's culture had no unique contribution to make to
Christianity in particular and humanity
generally. Indeed white liberal Christians
understood integration to mean assimilation, that is, blacks rejecting their cultural
past by adopting Euro-American cultural
values. The assumption behind the white
definition of integration was the belief that
African cultural retentions among North
American blacks were completely destroyed
during slavery. Therefore, if blacks were to
develop a cultural knowledge of themselves,
they had to find it in their identification with
white American values.

Contrary to the dominant view, the black
scholar Joseph Washington contended that
there was a unique black culture, including
a distinctive black religion that could be
placed alongside Protestantism, Catholicism, Judaism and secularism. Black religion
is not identical with white Protestantism or
any other expression of Euro-American
Christianity. Washington, however, was not
pleased with the continued existence of
black religion, and he placed the blame
squarely upon white Christians. He contended that black religion exists only
because black people have been excluded
from the genuine Christianity of white
churches. Because blacks were excluded
from the faith of white churches, black
churches are not genuine Christian
churches. And if there are no genuine Christian churches, there can be no Christian
theology. Blacks have only folk religion and
folk theology. In Washington's own words:
'Negro congregations are not churches but
religious societies – religion can choose to
worship whatever gods are pleasing. But a
church without a theology, the interpretation of a response of the will of God for the
faithful, is a contradiction in terms (*Black
Religion*, pp. 142f.).

Although Washington's *Black Religion*
was received with enthusiasm in the white
community, it was strongly denounced in
the black church community. Indeed, black
theology was created, in part, to refute
Washington's thesis. Black preachers
wanted to correct two misconceptions: 1.
that black religion is not Christian and
thus has no Christian theology; 2. that the
Christian gospel has nothing to do with the
struggle for justice in society.

(c) *The black power movement.* After the
March on Washington in August 1963, the
integration theme in the black community
began to lose ground to the black nationalist
philosophy of Malcolm X. The riots in the
ghettoes of US cities were shocking evidence
that many blacks agreed with Malcolm X's
contention that America was not a dream
but a nightmare.

However, it was not until the summer of
1966, after Malcolm X's assassination
(1965), that the term black power began to
replace the word integration among many
civil rights activists. The occasion was the
continuation of the James Meredith's
'march against fear' (in Mississippi) by
Martin   Luther   King,   Jr,   Stokely

Carmichael, and other civil rights activists. Stokely Carmichael seized this occasion to sound the black power slogan, and it was heard loud and clear throughout the US.

The rise of black power had a profound effect upon the appearance of black theology. When Carmichael and other radical black activists separated themselves from Martin King's absolute commitment to nonviolence by proclaiming black power, white church-people, especially clergymen, called upon their black brothers and sisters in the gospel to denounce black power as un-Christian. To the surprise of white Christians, black ministers refused to follow their advice and instead wrote a 'Black Power' statement that was published in *The New York Times*, 31 July 1966.

The publication of the 'Black Power' statement may be regarded as the beginning of the conscious development of a black theology in which black ministers consciously separated their understanding of the gospel of Jesus from white Christianity and identified it with the struggles of the black poor for justice. Radical black clergy created an ecumenical organization called the National Conference of Black Churchmen (NCBC) as well as black caucuses in the National Council of Churches and almost all white churches. Black clergy denounced white racism as the antichrist, and were unrelenting in their attack in its demonic presence in white denominations. It was in this context that the phrase black theology emerged.

2. *Black Theology as Liberation Theology.* It is one thing to proclaim black theology and quite another to give it theological substance. Many white Christians and almost all white theologians dismissed black theology as nothing but rhetoric. Since white theologians controlled the seminaries and university departments of religion, they made many blacks feel that only Europeans and persons who think like them could define what theology is. In order to challenge the white monopoly on the definition of theology, many young black scholars realized that they had to carry the fight to the seminaries and universities where theology was being written.

The first book on black theology was written by James Cone under the title of *Black Theology and Black Power* (1969). The central thesis of that book was its identification of the liberating elements in black power with the Christian gospel. One year later Cone wrote *A Black Theology of Liberation* (1970), and made liberation the organizing centre of his theological system. He wrote: 'Christian theology is a theology of liberation. It is a rational study of the being of God in the world in the light of the existential situation of an oppressed community, relating the forces of liberation to the essence of the gospel, which is Jesus Christ' (p. 17).

After James Cone's works appeared, other black theologians joined him, supporting his theological project and also challenging what they regarded as his excesses. In his *Liberation and Reconciliation: A Black Theology* (1971), J. Deotis Roberts, while supporting Cone's emphasis on liberation, claimed that he overlooked reconciliation as central to the gospel and black-white relations. A similar position was advocated by Major Jones' *Black Awareness: A Theology of Hope* (1971). Other black theologians claimed that Cone was too dependent upon white theology and thus was not sufficiently aware of the African origins of black religion. This position is taken by Cone's brother, Cecil, in his *Identity Crisis in Black Theology* (1975), and it is also found in Gayraud Wilmore's *Black Religion and Black Radicalism* (1972).

While James Cone's perspective on black theology was challenged by other black scholars, they supported his claim that liberation was the central core of the gospel as found in the scriptures and the religious history of black Americans. For black theologians the *political* meaning of liberation was best illustrated in the Exodus, and its *eschatological* meaning was found in the life, death, and resurrection of Jesus. The Exodus was interpreted to be analogous to Nat Turner's slave insurrection and Harriet Tubman's liberation of an estimated 300 slaves. Slave songs (often called 'Negro Spirituals'), sermons, and prayers expressed the futuristic character of liberation found in the resurrection of Jesus.

During the beginning of the 1970s, black theologians of North America began to have some contact with other forms of liberation theology in Africa, Latin America, and Asia. Black theology in South Africa became a natural ally. Although Latin

American theologians emphasized classism rather than racism, black and Latin theologies became partners in their identification of the gospel with the liberation of the poor. A similar partnership occurred with black and Asian theologians regarding the importance of our culture in defining theology. Recently a feminist consciousness has also emerged among black women, and this has led to the beginnings of a black feminist theology (*see also* **Feminist Theology**).

On the basis of their mutual concern of defining the gospel as identical with the liberation of the poor, black and other Third World theologians organized the Ecumenical Association of Third World Theologians (1976) and have held several conferences in their attempt to develop a liberation theology common to us all. It has been within the context of black theology's dialogue with Third World theologies that the universal character of the gospel has been reaffirmed, because black Christians believe that no one can be free until all are set free.

See also **Liberation Theology.**

James H. Cone, *God of the Oppressed*, 1975; *My Soul Looks Back*, 1982; J. Deotis Roberts, *Liberation and Reconciliation: A Black Theology*, 1971; Joseph Washington, *Black Religion*, 1964; Gayraud S. Wilmore, *Black Religion and Black Radicalism*, 1972; Gayraud S. Wilmore and James H. Cone (eds.), *Black Theology: A Documentary History, 1966–1979*, 1979.

JAMES H. CONE

Blasphemy

Verbal assault on the sacred is judged severely in many societies, often with legal penalties. The injunction against reviling God in Ex. 22.28 has been formative theologically, and reference to its Mosaic penalties in Lev. 24.10–23 has influenced its treatment as a capital crime in some periods of Western history. Cases of blasphemy and the execution of punishment for it (by stoning) were rare in Hebrew history and rendered virtually impossible in rabbinic interpretation. In the Christian era the term expanded beyond the original meaning of abusive utterance against deity to include other perceived defamation of God's purposes including heterodoxy. N T accounts of Christ before the Sanhedrin (Mark 14.53–65), in the portico of Solomon (John 10.22–

33), healing the paralytic (Mark 2.5–12), Stephen's execution (Acts 6.11–14), and the association of it with unsound teaching (I Tim. 1.13; 6.1; Titus 2.5) were interpreted as warrants for linking blasphemy and heresy *, and punishing them with ecclesial sanctions that ran from censure to excommunication in early Christianity. Later an established church used the powers of the state to enforce more stringent measures against 'heretics and blasphemers', with the former becoming the encompassing identification for religious deviance. Some theologians sought to make distinctions between blasphemy as ill-will against God and unbelief, but others like Aquinas viewed blasphemy as a species (like heresy) of unbelief, the most grievous. As only professing Christians could be declared heretics, the specific charge of blasphemy was sometimes reserved for non-Christians, especially Jews, whose theological indictment was used to justify popular reprisals and subsequently pogroms carried out in conjunction with the crusades.

At the Reformation * blasphemy replaced heresy as the principal charge against religious belief that was seen as undermining both faith and society. It became a common epithet for error in doctrinal controversy. In the seventeenth century the state began to police doctrinal deviation, linking it with sedition. In that period in England, Puritan and Independent fell under the Star Chamber's campaigns against blasphemy, but later were themselves party to the Acts of 1648 and 1650 which designated it as a capital crime, having in view Anabaptists, Socinians, Familists and Ranters. The Restoration continued to treat blasphemy as a punishable crime but separated it from sedition, deliminating it to execrable words against the deity, but conceived so as to include heresy.

The blood spilled in the prosecution of dissent labelled blasphemous finally evoked counter-movements for both intellectual freedom and religious liberty * that have left their mark on doctrine and political charters. However, blasphemy laws may still be found on British and American statutes, now drastically altered from theological to psychological categories: the giving of public offence to the religious sensibilities of any group in the nation. Attempts to prosecute in the United States in 1971 and England in

1978 resulted in a token fine in the latter case and withdrawal of suit in the former.

Christian theology today, if it uses the term at all, tends to employ it either in the restricted sense of abusive language towards God (to be distinguished from profanity) or as radical opposition to the purposes of God such as 'the blasphemy of nuclear war', or the unforgiving heart that is 'blasphemy against the Holy Spirit' (Matt. 12.31; 6.12), to be countered not by sanctions of the state but by personal witness and ecclesial mission.

W. K. Jordan, *The Development of Religious Toleration in England*, 4 vols., 1932–1940; L. W. Levy, *Treason Against God: A History of the Offense of Blasphemy*, 1981.

GABRIEL FACKRE

Blood of Christ

The word 'blood' in the OT, apart from the everyday physiological meaning, is generally associated with the idea of death, violent death in particular. Certain scholars have urged (Milligan, Westcott, Hicks, Vincent Taylor, to name but a few) that the term means life rather than death, thereby emphasizing that the central idea of sacrifice* is the offering up of life, a view that is by no means universally accepted. When the word 'blood' is associated with atonement*, or with the cultus, the prime emphasis is on death not on life, or if with life, it is a life offered in death. Similarly in the NT, the word 'blood' is mostly indicative of violent death. Associations with sacrifice are confined to the Epistle to the Hebrews. Other references are mainly to Christ's death, in particular the death of the cross (Rom. 5.9f.; Col. 1.20; Eph. 2.13; I John 5.6; Rev. 1.5). It is difficult to come to any other conclusion than that these passages mean the death of Christ on the cross within a framework of salvation doctrine. It is not certain what the scholars mentioned above are arguing when they write that in the death of Christ his 'life' was 'liberated' and 'made available' for man. If by that is meant that the life of the Risen Lord is true life because his death is in it, that is true, but this subtlety, even when true, must not be allowed to becloud the plain fact that Christ laid down his life in sacrifice on the cross. In fact, the phrase 'the blood of Christ', like the word 'the cross', is nothing but a pregnant phrase for the death of Christ in its salvation meaning.

There is a finality and a once-for-all-ness about this death. It is the blood of the New Covenant (Matt. 26.28; Mark 14.24; Luke 22.20; I Cor. 11.25; II Cor. 3.6; Heb. 9.15 etc.), foretold by Jeremiah (Jer. 31.31). It further connotes at once both the fulfilment of the old covenant and its cessation. Jesus is both sacrifice and high priest in one, God's servant whose blood has everlasting atonement for all, and who has sealed the covenant* relationship between God and his people for ever. The power of Jesus' blood to effect salvation* comes to expression in several forms in the NT: it cleanses from sin (I John 1.7; Heb. 9.14; Rev. 1.5; 7.14): it sanctifies (Heb. 10.29); it offers forgiveness (Eph. 1.7); it re-establishes the people of God (Eph. 2.13); it redeems (Rev. 5.9). Already in the NT the blood is associated with the Holy Communion (I Cor. 10.16; 11.26), but not in any *ex opere operato** sense. It is always bound up with ideas of repentance (Rom. 3.25; 5.9; Col. 1.20–23), confession of sin (I John 1.7–10), and turning to God in faith (Heb. 10.19).

See also **Precious Blood.**

JAMES ATKINSON

Body

Two pressures in the nascent Christian churches prompted patristic* authors to give attention to the explication of their views on the human body and the relation of body and soul* in human beings. On the metaphysical side, Gnostic* doctrines of the creation of the body and the material world by an evil demiurge* (*see* **Gnosticism**) caused Christian authors to affirm in opposition the permanent goodness and integrity of the body by insisting on the centrality to Christian faith of the doctrines of creation* of the material world by God, the incarnation* of Jesus Christ in a fully human body, and the ultimate resurrection* of the body. On the practical side, the threat of martyrdom in the first three centuries and the strong ascetic tendencies in the fourth-century Christian churches forced Christians to clarify the role and meaning of the body in salvation, the Christian life, and death. For the religion of the incarnation, the human body became a problem. No longer, as in the Gnostic groups and Hellenistic philosophies, morally indifferent and to be understood biologically, the human body could not be described as the lowest component in human being, towards which an attitude of indifference was to be cultivated. Early Christian authors, struggling to define the meaning and value of the body, often seemed to find no contradiction in simultaneous metaphysical affirmation and practical instructions to ascetic practices that seemed to posit the enmity of body and soul. Christian history in the West has inherited this pervasive ambivalence concerning the body, an ambivalence that is frequently heightened by the use of careless terminology in which the Pauline distinction of 'flesh' and 'spirit' is confused with descriptions of body and soul. In Pauline usage, 'flesh' refers to the whole human being as oriented to sin, while 'spirit' designates the whole human being in orientation to God; 'body' and 'soul' are not synonymous with 'flesh' and 'spirit'.

1. Contemporary understanding of the views held by historic Christian authors about the human body is complicated by our Cartesian understanding of the body as possessing its own animation and psychological characteristics. For authors before Descartes, the body was dependent on the soul for animation and involuntary as well as voluntary motion; the soul's first duty was understood to be that of giving life to the body. 2. Historic authors often write very differently about the body according to their purpose in the particular context. Although no Christian author can completely ignore or deny Christian doctrines that insist on the goodness and permanence of the body as an essential part of human being, an author may write in one context of the body as *contrast* for the greater beauty and value of the soul. The same author in another context may present the body as *problem*, or in yet another context as *condition* for human learning, trial, salvation and resurrection to eternal life.

Despite this range of valuations and locutions concerning the body, Christian authors from the documents of the NT to our own time have consistently recognized the body as the appropriate model and symbol for the interdependence of Christians with one another and with Christ in the church, the body of Christ. The nourishment of the human body has also been understood as the basis for Christian interpretations of the eucharist as the participation of Christians in Christ's body and blood in the elements of bread and wine, a central activity of Christian worship. Contrary to a popular tradition that assumes the negativity of Christian authors' attitudes to the human body, historical exploration reveals that Christians were not only intensely interested in but also overwhelmingly affirming of the goodness, theological significance, and permanence of the body in human being.

Charles Davis, *Body as Spirit*, 1976; Margaret R. Miles, *Fullness of Life: Historical Foundations for a New Asceticism*, 1981; James B. Nelson, *Embodiment*, 1978.

MARGARET R. MILES

Body Theology

In a general sense, all Christian theology is body theology in that its distinctive characteristic is affirmation of the permanent integrity of the human body as given in creation*, affirmed in the incarnation* of Jesus Christ, nourished in the sacraments of the Christian churches, and to be glorified in the resurrection* of the body. However, in our time the term has come to carry a more specialized meaning, i.e. those theological statements that specifically address questions related to personal and social attitudes towards the body, moral decisions regarding one's own body and those of other human beings, and theological concern about the physical conditions in which human beings live and work. Liberation theologies* advocate the alleviation of oppressive political structures and reject the spiritualization of the Christian message. Feminist theology* urges awareness and change of sexist language and social institutions. Other concerns of body-integrative theology include recognition and respect for sexual-preference minorities, medical ethics and medical care for whole human beings, theologically-oriented ecology with concern over the abuse of the body of the earth, and theologically-motivated concern over the build-up of nuclear weapons. All of these theological statements take as their starting point a Christian evaluation of the value and significance of the human body as the good creation of God, worthy of respectful care.

James B. Nelson, *Embodiment*, 1978; Rosemary Ruether, *To Change the World*, 1981.

MARGARET R. MILES

Boundary Situation
see **Limit Situation**

Calendar, Liturgical

The church's calendar comprises three cycles: weekly, annual and daily. This temporal preoccupation testifies to a Jewish heritage, which takes time with great seriousness as the theatre of divine activity. Each of these three cycles turns on the same event, the resurrection of Jesus on the first day of the week, at Passover, and early in the morning.

The weekly Lord's Day (Sunday) reorients the Jewish week around the first rather than the last or Sabbath ('seventh') day. This effectively brings into play the Jewish 'eighth day' symbolism.

The Gospels document the resurrection * as occurring at the annual Passover season, notwithstanding divergence in detail between the Synoptics and the Fourth Gospel. This resulted in the continuing celebration by the church of the Jewish *Pascha* (Passover) and Pentecost, and by the second century they were transferred to the Lord's Day, now known as Easter and Pentecost.

The Gospels also locate the resurrection as occurring early on the first day of the week. This timing accords with the Jewish reckoning of 'day' as 'evening and morning' with its sequence of light out of darkness.

The Christian calendar therefore marks the natural divisions and progressions of time (*chronos*) with repeated celebrations of an event which is both above that time and constitutive of another kind of time (*kairos*) which is every bit as fulfilled as the other is fragmented. This liturgical time looks back to the Lord's resurrection and forward to the Lord's return, itself a trans-temporal event. This liturgical time is the church's unique time: 'It is no longer the time of Easter, and it is not yet the time, i.e., the moment of His return. The community moves from the one point to the other like a ship – a constantly recurring picture – sailing over an ocean a thousand fathoms deep' (Barth, *CD* IV/1, p. 728).

How did the early church observe these three cycles? The daily round was marked originally by a synagogue-like combination of scripture reading and prayer originally in church or cathedral, though later only in monastery or by secular clergy and religious. The weekly meeting was a combination of scripture reading, preaching and the Supper. The annual *Pascha* was marked by all of these together with rites of initiation: baptism and confirmation, in anticipation of which there was a forty-day fast now known as Lent. This threefold pairing of the daily cycle with prayer, the Lord's Day with the Lord's Supper and the *Pascha* with initiation, merit careful attention today for the enterprise of liturgical and lectionary reform.

Certain ancillary practices, days and festivals have attached themselves to these three cycles. To the daily there has been added in the West the celebration of the eucharist *, thus depriving it of its relation to the day of resurrection. To the weekly Lord's Day there have been added fast days, and in some Protestant traditions the Sabbath mentality has overtaken the joy of the Lord's (eighth) Day, either by dropping the Supper or by converting it into a passion instead of resurrection remembrance. To the annual cycle the Eastern church has contributed Epiphany (6 January) as a celebration of the baptism of the Lord, and the Western church, Christmas (25 December) as a celebration of the nativity of the Lord. These two festivals of rather unclear origins (although Christmas is thought to derive from an attempt by the Roman Church to Christianize the Roman winter solstice), in their interaction drew to them (by analogy to the Lenten preparation for Easter) a preparatory season now known as Advent. Its origins are mixed and reflect a certain indecision as to whether it concludes the Christian year in anticipation of the second coming or begins the year in anticipation of the nativity. This indecision is still reflected in a mix of penitential and festal customs and music. Its length (now approximately four weeks in the West) has also varied considerably, possibly depending on whether its *terminus ad quem* was Christmas or Epiphany.

Another addition to the annual cycle was the universal adoption of the 'stational' rites of Jerusalem for the days preceding Easter such as the triumphal entry, the institution of the supper and the crucifixion, which now comprise Holy Week. These developments eventually supplanted the Easter vigil and became the focus of Lent with its heavily penitential emphasis.

Recently revised rites reflect the ancient patterns, as does the lectionary recommended by the post-Vatican II Roman church, now widely used by Anglican and Protestant churches as well.

H. T. Allen, Jr, *A Handbook for the Lectionary*, Part I, 1980; G. Dix, *The Shape of the Liturgy*, 1945, ch. XI; Marion J. Hatchett, *Sanctifying Life, Time and Space*, 1976; A. A. McArthur, *The Evolution of the Christian Year*, 1953; W. Rordorf, *Sunday*, ET 1968.

H. T. ALLEN JR

Calling

The words for 'call' and 'calling' (sometimes translated 'vocation') occur frequently in a general sense throughout both OT and NT, often with the Hebraic overtone that a call, and certainly a call by name, can have the effect of bringing to pass what the caller intends; especially, to call someone by name is frequently to invest them with the qualities which the name connotes.

The notion of God's calling, in particular, is inherent in the whole of biblical religion; and God's calling is supremely effective in the fulfilment of his purposes through those whom he calls.

So God calls Moses (Ex. 3.4), Samuel (I Sam. 3.4) and the prophets (Isa. 49.1); and through the prophets God calls individuals and peoples, and especially the people of Israel (Isa. 41.8–9; Hos. 11.1).

In the NT God's calling, in addition to giving a name to the son of Mary (Luke 1.31f.) and to Simon bar-Jonah (John 1.42), takes on the specific sense of an invitation to enter the kingdom (Matt. 22.1–14; I Thess. 2.12) and to participate in the blessings of salvation (Rom. 1.6; Gal. 1.6). Within the scope of this call, those who believe are called into the fellowship of Christ (I Cor. 1.9), into the peace of Christ (Col. 3.15), and into freedom (Gal. 5.13); and some of them are called to particular tasks, such as that of apostleship (I Cor. 1.1).

All are called (Matt. 9.12–13; Luke 14.23; Rom. 11.29–32), and Christ is the power and wisdom of God to those who are called (I Cor. 1.24). Those whom God calls he justifies, and gives to them his glory (Rom. 8.30).

God's call is received and obeyed in faith, and those called out of darkness into light are to evidence their calling in their manner of life (I Peter 2.9–25). But in the NT there is no advice to the called to attempt a change in their social condition. Probably in view of the imminence of the End, those who were slaves when they were called are to be content with their condition and to evidence their calling within that condition (I Cor. 7.17–24; I Peter 2.18–21).

There is a close relation in the NT between 'calling' and 'election' * (II Peter 1.10; cf. Matt. 22.14). In post-biblical times 'calling' was reinterpreted (*see* Vocation).

E. Diserens, 'Calling', in J.-J. von Allmen, *Vocabulary of the Bible*, 1958; G. Wingren, *The Christian's Calling*, ET 1958.

RUPERT DAVIES

Calvinism, Calvin

John Calvin (1509–1564), leader of the Reformation * in Geneva and pre-eminent among Reformed theologians, was the son of a notary with advantageous connections. Calvin in boyhood received benefices which provided for his schooling. At fourteen he was sent to the University of Paris, where his brilliant gifts were developed under the influence of scholars who represented both the methods of scholasticism * and the new humanist learning. By a decision of his father he gave the years 1528–1531 to legal studies at Orleans and Bourges, incidentally acquiring Greek. But he turned from a legal career to pursue a passionate interest in Greek, Latin and Hebrew, taking advantage of the new foundation of the Royal Lecturers in Paris. Little beyond conjecture is known about his religious attitudes before his twenty-fifth year (1533–1534). His statement made in 1558: 'God by a sudden conversion subdued my heart to teachableness' almost certainly refers to an experience of this period. In the spring of 1534 he visited Jacques Lefèvre, the inspirer of a French Christian humanist movement in which some of Calvin's friends were active, and then journeyed to Noyon and resigned his clerical benefices (4 March). None of his writings prior to this is convincingly Protestant, while everything that he wrote thereafter is unambiguously so.

Calvin's conversation involved an unreserved commitment to the intense study of the Bible as the source of authority for the church and for the Christian life. It meant a rejection of the old order of the church under the papacy but therewith a devotion to the holy catholic church which is invisible and to the work of church reform that would follow a pattern based on scripture. The rich resources of learning, and the scholarly habits previously acquired, became a priceless asset in the formulation and communication of theological thought. His conversion, though scantily documented, must be regarded as a transforming experience that was essential to the making of the Calvin of history. With singular constancy he pursued through later years the direction then taken.

A period of withdrawal in Basle bore fruit in the *Christianae religionis institutio*, 1536; later progressively enlarged editions to 1559 bore the title *Institutio Christianae religionis*. He was soon drawn from the retirement he loved to bear a heavy load of practical duties in Geneva and to stand in the embattled line of the Reformation in Europe. At the price of great effort amid tasks of teaching, preaching, counselling and controversy, he maintained a high standard of excellence in his writings with respect to knowledge, argumentation and style. While we find in his pages some deplorable lapses into vituperation, any extensive reading of his works will make us aware of his animating sense of the living and ever-present God, who commands his adoration and his service, the Creator of all things, the source of all truth and of man's powers of thought, the Redeemer and inspirer of his elect. This lofty conception of deity, divinely revealed in holy scripture, is in accord with the evidence of the created world. Calvin without embarrassment appropriated the traditional doctrine of the Trinity*. On the person of Christ he is in full accord with the Chalcedonian formula, and he finds scriptural warrant for the Western 'filioque*' teaching. He lays emphasis on the Spirit's inspiration of scripture and the secret witness (*testimonium internum*) by which the Spirit makes effective for the devout reader the message of scripture.

The whole of the canonical Bible is linked together by the analogy of faith, so that the OT is freely employed to support the gospel. 'Moses' only intention,' he declares, 'was to call all men straight to Christ ... Without

Christ the law is empty and insubstantial ... The Scriptures should be read with a view to finding Christ in them' (*Commentary on St John*, 5.38,39). The ceremonies of the old covenant were types or foreshadowings of the realities of the gospel and are discarded, having no function, since the full light of Christ has shone. While he takes pains to state in detail the advance beyond the OT made in the NT, yet his principle of interpretation assures a firm view of the unity and continuity of scripture.

The question whether Calvin affirms a natural theology* has been vigorously answered in the negative by Karl Barth. If natural theology implies the ability of man, unaided by grace, to know God through the created world, Calvin repudiates it. But if it means that to the Christian mind aided by the 'spectacles' of scripture, observation of the created world provides an enhancement of the knowledge that is explicitly scriptural, the term cannot be fairly excluded. Innumerable statements of Calvin show him to have been intensely appreciative of the evidence of God's glory in the beauty, power and orderliness of the universe. He likes to say that man has been placed in this most glorious theatre of the world to be a spectator of God's works. He recognizes an awareness of divinity (*divinitatis sensus*) natural to the human mind, and in fallen man's darkness some remaining sparks of light, whose feeble glow is, however, wholly insufficient to afford an adequate knowledge of God.

Calvin's early casual interest in predestination* gave place in controversy, and under increasing influence from Augustine and Bucer, to the full-fledged doctrine of double predestination which has sometimes been regarded as the heart of his theology. Though he shudders at the decree of reprobation, he holds it an unavoidable inference from scripture. The efficacy of election* is such as to exclude a lapse from the state of salvation. Calvin warns against speculation on the mystery of election, but it clearly entails repentance, faith and sanctification. Holiness is not sought in detachment but in the society of believers and in active pursuit of the daily calling which is accepted as a station appointed by God. The inculcation of a personal and social piety is linked with a high doctrine of the holy catholic church and of the (two scriptural) sacraments. The holy mystery of the Lord's Supper requires that it be protected from profanation, and here lies the basis of the discipline by which the Reformed Church is historically characterized.

The term Calvinism is used historically, apart from its application to Calvin's own teachings, in two senses. 1. It signifies the doctrines emphasized by seventeenth-century Calvinist scholars, especially the 'five points of Calvinism' affirmed by the Synod of Dort (1618/19), which ended the bitter doctrinal controversy over Arminianism *. 2. It is applied broadly to the churches which took their rise under Calvin's influence, and to their impact upon society and culture. Inherent in Calvinism in the latter sense is a certain dynamic quality which is still in process of interpretation.

––––––––––

For Calvin's works, the series, *Joannis Calvini opera quae supersunt omnia*, ed. G. Baum and others, 59 volumes, 1863–1900, is now being enlarged by the collection, mainly of sermons, *Supplementa Calviniana*, ed. Erwin Muhlhaupt and others, 1961– ; *Calvin: Institutes of the Christian Religion*, ed. J. T. McNeill, ET F. L. Battles, 1960; E. A. Dowey, *The Knowledge of God in Calvin's Theology*, 1952; W. Niesel, *The Theology of Calvin*, ET 1956; F. Wendel, *Calvin, the Origins and Development of His Religious Thought*, ET 1963.

On Calvinism see J. W. Beardslee (ed), *Reformed Dogmatics*, 1965; J. H. Bratt, *Rise and Development of Calvinism*, 1964; W. Hastie, *The Theology of the Reformed Church in Its Fundamental Principles*, 1904; H. Heppe, *Reformed Dogmatics*, ET 1950; G. L. Hunt (ed), *Calvinism and the Political Order*, 1965; J. T. McNeill, *The History and Character of Calvinism*, 1967.

J. T. MCNEILL

Cambridge Platonists

A group including Benjamin Whichcote (1609–1683), John Smith (1618), Henry More (1614–1687) and Ralph Cudworth (1617–1688), with an unflagging faith in reason, believing that purified reason could bring the soul to the vision of God, rather than that human nature was a mass of perdition. Their theology laid particular stress on ethics and spiritual joy.

––––––––––

Rosalie L. Colie, *Light and Enlightenment.*

A Study of the Cambridge Platonists and the Dutch Arminians, 1957; C. A. Patrides (ed), *The Cambridge Platonists*, 1980.

GORDON S. WAKEFIELD

Canon

The word comes from an Egyptian word meaning a reed used for measuring, and in the ancient world it was used in a great variety of meanings, for example, rule, standard, ethical norm, list, rent paid for land to the Roman Emperor, ecclesiastical law. In the Middle Ages it was used to describe secular clergy who lived together in a group observing a certain rule, and from this derives its modern use as an ecclesiastical title. The word is not used for the list of authoritative scripture until the *Festal Letters* of Athanasius in the fourth decade of the third century, but the concept of a list of authoritative writings connected with the new dispensation given in Christ can be found long before that date. The list of writings of the OT had always been relatively fixed in the Christian church, for the vast majority of Christians accepted the Apocrypha * as part of the Bible. But it was only gradually and in a piece-meal fashion that the canon of NT scripture grew up. It is probable that a nucleus of the later NT was widely acknowledged as early as between 120 and 130, consisting perhaps of the Synoptic Gospels, ten Pauline letters, Hebrews and perhaps Acts. The Fourth Gospel began to be widely known between 140 and 160 but was not fully recognized as authoritative till the time of Tatian, Theophilus of Antioch and its great champion Irenaeus (*c.* 135–199). The recognition of the Pastoral Epistles, of I Peter and of Revelation was achieved perhaps a little earlier than this. The acceptance of the other books (Jude, II Peter and the Johannine Epistles) was only effected slowly by a process lasting into the fourth century. The Western Church had considerable doubts about Hebrews during the third century and the Eastern Church about Revelation during the third and early fourth centuries. The discovery of the Gnostic *Gospel of Thomas* and *Gospel of Truth* (both of which in their original form probably pre-date Marcion's activity) has badly shaken the theory of A. Harnack (till then almost universally accepted) that Marcion's treatment of the Gospels and Epistles forced the church to form the canon of scripture. Even up till the fourth century the limits of the canon were regarded by all as fluid. The Codex Alexandrinus and the Codex Sinaiticus include in their NT other works besides those which we now call canonical, e.g. Hermas' *Shepherd* and the *Epistle of Barnabas*. The early Christian Fathers, such as Clement of Alexandria, Tertullian and Origen, do not regard the NT canon as a hard and fast line, but quote quite freely apocryphal gospels and apocryphal sayings attributed to Jesus. During the second half of the second century references to the inspired nature of the NT scriptures appear and by about 250 most of them are regarded as enjoying divine inspiration of much the same kind as the OT scriptures were thought to possess.

It was under the guidance of the Holy Spirit that the church gathered together a collection of documents authoritatively witnessing to the advent of Jesus Christ and to the significance which was attached to him in the earliest period of the church's existence. But the nature of the documents themselves, as well as the manner in which they were canonized, make it very difficult, if not impossible, to describe each of these documents as possessing some quality of inspiration lacking in other Christian documents. There is, for instance, no obvious quality of inspiration present in II Peter but lacking in *I Clement* or the letters of Ignatius, which, incidentally, are earlier than II Peter. If the NT is regarded as a collection or corpus made in order to give witness, this difficulty disappears. As a collection it is unique and irreplaceable, even though some parts of the collection may have much less value than others. For the same reason it would be pointless to attempt to add to or to subtract from the NT canon.

The canonical hours or services appointed for particular times and days were those officially ordered by ecclesiastical or monastic authorities. A canon was (and is) a person who lived according to the rule of the institution to which he belonged, e.g. a Cathedral Chapter or a Collegiate Church. From the earlier Middle Ages women who had taken religious vows were sometimes styled 'canonesses'.

See also **Canon Law.**

James Barr, *Holy Scripture: Canon, Authority, Criticism*, 1983; H. von Cam-

penhausen, *The Formation of the Christian Bible*, ET 1972; F. V. Filson, *Which Books Belong to the Bible?*, 1957; R. P. C. Hanson, *Tradition in the Early Church*, 1962; F. G. Kenyon, *Our Bible and the Ancient Manuscripts*, [4] 1939; A. Souter, *Text and Canon of the New Testament*, [2] 1954.

R. P. C. HANSON

Canon Law

The term used of that body of law which is made by the church for itself as distinct from ecclesiastical law, which is law made for the church either by the state alone or by church and state acting together. In the later Middle Ages the canon law of the Latin Church was gathered together in the *Corpus Juris Canonici*, which contains both the canons of councils and papal decretals. It forms the background of the canon law both of the Church of England and of the RC Church. In the Church of England the code of canons promulgated in the seventeenth century has been replaced (with one exception) by a new code completed in 1969 but revised and supplemented from time to time as need arises. In the RC Church a comprehensive new *Codex Juris Canonici* was promulgated in 1917 but has now been replaced by a new code promulgated in 1983.

Insofar as any of these collections include statements of the natural law or the divine law they are held to be unchangeable. With that qualification a main characteristic of canon law has always been its flexibility as compared with most systems of secular law. This has been achieved principally by allowing the operation of two factors, custom and dispensation*, which allow the requirements of the law to be adjusted to the needs of particular times and places.

The canon law of the Eastern Churches consists mainly of the decrees of councils. Collections of these have been made at various times but there is nothing corresponding to the collections of canon law of either the RC Church or the Church of England. At Rome a code for the Uniate Churches has been long in preparation but shows no sign of completion.

By and large the Protestant churches have rejected the traditional concept of canon law, though they have regulations for their own internal affairs and are subject to the ecclesiastical law of the states in which they exist.

The sanctions available to the church for the enforcement of canon law vary greatly from place to place and depend much upon the extent to which the state is willing to support the church's courts and the extent to which the church is prepared to seek for or accept the state's support.

E. W. Kemp, *An Introduction to Canon Law in the Church of England*, 1957; E. Garth Moore, *An Introduction to English Canon Law*, 1967; R. C. Mortimer, *Western Canon Law*, 1953.

E. W. KEMP

Cappadocian Fathers

Three of the most significant Fathers of the Greek Church were natives of Cappadocia (Eastern Turkey): Basil of Caesarea (known as 'the Great'), Gregory of Nazianzus (known as 'the Theologian') and Gregory of Nyssa. They were closely connected, Basil being the older brother of Gregory of Nyssa and the student friend of Gregory Nazianzen. Convinced Nicenes yet theologically raised upon Origen, they were able to reach the theological synthesis needed in the East in the aftermath of the Arian struggle (*see also* **Arianism**), and were sufficiently independent of the Origenist tradition not to be tainted by association when his name fell into disrepute. Basil became bishop of Caesarea, the Cappadocian capital, and defended Nicene orthodoxy from this position of strength, unfortunately dying a couple of years before its triumph at Constantinople in 381. Soon after his death, his friend Gregory was invited to Constantinople where, by his brilliant preaching (especially the *Five Theological Orations*), he built up the Nicene party only to find himself superceded at the Council; but Basil's brother reached a position of considerable political influence in the ensuing decade, consciously adopting his brother's mantle. It was the Cappadocian Fathers who gave classic shape to Eastern Trinitarianism, by defending the divinity of the Holy Spirit *, confuting the Neo-Arian Eunomius and achieving a rapprochement between the homoeousians * and the homoousians. The term *homoousios* * was given a generic interpretation: thus Father, Son and Spirit were of the same *ousia* (*see* **Substance**), sharing divinity as Peter, James and John shared humanity. Yet this did not imply tritheism

because the divine *ousia* was indivisible, unchangeable and infinite. Eunomius' assertion that God was simple, uncompounded and indivisible, and therefore knowable as by definition the one ingenerate being, was disposed of on logical and religious grounds. God was incomprehensible, yet revealed as indivisible Trinity *. The two Gregories were also instrumental in assembling arguments against Apollinarius and defending the complete humanity of the Christ. Yet the contribution of the Cappadocian Fathers was not confined to the dogmatic arena. Basil's *Rules* tempered and ultimately shaped Eastern monasticism, and it is probable that the liturgy still in use which bears his name goes back to him in its essentials. His brother's devotional and exegetical writings which were profoundly influenced by Neoplatonism *, anticipated the spirituality of Dionysius the Areopagite, though the genesis of his thinking may not have been mystical experiences so much as Origenist allegorical habits and engagement with the issues of religious knowledge, religious language and of eschatology raised by the theological controversies of his time. All three, being formed by the educational traditions of the Graeco-Roman world and imbued with its rhetorical heritage, were influential in their contribution to the marriage of Christian religion and classical culture which was effected in this period.

FRANCES YOUNG

Casuistry

The application of moral principles to particular situations or to individual circumstances. The necessity for it arises from the fact that it is never possible to frame a general ethical principle which will be relevant to all the circumstances of the individual practitioner without exception. The rise of formal casuistry in the Christian church begins with the development of the practice of private penance from the seventh century onwards, and by the Middle Ages the Christian church possessed a fully articulated volume of casuistical analysis of human conduct. Some features of this body of casuistical theory have been responsible for the term 'casuistry' coming to have a pejorative meaning, but important theological issues are nevertheless at stake: nothing less than the doctrine of the incarnation and its implications, particularly an incarnation which is interpreted in terms of *kenosis**. This latter involves for the believer a continual exposing of himself to the ambiguity and imperfections of finite existence as a way of doing homage to the manner of the incarnation itself. An impatience with the particularities and partialities of finite existence is the mark of a gnostic turn of mind (*see* **Gnosticism**), and casuistry is involved in any tradition which is willing to take human existence in all its finitude seriously and sacramentally.

J. C. Ford and Gerald Kelly SJ, *Contemporary Moral Theology*, 1960; K. E. Kirk, *Conscience and its Problems*, 1927; Paul Lehmann, *Ethics in a Christian Context*, 1963.

E. J. TINSLEY

Cataphatic Theology
see **Apophatic Theology**

Catechesis

This has been broadly defined as 'a dialogue between believers'. Fuller descriptions are: 'All activity which makes divine revelation known and which aims at awakening and developing faith' (Van Caster, *The Structure of Catechesis*, 1965, p. 12); 'Throwing light on the whole of human existence as God's salvific action by witnessing to the mystery of Christ through the word, for the purpose of awakening and fostering the faith and prompting men to live truly in accord with the faith' (Higher Catechetical Institute of Nijmegen, *Making All Things New*, 1966, p. 88). The object of catechesis is therefore seen to be to lead people to communion with Christ, to build up the community of believers, and to strengthen the missionary activity of the church. It is concerned both with teaching the faith and opening the heart to conversion, so as to lead to the following of Christ.

The word catechesis derives from a Greek verb meaning 'to resound, to echo'. It is used in the NT in a transferred sense to mean oral teaching. Only later did it acquire a specifically religious meaning. In the course of the second and third centuries it came to be applied to the instruction given within the catechumenate to those preparing for baptism (baptismal catechesis) and to those recently baptized (mystagogical catechesis). The latter is richly illustrated by the writings

of, for example, Tertullian, Cyprian, Cyril of Jerusalem, Ambrose, Theodore of Mopsuestia, Augustine, John Chrysostom. The context of the catechesis was the liturgy, its method was preaching, its content was both doctrinal (based on the creed) and moral (the twofold law of love and the commandments).

As the practice of infant baptism became more widespread, the catechumenate – the structure within which the adult convert was initiated into the full life of the church – gradually disappeared, and because of the close link between this and catechesis this early form of Christian teaching also disappeared. With the emphasis now on teaching children rather than adults the method also changed. Classroom-type instruction and catechisms took the place of homilies and liturgies. A number of important catechisms were produced, for example, by Luther (1529), Canisius (1556), Bellarmine (1598), and the Council of Trent (1566) (the last being principally for the parish clergy). In the RC Church in Britain the 'penny' catechism based on one prepared by Bishop Challoner (d. 1781) has been in almost continuous use for more than a century. The stress in this, as in similar catechisms of the same period, is on doctrinal formulation and memorization.

By the end of the first quarter of the twentieth century a movement for a fundamental change in the approach to catechesis had begun; leaders in this were Drinkwater in Britain, Jungmann in Germany, and Hofinger through the Catechetical Institute in Manila. The inadequacies of reliance on a 'catechism' approach to education in faith became more apparent. Faith is not passed on merely by learning; doctrine is but one element in the content of catechesis; growth in faith is a lifelong process; the task of catechizing belongs to the whole Christian community.

There are four principal sources of catechesis, each with its distinctive content and method: scripture, doctrine, liturgy and experience. Scripture as the Word of God is normative, permanent and central. Doctrine is the formulation of the rational element of faith. Liturgy is the way the believing community expresses its faith in worship. Experience is the context of daily living within which faith takes root. Catechesis is thus a holistic process, addressing itself to the whole person, 'mind, heart, hand', in both cognitive and non-cognitive ways. There are currently two approaches to these languages of faith. One sees them as together conveying the fullness of faith; the other sees scripture, doctrine and liturgy as 'interpreting, purifying and enriching the existential situation of the pupil that we call experience' (D. J. O'Leary).

The opportunity for continuing catechesis throughout life should be available to all Christians. There is a catechesis proper to people of different ages (e.g. children, adolescents, the elderly); at key moments of their lives (e.g. preparing for confirmation or marriage, times of bereavement); in a particular condition of life (e.g. the handicapped, the persecuted, the sick); and with particular responsibilities (e.g. parents, politicians, clergy).

All members of the church take part in the work of catechesis according to their particular gifts and responsibilities. Various programmes for the preparation of children for the eucharist, confirmation and reconciliation ensure the involvement of parents, clergy and other members of the local community in the process (e.g. Brusselmans, *We Celebrate the Eucharist*, 1975; Saris, *Together We Communicate*, 1982). For adult catechesis the *Rite of Christian Initiation of Adults* (1972), though intended for adult catechumens, provides a valuable instrument for continuing growth in faith. Its emphasis is on faith as a journey made in company with other members of the local parish who welcome, support, instruct and pray with the adult, and so lead him to a deeper relationship with God.

T. H. Groome, *Christian Religious Education*, 1980; K. Nichols, *Cornerstone*, 1978; R. M. Rummery, *Catechesis and Religious Education in a Pluralist Society*, 1975; W. Saris, *Towards a Living Church*, 1980.

D. KONSTANT

Categorical Imperative

This is a principle to which Kant gives several different formulations in his *Groundwork of the Metaphysic of Morals* (1785). The first formula is, 'Act only on that maxim through which you can at the same time will that it should become a universal law', which he restates a few sentences later as, 'Act as if the maxim of your action were to become through your will a *universal law of nature*.' The second formula is, 'Act in such a way that you always treat humanity, whether in your own person or in the person of any other, never simply as a means, but always at the same time as an end.' A third formula is that one should 'never perform an action except on a maxim such as can also be a universal law, and consequently such that the will can regard itself as at the same time making universal law by means of its maxim'. In *Critique of Practical Reason* (1788), Kant states the categorical imperative as follows: 'So act that the maxim of your will could always hold at the same time as the principle of a universal legislation.'

While at first glance the categorical imperative might appear to be a formal principle that is devoid of specific moral content, Kant believes otherwise. For example, in the *Groundwork* he asserts that the categorical imperative precludes such things as suicide and securing a loan under false pretences. And in 'Perpetual Peace', he calls for the abolition of standing armies, stating that 'to pay men to kill or to be killed seems to entail using them as mere machines and tools in the hand of another (the state), and this is hardly compatible with the rights of mankind in our own person'.

Kant contrasts the notion of a categorical imperative, which represents an action as objectively necessary in itself quite apart from any relationship to a further end, with hypothetical imperatives, which declare that certain acts are practically necessary as means of attaining something else that one wills. To say that something should be done because it would contribute to happiness, for example, would be a hypothetical imperative. To base moral judgments, in whole or in part, on the desire for happiness or any other desire or inclination, Kant suggests, results in heteronomy*. While autonomy* involves the will giving itself the law independently of any property of objects of volition, heteronomy entails something other than the will giving it the law. Kant contends that the only thing which can be taken as good without qualification is a good will. Hence, only that which is willed autonomously – i.e., the categorical imperative – is unquestionably good, and everything that is willed heteronomously represents a spurious principle of morality.

Quotations from Kant's *Grundlegung zur Metaphysik der Sitten* (*Groundwork*) from the ET by H. J. Paton (1950); from *Critique of Practical Reason* and 'Perpetual Peace', ET by L. W. Beck (1949).

DANIEL E. LEE

Catholicism

The word catholic is probably derived from the Greek adverbial phrase *Kath' holou*, which means 'on the whole'. Its first appearance as a description of the Christian church is in the letter of Ignatius of Antioch to the church in Smyrna, written probably in AD 112. 'Wherever the bishop appears there let the people be, just as wherever Jesus Christ is there is the Catholic Church' (ch. 8). The word here describes the church as universal and widespread, the whole being represented in each local church. To the meaning universal there came to be added the meaning orthodox in contrast with heretical bodies. This use of the word is prominent in Augustine's writings, where in contrast with the church of the Donatists* the Catholic Church meant the church which is both universal and adhering to the true faith (cf. *De Fide et Symbolo* 10). But the word had meaning deeper and wider and this is drawn out in a striking passage in the Catechical Lectures of Cyril of Jerusalem. He wrote: 'The church is called Catholic because she is throughout the whole world, from one end of the earth to the other; because she teaches universally and without fail all the doctrines that ought to be preached to the knowledge of men concerning the visible and invisible, in heaven and on earth; because she subjects to her faith the whole of mankind – rulers and their subjects, educated and uneducated alike; because she is the universal physician and healer of sins of every kind, sins of soul or body, and possesses in herself every form of excellence that can be named in deeds and words in spiritual gifts of every kind' (XVIII.23).

Not surprisingly, catholic finds its way into the creeds* as a description of the church along with the words one, holy and apostolic. In the East the word appears in the Creed of Cyril of Jerusalem, the Creed of Epiphanius, and the Creed connected with Constantinople which came to be called the Ecumenical Creed and to be used in the Liturgy in both East and West. It is through this creed that the description of the church as catholic as well as holy and apostolic came to be familiar in liturgical worship throughout Christendom. In Western creeds the first occasion of the word catholic is in the Creed of the Dacian Bishop Niceta of Remesiana, and his comment is significant: 'The Catholic Church is nothing less than the congregation of all the saints.'

As the church in the West passed from the age of the Fathers into the mediaeval era with its unity of institutional life and doctrine under the leadership of the See of Rome, the word catholic came to express powerfully the themes of universality, institutional wholeness and orthodox belief. But the schism of West and East, sealed by the anathemas of 1054, began the controversial diversities of the use of the word which are still with us. Both the West, which accepted the leadership of the See of Rome, and the East which rejected it, claimed to be the one true church. Thus in the West catholic denotes the church in communion with the See of Rome, while in the East the phrase 'Holy Orthodox Church' came to be the more characteristic usage. When the Reformation* brought further divisions in the West, the words Catholic and Protestant came to stand out in contrast both in literature and in popular use, describing on the one hand the church in communion with Rome and on the other hand the churches of the Reformation which repudiated papacy. The words Protestant and Catholic have remained through the centuries with these same associations.

In the post-Reformation centuries 'Catholicism' has entered the English vocabulary. While some historians have used the word to describe institutional Christianity in contrast with a supposedly simple and non-institutional Christianity in primitive times, the most familiar use of the word has been to describe the Roman Catholic Church and its structure, doctrine, spirituality and culture. Theologians have also used catholic as a desired criterion of a church or doctrine or a feature of Christian life, as claiming that a particular church possesses it or lacks it. In particular two questions have been asked: Where is the Catholic Church now to be seen on earth? What are the characteristics which properly belong to the word catholic?

1. The Roman Catholic Church identifies itself with the one true Catholic Church, while teaching also that all baptized Christians in other bodies mystically belong to the true church. The decrees of the Second Vatican Council make much acknowledgment of Christian spiritual life in communions outside the boundary of the Church of Rome. The Holy Orthodox Church (often popularly known as the Eastern Orthodox Church) also claims to be the one true church and also acknowledges spirituality outside its borders. The Protestant churches reject the claims both of Rome and of the Orthodox and for the most part teach that the church includes all those Christian communions where the gospel is preached and the sacraments duly administered. The Anglican communion, while it refrains from unchurching other bodies, has claimed catholicity through retaining the scriptures, creeds, sacraments and historic episcopate* in continuity with the ancient church.

2. As to the characteristics of catholicity, theologians have been eager to explore both early traditions and later understandings. What is meant by ascribing the word catholic to a church or a doctrine or a custom or indeed to Christianity itself? Here much has been made of the test formulated by Vincent of Lerins in his *Commonitorium: Quod ubique, quod semper, quod ab omnibus creditum est*, what is believed everywhere, always and by all. This test has involved an appeal to the ancient church for discovering the norms of catholicity, and in this connection it has been customary to speak of scripture, creeds, sacraments and ministry as norms of catholicity. In modern times some theologians have been concerned with the interpretation of past traditions in relation to changing forms of thought and language and have asked what are the factors in Christian experience which can claim to be universal and normative for Christian identity.

Amidst the controversies about the identity of the catholic church and about the tests of catholicity there has been in recent times a reviving concern for the idea of wholeness. Within the ecumenical movement it is often urged that the recovery of Christian unity is inseparable from the realization of truth which is in turn inseparable from the deepening of holiness and self-giving amongst Christians. It is also urged

by some that catholicity, like the other notes of the church, belongs both to history and to eschatology* and is both present possession and future realization. Already possessing unity, truth and holiness, the church moves towards their complete realization. Some passages in the decrees of the Second Vatican Council refer to this concept using the phrase 'the Pilgrim Church'. This presentation of catholicity recalls the prayer of Jesus in John 17, where the unity of the disciples is linked with their consecration in the truth and their mission in the world, seen as present possession and as growth into future realization.

W. M. Abbott (ed), *The Documents of Vatican II*, with notes by Catholic, Protestant and Orthodox authorities, 1967; J. N. D. Kelly, *Early Christian Doctrine*, 1958; H. de Lubac, *Catholicism*, 1950; H. B. Swete, *The Holy Catholic Church*, 1915.

A. M. RAMSEY

Causality

Aristotle* (*Metaphysics*, 1013) taught that there are four *aitiai*, often translated 'causes', which make things to exist and to have the characteristics they do – the material cause (the matter out of which the thing is made), the efficient cause (the object which brings the thing about), the formal cause (the 'form', i.e. shape and mode of operation imposed upon the matter), and the final cause (the purpose for which the thing is made). Thus, to use an example from Aristotle – the material cause of the statue is the bronze out of which it is made, its efficient cause is the chisel or sculptor who yields it, the formal cause the shape given to the bronze, and final cause the purpose for which the sculptor makes his statue – e.g. to decorate the square. Since Aristotle, the matter and form of things have come to be seen as integral to those things and not as causes. The causes are what make those things thus, i.e. the efficient and final causes. Later Greek and mediaeval science and philosophy assumed that every coming into being of a thing and its properties (and the continuing existence of every contingent thing) had both an efficient cause and a final cause. When the efficient cause is a person who brings about something intentionally, we too in the twentieth century naturally think in this way – the sculptor makes the statue for a purpose. But when the efficient cause is an inanimate thing – say, a cloud causing rainfall – we do not think of the effect as having a final cause also. The mediaevals thought of the further consequence normally brought about by some effect of an inanimate efficient cause as the final cause of that effect. The final cause of rainfall is watering the ground. (Efficient and final causes may be immediate or more remote. If A causes B, and B causes C, B is the immediate and A a more remote cause of C. If C occurs in order than D may occur and thereby E may occur, D is the immediate final cause, and E the more remote final cause of C. Mediaeval philosophers taught that God was the first, i.e. most remote, efficient cause of everything in that by his present action, he caused everything to have its present effects; and also the last final cause of all things, since all things were brought about for his sake.) There is, however, an obvious difference between a final cause which is so by being the normal consequence of some effect, and a final cause which is so by being a person's chosen purpose. From the sixteenth century onward this difference was brought out by talking of events not caused by purposive agents as having only efficient causes, producing their effects in accord with 'laws of nature' which dictate both the effect of the efficient cause and (for given circumstances) its further consequence, e.g. watering the ground. Final causes operated only when persons had conscious purposes. Theists* then claimed that events not brought about by humans nevertheless had a final cause, since brought about (through the operation of laws of nature) for a purpose by a personal God; atheists denied this. An enormously influential account of causation in the inanimate world was given in the eighteenth century by David Hume. For Hume the efficient cause, now called simply the 'cause', was an event, not an object (e.g. the ignition of the gunpowder, rather than the gunpowder itself). To say that the cause (e.g. the ignition of the gunpowder) caused its effect (e.g. the explosion) was simply to say that events like the former were followed regularily by events like the latter. The 'necessity' previously supposed to be involved in causation was simply regular succession. Laws of nature were simply statements of regular

succession. Hume, and in a much more systematic way some of his twentieth-century followers (e.g. D. Davidson), sought to fit purposive agency also into the Humean pattern. On this scheme, when a person brings about an effect for some purpose, all that happens is that a previous state of the person, his desire to produce the effect, causes that effect; and to say this is to say that that sort of desire is normally followed by that sort of effect. Other contemporary philosophers (e.g. Richard Taylor) have disputed this analysis, claiming that there is more to purposive action than passive and so unavoidable states, like desires, causing effects; the person has to endorse his desires (rather than hold them in check) before an intentional action occurs. On this view, the person himself, not some state of the person, is the cause and the purposive element in causation by persons is not eliminable; personal causality is different in kind from inanimate causality. Many modern philosophers (e.g. R. Harré and E. H. Madden) have held to varying degrees that Hume's account of causation in the inanimate world is mistaken. There is, they have held, a necessity in nature (the stone does not just happen to fall, if you drop it; it necessarily falls). Causation involves this necessitation; it is more than mere regular succession. Likewise, some hold, objects, not events are the causes of things. It is the brick, not the motion of the brick, which causes the window to break.

D. Davidson, 'Actions, Reasons, Causes', in *Essays on Actions and Events*, 1980; R. Harré and E. H. Madden, *Causal Powers*, 1975; D. Hume, *A Treatise of Human Nature*, Book I, Part III, Sections 1–7 and 14–16; J. L. Mackie, *The Cement of the Universe*, 1974 (a developed Humean account of causation); R. Taylor, *Action and Purpose*, 1966.

R. G. SWINBURNE

Celibacy

Celibacy may be defined as life-long abstinence from marriage. The practice of celibacy in the primitive church was hindered for two reasons: 1. Jewish law required every healthy male to procreate; 2. Roman laws discouraged celibacy, placed penalties on bachelors and rewarded women who gave birth to three or more children. There is debate over the question whether the Essenes, the Therapeutae and the members of Qumran practised celibacy: more likely this was temporary continence.

Although there is no evidence at all that Jesus was married, early Christian literature bears witness that the 'Twelve' (including John) were. There are also five references to Paul as a married person (Origen, Tertullian, Methodius of Olympus, Clement of Alexandria and Ps. Ignatius). Therefore the primitive church placed more emphasis on continence than celibacy. This seems the most appropriate interpretation of Paul's teaching on marriage and abstinence in I Cor. 7 and also of Jesus' teaching about eunuchs in Matt. 19.10–12. However, the texts are debated. Paul encourages widowhood for both men and women on account of the *eschaton*.

It is important to note that celibacy was not originally associated with any ecclesiastical office. In the deutero-Pauline epistles a bishop/presbyter was obliged to be a married person who could govern his own family. He and his wife may have been the host and hostess in house churches in apostolic days. In the Bible there is no juridical connection between celibacy and the clerical office: indeed, according to the Hebrew scriptures an unmarried man could not be a priest. It was some centuries before this association was made.

About the third or fourth century Christian writings begin to teach that marriage is good but that celibacy is better. There may be some association with the fact that as Christianity began to spread more and more into the pagan world, the link between ritual impurity and sacrifice affected Christian thinking. This is most pronounced in the heterodoxical texts (*see* **Virginity**). The Council of Nicaea (AD 325) refused to make celibacy obligatory among clerics, although it was highly esteemed for the higher offices. In the fourth century the Eastern church chose their bishops exclusively from monks. In the sixth century Emperor Justinian decreed that a person who had children could not be a bishop, and a married cleric must live with his wife as with a sister. However, the main reason for this was to avoid church possessions being divided among the children of clerics. In the seventh century, at the synod of Trullo, the Eastern church made a definite law about celibacy for higher clergy. The West, apparently, did not raise any objection.

A law making marriage an obstacle to ordination is found in the Council of Elvira (fourth century). Then the synods of Orange (441) and of Arles (524) required a promise of celibacy before appointment to the diaconate. However, here we are dealing with abstinence within marriage, not celibacy *per se.*

The actual laws of celibacy prior to ordination* arise only in the twelfth century. At the Second Lateran Council (1139) under Pope Alexander II marriages of clergy after ordination were definitely declared invalid. This was reaffirmed by Alexander III in 1180 and by Celestine II in 1198. However, some opposition, both from clergy and laity, followed even in the fourteenth and fifteenth centuries. By then celibacy was practically free from pagan cultic superstitions, but child inheritance and nepotism were still serious problems. The formation of seminaries in the seventeenth century made the law of celibacy into a reality. In the nineteenth and twentieth centuries some Anglicans adopted the practice for both men and women.

From the above account it can be seen that the contemporary crisis about celibacy is not at all an innovation.

While one cannot deny a certain misogyny related to clerical celibacy the main reasons for its practice are: for the sake of the kingdom of God; so that a man or woman may extend their love to a greater number of persons than spouse and children and also to embrace the same state as Christ and the Virgin Mary. Hence celibacy combines in a special way the two great precepts of charity, love of God and of neighbour. In the Middle Ages great importance was placed on celibacy as a vehicle for evangelization.

However, it must be pointed out that the church never requires anyone to be ordained and thus never imposes celibacy on a Christian. Vatican Council II speaks of celibacy as an easier, but not higher, means of serving God and his/her people. It also asserted that celibacy is not essentially bound up with the priesthood.

H. C. Lea, *History of Sacerdotal Celibacy in the Christian Church,* 1932; E. Schillebeeckx, *Celibacy,* 1968.

J. M. FORD

Certainty

Either 1. a subjective state of complete or unqualified assurance, or 2. a relational property of a proposition. Descriptively the subjective state of assurance can be independent of the objective relational property, but it is generally agreed that the latter cannot be totally independent of the former. Although there has been a long 'ethics of belief' tradition in philosophy, according to which the degree of assent one gives to a proposition ought to be proportioned to the justifying evidence available, there has been no consensus on what constitutes 'sufficient' evidence for a justified state of certainty. One clear source of warranted certainty is found in demonstrative arguments (logical syllogism or mathematical demonstration), and some philosophers have maintained that in the absence of such demonstration only a judgment of probability is legitimate. Others, however, have followed a tripartite division made by David Hume between 'demonstration' (or 'knowledge'), 'proof', and 'probability' (*Treatise*, Bk. I, III, xi; *Enquiry*, VI). They argue that a second and equal source of certainty is found in 'proofs' – i.e., those arguments from experience which, as Hume noted, leave 'no room for doubt'. The distinction between doubt that is logically possible, doubt that is reasonable, and doubt that is unreasonable in a given case can be employed to back the claim that to be 'conclusive' an argument need not be secured against even unreasonable doubts; certainty can be justified when, though it is possible to doubt, it is nevertheless unreasonable to do so. The possibility of such warranted certainty is also supported by contemporary responses to scepticism which argue that certainty requires neither that the agent be infallible (incapable of error) nor that the belief be incorrigible (incapable of being corrected or amended).

Theological discussions of certainty often make use of the category of 'moral' certainty to refer to the certainty possible in nondemonstrative cases and necessary and/or sufficient for religious belief. (Some accounts of religious belief, however, consider certainty as either unnecessary or inappropriate – *see* **Doubt**.) The status of such 'moral' certainty, however, differs in various accounts. For example, in seventeenth-cen-tury British debates between Catholics and Protestants concerning infallibility, 'moral' certainty was generally understood by Protestants to refer to 'practical' certainty – namely, that degree of conviction sufficient for acting on a belief. Two centuries later, however, J. H. Newman carefully distinguished between the 'practical' certainty sufficient for acting on a belief and the 'moral' certainty (possible to and required for faith) that a particular proposition is true; he claimed that such 'moral' certainty is an unqualified theoretical or speculative certainty, even though it issues from nondemonstrative argument. This has been more often the Catholic position, and it can perhaps be illuminated by reference to the distinction noted above concerning unreasonable doubt.

The standard philosophical treatments can be found in R. Descartes, *Meditations*, 1641; D. Hume, *Treatise of Human Nature*, 1739–40, and *Essays Concerning Human Understanding*, 1748; J. Locke, *Essay Concerning Human Understanding*, 1690. Among a large number of recent works on scepticism and certainty are A. J. Ayer, *The Problem of Knowledge*, 1956, and L. Wittgenstein, *On Certainty*, 1969.

M. JAMIE FERREIRA

Chalcedon *see* **Christology**

Character

1. Sacramental character is the special effect predicated of baptism, confirmation and holy orders. It is regarded as a supernatural and indelible mark impressed upon the individual recipient which cannot be effaced either by sin or apostasy. Foreshadowed by the concept of the 'seal' (cf. Eph. 1.13) or identification mark, the idea was given currency by Augustine*, who distinguished between the grace conveyed and the character imprinted by a sacrament. He contended, in his debate with the Donatists*, that baptism is valid even when administered in schism* but conveys no benefit; it is not necessary to repeat it when the schismatic returns to the church, but it is only then that it fructifies. He was also prepared to extend this idea to ordination, in an effort to smooth the path for returning Donatists.

The concept of character was developed by the Scholastics*, for example, by Scotus, who maintained that it was a kind of quality and, on the basis of Aristotle's categories of quality, that it was something akin to the genus of quality called power. This teaching was endorsed by the Council of Florence (1438–45) and solemnly defined by the Council of Trent* (1545–63): 'If any one shall say that in three sacraments, namely baptism, confirmation and holy orders, there is not a character impressed upon the soul, that is a certain spiritual and ineffaceable mark (*signum*), whence these sacraments cannot be repeated, let him be anathema' (Conc. Trid. Sess. ult., can. 7).

Acceptance of the indelible character of holy orders has issued in the phenomenon of *episcopi vagantes* (wandering bishops). Since the character cannot be lost, even a bishop who has been excommunicated by the church retains the episcopal 'character' and therefore can and does ordain.

Most Christian churches would acknowledge the indelible character imparted in baptism, in the sense that it is an unrepeatable act, the principal exception being the Baptists who, rejecting infant and insisting upon believers' baptism, would re-baptize. But many Christians would not accept the indelible character of orders – such a view is repudiated, for example, by the Eastern Orthodox churches – on the grounds that ordination conveys authorization rather than an imprint, and hence if a person ceases to be competent to perform the function for which he was given authority, say, by excommunication, he forfeits his orders.

2. Moral character was regarded by some in the patristic period as being directly related to the administration of the sacraments. The Donatists, following Cyprian in part, maintained that the validity of the sacraments depended upon the worthiness of the minister. Hence they contended that episcopal consecrations performed by a *traditor*, that is, one who had handed over the scriptures in the Diocletian persecution and had thereby revealed his apostasy, were unacceptable. Optatus of Milevum, writing *c.* 366, argued against this on the grounds that the sacraments derive their validity from God and not from the person administering them. It is this latter view that has generally prevailed, as otherwise, since a person's moral character is only fully known to God, no one would ever know whether a baptism or a celebration of the eucharist had or had not been impaired by the unworthiness of the minister.

————

B. Leeming, *Principles of Sacramental Theology*, 1960, pp. 129–282.

J. G. DAVIES

Charismatic

In a general way, the word refers to the grace dimension of Christianity and of the church as distinguished from the institutional or hierarchical dimension. Without pushing the distinction too far, we can say that 'charismatic' designates the Christian community as guided by the Holy Spirit, as functioning according to the gifts of the Spirit (including the charisms), and as bonded by the love poured into the hearts of the faithful through the Spirit. The Pauline letters show clearly the integration of the charismatic and the institutional aspects of the church (see especially I Cor. 12; 13; 14; Rom. 12; 13; Eph. 4; 5; 6). The Pauline theology of Christian community, after beginning with the fact of the unity of the body of Christ in one Spirit, proceeds to the diversity of charisms in the body according to the graces given to each member ('the body is one and has many members; ... there are many different members, but one body' (I Cor. 12.12). There follows a discussion of the role of the gift of love in the community; love gives life to the church; without love, the charisms have no value. Finally, order and harmony in the body follow from the unity-in-diversity assured by the operation of the love given us through the Spirit; and so we must strive in the Spirit for peace among ourselves and with civil authority (Rom. 13.1–10), for domestic peace and order (Eph. 5.22–6.9), and for peace in our assemblies (I Cor. 14).

More specifically, 'charismatic' refers to those gifts of the Spirit called charisms, to the charismatic gifts. And it refers to the movement in the church that emphasizes the renewal of charisms: the charismatic renewal. The charismatic renewal is part of the Pentecostal movement (*see* **Pentecostalism**). The whole Pentecostal movement, including the charismatic renewal, has its historical roots in the Holiness Movement which separated from Methodism in the United States near the end of the nineteenth century. On the first day of 1901, in Topeka, Kansas, a woman student at the Bethel Bible Institute asked the head of that Institute, a

Methodist minister, to lay his hands on her head and to pray that she receive the gift of the Spirit. She experienced a transforming grace that filled her with joy, peace and praise, and – at the same time – she received the gift of praying in tongues. In the following days, the faculty and student body at the school received the same 'baptism in the Holy Spirit'. Pentecostalism spread rapidly, emphasizing the baptism in the Holy Spirit, marked by the reception of the gift of tongues and other charisms. Rejected by their churches, the Pentecostals formed their own assemblies. The Assemblies of God took shape in 1914, and since then many other Pentecostal churches and assemblies have been formed. This 'classical Pentecostalism' did not have a marked effect on the more traditional 'historic' Christian churches until 1960. Since it began to penetrate the main-line Reformation churches, the Anglican and Orthodox churches, and finally (1967) the Roman Catholic Church, Neo-Pentecostalism, or the charismatic renewal, has spread rapidly and now forms a strong current in Christianity. It manifests itself principally in the practice of praying for the baptism in the Holy Spirit, in the exercise of the charisms – such as prophecy, praying for healing, tongues (*see* **Glossolalia**), teaching, evangelization – in prayer groups, and also in the foundation of new 'covenant communities' of persons who, having experienced the power of the Spirit through charismatic renewal, seek to live in that Spirit in community (usually non-residential) with brothers and sisters who share the same experience.

See also **Pentecostalism, Spirtual Gifts.**

Francis A. Sullivan, *Charisms and Charismatic Renewal*, 1982.

ROBERT FARICY

Chastity

Here 'chastity' will be treated as 'continence', that is, refraining from sexual intercourse for a variety of religious reasons but not for one's entire lifetime. Continence was practised in Judaism mainly for three reasons: 1. in battle; 2. for certain cultic occasions, e.g. the high priest on the Day of Atonement; 3. as a sign of mourning on fast days or on bereavement. The members of the Qumran community prohibited second marriage and perhaps divorce.

Christian continence was not emphasized by Jesus except when he spoke about eunuchs for the sake of the kingdom (Matt. 19.10–12); many modern exegetes think that this text refers to abstinence from second marriage. Paul also spoke about temporary continence in marriage for the purpose of prayer (and fasting), but he cautioned against abuse of this practice. He also taught that abstention from second marriages, while not mandatory, was highly commendable, especially in the light of the expected parousia *. In the early church, certain Christians, of whom Tertullian is a prime example, deemed that marriage was for eternity, all second marriages were sinful and thus widows and widowers were obliged to remain continent. However, this was never approved by the whole church.

In I Tim. 5.3–16 one learns about a formal institution of continent women, namely, widows: of their qualifications, enrolment and duties. Younger widows (probably teenage girls) were advised to remarry. Gradually an order of widows developed within the church. Several times the Alexandrian writers of the third century list widows with bishops, presbyters and deacons. Some writers interpreted 'washing the feet of the saints' to mean that widows should be official teachers of women. The main task of a widow was prayer and fasting, and her prayers were thought to be especially efficacious. The *Testamentum Domini* has four chapters on widows. It speaks clearly about their qualifications and their ordination and treats this ceremony in a way similar to that of bishops, presbyters and deacons. The widows occupied special places near the bishop * in church. They joined the clergy during the oblation of the eucharist. They seem to have had a rank equal to deacons *. The text mentions that a widow should be visited by the Holy Spirit: this seems to suggest that she is a vehicle of revelation. Further she has considerable pastoral responsibility: teaching catechumens and the ignorant, visiting the sick, encouraging those practising continence and virginity * and gathering them together to pray. The order of widows declined in the fourth century, but the order of deaconesses * seems to have stemmed from it.

An interesting aspect of continence is the controversial practice of *virgines subintroductae* or *agapetai*. These were men and women who lived in marriage as brother and sister. From the second to the fourth centuries, this practice was adopted by many clergy, but it led to abuses and was condemned by the church.

A very intriguing aspect of continence is found in the Syriac church, where there is a clear distinction between continence and virginity (*betuluta*). Of note are a group of ascetics who appear to have lived in continence. They were called *benai qeiama* and *benat qeiama*, sons and daughters of the covenant, respectively. They were often children who were dedicated to God and then educated in monasteries. The *chorepiscopus* consecrated them through prayer, imposition of hands and blessing. They were clearly distinguished from monks but linked closely to them, although some were attached to churches. Provisions were made for betrothed people who might wish to embrace this state. The children of the covenant appear to have enjoyed certain privileges in that priests and deacons could not constrain them to do certain work, or impose tribute on them or demand interest. These ascetics were permitted to live only with relatives or within their own groups, but not with lay people. They had some authority in town churches as they were educated in scripture and especially the psalms. From the *benat qeiama* were sometimes selected deaconesses and from the *benai* deacons or priests. They were obliged to meet with the bishop twice a year. Some scholars have compared them with the members of the Qumran community.

Yet the Syriac church also showed more extreme, indeed, heterodoxical strains with regard to continence. This is found especially among the Encratites. Virginity and continence were almost identified with the proclamation of the gospel. Some baptized only married persons who would not live in continence. The term 'holy' became used for such continent people. The ascetic was seen as a combatant in the holy war fighting against evil. These trends led to much misogyny.

Roger Gryson, *The Ministry of Women in the Early Church*, 1976; A. Vööbus, *History of Asceticism in the Syrian Orient*, 1958.

J. M. FORD

Chiliasm

The word (from Greek *chilioi*, a thousand) is the equivalent of **Millennialism***, the belief that Christ will reign on earth for a thousand years before the final consummation of all things (cf. Rev. 20.1–5).

ALAN RICHARDSON

Chrism

From the Greek *chrio*, the word designates a fragrant, blessed oil which is used in the sacramental rituals of baptism*, confirmation* and ordination*. Chrism is also used in other solemn ceremonies of dedication (of altars, churches, etc.). The Church of England has retained anointing* for the coronation of a monarch. Protestant churches have discarded it, although it is undoubtedly ancient, chiefly because of the obscurity of its symbolism and its lack of sufficient NT authorization.

ALAN RICHARDSON

Christ *see* Messiah

Christ Event

The phrase evokes a rich ambiguity. Historical-critical research into the life of Jesus* has shown a wide chasm between the Jesus presented by research and the Jesus projected by the NT authors. In the NT Jesus' death is the event that brings about salvation for the world. But a study of the death of Jesus as a historical happening may produce the description of a tragic, or even uncalled-for, crucifixion. It would be incongruous, therefore, to claim that what historical research establishes is at the basis of the Christian faith. Yet Christianity has consistently claimed to have a historical foundation.

Besides, what the disciples of Jesus proclaimed after his death and resurrection was neither something he had taught or done, nor a new interpretation of the messianic expectations that would allow them to show Jesus as Messiah. *'Jesus' having come was itself the decisive event* through which God called his congregation (church)' (R. Bultmann, *Theology of the NT*, ET I, 1951, p. 43). Thus the first disciples at Easter already were pulled together by the realization that God's activity was to be seen in Jesus' coming as a whole, and not in any singular aspect of it.

The Christ event is both the coming of

Jesus which the disciples proclaimed – that is, the content of the *kerygma**, and the formation of the Christian community on the basis of Easter – that is, the occurrence of their faith. The Christ event signifies for the disciples both the new understanding of Jesus as Messiah*, and of themselves as new creatures. There is in this doctrine, then, a real tension between the continuity and discontinuity of Jesus and the post-Easter community.

R. Bultmann, *History and Eschatology*, 1957, pp. 138–55; G. Ebeling, *The Nature of Faith*, ET 1959, pp. 19–30.

HEROLD WEISS

Christendom

The word means 'the Christian world'. It is strictly applicable only to that period of the Middle Ages when the church could enforce obedience to its discipline both in belief and in practice. Its zenith was the pontificate of Gregory VII (1021–1085), who wrote to the nations to remind them that from the time of St Peter the See of Rome had been their overlord, and who humbled the Emperor at Canossa. The disintegration of Christendom began at the close of the Middle Ages with the rise of nationalism, the Reformation* and the inevitable secularization* of society which followed the Renaissance. The Reformers themselves hardly foresaw the break-up of Christendom which was to come, for even in the Protestant countries the reception of the sacraments was still enforced by the magistrates, and heresy and even dissent were offences against the state. But the mediaeval ideal of Christendom – one church, one state – could not survive the attainment of freedom by men come of age at the Renaissance and the Age of Enlightenment*. The French Revolution heralded the secular state. The newly independent colonies in America set up a constitution which strictly separated church and state. Only the reactionaries, to the immense disservice of the Christian cause, tried to keep the civil and lay society in tutelage to the hierarchy of the church. 'Christendom' was a magnificent ideal, and its realization in mediaeval Europe created a great civilization in the lands which the barbarian invaders had despoiled. But it could not last, for it was not the answer to the human quest for freedom. Today it lingers only as a memory. Its passing did not solve the problems of humanity; it only created new ones.

ALAN RICHARDSON

Christening

From Anglo-Saxon *cristnian*, the word is more popular in general English usage than 'baptism', with which it is almost synonymous. It carries, however, an overtone of 'naming with a Christian name', and in vulgar speech 'to christen' often means to name or to nick-name, without religious reference. *See* **Initiation, Christian.**

ALAN RICHARDSON

Christian, Christianity

The name 'Christians' seems to have arisen as a nickname (cf. 'Methodists', 'Quakers') for an unpopular sect (Acts 11.26; cf. 26.28; I Peter 4.16; Tacitus, xv, 44). It eventually took the place of such other designations as 'disciples', 'brethren', 'saints', or 'those of the Way', and became generally used by Christians themselves. It differentiated them from pagans and Jews, as now it differentiates them from Muslims, Buddhists, Hindus, etc. Today it is a generic description of all Christian churches and sects, though in the nineteenth century some Unitarians* rejected it. The name of Christ (as distinct from the reputation of the church) has become so revered in Western civilization that many people who hold no definite Christian beliefs would be offended if they were told that they or their actions were unchristian. But while 'Christian' is thus held to apply to certain ethical standards of behaviour, 'Christianity' remains a synonym for the Christian religion as distinct from other religions or philosophies of life (e.g. humanism, Marxism, etc.).

ALAN RICHARDSON

Christianity and Other Religions

The Christian attitude to other religions has been the subject of much discussion in recent years. The weight of opinion has moved from the predominantly negative attitude of the nineteenth century to a growing recognition that God's saving activity is not confined to the Judaeo-Christian tradition.

1. *Biblical material* is itself ambiguous. In the OT the gods of other nations were usually regarded as idols. They were snares, objects of scorn to be destroyed whenever possible.

The people of Israel were conscious that God had rescued them from Egypt and made a covenant* with them by which they became his chosen people. This could encourage an exclusive attitude, but it was sometimes recognized that the God of Israel was the One God of all mankind. The covenant with Noah and his descendants was understood as a universal covenant of God the Creator with all living creatures (Gen. 9.8). His choice of Israel was that they should bring his blessing* to all people (Gen. 12.3; Isa. 49.6; 66). He was active in the history of the nations (Isa. 10.5).

In the NT heathen gods are again regarded as idols (I Cor. 8), but there is some recognition that Gentiles may be aware of the One God known to Israel (Acts 18.24; 10.34; Rom. 1.19). In any case, as Paul insisted, Gentiles should be free to become full members of the Christian church.

The emphasis in the NT is on the salvation offered through Jesus Christ and this is often expressed in exclusive terms (Acts 4.12; John 14.6). These texts cannot, however, be simply applied to contemporary questions without discussion of their context and the purpose of the Fourth Gospel.

Jesus himself said little about pagan religion, but rejected the nationalist and exclusivist attitude of some of his Jewish contemporaries. Gentiles, he said, would share in the kingdom* of God (Matt. 8.11) and be judged on the same basis as the Jews (Matt. 25.31).

The reference in the prologue to the Fourth Gospel to the 'real light' that 'enlightens every man' which became flesh in Jesus has been interpreted to mean that the God who reveals himself in Jesus confronts every person in their conscience. This has given rise to a Logos* theology and talk of the 'Anonymous Christ'. There are also hints in Paul of universal redemption* (I Cor. 15.28; Rom. 11.32).

2. *Early Christian writers* were primarily concerned to show that Christ was the true Messiah* who fulfilled the OT. They argued that the church was the new Israel and the inheritor of the covenant. Their arguments, which may have encouraged antisemitism, are now being re-examined. In any case they cannot be used to determine the attitude of Christianity to other religions because of the particular relationship of the church to the Jewish people. Some writers, such as J. Parkes, argue that God's new covenant did not annul his covenant with Israel and that Christianity and Judaism should regard each other as sister religions. Other writers do not go so far, but Christians today look back with penitence on the church's shameful treatment of the Jews and are gradually building more friendly relationships.

Early in the second century, pagan writers began to attack Christianity as irrational, immoral and subversive. The Apologists (*see* **Apologetics**) responded to these attacks and explained why Christians could not join in the pagan cults or venerate the emperor. Pagan polytheism was to them the work of demons who were rebellious spiritual beings. The task of Christians was therefore to destroy paganism, which they eagerly did once the emperor had been converted. This continued to be the Christian attitude to paganism as the faith spread into Western and Northern Europe. At the same time worship of the Lord Jesus made it impossible for Christians to regard the emperor as Lord – and many paid for their refusal with their lives.

Yet although paganism was to be destroyed, a few writers, who appreciated Greek philosophy, saw that it was part of God's plan and one of the stages through which mankind was to be brought to Christ (e.g. Clement of Alexandria, *Stromateis* 1.5). It was also held that because man is created in the image of God, he participates through his reason in the Logos*. The more closely he responds to the Logos, the nearer, unconsciously, he is to Christ (Justin Martyr, *First Apology*, 46).

3. *The rise of Islam*, with its inroads into Christendom*, was met by the physical and spiritual hostility of Christians who often regarded it as a Christian heresy. The enmity came to a head with the Crusades, the bitter memories of which still mar Christian–Muslim relations. There were exceptions such as Raymond Lull (*c.* 1232–1315), a mystic and missionary to the Muslims, or St Francis (*c.* 1181–1226), who went to see the Sultan of Egypt. Thomas Aquinas (*c.* 1225–1274) wrote that as Muslims do not share any scriptures with Christians, arguments with them had to be based on natural reason alone. By unaided reason man could come to a knowledge of God's existence and

of some of his attributes. Aquinas, therefore, and many R C writers after him, have recognized in the world religions some truth – 'natural revelation' – which needs to be corrected and amplified by biblical revelation.

Martin Luther also, despite his vitriolic attacks on the Jews, made some study of Islam and edited a German translation of the Quran. Cardinal Nicholas of Cusa, in the fifteenth century, in his *De Pace Fidei* suggested that behind all religious differences there was one universal religion on which Jews, Christians and Muslims could agree. Few shared this view, and the dominant Christian attitude at the time to Jews and Muslims was one of hostility and opposition. Soon, in the sixteenth and seventeenth centuries, Christians were to show a similar hostility and opposition to each other.

4. *The Expansion of Europe.* Although the intellectual and physical battles of the Reformation* and Religious Wars absorbed much energy, European explorers of Asia and the New World were followed by Christian missionaries. From the sixteenth to the eighteenth century these missionaries were nearly all Roman Catholics. The general view of the Spanish missionaries in Latin America and the West Indies was of the *tabula rasa* – the view that in non-Christian life and systems there is nothing on which the missionary can build and that everything must be levelled to the ground. This was the approach Francis Xavier (1506–1552) at first adopted with the simple and illiterate fishermen of South India; but in Japan he met a civilization of considerable sophistication and saw that the gospel had to transform and recreate it, but need not reject everything that came before as worthless. This approach was adopted by other Jesuits such as Matthew Ricci (1552–1610) in China, who seems to have spoken of St Confucius, or Robert de Nobili (1577–1656) in India. Robert de Nobili adopted the ochre robe of a Hindu holy man (*sannyasi*). Learning Tamil and Sanskrit he presented the gospel in Indian terms. 'The law which I preach is the law of the true God, which from ancient times was by his command proclaimed in these countries by sannyasis and saints.' He met with some success, but his methods, and particularly his attitude to caste, were much criticized by other Christians. The arguments about this approach were to be repeated many times on the mission field and reflected different moral and theological evaluations of indigenous religions.

From the first, Protestant missionaries also adopted various approaches. Although it has become commonplace to think that nineteenth-century missionaries regarded other religions as nothing but the work of the devil, the reality is more complex. Some mission hymns such as

'Trumpet of God, sound high
Till the hearts of the heathen shake',

or,

'Rescue the perishing
Care for the dying
Snatch them in pity from sin and the
grave',

reflected the views of many missionaries, especially of those who worked in rural areas and who had no contact with higher forms of Hinduism or Buddhism. Indian society, as many Hindus would admit, was degenerate at the beginning of the nineteenth century. Bishop Heber, however, appreciated some aspects of Indian culture and renounced the Calvinist view that all Indians were under 'sentence of reprobation' from God. He advised his fellow missionaries to avoid all 'bitter and contemptuous words about the objects of idolatry'. J. J. 'Pundit' Johnson of Benares achieved a rare fluency in Sanskrit. Others, although their motive was to 'gain all information of the snares and delusion in which the heathen are held', studied the languages and religion of their area. William Carey (1761–1834), for example, produced a Sanskrit grammar and translated the Hindu epic the *Ramayana* into English, whilst William Ward (1764–1823) wrote a good guide to the manners and customs of the Hindu.

By the end of the nineteenth century, despite the evangelical revival of the closing years, knowledge of world religions was increasing and a sympathetic attitude was expected of missionaries. Even such a staunch evangelical as the Scotsman John Murdoch could 'cheerfully' admit 'that Hinduism contains some great truths, more or less clearly expressed'. The replies of missionaries before the Edinburgh Conference of 1910 lay emphasis on the necessity that the missionary to Hindus should possess, and not merely assume, a sympathetic attitude towards India's most ancient religion. In Britain Thomas Carlyle in 1840 lectured on Mohammed, insisting that he was not a 'scheming Impostor, a Falsehood incarnate' but a messenger 'sent from the Infinite Unknown with tidings to us'. Five years later F. D. Maurice lectured on *The Religions of the World in their Relations to Christianity*, in which he treated the world of religions as a whole. They all reveal something of the relationship of man to God, although only Christ can answer their deepest longings. By the end of the century, *The Sacred Books of the East*, edited by Max Müller, were appearing, and the science of religions was establishing itself in continental universities. Even so, there was still the optimistic hope that the world could be won for Christ in that generation.

5. *The Twentieth Century*. Many factors have helped to modify the Christian position in this century and a bewildering variety of views are now held by Christians.

European self-confidence has declined and, from early in this century, some artists and thinkers began to be influenced by non-European cultures. The Second World War resulted in a major shift of political and economic power away from Europe.

Thanks to the work of many scholars of world religions – sometimes called 'comparative religion' – knowledge of other religions has increased rapidly. Their scriptures, and books about them, are readily available. World religions are now taught in many colleges and schools and featured on television – although as W. Cantwell Smith points out, the real object of study is the faith of other people, as terms such as Hinduism or Buddhism are European abstractions. All this has helped many Christians to a sympathetic appreciation.

At the same time there has been increasing personal contact, and Christians have learned to respect the holy and moral lives of members of other religions. During the war, many Europeans were posted abroad and subsequently travel for business and pleasure has increased rapidly. Also, since the war, largely because of migration, other faith communities have established themselves in Western Europe and the USA. A Sikh or Muslim may now be a neighbour, or workmate, or school friend, not someone who lives in a far-off land across the sea.

This century has seen a great revival and renewal within the world religions. The influence of figures like Rabindranath Tagore, Aurobindo, Mahatma Gandhi, the Dalai Lama or Rev. Niwano has been worldwide. At a time when many Westerners have become disenchanted with Christianity, teachers of Eastern religions have attracted a number of Western followers.

There have also been changes in the theological climate. There has been much discussion of the authority and historicity of the Bible. Many question, for example, whether the Fourth Gospel records the actual words of Jesus. If it does not, his exclusive claims recorded there have to be re-evaluated. Preachers have emphasized the unbounded love of God – who must be concerned for all his children – and the concepts of judgment and damnation have retreated into the background. Recently, too, the witness of Asian, African and Latin American theologians has been heard more clearly.

Amongst Fundamentalists and Conservative Evangelicals, the dominant nineteenth-century view, that the only hope of salvation for members of other faiths was to be converted to Christ, has persisted. The Frankfurt Declaration of 1970 said that 'the adherents of the non-Christian religions and world views . . . must let themselves be freed from their former ties and false hopes in order to be admitted by belief and baptism into the body of Christ' (para. 6). 'In him alone is eternal salvation promised to them' (para. 3). Christianity is the true religion, all others are false. In more sophisticated form this was the position of the very influential Swiss theologian Karl Barth. He distinguished sharply between religion and faith. Religion as the human search for God is unbelief, the great concern of godless man, in contrast to faith, which is human powerlessness before the Word which reveals the judgment and grace of God. Emil Brunner was less categorical in denying the possibility of revelation outside 'the Word', but also treated the world of religion as evidence of human pride and rebellion. Similarly, the very influential missionary theologian Hendrik Kraemer, whose complex book *The Christian Message in a Non-Christian World* was at the centre of discussion at the 1938 Tambaram meeting of the International Missionary Council, stressed the discontinuity of the gospel. 'Biblical Realism', the message of God's forgiveness, salvation and judgment is quite different from all non-Christian religions which are attempts by man to raise himself to the Divine.

Kraemer had a deep knowledge of world religions, especially of Islam. Other Christian scholars who formed more sympathetic judgments of world religions were equally emphatic that Christ was the crown of all religions and that salvation required faith in him.

J. N. Farquhar, whose *Crown of Hinduism* (1913) became well known, devoted much attention to the careful and sympathetic study of Indian religion and society but argued that Hinduism provided at best only 'outdated' answers to the questions it asked. Their true answer was to be found in Christ – Christianity being the 'evolutionary crown' of Hinduism. Bishops Stephen Neill and Lesslie Newbigin, both with intimate knowledge of other religions, insisted that there could be no compromise on the question of salvation.

The desire to appreciate and understand other religions gave rise to the approach of dialogue. The need to listen as well as to speak was emphasized. The World Council of Churches, the Vatican and several denominations set up agencies for official dialogue. The purpose of dialogue could, however, be variously understood and did not necessarily imply a change from the traditional claim that salvation is only in Christ.

A growing number of Christians, however, came to recognize that God's grace was evidently at work in some members of other faiths. Their holiness and devotion was evidence of 'uncovenanted' mercy. The philosopher and missionary A. G. Hogg, well aware of the differences between the teachings of religions, held that some members of other faiths 'by the narrowest and crookedest of doctrinal bridges, win across the gulf of doubt to that trustful and obedient faith which the Father loves to reward' (*The Christian message to the Hindu*, 1947, p. 123). Bede Griffiths argued that God speaks to every man in his conscience and that his grace is available to all. 'Good' Hindus or Buddhists or Muslims might therefore be called (although they might not recognize themselves as such!) 'anonymous' Christians, members of the invisible church through 'baptism by desire' (*see also* **Anony-**

mous Christianity). Building on this Logos doctrine, there was talk too of the Hidden, Incognito, or Unknown Christ active within the world religions.

This led some to recognize that the world religions themselves might be channels of God's grace. In traditional society it was too individualistic a view to expect people to discover God's salvation apart from their ancestral faith. Fr Neuner therefore spoke of non-Christian religions as 'the ordinary way' of salvation. Karl Rahner likewise holds that traditional religions contain not only natural but supernatural, grace-filled elements and therefore, despite their undoubted errors, are lawful religions.

These concessions, charitable as they are, suggest to John Hick the need for a more radical revision. They indicate a recognition that God is at work in the world religions, but this cannot easily be combined with traditional beliefs that outside the church there is no salvation. Hick argues the need for a Copernican revolution, a shift from the dogma that Christianity is at the centre to the realization that it is God who is at the centre and that all religions of mankind, including our own, serve and revolve around him. This is to recognize the parity of status of all religions and marks a break with the views of those who, in however tolerant and liberal a form, hold on to a belief in the superiority or finality* of Christianity.

It is the position adopted earlier by Unitarians* and similar to the position Ernest Troeltsch reached towards the end of his life and that held by Friedrich Heiler or Arnold Toynbee. It is also widespread in the Interfaith Movement.

The difficulty is that the unity of religions may amount to a few generalities, whilst the important differences between religions are ignored. Further, each religion is a whole in which doctrine, ritual and ethics relate together to a core experience or event. Extracted from their context religious beliefs and practices are distorted. The American Roman Catholic R. E. Whitson therefore has argued that each religion is unique *and* universal. In a similar manner Bishop George Appleton, in a sermon preached in Canterbury Cathedral, said, 'Each religion has a mission, a gospel, a central affirmation. Each of us needs to enlarge on the gospel which he has received without wanting to demolish the gospel of others.' The hope of a growing convergence of religions – not dissimilar to the reconception suggested in the 1930s by the philosopher W. E. Hocking – is implicit here.

Such an approach, it is claimed, allows for the total commitment necessary for religious faith to the truth as far as it is already known, with an openness to further truth. It allows the Christian to witness to the revelation of God that he has recognized in Jesus Christ, without having to make negative judgments on the claims of others. It affirms that God in his universal love has no favourites, so that Christianity cannot be the basis of exclusivism and cultural pride. It allows the Christian to see that other religions have a place in God's plan and to recognize a dynamic convergent purpose in the religious history of mankind. It makes Christ, in the words of the missionary to India C. F. Andrews, 'more central and universal . . . because more universally human'.

It remains to be seen, however, whether the majority of Christians are content to affirm their experience of salvation in Christ without also asserting that this must be the way of salvation for all people. The answer will help determine whether the growing meeting of religions is in a spirit of competition or fellowship.

N. Anderson, *Christianity and Comparative Religion*, 1970; A. C. Bouquet, *The Christian Faith and Non-Christian Religions*, 1958; M. Braybrooke, *Interfaith Organizations, 1893-1979*, 1980; K. Cragg, *The Christian and Other Religions*, 1977; J. Hick, *God Has Many Names*, 1982; S. Neill, *A History of Christian Missions*, 1964; *Relations with People of Other Faiths: Guidelines on Dialogue in Britain*, BCC Report 1981; E. J. Sharpe, *Comparative Religion. A History*, 1975; *Faith Meets Faith*, 1977 (includes a bibliographical survey); W. Cantwell Smith, *Towards a World Theology*, 1981; O. C. Thomas (ed), *Attitudes Toward Other Religions*, 1969.

MARCUS BRAYBROOKE

Christocentrism

A christocentric theology is normally thought of as one in which controlling and definitive significance is accorded to the person and work of Christ. But this could plausibly be said of any Christian theology worth the name, and so 'christocentrism' is sometimes defined as the refusal to allow that there is any saving knowledge of God independently of his revelation in Christ. Barth's theology appears to be the most obvious modern example of a christocentric approach in this sense; but it should be remembered that for Barth the important point is not so much a concentration on the incarnation * as such, but the lordship and primacy of the Word of God which manifests itself freely and sovereignly in the 'concentric circles' of the life of Jesus, the witness of scripture, and the church's preaching. Not even in the life of Christ do we have an interweaving of God and the world in any way that would make it possible for the figure of Jesus to act as the interpretative coping-stone of a dogmatic *system*.

Something more like this could be found in the Eastern Christian tradition. Maximus the Confessor (seventh century) develops a scheme in which the incarnation is the means of repairing a whole sequence of disastrous rifts in the created order itself and between creation and God. As in Christ all things are 'ordered' at creation, so are they all reconciled in his divine-and-human incarnate form. Modern Orthodox writers (especially V. N. Lossky) have made much use of Maximus, and have employed the Chalcedonian antithesis of nature and hypostasis *, and the model of hypostatic union *, to work out a trinitarian theology, an anthropology and an ecclesiology: all heresy, in this perspective, is a form of christological heresy. However, such theologians are eager to avoid what has been dubbed (e.g. by N. Nissiotis) 'christomonism', which they regard as a typical Western aberration, minimizing the role of the Holy Spirit * by an excessive and forensically-dominated concentration on the work of Christ.

The 'death-of-God' * theologians (some of them ex-pupils of Barth) who argued for a kind of Christ-dominated atheism (Altizer, Pelz, van Buren) evidently appeared to some theologians, especially in the English-speaking world, to show the nemesis of 'christocentrism'. *The Myth of God Incarnate* (1977) represents one cluster of possible responses, tending to see the figure of Christ as *illustrative* (rather than finally *definitive*) of the nature and purposes of God.

Apart from the cosmic Christ-mysticism of Teilhard de Chardin, probably the most creative 'christocentric' essay to come from

RC circles in recent decades is the massive work of the Swiss Hans Urs von Balthasar, *Herrlichkeit* ('Glory'); subtitled 'A Theological Aesthetics', it is an attempt to show how the 'form' of the incarnate Christ, the pattern of his life and death and dereliction and return, can be seen as the norm of *beauty* and thus the hidden goal of desire in a vast range of religious and cultural phenomena, pre-Christian and (would-be) post-Christian: all human art is drawn magnetically to that point where the finite world in all its helpless tragedy is transparent to the beauty and glory of God. Intelligibility and beauty (desirability), understanding and love, unite in the vision of the central, revealed image of Jesus. Balthasar has an obvious debt to Barth; but his affinities are perhaps more obviously with Maximus (on whom he has written). Yet, as with Barth, vision rather than system is to the fore; and perhaps this is the least ambivalent way for 'christocentrism' to find theological expression.

H. Urs von Balthasar, *Love Alone: the Way of Revelation*, ET 1968; K. Barth, *Dogmatics in Outline*, ET 1949; John Hick (ed), *The Myth of God Incarnate*, 1977; Leslie Houlden, 'The Place of Jesus', in M. Hooker and C. Hickling (ed), *What About the New Testament?*, 1975; Vladimir Lossky, *In the Image and Likeness of God*, ET 1974; Jean Milet, *God or Christ?*, ET 1981; W. and L. Pelz, *God is No More*, 1963.

ROWAN WILLIAMS

Christology

1. *Introduction*. The pages of the NT cover a wide variety of topics, but nothing like as wide a range as appears in the OT. There is a tremendous concentration on one man, Jesus * of Nazareth. If there had been no such concentration, or if the texts had been uniform in the nature of their descriptions, there might perhaps have been no need for christology, for critical enquiry into the significance of Jesus Christ for Christian faith. But there is this concentration, and the terms in which the subject is expressed are extremely varied.

The centre of the Synoptic Gospels is the story of a man's life.

There were shepherds in the fields with their flocks. They were afraid, but the angel said, 'Do not be afraid. Today in the city of David a deliverer has been born to you, the Messiah, the Lord' (Luke 2.10). An age-old expectation has been fulfilled. For the Pauline community the child of Bethlehem has become the Lord. 'It is not ourselves that we proclaim: we proclaim Christ Jesus as Lord, and ourselves as your servants, for Jesus' sake. For the same Lord who said "out of the darkness let light shine" has caused his light to shine within us to give the light of revelation, the revelation of the glory of God in the face of Jesus Christ' (II Cor. 4.5f.) The Johannine Christ is himself the incarnate Word. 'So the word became flesh; he came to dwell among us and we saw his glory, such glory as befits the Father's only Son, full of grace and truth' (John 1.14).

The man Jesus and the Christ of faith are understood and portrayed in the NT in a large number of different ways. Throughout the history of the church hundreds, if not thousands of answers have been given to the central question: What think ye of Christ? We in turn will inevitably be influenced by the fact that the question is not asked in our day for the first time. Christology, the doctrine of Christ, is enquiry into the significance of Jesus for Christian faith. In the classical Christian tradition, faith is understood as faith in the person of Jesus Christ. Where the symbol, principle or idea of the gospel is differentiated from the man, one can speak of faith like Jesus' faith, or faith because of Jesus, but not of faith in Jesus, in the sense that in his person and history he does not simply bring or represent the truth of salvation, but *is* the truth, the ground of salvation. It is this stronger claim that is at once the glory and the problem of classical christology.

What are the grounds for faith in Jesus Christ? Basic questions arise. How can faith *, which involves trust without reservation, be based on anything so complex and so relative as a cluster of events in history, on the ever shifting sand of what is known as the quest of the historical Jesus? It will not do simply to say that what matters is not Jesus the specific historical individual but the kerygma * or proclamation of the early church. The NT writers were not preoccupied by modern notions of historicity. But they were reporting things which they believed to have happened. It would hardly be true to say that only the professional historian can have any knowledge of the person and history of Jesus. Christians usually work from the understanding – which constantly needs to be tested – that a basic outline at least of the life and activity of Jesus is available to us. This information is an important part of the data from which faith arises.

Christology involves the reflection of faith upon its own grounds. We cannot begin, it may seem, by presupposing the validity of a doctrine of Christ and then trying to understand it, moving as it were from above to below, from the trinitarian God above to the man Jesus below. Rather, we must begin from the man Jesus and try to spell out the meaning of the Christ from below, where we ourselves are. Though God may be before us in the order of being, we are concerned with the order of our knowing. Yet things are not so clear cut. When we speak of God in relation to Jesus and to all humanity there is an element of 'from above' wherever we choose to begin. In most critical investigation we begin from what we take to be 'the facts of the case', even though we seek a new appraisal of the 'facts'. Christian faith involves the claim that through Jesus human beings are brought into a deepened relationship with God their creator. Faith arises from the life and worship of the community as a gift of grace, and God does not offer us empirically verifiable proofs of his activity and presence. But without supporting evidence faith would be no more than blind credulity.

2. *The New Testament.* Here Jesus is portrayed as a witness to God. He speaks with authority, as the OT prophets had spoken. This authority is more than that of a prophet. 'You have heard that it was said . . . but I say to you' (Matt. 5.21). He proclaims the breaking in of God's kingdom *, which has come in his presence. He calls for repentance, and God's forgiveness is granted to those who will follow him. He speaks strikingly of God as his Father. His friends and followers were to go further, calling him the Messiah, the Lord. But his life has never been the sole ground for belief in him, for the disaster of his execution put all that he was into question. Whatever may have happened after his death, around what the tradition called the resurrection *, this was part of the ground for belief in Jesus in the apostolic communities. We are invited to

believe not in the dead Jesus but in the living Christ.

Paul can speak of seeing the glory of God in the face of Jesus Christ (II Cor. 4.6). For the author of the Fourth Gospel, 'When a man believes in me, he believes in him who sent me rather than me; seeing me he sees him who sent me' (John 6.29; 17.8). This belief in God is directed towards the man Jesus. The man is not the same as God: he speaks of his Father in heaven. He is not good, but only his Father is perfectly good. He is and remains a man, and still participates in the life, thought and action of his Father. He is at the same time the glory of God and the glory of man.

This unique relationship of Jesus to God was expressed by the various NT communities in a number of titles of honour – the Messiah, the Lord, the Word of God, the Son of God. As Messiah Jesus completes and fulfils the expectations of Israel, yet in completing transforms them. Christ is the end of the Law, it has been said. As the Johannine Word of God Jesus is not only the messenger but is himself the source of true life. The most striking claim of all is that Jesus is God's only Son (John 3.16f.). God has come into humanity in the person of his son. But how can Jesus be a man and at the same time the only Son of God? We are led straight into the central problem of christology.

It is natural that Christians in the modern world should wish to understand the essence of the gospel in terms which they can recognize and relate to the world in which they live. This search has brought drastic reinterpretation. The notion of God sending his Son into the world suggests that God is from eternity Father, Son and Spirit, and this ties up with the Pauline idea of the pre-existent son of God. An obvious move has been to regard the concept of an eternal son who comes into humanity as mythological in character. Christology then turns on the significance of Jesus for human existence. The relation of Jesus to God the creator of the universe remains unexplored. Critics have made the point that, at least in the NT, the coming of Jesus brings more than a new understanding of the world: something has happened in the history of creation.

A christology which attempts to preserve the breadth of its traditional scope would then seem to be faced with two tasks: 1. to express and explain the presence of the full divinity of God in the man Jesus, showing how he is both truly God and truly man; 2. to bring out the full differentiation between God and man in Jesus, avoiding the sort of confusion in which Jesus would be neither fully divine nor really human.

The classic solution was on the following lines. The full presence of the divine and so the unity of the divine and human in Christ takes place through a continuous giving on God's part and a continuous human receiving by Jesus. Jesus is the person he is only through his constant receiving of God's gift, and even his devotion to God from whom he receives is a gift of God. As far as the traditional doctrine that the man Jesus has no independent human nature intends to make the point that Jesus to be himself is always totally dependent on God, then this must be right. But the expression remains problematic. For this dedication to God involves an individual, who gives himself to God and receives God's gifts in a truly human way, in faith, prayer and obedience.

In this interpretation God, without ceasing to be God, comes into human existence, into vulnerability to temptation, openness to suffering, actual suffering. He does this precisely through his power as God, for the infinite is capable of assuming finitude, abandoning himself for mankind. This self-giving, of which only God is perfectly capable, is seen on the cross. Self-giving is brought to self-fulfilment in the resurrection.

For Jesus of Nazareth the meaning of the incarnation* is that God gives him participation in his divine nature, within the limitations of the human. He participates in God's power to heal the sick, to forgive and to renew. In devoting himself to his Father he receives the power to act in the way he does for the salvation of mankind. The full divinity of God is united with the man Jesus, but in such a way that the divinity is not changed into humanity; and man is not in any way divinized. Jesus is at once the bearer of the presence of God and the medium of its hiddenness. God does not force himself upon us: we become aware of his presence through faith. This mystery of union is complex beyond our comprehension, but we must continue to seek the best available explanations. In such an approach we come to understand who Jesus was by looking at his whole life and activity. (For the work of Christ and the nature of reconciliation *see* **Soteriology**.) Through life, death and resurrection there takes place a costly reconciliation, in which the relationship between God and man is renewed, to await the perfection of the eschatological peace of God.

3. *Doctrinal development*. Who was this Jesus Christ, the subject of the church's confession? Was he human or divine or both, partly the one and partly the other? From the earliest times to the present there have been those who have seen Christ as a divine being walking the earth in human disguise. The Docetists*, as they were called, understood Jesus' historical existence as appearance (*dokein*, to appear) rather than reality. In much Hellenistic thinking the world of the flesh is inferior to the world of the spirit. Ebionitism, on the other hand (a word possibly derived from a Hebrew word meaning 'poor') reflected the central problem facing Christians of Jewish background, of how to reconcile their Christian faith with the strict monotheism of Israel. Jesus' humanity was not in question, but divinity was played down: some suggested this was a special dignity which descended on Christ at his baptism. Both in Hellenic and in late Jewish thought – and it is artificial to see these as either distinct or uniform, for both overlapped and were pluriform in themselves – there was an important distinction between the earthly and the heavenly realm, between creator and creation.

One important answer to the central question had roots in the Palestinian background. Jesus was God's messenger, his word, his Logos*. The word became flesh and dwelt among us. But the Logos was also the all-pervasive rational principle of the universe in Stoic philosophy. So Justin Martyr, writing in Rome in the middle of the second century, when accused of blasphemy for worshipping not God but the man Jesus, could say that Jesus Christ was not merely a man, but the eternal and universal Logos of God from which all order and rationality were derived. His birth and conception were unique. He had indeed a body, soul and spirit, yet it was right to call him lord and to worship him, for this man was the Logos of God. Here was Logos christology.

Still, within this conceptual framework the Logos was secondary, in some ways inferior to God. Faith and worship seemed to involve that God was in Christ in such a way that there was no inequality. The problem was how to express this state of affairs, which arose in the realm of worship and commitment, in a conceptual framework. All kinds of variations on Logos christology arose. Paul of Samosata thought that the man Jesus united with the divine Logos by willing the same things – one in will with God. His opponents argued that the very essence*, and not just the will, of the Logos is incarnate. But where in a human being do you locate essence? How could you combine the essence of the nature of God, who did not change, with the nature of a man, who was crucified, dead and buried?

One important approach was that of Arius, which has been put like this (*see also* **Arianism**). Christ was the incarnate Logos: Christ was subject to change. Therefore, the Logos was subject to change. But, granting that God the creator was impassible, that he did not change, the Logos could not be identified with God. The Logos suffered in Jesus, while God remained unchanged. The main advantage of this approach was that it preserved the emphasis of the school of Antioch on the solidarity of Jesus with authentic human nature (*see also* **Antiochene Theology**). The disadvantage, pressed by the school at Alexandria, was that what was seen in Jesus was something less than God (*see also* **Alexandrian Theology**). This destroyed the defence against the charge of worshipping a man rather than God. It left Jesus as neither God nor man but something in the middle. Arius' theology was indeed a theology of the incarnation, but the incarnation of the Logos rather than of the creator in the created order. The Council of Nicaea (325) insisted that the Logos or Son was of one essence (*homoousios*,* *see also* **Substance**) with the Father. This was not a final solution, for it could lead to a minimizing of Christ's humanity and a confusion of divine and human natures.

Apart from putting Jesus in a somewhat ambiguous position, the Arian solution raised difficulties concerning the nature of salvation. A central point of patristic* christology was that God became man, took flesh, in order to redeem humanity to a new human nature in Christ. In Gregory of Nazianzus' (*see* **Cappadocian Fathers**) famous phrase, what is not assumed is not redeemed. If God did not himself come right into human life, then we remain imprisoned in our sins; in Pauline terms: the incarnation did not work. Fully aware of this difficulty, Apollinarius of Laodicea proposed that in the incarnate Christ the place of the human mind was occupied by the divine Logos. It is indeed perfectly possible to hold that the incarnation of God did not involve any sort of quasi-mechanical replication of creator in creation. But within the anthropology presupposed, of body, soul and spirit, Apollinarius' solution inevitably looked like a diluted christology at two-thirds strength, and was accordingly rejected. Without solving the problem, Nicaea made it clear that Christ was in no sense a part of the creation, subordinate to God, but that he was equal with God, of one substance with the Father. The discussion of the next century was concerned with understanding the relation, given this equality, of the divine and human in Jesus.

The upshot of the debate was the Chalcedonian Definition of AD 451, which said among other things: 'We confess one and the same our Lord Jesus Christ, the same perfect in Godhead, the same perfect in manhood, truly God and truly man, the same of a rational soul and body, acknowledged in two natures, without confusion, without change, without division, without separation, the difference of the two natures being by no means taken away because of the union but rather the distinctive character of each nature being preserved and combining in one person (*prosopon*) or entity (*hypostasis*).' Two natures in one person. It was thought, with some reason, that you could not have nature (*ousia*, *see* **Substance**) without person (*hypostasis*): no universals without particulars. This led on the one hand to Nestorianism (dualism in Christ's person) or (if only one and one) to Monophysitism, which made all divine and left no room for Jesus' human nature.

Chalcedon broke the rules and is on the face of it a bad compromise: two natures in one person. Some modern scholars would say that this move simply indicates the logical impossibility of the project. Yet within the terms available it was the best option. Two natures are affirmed, so stressing the full humanity of Jesus at a time of pressure to lose everything in divinity. At the same time Christ is only one person – there is no duality, he is one. The oneness is described in terms of *prosopon** and *hypostasis**, another diplomatic compromise because the terms could have slightly different meanings, but the main points which faith seemed to require were made.

There is, then, in the Christ of Chalcedon a human nature, but no separate human hypostasis (a solution echoed in recent times e.g. by Barth, *CD* IV/2,49ff). Some went on to say that the human nature of Christ had no hypostasis at all – it was a *physis anhypostatos**. One important further suggestion was made by Leontius of Byzantium at the beginning of the sixth century. Though the human nature of Christ has no hypostasis of its own it is not on that account completely *anhypostatos*. It is rather a *physis enhypostatos* – it finds its hypostasis in the hypostasis of the Logos. The distinguishing features of the particular man who Jesus was are then attributed to the divine hypostasis as well as the essential qualities of the species (mankind) to which he belongs. These ideas were to be further refined in a distinguished line of Orthodox theologians in the East. In the West Chalcedon was transmitted through the theology of Augustine. The Reformation* and the Enlightenment* were to produce pressure for other perspectives, first as alternatives and then as replacements. Chalcedon marks out as it were the limits of useful discussion within the classical framework of reference. It shows how the Christian tradition, out of which to some extent at least we must work, has arisen, enabling us to relate the biblical narratives and present circumstances to past Christian experience.

Christology did not stop between Chalcedon and Albert Schweitzer (*see* **Jesus**). Broadly speaking, the mediaeval christologies of the West, following Augustine, tended to be interested not so much in the nature and person of Christ as in the salvation brought by Christ to men (*see* **Soteriology**). Luther's classic question at the Reformation was 'How can I find a gracious God?' and the Reformers concentrated on the nature of the gift of the divine presence, especially in the understanding of the eucharist. Luther supported his doctrine of the real presence with the patristic theory of *communicatio idiomatum** (exchange of

divine and human attributes*); Calvin stressed the divine transcendence, in his famous *extra Calvinisticum*. The Lutheran tradition developed a new christology of the two states of Christ's humiliation and exaltation in cross and resurrection, in accounting for the biblical stress on historical contingency in incarnation. Humiliation and condescension led to further reflection on *kenosis**, self-emptying, in Jesus and in God. Though the great watershed of the Enlightenment* was to put christological discussion, for many Christians at least, in a quite new light, the previous tradition remained deeply influential, at times inhibiting and at other times enriching the discussion.

4. *Modern christology* may be said to begin in the European Enlightenment, at a time when all sorts of new questions had arisen concerning the nature of man and his world, in relation to God, questions to which the classical categories seemed to provide no relevant answer. To meet this challenge a new christology was produced, notably in the work of Schleiermacher and Ritschl. It sought, following a suggestion from Herder, to look for the divinity of Jesus in the unique quality of his life on earth. The focus is a picture of a man of pure compassion and kindness, who set a moral example in all that he did. He began the work of the kingdom of God, which we may carry on by acting in love towards our fellow men. Usually there was much more to this christology than twentieth-century critics have allowed. Though we may laugh at Victorian pictures of gentle Jesus meek and mild, after the manner of Sir John Seeley's *Ecce Homo*, at least here was a genuine attempt at communication in contemporary terms. In part at least, the impression that later christologies were better may be due to the fact that we have had less time to find out the difficulties involved in them.

Still, there could be no going back. By 1910 it seemed clear that the Jesus of much nineteenth-century piety, the leader of a moral kingdom of God in which we might cooperate, was not to be found in the Gospels. As rediscovered by Johannes Weiss and Albert Schweitzer, the Jesus of the NT preached an eschatological message, warning of the imminent end of the world. God will bring in his kingdom, and human moral effort has nothing to do with it. Critics argued that though the example of Jesus could easily be related to the private moral duties of the individual and his family and friends, the old classical understanding of the Christ who makes a radical difference to the way the world is – however unintelligibly described – had largely gone. It was left to Marx and Engels to provide an account of alienation*, of sin, of the gulf between the actual and the desirable state of the population of the nineteenth-century world, which was much less shallow than that of many Christian assessments.

(a) It was in reaction to this scene that the so-called dialectical* theology arose, the foremost exponents of which were to be Barth, Brunner and Bultmann. For Karl Barth, the Swiss pastor, it was the German theologians' glorification of the First World War (British scholars, it must be said, were no better!) that sparked off rebellion. For Bultmann it was the collapse of the liberal pictures of Jesus when compared with the latest NT scholarship. Barth's God at this time is the wholly other, who in Christ reveals himself as and when he wishes. For Bultmann, Jesus is the one who confronts man with the eschatological message, demanding response in existential commitment. For Barth there is a return to the high classical christology, for Bultmann a renewal of the attack on 'metaphysics' and concentration on obedience to God's will as revealed through Jesus' message. Barth's thought, perfected in the symphony of the *Church Dogmatics*, is perhaps most easily caught in *Dogmatics in Outline*. Jesus Christ is a unity, a single word of revelation. Therefore we cannot move from the historical Jesus to the Christ of faith, nor from the man Jesus to the divine Christ. In Jesus the old covenant* promise, that God wills to be with his people, is fulfilled. The Jewish background is essential. But Jesus is not just the hope of Israel. He is God's only son. 'Either in Jesus we have to do with God or a creature, and if with God, we have to affirm what Nicaea affirmed.' Jesus Christ is *the* man, the measure of all human being. This truth does not depend on our acknowledging it. It is because he is that he can be known as such. Incarnate by the Holy Ghost of the Virgin Mary, he lived a life of obedience as the son of God and the son of man. Humiliated, murdered by the judiciary, dead, he is exalted by the empty tomb to be the eternal source of salvation. Barth's grand symphony is clearly not the only possible music in theology, but its intrinsic merit already makes it a classic.

In principle Barth accepted the modern critical approach to the Bible: in practice he often ignored its implications. More recent scholars, aware that we might have only a dozen or so of the *ipsissima verba* of Jesus, have produced rather different christologies, building upon what are taken to be the reflections and liturgies of the early communities. Where Barth saw lineaments of the classical christology of Chalcedon in the Bible, others have drawn very different conclusions. Partly through the influence of the philosopher Heidegger, Rudolf Bultmann developed an existential* understanding of the NT, interpreting the message of Jesus for the modern world in order to produce a contemporary invitation to commitment. Before the message can be accepted it must be understood, through demythologizing*, by discarding the wrappings of ancient culture and expressing the gospel in truly contemporary terms. Faith for Bultmann has its origins in the *kerygma** or event of proclamation, rather than in value judgments concerning an historical portrait. Some of his pupils (notably Käsemann, Ebeling and Fuchs) developed a 'new quest' of the historical Jesus (*see also* **Jesus**), accepting the importance of *kerygma* but seeking to relate it again to history.

Bultmann and his disciples have been criticized for adopting solutions which are just as 'abstract' and 'metaphysical' as those which they rejected. There is then scope either for a reaffirmation of metaphysics, of a more or less traditional sort, or else for a more determined attempt to get beyond metaphysics. Yet Bultmann, along with Barth, and perhaps Troeltsch and Rahner, must count as a major contributor to christology in the modern world. In the work of Barth and Bultmann it is possible to see most of the elements of post-Enlightenment christology in interaction. Tens of thousands of volumes on christology have appeared since 1800. Here only one or two of the most significant thinkers can be considered.

(b) British christology in the twentieth century has been centred in large measure on the classical doctrine of the incarnation and attempts to reinterpret it. Theories of *kenosis*, of the self-emptying of Christ, were an important vehicle for the understanding of Christ's human nature in the work of Gore, Weston, Forsyth and others. Kenosis in turn has been much criticized, then used again successfully by Barth and Rahner. In Scotland Donald Baillie's paradox christology provided an important holding perspective between classical christology and concern for the humanity of Jesus, though the details could not be pressed without dissolving the paradox. In Anglican theology the continuing debate with the Fathers was pursued especially in discussion arising from the Modern Churchman's Conference of 1921, on the relation between the humanity and the divinity of Christ. The divinity of Christ was explored by Eric Mascall, the humanity by John A. T. Robinson. A more traditional christology of the incarnation was worked out by Creed, Quick, Mozley, Hodgson and Ramsey, and attacked by the authors of *The Myth of God Incarnate* symposium, notably John Hick and Maurice Wiles. Lively discussion continues. In Scotland significant and contrasting contributions were made by John McIntyre and T. F. Torrance.

(c) On the Continent as in Britain all the elements of christology are subject to continuing reappraisal. In the tradition of Barth, Jürgen Moltmann and Eberhard Jüngel see the cross of Christ as the key not just to christology but to all legitimate Christian talk of God. On the cross God suffers. There is death in God, though not the death of God. From this suffering relationship between Father and Son we may understand the Trinity*. Through the cross we may share in God's identity with men and women crushed by evil. 'Even Auschwitz is taken up into the grief of the Father, the surrender of the Son and the power of the Spirit.' Such a theology of solidarity with suffering has had powerful echoes in liberation* theology.

Where the cross is absent, strange things happen to faith. On the other hand it can be argued that the centre of Christianity is not the cross but the love of God. Evil is to be opposed firmly rather than accepted *sub specie crucis*, through the gift of the grace of resurrection. It is interesting that British and Continental theology have taken such opposing paths in meeting the same challenge

of the complexity and often the tragedy of the modern world, the one in abandoning and the other in reaffirming the classical doctrines of Incarnation and Trinity. God's hidden presence is not easily to be read off our theological measuring devices.

Wolfhart Pannenberg has produced the most comprehensive of modern christologies after Barth. He is radical in rejecting the theology of the Word of Barth and Bultmann, in deciding that the incarnation is definitely not the correct starting point, and in stressing the need to do christology from below, or in a sense from before, through eschatology. Yet he takes a fairly traditional view of resurrection*. Pannenberg stresses a need both for rationality and for an apocalyptic* framework: it is hard to see how these criteria can coincide. But his work is of major significance, taking up, almost alone among the writers mentioned so far, the concern for the correlation* of theology and history, and the problem of historical relativity, pioneered by the great Ernst Troeltsch (*see also* **Cultural Relativism**).

(d) Catholic theology has been extraordinarily fertile in the field of modern christology, especially in the work of Rahner and Schillebeeckx, Küng and von Balthasar. Karl Rahner displays an almost unique versatility in criticizing the ancient formulas, reinterpreting them radically in line with a post-Enlightenment anthropology, and then still using them to interpret the centre of christology. The doctrine of man which is his genius is also, it is sometimes thought, his Achilles heel: why should we accept a general anthropology any more than a particular apocalyptic framework as definitive? But Rahner's insights are many and varied. For Karl Rahner, God alone can become something. He who is unchangeable in himself can become subject to change in something else. Giving himself away, God posits the other as his own reality. Humanity is the medium of God's kenotic presence in the world: the word becomes flesh. The nearer one comes to God, the more real one becomes. As men and women open themselves to one another, and so to themselves, they may become 'anonymous Christians' (*see also* **Anonymous Christianity**). There is a reciprocity between selfhood and dependence in man and in God. 'The only way in which Christ's concrete humanity may be conceived of in itself as diverse from the

Logos is by thinking of it in so far as it is united with the Logos. The unity of the Logos must constitute it in its diversity from him, that is, precisely as a human nature: the unity must itself be the ground of the diversity' (*Theological Investigations* 1,5,181). Such a solution may be thought, like Chalcedon, to mark out the parameters of a problem rather than to offer an explanation. This level of explanation may sometimes be all that the theological mystery allows, and is certainly valuable. But we shall no doubt always look for other levels of clarification, at least in part. Such another level may be seen in the exegetical struggles with historical evidence which characterize the work of that other major Catholic christological interpreter, Edward Schillebeeckx.

Like Rahner, Schillebeeckx is concerned to take account of the whole of the church's tradition. But unlike Rahner he settles firmly for a decisive shift away from incarnation and Chalcedon to stress on Jesus, the Mosaic-messianic 'eschatological prophet' as the basic NT model from which all others are derived. This 'maranatha' christology is the centre, a centre of experience by man of God and the world, then and now. Christology is to be done by reflection on experience of life in modern society, and the impact of the Christian tradition on this reflection. We may not simply 'apply' biblical models to the modern world in the hope of illumination. We look to Jesus' own experience, the experience of his followers and the experience of God in community ever since. (The appeal to experience * is characteristic of modern christologies, producing different results in different traditions.)

For the community represented in the NT by the Gospel material common to Matthew and Luke (the Q community) there is experience of Jesus as present now and soon to come. Resurrection is important, centred not on the person of Jesus but on the experience of his presence in community. Repetition of this saving experience leads to transformation of human life, and to a challenge, not about formulas but about our social structures. Christology is 'concentrated creation'. Christology 'can only be understood as a specific way of making belief in creation more precise'. It is not yet entirely clear, perhaps, on Schillebeeckx's account, what difference it makes to God the creator that he is involved in incarnation in human life. But real progress is made in filling out further our understanding of the human significance of Jesus and his relationship to us.

(*e*) *Process* christology looks back in the tradition to Irenaeus, and attempts to achieve a better understanding of the relation between creation and redemption, seeing incarnation as the consummation of creation in an ongoing process. A. N. Whitehead's philosophy of process, and C. L. Morgan's philosophy of emergent evolution, provided a theoretical framework, first explored by L. S. Thornton in *The Incarnate Lord* (1928) and more recently, especially in America, by Norman Pittenger, D. D. Williams, John Cobb, David Griffin and others. Pittenger understands the Logos as 'the self-expressive principle of God at work in the whole creation'. The incarnation of God in Christ is the culmination of the process. Christ is not a 'divine intruder' but one who emerges from humanity. He is the fulfilment of man's capacity for God and of God's purpose for man. It may well be possible for those who find it hard to accept general theories of dipolar theism to learn from the imaginative insights into the relation between creator and creation which process thought provides (*see also* **Process Theology**). Again it is notable that Logos and incarnation, suspect in some avenues of recent thought, are quite acceptable in others.

Nothing has been said so far of the increasing amount of theology being produced in the so-called Third World, by such scholars as Cheng Song in Asia, John M'biti in Africa, James Cone in the United States (*see* **Black Theology**), and by liberation theologians *, mainly in Latin America. In its commitment to love for the poor and the dispossessed, liberation theology relates incarnation to salvation * in the most direct possible way. In L. Boff's christology we are concerned supremely not with a heavenly Christ who lives in and belongs to another world, but with the Jesus of history who is engaged in all the continuing conflicts in history. God's humanity in Jesus Christ is a fact which we are urged to consider with new urgency.

5. *Conclusion.* At the end of his article in the previous edition of this dictionary,

George Hendry concluded that 'Christological thought is fluid at the present time, and no one can predict what course it will take in the future.' With this we may safely agree. Not all, however, is complete confusion. Let us imagine an account along these lines. The parables of Jesus, his life and his teaching, are *the* examples for Christians of self-giving love. Kenosis is incarnation and service is the way of the cross. Through the suffering humanity of Jesus Christ in humiliation comes resurrection. God is compassionate and creates compassion in us. Jesus Christ is God for us, answering God's self-emptying in his own life of sacrifical love, a love eschatologically effective through resurrection. Such an account says more than a little about Jesus, about God and man, and the way of discipleship in the world today, and most Christians would agree on it. The task of constantly improving construction and design in detail is left to the professional skill of theologians to work out in creative tension and discussion. This may be no bad thing. Complete unanimity often indicates the death of a subject, or of freedom of thought.

D. M. Baillie, *God was in Christ*, 1948; K. Barth, *Church Dogmatics* IV, *The Doctrine of Reconciliation*, ET 1956; D. Bonhoeffer, *Christology*, ET 1966; R. Bultmann, *Jesus Christ and Mythology*, ET 1960; P. T. Forsyth, *The Person and Place of Jesus Christ*, 1909; C. Gore, *The Incarnation of the Son of God*, 1891; M. D. Goulder (ed), *Incarnation and Myth*, 1979; J. Hick (ed), *The Myth of God Incarnate*, 1977; W. Kasper, *Jesus the Christ*, ET 1976; G. W. H. Lampe, God as Spirit, 1977; J. Moltmann, *The Crucified God*, ET 1974; G. M. Newlands, *Theology of the Love of God*, 1980; W. Pannenberg, *Jesus, God and Man*, ET 1968; N. Pittenger, *The Word Incarnate*, 1959; K. Rahner, *Theological Investigations*, passim, ET 1961–1982; J. A. T. Robinson, *The Human Face of God*, 1973; E. Schillebeeckx, *Jesus*, ET 1979; *Christ*, ET 1980; S. W. Sykes and J. P. Clayton (eds), *Christ, Faith and History*, 1972; P. Tillich, *Systematic Theology* 2, 1957; F. Weston, *The One Christ*, 1914.

GEORGE NEWLANDS

Church

The word itself is derived immediately from the Greek *kyriake* ('belonging to the Lord')

and *ekklesia* ('assembly'). In its primary sense, therefore, the church is the worshipping assembly called forth by God. The theological study of the church is called ecclesiology.

The word *ekklesia* was not at first identified exclusively with the Christian community. Not until the admission of the Gentiles did the distinction between the church and Judaism become acute. Thereafter, the word *ekklesia* applied to the Christian assembly alone.

The church of the NT was richly diverse. Indeed, the noun has always had a plural as well as a singular form: the great church (or church universal) and the churches. There were at least three kinds of post-Pauline communities: those reflected in the Pastoral Epistles, with their emphasis on teaching, structures, pastoral care and the survival of the Christian community; those reflected in Ephesians and Colossians, with their emphasis on the church as the fullness of Christ, his body, and his spotless bride; and those reflected in Luke/Acts which combined the previous two forms, stressing both the institutional and the charismatic, i.e. the unpredictable intervention and guidance of the Holy Spirit. There were also two forms of Johannine communities, neither of which paid much heed to structure and apostolic succession but emphasized instead the equality of disciples living in community with the Father and the Son, under the tutelage of the Paraclete. There was, in addition, a community related to I Peter shaped by Jewish symbolism (especially the Exodus) and perceiving of itself as the new Israel and the new people of God. The Matthaean community, with its mixture of Jews and Gentiles, revered both the Law and Peter. A strongly Jewish community related to the epistle of James practised works of piety on behalf of widows and orphans and assembled for worship in Christianized synagogues. And there were yet other communities associated with Mark, Hebrews and Revelation, as well as those connected with non-NT writings such as the Didache, I Clement, and Ignatius of Antioch.

Despite all local differences, however, certain common elements stood out clearly: faith in Jesus as Messiah and Lord; the practice of baptism and the celebration of the eucharist*; the apostolic preaching and instruction; the high regard for communal love; and the expectation of the coming kingdom of God *. Freedom was allowed in other matters.

The mission of the church, then as now, centred on the kingdom of God, with the church located somewhere between-the-times, i.e. between the time when the kingdom was first proclaimed and manifested in Jesus Christ and the time when it is to be realized in all its fullness at the end. The church is both sign and instrument of this kingdom. It is 'the initial budding forth of the kingdom' (Second Vatican Council, *Lumen gentium*, n. 5) and the means by which the gospel * is proclaimed, disciples are drawn together, sins are forgiven, and the power of Satan is broken.

The extension of this mission beyond the original Jewish community of Jerusalem provoked the first great crisis in the history of the church (Acts 10; 11; 15). Gentile converts need not be circumcised, it was decided, nor be subjected to Jewish dietary laws. Thus ended the first great moment in the church's history, its Jewish phase, and the beginning of the second, its Gentile phase.

As the church spread through the Roman Empire, it adapted itself to contemporary social and political structures. By the latter half of the second century organizational complexification had occurred in the form of synods and councils, and in the emergence of the monarchical episcopacy *. The latter was especially linked with the effort to combat certain rigorist movements. Among the major bishop-theologians who fashioned an ecclesiology over against Gnosticism *, Novatianism and Donatism * were Irenaeus, Cyprian and Augustine * respectively. Against the Gnostics Irenaeus taught that the church is the unique sphere of the Holy Spirit *, possessing the canon * of truth in apostolic succession * focussed in the Roman church. Against the Novatians Cyprian insisted that the unity of the Catholic church is rooted in the oneness of God, and that orthodoxy alone is insufficient for union with the one church. True membership requires unity with the bishops on whom the church is founded, with the successors of Peter at their centre. And against the Donatists Augustine declared that the holiness of the church, too, is derived from God, not from its members. The church is a fel-lowship of love, and schism * is diametrically opposed to its essence. On the other hand, the church is also a mixed community, including good and bad alike. The sorting out will be left to God at history's end.

Augustine's distinction between those who truly belong to Christ and therefore to the essence of the church and those who belong only outwardly to Christ and his church was carried forward in various forms. Martin Luther *, for example, distinguished between the church as a visible fellowship including saints and sinners and the church as a hidden community of true Christians. John Calvin *, also following Augustine, insisted that God's elect are a minority not only within the world but within the visible church itself. But neither Luther nor Calvin entirely depreciated the visible church. Luther saw the visible church as the embodiment of the gospel which comes into being wherever the gospel is proclaimed. He enumerated seven external marks of the earthly church: the preached word, baptism, the Lord's supper, the administration of church discipline (the keys), the public ministry, prayer and worship, and identification with the cross of Christ through suffering. Calvin, too, acknowledged that we can know the visible church by its preaching of the word and celebration of its sacraments.

The teaching of both Luther and Calvin influenced, in turn, the nineteenth article of the Thirty-Nine Articles * of the Church of England, which defines the visible church as 'a congregation of faithful men, in which the pure Word of God is preached, and the sacraments duly administered according to Christ's ordinance'. Eastern Orthodox ecclesiology meanwhile continued to understand the church primarily as the community gathered around the bishop at the eucharist. Each bishop is the representative of his local church and with all other bishops shares in the Petrine succession and primacy. Eastern Orthodoxy, however, does reflect the same tension between the earthly and the heavenly churches, with the balance tipped on the latter side. The eucharistic gathering is primarily eschatological * in nature. It is the banquet of the kingdom of God and the ecclesial community which celebrates the eucharist somehow already experiences heaven.

Between the mediaeval period and the middle of the twentieth century RC ecclesiology had been shaped largely in reaction against challenges to ecclesiastical authority both from the state and from groups within the church itself: first the conciliarists, then the Reformers, and finally the Gallicans and other nationalist movements. Against the conciliarists, church law was codified to support the new network of papal authority which had developed especially during the pontificate of Innocent III (1198–1216), and a spirit of legalism intruded itself in the church's self-understanding. By the middle of the thirteenth century the canonical, juridical, papal-hierarchical concept of the church was so firmly established that when popes assumed their office, they were crowned like emperors – a practice in force until 1978, when Pope John Paul I abandoned the coronation rite. Counter-Reformation* ecclesiology remained in effect through the anti-Gallican First Vatican Council (1869–1870), with its definitions of papal primacy and papal infallibility*, but at the Second Vatican Council (1962–1965) a new ecclesiology emerged which was at once biblical, ecumenical and socially progressive.

Guided by the charismatic leadership of Pope John XXIII, the council officially described the church as a mystery or sacrament ('a reality imbued with the hidden presence of God', as Pope Paul VI put it), as the whole people of God, as a collegial reality, i.e. a college of local churches each embodying the corporate presence of Christ, as an ecumenical reality embracing Catholics, Anglicans, Orthodox and Protestants alike, and as having a mission not only to proclaim the kingdom of God in word and sacrament, but to be itself a credible sign and example of that kingdom as well as an instrument of its realization in the world at large through its service on behalf of justice and peace.

Catholicism's understanding of the church, therefore, is rooted in three theological principles: sacramentality, mediation, and communion. 1. The church is above all a living sign of God's presence in Christ through the empowerment of the Holy Spirit, so that even the church itself is an object of faith. 2. The church is an efficacious sign, i.e. it actually causes what it signifies. Through the word, the sacraments and its various ministries, the church mediates to its own and to others the saving grace which it embodies. 3. The church is a corporate or communal expression of the union and unity which God wills for the whole human family. The church, or the gathering of a redeemed community, is the sign and instrument of what God is in fact doing for all.

Yves Congar, *L'Église de saint Augustin à l'époque moderne*, 1970; Avery Dulles, *A Church To Believe In*, 1982; James D. G. Dunn, *Unity and Diversity in the New Testament*, 1977; Hans Küng, *The Church*, 1968; Richard McBrien, *Catholicism*, 2 vols, 1981; Jürgen Moltmann, *The Church in the Power of the Spirit*, 1977; Jean Meyendorff, *Orthodoxy and Catholicity*, 1966; Karl Rahner, *Concern for the Church*, 1981.

RICHARD P. MCBRIEN

Circumcision

The surgical removal of the foreskin of the male organ, widely practised for ritual reasons and virtually universal in the Near East until the Persian conquest. Though generally a puberty rite, among Jews it is performed on infants, normally at eight days old (Gen. 17.12; 21.4; Lev. 12.3; cf. Luke 1.59).

Its introduction to the people of God is attributed to Abraham in Gen. 17.10–14. Ex. 4.24–26 and Josh. 5.2–9 have been interpreted as alternative accounts of its introduction. Gen. 34 attests the practice in pre-Mosaic times. Its true origins are lost in antiquity. The use of flint knives (Ex. 4.25; Josh. 5.2) suggests a pre-Bronze Age origin.

Jewish circumcision is an initiation rite, signifying incorporation into the people of God. It was imposed on slaves and demanded of proselytes. By the Priestly Writer it is seen as a sign of the covenant* (Gen. 17.10–14). The figurative use of the idea, as signifying moral cleansing, is found as early as Jeremiah (4.4) and Deuteronomy (10.16; 30.6) and becomes widespread (Lev. 26.41; Rom. 2.25–29; Col. 2.11; Manual of Discipline 5.4; 5.28).

In the Greek period some Jews were embarrassed by their circumcision and tried to efface its effects (I Macc. 1.15; Josephus, *Antiquities*, XII, v.1; cf. I Cor. 7.18). Antiochus Epiphanes' prohibition of the rite was a chief cause of the Maccabaean revolt (I Macc. 1.48; II Macc. 6.10), as its later prohibition by Hadrian led to the revolt of Bar Kochba.

The church early had to decide whether circumcision was to be required of Gentile Christians. The Council of Jerusalem's ruling (Acts 15) that it was not essential did not immediately settle the matter. Paul argues forcefully against its necessity in Galatians (5.2ff.; 6.15) and elsewhere (I Cor. 7.17–19; Rom. 2.25–29, cf. Col. 2.11), but his own behaviour seems not to have been altogether consistent. He circumcised Timothy (Acts 16.3) but not Titus (Gal. 2.3).

R. Meyer, '*Peritemno*', etc., in G. Kittel (ed), *TDNT* 6, 1968, pp. 72–84; R. de Vaux, *Ancient Israel, its life and institutions*, ET 1961, pp. 46–8; 'Circumcision', *Encyclopaedia Judaica* 5, 1971.

H. MCKEATING

Cognition, Modes of

Traditionally the centre stage of the discussion surrounding the nature of human thought was dominated by the rationalist v. empiricist debate (*see* **Empirical Theology, Rationalism**), with sceptics, intuitionists and existentialists* playing minor parts. A mediating presence was that of Kant, who sought to synthesize these two postures by grounding cognition in the structuring activity of the mind *vis à vis* sensory perceptions. Although Kant's insights were largely ignored by philosophers of nearly every stripe in both the nineteenth century and the first quarter of this century, in the last thirty years he has surfaced as a central figure, albeit in a slightly different garb.

The debate over the nature of cognition still has a rationalist v. empiricist character about it, but now it is cast in a psycholinguistic mould, rather than the traditional epistemological one. Today the empiricist position is defended by thinkers like B. F. Skinner, who contends that cognition (including speech) is just another term for complex animal behaviour, behaviour that is the result of conditioning processes based in positive reinforcement. The rationalist position is expressed by thinkers like Noam Chomsky, who stresses the role of certain innate capacities, especially for language, in structuring our cognitive experience.

Obviously, there is a certain amount of Kant reflected in Chomsky's approach, for it emphasizes the crucial function of the mind over against Skinner's almost exclusive emphasis on external input. Nevertheless, the fact remains that both rationalism and empiricism, whether traditionally or contemporaneously conceived, as well as Kantianism in nearly all of its form, understand cognition (or deny it, in Skinner's case) as strictly a function of the mind as distinct from the body. There are three important thinkers who in recent years have challenged this 'mentalism'.

From a psychological perspective, Jean Piaget (*The Language and Thought of The Child*, ET 1932) has worked towards establishing the bodily basis of human cognition. His experiments with children have led him to the conclusion that we think with our bodies before we think with language; that it is by means of the interaction of our psycho-physical endowment with our physical environment that we develop cognitively. Piaget has worked out what he takes to be the successive stages of this cognitive development, from infancy through adolescence. This is Kantianism with a 'somatic twist'.

On a more broadly philosophical basis, Maurice Merleau-Ponty (*The Phenomenology of Perception*, ET 1962) has also constructed an understanding of cognition which places bodily activity at the axis. Drawing on the phenomenological* approach of Edmund Husserl, Merleau-Ponty argues that it is the embodied character of our existence which significantly determines the way in which we perceive and act in the world. He specifically indicts empiricism and rationalism for failing to account for the unitary and vectoral character of cognition; according to Merleau-Ponty, we encounter and gear into the world synaesthetically, as embodied, meaning-seeking agents. In short, he is opposed to the atomistic and static nature of traditional accounts of cognition.

Finally, Michael Polanyi (*Personal Knowledge*, 1958) is a contemporary thinker who makes a case for both the legitimacy and the primacy of what he terms 'tacit knowing'. Explicit knowing arises out of the interaction between focussed awareness and conceptual activity, being characterized by isolating definitions and inferential reasoning. Its meanings and justifications can be articulated. Tacit knowing, on the other hand, arises out of the interaction between subsidiary or subliminal awareness and bodily activity, and is characterized by holistic meanings and integrative acts, the particulars of which cannot be articulated. In Polanyi's words, 'We always know more than we can say'.

The more radical ramifications of this perspective on cognition pertain to its primordial nature. All knowing is tacit in the sense that all cases of explicit knowing are grounded in skills and commitments which can neither be specified nor justified by explicit processes. In the end, according to Polanyi, our cognitive powers are based in our mode of existence, a mode which needs neither defence nor lament, but merely acknowledgment.

JERRY H. GILL

Coincidentia Oppositorum

Although its complex root system extends far back in the history of both Eastern and Western thought, the notion of the *coincidence of opposites* seems first to have come to critical self-consciousness as a metaphysical principle in the thought of Nicholas of Cusa (1401–1464). He perceived the finite world with its variety and multiplicity (opposites) as finding resolution and knowability only in a transcendent unity or truth. Infinity, the Absolute Maximum, God, is completely beyond human reason, whose basic principle of operation is the Aristotelian* logic of mutually exclusive contradictories. Reason's limits can be surpassed only by the mystical vision of 'learned ignorance', a unifying, contradiction-resolving intellectual glimpse of the Infinite. This 'seeing' is darkness to the reason, but it is nevertheless in its 'light' that reason functions at all.

The *coincidentia oppositorum* also enables Nicholas of Cusa to name God the *complicatio* (enfolding) whose *explicatio* (unfolding) is the created world. This reconciliation of creator and creation is completed in the incarnation, a *coincidentia oppositorum* uniting divine and human, infinite and finite. The principle also finds application in his resolution of the problem of the world religions: religion is one, although existing in a variety of rites.

Meister Eckhart, Bonaventure and Pseudo-Dionysius are the principal and immediate Christian sources of these ideas, but they are also evidenced in the Victorines and the Greek Fathers. In modern times they have found their chief development in Hegelian* dialectic and Jungian* psychology. Outside the Christian West, Proclus, Parmenides, Heraclitus, Shankara and Lao Tzu reflect this view, which Mircea Eliade regards as fundamental to the structure of all hierophany and '*the* cardinal problem of any religion'.

Nicolai de Cusa, *Opera Omnia*, 1932—; E. Cassirer, *Individuum und Kosmos in der Philosophie der Renaissance*, 1927; E. Cousins, *Bonaventure and the Coincidence of Opposites*, 1978; M. Eliade, *Patterns in Comparative Religion*, 1958.

JAMES E. BIECHLER

Coinherence

Coinherence (Latin: *circumincessio, circuminsessio*; Greek: *perichoresis*) is the doctrine denoting the mutual indwelling or interpretation of the three Persons of the Trinity* whereby one is as invariably in the other two as they are in the one. The term *perichoresis* does not occur before Maximus the Confessor (seventh century) and it is then applied to the reciprocal action of the two natures of Christ. Its transference to trinitarian doctrine is completed by John of Damascus. The idea expressed in similar words from the same root is familiar in earlier times (Irenaeus, Cappadocians). Based on John 10.28–38 and adumbrated, for example, by Novatian, the doctrine became important from the fourth century onwards as the reciprocal of the *homoousios*. Each person belongs to the others (Athanasius, Cyril of Alexandria). It is especially important for the Cappadocian Fathers* with their strong pluralism. As three sciences interpenetrate each other and the omnipresent God permeates the universe, so much the more each Person interpenetrates the others. In the West it is emphasized by Hilary and Augustine*. Each Person is the mirror of the others (Hilary). Each Person is relative to the others; the Spirit is the bond of love (*vinculum amoris*) of the Father and the Son (Augustine). The key to the doctrine is mysticism rather than the logic of the divine relations. In modern trinitarian theology it is used both by monists (Barth) and pluralists, for whom it is of even greater importance.

H. E. W. TURNER

Communicatio Essentiae

In Western theology, this is the doctrine that the Son receives his essence from the Father and the Spirit his essence from the Father and the Son, though this takes place within the single essence of God. (The equivalent exists in Eastern theology, though because there is no double procession*, it takes a different form.) It is inferred from the *homoousios**, the divine monarchy (*see* **Monarchianism**) of the Father considered as the fount of the whole Trinity and the relations of origin (*see* **Generation; Procession[s]**). Calvin argues vigorously against the view that the Father is the *essentiator* of the Son and the Spirit and claims that the essence of God belongs to the one true God alone (and not, therefore, of sole right to the Father and by derivation from him to the Son and the Spirit). His frequent use of *autotheos* of the Son or his reference to his *autousia* was sharply criticized by contemporary R C theologians as a denial of the 'God from God' of the Nicene Creed and of the eternal generation of the Son by the Father. Calvin, however, denied neither and did not maintain the heresy called 'Autotheism' (the view that Christ was God *a se ipso, non a Patre*). Christ may be said to be from another either by production or by communication of essence. In his repudiation of the former view (an extreme type of subordinationism*) he used language which might appear to exclude the latter, which he clearly accepted. Bellarmine held that Calvin here errs not in judgment but in form of words. Calvin's followers were more guarded: 'We do not deny that the Son received his essence from the Father but we deny that his essence is generated.' This is in line with the scholastic maxim, *Essentia nec generat nec generatur* (an essence neither generates nor is generated). Karl Barth (following Calvin) treated the doctrine with great reserve on different grounds. The relations of origin are attempts to express the ineffable (a view for which he cited good patristic precedent). He accepted the *communicatio essentiae* as a statement of the dependence of God's existence as Son and Spirit upon his existence as Father (*see* **Person[s]; Modes of Being**); but hesitated on the question of origin. The Father is the presupposition or ground of the Son and the Spirit. This is bound up with the doctrine of the Divine Persons as modes of being or 'styles' of God's being God.

The phrase *communicatio essentiae* safeguards the monarchy of the Father as the source of the whole Trinity. If, however, communication is glossed by production or the essence shared by the Son and the Spirit regarded as subordinate because it is derived, it might lead to subordinationism. Calvin's exaggerated protest against such misunderstandings was intended to safeguard the full divinity of Christ, not to deny his relation or origin to the Father.

See also **Trinity, Doctrine of the.**

H. E. W. TURNER/FRANCES YOUNG

Communicatio Idiomatum

'The sharing of the attributes or properties' is a christological* term used to describe the transference of epithets appropriate to the human or the divine nature of Christ either to each other or to the total unitary subject of the incarnation*. It had a long history in patristic christology with a notable example in the *Tome* of Leo. The principle was set against a tight doctrinal background in Alexandrian* christology but was deeply suspect (though not completely excluded) by Antiochene* christologians. The controversy over the title *Theotokos* (Mother of God) between Cyril of Alexandria and Nestorius centred on the legitimacy of this principle. Monophysitism* gave it an ontological ground. Nestorianism*, with its sharp separation of the two natures, went even further than Nestorius himself in its repudiation. In Reformation times the Lutheran doctrine of the eucharist demanded the transference of the attribute of ubiquity from the divine to the human nature of Christ. The principle of the *communicatio idiomatum* was therefore invoked and interpreted as a real participation in attributes. This clearly tended towards Eutychianism, and Melanchthon abandoned the attempt to clarify the doctrine of the eucharistic presence in this way. The Reformed tradition which (unlike Luther) held that the finite could not contain the infinite regarded the principle as valid as a turn of speech but not as describing a real transference or sharing of qualities.

H. E. W. TURNER

Communicatio Operationum

Communicatio operationum (participation in operations) is the term used in second generation Lutheranism by Chemnitz to express and to delimit the realist interpretation of the *communicatio idiomatum*.

H. E. W. TURNER

Communion of Saints

Communio sanctorum apparently first occurs in a sermon of Nicetas of Remesiana (d. *c.* 414), where it is treated as a masculine plural. The phrase is not actually used in the NT, though the conception is there of course, e.g. Col. 1.12. Compare also I John 1.3f., where we find the NT emphasis that the communion of saints is based on their communion with the Father through the Son. In II Cor. 13.13 we are reminded that this communion is in the Spirit. There is not much light to be found in the NT on the question of how faithful Christians who have died are joined in communion with Christians on earth. All are in Christ. The practice, attested in Corinth, of being baptized for the dead (I Cor. 15.29) would seem to imply that what we do on earth can affect them, but it is an obscure passage. The Book of Revelation shows us the martyrs worshipping God in heaven; in 6.9 they cry out for judgment on those who have murdered them, which presupposes a knowledge of what is happening on earth.

It is no coincidence that the book in the NT which is most concerned with martydom contains these passages, for it is in connection with local saints, mostly martyrs, that we find the first examples of requests for the prayers of the saints. These occur in the third century, mostly on tombs or in the catacombs. Invocation of the Blessed Virgin Mary is very rare until well after AD 300. The earliest known prayer to her occurs in a third-century papyrus: 'Under the shelter of thy mercy we take refuge, O Mother of God; lead our prayer not into temptation, but deliver us from evil, thou who alone art chaste and beloved.' The practice of invoking the saints became officially countenanced during the fourth century. The first known introduction of an invocation of St Mary into the liturgy occurs about 480 (*see also* **Mariology**). Gregory the Great offers us a good example of the theological justification which was provided for the practice of invocation of the saints: 'The saints inwardly see the brightness of Almighty God, and therefore we cannot believe that

they are ignorant of anything outward' (*Moralia in Job*, 12.12). At the Second Council of Nicaea in 787 an attempt was made to define the various degrees of reverence which ought to be paid to God and the saints respectively. The final schema ran thus: to God alone must *latreia* be offered; to the Blessed Virgin *hyperdouleia* may be rendered; to the saints *douleia*, and to icons *proskynesis*.

The veneration of saints would seem at first sight to be an issue between the Catholic and the Reformed which cannot be resolved. There are certainly features in connection with the veneration of saints which responsible Catholic theologians would not claim to defend, such as the making of specific requests to them – frequent as this practice is in popular devotion. The following sentence occurs in S. Bulgakov's *The Orthodox Church* (1935): 'It is naturally necessary for us to hide ourselves in awe before the Judge of all, and here we take refuge beneath the protection of the Virgin and the saints' (p. 142). This sentiment could easily be paralleled in the piety of the Counter-Reformation*. It is doubtful if the theologians of the *aggiornamento* would readily endorse such a suggestion.

It is possible, however, that the concept of *comprecation* may provide at least a means of mutual comprehension. Cyril of Jerusalem (d. 386) writes: 'We make mention of those who have fallen asleep before us, first of patriarchs, prophets, apostles, martyrs, that God would at their prayers and intercessions receive our supplications.' This is explained by Max Thurian in the following terms: 'There is a theological necessity to recall the saints in the liturgy of the Church. They are a reminder of the mediation of Christ in the universal Church of all time. The Son of God has willed to be present in the incarnation to men by the mediation of his humanity. The risen Christ has willed to leave certain signs which recall and realize this mediation . . . The saints are therefore the signs of the presence and of the love of Christ . . . It is thus that in the ancient Church prayer for the apostles, prophets, and martyrs became after their death a prayer *with* them in the communion of saints on behalf of the whole Church' (*The Eucharistic Memorial*, ET 1961, p. 23). Compare also B. Häring: 'The prayer dialogue with the saints, by comparison with our direct adoration of God, is a prayer only in an analogical sense. It is communication corresponding to the communion of saints' (*The Law of Christ*, II, p. 534). But if there is to be genuine mutual comprehension on this issue there is much questioning of popular devotion still to be undertaken.

D. Bonhoeffer, *Sanctorum Communio*, ET 1963; S. Bulgakov, *The Orthodox Church*, ET 1935; B. Häring, *The Law of Christ*, ET 1963; Daniel Jenkins, *The Gift of Ministry*, 1947; K. Rahner, *Theological Investigations* 2, ET 1967, 91–104; 8, 1971, pp. 3–23; Max Thurian, *The Eucharistic Memorial*, ET 1961.

A. T. HANSON

Comparative Religion
see **Christianity and other Religions**
Religionsgeschichtliche Schule

Conciliarity
This word seems to have been coined in French, by Fr Sergei Bulgakov, around 1932, to translate the Russian word *Sobornost*, the root idea of which is 'unite', 'assemble'; the cognate word *Sobor* means both 'church' and 'council'. To believe in the 'catholic (in Slavonic *Sobornaïa*) church', means to believe both in a church which assembles and unites in time and space, but also in a conciliar church, a church in which 'the supreme authority lies in the Ecumenical Councils' (P. Bratsiotis)' Further, the decisive criterion of an Ecumenical Council is its reception as such by the church as a whole and so, in the words of the Patriarchal Encyclical of 1848, 'The guardian of religion is the very body of the church, that is, the people (*laos*) itself.'

The 'conciliarity' of the church is underlined by the use of the plural 'the holy churches of God' in the liturgical formulae. For the Orthodox the Catholic Church is the gathering of many autonomous local communities which, while professing the same faith and celebrating the same sacraments, are independent in their administration. ·

On the other hand each local church as it celebrates the eucharist united under its bishop is the church of Christ in all its fullness. In the great diversity of local churches with their many differences of language and culture there is a fundamental unity. Put another way, the idea of conciliarity expresses the belief that the church is an earthly icon * of the Holy Trinity *. Just as in the One Godhead there are three distinct and autonomous persons, so in the one church there are distinct and autocephalous local churches with no one church claiming authority over the rest.

SYMEON LASH

Concomitance
(Literally 'accompaniment'.) A term used in RC eucharistic theology in justification of: 1. the belief that the whole Christ, and not just his body and blood, is present in the eucharist; 2. the practice of communion under one kind. In the classic exposition of the theory by Thomas Aquinas (*ST* III, 76, 1 and 2) 'by virtue of the sacrament' the bread is changed into Christ's body and the wine into his blood; but 'by natural concomitance' Christ's soul and divinity are inseparable from his body and blood. For according to Aquinas the divinity never departed even from Jesus' dead body; his soul, though separated from the body at death, must also be present in the eucharist since it is the risen Christ that we receive. By virtue of the sacrament the bread is changed only into Christ's body; but, as the blood as well as the soul and divinity are present by natural concomitance, Christ is received in his full reality even under the single species of bread.

The theory has the merit of insisting that it is the whole living and risen Christ who is received in the eucharist. But, in so far as it is intended as a metaphysical explanation of the mode of Christ's presence, it seems open to the criticism that the presence is conceived in too static and physical a way, and the eucharistic words interpreted too literally.

E. J. YARNOLD

Concrescence
'Concrescence' and 'transition' are the two types of process distinguished by Alfred North Whitehead. Transition is the temporal movement from moment to moment or 'occasion' to 'occasion'. Concrescence is the non-temporal process whereby a single occasion becomes actual or concrete. It is the process in which the many given entities

making up the actual world come into novel unity. It is best understood by consideration of how in a moment of human experience the influence of one's past and many fresh stimuli are unified.

Whitehead analyses the process of concrescence into the conformal phase and the supplementary phases. Conformation to the past insures the reality of efficient causality, but concrescence is governed by final causation as well. Every occasion realizes an aim that is particular to itself. Whereas in occasions that make up such physical objects as atoms, conformation to the past is dominant, in occasions of human experience the supplemental phases are important. Here elements from the past are integrated with possibilities not derived from the past in such ways as to give rise to conscious thought.

The supplemental phases involve radical novelty. Whitehead attributes the effective relevance of novel possibilities to God. God is also a concrescence, but in God's case the concrescence is primordial and everlasting. It synthesizes all possibility and all actuality in the inclusive unity of the divine life.

Elizabeth M. Kraus, *The Metaphysics of Experience*, 1979; Alfred North Whitehead, *Process and Reality*, corrected edition, 1978.
JOHN B. COBB JR

Concupiscence

The Latin word *concupiscentia* was used to translate various words in the Bible covered by the English word 'desire'. It is used by Paul to refer to the commandment against covetousness (Rom. 7.7f.), and occurs in the plural in Mark 4.19; Gal. 5.24. James 1.14f. makes desire the first step in the chain of evil: every man's own desire leads him to be tempted; desire begets sin, and sin death (cf. I John 2.16f.). The word is often used of sexual lust, the normal non-theological meaning of concupiscence. However, *concupiscentia*, like desire, is sometimes used of necessary human desires (for food, Wisdom 16.3) and of the desire for good: 'The heart of a wise man exercises its judgment in wisdom, and a good ear listens for wisdom with all its desire' (Ecclus. 3.31 Vulgate; cf. 3.29 LXX; 6.37; Wisdom 6.18, 21).

In Augustine concupiscence is the opposite of love; desire corrupts the enjoyment of things and of other people, because they are not loved in relation to God. This desire is the result of the Fall* and is made known by the law.

The Council of Trent* said that the whole of sin was taken away at baptism; only concupiscence (desire), the incentive to sin, remained. Calvin replied that the desire which remained was truly sin; but this sin is not imputed and its guilt is abolished. The difference seems to be that Trent conceived of the possible loss of salvation through failure to resist desire, while Calvin believed that the long course of 'putting off the old man' would be successful in the elect.

Karl Rahner, 'The Theological Problem of Concupiscentia', *Theological Investigations*, 1, ET 1961, pp. 347–82.
J. C. O'NEILL

Confession(s), Confessionalism

In the ancient church *confessio* meant the profession of faith made by a martyr* (or 'confessor', who had withstood persecution for his faith; cf. I Tim. 6.13; II Cor. 9.13). The word thus came to mean a firm declaration of religious convictions with or without reference to persecution. (The word is also used of the tomb or shrine of a martyr or confessor; e.g. the *confessio* of St Peter in the Vatican.) It could also have a still more general sense, namely the biblical sense of praising God. e.g. Augustine's *Confessions*, in which Augustine blesses God for his conversion.

From this second sense of *confessio*, the declaration of what is believed, arises the use of the term in the churches of the Reformation* during the sixteenth and seventeenth centuries for their credal statements ('confessions') or professions of faith as over against Rome. They were not intended as alternatives to the ancient ecumenical creeds* (the Apostles' or the Nicene) but rather as statements of how the traditional creeds ought to be understood. Their aim is to make clear what is meant by proclaiming that 'Jesus is Lord' and to show that this affirmation can be made only in the light of the doctrine of justification by faith*. They were confessions of the church rather than of individual theologians. The earliest of them was the Augsburg Confession (1530); among the latest is the Westminster Confession (1643), which became the formulary of the Church of Scotland in 1689. The decrees of the Council of Trent* (1545–63) may be thought of as a 'confessional' reply of the Roman Church to the principles of the Reformation as enunciated in the various Protestant Confessions. Although the Anglican communion is often regarded as one of the 'confessional' churches, this view is not strictly correct. The Thirty-nine Articles* are not a confessional statement in the above sense; they were not so much the work of theologians defining a confessional position as an attempt to reconcile conflicting confessional points of view in the interests of a comprehensive church unity; and in any case they are not binding through the various provinces of the Anglican communion. It should be added that the Declaration of Barmen (1934), the foundation document of the 'Confessing Church' in Germany, is not strictly a 'confession' in the above sense, since it does not seek to distinguish one *church* from another but rather Christian faith from its denial.

H. Bettenson, *Documents of the Christian Church*, 1943; A. C. Cochrane, *Reformed Confessions of the 16th Century*, 1966; G. S. Hendry, *The Westminster Confession for Today*, 1960; B. J. Kidd, *Documents Illustrative of the Continental Reformation*, 1911; John H. Leith, *Creeds of the Churches*, 1982.

ALAN RICHARDSON

Confirmation

The earliest attestation of the ceremony which ultimately came to be called 'confirmation' (Lat. *confirmatio*, Greek *bebaiōsis*) is to be found in the baptismal rites of Hippolytus' *Apostolic Tradition* (AD 215) and Tertullian's treatise *De Baptismo* (AD 198). Both works attest a ceremony after baptism* consisting of a prayer said by the bishop* with his hands extended over the candidates, the anointing* of the candidates on the forehead, the imposition of the hand on the head of each and the sign of the cross on the forehead.

Originally no distinction was made between infants and adults in the use of this post-baptismal ceremony. When infants were baptized they were also anointed and hands were laid on them. But the requirement of the Roman and African churches that the anointing and imposition of the hand be reserved to the bishop came to

result in the separation of these actions from baptism, for infants and adults alike. In cases of emergency baptism, administered by a priest, or when bishops were no longer able to preside over all baptisms, the post-baptismal ceremony was inevitably delayed until the candidates could appear before a bishop. This separation between baptism and confirmation, which was originally imposed on the church by practical necessity, came ultimately to be regarded as the normal practice, and led to a situation in which baptism was thought to be appropriate to infancy and confirmation to later years.

Although in the Roman rite the ceremony was associated with the gift of the Holy Spirit,* it is not clear that this was the case with the other rites of the Latin West. These provide for a simple post-baptismal anointing of the forehead, which in Gaul and Spain was performed by the priest who baptized with oil which had been consecrated by the bishop. But in rites which were unaffected by Roman influence there is nothing to indicate that the bestowal of the Spirit was understood to be the purpose of the anointing.

1. *Origins.* According to the Council of Trent*, confirmation is one of seven sacraments instituted by Christ. RC theologians define the matter of the sacrament variously as chrism,* the imposition of the hand, or the combination of both. The form used throughout the RC Church is as follows: 'I sign thee with the sign of the cross, and I confirm thee with the chrism of salvation, in the name of the Father and of the Son and of the Holy Spirit. Amen.' A distinction is commonly made between the grace of baptism and that of confirmation: in baptism the Holy Spirit is given for pardon and new birth, in confirmation for strength to preach the gospel and to live the adult Christian life. Such a distinction does not seem tenable in the context of infant confirmation, and appears to have originated in the Middle Ages as a rationalization of the situation when baptism was administered in infancy and confirmation in later years.

The ablutionary customs of the ancient world called for the use of oil as well as water in bathing, and it has therefore been suggested that confirmation may have originated in the oil which would commonly have been used after the baptismal bath. Passages in the NT which have been thought to refer to the use of oil or chrism in initiation include II Cor. 1.21 and I John 2.20, 27; but the anointing to which these texts refer may be nothing more than a metaphor for the gift of the Holy Spirit in baptism.

Another explanation for the origin of confirmation has been sought in the complexity of the Gnostic* and mystery* religions in which candidates proceeded from one stage in initiation to higher and more advanced stages.

2. *The name.* To many people today the word 'Confirmation' connotes the fact that candidates confirm their baptismal vows at confirmation. This interpretation of the word dates only from the Reformation and takes no account of such prayer-book expressions as 'to be confirmed by the bishop', which go back to a higher antiquity. The words *confirmatio, confirmare*, began to be used of the post-baptismal anointing or hand-laying in the early fifth century in the sense that the bishop then ratified or completed what had been begun in baptism. At a later stage, when the church had accepted the doctrine that this rite supplied strength for the adult Christian life, it was natural that the word *confirmation* came to be understood as 'strengthening'.

See also **Initiation, Christian**.

A. D'Ales, *De Baptismo et Confirmatione*, 1927; J. D. C. Fisher, *Christian Initiation. Baptism in the Mediaeval West*, 1965; *Christian Initiation. The Reformation Period*, 1970; P. J. Jagger, *Christian Initiation, 1552-1969*, 1970; G. W. H. Lampe, *The Seal of The Spirit*, 1951; A. J. Mason, *The Relation of Confirmation to Baptism*, 1893; L. L. Mitchell, *Baptismal Anointing*, 1966; S. L. Ollard (ed), *Confirmation or the Laying On of Hands*, 1926; E. C. Whitaker, *Documents of the Baptismal Liturgy*, 1970; J. Ysebaert, *Greek Baptismal Terminology*, 1962.

E. C. WHITAKER

Congregational Theology

The historic Congregational churches, now largely incorporated in united churches, have been among the most theologically active parts of the Christian community. While their emphasis on the overriding authority of the Bible and on the freedom of the Spirit has made them reluctant to make acceptance of the classical creeds* a condition of membership, they have produced many corporate declarations of faith. Their earliest such declarations, the Massachusetts Cambridge Platform of 1649 and the English Savoy Declaration of 1658, were Calvinist, reproducing the mainly Presbyterian Westminster Confession of 1621 except for those sections which dealt with church order.

Those differences, however, did point to a difference in spirit. Congregationalism's 'decentralized Calvinism' meant that they recognized not only the autonomy of particular congregations but also the importance of the Spirit both in calling churches into being and in providing gifts for their upbuilding. This gave them links with the more radical forms of Protestantism as well as with Presbyterianism. At the same time, the two chief statements of Congregational polity in the seventeenth century, John Cotton's 'Keyes of the Kingdom of heaven and the Powers Thereof' (1644) and John Owen's 'The True Nature of a Gospel Church and its Government' (posthumously published in 1689) make clear that Congregationalism was not an expression of spiritual individualism and institutional voluntarism but a re-interpretation of classical church order. It emphasized the church's corporate nature in its most specific form, that of the local congregation, but insisted that all the means of grace were necessary before it could claim to be independent, while recognizing the importance of the communion of the churches with each other. That a church must be a 'gathered church' did not mean that any ordinary associations of Christians could claim that title but that it was the Spirit who gathered God's people and prompted them to enter into a covenant to walk together in church order. Their emphasis on the gathered nature of the church was an attempt to assert the 'crown rights of the Redeemer' against Anglican Erastianism. In New England, a full and detailed conception of what a 'godly commonwealth' should be was worked out.

The Calvinism of Congregationalists was always of the 'open' sort and this made them sensitive to new movements of thought. In the eighteenth century, the influence of rationalism* and later of the 'Great Awakening' in America and of Methodism in England produced a modification of Calvinism. The comprehensive scope of the work of Jonathan Edwards, the outstanding American theologian, and the hymns of Isaac Watts showed that this did not mean any loss of an awareness of the cosmic range of the gospel. This, and its emphasis on the affective element in religion, reflected in Philip Doddridge's 'Rise and Progress of Religion in the Soul' (1745), helped to prevent most Congregationalists going the way of Presbyterianism towards Unitarianism* in eighteenth-century England. Many more American Congregationalists did become Unitarians early in the nineteenth century, and even among those who did not, theological liberalism became influential. The work of Nathaniel Taylor and, in particular, that of Horace Bushnell on the atonement and in his *Christian Nurture* (1847), helped to change the Congregational attitude towards conversion and growth in the Christian life. The so-called Kansas City Creed of 1913 registered the extent of American Congregationalism's departure from its Calvinist origins.

Broadly similar influences were also at work in England, but the influence of Anglicanism and a more pronounced Evangelicalism were stronger countervailing forces. The work of a representative nineteenth-century figure, R. W. Dale, in his restatement of the doctrine of the atonement* and of Congregational principles, as well as in his preaching and social teaching, carried forward rather than broke with the tradition. By the end of the century, P. T. Forsyth was beginning his critique of theological liberalism in a way which remarkably prefigured the work of Barth. His *Faith, Freedom and the Future* (1912) is still influential.

It prepared the way for the welcome which neo-orthodoxy* received in British Congregationalism later in the twentieth century, leading a whole group of well-known theologians to a restatement of classic Congregationalism in an ecumenical context. The influence of neo-orthodoxy was not, perhaps, as strong in the USA but it was considerable and was a factor in achieving the union of the Congregational-Christian churches with the more conservative Evangelical and Reformed Church in 1961, a church of German origin which included Reinhold and Richard Niebuhr and Paul Tillich among its theologians.

The readiness with which Congregational churches in many parts of the world have united with other bodies, together with the outstanding service rendered by many of its ministers to the wider ecumenical movement, strengthens their claim to have a genuine, if incomplete, vision of catholicity. Whether what is distinctive of Congregationalism can be retained in the more centralized bodies which have been produced by these mergers remains to be proved.

DANIEL JENKINS

Conscience

The complex human capacity, utilizing people's understanding of moral life and their decision-making ability, to live in conformity with those principles it deems acceptable and good. In a morally informed and psychologically balanced person, the conscience serves as a guide or a monitor of life, enabling the individual to evaluate and choose potential courses of action and thought in the light of his or her values and commitments. Though the Bible does not contain a fully developed theory of conscience, the NT implies that this capacity is an integral part of the human personality and that its violation results in great harm to the individual's innermost being. For Christians, the conscience is not the sole guide to moral life; rather, informed by scripture, nurtured by grace, inspired by the Holy Spirit, and enacted in love for others, the conscience serves as a flexible and fallible evaluator of one's own actions in light of one's understanding of God's will. Thus, the 'good conscience' in Christian terms is continually open to new information and leads one's actions to exhibit love and compassion for others and respect for one's own dignity as a creature of God.

LEWIS R. RAMBO

Consecration

This liturgical act is a prayer of petition that asks God to bless, sanctify and transform that which is set before him. In the West, consecration itself is attributed to the power of Christ; in the East, it is seen as an act of the Holy Spirit. Consecration in either understanding is always the action of God upon what is presented.

The Hebrew scriptures give varied witness to this transforming initiative: the hovering spirit at creation (Gen. 1.2), the bow as the pledge of the covenant* (Gen. 19.3); the blood on the doorposts at the exodus (Ex. 12.22). Kings are anointed* by God (I Sam. 16.13); priests are ordained and consecrated (Ex. 29.1–9); elders are given a share of the spirit that was upon Moses (Num. 11.17); and the prophets proclaim the day when God's own spirit will be placed in every human heart (Ezek. 36.27).

In the NT the transforming action of God is directed first to Jesus himself. This is most manifest in the narratives of Jesus' baptism, transfiguration* and resurrection*. At the heart of the gospel* is the proclamation* that God has responded to Jesus' life of obedient offering by transforming death into life and the old creation into the new. The Christian church was formed, and its imagination shaped, by this definitive act of God which it recognized to be not only on Jesus but even more on all who believe, and by baptism are united with him.

All Christian prayer is rooted in the Hebrew concept of remembrance. Israel narrated the mighty acts of God in order that God would remember and act once again. That theme recurs in the eucharist* (*see also* **Anamnesis**, **Epiclesis**). In Christian prayer, to remember is to activate once again the eternal victory that is Jesus Christ. No part of creation cannot be touched by God's transforming act, and the ultimate goal is the transformation of all creation (Rom. 8).

The principal ritual gestures to have arisen in the church's prayer for consecration are anointing with oil and the laying on of hands. The primary rituals to employ these gestures of consecration are those of initiation*, eucharist and the assignment of ministries or ordination.

B. S. Childs, *Memory and Tradition in Israel,* 1962; P. Fink, 'Investigating the Sacrament of Penance: An Experiment in Sacramental Theology', *Worship* 54, 3, 1980, pp. 206–20; J. Meyendorff, *Byzantine Theology,* 1974; D. Ritschl, *Memory and Hope,* 1967.

PETER E. FINK

Consubstantiality

The doctrine developed in the fourth century to express the full divinity and the full humanity of Christ. It is derived from the Latin term *consubstantialis*, which was used by the fourth-century Latin fathers to translate the Greek term *homoousia* (one substance, or the same substance).

The doctrine was anticipated in the third century by the Alexandrian* theologians, Clement and Origen. Origen, in his commentary on Hebrews, applied the term *homoousia* to the relationship of the Son to the Father. Despite some reservations on the part of late third- and early fourth-century theologians, it was adopted by the Council of Nicaea in 325 in order to exclude the Arian belief that the Son belonged to the created order and was not fully God. Gradually in the fourth century the doctrine was refined to affirm an absolute identity in essence or being between the Son and the Father, while maintaining a distinction of persons* (*hypostasis*).

The Greek philosophical term *ousia** (essence, or being) was translated in the West by the Latin term *substantia* (essential nature). Thus developed the Western formulation: 'being of one substance (*unius substantiae*) with the Father'. In the Latin West the divine substance was the principle of unity, and all three persons of the Trinity* equally possessed the divine substance and so were consubstantial.

The doctrine of consubstantiality was used at the Council of Chalcedon in 451 to affirm the full humanity of Christ (two natures in one person), and that his divinity was consubstantial with his humanity. In this double consubstantiality the Son has numerical identity with the Father, while the divinity of the Son has only specific identity with humanity.

From the fourth century on the doctrine of consubstantiality was used to express the mystery of the incarnation* and became orthodox doctrine in both the Eastern and Western churches.

See also **Homoousion**.

J. N. D. Kelly, *Early Christian Creeds,* ²1960; *Early Christian Doctrine,* ²1960; B. Lonergan, *De Deo Trino,* 2 vols., 1964.

WILLIAM J. COURTENAY

Consubstantiation

The doctrine that in the eucharist*, after the consecration, the substance of bread and wine remain alongside the substance of the body and blood of Christ in such a way that the latter are in, with and under the substances of bread and wine. Unlike simple 'remanentism', in consubstantiation the substances of bread and wine and the substances of the body and blood of Christ are in some manner joined.

This view, without actually being called consubstantiation, was discussed but seldom adopted in the late Middle Ages. It was, however, rarely affirmed. In the sixteenth century it became a term used to describe, somewhat inaccurately, the eucharistic teaching of Martin Luther. The Council of Trent* reaffirmed the doctrine of transubstantiation*, which states that after consecration the substance of bread and wine cease to exist, either because the substance of the body and blood of Christ are produced out of them (Thomas Aquinas' view) or because the body and blood of Christ take the place of the substances of bread and wine (the view of William of Ockham and Gabriel Biel). In all cases both Catholic and Protestant theologians maintain that the accidents of bread and wine (the shape, taste, texture, etc. of the bread and wine) remain after consecration.

WILLIAM J. COURTENAY

Contemplation

In popular usage the word can indicate either thinking about some subject or gazing upon some object. In Christian spirituality it is the latter meaning that is uppermost: thinking about God gives place to a simple, loving, looking towards him, and this is contemplation. A distinction is sometimes made between acquired, active, ordinary contemplation and that which is infused, passive and extraordinary. The word 'acquired' is not a happy one, for all prayer is the gift of God, but it indicates that there is a form of contemplation open to all believers. This occurs when habitual meditation, in which the mind and imagination are used (discursive prayer), no longer seems enough. Either there is a positive desire to reach out to God for his own sake or the person finds no satisfaction in discursive prayer. This dry state, sometimes called the dark night of the senses, is usually taken by spiritual directors as a sign that God is calling the person to a 'prayer of loving attention' (St John of the Cross). Other names are 'Prayer of simplicity' (Poulain) and 'Prayer of simple regard' (Bossuet). St John of the Cross wrote: 'The soul must be lovingly intent upon God, as a man who opens his eyes with loving attention.'

Infused, passive extraordinary contemplation refers to the higher stages of the mystical life. Indeed, St Teresa, in contrast to other writers, reserves the word contemplation for those stages of passive union and spiritual marriage. Although the distinction between this and the prayer of loving attention was not made until the seventeenth century, it reflects a genuine difference between the contemplation which is accessible to all who are faithful in prayer and the contemplation which is a special gift and vocation.

In the eighteenth and nineteenth centuries it was assumed that lay people would be limited to discursive prayer and this was contrasted with the prayer of the mystics. At the end of the nineteenth century a new emphasis on contemplation as accessible to all believers emerged and this view has continued to gain favour.

Dom Cuthbert Butler, *Western Mysticism*, 1922; Richard Harries, *Turning to Prayer*, 1978; Michael Ramsey, *Be Still and Know*, 1982.

RICHARD HARRIES

Contingency

In the senses most relevant to the philosophy of religion, an event or an entity may be called 'contingent', if it could have *not* happened or *not* existed; if it is conditional (or dependent) on some other event's occurring or some other entity's existing. The argument to God *e contingentia mundi* (an important form of the cosmological argument, *see* **Arguments for the Existence of God**) claims that not everything can be contingent and that one being – God – must be 'necessary'. But what exactly can 'necessary' mean here? Some critics of the argument (e.g. Hume) have denied that the existence of any being is necessary; and have claimed that no *contradiction* at any rate is ever involved in denying the existence of anything. 'God does not exist' could be contradictory only if the concept of God itself included 'existence' as one of its essential constituents. That the concept *does* include 'existence' is an essential, and much disputed, claim of the *ontological** argument. 'Existent' has a very different logic from 'omniscient' or 'all-loving'. Unlike these, it does not describe or characterize: and thus it is hard to see how it could play the role the argument requires it to play.

The contingent-necessary distinction can, however, be interpreted in more ways than one. 'A sense of contingency' may be a sense of dependence, derivativeness or creatureliness. With these as starting-points an argument may be attempted to God as Cause or Creator and Sustainer. Alternatively, step-by-step argument may be by-passed in favour of an alleged direct 'insight' or 'intuition' of God as the source of our contingent being. Each path has its pitfalls. In the first case the concept of 'cause' is strained to the limits of meaningfulness, and perhaps beyond them. In the second, the problem is how to test whether or not there is a genuine cognitive act, or only the appearance of one, in an experience that may be predominantly emotional.

On the contrast 'necessary'/'contingent', see R. Swinburne, *The Coherence of Theism*, 1977, chs. 13 and 14.

R. W. HEPBURN

Continuity

Throughout patristic* and mediaeval times Christians were united in believing the Christian faith to be unchanging. They were naturally aware that their codes of conduct and forms of worship, and the way they expressed themselves in creeds and dogmas, often went beyond anything expressly contained in scripture; but they believed that these elaborations, necessitated by the need to explain the faith to outsiders and to define it against the misunderstandings of heretics, had added nothing to the original gospel. The way they understood the matter is clear from the analogies they used, e.g. the logical analogy of making explicit what had hitherto been implicit, or the analogy of a man's becoming aware of beliefs and assumptions which he then recognizes as having already been present in his mind in an inchoate form and having thus shaped his outlook and attitudes. The Reformation* made little difference in this connection: the Reformers' complaint against the Catholics was precisely that they had introduced novelties where no change was admissible, while the Catholics felt that the Reformers were excluding vital elements which had been part of the faith from the beginning, and so were guilty of attempting to change the unchangeable.

In spite of efforts to maintain it, some of which persist right up to the present time, such an attitude could not in fact survive the rise of modern science, which showed the error of many biblical and traditional beliefs about the nature and origins of the natural world, or the emergence of the modern historical outlook, which not only cast doubt on a good deal in the traditional picture of the past, but demonstrated the existence of real differences of belief and practice between different Christian epochs. It gradually became clear that it was no longer possible to talk of an unchanging gospel, in the sense in which the phrase had been used hitherto; and thoughts turned from the idea of Christianity as a faith identical at all times to the idea of it as a faith held in different forms, and expressed in different ways, at different times and places. It then became a crucial question what it is that unites these different forms of the faith and constitutes each of them genuinely Christian.

Among the ways that have been suggested for dealing with this problem, three may be mentioned.

1. To seek for some inner core which has been the essence of Christianity in all periods (e.g. the belief in the fatherhood of God and the brotherhood of man or the sense of absolute dependence), and to argue that the various philosophical and cosmological beliefs with which this essence has been associated at various times have been due to the influence of the different cultural milieus in which Christianity has found itself. On this view primitive Christianity was, as Whitehead put it, 'a religion in search of a metaphysic', and its alliance with Platonic thought in patristic times was a contingent, and in many ways unfortunate, development. There is therefore no obligation on Christians to continue to maintain that, or any similar, alliance; the only sort of continuity with the past which is required being the acceptance, and practical working out, of the essence of Christianity, however defined.

2. To take more seriously the full range of the traditional, or at any rate the NT, belief-system, while emphasizing the importance of interpreting correctly the language in which it was formulated. An example of this approach is the position of Rudolf Bultmann, who insisted that a proper continuity with the past involves no obligation to take

the various cosmological and metaphysical claims in the N T at their face value as objective statements about the way things are. On the other hand, they are not to be discounted, but interpreted as so many ways – natural enough at that particular stage of cultural development – of making clear how man must respond to his total environment and to the future, if he is to attain the authenticity which modern existential analysis shows to be necessary but cannot make possible. Where Bultmann attempted to translate the N T proclamation into the language of existentialism * (*see also* **Demythologizing**), others have attempted a comparable translation into other contemporary 'languages'. What is common to all theologians of this way of thinking is the claim that the original gospel is still intelligible and acceptable in changed cultural circumstances, if only it is properly interpreted (*see* **Hermeneutics**).

3. To lay under contribution the modern ideas of evolution and organic development. Christianity is seen as a developing reality informed by a kind of continuity comparable to that between an acorn and the oak sapling or the full-grown tree which spring from it. This suggestion was explored by J. H. Newman in his *Essay on the Development of Christian Doctrine* (published in 1845, just at the time when he was moving from the Church of England to the Roman Catholic Church) as a way of explaining how he could now accept teaching and practices in contemporary Roman Catholicism which were not to be found in the Bible or the early church. According to his analysis, the novelty of these beliefs and practices was of a very special and strictly limited sort; but others who have used this developmental model have been impressed by the extent to which every belief-system is conditioned by its cultural context, and argued for a much more radical type of development in Christianity (*see also* **Development, Doctrinal**).

Two difficulties are frequently voiced about this type of approach: (*a*) It is not clear what exactly it is that develops – Newman's characterization of Christianity as a developing 'idea' is characteristically subtle and hard to pin down. (*b*) It is difficult to distinguish true development from false. The seven tests which Newman proposed in this connection have provided little practical help in discriminating between the

various proposals that have been made for modifying Christian doctrine – sometimes quite radically – in the light of modern scientific knowledge and historical study. What corresponds in Christianity, critics ask, to the regulating mechanism which ensures that an acorn should develop into an oak and not, for example, into a beech or a fir?

Although these difficulties are real, it may still be the third approach which promises most for the future.

R. Bultmann, Essays in *Kerygma and Myth*, Vol. 1, ed. H.-W. Bartsch, E T 1953; O. Chadwick, *From Bossuet to Newman*, 1957; A. Harnack, *What is Christianity?*, E T 1901; A. F. Loisy, *The Gospel and the Church*, E T 1903; J. Pelikan, *Historical Theology*, 1971; E. Troeltsch, *The Absoluteness of Christianity* (1901), E T 1971; *Writings on Theology and Religion*, E T 1977, esp. ch. 3.

DENNIS NINEHAM

Conversion

In the Bible the words translated as conversion – Hebrew: *shub*; Greek: *epistrephein, strephein* and *metanoia* – mean merely to turn, to turn again, or to return. Though these words carry no specifically religious meanings, they connote the alteration that is made in people's lives when they turn from idols to the living God. In the N T conversion refers specifically to the call of God in Christ, at first to Jews and later to Gentiles as well.

Present-day meanings of the word conversion refer to a variety of kinds of changes, or turnings.

1. Traditional transition. This is the decision of an individual or a group to change affiliation from one major religious tradition to another, for example, from Buddhism to Christianity or from animism * to Islam. Such conversion is typical in the missionary context.

2. The transition from one denomination to another within a major tradition. Motivations for this type of conversion vary from mere convenience to the conviction that the truth of the gospel is more perfectly embodied within a particular group.

3. Conversion from non-involvement in religion to affiliation with a religious group. Given the fact that more and more people are being raised within totally secular

families, this type is becoming increasingly more prominent.

4. Perhaps the most numerically significant kind of conversion is intensification, i.e. the deepening of feeling experienced by individuals who change from nominal or apathetic members of a religious group to ones whose religion is a central part of life.

In the past, the word conversion referred to the initial turning to a faith or religious organization. Recently, however, some theologians have emphasized the importance of conversion as an on-going process, and nowadays in the study of this phenomenon the stress is on the conversion of the whole individual over an entire lifetime. In this perspective particular reference is made to effects of the process in the domains of the intellect, morality and emotions, as well as the realm of religious experience. Thus, the person undergoing conversion is seen to be transformed through a combination of deep intellectual activity, emotional maturation, increasing ethical vigour and sensitivity, and an intensifying of the religious love of God and humanity.

A. D. Nock, *Conversion*, 1961; A. J. Krailsheimer, *Conversion*, 1980; Lewis R. Rambo, 'Current Research on Religious Conversion', *Religious Studies Review* VIII, 1982, pp. 146–59; 'Charisma and Conversion', *Pastoral Psychology* XXXI, 1982, pp. 96–108.

LEWIS R. RAMBO

Corredemptrix, Co-Redemptrix

This title, applied to Mary, the mother of Jesus, implies that Mary closely co-operates with her son in the work of redemption*. By her 'let it be done to me according to thy word' in the annunciation, Mary assents to the incarnation. In her sufferings on behalf of Christ, culminating in the cross, Marian piety sees her as co-offerer of the oblation of his death (John 19.26–27). Mary's role is subordinate to that of Christ, but her unique co-operation with the work of Christ makes her a co-author of salvation for Christians. Mary's role as co-operator with redemption can also be seen as an archetype of the role of all Christians as co-operators with Christ's grace (II Cor. 6.1). The title thus depends on an anthropology which stresses the synergistic relationship (*see* **Synergism**)

between Christ's redeeming work and human response.

R. R. RUETHER

Correlation

The method of correlation is described as 'the subject of all sections' of Tillich's system (*Systematic Theology* 1, 1951, p. x) but it does not fully define either his view of theological method or the *methods* he actually employed. Its origins are found in 'The Idea of a Theology of Culture' and probably earlier. Like the young Schelling's, Tillich's aim was an ideological one. This wider reference of the method is not as obvious in *Systematic Theology*, where the emphasis is more on the correlation of philosophy and theology. Yet not only is it the point of departure for the development of his thinking: it remains its inspiration despite the changes.

Tillich describes the task of theology as 'mediation between the eternal criterion of truth as it is manifest in the picture of Jesus as the Christ and the changing expressions of individuals and groups' (*The Protestant Era*, ET 1948, p. xxvii), 'a way of uniting message' and the correlation of 'the questions implied in the situation with the answers implied in the message' (*Systematic Theology* 1, 1951, p. 8). Furthermore, the method of correlation is said (ibid. p. 68) to reflect the various ways in which correlation is used in ordinary language. Tillich's account of the method thus displays very clearly the confusions and the exploitation of ambiguity with which his critics charge him; but throughout it too shines a vision of theology that is radical – an attempt to offer penetrating analyses of the dynamic and form of modern culture and a real effort to present to that culture as a challenge the paradoxes of the Christian gospel.

J. HEYWOOD THOMAS

Cosmogony

In theology and religions generally, the term refers to the creation of the world or, more specifically, to accounts of the world's creation (from the Greek *kosmos*, ordered world and *ginesthai*, to become). Cosmogonies are usually in narrative or mythical form, and are as diverse in content and motifs as they are widespread among religions of the world. They may be viewed, however, as falling into several types.

One common type may be designated

'emergence myths', because the earth – Mother Earth – is portrayed as containing within herself all the potentials of life; here the potency of the female element is prominent, for although the male element is present, it plays a minor or even insignificant role. The symbolism of the womb, growth and life stands out, for the Mother Earth is the source whence creatures come, their nourishment while alive, and their destiny after death as they make their way from the womb to the tomb and find the end of life to be identical to its origin. Another type of cosmogony portrays two figures, one male and the other female, who, though opposite, come together to produce reality as human beings know it. In yet another type of myth, the world emerges from a cosmic egg, within which all potency and all potentiality is contained. Another common myth has divine beings dive into water to acquire the particles from which the earth will be shaped, while yet others show a primordial sacrifice occurring at the origin of the world. A final type of myth consists of those accounts in which the world is not merely shaped or fashioned by a deity from already existing materials; the very materials from which reality is shaped are themselves brought into existence by an agent who is not created and yet is sufficiently powerful to create all reality except itself.

These types of myths suggest that the various cosmogonies come from diverse social and cultural situations and religious traditions. Although 'myth' often has been relegated to a pre-scientific and presumably surpassed intellectual history, a deeper meaning may be discerned, a meaning which shows that mystery is apprehended as the origin from which order and pattern are derived. If scientific language is useful to describe and predict the operations and events of the existing world, the language of myth may fruitfully be understood as attempting to express the absoluteness and the plenitude, the richness and the mystery of existence itself, existence which is human but also organic and material. In the cosmogony of a given society or religion it may well be possible to discover what is most important to the people who believe the myth and to learn something of the way they orient themselves to reality. If the content of the myths expresses an attitude or particular view with regard to reality, the literary form of myths is most usefully

viewed as a narrative of events which brought about reality as it is known and experienced. To think of cosmogonies as bad science or early psychology misses one of their crucial features: the acts of beings who are neither human nor animal, but divine. And how the divine beings perform their deeds is significant for the world they create and the creatures who inhabit it.

In Christianity there is but one being properly called God. To this God are ascribed the characteristics of creator and redeemer, with the interest in the divine act of creation serving not so much as the basis for cosmological speculation but as a sign of the redemptive character of God's acts (*see* **Creation**).

See also **Myth**.

Mircea Eliade, *Cosmos and History*, 1959; *Myth and Reality*, 1963; H. and H. A. Frankfort, John A. Wilson, and Thorkild Jacobsen (eds), *Before Philosophy*, 1951; James B. Pritchard (ed), *Ancient Near Eastern Texts Relating to the Old Testament*, 1969; Gladys A. Reichard, *Navaho Religion: A Study in Symbolism*, 1950.

LARRY J. ALDERINK

Cosmological Argument
see **Arguments for the Existence of God**

Cosmology

The most general sense of the term indicates a view of the world or universe, and particularly its order and arrangement. The Greek *kosmos* means 'world' and *logos* means 'speaking about a thing' as well as 'reason' or 'doctrine'. Since 'cosmology' in its larger sense is not a biblical term, but is to be traced to Greek religious and philosophic roots, examination of the origins will help understand the large role cosmology has come to play in Christian theology. The Bible does deal with cosmological matters, but largely in terms of creation*.

In Greek religion and philosophy, *kosmos* came to have connotations of system or order. The Ionian philosophers (Thales, Anaximander and Anaximenes) sought something permanent beneath the chaos and change perceptible through the senses; by asking what the world is made of, they pointed in the direction of substance, which is permanent, and also provides unity and stability to the world of appearances. In addition to the issue of permanence, cosmology raises the issue of reality. To the question, 'What is real?' Parmenides responded by saying that only that which abides and does not change qualifies for the designation 'real'. Heraclitus, in distinction, answered that reality is always and only changing. Between these two extreme positions, Plato* and Aristotle* set the main options for subsequent Western thought, scientific as well as theological and philosophical. Plato's cosmology, expressed most clearly in the *Timaeus*, holds that the visible world and all existing things and creatures in it are interrelated through a universal order which is but a reflection or manifestation of the ideal world of Forms which was used by the god or demiurge* as a model to fashion the visible world. Aristotle's cosmology, on the other hand, views the universe as a spherical body within which is our unmoved and unmoving spherical earth; further, the cosmos lacks beginning and end, and thus is eternal.

Christian theology has been heavily influenced by Greek thought, but has also moved beyond it. Christian theologians have generally held that a gulf separates the creator from the creation, with the consequence that the world is a creation by God rather than a development or emanation from deity; Christian cosmology holds that the world is a product of divine activity. Christian theologians also have held that God acts *on* the world in bringing it into existence and *in* the world to redeem it, with the consequence that the world and its creatures are both the scene of divine activity and the recipients of divine love; Christian cosmology holds that God loves the cosmos.

Several themes have pervaded theological views of nature*. Among the most important is the belief that the relation between God and the world is one of Creator to creation/creature, a view already prominent in the biblical materials. To say that the world is created is to say that its reality is derived and dependent; to say that God is Creator is to say that divine reality is original and independent. From this central and foundational idea, two further ideas are derived. 1. Since the world is created, it cannot be divine; hence, the world is not a proper object of worship. 2. Since the world is created by God, it cannot be the scene of conflicts among gods or the location of mysterious and divine powers; rather, the world is subject to God and, therefore, rational, orderly and patterned. The world is, moreover, a place in which human beings can be confident rather than fearful. Neither worship nor fear is inspired by the created world.

Several further issues call for brief attention.

1. Ideas of determinism and freedom have exercised the theological imagination with regard to cosmology. Assuming the universe and human creatures to be subject to laws, how can determinism be avoided? Yet determinism deprives humans of responsibility. On the other hand, assuming humans to be free and responsible, does it follow that the world is chaotic and meaningless? In order to avoid the regrettable results of either extreme, theologians have asserted both that the world is orderly and patterned, and that humans are responsible.

2. The influence of scientific views on theological doctrines is indisputable; as the Ptolemaic cosmology gave way to the Copernican cosmology, and as the Newtonian view was succeeded by relativity, and as evolution came to be accepted, theologians often have registered opposition at first but eventually accommodated new knowledge and Christian faith.

3. A final issue concerns the relation between church and world. Two temptations have exercised a strong appeal but nevertheless have been evaluated as theologically defective. The first is to view the world as raw material for the church's activity and the church as charged with the task of incorporating the world into itself. The second is to view the world as evil and beyond redemption, and the church as isolated from worldly concerns and responsibilities. The belief in creation and redemption by God has served to prevent a union with or a separation from the world; a distinction between church and world, as between theology and science and theology and philosophy, has encouraged a fruitful relationship.

———

Aristotle, *Metaphysics* and *De Caelo*; Augustine, *Confessions, On Free Will, On Order*, and *Soliloquies*; John Calvin, *Institutes of the Christian Religion*; Martin Luther, *On the Bondage of the Will*; Plato,

Timaeus; Thomas Aquinas, *Summa Theologiae*, esp. I.

LARRY J. ALDERINK

Counter-Reformation

The phenomena usually treated under this head include much more than the reactions within Roman Catholicism to the Protestant Reformation. Out of Spanish mystical piety came the work of Ignatius Loyola (d. 1556) and the world-wide missions and educational efforts of the Jesuit Order. Numerous other Orders, chiefly in Italy, engaged in work of clerical reform, preaching, hearing confessions and service to the poor. A large body of controversial writing reaffirmed against Protestantism scholastic doctrines and papal authority. Paul III (1534–49) was the first of a series of reforming popes. Under him the Council of Trent began its sessions. It was to meet intermittently over a period of eighteen years (1545–63) and to produce documents that formed a new basis for the modern advance of the church. Among the representative writers of the Counter-Reformation may be named: John Fisher, bishop of Rochester; John Eck, John Cochlaeus, Josse Clichtove, Alfonsus de Castro, Melchior Cano, and at the later stage Cardinal Carlo Borromeo, chief author of the Catechism of Trent (1564), Philip Neri, founder of the Oratory (1564) and the learned Caesar Baronius, author of the *Ecclesiastical Annals*.

E. M. Burns, *The Counter-Reformation*, 1964; A. G. Dickens, *The Counter Reformation*, 1968; B. J. Kidd, *The Counter-Reformation*, 1933.

J. T. MCNEILL

Covenant

The term has come to categorize the two phases of religious life and experience reflected respectively in the major divisions of the Bible. The Old Covenant, or 'Testament' (via the Latin *Testamentum* = oath, covenant), refers to the religious order instituted by God through Moses with the people of Israel (cf. Exod. 19.5–6). This comprises the 'Israelite', or 'Jewish', covenant attested in the literature of the OT. The New Covenant (= Testament) then describes the renewal and extension of this through the death and resurrection of Jesus of Nazareth, celebrated in the eucharist (cf. Luke 22.20; I Cor. 11.23–25).

Although the entire religious order prevailing between God and Israel from the time of Moses is described as one of covenant, the use of the actual terminology (Heb. *bᵉrīt*) in the literature of the OT is very uneven in its distribution. It appears most prominently in a particular strand of the history, Joshua – II Kings (the so-called Deuteronomistic History), particularly II Kings 22–23 and the book of Jeremiah (cf. especially Jer. 11.1–8). This would indicate that the term acquired a special popularity to describe the unique religious bond existing between God and Israel during the late seventh and sixth centuries BC. This feature forms a major point in the important study by L. Perlitt, *Die Bundestheologie im Alten Testament*, 1969). Perlitt accordingly views this special religious usage as a product of this period, and almost certainly related in a direct way to the threat of exile and destruction. Other scholars argue that a much older idea of covenant received a new emphasis at this time and underwent a substantial change of meaning (W. Eichrodt, N. Lohfink, D. J. McCarthy).

Besides the covenant with Israel inaugurated through Moses, the OT speaks of a covenant with Abraham (Gen. 15.18) in which the promise of possession of the land of Canaan plays a central part. The vesting of the kingship of Israel in the Davidic dynasty is also described as a covenant (II Sam. 23.5; Ps. 132.12). However, it is most of all the prominent use of the term to describe the relationship between God and Israel instituted through Moses which makes it a major theological concept of the OT. In this relationship the obligation to observe the demands of the Ten Commandments (Exod. 19.2–17; Deut. 5.6–21) takes a very central place, so that these commandments themselves come to be viewed as the conditions of the covenant (we may compare further the 'Book of the Covenant' in Exod. 20.22–23.19).

Alongside the important work of L. Perlitt, two major theses have dominated recent discussion regarding the origin and significance of the term 'covenant' in the OT. The first has been propounded by G. E. Mendenhall and draws attention to the similarities in form, character and idiom between the Israelite covenant, focused on the Ten Commandments and the vassal treaties by which an imperial suzerain bound his vassal kings and kingdoms to himself. These are especially known from the Hittite empire of the second millenium BC, but are found later also in the Assyrian sphere. Mendenhall draws the conclusion that the Israelite usage was a consciously planned adaptation from this wider sphere, originating early and almost certainly from the figure of Moses himself.

Beginning from a different starting point, and concentrating largely on an examination of the vocabulary used to describe 'covenants' (the Hebrew uses a phrase meaning 'to cut a covenant ($b^e r\bar{\imath} t$)'), E. Kutsch (*Verheissung und Gesetz*, 1972) reaches very different conclusions. He argues that the terminology did not at first signify the making of a bilateral 'pact', or 'accord', but rather expressed the idea of imposing an obligation. Only later, when it had come to refer to an arrangement involving the mutual imposing and acceptance of obligations by two, or more, parties did it come close to indicating the idea of 'covenant' as later understood.

The belief that the covenant order, established in Israel through Moses, would eventually be superseded by a new order, with a new covenant, is referred to only once in the OT (Jer. 31.31–34). However, this expectation of a new covenant proved to be of great importance to later Judaism and the early Christian church, since the latter was able to use it to express its conviction that this new order had been established by God through the death of Jesus, with the consequent abrogation of the old covenant order (cf. Heb. 7.1–22. Heb. 8.8ff. identifies the 'New' Covenant made in Jesus with the promise of Jer. 31.31–34). The Jewish community of Qumran also viewed its special status as a revitalized religious community as fulfilling the promise of the 'New' Covenant of Jer. 31.31ff.

In the NT the majority of the occurrences of the word 'covenant' (Greek *diathēkē*) refer to the covenants of the OT. Supremely for the Christian church the celebration of its new covenant with God is focussed in the Lord's Supper, which thereby compares closely with earlier ideas of a covenant meal (cf. Matt. 26.28; Mark 14.24; Luke 22.20; I Cor. 11.25). Gal. 4.21–28 contrasts the covenant of promise made to Abraham with the covenant of law made on Mount Sinai

and sees the former as the foreshadowing of the New Covenant made in Jesus.

Within the development of Christian doctrine the biblical concept of a covenant between God and man has received strongest attention in the Protestant tradition since the Reformation. Initially this was to be seen in the work of J. H. Bullinger (1504–1575), and then more fully in the work of a number of theologians, especially those of the Genevan tradition, culminating in its extensive employment in the writings of the English Puritans of the sixteenth and seventeenth centuries, among whom we should particularly single out William Perkins (1558–1602), John Owen (1616–1683) and Richard Baxter (1615–1691). It also appears prominently as a category for describing the unity of the biblical revelation in the Westminster Confession of 1647 (ch. vii). In this regard, its emphasis upon 'one covenant under different administrations' (West. Conf. vii, 5, 6) has lent to this aspect of the Reformed tradition a strong regard for the gracious elements of the OT administration and a rejection of the notion that it presents a 'covenant of works'.

We should also note the extensive use of ideas of covenant in the writings of Johann Koch (Cocceius, 1603–1669), who developed a distinctive 'federal theology*' around the notion of God's self-limitation through his entering into covenants with mankind. In a different direction the writings of the Puritan William Ames (1576–1633) laid stress upon the different 'dispensations' through which God had administered his one gracious covenant with mankind.

In the religio-political sphere this concern in the Reformed Genevan tradition with concepts of a mutually agreed covenant led to the emergence in Scotland of the 'Covenanters' and to the National Covenant of 1638 in opposition to the attempt of Charles I to impose a Scottish Prayer Book. Similarly, the alliance between Scottish Presbyterians and the English Parliamentarians in 1643 was established through a Solemn League and Covenant. From Puritan roots, concepts of covenant came to play a prominent part in the political thinking of the early settlers in the New World, where various forms of federation (from the Latin *foedus* = covenant) bound communities together through mutually accepted rights and obligations. Most recently the *Proposals for a Covenant* adopted at the Nottingham Faith and Order Conference of the British Council of Churches in 1964 has brought similar concepts of covenant, conscious of its biblical origins, into the forefront of ecumenical negotiation.

K. Baltzer, *The Covenant Formulary in the Old Testament, Jewish and Early Christian Writings*, ET 1971; J. Bright, *Covenant and Promise*, 1977; D. R. Hillers, *Covenant: The History of a Biblical Idea*, 1969; D. J. McCarthy, *Treaty and Covenant*, 1963; ²1978; G. E. Mendenhall, *Law and Covenant in Israel and the Ancient Near East*, 1955.

R. E. CLEMENTS

Creation

The doctrine of creation has suffered through its association with literal interpretations of the first chapters of Genesis, and through the belief that it ought somehow to be 'proved' by science. Like all Christian doctrines it is essentially a statement about God, and in particular about God's relationship with the world. It asserts that this relationship is one of dependence and that every existing thing depends upon God for its existence, whereas God depends upon nothing outside himself. The history of the universe, the interactions between the different entities of which it consists, and the multitude of theories about how things have come to be, all presuppose a prior and more fundamental question about why anything should exist at all. It is to this question that, in philosophical terms, the doctrine provides an answer.

Its roots are not in philosophical enquiry, however. Biblically speaking, it is a corollary of belief in the sovereignty of God, a sovereignty which in its fully developed form is seen as extending from lordship over human history to the universe as a whole. It is God who 'stretches out the skies like a curtain ... and makes all earth's princes less than nothing' (Isa. 40.22–23). Belief in this sovereignty provides assurance that, despite defeats and disasters, life is not meaningless. Fundamentally the world is ordered and reliable, because it is God's world; and it is this perception which is given authoritative expression in the Genesis stories. To say that 'God saw all that he had made, and it was very good' (Gen. 1.31) required a high degree of faith in a world where much was mysterious, painful and threatening. In Christian terms this faith received its final vindication in the person and work of Jesus, in whom God's faithfulness and ultimate purposiveness were revealed in the face of all that might seem to deny and destroy them. In orthodox Christian theology, therefore, the doctrines of creation and redemption * are inseparably linked. Creation stands secure because God's faithfulness has been demonstrated on the cross.

These two approaches to the doctrine, philosophical and biblical, should ideally complement one another, but in practice their different emphases can lead to internal strains.

Thus the Thomist conception of God as the First Cause, the Unmoved Mover etc., has been criticized, not only by post-Kantian philosophers, but by theologians who see it as incompatible with the dynamic biblical understanding of him as deeply and continuously involved in his world (*see* **Arguments for the Existence of God**). Furthermore evolutionary ideas have given new prominence to the belief that creation is a continuing process rather than a once-for-all event (*see also* **Evolution**). A substantial body of process theologians, particularly in the USA, have developed these criticisms to the point at which belief in creation's total and one-sided dependence on God seems threatened (*see also* **Process Theology**). Their ideas have proved especially popular among writers on science and religion. Charles Birch, for example, makes much of the idea of God 'luring the world to completeness' by his immersion in its struggles.

An alternative style of criticism deplores the extent to which present-day theology has concentrated on human feelings and predicaments, and person-to-person relationships, to the exclusion of any systematic concern about the natural world in its own right. Within the familiar triad of nature, man and God, nature is often treated, if at all, only in its relation to man. In fact in one of the most massive works of modern popular theology, Hans Küng's *On Being a Christian* (1977), neither creation nor nature rate a single entry in the index. A practical consequence of this lack of concern is the relative failure of Christian thinkers to contribute significantly in current debates on ecology, conservation and the uses of technology.

Biblical hints that nature as such has a significance for God, even apart from its relationship to man, are to be found especially in the Book of Job. But a strong and satisfactory doctrine of creation has to go further than this in positing ways in which God makes his being known through the whole of reality, human and non-human (*see also* **Nature and Theology**). Such a doctrine needs the support of philosophical insights about existence as dependent on the creative will of God, as well as biblical assurances about the superabundance of God's grace. The created world thus conceived is both intelligible and contingent: intelligible because God is a God of order; contingent because his actions spring, not from necessity, but from his gracious will. As such it is particularly amenable to scientific study. In Torrance's words, 'The intelligibility of the universe provides science with its confidence, but the contingence of the universe provides science with its challenge.'

A distinctive feature of Christian doctrine is that God creates *ex nihilo*, i.e. 'out of nothing'. This was originally affirmed in opposition to, e.g. Gnostic, ideas of a dualistic kind in which creation was seen as a struggle by God against intractable or evil material (*see also* **Dualism, Gnosticism**). Some modern theologians, notably Tillich, have interpreted 'nothing' as 'non-being' in an attempt to revive the notion of struggle as an element of creatureliness. It seems preferable, however, to treat the phrase as a reminder that the analogy of human creativity breaks down when applied to God. There is a qualitative gulf between man who creates out of what God has given him, and God who creates *ex nihilo*.

The familiar, if naive, question 'what happened before creation?' hardly arises if the doctrine is seen as describing a relationship and a process rather than an event. If an answer is to be given in its own terms, however, Augustine's reply that time is itself part of creation is probably the best, and has been given added significance by Einstein's concept of the universe as a continuum in which space and time are inseparable (*see also* **Time and Timelessness**).

K. Barth, *Church Dogmatics III: The Doctrine of Creation I*, ET 1958: L. C. Birch, *Nature and God*, 1965: D. D. Evans, *The Logic of Self-Involvement*, 1963: E. L. Mascall, *The Openness of Being*, 1971: A. R. Peacocke, *Creation and the World of Science*, 1979: T. F. Torrance, *Divine and Contingent Order*, 1981: G. F. Woods, *Theological Explanation*, 1958.

JOHN HABGOOD

Creationism

Creationism refers most generally to the doctrine that the world has been created by God, in distinction from its being illusory, self-existent, an emanation* from God, or identical with God (*see* **Creation**). Creationism has also named the doctrine that each soul is separately created by God against the Platonic view of the pre-existence of the soul, the idea that the soul is an emanation from God, and Tertullian's doctrine of traducianism according to which the individual soul comes into being from those of its parents (*see also* **Soul**).

With the rise of evolutionary thinking (*see also* **Evolution**), creationism has come to refer primarily to the doctrine that the world was brought into being by acts of God discontinuous with the antecedent situation. Contemporary creationists believe that the Genesis account of creation can be so interpreted as to fit modern scientific evidence and has equal warrant with evolutionary theory as an explanation of the origins of our world. In the United States they want both theories taught in the public schools. Most scientists hold, in contrast, that the evolutionary understanding is overwhelmingly probable and that the teaching of creationism would infringe on the separation of church and state. Many church leaders agree, holding that the biblical account of creation* should not be confused with science.

Many creationists suppose that the only alternative to their doctrine is the exclusion of God's creative activity altogether. But from the beginning of evolutionary thinking some theologians have seen God's continuous activity as essential to the evolutionary process. Recently Teilhard de Chardin has done much to develop this view along with Wolfhart Pannenberg and process theologians influenced by Alfred North Whitehead.

Some who accept biological evolution nevertheless hold to the creationist view of the human soul. In their view, at some point in the evolution of our animal ancestors God began creating for them human souls; similarly, in the development of each human foetus, at some point God injects a soul. Those who hold this view believe that once the soul has been added to the foetus, abortion is tantamount to the killing of a human being.

Arlie J. Hoover, *Fallacies of Evolution: The Case for Creationism*, 1977; A. R. Peacocke, *Creation and the World of Science*, 1979; Eric R. Rust, *Evolutionary Philosophies and Contemporary Theology*, 1969.

JOHN B. COBB

Creeds

Christianity has always been a credal religion. Creeds have been used both to express devotion and commitment to God and to explicate the faith. Christian creeds are rooted in the theological tradition of ancient Israel with its confessions of God's activity in history (Deut. 26.5–9) and its declaratory affirmations of faith (Deut. 6.4–5). Creed-like statements appear in the earliest NT writings (Mark 8.29; I Cor. 12.3; I Tim. 3.16; I Cor. 8.6; 15.3–7; II Cor. 13.14). No non-theological Christianity has ever survived.

The need for creeds is established in the nature of human beings as intelligent persons and also in the nature of the faith itself. In the long run only those convictions which can be thought through critically and which can be stated with clarity and coherence can command the allegiance of human beings. Furthermore, Christian faith itself seeks understanding, that is, intelligibility.

Creeds have their origin in history. They develop out of the life of the Christian community itself and also out of the response of the Christian community to forces which threaten its existence. Hence creeds always reflect the time and place they were written. Once creeds have been written and established in the community, they begin to shape history and the communities that produced them.

Christian creeds are catholic, that is to say, they intend to express the Christian faith. Protestant creeds and confessions in particular are aware that no creed is final. Yet creeds are in intention catholic, not sectarian.

Creeds and confessions are communal.

Even those few creeds such as the Second Helvetic Confession that were written by one person are rooted in the common life of the church. Some creeds such as the Apostles' Creed are anonymous, growing out of the life of the church. Those creeds which have more specific authorship are replete with language and content that belongs to the church, not to an individual theologian.

Creeds served many functions in the church. They played a central role in the liturgy of the church. In the form of 'rules of faith', they were a guide for preaching. The confession of faith itself is an essential moment in worship as the response of the community to the Word of God. The inclusion of confession as a specific act of worship was natural and inevitable, particularly in the liturgy of the Lord's Supper. Credal statements were from the beginning associated with baptism, first in interrogatory form as questions to the person being baptized. Later in the third century in Rome, a declaratory form of the creed appeared as a part of the preparation for baptism. It was used in the dramatic moment when the faith was 'traditioned' and then 'rendered' back by the baptizand.

Creeds also played a significant role in the teaching of the church. They served as bases for the famous catechetical lectures such as those of Cyril of Jerusalem. The rules of faith which we find in the writings of Justin Martyr, Irenaeus, Tertullian, Clement and Origen were a basis for the teaching ministry of the church; and they all intended to transmit the faith of the apostles.

Creeds had from the beginning a hermeneutical* function in the work of the church. This was as true after the fixing of the canon as before. Every interpreter has to distinguish between the central data and what is derived from it. Hence every student of scripture or of the tradition has to have a rule of faith. In a fundamental sense the creed is simply the way the church reads scripture.

The rise of heresy* was another occasion which required creeds. Heresy is such an important factor in the rise of creeds that it has been easy to exaggerate its role. As was said long ago, creeds are signposts to heresies. The task of the creed was to defend the church against heresies. Yet it is a mistake to attribute creeds to heresies alone, for there would have been creeds if there had been no heresy. Creeds were made better because of heresy, for the heretics required that the church think through its faith with care.

Creeds have also served as a battle cry, a standard. The early church found them helpful in times of persecution. In the twentieth century the rise of National Socialism in Germany was the occasion for the raising of a standard against an alien philosophy and power. In this sense the creed is a marching song, a battle cry.

The best known creeds of the ancient catholic church are the Apostles' Creed, the Nicene Creed and the Athanasian Creed. The Apostles' Creed had its origin in the baptismal creed that was in use in Rome at the beginning of the third century. As one of the daughter creeds which developed in the area within Rome's influence, the creed received in south-western France near the end of the seventh century the form in which it is now used, Charlemagne standardized its use in his realm, and it was adopted by Rome, becoming the common creed of Western Christendom.

The Nicene Creed was promulgated by the Council of Nicaea in 325 and was as such the first conciliar creed. Its intention was the rejection of Arianism*, the doctrine that Jesus Christ was God by courtesy, not in fact. It achieved this rejection by adding to a local Palestinian creed four phrases with Arians could not repeat. The creed that is now known as Nicene is related to the Council of Constantinople (381) and contains an affirmation of the deity of the Holy Spirit. The Nicene Creed, used in Eastern as well as Western Christendom, can be designated the most universal Christian creed. It also expressly deals with the decisive Christian affirmation and rejects the most serious Christian heresy.

The Athanasian Creed was not written by Athanasius but by some Augustinian theologian some time after the middle of the fifth century. Its use has declined because of its anathemas, but recent studies by J. N. D. Kelly have pointed to its theological excellence. The Definition of the Council of Chalcedon (451) was the definitive statement of the ancient church on the person of Jesus Christ, but was never used in worship as were the other three creeds.

The development of theology in the mediaeval church set the stage for new creeds. The fluid theological heritage of the mediaeval church was funnelled into the modern world by the Council of Trent* (1545–1563) and the Protestant Reformation*. The Canons and Decrees of the Council of Trent have shaped Roman Catholicism until Vatican II. Some of the early Protestant creeds were brief theses centring upon points most at issue at the moment (e.g. Ten Conclusions of Berne, 1528). Later Protestant confessions were even more comprehensive statements of Christian faith, based upon the whole Bible, than the Decrees of the Council of Trent. Such 'complete' statements of faith would not have been possible apart from the theological development of the preceding centuries (e.g. Book of Concord, 1580; Second Helvetic Confession, 1566; the Westminster Confession, 1646).

The final Protestant confessions as well as the Canons and Decrees of the Council of Trent were done with such care that they seemed for a time to put an end to the need for the writing of new creeds. In the twentieth century the writing of creeds and confessions has become a very common practice in the churches, but no contemporary creed has attained influence approaching that of the earlier creeds. The only exception is the Barmen Declaration proclaimed in 1934 by the confessing churches in Germany in response to the rise of the Third Reich and 'German' Christianity.

J. N. D. Kelly, *The Athanasian Creed*, 1964; *Early Christian Creeds*, [3]1972; John H. Leith, *Creeds of the Churches*, [3]1982.

JOHN H. LEITH

Crisis Theology

The title of that type of theology initiated immediately after the First World War by several theologians under the leadership and inspiration of Karl Barth (1886–1968). The term 'crisis' may be legitimately interpreted in several ways. 1. As indicating the critical point in an illness; Barth and his colleagues were convinced that nineteenth-century anthropological, immanentist, optimistic theology had shown itself to be dangerously unhealthy by the second decade of the twentieth century, and that the time was now ripe for a new, healthy and vigorous type of theological thought. 2. As referring to the *critical* times through which Christian theology was passing, in the light of the approval which had been given by distinguished German liberal theologians to the German government's war policies in 1914. But, most significantly of all, the term 'crisis' refers quite literally to the *judgment* (Greek *krisis*) of God emphasized by Barth and his fellow crisis theologians in their new theological emphasis, a judgment regarded as falling uniformly and severely upon all merely natural and human endeavours and enterprises, including moral and religious ones. The main influences upon Barth are usually taken to be the Pauline writings of the NT, the thought of the sixteenth-century Reformers (of Calvin especially), and the writings of certain nineteenth-century critics of bourgeois liberal Christianity, most especially Kierkegaard and Dostoievsky. In the early years of his new theological programme Barth was closely associated with other theologians, for example, with Eduard Thurneysen, Friedrich Gogarten and Paul Tillich.

Crisis theology (sometimes known as dialectical * theology) made rapid progress towards becoming continental theological orthodoxy during the 1920s and particularly during the 1930s, and its influence soon came to be felt strongly in Britain and in the USA. Two episodes in the career of crisis theology in the 1930s deserve brief mention here. 1. It made a significant contribution to the cause of the German Confessing Church in its struggle for doctrinal purity and autonomy against the so-called 'German Christians', that section of German Protestantism which was prepared to synthesize Christian doctrine with German National Socialist racist ideology. The strong influence of crisis theology can be clearly seen in the teaching of the Declaration of Barmen (May 1934), which, over against the doctrine of the German Christians, explicitly denied the existence of 'subordinate revelations of God' (e.g. in history, nature or race), apart from God's only and sufficient revelation in Jesus Christ as witnessed to in the church by scripture. 2. There was the celebrated dispute between Barth and Emil Brunner in 1934, over Brunner's suggestion that there was a limited place in Christian theology for natural theology *, a suggestion that evoked from Barth his celebrated pamphlet *No! An*

Answer to Emil Brunner, in which Barth reiterated the fundamental negative tenet of crisis theology that there was absolutely no 'point of contact' between human nature and God's revelation, and hence that *all* natural theology is an impossibility.

The *direct* influence of crisis theology has declined gradually since 1945, although it has left a deep mark on postwar theology in continental Europe, in Britain and in the USA. Dietrich Bonhoeffer (1906–1945), for example, was decisively influenced in his formative years by crisis theology; his later revolutionary views (as expressed in his *Letters and Papers from Prison*, ET 1953, ³1971) are almost unintelligible if they are interpreted in isolation from this seminal influence.

See **Dialectical Theology; Liberal Protestantism.**

E. Busch, *Karl Barth*, ET 1976; A. I. C. Heron, *A Century of Protestant Theology*, 1980; H. R. Mackintosh, *Types of Modern Theology*, 1937 and 1963; J. Macquarrie, *Twentieth-Century Religious Thought*, ²1981; James Richmond, *Faith and Philosophy*, 1966; Paul Tillich, *Perspectives on Nineteenth and Twentieth Century Protestant Theology*, 1967.

JAMES RICHMOND

Criteria, Theological
see **Method, Theological**

Critical Theory

A form of social theory, belonging to Western Marxism and originating in a group of thinkers associated with the Institut für Sozialforschung (Institute of Social Research) at the University of Frankfurt. The Institute was founded in 1923, with Carl Grünberg as Director. He was succeeded in 1930 by Max Horkheimer (1895–1973), who had a major impact upon the work of the Institute and gathered around himself a varied and unusually talented group. Among the leading figures were Theodor W. Adorno (1903–1969) and Herbert Marcuse (1898–1979). Though Walter Benjamin (1892–1940) became a research associate and had considerable intellectual influence, especially upon Adorno, he was never a close member of the group. With the rise to power of the Nazis, the Institute went into exile, first to Geneva (1933) and then to

Columbia University, New York (1935). It was transferred back to Germany in 1950. The notion of a particular school of thought developed during the exile, but only after the return to Germany did the term 'Frankfurt School' come into use to designate certain members of the Institute. It suggests a greater unity than there ever in fact was. At best, 'the Frankfurt School' can be used only of five thinkers: Horkheimer, Adorno, Marcuse, Leo Lowenthal and Friedrich Pollock. It is the first three who have attracted widespread attention in the English-speaking world.

A second generation of critical theorists has formed around the figure of Jürgen Habermas (b. 1929). Habermas turned to critical theory in the 1950s, under the influence of Adorno, whose assistant he became. He taught first at Heidelberg, and then in 1964 was appointed to a chair in philosophy and sociology at the University of Frankfurt. In 1971 he moved to the Max Planck Institute in Starnberg. In 1981 he resigned from the Institute and is now again at Frankfurt. Although his work is too original to be seen simply as a continuous development of earlier critical theory, he himself has presented his thought as a reworking of critical theory. His collaborators have included Claus Offe (political scientist and sociologist), Albrecht Wellmer (philosopher) and Klaus Eder (anthropologist).

Critical theory is defined by contrast with traditional or positivist social theory. Positivism * holds that all forms of knowledge have the same structure and that this structure is exhibited paradigmatically in the natural sciences. Scientific method as applied to social phenomena aims therefore at the discovery of universal laws, the truth or falsity of which is determined exclusively by comparing them as hypotheses with empirical data provided by observation. The objectivity of science for positivists does not allow any consideration of moral and political values. Scientific knowledge is morally and politically neutral. For critical theory, social science conceived in that way misrepresents historically relative and alterable social structures as natural and unchanging, and its purely technical, allegedly value-free use of science to organize society becomes repressive and manipulative. What, then, distinguishes critical theory is its explicit recognition of the link between knowledge and human interests. Critical theory itself as knowledge is guided by a fundamental practical interest, namely emancipation. Its aim is to become part of a self-reflective movement towards a more rational society. It studies existing social and political conditions, in order to identify the present possibilities for change and move towards a society where human beings, free from relations of domination, exercise a self-reflective conscious control over social processes.

In developing their thought, critical theorists have drawn upon a wide variety of thinkers, entering frequently into a detailed discussion of their thought. Besides Marx, especially the early Marx, Kant, Hegel, Weber, Lukács and Freud have been thoroughly put to use. Habermas has extended the range to include Anglo-American philosophy, especially in his study of language. In the choice of themes, critical theory marks a shift from the focus of orthodox Marxism upon the economic base and the critique of political economy to concern with the superstructure and with the introduction of a wide-ranging cultural criticism into Marxist social theory. An example is the attention given to an aesthetics of mass culture.

The critical theorists do not in general share the view of the early Marx that religion has no content of its own and simply expresses social contradictions. They consider it important to preserve what they refer to as the utopian content of religion against the reduction of society to a totally administered system, governed by a purely instrumental or technical rationality. All the same, they regard the age of religion as past without recall and reject all religion as obsolete. In his later years, Horkheimer modified his religious stance, contending that all politics and critique had to have a theological moment, namely an awareness of the transcendent or Wholly Other. He tried to develop an areligious theology, an extreme form of negative theology, which denies any certitude about God, but gives the thought of God the important function of confirming our finitude. Theology enables us to transcend the empirically given world in a yearning for a free and just community. It is the hope that injustice does not have the last word, the longing that the murderer may not triumph over his victim. Other critical theorists have not followed Horkheimer into his theological speculations.

Critical theory has entered in diverse ways into theological debate. It was a factor in the emergence of the new political theology of Johann Baptist Metz and Jürgen Moltmann. It influenced the Kritischer Katholizismus movement, which no longer exists, but which produced some valuable theological writing. Critical theory has been discussed by various Continental theologians, such as Schillebeeckx and Pannenberg. Helmut Peukert, adapting the procedure of Habermas, who makes an analysis of communicative action, that is personal interaction, the basis for a theory of society, proposes a theological theory of communicative action as a new fundamental theology*. The reception of critical theory in North America through translations is attracting considerable theological attention. Its methodological concerns are being related to the action-oriented theologies of liberation.

Charles Davis, *Theology and Political Society*, 1980; David Held, *Introduction to Critical Theory: Horkheimer to Habermas*, 1980; Martin Jay, *The Dialectical Imagination: A History of the Frankfurt School and the Institute of Social Research 1923–1950*, 1973; Thomas McCarthy, *The Critical Theory of Jürgen Habermas*, 1978.

CHARLES DAVIS

Cross, Theology of the

1. Theology of the cross (*theologia crucis*) is the short formulation of true faith chosen by Martin Luther in the early period of the Reformation. In the *Heidelberg Disputation* (1518) he makes a schematic contrast between his *theologia crucis* and the *theologia gloriae* which had been dominant hitherto, with its scholastic and mystical speculation: God is known in the cross of Christ and experienced through suffering. *Theologia crucis* is revelation theology in the strictest sense. God's revelation takes place indirectly and in a hidden way, not in the works of creation or in human good works; God is known 'only through suffering and cross' (*per passiones et crucem, WA* I, 354). Only faith can understand the real work (*opus proprium*) of God in the cross as the strange work (*opus alienum*) of the hidden God (*deus absconditus*): the justification of the godless person, for whose sake God goes his way in the lowliness of the cross. Thus *theologia crucis* means indirect knowledge of God; the cross of Jesus Christ is the epistemological principle for any divine action. However, not only God's work but also his being is known in the cross; thus the cross is no less an ontological principle. So Luther's doctrine of God, with the distinction between the hidden and the revealed God (*deus absconditus* and *revelatus*), Luther's christology, which sees the heart of the loving God in the sacrifice of the crucified Christ, and his anthropology, according to which the depth of guilt is first disclosed in the cross and man first comes to himself in justification faith, are all grounded in the cross and are aspects of the all-embracing theology of the cross: 'the cross is the criterion of all things' (*crux probat omnia, WA* V, 179).

2. By stressing that revelation has the character of humiliation and emphasizing the love of God which shows itself in the cross and passion, Luther is going back to a central theme of the Bible. Already according to the OT, God chose for himself the smallest of all the peoples (Deut. 7.7), and thus exposed himself to the mockery of the powerful (Ps. 115.2). The power of the Lord is manifest in a hidden way in the suffering servant of God (Isa. 52.13–53.12), and the mercy of Yahweh is there in particular for the oppressed, the hungry and the prisoners (Ps. 146.7). Jesus stands in this tradition when he welcomes the humblest (Matt. 11.2–6) and brings the kingdom of God to those who are poor in every respect (Luke 6.20). The mystery of the kingdom of God is God's present appearance in the activity and the person of Jesus; this is a mystery which is revealed by God only to the disciples (Matt. 13.16f.) and remains hidden from the 'wise and understanding' (Matt. 11.25). For it is not just Jesus' death but the whole of his life which stands under the sign of humiliation. It is here that the notion of the messianic 'secret', which Mark uses to stylize the hiddenness of the eschatological revelation of salvation, has its historical basis. Paul, to whom Luther principally refers, is by no means alone in primarily proclaiming the gospel as the 'word of the cross' and developing a 'theology of the cross'. Here he is concerned to demonstrate the saving significance of the cross, which under Roman rule represented the most fearsome torture and death for slaves and

rebels. In this deepest humilation Christ, obedient to the will of the Father, achieved the work of redemption (Phil. 2.8). For Jews and Greeks that is such an unimaginable scandal that the 'word of the cross' is contrasted, in a way which cannot be resolved, with the wisdom of the world (I Cor. 1.17f.). The cross of Jesus Christ is the only boast of the apostle (Gal. 6.14), who can take up his cross and follow Christ (cf. Mark 8.34), because he knows that the grace and power of God are made perfect in weakness (II Cor. 12.9f.).

3. It is the testimony of the whole of scripture that the centre of Christian theology can never be anything other than 'theology of the cross'. However, this position has not always been maintained in Protestant theology since the Reformation * period. Of particular importance is the Anglican theology of passibility dating from the end of the nineteenth and beginning of the twentieth century. Its basic approach is to take the eucharistic sacrifice, the cross on Golgotha, and the heart of the triune God together and thus to develop anew God's power to suffer as the omnipotence of suffering love (C. V. F. Storr, C. E. Rolt, J. K. Mozley, B. R. Brasnett). Generally speaking, the twentieth century has returned more markedly to the theology of the cross. Accounts from the Catholic side (K. Rahner, H. U. von Balthasar, H. Mühlen) and from the Orthodox side (N. Berdyaev, S. Bulgakov, P. Evdokimov and D. Staniloae) show that the Reformers' concern for the *theologia crucis* no longer need be a factor which divides the churches. From the Protestant side, K. Barth, H. Vogel and H. J. Iwand above all have deepened Luther's theology of the cross: the divinity of Jesus is revealed specifically in his humiliation to the point of death on the cross, while his manhood is manifested in his exaltation. At the end of the Second World War, the Japanese theologian K. Kitamori and the German theologian D. Bonhoeffer simultaneously discovered the significance of the 'pain' or 'suffering of God in the world'.

4. However, the significance of the cross must not be limited to soteriology *, if otherwise God's being is left untouched by the death of Jesus. To think of God in the death of Jesus must therefore also lead to a change, to thinking of the death of Jesus in the being of God: indeed the cross of Jesus

Christ stands in the centre of the divine Trinity * as a divide between God and God (Mark 15.34). The Son offers himself (Gal. 2.20) and endures dying in being abandoned by God on the cross; the Father leaves the Son, offers him up (Rom. 8.32) and suffers the death of the Son in the pain of love. Because the suffering of the Son is different from the suffering of the Father, one cannot simply speak in theopaschite terms of 'the death of God', as happens in the 'death of God' * theology. In the light of the cross we must rather talk, in trinitarian terms, of a patricompassianism. In the common readiness for offering, this gives concrete expression to the community of existence in the divine nature, and the nature of God as love. The biblical foundation for the theology of the cross as the theology of the divine passion may be found in I John 4.16. The doctrine of the Trinity understands the trinitarian nature of God in terms of a shortened form of the account of Christ's passion, and is at heart none other than a *theologia crucis*. This notion is represented in contemporary Protestant theology above all by J. Moltmann and E. Jüngel.

The theology of the cross also has a political significance. It is a radical questioning of all religious images of God which seek to understand the being of God unhistorically and without the element of suffering, as happened in antiquity. The theology of the cross is also the sharpest attack on all political idols: 'the crucified God' calls as the God of the poor, the oppressed and the humiliated for a demythologizing * of all earthly authorities, and frees men and women to follow Christ in faith, love and hope. For just as the cross of Christ and the passion of God can never be thought of without the resurrection, so too the suffering of the Christian and the enduring of creation carries within itself the promise of redemption. Thus the identity and relevance of Christian faith are rooted in the cross of Christ.

D. Bonhoeffer, *Letters and Papers from Prison* (1953), ET ³1971; E. Jüngel, *Gott als Geheimnis der Welt*, 1977; K. Kitamori, *Theology of the Pain of God*, 1966; P. Evdokimov, *Christus in russischen Denken*, 1977; J. Moltmann, *The Crucified God*, ET 1974; J. K. Mozley, *The Impassibility of God. A*

Survey of Christian Thought, 1926; W. von Loewenich, *Luthers Theologia crucis*, [5]1967.

JÜRGEN MOLTMANN

Cult

The word has a number of mutually exclusive meanings largely dependent on the context in which the word is used. In its broadest sense, cult refers simply to a system of religious beliefs and rituals or to that system's body of adherents. More specifically, a cult is a particular form or pattern of ritual or worship. Thus, scholars and theologians refer to 'the cult of the saints' or 'the cult of the Virgin Mary', meaning forms of worship dedicated to the adoration, service and honour of these persons or a deity. In a theological context, cult can mean a specific group outside that one accepted as primary by the speaker or writer; in this sense, some Christians consider Mormons, Jehovah's Witnesses and other such firmly established groups to be cults.

In modern usage, however, the word cult most frequently denotes a group, usually religious or pseudo-religious in nature, that exhibits the following characteristics: it deviates sharply from and strongly rejects the prevailing culture; it is dominated by a highly charismatic leader who often proclaims him- or herself to be divine or to have special access to the divinity; it exacts total commitment from its followers including the commitment of time and money; it is rooted in a comprehensive ideology, touching on every facet of the adherents' life; and, finally, it is aggressive in its efforts to recruit new members, sometimes resorting to manipulative techniques of persuasion, as opposed to the conversion, of potential adherents.

Within the decade of the 1970s, the word cult came to be used to refer to the proliferating new religious movements that many traditional-minded observers deemed pernicious. Their judgments hinged on the methods of recruitment, the eccentric style of leadership found in these groups, the esoteric theology they exhibit, the rigorous discipline they impose on members, and the unusual life-styles both their leaders and adherents affect. More cautious critics avoid judging adherents but focus on the leaders of these new groups, suggesting that they are more self-serving and power-seeking than sincerely committed to providing spiritual guidance. Some social scientists view these cult groups as genuine responses to the modern world in which secularization, urbanization and technology have stripped traditional religious groups of their viability and left individuals without resources for spiritual succour. In this context, the cults are seen to provide intensive group support, comprehensive and compelling interpretations of the world, and a means of relieving the frustrations and anxieties produced by modern life.

It is important to note that not all groups are cults in the negative sense of the term, and that the definition is often as dependent on the nature of the definer as on the group in question. In fact, given the variety of ways in which the term is used, it is possible to define *cult* simply as 'any group you don't like'.

LEWIS R. RAMBO

Culture

If human culture is understood as a corporate undertaking in which people succeed in establishing a distinctive style of living based on common values, it can be seen that much of what is distinctive in Christian faith emerges from its dialogue with it. This dialogue is inherent in their relationship and takes place not only between Christians and those who do not share their faith but also among Christians themselves. This was clearly and self-consciously grasped from the beginning of the Christian story. The first account of creation in Genesis can be legitimately thought of as the imposition by God of an order, which implies a cultural pattern, upon primeval chaos. The earth is separated from the shapeless waters. The creatures are distinguished from each other, named and set in relationship. Man is given dominion. Yet we are immediately confronted with the second account, in which man, dwelling in the Garden, is seduced through the woman from that obedience to God from which he derives his dominion and surrenders himself to the serpentine power of the world about him, whose independent existence is not explained and which offers him an apparent freedom to manage his own life without reference to God. The result is that man and woman are cast out of paradise and their work now becomes not the enjoyment and celebration of God's gifts but a painful struggle for survival.

This two-sided attitude to culture expresses itself throughout the OT. Babel, the representative institution of the religion and culture of the ancient Middle East, is confounded. Zion, the true city of God, is contrasted with Babel, but Zion herself also quickly becomes ambiguous. When, through the Exodus and the discipline of the Torah, Israel is able to settle in the promised land, she becomes vulnerable to the cultural complacency which besets all settled societies. This complacency was, to some extent, the consequence of her success, just as the desire to have a king and to have a glorious temple to house the traditionally mobile ark of the covenant * were partly the fruit of a genuine desire to serve and magnify God. Yet the danger, which the great prophets saw so clearly, was that the life of Israel should become an end in itself and her faith turn into a self-enclosed culture-religion. The essence of that faith lay in her dependence on her Lord and her continual openness to fresh disclosures of his will from the One who is only really known in the commitment of venture into the unknown. Once that openness was lost, Israel had no barrier against cultural assimilation to the nations around her and no distinctive purpose and no power of self-criticism. This is the point of the insistence on the jealousy of God, of the eloquent rhetoric of Deuteronomy about the dangers of prosperity and of the denunciations and lamentations of the great prophets. Israel can enjoy the Law and the cultus and the kingship, but only if she realizes their relativity to the will of a God who stands over against her and who may at any time ask her to forsake them and to go on her travels again. It was their realization of this which made the prophets see the Exile, not as the catastrophe which it otherwise would have been, but as a corrective punishment, designed to recall Israel to the terms upon which she could alone keep covenant with God.

It is facts like these which give substance to the contention of the writer to the Hebrews that the people of faith of the OT sought a city with truly durable foundations, which they never identified with the earthly Jerusalem. They always strove to realize what Abraham was made to see at the beginning of their history, in the great story of the sacrifice of Isaac, that the way of life for Israel consisted always in being prepared to lose her life and that she must always love her Lord even more than the precious gift of the community of Israel which she has received from him as the fruit of the covenant.

This prophetic interpretation is intensified and fulfilled in the experience of Jesus. The cultural anthropologist would describe him as a man who was fully identified with the community of Israel. He grew up in obedience to the Law, a member of the house of David, and, as the story of the temptations implies, he discovered and defined his own task through sustained meditation upon the meaning of the tradition of Israel. Yet all this led him to reject the cultural forms through which Israel expressed her distinctive identity in his time, which, in its turn, meant his complete repudiation by the official representatives of Israel. It was not simply that he preached that the Sabbath was made for man and not man for the Sabbath, which meant that the Law must be seen as relative to man's highest good, which always has to be freshly defined; it was much more that he wanted Israel to see that the way in which she now thought of herself had become the greatest barrier to entry into the kingdom * of God.

This is the point of Jesus' much misunderstood teaching about the rich man and the kingdom. The rich man is primarily Israel herself, blessed in the things of God – the Law, the cultus and the promised land. But these very fruits of past faith produced a self-sufficiency which prevented her from seeing her real relation to God and discerning God's will for her present situation. This was why the spiritually impoverished publican was in a more hopeful situation. Jesus believed himself called to be the true representative of Israel, the one who was most conscious of her richness, who found that he could only fulfil the vocation of Israel by becoming poor. In becoming accursed for his brethren's sake, he accepted God's rejection of the empirical form of Israel's life and trusted in God's ability to establish a new way of life for his people. His death and resurrection are the exemplification of the truth proclaimed in the Sermon on the Mount which says that it is only as we first seek God's kingdom and his righteousness that the good fruits of human culture will be added to us and which concludes with the warning that only the house built on the rock of the faith celebrated in the Beatitudes, with their transvaluation of human values, is able to endure when the storms come.

Paul, who was also acutely conscious of what was involved for Christian faith in its break with the cultural tradition of the old Israel, underlined the fact, in Galatians and elsewhere, that the possession of the gifts of the Spirit means a rejection of the old patterns and a new outburst of cultural creativity, which must at all costs reflect the freedom of the Spirit. He was, however, so conscious of the imminence of the End and, in his later writings, was so caught up in turbulent events, that he had little incentive to deal with the kind of problem which arose when the rich community life of those who dwelt together in the mutual dependence and the *agape* which he described in classic terms became sufficiently articulated to have a well-defined cultural pattern of its own. Persecution prevented this from being a very living issue for the other NT writers also, except partly in the Pastoral Epistles and I Peter, but as the church established itself in the world, and particularly in the post-Constantinian era, it became more and more inescapable. So pervasive, in fact, has it became that, in his well-known book *Christ and Culture*, Richard Niebuhr was able to distinguish five different types of attitude towards human culture which have received significant expression in the history of the church. He describes them as those respectively of Christ against culture, of the Christ of culture, of Christ above culture, of Christ and culture in a relationship of paradox, and of Christ as transformer of culture.

Niebuhr sees Tertullian and Tolstoi as the chief historical exemplars of the first attitude, which emphasizes the opposition between the claims of Christ and those of all forms of human culture. These Christians, it is asserted, do not see it as part of their responsibility to try to build a stable order of society in accordance with the divine command for the ordering of human life. Their duty is to withdraw into a community of their own, in which they do their best to minimize their earthly desires and reduce their contacts with those outside the saved community as much as possible. To possess many material goods or to exercise secular power is a form of disobedience.

The second attitude moves in the opposite direction, rejecting the first attitude as both inconsistently impracticable and unworthy, a denial of the promise of the gospel. Christ is the supreme example of universal human goodness and the fulfilment of cultural aspiration. This attitude is exemplified in different ways by Gnosticism* in the early centuries, by Abelard in the Middle Ages and, in particular, by Schleiermacher and the whole liberal* theological movement which has become widespread in modern Protestantism*. All who share this attitude take a positive view of human cultural achievement but believe that it cannot be true to its best ideals except through obedience to Christ.

The third attitude, that of Christ above culture or, better, of Christ and culture in synthesis, has affinities with but also important points of difference from the second. It sees a clear distinction between the spirit of Christ and that of culture but does not believe that their relationship needs to be one of opposition. When culture fulfils its proper role, their relationship is complementary and a synthesis between them is possible. This is the attitude which has, perhaps, won most favour in the course of Christian history and it has inspired notions of Christendom* and 'Christian civilization'. Its outstanding representative is the Roman Catholic Church in the Middle Ages, with Thomas Aquinas as its intellectual exponent. Clement of Alexandria in the ancient world and Bishop Butler in modern Anglicanism (Niebuhr might also have added Richard Hooker) are also good examples of synthesists. Those who hold this view lay great stress on the importance of law, which they see as natural law rather than revealed Torah, although with the recognition of a close relationship between the two. This law all people can see, but it is qualified and illuminated by the light of the gospel.

The fourth attitude, which sees Christ and culture standing in a relation of paradox, is exemplified by such great figures as Paul himself, Luther and Kierkegaard. Like those who see Christ and culture in opposition, they are acutely conscious of the distinctive character of the claim of Christ, but they accept realistically their inescapable involvement in the life of human culture, because they too are human beings. They take both faith and culture too radically to find it possible to achieve a stable synthesis of them. They have to follow Luther's para-doxical injunction, *Pecca fortiter*, par-ticipating fully in human culture, conscious of its ambiguity, yet recognizing the in-escapability of commitment and trusting to the forgiving mercy of God, which will open up the way of obedience to them in forms which cannot be foreseen. The tension in which people stand between the will of God and human culture cannot be relaxed except eschatologically, but this does not en-courage a defeatist attitude in relation to the cultural possibilities of life on this earth. On the contrary, it encourages vigilance and self-criticism and stimulates creativity.

The last attitude is the conversionist one, which sees Christ as the great transformer of culture. Human culture on its own stands opposed to Christ, as part of a fallen world, but he gives us power to remove the threat to his lordship which all culture contains and to establish it on a different basis. Augustine, Calvin and, in modern times, F. D. Maurice are held to be representative conversionists. The world of culture has its demons, but they can be exorcized, and something like a new Christendom becomes a possibility, not through synthesis but through radical transformation.

While these five attitudes can be distin-guished in history and it is helpful to see an otherwise almost intractably complicated story in their terms, it must be remembered both that these attitudes cannot in practice be so sharply distinguished from each other and that they are much more clearly ex-emplifed by outstanding theologians and churchmen than by ordinary church people. Thus, while the first and the last two have a powerful impact and very considerable indi-rect influence, they have never been any-thing like as widespread as the second and the third. It is obvious that to maintain a consistent attitude of opposition to the ordinary life of the world is very hard, and all kinds of compromises will have to be made. To live in the situation of paradox as between Christ and culture is possible only to people of quite exceptional independence and insight, who are always few and far be-tween. The whole drive of cultural achieve-ment is, quite properly on its own terms, to reduce the tension and to try to make life in the tents of our earthly pilgrimage as com-fortable and self-sufficient as possible. This means that, to the extent that the faithful

live successfully in the paradox, they become rich, like the old Israel, and they, or still more their children, develop a synthetic or a cultural Christianity. Thus, Lutheranism *, which, originally developed a theology of the orders of creation on the basis of a theo-logy of paradox, quickly found itself subtly giving a much more positive status to such orders as the state and the family and thus transforming itself into a form of conser-vative culture-Protestantism.

A similar danger confronts 'conver-sionists' in their attitude towards culture. The transformation of culture into the image of Christ is authentic only when it carries with it a prophetic challenge and risk. But when the transformation takes place in a particular situation, it is natural that it should lead to celebration and enjoyment, which in their turn lead to a relaxation of tension and an emphasis on consolidation of hard-won gains. This is why transforma-tionists' vision of the kingdom of Christ must always be radically eschatological *, making them dissatisfied with their achieve-ments and acutely aware of the relativity of all earthly forms. Otherwise, to the extent to which they are serious, they cannot escape the dangers of theocracy *, where humanity is set in the place of God, and this in turn leads to a form of culture-Christianity, which may be repressive or 'soft-centred' according to circumstances. Christian ex-perience through history suggests that a healthy relation cannot exist between faith and all forms of culture, including 'Christ-ian' culture, without a measure of tension.

It is important to bear in mind the com-plicated history of the relation of faith to culture and the various attitudes which have seemed right at various times in considering the theological discussion inspired by the ideas of Dietrich Bonhoeffer, those of 'secu-larity', 'coming of age' and 'speaking to man in his strength'. To take a positive view of 'secularity', the recognition that it is in this world and no other that we have to work out our present Christian obedience, can be seen as an act of faith in the transforming power of Christ. We should rejoice in hu-manity's strength and not feel under the necessity of trying to demonstrate that it is really weakness in order to make room for God. Like the riches of the Bible, this strength should be gratefully accepted as a gift from God, together with the freedom for creative action which it makes possible (*see also* **Secular Christianity**).

But the Bible and history make abundantly clear to us the perils of riches, and they are perils which are particularly acute in the modern world. If it is true that humanity has 'come of age', this appears, Christians believe, only 'in Christ'. The human power of self-direction is not, therefore, something which can be taken for granted as a natural right, but a gift which has constantly to be renewed and which prompts us to choose one course rather than another. When, as the fruit of faith, people succeed in establishing a new cultural pattern, they are in danger, as we have seen, of slipping out of the situation of tension in which Niebuhr's 'paradoxical' school sees them to stand and of ignoring the perpetual challenge and risk of which his 'conversionists' are aware. When this happens, they are in danger of creating a new form of cultural Christianity or, at best, of achieving a new Christian synthesis which fails to do justice to the radicalism of the Christian claim. This is why the church always needs to recall itself to the significance of the cross and resurrection of Jesus Christ and to see that all human culture, including 'Christian culture', has always to be revalued anew in their light.

Christopher Dawson, *The Historic Reality of Christian Culture*, 1960; H. Richard Niebuhr, *Christ and Culture*, 1952; Paul Tillich, *Systematic Theology*, Vol. 3, 1964, ch. 27; A. T. Van Leeuwen, *Christianity and World History*, 1964.

DANIEL JENKINS

Curriculum, Theological

The organization of the studies required for church leadership, whether in the priesthood, the ministry or education. Uniformity of practice throughout Christendom is hardly to be expected. The structure of the curriculum varies according to time, place, denomination, and specific vocational goals; and it is inseparable from questions about the ministry itself and the nature, task and divisions of theology. Hence it is not surprising that reform of the theological curriculum has been a perennial issue throughout the history of the church. Partly by way of reaction, some religious groups view the entire enterprise of theological education with suspicion, preferring either an exclusive biblicism or else a conception of ministry as charismatic rather than professional. There has also been no shortage of individual protests against elaborate 'academic' preparation for a supposedly 'practical' task.

1. *Before modern times.* Beneath the divergent practices, some constants have no doubt been present. In particular, there has been a general continuity with respect to the tasks assigned to 'ministry' (the term will be used here inclusively for all forms of church leadership). Ministry has always embraced the administration of the sacraments, preaching* or teaching, discipline or oversight, and pastoral care. True, at various times and in various places there has been a tendency to rank one function above the others in importance, e.g. the administration of the sacraments in the mediaeval church, or the proclamation of the word in the Reformation churches; and sometimes the functions have been parcelled out among several offices, e.g. in Calvin's fourfold scheme of pastors, teachers, elders and deacons. But however differently the priorities may be ordered, an adequate theological curriculum has had to take account of all the constant ministerial functions.

Until the twelfth century, the material of theological study was largely exegesis*, and the best-trained clergy of the early Middle Ages were mostly educated in monastic schools. The *Four Books of Sentences* of Peter Lombard (d. 1160), a collection of systematically arranged statements from the Fathers and masters, then became the official theological textbook of the universities. Lombard's dialectical method – the juxtaposing of authorities and the attempt to reconcile apparent contradictions – was influenced by Peter Abelard's (d. 1142) *Sic et Non* and in turn shaped the pattern of later theological instruction. The schoolmen continued to write biblical commentaries, as well as commentaries on the *Sentences*, but it was the dialectical method that formed the mediaeval 'summas*' and it displaced exegesis as the crown of theological studies. The greatest of the mediaeval systems, the *Summa Theologiae* of Thomas Aquinas (d. 1274), eventually supplanted Lombard's *Sentences* as the favoured textbook of theology.

The beginnings of the Protestant Reformation * were closely tied up with the cause of curricular reform at Wittenberg University. Partly under the influence of Renaissance scholarship, interest swung back from scholastic theology to biblical exegesis, to which Martin Luther (1483–1546) devoted a large part of his career. Understanding the scriptures in the original languages became the heart of theological study. But in his *Open Letter to the Christian Nobility*, in 1520, Luther showed himself willing to have the Fathers and even the *Sentences* included in the preliminary stages of theological education, and in the same year Philipp Melanchthon (1497–1560) proposed that history be made a subject in its own right.

2. *The modern curriculum*. With the eighteenth century, the distinctively modern problem of the theological curriculum began to emerge: the fragmentation of theology into several autonomous disciplines. Learning became increasingly specialised, and scholars in the historical fields – OT, NT, church history, history of doctrine – asserted the strictly scientific character of their method and claimed independence from the churchly and confessional enterprise of dogmatics. Moreover, the demands of scholarly specialization led even to the separation of the historical fields from one another, and each tended to spawn its own subdivisions (such as patristics *) or ancillary disciplines (such as archaeology). In everyday usage, 'theology' no longer named the total enterprise of the curriculum but became one field among several.

The appearance of 'theological encyclopaedias' * in nineteenth-century Germany was largely an attempt to locate and preserve the lost unity of the theological curriculum. But in practice they tended only to confirm the fourfold division of Protestant ministerial education into biblical studies, church history, systematics (including both dogmatics and ethics) and the practical arts of ministry. A similar division became the rule in the RC curriculum, except that there Bible and church history are generally placed together as 'historical theology', and as preface to the resulting three disciplines – historical, systematic and practical – 'fundamental theology' lays out the basis and presuppositions of them all. The usual subdivisions of practical theology in the RC curriculum are pastoral theology, liturgics, catechetics, homiletics and church law.

The fragmentation of the theological curriculum has been made still more acute by the mushrooming of the practical field. Preparation for ministry has come to be widely understood as essentially the impartation of skills for the performance of the ministerial functions, partly in dependence on current educational theory, psychology, business administration, and so on. 'Theology' may then be viewed, not as the defining characteristic of the curriculum and of ministry itself, but as one component of the 'academic' side of ministerial education, often perceived as sharply opposed to the 'practical'.

The impact this opposition makes on the theological curriculum is particularly visible in North America. A contrast may usefully be drawn at this point between two institutional forms of training for ministry, of which America and Germany provide the typical illustrations. In Germany, theological education is divided between academic study in a university and subsequent practical training in a parish and a church seminary; and for the academic part there is, strictly speaking, no curriculum at all, the students simply preparing themselves for comprehensive examinations as they think best. In the United States, by contrast, theological education typically occurs in a seminary for students who have a bachelor's degree in a subject other than theology. Since it can no longer be expected that every student will later serve an assistantship, the three-year seminary curriculum is designed to be complete, including practical experience through 'field work' (or, less often, an 'internship') in a congregation, hospital, prison, or community agency. Recent emphasis on specialized ministries, such as care of the emotionally disturbed, tends to heighten the expectation that a seminary training will furnish the special skills and experience needed for a special job; the role of the traditional academic fields in this preparation may be far from obvious.

Plainly, the curricular split between the academic and the practical and the fragmentation of both are not likely to be overcome unless the end-product of a theological education is redefined, and unless the dividing lines are redrawn to cut across the entrenched fields. The reason why we speak of a *theological* curriculum at all is because the chief requirement of Christian ministry is

neither a tool kit nor a walking encyclopaedia, but a person who has learned a
certain way of thinking that cannot be better
described than in Paul's phrase 'bringing
every thought into captivity to the obedience
of Christ' (II Cor. 10.5). The themes of such
reflection may perhaps be summed up as
'message', 'church' and 'world'. The question of curriculum is then what each of the
existing academic fields has to contribute on
these three themes; and the practical component is less a fourth field (though it is
bound to be that, too) than the constant
and explicit telos of all the fields, insofar as
they are genuinely united in a single enterprise. It must be admitted, however, that
attempts to reformulate the theological curriculum along some such lines as this have
usually foundered on the vested interests of
the individual fields, or have simply yielded
to such pragmatic – and perhaps equally
intractable – questions as how much Hebrew
and Greek a candidate for ministry can be
expected to absorb in the three years of a
packed agenda.

Much of the best thinking on theological
curriculum has to be gleaned from oral tradition, departmental minutes, and the bul-
letins or catalogues of seminaries and divinity schools. The underlying problems and
principles are usefully explored in the following: Gerhard Ebeling, *The Study of
Theology*, ET 1978; Edward Farley, *Theologia: The Fragmentation and Unity of Theological Education*, 1983; Kenneth E. Kirk (ed),
The Study of Theology, 1939; H. Richard
Niebuhr, *The Purpose of the Church and Its
Ministry: Reflections on the Aims of Theological Education*, 1956. H. Richard Niebuhr
and Daniel D. Williams (eds), *The Ministry
in Historical Perspectives*, 1956. On the relationship between theological education and
the newer programmes in religious studies,
see Claude Welch, *Graduate Education in
Religion: A Critical Appraisal*, 1971. A continuing forum for the discussion of curricular and related issues is the quarterly
Theological Education, published by the
Association of Theological Schools (ATS) in
North America.

B. A. GERRISH

Damnation

The idea of damnation has not been much
in fashion in the theological writing of this
century, although there can be no denying
that it is to be found in the pages of the NT
including the sayings of Jesus. Perhaps as a
consequence the belief in the possibility of
eternal damnation has appeared and reappeared in the history of the church although the 'Westminster' Confession of
Faith (1646), which is still the subordinate
doctrinal standard of the Church of Scotland, does overstate the case in its assertion
that 'The entire Christian Church, Greek
and Roman, Lutheran and Reformed, have
agreed in holding this truth that the penal
sufferings of the lost are to last for ever'.

Many fundamentalist groups and
branches of the church would certainly agree
in holding such a view, but many theologians and believers have offered theological
arguments for rejecting it. Most notably
Paul Tillich has pointed out that, 'The doctrine of the unity of everything in divine love
and in the Kingdom of God deprives the
symbol of hell of its character as "eternal
damnation".'

The difficulty, or even embarrassment,
felt over this doctrine clearly exemplified by
Tillich's discussion, has its roots in a very
interesting and important phenomenon of
European and Western culture. F. D. Maurice well illustrates the point, for alongside
his writings on the application of Christian
ethics to questions of social reform, he is
also remembered in part for his attack in
Theological Essays (1853) on the doctrine of
eternal damnation. In Victorian England
this caused quite a sensation and led to his
resignation from the Chair of Theology in
King's College London. In essence Maurice's opponents were protesting at the use of
moral criteria to evaluate theological beliefs.
The discomfort which many Christians feel
over the doctrine of eternal damnation, and
their grounds for rejecting it, are in the end
rooted in their moral beliefs, and the consequences of these beliefs for their understanding of what God would and would not
include in his providence *. The presence or
absence of a doctrine of eternal damnation
in a creed or theology tends to be closely
correlated with this point.

An interesting recent approach to the
matter rather stands on its head this tradition of rejecting the doctrine on moral
grounds. In his *A Rumour of Angels*, Peter
Berger offers as one of the pointers to an
awareness of 'the supernatural', an 'argu-

ment from damnation'. His counter-suggestion to liberal* theology is that on *ethical* grounds, some behaviour or deeds do call forth 'a curse of supernatural dimensions', and that as in the case of an Eichmann, 'a refusal to condemn in absolute terms would appear to offer prima facie evidence not only of a profound failure in the understanding of justice, but more profoundly of a fatal impairment of *humanitas*'. Perhaps, it is argued, only the idea of damnation which is to be found in a religious context, offers the outline of a response to the massacre of the innocent which avoids moral evasion.

P. L. Berger, *A Rumour of Angels*, 1970; P. Tillich, *Systematic Theology*, Vol. III. ch. XLI, 1964.

STEWART SUTHERLAND

Deacon

In the NT a 'deacon' (*diakonos*) is someone who 'serves' (*diakoneō*) or renders 'service' (*diakonia*). The words refer to assisting or helping through such actions as waiting on tables or attending to someone's personal needs. A deacon is a 'helper' who serves through acts of service. Accordingly, Jesus' whole ministry is one of 'serving' (Matt. 20.25–28), and that is to be the case with his followers (Mark. 9.35). However, while the word *diakonos* appears twenty-nine times in the NT, only in Phil. 1.1; I Tim. 3.8–13; Rom. 16.1 does it clearly refer to a designated church office. Acts 6.1–6, which has commonly been associated with the office of deacon, does not use the word *diakonos*. In sum, what had been an ordinary term for helpers or servants is used rather flexibly to describe the ministry of Jesus, the task of his followers, the mission of the church in the world, and an ecclesiastical office.

During the second century a definite church order began to emerge. Ignatius suggests an ordered ministry of bishops*, presbyters and deacons. According to the *Apostolic Tradition* of Hippolytus, deacons are to assist the bishops. During the third century, Rome was divided into seven administrative districts, each under a deacon. As deacons undertook various administrative, liturgical and pastoral tasks, their ministry was understood to be significant and lifelong, though occasionally deacons were elected to become bishops. Nevertheless, as early as the Council of

Nicaea in 325, there were specific restrictions placed upon the growing extent of diaconal functions. Hence, although the lifelong diaconate persisted in the Eastern churches, during the Middle Ages in the West the diaconate gradually became subordinate, temporary and largely ceremonial in function. Deprived of major significance, it became simply a brief step on the ladder to the priesthood*. As a result, an office which had evolved to order and incarnate usefulness became a fleeting symbol of hierarchical subordination.

During the sixteenth century, John Calvin and others sought to restore the diaconate to what they understood as its scriptural and lasting charitable and administrative functions. Other Protestants (such as the Congregationalists and Baptists) attempted to recover its liturgical functions. More recently, there have been various movements to reform the diaconate. Among the churches, Vatican II acted formally to open the way towards a reinstatement of the 'permanent' diaconate, with a variety of functions and open to married men of mature years. Meanwhile, the 'temporary' diaconate continues for celibate candidates for the priesthood. Other churches are devising other patterns; and the Faith and Order Commission of the World Council of Churches has explored diaconal ministries theologically. All the while, and underlying many of the recent changes, there is a growing rediscovery of the diaconal character and function of the whole 'people of God' as they are called to minister to the world.

Baptism, Eucharist and Ministry, WCC Report, 1982; Edward P. Echlin, SJ, *The Deacon in the Church*, 1971; James I. McCord and T. H. L. Parker (eds), *Service in Christ*, 1966; Lukas Vischer (ed), *The Ministry of Deacons*, 1965.

JOHN E. BURKHART

Deaconess

A deaconess is a member of an Order of women which some believe to have originated in the apostolic age and others in the third century, having been developed in the East from the active widows. Her duties were: 1. pastoral: she had to visit sick women in those heathen households where a male deacon might not fittingly enter; 2. liturgical: she administered the pre-baptismal unction to women candidates; she gave instruction to women after baptism; she kept the women's door at the eucharist and carried the reserved sacrament afterwards to sick women. The purpose and function of the Order, as understood in the patristic period, was clearly expressed by Epiphanius: 'Although there is an Order of deaconesses in the church, yet it is not for priestly service, nor to undertake anything of the sort, but on account of the modesty of the female sex with a view to either the occasion of baptism, or of inspection of illness, or of suffering and when the woman's body is bared, so that it might not be seen by the men officiating, but by the deaconess, who is directed by the priest to see to the woman when her body is bared' (*Adv.Haer*. iii.2.79).

In the nineteenth century the Order, which had fallen into abeyance in the early Middle Ages – it was abrogated by the councils at Epaon (517) and Orleans (533) but is found in some centres as late as the eleventh century – was revived in the Church of England, the Church of Scotland and by the Methodists, Mennonites and Lutherans. The functions of a deaconess at the present day are variously defined; e.g. they may include reading certain services, giving instruction and preaching. However, while, in the Church of England, she is admitted by the laying on of episcopal hands and acquires a lifelong status, it is by no means evident what the extent and limitations of her ministry should be. The circumstances that appear to have operated in the patristic * period to bring about the inauguration of the order – the seclusion of women and their nakedness at baptism – no longer obtain in the West. This does not mean that the Order is not required in modern circumstances, and many would assert its value within the overall ministry of the church. However, discussion of its future has become very much bound up with the question of the ordination of women to the priesthood. Until the resolution of this issue, no denomination can expect to be precise about the status of the order.

J. G. Davies, 'Deacons, Deaconesses and the Minor Orders in the Patristic Period', *JEH* XIV, 1963, pp. 1–15; J. Grierson, *The Deaconess*, 1981; Church of England, *The Ministry of Deacons and Deaconesses*, 1977.
                                    J. G. DAVIES

Death

From the OT perspective death is simply part of the natural order. Man is 'like the beasts that perish' (Ps. 49.12), 'the grass that withers and the flowers that fade' (Isa 40.7), and as such must expect to 'perish for ever like his own dung' (Job 20.7). This way of thinking derives naturally from the Hebrew insistence that man is not an incarnate soul * but an animated body, an irreducibly physical being whose only possible life is on this earth. And though some passages speak of the soul departing at death or of the spirit returning to God, the consensus of Hebrew scholarship is that in their original context such language does not imply any kind of belief in personal survival but refers solely to God taking back to himself his own life-sustaining spirit.

For much of Israel's history this view of death posed no religious threat because Jewish faith was initially understood in terms of a bond between God and the whole nation of Israel. But when stress came to be placed on personal fellowship between the individual and God, death was seen as undercutting the reality of that relationship and challenging the nature of God's concern (Eccles. 9.1–10; Job 10.8–13). This led some of the later psalmists towards a repudiation of the finality of death and towards a belief that God's power must extend beyond death (Pss. 16; 49; 73). But no unequivocal statement of a future hope occurs in the OT except for two very late passages (Isa. 26.19; Dan. 12.1) which affirm bodily resurrection. However, during the inter-testamental period resurrection * faith became more common, while simultaneously (possibly under Greek influence) some abandoned the old Hebrew anthropology in favour of body-soul dualism, and belief in the soul's immortality (Wisdom 3. 1–5). By the time of the NT at least four conflicting attitudes towards death can be discerned in Jewish thought: the Sadducees continued to equate death with personal extinction, the Pharisees looked for literal bodily resurrection at the last day, the Essenes taught the immortality of the soul, while the Covenanters of Qumran appeared to have embraced a doctrine of resurrection which did not entail the resuscitation of the corpse, but looked instead for a mode of existence in which people would be 'like angels in heaven'.

The NT sees death as a profoundly hostile force. According to Paul, death is the consequence of Adam's sin (Rom. 5.12), and the last enemy to be destroyed (I Cor. 15.26). He believes that Christ's resurrection has released man from the power of sin and death and expresses total confidence that death no longer has dominion (Rom. 6–9 and I Cor. 15 passim). There is no consistent anthropology in the NT nor even in the writings of individual authors. Paul's dominant theme is the resurrection of man into a 'spiritual body' (I Cor. 15.44), but at other times he almost seems to embrace a body-soul dualism (II Cor. 5.8). Jesus appears to have endorsed the notion of a quasi-angelic future life (Mark 12.25), yet the Gospel accounts of his resurrection imply a very much more literal understanding of what resurrection means. But whatever view is taken of the NT's anthropologies – and these are matters of fierce contention in contemporary scholarship – there is no doubt that the resurrection of Jesus is the central theme of the NT and that it transformed the first disciples' attitude towards death. It generated a sense of certainty about life after death which far transcended any earlier expressions of hope for a future life.

During the early centuries Christians became well-known for their fearlessness of death and their apparent certainty about life beyond it. Tertullian's expression 'the blood of the martyrs is the seed of the church' may be cited as one example of the converting power of this new conviction, while Bede's account of the conversion of Northern England provides another instance. However, from the sixth century onwards death assumed a more sinister aspect as the concepts of judgment, purgatory and hell began to loom ever larger in Christian thinking. Fear of death became a dominant theme of mediaeval religion and the contemplation of death a striking feature of Christian spirituality.

The classic Christian anthropology represents a blend of Hellenistic and Hebrew thinking. It assumes that the soul is a divine creation and destined for immortality, yet it stresses that the body is of crucial importance to us and that its resurrection is a *sine qua non* for any genuinely personal future existence. Death is seen as the 'parting of soul and body' and as setting a limit to our moral and spiritual development prior to the last judgment.

The validity of this picture has been seriously challenged in recent centuries by advances in the natural sciences which place man firmly within the natural order and call in question both the concept of the soul and the intelligibility of bodily resurrection. Consequently it has become increasingly common in both secular and Christian thought once more to see death as the end-point of the natural process of life and to eschew any serious thought concerning anything beyond our present existence. Certainly neither the mediaeval emphasis on the fear of death nor the confident hopes of the early Christians are much in evidence today. And though few churchmen explicitly repudiate belief in a future life, the virtual absence of reference to it in modern hymns, prayers and popular apologetic indicates how little part it plays in the contemporary Christian consciousness.

On the other hand, death is an issue of central significance in modern existentialist * philosophy which urges that awareness of our finitude is crucial to any truly authentic approach to life. At a popular level reports of the 'near-death experiences' of resuscitated persons have stimulated renewed interest in the possibility of human survival. And in the philosophies of mind and of religion there is a vigorous on-going debate concerning the intelligibility of belief in a future life and the importance of such belief to any coherent Christian theism.

See also **Identity, Life after Death**.

Paul Badham, *Christian Beliefs about Life after Death*, 1976; P. and L. Badham, *Immortality or Extinction?*, 1982; W. Eichrodt, *Theology of the Old Testament*, ET 1961, 1967; John Hick, *Death and Eternal Life*, 1976.

PAUL BADHAM

Death of God Theology

The theme of the death of God begins with J. P. F. Richter (d. 1825), better known as Jean Paul, and the 'Speech by the Dead Christ . . . that there is no God' in his *Siebenkäs* (1796/7). It was to fascinate the mind of the romantics. As early as 1802, Hegel had spoken of the Good Friday experience of the death of God as the basic religious awareness of modern times. In his philosophy the god-forsakenness of the world is a necessary element in the dialectical process, but not the final word. For Kierkegaard, contempt for outward things as godless, meaningless and absurd goes hand in hand with the existential inner life of subjective piety. For Nietzsche, God is dead and men have killed him; they must therefore themselves be gods or supermen. Man takes charge of history which he now builds on the corpse of God; the cross is the symbol of man's victory over God. In Feuerbach and Marx all the qualities which metaphysics has attributed to God are attributed to man, and theology becomes anthropology.

In the 1960s 'the death of God' served as a slogan for a number of 'radical' theologians, particularly in the USA, the most notable of whom were T. J. J. Altizer and Gabriel Vahanian, resulting in regular references to 'the death of God theology'. However, writers thus referred to had little in common other than acceptance of the label. Vahanian's *The Death of God* (1961), for example, was concerned with the death of God as a cultural fact; Altizer's *The Gospel of Christian Atheism* (1967) went back to Hegel's dialectic; theologians like William Hamilton and Paul van Buren adopted other approaches. One direct cause for theologies of this kind was Karl Barth's rejection of all natural theology *, leaving disillusioned pupils who could not share the positive side of his theology with little to fall back on. Being too simplistic, the term has virtually fallen out of current use.

T. J. J. Altizer and W. Hamilton, *Radical Theology and the Death of God*, 1966; Paul van Buren, *The Secular Meaning of the Gospel*, 1963.

ALAN RICHARDSON/JOHN BOWDEN

Decretals

In the wider sense a decretal was any letter containing a papal ruling, especially in matters affected by canonical discipline. In the strict sense decretals were papal rescripts which were canonically significant and issued in response to some appeal or particular enquiry (whether coming from an individual or from a whole province of the church). From the time of Damasus (d. 384) or at least Siricius (d. 399) popes began to issue such decretals. With Gregory VII in the mid-eleventh century the Western church became more centralized and de-

cretals increased in number. After the Middle Ages the term was limited to such solemn documents as those concerned with the canonization of saints or dogmatic definitions of faith.

Among early collections of decretals that of Dionysius Exiguus (*c.* 520), along with the *Hadriana Collectio* (774) and the *Hispana Collectio* (sixth–seventh century), enjoyed a long influence. In his *Decretum* (*c.* 1140) Gratian systematized canon law * and besides other documents incorporated decretal letters in his work. He took over some items from the *False Decretals*, a collection which among other things contained papal letters forged and assembled in France around 850.

Three later collections of decretals were to make up the official corpus of canon law: the *Decretales* of Gregory IX (1234), the *Liber Sextus* of Boniface VIII (1298) and the *Constitutiones Clementinae* of Clement V (1305–1314).

GERALD O'COLLINS

Dedication *see* **Consecration**

Deification

Deification (Greek *theosis*) is for Orthodoxy the goal of every Christian. Man, according to the Bible, is 'made in the image and likeness of God' (cf. Gen. 1.26), and the Fathers commonly distinguish between these two words. The image refers to man's reason and freedom, that which distinguishes him from the animals and makes him kin to God, while 'likeness' refers to 'assimilation to God through virtues' (St John of Damascus). It is possible for man to become like God, to become deified, to become god by grace. This doctrine is based on many passages of both OT and NT (e.g. Ps. 82 (81).6; II Peter 1.4), and it is essentially the teaching both of St Paul, though he tends to use the language of filial adoption (cf. Rom. 8.9–17; Gal. 4.5–7), and the Fourth Gospel (cf. 17.21–23).

The language of II Peter is taken up by St Irenaeus, in his famous phrase, 'if the Word has been made man, it is so that men may be made gods' (*Adv. Haer* V, Pref.), and becomes the standard in Greek theology. In the fourth century St Athanasius repeats Irenaeus almost word for word, and in the fifth century St Cyril of Alexandria says that we shall become sons 'by participation' (Greek *methexis*). Deification is the central idea in the spirituality of St Maximus the Confessor, for whom the doctrine is the corollary of the Incarnation: 'Deification, briefly, is the encompassing and fulfilment of all times and ages, and of all that exists in either. This encompassing and fulfilment is the union, in the person granted salvation, of his authentic origin with his real authentic consummation' (*Philokalia*, Vol. 2, ET 1981, p. 240), and St Symeon the New Theologian at the end of the tenth century writes, 'He who is God by nature converses with those whom he has made gods by grace, as a friend converses with his friends, face to face.'

In reading these texts it is important to bear in mind the distinction traditionally made in Orthodox theology between God's essence* and his energies. The former remains totally mysterious and inaccessible (cf. I Tim. 6.16) to any created being; deification, sharing in the divine nature, means sharing in God's energies which, however, are truly God in his action and self-disclosure. As St Basil says, in knowing God's energies it is truly God whom we know.

Finally, it should be noted that deification does not mean absorption into God, since the deified creature remains itself and distinct. It is the whole human being, body and soul, who is transfigured in the Spirit into the likeness of the divine nature, and deification is the goal of every Christian, to be reached by the faithful following of Christ in the common life of his body the church.

Clear treatments of this are to be found in V. Lossky, *The Vision of God*, ET 1963; *The Mystical Theology of the Eastern Church*, ET 1957; K. Ware, *The Orthodox Church*, 1973.

SYMEON LASH

Deism

Etymologically this word (from the Latin *deus*) is parallel to 'theism' (from the Greek *theos*), and would seem simply to indicate belief in the existence of a god or gods. Although in the seventeenth century the words were sometimes used interchangeably as the contrary to 'atheist', in practice they have come to have separate connotations. 'Deism' is now used to refer to belief in the existence of a supreme being who is regarded as the ultimate source of reality and ground of value but as not intervening in natural and historical processes by way of particular providences, revelations and salvific acts. The common use of 'theism'*, in contrast, does not have these negative implications.

In the history of thought the description deism designates a movement, largely British, which flourished in the latter part of the seventeenth and through the eighteenth century. The designation, though, is vague because it refers to a general attitude or approach to religious understanding much more than to a specifiable set of doctrines. In many respects its descriptive content is as imprecise as current uses of the word 'radical'. Although the term is used pejoratively, what is being disapproved of thereby depends upon the positions of the persons using it. All that may safely be inferred is that they consider the person or movement so described as challenging what ought to be accepted with confidence. Generally though, the deists may be said to be those at this time who apply the principles of the Enlightenment*, and especially the canon of reason, to religious belief in a critical way in order to establish what it is and what it is not reasonable to believe about God. As a consequence they tend to stress the importance of following reason, the sufficiency of natural religion and the need for toleration. Negatively they are likely to express doubts about belief in mysteries such as the Incarnation and the Trinity, in the reality of immortality, revelations and miraculous interventions, and in the authority of the Bible and of the priesthood. It must be stressed, though, that there is no set of ideas which links the deists together. According to Edward Stillingfleet (1639–1699), a deist accepts 'the Being and Providence of God' but has 'a mean esteem' of Christianity and the scriptures. Samuel Clarke (1675–1729), though, distinguishes four sorts of deists in his Boyle Lectures for 1705: some hold God exists but has no dealings with the world; others maintain 'the Providence of God' but deny that he is concerned about morality; a third group entertains 'right Apprehensions' about God but rejects belief in immortality; finally there are 'the only True Deists' – these will accept only what is 'discoverable by the Light of Nature' and refuse all reference to revelations. As for Daniel Waterland (1683–1740), he regards contemporary deism as *de facto* atheism, characterized by individualism, 'libertinism' and 'irreligion'.

Just as it is impossible to define deism

clearly by reference to doctrines, so it is difficult to decide who is to be classed as a deist and who not. It is hard, for example, to see where to draw the line between some supposed deists and such upholders of self-consciously rational views of Christianity as Ralph Cudworth (1617–1688) and other Cambridge Platonists *, John Locke (1632–1704) and John Tillotson (1630–1694). The last-mentioned is described by Anthony Collins (1676–1729), an undisputed deist, as one who is acknowledged as their head by 'all English free-thinkers', and yet this arch-bishop's printed sermons enjoyed consider-able popularity in church circles for several decades after his death. In the end it seems that to a large extent the traditional canon of deistical writers was determined by early critical commentators on this supposed movement – notably Thomas Halyburton (1674–1712), Philip Skelton (1707–1787) and, above all, John Leland (1691–1766) in his *View of the Principal Deistical Writers* (first published in 1754). According to the usual lists the deists, beginning with Edward, Lord Herbert of Cherbury (1583?–1648), include Charles Blount (1654–1693), John Toland (1670–1722), Anthony Collins (1676–1729), William Wollaston (1660–1724), Matthew Tindal (1657?–1733), Thomas Woolston (1670–1731), Bernard Mandeville (1670–1733), Anthony, Earl of Shaftesbury (1671–1713), Thomas Chubb (1679–1746), Thomas Morgan (?–1743), Henry St John, Viscount Bolingbroke (1678–1751) and Peter Annet (1693–1769). Leland's review also has a long discussion of David Hume (1711–1776), but it is ques-tionable whether he ought to be regarded as belonging to the deist movement. Although his essays on miracles, on a particular pro-vidence and a future state, and on the origin of religion may be seen as deistic, the basic thrust of his work is to cast doubt on all arguments which purport to show the reas-onableness of belief in God. He is therefore better classed as a sceptic whose penetrating criticisms threatened the foundations of de-istic as well as of more orthodox beliefs. As for challengers to deism on behalf of more or less traditional understandings of Christ-ianity, the leading apologists include Samuel Clarke, Richard Bentley (1662–1742), George Berkeley (1685–1753), Joseph Butler (1692–1752) and, at the end of the period, William Paley (1743–1805) together

with others, such as William Law (1686–1761) and Henry Dodwell (?–1784), who raised doubts about the normative status of reason in matters of religious belief. On the Continent leading deistic writers in-clude Voltaire (1694–1778) and Jean-Jacques Rousseau (1712–1778) in France, and Hermann Samuel Reimarus (1694–1768), Gotthold Ephraim Lessing (1729–1781) and, at least in certain respects, Immanuel Kant (1724–1804) in Germany. Across the Atlantic Benjamin Franklin (1706–1790), Thomas Jefferson (1743–1826), and George Washington (1732–1799) can be placed in this movement. Its most vigorous proponent there, however, was Thomas Paine (1737–1809), who initiated a new phase of popular artisan deism which, connected with radical politi-cal movements, extended the deist move-ment well into the nineteenth cen-tury.

The variety of positions, sometimes mutually conflicting, maintained by the above authors strongly suggests that the label deist is of dubious value for studies of seventeenth-and eighteenth-century thought, especially when it is supposed to designate a coherent movement opposing Christianity. What per-haps it can be held to indicate is the more critical, at the extreme virulently critical, flank of a broad movement which attempts to interpret religious belief in ways that avoid the bigotry of unreflective faith and the doubts of utterly sceptical reason. For some it involves an attempt to replace Christianity by a more 'reasonable' faith; for others its pur-pose is to produce a more 'reasonable' version of Christianity. As such it is an important, though neglected, early chapter in the story of the modernizing, secularizing and uni-versalizing of belief in God.

Gerald R. Cragg, *From Puritanism to the Age of Reason, A Study of Changes in Re-ligious Thought within the Church of Eng-land, 1660–1700,* 1950; Gerald R. Cragg, *Reason and Authority in the Eighteenth Cen-tury,* 1964; Paul Hazard, *European Thought in the Eighteenth Century,* ET 1954; Herbert M. Morais, *Deism in Eighteenth Century America,* 1934; John Redwood, *Reason, Ridicule and Religion, The Age of Enlighten-ment in England,* 1976; Leslie Stephen, *His-tory of English Thought in the Eighteenth Century,* 2 vols, ³1902; Roland S. Stromberg, *Religious Liberalism in Eighteenth-Century England*, 1954.

DAVID A. PAILIN

Demiurge

In his myth of the creation of the world Plato in the *Timaeus* spoke poetically of the Creator as a craftsman (in Greek, *demiourgos*). The Greek Fathers naturally (though hardly accurately) hailed Plato as the Greek Moses (Moses, of course, was assumed to be the author of Genesis). Hence the word passed into Greek Christian usage as the equivalent of 'Creator'. But it fell into disrepute as a consequence of its having been adopted by the Gnostics * as the designation of the inferior deity who had made the world and had made it badly.

ALAN RICHARDSON

Demonology, Demons

'Demon' derives from the Greek *daimōn* or *daimonion*. The later Platonists placed *daimonia* in an ontological level between gods and humans. The apocalyptic writers and the Christians coalesced *daimonia* with the Hebrew *malakim*, Greek *angeloi*, 'messenger' spirits, and established a new division into good spirits ('angels') and evil ones ('demons'), a term that now became pejorative). In the NT, demons aid the Devil's opposition to God's saving grace by harming humans, but God's power limits and repels them, the most common miracles of Christ being worked against demons. The Fathers defined the demons as the fallen angels, who had joined Satan in his revolt against God and share his functions as tempters and punishers. Some Fathers contrasted a mystical body of Satan, composed of fallen angels and wicked humans, to the mystical body of Christ. Theologians identified the pagan gods as demons and also associated Mediterranean and Northern nature-spirits to the concept. The distinction between Satan, the chief of all evil powers, and his demon subordinates remained theologically firm, but in homilies, exempla, folklore, and popular usage the terms were often confused (French *le démon* can mean 'Devil', and English usage permits 'devils' for 'demons'). The Desert Fathers, whose influence persisted through the Middle Ages and Reformation, perceived demons as swarming thickly, always and everywhere alert to every opportunity of harming humans and spiting God. Demons 'obsess', attacking a person from without, or 'possess', entering the body and seizing it from within. They cause disease, accidents, madness and death; they also hurt animals and causes natural disasters. Their greatest joy is temptation, which is aimed at the corruption of the soul. Evagrius described how demons watch every thought, and whenever they see someone opening even a tiny hole in the mind to sin, they rush through the breach. God never gives demons the power to tempt beyond our ability to resist, and they may be repelled by calling on God's power through repentance, prayer, the sign of the cross, exorcism, or the immediate intervention of a holy man or woman. Literal belief in swarming hordes of demons was dominant from the fourteenth to the seventeenth century, fuelling the witch-craze. But from the late seventeenth century belief declined rapidly owing to reaction against the excesses of the witch-craze, to the Reformers (who had more theological use for the Devil than for demons), and to rationalism, liberalism and empiricism, which attributed most of the activities hitherto associated with demons to natural causes. The growth of interest in the Devil since 1939 has not extended to demons, except among certain evangelical groups who, relying upon the undeniable NT support for the existence of demons, have revived exorcism.

N. Cohn, *Europe's Inner Demons*, 1975; H. A. Kelly, *The Devil, Demonology, and Witchcraft*, [2]1974; E. Langton, *Essentials of Demonology*, 1949; D. P. Walker, *Unclean Spirits*, 1981.

JEFFREY BURTON RUSSELL

Demythologizing

A method of interpreting the NT (German: *Entmythologisierung*). The term was used by Rudolf Bultmann in 1941 in an essay entitled 'New Testament and Mythology'. Bultmann was concerned that the central proclamation of the NT cannot reach people today because it is so much covered up in mythical trappings from the first century – voices from heaven, angelic visitors, demon posessions, a coming end of the world, ascension into heaven and so on. No doubt people today are credulous in many ways, but their outlook has been sufficiently influenced by science and technology as to make such events seem incredible. These mythical trappings constitute an obstacle or scandal in the way of hearing and responding to the gospel, but it is not the genuine scandal which, for Bultmann, is the surrender of self-centredness and self-sufficiency and to live by God's grace. So if the gospel is to be heard by modern persons, it must be set free from mythology. Perhaps the word 'demythologizing' was unfortunate, since it would most naturally be taken to mean the elimination of myth from the NT, and that would demand such severe surgery that very little would be left. But this is not what Bultmann has in mind. Indeed, he is critical of nineteenth-century liberal theologians who simply ignored the mythological parts of the NT, and reduced the gospel to some simple formula like the fatherhood of God and the brotherhood of man. The mythology is saying something important and cannot just be eliminated, but it needs interpretation if men and women today are to hear what it is saying. Bultmann believes that mythology gives expression to a self-understanding*. The myth of creation, for instance, expresses the human sense of dependence on a transcendent reality. So the work of demythologizing consists in making explicit the self-understanding concealed in any particular piece of mythology. It will be seen that his approach to the NT has a strong ethical slant. According to Bultmann, the right question to put to the sacred texts is: Into what self-understanding does this direct me? Thus, to believe in the cross of Christ and its saving efficacy is not to accept some theory of ransom or sacrifice or satisfaction, but, in Bultmann's words, to make Christ's cross one's own, that is to say, to die to oneself and enter on the new life of love and self-giving. But to be able to ask the question of human self-understanding implies that one must already have a language in which to express it, other than the language of mythology. This is where Bultmann's interest in existentialism* comes in, and demythologizing might have been better described as 'existential interpretation'. Existentialist philosophy, especially the early philosophy of Martin Heidegger, supplies Bultmann with a terminology into which the mythology of the NT can be translated. The story of the divine being who comes down from heaven and atones by his blood for the sins of mankind is interpreted in terms of the Crucified One who speaks the ultimate

word that summons human beings to their authentic existence. While Bultmann's demythologizing has undoubtedly given to the NT and its message a new relevance and vitality for some people, it gives rise also to some difficult questions. Does it not mean that the Christian proclamation can be dissolved into a philosophy of authentic human existence, in which there is no need to mention God or Christ? Bultmann vigorously denies this, claiming a decisive role for Christ as the one who brings God's word to man, but to claim this, one would need to go beyond an existential interpretation of the NT. Again, is God subjectivized in an existential interpretation? Bultmann denies this, too, but it is instructive to note that Tillich remarked that while he agreed with Bultmann on the need for demythologizing, this calls for an ontological as well as an existential interpretation (*see also* **Ontology**). Finally, one may ask whether – as in the idealist* philosophy of an earlier time – the gospel message has become the proclamation of a timeless possibility of salvation, set free from its place in history, so that nothing is left of the vaunted historical character of Christianity or of the 'once for all' work of Christ or of his coming in the fullness of time. Bultmann does in fact assert the historical reality of Jesus, but he so devalues objective historical events that they do not seem to retain any importance in his theology.

See also **Myth, Hermeneutics**.

R. Bultmann, *Jesus Christ and Mythology*, ET 1958; H-W. Bartsch (ed), *Kerygma and Myth* (Bultmann's original essay with critical responses), ET 1953; J. Macquarrie, *An Existentialist Theology*, 1955.

JOHN MACQUARRIE

Dependence

The Christian doctrine of creation*, avoiding pantheism* and dualism*, has usually asserted that God, in his unique and distinctive order of being, creates the world *ex nihilo*. This means that all existents, belonging to a different order, viz., that of created being, depend utterly and ultimately on God for their original and continued existence. Without God's purposive willing and creating, there would be nothing. Human beings belong to this *dependent* order.

But the doctrine of creation also affirms

that a relative freedom or *in*dependence is part of what God creates in and for the world and for human beings. In their independent order of being, persons are vouchsafed some liberty – to act, to invent, to fulfil God's purposes. 'He has committed some of the power of causation to the persons whom he has made' (L. H. De Wolf). The proper human response to God's gift of freedom is, therefore, the active continuation of his purposes in the human sphere.

In some traditions of piety and theology this notion of dependence upon God is, however, interpreted in terms of an extreme, even servile, submission to God in matters large and small. Here the creature's selfhood is constantly overwhelmed by the Creator who has perhaps already predetermined the creature's ultimate fate. This relationship is rendered even more dependent by a sense of the impotence caused by human sin * and by the need for total reliance upon divine redemption *. Such a theology or piety will often treat human effort and achievement as irrelevant or spiritually suspect. Because of his incompatibility with the idea of an *in*dependence given to humans by God, 'this is the God Nietzsche said had to be killed because nobody can tolerate being made into a mere object of absolute knowledge and absolute control' (P. Tillich).

A radically submissive view of human life is also sometimes reflected in the idea of 'orders of creation' (the state, the family etc.) which themselves demand from human beings dependent conformity. This can provoke excessive deference towards, for example, the *status quo* in the political realm, and immobility in the social order.

Instead, we should see no theoretical incompatibility between human dependence and relative human freedom or autonomy *. God as Creator creates, among other things, human freedom to create. Human beings may draw upon that freedom in order to initiate new forms of individual and collective history in accord with the normative design of God. But in practice sin deprives human beings of their relative independence, making them victims of all kinds of impairment. Paradoxically, distance from God leads to unfreedom rather than to freedom. And so redemption in and by Christ, with its renewed gift of freedom, strengthens and enables human capacities of action and creation.

Though these assertions may sound fine in principle, distinctions between dependence, autonomy and sin are difficult to handle amid the contingencies of history and the manifold ambiguities of human existence. But it is clear that dependence upon God *need* not lead either to that alienation * from terrestrial effort of which Marxism often accuses Christianity or to that condition of enervating over-dependency identified by psychology. However, it must be admitted that, in practice, Christians have often traded excessive dependence for the reward of an alleged security and that collective Christianity has frequently been the natural ally of reaction. As with the human child, individual and corporate growth to maturity before God and other persons hangs upon a subtle interplay of firm dependence and actual, though limited, freedom.

Gordon D. Kaufman, *Systematic Theology*, 1968, Parts 2 and 3; Karl Rahner, *Theological Investigations* 2, 1963, pp. 235–63; Richard Rubenstein, *The Religious Imagination*, 1968, chs. 5–8.

A. O. DYSON

Deposit of Faith

The classical term for the definitive revelation of God given in Jesus Christ and entrusted to the church to be preserved and proclaimed with fidelity.

Jewish, Greek and Roman law allowed for contracts whereby someone could entrust to another a *depositum* or *paratheke* which was to be guarded faithfully. The Pastoral Letters apply this legal term analogously to the apostolic tradition (behind which was the divine self-revelation in Christ) that had been committed for safekeeping and preaching to the disciples of Paul (I Tim. 6.20; II Tim. 1.12, 14).

The analogy can be and at times has been taken up wrongly either by reifying revelation and/or by reducing the church to the 'hierarchy' *. First, revelation means the personal disclosure of the triune God through the incarnation, life, death and resurrection of Christ, and the coming of the Holy Spirit. It is not to be reified as if it were merely a set of divinely revealed teachings that should be repeated mechanically till the end of time. Fidelity to the living presence of Christ demands fresh understanding and interpretation as new situations and challenges arise. Second, in different ways all believers have the help of the Holy Spirit to carry out their responsibility of maintaining and sharing with others the good news of God's final revelation in Christ. They all enjoy the 'instinct of faith' (see **Faith**) to preserve faithfully the 'deposit of faith'. Within the community of Christians, bishops have a special duty of 'authentically' preserving and proclaiming that 'deposit'.

Article 10 of Vatican II's Dogmatic Constitution on Divine Revelation (*Dei Verbum*), which speaks three times of 'the deposit of faith', does so dynamically to portray it as the word of God to be 'held to, practised and professed' by the whole church.

See also **Revelation, Tradition**.

Yves Congar, *Tradition and Traditions*, ET 1966, pp. 19ff., 237ff.

GERALD O'COLLINS

Depravity, Total

The Reformed doctrine, given classical expression by John Calvin *, of the 'depravity and corruption' of all man's faculties, natural and supernatural, as a consequence of the Fall.* Thus Calvin claimed that since the Fall man is depraved 'by nature', though he recognized a primary sense of 'nature' – before the Fall – in which man is good. Apparent manifestations of 'good nature' or virtue in unregenerate men (pre-Christian pagans, unbelievers) are illusory and worthless, the consequence of God's 'restraining grace' to preserve society which otherwise would be overwhelmed by 'many kinds of foulness'.

Calvin recognizes the survival in man of some natural gifts, in particular reason, by which man is distinguished from the beasts, but because of its dullness, the mind cannot come to know God by nature, though God is revealed in the natural order. Nevertheless, human beings may excel in the arts and sciences, which are natural gifts, though this excellence is itself the work of the Holy spirit displaying God's special grace in 'common nature'. Calvin's use of 'common grace' to moderate the consequences of his teaching on depravity has remained a difficult area for Reformed theology and has affected Prot-

estant attitudes to the natural world and 'secular activity'.

The Reformed doctrine of depravity contrasts strongly with mediaeval and Tridentine R C teaching on the freedom of the will (see **Free Will**): Calvin denied any freedom to the unregenerate will except the freedom to sin. Man is not compelled by any force outside himself to sin; he himself naturally gravitates to sin because of his corruption. In this limited sense only is he free.

Calvin, *Institutes of the Christian Religion*, Book 1, 1–5; 2, 1–5, LCC, 1960.

EAMON DUFFY

Descent into Hell, The

There are only two places in the NT where Christ's descent into hell is absolutely explicitly referred to, and one of these has often been interpreted differently. These are I Peter 3.19f.; 4.6 and Eph. 4.9f. The author of I Peter certainly represents Christ as preaching to the spirits that are in prison, whether this means those who died in the Flood or the rebellious angels. The author of Ephesians very probably refers to Christ's triumph over the elemental spirits in his interpretation of Ps. 68. But there are several other passages in the NT where Christ's presence among the dead, or his victory over the realm of the dead, is at least alluded to; compare Matt. 27.52; Luke 23.43; Acts 2.27, 31; Phil. 2.10; I Tim. 3.16; Rev. 5.13. The main emphasis in the NT references is on the completeness of Christ's victory by means of the cross and resurrection *. The I Peter passage introduces another motif: the doctrine of the descent helps to answer the question: 'what of those who have died before the incarnation?' This is undoubtedly how we should interpret the article in the Apostles' Creed, 'He descended into hell'.

Owing to Augustine's failure to distinguish between Hades (the place of the dead) and Gehenna (the place of punishment), theologians in the West have occasionally interpreted the descent into hell as meaning that Christ underwent the punishment, or at least the experience, of condemned sinners. Calvin is the most famous exponent of this view, and Karl Barth has adopted a modified form of it. But there is no justification of this in scripture. Apart from Barth, modern theologians have tended to adopt one of three methods of dealing with this latecomer to the Creed. They can reject it altogether: for example, F. W. Beare calls it 'a fantastic dream'; or they may follow the main N T tradition and say that it underlines the completeness of Christ's victory; or they may take it as emphasizing that Christ really died as man, as contrasted, for instance, with the Muslim claim that he never really died. This last is no doubt legitimate, but has no more claim to scriptural support than Calvin's interpretation. The suggestion found in I Peter that the descent gave an opportunity for those who died before Christ to hear the gospel is rather too mythological for modern minds, but it may be regarded as a hopeful symbol of the destiny of those who have died without ever having heard the good news of Christ. Some means must be found for safeguarding the insight that the generations before Christ were not deprived of the gospel.

Commentaries on I Peter, especially those by E. G. Selwyn (1946) and F. W. Beare (1947). Since E. H. Plumptre's *The Spirits in Prison* (1871), no single book of the subject in English has appeared but the following is relevant: H. A. Blair, *The Creed Behind the Creeds*, 1955; see also A. T. Hanson, *The New Testament Interpretation of Scripture*, 1980, pp. 122–56.

A. T. HANSON

Design, Argument from
see **Arguments for the Existence of God**

Determinism

This term is used in a variety of ways, and is often found combined with other words. Two of these combinations are of special importance for theology: theological determinism and physical (or scientific) determinism. In both cases the root idea is that there is an inevitability or necessity in events, although when it is asked what this inevitability means the answer is often unclear. Usually, though not always, this inevitability is linked with the theoretical possibility of total predictability.

Theological determinism is implicit in many parts of the Bible, and has often been held to be a necessary consequence of the sovereignty of God. For example, Amos sees the fall of a city as determined by God (3.6). Calvin's theology is an example of this view, in which 'not a drop of rain falls without the express command of God' (*Inst*. I, XVI, 5). However, if God directly controls every event, two major problems arise. 1. How can man be genuinely free and responsible, as the Bible also assumes? 2. How can it be *meaningful* to say that God is good (since his sheer will is to decide what counts as good and bad)? In the light of these difficulties most theologians have tried to combine a doctrine of sovereignty that is less extreme than Calvin's with some degree of autonomy in the world order, and especially in man. Aquinas' doctrine of secondary causality is one such attempt. Some more radical thinkers, including process philosophers, have been led to limit the area of God's sovereignty, and have allowed for a radical contingency in events, at least in the short run (*see* **Process Theology**).

Although physical determinism has antecedents, as in the philosophy of Democritus, it has only been a major concern of theologians since the rise of modern science, which raises the question 'What room can a universal causality leave for human freedom, especially when it is applied to human thought and action, as in modern behaviourism?' In the debate on this issue some important distinctions must be born in mind. 'Hard determinism' is used to indicate the view that all events are rigorously determined *and* that moral categories (such as 'ought' and 'guilt') are really meaningless. 'Soft determinism' also holds that all events are determined, but claims that moral categories still have a significant meaning (e.g. they are important aspects of social engineering). 'Indeterminism' is sometimes used as another term for belief in free will, or 'libertarianism', but this can be misleading. Since around 1925, and the advent of quantum mechanics, many physicists have believed in the indeterminism of matter at the subatomic level. However, they have disagreed profoundly as to whether this indeterminacy, or randomness, is a purely epistemological one, or whether it reflects what is sometimes called an 'ontological indeterminism'. Any ontological indeterminism can be just as much a threat to free will as can classical determinism, so that it is better to distinguish belief in free will from both determinism and indeterminism.

See also **Causality**, **Foreknowledge**, **Freewill** (including bibliography), **Predestination**.

M. J. LANGFORD

Deus absconditus

Deus absconditus, 'the hidden God', is a phrase peculiarly associated with the theology of Luther. It is the common testimony of the religious consciousness that God transcends human understanding. As Augustine said, if we understood God, then that would not be God any more. Some theologians have gone to very great lengths to preserve the mystery of God. The negative theology, which contents itself with saying what God is *not*, was developed by Clement of Alexandria, Dionysius the Areopagite and others, and was held to be more fundamental than any affirmative theology. Yet, if carried to excessive lengths, how would belief in a hidden God differ from atheism *? Again, how can the doctrine be reconciled with God's revelation * in Christ? It might be replied that the revelation of God in the finite must also be a veiling, so that the *Deus revelatus* is at the same time a *Deus velatus*. But theologians willing to admit such a veiling, e.g. Karl Barth, are still critical of Luther's 'hidden God', for that seems to envisage the possibility of something in God which contradicts the revelation in Christ. On the other hand, Otto has defended Luther, holding that the *Deus absconditus* is no *Deus ignotus*, the 'unknown God' of the Athenians, and that the use of the phrase testifies to Luther's deep sense of the numinous character of God. It could be argued that a decent silence about God is in many cases preferable to an over-familiarity.

See also **God.**

JOHN MACQUARRIE

Deus a se *see* Aseity

Deus Pro Nobis

The phrase means 'God on our behalf' or 'God for us', or in the singular, 'God working on my behalf'. In addition to the Pauline sense of God identifying himself with man for the purpose of man's redemption * here on earth and in eternity (Rom. 8.31), it has the clear reference to what is generally called the substitutionary theory of the atonement * (II Cor. 5.21; Gal. 3.13; Eph. 5.2; I Thess. 5.10; Titus 2.14; Heb. 6.20; 9.12, 24; 10.20; I Peter 2.21; 4.1). The idea goes back to Christ himself, 'The Son of Man . . . came not to be served but to serve, and to give his life as a ransom for many' (Mark 10.45). The significance lies not only in the word ransom but in the 'for many' (Greek *anti pollon*). The meaning of *anti* is 'instead of' and cannot properly be escaped or explained away. The thought is echoed in I Tim. 2.6 with its use of *antilutron* and perhaps also in Titus 2.14, where the verb *lutroō* occurs. It can hardly be doubted that Isa. 53, and indeed the 'servant passages' generally, have had considerable influence on the interpretation of Christ's death as a substitution. The doctrine was preserved in the mediaeval theories of atonement and further underwent a strong revival under Luther. Luther argued, 'This "for me" or "for us", when believed, constitutes true faith, and differentiates this faith from every other kind of faith, which merely hears the facts of history' (*WA* 39.1.46.7–8). Luther was arguing for a true faith (*fides vera*) which puts its whole trust in God, over against an historic faith (*fides historica*) or mere acceptance of fact (*frigida opinio*). Barth's energetic maintenance of the idea, which was actually a revival of Luther's theology, has had considerable influence on much contemporary theology. The doctrine has always been an essential plank in the militant evangelical platform, and has had a not inconsiderable influence in existentialist * circles, particularly in Germany.

JAMES ATKINSON

Development, Doctrinal

To say that Christian doctrine has a history is to say that it has changed. And a constant factor in the promotion of or resistance to doctrinal change has been a concern to maintain the identity of Christianity, to proclaim no other message than the gospel once delivered. Mere repetition of ancient words has never seemed a sufficient condition of maintained identity of meaning: not to those who fought for or against the '*homoousios* *', nor to the Schoolmen writing theologies of history or elaborating doctrines of the 'senses' * of scripture. Until quite recently, however, it was change that was problematic and maintained identity a value to be protected. Today, identity is sought with difficulty across the pervasiveness of change. The rise and fall of theories of 'doctrinal development', most in vogue in RC theology in the first half of the twentieth century, marked the transition from a 'modern' to a post-modern perception of the problem.

In the apologetic mood of seventeenth-century theological polemic, 'novelty' was the charge levelled at each other by Catholics and Protestants. Catholics had corrupted the ancient faith by addition, Protestants by departing from perennial belief and custom. Both Catholics and Protestants knew, however, that what each of them said today was not identical with what had been said in the past. In the seventeenth and eighteenth centuries, both traditions thus sought to ease the problem by appeal to sharp distinctions between immutable revelation and a progressive understanding of that revelation in the light of better scholarship or through processes of deductive inference.

In the 1830s, J. H. Newman's polemic against Roman Catholicism still focussed on the charge that Catholics had 'added' to the ancient faith. This was the charge he sought to rebut when, in 1845, he wrote the *Essay on the Development of Christian Doctrine* to account for his decision to become a Roman Catholic. The *Essay* was treated with considerable respect, less understanding and a little suspicion, by twentieth-century elaborators of 'theories' of doctrinal development. Newman did not, however, have a 'theory' of development in the modern sense: it was the *fact* of 'development' which he offered as a 'hypothesis', alternative both to an 'immutability' rendered untenable by historical scholarship and a recognition of the pervasiveness of change, and to a 'corruption' amounting to loss of identity. He was not a liberal, arguing for doctrinal 'progress'; his argument was that, of all forms of nineteenth-century Christianity, Roman Catholicism could be seen, in the light of his guiding hypothesis, to be the *least unlike* the church of the Fathers.

In recent decades, the notion of 'development', with its overtones of nineteenth-century 'evolutionary' accounts of social and intellectual history, has come to seem more like a statement of the problem than a programme for its solution, thought it may still serve as a reminder that there is an element of irreversibility in doctrinal history. But the focus has shifted. Increasingly, general philosophies of historical existence and interpretation, or 'hermeneutics'* provide the framework within which both Catholic and Protestant theologians seek to negotiate the 'gap' between, on the one hand, Christian origins and their subsequent developments and, on the other, whatever it is that we might seek to say and think and do, today, in attempted fidelity to the truth of the gospel and its history. (*See also* **Doctrine, Theology, Tradition**).

O. Chadwick, *From Bossuet to Newman*, 1957; N. L. A. Lash, *Change in Focus*, 1973; *Newman on Development*, 1975; M. F. Wiles, *The Making of Christian Doctrine*, 1967.

NICHOLAS LASH

Devil

The word derives from Old English *deofel*, Latin *diabolus*, Greek *diabolos*, a direct translation of Hebrew *satan*, 'adversary, opponent, one who obstructs'. In Christianity the Devil is called Satan, Lucifer, less frequently Beelzebub, Belial, etc. Most other religions posit ambivalent deities rather than a chief of all evil; Iranian dualist Mazdaism is an exception. In ancient Hebrew religion Yahweh was originally perceived as ambivalent, but in time only good qualities came to be ascribed to the Lord, evil being attributed to Satan. This distinction began in the OT but became markedly dualist only in apocalyptic Judaism. Influenced by Mazdaism and Hebrew apocalyptic* some early Christians, e.g. the Gnostics*, became strongly dualist, but most Christians hewed to the monist view that the Devil was a creature, not an independent principle. Rabbinical Judaism reacted against apocalyptic and minimized Satan's role, but he continued important in Christianity. The NT assumes the reality of Satan, though vaguely defined: he is Christ's tempter in the wilderness and prince of this world (*aiōn, kosmos*), lord of the old age that comes to an end with Christ. The Fathers offered further definition: Satan was created by God with a good nature; he was a great angel who fell of his own free will, convincing many angels to join him; he was cast out of heaven with his followers down to the lower air, earth, or underworld; he tempted humanity to original sin; he ruled the world under God's permission, testing and punishing. His power was broken by Christ, yet God allows him limited scope till the end of the world, when he will be defeated for ever. The Desert

Fathers felt his presence everywhere. Mediaeval writers addressed problems left unresolved by the Fathers: the question of the freedom of man and angel *vis-à-vis* the predestining omnipotence of God; the role of Satan in salvation theory (Anselm emphasized sacrifice over ransom, diminishing Satan's role). Homilies, exempla and folklore popularized the sense of a powerful, ubiquitous Devil, a view enhanced by the spread of Cathar dualism from the twelfth century. From the fourteenth to the seventeenth century belief in Satan's power increased to the level of mania. Luther's emphasis upon guilt and Calvin's upon sin helped fix the Devil as firmly in Protestantism as in Catholicism. The fuel of the great witch-craze was this belief in the omnipresence of the Devil. The excesses of the witch-craze provoked a reaction that was reinforced by Rationalists *, the Enlightenment *, and emphasis upon human moral responsibility. In the nineteenth century scientism and liberal Protestantism dealt belief in the Devil further blows, though Romanticism * briefly revived him, sometimes as a positive, Promethean figure. The Devil reached his nadir in the 1920s and 1930s, but the concept has regained strength (at least as metaphor) owing to the horrors of the period since 1939 and to an increasing sense that the destructive impulses of humanity may be intractable.

H. A. Kelly, *The Devil, Demonology, and Witchcraft*, ²1974; J. B. Russell, *The Devil*, 1977; *Satan*, 1981.

JEFFREY BURTON RUSSELL

Dialectic

Dialectic is a term of very ancient philosophical lineage, receiving its first explicit definition in Plato. Meaning (etymologically) 'argument', or 'debate', it was thought of by Plato as the necessary method of philosophy itself, characterized by the philosophical genre of the 'dialogue'.

At a deeper level Plato thought of the dialectic as having an objective character, for in his view the world itself was a structure of 'dialogue' or 'argument' between appearance and reality. In Plato's view, the world of sense-perception or appearance is less than fully real, and if taken to be the real is a source of illusion. The reality of the world of appearance consists in the extent to which

it participates in or imitates the real world of Forms or Ideas and is available to knowledge only as a result of a critical dissection of appearance (*see also* **Platonism**).

The contemporary uses of the word, however, while retaining their roots in the conflict between appearance and reality, owe more to Hegel * than to Plato. For Hegel, the dialectic is the necessary structure of rational thought because reality itself is structured in conflict and contradiction. All that is, is Absolute Spirit (God). God in affirming himself (thesis) necessarily affirms the other than self (antithesis) in the form of the world, and achieves his fullness of self-identity in the overcoming of the contradiction between himself and the world. This 'negation of the negation' is for Hegel the fulfilment of ultimately rational processes within history but finds its symbolic expression in self-alienation of God in the man Jesus whereby man is redemptively restored in God.

The term has secondary uses in Marx, who claimed to have accepted the rational structure of Hegelian dialectic but to have turned it 'upside-down'. In Marx the dialectic becomes the contradictory structure of capitalist society itself which simultaneously affirms itself as capitalist and in doing so generates the proletarian class which is its revolutionary opposite, thus producing a contradiction which can be resolved only in a communist society.

Today the term is more widely used to designate a method of argument than any claims about the structure of reality, and as such the term has passed into contemporary theology through the 'dialectical theology' * of Karl Barth.

DENYS TURNER

Dialectical Theology

An alternative title for crisis theology*. Rejecting the classical Catholic threefold method of gaining knowledge of God (the *via affirmativa*, the *via negationis**, and the *via eminentiae**), Karl Barth and his colleagues insisted that only valid theological method was the *via dialectica*; this was the method of statement and counterstatement, of 'yes' and 'no', of paradox, in which polar pairs (whose unity cannot be thought) are held together only in the response of God-given faith – finite and infinite, time and eternity, wrath and grace. God thus transcends rational comprehension and, it must be stressed, dogmatic formulation. It follows from the *via dialectica* that is impossible to identify divine truth with a set of dogmatic propositions, God's Word with a written theology.

See also **Word of God.**

JAMES RICHMOND

Disciplina Arcani

The practice of keeping the rites and some of the doctrines of the church secret so that they are divulged only to communicants and not to catechumens or pagans. There is no satisfactory evidence for this practice until the fourth century, when it was occasioned partly by imitation of the mystery religions and partly by the increased interest in Christianity taken by pagans.

R. P. C. HANSON

Discipline

A term used in the Christian tradition in four main senses. 1. It can be used of the way of life which is prescribed by the church and embodied in various regulations and rules, expecially as these are backed, as they often have been, by the power of the state. 2. It is used as a term covering all those forms of asceticism and mortification which one associates for instance, with the monastic tradition. 3. Arising out of this, discipline is used in a quite precise and technical sense for the scourge, a kind of whip of knotted cords, used in monastic practices of discipline. 4. It is used, in a way which is closely akin to the first sense, of a way of life prescribed by the church and enforced upon its practitioners. Examples of this are the discipline laid upon the life of the Christian community by Calvin in Geneva, and the discipline, in the same way, of the Scots Presbyterians.

E. J. TINSLEY

Dispensation

The term is derived from Latin *dispenso*, to weigh out, to administer as a steward. In theological usage it is the system established by God to regulate men's obedience towards him in matters of religion and morality, e.g. 'the Mosaic dispensation' or 'the dispensation of Law' (the Old Covenant) as contrasted with 'the dispensation of Grace' (the New Covenant of Jesus Christ). From at least the fifth century 'dispensations' were licences granted by a bishop or other eccles-

iastical authority permitting some act which would in the absence of such dispensation be illegal according to canon law*.

ALAN RICHARDSON

Dispensationalism

A system of biblical interpretation put forward in the nineteenth century to help believers who studied the Bible alone or in groups and Bible schools to master the Bible as one book. 'No particular portion of Scripture is to be intelligently comprehended apart from some conception of its place in the whole' (C. I. Scofield, 1843–1921). Dispensationalists trace their origins to the preaching and writings of John Nelson Darby of Dublin (1800–1882), one of the early leaders of the Plymouth Brethren. The most popular form of the system is in the Scofield Reference Bible (1902–1909, revised 1917, 1966). Although the Bible testifies from beginning to end to the one redemption by Christ, God progressively dealt with man in seven dispensations, in each of which man was set a specific test, which continues as an abiding truth into subsequent dispensations. The dispensations are: Innocence (Gen. 1.28) to the expulsion from Eden; Conscience or Moral Responsibility (Gen. 3.7) to the Flood; Human Government, in which God delegated areas of his authority and said 'Render to Caesar' (Gen. 8.15) up to the call of Abraham; Promise, the test of Israel's stewardship of divine truth (Gen. 12.1) to the giving of the Law on Sinai; Law, disciplinary correction (Ex. 19.1) to the death of Christ; The Church, the Dispensation of the Spirit (Acts 2.1) to Christ's return; the Kingdom for 1,000 years (Rev. 20.4) to the eternal state.

J. C. O'NEILL

Dissonance, Cognitive

This theory, developed in the 1950s by Leon Festinger, seeks to analyse responses to disconfirmations of attitudes, beliefs or expectations brought about by counter-information or experience. Disconfirming evidence is said to produce dissonance among individuals or groups. Attempts are made to deny such disconfirmation or to reinterpret either the dissonant information or the original set of beliefs in order to restore consonance between it and reality. Dissonance resolution is a psychological mechanism which brackets unpleasant truths and protects individuals or groups from the necessity of having to change the belief system. Using questionnaires, forced compliance tests and other investigative techniques of social psychology, cognitive dissonance theory sets out a number of predictions about the ways in which responses are made to dissonance inducing experiences. According to the theory, people always seek psychological equilibrium, so dissonance-arousing factors need to be controlled, if not avoided altogether, in ways which will reconfirm the original set of attitudes, beliefs or expectations. Where the facts of experience contradict attitudes, beliefs or expectations, it is the facts which may require explanation rather than the beliefs which need to be changed. The ways in which consonance may be maintained between attitudes and new information or experience are numerous, but may be reduced to three categories here for convenience: group solidarity which permits the avoidance of dissonance-arousing information in the first instance or provides support in the face of such disconfirmation; schemes of rationalizing explanations which neutralize dissonance; proselytizing movements which seek to confirm original attitudes, beliefs or expectations by increasing the number of adherents of such views. Number adds strength to conviction, because the more people who think in the same way the less force dissonance can generate.

The theory generated many research programmes in the following decades and was made more sophisticated by numerous studies. Its main contribution to modern thought lies in market research and the psychology of attitude change. But it also includes work on groups of devotees gathered together around expectations of imminent future bliss or disaster and, in analysing such groups and their responses to failed expectations, the theory developed a perspective on messianic-type beliefs and expectations. Such a perspective takes the theory into the field of biblical and theological studies where it has been utilized in the analysis of prophecy (Carroll) and aspects of the NT (Gager). Although the theory cannot be applied directly to biblical studies without serious critical analysis, it can yield useful analytical tools for investigating some of the more difficult areas of biblical interpretation. Elements of response to dissonance may be detected at certain points in the prophetic traditions (e.g. Zech. 6.11, 14), along with evidence for group response to failed expectations (e.g. Isa. 8.16–18). Part of the complex reinterpretations of prophecy within the traditions may reflect the principle 'dissonance gives rise to hermeneutic' (Carroll). In the NT it is possible that dissonance created by the crucifixion of Jesus may have been resolved by the development of belief in his resurrection * and Paul's transformation of that disastrous death into the saving power of God (e.g. I Cor. 1.18–25). The strong sense of mission in the early church may also indicate one of the standard responses to dissonance: reinforcement of belief by multiplying its numbers of adherents (Gager).

Robert P. Carroll, *When Prophecy Failed: Reactions and responses to failure in the Old Testament prophetic traditions*, 1979; Leon Festinger and others, *When Prophecy Fails*, 1956; Leon Festinger, *A Theory of Cognitive Dissonance*, 1957; John G. Gager, *Kingdom and Community: The Social World of Early Christianity*, 1975.

ROBERT CARROLL

Distinction, Method of

Mediaeval thought is particularly noted for its concern in making the most careful of distinctions in all matters. The practice derives from the tradition in classical philosophy of defining, and thus knowing, an object through its genus and specific difference; it is the definition which distinguishes one sort of thing from another. Among the most important of the distinctions are 'formal' and 'material'. The former signifies that two things differ in species; the latter means that two things differ in number. Another important set of distinctions is the 'real' distinction that obtains in reality and the 'rational' distinction which is produced solely by the mind. Mediaeval theology abounds in a myriad of distinctions and subdistinctions on almost any topic. This tendency to split an issue into a multiplicity of facets permitted mediaeval thinkers to resolve the thorniest of problems (as, for example, the unity and the trinity of God), but also contributed to the impression that later scholasticism was merely a system of logic-chopping.

JAMES P. ETZWILER

Docetism *see* **God**

Docetism

Docetism (from Greek *dokeo* – I seem) refers to the doctrine that the manhood of Christ was apparent not real, that as in some Greek myths, a divine being was dressed up as a man in order to communicate revelations, but was not really involved in the human state and withdrew before the passion. Already opposed by Ignatius in the early second century, and possibly by the Johannine Epistles, this christological heresy was a feature of most Gnostic systems. The term is now often applied to christological assumptions or proposals which by implication undermine the full manhood of Christ: thus much traditional and popular christology, even the position of Athanasius, may be described as docetic in tendency. It is the principal concern of modern revisionist christologies to avoid any form of docetism.

See also **Christology**.

FRANCES YOUNG

Doctrinal Criticism

The critical assessment and appraisal of doctrine is a continuing feature of all religious traditions. Christianity is no exception. In Britain the term is often associated with the work of the late G. F. Woods, who saw doctrinal criticism as the critical study of the truth and adequacy of doctrinal statements. Observing the development in the nineteenth century of biblical criticism*, he believed that the time had now come for a scientific discipline of doctrinal criticism. The historical study of doctrine tended to impede the work of critical systematic theology. Doctrinal fundamentalism was widespread. How do we come to speak of revelation? How does a revealed statement differ from one which is unrevealed? Since any doctrinal statement must be intelligible in order to be effective, none is exempt from doctrinal criticism.

The language we use to express experience of the transcendent will have inevitable limitations. We have to use our imagination, not in passive contemplation but in active interpretation of images of the divine within our human framework. This does not make the transcendent unthinkable. The doctrinal critic will seek to analyse the great affirma-tions of the faith, exploring the various separate dimensions of which they are a single complex expression. His concern is always the pursuit of truth. A doctrinal system may be logically flawless and yet untrue to the facts. Some measure of paradox may be inevitable in speaking about God. Different areas of doctrine may develop in different ways. 'There can be no true defence of the faith which is not ultimately the same as the defence of the truth.'

Woods' criteria have been developed and discussed by Maurice Wiles, Brian Hebblethwaite and others. The last twenty years have seen a considerable interest in systematic theology, and an appraisal of Christian doctrine which has sought to be at the same time critical and constructive. A major instance of this may be seen in the long discussion following the publication of *The Myth of God Incarnate* in 1977.

In Britain the influence of linguistic philosophy has contributed to a distrust of general theories and grand systems of doctrine. The approach is more often one of building up a cumulative rational case on the basis of analysis of the various components of a given doctrinal affirmation. Realization that 'metaphysics'* may not always be a bad thing has been coupled with caution. On the Continent from at least the time of Albrecht Ritschl in the nineteenth century there was a parallel attack on 'metaphysics'. This has in no way deterred scholars in all ecclesiastical denominations from producing comprehensive doctrinal systems, often with the metaphysical structure implicit rather than explicit, and so, often unexamined. Genuine dialogue between British and Continental scholars in this area is limited, though there are some signs of hope.

Among recent approaches to doctrinal criticism which have attempted to take advantage of a number of different techniques, mention may be made especially of David Tracy's *The Analogical Imagination*. In this study, subtitled 'Christian Theology and the Culture of Pluralism', Tracy develops criteria for his own theology in dialogue with other approaches to method. He considers doctrine under the image of the classic, a work of art or an event in which persons express themselves in a manner that has universal significance. The classic provokes new insights and leads to decisions. The Christian classic is God's self-manifestation in Jesus Christ. Through reflection on the pluralism of approaches to the events concerning Jesus we may reach a deeper understanding of the divine presence in the world. Tracy's work provides support for the suggestion that doctrinal criticism is important both for its own sake, as part of the search for intellectual truth, and for its place in the continuing human search for a deeper understanding of the meaning of God's salvation. Doctrinal criticism may lead to doctrinal construction, which in turn will provoke further critical questioning of previous assumptions.

Our understanding of doctrinal criticism will depend to some extent on what we mean by doctrine *. In the N T *dogma* can refer to a decree, or to the O T law. If we were to regard this as normative for our understanding, we should already be taking a doctrinal decision, which would in turn be a proper subject for doctrinal criticism, in order to produce the best available rational basis for our doctrinal choices.

Doctrine overlaps with faith, information, worship, the philosophy of religion, apologetics, reflection on personal faith, reflection on an historical tradition. But it coincides with none of these. We may perhaps regard it as the formulation, with the maximum precision, of the significance of the Christian gospel in the history of mankind. Its sources lie in the Bible and in the tradition of the church, in personal faith, in the contemporary Christian community, and in the development of reason through the experience of and reflection upon modern society. Understanding of God is always a gift of God. Yet it is human doctrine, with all its provisionality and possibility of error. As the study of human response to the gospel, it is something that Christians cannot do without. They need doctrine, critical doctrine and doctrinal criticism.

B. L. Hebblethwaite, *Theology*, 1967, pp. 402f. (on Woods); *The Problems of Theology*, 1980; Van Harvey, *The Historian and the Believer*, 1967; G. Kaufman, *God the Problem*, 1972; N. L. A. Lash, *Theology on Dover Beach*, 1979; B. Lonergan, *Insight*, 1957; B. Mitchell, *The Justification of Religious Belief*, 1973; D. E. Nineham, *Explorations in Theology* 1, 1978; S. W. Sykes, *Christian Theology Today*, 1971; D. Tracy, *The Analogical Imagination*, 1981; K. Ward, *Rational*

Theology and the Creativity of God, 1982; M. F. Wiles, *The Making of Christian Doctrine*, 1967; *The Remaking of Christian Doctrine*, 1974; G. Woods, 'Doctrinal Criticism' in *Prospect for Theology*, ed. F. G. Healey, 1966, and *Theological Explanation*, 1958; S. W. Sykes (ed), *England and Germany: Studies in Theological Diplomacy*, 1982.

GEORGE NEWLANDS

Doctrine

Doctrine means 'teaching'. In Christian tradition the word is used in a broad sense to describe the whole body of Christian teaching, or in a narrower sense to describe what Christians believe about particular aspects of their faith: the doctrine of God, human nature and destiny, Christ, salvation, the Holy Spirit, the church and the like. Christian doctrine is not the object of Christian faith. Christians do not believe in this or that doctrine or doctrinal system but in God. Nevertheless doctrines and doctrinal systems are the result of their attempt to reflect rationally and consistently *about* the God in whom they believe and thus to explain and defend their faith and way of life.

All Christians agree that the original statement of Christian doctrine is found in the Bible. But the history of the church is (among other things) the history of the doctrinal *interpretation* of scripture by preachers, teachers and theological scholars speaking for themselves; and by church leaders, councils and assemblies speaking for a whole Christian body. From the beginning Christians and Christian traditions have differed in their understanding of the relationship between biblical teaching, the doctrinal interpretations of individual thinkers, and the official doctrinal formulations (dogmas) of the church.

1. *Scripture and tradition.* Although the issue was not new at the time of the Reformation, it was at this time that the church in the West split over the issue whether the source and norm of true or correct doctrine is biblical teaching *and* the past and present teaching of the church (the R C position) or scripture *alone* (the Reformers' position – by which they did not deny the necessity of church formulations of doctrine but did insist that the authority of such formulations can only be subservient and not equal to that of scripture). This is still an unresolved issue, but the conflict between the Catholic

emphasis on tradition and the Protestant emphasis on scripture is no longer as great as it once was. Contemporary Roman Catholics are more open to acknowledge the superior authority of scripture. Protestants have learned that scripture itself is the result of developing traditions in ancient Israel and the early church, and in turn part of the developing tradition of the church.

2. *Other authorities.* In the history both of the Catholic and various Protestant traditions there has been an ongoing debate about the extent to which the interpretation of scripture and the formulation of doctrine should be shaped by the insights of reason, intuition, conscience, the natural and social sciences, or personal, political, economic and cultural experience. Disagreements about how Christian doctrine can be both faithful to scripture and relevant to the experience and 'secular' wisdom of people in different times, places and situations have been one of the main causes for lack of doctrinal consensus among Christians.

3. *The individual and the church.* Who decides what 'correct' doctrine is? Classical Roman Catholicism and some forms of strongly confessional Protestantism believe that the church establishes orthodox belief with its dogmas and confessional standards. This position denies individual Christian freedom and makes the church rather than scripture the final authority.

Some Protestants have gone to the opposite extreme and argued that each individual Christian has the right to decide for himself or herself what true Christian doctrine is – either by appealing to the exclusive authority of scripture or by appealing to rational, experiential, moral, scientific or politically-economically relevant interpretation of scripture and critical evaluation of church tradition. Both in its conservative and liberal forms this position makes individual preference and opinion rather than either scripture or church to be the final authority.

Most Christians today seek an intermediate position between ecclesiastical and individualistic absolutism. In various ways they argue for the relative authority of church dogma and confessional standards and for the relative freedom of individual interpretation. On the one hand, dogmas and confessional formulas of the church are viewed as subject to criticism, correction and further development in the light of the normative authority of scripture and the needs and problems and insights of the church and society in new situations. On the other hand, individual interpretations of doctrinal truth are to be critically evaluated in the light of both biblical teaching and church tradition, but in turn may contribute to the reformation of traditional biblical interpretation and church doctrine. While this position does not solve the problem of authority, it does try to make room at the same time for the authority of scripture, Christian consensus and individual freedom.

Despite the differences among Christians and Christian traditions, there is more agreement among them than appears at first glance. All Christians acknowledge the Bible to be the primary source and norm of Christian doctrine. Most agree that true Christian doctrine follows the teaching of the ancient church concerning the Trinity* and the person and work of Christ (*see* **Christology**). Most Christians can confess together the summary of Christian doctrine in the Apostles' Creed.

SHIRLEY C. GUTHRIE, JR

Dogma

In classical times the term (Greek for 'opinion') was applied to the teaching of various philosophical schools or to some practical decree coming from those in authority (Luke 2.1; Acts 15.29; 16.4). After a chequered history, by the end of the nineteenth century the word came to bear the precise meaning of (i) a divinely revealed truth, (ii) proclaimed as such by solemn church teaching (for Roman Catholics by the infallible authority of the magisterium*), and (iii) hence binding now and forever on the faithful.

In these terms, dogmas, precisely as such, are not found in the constitutive period of foundational revelation which climaxed and ended with Christ and the apostolic age and which received its literary expression in the books of the NT. Rather, from the Council of Nicaea on (325), clearly defined dogmas like the one person of Jesus Christ in two natures (Council of Chalcedon, 451) have emerged in the interpretative period of dependent revelation. This means that dogmas cannot and should not be treated as ultimate norms. 'The supreme rule of faith' is found rather in 'the Scriptures, taken together with sacred Tradition' (Vatican II, Dogmatic Constitution on Divine Revelation, *Dei Verbum*, n. 21), which witness to the original experience, faith and preaching of the apostolic church.

To cover certain essential truths (such as that of Christ's being universal redeemer) which have never been explicitly and authoritatively proclaimed in the way indicated above, theologians also speak of 'non-defined dogmas'. For Roman Catholics the ordinary, universal magisterium teaches such 'non-defined dogmas' when (i) the bishops throughout the world in union with the Bishop of Rome, (ii) representing the whole church and proclaiming the truth to the whole church, (iii) unanimously teach as such some revealed truths to be held now and forever (Vatican II, Dogmatic Constitution on the Church, *Lumen Gentium*, n. 25).

As a special form of teaching, dogmas fall within the much wider circle of church doctrines, whether present or past. All dogmas are doctrines, albeit of a particularly solemn kind, but obviously not all doctrines have reached or ever will reach dogmatic status.

Dogmatic development has been part of the wider development* of doctrine, while doctrinal development itself belongs within that wider context of change, growth, decline and reform which characterizes Christian life and history in their entirety.

In interpreting dogmas one should recognize the ways in which they were historically and culturally conditioned. Usually formulated as answers to particular distortions in Christian teaching and belief, they were often more explicit in what they ruled out than in what they positively affirmed. Some dogmas (like the christological ones) were and remain more important in the 'hierarchy of truths' than others (e.g. the dogmas concerned with the church). In all cases dogmas do not excuse Christians from the task of reflecting further. No dogmatic statement can ever exhaustively express the mystery of God's self-communication in Christ. Here as elsewhere faith must continue to 'seek understanding' and appropriate new formulations. Apropos of the christological dogmas, Karl Rahner rightly declared: 'The clearest formulations, the most sanctified formulas, the classic condensations of the centuries-long work of the Church in prayer, reflection and struggle

concerning God's mysteries: all these derive their life from the fact that they are not end but beginning, not goal but means, truths which open the way to the ever greater Truth' (*Theological Investigations* I, p. 149).

See also **Creeds**; **Development, Doctrinal**; **Doctrine**; **Infallibility**; **Revelation**; **Truth**.

———

Gerald O'Collins, *Has Dogma a Future?*, 1975 (US title *The Case Against Dogma*); Wolfhart Pannenberg, 'What Is a Dogmatic Statement?', *Basic Questions in Theology* I, 1966, pp. 182–210; Karl Rahner and Candido Pozo, 'Dogma', *Sacramentum Mundi* II, pp. 95–111.

GERALD O'COLLINS

Dogmatic Theology

This term (which later acquired as its synonym 'dogmatics') first emerged in the seventeenth century, but from the twelfth or certainly from the thirteenth century the reality was already there in the great syntheses of Thomas Aquinas and others. Where dogmatic theology is distinguished from systematic theology, this is generally done not because the former is less methodological or systematic than the latter, but because 'systematic' is used as a wider term to embrace not only dogmatic theology but also moral theology*, fundamental theology* and apologetics* (see Paul Tillich's *Systematic Theology*, 1951–1964). Some, like John Macquarrie, note the pejorative overtones of 'dogmatic' in ordinary speech and avoid the term 'dogmatic theology'. His 'symbolic' and 'applied' theology, taken together, cover much the same ground as others cover in dogmatic theology (see *Principles of Christian Theology*, 1977).

Dogmatic theology aims to examine and present coherently and systematically all major Christian doctrines (on the Trinity*, the Incarnation*, redemption*, sin* and grace*, the church*, the sacraments*, the eschaton*, etc.). It accepts and draws on the data of revelation to do its work in the light of faith. As the title of Karl Barth's monumental *Church Dogmatics* (1932–1967) suggests, dogmatic theology is essentially ecclesiastical. As a service undertaken within the church and for the church, it reflects on the community's official faith. Nevertheless, while it is a discipline practised by believing scholars, dogmatic theology does not entail a refusal to question, investigate, and think critically as well as constructively.

Typically, dogmatic theology expresses a dialogue between the historical faith of Christians and (philosophical) reason. On its 'positive' side it draws on the scriptures, official church teaching, the history of theology, liturgical texts and other items which make up the lived tradition of the believing community. To bring this data into a coherent system, dogmatic theology in one way or another will take up questions, concepts, terms and schemes for understanding oneself, society and the world which have been elaborated in philosophy (understood fairly broadly). Of course, such philosophical material will always be adjusted. For instance, what the revelation which climaxed in Christ indicates about the origin, nature and destiny of human life must modify any 'anthropologies' drawn from Aristotelianism *, existentialism * or some other school of philosophy. Philosophical notions cannot be expected to move unchanged straight into theology. All the same, whether blatantly or more discreetly, dogmatic theology has consistently used philosophical reason to clarify, elaborate and systematize the data of faith (see also **Philosophy of Religion**).

In *The Analogical Imagination* (1981), David Tracy draws attention to ways in which theological standards, criteria, methods and norms will be affected by one's setting and audience. A 'good performance' in dogmatic theology will be partly determined by its public – a seminary, a monastery, a diocese, the church at large, a university, academics in general, or simply society at large. To Tracy's list of settings we should add the gaol. Thomas More, Dietrich Bonhoeffer and other Christian theologians did some of their finest theological work as prisoners writing for a tiny circle of relatives and friends. All the same, Tracy's approach is valid and valuable. Standards of meaning, truth, language and success in various dogmatic theologies should at least partly be judged in terms of such questions as: For whom and to whom are these theologians speaking? Where are they doing their work?

See also **Dogma**, **Systematic Theology**, **Theology**.

Karl Barth, *Church Dogmatics* I/2, ET 1956, pp. 758–884; Gerhard Ebeling, *The Study of Theology*, ET 1979, pp. 125–38.

GERALD O'COLLINS

Donatists

Persecution produced not only martyrs * but schisms *. Donatism arose in North Africa after Diocletian's persecution (beginning of the fourth century) when certain purists refused to accept as bishop a man thought to have been consecrated by traditors, i.e. persons suspected of having surrendered the scriptures to be burned by the authorities. The schism was named after an early rival bishop, Donatus. It lasted in strength for over one hundred years, and was not eliminated until the coming of Islam. It was a major force against which Augustine * struggled. Although orthodox in doctrine, the sect was rigorist in its view of the church, regarding holiness and purity as essential. Its power lay to a fair extent in its appeal to anti-Roman nationalism in North Africa.

W. H. C. Frend, *The Donatist Church*, 1952.

FRANCES YOUNG

Donum Superadditum

The concept *donum superadditum* (supernatural or additional endowment), suggested by Athanasius and most fully developed by Aquinas, distinguishes between certain natural endowments that humanity has from God and which it retains after the fall and the supernatural or additional endowments which were lost in the fall. The *donum superadditum* included the powers that enabled people to know God, to live according to God's will and thus to retain immortal life. When these powers were lost in the Fall *, humanity's natural powers of reason, conscience, etc. were weakened but not destroyed. As such they are the image * of God within fallen humanity. Fallen humanity thus still has the power to practise the natural virtues of prudence, justice, courage and self-control but has lost the ability to attain a vision of God or to live the Christian virtues of faith *, hope * and love *. Fallen persons can regain these lost abilities only through the grace that comes through the sacraments of the church.

The Protestant Reformation * generally denied any distinction between natural and supernatural endowments. The Fall, it declared, resulted in the corruption of the whole of a person and not in the loss of supernatural endowments. Calvin in his *Institutes*, ii. 2, came as close to the concept of the *donum* as did any Protestant. He argued that certain natural talents had been corrupted by sin but that certain 'celestial' talents were totally lost. Thus sinful and fallen humanity still retains an ability for political order and general reason and Calvin suggests that in such areas Christians can learn from pagan philosophy. But in coming to know about God and the way of salvation, Calvin found that 'the most sagacious of mankind are blinder than moles'. In this way Calvin could argue that even sinners are able to live on a level above the animals but cannot, by their own efforts, do anything to aid their salvation.

See also **Anthropology**.

WILLIAM HORDERN

Double Procession

The doctrine that the Holy Spirit * proceeds both from the Father and the Son (credally expressed in the *Filioque* *) is a marked feature of Western theology (Augustine) which always held firmly to the unity of the Godhead and emphasized the relations between the Persons. The East preferred the doctrine of the single Procession from the Father, which seemed to secure better the unity of the Godhead. They endeavoured to express the operation of the Son with regard to the Spirit either by the use of an additional verb (send, receive from) or by a change of preposition (proceeding from the Father *through* the Son).

See also **Trinity, Doctrine of the**.

H. E. W. TURNER

Doubt

Part of the legacy of classical Greek and Cartesian scepticism has been a long history of concern with the question of both the descriptive and prescriptive relation between doubt and religious faith. This concern has generated a wide variety of responses which can be usefully reduced to three main types. 1. The claim that 'faith embraces doubt'. The requirements of self-criticism and autonomy are said to necessitate the normative compatibility of faith and doubt. 2. Faith and doubt are not compatible because religious faith must transcend categories of rational justification altogether if it is to retain its distinctive character. Rational justification cannot be allowed to be relevant

to faith because it (and its obverse possibility of doubt) precludes the freedom, the unconditionality, and/or the passion of genuine faith. 3. Faith and doubt are incompatible, yet rational justification is relevant and appropriate to faith. In addition to these three types of account of the relation, faith and doubt are sometimes said to be compatible precisely because faith is viewed as non-propositional – i.e., faith is not understood as 'belief that something is true'. Holding such a view, Paul Tillich, for example, contrasts 'methodological' doubt (about facts and conclusions) and 'sceptical' doubt (an attitudinal rejection of the possibility of any certainty) with 'existential' doubt. It is questionable, however, whether such 'existential' doubt can ultimately be independent of propositional beliefs.

With respect to propositional accounts of faith, 'doubt' can refer either to 1. uncertainty concerning a belief or proposition, or 2. suspension of assent or judgment. In the first case one assents to the proposition in question, but with reservations; in the second case, one withholds assent from both the assertion of the proposition and its negation. Descartes made the second kind of doubt the starting point for his entire programme of finding indubitable foundations for belief (*Meditations*). The doubt that consists in withholding assent from a proposition p is by definition incompatible with assent to p. To argue the compatibility of faith and doubt in this sense would be to argue that we can do both X and not-X at the same time. The important question then concerns the first kind of doubt: what kind of uncertainty is being ruled out or allowed by the types of responses noted above, and what kind of critical investigation is being legitimated or proscribed?

Critical investigation can lead to suspension of assent; moreover, the legitimation of critical appraisal at all also legitimates some suspensions of assents because while investigating p we necessarily suspend assents to particular propositions being considered as evidence for p (though we do not suspend assent to p). Nevertheless, to argue that doubt (withholding assent) is incompatible with faith does not imply that investigation or critical appraisal is also thereby ruled out.

A proposition is dubitable in a strictly logical sense if the negation of the proposition is not a logical contradiction. Doubt can, however, be 'unreasonable' in cases where it is logically possible, and even in cases where it is more-than-logically possible. The distinction between doubt that is impossible and doubt that is unreasonable in a given case is crucial to any attempt to determine the normative relation between faith and doubt and to evaluate contrasting accounts of that relation.

See also **Certainty**, **Faith**.

A useful general background to Cartesian scepticism can be found in Richard H. Popkin, *The History of Skepticism*, 1979. Some especially useful treatments of doubt in religious cases are K. Barth, *Evangelical Theology*, ET 1963, ch. 3; J. H. Newman, *Grammar of Assent*, 1870; P. Tillich, *Dynamics of Faith*, 1957; L. Wittengenstein, *Lectures and Conversations on ... Religious Belief* (1938), 1972.

M. JAMIE FERREIRA

Dualism

Metaphysical dualism is the view that reality is of two distinct and irreducible kinds, as in Plato's distinction between the sensible and intelligible worlds, Descartes' distinction between thinking and extended substances, and Kant's distinction between the realms of phenomena and noumena. In Christian theology the use of the term dates from 1700, where Thomas Hyde (*Historia religionis veterum Persarum*, ch. 9, p. 164) refers to the dualism of good and evil. From its biblical beginnings onwards, however, Christian thought reflects a qualified dualism between God and the creation, whereby an irreducible difference is related through an indissoluble bond. God creates the natural world from chaos, but with the mark of the divine order so that God pronounces it good. God then shapes humankind from the dust of the earth and breathes spirit (*nephesh*) to create human life made in the image of God. The freedom to sin marks humanity's distinction from God but cannot destroy God's claim on humanity as children of the divine image. Among world religions this qualified dualism contrasts both with the radical dualism of Zoroastrianism, where the distinction between light and dark, good and evil, is absolute, and with the Hindu tradition of *Ādvaita Vedānta*, where all metaphysical difference is the

unreal effect of *māyā* (illusion). Philosophically it is close to the qualified non-dualism of Rāmānuja's *Viśiṣṭādvaita* in Hindu thought.

Although metaphysically inchoate, Christian qualified dualism is historically dynamic, providing both difference and relation between good and evil, God's grace and humankind's sin, the tragedy of the fall* and the final fulfilment of the kingdom of God. A qualified dualism is philosophically required by the Christian affirmation that God works in history as both transcendent (i.e. *sui generis*) and immanent (i.e. related to humankind in a non-accidental way) in the incarnation* of Jesus the Christ.

John Herman Randall, Jr, *Hellenistic Ways of Salvation and the Making of the Christian Synthesis*, 1970; Harry A. Wolfson, *The Philosophy of the Church Fathers*, 1956.

LEROY S. ROUNER

Dysteleology

The word is derived from Greek *dys*, bad, *telos*, an end: evidence of disharmony or purposelessness in creation.

See **Teleology**; **Evil, Problem of.**

ALAN RICHARDSON

Eastern Orthodox Theology

'Eastern Orthodoxy' is one of the currently used names of the church which identifies itself with the One Holy Catholic Apostolic Church of the seven Ecumenical Councils of Christianity. It is also known as the Greek Orthodox Church, the Eastern Church, the Eastern Orthodox Church, the Orthodox Church, the Greek Church, etc. The Orthodox Church sees itself as continuing into the present day the spiritual life, worship, faith, doctrines and moral teaching of the catholic and undivided church of Christ of the first eight centuries. Its life is rooted in the patristic* spirit and there is no understanding of it unless that fact is kept prominently in mind.

Eastern Orthodox Christianity perceives its history as beginning with Jesus Christ and the apostles. It traces its history from Pentecost through the apostolic period, the church of the apologists, and the Constantinian synthesis. It recognizes as the major disruption in its life the process by which the Western portion of the church was divided from itself through the Great Schism (the tenth to the early thirteenth centuries), thus producing a divided Christendom. Historically and spiritually, in consequence, Eastern Christianity differs qualitatively from Western Christianity, now divided into Roman Catholicism and Protestantism.

The polity of the Orthodox Church, reflecting its strong trinitarian theology, is both episcopal and collegial at once. Within local churches, the bishop is the centre of church unity: he functions as the centre of the church's life of worship, especially in the eucharist; as the chief responsible agent for the purity of faith and teaching; and as the canonical link with the other local churches. The ecclesiastical principle of territoriality gathers several local churches into more or less autocephalous (self-governing) churches. The bishops at the head of the autocephalous churches are variously named Patriarchs, Metropolitans or Archbishops. All, as heads of churches, are deemed equal in authority, though a primacy of honour is accorded to the Patriarch of Constantinople. There is, however, no supreme pontiff in the Western sense. The church governs itself on all levels through councils (Synods, *Sobor*). The highest and most authoritative council is the Ecumenical Council, whose decisions on dogmatic questions (*horoi*) are held by the Orthodox to be unchanging formulations of divinely revealed truth (*see also* **Conciliarity**).

The theological and doctrinal teachings of the Orthodox Church carefully avoid both rationalistic propositionalism and vague pietistic anti-intellectualism. The approach to theological knowledge is at once highly sensitive to the mystery of transcendence and to the ability of human beings to know in truth the immanent God. This viewpoint is usually articulated in the approach to theological epistomology embodied in the terms apophatic theology * and cataphatic theology. Eastern Christian theological perspectives take the unknowability of God with utter seriousness. As completely unknowable in the divine essence, there is no ontological or genuine conceptual analogy between the uncreated God and created existence. It is impossible to reason from created existence, experience or relations to the essence of the uncreated divine reality. The fundamental attitude of the creature before God, then, is not comprehension or understanding but awe and reverence, that is, worship, trusting belief, repentance and obedience. This negative theological approach, 'apophaticism', affirms the irreducible mystery of God's reality for the human mind. St John of Damascus said, 'God is unknowable and incomprehensible and the only thing knowable of God is his unknowability and incomprehensibility' (*De Fide Orthodoxa* I, iv).

But the unknowable God (according to the essence) has communicated himself to created beings through his energies. Orthodoxy rejects the idea of 'grace' as a substance or thing (which it describes as 'created grace'). Grace is the self-giving action of God as he brings into being created reality and enters into communion and relationship with it. His energies *are* uncreated grace. As we participate in them we have true experience of God and know God in a way which is sufficient for salvation but which never goes beyond the paradox and mystery that is inevitable when finite creatures seek to articulate in limited and inadequate terms the experience of God's energies. This theology, contingent and inadequate to its subject as it may be, is necessary to articulate the message of salvation on the basis of God's self-disclosing revelation. It is called 'cataphatic' or positive theology. Apophatic theology keeps cataphatic theology from absolutism. Cataphatic theology keeps apophatic theology from subjectivism. Apophatic theology requires a personal experience of God, and cataphatic theology demands faithfulness to revealed truths. Together, they bridge the subjective-objective gap in the experience of the divine, though never to the point where the tension is dissolved.

The purpose of cataphatic theology is to preserve the revelation of God from error, to provide direction and guidance for Christian thought, practice and worship, and to lead the believer in the fullest possible communion with the living God. Some of the major themes of cataphatic theology, as formulated in the dogmas, received theological teaching and thought of Eastern Orthodoxy follow.

Our human experience of God is made possible by the self-disclosure of God, i.e. his revelation *. God has revealed something of himself in created reality. What he has revealed, however, is quite modest: that he exists, that he is provident, that he has ordered the creation physically and in a most elementary manner, morally. Thus, there is a low-level natural theology* and natural moral law to be discerned in created reality. However, this revelation barely serves the most elementary ordering of human life and is far from providing saving knowledge.

Eastern Christian theologians all acknowledge that God has concretely revealed himself to humanity in the first instance through the Hebrew people (his chosen race) and through Jesus Christ. The witness and record of revelation to the Hebrews is the OT. The written witness to the revelation in Jesus Christ is the NT. The (originally) unwritten witness to the revelation in Jesus Christ was the apostolic tradition, including not only teachings and practices, but more importantly a mind-set or ethos, the whole of which is perceived as being guided by the Holy Spirit* and known as holy tradition. Often, however, some Orthodox theologians will include (systematically) scripture within the concept of holy tradition. This is because the Holy Spirit is the guarantor of truth in both: scripture and holy tradition. Holding to a doctrine of inspiration of scripture, Orthodox theology rejects both the literalistic approach of inerrancy and the literary approach which sees scripture as a merely human document. As a divine-human document, it is true in its record of God's revelation of the truths of God and his relationships to humanity, while embodied in forms and expressions which reflect the human condition of its divinely inspired authors.

The Eastern Orthodox Christian doctrine ·of God is trinitarian from the outset. Experientially, God has revealed himself, first, as a Trinity* of persons rather than as a philosophically defined unity. He has revealed himself as creator, as redeemer and as sanctifier. The Father is understood in Orthodox theology as the unique source (arche¯*) of divinity within the Holy Trinity. The second person of the Holy Trinity is eternally born of the Father and the third person of the Holy Trinity eternally proceeds from the Father. All three, Father, Son and Holy Spirit, are fully persons. The unity (oneness) of God and the multiplicity (trinity) of God are understood as a mystery (paradox, autonomy, mysterion) which cannot be subjected to human categories of logic but which is required if human beings are to approach the mystery God as he has revealed himself. The formula which most adequately describes this mystery is that of the fourth Ecumenical Council of Chalcedon (451). God is one divine essence (ousia*) in three hypostases or persons. This formula describes the mystery of the Trinity – but it does not, nor can it ever be possible to explain the mystery in human rational terms. Any attempt to do this inevitably results in a distortion in which the transcendence of God is compromised.

That transcendence is articulated most clearly in the Eastern Orthodox doctrine of creation*. There is a very sharp and clear line of demarcation between God as Creator and that which he has created. As noted above, no analogies can be postulated by reasoning from created reality to the uncreated essence of God. Even those concepts which appear to apply to God by analogy from creation are not in fact positive statements, but negations, i.e. infinite means without limit and eternal means without the limits of time. Only as we perceive and experience the outreaching energies of God do we come close to a more positive statement about the being (ontotēta) of God. Thus, the only NT 'definition' of God is relational – 'God is love' (I John 4.8). God created everything else that exists other than himself, out of nothing. There is no analogy, emanation, procession or effluence from the uncreated God. This creation as it came into being was a concrete act of creation – it could have been created differently with different forms, laws, etc. It is fully and completely subject in its constitution and laws to the creative will of the Holy Trinity. God the Father, through the Son, in the Holy Spirit created and ordered this concrete created reality. Thus, for Orthodox Christianity, science studies this particular created reality and describes it, but its descriptions cannot provide much knowledge, if any, of divine reality.

This, however, does not mean that God is unrelated to his creation. God's energies sustain the creation and provide for its continuous existence in his providence. In communion with him, through his energies, the created world fulfils its purposes. This is more fully apparent in reference to the conscious and intelligent creation – angels and humanity. The bodiless angelic world exists in order to be in communion with God, to serve him and to realize their own natures through participation and relationship with God. Having been created as free and self-determining, some broke the relationship appropriate to them and God and fell, resulting in a permanent distortion of their natures. Having been created good, they were transformed by choice into demonic opponents of God and his will.

Human beings, composed of body and soul, are unique in that they not only share both in the spiritual and material worlds, but also, they have been created by God in his own image and likeness. Eastern Christianity interprets these terms through the patristic tradition to mean that humanity was endowed with certain God-like capacities and with the potential to fulfil and complete them through communion and participation with God. Humanity was created potentially perfect – what was required, however, was humanity's exercise of self-determining freedom (*autexousion*), also a part of the divine image, in the direction of communion, fitting relationship and participation with God. In other words, the achievement of full humanity requires that human beings be 'communicants of divine nature' (II Peter 1.4). The Fall* is understood in Eastern Christianity as the condition arising from the breaking by human beings of the necessary and fitting communion between human nature and God in whose image humanity was to have found its fulfilment. The condition, described as 'original sin', destroyed the potential for full communion and participation with God and distorted the image of God in humanity, but did not destroy it.

The broken relationship could only be restored by God's initiative, which human beings are still free to accept or reject. The work of redemption* begins with God's relationship with the chosen people and the promise of a Messiah as recorded in the prophecies of the OT. However, it was fulfilled and completed by Jesus Christ. The second person of the Holy Trinity, the Son who is eternally born of the Father, in time was incarnated, taking on all of human nature, except sin. He was perfect (complete) God and perfect (complete) man in one person or hypostasis*. The doctrinal formula which expresses this mystery was articulated at the First and Second Ecumenical Councils (Nicaea, 325; Constantinople, 381) through the development of the phrase *homoousios to patri* to indicate that the incarnated Son was of one substance with the Father and through the term *enanthropēsas* (literally, 'enhumanized') to indicate that he took on the total human nature. The relations of the divine and human natures in Jesus Christ were doctrinally formulated in the Third and Fourth Ecumenical Councils (Ephesus, 431; Chalcedon, 451). The separation of the two natures was rejected in the Council at Ephesus and their confusion or intermingling was rejected at the Fourth Ecumenical Council. The formula expressing this mystery was 'one ... Christ ... in two natures, without confusion, without change, without division, without separation' and, more succinctly 'two natures in one hypostasis'. The Sixth Ecumenical Council (Constantinople, 680) affirmed the existence of both divine and human wills in Jesus Christ with the divine will taking precedence, leading and guiding the human will.

Eastern Orthodoxy has not adopted a single view of the saving work of Christ. The many images of that work in scripture are accepted and used without systematization. The whole Christ-event was a saving work: incarnation (*kenosis*), teaching (prophetic role), miracles and commands (kingly role) and especially the cross and the resurrection (high-priestly role). However, the dominant view in Eastern Christianity is the 'Christus Victor' theme, embodied in the liturgy of Holy Week. Jesus Christ assumed human nature to redeem it. His incarnation, his endurance of created existence and his death on the cross caused him freely to accept, on humanity's behalf, the consequences of the fall – sin, evil, demonic influence and death. Jesus Christ's bodily resurrection overcame all these demonic consequences and destroyed their power over human beings, thus redeeming all mankind from their necessary dominion. The Paschal dismissal hymn embodies this understanding of the saving work of Jesus Christ: 'Christ is risen from the dead, by his death destroying Death, and to those in the tombs he gives life.' This act of redemption restores to all humanity the potential to achieve full communion with God once again and to realize the 'image and likeness of God' in human life (*see also* **Icon**). For this reason the broadest Eastern Orthodox perspective on salvation is Athanasius' dictum 'God became man so that man might become divine'.

Because of this, the goal of all human life, and in particular, the goal of the Christian life, is to become that which we were created to be: 'The image and likeness of God.' The theological term used to describe this ultimate human purpose is 'deification *' or 'theosis'. The appropriation of the work of Christ by humanity is the consequence of the work and indwelling of the Holy Spirit. The work of the sanctification of humanity takes place through the church, which is guided and empowered by the presence of the Holy Spirit given to it at Pentecost. Through the church the good news of redemption (euaggelion) is preached and communicated to the world. Persons are incorporated into the church through the threefold sacramental experience of baptism, chrismation and eucharist. In baptism the believer shares in the death and resurrection of Christ through triple-immersion and thus personally appropriates the consequences of Christ's victory over death, sin, evil and the Devil. The 'gift of the seal of the Holy Spirit' begins the road of growth towards theosis. The eucharist incorporates the communicant into Christ, uniting the believer with his 'very body and very blood' and with all others who form the people of God, the church, which is also the body of Christ. The concept of sacrament is also not precisely defined. Additional sacraments are identified, such as penance, matrimony, orders and unction, but the church is replete with other expressions of worship and life which embody the transfiguring dynamic of theosis. All of life, for the Christian growing in the development of the divine image and likeness, is thus a sacrament or mysterion.

The church is one, holy, catholic and apostolic. The historical continuity of the church in its earthly reality is defined by its adherence to the apostolic faith and tradition, its maintenance of the apostolic orders in the continuous succession of the episcopacy and in its maintenance of eucharistic and sacramental communion by which the whole church is united. These conditions are met in their fullness only within what is now commonly referred to as the Eastern Orthodox Church, but Orthodox Christianity acknowledges that in greater or lesser degree they are to be found in all who profess the Trinity and who are committed to Jesus Christ. This allows the Orthodox to seek the unity of Christianity in the ecumenical movement.

The church, then, is the workshop in which people are guided, directed and assisted in their growth towards theosis. The necessary presupposition is the saving work of Jesus Christ and the presence of the Holy Spirit. But, each human being must also respond to what is offered through God's energies, through free and unconstrained co-operation with the divine gift (energies, grace). Each Christian uses his/her self-determining powers (autexousion) to enter into an ever-increasing relationship of conformity with God's will, of growth in communion with God, of Christ-likeness in relationship with others. This requires on the part of human beings spiritual and moral struggle (agōna) and exercise (ascesis). It implies a mode of behaviour which respects those courses of action which are in harmony and appropriate to the God-like life. This life is not mere overt obedience to externally imposed rules, for it is motivated by inner dispositions which are fitting to the divine-human relationship. The fullest embodiment of the God-like ethos in life is experienced in the reflection in human life of divine love – seen as selfless concern for others (agape) and intimate communion with God through loving participation in the trinitarian existence (theion eros). Thus, in Orthodoxy, ethics, spirituality and mystical experience are one with the experience of redemption and sanctification.

This earthly experience of the saving work of God embodies in part that which already exists in heaven – the kingdom * of God. The kingdom is the ultimate expression of the participation of creation in the life of the uncreated God. Thus, in a real sense, all that has preceded in this account is eschatological * and points towards its fulfilment in the kingdom. In as much as the work of Father, Son and Holy Spirit is accepted and shared in by creation, the kingdom is manifested on earth. The Orthodox hold that upon death each person experiences a foretaste of his/her eternal destiny. This is referred to as the partial judgment. Those who have been in fuller communion with God, the saints, may and do intercede before the throne of Christ, for those still struggling towards theosis. Concurrently, those on earth may and do offer prayers for the rest of the souls of those of their company who have died. No claims of effectiveness, however, are made for these prayers, other than a measure of loving, yet undefined, 'help'. The Orthodox anticipate the second coming of Jesus Christ at the general judgment. He will return to judge the living and the dead, who will be resurrected. His return will also be a redemption of the cosmos.

The cataphatic articulation of this theology is never understood as providing an absolute description. The acts, words and images used to describe the divine and human mysteries are adequate for the direction of human thought and action and therefore a fitting and appropriate canon of faith (orthodoxy* as 'true belief' and 'true worship' and orthopraxis* as 'true behaviour'). But as created beings seek to penetrate the divine darkness, the cataphatic approach breaks down – its conceptualizations fail, and its words turn to silence. As the heart is purified and approaches the divine mystery, there is only apophatic reality, the divine mystery. Before the Indescribable One the only genuinely appropriate and fitting response is worship. The Orthodox liturgy thus prays 'Holy God, Holy Mighty One, Holy Immortal One, have mercy on us.' This attitude of prayer and repentance is the beginning and the end of all theology.

Georges Florovsky, *Bible, Church, Tradition: An Eastern Orthodox View*, 1972; *Creation and Redemption*, 1976; John Karmiris, *A Synopsis of the Dogmatic Theology of the Orthodox Catholic Church*, 1973; Vladimir Lossky, *The Mystical Theology of the Eastern Church*, 1957; A. J. Phillipou (ed), *The Orthodox Ethos: Studies in Orthodoxy*, 1964; Dumitru Staniloae, *Theology and the Church*, 1980.

S. HARAKAS

Ebionitism *see* **Christology**

Ecclesiology *see* **Church**

Economic Trinity
see **Trinity, Doctrine of the**

Economy

This term (Greek *oikonomia*, management,

organization, dispensation) has two principal and distinct meanings in Orthodox theology.

1. Although Tertullian, followed by Hippolytus, had used 'economy' to refer to the eternal law of God's being, classical patristic usage distinguishes 'economy' from 'theology', the former being concerned with the 'exterior' manifestation of God's being and purposes while the latter refers to the inner life of the most holy Trinity*. This use of the term has its source in the expression 'the economy of the mystery which has been hidden in God from eternity' (Eph. 3.9; cf. 1.10), which refers to the carrying into activity in the temporal sphere of the eternal purposes of God. Hence it comes to mean in general God's gracious dispensation in creation and salvation under both the old and the new covenants and in particular the incarnation* as the supreme manifestation of God's loving purpose for his creation. Nestorius can speak of the '*prosopon* or person of the economy' and St Maximus the Confessor of 'those who divide Christ into two persons, thus denying the economy', while St John of Damascus refers to 'those things which can and cannot be known of the theology and of the economy', where the context clearly shows that 'economy' refers to the incarnation. The word is used of the life and work of the Incarnate Word, in particular the passion and resurrection. Since the dispensation of God continues in the church, economy can also signify the grace of God which is at work in the mysteries of baptism and the eucharist, through the operation of the Holy Spirit*. Hence one may also speak of the economy of the Holy Spirit with reference to his activity in the church and the world: 'The church is founded on a twofold economy: the work of Christ and the work of the Holy Spirit, the two persons of the Trinity sent into the world' (V. Lossky).

2. Economy is also used in Orthodox theology to refer to dispensations or concessions made by the church to human sin or weakness. It is opposed to *akrivia*, or strict adherence to the letter of the law, and since for the Orthodox the disciplinary canons of the Ecumenical Councils have binding authority, derogations from them may only be granted by economy. The use of economy is based on the words of Christ to the apostles about binding and loosing in

Matt. 18.18. Thus the Orthodox church, while it disapproves of divorce and even of remarriage after the death of one of the partners, also recognizes that because of human sin or weakness a marriage may break down irretrievably, and so, in certain circumstances (cf. Matt. 19.9), by economy allows divorce and remarriage. Again, baptism in the Orthodox church must be performed by a priest with triple immersion, but by economy in cases of extreme emergency an Orthodox layman may baptize, even by affusion. As early as the Didache we find similar dispensations from the strict practice of baptism in fresh running water where that is not available. The Orthodox principle of economy thus corresponds in many ways to the Western idea of dispensation *, but the Orthodox understanding is more far-reaching, because since the church considers herself to be the mistress of the sacraments she may also, by economy, declare valid that which is invalid, though clearly this could not be done if thereby the fundamentals of the faith were to be affected. The general principles are to be found in St Basil the Great who declares, for example, that since some Asian bishops have accepted the baptisms of the Novatianists they should, through economy, be accepted (*Ep.* 188, can. 1), though they are strictly invalid.

The following passage puts the matter clearly:

'This conception of economy has not been authoritatively defined, but historically is accepted as having been the practice of the Church, in that one and the same Sacrament is seen to have been sometimes valid and sometimes invalid. In principle, however, the Orthodox Church does not recognize sacraments administered outside itself, for the acceptance of non-Orthodox sacraments involves the recognition of a Church outside the Orthodox Catholic church. It is apparent that the Orthodox Church places greater importance on the connection between right faith and right Sacraments than does the West' (Archbishop Methodios Fouyas, *Orthodoxy, Roman Catholicism and Anglicanism*, 1972, p. 182).

SYMEON LASH

Ecstasy

A sense of being taken out of oneself, caught up, like Paul, into the third heaven, and united with some higher power. The word is often used to describe the raptures of sexual intercourse, which, as in Donne's poem 'The Ecstasy', is not simply a 'transport of delight', but enables the lovers to penetrate the mystery of love itself. Such union is the climax of contemplation more than of physical or mental activity and provides an analogy of the type of mystical experiences, which e.g. Plotinus describes, though unlike Donne, the Neoplatonist * finds ecstasy in deliverance from the body rather than in psycho-somatic harmony. Ecstasy is not always of God or of joy. English literature knows of an ecstasy of terror and anxiety. Philo distinguishes four types, and the fourth is not mystical union but prophetic inspiration. The Divine Spirit 'evicts' the mind and the result is inspired frenzy. This is not a perpetual state, but transient, for a purpose. When the ecstasy passes, the prophet becomes a normal, rational being, with no supernatural knowledge.

Some Christian teachers, mystical and otherwise, are suspicious of ecstasy. Paul sets greater store by his 'thorn in the flesh' than by his mystical rapture (II Cor. 12), and warns the Corinthians against mistaking elation for grace. For Gregory of Nyssa, ecstasy is non-attainment rather than attainment. 'This truly is the vision of God; never to be satisfied in the desire to see him! But one must always, by looking at what he can see, rekindle the desire to see more' (*Life of Moses* 239).

Augustine finds in ecstatic experience a fleeting glimpse on earth of the joys of heaven, but he also writes of ecstasy as that flash of the divine light and beauty which arouses our longings and is, in fact, the beginning of the quest. Luther knew of moments of an ecstasy in which 'through faith a man is raised above himself that he may behold good things in the future' (*WA* 4, 273). For the Cambridge Platonists * contemplation is not the goal. Ecstasy inspires to action; it must have moral consequences. Henry More, using a much-employed metaphor, speaks of the soul 'inebriated as it were, with the delicious sense of the divine life', but this is a state, more sober than sobriety, which restores man to rationality and virtue. There is a Puritan 'devotion of rapture' found in the lyrical passages of many sermons and prayers and linking the seventeenth and eighteenth centuries. The age of reason was also the age of rapture. Joseph Butler can soar as high as the loftiest flights of contemplative devotion. Wesley, like Addison, can be 'lost in wonder, love and praise', while for Doddridge, 'delight is not calm, it is rapture, transport, even ecstasy' (G. F. Nuttall).

Ps. Denys the Areopagite is not afraid of erotic language to describe the ecstasy which he finds in Paul's words: 'I live, yet not I, but Christ lives in me.' But he also dares to speak of the ecstasy of God himself. It is no illegitimate extension of his thought to say that creation, providence, incarnation are all of the divine ecstasy, of God himself inspired, taken out of himself, made man so as never to be unmade more, united with us for ever by his own initiative of love, which antedates the worlds.

Anne Freemantle (ed), *The Protestant Mystics*, 1964; Marghanita Laski, *Ecstasy*, 1961; Andrew Louth, *The Origins of the Christian Mystical Tradition*, 1981; Gordon Rupp, 'A Devotion of Rapture in English Puritanism', in *Reformation, Conformity and Dissent*, ed. R. Buick Knox, 1977; R. C. Zaehner, *Mysticism, Sacred and Profane*, 1957.

GORDON S. WAKEFIELD

Ecumenism

This is a new word to refer to an old phenomenon in Christian life – the sense of the importance of reuniting separated churches. In mediaeval times, there were attempts (Councils of Lyons, 1274, and Florence, 1438–1439) to bring together the Eastern and Western churches, and the first stages of the Protestant Reformation were closely followed by attempts to heal the new wounds. In England, the later seventeenth century saw unsuccessful moves to 'comprehend' the dissenting bodies within the established church. The theologico-political concept of 'the national church' provided much of the motivation for these negotiations, as it still did for the ideas of Thomas Arnold in the first half of the nineteenth century, though now in a mould affected by the Romantic Movement (*see* **Romanticism**).

There were comparable sporadic movements between Anglicans and Roman Catholics, for example the negotiations between Archbishop Wake of Canterbury and French theologians in the early eighteenth century. Here the theological basis was a combination of shared faith and traditional ministry with the non-papalist propensities of the Gallican leaders. On this side too, Romanticism provided a new impulse in the nineteenth century, and there were dreams of the corporate reunion of the Church of England with the main body of the Western Church, seen in the light of return to historical roots or the fulfilment of God-given destiny. In the setting of a strong sense of historical continuity and of the organic development of institutions, ecclesiology moved, for many, to the centre of theological concern. This movement of thought bore fruit in unofficial negotiations in the 1890s and 1920s (Malines Conversations) and, ultimately, in a more widely based theological framework, the official discussions which have issued in the *ARCIC Final Report* and the Papal visit to Canterbury, 1982.

But in practical terms, ecumenism has been predominantly a phenomenon of the twentieth century and, until recently, of Protestantism. It is essentially a spiritual mood or religious commitment rather than a single clearly worked out theological position; and moreover, much of its impulse has always been pragmatic: the wasteful and scandalous rivalries and duplication of effort in the missionary work of the churches, especially in India and Africa; the clear need for cooperation in areas of social witness; the declining resources of the smaller churches in a country like England; the increasingly 'sect'*-like character of all Christian bodies in more plainly secular societies (cf. B. Wilson, *Religion in a Secular Society*, 1966), giving even to established churches a greater self-consciousness as they have ceased to occupy a central role in relation to political and cultural life in general.

But theology has played its full part. The diffuse movement known as biblical theology*, deeply affecting Protestant and, subsequently, R C thought in recent decades, led to a sense of the organic and unified nature of the Christian community, as described particularly in the Pauline and Johannine writings, and to the idea of an essentially single 'people of God', the instrument of his purposes throughout history, from the beginnings of ancient Israel onwards. In this perspective, some of the traditional reasons for division between Christians seemed to fall away and came to be seen as the product of particular historical circumstances, now long past. Both new needs and a realization of deeper doctrinal roots, shared by all Christians, have led to a sense of the divine will impelling the churches towards not only closer cooperation as institutions but also visible unity as a sacramental expression of God's own life and purpose. Oneness in Christ is the foundation on which all rests. Thinking of this kind (stemming from the Faith and Order Movement after the First World War) has borne fruit in many different settings: notably in the establishment of the World Council of Churches in 1948; in the close doctrinal rapprochement between Catholics and Protestants in Germany (cf. Karl Rahner, *Theological Investigations* 17, Part 4, ET 1981) and other parts of Europe; in the inauguration of the Church of South India in 1947; and in the numerous and varied reunion schemes which have been embarked upon in many parts of the world. Apart from examples of organic unions of churches, by far the greatest achievement of ecumenism has been the growing commitment of the RC church to the cause of unity, exemplified in the Decree on Ecumenism of the Second Vatican Council (ed. W. M. Abbott, *Documents of Vatican II*, 1966). Also remarkable has been the strong participation of the Orthodox churches in the work of the WCC in recent years and in conversations with other churches.

However, more traditional lines of thought persist. The theological vision which has marked much ecumenical thinking still meets competition, especially in catholic Anglican circles (*see also* **Anglo-Catholicism**), from an emphasis on historical and sacramental concepts of the church as centred on its traditional ministry, in particular the historic episcopate. Though the motivation is partly tactical (in that it is feared that dilution on this matter for the sake of unity with non-episcopal churches will render more difficult the attaining of the greater goal of union with Rome and the East), there is here a genuinely distinct theological position. Looking back to the Tractarians and beyond, and to the nineteenth-century hopes for corporate reunion with Rome, its scholarly appeal is patristic rather than biblical. In the present theological world, it is increasingly isolated. Though

it has some points of coincidence with traditional thought in the RC church, it fails to satisfy the papal criterion and is in effect an almost solely Anglican phenomenon. It continues to have bite, especially in the Church of England itself, as the defeat of the scheme for unity with the Methodist Church (1972) and the proposals for Covenanting (1982) clearly shows. It retains the hope that its 'mid-way' position with regard to the church's ministry (historic episcopate with a modified papacy) may yet prove a more satisfactory framework than any other within which to achieve the wider kind of institutional unity. The history of ecumenism, now embracing all the older churches, lends some support to this hope.

Two other factors are worth noting. First, the Christian world includes many evangelical and Pentecostalist* bodies which remain quite outside the widest reach of the umbrella represented by the WCC and form a kind of 'alternative' ecumenical movement. Second, there are many signs that relations between Christians of different traditions are becoming closer quite apart from the official efforts of the churches, that is, on a personal or local basis, with church discipline much less to the fore. Many Christians have come to take ecumenism for granted and to act upon it as opportunity offers.

H. E. Fey (ed), *A History of the Ecumenical Movement II (1948–1968)*, 1970; R. Rouse and S. Neill (eds), *A History of the Ecumenical Movement I (1517–1948)*, 1954. See also S. Neill, *The Church and Christian Union*, 1968; T. Sartory, *The Oecumenical Movement and the Unity of the Church*, 1963.

J. L. HOULDEN

Efficacy

A term used in discussion of 1. the type of causality exercised by a sacrament; 2. the validity of a sacrament. 1. Sacraments are generally understood to be not mere signs expressing or arousing faith (as Zwingli taught), but 'effectual' means of grace (Article XXVI), which 'contain the grace which they signify' (Trent, Denz. 1606). In scholastic* theology there was much debate over the way in which the gift of grace is effected: whether sacraments are occasions of grace (Ockham), moral causes which move God to give grace to the recipients

(Bonaventure), or instrumental (sometimes misleadingly called 'physical') causes. In recent theology there has been a tendency to link the efficacy of a sacrament more closely with the fact that it is a sign: God's grace works through the psychological power of the symbols. 2. The efficacy of a sacrament is distinguished from its validity*. A sacrament is valid if the sign established by Christ has been duly performed; it is efficacious if through it there is conferred the grace of which the sacrament is the divinely instituted means. But whereas a valid sacrament must be efficacious unless the recipient resists the grace, it does not follow that an invalid sacrament is inefficacious, for 'God is not confined to the sacraments'. Hence the flaw in the not uncommon argument: 'I know the sacraments I administer are valid because I can see God's grace working through them.'

See **Ex opere operato.**

B. Leeming, *Principles of Sacramental Theology*, 1956, ch. 9; K. Rahner, *The Church and the Sacraments*, ET 1963, pp. 34–40.

E. J. YARNOLD

Elder

The word elder, derived from the Old English, is synonymous with presbyter derived from the Greek. In contemporary usage, however, the two words tend to be distinguished, a presbyter being an ordained minister of word and sacraments and an elder being a layman set apart by ordination to assist the presbyter in his administration and government of the church. This differentiation corresponds in the Presbyterian Churches to the two types of elder defined by Calvin: 1. Teaching elders, that is, presbyters with pastoral functions, and 2. ruling elders, that is, elders with administrative functions.

In the *Book of Common Order of the Church of Scotland* the duties of elders in the second sense are listed as follows: 'to set the example of a virtuous and godly life, and of regular attendance at public worship; to take part with the Minister in administering the care and discipline of the parish; and to represent their brethren in Presbyteries, Synods, and General Assemblies, when commissioned thereto'. The office of elder, somewhat similarly conceived, is also found in Christian bodies other than the Presbyterian, for example, the Disciples of Christ and the Moravians.

Whether or nor Calvin's distinction has any NT basis may be questioned, but as a means of allowing the laity a greater part in church affairs the eldership may be said to have much to commend it.

J. G. DAVIES

Election

'Choose' and 'elect' are translations of the same verb in the original Hebrew and Greek of the Bible; 'election' is the usual translation of a noun which could equally well be rendered 'choice'.

The OT consistently asserts that God chose Israel to be his people, and that this was an act of his sovereign grace. The choice was not on the ground of Israel's merits; it was made, in spite of Israel's faults and small size, because God freely decided to make it. The Deuteronomist (Deut. 4.37) says that God chose Israel because he loved it, but gives no reason for that love. But he had a purpose in mind: it was that Israel should fulfil the role of his servant within his plan of salvation. The choice brings certain privileges, but also heavy responsibilities, and at the same time dire penalties for disobedience (Amos 3.2), the direst of all being the exile in Babylon. Yet the choice is never withdrawn; when the majority of the people fails, the faith remnant inherits the privileges and responsibilities (Isa. 4.3).

Jesus in the Gospels chooses his apostles just as freely and just as irrespectively of merit. He is also said to 'call' them, and in many passages of the NT 'choice' and 'call' go together (n.b. the enigmatic comment in Matt. 22.14; *see* **Calling**). In the Pauline writings the church is called and chosen by God, as the new Israel (so also I Peter 2.9). It is composed of humble and despised people, lest anyone should boast of his position (I Cor. 1.27–31). Those chosen are entrusted with the task of witnessing to the world. The choice is 'in Christ'; and in Ephesians (1.4) it is said to have been made before the foundation of the world.

Paul has virtually nothing to say about any who may be rejected by God, or who themselves reject his choice. But there are sentences in Romans (8.20, 29, 30; 9.13) which, together with Eph. 1.4, later thinkers hardened into a doctrine of double predestination (*see also* **Predestination**). Augustine, through his deep conviction of God's sovereignty, came gradually to conclude that God foreknew from eternity those who would have faith (including Christ) and those who would not; that he created their faith or lack of it; and that he foreordained their salvation or damnation. In answer to his critics he urged that God's will is not to be questioned.

The Pelagians* and semi-Pelagians* asserted the human right to resist the grace of God, but were judged to over-emphasize human capabilities. Aquinas sought to reconcile human free will with double predestination, but cannot be said to have succeeded. Calvin in this connection abandoned free will, and insisted on the full Augustinian doctrine, which he held to be required by scripture.

There have been many later attempts to do what Aquinas failed to do, as by Arminius in the sixteenth century, and by John Oman and Karl Barth in the twentieth. The unassailable but not wholly consistent propositions are these: God in his free and sovereign grace chooses and calls all people, but does not coerce them; to those who accept his choice and call he gives the freedom which belongs to his children.

K. Barth, *Church Dogmatics* II/2, *The Doctrine of God*, ET 1957, ch.7; A. M. Hunter, *The Teaching of Calvin*, chs. IV to VII, 1950.

RUPERT DAVIES

Emanation

The word is used of ways of thinking which understand God's relationship to the world of which he is the origin in terms of outflow or irradiation, like light from the sun, rather than of an artisan's relationship to the artefact which he makes. Emanationist language was used by the Gnostic* sects of the first centuries AD, but its real significance is not always clear and the influence of Gnostic emanationism on Christian theology has been minimal. More important was its use by Plotinus and the other Neoplatonists* from the third to the sixth centuries AD. This has had considerable influence on some forms of Jewish, Christian and Islamic thought about God and his creation. But most Christian theologians have regarded it with dislike and suspicion and tended to accuse the Neoplatonists and Christian

thinkers deeply influenced by them in this respect (e.g. Eriugena) of 'pantheism'*. They have generally preferred the artisan model of creation, in which God freely and deliberately makes a world of objects quite separate and distinct from himself. However, recent studies of Neoplatonism, notably by Jean Trouillard, have made the thought of the Neoplatonists in this matter much clearer, and made it possible to speak of them and of Christian thinkers influenced by them with much more justice and understanding. The emanation-metaphors which they use are of two kinds: physical (light from the sun, heat from fire; derived perhaps from Platonized Stoicism) and mathematical (generation of numbers from the monad; derived from Neo-Pythagoreanism). They prefer them, though well aware that, like all language, they are inadequate in speaking of the outgoing or procession of all things from the One*, at least partly from a strong dislike of what seems to them the anthropomorphic crudity of the artisan model of creation. But they use them much more critically and subtly and with much greater care than has generally been supposed. The principal points which need to be noted are these. There is no confusion of the source with its derivatives. The source, God, the One or Good, ineffably transcends all that proceeds from him and is unchanged and undiminished by his giving out. This giving out is not due to any kind of necessity. The Neoplatonists use their metaphors of natural process as the best language they can find to express the absolute, eternal, undeliberate, spontaneous generosity of the Good. God is beyond freedom and necessity as the cause of both. But if one must think of him in terms of one or the other, it is better to think of him as absolutely free (Plotinus *Ennead* VI, 8 [39]). And there is freedom also on the side of the creature. In the case of spiritual beings (including man) what is given out is not the completed being but the power which enables the being to make itself, to bring itself to completion by returning in contemplation to its source. And though the Neoplatonists' hierarchies of being are elaborate, they always insist that the source of being, the Good, is creatively present at every level and to every being.

A. H. Armstrong (ed), *The Cambridge His-*

tory of Later Greek and Early Mediaeval Philosophy, 1970; J. Trouillard, *Le Néoplatonisme*, 1981; R. T. Wallis, *Neoplatonism*, 1972.

A. H. ARMSTRONG

Empirical Theology

The roots of efforts to shape an empirical theology lie in such diverse movements as Schleiermacherian theologies of experience, British empirical philosophies and naturalism. Several major centres of empirical theology emerged on the American scene in the early twentieth century as part of the broader movement of theological liberalism * within Protestantism. The empirical theologians were attempting to answer the challenges of atheism * and humanism * on the common ground of human experience and scientific knowledge. Both historical-critical and systematic-constructive methods were employed. They were basically involved in an apologetic task, for they sought to reinterpret Christian theological symbols so as to make them intelligible and effective in a scientific-industrial age, but their work placed them on the theological left. They were influenced by pragmatism *, and by the rigorous insistence on empirical data so important in various schools of historical, sociological and philosophical inquiry.

Important developments in empirical theological thought took place at the Divinity School of the University of Chicago under the leadership of Shailer Mathews (1863–1941). A graduate of Colby College and Newton Theological Institute, Mathews studied history and political economics in Germany, and began his teaching at Chicago in 1894 in the field of NT history, later shifting to historical and systematic theology. A leader in the application of social historical analysis to Christian life and doctrine, he avoided any appeal to religious authority but insisted on a fully scientific, rigorously empirical, inductive method in the theological disciplines. In *The Growth of the Idea of God* (1931) he insisted that the starting point for religion is 'a relationship with the universe described by the scientist', and defined God as 'our conception, born of social experience, of the personality-evolving and personally responsive elements of our cosmic environment with which we are organically related'.

Henry Nelson Wieman (1884–1975) was also a central figure in the 'Chicago school'; his approach was primarily systematic-constructive, under the influence both of the pragmatism of Dewey and the metaphysics of Whitehead. A graduate of Park College, San Francisco Theological Seminary and Harvard University, he came to Chicago in 1927, in search of a theocentric as against an anthropocentric religion. In his early writings, he maintained that God must be known as any other object in experience, by means of scientific observation and reason. Following the clue of defining God as the source of values disclosed in experience, he came to characterize God as a delicate system of complex growth, that is, as the development of meaning and value in the world. In his major work, *The Source of Human Good* (1946), he asserted that his religious thought was within the Christian tradition, and developed certain christological, ecclesiological, and eschatological positions. 'Salvation through Jesus Christ' was presented as 'a transformation in the life of man which is accomplished not by human intelligence and purpose but by certain happenings in history centering in the man Jesus'.

Douglas Clyde Macintosh (1877–1948), born in Canada and educated at McMaster University, received his doctorate at Chicago in 1909, and began a lifetime of teaching at Yale Divinity School. As philosopher of religion, Macintosh insisted on a solid empirical basis for assertions. His *Theology as an Empirical Science* (1919) was a classic statement of the empirical movement. But he also allowed room for a realm of 'over-beliefs', which are not determined by evidence gathered through scientific methods but by what we need to believe in order to live as we ought. Such beliefs, however, would be reasonable and consistent with what we learn by empirical approaches. Holding to a position of 'moral optimism', he defended an understanding of God as a supreme personality of intelligence and goodness, and argued for personal immortality.

In 1931, Macintosh edited and contributed to an important volume, *Religious Realism*, which sought to resist the romantic subjective tendencies of earlier liberalism. His procedure involved proving the existence of God in essentially that religious sense in which the term has been used throughout history, 'and proving this by a new and regenerating experience'. To this symposium intended to affirm the objectivity of a divine ground of faith, Wieman also contributed, as did Eugene W. Lyman.

Lyman (1872–1948) was educated at Amherst and Yale, and after study in Germany, he began a teaching career that climaxed in a professorship (1918–1940) in the philosophy of religion at Union Theological Seminary, New York. In *The Meaning and Truth of Religion* (1933), Lyman argued for the realistic trend then current in the philosophy of religion, indicating that in 'intuition' the depths of reality are really present. Intuitions are 'perceptive', 'synthetic', and 'creative'; they discover truth while reason tests and establishes truth. As with most empirical theologians, Lyman was concerned about the social order, and sought to bring religious resources to bear on the problem of modern living.

The empirical movement in American theology exerted influence on many thinkers who never fully accepted its tenets, among them such figures as John C. Bennett, Robert L. Calhoun and Walter M. Horton. The realistic movement in the 1930s tended on the whole to provide a transition to neoorthodox trends, and empiricism in theology fell under sharp attack, especially from Reinhold and H. Richard Niebuhr.

Kenneth Cauthen, *The Impact of American Religious Liberalism*, 1962; William R. Hutchison, *The Modernist Impulse in American Protestantism*, 1976; Sydney E. Ahlstrom, 'Theology in America: A Historical Survey', and Daniel D. Williams, 'Tradition and Experience in American Theology', *The Shaping of American Religion*, eds. J. W. Smith and A. L. Jamison, 1961, pp. 232–321, 443–95.

ROBERT T. HANDY

Encyclopaedia, Theological

This literary genre emerged out of eighteenth-century German theology largely as a pedagogical remedy for the fragmentation of theological studies. Rapid growth in the number, scope and matter of the theological disciplines made general introductions to the study of theology an urgent necessity. Two kinds of introduction were developed: the 'material encyclopaedia' offered basic in-

formation about the state of the individual disciplines, and the 'formal encyclopaedia' established the unity of the disciplines as parts of a single whole. An influential mixture of the two kinds was written by Karl Rudolf Hagenbach (1801–74), who adopted the four-fold division of theology into exegetical, historical, systematic and practical disciplines, a scheme that was virtually canonical in the German universities and exercised a powerful hold on theological study in Britain and America as well.

Brilliant but too idiosyncratic to win many imitators was the earlier outline by Friedrich Schleiermacher (1768–1834), in which all three of the classical fields – Bible, church history and dogmatics – were placed together under the rubric 'historical theology' as the actual body of material. 'Practical theology' followed historical theology not as an extrinsic appendage to it but as the unifying goal of all the theological studies, apart from which they would scatter to the corresponding secular disciplines (history, linguistics, etc.). 'Philosophical theology', divided into apologetics and polemics, preceded historical theology as the critical discipline that established the normative essence of Christianity unfolded in Christian history. In this way, Schleiermacher offered a tight, threefold organization strikingly different from the conventional pattern of four more or less autonomous parts; and he was a pioneer in his recognition that theology as such, not just in certain of its parts, is essentially historical by reason of its subject matter, which is the church as a phenomenon of change.

Introductions expressly titled 'encyclopaedia' have gradually disappeared, but the problem has not; if anything, it continues to grow. The encyclopaedic model lies behind such recent works as Gerhard Ebeling's *The Study of Theology*; and in the English-speaking world collections of essays have occasionally been edited to meet the same need, each discipline having its own chapter by a specialist. It is evident, however, that a collective volume cannot cure the problem but is itself a symptom of it, demanding more of theological students than is expected of their teachers.

See also **Curriculum, Theological.**

George R. Crooks and John F. Hurst, *Theological Encyclopaedia and Methodology* on the Basis of Hagenbach, rev. ed., 1894; Gerhard Ebeling, *The Study of Theology*, E T 1978; Friedrich Schleiermacher, *Brief Outline on the Study of Theology* (1811, ²1830), E T 1966.

B. A. GERRISH

Enhypostasia

Enhypostasia is the doctrine that the *hypostasis* (i.e. person) of the Godhead, which was incarnate in Christ, included all the attributes of human nature as perfected, and that therefore the one person of Christ, though divine, is fully human. In the patristic age the term was introduced by Leontius of Byzantium (*c.* 550) and later taken up by John of Damascus (d. *c.* 749). In the present century the doctrine has been revived by H. M. Relton in *A Study in Christology*, 1917.

ALAN RICHARDSON/
JOHN MACQUARRIE

Enlightenment

'The Enlightenment' (German, Aufklärung; French, 'L'illumination') is a title given in the history of thought to the dominant intellectual tendency in Western culture in the eighteenth century. The application of this title is sometimes extended to cover also the prevailing current of thought in the previous century, in which case its use can either overlap or be identical with what others call 'The Age of Reason'. Among the major formative influences on this movement are the works of John Locke (1632–1704), Gottfried Wilhelm Leibniz (1646–1716) and Pierre Bayle (1647–1706). Its basic attitude was popularized and applied to religious belief in such works as those of the English deists *, the German Wolffians (cf. Christian Wolff, 1679–1754), and the French *philosophes*, particularly Voltaire (1694–1778) and the 'Encyclopaedists'. Although as a cultural movement the Enlightenment found expression in a great variety of ways, some of which are not mutually compatible, it was largely orientated by four fundamental notions.

1. A commitment to reason as the proper tool and final authority for determining issues. Although there were disputes about the extent of reason's competence and about what it was 'reasonable' to affirm, it was widely considered that reason acts in substantially the same way in all persons once they are freed from the corrupting influence of an unenlightened cultural environment. Locke expresses, therefore, a fundamental principle of the Enlightenment when he declares that a person 'governs his assent right, and places it as he should, who, in any case or matter whatsoever, believes or disbelieves, according as reason directs him'. It was also to a great extent due to Locke's *Essay concerning Human Understanding* (1690) that reason was largely regarded as primarily a matter of reflection on experience and not a development of innate ideas.

2. Stress on nature and the appeal to what is 'natural'. On the one hand there is widespread interest in and respect for what natural scientists, using empirical methods, were discovering about the natural world. Here the example of Isaac Newton (1642–1727) had considerable influence. According to Alexander Pope,

> Nature and Nature's Laws lay hid
>   in Night:
> GOD said, *Let Newton be!* and all
>   was Light.

On the other hand there is a widespread conviction that what is 'natural' is what is right – although there is considerable disagreement about whether the 'natural' is to be discerned by empirical methods or rather is a matter of establishing what ought to be the case and would be if the real world ceased to be subjected to corrupting forces.

3. A widespread acceptance of an idea of progress. Although there is some pessimism about the pattern of events (cf. Voltaire's *Candide* for a bitter comment on Leibniz's doctrine that everything is for the best in the best of all possible worlds), the present is generally regarded as an improvement on the past. Furthermore, by the use of reason under the guidance of education, enlightened humanity is expected to move into an even better future. In literature this attitude finds expression in the battles concerning the superiority of moderns over ancients.

4. Rejection of the authority of tradition. So far as the past is concerned, historical investigations are held to indicate that the evidence often does not warrant the claims made about it. As for current positions, they are to be justified by their manifest reasonableness, not by their antiquity. In this respect there is suspicion of the viability of grand metaphysical systems of understand-

ing but considerable interest in epistemology *. There is also great concern for morality, 'natural rights' and justice. A number of thinkers attempt to show how ethics is to be seen as independent of metaphysics and theology. In political thought this moral concern is often expressed, as by Locke and Jean-Jacques Rousseau (1712–1778), in social-contract theories of the state, although others prefer policies of enlightened despotism.

Immanuel Kant (1724–1804) sees his age not as one which is enlightened but as one which is in process of enlightenment. He sums up this process as one of 'man's release from his self-incurred tutelage'. This latter is the state of refusing, through laziness and cowardice, 'to make use of his understanding without direction from another'. The prerequisite of Enlightenment, then, is freedom; its motto is *'Sapere aude!* Have courage to use your own reason!'; its goal is humanity become 'of age'.

The Enlightenment's criticism of the authority of tradition * led to increasing secularization * in attitudes and ideas. Nature is seen as an ordered whole rather than as a stage for divine interventions and supernatural happenings. So far as religious beliefs are concerned, claims to revelation are acceptable only when they are rationally justified and their contents subject to reason's judgment. Biblical stories and accepted doctrines are not immune from criticism. Works like Bayle's *Historical and Critical Dictionary* and Voltaire's *Philosophical Dictionary* highlight the faults of revered figures and the questionability of standard doctrines. Historical and literary investigations into the Bible develop. Reports about miracles, especially that of the resurrection, give rise to considerable discussion. There is great hostility to priestcraft and suspicion of ecclesiastical pretensions to guide human understanding. Awareness of non-Christian religions adds to the growing sense of the cultural relativity of religious commitments. As for theology, Voltaire describes 'a real theologian' whom he knew: 'the more he grew truly learned, the more he distrusted everything he knew . . . and at his death he confessed he had squandered his life uselessly.'

Although the Enlightenment's attitude is generally hostile to traditional Christian faith, its adherents vary in their own com-

mitments from the materialist atheism of a Baron d'Holbach (1723–1789) or a Julien Offray de la Mettrie (1709–1751), through various forms of scepticism and of deistic belief, to attempts to produce a 'reasonable' version of Christianity. Locke represents the Enlightenment's attitude to religion when he states that 'I believe, because it is impossible, might in a good man pass for a sally of zeal; but would prove a very ill rule for men to choose their opinions or religion by.' He judges, however, as do many, that an enlightened, i.e. 'reasonable', understanding of Christianity is possible. Others, such as David Hume (1711–1776), are not convinced. For them enlightened criticism shows fallacies in all the arguments used to justify theistic, let alone Christian, beliefs. It must not be forgotten, though, that the period of the Enlightenment was also a period in which traditional forms of Christianity not only survived but also produced the evangelical revival in Britain and America and the growth of pietism * in Germany.

Ernst Cassirer, *The Philosophy of the Enlightenment*, ET 1951; Gerald R. Cragg, *From Puritanism to the Age of Reason, A Study of Changes in Religious Thought within the Church of England, 1660–1700*, 1950; Gerald R. Cragg, *Reason and Authority in the Eighteenth Century*, 1964; Peter Gay, *The Enlightenment: An Interpretation*, 2 vols., 1966, 1969; Norman Hampson, *The Enlightenment*, 1968; Paul Hazard, *The European Mind 1680–1715*, ET 1953; Paul Hazard, *European Thought in the Eighteenth Century*, ET 1954; Henry F. May, *The Enlightenment in America*, 1976; John Redwood, *Reason, Ridicule and Religion, The Age of Enlightenment in England, 1660–1750*, 1976.

DAVID A. PAILIN

Eph hapax   see **Finality**

Epiclesis

That section in the anaphoras * of classic Christian eucharistic liturgies East and West which petitions God to continue his past benevolence towards humanity into the present. The petition, which may have euchological roots in the third of the after-meal *Birkat-ha-mazon* of Tannaitic Judaism ('Have mercy, O Lord our God, on thy people Israel . . .'), is first noted in *Didache* 9 and 10 ('Remember, Lord, thy church . . .') where it asks that God deliver the church from evil, perfect it in love, and gather it in oneness into the kingdom *. Of this gathering the eucharistic bread made of many grains and the wine made of many grapes are the image. Subsequent eucharistic traditions develop this sense, specify it in different ways, and locate it at different points in the anaphora's structure. In West Syria the petition was located after the anamnesis * where it remains in the Byzantine family of rites as a request for the Holy Spirit to make the elements the body and blood of Christ for the common spiritual benefit of the participants. In the Egyptian anaphora of Serapion there was a petition before the institution account for the Son and Spirit to enlighten and strengthen the church in proclaiming the gospel, and a petition after the institution account for the Logos * to come upon the elements and bless the participants. In the Roman anaphora before the institution account there was a petition for consecration directed to the Father, and another after the anamnesis, asking for the favourable acceptance of the entire sacrifice by the Father so that its spiritual benefits might be shared by the participants: in neither petition was the Holy Spirit mentioned. Recent Roman reforms have added pneumatic epicleses before and after the institution narrative according to Egyptian structure.

L. Finkelstein, 'The Birkat-Ha-Mazon', *JQR* 19, 1928–1929, pp. 211–62; L. Ligier, 'The Origins of the Eucharistic Prayer: From the Last Supper to the Eucharist', *Studia Liturgica* 9, 1973, pp. 176–85; T. Talley, 'From *Berakah* to *Eucharistia:* A Reopening Question', *Worship* 50, 1979, pp. 115–37.

AIDAN KAVANAGH

Epicureanism

A philosophy widely current in the Roman Empire before, during and after the NT period (cf. Acts 17. 18). Founded upon the teaching of Epicurus (342–270 BC), it accepted the theory of the Greek Democritus that reality consisted in the swirling movements of particles of matter in motion. At death the human soul disintegrates and there is no immortality.

Epicurus conceived of this teaching as a real liberation from the fear of Hades and of the revenge of the gods upon human beings who had failed to satisfy their demands for craven flattery. Epicurus and his followers did not deny the existence of the gods (they were made of very refined atoms); they taught that the gods in their state of bliss were totally uninterested in the doings of the human race. Nor did the Epicureans teach the kind of vulgar hedonism which has so unfairly been attached to their name. They held, indeed, that pleasure was the chief end of human life, but not in the sense of merely sensual pleasure. The principal virtue was prudence, because without wisdom and self-control true happiness or pleasure could not be attained or sustained. The Roman poet Lucretius at the end of the first century AD gave memorable expression to the Epicurean attack upon superstition (i.e. religion) in his philosophical poem *De Rerum Natura*. It will be readily apparent from the above brief description of the Epicurean philosophy why it did not exert any influence upon the development of Christian thought comparable to that of Stoicism *.

C. Bailey, *The Greek Atomists and Epicurus*, 1928; R. D. Hicks, *Stoic and Epicurean*, 1910; A. E. Taylor, *Epicurus*, 1910.

ALAN RICHARDSON

Epiphany

The Greek word means 'manifestation'. The word 'theophany' is sometimes used, meaning 'manifestation of a god (or God)'. In polytheistic religion nature is full of local manifestations of the gods. In popular Greek religion a deity might manifest himself in a 'divine man', a prince (e.g. Antiochus Epiphanes), a miracle-worker (Simon Magus, Elymas), and so on. In Greek philosophy epiphany-religion is the foundation of a natural theology which discerns manifestations of the eternal present (or of the divine) in all things. But in biblical religion direct epiphanies of God are spoken of with reticence, though they do occur, as notably at the burning bush (Ex. 3.2). Usually God manifests himself in the paradoxical act of veiling himself, supremely of course at the incarnation.

ALAN RICHARDSON/
JOHN MACQUARRIE

Episcopacy

In Christian church history the term denotes the office and function of an individual bishop, or the kind of church order characterized by the governance of bishops. Episcopal churches trace the office of bishop* to the earliest phase of Christian history, seeing its origin in the ministry called *episkopos* in the NT. Though *episkopos* is not distinguished from *presbyteros* in the NT, by the second century it had emerged as the ordinary term for the chief leader of the Christian community in a particular place. Episcopacy became the accepted form of church order in the Orthodox Church of the East and the RC Church of the West, as it still is today. In the theology of these churches, the bishops collectively are believed to be the successors of the apostles, and this is the basis of their authority in doctrinal, liturgical and legislative matters (*see also* **Apostolic Succession**).

With the Reformation*, episcopacy became a matter of great controversy, as the majority of Protestants repudiated it. Churches of Calvinist* orientation, for example, turned strongly to presbyterian and congregationalist models of church polity, convinced that episcopacy was little more than 'prelacy', which term means that bishops are seen as worldly potentates rather than evangelical ministers. Christians of the sect* tendency, such as the Anabaptists, also rejected emphatically the hierarchy of the pre-Reformation period.

The Church of England, on the other hand, retained episcopacy, believing it to be not merely an administrative expedient of contingent historical origin but an essential part of the church as founded by Christ. (In recent times, some Anglican theologians have questioned whether it should be termed absolutely or relatively essential.) Anglican ecclesiology has a strong conviction of being in continuity with the historic ministry of the Church Catholic, including the apostolic succession as held in the Orthodox and RC churches.

Among Lutheran churches, though Luther's own theology did not favour the preservation of episcopacy, church polity has varied considerably by nationality. The churches of Sweden and Finland retained bishops and the conviction of being in continuity with the apostolic succession, while in Denmark the title bishop was retained without the doctrine of apostolic succession. German Lutheranism did not see fit to retain the episcopate, though the title was revived for the superintendent of the church in 1927. Some major Lutheran bodies in North America use the title bishop for their chief executive officers.

A few other Protestant churches have preserved the title bishop. Thus, the Moravian Brethren use the term bishop for certain of their leading ministers, and Methodists in the United States use this title for their superintendents, though not conceiving of them in the Orthodox, RC or Anglican sense. It is episcopacy in the latter sense that remains a prominent issue in ecumenical discussion between episcopal and non-episcopal churches.

See also **Bishop**.

K. M. Carey (ed), *The Historic Episcopate*, 1954; T. Cranny (ed), *The Episcopate and Christian Unity*, 1965; K. E. Kirk (ed), *The Apostolic Ministry*, 1946.

R. F. COSTIGAN

Epistemology

The theory of knowledge. At the general level, it deals with such questions as: What is knowledge?, What is the scope of human knowledge?, and What are its sources and criteria? Distinctions have been drawn between knowledge by acquaintance and knowledge by description, and between knowing someone or something, knowing how to do something, and knowing that something is the case. In modern philosophy propositional knowledge is usually defined as justified true belief, the main problems arising over what is to count as justification. Clearly this will differ according to different areas of purported knowledge – everyday knowledge of the world around us, scientific knowledge, personal knowledge, historical, legal, political or aesthetic knowledge, mathematical knowledge, moral knowledge, or religious knowledge.

In philosophy, the general questions of epistemology have constituted one of the main topics of study since the time of Plato. We may distinguish, in the history of epistemology, between the rationalist strand, stressing the power of human reason to deduce and grasp the basic truths about man and the universe (and God), and the empiricist strand, stressing rather the foundation of all factual knowledge in the data of sense. Kant is particularly important in this connection for his recognition of the way in which both sensing and thinking must combine to produce knowledge and particularly for his theory of the way in which our faculties determine *a priori* both what can be known by us and the basic forms such knowledge can take. In modern philosophy, a sharpened empiricism, known as logical positivism, has restricted the scope of knowledge and belief to logical truths and truths capable of verification by the senses, and a sharpened Kantianism has encouraged the 'constructivist' view that the world of so called human 'knowledge' is largely a product of the human mind. But these are only two of the many different epistemologies into which modern philosophy has fragmented. We may also mention hermeneutics,* phenomenology* and existentialism*, all of which have tried to spell out from within the nature and content of human experience, both collectively and individually, and also the more practically orientated epistemologies of Marxism*, pragmatism* and critical rationalism. The linguistic philosophy associated with Ludwig Wittgenstein has helped to widen the scope of purported knowledge once again through its analysis of many different kinds of 'language-game'. The philosophy of Karl Popper has encouraged us to see the human mind as more like a tool or searchlight probing what is there to be known than a passive receptacle of data. The philosophy of Michael Polanyi has encouraged us to note the degree to which personal knowledge and tacit awareness enter into all knowing, even in science.

In the philosophy of religion*, the special problems that attend purported knowledge of God* or the Transcendent have constituted the main focus of religious epistemology. The relation between faith and knowledge and the alleged sources of religious knowledge – experience*, revelation* and history* – and the relation of all these to reason, have received repeated scrutiny. Inevitably the prevailing philosophical climate has tended to dictate the terms of the epistemological debate in the philosophy of religion. Thus for many years in England, confronted by the hostile critique of logical positivism, philosophers of religion sought to show the meaningfulness of religious knowledge-claims by pointing to broader conceptions of experience, 'disclosure situations', the possibility of 'eschatological verification' and so on. Now the emphasis is more on the question of truth and the justification of religious belief. Much sophisticated work on the arguments * for the existence of God * is being done, and the idea of a 'cumulative case' for religious belief developed. Considerable interest is also being shown in the bearing of the continental hermeneutical tradition on problems of religious knowledge.

In Christian theology, there is a sharp divide between the Thomist * tradition (congenial to English philosophers of religion), which maintains a viable place for natural theology in the justification of religious belief, and the twentieth-century Barthian tradition, which asserts the sole basis in revelation for knowledge of God. For Barth, God creates the conditions of his own knowability by revealing himself to the faith of the believer. Barth's own emphasis was on the objective pole of this divine self-revelation in Jesus Christ. T. F. Torrance has emphasized as well the subjective pole of this faith-revelation relation in terms of the 'epistemological relevance of the Spirit'. However, since alleged revelation must be received by human beings, expressed in human language, and tested by human reason and experience, it does not seem possible to by-pass the problems of religious epistemology in this way. For all the theological power of a Barthian epistemology, the rationality of religious knowledge or belief is still open to critical debate amongst holders of any faith or none.

A. J. Ayer, *The Problem of Knowledge*, 1956; J. H. Hick, *Faith and Knowledge*, 1966; W. Pannenberg, *Theology and the Philosophy of Science*, ET 1976; T. Penelhum, *Problems of Religious Knowledge*, 1971.

                                    BRIAN HEBBLETHWAITE

Epoche *see* **Phenomenology**

Eschatology

It is significant that the word first occurs apparently in 1844, where it is used in a disparaging sense. This is because the traditional account of Jesus' career and teaching really had no place for eschatology, except as a description of what is yet to happen at the end of human history. Traditional Christian theology, proceeding on the assumption that Jesus throughout his time on earth had divine foreknowledge of all events, relegated all his references to the future into one of three categories: some of his prophecies referred to his presence with the church from the time of Pentecost onwards (e.g. Mark 9.1); some referred to the fall of Jerusalem (e.g. Luke 21.20); and some to his final coming in glory (e.g. Matt. 24.37ff.). This scheme worked well enough when applied to all the teaching attributed to Jesus in the Gospels, since this is no doubt the significance it bore for those who recorded it. But it only applied in a very unsatisfactory way to the strong expectation of an imminent *parousia* * which runs through most of Paul's letters. Already as early as the time of the writing of II Peter (*c.* AD 120) we can see the embarrassment caused by this expectation (*see* II Peter 3.3–9). Traditional theology could only answer the complaint that the *parousia* (coming) had not arrived as expected by saying that, since we do not know the day or the hour, it might occur at any time, probably would occur very soon, and that we must live as if it would take place immediately.

The rise of the critical study of the NT, which only began to affect English theology in the second quarter of the nineteenth century, altered all this. Once you have abandoned the belief that Jesus knew all about the future by means of a divine foreknowledge, you are at once faced with the question: What precisely did he mean by the kingdom * of God? The kingdom obviously plays an essential part in his thought; if you cannot necessarily assume that he had in mind the Christian church as it actually developed in history, what did he have in mind? The first attempts to answer this question (mostly emanating from Germany) were based on the assumption that it was possible to penetrate behind the dogmatic constructions of the early church in order to find and vindicate 'the Jesus * of history', the real human figure with his original teaching. In the course of this attempt the kingdom tended to be represented as a largely immanental one, a spiritual condition available to those who associated themselves with Jesus or who accepted his teaching about God. The eschatological

traits, the prophecies about future woes, the descriptions of the coming world cataclysm, all these were usually dismissed as the products of the fervent apocalyptic * atmosphere in which the early Christians moved. Thus eschatology, along with christology * and the doctrine of the church, appeared to be part of the dispensable wrappings in which the Jesus of history was encased.

Between 1901 and 1906 Albert Schweitzer may be said to have placed a bomb under this imposing structure. In two books he effectively argued his thesis that critical scholarship is bound by its own premises to give to the eschatological teaching of Jesus not a peripheral, but a central position. He maintained in fact that Jesus' eschatology is the key to a right understanding of his life; only by means of a consistent application of the eschatological category can we understand Jesus at all. Jesus, says Schweitzer, came in order to proclaim the approaching eschatological climax. He originally believed that by sending out the Twelve he would bring the crisis to its consummation. When this failed to happen, Jesus decided that he must deliberately take upon himself the apocalyptic woes and offer himself as the ransom which would enable God to grant the New Age. He went up to Jerusalem, therefore, with one aim only, to die in order that history might end, and God's great act of consummation might take place after his death. His cry on the cross leaves us doubtful whether he maintained this conviction to the very end. Schweitzer insists that, with the collapse of the attempt to rediscover 'the Jesus of history', critical scholarship is left with only two alternatives: either to accept his theory of consistent eschatology, or to relapse into almost total scepticism about the life and significance of Jesus.

Schweitzer's thesis has had a lasting effect on the study of the Gospels. Nothing can be quite the same as it was before. But this does not mean that his theory is universally accepted in all its details today. He put too much emphasis on contemporary Jewish apocalyptic; his disparagement of the value of rabbinic sources has not been justified; the Qumran documents have shown how much more complicated were the various messianic expectations than Schweitzer realized. In the 1930s C. H. Dodd restored the balance to a considerable extent by his concept of 'realized eschatology'. Beginning from the undeniable fact that in Acts and the Pauline letters the kingdom is represented as something which is very much present in power already, he argued that much of Jesus' teaching suggests a kingdom that is already accessible. He therefore claimed to be reasserting Jesus' central emphasis when he said that with Jesus the kingdom in all essentials had come already. Jesus brought the kingdom and was the kingdom; the whole complex of events comprising Jesus' ministry, teaching, death and resurrection themselves constitute the coming of the kingdom. Concentrating mainly on the implications of 'the parables of the kingdom', he argued that Jesus was not greatly concerned with the future, and suggested that some at least of the apocalyptic prophecies attributed to him in the Gospels are the product of the early church.

Since then various mediating positions have been taken up. The clearest in English was set forth in a book, *The Mission and Achievement of Jesus* (1954), by R. H. Fuller where he makes out a strong case for what might be called 'inaugurated eschatology': Jesus saw the kingdom as connected with his ministry, but not as being fully revealed and operative till after the great crisis which his death and subsequent vindication were to bring about. The attempt to decide what was Jesus' teaching about the kingdom is, of course, inextricably bound up with the whole problem of the historical Jesus. It may be said generally that the more radical form critics, whose foremost representative was Rudolf Bultmann, much though they insisted on the impossibility of recovering many authentic details about Jesus' life and teaching, tended to accept the validity of Schweitzer's thesis, inasmuch as they agreed that in Jesus' mind there was to be no interval between his death on the one hand and the full consummation of the New Age on the other. They did not believe that Jesus foresaw an era in which the church was to live and develop in the midst of an on-going world. It should also be noted that C. H. Dodd's thesis had some defenders among British scholars: T. F. Glasson and J. A. T. Robinson both wrote books in which they maintained that Jesus was not expecting an immediate and supernatural return from the heaven after his death. The whole question is bound up with the debate as to the meaning of the phrase 'the Son of Man'. On the whole the tendency during the last decade has been towards the conclusion that Jesus did use this phrase of himself, but that he did not connect it with the figure in Dan. 7. But most scholars would hesitate to say that the phrase as used by Jesus had no eschatological overtones whatsoever.

In one sense Schweitzer's diagnosis may be said to have been justified: he said that the choice was between consistent eschatology and scepticism. But it is scepticism that has been winning the field, to judge by present trends in the study of the Synoptic Gospels. As more and more of the material in the Synoptic Gospels is being attributed to the early church rather than to Jesus himself, it becomes easier and easier to relegate to the same source the eschatological sayings attributed to him. This does not mean, however, that a non-eschatological message of Jesus emerges, but that we are precluded from ever discovering what his message was, since we cannot hope to penetrate behind what the early church said it was. The logical (and absurd) conclusion is a Jesus who (for reasons which we can never hope to discover) was the cause of an outbreak of extensive eschatological expectaton among the first Christians. More hopeful as far as positive conclusions are concerned is the general recognition among scholars that the theology of the NT is based upon a realized eschatology. Whatever their expectations about the future, the writers of the NT proclaim their message on the assumption that the all-important event has happened; we are they 'upon whom the end of the ages has come' (I Cor. 10.11); we have 'tasted the powers of the age to come' (Heb. 6.5). This conclusion is already having a reinvigorating effect on the theology of the church* and the sacraments*, and should begin to affect the theology of the ministry*.

In the meantime a substantial part of Christendom, that part which is often described by the epithet 'conservative evangelical', continues with the concepts and expectations of traditional theology, deliberately eschewing all critical speculations. One of the consequences, however, of the divorce between traditional theology and critical thought is that the former is more vulnerable than it was to adventism. Theologians and others have always been prone to the conviction that they could calculate the exact time of the *parousia*, but up till the rise of critical thought adventist speculations were to some extent checked by the disapproval of the majority of Christian scholars, whom the adventists themselves still regarded as orthodox. Now that the bond of orthodoxy no longer links catholic and evangelical to the same extent, the conservative evangelical is more strongly tempted by adventism. Sects now flourish which originated in a claim to know the time of the *parousia*, and then, when that claim proved to be mistaken, adapted their theology to a 'spiritual' advent. This is true of both Seventh Day Adventism and the Jehovah's Witnesses. Naturally the cataclysmic possibilities latent in nuclear weapons have produced a strong conviction among some Christians that we really have now reached the age when the *parousia* is very close.

Along with adventism often goes Millenarianism (Chiliasm)*, the belief in a thousand-year reign of Christ and the redeemed on earth in the future. It seems probable that Millenarianism, basing itself on one distinctive element in Jewish apocalyptic thought, originated in Asia Minor. It is represented in the Book of Revelation, in Papias, and in Irenaeus. It is an element in the NT which modern critical theology has not attempted to incorporate, and is therefore left to the adventists and literalists to expound. The same could be said of the Antichrist, who plays some sort of part in Paul's thought, and a much more profound one in the Apocalypse. Adventist speculation has never lacked a contemporary figure with which to identify him, whether Mohammed, the pope, Napoleon, or Hitler. Here, however, modern critical theology has occasionally attempted a reinterpretation. As long as it is realized that Antichrist is not exhausted in any one historical individual, but is to be found in various forms in every generation, there is no reason why this compelling symbol should not play a fruitful part in Christian theology.

M. Casey, *The Son of Man*, 1979; C. H. Dodd, *The Apostolic Preaching and its Development*, 1936; R. H. Fuller, *The Foundations of New Testament Christology*, 1965; *The Mission and Achievement of Jesus*, 1954; T. F. Glasson, *His Appearing and His Kingdom*, 1953; *The Second Advent*, 1945; A. E.

Harvey, *Jesus and the Constraints of History*, 1982; J. Moltmann, *Theology of Hope*, ET 1967; J. A. T. Robinson, *In the End God*, 1950; A. Schweitzer, *The Quest of the Historical Jesus*, ET 1910, [3]1954.

A. T. HANSON

Essence

This represents the Latin word *essentia*, which was introduced to stand for the Greek word *ousia* ('being'); *essentia* thus at first had the same range of meanings as *substantia* (*see* **Substance**). The Nicene Creed defined Christ as 'one in being' with the Father (*homoousios**), and this could be rendered either 'consubstantial' or 'coessential'. *Essentia* was at first little used; when revived in the fourth century it acquired a more precise meaning than *substantia*, which too easily suggested 'material stuff', like the English word 'substance'*. Augustine therefore preferred *essentia* to designate God's being. In particular it reflected Aristotle's conception of a formative or constitutive principle in things, suggesting that living beings were controlled by a formula or character which their definition expressed. Some thought this applied even to individuals. Mediaeval philosophers used the alternative term 'quiddity' to denote the unchanging character which prescribes what e.g. Socrates is and does. 'Essence' could thus express the unique unchanging reality of God, as opposed to his particular 'energies' or activities; the 'energies' could in some degree be known, the essence remains a mystery.

Mediaeval philosophers adopted the term 'existence' to distinguish the actual being of a thing from its essence, its nature or individual character. It was held that God's existence, uniquely, is identical with his essence; one cannot distinguish between his actual being and his ideal nature, since he is himself the source of all perfections. In other cases it is still sometimes debated whether essence is prior to existence or vice versa. Many modern philosophers, however, have developed a new concept of existence and regard the term essence as obsolete.

See **Substance**, with bibliography.

CHRISTOPHER STEAD

Essential Trinity

As a term, essential or immanent Trinity is intended to convey the conviction that God is triune in God's inner essence or being and not just in creative and salvific outreach to the world. So expressed, a distinction tends to emerge between essential and economic Trinity which was almost certainly absent during the formative centuries of trinitarian theology, and which, once it has more recently emerged, invites those calls for identity of economic and immanent Trinity so often heard in contemporary theology: 'the immanent Trinity *is* the economic, and vice versa', 'God corresponds to himself'. The case for this identity, or at least reunion of immanent and economic, is of two different kinds. In Rahner and Moltmann, for example, it takes the form of a kind of parallelism between the relations and interactions of the three 'persons' 'within' the divinity, on the one hand, and on the other those between the Father, Jesus and the Spirit of Jesus embodied still in the world. In Barth the parallelism is rather between the utterly hidden nature of God which even biblically authorized trinitarian terms do not allow us to know, and the sovereign freedom and therefore the hiddenness still of God in his very acts of salvation/revelation. These contemporary calls for identity are probably justified as protests against some who seemed so daunted by the difficulties with essential trinities that they opted for economic ones *instead*. But neither form of protest seems sufficiently retentive of a more ancient piece of Christian (and Greek) wisdom which said that God's inner essence or being remained veiled from us while *in via*, in a way in which God's outreach did not. From that more ancient point of view it seems best to say that trinities (or binities) primarily, to the extent that they are or were at all successful, point to God's being in outreach to us and as such suggest some self-differentiation in God which, however, we are quite unable to describe.

See **Trinity, Doctrine of the.**

J. P. MACKEY

Eternity *see* **Time and Timelessness**

Ethics, Christian *see* **Moral Theology**

Eucharistic Theology

Theological interpretations of the eucharist have varied through the Christian centuries, reflecting the variety of liturgical forms and philosophical modes of thought that have predominated in various historical periods. Nevertheless, there are some basic elements of eucharistic worship which have been found in all periods, and there is a fundamental continuity to be found in the historical development of eucharistic worship and theology.

The word itself derives from the Greek *eucharistia*, meaning thanksgiving, which was used in NT times to translate the Hebrew *berakah*, blessing*. Shortly before his death, Jesus shared a last supper with his disciples, in the course of which he offered praise and thanks to God in the Jewish manner customary on ceremonial occasions. According to the NT traditions (I Cor. 11.23–25 and Luke 22.14–20 seem to represent one tradition; Mark 14.22–25 and Matt. 26.26–29 another), Jesus pronounced this blessing (*berakah*) over the bread and wine and identified himself with the food thus being offered to God and shared by his followers.

Whether or not that last supper was actually a Passover meal, its proximity both to the Jewish feast and to Jesus' crucifixion gave it both paschal and sacrificial* connotations which Christians utilized to interpret the meaning of the event. Moreover, they continued to 'break bread' (Acts 2.46) in memory of Christ's redemptive suffering and death, believing in his resurrected presence among them, especially in celebrations of the 'Lord's Supper' (I Cor. 11.20). It is problematic whether the earliest Christians associated Christ's presence with the elements of bread and wine or with the action of blessing and sharing them (the synoptic and the Pauline texts allow for both interpretations), but the Bread of Life discourse in John 6.26–66 suggests that by the end of the first century Christians were identifying the bread and wine themselves with the flesh and blood (Greek *sarx, haima*) of Christ.

By the middle of the second century, the full commemorative meal had become a symbolic sharing of bread and wine in most Christian communities, the dinner itself (Greek *agape*) being held separately if at all. To the brief actions of blessing and sharing were joined prayers, scripture readings and a homily by the bishop or presbyter. Some of the earliest accounts of this practice are found in the Didache (9 and 10) and in the writings of Justin Martyr (*Apology* 1, 65–67). Justin referred to both the service and the elements as 'eucharist', a usage which would continue in Christian theology.

During the second century as well, it began to become common to interpret eucharistic worship as sacrificial in nature, both commemorating and making present the sacrificial action of Christ's redemptive offering of himself to the Father (cf. Clement, *Letter to the Corinthians* 40; Irenaeus, *Against the Heresies* 17, 5; Tertullian, *To Scapula* 2). In conjunction with this, the strong identification of the bread and wine which were offered and shared with the body and blood of Christ who was both priest and victim became orthodox church doctrine and was defended as such by the third century (cf. Ignatius, *Letter to the Smyrnaeans* 7, 1; Irenaeus, *Against the Heresies* 4, 18; 5, 2; Cyprian, *Letters* 63, 4; *Didascalia Apostolorum* 2, passim). The *Apostolic Tradition*, composed by Hippolytus of Rome around the year 215, contains eucharistic liturgies whose words signify that what is being performed is interpreted as a sacrificial offering of Christ, represented by his body and blood, to God.

This theological interpretation of the eucharistic action and elements remained orthodox throughout the patristic* period, even though there was no standard philosophical explanation of how the action represented Christ's sacrifice nor of how the elements were transformed into his body and blood. In contrast to this fundamentally uncomplicated theology, the eucharistic liturgy itself, after the sanctioning of Christianity by the Roman Empire, developed into an elaborate and complex ceremony replete with processions, ecclesiastical vestments and antiphonal chanting. To counter the Arian* and other heresies* of the fourth century, moreover, great emphasis was placed on the divinity of Christ in the eucharist, with the double result that as reverence for the sacrament grew the reception of communion by the faithful declined (cf. Ambrose, *On the Sacraments* 5, 25; Augustine, *On the Psalms* 98, 9; Chrysostom, *Homily on Ephesians* 3, 4).

During the early Middle Ages, the elaborate patristic liturgy was shortened into a more simple form commonly called the mass, which could be performed by a single priest with or without assistants. Since it was recited in Latin, a language which was now foreign to most believers, the role of the congregation at eucharistic worship was reduced to silent spectatorship while the priest offered the holy sacrifice to God. Writers and preachers such as Amalarius of Metz attempted to explain the mass to the faithful by giving allegorical significance to each of its parts, but speculative interest focussed on the words of institution ('This is my body ... This is my blood ...') and the consecrated bread and wine. In the ninth century, Paschasius Radbertus and Ratramnus both published works entitled *De Corpore et Sanguine Domini*, in which they debated whether the eucharistic elements should be regarded as symbol (*figura*) or reality (*veritas*) when they are called Christ's body and blood. Most mediaevals, however, took the words of institution literally, as is evidenced by the condemnation of the opposing view held by Berengarius of Tours (cf. Denzinger-Schönmetzer, *Enchiridion Symbolorum* 690, 700).

The introduction of Aristotelian* philosophy to European universities in the thirteenth century gave scholastic theologians such as Albert, Aquinas, Bonaventure and Scotus a metaphysical system which they could use to interpret both secular realities and sacred mysteries, such as the sacraments. Various theories were put forth to explain how the bread and wine were changed into the body and blood of Christ, the majority of theologians siding with Aquinas in favour of transubstantiation*, the explanation being that the substances of bread and wine were transformed at the time of consecration into the substance of Christ's body and blood, even though the outward appearances of the eucharistic elements were not altered. By the end of the Middle Ages, this philosophical interpretation of the eucharist was so commonplace that it was assumed by many to be Catholic dogma.

An alternative to transubstantiation was consubstantiation*, the explanation here being that after the words of institution were spoken, there were two realities copresent under the appearances of bread and wine: the foods themselves, which could be touched and tasted by the senses, and Christ himself, who could be known by faith and experienced through the power of grace. Martin Luther adopted this theory, for which he was condemned by the Council of Trent, but Luther also argued that Christians should participate more actively in eucharistic worship and receive the sacrament more often. Towards these ends he translated the mass into German and denied that it was a sacrifice that could be offered by a priest on behalf of others. Additional alternative interpretations of the eucharistic action and elements were developed during the Reformation * (the Reformers preferring to call them the Lord's Supper and Communion), with the majority of Protestants eventually settling either on the notion that they are merely commemorative and symbolic in nature, or on the explanation that Christ is spiritually received by the believer in some way when communion is devoutly taken. The Roman church insisted on the validity of the traditional doctrines of the real presence of Christ and the sacrificial nature of the mass. The Anglican church has tolerated both Catholic and Protestant interpretations of the eucharist.

The eucharistic theologies of most churches today reflect to a greater or lesser extent the official positions formulated during the Reformation and its aftermath, but the ecumenical impetus of the mid-twentieth century has encouraged a greater tolerance for opposing interpretations. Modern scriptural and patristic studies have awakened interest in pre-mediaeval records of the eucharist, and have freed them somewhat from the doctrinal assumptions of later periods. In addition, the liturgical movement *, which has led to a revision of the eucharistic rites in the Roman, Anglican, Lutheran and other churches, has thereby encouraged a renewed perception of what it is that eucharistic theology is supposed to explain.

Put succinctly, the fundamental question in eucharistic theology is: What is happening during eucharistic worship? To answer that question, contemporary theologians both Catholic and Protestant rely not only on the doctrinal formulations of their respective churches but also on the revised texts of the liturgies, the findings of scriptural and historical theology, insights into the individual and social experience of eucharistic worship, and suggestions from a variety of modern philosophies. In Roman Catholicism alone, for example, the fact that the eucharist is celebrated in diverse cultural contexts (European, American, Latin, African, etc.) is leading to the development of eucharistic

theologies which are not always compatible with each other nor with established church teachings. Similarly, the use by Catholic theologians of modern philosophical systems (existentialism *, phenomenology *, process * thought, even Marxism *) is leading to the development of intellectual alternatives to the traditional scholastic theology.

It would be a mistake, therefore, to suggest that in contemporary Christianity there is a small set of stable eucharistic theologies which may be conveniently labelled 'Catholic', 'Protestant', and so on. Indeed, the trend seems to be in the direction already found in the Anglican communion, namely, that of tolerating a diversity of intellectually honest attempts to understand the meaning and reality of eucharistic worship. Nevertheless, some fundamental factors remain central to all such attempts, in particular the relatedness of such worship to the last supper, to Christ's death and resurrection, to the mysteries of incarnation and redemption, to the local Christian community, and to the universal church.

In any denominational setting, the eucharist is a memorial of Jesus' last supper with his disciples as it has been preserved in the scriptures. The Gospels portray Jesus as giving himself to his followers through the blessing and sharing of bread and wine, an action which both culminates his ministry of self-giving and anticipates his death for the salvation of others. It is therefore the inauguration of a new covenant *, a new relationship between God and humankind, initiated by Jesus as Christ and continued in the church as the body under his headship. The key to that relationship is self-surrender to God the Father and self-sacrifice to others, opening the door to the eschatological kingdom (cf. Luke 22.14–20).

By its close association with the Jewish Passover and with Jesus' crucifixion, the eucharist is also a celebration of Jesus' own passing over from death to life, from ignominy to glory. The crucifixion was both self-willed and yet not wanted (Mark 14.26), but Jesus undertook it as a response to the Father's will and in anticipation of resurrection (Mark 14.28). In their recalling of his death and resurrection through their ritual re-enactment of his last supper, Christians are therefore reminded of their calling to live as Jesus did, and they are invited to share their lives and pour out their energies in the service of others, in the confidence that their sacrifice will likewise lead to new life and the belief that this is the paradigmatic way to enter the kingdom of God.

The eucharist thus resonates with overtones of the great christological * doctrines, for in traditional theology Christ is the incarnation * of God, the living Word spoken in human history who became flesh and blood in order to accomplish the redemption of the world. It is in this dimension that the eucharist lives up to its name of being a 'thanksgiving', a praising of the Father for the redemption wrought by the Son, and a thanking of both for the Spirit who has been released into history through the salvific sacrifice of Christ on the cross (cf. John 15.26; 16.7ff.). Being a sacramental celebration, moreover, the eucharist is a means of entering into that attitude of praise and thanks to the Father, of identifying with the transformed humanity of Christ 'the first born of many brothers' (Rom. 8.29), and of experiencing the workings of the Spirit 'who dwells in our hearts' (II Cor. 1.22).

It is the Spirit of Jesus, alive and active in those who are united under the Fatherhood of God, which permeates the Christian assembly, making it one body, the church. Although any act of worshipping together unites, to a greater or lesser extent, those who are gathered in common prayer, eucharistic worship since the earliest days of Christianity has been the liturgical expression and cause of church unity *par excellence*. It prophetically announces that Christians in community are one body, the body of Christ (I Cor. 11.28f., 12.12ff.), united as grains of wheat in one loaf of bread, which is likewise the body of Christ (Didache 9). It therefore calls Christians not only to unity in mind and heart but also to community in action and co-operation through its central symbolism, whereas in other church services unity in the body may be only an implicit or peripheral theme.

Finally, the theological dimensions of the eucharist expand outward to embrace the church universal in time and space. Historically it is a type of worship which has perdured in one form or another through all the Christian centuries, and today it is found in almost all Christian churches. Although confessional considerations still prevent intercommunion in certain cases (e.g., in the Roman Catholic and Eastern Orthodox churches), many Christians today recognize eucharistic worship as a sign of ecumenical unity which transcends denominational differences, and they acknowledge it as a reminder of the prayer of Jesus, recounted in the Johannine account of the last supper, 'that they all may be one' (John 17.21).

L. Bouyer, *Eucharist*, E T 1968; O. Cullmann and F. Leenhardt, *Essays on the Lord's Supper*, E T 1958; G. Dix, *The Shape of the Liturgy*, 1945; A. Higgins, *The Lord's Supper in the New Testament*, 1952; J. Jungmann, *The Mass of the Roman Rite*, 2 vols, E T 1951, 1955; E. Kilmartin, *The Eucharist in the Primitive Church*, 1965; T. Klauser, *A Short History of the Western Liturgy*, E T 1969; J. Powers, *Eucharistic Theology*, 1967; E. Schillebeeckx, *Christ the Sacrament*, E T 1963; *The Eucharist*, E T 1968; M. Thurian, *The Eucharistic Memorial*, 2 vols, E T 1960, 1961; J. von Allmen, *Worship: Its Theory and Practice*, E T 1965.

J. MARTOS

Eudaimonism, Eudemonism

The latter is the more common English form of the word, which derives from the Greek *eudaimonia*, lit. 'the well-being of the spirit (soul)'. As used by modern philosophers eudemonism is the theory of ethics which teaches that happiness or contentment is man's highest good. The word, however, goes back to Aristotle, who taught that *eudaimonia* was the criterion and end of right conduct. For Thomas Aquinas (*see* **Thomism**) *beatitudo* or blessedness consists in the vision of God (*see* **Beatific Vision; Vision of God**). This view has been questioned by more recent theologians on the ground that any form of cultivation of one's own spiritual life, or the making of one's own blessedness the goal of ethics, is a form of selfishness which leaves no room for the love of God for his own sake or of our fellow creatures as man's chief ethical end.

ALAN RICHARDSON

Euhemerism

The theory of Euhemerus (*c.* 315 BC), a Sicilian Greek philosopher, that the traditional (Homeric, etc.) beliefs about the gods originally developed from legends and traditions about human heroes of distant ages. The ancient Christian apologists (e.g. Lactantius, AD 240–320) were quick to seize upon this convenient explanation of the origins of Greek religion.

ALAN RICHARDSON

Eutychianism see Incarnation

Evangelical, Evangelicalism

Derived from *euangelion* (evangel, gospel, good news), the term came into use at the Reformation to identify Protestants, especially as they held to the belief in justification * by grace through faith and the supreme authority of scripture (often considered the material and formal principles of Reformation teaching). Subsequently, the meaning tended to narrow, with evangelicalism referring to those who espoused and experienced justification and scriptural authority in an intensified way: personal conversion and a rigorous moral life, on the one hand, and concentrated attention on the Bible as a guide to conviction and behaviour on the other, with a special zeal for the dissemination of Christian faith so conceived (evangelism). Anabaptism, Puritanism, Wesleyanism, Continental pietism, converts of the American Great Awakenings, and all their heirs represent variations on these themes. Today evangelical continues as an adjective in the names of some Protestant denominations and is also used in theology to identify Reformation doctrine (viz. Karl Barth's *Evangelical Theology*), but it is more generally associated with the aforementioned subsidiary meaning of interiorization and intensification as in 'born-again Christianity'.

Evangelicalism (second meaning) in the late twentieth century expresses itself in various sub-communities: 1. Fundamentalist * evangelicals, characteristically militant and separatist, view themselves as born-again Christians who have held unswervingly to the doctrine and practice of 'biblical inerrancy', and as such are loyal to the doctrinal propositions of the Bible, and the complete reliability of the accounts of events in nature and history (in the autographs and sometimes in the received texts themselves). Fundamentalists may be apocalyptic* or non-apocalyptic, apolitical or political. A form of apocalyptic political fundamentalism that makes extensive use of television and radio to spread its views has come to be known in the United States as the Christian Right. 2. 'Old evangelicals' are exponents of the life of personal piety. They are known for their stress upon the conversion experience and its evocation in either mass evangelism or individual witness, strict standards of personal morality and disciplined biblical study. 3. 'New evangelicals' share the convictions of old evangelicals but add an accent on the rational defence of faith and seek to relate piety more aggressively to social issues. Their increased visibility in the 1950s and since challenges stereotypes of evangelicalism as against reason or as unconcerned about the civil order. 'New evangelicals' and 'old evangelicals' may also espouse biblical inerrancy but interpret it in a wider sense (authorial intent). 4. 'Justice and peace evangelicals', also referred to sometimes as 'young evangelicals', represent a vocal minority within modern evangelicalism calling for a more radical critique of the systems and practices of oppression and war. Heirs of Anabaptist and high Calvinist traditions are linked in this movement which sometimes expresses itself in intentional communities. 5. 'Charismatic evangelicals' are identifiable by their stress on 'the baptism of the Holy Spirit' understood primarily, although not exclusively, as the gift of tongues (glossolalia *), and a fervent life of prayer, praise and personal testimony. These variations of evangelicalism may be found in combination, as in the charismatic political fundamentalism of some in 'the electronic church', as well as in major separate constituencies.

Controversy among evangelicals today is related to the focus on one or another of the two formative principles, justification and scriptural authority. Thus in 'the battle for the Bible' single-minded proponents of inerrancy, representing the cognitive side of evangelicalism (scriptural authority) are pitted against defenders of a 'soteric' interpretation related to the affective dimension of evangelicalism (justification) who view scripture as definitive in faith and morals and not so in cosmologies and chronologies. Further, the movement of many evangelicals towards the mainstream of Christianity, or their acceptance of a common ecclesial life with other Christians, is viewed as a sign of defection by rigorist elements within evangelicalism. Evangelicals and 'ecumenicals' now regularly share in efforts in evangelism and social witness, and have come together in major conclaves from time to time for the articulation of common concerns.

D. Bloesch, *The Essentials of Evangelical Theology*, 2 vols, 1978, 1979; G. W. Marsden, *Fundamentalism and American Culture: The Shaping of Twentieth Century Evangelicalism, 1870–1925*, 1980; D. F. Wells and J. D. Woodbridge (eds), *The Evangelicals*, rev. ed. 1977.

GABRIEL FACKRE

Evangelism

The word 'evangel' is a transliteration of the Greek word *euaggelion*, translated 'gospel' (Anglo-Saxon 'god-spell'), meaning good tidings, or good news (*see also* **Gospel**). The NT word had two basic uses, referring first to the good news Jesus preached (the proclamation of the kingdom* of God), and later to the good news about Jesus. The Greek verb *euaggelizesthai* means to bring or proclaim good news, specifically the gospel of Jesus Christ, who was both its bearer and its embodiment, and whose birth and life; words and work; and death, resurrection and exaltation are both its proclamation and its manifestation.

Simply put, then, evangelism is the proclamation of the gospel. The evangelistic activity of the early Christians, however, was not limited to preaching, for it informed and involved everything the church was called to be and do in its worship, fellowship and service. While evangelism is properly defined in terms of its message and not the recipients, the results, or the methods used, most definitions are more descriptive, such as the oft-quoted definition of the Church of England's Commission on Evangelism, adopted in 1918 and reaffirmed in 1945: 'To evangelize is so to present Christ Jesus in the power of the Holy Spirit that (people) shall come to put their trust in God through him, to accept him as their Saviour, and serve him as their King in the fellowship of his Church.'

Evangelism is not optional for the Christian church, which has a mandate from its Lord to proclaim the gospel. The climactic words of Jesus to his disciples at the end of each of the four Gospels are authority enough for most Christians: 'Go into all the world and preach the gospel to the whole creation' (Mark 16.15; cf. Matt. 28.18–20; Luke 24.47f.; and John 20.21–23; see also

Acts 1.8; John 17.18–21, and for Paul, II Cor. 5.19f).

The Greek noun *euaggelistēs* (evangelist) occurs only three times in the NT (Acts 21.8; Eph. 4.11; II Tim 4.5) and originally denoted a function rather than an office. The apostles* were evangelists, but not all evangelists were apostles. Paul charged his protégé Timothy to do the work of an evangelist.

The Protestant Reformers had little to say about evangelism. To John Calvin the term referred to an office which ranked next to the apostles, but like them was not meant to be perpetual, even though God occasionally raises up evangelists. 'The Office I nevertheless call extraordinary,' said Calvin, 'because it has no place in churches duly constituted' (*Institutes*, IV–3, sec. 4). The eighteenth century produced such powerful preachers as George Whitefield, the Wesley brothers, and Jacques Bridome of France, while the nineteenth century, beginning with the Great Revival of 1800 in America, followed with such renowned evangelists as Charles G. Finney, Dwight L. Moody, Billy Sunday, Hans Hauge of Norway, Johann Wichern of Germany and John Roberts, key figure 'in the Welch Revival of 1904–1906. A plethora of twentieth-century evangelists, spurred by the appeal of reaching millions around the world via radio and television, offer their commercially packaged versions of the gospel to more persons in a single broadcast than John Wesley preached to in his entire lifetime. The televised 'crusades' of Billy Graham made him one of the most familiar faces in the entire world, as well as the foremost revivalist of his time.

While certain persons will be called to preach, the church's evangelistic task belongs to all Christians, who have been empowered by the Holy Spirit to be Christ's witnesses to the end of the earth (Acts 1.8). The gift of the Holy Spirit is to enable the church to fulfil its mission. Thus evangelism is a function of the body of Christ, whose members use their individual gifts to help the church to be the evangelist. Christ's witnesses know, however, that the ultimate Evangelist is the Holy Spirit* and that they are only the instruments God uses to touch the hearts of those who are receptive to the gospel.

As in NT times and throughout history, so also today people respond in different ways to the message – some positively, some negatively, some indifferently. The word evangelism has itself become a source of controversy, as Christians argue about the appropriateness of particular methods. Pejorative images of overly-aggressive 'soul-winners' cause many Christians to reject all evangelism, as meaning and method are confused, whereas sensitive communicators of the gospel know that what may be an appropriate style for one setting or situation may not be proper for another. Others are concerned that a pietistic individualism may blind the personal salvationist to the issues of social justice which the gospel must address. The dichotomy between evangelism and social action is an unfortunate misunderstanding of the gospel, which demands that evangelism be both personal and social. The evangelistic approach that is concerned with reaching the whole person cannot overlook the social dimensions of a person's life, or the context in which that life is lived. What indeed is good news to the poor, the hungry, the oppressed, if it does not speak to their condition? More and more Christians are recognizing the need to address not only the symptoms of the world's social ills but the systemic evils that cause them (*see* **Political Theology**).

While the NT is the basis of the church's understanding of evangelism, it does not describe a model or define a programme for the kind of cross-cultural mission and inter-faith dialogue in which today's evangelists must engage. Jesus' mission was to Jews and Paul's to Gentiles of his own culture. The challenge to the contemporary church is how to do evangelism in a pluralistic world, how to be both ecumenical and evangelical at the same time, affirming the truth of other faiths without compromising the uniqueness of Christ, how to proclaim the gospel with integrity in a world which questions the validity of God-language, how to keep a church's desire to grow and its prophetic mission in proper perspective. Evangelism will have integrity when it is done by Christian congregations who understand themselves to be the servant people of God, called to seek first the kingdom of God and his righteousness and to follow where the Lord of the church leads them.

RICHARD STOLL ARMSTRONG

Evil, The Problem of

The 'problem of evil' is raised by the opening words of the Apostles' Creed: 'I believe in God, the Father, Almighty . . .' If God loves as a father loves his children, and if he is also omnipotent, why does he permit suffering and other forms of evil in the world? If God is good, he cannot be almighty; if he is almighty, he cannot be a God of love. This is a problem only for believers in a personal God (Jews, Christians and Muslims). For others evil is no problem: it is simply 'the way things are', although it would be possible to press them about 'the problem of good' – why certain things should appear more valuable than other things, if all things are simply the way they are. Where then does the illusion of value come from? Attempts at a solution of the problem of evil may be divided into four types.

1. *Evil as Non-being*. The 'perennial * philosophy' from Plato * through Neoplatonism * to Thomas Aquinas held that evil was non-being. God is *ens realissimum*, the source of all perfection; below him in the Great Chain of Being there stretch orders of being each less perfect and therefore less real than the one above it (cf. Aristotle's gradation from Form to Matter). As God is absolute reality and absolute perfection, so at the other end of the Chain evil is absolute imperfection and therefore absolutely non-existent. Various stages of perfection correspond to their equivalent degrees of being. Evil is nothing in itself; it represents only an absence of good. There is therefore in fact no problem of evil at all. Since every degree of perfection is necessary to the fulness of perfection as a whole, every form of imperfection in creation must necessarily exist, and the justification of its existence is that without it the wholeness of perfection could not be; but absolute imperfection cannot (logical 'cannot') exist. Various forms of idealistic * philosophy of the Hegelian * type similarly regard evil as an illusion, or at least as necessary to the perfection of the whole. The notion is sometimes given an aesthetic expression. The dark colours in a picture are necessary to the artistic perfection of the whole work; if we could but 'stand back from the canvas', we would realize that what looks like an ugly smudge seems thus only because of our bad perspective. Or again,

the profundity of tragic beauty could not be experienced unless evil in defeat encompassed also the destruction of the good: not only is an Iago necessary in 'Othello' but the very imperfection of Othello's love is necessary to the tragic defeat of evil. Life is tragedy or tragi-comedy; it is not melodrama, in which the unsullied good comes into conflict with the wholly bad and defeats it. The difficulty with this kind of 'solution' to the problem of evil is that it requires a long period of philosophical training before it can be appreciated, and in the twentieth century the philosophy involved does not seem so self-authenticating as it did in former centuries. It would be difficult to bring comfort to a bereaved parent or an incurable invalid by means of an explanation of the degrees of being and of perfection.

2. *Dualism* *. The above type of solution to the problem of evil is offered by philosophical monism. Another explanation is given by dualistic or pluralistic philosophies, which in some way limit the omnipotence of God. Zoroastrianism in ancient Persia envisaged the world as the scene of a struggle between light and darkness, good and evil. Crude dualism, however, is philosophically unsatisfactory, because there cannot (logical 'cannot') be two ultimate principles of reality. Similarly Satan cannot help to provide a philosophical explanation: how did the Serpent get into the Garden of Eden, after God had seen that the whole creation was 'very good'? Speculation about a 'premundane fall *' – a rebellion of angelic beings in heaven before the creation of the world – is unlikely to commend itself to thoughtful people in the age of demythologizing. No exception need be taken to the ancient symbolism, revived by Luther, of Christ's defeat of the powers of evil; indeed, the *Christus Victor* concept is rooted in the N T and in the ancient Fathers (cf. G. Aulén, *Christus Victor*, E T 1932). But this is not a philosophical explanation of evil; it is rather an affirmation that Christ has defeated evil and that we also can overcome in Christ. Christ came not to explain evil but to defeat it (cf. A. N. Whitehead, 'The Buddha gave his doctrine; Christ gave his life'). Pluralistic philosophies are no more intellectually satisfying than is dualism. A limited God, who is himself struggling not only *pro nobis* but *cum nobis* against the

forces of disorder in the universe, satisfies neither the reason nor the religious awareness of thoughtful Christians (e.g. H. G. Wells, *God the Invisible King*, 1917; William James, *A Pluralistic Universe*, 1909). Theories of a limited God, who is himself in process of overcoming the disorder of the universe of which he is himself a part, are again receiving favourable attention from some theologians (*see* **Process Theology**), but they seem to others more akin to gnostic speculation or sheer mythologizing than to the historic tradition of biblical and Christian thought. It would seem that the denial of the omnipotence of God does not offer a convincing solution of the problem of evil.

3. *Despotism*. In contrast to the views which limit the omnipotence of God are the views which emphasize it strongly. Such views are based on oriental conceptions of sovereignty. (The Greek *despotes*, master, owner, lord, does not necessarily imply 'tyrannical'.) What the Sultan wills is right, is law, simply because he wills it; he does not have to conform to any objective law or right external to himself. This, indeed, is not the Hebraic view of kingship; in Israel the king was judged entirely by his obedience to the divine will. Nor is it the O T view of God's sovereignty, since his sovereignty is identical with his righteousness (cf. Gen. 18.25). Yet in the O T there are found metaphors of God's sovereignty which imply an almost arbitrary despotism, e.g. the potter and the clay (Isa. 45.9; 64.8; Jer. 18.6); and in Rom. 9.20f. Paul states one side of the paradox of man's relationship to God. The most grossly oriental conception of the Godhead remains in Islam, in which an enervating fatalism is based upon the doctrine of 'the will of Allah'. Within Christianity Calvinism * has most strongly asserted the sovereignty of God and has developed the consequent doctrine of predestination *. Karl Barth, while he modified the harshness of the predestinarian teaching, nevertheless sternly refused to discuss the problem of evil. If God is God, how can we dispute his wisdom in making things as they are? The clay can have no just grievance against the potter. If God decrees from eternity that this man shall be saved and that one damned, his decree is just because he is God, and what God decrees is automatically right. Hence there can be no such thing as a problem of

evil: 'whatever is is right' because God wills it. This kind of attempt to solve the problem of evil by denying its existence is unlikely to appeal to thoughtful people today. For one thing, it loses sight of the fatherhood of God behind his sovereignty, whereas the essence of the problem is how to reconcile the fatherhood with the omnipotence. Secondly, the idea that a thing is right because God wills it rather than that it is willed by God because it is right will appear offensive to the moral sense of most Christians today.

4. *The Moral Theory*. In contrast to the view that God's power is subject to limitation and also to the view that it is absolute and constitutes right and wrong by decree there stands the mediating view that God's power is limited by his own character of righteousness, truth and love. According to this view God is not limited by anything external to himself (as in dualism or pluralism) but he is limited by the essential character of his own being. He cannot will the irrational or the morally wrong, because his nature is truth and righteousness. Because he is *God*, he cannot will two and two to be five; because of the nature of goodness (which is his own nature) he cannot create beings who are instantly free and good. This is because value to be valuable must be freely chosen; as every teacher knows, outward obedience can be enforced by iron discipline, but it is not genuine goodness. Goodness to be good must be freely chosen; value must be freely loved in order to be attained. God in creating mankind (and perhaps the whole evolutionary process which preceded it) desired to bring into existence beings who could freely choose the true, the beautiful and the good, and above all who could freely return the love which he had lavished upon them. The creation of a world in which this end was possible necessarily involved three things, which together constitute the problem of evil: (*a*) pain; (*b*) suffering*, and (*c*) moral evil. (*a*) The *biological* utility of pain is obvious: if the child did not hurt his hand when he touched the fire, he would quickly perish. There is also undoubtedly a corresponding *spiritual* utility of pain, which when bravely borne results in the formation of noble character. But against this it must be remembered that there is a great deal of physical suffering in the world which is not ennobling but on the contrary would seem to be soul-destroying and meaningless. (*b*) Suffering is wider than pain, though pain is often involved in it. It is probably the *irrationality* of much of the suffering in the world which causes moral revulsion – earthquakes, pestilences, famines, infants born deformed, insanity, etc. Undoubtedly character is formed in the struggle to overcome suffering; yet it is unconvincing to argue that a lot of people are starving or stricken simply in order that others may have the opportunity of character-forming unselfish relief-work. Even so, it is hard to see how distinctively human values could emerge in a world in which suffering did not exist. There is something in the insight that, if this world were created to be 'a vale of soul-making' (Keats) or 'a school of manhood' (Streeter), it serves its purpose fairly well. The insight is an ancient one (cf. e.g. Wisdom 3). If this world is a preparation for a future life, the problem of suffering is immediately alleviated (cf. Rom. 8.18). Nothing but the hope of 'the glory which shall be revealed' can make bearable the thought of the infinite wastage, suffering and pain of the centuries of evolution which had to pass before man as a free moral agent could exist: 'with a great sum I obtained this freedom'. (*c*) It is in moral evil that the problem of evil culminates – man's rejection of God and the divine law in order to put himself in God's place and create his own right and wrong. The parable of Gen. 3 (the Fall) succinctly delineates, though it does not explain, man's predicament as a fallen creature. The problem of evil is ultimately the problem of man's existence. As such it requires indeed a rational explanation, if that is forthcoming, and men will for ever go on searching for explanation because they are themselves rational beings. But while rational explanation can perhaps give us a glimpse, as through a mist, of the outline of an answer to the problem, it is possible for the Christian to understand existentially his own situation as in rebellion against God and yet as redeemed by God. He knows that he is himself the problem of evil and also that through the unmerited grace of God the problem has been solved in his existence. This is not indeed the kind of solution which can be explained philosophically to an interested intellectual, because it can be understood only in Christian faith and life. The ultimate solution of the pro-

blem of evil must lie in the fact that the God who created the world is also the God who has redeemed it; the Creator is himself in Christ the bearer of all creation's sin and suffering as he is the bringer of the redemption that shall be. But only the Christian can know that Christ has explained evil in the act of defeating it.

See also **Theodicy**.

John Cowburn, *Shadows and the Dark*, 1979; A. M. Farrer, *Love Almighty and Ills Unlimited*, 1962; John Hick, *Evil and the God of Love*, 1966; C. S. Lewis, *The Problem of Pain*, 1940; B. H. Streeter, *Reality*, 1926; W. Temple, *Mens Creatrix*, 1917; F. R. Tennant, *Philosophical Theology*, II, 1929.

ALAN RICHARDSON

Evolution

The theory of evolution provides the basis for two premises which lie at the heart of modern biology. The first is that all living things are related as part of the same family tree, a premise which has recently received spectacular support from molecular biology and the discovery that all known genetic systems are based on the same genetic code. The second is that the most fruitful questions to ask about the ways in which life has developed are in terms of the advantages which particular developments give to their possessors. Advantage, rather than purpose or design, is the key explanatory concept. In this general conceptual sense the theory is now treated as axiomatic.

The details of evolutionary history still contain many areas of uncertainty, and understanding of how evolution actually takes place is still incomplete, though it has advanced greatly in complexity and sophistication since Darwin's day. However, the twin principles of random variation and natural selection remain the pillars on which everything else is built. Since the beginning of this century the principle of random variation has been given precise content through the development of genetics, and latterly through advances in molecular biology. Natural selection is no longer thought of in terms of crude competition between individuals, but has been broadened to include populations of animals in complex inter-relationships responding in different ways to environmental change. Of particular interest to those concerned about the 'mean-ing' of the evolutionary process is the recognition that behavioural adaptation may be as important as genetic change in determining the success of an individual species. The idea that the story can be understood wholly in terms of chemistry, i.e. in the progress of 'the selfish gene', is a gross over-simplification.

Current debates about evolution have given some religious believers the mistaken idea that the theory itself is in doubt. So-called 'creation scientists' exploit selected, and often misinterpreted, evidence in the interests of demonstrating that Genesis provides a scientific account of pre-history, a conclusion which study of the history of the documents themselves renders highly improbable. Some of their more detailed and technical criticism is focused on the relative lack of fossil evidence for intermediate evolutionary forms. It is important to note, therefore, that for Darwin the fossil record only provided corroborative evidence, and could not be expected to do more on account of its paucity. The three main lines of evidence on which he relied were 1. the experience of animal and plant breeders; 2. the geographical distribution of different species; and 3. the possibilities of classifying species in a reasonable historical sequence. These, extended and refined in countless ways, remain the basis of the theory.

Apart from the problems created for fundamentalists *, there were other legitimate reasons for concern among Christians when Darwin's theory was first made public. For example, it stood the teleological argument for the existence of God (i.e. the argument from 'design', *see* **Arguments for the Existence of God**) on its head. Creatures were seen to be wonderfully adapted to their environment, not because they had been designed that way, but because only well-adapted creatures survived. Modern versions of the teleological argument concentrate, more wisely than earlier ones, on the intelligibility of the universe, an intelligibility to which the theory of evolution itself contributes, thus strengthening belief in the purposiveness of God as the author of a rational process.

Darwin's theory also put in question the unique character and dignity of man. T. H. Huxley's famous exchange with Bishop Wilberforce reached its sharpest point in repartee about Huxley's relationship to the apes. Nowadays it is less difficult for Christians to accept that human distinctiveness does not necessarily have to depend on the belief that humanity had a distinct and separate origin. Just as individual human beings emerge gradually into full personhood through a natural process of growth and development, so the fact that *homo sapiens* evolved through many millions of years does not detract from our present uniqueness. In fact it is a source of wonder and reassurance about the evolutionary process as a whole that it should reach a peak of significance in producing creatures capable of responding to God.

The mechanism of evolution, in particular the element of chance, has always caused difficulties for those who believe that the universe is the work of a loving creator. It is important, therefore, to distinguish between a random process and a process which contains a random element. A completely random process would be by definition meaningless. A process containing a random element, however, in which random possibilities are selected and developed in the light of previous developments and under the pressure of particular circumstances, may be highly purposive. In fact there is good reason to suppose that much creative activity takes place in precisely this way. Creativity entails the exploration of hitherto undreamt of possibilities, and randomization is one of the ways of generating these. In evolutionary terms, chance may thus be an expression of God's super-abundance. In Teilhard de Chardin's words, evolution 'means pervading everything so as to try everything, and trying everything so as to find everything'.

The success of Darwin's theory has led to the wide extension of the concept of evolution into other fields of study. The perception that most things are in process of change and development is one of his legacies. But how and why particular phenomena change, e.g. in cosmic evolution, may bear little relationship to the actual processes of biological evolution.

The application of evolutionary concepts to human behaviour, under the title of sociobiology, and the attempt to prescribe human norms in the light of evolutionary development, is a present source of major controversy. Earlier excursions into this field,

e.g. social Darwinism, have rightly been discredited.

See also **Arguments for the Existence of God.**

A. L. Caplan (ed), *The Sociobiology Debate*, 1978; Teilhard de Chardin, *The Phenomenon of Man*, ET 1959; J. S. Habgood, 'After Darwin', in *A Working Faith*, 1980; A. Hardy, *The Living Stream*, 1965; P. Kitcher, *Abusing Science: The Case Against Creationism*, 1982; J. Maynard Smith, *The Theory of Evolution*, 1958; A. R. Peacocke, *Creation and the World of Science*, 1979; W. H. Thorpe, *Purpose in a World of Chance*, 1978; R. Trigg, *The Shaping of Man: Philosophical Aspects of Sociobiology*, 1982.

JOHN HABGOOD

Exegesis

The term is a transliteration of a Greek noun, *exēgēsis*, namely the process of bringing out. The Greek verb that dominates the word-constellation to which exegesis belongs means to direct, to expound, to interpret. Hence exegesis is the process of bringing out the meaning of a text; the work of textual interpretation. Exegesis is generally understood to designate the praxis* of the interpretation of texts. Thus it is usually differentiated from hermeneutics*, frequently taken to refer to the theory of the interpretation of text, although in times past it was most often understood as a term which designated the general rules of interpretation as, for instance, those of the school of Hillel. Exegesis is also to be distinguished from eisegesis, the process of bringing in, commonly employed to designate the tendency to read meaning into a text rather than deriving meaning from a text itself.

One's pre-understanding* shapes the way that one interprets a text. In the third century, Origen (*c.* 185–*c.* 254), the biblical scholar and theologian, developed his notions on the interpretation of the scriptures in the fourth volume of the most important of his theological works, *Peri Archōn*. He held that just as man is composed of body, soul and spirit, so too there is a corporal, psychic, and a spiritual sense of the scriptures. The Alexandrian* Father's prime analogue is manifestly Platonic anthropology, but he found support for his three-fold approach to the scriptures by an allegorical* interpretation of such notions as that of the three loaves of bread of Luke 11.5. The first of Origen's senses, the corporal, grammatical, or historical, is present when the meaning of scriptures is given without the use of figures. Some passages were considered not to have a literal sense either because the language of the text was undeniably figurative or because the obvious literal sense was clearly unworthy of God. The psychic or moral sense has to do with the text's ability to edify the faith. Hence it was often considered by Origen to be the most important of the senses of the scriptures. The search for the pneumatic or spiritual sense of the scriptures was, in Origen's view, consistent with Paul's use of the OT, for example in I Cor. 10.11 and Gal. 4.24. This pneumatic sense was frequently an accommodation of the text; at other times it involved a metaphorical or typical use of the scriptures. Origen's hermeneutics seem to have consisted in three principal rules: 1. that the scriptural text be interpreted in a manner worthy of God, the author of all scripture; 2. that the literal sense be abandoned when it says anything impossible or unworthy of God; and 3. that the teaching of the church clarifies the meaning of the scriptures. True exegesis must serve the faith. Origen's appreciation of the scriptures is well summed up in his commentary on the *dramatis personae* of the Song of Songs: 'These things seem to me to afford no profit to the reader as far as the story goes; nor do they maintain any continuous narrative such as we find in other scripture stories. It is necessary, therefore, rather to give them all a spiritual meaning.'

Origen's notion of the many senses of scripture and his use of allegory, based on natural and biblical analogy*, was the beneficiary of the allegorical method of interpreting ancient texts, particularly Homeric texts, which had been developed in such centres of Hellenistic learning as Pergamum and Origen's own city of Alexandria. Origen's idea that there is more than one level of meaning of scripture as well as the notion that only that which is consistent with the divine nature can be ascribed to God was paralleled in the Western church two centuries later by Augustine of Hippo (354–430), who wrote in his classic work *On Christian Doctrine* that 'we must show the way to find out whether a phrase is literal or figurative. And the way is certainly as fol-

lows: Whatever there is in the word of God that cannot, when taken literally, be referred either to purity of life or soundness of doctrine, you may set down as figurative. Purity of life has reference to the love of God and one's neighbour; soundness of doctrine to the knowledge of God and one's neighbour.' Augustine was not, however, unaware that a correct interpretation of the scriptural text required that the interpreter be aware of the nature and extent of the canon*, that he evaluate the various readings in the ancient manuscripts, that he be familiar with the ancient languages in which the scriptural texts were written, and that he appreciate the variety of connotations of Hebrew and Greek terms especially as this was reflected in the different translations of the Bible.

Largely because of the influence of Origen and Augustine, the churches of the East and the West accepted the notion of the multidimensional senses of the scriptures well into the Middle Ages. Incorporated into the mediaeval catenae and glossae, the mediaeval notion that there are four senses* of scripture was classically formulated by Sixtus of Siena (1520–1569) who wrote that: 'the interpretation of sacred scripture is twofold, namely, historical and allegorical. Again, the historical is analogical, on the one hand, and aetiological, on the other. The allegorical interpretation is, however, three-fold: the first correlates the figures of realities with the present and retains the name of allegory; the second relates to conduct and is called tropological; the third relates to unchanging eternity and is called anagogical.' Although Jewish and Christian interpreters shared much methodology in common during the mediaeval period, Christian schoolmen often related the three-fold allegorical sense to the triple coming of Christ, in his church (the allegorical sense), in the soul (the tropological sense), and in glory (the anagogical sense). Since, however, the mystics were deemed to have a foretaste of the glory of Christ, the anagogical sense was sometimes taken as a spiritual or mystical sense and at other times as an eschatological sense. For the schoolman the scriptures were thus related to the life of the church and the systematic exposition of its doctrine.

During the Reformation* the interpretation of scripture according to the dogmas of the church was rejected in favour of the principle that scripture be interpreted according to scripture alone. Scripture is the sole authority for interpreting the scriptures, since it is only from the scriptures that the gospel* is heard and men and women are led to that faith which is alone justifying. *Sola Scriptura*, *solus Christus, sola fides*summarized the position of the Reformers. Within this perspective, the primary theological endeavour was the interpretation of the scriptures, whose sole purpose was the proclamation of the gospel. The Reformers attempted to improve the traditional method of exegesis by maintaining the principle, if not always the language, of the analogy of scripture. Scripture was to be interpreted in a fashion conversant with the scriptures themselves, *scriptura ipsius interpres*. Allegory was to be excluded, and the original meaning of the texts was to be sought. Both Luther and Calvin tried to elucidate the literal meaning of the scriptures. They shared the concern for the original texts and the preference for philological exposition which characterized all textual interpretation in the age of the Humanists.

In the wake of the Reformation, the interpretation of the scriptures was largely abandoned as a theological task by the leading theologians of both Protestant Orthodoxy and the Counter-Reformation*. The one side and the other sought scriptural texts in support of their doctrinal positions. Nonetheless some few scholars continued to be interested in the scriptural text for its own sake and thus paved the way for the historical critical interpretation of the scriptures. Richard Simon (1638–1712) is widely regarded as the father of OT criticism, but he was expelled from the Oratorians because of his various studies on the critical history of the scriptures and their interpretation. John Jakob Wettstein (1693–1754) was removed from his pulpit in Basel because his text-critical studies on the NT were deemed inconsistent with the church's confession. Thus the locus of the interpretation of the scriptures moved from the churches to the universities, where the historical critical method of interpretation was born as a child of the Enlightenment*.

During the Enlightenment, scholars sought to understand the scriptures in a rational way, independent of the doctrinal control of the churches. The distinction between scripture and the Word of God enabled biblical criticism to achieve autonomy. The texts of the scriptures were interpreted in a fashion similar to the interpretation of other ancient texts. Since the books of the OT are rooted in the history of Israel and the books of the NT in that of the early church, it was necessary for biblical interpretation to be historically oriented. Indeed during the nineteenth century history became the medium for understanding the texts of the Bible. The genesis of the biblical texts themselves was one focus of interest, while the history of Israel and the life of Jesus* provided another focus of research for biblical scholars. Exegesis could then be described as the scientific attempt 'to understand a text in its original context' (Willi Marxsen).

In the pursuit of such a goal, the first task of the exegete is to have the text at hand. The task is not an easy one since there no longer exists the original manuscript of any biblical text. The text upon which the interpreter is to base his or her exposition is one which must be reconstituted according to the principles of textual criticism on the basis of the tens of thousands of extant biblical manuscripts (and fragments thereof). Should the interpreter base his or her exposition upon a printed edition of a biblical book, textual criticism must still be used because the interpreter may well not agree with the judgment of the editors as to the preferable reading of one passage or another. The work of textual criticism must be considered as a necessary pre-condition for the work of exegesis itself. Thus textual criticism has sometimes been called 'lower criticism', while the term 'higher criticism' was reserved for the task of interpretation per se. Nonetheless textual variants often attest to the interpretation of a given biblical text at some moment in history, with the result that the practice of textual criticism sometimes provides a useful clue for the interpretation of the text itself.

To understand a biblical text within its context requires that the exegete be familiar with the literary and historical worlds (the macro setting) within which each of the biblical books arose. Since each book is a piece of religious literature, at least in the sense that it is a written document with religious themes, a comparative study of the biblical books and ancient religious literature will prove helpful. Since not all of the literary forms attested in the Bible are found uniquely in religious literature (for example the letter, or the speech), an understanding of the literary context of biblical texts requires an awareness of ancient Mediterranean and near-Eastern literature. An appreciation of the literature contemporary with the biblical books is also important for understanding the real connotation of the language of the Bible.

The books of the Bible were not written in a historical void. Rather, they are pieces of literature which a competent exegete can locate, with reasonable accuracy, in a given time and place. An appreciation of the social, economic, political and religious history of the time and place in which any biblical book was written is an essential factor in its interpretation. The great contribution of F. C. Baur and the school of Tübingen to the historical-critical interpretation of the NT was the notion that a book must be interpreted within its historical context if it is to be understood at all. The so-called History of Religions school of biblical interpretation (*see* **Religionsgeschichtliche Schule**) helped to clarify the meaning of the scriptures by comparing their content with extrabiblical but contemporary religious ritual, ideology and literature.

In the interpretation of a text the immediate context which must be studied in order that the text receive a correct interpretation is that of the text itself. Exegesis requires attentiveness to the language of a text as well as to the style in which it is composed. The exegete must therefore have such linguistic competence as will enable him or her to understand both the denotation and the connotations of the biblical text. An appreciation of the literary style of a biblical text will include not only an appreciation of the literary skill of its author(s), but also the choice of literary forms which are present in the text. Apropos the inevitable use of literary forms, it can be said that the medium is the message. The literary form corresponds to the set of social circumstances in which a text is composed and determines the content and manner of presentation of its 'message'.

A biblical text – whether the text be a single passage or an entire book matters little to the exegete since the entire book is the *de facto* literary context of any of its passages – also has its own particular history (the micro setting), to which the interpreter must be attentive in making an exegesis of the text. Most significant in this regard is the literary history of the text itself, to which the disciplines of source criticism and redaction criticism are especially devoted. Frequently biblical books exist in their present form because they were substantially composed by an author or authors (in one or more drafts) who have relied on extant documentary material as their source, but have since been modified by one or more later editors (redactors). Although redaction criticism may examine the modifications brought about by later editors of a text, it is principally concerned with the technique of composition (composition criticism) and the modification of traditional material (emendation criticism) used by the principal author(s) of a biblical book.

The biblical exegete will not, however, overlook the fact that much of the literary material contained in the Bible had a history which was broader than the history of successive literary compositions. The interpreter must take into consideration the oral traditions (including the liturgical traditions) to which the biblical documents give witness. To the extent that the task is practicable, the exegete will seek to determine the history of tradition of each of the various parts of the Bible.

By examining a text within its proper historical and literary context, exegesis seeks to clarify what the author of a biblical text intended to say to his particular audience. It seeks to elucidate his vision and his message. The historical-critical method of exegesis thus arises from the so-called romantic hermeneutics. It seeks to understand what the text meant at the time and in the circumstances in which it was written.

Some scholars restrict the meaning of the term exegesis to that historical and literary type of study which has been outlined above. In their estimation, the issue of the relevance of the biblical text for the present generation belongs to some other discipline. In this view, exegesis is a historical study; systematic theologians can raise the issue of the relationship between the meaning of the Bible and church teaching, and philosophers can examine how a text written in the past can convey meaning to a present generation (the hermeneutical question). Other contemporary scholars, however, query whether a narrowly-conceived historical-critical approach is adequate for the interpretation of the scriptures. Some consider that the systematic elaboration of biblical theologies is part of the task of exegesis. Many others hold that the scriptures claim to address their audience-readership, and thus the issue of the contemporary relevance of the scriptures arises from a consideration of the text itself. Still others would opt for a structuralist * reading of the biblical text or would include within the ambit of exegesis one or another of the various sociological political, and psychoanalytic readings of biblical texts.

See also **Biblical Criticism, Historical Criticism.**

B. S. Childs, *Biblical Theology in Crisis*, 1970; Raymond F. Collins, *Introduction to the New Testament*, 1983; John H. Hayes and Carl H. Holladay, *Biblical Exegesis*, 1983; Henri de Lubac, *Exégèse mediévale: Les quatre sens de l'Écriture*, Théologie XLI, XLII, LIX, 1959, 1961, 1964; O. Kaiser and W. G. Kümmel, *Exegetical Method: A Student's Handbook*, rev. ed., 1981; W. G. Kümmel, *The New Testament: The History of the Investigation of its Problems*, 1973; Stephen Neill, *The Interpretation of the New Testament, 1861–1961*, 1964; Beryl Smalley, *The Study of the Bible in the Middle Ages*, 1952; J. D. Smart, *The Interpretation of Scripture*, 1961; *The Past, Present, and Future of Biblical Theology*, 1979; P. Stuhlmacher, *Historical Criticism and Theological Interpretation of Scripture: Towards a Hermeneutics of Consent*, 1977.

RAYMOND F. COLLINS

Exemplarism

That view of the atonement *, called also the 'subjective' or 'moral' theory, associated with Abelard and H. Rashdall in the mediaeval and modern periods respectively, which holds that the value of Christ's atoning work lies in the moral and exemplary character of his love and self-surrender, stirring the imagination and will to repentance and holiness.

JAMES ATKINSON

Existentialism

This term is best taken as descriptive of a certain *type* of philosophical thinking rather than as the name of a unified *school* of philosophical thought. Although it is not uncommon to find theologians such as Augustine and Pascal, and novelists such as Dostoievsky and Kafka, classified as existentialists, it makes for clearer understanding if the term is reserved for those philosophers who have been influenced by and whose thinking stands in continuity with the thought of the Danish religious thinker Søren Kierkegaard (1813–1855). Although, as has been said, existentialists do not form a single school, and, as we shall see, existentialist thought is reconcilable with a wide variety of theological (and anti-theological) positions, there are sufficient themes common to existentialist thinkers to enable us to characterize the existentialist standpoint as a whole.

In general, existentialist thinkers have on the whole rebelled against many of the main trends of Western philosophy, especially in so far as this has been influenced by the thinking of 'the Father of Western philosophy', René Descartes (1596–1650). In so far as Western philosophy has concerned itself with the objective exploration of 'beings-in-general' and with the essential categories applicable to these, it has been held by most existentialists to be gravely defective. This is so for two reasons. 1. In investigating 'beings-in-general' it has tended to ignore the reality and problematical nature of truly personal existence. 2. In so far as it has attempted to grasp human being by those categories applicable to non-human being it has been gravely erroneous, since this approach overlooks the immense differences between human and non-human being. This second error was, *par excellence*, the error of Descartes and his school. Existentialists can therefore be described as anti-positivistic in standpoint; they radically disagree with the positivist * tradition that the methods of the empirical sciences are our only means of acquiring knowledge, precisely because these sciences are unable to grasp the reality of human existence, which requires radically different techniques for its elucidation.

Existentialists have accordingly placed a heavy stress on subjectivity (cf. Kierkegaard's celebrated aphorism: 'Truth is Subjectivity'). By this stress existentialists do not wish to relinquish the claim to objective truth, but rather to emphasize (i) that the only route to such truth in the sphere of human existence is through the human subject's own personal participation in being from, so to speak, the inside; and (ii) that man's knowledge of being must begin with his own personal being, since man himself is the only element in being which possesses self-understanding and hence understanding of being in general. But existentialists have deliberately refrained from giving detailed, concrete descriptions of what human existence involves, confining themselves to formal analysis of the structure of such existence. (The technical philosophical way of putting this is to say that they give ontological but not ontic descriptions.) They have done so because they hold that existential characteristics and possibilities are uniquely grouped in unique personal subjects and thus evade detailed analysis and description. The German philosopher of existence Martin Heidegger (1889–1976) thus isolates two categories of human existence – *Jemeinigkeit* (my existential characteristics and possibilities are inalienably and uniquely mine), and *Geworfenheit* (I am thrown [German: *geworfen*] into existence at a certain point in space and time, and therefore my existence has a unique givenness, a uniqueness which transcends general analysis, description and prescription).

Nevertheless, certain very general descriptions of human existence are not out of the question. Generally speaking, existentialists would assent to, in some sense or other, the proposition, 'existence precedes essence'. By this is meant that man, unlike natural things, objects and organisms, does not have his essential nature given to him as an already realized possibility (or as a possibility whose realization is inevitable), but that man's essential nature is one from which in his actual existence his is separated, one that as yet lies before him, yet to be laid hold of, grasped or realized. Hence the denial by existentialist thought that human essentiality can be grasped and communicated by the natural sciences (e.g. biology, physiology, psychology) or by the human or social sciences (e.g. anthropology, sociology). Rather, such essentiality can only be described as future existential possibility.

Closely linked with the claim that 'existence precedes essence' is the concept of what we might describe as 'fallenness'. By this is meant that empirical human existence is in greater or lesser degrees estranged from or fallen away from its true, genuine or authentic modes. Thus Heidegger speaks of 'inauthentic' existence, in which man flees from responsibility for his own self by sinking himself in the average or the typical, or by understanding his being purely by the categories of the sciences. The Jewish personalist* philosopher Martin Buber (1878–1965) speaks of man's sinking himself in the world of It, the world of objects, ideas and instruments, thus cutting himself off from the maturation of his personal being which is possible only in I-Thou relationships. Karl Jaspers (1883–1969) speaks of man's immersion of himself in the world of objectifiable things, an immersion which separates man from transcendent life. The French Catholic existentialist Gabriel Marcel (1889–1973) speaks of man's over-indulgence in the attitude and activity of egocentric 'having', at the expense of the mutual, reciprocal, communal activity of 'being'.

Conversely, all of these thinkers speak of the possibility of the transition from false to genuine modes of existence. Hence Heidegger speaks of man's transition to authentic existence. Buber holds that real personal being is possible through 'turning' from over-indulgence in It-relations to openness towards the Thou which alone constitutes man's true and essential being. Jaspers speaks of the achievement of a 'philosophical faith' in which man is linked to his genuine, transcendent self, and to God. Marcel points to the reality of personal existence which can come about through man's 'engagement' of himself to communal life and to God.

Generally speaking, in existentialist thought we also find importance being ascribed to the cognitive value of certain subjective affective dispositions, states and moods. It is denied by existentialists that such feeling-states are merely subjective or arbitrary; rather, it is asserted that they point to or bring to light certain aspects or dimensions of being which might otherwise be overlooked or ignored. Here might be cited the celebrated example of Jean-Paul Sartre's analysis of nausea (*La Nausée*), in which he tries by a series of evocative descriptions to communicate the feeling subject's convictions about the futile nature of much human existence and the ridiculousness of the world. But much more fundamental to existentialist thought is the great attention paid to the cognitive status of *Angst* * ('anxiety' or 'dread'), considered as an essential part of the structure of human existence. Anxiety is considered to be a fundamental part of humans because it is not evoked by this or that object or state of affairs within the world, but by the total situation of human being as such, disclosing man's awful freedom and responsibility as a being flooded by dissatisfaction with the empirical self he has become and by the awareness of the true, genuine self that he might become through the realization of his existential possibilities.

The roots of the significance attached to these affective cognitive states appear to be twofold. 1. There is the obvious influence of the brilliant analyses of anxiety and dread worked out by Kierkegaard in his *The Concept of Dread* (ET 1944) and *The Sickness Unto Death* (ET 1941). Kierkegaard's work here has been both philosophically and theologically influential. 2. There is the philosophical method of phenomenology *, pioneered by Heidegger's teacher, the German philosopher Edmund Husserl (1859–1938), a method which was adapted and developed by Heidegger in his work. Husserl attempted to work out a philosophical method which was purely descriptive, in which an attempt was made to elucidate and analyse the knowledge of pure universal essences which are inalienably present to human consciousness. According to Husserl, accurate description and analysis are possible only if certain techniques are employed in order to remove those particular (as contrasted with universal) elements which obscure and distort these essences. The phenomenological anlaysis of 'anxiety' or 'dread' which we find in Heidegger's work is a result of his application of the phenomenological method to human existence.

It follows that by and large existentialist thinkers have been highly critical of much in our modern and contemporary civilization and culture. In the sphere of civilization they have protested vigorously against contemporary mass-society, with its dreadful potentialities for obscuring or denying the reality of personal existence; they have criticized modern society's frightful abuse of mass-communication and its over-employment of modern man in industrial techniques which dehumanize and depersonalize him. They have laid bare the impersonality and anonymity of much modern life, and have warned us of the grave dangers to humanity implicit in totalitarian and collectivist societies. Martin Buber's *I and Thou* (ET 1937) and Karl Jaspers' *Man in the Modern Age* (ET 1933) are notable examples of existentialist writings which are critiques of modern civilization. In the sphere of culture, existentialists have protested against the sinister qualities of modern 'scientism', the idolization of science as the main (or the only) source of our knowledge about the world, a procedure which overlooks the significance of personal being within reality as a whole. Heidegger's *Being and Time* (ET 1962) can aptly be regarded as partly, at least, a critique of certain basic and insidious errors implicit in the history of modern thought and culture.

It goes without saying that the debate about the relationship between the philosophy of human existence and Christian theology is an immensely complicated one, bristling with disagreements and difficulties. The nature of this relationship can naturally be investigated fully in the context of the work of a theologian who has systematically tried to link existentialist thinking with Christian thought; for example, in the context of the work of Paul Tillich or Rudolf Bultmann. But certain general remarks can be made here. Certain theologians have been highly critical of the attempts to synthesize Christianity and the philosophy of existence. Certain conservative Protestant theologians have protested against the attempt, not infrequently on the grounds that to interpret Christianity in the light of *any* secular philosophy whatever must lead to distortion and impoverishment of the former. This is so, for example, of Karl Barth's criticisms of both Tillich and Bultmann. Sometimes there is combined with this type of objection the argument that existentialism is only a single cultural aspect of twentieth-century gloom and despair, understandable enough in the light of the century's frightful political and international history.

More specifically, hostile critics have tried to argue that existentialism is fundamentally humanistic, if not atheistic. They have pointed, for example, to Sartre's insistence that existentialism is fundamentally an expression of a humanism which has no room whatever for transcendence (*see* Sartre's *Existentialism and Humanism*, ET 1948). Much has also been made of Heidegger's leaving of the question of God open; it can be objected that Heidegger allows that man's transition from inauthentic to authentic existence is possible without any dependence upon grace, a position which is basically hostile to the Christian understanding of human nature. More specifically still, it can be argued that a careful examination of the content of fundamental existentialist categories such as inauthenticity, authenticity, fallenness and the like, demonstrates that this does not at all correspond with the content of their allegedly Christian counterparts. Again, critics can point out that when a theologian attempts radically and thoroughly to synthesize Christianity and existentialist philosophy, he may very well end by denying both divine transcendence and the idea of the special, particular action of God. Other criticisms of existentialist theologies may take up and develop the theological consequences of radical subjectivism, irrationalism and anthropocentricity.

On the other hand, existentialist theologians have had much to say in reply and defence. As apologetic, mediating theologians they have deplored the attempt to make theological constructions in isolation from and independently of contemporary philosophy. In particular, they have been able to argue that the philosophy of personal existence is a much more apt vehicle for conveying the meaning of Christian doctrine than, say, contemporary Anglo-Saxon empiricism or positivism. This is so, it can be argued, because most existentialist thinkers have been in greater of lesser degree influenced by Christian traditions: there is no denying the Protestant Christianity of Kierkegaard or the Catholicism of Marcel; Heidegger's anthropology has been deeply coloured by theologians like Augustine, Duns Scotus, Luther and Kierkegaard; the effect of the biblical tradition on Jaspers is clear. Gross distortion, it has been insisted, can be guarded against and avoided. Existentialism represents a salutary corrective against a shallow utopian optimism based on the idolatry of science or a belief in inevitable technological progress. This debate

is intrinsically of the first importance, because to engage in it enables us to perceive more clearly the inner nature both of Christian theology itself and also its relation to contemporary civilization, culture and thought.

See also **Angst; Demythologizing; Phenomenology.**

H. J. Blackham, *Six Existentialist Thinkers*, 1952; F. Copleston, SJ, *Contemporary Philosophy*, 1956; M. King, *Heidegger's Philosophy*, 1964; J. Macquarrie, *An Existentialist Theology*, 1955; *Existentialism*, 1973; D. E. Roberts, *Existentialism and Religious Belief*, 1957.

JAMES RICHMOND

Ex opere operato

The phrase (meaning 'through the performance of the work') is used in RC theology to express the belief that the efficacy * of a sacrament is derived from Christ's promise that he will confer grace when the sacramental sign is duly performed within the church. The contrasting term *ex opere operantis* would imply that sacraments depend ultimately on the merits of the minister or the recipient. The purpose of the expression, which first appears in the thirteenth century, is to emphasize that sacraments are fundamentally the acts of God and not of men; it is not denied that a sacrament will be morally effective only if the recipient has the right dispositions.

B. Leeming, *Principles of Sacramental Theology*, 1956, ch. 1; K. Rahner, *The Church and the Sacraments*, ET 1963, pp. 24–33.

E. J. YARNOLD

Exorcism *see* **Demon, Demonology**

Experience, Religious

1. *Meaning of terms.* The word experience has changed its meaning since the fifteenth and sixteenth centuries, when it was primarily concerned with testing in order to obtain proof. In Rom. 5.3f. 'tribulation worketh patience and patience experience' (AV/KJV) appears in the NEB as 'suffering trains us to endure and endurance brings proof that we have stood the test'. However, it also took on the meaning of a state of mind or feeling produced by environmental

influences – nature, man and God. This is the common meaning today.

Can these experiences be classified? Is there artistic, scientific, personal, religious experience? It is doubtful whether clear distinctions can be drawn, but at least the environment at any particular time favours an interpretation consistent with its own nature. Thus religious experience is conceived as a state of mind or feeling induced by factors beyond ordinary explanation, though it is most likely to occur in a context of religious expectancy or desire. Even when the experience appears to have been sudden and unexpected, there may well have been preparatory wrestlings and wonderings about ultimate realities. What is then called a religious experience may be the climax of a long drawn-out struggle or enquiry.

One other distinction needs to be made. Religious experience may be conceived as happening to an *individual* in privacy or solitude. There are innumerable records of those who have been lifted above their common concerns and become aware of some transcendent agent making an impact upon their own consciousness. Equally, there have been records of *corporate* gatherings where many present have become aware of being grasped by powers beyond their ordinary comprehension and control. The crucial question in both types of experience has ever been that of the nature of the transcendent agency: divine, demonic, psychedelic, hysteric, hypnotic? What are the criteria or tests by which an experience can be judged to have been truly religious?

2. *Case-histories.* In the Judaeo-Christian tradition, certain records have attained classic significance. In the O T, Moses' experience in the loneliness of the desert when he *saw* a bush burning but not consumed and *heard* a voice calling him to undertake a task (Ex. 3): Elijah's experience in the loneliness of a cave when a great storm raged around him, followed by 'a still, small, voice' issuing in a command to return to the troubled world (I Kings 19): Isaiah's experience in the temple when he *saw* the Lord, high and lifted up, and *heard* a voice bidding him go and bear witness to his people (Isa. 6). In each case there were outward phenomena which took on symbolic significance: at the same time a message defining a task was registered in the mind. In the wider

world there were situations of conflict and distress: the outcome of the individual's experience was a mission directed to the particular manifestations of that distress.

In the N T the experience of Saul of Tarsus on the road to Damascus became outstandingly significant in the history of Christianity. The blinding light and the compelling voice led an arch-persecutor to become a heroic witness to the faith he had once sought to destroy (Acts 9). The nearest parallel in later N T writings is that recorded of John the seer (Rev. 1–3) in which he saw a vision of one like a son of man and heard a voice conveying charges to churches living in a time of stress, even of persecution.

Besides these experiences dramatically recorded must be set the total experience of those who saw and heard and touched the 'word of life' (I John 1ff.). Clearly those who became disciples of Jesus believed that he was entrusted by God with a particular mission and in this sense their companying with him involved them in 'religious' experiences. There was the high-point of the discipleship of Peter, James and John on the mount of transfiguration (Mark 9.2ff.), but it seems to have made only a temporary impact on them. It was after the resurrection that disciples became aware of the transcendent significance of Jesus and in their encounters with him they became conscious of fully 're-ligious' experiences. Examples are those of the pair walking to Emmaus (Luke 24.13ff.) and of the ten in the upper room (John 20.19ff.). Here are the outward symbolic actions together with words of interpretation or commission. In all major biblical accounts of religious experience both visual and verbal symbols have a part to play.

What inferences may be drawn from these records? One in particular. The dominant feature of the experiences recorded is that they were vouchsafed to those destined to share actively in God's ongoing purpose for mankind. The experience was never self-enclosed: the enjoyment of a secret revelation or the excitement of a state of exaltation. Those who were granted visions were called to engage in the great conflicts between right and wrong in the world at large and to become agents in the working out of God's redeeming purpose. A searching criterion of whether an experience is truly religious is whether it issues in sacrificial service.

3. *General religious experience*. As cultures other than the Judaeo-Christian have become more widely known, the nature of experience in non-Christian religions has become a subject for concerned enquiry. When early Christian missionaries went out into the world of Hellenism they were compelled to consider the significance of the lofty ideals and religious aspirations of the inherited traditions of their contemporaries. So began a conflict which has continued ever since. Are the religious feelings and techniques belonging to non-Christian cultures to be regarded either as purely human phenomena or demonic deceptions? Or are they to be viewed as evidences of God's prevenient grace, stirring in human hearts and causing them to 'feel after him and find him' (Acts 17.27)?

In the course of Christian history answers to these questions have oscillated between the sympathetic and the suspicious. If sympathy is shown, the distinctiveness of the Christian revelation seems to be in danger: if suspicion, the all-embracing mercy of God seems to be questioned.

One of the most notable attempts made during the twentieth century to isolate a type of experience which, wherever found, could be termed 'religious', was contained in Rudolf Otto's book *The Idea of the Holy* (1923). Quoting records of experiences from many sources, he claimed that they included certain common elements. Primarily there was a sense of awe in the presence of that which could best be described as *numinous*. At the same time there was a sense of fascination overcoming any initial reaction to withdraw in fear. Wherever human beings had experienced concurrent feelings of mystery, awe, wonder, fascination, there, it could be said, they had been in touch with that which was beyond themselves, the Holy, the Transcendent, the Eternal.

Otto's book concentrated attention on elements in the objective and external world which had aroused feelings of otherness or distance in human hearts. A later writer, Paul Tillich, laid greater stress on the subjective feeling of what he called 'ultimate concern' as being characteristic of a truly religious experience. This feeling is not to be regarded merely as a sentiment; for Tillich it demanded also a decision of the whole personality. Nevertheless he allowed that it was possible for an individual to grow up within a community, sharing its ultimate concern, that is its religious experience, and continuing within the ambit of its values and aspirations without necessarily undergoing any crisis of commitment. Thus he defined two kinds of religious experience: participation in the religious life of a community, motivated and governed by an ultimate concern; being grasped in a critical way by a concern hitherto regarded either as illusory or unimportant but now recognized as of unconditioned seriousness.

Conclusion. Life for all human beings consists in a succession of experiences in which the individual is related to his or her environment, natural and social. Through these experiences, he or she learns to observe the structure and processes of the natural order and to interpret them either as being the result of forces whose character can be determined by human investigation or as being created and sustained by an ultimate agency. The latter conviction may be formed gradually: it may come as a sudden revelation. In either case, such a conviction is to be regarded as religious: the experiences which led to and maintained it may rightly be called religious experiences.

Further, an individual learns continuously the nature of the social order of which he or she is a member. Society may be regarded simply as having been moulded by multiple forces: climate, land resources, human inventiveness, migrations, charismatic leadership, competition and internecine struggles. Or it may be regarded as ultimately controlled by and accountable to the living God. Again the latter interpretation may be designated as religious and the experiences in life which lead to and confirm it may also rightly be called religious experiences.

Such experiences are most frequently mediated through the words and example of one who in an altogether outstanding way lived out and even died for the conviction that nature and society are (to use a metaphor) in the hands of the living God. It is the distinctive mark of Christian religious experience that it learns constantly, through the Christ of the NT and the witness of his disciples, reconciliation and hope. It does not deny the validity of other religious traditions where these have been conceived in a spirit of ultimate seriousness and with a willingness to recognize an ultimate centre of unity, giving vitality and significance to all its parts. It does not deny the validity of religious experiences claimed by individuals who have been constrained by a sense of awe and wonder in the presence of ultimate mystery. Nevertheless, it believes that the revelation through Christ has been the source and remains the effective instrument of a type of religious experience classically described in John 1.1–4, a sharing in eternal life with a consequent sense of fullness of joy.

J. Baillie, *The Sense of the Presence of God*, 1962; John Bowker, *The Sense of God*, 1973; *The Religious Imagination and the Sense of God*, 1978; F. W. Dillistone, *Religious Experience and Christian Faith*, 1981; Alister Hardy, *The Spiritual Nature of Man*, 1979; William James, *The Varieties of Religious Experience*, 1907; Ronald A. Knox, *Enthusiasm*, 1950; Marghanita Laski, *Ecstasy: A Study of some Secular and Religious Experiences*, 1961; H. D. Lewis, *Our Experience of God*, 1959; W. R. Matthews, *God in Christian Thought and Experience*, 1930; Rudolf Otto, *The Idea of the Holy*, ET 1923; H. Wheeler Robinson, *The Christian Experience of the Holy Spirit*, 1930; Paul Tillich, *Ultimate Concern*, 1965.

F. W. DILLISTONE

Faith

The centrality of faith for Christianity dates from the NT itself, where 'believers' often occurs as a short-hand term for those living according to the apostolic teaching (Acts 10.45, etc.) and 'the faith' for all that would later be termed 'Christianity' (Acts 6.7, etc.). The only actual biblical definition of faith (Heb. 11.1) does not encapsulate all that the Bible says on the subject, but indicates its main features: 'the assurance of things hoped for, the conviction of things not seen'. It is a confident, obedient trust in the reality, power and love of God known through his acts, and an awaiting of their future consummation.

The Bible contains a variety of emphases within this overall view. The noun 'faith' is comparatively rare in the OT, where (e.g. Hab. 2.5) it may indicate 'faithfulness' or 'loyalty' to God rather than purely passive reliance. But dependence on God as distinct

from human powers was important for Isaiah (7.9; 30.15), and while the OT so often sees faith concretized as obedient action (Deut. 6.1ff., etc.), the note of trust also resounds, especially in the Psalms. In the Synoptic Gospels, those who respond to Jesus' proclamation of the kingdom * and believe in his salvific powers are commended for their faith (Mark 2.5; 5.34); unbelief is a 'hardness of heart', refusal to accept the immediacy of God's saving power (Mark 6.1ff., etc.). In the Johannine writings a somewhat more reflective or even credal note appears: belief *that* Jesus is Son of God in the flesh (John 20.31; I John 5.1, etc.). For Paul, faith is the utter reliance on God's grace, of the man who knows that he cannot attain righteousness ('justification') by works of the law, but only by union with Christ crucified and *his* righteousness.

Faith being so central in Christian thought, yet comprising several layers of meaning, the theological tradition has produced certain tensions in its understanding. Thus:

1. *Belief in* and *belief that*. Corresponding to the question whether God's revelation * to man is the impartation of certain 'truths' about his nature and will, or is his personal self-giving in love, is the issue of whether faith is primarily the acceptance of doctrinal propositions, or the response of personal trust in God. Traditional Catholic theology has emphasized the former, and early Protestantism (as in Luther) the latter. But later Protestantism also took a very propositional turn, and some attempted to resolve the issue by a three-fold analysis of faith as the process of *notitia* (knowledge of what was to be believed), *assensus* (intellectual acceptance of its truth) and *fiducia* (personal commitment to that truth). More recently there has been a growing Catholic-Protestant consensus that while faith is primarily personal and relational there is a necessary reflective element in explication of its truth.

2. *Faith by which we believe* and *the faith which we believe*. Either the subjectivity of the believer, or the objectivity of that to which his faith attaches, is liable to emphasis at the expense of the other. Søren Kierkegaard, father of modern existentialism *, notably stressed the subjectivity of faith as decision, in reaction to a bloodless intel-

lectualism. Certain later existentialist theologians such as Bultmann have been accused of so stressing faith's subjectivity as to lose sight of the reality of the God in whom faith rests. Faith is passionate precisely because of the holiness and grace of the God whom it apprehends.

3. *Faith as human decision* and *faith as divine gift*. Faith being man's response to divine initiative, human decision, trust and understanding are involved. But much theology (especially Reformed) has also attributed faith to the creation of God through the Holy Spirit. Both emphases are necessary, otherwise faith is seen as a human activity independent of God and loses the sense of grace, or as a mechanical operation of God subverting the human will. The paradox can be viewed as analogous to human inter-personal relationships where both freedom and dependency operate in the growth of love.

There are also tensions between faith and other elements in Christian awareness. Thus:

1. *Faith* and *works* *. Paul's emphasis on the sole efficacy of faith for justification is already queried in the NT by the letter of James. But Paul was not antinomian. While righteousness cannot be achieved by works, faith being a unity with Christ in the Spirit naturally issues in love (Gal. 5.6). This was Luther's emphasis likewise. But there is a perennial danger that 'justification by faith' can be interpreted quietistically.

2. *Faith* and *reason*. This tension is especially evident where God's existence is itself at issue. Mediaeval Catholic theology (as in Aquinas) held that reason was capable of demonstrating the existence and to some extent the nature of God, although a full understanding had to rely on revelation. The Reformers, viewing the human intellect as involved in the fallenness of man, drastically restricted the scope of reason. Kierkegaard even saw faith as authentic precisely in its grasp of what was most absurd to reason, the incarnation. A number of modern theologians, both Catholic and Protestant, would view faith as neither dependent on nor contrary to reason, but as a commitment to a view of ultimate reality, regarding which reason by itself is neutral. Reason reveals the ambiguous nature of the universe. Faith involves a 'primal decision' that the universe is grounded in a transcendent reality, a decision which moves beyond 'rationality' but is not thereby 'irrational'.

3. *Faith* and *knowledge*. Faith claims a certain 'knowledge' of God, and therewith of the nature of the world and human destiny. But by its very nature as trust in a God transcending finitude, it requires an admission of much that is unknown and unknowable. In the NT, faith is contrasted with 'sight' which is reserved for eternity (II Cor. 5.7). In Christian tradition, faith therefore combines a certitude with an equal acknowledgment of mystery.

K. W. Clements, *Faith*, 1981; J. Hick, *Faith and Knowledge*, 1966; H. Küng, *On Being a Christian*, 1977; *Does God Exist?*, 1980; E. Maclaren, *The Nature of Belief*, 1976; W. Cantwell Smith, *Faith and Belief*, 1979.

KEITH CLEMENTS

Fall, The

The presumed historical accounting for mankind's actual condition of sinfulness and inadequacies and frustrations in life (*see* Original Sin). Gen. 3 tells a story of the first man and woman of the human race who, through their disobedience to a divine command, forfeited a paradisiacal and ideal existence in which they had first been constituted by their Creator and were reduced to the actual human estate with all its physical and social shortcomings. This is a use of ancient myth by the Yahwistic author of the Genesis traditions, who was much concerned with the aetiology * of the human situation and institutions. In Ezek. 28 essentially the same myth appears: here the theme of the decline of primordial man has been applied to the king of Tyre (i.e., the great mercantile kingdom of Phoenicia) to illustrate 'how have the mighty fallen'.

The Genesis myth accounting for the existing human condition is not taken up elsewhere in the Hebrew Bible, though there are obvious references to it in Ecclus. 25.24 and Wisdom 2.23f. (in which latter text the 'serpent' of Genesis has clearly been identified with 'the devil'). Rom. 5.12–21, on the contrary, has obviously made use of it in pairing off the 'one man' Christ through whom redemption has come to all with his 'type', the 'one man' through whom death and sin entered the world (contrary to Ecclus. 25.24, 'From a woman sin had its beginning, and because of her we all die'). Speculation on these scriptural data led to a long persuasion of Christian theology that by 'the sin of our first parents' the human race had been deprived of immortality, innocence, preternatural knowledge, etc., and that this deprivation together with, in some sense, the sinfulness attaching to this 'original sin' had been transmitted to every subsequent generation of mankind ('in Adam's sin, sinned we all'). Genesis was the historical record; Romans was its Christian confirmation and interpretation.

Critical interpretation of the Bible leads to other conclusions. The Genesis story is not history but an aetiological myth. In company with other Near Eastern myths of primordial man, it presents immortality not as a gift that has been lost but as an opportunity that was missed. There is no note of original wisdom (though there may be in Ezek. 28). It is a primitive attempt to offer an Aesopian explanation of how things came to be as they are. What it does want to say is that the disorder and evil in a world created in order and for good is the result of human frailty and not of divine caprice – a point that is never made in the more sophisticated Priestly theology of Gen. 1.1–2.4a; 6.11.

Rom. 5.12–21, which evidently took over the story of Gen. 3, did not, however, anticipate what later theology would make of it. The crucial v. 12 'in whom [Adam] all have sinned', translates better as ['because', or, 'because of whom'] all have sinned'. Despite the fact that the first alternative became common in the Western church, the almost universal earliest Christian exegetical tradition favours the latter.

In other words, the message of the Fall, as of original sin, is that a sinful world is not of God's design, that it has come to be through human failing, and that through this fact all human beings are born into a sinful world and, failing the grace of God, themselves become sinners.

BRUCE VAWTER

Fanaticism

We all know what fanaticism is, but it is very difficult to produce a helpful, formal definition that will cope adequately with the difficult questions of theologians and philosophers.

The derivation of the term is undoubtedly religious, from the Latin *fanaticus*, 'inspired by a deity', and through that from *fanum*, 'a temple'. Even in Latin, however, the sense of the word had extended to less overtly religious applications: *fanaticus* = 'enthusiastic, raving'. However, the religious source remained a dominant element of the meaning of the term. The essential problems in giving an adequate account of fanaticism lie on the one hand in suggesting criteria for the identification of fanatics, and on the other in the very idea of fanaticism itself.

The difficulty in identifying cases of fanaticism is that one man's fanatic is another's four-square saint. For example, Bishop Berkeley's reference in *Alciphron* (1732) to someone 'as fanatical as any Quietist or Quaker' tells us more about Berkeley and his times than it does about the essence of either Quietism or Quakerism. Equally, when in Daniel Deronda, George Eliot penned the following words, the notion of 'fanaticism' had moved about as far as it might from its original religious connotations of 'possession' as it can, without losing connection altogether: 'I call a man fanatical when ... he ... becomes unjust and unsympathetic to men who are out of his own track.' The notion had now become so tepid, and in its own way culture-bound, that few of us could hope to avoid completely the charge of fanaticism!

These simple examples point to the real source of the problem. The very idea of fanaticism, of disproportionate enthusiasm in the cause of religion, contains its own inherent difficulties. Can one, to be theologically blunt, be *too* enthusiastic in the expression and practice of one's faith? If religious belief is in some sense an aspiration to what is eternal and absolute how is it possible to be too enthusiastic? The theological answer here must be in the affirmative and on one of the following two grounds.

Over-enthusiasm is possible in a religious context where human limitation is forgotten. In the exploration which is faith there must remain some residual modesty on the part of the believer. This modesty is the continuing awareness of one's finitude. No matter how awesome and extraordinary the context of faith may be, no matter how much one believes oneself to be the vessel or even messenger of an almighty God, one is never either more nor less than a finite human being. As such one is fallible, and the risk of having misread or misinterpreted the situation is always present. To forget this in one's enthusiasm is to risk falling over the precipice of fanaticism, even where basically one's belief has sprung from roots which are true and firm.

Alternatively, the over-enthusiasm of fanaticism can arise not only from inappropriate grasp of the truth, but also from becoming attached through the forms of belief to an object of faith which cannot bear the weight of faith. This is the fanaticism which has attached itself not to God but to some false god. That such a distinction is possible is a condition both of understanding how some forms of fanaticism are possible, and also of the practice of theology itself. It is however, the correlated task of theology to make proposals about how to distinguish the true from the false god.

H. Ibsen, *Brand*, 1866; S. Kierkegaard, *Fear and Trembling*, 1843.

STEWART R. SUTHERLAND

Fathers, Christian
see **Patristics, Alexandrian Theology, Antiochene Theology, Cappadocian Fathers, Christology, Trinity**

Federal Theology
'Federal', from the Latin *foedus*, a covenant*. Federal Theology was a movement in seventeenth century Reformed theology to present a comprehensive history of salvation, working from the OT (see Westminster Confession chapter vii). Federal theology specifically refers to the theory of Johannis Cocceius (1603–1669), who taught mainly in the Netherlands and whose teaching threw the church into turmoil. Cocceius held that the original natural covenant of works was 'abrogated' in five steps in accordance with the super-natural covenant. The steps were: the Fall; the inner-trinitarian pact between God and the Mediator; the proclamation of the covenant of grace in the OT, fulfilled in the NT; the death of the body and sanctification; and the resurrection of the body. Federal theology deeply influenced pietism and all later philosophies of history.

J. C. O'NEILL

Feminist Theology
Feminist theology has had its primary development in the United States, although conferences, publications and teaching in this area are also taking place in Britain, Western Europe and Latin America. Much of feminist theological thought has been associated with the period after 1968, although feminist criticism of biblical exegesis and Christian theology can be traced to earlier roots. In 1667, Margaret Fell, influential early Quaker leader and wife of George Fox, founder of the Society of Friends*, wrote a tract entitled *Women's Speaking Justified, Approved and Allowed of by the Scriptures*. This tract attempted both a biblical hermeneutic* and theological anthropology of women's equality in Christ and consequent right to preach, teach and administer in the church of Christ.

In nineteenth-century America, Quakerism was an important source for feminist leaders who typically argued their case for women's rights from a biblical basis. In 1837, Sarah Grimké, a Quaker, an abolitionist and feminist, argued women's rights in society theologically and biblically. On the basis of Gen. 1.27, Grimké defined women's equality with men in the original creation, exemplified by their common possession of the *imago dei*. Both women and men were given dominion over nature, but men were not given dominion over women in the original creation. Patriarchalism was criticized as a sinful decline from this original place of woman in the divine plan. Grimké called upon church and social leaders to reform their institutional structures to rectify this injustice (Grimké, *Letters on the Equality of the Sexes and the Condition of Woman*, 1837). Nineteenth-century American feminists typically argued their case in biblical and theological terms and criticized the use of the Bible as an instrument of male domination (Elisabeth Cady Staton, *The Woman's Bible*, 1895–1898; Matilda Joslyn Gage, *Woman, Church and State*, 1893).

Feminist theology is not to be understood primarily as theological reflection on separate 'feminine' themes. Feminist theology takes as its first agenda the criticism of the masculinist bias of Christian theology. This bias has excluded women both from ordained ministry and from higher theological education throughout much of the church's history. Feminists therefore see Christian theology as having been done in exclusion of women's experience. Classical theology reflects a negative bias against women in its anthropological teachings (K. E. Borresen, *Subordination and Equivalence: The Nature and Role of Woman in Augustine and Thomas Aquinas,* 1968). Feminist theology seeks to analyse the effects of this exclusion of and negative anthropology about women in shaping the theological understandings of God, nature, sin, grace, christology, redemption and ecclesiology. Feminist criticism documents this male bias in theological doctrines and traces its effects in scripture, and in patristic, mediaeval and modern theologians (M. Daly, *The Church and the Second Sex,* 1968; R. Ruether, *Religion and Sexism,* 1974).

The second agenda of feminist theology aims at the discovery of alternative historical traditions supportive of the full personhood of woman and her inclusion in leadership roles in church and society. There are two approaches to this quest for alternative tradition. Some feminists concerned with religion and spirituality have given up on the Judaeo-Christian tradition. They feel that this tradition is inherently patriarchal. Women should abandon Judaism or Christianity and seek alternative traditions outside them, by returning to ancient religions with female symbols for the divine and by drawing on their own experience (M. Daly, *Beyond God the Father,* 1973; Starhawk, *The Spiral Dance,* 1979).

Other feminists wish to affirm the possibility of feminist theology within the Judaeo-Christian tradition. They seek to uncover the more fundamental meaning of concepts of God, Christ, human personhood, sin and redemption that can criticize the deformation of these concepts as tools of male domination. The vindication of an alternative feminist reading of Christian origins is particularly important. Early Christianity is read as a counter-cultural movement subversive of the traditional hierarchical religious and social relationships. This radical vision was gradually submerged as institutional Christianity reintegrated itself back into patriarchal and slave-holding society and justified these household relationships, not only for the church but as a metaphor of Christian submission to God

and to Christ. However, the radical vision of Christianity was not entirely extinguished, but continued to appear in both mystical and popular movements which affirmed the charismatic authority of women (E. S. Fiorenza, *In Memory of Her: A Feminist Theological Reconstruction of Christian Origins,* 1983; R. Ruether and E. McLaughlin, *Women of Spirit,* 1979).

Feminists engaged in recovering alternative traditions for women in theology do not intend merely to supplement the present male tradition. They are constructing a new norm for interpretation of what is 'true' and 'false' in the tradition. Justifications of women's subordination in scripture and theology are no longer regarded as normative expressions of the gospel. Rather, they are judged as failures to apply the norms of equality in creation and redemption authentically, as perversion of the good news into an instrument of oppression. The full personhood of woman is one of the touchstones for testing our faithfulness to the vision of redemption in Christ. By this norm much of mainstream tradition must be judged as deficient.

There is debate within feminist theology about the usefulness of traditional 'feminine' concepts in theology: Wisdom, Mother Church, Mariology, the 'bridal soul'. Some feminist theological writers, drawing on concepts of complementarity, particularly as influenced by Jungian* psychology, want to expand and develop these feminine symbols as central to female identity (Ann Ulanov, *Receiving Woman,* 1981; Joan Engelman, *The Feminine Dimension of the Divine,* 1979). Other thinkers are critical of these concepts in their traditional form. They see the historical feminine symbols as the underside of symbols of masculine domination. Such symbols simply direct women to the traditional feminine roles within patriarchy of passivity, subservience and receptivity to male control. For such feminists it is necessary to re-evaluate the psycho-dynamics of all the inherited symbols. Hierarchical patterns must be transformed into patterns of mutual service and mutual empowerment.

The re-evaluation of Christian symbols not only touches the masculine symbols for Christ and God and the feminine symbols for church and creaturehood; it also questions the shape given by concepts such as sin and grace. When, for example, sin is seen primarily in terms of overweening pride and grace as redeeming humility, one has a theological pattern that derives, sociologically, from the experience of men in power. But this pattern may be much less relevant to women or oppressed people, whose sin has been more the failure to affirm the self. For such people, 'humility' may suggest simply a continuation of subjection to unjust power, rather than the redeemed self. Thus all the basic Christian theological constructs need to be examined for their masculinist bias and redeveloped to include the different experiences of women (Judith Plaskow, *Sex, Sin and Grace*, 1980).

R. Ruether, *Sexism and God-Talk: Toward a Feminist Theology*, 1983; Sally McFague, *Metaphorical Theology*, 1982.

R. R. RUETHER

Fideism

The word was coined in the nineteenth century, probably by A. Sabatier and his modernist circle of Protestants in Paris, to denote the view that (as Kant has demonstrated) reason could not prove the truths of religion and that therefore believers could rely upon faith, which was a kind of religious experiencing. Dogmas were only the symbolic expression of religious feelings; this view stands in the general succession from Schleiermacher (and Ritschl). 'Fideism' has continued to be used especially by theologians of the Thomist tradition as a pejorative term for subjectivist theories which are based upon religious experience and which undervalue reason in theology. 'Wittgensteinian fideism' is the term that has been applied to the work of some theologians and philosophers of religion who claim that every form of life, including religion, develops its own autonomous language-game, and that it is neither necessary nor possible for it to be justified by anything outside of itself.

ALAN RICHARDSON/
JOHN MACQUARRIE

Filioque

Filioque is the Western insertion in the article on the Holy Spirit in the Niceno-Constantinopolitan Creed, 'Who proceeds from the Father *and the Son*', to express the doctrine of the Double Procession* of the Spirit. While the underlying theology had deep roots in the West from Augustine onwards and had formed part of official documents from the fifth century, the intrusion into the Creed is first evidenced in France in Carolingian times. Widely accepted in the West, it was only later received at Rome. This has been bitterly resented in the East both on canonical and doctrinal grounds.

See **Trinity, Doctrine of the; Holy Spirit.**

H. E. W. TURNER

Finality

The rabbis sometimes taught that God revealed all truth to Moses on Sinai, both the written and the oral instruction, and that what he learnt was definitive for mankind. Since Christianity originated within Judaism it was likely to have its own doctrine of finality. Jesus and his followers expected the present age to terminate and to be followed by the wonderful new age. Hence whatever happened through the work of God's agent of that transformation must be a final activity and he must be God's Son in a final sense, later to be expressed by a doctrine of incarnation*. His resurrection* was thought to prefigure the new age and hence his death was given final significance (Rom. 6.10; I Peter 3.18), especially in the Epistle to the Hebrews, where God finally shakes the world into shape (12.26–27), Jesus offers himself in sacrifice to remove sins and to consecrate followers (9.26–28; 10.10), and those who have tasted the powers of the age to come have no second chance if they fall away (6.4–5). Even so, the vigorous temporal imagery is supplemented by the equally forceful claim that the indestructible life of Jesus is the means by which we leave the shadow world in which we live and enter the heavenly world of reality. So also in the Johannine tradition where the present experience of eternal life has largely replaced the eschatological hope, 'no one has ascended into heaven but he who descended from heaven, the Son of man' (John 3.13). Yet the finality of God's activity and revelation in Jesus was contested by those who claimed experience of the Spirit (who are repudiated in the statement 'no one comes to the Father, but by me', John 14.6). Much of the doctrinal conflict in the first centuries of the church was prompted by disagreement between those who were reluctant to concede finality to God's revelation in

Christ, or to concede it in the language that had become conventional, and those who were determined to assert such finality and define it in terms that would exclude both variation within the church and the damaging intrusion of pagan religion and philosophy. No doubt the church's position as a minority group in the Roman empire strengthened its early claim to finality, which then provided it with a useful weapon when it came to power and moved towards dominance. A modern statement about Christ says that 'he is definitive in the sense that for Christians he defines in normative fashion both the nature of man (which he has brought to a new level) and the nature of God (for the divine Logos, expressive Being, has found its fullest expression in him)' (J. Macquarrie, *Principles of Christian Theology*, 1977, p. 305). Even such a modest claim, however, is now contested because of the church's weakened position and loss of confidence in face of critical enquiry, other world religions, the modern scientific revolution, and the cheerless political prospect for mankind. For the questioning of finality, see M. Wiles, *The Remaking of Christian Doctrine* (1974). For the transition from finality in Tertullian to universality in Eusebius, see J. Pelikan, *The Finality of Christ* (1965). The real question, however, may well be whether 'finality' is any longer a useful description for events, images and ideas that have permanent and creative force.

KENNETH GRAYSTON

Final Perseverance

The phrase is derived from Matt. 24.13: 'But he who endures to the end will be saved.' The theological question was whether Christian hope included the assurance of final perseverance. The writings of Paul could be cited on both sides: *for*, 'I am sure that he is able to guard until that Day what had been entrusted to me' (II Tim. 1.12); *against*, 'Therefore let any one who thinks that he stands take heed lest he fall' (I Cor. 10.12). The problem was sharpened by Augustine's *Treatise on the Gift of Perseverance*, in which he stated that 'the perseverance by which we persevere in Christ even to the end is the gift of God'; 'if this is given, one does persevere unto the end; but if one does not persevere unto the end, it is not given'. Augustine's argument hinged upon

the fact that Christians pray for perseverance, notably in the Lord's Prayer; if perseverance is asked for from God, it must be given by God. The Council of Trent * condemned anyone who said that he certainly by an absolute and infallible certainty had this great gift of perseverance to the end, except the person to whom this had been specially revealed. Calvin on the contrary affirmed the certainty of Christian hope; irresistible grace and the perseverance of the saints became two of the five points of Calvinism, disputed from within by the Arminians *. Ernst Bloch's statement of the (seemingly irrational) 'principle of hope' as the driving force in human life has helped revive theological interest in the question (Moltmann).

See also **Hope, Perseverance.**

J. C. O'NEILL

Five Ways
see **Arguments for the Existence of God**

Foreknowledge

The view that God knows the future has been an essential part of traditional Christian accounts of providence *, predestination * and prophecy *. The obvious problem has been to relate this foreknowledge with belief in free will * and human responsibility, and there have been various attempts to do this. In Christian thought one of the most important and influential approaches to the problem can be found in Boethius, though the origins of his views can be found in Neoplatonic * ideas. Boethius stresses the eternal nature of God's knowledge, whereby he sees all things in an eternal present. Therefore, although we can use *providentia* to refer to God's knowledge of the future, we should not use *praevidentia*, for this, he claims, can mislead us into likening God's eternal knowledge to human temporal knowledge through causes. This latter, he holds, would be inconsistent with human freedom. Similarly, he prefers to speak of God's *praesentia* rather than his *praescientia*, again in order to stress his eternal standpoint. Boethius' account became the source for most later views, such as that of Aquinas on the 'eternal now' in which God lives. It is less evident in the Reformers, however, many of whom had a doctrine of divine sovereignty which included a divine causation of all events, natural and human, and either a rejection of free will, or a theory that left it virtually empty.

While Boethius' view remains orthodox, there is a significant contemporary movement towards a reappraisal of divine foreknowledge. One aspect of this is a changed emphasis in prophecy, which is seen more and more as the 'forthtelling' of the meaning of the present, rather than as a looking into the future. As a result, significant prophecy no longer demands that the future be knowable in detail. Another, and more radical change is suggested by those who challenge the traditional idea of God's total changelessness, which underlies Boethius' account of foreknowledge. According to these thinkers, in freely choosing to make a temporal universe, God in some way committed himself to a temporal relationship with it. For example, according to Hartshorne, both God's knowledge of us and his love for us can only be meaningful if change of a kind is possible for God (*see* **Process Theology**). Omnipotence* and omniscience* are then reinterpreted to allow a radical contingency in the future, that is therefore unknown in detail, even to God.

See also **Time and Timelessness.**

Boethius, *De consolatione philosophiae*, V; C. Hartshorne, *Man's Vision of God*, 1964.

M. J. LANGFORD

Forgiveness

1. *Theological.* Forgiveness plays a central role in the Jewish and Christian understanding of the history of God's relationships with humankind. It is the divine correlative of human sin. The various Hebrew and Greek words employed in OT and NT, of which *salaḥ* and *aphiemi* are the most frequent, speak primarily of the divine action to remove or overcome human sin. Although prayers of petition and rites of atonement are associated with forgiveness among Israel's Assyrian and Babylonian neighbours as well as in Israel itself, the actual forgiveness remains the free gift of God. It is a theological reality. Self-justification is always excluded. Moreover, for Israel magical results are ruled out by the demand for repentance. The history of Israel is the history of a forgiving God in search of a repentant people. The repentance, fully human as it must be, also derives from the loving power of the forgiving God. Human love of repentance is derived from and dependent on the divine love of forgiveness (*see* **Love**).

2. *Christological.* In Jesus Christ the theme of forgiveness marked the introduction to his mission by John the Baptist (cf. Mark 1.4). It quickly became one of the decisive characteristics of his own teaching, activity and self-identification. Forgiveness of sin was a critical feature of the kingdom he announced. His own death was in view of this kingdom of forgiveness (Matt. 26.28; I Cor. 15.8). It implied repentance, itself a gift of God. It was available in unlimited fashion, 'seventy times seven' (Matt. 18.22), and impossible only for those who deliberately blasphemed by consigning the forgiving work of the Spirit of God to Beelzebul, the sin against the Holy Spirit (Matt. 12.31 par.).

The climactic prayer of Jesus on the cross for forgiveness for his enemies (Luke 23.34) reveals the range of divine power and human need. Forgiveness is from God and by God in Jesus' teaching and activity. Yet human forgiveness of one another plays a role equal to that of repentance as a 'quasi' condition for divine forgiveness. The Lord's Prayer, the warning about the gift at the altar (Matt. 5.23) and the parable of the unmerciful debtor (Matt. 18) highlight the intimate connection between God's forgiveness of human beings and their forgiveness of one another (cf. Matt. 6.14f.), parallel to the connection between divine and human loving. The forgiveness is theological. It comes from God. So do the repentance and the mutual human forgiveness. Yet it is part of the glory and terror of human beings that they must open up to these divine gifts which were expressed definitively in the person and mission of Jesus Christ.

3. *Ecclesial and sacramental.* The forgiving message and mission of Jesus reached beyond his own time and place to all times and places through the church. The Gospels record Jesus' commissioning of his disciples (Matt. 16.28; John 20). The early apostolic preaching by Peter and others confirmed this (Acts 2.38). Paul's presentation of forgiveness in terms of justification emphasized the availability of divine initiative in Jesus across all human barriers (cf. Gal. 3.28).

The early church practice emphasized the role of baptism and eucharist in mediating divine forgiveness. Incorporation in the church of the saints through baptism* and full community celebration in eucharist* involved sharing in the forgiving death and resurrection of Jesus. With experience of sinners in the church and the fading hopes of an imminent parousia*, further forgiveness and repentance became a need (cf. I Corinthians). The practice of public and subsequently even private penance* followed by reconciliation had an obvious ecclesial as well as christological and theological significance. The sacramental character of this practice of reconciliation proved divisive at the Reformation*. In more ecumenical times the forgiveness necessary and available through the church of Jesus Christ may be expressed in different ways and sacraments, including the sacramental rite of penance and reconciliation.

4. *Personal and social.* Although forgiveness through the church maintained its ecclesial and so social dimension, this social dimension became very attenuated. Currently there are significant efforts to restore it in baptism, eucharist and penance. The human fraternal forgiveness so closely allied to divine forgiveness in the NT has become even more individualistic. The need for reconciliation between classes and nations and races today has raised the prospects of political forgiveness or a 'politics of forgiveness' (Willmer). It promises new possibilities, provided it is not used by the powerful to exploit the weak; provided it is accompanied as always by repentance.

H. R. Mackintosh, *The Christian Experience of Forgiveness*, 1927; B. Poschmann, *Penance and the Anointing of the Sick*, 1963; M. J. Taylor (ed), *The Mystery of Sin and Forgiveness*, 1970; Hartwig Thyen, *Studien zur Sündenvergebung*, 1970; H. Willmer, 'The Politics of Forgiveness', *The Furrow*, 3, 1979.

ENDA MCDONAGH

Form Criticism

Form criticism begins from the observation that particular types of communication have particular preferred forms. When dealing with our own language and culture we find these forms readily recognizable. We do not confuse a hire purchase agreement with a love letter. But when dealing with a foreign or ancient language and culture we may need to study the forms of communication quite deliberately.

Some forms are very rigid (the limerick, the income tax declaration), others very flexible (the lecture). Many have stereotyped opening and closing formulae but are otherwise free (the letter). Form criticism further observes that particular forms are often strongly associated with specific social settings. E.g. the normal locus of the sermon is in church, that of the sports commentary is the radio or television.

1. *Uses of Form Criticism.* Use of the proper form is a signal to the hearer or reader, letting him know what to expect and how to evaluate the communication. A communication which begins 'Once upon a time ...' is not met with the same expectation as one which starts 'Here is the news', neither will we evaluate its contents in the same way. Identification of forms is thus fundamental to interpretation. We shall not get the best out of the book of Jonah if we fail to identify it as satire, and we shall misinterpret the Song of Songs if we fail to perceive that it is love poetry. This identification of forms is especially important when assessing the value of a text as historical evidence. Material identified as 'legend' will have a different kind of evidential value from material classified as 'royal annals'.

Study of forms may illuminate the settings in which they were used. Formal analysis of the psalms, for example, has thrown much light on Israelite liturgy.

In principle, the study of forms may help in the dating of particular pieces of tradition. In practice we rarely know enough about the history of biblical forms and the periods at which each was current to enable us to draw confident conclusions as to date. A notable attempt to do this was Mendenhall's work on the Sinai covenant formulations and the Hittite royal treaties (*see also* **Covenant**).

2. *Techniques of form criticism.* The form critic assumes that originally the units of tradition (i.e. individual stories, sayings, poems) circulated independently. It is necessary, therefore, to identify the units. The formulae which introduce and close each unit are important clues, though some forms are also distinguished by a distinctive structure. The next stages are to look for indications of the social setting and possibly also the geographical location in which the unit originated. The form critic also notes apparent secondary modifications to the unit

which may reveal something of the history of its transmission.

Form criticism was originally conceived as an attempt to trace the history of the biblical material before it was written down. In this sense form criticism begins where literary* criticism leaves off. But written materials themselves have their own customary forms, and form criticism does have an application to the literary as well as the preliterary phases of tradition.

3. *History of form criticism.* H. Gunkel is usually credited with the introduction of form critical methods to the OT with his commentary on Genesis (1901). He later went on to apply his methods fruitfully to the psalms. S. Mowinckel and other continental scholars built on his work.

In the NT field form criticism was pioneered by K. L. Schmidt, M. Dibelius and R. Bultmann, major works on the subject appearing from 1919 onwards (*see also* **Jesus**). NT form critics argued that the units of the Gospel tradition were preserved and transmitted primarily because they met the needs of the primitive church, and were sometimes modified in response to those needs. These scholars did not precisely agree in their classification of the Gospel materials, but they were united by their sceptical attitude to the historicity of the Gospel traditions. For some decades form-critical methods were therefore associated with historical scepticism. Perhaps for this reason they were for some time taken less seriously in the English speaking world than they deserved. It may be observed, however, that English-speaking OT scholars were also slow to take up form-critical techniques, even though in that field these techniques had not been put to use primarily in the interests of scepticism.

Though the principles of form criticism and its techniques are basically the same in the two Testaments, large differences in application arise because of the different time-scales involved. Most of the NT writings achieved their present form within a generation of the events to which they refer, whereas much of the OT material was handed down for some hundreds of years before reaching the form in which we now have it. The processes of transmission in the two cases inevitably involved quite different factors.

See also **Biblical Criticism, Jesus.**

K. Koch, *The Growth of the Biblical Tradition*, 1969; E. V. McKnight, *What is Form Criticism?*, 1969; S. H. Travis, 'Form Criticism', in I. H. Marshall, *New Testament Interpretation*, 1977; G. M. Tucker, *Form Criticism of the Old Testament*, 1971.

H. MCKEATING

Frankfurt School *see* **Critical Theory**

Freedom

The notion of freedom is central to the vocabulary of moral and religious thought in the Western tradition and, it appears, in non-Western traditions as well. It is not hard to understand why. If freedom, in relation to practical discourse or the language of human action, is understood as the capacity for deliberating and choosing among desired or valued courses of action, and pursuing the preferred course without restraint, that idea is presupposed in most utterances that prescribe or evaluate human action.

Insofar as human beings, in prescribing or recommending (or ruling out) a course of action, appeal, as they seem universally to do, to actions as 'good' or 'bad', 'right' or 'wrong', etc., and ascribe praise and blame accordingly, they assume a capacity for deliberative choice. Clearly, 'ought-language' or 'should-language' is invariably reserved for beings regarded as free to choose deliberatively. (In the Western tradition, we typically do not address animals, very young children or seriously incompetent individuals with 'ought' or 'should' statements. In cultures where some or all of these groups are so addressed, it is because they are believed, under some conditions, to possess the capacity for deliberative volition.) The same is true of locutions like, 'it would be good if you did this', or, 'doing that is a bad idea'. In short, practical language presupposes freedom in the sense that only those regarded as free, or as having the ability to consider, weigh, choose and then direct themselves accordingly, may intelligibly be addressed in such terms.

If an ability for deliberative choice is presupposed by the notion of freedom, a capacity for acting on the choice without coercive restraint goes with it. Although the idea of restraint or constraint imposed by other human beings is taken as the standard complement to freedom (particularly in the

liberal tradition), the idea is more complicated. Restraints may, in general, be
'internal' or 'external', as well as 'positive'
or 'negative' (Feinberg). Internal positive
restraints upon action may, for example,
consist of debilitating or disconcerting
compulsions or obsessions, while internal
negative restraints would be such things as
deficiencies in information, training, mental
activity, talent, perseverance, etc. External
positive restraints are things like coercion or
physical or psychological compulsion inflicted by other human beings, or restrictions imposed by 'natural causes'. Lack of
wherewithal for accomplishing desired
objectives would constitute external negative restraints.

But important as it is to recognize the
complexity of the kinds of restraint on freedom, it is even more important to acknowledge that the relation between freedom and
restraint depends on the particular view of
approved or desirable action that is accepted
in the first place. In other words, the relation
between freedom and restraint is normative
and not purely descriptive. Only after it has
been determined what course of action is
valuable, can the character of restraints on
freedom be identified and assessed.

For example, if human fulfilment is taken
to consist in the accumulation of great
material wealth, then whatever external or
internal, positive or negative restraints
retard the achievement of that end will
become significant precisely by constituting
unacceptable impediments to the 'free' pursuit of the desired end. By contrast, if asceticism is believed to be an indispensable part
of the ideal life, then opportunities for
material gain, especially if they tempt the
would-be ascetic, will be regarded as obstacles to the 'life of freedom'.

It is for this reason that Bertrand Russell's
well-known definition of freedom as 'the absence of obstacles to the realization of desires'
is unsatisfactory. The ascetic may well describe the acquisitive person who with ease
obtains considerable wealth as having
realized his desires in the absence of obstacles.
But the ascetic will not normally describe that
person as being 'genuinely free'. Only those
whose desires are in order can know what
freedom is as well as what restraints and
obstacles to freedom are all about.

It is also for this reason that John Stuart
Mill's much-repeated statement, 'All re-

straint, *qua* restraint, is an evil . . .' is at least
misleading. Since the relation between freedom and restraint depends on a prior determination of what is valuable or acceptable action, restraints which impede the
performance of valuable or acceptable
action would naturally be regarded as evil.
However, forms of restraint (certain laws,
acts of resistance, etc.) would not be
regarded as evil so long as they are believed
to prevent the pursuit of harmful ends.

These considerations lie behind and
illuminate the use to which the word freedom is put in specifically religious contexts.
The centrality of contrasts like 'freedom and
slavery', 'deliverance and captivity', 'liberation and imprisonment', in religious literature and experience attests to the preoccupation of religious practitioners with
the tensions between freedom and restraint,
and with the normative interpretations of
those tensions.

Roland Bainton, *The Travail of Religious
Liberty*, 1951; Christian Bay, *The Structure
of Freedom* 1958; Isaiah Berlin, *Two Con-
cepts of Liberty*, 1958; Maurice Cranston,
Freedom; A New Analysis, ²1954; J. C. Mill,
On Liberty, 1912; Bertrand Russell, 'Freedom
and Government', in Ruth N. Anshen (ed),
Freedom: Its Meaning, 1940.

DAVID LITTLE

Freethinking

In religious questions this means a rejection
of the control of authority over the reason.
In England the word comes from the late
seventeenth century, when it began to be
used in Deist * circles, notably by Anthony
Collins (1676–1729) in *A Discourse of Freethinking*, published in 1713. Seventeenth-
and eighteenth-century freethinkers denied
above all the Christian claim to the possession of a unique and final divine revelation *
which could be found in the Bible: they preferred the idea of 'natural religion', which
was accessible to reason. However, freethinking in the sense of a rejection of the
absoluteness of the authority of Christianity
was visible earlier: for example, Edward
Herbert (1583–1648) published *De Veritate*
in 1624, and similar attitudes are found in
France at that time in small groups devoted
to science and ancient philosophy. For most
of the seventeenth century the French used
the term 'libertin', but at the end of the cen-

tury they borrowed 'freethinker' from Britain, translating it as 'libre-penseur'. In the nineteenth century freethinking came much closer to militant atheism *: in England, for example, the National Secularist Society was founded in 1866 on a platform of aggressive freethought, and *The Freethinker* started publication in 1881 as 'an anti-Christian organ'. By that time, however, because of the growth of biblical criticism *, and the development of science *, it was the Christian theologian himself who faced with new intensity the issues of freedom of thought and publication, as was seen in the conflict between individual theologians and the Anglican Church after the publication of *Essays and Reviews* in 1860. In general, churches still maintain the claim to decide what is revelation and how it is to be interpreted: individual theologians who reject the concept of revelation, or reject the church's authority to prescribe their conclusions, may find themselves in difficulty.

E. Royle, *Victorian Infidels: The Origins of the British Secularist Movement 1791–1866*, 1974.

JOHN KENT

Free Will

The view that man has a capacity to choose between good and evil has been that of most Christian theologians, over against various forms of determinism * and logical positivism * (which holds that the terms free will and determinism are both literally meaningless). The central question involved is not 'How far should man be allowed to do as he wishes?', which is that of political freedom, but the much more radical question 'How far is man able to choose anything at all, except as a mechanical response to the genetic and environmental pressures that bear upon him?' However, human responsibility, and thus some kind of free will, is generally implicit in the Bible, and also in the Western tradition of *mens rea* (guilty mind), which is taken to be a precondition of criminal liability before the law. For theologians the problem is to reconcile this with God's omnipotence *, and with modern views of causality *.

In his *De libero arbitrio* Augustine argues forcibly for free will. Although God foreknows all things, this does not deprive us of freedom, he claims, for he foreknows what I shall freely choose. At the same time Augustine's account of the absolute necessity of grace in order for the will to be rightly moved, especially in the condition of fallen nature, appears to contradict his libertarian stand. Later theologians have sought various ways of resolving the contradiction. One of the most important attempts is that of Boethius who insisted that God's foreknowledge * is outside the order of time *, and is therefore quite different from human prediction based on knowledge of causes. By using distinctions of this kind most subsequent theologians argued that there could be both freedom and a divine providence.

Protestantism has generally taken a more negative view of free will than Catholicism, but the various positions must be stated with care. Some, such as Jonathan Edwards, positively denied 'free will', but still maintained that man had an essential 'liberty', and denied that God was responsible for evil. Most others paid similar lip service either to free will or to human liberty, at least in man's unfallen state, but their Augustinian doctrines of grace, foreknowledge and predestination made it even harder to give significance to freedom than in the Catholic tradition. In particular, the widespread doctrine of man's total depravity * following the Fall * made any freedom that he originally possessed virtually irrelevant. More recent Protestant thought has tended to accept more liberal positions, and some of the more radical thinkers have sought to limit, or at least to redefine, God's omnipotence and omniscience, in order to allow for a more positive account of free will. An important example of such an approach is the thought of Charles Hartshorne.

There are two principal arguments for the libertarian position. The first is the moral argument, for which Kant is the most famous spokesman. He claimed that although man is 'phenomenally determined', this is to refer only to the world of appearances, and human reason could see that this left open the possibility that in the order of true reality, or 'noumena', man is free. Since morality demands freedom as one of its preconditions ('ought implies can'), we must assume that man is noumenally free. Most recent defenders of the moral argument, while following Kant in arguing that a significant morality presupposes free will, have not accepted his theory of total determinism in the world of sense, which they tend to see as a relic from a more primitive age of science.

Another kind of argument for free will can be built on the nature of self-consciousness, with the emergence of which, it is claimed, we reach a new *level* of being, beyond the inorganic and the merely animal, and this level requires new categories of language, including the idea of free will, to describe. This level includes consciousness, creativity, the capacity to love, and free will, which can all be seen as mutually interdependent. Determinist arguments which seek to explain human choice through a lower level of being are therefore question-begging, because they already assume a stimulus-response, or a mechanical model, like that of the balance scale. But this is to accept determinism in advance, and to rule out the possibility that there is genuine novelty at the *human* level. Moreover, the argument goes on, the claim that any position is actually *true* appears to be meaningful only if we believe in a significant freedom. This applies equally to the paradoxical belief that determinism is true, for the determinist must believe that he is determined to believe this. It follows that if the libertarian position is correct, there cannot be an *explanation* of free will within the traditional physical sciences, but only from within the phenomenon of human consciousness.

See also **Predestination.**

Aquinas, *ST* 1a, Qs. 82–3; Augustine, *De libero arbitrio voluntatis*; C. A. Campbell, *In Defence of Free-will*, 1967; A. M. Farrer, *The Freedom of the Will*, 1958; S. Hook (ed), *Determinism and freedom*, 1961; J. Thorpe, *Free Will*, 1980.

M. J. LANGFORD

Freudian Psychology

1. Like Marx's 'opium of the people', Freud's 'universal neurosis' has come to epitomize, in the minds of most Christians, an attitude hostile to and dismissive of religious faith and practice. People are vaguely aware that Freud described religious ritual in terms of neurotic obsession, that he considered God to be the projection of fantasies of the omnipotent and menacing father (*see also* **Projection Theory**), that he saw conscience as the 'inner aggression' of the superego (the psychic mechanism for the repression of instinct); and there is, of course, the title of his late (1927) work, *The Future of an Illusion*, to confirm the general impression of a system deeply inimical to any kind of religion, and especially to the Judaeo-Christian tradition.

It is certainly true that Freud saw religion as a psychopathological phenomenon in human history overall, analogous to neurosis in the individual; and just as neurosis in the individual is the result of trauma and repression, with the return of repressed memories of fear and guilt in disguised forms, so the genesis of religion is to be understood as lying in primal events producing traumatic guilt. *Totem and Taboo* (1912–1913) postulates a father-dominated 'primal horde', in which the sons eventually slaughter the father to gain freedom of sexual access to the women of the group, and devour his body; the primitive religious ritual of a meal in which a totem animal is eaten is a recapitulation of the primal murder. It celebrates the defeat of the father, but also (involving as it does a lament for the 'sacred' victim, the source of power) articulates guilt for the deed and seeks some kind of reconciliation with the memory of the victim. *Moses and Monotheism* (1937–1939) argues a parallel process in the origins of Judaism: Moses – an Egyptian devotee of the one universal god, Aten – imposes monotheism on a group of Semitic tribesmen; he is murdered by the tribesmen, who deal with their guilt by associating the one Mosaic god with a local volcano deity, a projection of omnipotent wrath. The heavenly projection of the 'threatening father', the Moses who has been killed, makes it possible to forget the actual murder – at the cost of introducing a generalized guilt in place of the specific memory of Moses' murder, and obscuring the universal and ethical God of Moses himself with the worship of a vindictive and bloodthirsty local demon. It is the religion of Moses which the 'ethical monotheism' of the prophets finally reactivates as the foundation of the religious and moral system of classical Judaism, but without removing the element of pervasive guilt. Pauline Christianity, recollecting the murder of a 'son' who represents both the primal father *and* the guilty children, is a brilliant resolution of primal guilt, allowing the ultimate displacing of the father by the exalted son who has expiated in his own death the remembered murder of the father. The totemic meal of the eucharist is a 'reconciliation with the father' by eating the murdered son.

2. It hardly needs saying that, as anthropological or historical hypotheses, these accounts are painfully absurd; and they also presuppose the notion of an inherited memory of 'primal' events – which creates enormous theoretical difficulties. On his own resolutely materialistic account of the basis of psychic life, Freud would have had to assume a *genetic* modification resulting from the events described. What Freud is actually doing, with the help of various bits of nineteenth-century anthropology, is constructing a mythical correlative for his theoretical scheme. Wittgenstein (in the 'Conversations on Freud' reported by R. Rhees) noted that Freud's very *use* of myth (especially the Oedipus myth) is mythical – setting present reality in the context of an archaic predetermined narrative pattern, and so giving it the dignity of a classical tragedy.

In other words, Freud believes that he is giving explanations of a scientific and materialistic kind where in fact he is constructing imaginative frameworks of interpretation. Freudian theorists still disagree vigorously about the nature and possibility of 'explanation' in psychoanalysis, but recent decades have seen a marked increase in the number of those prepared to see analysis as a linguistic process, a conversation about possible meanings for the subject undergoing the analysis, a suggestion of viable stories to tell about oneself in a way that opens up further growth. What is *not* being offered is scientific explanation: the Freudian theoretical structure is a therapeutic myth. Jacques Lacan in France, Roy Shafer in the USA, James Home and Charles Rycroft in Britain have all developed variations on this basis recognition, and 'existential' psychology (R. D. Laing, T. Szasz) has some important, though limited, affinities with this approach.

3. At first sight, it would appear that the surrender by psychoanalysis of any claims to explanatory force is a welcome relief for religious language. No longer is it to be subjected to a grossly reductionist account of its origins; it is not taken for granted that (like any other pathology) it demands explanation – and cure. However, things are not so simple. On the one hand, the 'interpretation' model of psychoanalysis involves a theory of language which brackets the whole issue of descriptive truth: the validity of myth is its therapeutic resourcefulness, no more. No less serious a question is put to Christian theology by this scheme than by Freud's cruder scientism. On the other hand, and following from this first point, the analytic interpretation may still diagnose religious language as a malfunction of the subject's speech, insofar as religion's claims to objective, superpersonal truth are a means of alienating the subject from his or her own life and language, so that (in Erich Fromm's phrase) the self only 'has access' to itself via the alien, external reality of God. Such a grounding of identity in what is objectively other is a stage in psychic development which has to give way to symbolic identification with the other, internalized in one's own psychic processes – the resolution of the problems set up in what Lacan calls the 'mirror stage' of infant development.

This brings us back to the central and abidingly important feature of Freud's critique of religion. Religion attempts to deal with the powerlessness of the human subject; but rather than being itself a means of empowerment, it projects unrestricted power on to an alien reality and fixes the self in a permanent state of impotence and alienation. Power (divine power) is accessible only through self-abasement and self-devaluing. Freud recognized no other significant manifestations of religion; for him it was invariably and intrinsically alienating, self-destructive.

Some of his followers and interpreters have been less confident about this. The American writer Erich Fromm (notable for some bold early attempts at marrying Freud to Marx, and so an important figure in the development of the New Left synthesis of the 1960s and 1970s) argued for a distinction between 'authoritarian' and 'humanistic' religion. The latter is rather loosely defined, but seems to involve elements of cosmic mysticism, a sense of dependence that is also a sense of belonging in the universe, and a capacity for loving based on inner strength and integrity. Spinoza and certain aspects of Buddhism play a significant role in Fromm's exposition: God is indistinguishable from the 'process of being'.

Others have been more sceptical. Philip

Rieff and Ernest Becker have protested that Fromm's reconciliation (not to mention the mystical religiosities of Reich or Jung) is too facile: Freud's view of the human condition is almost entirely tragic, and allows little place for the consolations of union with cosmic energy or even the 'process of being'. Our existence is at every level precarious, the ego is an uneasy compromise between instinct and repression, desire and death. 'The process of being' is in danger of becoming another alienating myth if we fail to recognize that it includes contradiction, limit and mortality. Traditional religion, which breeds a healthy suspicion of human aspirations to heroic self-deification, and which unashamedly counsels receptivity, waiting, humility, is actually a more honest, less delusory project – more in line, strange as it may seem, with the scepticism and stoicism of Freud himself.

This approach, most eloquently argued by Becker (with much indebtedness to Freud's collaborator, Otto Rank), assumes (i) that there is no way in which limitless power ever becomes available to humanity, i.e. that dependence is an immutable fact about the human condition; (ii) that recognizing this, recognizing that one's identity is not self-created and can never wholly be so, need not be alienation and self-loss. A God who is both radically other and radically hidden is not a competitor for power with the finite self; to depend for one's identity ultimately upon a hidden source of self-giving or self-sharing is to be as free as one can be within the tragic limits of the world.

4. Religion remains, in the purely technical sense, an 'illusion' in this perspective: mental health itself depends, Becker maintains, on the possibility of 'illusion' or myth or a narrative locating of the individual's problems. Nothing can be said by psychoanalysis about ontology* and truth, and the use of the word 'illusion' is not meant to prejudge such questions. The role of 'necessary illusion' (i.e. something other than mere fiction) in metaphysics comes into play here: to think about certain non-empirical questions, we need such intellectual and imaginative constructs. The error of certain sorts of metaphysics is to treat these as clearly-defined concepts which can be employed in deductive arguments. Thus metaphysics and religion stand in constant need of demythologizing: there must be kinds of critical

analysis which step in to question us when we think we have obtained a firm intellectual purchase on our images, our 'illusions'. Psychoanalysis has its use here; in showing us the ambiguous, domesticated, fantasy-ridden or self-indulgent functions of our religious language, it pushes us towards the purifications of a negative theology which is constantly suspicious of the religious temptation to seek for absolute knowledge (*see* **Imagery, Religious; Interiority**). It is at this level that it makes sense to see Freud (in Donald Evans' phrase) as a 'master of the contemplative way', because of his assault on the trivialized God who represents only the non-humanity of the human self.

Such at any rate is Paul Ricoeur's conclusion at the end of a classic and magisterial study of Freud. There is, he maintains, a way of reading Freud which – while fully aware of the inadequacies and imbalances of the Freudian system as a system – is yet a liberation into a richer, more nuanced, and more chastened style of religious and theological discourse. Freud presses us to work out the sense in which the image of God – and especially of God as Father – does not diminish but both founds and calls (or challenges, or draws out) our full humanity (which does *not* mean a transcending of human finitude, but the full range of receptive and compassionate response possible within human finitude). For the Christian, this is the point at which Freud poses essentially christological questions. 'The only thing that can escape Freud's critique is faith as the kerygma of love . . . his critique can help me discern what this kerygma of love excludes – a penal christology and a moral God – and what it implies – a certain coincidence of the tragic God of Job and the lyric God of John' (Ricoeur, *Freud and Philosophy*, p. 536); and compare this with Becker's summary of Rank, who 'saw Christianity as a truly great ideal foolishness in the sense that we have been discussing it: a childlike trust and hope for the human condition that left open the realm of mystery' (*The Denial of Death*, p. 204).

See also **Jungian Psychology, Psychology of Religion**.

(In addition to the works of Freud cited.) Ernest Becker, *The Denial of Death*, 1973; Erich Fromm, *Psychoanalysis and Religion*, 1950; Jacques Lacan (with Anthony

Wilden), *The Language of the Self*, 1975; R. S. Lee, *Freud and Christianity*, 1948; D. Z. Phillips, *Religion Without Explanation*, 1976; Paul Ricoeur, *Freud and Philosophy*, 1970; Ludwig Wittgenstein, *Lectures and Conversations on Aesthetics, Psychology and Religious Belief*, 1970.

ROWAN WILLIAMS

Friends, Religious Society of

The Religious Society of Friends, also known as the Quakers, was founded about 1652 by George Fox (1624–1691), son of a Leicestershire weaver, a wandering prophet and healer. He drew together several groups of North-country 'Seekers' who had rejected the institutional church and met privately to wait upon the will of God. The survival of the movement was due not only to its spiritual merits and courage but to Fox's own striking personality and to his genius as an organizer. Travelling almost as widely as John Wesley did later, Fox created a pyramid of local congregations or Meetings which reported their persecution or 'sufferings' upwards to a central Meeting for Sufferings in London, where Fox himself would remonstrate with government. Persecution was severe under Monarchy and Commonwealth, and some 450 Friends died in jail before Toleration was granted. Quakers' offence lay in their thorough-going nonconformity: they refused to attend the parish churches or to accept any approved form of worship or creed, to take up arms on either side in the Civil War, to take oaths or to use respectful forms of address to their social superiors. As today, their Meetings consisted of silent prayer punctuated by such messages as members felt moved by the Spirit to utter. They had, and continue to have, no outward liturgy, sacraments or priesthood. Where a decision of the Meeting is needed, Friends never vote but try to arrive prayerfully at a unity. Fox and his generation were firmly rooted in Puritan, biblical Christianity. But they felt the church was using doctrine to blackmail the people and restrict the movement of the Spirit. Fox's great insight was that of the Inner Light*, the Spirit of Christ in everyone to which everyone could gain access without intermediary or ceremony. This gave the early Friends a great sense of joy and freedom from sin. They were dubbed Quakers, and accepted the title, because it was said

they quaked at the power of the Lord.

During much of the eighteenth and nineteenth centuries Friends had a reputation for quietism, separation and plain living. However, they became successful in industry, trade and banking, where their integrity won them respect; and later they became prominent in social concerns like the abolition of slavery, prison reform, the humane treatment of the mentally ill, international relief work, wartime ambulance work and campaigns for peace and disarmament. One of the few things on which Quakers are dogmatic is their pacifism.

Today's Quaker is likely to live and dress much like anyone else, to be a teacher or member of another profession and to have joined the Society from some other church background. Membership in Great Britain and Ireland is around 20,000. In North America, which Fox himself and William Penn evangelized, there are some 100,000 members (some of whom employ professional ministers and structured services). There are about 45,000 members in East Africa and some hundreds in Australia, New Zealand and Germany.

The basic book is Fox's *Journal* (1694 and several later editions). Robert Barclay's *Apology for the True Christian Religion* (1678) sets out a more developed theology. See also the Society's own *Christian Faith and Practice in the Experience of the Society of Friends*, 1972; A. Neave Brayshaw, *The Quakers*, 1969; Elfrida Vipont, *The Story of Quakerism 1652–1952*, 1970; Harold Loukes, *The Quaker Contribution*, 1965.

GERALD PRIESTLAND

Fulfilment
see **Promise and Fulfilment**

Functional Specialization

As 'field specialities' in theology (OT, patristics, etc., and their subdivisions) proliferate, the relevance of each to that understanding of faith as a whole which is the business of theology becomes increasingly obscure. To meet this difficulty, Lonergan has proposed a division of theology into functional specialities, which deliberately articulate a faith whose source is in ancient documents, and apply it to life in the present and future. *Research* establishes what is in the relevant documents; *interpretation* understands their original meaning; *history* embeds authors, texts and meanings in an account of what was going forward; *dialectics* determines their value for better or worse. *Foundations*, where attention shifts to the present, clarifies the nature of religious conversion; *doctrines* sets out the judgments of fact and value to be believed by the converted person; *systematics* works the doctrines into a coherent and integrated whole; *communications* brings home the doctrines as systematically understood to each person in each situation.

B. Lonergan, *Method in Theology*, 1972.

HUGO MEYNELL

Fundamentalism

The term is derived from the title of a series of booklets, *The Fundamentals*, published in the USA between 1910 and 1915. 'The fundamentals' referred to central elements of the traditional Christian teaching, such as the divinity of Jesus Christ, the Second Coming, heaven and hell, and the inspiration and authority of the scriptures. Subsequently the term was applied to a current of Christianity, existing alongside and within the traditional churches, commonly called evangelical, and characterized by a doctrine of personal salvation and a literal interpretation of the scriptures.

As a specific movement fundamentalism is, however, not so much characterized by the authority which it attributes to the Bible and a literal interpretation of the biblical texts as it is by its claim of biblical inerrancy. Fundamentalists hold that the Bible in its entirety and in each of its parts speaks the truth. Thus fundamentalist preachers often speak of the claims of the Bible as if the only acceptable response is assent, understood as assent to the truth, any other response being equated with disbelief. This approach to the scriptures does not take into consideration the variety of literary forms in which the 'biblical message' is phrased nor is it sufficiently attentive to the various modes of human discourse, principally the referential, the attitudinal and the performative.

Fundamentalism is basically an attitude whose major tenet is that the Bible is inerrant. The central tenet is supported by two others, namely the verbal inspiration of the scriptures at their origin, and the literal interpretation of the scriptures in their use.

Since fundamentalists hold to the verbal inspiration of the scriptures, the scriptures are presented as the word of God. Faith in God is essentially assent to the 'truth' of the scriptures. Within this perspective the *Scofield Reference Bible*, whose text is that of the AV/KJV but whose notes and textual divisions derive from the American C. I. Scofield, is particularly important insofar as it is claimed to convey the word of God. Although fundamentalists professedly hold to the literal interpretation of the scriptures, the literal sense is sometimes expanded metaphorically in order that the basic tenet of scriptural inerrancy be maintained. Thus the days of creation of Gen. 1 are often interpreted, metaphorically, as eras in which the various stages of creation took place. Moreover, the literary sense of the scriptures is often equated with the meaning of the scriptures exposited by such fundamentalist authorities as John Stott and K. A. Kitchen.

Because of its insistence that the scriptures are the word of God, fundamentalism stands in radical opposition to Roman Catholicism, and the historical–critical method of biblical interpretation, the former because of its insistence on 'human' tradition, the latter because it understands the scriptures as works of human literature. The roots of fundamentalism go back to the denominational orthodoxies of the seventeenth century and the revivalist movements of the eighteenth and nineteenth centuries. The conservative evangelicals or fundamentalists of the present era share with their forbears an apologetic mode of theology reflecting an historicist notion of truth as well as an insistence on the 'fundamentals', especially creation, sin and redemption, the second coming, personal salvation, the Virgin Birth and the divinity of Jesus, and a literalist interpretation of miracles. Their point of view is represented through preachers such as Billy Graham and Hubert Armstrong, as well as through the press, for example, *Bibliotheca Sacra*, the *Evangelical Quarterly*, and the publications of the Inter-Varsity Press.

James Barr, *Fundamentalism*, 1977; 'The Fundamentalist Understanding of Scripture', *Conflicting Ways of Interpreting the Bible*, *Concilium* 138, ed. Hans Küng and Jürgen Moltmann, 1980, pp. 70–4; G. I.

Packer, *Fundamentalism and the Word of God*, 1958.

RAYMOND F. COLLINS

Fundamental theology

As the name suggests, this studies utterly basic issues which affect the whole of Christian theology. As such it does not use the data of revelation to discuss and decide particular questions in the way christology, ecclesiology and other branches of dogmatic (or systematic) theology do. Fundamental theology has at least four essential themes to reflect on critically.

1. It investigates that divine *self-revelation* (communicated through the history of Israel and Jesus Christ) which forms the primary reality for Christian faith and the foundation for all further theological study. This enquiry covers such questions as: Did this revelation take place through deeds (the indirect revelation through the exodus, Jesus' resurrection, etc.) or also through speech-acts (the direct revelation through the words of prophets, apostles, Jesus himself, etc.)? In what sense did the divine self-revelation end with the apostolic age and in what sense does it continue? How should we relate the absolute revelation through Christ to the knowledge (or revelation?) of God available 'elsewhere' (e.g. through non-Christian religions and the works of creation)?

2. It also asks about the *subjects* who can and do receive the divine self-communication in faith. What makes human beings potential 'hearers of the word' (Karl Rahner)? What constitutes the religious dimension in human experience that makes it possible to receive God's self-communication? How should we 'correlate'* (Paul Tillich) the questions which arise from existence with the response which is revelation? What are the basic structures which form faith? It should be noted that many practitioners of fundamental theology prefer to deal with this 'a priori' religious element in human existence *before* treating the 'a posteriori' historical divine self-revelation itself.

3. It also studies the case for believing, provided by those signs and witnesses which can legitimate faith as a reasonable (although not strictly demonstrable) option. In developing such an 'apologetic' meeting between faith and reason, fundamental theology must attend to contributions and challenges coming from philosophy, history, sociology, contemporary ideologies, etc. Even more than other sectors of theology, fundamental theology stands at the frontier in dialogue with a variety of other academic disciplines and modern movements.

4. Its task is also to examine in general how the apostolic church handed on to later generations its experience of the supreme divine self-communication in Christ. This entails reflecting on tradition, the writing of the inspired scriptures, their truth, canonicity and manifold interpretation (through creeds, doctrines, dogmas, the teaching of church leaders, the work of theology, Christian art, etc.).

In *The Study of Theology* (1979) Gerhard Ebeling suggests further basic issues which could also be handled in fundamental theology: the language of theology, the general conditions for verifying any theological propositions, the scientific nature of theology, etc. David Tracy has questioned the place of faith in this discipline, arguing that at least for fundamental theology Christian faith is not necessarily a prerequisite. But this seems to confuse the philosophy of religion (where such faith is not presupposed) with fundamental theology (which like all theology is an exercise of 'faith seeking understanding'). Lastly, philosophical theology (as practised by John Macquarrie and others) often coincides with the way this article interprets fundamental theology.

See also **Apologetics, Dogmatic Theology, Inspiration, Revelation, Systematic Theology, Tradition.**

Heinrich Fries, 'Fundamental Theology', *Sacramentum Mundi* II, pp. 368–72; René Latourelle, 'A New Image of Fundamental Theology', in *Problems and Perspectives of Fundamental Theology*, ed. René Latourelle and Gerald O'Collins, 1982, pp. 37–58; Johann Baptist Metz, *Faith in History and Society. Toward a Practical Fundamental Theology*, ET 1980; Gerald O'Collins, *Fundamental Theology*, 1981; Jean-Pierre Torrell, 'New Trends in Fundamental Theology', *Problems and Perspectives of Fundamental Theology*, pp. 11–22.

GERALD O'COLLINS

Generation

Generation (Greek: *gennēsis*; Latin: *gener-*

atio) is the term used in Cappadocian * theology and thereafter to denote the differentiating characteristic of the Son. The term arose naturally out of the NT's Father–Son language, and although careful to exclude crude sexual connotations, the Cappadocians endeavoured to give more force to this term than mere analogy. The use of 'ingeneracy' to characterize the Father's nature and 'generation' to characterize that of the Son arose out of important clarifications occasioned by the Arian * controversy. 1. A distinction was made between 'uncreated' and 'unbegotten' (*agenētos* and *agennētos*, see **Ingeneracy**), so that both could be predicated of the Son whose generation was eternal, a doctrine first taught by Origen: thus the Son never came into being (there never was a when he was not), but yet derived his being from the Father, being begotten not made. 2. *Agen(n)esia* was disallowed as a definition of the divine substance which was indefinable, and appropriated to the Father as signifying the essential difference between Father and Son.

FRANCES YOUNG

Glossolalia

Glossolalia (or speaking in tongues) is a religious practice which is known inside and outside Christianity. It 'is a commonplace in human cultures from Asia to America and Siberia to Africa' (Christie-Murray). There are comparable phenomena in the OT, in Shamanism and in Islam (Williams). However, it has been socially unacceptable in European/American main-line churches for many centuries. With the emergence of the Charismatic * Movement it has gained some acceptance.

1. *Phenomenologically* it is a kind of atmospheric communication like music, dream and dance and therefore able to express pre-conscious insights, but it is also open to ambiguities. Glossolalics are not abnormal or especially excitable persons. Due to our social and cultural climate they may be considered as such, but this says more about the observer than about the observed (Vivier, Samarin). That which we consider to be inarticulateness is not identical with absence of meaning. The function of language is not restricted to conveying information, for it can be used to express a relationship or to create ties of union. Glossolalia can thus be a reminder of that important and deep dimension of language which we tend to suppress in our discussion on language and without which language ceases to exist (Williams). It is 'yet another kind of communication' (Christie-Murray).

The area of actual foreign languages spoken by people who have never learned them is not yet sufficiently examined. Many of the cases mentioned in the literature are not sufficiently documented in order to make a case. However, the stubborn fact remains that some cases evade all rational explanation. And these are of course the interesting ones (Williams). 'There is room for experiment'; however, 'the very frame of mind which wants to capture and study such evidence may inhibit the phenomena and upset the delicate conditions in which they occur . . . It might be equally hard to prove the existence of lightning to those who demanded for its proof photographs of it taken only on film that would be ruined by its flash' (Christie-Murray), which might suggest that perhaps we need film with a different kind of sensitivity.

2. *Ecumenically* the importance and significance of glossolalia has not yet been explored. This is astonishing, as it plays a natural role both for liturgy and theology in many Third-World churches.

3. *Doctrinally* the charismatic movement and the Pentecostals * have blurred the issue by the doctrine of the so-called 'initial evidence', i.e. the doctrine that glossolalia is the initial evidence of the baptism of the Spirit. This doctrine necessarily divides Christians into two classes, those who have received Spirit-baptism and those who have not, the differentiation being the exercise of glossolalia. The reconsideration of this doctrine (which is slowly emerging in Pentecostal and charismatic circles) is therefore a necessity.

4. *Theologically* glossolalia must (according to I Cor. 12–14) be judged on its usefulness *pros to symphéron*, for the common good (of the church or of society?) and on the willingness of its practitioners to submit their *public* practice to the judgment 'of the others', both Christian and *idiotai*. Many have found in *private* glossolalia a source for prayer on a level which borders on the pre-conscious – an experience with which Paul was familiar. A theology of glossolalia would have to be developed with the following question in mind: How can *human* (and

even pre-Christian) faculties (such as glossolalia, healing by laying on of hands, and also intellectual, analytical and artistic faculties) be of liturgical, ecumenical and theological use? Against the harsh judgment of R. A. Knox (*Enthusiasm, a Chapter in the History of Religion*, 1950) Joseph Haroutunian's statement will be borne in mind: 'It is not justified to draw a sharp line between the Christian's joy in sanctification and "enthusiasm".' Why should the Christian experience his religion only with the mind and not equally with the heart, with his pre-conscious faculties? The criteria of its genuineness are not purely phenomenological but rather functional, as the American Benedictine K. McDonnell says: 'A gift of the Spirit is not a "what" but a "how".'

D. Christie-Murray, *Voices from the Gods. Speaking in Tongues*, 1978; W. J. Hollenweger, *The Pentecostals*, ET 1972; *Conflict in Corinth*, 1982; W. J. Samarin, *Tongues of Men and Angels. The Religious Language of Pentecostalism*, 1972; L. M. Vivier, 'The Glossolalic and his Personality', in: T. Spoerri, *Beiträge zur Ekstase*, 1968, pp. 153–75; Cyril G. Williams, *Tongues of the Spirit. A Study of Pentecostal Glossolalia and Related Phenomena*, 1981.

WALTER J. HOLLENWEGER

Gnosticism

1. *Definition*. Gnosticism is the term used to describe a religious movement of the early Christian centuries which laid a special emphasis upon knowledge (Greek: *gnosis*) of God and of the nature and destiny of man. This knowledge, 'of who we were or where we were placed, whither we hasten, from what we are redeemed, what birth is and what rebirth' (Clem. Alex., *Excerpta ex Theodoto* 78.2), was believed to have redeeming power, liberating the soul from the sway of cosmic forces. The earliest information about this movement came from the work of Christian opponents (Irenaeus, Hippolytus, Epiphanius, Tertullian), who regarded it as a Christian heresy, and it was so treated down to the nineteenth century. Harnack in a famous phrase called it 'the acute Hellenization of Christianity'. Study of other religions of late antiquity, however, led Reitzenstein and Bousset, and later Bultmann and other scholars, to argue that even before NT times there was already a

system of *gnosis*, knowledge of the divine origin of the soul and of the way of redemption from this world. By combining material from diverse sources it was possible to reconstruct a myth of a Primal Man who descended into this world and was in some way imprisoned there, divided into a multitude of sparks of light which are individual souls. These sparks have to be delivered and re-united by a Redeemer from above. The full form of this 'Heavenly Man Redeemer Myth', however, appears only in Manichaeism* in the third century AD, and it is more likely that the Manichaean myth is the end-product of a long development than that the scattered pieces of the postulated myth found earlier point to the existence of an older myth of which they were originally part.

2. *Origins*. As already indicated, there have been two main views about the origins of this movement. The 'traditional' theory, still powerfully argued by some scholars, saw in it a Christian heresy originating in the early second century, as the result of the fusion of Christianity with elements from other sources (e.g. Greek philosophy). The difficulties here are (*a*) to explain the apparently sudden emergence of the movement, if there was nothing to prepare the way, and (*b*) that this view takes no account of certain anticipations of later gnostic ideas, e.g. in the works of Philo of Alexandria or in the NT itself. Adherents of the traditional view themselves admit the existence in the first century of 'trends and tendencies' already moving in the direction of the later Gnosticism. On the other hand the broader view, the representatives of which often speak of Gnosis rather than of Gnosticism, suffers from the fact that we have no documentary evidence for any developed *system* prior to the rise of Christianity. Moreover the 'evidence' for a pre-Christian Gnosticism (or Gnosis) has on occasion been found by interpreting NT or other material in a gnostic sense, and then assuming that the presence of 'gnostic motifs' is indicative of the existence of a full-scale gnostic system. This is to read first-century documents with second-century spectacles, and entails the danger of importing into the material the 'evidence' that we wish to find. The fact that we have no documents for any 'pre-Christian' gnostic system does not of course mean that there

was no such thing. It merely means that in this area we are reduced to hypotheses, and must proceed with caution. More recent studies have tended to speak of development, of 'trajectories' leading from earlier movements such as Jewish apocalyptic or the Wisdom literature to the developed Gnosticism of the second century A D.

An easier and more profitable exercise is to identify the sources from which the gnostics drew their material. Reference has already been made to Jewish apocalyptic, the Wisdom literature and Greek philosophy, as well as to Philo of Alexandria. The gnostics also made quite extensive use of the O T, especially the early chapters of Genesis, and in some systems there is considerable influence from Christianity, evidenced for example by N T quotations. Other relevant material has been found in the Qumran scrolls, or in documents of Jewish mysticism. This does not mean that any of these can be claimed as *the* source of Gnosticism, merely that they have in some way contributed. Here we must note the characteristic transmutation which some of this material underwent when it was used in a gnostic context. It is this that makes any reading back dangerous: we have no grounds for assuming that terms and concepts which in a gnostic context have some technical significance already carried that significance at an earlier stage. Such an assumption may lead to distortion of the earlier evidence.

3. *Source materials.* The earliest information, as already noted, came from the works of Christian opponents, which were of course to some extent suspect as hostile propaganda. Modern studies, and comparison with new material, have, however, vindicated the essential reliability of the reports of Irenaeus. A convenient anthology of patristic material is provided by the first volume of W. Foerster's *Gnosis.* Down to 1955 our only other sources were some Coptic texts (Pistis Sophia, the Books of Jeu, and an anonymous treatise) from a late period when Gnosticism had already run to seed. In that year W. C. Till finally published a Berlin Coptic codex, known as far back as 1896, which contained much older material (the Gospel of Mary, the Apocryphon of John [Apoc. Joh.], the Sophia Jesu Christi [S J C]). A new era was inaugurated by the discovery in 1945 of the Nag Hammadi library (see below), the first text from which appeared in 1956 (the Gospel of Truth). Though progress at first was slow, a complete translation is now available (see *The Nag Hammadi Library in English*). It includes further copies of Apoc. Joh. and S J C, and makes it possible for the first time to study gnostic ideas on the basis of original gnostic texts.

4. *Characteristics.* Gnosticism in the past has often been characterized as bizarre and even perverse, a distortion of Christian theology. Bigg wrote in 1886: 'The ordinary Christian controversialist felt that he had nothing to do but set out at unsparing length their tedious pedigrees, in the well-grounded confidence that no one would care to peruse them a second time'; but he went on to add: 'It was an attempt, a serious attempt, to fathom the dread mystery of sorrow and pain, to answer that spectral doubt, which is mostly crushed down by force – can the world as we know it have been made by God?' (*The Christian Platonists of Alexandria*, p. 28). This last aspect has been amply confirmed by the new documents, which often show what Gnosticism meant *to a gnostic*, a religion not of despair and hopelessness but of deliverance and release, of light instead of darkness, day instead of night.

In contrast to other attempts to deal with the human predicament, the developed Gnosticism begins by rejecting this world itself as evil. It is the creation not of the supreme God, but of some inferior being or beings. The chief characteristics are: 1. a radical cosmic dualism * (dualism in itself is not necessarily gnostic, since there are different kinds); 2. a distinction between the unknown transcendent true God and the creator (here we can trace a development: in the earliest Christian gnostic systems the world is made by angels, but later we find a Demiurge * or Creator, commonly identified with the God of the O T); 3. the belief that man in his true nature is essentially akin to the divine, a spark of heavenly light imprisoned in a material body; 4. a myth, often narrating some pre-mundane fall, to account for man's present state and his yearning for deliverance; and 5. the saving *gnosis* by which that deliverance is effected and man awakened to recognition of his true nature and heavenly origin. One of the problems is that gnostics may use the same language as orthodox Christian writers, but give it a different meaning. The creation story in Genesis, for example, becomes the story of an attempt by the hostile Demiurge to hold mankind in subjection. Some terms, in themselves neutral, are given a specific application in a gnostic context, and gnostic imagery on occasion requires a knowledge of gnostic systems for its decoding.

5. *Some Gnostic systems*. The main target of Irenaeus' refutation was the Valentinian system, but there were several other schools, all showing the basic characteristics listed above but in a sometimes bewildering variety of myths and forms. Valentinianism itself underwent development, from the original system of Valentinus to more elaborate forms of a 'Western' type represented by Ptolemy and Heracleon and an 'Eastern' represented by the extracts preserved by Clement of Alexandria from Theodotus. In broad outline, the system postulates a primal Ground of Being from whom emanate a succession of aeons, to the number of thirty (the 'pleroma'). The last of these aeons, Sophia, is guilty of a fault, variously described, which leads to the appearance of the Demiurge, and so to a re-interpretation of the Genesis creation story. The inbreathing of the breath of life into Adam is part of Sophia's attempt to recover the divine element which the Demiurge derived from her, the 'coats of skin' are the Demiurge's device for holding mankind captive.

This system appears to be a development and elaboration of an earlier system represented in Apoc. Joh. and its parallel in Irenaeus. Here the Christian element sometimes has the appearance of being secondary, and it has been noted that the figure of Jesus could be lifted right out of the book without making any essential difference. It is the *gnosis* he brings which is the real saving power. Other documents also appear to show signs of secondary Christianization, and this is especially clear when SJC is compared with another Nag Hammadi document, the Epistle of Eugnostus. This, together with the presence of some non-Christian gnostic texts in the Nag Hammadi library, lends support to the view (see 2. above) that this movement was not merely a second-century inner-Christian heresy, but goes back at least into the first century. On the other hand, it should be remembered

that the older 'non-Christian' forms in these cases can sometimes only be reconstructed by eliminating the Christian elements from our present texts. We do not have the 'non-Christian' originals. The alternative, that the movement was one away from Christianity, and the existing non-Christian texts the result of de-Christianization, suffers from the difficulty that the process would have to be regarded as so thorough that no vestige of Christian influence remains. Moreover it would play havoc with all we know of the relative chronology, since some of these texts appear to belong to a fairly early stage. The possibility should, however, be borne in mind that there was de-Christianization in gnostic literature as well as Christianization, although in the nature of things it is more difficult to prove.

Another system is that of Basilides, who according to Hippolytus (here differing from Irenaeus) postulated a non-existent god who resolved to create a world. The first stage was the depositing of a seed containing a threefold Sonship. The first Sonship immediately returned to the non-existent. The second took the Holy Spirit as a wing, and also ascended, but the Spirit, not being consubstantial with the Sonship, could not remain in the non-existent and was left in the intermediate confines as a type of man's yearning for better things. The third Sonship remained in the seed, and requires to be restored to its place with the others. When that time comes, all the lower orders will be seized with ignorance, so that they do not desire what is above, for to them such desire is death. The report in Irenaeus presents a rather more conventional gnostic system, which includes one of the 'docetic' re-interpretations of the crucifixion, that it was not Jesus who suffered but Simon of Cyrene. This appears in various forms in other gnostic documents (e.g. 2 Log. Seth), and in a tenth-century Moslem text once thought to be based on a Jewish-Christian source.

Another independent and original form of Gnosticism, the Book Baruch of the gnostic Justin, begins with three primal beings, two male and one female. The highest, 'the Good', has no contact with the lower world. From the union of the other two, Elohim and Eden, are born twenty-four angels, twelve on each side, who create Adam and Eve, in whom Eden sets the soul

and Elohim the spirit. Elohim ascends to see
if anything is wanting in his creation, and
only then discovers the Good above him.
He is commanded to leave the created world
with Eden, and remain with the Good. Eden
seeks revenge by tormenting the spirit of
Elohim in man, and Elohim's efforts to help
by the agency of his angel Baruch (through
Moses, the prophets and Heracles) are
thwarted by Eden's angel Naas, until Baruch
at last finds Jesus, whom Naas cannot lead
astray.

These are but a few examples, but may
serve to show the nature of gnostic systems,
and the way in which the characteristic
features listed above are worked in. In all of
them there is a fusion of biblical and other
elements, drawn from Greek philosophy or
other pagan sources, or from Jewish legend
and inter-testamental speculation.

6. *Gnosticism and the New Testament*. This
heading covers two distinct questions, one
of which is comparatively easy, the other
the subject of much debate. The first is that
of gnostic use of the N T, which can be readily
documented from the occurrence of quotations and allusions in the gnostic texts.
Problems arise here only when motifs are
shared by the N T and other systems of
thought, and it is not certain whether in any
given case we have an actual borrowing.

The more difficult problem is that of possible gnostic influence in the N T itself. Those
who regard Gnosticism as a second-century
heresy of course deny any such thing, but
have to admit the 'trends and tendencies'
already mentioned (see 2 above). On the
other side there is the danger of anachronistically identifying as 'gnostic'
motifs which are certainly found in the
second-century systems, but which admit of
another interpretation at the N T stage. The
safest course is to begin where the situation
is fairly clear, and work back into the more
obscure areas.

The First Epistle of John is generally
recognized to be directed against some incipient form of Gnosticism, although it is
not possible to identify the opponents definitely with any known school (there are similarities to the views of Cerinthus). This
brings the Fourth Gospel into consideration, although some are appalled at the very
idea that a Gospel so deeply loved could
suffer any taint of heresy. At this stage,

however, the line between orthodoxy and
heresy is only beginning to be drawn. It is a
mistake to think of an original pristine orthodoxy, preserved intact in one tradition
while in others the heretics fell away. Rather
there was initially a variety of possible formulations of the faith, of which some were
eventually retained while others were discarded as inadequate. Due attention must
be paid to diversity in the N T as well as to its
unity, and of this diversity the element later
stigmatised as gnostic forms a part. At any
rate, John avoids the term *gnosis*, although
the verb 'to know' has a significant place in
his vocabulary.

There are fairly clear indications of developing opposition to 'gnostic' ideas in the
Pastorals and in the later N T books generally. I Tim. 6.20 provides the phrase
quoted by Irenaeus which gave the movement as a whole its name: the falsely so
called *gnosis*. II Tim. 2.17f. mentions the
error of Hymenaeus and Philetus, who
claimed that the resurrection was past
already. References to 'myths and endless
genealogies' (I Tim. 1.4; cf. II Tim. 4.4;
Titus 3.9; II Peter 1.16) readily recall the
long successions of aeons in the gnostic systems, while the references in Revelation to
Balaam and the Nicolaitans (2.14f.) and to
Jezebel (2.20) also appear to have some connection with gnostic groups. By the end of
the first century there was thus an emergent
Gnosticism which was being firmly rejected
by other Christians. It should, however, be
noted that a 'false' *gnosis* implies the existence of a true, which only adds a further
complication. For Clement of Alexandria
the true gnostic is a Christian who has penetrated more deeply into the faith than the
simple believer.

The real problems begin when we seek to
go further back: was the Colossian heresy
really gnostic? Was there Gnosticism in
Galatia? How gnostic were the Corinthians?
A. S. Peake in the *Expositor's Greek Testament* long ago claimed to explain the Colossian situation on a purely Jewish basis. The
attempts of Lütgert, J. H. Ropes and W.
Schmithals to find Gnosticism in some form
in Galatia have not commanded the full
assent of scholars, while a case has been
made for distinguishing Paul's opponents in
II Cor. from those opposed in the first letter.
On the one hand it must be said quite bluntly
that there is as yet no evidence for a de-

veloped gnostic system at this stage. On the other, it would be a serious error to ignore the trends and tendencies in a gnostic direction which are already present. At the very least, 'Paul's Corinthian correspondence shows into how congenial a soil the seeds of Gnosticism were about to fall' (R. Law, *The Tests of Life*, p. 28).

The issue would be settled if, as some scholars have argued, Simon Magus was already a gnostic before coming into contact with Christianity; he appears in Acts even before the conversion of Paul. However, the question is not quite so easy. Irenaeus calls Simon 'the father of all heresies', but how far do later Simonian doctrines go back to the historical Simon? It is possible that a later gnostic group, looking for a 'founder' in the early days, settled upon Simon and fathered upon him their own later teachings. Altogether it is best to recognize that in the NT period the situation is still fluid: ideas later stigmatized as gnostic and heretical could for the moment co-exist with what later crystallized into orthodoxy. The history of the first Christian century is rather more complex than is sometimes thought.

7. *Nag Hammadi*. The extant texts (over forty in all, excluding duplicates) are Coptic versions written in the fourth century of older Greek originals, some of which go back to the early second century. They do nothing to solve the problem of gnostic origins, but they provide the basis for a better understanding of Gnosticism and of the development of gnostic literature. The nature and origin of the collection is not entirely clear (the library of a gnostic group, or a collection for heresiological purposes?), but the texts have been classified under four main heads: 1. non-Christian gnostic works (e.g. Zostrianos, Allogenes); 2. Christian gnostic works, sub-divided into (*a*) Christianizations of older texts (Apoc. Joh., SJC) and (*b*) original Christian gnostic works (Gospel of Philip, Gospel of Truth); 3. Hermetic texts (interesting because of the long debate as to whether Hermetica should be counted gnostic) and 4. wisdom teachings and philosophical writings (the Sentences of Sextus). Some of the texts, particularly of the last group, are not gnostic at all, but were evidently congenial to the users of the library. Perhaps the most famous is the Gospel of Thomas, a collection of 'sayings

of Jesus' which incorporates all the material of the three Logia papyri found at the beginning of this century at Oxyrhynchus. The literature on these texts is already extensive, but much remains to be done, and much to be discovered.

Introduction: R. M. Grant, *Gnosticism and Early Christianity*, [2]1966; main ideas: Hans Jonas, *The Gnostic Religion*, 1958; K. Rudolph, *Gnosis*, 1977 (ET 1983); cf. also B. Layton (ed), *The Rediscovery of Gnosticism*, 1980–1981; also J. M. Robinson and H. Koester, *Trajectories through Early Christianity*, 1971; R. McL. Wilson, *The Gnostic Problem*, 1958; *Gnosis and the New Testament*, 1968, and 'Gnosis/Gnostizismus', in *TRE*; E. M. Yamauchi, *Pre-Christian Gnosticism*, 1973. Texts: W. Foerster, *Gnosis* (ET 1972, 1974, Vol. 1 has patristic texts; Vol. 2 Coptic and Mandean material). ET of the Nag Hammadi material in *The Nag Hammadi Library in English*, ed. J. M. Robinson, 1977. Bibliography: D. M. Scholer, *Nag Hammadi Bibliography 1948–1969*, 1971, up-dated annually in *Novum Testamentum*.

R. MCL. WILSON

God

1. *Introduction*. The Christian understanding, knowledge and doctrine of God may most conveniently be gathered from the creeds* and confessions* of the Christian church. Thus the Apostles' Creed, which is an expansion of the old Roman creed and has yet proved itself serviceable to the contemporary ecumenical movement and which again and again in the history of theology has provided the text and ground-plan of more elaborate expressions of the Christian faith, declares its belief in 'God the Father almighty, creator of heaven and earth'. Although more extensive creeds such as that commonly called the Nicene are manifestly concerned to define as explicitly as possible specifically Christian belief, not simply in God, but in God in Christ, they none the less affirm a basic belief in 'One God the Father almighty, maker of heaven and earth, of all things visible and invisible'. (This interest is not, of course, entirely absent from the Apostles' Creed, which in describing God as Father probably means the Father of all people, the Father of our Lord Jesus Christ, and indeed the Father and creator of the universe; but a distinction can be drawn

between creeds which in origin sought to summarize faith and creeds designed as tests of orthodoxy.) According to the Thirty-nine Articles* of the Church of England, 'there is but one living and true God, everlasting, without body, parts or passions; of infinite power, wisdom and goodness; the Maker and Preserver of all things both visible and invisible'. The Augsburg Confession declared that there is one divine essence which is called and is God, eternal, 'without body, indivisible, of infinite power, wisdom and goodness'; while the Westminster Confession held that God 'hath all life, glory, goodness, blessedness, in and of himself; and is alone in and unto himself all-sufficient, not standing in need of any creatures which he hath made, nor deriving any glory from them, but only manifesting his own glory, in, by, unto and upon them: he hath most sovereign dominion over them, to do by them, for them or upon them, whatsoever himself pleaseth'. Again, the Profession of the Tridentine Faith (*Professio Fidei Tridentina*), sometimes called the Creed of Pope Pius IV, re-iterated in its first article the whole of the Nicene Creed.

Such credal affirmations, however, are very summary statements indeed and each arose out of a particular historical situation. In certain respects, therefore, they are like the intermittent ripples that appear here and there on the surface of the stream. In order to grasp more adequately the church's thought and conviction in their fullness and continuity it is necessary to take into account also the underlying currents and cross-currents of theological opinion, and, no less, the source of the church's life and thought in the religion of the Bible.

2. *Biblical faith in God.* To begin at the beginning is to begin with that complex of events and messages which arose within a particular strand of history and which are recorded together in the scriptures of the OT and NT. Even a long familiarity cannot finally obscure the grandeur and profundity of the Jewish religion and the Christian faith in which, from a Christian perspective, it culminated; and the development of thought and belief which is here involved is on any reckoning a most remarkable one. Its distinctive note is sometimes said to be that of monotheism*; and certainly, while in this respect it may not claim to be absolutely unique since there are adumbrations of a practical and ethical monotheism in the great poets of ancient Greece and of a speculative but still largely ethical monotheism in the philosophy which flourished on that same soil, these foreshadowings are as fumblings in the dark which do not share the firmness of apprehension characteristic of Hebrew-Christian religion.

Monotheism, however, is not by itself the distinctive stress of biblical religion. One theologian has even said that 'monotheism is neither a characteristically Christian view nor even a biblical one, save as an inference derived from the truth that God is the Lord' (E. Brunner, *Dogmatics I: The Christian Doctrine of God*, 1949, p. 137). Not even the characterization of biblical religion as ethical monotheism adequately grasps its peculiar outlook. It is rather as if the unity of God cannot be affirmed without attracting to God alone all the hopes and fears of all humankind. For the Bible, the divine unity is not an abstract speculative principle so that its first implication is that polytheism is an error. Rather the divine unity already means that God alone is the ultimate authority in human life and the ultimate refuge amid all the perils of historical existence. The worshippers of idols are not only in error – the falseness of their gods mean also, inseparably, that the claims of these gods are a pretence and their promises illusory. It is as if the Bible declared in one and the same breath that God is one, that he is holy and just and good and that he is love. Even so, we have missed the essential part if we do not think of God as active. He is the creator and in his loving-kindness he takes the initiative. He chooses his own people out of all the families of the earth and they in their turn look for the coming of the Messiah. Accordingly, this dynamic outlook finds its fulfilment in the new covenant* and specifically in what the NT calls 'the grace of our Lord Jesus Christ'.

Such is the origin of the Christian doctrine of God, the source from which the stream of Christian thought takes its rise; but a conception of God which could be expressed, with its own adequacy, in the simple words of the prayer 'Abba, Father' was to be the subject of an extensive and often debatable elaboration as the church in its historical situation sought both to articulate more fully the saving truth of the gospel and to repel insidious but serious error. More-over, although it may seem a far cry from the Sermon on the Mount to the findings of the Council of Nicaea or the Chalcedonian Definition (*see* **Christology**), it is important to remember, on the one hand, that the intellectual demand for systematic elaboration was legitimate and inevitable, and, on the other hand, that for the most part the work of elaboration was regarded by those who performed it as precisely that, a work of elaboration and not a fresh construction. Further, such work was often undertaken with an acute sense of unworthiness for the task, in the very spirit of the prayer, 'Abba, Father', and in a context of worship and mystery.

3. *The Hebraic Experience and the Greek Understanding.* If it was the Hebrew religion which culminated in the work of Christ which provided the church with the substance of its faith and of its knowledge of God, that religion did not supply the intellectual concepts and categories for the systematic articulation of this knowledge. These were, however, available in the Greek philosophical tradition; and if the philosophy of ancient Greece failed to become an alternative and rival to the monotheistic faith of Israel it did contrive to become at least the handmaid of Christian theology. If Christ conquered the ancient world in the sphere of religious faith, it was Greek philosophy which had prepared minds for the theological task of understanding, so far as possible, the redemptive reality by which they had been apprehended. This is what happened. One might even say that this is what had to happen, nothing else is conceivable. Yet from a much later perspective two opinions have been held of the process, for some see in the philosophical constructions of ancient Greece something hardly less than a *praeparatio evangelica*, a preparation for the gospel, while others see in them the source of a radical distortion of Christian faith, the Hellenization of the gospel.

Whatever be the truth in the area covered by these conflicting verdicts the fact remains that Greek philosophy provided the instrument with which Christian theology set about its task, particularly the philosophy of Plato and Aristotle. It would be misleading to assume either that this philosophical influence was itself a single stable and un-changing factor, or that its effect on the Christian understanding of God was a solitary and permanent achievement. On the contrary, so far as the latter is concerned, a distinction may be drawn between the concept of God on the one hand and the method by which it is reached on the other; and it was in the former direction that first of all the influence of Greek thought made itself felt explicitly and extensively, and this especially in the form it assumed in certain aspects of Platonism* and in Neoplatonism*.

4. *The Augustinian* View.* One of the key figures in this connection was undoubtedly Augustine; and it is important to realize that, although in the modern period many Christian thinkers have been attracted to the teaching of Plato and have made frequent use of it, it was not exactly in the same way that Augustine found it congenial. Rather it was through the Neoplatonist Plotinus that Platonism came into Augustine's theological outlook. Every student of Greek philosophy knows that one of the distinctive Platonic doctrines was that of the Forms or Ideas: beyond the world of sensible objects there is a world of unchanging essences, more real than the world of sensible objects; it is through participation in the world of essences that sensible objects have whatever reality they possess; and knowledge of them is possible to the extent that such participation is possible. Moreover, supreme among the Ideas or Forms, according to Plato, is the Idea of the Good. No doubt it is tempting to regard the Good as divine, although in fact Plato does not seem ever to have identified God and the Good (in spite of the *Republic*, 517). On the contrary, in Book X of the *Laws* he spoke of God as a divine soul who is the self-moved mover and the cause of the basic and regular movements of the heavenly bodies. God in this sense is not the Good but has knowledge of it and indeed seeks its realization in all his causal activity; and it is this Platonic God who has appealed strongly to many Christian thinkers in the modern period, in spite of the fact that on this statement of the case the Good is metaphysically independent of God and in the *Timaeus* is even represented as superior to God. It was not, however, this Platonic God who directly attracted the mind of Augustine but rather the teaching of Plato

as seen through the eyes of Plotinus. According to Plotinus God is identical with the Good, not a divine Soul, but the source of all being and knowledge of whom nothing at all can be predicated (for otherwise his unity would be destroyed), but rather from whom everything else derives as regards both its essence and its existence. This relation of one-way dependence was called emanation *. It did not imply antecedence in time and was in fact consistent with the belief that the world was eternal, and this has led some commentators to conclude that the worlds of Plotinus and of Christianity are not comparable. Yet it was in terms of the world of Plotinus that Augustine had to give expression to his firm grasp of Christianity and in doing so he inevitably gave to it what may be called an 'essential' rather than an 'existential' slant. Thus the divine is identified with pure being and is marked by immateriality, intelligibility, immutability and unity. This does not mean that Augustine's grasp of the Christian faith was any less sure. He could wage unremitting warfare against Pelagianism * as others had fought the Arian thesis (see **Arianism**); he could provide the distinctively Christian doctrine of the Trinity with something like a completed statement, and he could supply what was to prove in due course an important warrant of the Protestant Reformation. But it does mean that in the permanent background of the church's thought there was a conception of God which was in certain respects, some would hold, basically alien to the Christian faith, which led, for example, to Augustine's privative view of evil and which identified the sphere of the divine with that of the true, immutable, unchanging and timeless *, in stark contrast with the realm of change and decay.

Moreover, in the shadow of this conception of God there is the other topic already distinguished, the question of method, in particular the attempt to prove or demonstrate by rational argument the existence of God. There can be no doubt that Augustine was one of the very great figures in the history of Christianity, and it is remarkable how many diverse and sometimes mutually conflicting movements can with more or less justice claim something of his authority. Perhaps not the least noteworthy of such facts in the field of thought is that two famous arguments, Anselm's ontologi-

cal * proof of the divine existence and the *cogito ergo sum* of Descartes, were foreshadowed in Augustine. The self and God, these were indeed the great objects of all Augustine's intellectual life: '*Deum et animum scire cupio. Nihilne plus? Nihil omnino*' (*Soliloquies* i.2.7). So far as the divine existence is concerned, the core of the type of argument favoured by Augustine himself involved an ascent (which was also an escape) from the changing world of sensible things to the possession of truth in the mind and a further ascent (which was, however, a fulfilment rather than an escape) from this truth to Truth itself, its one and only possible source, the unchanging Truth which is God. If such an argument were treated as a self-sufficient exercise and a detached demonstration, it might not seem entirely satisfactory, for if one begins by positing Truth as the only possible source of truths one would then be making no advance to argue from truths to Truth and the attempt to do so might well appear as circular. In the case of Augustine, on the other hand, it must be recognized that again and again he emphasized that the human mind is so darkened by sin that human beings could not of themselves make the ascent to Truth. Accordingly, he consistently taught that we can learn only by grace and must believe in order that we may understand. Thus, 'no-one can become fit to discover God unless he shall have first believed what he is later to come to know' (*De Libero Arbitrio* 11.2.6), and there is no doubt that the constant conjunction of this teaching alongside a proposed rational demonstration of God's existence sets up a tension which is not readily resolved, which it may not be possible to resolve so long as the priority of intellect is taken for granted.

5. *The Ontological Argument*. Be that as it may, it is a fact that some six hundred years after Augustine's death another saint, Anselm (1033–1109) was to be found teaching the same view that in order to understand one must believe (*credo ut intelligam*), and also insisting that one can none the less by reason demonstrate the existence of God – in this case by the famous ontological argument. The ontological argument is Anselm's argument and, ever since he devised it, it could scarcely have had a more chequered history. Thomas Aquinas, who

was not averse to rational demonstrations of the divine existence, who on the contrary gave definitive and classical form to the natural theology of which proofs of God's existence are a fundamental and substantial part, none the less rejected this one. Yet in the sphere of philosophy it re-appeared in the work of René Descartes and was later rejected by Immanuel Kant; but, curiously, it has provoked lively discussion in twentieth-century philosophy of religion, proving itself 'many-faced' (e.g. John Hick and Arthur McGill, eds, *The Many-Faced Argument*, 1968).

The ontological argument reflects the general type of argument favoured by Augustine; but, as Anselm framed it, it takes its start neither from sensible things nor from the possession of truth, any truth in the mind, but from a concept or definition of God. According to Anselm, God is that than which nothing greater can be conceived; and, therefore, Anselm concludes, God must exist, since if he did not exist, he would not be that than which nothing greater can be conceived, that which exists in reality being 'greater' (in the sense of 'more perfect') than that which exists in the understanding only. God, not existing, might have all conceivable forms of greatness but he would still fall short in respect of greatness of the same God having all these forms of greatness and, into the bargain, existing. Consequently, if God is that than which nothing greater can be conceived, existence cannot be taken away from him, he must exist. Anselm went on to claim that from this definition, God cannot even be thought of as not existing (i.e. he exists necessarily) since what exists necessarily is greater than that which can be thought of as not existing.

As already indicated, opinions have varied widely on the validity of this argument. In Anselm's own lifetime it was pointed out by Gaunilo of Marmoutiers that if a lost island is said to be wealthier and better than any inhabited island the argument would be invalid which sought to suggest that this lost island must exist, on the ground that otherwise it would not really be richer than all inhabited islands. Centuries later, Kant was to use a somewhat similar argument concerning not an imaginary island but an imaginary hundred dollars. But Anselm had already pointed out in reply

that his demonstration is not applicable to a whole class of concepts but to the one unique concept to which his definition of God refers, and certainly no critical assessment of the ontological argument has really reckoned seriously with it if it has not taken account of the peculiarity of the concept of God. Few modern commentators would claim that the argument succeeds in proving God's existence. What is claimed for it is that is can clarify the concept of God, even to the extent of showing, according to Charles Hartshorne, that 'the only admissible way to reject theism is to reject the very idea of God as either contradictory or empty of significance'. When the ontological argument is confronted on this more profound level it becomes apparent that the verdict depends to some extent on the presupposition entertained regarding the function and competence of reason and logic. If the function of reason is to order and so to comprehend the reality that confronts us in experience (which may in turn be narrowly or broadly conceived), then reason may indicate that something cannot be but not that something must be, whereas if reason is also such that it has its own opening upon reality, either through some power of intellectual intuition distinguishable from experience no matter how broadly conceived, or because reality is just not constructed on rational lines but is itself of the very stuff of reason, this restriction would not apply. To accept the ontological argument involves the defence of one or other of these two possibilities covered by the latter main alternative; and neither is easy. On the other hand, if one were confronted by God in his self-revelation as the one who exists out of himself in sheer necessity and who conveys existence to everything else, one might well have a concept of God of which the ontological argument is perhaps an elucidation. It is clear, however, in that case, that one's belief in the existence of God does not rest ultimately upon a demonstration but on the revelation.

Even if the ontological argument as a piece of pure reasoning is of questionable validity, it did give shape and substance to a natural* theology, a theology based on reason independently of all revelation. It was this that in the thirteenth century was re-fashioned and given its completed form by Thomas Aquinas. Indeed it was not only natural theology but the entire contribution of Greek philosophy to Christian thought which received definitive expression from the Angelic Doctor. It is important to realize, however, that what did receive definitive expression in this way was something for which the pattern had already been set, in the shape of a speculative method and an abstract conclusion. This seems to remain basically true whether one minimizes or magnifies the change that was then taking place. It also seems to remain basically true, whether we agree with Benjamin B. Warfield's criticism that the whole history of the Church of Rome 'since the second Council of Orange (529) has been marked by the progressive elimination of Augustinianism from its teaching' or with Etienne Gilson's thesis that 'Saint Augustine . . . had reached . . . the limit of Greek ontology itself' and that 'a new and decisive progress in natural theology was made only through Aristotle and Aquinas' (*God and Philosophy*, 1941, p. 62).

6. *The Cosmological and Teleological Arguments*. The change of emphasis which made itself felt at this time was a change from essence to existence, from the sphere of 'what' to the sphere of 'that', and, consequently, so far as the proofs of the divine existence are concerned, a change from *a priori* argument to *a posteriori* argument, from arguments taking their rise in ideas and concepts to arguments taking their rise in facts and things. For Aristotle the supreme reality was not a static essence, no matter how remote, no matter how abstract, but an act of thinking, a pure act of self-thinking; and what Thomas Aquinas did was to transpose this teaching from the key of knowing and thinking to that of existence. This may well seem a radical transposition, and there is no doubt that Aquinas was enabled to make it only in the light of what he had learned from the biblical revelation and in particular from the name by which God had made himself known to Moses, namely, 'He who is' (Ex. 3.14). Yet once the transposition has been made the resultant insight is deemed able to stand upon its own feet as a properly rational theology. As one Thomist scholar expressed it, it is 'difficult for us to see that "it is" ultimately points out, not that which the thing is, but the primitive existential act which causes it both

to be and to be precisely that which it is. He who begins to see this, however, also begins to grasp the very stuff our universe is made of. He even begins obscurely to perceive the supreme cause of such a world' (E. Gilson, *God and Philosophy,* pp. 69f.).

If the act of existence or the existential act is understood to cause anything 'both to be and to be precisely that which it is', primacy is in effect being given to 'existence' over 'essence'; attention is drawn from ideas to sensible objects, and the way is paved for an *a posteriori*, as distinct from an *a priori* proof of the divine existence. As a matter of fact, Thomas offered not one but five proofs of the existence of God, known as the Five Ways; but by and large they cover much the same ground as the argument provided by Plato in the *Laws*, xii, and are in turn comprehended by the two lines of proof which theology has come traditionally to distinguish as the *cosmological* argument and the *teleological* argument. The latter argues from the evidence of design in the universe to an originating intelligence, and this is what Aquinas also does when, from the orderliness of the universe, he infers the existence of a supreme intelligence whom everyone understands to be God. Different writers may look in different directions for the evidence of order and design. Thus Paley, writing as late as 1802, says, 'For my part, I take my stand in human anatomy.' Plato, writing about 350 BC, may be said to take his stand in mathematical astronomy. Others have taken their stand elsewhere, for example in the varied field of entomology; but perhaps the distinctive feature of the Thomist form of the argument is that here the final appeal is to order over the whole extent of the universe. Indeed, although basically it is the same argument, the difference between these two forms of it, that which appeals to order over the universe at large and that which looks to order in some more limited and compact sphere, points to the proper assessment of the argument; for the choice of a restricted sphere where order can be detected and explored in detail is always somewhat arbitrary, whereas the orderliness of the whole is rather a postulate than attested fact. Accordingly, the argument has at the most a fairly high degree of probability, and it functions more readily as the articulation of a belief in God than as a demonstration *de novo*. By itself it may raise a question and suggest an answer without creating a conviction.

Three of the remaining four ways of Aquinas clearly cover the ground of the cosmological argument which infers from the causal series a first and uncaused cause. This is precisely what Aquinas argues in respect of three features of anything to be found in the causal series, the fact that it may be in motion for which it cannot account, the fact that it falls within this series, and the fact that in or out of the series it enjoys only a contingent existence and does not exist out of itself. In all three respects it is either assumed or affirmed as a self-evident truth that an infinite regress in the series of causes is not possible, and consequently it is concluded that at the beginning of the series there stands a first and unmoved mover, a first and uncaused cause and an absolutely necessary being, whom in each case, Aquinas affirms, all men understand as God.

The fourth way is rather more difficult to understand, and there are in fact considerable differences between the two expositions of it which Aquinas gives in the *Summa contra Gentiles* and in the *Summa Theologiae*. The aspect of sensible objects from which this proof takes its start is what is called 'the degrees of being', and this in itself is not easy for a modern reader to grasp, because the idea brings under one category and into one class 'real' qualities and normative ones, and treats both as somehow residing in the object or even thinks of the object as having these qualities by participation (a Platonic idea) in their supreme form. If, however, we can think of reality in this way, we can, Aquinas would say, further infer the existence of a supreme cause in which all being and perfection is to be found. It is true that not only is this a more difficult argument but also it is one which can readily be interpreted as if Aquinas were arguing from the perfection of essence or being to existence in a way reminiscent of the ontological argument of Anselm. However, we probably keep much closer to his mind if we think of all five arguments as taking their rise in sensible objects, as employing the Aristotelian analysis of causation in terms of material, moving, formal and final causes, and as arguing that, since an infinite regress is not possible, each type of cause must lead us to the thought of God, who into the bar-

gain must be further deemed self-existent or else the causal series could never get under way. Thus when set against the Aristotelian fourfold analysis and Aquinas' own concept of, and emphasis upon, existence, the five ways can be seen to form a unity which subsequent reflection has broken up into two main arguments, the cosmological and the teleological.

This is not the only view of the inter-relationship of the five arguments. Another is that although the structure of the five proofs is identical, forming one whole, each approach discloses a different aspect of the divine causality. It is important, then, to see that the validity of this unified fivefold argument depends on the correctness of Aristotle's fourfold analysis of the causal nexus and the distinctive emphasis upon existence imparted by Aquinas himself.

7. *The Thomistic* View.* On the face of it a philosophy of existence such as Aquinas favoured is more congenial to the modern mind than the kind of philosophy of essence that lay behind the Christian thought of Augustine, and its conception of causality seems nearer to the Christian belief in creation than is the idea of emanation inherent in Neoplatonism. Aquinas, however, meant a great deal more by existence than appears at first sight. It is tempting to think that, since we know what we mean when we say that a tree exists, we must know now what we mean when we say that God exists, even if we realize that unlike a tree God exists out of himself and so necessarily; but if we mean by God's existence the existence of something else over and above all mundane existing things, we have not properly grasped what Aquinas really means. To put it thus is to imply a distinction between what God is and his self-existence, whereas it is precisely this distinction that Aquinas rejects when he says, *Deus est suum esse*; or, as he has been expounded, 'Like whatever exists, God is by his own act-of-being; but, in his case alone, we have to say that *what* his being is is nothing else than that by which he exists, namely, the pure act of existing' (E. Gilson, *The Christian Philosophy of St Thomas Aquinas*, ET 1957, p. 91). In other words, God is 'an act of existing of such a kind that his existence is necessary'; and as such he is the source of everything both in respect of what it is and in respect of the

fact that it is. Moreover, for Aquinas this conclusion of natural theology that God is 'nothing else than . . . the pure act of existing' is confirmed by God's revelation of himself in scripture where in reply to Moses he names himself as 'He who Is' (Ex. 3.14); and so a link is forged between natural and revealed theology.

Since the 'what' and 'that' of God's being are identical, since God is nothing but what has been called a pure act of existing, theology is compelled to speak of the *simplicity* of the divine nature, and by that it means to do justice to the purity of the act and therefore to the total lack of composition, division and qualification in the divine nature. To say anything more of God than that he is is to misrepresent him by denying his simplicity. Yet theology is bound to try to say more, although this it can do only if it is prepared to follow what was called the way of negation, that is, by saying what God is not. Accordingly, theology can and must deny of the divine being all the imperfections of creaturely reality and so speak of God's perfection. The idea of degrees of being or perfection is not an easy one for the modern mind, and it may well seem that to eliminate all the varied content of creaturely existence is to end with an abstract and nearly empty idea, the idea of pure being. Some Thomists would admit that their view can appear as the emptiest of philosophies, but they would also argue that to follow Aquinas faithfully in his interpretations of the identification of the 'what' and the 'that' of God from the side of the 'that', in contrast to its interpretation in Augustinianism from the side of the 'what', is to turn it at once into the fullest of philosophies. Moreover, to say that God is marked by simplicity and perfection in this sense is to say that he is infinite, omnipotent, immutable, eternal and one. Indeed all these characteristics are but hedges to secure and safeguard the purity and uniqueness of his existential being.

On the other hand, sensible things are God's effects and the nature of these effects should tell us something positively about God. Yet care must be exercised in claiming any knowledge of God in this way. Even if we consider the chief perfections to be found in the universe, that is, in the sphere of God's effects, such perfections as intelligence and will and life, we cannot simply and naively attribute these to God. They are God's effects and not God himself. Yet, according to Aquinas, we can affirm these perfections of God in an eminent and inconceivable way, that is, in a way and degree which does not conflict with the simplicity of the divine nature or the identity of essence and existence in God. When we thus predicate perfections of God, we do so not univocally but equivocally, yet in a way which, as Aquinas says, is not altogether equivocal; and the knowledge of God we thus have he calls analogical. Moreover, these attributes of intelligence, will and life, analogically predicated of God, include what on a mere matter-of-fact level would come first to mind, the goodness of God and the love of God. God's goodness is his perfection, and his love is his willing of the good; and both are identical with his pure act of being.

8. *Reformation Views.* It would be too much to say that this conception of God is not a specifically Christian one. On the contrary two facts must be noticed, first, that this conception provided the substructure on which were raised the specifically Christian doctrines of christology * and the Trinity *; and, secondly, that the conception itself was developed under the guidance of the biblical revelation, especially that of the OT and, in particular, of Ex. 3. On the other hand, in order to appreciate the full effect of the Reformation * on this sphere of Christian belief, it is necessary to keep in view the complete development in this direction. It is true that the Council of Trent * was content to reaffirm the Nicene Creed, and that the doctrine of God was not made a matter of dispute by the churches of the Reformation. None the less there was an underlying process of shaking loose which is evidenced by an elusive but real change of atmosphere. Thus, while the Augsburg Confession continues to speak of a 'Divine essence', the Scots Confession, 1560, is content to declare that 'we confess and acknowledge only one God to whom only we must cleave, whom only we must serve . . .', adding the attributes 'eternal, infinite, unmeasurable, incomprehensible, omnipotent, invisible'; and, although the Westminster Confession extends considerably the list of attributes, each is attested by a scriptural reference. It is noteworthy, too, that in none of these documents is the simplicity of the divine being mentioned. The affirmations tend to be

more directly biblical and not to depend so clearly on the systematic presuppositions of a given philosophy.

There is, then, a recognizable change of atmosphere; but the completed mediaeval doctrine of God contained not only a certain conception of God but a well-established speculative method, a natural theology, and here the beginnings of drastic change can be observed. It is true that even John Calvin retained a natural theology as something 'not to be controverted'. He retained it, however, only to secure man's responsibility for his total sinfulness and depravity, and, so far from being expounded in detail as an independent theme worthy of elucidation, it became nothing more than a thoroughly obscured natural knowledge, and even natural sense, of God. For neither Calvin nor Luther was God basically an abstract essence or a pure act of existing. For the latter he was fundamentally our heavenly Father and for the former our sovereign Creator. Moreover, under this silent untrumpeted revolution, this *fait accompli*, one may not be wrong in detecting another, radical but as yet only implicit. This was an instinctive decision in favour of the priority of will in contrast to the prevailing assumption in both Augustinianism and Thomism of the priority of the intellect.

None the less what was implicit did not immediately become explicit. Instead, the age of the Reformers was quickly followed by the development of a Protestant scholasticism in the seventeenth century in which natural theology came once again into its own. Even as late as the second half of the nineteenth century, in the influential theological work of Charles Hodge and his son A. A. Hodge, a place was found for the various proofs of the divine existence. The latter, for example, even included the ontological argument in the form given to it by Descartes, although assigning it only a very ambiguous validity as enhancing the credibility of other arguments. More generally, Hodge held that the various arguments gave '*confirmatory* evidence that God *is* and *complementary* evidence as to *what* God is'. It is noteworthy, too, that Hodge gave importance to the topic known as the evidences of Christianity, by which he meant a rational proof that the God whose existence has already been proved is likely to reveal himself and that this revelation is to be found in

the pages of the OT and NT. Thus, the logical continuity of the theological system is maintained in this strand of post-Reformation theology, and the arguments from the occurrence of miracles in connection with the biblical revelation, from the fulfilment of prophecy therein, from 'the miraculous harmony of all the books', and from the moral character and spiritual power both of Christianity and of Christ take the place of Ex. 3.14 ('He who Is') in providing the link between what can be learned by reason and what is taught by revelation.

9. *Kant and the Moral Argument*. It is impossible in the space of this survey even to mention every school of thought relevant to the topic, such as the teaching of the Cambridge Platonists* and the work of the Deists*, both in the eighteenth century. On almost any reckoning, however, the contribution of Immanuel Kant in the same century must receive attention, in the last resort on the ground that, if indeed in the Reformation there was a radical, but as yet implicit revolution in the silent affirmation of the priority of will over intellect, this affirmation was made explicit by Kant, not in the sense of pragmatism, but in that of Kant's famous principle of the primacy of the practical reason. Kant's contribution was both massive and varied, and for this reason estimates of it are apt to be widely diverse. It may be that some degree of objectivity can be achieved if the two main sides of his philosophical system are kept in view. On the speculative side (which made contact not only with Protestant scholasticism but with the whole history of theology), it is well to recall that, at an earlier stage of his own career, Kant had believed in the possibility of natural theology and favoured an argument which curiously combined elements of both the ontological and the cosmological proofs and which, according to Kant, justified belief in a supreme being and Creator 'one, simple, immutable, and eternal'. He even allowed a certain validity to the teleological argument in proving the Creator 'one, wise, and good', but held that the evidence of order in the universe was not sufficient to justify the traditional concept of God. All this, however, came before the development of his distinctive critical philosophy. In this, on the speculative side, Kant maintained that in

principle there are three types of theistic argument: the ontological (which is based on ideas and takes no account of what exists), the cosmological (which makes use of the fact that something does exist), and the teleological (which takes some account of what it is that does exist). Of these, he dismissed the first as an illegitimate attempt to move directly from what is intelligible to what actually exists. It is, however, the remaining two arguments which constitute the real strength of speculative theism. Both employ the category of causality *, and it is against this common element that Kant concentrated his attack. According to him the category of causality is imposed upon experience by the human understanding and is therefore applicable only to the world of appearance as it presents itself to us in our experience. It may not conceivably be given an application, as in the two arguments, which would transcend the limits of that world and lead to affirmations concerning reality itself.

This is the basic contention of Kant's demolition of natural theology and the speculative method in theology. Now the odd thing about this demolition is that, widely as the conclusion has been accepted, the premise on which it was based has been no less widely rejected. Kant's radical separation of a world of appearances or of experience from a real world of things in themselves simply will not do, especially when it means a similar separation between the real 'I' and the empirical 'I'; and yet the rejection of this division has not led to the reinstatement of speculative theism. The criticism of the causal argument can be stated independently of the distinction between appearance and reality; and then it affirms that, while it is legitimate and significant to inquire of anything within the causal series or system what its cause is, it is not legitimate and significant to make the same inquiry regarding the causal series or system itself.

This odd state of affairs draws attention to the massive complexity of Kant's thought and if he denied what he called knowledge he did so to make room for what he called faith and so to give substance to his principle of the primacy of the practical. In other words, if he rejected the three speculative theistic arguments, he immediately replaced them by what has come to be called the

moral argument. For Kant the complete good was one in which virtue received its due reward of happiness and yet the good will must act virtuously whatever the consequences. This is the antinomy * at the heart of the moral life, that morality shines out most clearly when it suffers the persecution of fate, and yet no less clearly these things ought not so to be. To this antinomy there is only one solution, the postulate by the practical reason of a God, wise and holy, who ordains the complete good. In more general terms, the situation in which the claim of morality is not vindicated is, it is argued, morally intolerable, and is, on Kant's interpretation, an absurdity of the practical reason in which it would be illogical to rest.

Kant's rejection of a speculative natural theology, then, has gained a much wider acceptance than the argument with which he supported it, and, in turn, his moral argument has also had a wider influence than the severely rational interpretation of morality which makes it most convincing. As a matter of fact, although all the credit cannot by any means be given to Kant, the theistic outlook which the moral argument suggests has had an even wider effect than the argument itself; and a belief in God as the supreme being, personal, all-wise, all-holy, and all-loving, established itself as the form of theism characteristic of the later nineteenth century and the early part of the twentieth. It may be that this outlook can claim a longer lineage than has so far been suggested and that it can find its ancestry in Greek philosophy; but, if so, it is in the Platonism of the *Laws*, not in Neoplatonism nor in the teaching of Aristotle nor in the so-called 'existentialism' of St Thomas. Even so it has acquired a wealth of content in the interval, to be measured by the difference between the divine soul and the Personal Spirit or Absolute Person. Into the bargain it has received powerful reinforcement from a contemporary movement wherein supremely revelation has come to be conceived in terms not of propositions or divinely guaranteed information but, precisely, of a unique person.

10. *Developments since Kant.* If, however, in the Christian thought of God the absolute has taken the place of the one that is marked by utter simplicity, it has brought its own

peculiarly difficult problems and especially the question of immanence * and transcendence *; but it has done so not by itself but in conjunction with a changed view of the universe. No longer does the latter appear as a panorama of diverse existents, each perhaps possessing what reality it has by virtue of its participation in some eternal and unchanging form. No longer does it appear as a vast collection of different classes of different objects. Rather it confronts modern man as a process, and if he is a theist, he finds the origin of the process in God; but then the question faces him whether God transcends the process or is wholly immanent within it. It is well known that Hegel developed the thought of Kant in the latter direction, and the movement of absolute idealism *, which had studied long in the school of Hegel *, exercised a wide influence on the Christian thought of God. On the other hand, the Christian mind, the more it is governed by the fact of revelation rather than by the logic of philosophical presuppositions, does not readily rest in any such thesis. Theism asserts that the process of nature is pervaded, sustained and directed by the intelligent purpose of mind. But the question arises whether the mind is entirely expressed in the process, such that it has its whole being in it, or whether it is something over and above the process. Christian thinkers are inclined to insist on the latter, i.e. that it transcends the process of nature, even while it is immanent within it.

The twentieth century has made its own distinctive contribution to this development in the Christian thought of God, a contribution which, without achieving anything like finality, is definitive of a phase in that development; and those who see the situation in this light would probably agree that it is largely the work of one man, Karl Barth. The traditional view posited, as we have seen, both a speculative method and a set of conclusions; and, since the end of the fifth century, through the writer known as the pseudo-Dionysius, this view has been associated with the three-fold way of knowing, the way of negation, the way of analogy (eminentia) and the way of causality, although so far as the divine nature as distinct from the divine existence is concerned, the last of these has played little part as an independent avenue. Accordingly the knowledge of God as understood by the

traditional system can be expressed in the words, 'We learn what God is, partly by removing from the idea we form of him all perfections which belong to creatures, partly by attributing to him, in a more excellent form, all the perfection we find in them' (W. E. Addis and T. Arnold, A Catholic Dictionary, [15]1951, p. 373). Now in a sense, but in a very different one, Barth has his way of negation and his way of analogy. They are, however, ways which have their origin in God's condescension rather than in man's searching aspiration. The element of negation consists in the negation of all natural man's understanding and especially his natural theology. 'This negation,' Barth has said (CD, I/2, 1956, p. 260), 'the negation of man through God's eternal grace and mercy, is only the obverse of his position as a child of God, as a member of the covenant between God and man'; and he has claimed that the Theological Declaration of the Synod of Barmen in 1934 was 'the first confessional document' to make this clear (CD II, 1, pp. 172ff.). On the other hand, there is still a place for analogy *, but it is not the traditional analogy of being (analogia entis) but the analogy of faith (analogia fidei). What this means is that, not directly, but through his works of mercy, God has allowed man to know him and has permitted man to see him through his Word and through it alone; but this human knowing and seeing and apprehending always fall short of what is truly given to man. 'This being known, the divine possibility, even in the Christian remains distinct from the human possibility of knowing: the latter cannot exhaust the former; the resemblance, the analogy remains' (CD, I/1, p. 279); but by the nature of the case it is the analogy of faith, not 'an already existent analogy' but 'an analogy to be created by God's grace and faith' (CD, II/1, p. 85). Moreover, this means that the Christian knowledge of God is not one for which the trinitarian aspect is a further instalment. Rather it is knowledge of God which from the beginning is the knowledge of God as 'Lord, Creator, Reconciler and Redeemer' (CD, II/1, pp. 79ff.). More than that, while this theological approach can speak of the divine simplicity, it rejects the traditional idea and declines to allow it to be 'exalted to the all-controlling principle', holding that it led, not to the abandonment of biblical themes, but to an improper hesitation in their affirmation (*CD*, II/1, pp. 327ff.). In place of the idea of simplicity appropriate to the idea of God as pure being it speaks of 'the multiplicity, individuality and diversity of the divine perfections' in the inviolable unity of the divine being. Similarly, another traditional attribute, the divine incomprehensibility, changes its status, achieving, however, in this case and unprecedented status and indeed 'a basic and determinate position' (*CD*, II/1, pp. 184ff.).

With his stress on revelation to the extreme detriment of reason and on transcendence to the extreme detriment of immanence, Barth seemed to bring to completion a phase, or rather a strand in post-Reformation thought; and yet finality could not be claimed for his massive contribution to theology, even in its broad outlines.

In the second half of the twentieth century, there have been significant developments. Theology never survives long in isolation from contemporary thought, and contemporary movements have indeed influenced Christian thought about God. Under the influence of existentialism*, objective knowledge of God was altogether denied, transcendence being so stressed as to reduce God to the unknown cause of identifiable effects (Rudolf Bultmann). For Paul Tillich, God was identified with the power of being itself. Under the influence of empiricism and linguistic analysis, all metaphysical structures were eliminated, attention being focussed on how the word 'God' functions in human language and traditional formulations being seen as metaphorical or symbolical representations of human and historical possibilities. Under the influence of secularism*, all 'otherwordly' language was to be replaced by the articulation of a particular historical perspective, even if this meant the demise of transcendence or of the very concept of God.

In stark contrast both to this extreme and, it now appears, temporary phase and to the Barthian and neo-Orthodox ban on natural theology, the older tradition of philosophical theology has also seen lively developments. For example, Anselm's ontological argument has not lacked able and eloquent defenders (e.g. in John Hick and Arthur McGill, eds, *The Many-faced Argument*, 1969); and the Thomist outlook has shown itself capable of adaptation to certain pervasive presuppositions and approaches of modern thought. One of these characteristically modern ways of thinking is that which substitutes apprehension for argument, and monstration and manifestation for demonstration; and it is precisely this change that Thomism has proved itself capable of making in the hands of some of its contemporary expositors. For example, it has been argued that the five ways of Aquinas are not really five separate proofs of the divine existence – otherwise it is difficult to see why, if valid, they do not prove the existence of five separate beings – but rather five ways of looking at the world around us, five aids in jockeying for a position and perspective, so that we see finite being as totally incapable of accounting for its own existence, so that indeed we apprehend God over the horizon of the finite world as the One who not only exists out of himself but accounts for the existence of everything else. Moreover, on this view, the primacy of intellect over will is once again posited, God is understood basically as the self-existent One, and a revised natural theology is enabled to make contact with the God of revelation through the OT name of God, 'I am that I am', or, in the old philosophical tradition, 'He who is'.

A different kind of natural theology has developed under the influence of so-called 'process' thought, particularly of A. N. Whitehead and Charles Hartshorne (*see also* **Process Theology**). Here a di-polar concept of God is offered, in terms of which God is thought of as having a primordial nature and a consequent nature (Whitehead) or an abstract aspect and a concrete aspect (Hartshorne). Without attempting to expound the details of this approach, one may say that a conceptuality is developed which enables God to be understood as the purposive provider of creative possibilities for finite creatures, who is changeless and necessary in some respects (e.g. his wisdom, goodness, unsurpassability by anything other than himself) but capable of change and contingent in others (his relation to finite creatures as he reacts to actual events in the cosmos, the particular ways in which his goodness is expressed and his purpose pursued). This is a radical revision of traditional theistic thought, but even if the whole apparatus of 'process' metaphysics has not found wholesale favour with many theologians, some of its features have proved of considerable service to Christian thinkers. In this perspective it is impossible to think of God except as intimately related to everything that is, capable in some sense of experiencing, responding to and suffering with what goes on in the world. Consequently, this concept appears to some to be more consistent with the God of the Christian gospel than the immutable, impassible, static associations of the classical concept.

It also, incidentally, makes it easier to speak of God as 'personal'. This has indeed been one of the recurring emphases of the twentieth-century contributions: that even although God 'as he is in himself' is incomprehensible by the human mind, even although he may not be objectified as 'a person' (in the sense of 'A is a person, B. is a person, God is a person'), yet the concept of God must be such as to enable him to be addressed, responded to and known in personal terms. Knowledge of God is more and more recognized as being much more like personal knowledge than neutral, abstract or theoretical knowledge. In other words the appropriate response to him and the appropriate attitudes involved in such response are much more likely to emerge when he is conceived in personal rather than impersonal terms. Although the term 'personal' as used here in its modern, psychological sense is not to be confused with the use of the term 'person' in its older, logical sense as it appears in trinitarian doctrine, the extent to which the latter is presupposed by the former is one of the questions implicit in some contemporary discussions of Christian teaching on the Trinity *.

11. *Conclusion*. This summary account of the movement of Christian thought around the concept of God is not intended to yield conclusions, but it does underline certain basic questions: the question of method which involves the question of the primacy of intellect or will; the resultant concept of God and the contexts in which it arises; and, finally, the question of the relationship and the connection between reason and revelation – or between revelation and will. Historically, different answers have been given to each of these questions, and this in the course of a highly complex movement of human thought from the primitive witness

of scripture, 'Abba, Father', to the much more sophisticated theological dictum that 'God cannot be expressed but only addressed' (M. Buber, *I and Thou*, 1937, pp. 127, 133).

See also **Arguments for the Existence of God; Atributes, Divine; Revelation; Trinity.**

K. Barth, *Church Dogmatics*, II/1, 1957; C. Hartshorne, *The Divine Relativity*, 1948; G. Kaufman, *The Theological Imagination: Constructing the Concept of God*, 1981; A. J. P. Kenny, *The God of the Philosophers*, 1979; H. Küng, *Does God exist?*, 1980; E. L. Mascall, *The Openness of Being*, 1971; S. M. Ogden, *The Reality of God*, 1967; H. P. Owen, *Concepts of Deity*, 1971; R. Swinburne, *The Existence of God*, 1979; K. Ward, *The Concept of God*, 1974.

N. H. G. ROBINSON/D. W. D. SHAW

God of the Gaps

The phrase is used, generally in a derogatory sense, to describe the policy of locating the activity of God in those phenomena of which science is not yet able to give a satisfactory account. A religion relying on such 'gaps' for its plausibility is forced into a posture of defensiveness against science, punctuated by ignominious retreats.

Sometimes the gaps are crudely stated, as in Newton's claim that his celestial mechanics required continual minor adjustments by 'the divine arm', or in assertions that the origin of life necessitates belief in divine intervention. Sometimes they are less apparent, as when there is failure to acknowledge that direct inspirations of the Holy Spirit have sociological and psychological concomitants.

It is theologically more satisfactory to look for evidence of God's action within natural processes, rather than apart from them, in much the same way that the meaning of a book transcends, but is not independent of, the paper and ink of which it is comprised.

JOHN HABGOOD

Good

To ask what 'good' means is not the same as to ask what really is good; though religious people are inclined to answer 'God' to both questions. They want to affirm that all goodness is grounded in God who is the only source of value. As Brunner put it, 'the

Good is that which God does' (*The Divine Imperative*, ET 1948, p. 55).

It is important that the philosophical difficulties in this affirmation should be understood. Plato's *Euthyphro* dialogue sets an intractable problem for theological moralists about the meaning of 'good'. Socrates asks (9e) 'whether the pious or holy is beloved by the gods because it is holy, or holy because it is beloved by the gods'. It sounds pious to define 'good' as 'what God wills'; but on the contrary, unless we have some distinct idea of what 'good' means in its own right, we are not saying anything when we affirm 'God is good'. The philosophical dogma of the autonomy* of ethics is not an anti-religious dogma. To insist that 'good' cannot be defined as anything whatsoever other than itself is meant to safeguard what is special about *value* against every kind of 'reductionism'.

Since G. E. Moore warned philosophers against the 'naturalistic fallacy' of trying to define 'good', whether in terms of nature, or happiness (one's own or someone else's), or God's will, or anything else, there has been much discontent with his positive view that goodness is 'a simple non-natural quality'. More recently 'good' has been, not defined, but explained in terms of the work the word does (cf. Wittgenstein's dictum, 'Don't ask for the meaning, ask for the use'). This approach need not be as subjective as it was at first (A. J. Ayer, C. L. Stevenson). 'Good' need not be analysed as merely the expression of liking or even approval. The most responsible theory in this field is 'prescriptivism' (R. M. Hare), which emphasizes that 'good' is used to *guide choices*. It is worth noting that the OED 'defines' it as 'the most general adjective of commendation'.

Theologians cannot be entirely content with these developments: not because of the refusal to define 'good' as something else, but because of the difficulty of giving supremacy to a personal God. Are creatures to 'commend' God for being good? But if 'good' is 'what God commends', might God have commended anything? Have we not built in a hopeless arbitrariness instead of what our best understanding knows that goodness really is?

The best hope for a Christian answer must be to start with something given and affirm that as comprehensively as possible, in the faith that truth will sooner or later mean convergence. For some the conviction that God as known to human beings is good will illuminate what goodness means. For others the conviction, as serious though less immediately personalist, that the pursuit of goodness is all-important is not remote from worship. For such as these, personalism and maybe theism could come in at the stage when the question is asked, not what goodness means, but where the search for it comes to rest.

D. M. Mackinnon and H. Meynell, 'The Euthyphro Dilemma', *Proceedings of the Aristotelian Society* Supplementary Vol. 1972; G. E. Moore, *Principia Ethica*, 1929; I. Murdoch, *The Sovereignty of Good and Other Essays*, 1970; H. Oppenheimer, *The Character of Christian Morality*, 1974, ch. III.

HELEN OPPENHEIMER

Good Works

Bitter controversy has raged here, with scant regard to the principle that antagonists are apt to be right in what they say positively and wrong in what they say negatively. It is agreed that we are saved by grace through faith and this is not our own doing (e.g. Eph. 2.8). It is agreed that faith must bear fruit in works (e.g. Gal. 5.22–23). Disastrously, some Christians have been so seized of the dangers of lawless abandon as to revert to legalism, and even succumb to a kind of commercialism in which salvation is to be earned. Other Christians have so deplored 'works-righteousness' as to deny all point to human activity. The Thirty-nine Articles* of the Church of England seem to go this way in Article XIII: 'Works done before the grace of Christ . . . are not pleasant to God' but even 'have the nature of sin'.

Where stereotypes are embattled, compromise looks like an improvement on intransigence but may lose what both mind about. The attempt at a balance which takes both sides to heart and tries to go beyond contradictions ought to be a Christian exercise. A Johannine affirmation that it is God who works (John 5.17); a Pauline conviction that we work because God works in us (Phil. 2.12–13); a Protestant reminder that we have *nothing* that we have not received and that self-righteousness is more dangerous and corrupting than transgression; a Catholic insistence that we are made for perfection and will be able at last to fulfil our Maker's purposes: these are the foundations for a grasp of the paradox that 'when God crowns our merits he crowns nothing but his own gifts' (Augustine, *Ep.* 194.19). St Paul called death 'the wages of sin'; but eternal life he will not call wages, even the wages of sanctification, but charisma, free gift (Rom. 6.22–23).

J. Burnaby, *Amor Dei*, 1938, pp. 235–41, 277; S. Laws, *The Epistle of James*, 1980, on James 2.14–26; H. Thielicke, *Theological Ethics*, 1968, Vol. I Part Two, A 5.

HELEN OPPENHEIMER

Gospel

The English word comes from Old English *gōdspel* (*gōd* good, *spel* recital) as a rendering of the mediaeval Latin *bona annuntiatio* and hence of the Greek *euangelion*, originally the reward for good news and then good news itself. The secular use of the noun in late antiquity is not significant and its sparse religious use not markedly important. The corresponding verb appears at significant points in Deutero-Isaiah's message of divine restoration (Isa. 40.9; 52.7; 60.6; 61.1), to which reference is made in the report of Jesus' reply to the Baptist (Matt. 11.5; Luke 7.22), in Luke's account of the synagogue sermon (Luke 4.18), and in Paul's quotation in Rom. 10.15–16. But in the NT the noun, very common in Paul and frequent in Mark, is an important standard word of their missionary vocabulary. (John lacks both verb and noun; Luke lacks the noun which occurs twice in Acts; Luke moves wholly within the Hebrew thought of benefits offered, and Acts thinks of the missionary proclamation of the kingdom of God and of Jesus as Christ and Lord.) Paul's use is defined in Rom.1.3–4: the gospel is the disclosure of Jesus Christ as God's Son and our Lord by his resurrection from the dead. This disclosure implies the ending of one world and the beginning of a new one (in the eschatological credo of I Thess. 1.9–10) and the dismissal of sins (in the traditional *kerygma**, of I Cor. 15.1–5). Thus the gospel is also the disclosure of God's righteousness (i.e. his restorative activity) for everyone who has faith, both Jews and Greeks (Rom. 1.16). In this new world all may be included in the divine salvation (Gal. 1.11, 16; 2.16). At least to those whose minds are not blinded, the gospel gives 'the knowledge of the glory of God in the face of Christ Jesus' (II Cor. 4.3–6). Mark's use of gospel (avoided by Matthew and Luke) is simpler. He labels the first part of his narrative, which includes Jesus' great deeds, parables and conflicts, as preaching the gospel of God, announcing that the kingdom of God is at hand, and calling to repentance. In the second part of the narrative, where the suffering of the Son of man is prominent, the gospel demands renunciation, endurance, and honouring of Christ in his death (Mark 8.35; 10.29; 13.10; 14.9). The general Pauline sense is continued for a while by the post-apostolic writers, but by the time of Justin *euangelion* begins to mean a book dealing with the life and teaching of Jesus. By the time of Clement of Alexandria, gospel was the written book or the general system of Christian morality. In modern times 'gospel' is popularly associated with evangelical preaching and views of personal salvation. It plays small part in books of NT or systematic theology, but a change may be on the way. 'Whereas in the past appeal would have been made primarily to 'the church', in current Christian usage – both ecclesial and ecumenical – it is now customary to invoke 'the gospel' (E. Schillebeeckx, *Jesus*, 1979, p. 105) – though that welcome judgment needs to be supplemented by considering the absence of 'good news' language from John.

See also **Evangelism.**

E. Käsemann, *Commentary on Romans*, ET 1980, 6–10, for survey and bibliography.

KENNETH GRAYSTON

Grace

The word translates the NT term *charis*, which refers to God's graciousness towards mankind. *Charis* in the LXX usually translates the Hebrew word *ḥēn*, which frequently denotes God's undeserved election of his people manifested in the covenant. The NT also employs other terms to describe God's gracious giving. Christians receive a new birth (cf. John 1.13; 3.3), become sons of God through the Spirit of adoption and so pray to God as Father (Rom. 8.14–16), become members of Christ's body (I Cor. 12.27) and partakers of the divine nature (II

Peter 1.4); abiding in Christ we can bear much fruit, but apart from him we can do nothing (John 15.5).

Later tradition used the term grace in this wider context. Grace, therefore, is not conceived as a thing: it is the transformation (as the Greek Fathers boldly said, the deification, *theōsis*) of human life. Therefore grace is a gift of God distinct from his gift of human life. It consists of God giving himself to men, so that they can know him and love him, so entering into a relationship with him which totally exceeds the relationship of creature to Creator, and is therefore totally undeserved. In this sense RC theology is accustomed to characterize grace as 'supernatural'. Nevertheless grace is not 'extrinsic' to human nature: unless God had implanted in men an affinity for or aptitude for grace, grace would be irrelevant to human nature and not a transformation of it. Thus Barth, though denying that revelation finds any point of contact in human nature, still held that God created human nature expressly in order to enter into a covenant with man.

However, God's gracious relationship with human beings is always a relationship with sinners: it therefore involves forgiveness as well as participation in the divine life. These two aspects of God's grace correspond closely to the distinction between justification and sanctification. The Catholic and Orthodox traditions have taken the fundamental gift to be that of sanctification; the Protestant tradition emphasizes the fact that before grace can be sanctifying it must justify the sinner in the sight of God. Recent ecumenical writers have attempted to show that the Catholic/Orthodox and the Protestant positions are not opposed as sharply as is often believed.

The false views of grace which the church came to reject throw light on the positive meaning of the doctrine. Pelagianism * held that human nature was sufficient for salvation without the further gift of God's grace. Semi-pelagianism * held that grace was given only when a man by his own powers made the first movement towards God.

Various terms have been used to describe the different aspects of grace. Uncreated grace is God's gift of himself; created grace is the transformation of human nature which this gift brings about. Habitual or sanctifying grace is created grace seen as a permanent principle of new life in the Spirit; actual grace is the effectiveness of that new life for particular needs, often experienced as God-given strength. Elevating grace is the participation in the divine nature; healing grace is that participation healing the effects of sin. Prevenient grace is God's grace anticipating any movement by man towards God. Efficacious grace is God's offer of grace to which man responds; (merely) sufficient grace is God's offer of grace which man rejects.

D. M. Baillie, *God was in Christ*, 1961; P. Fransen, *The New Life of Grace*, 1969; H. de Lubac, *The Mystery of the Supernatural*, ET 1967; C. Moeller and G. Philips, *The Theology of Grace and the Ecumenical Movement*, 1961; H. Rondet, *The Grace of Christ*, ET 1967; E. J. Yarnold, *The Second Gift*, 1974.

E. J. YARNOLD

Guilt

The term may be used in different contexts with differences in meaning. Government authorities define guilt precisely in terms of legal codes, and apportion penalties to correlate with the seriousness of the crime and the amount of responsibility involved. Ethical guilt is not synonymous with legal guilt. We may judge a person to be ethically guilty even when he or she is legally innocent. Persons are normally judged ethically if, through free choice, they violate a moral law that they know. Another dimension of guilt occurs in personal relationships where one violates a relationship with another person and experiences guilt in terms of estrangement from the other. This differs from both legal and ethical guilt. An alcoholic drinks from compulsion and not from free choice so that, ethically speaking, we may say there is no guilt. But the alcoholic experiences guilt as estrangement from the members of his or her family because the harmony of relationships with them has been broken.

Theological discussion needs to notice the different meanings of the term guilt. In theology guilt has a connotation that is more analogous to guilt in personal relations than it is to guilt in either ethical or legal contexts. Before God we experience guilt in the form of estrangement from the righteousness of God. We know ourselves to be unworthy of fellowship with God. Our problem is not primarily the fact that we have broken God's laws so it is useless to plead that our sins have been 'small ones'. Our primary guilt lies in the fact that we are prodigals in a far country. Our guilt can only be removed when the Father's forgiveness receives us home as a child. Jesus equated the guilt of a man who has lust in his heart with the guilt of a man who actually commits adultery (Matt. 5.28). To understand this, we must see that Jesus is speaking theologically. Ethically and legally, of course, there is a vast difference between the guilt in the two cases. Jesus' point is that both men are equally alienated from God.

When Protestantism rejected the Catholic distinction between mortal and venial sins, it was thinking in theological terms. Protestants recognize that particular sins may differ in terms of their seriousness if weighed legally or ethically. But in so far as guilt means a separation from God, all sinners are equally guilty (*see also* **Mortal Sin**).

In the history of theology it has been widely held by both Catholics and Protestants that each child inherits Adam's guilt. Where this is held, baptism is often seen as necessary to remove the inherited guilt. If children die unbaptized, it may be impossible for them to go to heaven. This doctrine has been widely rejected in modern theology. It is never just to hold a person guilty of what happened before he or she was born. Today Protestants and Catholics are almost unanimous in rejecting the view that Jews living today are guilty of crucifying Jesus. Increasingly theologians who defend the doctrine of original sin* are desirous of dividing between inherited guilt and sin. We may inherit the nature and/or the situation in which sin is inevitable, but we do not become guilty until we act to alienate ourselves from God.

With the rise of political and liberation theologies, sin has been interpreted politically. These theologies argue that traditional theology concentrated on sin and guilt in terms of individual actions. However, when we are members of an unjust society and profit from its injustices, we share guilt for those injustices. When Isaiah confessed his sin he confessed not only his own 'unclean lips' but also that he lived among a people of 'unclean lips' (Isa. 6.5).

The political interpretation of sin brings a new interpretation of original sin. Human beings are not born in a vacuum but in a concrete social context with a long history. Being dependent upon the stimuli that come to them from their society, human beings naturally accept the basic values of their society. Sin, therefore, consists in collaborating with the inherited social values and incurs guilt for the injustices arising from those values. Repentance means that the Christian will work to remove the unjust structures of the inherited society.

R. Niebuhr, *The Nature and Destiny of Man*, I, 1941, chs. 8–9; Dorothee Soelle, *Political Theology*, 1971, ch. 7.

WILLIAM HORDERN

Habit

Aristotle is the main source for much of the mediaeval reflection on the concept of habits, a notion that formed a principal part of mediaeval psychology and ethics. A habit was conceived of as a firm disposition to act in a certain way. Because they are ingrained in one's character, habits are difficult to change. There were considered to be two sorts of habits, those of intellect and those of will and emotion. Chief among the habits of intellect are 'art' (the fixed ability to make things correctly), 'prudence' (the right way to behave), 'science' (the capacity to reason correctly) and 'wisdom' (the ability to grasp ultimate truths). The habits of the will and of the emotions, principally the concupiscible (*see* **Concupiscence**) and irascible appetites, comprise all the numerous stable tendencies one develops to act either for good or for ill. Thus, the concupiscible appetite may be governed either by a habit of sobriety (the virtue) or of drunkenness (the vice). Or again, either courage (the virtue) or cowardice (the vice) controls the irascible appetite. Following Aristotle's lead, mediaeval moralists centred the study of moral theology on the habits, for only actions proceeding from a habit can be judged good or bad. Other acts are merely accidental, out of character we might say, and so do not make one either a good or an evil person. In dogmatic theology the notion of habit was borrowed to explain the ontological* effect of salvation in the soul. Grace was viewed as a habit elevating the soul to a supernatural plane, thereby enabling one to perform acts of faith, hope and charity which consequently took on a supernatural character.

Thomas Aquinas, *Summa theologiae*, I–II, questions 44–89; Robert Brennan, *Thomistic Psychology*, 1941.

JAMES P. ETZWILER

Hagiography, Hagiology

Derived from the Greek words *hagios*, 'holy', 'saint', *grapho*, 'to write', and *logia*, 'discourse'. These words connote the writing of the lives of the saints and the study of them. This was a considerable industry from early times until the close of the Middle Ages; legendary and indeed totally fictitious elements abounded, until in the seventeenth century a critical attitude began to develop among the Bollandists (the Jesuit editors of the *Acta Sanctorum*, so called after the originator of the series, John van Bolland, 1596–1665). *Foxe's Book of Martyrs* (1563) might be regarded as a kind of Protestant hagiography; but in general Protestants have not encouraged the cult of the saints *, believing that it observes the unique mediation of Jesus Christ.

ALAN RICHARDSON/
JOHN MACQUARRIE

Heaven *see* Life after Death

Hegelianism

As expounded in the work of G. W. F. Hegel (1770–1831), this is a version of idealism * which is best understood as arising out of dissatisfaction with Schelling's doctrine that the ultimate reality or the Absolute is the eternally present, pre-given source and origin of the realms of both nature and spirit and as such is at any time accessible by means of 'intellectual intuition'. In contrast, Hegel argues that knowledge of the ultimate nature of reality is possible only by means of what he calls 'dialectic'. The dialectical process begins with the simplest or most undifferentiated moment or level of experience (e.g. sense-perception or 'being'); then this and each higher or more complex moment or level is shown on analysis to manifest its own inadequacy ('negativity') as an account of the real; thus the whole series of levels or moments becomes accountable only as a series of moments or levels in the unity of all, the Absolute *. For Hegel, then, the Absolute is not an intuited or presupposed given, but is a product. In

The Phenomenology of Spirit (1807) he attempts to show that his account of the Absolute is the proper and inevitable issue of the entire previous historical development (dialectical progression) of Western society and philosophy and Christian theology. In the ensuing *Science of Logic* (1812–1816) he assumes the reality of the Absolute and attempts to re-think the nature of logical concepts and categories in that light. In Hegel's view, the logical order of thought is a dialectical recapitulation of the order of Western philosophical reflection up to his own day. Logic is to be understood not as a theory of the relation of propositions but as a theory of the order of the world. Hence, in both its historical and logical forms, the dialectical method is not a formal method divorced from its contents; rather, it shows that the nature of reality is identical with the rational order which it reveals.

As an indication of the massive influence which Hegelianism has had on subsequent thought, two features can be stressed.

1. Hegel identifies theology with (or subsumes it under) his doctrine of the Absolute – a doctrine which maintains that the finite is an expression or manifestation of the infinite. It is this doctrine which in christology * provides the impetus for D. F. Strauss's claim that the incarnation occurs not in one man but in the race as a whole. Moreover, it allows Ludwig Feuerbach to regard Hegel's metaphysics as a disguised theology, and invites his 'reversal' of both, in which the infinite is regarded, not as manifesting itself in the finite, but as the illusory projection of finite man. Not surprisingly, much theology since Hegel has been concerned to find either an alternative philosophical anthropology, or a non-metaphysical locus, for itself.

2. Hegel is the first philosopher to give history a central place in his thought. And this allows Marx to develop Feuerbach's reversal, i.e. to regard philosophy as an expression of material or socio-economic conditions (the historical dialectic). Indeed, since Hegel the relationship of philosophy and theology to history has become a central issue. His influence is evident in the work of Benedetto Croce and R. G. Collingwood; in the Hegelian Marxism of G. Lukács; in the 'critical theory *' of T. W. Adorno, H. Marcuse and J. Habermas; and in the theologies of Pannenberg and Moltmann (for

instance), as well as in 'political' * theology So pervasive is his thought that it has been suggested that subsequent thinkers can best be understood in relation to a particular chapter of the *Phenomenology* – e.g. Marx in relation to the section on 'Master and Slave' and Kierkegaard to that on the 'Unhappy Consciousness'.

In Britain Hegel's influence can be seen in the work of the British Idealists (*see* **Idealism**) and through them on late nineteenth- and early twentieth-century British theology. Yet none of the members of this movement accept Hegel's dialectic in either its historical or logical form; their relation to him is best understood in the context of native developments. The same is true of the American idealist philosophers Josiah Royce (*see* especially his *Problem of Christianity*, 1913) and Brand Blanshard (*Reason and Belief*, 1974).

K. Barth, 'Hegel', *Protestant Theology in the Nineteenth Century*, ET 1972, pp. 384–421; J. S. Boys-Smith, 'The Interpretation of Christianity in Idealistic Philosophy in Great Britain in the Nineteenth Century', *The Modern Churchman* XXI, 1941, pp. 256–73; J. E. Erdmann, *A History of Philosophy*, vol 3, *German Philosophy Since Hegel*, ET 1890; T. Langford, *In Search of Foundations: English Theology 1900–1920*, 1969; Q. Lauer, *Hegel's Conception* of God, 1982; K. Löwith, *From Hegel to Nietzsche*, ET 1965; G. Lukács, *The Young Hegel*, ET 1975; H. Marcuse, *Reason and Revolution: Hegel and the Rise of Social Theory*, 1955; W. Pannenberg, 'The Significance of Christianity in the Philosophy of Hegel', *Basic Questions in Theology*, vol 3, 1973; C. Taylor, *Hegel*, 1975.

JAMES BRADLEY

Heilsgeschichte

The German word 'redemptive history' or 'history of salvation' was made a prominent technical term by J. C. von Hofmann (1810–1877) and the Erlangen School, which deeply influenced pietism *. Hofmann argued that as a historian could deduce from the legal circumstances of a period all the preceding facts responsible for that situation, and as a scientist could deduce from a series of natural changes the causes of those changes, so the theologian finds in the fact of [his own] conversion the whole sacred

history. The inner-trinitarian decision to commit itself to historical self-fulfilment in the appearance of Jesus Christ set in motion the history of salvation. The nation Israel received a call to play its part in salvation history solely in order to provide the place for the appearance of Jesus and the beginning of his church. The whole content of salvation history (from the inner-trinitarian decision to the virgin birth, the death, resurrection, ascension and return of Christ) is the presupposition of the personal relation to God we have in Christ, of which we are certain through personal experience.

The term was used by Bultmann to describe the way Paul, John and Luther transformed mythological cosmological ideas to bring home to the sinner that he could only live by grace; Paul, for example, 'strove to make the mythical cosmology into *Heilsgeschichte*'. Oscar Cullmann revived the wide theological use of the term by his statement 'The "Biblical history", which we ... can also designate as "revelatory history" or – since indeed all revelation is God's love – as "redemptive history [*Heilsgeschichte*]", is the heart of all NT theology' (*Christ and Time*, ET 1946). The theme of von Rad's *Old Testament Theology*, ET 1957, 1960, was that Israel's faith is based on the ever-renewed actualization of the saving historical facts; he said that Deut. 26.5–9 is one of the oldest presentations of *Heilsgeschichte*. Wolfhart Pannenberg and others in *Revelation as History* (1961) made cautious use of the term; see U. Wilckens, *Commentary on Romans* (1978–1982).

J. C. O'NEILL

Hell *see* **Damnation, Life after Death**

Henotheism

The term has been used to describe the exclusive worship of one god, whilst at the same time retaining a belief that other gods exist and may be worshipped by other peoples. As such it has been applied to the religion of Israel from the time of Moses until a fully developed monotheism * emerged with the prophet Deutero-Isaiah in the sixth century BC. It would then affirm the solemn obligation on the part of Israel to worship its own God Yahweh exclusively (cf. Deut. 6.4–5), without denying that other gods may exist and be worshipped by other nations (cf. Deut. 32.8–9). In this way a number of scholars have endeavoured to trace a development in the emergence of a theological monotheism. Other scholars have, more recently, argued that monotheism did not develop in clear-cut stages in this fashion, and in any case such a concept of henotheism fails to do justice to the prominent sense in Israel that Yahweh was superior to all other deities. H. H. Rowley preferred to describe the Mosaic religious inheritance as 'incipient monotheism', and the sense of Yahweh's superiority to other gods has been shown by C. J. Labuschagne to have arisen in Israel at a very early stage, long before Deutero-Isaiah (*The Incomparability of Yahweh in the Old Testament*, 1966, esp. 64ff.). From a wider study of ancient religion it has also become increasingly evident that polytheism * and monotheism do not represent distinct stages in a progressive intellectual development, but rather indicate contrasting emphases in a very complex pattern of religious traditions.

O. Keel, *Monotheismus im Alten Israel und seiner Umwelt*, 1980; H. H. Rowley, 'Moses and Monotheism', *From Moses to Qumran*, 1963, pp. 35–66.

RONALD CLEMENTS

Heresy

The traditional meaning of the term was rigorously defined in mediaeval canon law * to signify the sin of a person who, having been baptized and calling him or herself a Christian, denies a defined doctrine of the faith even after having been formally instructed. 'Formal' heresy is such persistent adherence to erroneous teaching; 'material' heresy means adherence to error, without any culpability (for example, because the truth has never been presented as such). The definition of heresy is logically dependent, therefore, on that of defined doctrine. It presupposes that Christian truth may be known in such a way that one can recognize doctrines bearing a certain resemblance to the truth, but denying its substance.

The Greek word *hairesis* (literally 'choice', or 'thing chosen') was applied to the doctrines of philosophical schools. But already in I Cor. 11.19 and Gal. 5.20 Paul uses the term in a negative sense to mean a divisive faction. In the works of Ignatius of Antioch (*c.* 35–*c.* 107), that is, even before the days

of the conciliar definitions of Christian faith, it denotes theological error. Tertullian (*c.* 160–*c.* 225) identifies the root of heresy as the wilful choice of philosophical opinion over revealed Christian truth.

Churches in the modern period which retain canonically enforced normative statements of doctrine have little difficulty in continuing to identify heretical opinions. Two developments, however, are of interest. In the first place historical scholarship has been increasingly willing to accept the fact that the risk of material heresy at least seems an inevitable consequence of theological activity. Only if theologians are willing to say things which have never been said in precisely the same way before would it be possible for theology to meet new intellectual challenges. Secondly, with the developing realization of the plurality of special fields with their own canons of judgment, theologians have been increasingly unwilling to identify Christian truth with the grammatical meaning of a single text or series of texts. The application of strictly legal methods to the interpretation of religious texts artificially restricts the range of possible meanings in Christian symbolism. The identification of formal heresy has consequently become a more questionable and inherently disputable process.

The radical denial that heresy could exist, or if it existed, could be identified, seems to be based on a sociological misunderstanding. The fact that the boundaries of a religion may be difficult to determine with precision does not mean that a religion has no boundaries. Religious commitment depends upon both affirmations and denials. Heresy, accordingly, belongs in the ambiguous realm between what is affirmed and what is denied, preserving the appearance but not the substance of the former.

S. W. SYKES

Hermeneutical Circle

In pursuit of the meaning of any expression or text – a poem, narrative, parable, etc. – we must begin with sufficient prior understanding of what the text is about in order to enter into a dialogue with it in which our understanding is subsequently enlarged. We put questions to the text which are, in turn, reshaped by the text itself. This process has come to be called the 'hermeneutical circle'. The term is also used of the related process by which we interpret parts of a text on the basis of a grasp of the whole work while our grasp of the whole requires that we have at least some understanding of the parts. In theological usage the 'circle' appears in the dialectic of faith and understanding. To understand, it is necessary to have faith; to have faith, it is necessary to understand. Differing forms and applications of the notion of the circle appear in the works of Schleiermacher, Dilthey, Heidegger, Bultmann, Gadamer and others.

The prior understanding with which we enter the circle may take many forms. It may consist simply in our being at home in the language in which the text is written. Or it may lie in a certain existential experience or disposition. Or it may be the knowledge of a certain history of events, or certain cultural and literary tradition, which the text at hand presupposes: e.g. the NT presupposes the Israelite and Jewish tradition, which we need to understand to grasp the basic NT terminology.

It is sometimes claimed that acknowledgment of the function of prior understanding and of the resulting dialogue between interpreter and text 'enforces an anthropocentric perspective on all interpretation because it makes human experience the measure of truth' (A. C. Thiselton, *The Two Horizons*, 1980, p. 197). Yet Gadamer stresses that the text must 'break the spell' of the presuppositions which have given us a point of entry into its meaning. The subject-matter of the text effects the correction, revision, even the effacement, of our preliminary understanding. Acknowledgment of the circle is thus compatible with acknowledgment of the priority of the message. 'To understand the text, it is necessary to believe in what the text announces to me; but what the text announces to me is given nowhere but in the text' (Paul Ricoeur).

See also **Hermeneutics**.

LEWIS S. MUDGE

Hermeneutics

Although contemporary usage of the term varies, 'hermeneutics' generally means the theory of the interpretation of texts. Hermeneutics is thus the science of the interpretative process which begins with determination of the original meaning of a text (exegesis) and leads to elucidation of its sense for modern readers (exposition, paraphrase or sermon). Because of the nature of the problems involved, hermeneutics has from classical times involved philosophical inquiry, in addition to calling upon lexical, linguistic, literary, and other disciplines.

The origins of the word lie in the Greek *hermeneuein*, 'to interpret' (cf. *hermeneia*, 'interpretation', *hermeneus*, 'an interpreter', and other cognates). The root is apparently derived from (or conceivably reflected in) the divine name Hermes, the messenger of the gods who makes intelligible to human beings that which otherwise cannot be grasped. The Greeks associated Hermes with the discovery of language and writing, the indispensable tools of understanding. The verb is common in classical literature in such senses as 'to express aloud', 'to explain', or 'to translate', and often appears in contexts which stress the responsibility of human beings rightly to interpret ancient writings thought to contain messages from the gods. The importance of the notion for philosophical reflection can be seen in Aristotle's treatise, *Peri hermeneias*, 'On Interpretation', a work which remains of fundamental importance for some phases of contemporary discussion. If the meaning of the word be derived from the classical usage of its root, hermeneutics is the art and science of elucidation of the meaning of texts or oracles: especially ancient messages held to contain divine truth.

These general notions comported well with late Jewish and early Christian understandings of the interpretation of sacred scripture. In the NT we find *hermeneuein* and its cognates used in reference to the translation of unusual or specially significant terms and proper names (John 1.38, 42; 9.7; Heb. 7.2), and to the interpretation of 'tongues' (I Cor. 12.10; 14.26–28). Paul, at Lystra, is called 'Hermes' because he is the chief speaker (Acts 14.12). But by far the most significant instance theologically is to be found at Luke 24.27, where we read of the risen Christ at Emmaus that '. . . beginning from Moses and from all the prophets, he interpreted (*diermeneusen*) to them in all the scriptures the things concerning himself'.

Prior to the Enlightenment * (and, in conservative circles, afterwards as well) the Western church understood the interpretation of scripture as a matter of following rules which would yield a correct sense. For the most part the different schools of interpretation and the different modes developed within the schools (e.g. the literal, allegorical, analogical and anagogical methods recommended in the Middle Ages, *see* **Senses of Scripture**) appear to us today innocent of much sense of historical relativity either of the texts interpreted or of the presuppositions of the interpreters (*see* **Historical Criticism, History**). Soon after 1800, the situation for theologians in touch with the larger intellectual world began to change. The early development of historical-critical method as well as the beginning of scientific historiography raised the question whether the interpretation of human signs, as inscribed in the texts of other cultures and other times, could be the subject-matter of a 'science' analogous to that involved in the study of nature.

The first Christian scholar to give substantial attention to this issue was Friedrich Schleiermacher (1768–1834), whose work decisively transformed the hermeneutical question from one of devising adequate 'rules' for accurate exegesis to realization that the real issue is how any understanding of another mind or culture through written communication is possible. Schleiermacher identified many issues still salient in discussion today, e.g. the relation between comprehension of the whole of a work and interpretation of its parts, the role of prior understanding of the subject-matter of a text in the process of understanding it (*see* **Hermeneutical Circle**), and the relation between language and thought. Despite his early inquiry into the possibility of a language-centred hermeneutic, Schleiermacher seems finally to have understood hermeneutics as reconstruction of the author's mental process and to have understood this as a reality distinct from his or her language. Schleiermacher's work was continued most notably by Wilhelm Dilthey (1833–1911). Dilthey developed the concept of 'understanding' (*Verstehen*) as key to the *Geisteswissenschaften* (the sciences of the human as opposed to the sciences of nature), whose object he saw as the recovery from historical texts the fullness of lived experience: indeed the attempt 'to understand the author better than he understood himself' through the study of the objectification of experience in the work of literary or other art.

After World War I, the work of the 'dialectical' or 'neo-orthodox' theologians put the hermeneutical question in a new light. The work of Karl Barth (1886–1968) and Rudolf Bultmann (1884–1976) made clear that, far from being a mere artifact of the modern era, the hermeneutical issue is inherent in the nature of Christianity as a historical religion. The issue for these writers, however, was no longer the essentially 'romantic' one of recovering the consciousness of past cultures and persons, but rather that of the relation between the biblical text as such and the 'kerygma*' that God has drawn near to us in Jesus Christ. This formulation went with a certain agnosticism about our ability to recover much information about Jesus' mental processes from the Gospels, as well as a desire that the proclamation of the Word be essentially independent of the results of historical, cultural, or psychological inquiry (*see also* **Dialectical Theology, Jesus, Word of God**).

In Bultmann's work, particularly, the hermeneutical implications of this stance are drawn out in a programme of demythologization*, in which the attempt is made to disengage the essential message of the gospel from the mythological* and eschatological* presentation of reality in which it is clothed. This disentanglement is accomplished with the help of existentialist* categories derived from the earlier work of the philosopher Martin Heidegger: categories thought to correspond closely to the experience of the gospel as a demand for radical decision in the face of the threat of loss of our being. In the hands of colleagues and pupils of Bultmann such as Gerhard Ebeling, Ernst Fuchs, and others, the existentialist* programme has been carried forward with the aid of Heidegger's later reflections on language as disclosure of being in the direction of the concept of 'word-event', the manifestation of being in history through language and action which can change the course of history. Through appropriate interpretation, these scholars argue, the scriptural record of the word-event of Jesus Christ can become word-event once more. The use of existentialist categories helps bridge the cultural distance between then and now. It is this understanding of history, we are told, which helps us grasp what the NT writers truly intend to convey. Existentialist hermeneutics thus leads to what James M. Robinson calls 'the new quest of the historical Jesus', the effort to get at Jesus' historicity not as a chain of outward events or of inner states of mind but as a fundamental disposition of personhood in which Jesus' words and actions are seen to be one (*see also* **Jesus**).

We may fairly represent the state of the hermeneutical question since the 'new quest' in terms of the paradigm given it by Hans-Georg Gadamer. The German scholar speaks of the goal of hermeneutics as a 'fusion of horizons'. Our 'horizon' is the limiting circle of our vision, or of our thought, as determined by the place where we stand. In the interpretative process the horizon of the interpreter is to be reconstituted, reoriented, transformed, by the horizon of the text. What issues are raised when we try to understand how this happens? Gadamer himself seeks to connect the pre-understandings, preconceptions and 'prejudices' we bring to texts with our participation in tradition. Human beings do not and cannot stand outside the flow of history and culture*. Our capacity to understand is governed by projections of possibilities already embedded in the tradition which we represent. That which we try to understand, whether it be person or culture or text, is sense or content which likewise is embedded in, an expression of, some body of tradition. Gadamer thus abjures the notion of an empathy which mysteriously connects reader with writer. A 'fusion of horizons' can occur only within and through language in a process which is virtually identical with the movement of history. Tradition is essentially linguistic. It is by means of language that the world as historic phenomenon is given duration from generation to generation.

Work done since Gadamer's great book *Truth and Method* has tended in various ways to emphasize the cultural distance between the biblical world and our own. If Gadamer is taken seriously, it becomes plain that the consciousness of ancient writers cannot be detached from their ancient cultural and linguistic contexts. Rather, these contexts must be studied for what they are. Dennis Nineham, for example, has called in question the very possibility, in some cases, of finding modern equivalents for biblical meanings. An array of 'human science' methods – sociological, psychological, anthropological – has now been brought to bear on the biblical data, with the general result of objectifying the cultures they represent and emphasizing their specificity and remoteness. Such work casts doubt on the feasibility of any significant empathetic recovery of the ancient life-world, much less of knowing the original writer's mind better than he did himself. At the same time, we find a new interest in what Paul Ricoeur has called the 'career' of the biblical texts after they leave their authors' hands. The question of how the text as a literary object contains meanings and conveys them independently of authorial intention now stands close to the centre of hermeneutical debate.

Literary studies, including generative grammar, semiotics, genre research, structuralist* analysis, and inquiry into the formation and meaning of the canon now illumine our understanding of how the Bible came to be as well as of how it may be interpreted today. Each stage in the growth of the biblical tradition is, in effect, an interpretation of some body of prior tradition. The different scribal traditions underlying the Hebrew scriptures are interpretations of already existing oral and written materials, designed to make them applicable to new political and cultural conditions. What we call the 'Christ event*' is what it is, even for eye-witnesses, because it enters into what Ricoeur calls a 'network of intelligibility', supplied by the Hebrew scriptures and other Jewish traditions of the time. With the writings of Paul, this 'apostolic' interpretation of Hebrew scripture is in turn made to decipher – typologically – the meaning of human existence: the death of the old humanity and the appearance of the new are understood under the signs of cross and resurrection (*see also* **Allegory and Typology**). The four Gospels are, in turn, interpretations of this intelligible event under the control of the apostolic witness through the oral and written materials to which the event gave rise. And finally, the results of this complex process form a written text which goes on to have a hermeneutical history of its own: bearing its message in a medium marked by the cosmological and cultural traits of its place and time and encountering the presuppositions of other places and times. To grasp the meaning of this process we must ask what hermeneutical assumptions are at work at each stage. We must ask how the gospel meanings are related to their different media, from Hebrew traditions to our own attempts to articulate them in teaching and preaching.

The treatment of biblical tradition as itself a complex literary process makes us aware that our notion of 'revelation *' must not be allowed to rest on too narrow a conception of the way the biblical materials convey sense. Literal dictation theories of biblical authority tend to follow a particular understanding of the literary form of the prophetic oracle ('And the Lord said . . .'). But there are many other genres in the Bible, each with its own sociologically understandable roots and its own way of embodying the gospel. Each has had, and will have, its own 'career' in culture and church. An adequate 'hermeneutic' will now study with care the range and richness of these many meaning-processes.

Likewise, we become increasingly aware of the pluralism * of contemporary contexts in which the Bible is interpreted. No longer can the hermeneutical presuppositions and practices of northern Europe and North America be considered normative in the Christian church. Within these cultures the perspectives of minority groups and of women enlarge, enrich and challenge traditional understandings (*see also* **Cultural Relativism**). The churches of Latin America, Africa and Asia now interpret scripture in a wide variety of cultural and political settings. The different forms of Eastern Orthodoxy *, heirs to a history which in many ways bypassed the Enlightenment and its aftermath, now vigorously enter the dialogue.

It may, then, be fruitful not only to study these many interpretative processes as objectively as possible, but also to see our own attempts to interpret the Bible as representing but one 'horizon' among many. In this work the 'human sciences' of anthropology, sociology, psychology, linguistics, and so on – those contemporary forms of the *Geisteswissenschaften* – will increase in importance. We may begin to see the human sciences less as attempts at empathy with other times and places, as Schleiermacher and Dilthey tended to do, and more, with Paul Ricoeur, as our own attempts to read the 'texts' of our times in terms of traditions of meaning which summon us. If so, we could construct alongside the hermeneutic of actual texts a hermeneutic of the human world seen from various points of view as text-like, thus permitting a comparative study of the many forms of engagement of the gospel with the human situation.

Hans-Georg Gadamer, *Truth and Method,* ET ²1979; E. D. Hirsch, *The Aims of Interpretation,* 1976; Van A. Harvey, *The Historian and the Believer: The Morality of Historical Knowledge and Christian Belief,* 1965; D. E. Nineham, *The Use and Abuse of the Bible: A Study of the Bible in an Age of Rapid Cultural Change,* 1976; R. E. Palmer, *Hermeneutics: Interpretation Theory in Schleiermacher, Dilthey, Heidegger, and Gadamer,* 1969; Paul Ricoeur, *Interpretation Theory,* 1976; A. C. Thiselton, *The Two Horizons, New Testament Hermeneutics and Philosophical Description,* 1980.

LEWIS S. MUDGE

Hermetic Literature

A collection of Greek and Latin writings representing a noble religious philosophy of the Hellenistic period (the chief work is the 'Poimandres'), fusing together Platonic and Stoic teachings with oriental elements. The writings were ascribed to Hermes Trismegistus, a name for the Egyptian god Thoth. The best introduction to the subject will be found in C. H. Dodd, *Interpretation of the Fourth Gospel* (1953), pp. 10–53. W. Scott's four-volume *Hermetica* (1924–1936) is for scholars only. Critical text ed. by A. D. Nock and A. J. Festugière, with French trans., *Corpus Hermeticum,* 4 vols., 1945–1954.

ALAN RICHARDSON

Heterodox

From Greek *heteros*, other, and *doxa*, opinion. Contrary to the received opinion; unorthodox.

ALAN RICHARDSON

Heteronomy

The term was used by Kant of both the state of the individual rational will related by some law or authority from the outside and a system of ethics which derives ethics from anything but the nature of the rational will as such. Neither private interest nor personal feeling can be the ground of the moral imperative; nor can either metaphysics or theology. Tillich modifies Kant's decision in various ways, the most obvious being that he uses it to develop what is essentially an ontological foundation of ethics. This he does by introducing a third term, theonomy. 'Autonomy asserts that man as the bearer of universal reason is the source and measure of culture and religion – that he is his own law. Heteronomy asserts that man, being unable to act according to universal reason, must be subjected to a law, strange and superior to him. Theonomy asserts that the superior law is, at the same time, the innermost law of man himself, rooted in the divine ground which is man's own ground: the law of life transcends man, although it is, at the same time, his own.' The concept of heteronomy relates to the political interest which is much more obvious in Tillich's early than in his later work. In the essay 'Protestantismus und Politische Romantik' (1932) he outlined a classification of political ideologies which was developed in the *Socialist Decision* (1948) – ideologies of origin and ideologies of autonomy. The drive for autonomy is rooted in the experience of the unconditional demand for justice. The danger of autonomy is that it becomes empty and that vacuum is a space to which the authoritarian forces will return. Thus nationalism, without the proper qualifications, is a heteronomy. Similarly in his doctrine of the kairos* Tillich admits that there can be an element of heteronomy in a potential theonomy.

It would be quite wrong to suggest that Tillich's later theology was different in any radical sense from his earlier, as is illustrated by the importance of the concept of heteronomy for systematic theology. In *Systematic Theology* Vol. 1 (1951) he is concerned to point out the wider implication of the preoccupation of modern philosophy with epistemology. That 'victory of technical reason' has encouraged the treatment of human beings as means rather than ends and opened the way for the erosion of human values in the societies dominated by liberal capitalist communism or a Stalinist terror. The former Tillich calls a world of empty autonomy and the latter a world of destructive heteronomy. Autonomy and heteronomy are rooted in theonomy; but there is no complete theonomy under the conditions of existence. Under the conditions of human existence the reason is subject to the polarities of the conflicts between autonomy and heteronomy which are in turn produced by the polarity of structure and depth within reason. So Tillich relates his anthropology to both his epistemology and his political theology.

J. HEYWOOD THOMAS

Heuristics

A heuristic proposition is a hypothesis used to give guidance or direction in a process of discovery. The term comes from the Greek *heuriskein*, 'to find', the first person singular *perfect* form of which is the familiar *heureka*, 'I have found (it)'. The English word first appears in the nineteenth century (e.g. Whewell, 1860) with reference to the art of scientific or philosophical discovery. Edward Caird applies the term, more specifically, to the thought of Kant, saying (1877) that this philosopher's 'ideas of reason are heuristic, not ostensive; they enable us to ask a question, not to give the answer.'

But the idea behind the word is much older than the word itself. In the *Meno*, Socrates seeks to ascertain 'what virtue is'. Now this, he says, means enquiring into something whose nature he does not yet know, which in turn requires a conception whose function is to guide the enquiry, 'a hypothesis which may assist us in forming a conclusion' (Jowett). There are also theological uses of the idea. A heuristic method is embedded in the formula *fides quaerens intellectum*, 'faith seeking understanding'. Our approach to a biblical or other text with prior understanding which gives us a clue to its meaning, an understanding then deepened dialectically by our continued encounter with the work, is likewise a heuristic method (*see Hermeneutical Circle*).

Heuristic procedures abound in modern methods of enquiry. The scientific hypothesis, the 'model'* in the human sciences, the 'paradigm' informing a whole epoch of research, are all heuristic devices. In contemporary mathematics, 'heuristics' is the study of the methods used in problem-solving. As a given conception in any field is used to guide the search for truth, discoveries and insights inevitably modify the original heuristic idea and the process begins anew. Many would say that all knowledge is acquired in this manner, with the implication that there is no end to the heuristic process and that the knowledge available at any given time is tentative and relative to the procedures by which it is achieved.

LEWIS S. MUDGE

Hierarchy

From the Greek *hieros* 'sacred' and *arche*
'origin' or 'rule'. The idea of the divine principle of order as it can be discerned in the
whole created universe and should therefore
also inform human society, and not least
the church, is a recurring theme in Christian
theology. It is found in Clement's (First)
Epistle to the Corinthians (XIX–XX, XXIV,
XL, XLIV) and is most fully expounded by
Dionysius the Pseudo-Areopagite. He
teaches that in the divine economy the invisible and eternal emerges through the
sacramental system into the visible and
transient world, elaborates its purpose
and returning to God achieves its final destiny. The nine-fold order of the *Celestial
Hierarchy* (Seraphim, Cherubim, Thrones;
Dominions, Virtues, Powers; Principalities,
Archangels, Angels) is faithfully reflected on
a lower plane by the *Ecclesiastical Hierarchy*
extending through the mysteries (sacraments), the initiators (clergy) and the initiates (laity) down to the animals, plants
and inanimate creation – each in turn
moving towards fullness of being by the
three stages of purgation, illumination and
union.

This concept of hierarchy not only deeply
influenced Eastern and Western theology
and teaching on prayer but also inspired
much mediaeval political and social
thought. In RC doctrine on the church's
ministry two forms of hierarchy came to be
distinguished – the *hierarchia ordinis* of
bishops, priests and deacons established by
divine law and entered by ordination which
is indelible, and the *hierarchia jurisdictionis*
of Pope, bishops and other pastoral offices
which belongs to ecclesiastical law and is
entered, not necessarily permanently, by
canonical election, licensing or appointment.

D. Rutledge, *Cosmic Theology: The Ecclesiastical Hierarchy of Pseudo-Denys*, 1964.
                                   VICTOR DE WAAL

Historical Criticism

With rare exceptions, Christian faith in the
period up to the eighteenth century was
based on unquestioning acceptance of the
entire contents of the Bible. In particular,
complete credence was given to the biblical
accounts of the past, and their interpretation

of it as a series of 'wonderful works of God'
through which the salvation of mankind was
accomplished. Apart from the need to harmonize a few apparent discrepancies, theologians felt able to accept the biblical story
at its face value and to concentrate on an
attempt to draw further implications from it
and to weld the whole into a comprehensive
and coherent account of reality, with the aid
of ideas and categories derived from Greek
philosophy. So far as the conclusions of this
process seemed valid, and fitted in with the
tendencies of contemporary piety, they were
accepted almost as implicitly as the biblical
records themselves. Such an understanding
of things still has its defenders today.

However, from the later Middle Ages onward a considerable change has come over
scholarly attitudes towards the past. By the
sixteenth century, although the contents of
the Bible were rarely, if ever, challenged, it
was clear that many of the sources on which
the Middle Ages had relied for a knowledge
of the past (including such ecclesiastically
important documents as the *Donation of
Constantine* and the *Isidorean Decretals*)
were spurious or inaccurate in whole or part.
The need was increasingly felt for methods
and criteria which would make it easier to
distinguish the true from the false in traditional accounts, and by the nineteenth century historians had worked out a self-conscious and sophisticated approach to their
sources, which had as its aim the recovery
of the past, 'as it actually happened' (von
Ranke), i.e. in distinction from the way it
was reported in the sources.

The initial scepticism towards the evidence which this approach involves has
sometimes been misunderstood by theologians, so it is important to understand its
basis in the historian's thinking. His contention is that once an event is past there can
be no direct access to it or relationship with
it. Nothing is available except data relating
to it. These may be of various kinds, e.g.
words, written or spoken, archaeological
remains or later events needing earlier
events for their explanation; but whatever
they are, they can never be more than data,
and no datum is above suspicion. Even eye-
witnesses' memories of events in which they
took part may well turn out on investigation
to be partial or distorted. Consequently, just
as a law court cannot allow the evidence of
any one witness to be exempted from criti-

cism, but must insist on the rigorous cross-questioning of all witnesses, so the historian must approach all his data with an initial scepticism. He must make sure that he has taken account of all the available data, some of which may not reveal their relevance at first sight, and then he must 'torture them' (Collingwood) i.e. sift them, analyse them, compare and contrast them, in fact do to them everything possible that will make them yield all that they have to disclose about the events to which they relate (cf. Bacon's instruction to the scientist to 'put nature to the question').

In this way the historian seeks to establish the facts, and it should be noted that the account he arrives at seldom, if ever, coincides exactly with that given by any one of his sources. The 'facts' as thus 'established' may often approximate closely to the event, but they must be clearly distinguished from it. An event can never be fully encompassed in any structure of words, so any one historian can only bring out certain aspects of it. Moreover, an event, once it has occurred, does not change, but it is different with the so-called facts. The facts as established by one historian hardly ever commend themselves in their entirety to his fellow-workers; and even if they do, historians are well aware that their accounts will in all likelihood be modified by their successors in the light of further evidence and new categories of explanation.

The *provisional* character of historical reconstructions is thus fully admitted, the more so because it is fully recognized today that the explanatory categories on the basis of which an historian constructs his account of the past are always those of the particular cultural context to which he belongs; e.g. an ancient Greek writer might explain a deterioration in the climate of his area as due to the anger of the gods; a modern writer will attribute it to the meteorological effects of large-scale deforestation. It is no accident that the modern account in that example is based on natural causes, because the modern historian's process of testing the evidence is essentially based on the presupposition that people and things in the past exhibited broadly the same character and modes of behaviour as the people and things of the present. Nothing the historian meets in the course of his normal work puts that presupposition in question; he is not normally con-

fronted with allegedly miraculous, or strictly unique, events. If he is, he is in no position to deny *a priori* that such events can have occurred; on the other hand, if a miracle does occur it robs him of the possibility of testing it and the accompanying events in the normal way, and pronouncing for or against their historicity. If, like most of his contemporaries, the historian has never himself experienced an unequivocal instance of the miraculous, or known anyone else who has, he will require an overwhelming weight of evidence before he accepts the occurrence of a miracle – in fact a weight so overwhelming that in practice it could never be forthcoming. His reaction to the idea of providence will be somewhat different. He will insist, again on the basis of experience, that all events appear to be parts of an interrelated web of scientific and historical causality, and that any event can be sufficiently accounted for on the basis of some combination of physical causality and human intentional behaviour. When he has explained an event in those terms he feels that, as an historian, he has fulfilled his task; if the suggestion is made that these factors in their turn are under the control of 'primary' causes which direct them towards some pre-determined end, he will feel that such questions lie outside his professional competence.

Naturally enough, the implications of this development for Christianity have been widely debated, though so far without any very conclusive results. At the risk of serious over-simplification, four main responses to the situation may be distinguished.

1. Initially, many believers denied outright that historical criticism was relevant to the Bible and the story of Christian origins, on the ground that the biblical accounts, being inspired, are exempt from all error of fact or interpretation. In that extreme form, this position has proved untenable, but claims originally associated with it are still put forward, e.g. that biblical passages such as Gen. 1–2, which appear to be advancing historical claims, cannot be convicted of error because, in spite of their historical form, their real concern is simply with theological truth.

2. A second response is to take over modern historical method (in fact quite largely hammered out in connection with work on biblical texts) *in toto* and apply it

to the Bible and the literature of the early church in exactly the same way that it would be applied to any other historical source. When this is done, the account which emerges tends to be framed in terms of normal or 'natural' factors; e.g. Jesus* is interpreted as an essentially human figure, even if he is held to have embodied in his life and teaching the perfect human relationship to God and the neighbour. By exponents of this approach the interpretative categories employed by the biblical and patristic writers (e.g. eschatological kingdom* of God, substance*, Incarnation*) are seen as part and parcel of the cultural milieu of the time, and so as needing to be modified or replaced, given the very different cultural conditions of the modern West.

If so, the implications of historical criticism for Christian doctrine are considerable, and some of them problematic. As explained above, historical reconstructions are always provisional, and in the case of the Bible, the quantity and quality of the evidence are such that reconstructions based upon it must often be very provisional indeed. For example, the evidence of the Gospels, when subjected to historical criticism, turns out not to provide the basis for anything like a full picture of Jesus, or indeed for any picture of him which commands a full consensus of competent scholarly opinion. How, it may be asked, can the shadowy and provisional figure which does emerge form the object for Christian faith and devotion?

More generally, traditionalists feel that this approach begs the essential question right from the start. As we have seen, it treats the Bible exactly in the same way as any other text and asks what would be deduced from it had it concerned ordinary figures of the past; but the claim of orthodoxy is precisely that the Bible is *not* an ordinary book and that the events it reports were *not* ordinary events. If this is right, any investigation which starts out with the contrary assumption is bound to be misleading both in its conclusions and its handling of evidence. Such a contention is obviously not without force, and it helps to explain a third way of trying to resolve the underlying problem, associated with the so-called 'mediating theology' which originated in Germany in the nineteenth century (H. J. Holtzmann) and has subsequently been popular in England.

3. On this view, it is perfectly proper to apply historical criticism to the Bible, but since God was uniquely at work in the events it relates, they may be expected to exhibit unusual, and indeed unique, characteristics; and historians must take account of this in applying their method to them. On such a basis it proves possible to accept much more of the biblical story at its face value – for example to arrive at a picture of Jesus broadly similar to that portrayed in the Gospels and requiring something like the explanatory categories of the NT itself to do him justice. The element of the provisional in the results arrived at is greatly reduced, and so are the general implications of historical criticism for religious faith.

However, the approach of this group of scholars is by no means free of difficulties, the nub of the matter being the *status* of the reconstruction they put forward. This reconstruction can hardly be described as 'historical' in the usual sense of having been subjected to the full rigour of historical criticism; for it is arrived at by weighting the evidence in favour of one particular interpretation in a way that can only be justified on the basis of a faith claim about the unique status of the events under investigation. Once again, the conclusion has already been smuggled in along with the premisses.

4. Partly for that reason a quite different way of dealing with the problem has been proposed, mainly by Lutheran scholars among whom are Barth, Bultmann and Tillich. These scholars fully concede the impossibility of arriving at any full or reasonably well-assured historical account of Jesus (see on 2, above). They go on to claim, however, that it has always been the Christ of the proclamation, and not the events of Jesus' earthly life, which has been regarded as the proper object of faith. Despite the fact that we can no longer reconstruct the detail of Jesus' life, it is perfectly reasonable to believe that God used it as the occasion for making available forgiveness and salvation. This is particularly the case if, as some of these scholars believe (e.g. Bornkamm, Käsemann, Fuchs), we can discover enough about Jesus to make clear how appropriate an occasion his life constituted. The decision whether to accept the proffered salvation has always to be made *sola fide*ature*, that is, by a pure act of faith which makes no attempt to establish or buttress itself on the essen-

tially partial and provisional findings of the historian. Consequently, however drastic the impact of historical criticism may be on the possibility of knowledge of the historical Jesus, it leaves completely untouched the possibility of faith-response to the Christ of the preaching.

It is difficult to disentangle the relative contributions of historical criticism, Lutheran theology and nineteenth-century German philosophy to the emergence of this approach, but the sharp distinction it makes between the gospel and the events which were the occasion of its proclamation marks it off very distinctly from traditional Christianity, and even from traditional Lutheranism. It has been attacked on the ground that it involves a 'flight from history' and a betrayal of the traditional insistence that it was through just the events reported in the Bible that salvation was accomplished, and that therefore the truth of Christianity stands or falls with the historical actuality of those events. To this the counter-charge is that such reliance on the historical actuality of contingent facts betrays a faithless dependence on the flesh which undermines the character of faith as faith.

It will thus be clear that no one has yet succeeded in finding a really satisfactory way of combining Christianity, in anything like its traditional form, with a thoroughgoing application of modern critical method to its historical title-deeds. Whether the conclusion to be drawn from that is that traditional Christianity needs radical rethinking, or that modern historical method needs purging of one or more false presuppositions, perhaps derived from the antireligious philosophy of the Enlightenment * is something which calls for further study and debate.

See also **Biblical Criticism**.

Marc Bloch, *The Historian's Craft*, 1954; R. G. Collingwood, *The Idea of History*, 1946; C. H. Dodd, *History and the Gospel*, 1938; Van Harvey, *The Historian and the Believer*, 1967; D. E. Nineham, *Explorations in Theology* 1, 1977, esp. chs. 6, 8 & 10; *The Use and Abuse of the Bible*, 1976; Alan Richardson, *History Sacred and Profane*, 1964.

DENNIS NINEHAM

History

In the late Middle Ages the scholar's attitude to history began to change. He no longer accepted the myths, the stories and other remnants of the past so much at their face value. He began to ask questions: who wrote this document, when did he write it and why; who read it and what did they think of it? He now looked for evidence which would support or refute possible answers to his questions. One of the earliest triumphs of the method was the demonstration of the spuriousness of the so-called *Donation of Constantine* in 1440 by Lorenzo Valla (1406–1457), an Italian humanist. Asking questions (which meant doubting received authority), asking for evidence, and accepting the results of free enquiry wherever they seemed to go, were always at the heart of the historical method. Of course, the questions were not always innocent questions: Valla, for example, wanted to attack papal power. Another landmark in the growth of the approach was the questioning of the Mosaic authorship of the Pentateuch by the Catholic scholar, Richard Simon (1638–1712). By the eighteenth century historians had begun to ask very general questions (about the rise and decline of states, for example), to which it was very hard to give sufficient answers. The professional historian was not, however, as is sometimes suggested by theological writers, automatically committed to disbelief in the possibility of the supernatural or the miraculous; his position required him, in the case of any allegedly miraculous event, to ask for the grounds of such claims, and, as Ernst Troeltsch (1865–1923) argued forcefully in *The Absoluteness of Christianity* (1901), he was bound to apply the same rules of criticism to Christian claims which he applied to alleged miraculous events in the history of other world-religions, miracles * which Christian writers themselves normally rejected, at least in part on the same grounds as those used by professional historians.

From the late eighteenth century onwards the study of history, stimulated by the Enlightenment's scepticism * about authority, was giving scholars a new understanding of time in terms of change, so that the OT and NT no longer seemed perpetually contemporary documents whose events could be pictured in the dress of one's own time, but had become documents from a dateable past which could be examined by normal historical methods. The historicization of the

Christian sacred writings was a slow process, not even now fully accepted by all theologians (*see also* **Biblical Criticism**). For much of the nineteenth century, in fact, Christian scholars who applied historical method to the Bible did so on the assumption that in the long run there would emerge an agreed account of the historical Jesus*, whose teaching and example would prove to be acceptable by 'modern man'. Historical method would both clarify and confirm the truth of Christianity in its essentials. However, such an agreed outcome – 'the results of NT criticism' – was never likely. Already in the eighteenth century Hermann Reimarus (1694–1768), a Deist* intellectual, had interpreted the career of Jesus, as described in the NT, as that of a Jewish politician who failed to seize power in Jerusalem; it was only after his death that his disciples built the system of a spiritual suffering saviour of the whole human race. Reimarus showed, once and for all, that one could give a coherent historical interpretation of primitive Christianity without any appeal to the supernatural, and his work in this direction was followed by that of D. F. Strauss (1808–1874), Ernest Renan (1823–1892), and F. Nietzsche (1844–1900). Reimarus and Strauss emphasized the creative role of the community, Renan and Nietzsche the brilliance of an isolated religious personality, but none of them thought it necessary to use the idea of a unique, divine, incarnational intervention in the series of historical events (*see also* **Jesus**). Nietzsche emphasized that the absence of adequate parallel non-Christian material from the primitive period, together with the briefness of the NT itself, made the historian's task virtually impossible in the strict sense: there would always be more hypotheses than available evidence. It was inevitable that Christian theologians should react against a historical process which was secularizing the sacred books, and which could be summed up in the axiom of the German philosopher, G. E. Lessing (1729–1781), the editor of Reimarus' work, that no accidental truths of history could ever become the proof of necessary truths of reason. Lessing had rejected Christianity because it required unconditional assent to allegedly historical events, like the resurrection* of Jesus, which could not be given the absolute certainty required before one could make

them the basis of religious commitment.

In reply, the Danish theologian, Søren Kierkegaard (1813–1855), tried to reduce the dependence of Christianity on history to a minimum: 'If the contemporary generation had left nothing behind them but these words: "We have believed that in such and such a year the God appeared among us in the humble figure of a servant, that he lived and taught in our community, and finally died," it would be more than enough' – more than enough, because it would set the modern seeker on the track of the self-revelation which God would give in response to faith. There was no historical problem because Christianity had no history, because salvation came through the immediate encounter with a Christ who is always our contemporary: 'there is no disciple at second-hand'. Kierkegaard's argument, that all we historically need, and what we have, is a record of the faith of the first disciples, has often been repeated in one form or another down to the present day.

The argument is obviously not decisive, because it does not really break completely with a historical base. The critical historian may say, for example, that although the events of Jesus' career might have seemed to demand interpretation in terms of a unique and final divine intervention if they were experienced through the presuppositions of some parts of the Jewish culture of that time, they would not necessarily demand that interpretation, given observers with different presuppositions. Indeed, critics have even raised the further question as to whether it is really possible for twentieth-century observers to enter empathetically into the alien culture of the ancient world in which the Gospels are embedded (see, e.g. D. E. Nineham, *New Testament Interpretation in an Historical Age*, 1976). This is why, in the first half of the twentieth century, Protestant theologians like Karl Barth said that it was only as a consequence of the gift of faith* that a scholar was enabled to grasp the true meaning of the text of the NT; the historian could only write footnotes to the insights of faith, which itself guaranteed, for example, the truth of the assertion of the resurrection* of Jesus, whatever comment the historian might make. A more cautious version of this position, popular in England, has held that the presuppositions of faith are at least as plausible as those of the sceptical historian. This view sounds reasonable as long as the issue is defined by the parameters of Western culture, religious and secular, but loses much of its cogency if the historian insists that the history of Christianity must be related to the history of other world religions which make similar claims (*see also* **Christianity and Other Religions**). In any case, to say that a presuppositionless examination of the NT is not possible is not automatically to justify whatever tradition of dogmatic interpretation the theologian may hold.

The development of historical studies during the eighteenth century also came into conflict with the overall Christian theological understanding of history*. The classical Christian view, which derived from the Bible via Augustine's *City of God* (413–426, *see also* **Augustinianism**), thought of human history as a process moving in a linear direction from creation and fall to a triumphant, restitutionary conclusion which lay outside the temporal sequence in a community of resurrected believers united in the faith of Christ. This picture of history assumed recurrent divine intervention. For Augustine, the secular history of man, the life of the earthly city, was only a detour in the movement towards the final salvation and judgment. The historians of the Enlightenment* rejected these Christian presuppositions, but did not altogether succeed in substituting their own. They were so deeply influenced by the Christian tradition that they still thought that history must have unity, a meaning and a goal which could be worked out from the study of history itself. A new, speculative, non-Christian history flourished, especially in the writings of Hegel and Marx, both of whom believed that they could show how an autonomous* historical process would finally generate a perfect social and individual freedom. In the course of the nineteenth century, however, confidence in such speculative systems, however elaborately related, as in the case of Karl Marx, to historical data, waned steadily; twentieth-century historians work with regulative ideas, but they no longer expect to organize these into coherent systems of universal explanation. (In the case of Marxism, see E. P. Thompson, *The Poverty of Theory*, 1979, for a devastating attack on its theoretical rigidity.) It is partly because of this, and partly because of the chaos of the

period, that Christian interpretations of history, usually close to the Augustinian model, have reappeared in the twentieth century. Among the theologians and historians involved have been Nicholas Berdyaev, Herbert Butterfield, Christopher Dawson, Karl Löwith, Reinhold Niebuhr and Arnold Toynbee. These authors generally agreed in criticizing secular theories of human history on the ground that they were satisfied with finite, immanent meaning to the exclusion of any transcendent dimension to human life. The Christian thinkers asserted, on the contrary, that the historical process did not make sense in its own terms – that it accumulated, instead of solving, the problems of human existence, and that only by accepting the transcendent standpoint of Christian eschatology* could one glimpse the meaning which God gave to human history when he intervened to bring it to a halt in a final judgment. The Catholic historian, Lord Acton (1834–1902), said that if one believed in God one had to believe in some degree of progress in history, however slight; but his successors, like Augustine in the days of the collapsing Roman Empire, were tempted to give up hope in the present age and to look for a transcendent meaning which lay beyond, not in, history.

Finally, the historical approach has inevitably been applied to theology itself, as part of the history of ideas (*see also* **Historical Criticism**). The traditional view was that only the theological history of the theoretically undivided ecclesia – down to AD 451 – mattered, and that this contained a sufficient elucidation of scripture and tradition. This position remained embedded in early twentieth-century British degree courses in theology, but since 1945 the importance of the historical study of what has happened to Christian theology in the modern period, that is, since about 1700, has been slowly recognized. Theologians face the problem: does Christian theology develop in history, and if it does, are the changes which take place more than a question of restatement in language adapted to a particular period (*see* **Development, Doctrinal**)? J. H. Newman, in his *Essay on the Development of Christian Doctrine* (1845), put the conservative case for development by addition: new dogmas* – infallibility*, for example – developed in the living ecclesia over long periods of time until it was possible for the whole body, in which Newman included the laity (though the Vatican did not) to affirm the dogma through the appropriate institutions. There was no question for Newman of subtracting from the inherited dogmatic system, and the demand for this – notably for the abandonment of the concept of eternal punishment – was characteristic of Liberal Protestantism * and the Catholic Modernists * at the start of the twentieth century. Orthodox theologians maintain that revelation, once given, has no essential history and there is no ground for abandoning given dogma; thus the documents of the twentieth-century Ecumenical Movement assert that the Holy Spirit works through ecclesiastical institutions, especially the episcopate, to maintain the faith which has been handed down. It is the critical theologian (it would be said) who is susceptible to 'history': this is the source of his errors. There is little common ground between this position and that of the critical historian of theology who, at least since Ernst Troeltsch, has argued that orthodoxy has been as historically conditioned as its counterpart. The critical historical view was always latent from the sixteenth century in the conflict between Roman Catholic and Protestant apologists.

H. Butterfield, *Christianity and History*, 1943; Van A. Harvey, *The Historian and the Believer*, 1967; H. S. Hughes, *Consciousness and Society*, 1958; S. Kierkegaard, *Philosophical Fragments*, 1967; K. Löwith, *Meaning in History*, 1949; J. Maritain, *On the Philosophy of History*, 1957; H. Meyerhoff, *The Philosophy of History in our Time*, 1959; R. Niebuhr, *Faith and History*, 1949; H. Palmer, *The Logic of Gospel Criticism*, 1968; K. R. Popper, *The Poverty of Historicism*, 1957; A. Richardson, *History Sacred and Profane*, 1964.

JOHN KENT

History of Religions School
see Religionsgeschichtliche Schule

Holy, The

Except for those views which stress radical discontinuity between Christianity and culture, Christian understanding of holiness includes general religious claims as well as specific Jewish claims about the holy, yet goes beyond them in relating all holiness to Jesus Christ.

In general culture, the holy designates the peculiar quality of the 'religious' and indicates a sharp distinction between the ordinary and the special by virtue of the threatening or benevolent presence of a non-human power. That presence provides order, orientation, life, sustenance and meaning to existence in space and time, a dimension of 'otherness', primal and foundational, upon which everything in creation depends, yet which is not subject to human manipulation or control. It is 'wholly other', in that space and time receive an orientation and meaning from the outside which qualify and relativize the level spectrum of equal 'spaces' and 'moments': an axial centre to space (*axis mundi*) and a decisive moment to time (*illud tempus*). The primal, altogether 'other' quality of holiness entails both an ultimate *threat* and an ultimate *blessing*, giving rise to a distinction between the sacred and the profane. The profane is the ordinary and possesses only the power or significance it generates on its own. The sacred is that which is infused with the holy and draws persons into a power/significance that is given and indestructible, not subject to human designations and achievements in ordinary space and time. Hence, there are specific holy places, holy persons, holy ceremonies and holy events. Holiness requires these designations, but they function as holy only because these 'special' centres of power and presence recreate or recover primal and foundational dimensions for ordinary existence. Rudolf Otto suggested the words *numen* and *numinous* for this definitive and peculiar quality of the religious, describing it also as overwhelming and fascinating mystery (*mysterium tremendum et fascinans*).

Judaism gives special content to holiness, particularly through the text of Leviticus ('You shall therefore be holy, for I am holy,' Lev. 11.45) and the explicit combining of the category of goodness (morality) with that of holiness in Isaiah: 'Holy, holy, holy is the Lord of hosts ... the whole earth is full of his glory ... Woe is me! for I am lost; for I am a man of unclean lips and I dwell in the midst of a people of unclean lips; for mine eyes have seen the King, the Lord of hosts' (Isa. 6.3, 5). For Judaism, holiness becomes the peculiar designation of God and the most decisive and comprehensive requirement upon the covenant people. In the Isaiah passage, the relation of the holy to morality becomes explicit, not as if morality is added to the *numinous*, but because holiness includes morality although it is more than morality, and because the 'lostness' of the prophet, mentioned immediately afterwards, includes unworthiness, although it is more than unworthiness. Otto makes that relation clear when he describes the holy as a complex category containing the moral, aesthetic and rational along with the non-rational category of the *numinous*. Further, in Judaism, there is a critical shift from space to time as the dominant locus of the manifestation of the Holy. The Exodus/Sinai event and the enacting of a covenant between God and God's people is an event within time breaking a temporal cycle and giving time the quality of irreversibility: past, present and future. The Jews cannot return to prehistory nor can they hasten the coming of the future reign of God. But they are marked as a people by a revelation which calls them to prepare for and await the coming of the Messiah *, the dawn of the messianic age. They live between creation and redemption and they are given a revelation in a 'holy event' in time (Martin Buber).

Whereas Judaism responded to the holy under the dominance of vocation and expectation, Christianity makes new claims for the holy under the dominance of realization, without, however, excluding vocation (*ekklesia*) and expectation (hope). For Christians, holiness is supremely manifest in the mystery of Jesus the Christ, in whose life, teaching, death and resurrection the powers of righteousness and love of God's kingdom are already present. Everything that sustains and redeems the creation as well as everything that cleanses and purifies and fulfils, that empowers faith, hope and love, is understood in relation to the holiness manifest in Jesus Christ. For the Christian community, both the culturally specific and the most general and universal dimensions of history have their centre in the holiness of Jesus Christ. Handel chose the words from Rev. 6.15; 19.6, 16, to express this in the Hallelujah Chorus of *Messiah*. Until the full coming of God's kingdom, however, there remains much tension within Christianity between an exclusivistic emphasis on belief in Christ as the only way to the holiness of God and an inclusivistic emphasis on God's

holy love for all people which the church knows and serves in and through Jesus Christ. In either case, holiness is acknowledged as hovering over all claims to power, beauty, goodness and truth, confirming and purifying them and pointing them towards God, the Holy One, as their creative ground and final sanction.

M. Buber, *The Prophetic Faith*, ET 1949; M. Eliade, *The Sacred and the Profane*, 1957; R. Otto, *The Idea of the Holy*, ET 1917; *Religious Essays*, ET 1931; G. van der Leeuw, *Sacred and Profane Beauty*, ET 1963.

JACK S. BOOZER

Holy Spirit

The Holy Spirit (*to pneuma hagion*) is understood by Christians as the divine agent who brings about the transcreation, or the culmination of human and cosmic liberation, since he perfects the Father's creative and the Son's recreative mission in history. For this reason, the Spirit is confessed as antecedently in himself the Transcreator who is identical in being with the Father-Creator and the Son-Recreator. Pneumatology is the theological science which seeks to relate in a consistent manner and to situate in a soteriological context both the temporal function and the eternal essence of the Holy Spirit. Many scholars ascribe the previous neglect of this discipline to the particularly controversial debates it has fomented among various Christian groups through the centuries; early strife concerning the nature of the Spirit was settled, but later discord was foreshadowed in the Symbol of the Council of Constantinople in AD 381: 'And we believe in the Holy Spirit, the Lord and Giver of life, who proceeds from the Father (and the Son), who together with the Father and the Son is worshipped and glorified, who has spoken through the prophets.' Besides the schism between Eastern and Western Christianity, caused in part by the words in parentheses which theologians in the West later added in the form of the Latin word *filioque* *, the ambiguous definition of the Holy Spirit as Giver of life continues to divide Catholic and Protestant theologians. The former tend to stress that the scriptures themselves recognize a universal, life-giving and salvific function of the Spirit of the Father before and after the Christ-event *, while the latter generally respond that the

Spirit's vivifying function rightly affirms his essential submission to the Son; as the Giver of life, the Spirit of Jesus Christ is properly the source only of the new, redeemed existence granted to Christians.

Despite these persistent problems, there is a growing consensus among Christian theologians that they can gain new insights into the ontological* or immanent nature of the Holy Spirit only through constant analysis of his salvific or economic activity within cosmic and human history. Therefore, contemporary pneumatology must provide an ecumenical clarification and harmonization of the three concomitant domains in which the Holy Spirit acted and acts: first, in creation itself which includes the history of religions and the special place of Judaism; second, in the initiation, success and prolongation of the Christ-event; and third, in the world at large within which Christians live in faith, serve in love and wait in hope until the consummation of all things. Consequently, any adequate theology of the Holy Spirit must explain how the one Giver of life is he who speaks for the Father-Creator through religion and through the prophets (*Spiritus Patris*), facilitates the mission and glorification of the Son-Recreator in history (*Spiritus Christi*), and continues to animate the church's message, sacraments and pilgrimage in society, all of which already prefigure and are oriented towards a final goal, everlasting participation in the kingdom of God (*Spiritus Redemptor*). For these reasons, instead of following the usual practice of treating biblical, patristic and doctrinal data separately, this presentation of the Holy Spirit sets out to integrate the traditional material within a discussion of the currently debated issues, and thus to adhere to the scheme Creator-Recreator-Transcreator with regard to the Spirit's mission and being.

1. *The Holy Spirit as Spiritus Creator.* Recently both Catholic and Protestant theologians have reacted against an exclusively christocentric* approach to pneumatology, since such a starting point usually emphasizes the valid pedagogical and governing, but not the primary life-giving and sanctifying activities of the Holy Spirit. When Christian pneumatology begins, however, with reflections taken from the ethnology and sociology of religion, it can rest its intellectual foundation on documented findings that in many cultures an inchoate notion of the immanent spirit of divine mystery produces greater social unity and clearer understanding of the cosmos and of life. Spirit can be described as the outreaching, intercessory and unifying power of the divine which affects matter from within, so that the forms of life can emerge and so that human existence can be spiritual and free. Whatever name it gives the transcendent reality, tribal religion does not perceive it as disinterested in the universe or in human community but, in paradoxical fashion, as directly present to all things through their mediation. In this immediate-mediate way, divine power can especially enliven and renew human beings, while it directs them and all things to itself. The religious person spontaneously intuits this spiritual presence in such gratuitous human undertakings as art, law-making, ethics, religion and worship, without which groups of persons might resort to socially retrogressive egoism (magic) rather than strive for that cohesion with matter, among themselves and with other communities, which befits human existence as corporeal, interpersonal and transtribal reality (prophecy). At a time when it is imperative to lead modern persons to the credibility and practicality of faith in God as Spirit, a Christian pneumatology in dialogue with the social sciences yields perceptions of various independent concepts of the presence of divine spirit in human society itself, and thus places religion and pneumatology in a global and communitarian context from the outset.

Furthermore, this anthropological approach to the reality of the immanent spirit of the transcendent is central to the thought process of the scriptures. The OT authors made a consistent effort to situate the spiritual renewal arising from the Exodus-event within a wider salvific framework; they find the basis of Yahweh's regenerative work in his previous and continuing nearness to all animated things as life-giving breath (*rūah*). Similarly the NT attempts to root the unwarranted newness of life bestowed on Christ's followers at Pentecost in the Spirit's enduring vitalization of humanity and especially of Israel; the intense renovative activity of the Father's Spirit in Christ and in the church finds its condition of possibility in a widely diffused pneumatic presence. Thus, in making the transition from a universal to a particular concept of spirit, Jewish and Christian theologians concede the precedence of the *experience* of the Spirit's recreative power over *reflection* on its overarching creative function. Yet, logic itself demands that consideration of the Spirit's cosmic role in the created order (natural theology) form the background against which its specific role in behalf of humanity's recreation (revealed truth) can be grasped and appreciated. Along with Judaism, Christianity not only recognizes the identity of the Spirit of the covenant with the Spirit of creation, but also insists that the former mode of acting presupposes the latter as its very ground. In effect, the revealed data concerning the Spirit confirm the validity of a natural or implicit pneumatology; the ubiquitous presence of the Spirit as life-giver proves to be the substructure of its revelatory capacity as life-restorer; if this were not the case, the divine Spirit would be the transcendent and immanent goal, but not the correspondingly omnipotent source of human life.

Thus, in the OT the Spirit of Yahweh is viewed both as the identifiable agent of Israel's achieved as well as awaited redemption, and as the hidden divine agent of humanity's very life and innate knowledge of the transcendent. As the revealed power of Yahweh, the Spirit strengthens the judges, anoints the kings and inspires the prophets in order to bring the covenant, the divine alliance with humanity (creation), to ever greater fulfilment within Israel's history (recreation); since the definitive attainment of redemption was gradually projected further into the future messianic time, the Spirit also took on an eschatological role in Judaism (transcreation). Numerous prophetic passages foretell an unprecedented outpouring of the Spirit which will renew Israel when the charismatic servant appears as the inaugurator of an endless period of religious and national prosperity. It is notable that the Spirit of Yahweh will effect not only the interior rebirth of persons but also the material and political well-being of the entire people, since the Hebrew notion of salvation invariably involves justice and community. Interwoven in this specific story of liberation, however, is the Spirit's accompanying function as the hidden agent of

human life and holiness. As the breath of the Creator and as his wisdom, the Spirit acts within as well as beyond Israel to accomplish a single end, yet in different, co-ordinate ways. Consequently, in Jewish pneumatology the power of Yahweh is attributed creative, recreative and trans-creative roles, all of which manifest the divine intention to lead persons, along with the matter which sustains them and the social structures which they fashion, through history to a transhistorical share in divine life and holiness.

Moreover, Jewish pneumatology, both in its covenantal and sapiential traditions, links the divine *rūah* with another attribute of Yahweh, that is, his Word or communicableness (*dābār*). These two descriptions of Yahweh's outreach to Israel and to humanity are inseparable, since on the one hand the Spirit acts to elicit the creature's hearing and acceptance of the Word, and on the other the Word acts to fulfil the creature's attentiveness to and receptability for it through the Spirit's immanent mediation. Through the joint exercise of these divine properties, Yahweh can communicate himself to and be assimilated by human persons, with the result that their minds and hearts, by sharing in divine being, come to self-possession and are freed to know and love the world as the Creator's gift. In the context of Judaism's strict monotheism*, these two qualities of Yahweh's inscrutable essence, despite their ability to advance human personhood, cannot be considered personal in any sense. Yet, Christian theologians claim that the human spirit is an image of the personal character not only of Yahweh (memory) but also of his Word (knowledge) and his Spirit (love), so that Augustine's psychological model of the Trinity* serves to show that in the structure of human personality there is a divinely intended means to help humanity arrive at the reasonableness of revelation. In similar fashion, mediaeval thinkers such as Aquinas maintain that the *vestigia trinitatis* in creatura*, traces of God's one-in-threeness inherent in the creature and implicitly acknowledged in the Jewish writings, affords the basis of human apprehension of the Trinity. K. Barth, however, restates the classical Protestant stance concerning the *vestigia creaturae in trinitate*, opposing natural theology's penchant for grounding in reason a mystery that can be known solely through faith; revelation attests that there is in the triune God's being a vestige of the creature, and not vice versa.

Irenaeus was the first Christian theologian who systematically attempted to expound the collaboration of the Word and the Spirit in all Yahweh's actions by employing the graphic image of the 'two hands of God'. K. Rahner follows in this tradition by proposing for the same purpose a paired series of terms which are derived from experience: origin and future, history and transcendence, gift and acceptance, knowledge and love. The second term of each pair yields insight into the specific identity and activity of the Spirit of the Creator. As the *future* of the Word's being and acting for creation, the Spirit is sent by Yahweh from the beginning of time to guarantee that the eventual glory of the Word who originates all things is proleptically operative in them. As the *transcendence* of the Word, the Spirit of Yahweh furnishes creation with a perduring state of readiness and reciprocity, so that the advent of the Word in space and time be prepared, actuated and perpetuated. What is given is effective only if it is received; as the intradivine *acceptance* of the Word, the Spirit acts as such in history by rendering creation innately capable of freely accepting the self-gift of Yahweh which is never imposed but always offered to it. What is known is appropriated to the self only if it is loved; as in himself the divine *love* of the Word, the Spirit subsequently accompanies Yahweh's self-communication as Word in history, so that the human spirit is enabled to be not only a receptacle of the knowledge of the Word but also a channel of its propagation through love. Such reflections, admittedly informed by the Christ-event but aimed at presenting the subtle and self-effacing activity and nature of Yahweh's Spirit, interpret the Giver of life first of all as the cosmic *Spiritus Creator* whose essential union with the Word, though sometimes not evident, is always operative and efficacious. When other Christian theologians, such as P. Tillich, C. F. D. Moule and H. Mühlen, also underline the universal dimension of Jewish and Christian pneumatology by affirming that the Spirit is sent to all humanity by the Father (*ex patre*), they do not do so at the expense of the *filioque* tradition. Their purpose is to urge Christian theologians to consider humankind's renewal by the Spirit of the Son as an entirely unmerited gift, but nevertheless as one always capable of being received because of the cosmic activity of the same Spirit in his capacity as animating power of the Creator.

2. *The Holy Spirit as Spiritus Recreator.* Another related factor in contemporary pneumatology is the rediscovery of the primary model by which the NT authors comprehend Jesus Christ's being and mission: Spirit christology. To counterweigh the dominance of Word christology in the West, scholars are re-evaluating and developing the main advantages of viewing Jesus of Nazareth against a decidedly pneumatic and universal horizon. First, this approach is faithful to the Synoptic and Johannine presentations of Jesus as the one anointed without measure by the Holy Spirit of Yahweh; as the privileged bearer of the Creator's power, Jesus is the unique Recreator who through his ministry, suffering and exaltation becomes in turn the sender of the Spirit-Transcreator. Second, this model, while not negating the central tenet of Word christology – that Jesus' flesh is united substantially to the person of the Word from his conception – does account for the process of growth which the human nature of Jesus undergoes as he *becomes who he is*. This evolution, not in Jesus' divinity but in his humanity, is the work of the Spirit, since only Yahweh's creative love can join the Word to human flesh so that humanity itself is pervaded and renewed by divinity; it is the sanctification of human nature which patristic writers, such as Theodore of Mopsuestia and Hilary of Poitiers, regarded as the proper salvific activity of the Spirit in the human flesh assumed by the Word. Third, as the intradivine future, transcendence, acceptance and love of the Word, the Spirit permits the Word who enters history to have a lasting, temporal, free and heartfelt effect on the flesh to which he is joined; in Jesus Christ the recreative intention of Yahweh comes to humankind once for all, while at the same time his humanity accepts this offer in the name of all. In effect, Yahweh is the giver, the Word the gift, and the Spirit the giving; in the Spirit Yahweh gives his Word to humankind, and in the Spirit humankind

gives its acceptance to Yahweh's Word. The Spirit thus allows Jesus of Nazareth to become who he is, both the Recreator and the Recreated, in one person the Word historically offered and the Word effectively received.

A pneumatic christology also explains how the Spirit, in sanctifying Jesus' flesh, communicates to him, and through him to all humanity, the identity of Yahweh as Abba, or intimate Father. The Spirit is the transcendent-immanent medium which permits the incarnate Word to be, to know himself and to be known as united to the Father in a special filial bond; thus the Spirit-filled human nature of Jesus is indispensable in revealing the divine and personal identity of the Word as the Father's only Son. Moreover, these historical disclosures which are made possible through the intercessory power of the Spirit raise the further question about the essential nature of this divine mediation. Can the power of the Father which acts in history as the necessary medium through which the Son in the flesh exists, knows himself and is revealed as such, be anything less than divine and personal? The Macedonians or Pneumatomachians (opponents of the Spirit) responded by advancing a variation on Arius' position regarding the Son; they asserted that the Spirit is a godlike creature inferior both to the supreme Father and to the first of created beings, the Word. A revitalized Spirit christology, it seems, can illumine and confirm the correctness of the definition concerning the personal divinity of the Spirit which was proclaimed at Constantinople. If the economic role of the Spirit is that of personally assuring that the incarnate Word be revealed as Son of the Father, the Spirit must previously, or in himself, or immanently be the divine and personal intermediary, since how the Spirit *acts* depends on who the Spirit *is*. The Spirit could not function in the economy of salvation as the mediator between the Father and the Son if on the ontological level the Spirit were not the personal relation of the Father to the Son and vice versa. In other words, if either the function or the being of the Spirit were not divine and personal, salvation could not reach humankind, since the being and action of the Father and the Son would prove themselves ineffective in human history, and thus antecedently powerless in themselves.

Admittedly, Word christology often overlooks the Spirit's sanctifying activity in the humanity of Jesus by insisting on the absolute difference between him and all other bringers of salvation. Yet, Spirit christology can lead to an equally inadequate result, namely Ebionism (*see* **Christology**) or Adoptionism*. This early Jewish-Christian position accented a soteriological theme; it held that Jesus stood on humanity's side in the struggle with evil, merited his glory, and became the Messiah as his purely human nature was guided by the Spirit towards ever greater appropriation of salvific and divine status. In effect, Word christology tends to be solely a Father-Son theology which, while preserving the Spirit's action from above at the incarnation, practically excludes the Spirit from the historical dialogue between the incarnate Word and the Father; Spirit christology, in turn, is prone to be simply a Father-Spirit theology which, though it safeguards the Spirit's soteriological action from below until the glorification of Jesus, neglects the ontological role of the Word in the Father's messianic design, and attributes it instead to the Spirit. Pneumatology is currently much discussed, since it promises to offer a solution to the impasse caused by two conflicting viewpoints: one states that there is no becoming whatsoever in Jesus, since he is from the moment of his conception the absolute saviour whose humanity is already sanctified by union with the Word; the other claims that Jesus has in some sense freely to engage in an inter-personal transaction with the Father, that his fidelity earns his eventual promotion, and that he becomes that which he is not beforehand, if it is really humanity which is saved absolutely in his person and mission within creation. Not all theologians would agree with the above-mentioned compromise: by the power of the Holy Spirit, the Word *becomes* in the flesh (functional aspect) the one who he always *is*, the Father's only Son (ontological aspect). G. W. H. Lampe would veer from such a trinitarian to a unitarian interpretation of the Spirit's work in Christ; God is simply Spirit, so that insofar as he is divine in himself he is called Father, and insofar as he acts divinely in Jesus he is called Son. P. Schoonenberg and others criticize this merely functional or adverbial (acting divinely) description of Jesus' person and mission which is based on a thoroughly pneumatological concept of God.

Theologians employ such triads as Fashioner-Refashioner-Transfashioner or Creator-Recreator-Transcreator to speak not only of the Father, the Son and the Spirit respectively, but also of the Spirit either in relation to the Father, to the Son, to both, or in himself. The need for these terms reflects the difficulty of adhering to Christian monotheism * and trinitarianism while at the same time not advocating unitarianism or tritheism. One root, like fashioner or creator, is repeated three times so as to indicate the unity not only in divine being itself but also in divine revelation, while two different prefixes are added in order to explain the threeness within the Godhead which must be posited because of the three different roles the one God assumes in the drama of salvation. With such linguistic innovations, theologians reiterate the One Nature * and the Three Persons * of traditional dogma in a more contemporary and understandable vocabulary. In modern times the technical word Person, which originally did not connote an individual being but a state of being-in-relation, has become particularly problematic since it usually implies independence and singularity. To offset any suspicion that Christianity in effect espouses tritheism, K. Barth translates Person as 'way of being', and K. Rahner opts for 'way of subsisting'. These major twentieth-century theologians fully intend to avoid Modalism *, the view that there is a fourth, real God behind the Father, Son and Spirit, and that the latter are only modes in which the hidden God partially reveals himself, but not essential relations which belong to him. Despite their assurances that this is not what they mean, both thinkers are accused of failing to appreciate the rich denotations of the concept Person, and of dwelling instead on its troublesome ambiguity. J. Moltmann and W. Kasper suggest that theologians seriously reappraise G. W. F. Hegel's understanding of person which centres on the intuition that, the more one enters into community, the more one is oneself. Thus, the Word and the Spirit, as well as the Father, are persons in the fullest, communitarian sense of the term. The unoriginate Father does not duplicate his personhood twice because he ceaselessly generates the Son, and with him eternally breathes forth the Spirit. Rather, the intra-divine processions correspond to revelation, since they point out that true personhood consists in total self-giving. As Creator-Recreator-Transcreator, the one God is the essence of being-in-community and thus both the origin of personhood itself and the sole end to which all persons are called.

3. *The Holy Spirit as Spiritus Transcreator.* Contemporary pneumatology also stresses the forward thrust towards the fully realized kingdom which is contained in the third credal section. Ironically Christian theology largely ignores the Spirit's eschatological activity in its interpretation of the very articles of faith referring to his transforming power. Orthodox theologians, like N. Nissiotis, often lament the absence of pneumatological perspectives in Catholic and Protestant treatises on the church, the sacraments and the eschaton; it is imperative that the pneumatic model of christology exert a determining influence on ecclesiology; after the Christ-event, the Spirit must be regarded as acting in the church, until the consummation of the world, in a way parallel to his activity in Jesus. If the tendency to christomonism is to be overcome in the West, pneumatology and ecclesiology can no longer be understood as mere corollaries to christology (the Spirit empowers the magisterial and gubernatorial role of Christ's church); rather, the existence of Christ and of Christians should be treated within the framework of an eschatologically oriented pneumatology (the Spirit directs Christ and his church towards the eschaton). Thus, J. Moltmann proposes that Christian theology, while it admits the validity of placing the Spirit last in the originative movement of the Trinity (Father → Son → Spirit), should not view the Spirit as simply submissive to the Father and the Son. After Pentecost, the Spirit-Transcreator furthers the mission of the Creator and the Recreator by adjoining to the originative an eschatological movement of the Trinity (Spirit → Son → Father). Seen in this way, the Holy Spirit enjoys the pivotal historical role as the culmination of the originative movement from the Father and the Son and as the initiator of the eschatological movement towards the final coming of the Son and the full revelation of the Father. Thus the Creator and the Recreator first meet and then redirect the human person through the mediation of

the Transcreator; the Spirit not only facilitates the openness of the Father and the Son to creation but also prepares humanity for its future in the divine community as he leads all things back to the Son (or forward towards him), and with him, into the glory of the Father.

Without denying that Christ is the primary sacrament both of the Father's redeeming love in history and of the human person's redeemed response to it, it can be said that the Holy Spirit is the equally important sacrament of the Father's end-time glory and of the person's participation in it. Precisely as the sacrament of the kingdom, the Transcreator is divine; if he were not, humanity's definitive redemption by the Father and the Son would remain an objective historical truth but not an interior transformative reality now and in the future. The soteriological argument presented here is an eschatologically formulated variation on the Cappadocians' * and Athanasius' theological defence of the divinity of the Holy Spirit. As the sacrament of the end-time, the Spirit creates in the world the charismatic * and institutional community of saints which is in itself a prelusive realization of the eschaton. Enlivened by the Spirit, the church is both already one, holy, universal and apostolic, and not yet fully such. Ecclesial existence in the time between the times, that is, between Christ's first and last advents, is a new existence only in the Holy Spirit, since in himself the Transcreator is the eschatological power of the triune God, and thus the divine pledge of the parousia's ultimate arrival. It follows that each of the main tasks of the church is in itself a pneumatic or eschatological action: preaching the Word is announcing and extending the continuous and final exaltation of the New Man, Jesus Christ; celebrating the sacraments is prefiguring in time the Omega's recreation of the heavens and the earth; building and maintaining a community of love in history is anticipating the reunion of all humanity with the risen Christ in the Father's glory. These rediscovered pneumatological perspectives account for the many recent works on baptism as a foretaste of eternal and just life, and on the eucharist as an antepast of the heavenly and fraternal banquet, both of which spur Christians to a just and fraternal style of living. Even the Catholic position on transubstantiation *

might find broader acceptance if it were explained as a pneumatic event through which consecrated matter participates in its own final destiny. Instead of seeking to escape the world by entering into the totally sacred dimension, recipients of the new creation in its sacramental form engage themselves in the Spirit's epicleptic mission for the transformation of society.

With the emergence of inculturation and liberation as theological issues, the Christian churches are being challenged to discern what their role in the cultural and social spheres should be in the light of what the Spirit might be accomplishing beyond their evangelical and sacramental ministries. For Luther, the question of the believer's responsibility for the secular realm properly belongs under the first and not the third article of the Creed; since the Spirit's universal task is solely that of bringing the justification won by Christ to existential recognition and acceptance, it is rather the Father's work in the created order that Christians should foster. Modern Protestant authors, like H. Berkhof and W. Pannenberg, do attribute to the Spirit a wider cosmic mission as the agent of the consummation of all things; what he accomplishes first and foremost in the church, the Spirit also works to realize, and perhaps at times anticipates, in every authentic social movement aimed at human freedom. The Catholic and Orthodox communities generally consider the life of grace (created experience of the Spirit), which is available to all persons and comes to full expression in the liturgy of the church, as the primary work of the Spirit (uncreated grace in person), but immediately add that the efficacy and credibility of grace necessitate an active commitment on the part of its recipients to public life where the Spirit is groaning with suffering humanity. Though P. Teilhard de Chardin does not insinuate, as do Joachim of Fiore and G. W. F. Hegel, that the Spirit is still arriving or becoming himself through the evolutionary process, he does point to the divine Spirit's immanent transforming presence in the geosphere, the biosphere and the noosphere as the foundation of Christian secular involvement and as its transcendent guarantee of success. Other Catholic theologians, such as B. Lonergan, J. B. Metz and J. Segundo, would conclude from diverse starting points that the self-transcendence of humanity, in the form of consciousness, culture and politics, is a genuine experience of the Spirit's transcreative power. Christians judge the validity of an experience of the Spirit by discerning whether or not it induces individuals to find themselves only in giving way implicitly or explicitly to the supremacy of Christ, the fullness of truth, justice and peace.

What further theological research is needed to ground the Spirit's cosmic function of advancing the final glory of the Son and the Father, a biblical and patristic theme greatly disregarded in the past, but now prominent because of the modern concern for the future of human history? Three areas seem to demand attention: fundamental reflection on pneumatology within the matrix of a future-oriented metaphysics; historical analysis of the secular ramifications of belief in and action based on the Spirit's transcreative power; concrete inculturation of Spirit theology in diverse regions with a view to a cross-cultural Christian effort to shape social structures in a way which reflects humanity's fulfilment in the just and fraternal reign of the Trinity. No doubt, previous speculation about the proximity of the parousia led to utopian*, chiliastic* and enthusiastic* distortions of Christian pneumatology; the constant and painful Christian ministry of overcoming the human misery caused by injustice and hatred is not a central theme in such millenarian visions as those advocated by the Spiritual Franciscans or the Moravian Brethren. Yet, not to probe deeper into the content of Christian hope, the anthropological dimension of pneumatology, would be to leave unanswered not only atheistic denials of the relevance of eschatological faith, but also overly optimistic views of human progress on the part of many sincere believers. Since pneumatology is the theological specialization which accounts for Christian hope as divine gift (orthodoxy*) and as a divinely guided enterprise (orthopraxis*), theologians must investigate reality itself, and especially human ingenuity, in terms of revelation's claims about the graced coresponsibility of humanity with the Spirit in achieving its final end; a Christian teleological ontology, along the lines of that proposed by E. Bloch, could provide the substratum for a future-oriented theology of the Spirit which does not overlook the social forms of sin. So would detailed studies of the effect which Christian prophetic movements have had on the betterment of international understanding and collaboration. Furthermore, Christian theologians can answer the perennial objection that pneumatology is an abstract and irrelevant field only if they pursue this discipline in conjunction with reflection on the inequities in their given societies and refuse to give up the conviction that the Holy Spirit stands on the side of righteousness.

Karl Barth, *Church Dogmatics* I/1, ET 1936, rev. ed. 1975; Hendrikus Berkhof, *The Doctrine of the Holy Spirit*, ET 1964; Ernst Bloch, *Das Prinzip Hoffnung*, 1965; Ewert Cousins, 'Teilhard and the Theology of the Spirit', *Cross Currents* 19, 1969, pp. 159–77; James D. G. Dunn, *Jesus and the Spirit: A Study of the Religious and Charismatic Experience of Jesus and the First Christians as Reflected in the New Testament*, 1975; Norman Hook, 'A Spirit Christology', *Theology* 75, 1972, pp. 226–32; Walter Kasper, *Jesus the Christ*, ET 1977; Geoffrey W. H. Lampe, *God as Spirit*, 1977; Bernard Lonergan, *Method in Theology*, 1972; Johannes B. Metz, *Theology of the World*, ET 1969; Jürgen Moltmann, *The Church in the Power of the Spirit*, ET 1977; *The Trinity and the Kingdom of God*, ET 1981; C. F. D. Moule, *The Holy Spirit*, 1978; Heribert Mühlen, 'Die Epochale Notwendigkeit eines Pneumatologischen Ansatzes der Gotteslehre', *Wort und Wahrheit* 28, 1973, pp. 275–87; Nikos Nissiotis, 'Pneumatological Christology as a Presupposition of Ecclesiology', *Oecumenica* 2, 1967, pp. 235–52; Wolfhart Pannenberg, *The Apostles' Creed in the Light of Today's Questions*, ET 1972; K. Rahner, *The Trinity*, ET 1974; *Foundations of Christian Faith: An Introduction to the Idea of Christianity*, ET 1978; Juan Luis Segundo, *The Community Called Church*, ET 1973; Piet Schoonenberg, 'Spirit Christology and Logos Christology', *Bijdragen* 38, 1977, pp. 350–75; J. V. Taylor, *The Go-Between God: The Holy Spirit and the Christian Mission*, 1972; Pierre Teilhard de Chardin, *The Phenomenon of Man*, ET 1965; Paul Tillich, *Systematic Theology* III, 1963; Geoffrey Wainwright, *Eucharist and Eschatology*, 1971.

PHILIP J. ROSATO

Homiletics, Homily

Homiletics is the art of preaching. The derivation of the word is from the Greek *homileticos*, from *homilein*, to consort or hold converse with. As taught to preachers, homiletics is concerned with the sources of sermons, their doctrinal and ethical content, progression of thought, structure, illustrative material, language, preparation for the pulpit and delivery. The subject cannot be taught with complete objectivity, for though guidelines in the areas referred to can be invaluable, the preacher's ability and temperament will considerably affect both the preparation and delivery of the sermon. Homiletics has a long history, and throughout it practitioners have not always felt it wrong to keep the rules in spirit rather than in letter.

A homily is a short discourse addressed to a congregation with a view to its spiritual edification. It is usually closely related to a passage of scripture and is a commentary upon it. Homilies were used in Jewish synagogues and the early church took over the practice. They can be found, for example, in Origen, but the Clementine Homilies are a different genre and the title is a misuse of the word. Homilies were produced in the Middle Ages for the benefit of the unlearned clergy. In England the homily is associated with the Books of Homilies, the first of which was issued in 1547 for the use of disaffected and illiterate clergy. It contained twelve homilies, each on a subject of theological or ethical concern. A second book, with a further twenty-one homilies, followed in 1571. Today the homily tends to be subsumed under the sermon (*see* **Preaching**).

JOHN STACEY

Homoeans

The term was used to describe the conciliatory Arians * whose watchword, that the Son was *homoios* (like the Father), was adopted in a series of formulae from the years 359–360 as the official ecclesiastical policy of the Emperor Constantius.

See **Trinity, Doctrine of the; Anhomoeans; Homoeousians.**

H. E. W. TURNER

Homoeousians

Homoeousians were the middle party between the full Nicenes and the conciliatory Arians * (*see* **Homoeans**), otherwise called the Semi-Arians or Semi-Nicenes. Under their leader, Basil of Ancyra, they proposed the term *homoiousios* (of like substance with the Father) to describe the status of the Son.

See **Trinity, Doctrine of the; Anhomoeans; Homoeans; Homoousios.**

H. E. W. TURNER

Homoousios

Prior to the Council of Nicaea (325), the term *homoousios*, meaning literally 'of the same substance' or 'being', did not occupy a prominent place in the Christian theological vocabulary. Valentinian gnostics * had employed it to indicate affinity or community of nature among the members of each of their categories of being: spirit, soul, and flesh. Origen employed it in a trinitarian connection to express the kinship between source and emanation * or parent and offspring. In general it appears to have connoted fundamental, or at least significant, likeness.

The reason for the introduction of *homoousios* into the creed of Nicaea has been a subject of scholarly debate. Many have argued that its use there to describe the relation of Son to Father reflects a Western and Latin belief that Father, Son and Spirit are 'one substance *' (*una substantia*) – i.e., that they share a single form of being. There is, however, little evidence to show that this conviction was expressed by the use of *homoousios* or a Latin equivalent. On the other hand, Eusebius of Caesarea understood the term to mean (*a*) that the Son is 'in every way like' the Father (and so not 'like' creatures) and (*b*) that the Son is 'from the Father' (i.e., an offspring and not something externally caused). This understanding is consonant with the word's usual sense; but if it is correct, the term was used at Nicaea in a sense vaguer than has sometimes been thought. The later idea – that *homoousios* expresses a strict unity and identity of being in the divine persons – must then be seen as an interpretative development of the position explicitly taken at Nicaea.

See also **Christology, Trinity.**

R. A. NORRIS

Hope

1. The European history of the concept of hope is shaped by the tension between Greek

philosophy and biblical, Christian under-standing.

In Greek antiquity, hope has a formal reference to the future as a neutral expecta-tion, the content of which can be either pleasant or unpleasant. This ambiguous reference to the future therefore appears under different aspects: (*a*) as an illusionary acceptance; (*b*) as a rational prospect; (*c*) as existential confidence; or (*d*) in Plato as the reaching out of the soul to the future in a transcendent dimension. While in the ongo-ing history of Greek thought hope is in-creasingly interpreted in a positive way, the undertones of uncertainty and unrest in a negative sense still remain.

By contrast, biblical thought always understands hope as the expectation of a good future which rests on God's promise. Because hope is moulded by the way in which God is understood, and determined by a relationship with God, it is unambigu-ous. The foundation of hope is the experi-ence of the liberating action of God in the exodus of Israel from slavery and in the overcoming of death in the cross and resur-rection of Christ. The goal of hope is the eternal presence of God himself in the king-dom of glory which renews heaven and earth. Of course in the O T the pious look for earthly benefits like health and peace from the blessing of Yahweh, but these particular hopes are to be found in a context of con-stant reinterpretation and eschatological realization, as are the universal promises of the exilic and post-exilic period (the return home, Ezek. 37; the reunion of Israel and Judah, Jer. 30f.; the messianic king of salva-tion, Isa. 9.1–6; peace for the nations, Isa. 2.2–4; peace among the animals, Isa. 11.6–9; the overcoming of death, Isa. 25.8; a new heaven and a new earth, Isa. 65.17ff.). Any historical, earthly fulfilment is understood as a pledge of a greater hope and taken to be an anticipation of God's eschatological future.

This tension between the fulfilment of earlier promises and the arousing of new hopes is also preserved in the N T. Christo-logically oriented in form and content, earliest Christian hope is directed as a result of the proclamation of Jesus towards the parousia * of the one who is to come and the kingdom * of God as the embodiment of the common future of God, man and the world.

Thus the structure of hope common to the two Testaments is sharply different from any extra-biblical expectation: the act of hope is not an extrapolation of the present into an expected future, but is the anticipa-tion of the promised future itself. This future is already at work in the present in hope for the future of God.

2. Significantly, the theme of hope plays only a subordinate role in patristic * theo-logy. Augustine individualizes hope – in accordance with his concentration on the relationship between God and the soul – so that it becomes the expectation of the indi-vidual: happiness hereafter (*vita beata*), the vision * (*visio*) and the enjoyment (*fruitio*) of God. The apocalyptic * elements of N T hope were transformed and accentuated by the interpretation of the thousand-year king-dom (Rev. 20) in terms of the Roman state church. Hope itself is later mentioned by Thomas Aquinas alongside faith and love as one of the supernatural cardinal virtues *. However, Thomas too attributes only a limited certainty to hope. Luther criticized this lack of certainty sharply. On the basis of the certainty of justifying faith * he stressed the totality of hope as described by Paul: it is the offering of existence to the future of the kingdom of God. However, even for Luther the content of hope is oriented on the faith of the individual; the all-embracing expectation of the kingdom of God is neglected.

Modern rationalism has been shaped by this individualism and ends up either at a completely negative estimation of hope (Descartes, Hobbes, Spinoza: hope is illu-sionary, disruptive, dubious) or in the case of Kant and the existentialism * of Kier-kegaard, Heidegger and Bultmann at a re-duction of the content of hope to the act of hope. G. Marcel and P. Teilhard de Chardin worked towards opening up this restricted concept of hope, but it was E. Bloch, going back to biblical and Marxist traditions, who first made the 'Principle of Hope' (his book, *Das Prinzip Hoffnung*, 1959) a central sub-ject of philosophical and theological con-cerns. In the mediation of anthropological hopes and material tendencies through society, Bloch's 'ontology of not-yet-being' aims at overcoming the alienation of man and nature. In his *Theology of Hope* (1964), following the biblical tradition, J. Molt-mann stresses the future-related and all-embracing character of the whole of Christ-ian faith and action.

3. The new eschatology also focusses attention on the apocalyptic and chiliastic* groups standing at the fringe of church history. Thus for example the Montanism of the second century, the heretical movements at the end of the first millennium and the Franciscan spiritualists who followed the abbot Joachim of Fiore in the thirteenth century were all concerned with God's future. Enthusiasts and Baptists in the sixteenth century looked for the dawn of the eschaton by actively seeking to transform their oppressive present. Of course the cross of Christ, as the sign of hope for those who live in the shadow of the cross, is also the criterion for all dreams and fantasies about the future. The hope which is born of the cross distinguishes Christian faith from supersitition and unbelief.

Just as faith ties a person to the crucified Christ, so hope opens up this faith to the all-embracing future of the risen Christ. In hope for the kingdom of God the Christian also experiences the contradiction between resurrection* and life and a world of evil and death. Faith which opens itself to hope does not bring peace, but disquiet. In contrast to the reality that we experience, love accepts the earth because it hopes for the new creation. Thus hope draws believers into the life of love and frees them for solidarity with the whole of suffering creation.

A theology of love was developed in the Middle Ages and a theology of faith at the time of the Reformation; now it is important to develop a universal theology of hope which directs the church and mankind, mankind and nature, towards the kingdom of God and prepares them for it.

R. A. Alves, *A Theology of Human Hope*, 1969; E. Bloch, *Das Prinzip Hoffnung*, 1959; G. Marcel, *Fresh Hope for the World*, 1960; J. Moltmann, *Theology of Hope*, ET 1967; J. Pieper, *Über die Hoffnung*, 1949; K. M. Woschitz, *Elpis, Hoffnung, Geschichte, Philosophie, Exegese, Theologie eines Schlüsselbegriffes*, 1979.

JÜRGEN MOLTMANN

Horizon see Hermeneutics

Humanism

In the broadest sense, the term includes any philosophy or teaching which emphasizes the worth and dignity of human beings, seeks the welfare of the human race and rejoices in human achievements. It might seem that any human being would be committed to such attitudes, just in virtue of being human. But this is not so, and the human race has often been denigrated, sometimes by religious teachings which contrast human sinfulness with the divine goodness, and sometimes by secular worldviews which see man as a mere accident or even misfortune in the cosmos.

The Renaissance was an age of humanism. The term refers here chiefly to the rediscovery of classical culture* in all its branches – its learning, literature, sculpture, architecture, political institutions and so on. That classical culture was, of course, pre-Christian, so that the new admiration for its achievements carried with it implicitly the belief that man, even without Christianity, is not merely a sinner but possesses some natural virtues. Even at this stage, a certain tension between humanism and the church was emerging, for instance, in the beginnings of critical study of the Bible by humanists (*see* **Biblical Criticism**). While humanism contributed to the Reformation, the underlying tensions can be seen in the controversy between Erasmus, who upheld the freedom of the human will (*see* **Free Will**), and Luther, who believed it to be in bondage to sin*. However, most Renaissance humanists were within the Christian fold, though they were seeking a version of Christianity that would do more justice (as they supposed) to the human element.

By contrast, modern humanism since the Enlightenment* has been marked by anti-religious and anti-Christian feeling. The new spirit was clearly expressed by Feuerbach, who attacked Luther's teaching as a glorification of God and a lampoon on man, and declared that the true object of devotion is an idealized humanity. Man must abolish the alien God and repossess his true humanity. Auguste Comte went so far as to found a religion of humanity with its own liturgy and festivals, and even today some humanists have quasi-religious rites to celebrate the major events of life and death.

But the more typical humanism eschews even the appearance of being a religion. It claims that values such as love are purely human values and need no religious support. There are various forms of humanism. Scientific humanism seeks to found its values on science, while for existentialist humanism, the chief value is freedom, and God is seen as an obstacle to the exercise of such freedom. But not all humanists are anti-Christian, and perhaps increasingly humanists are stressing the affirmative elements in their position and recognizing that on matters like the quest for peace and opposition to tyranny they should co-operate with Christians and others.

We can see corresponding differences on the Christian side. In the earlier part of this century, theologians were strong in their attacks on humanism. Man's attempt to live without God and to rely on his own wisdom and virtue was held to have led to many of the severe problems of contemporary society. But that attitude has been changing in the later half of the century. Protestant theologians such as Bonhoeffer and the advocates of 'secular * Christianity' have called for a new respect for human institutions and achievements, for a more mature relation to God, and, as a consequence, for a closer co-operation with secularists who are seen to be seeking the enhancement of human life. Catholic theologians, notably Rahner, have likewise been developing a more humanistic or anthropological style of theology, and Vatican II has encouraged contacts with secular groups that are inspired by humanist aims.

R. L. Shinn has made a useful distinction between a 'closed' humanism and an 'open' humanism. The former takes man as the measure of all things, is explicitly atheistic and tends to regard Nature as of interest only for human exploitation. The latter sets man in a wider context, though it may remain agnostic * about God. It would be hard for Christianity to come to terms with the former of these positions, but there is a good deal of common ground with the latter and many areas for practical co-operation. Nevertheless, a Christian is bound to maintain that in the long run a humanism which aims at the full achievement of human potential will include in its sights the relation to God, without which man remains incomplete. Indeed, Christianity holds that the full stature of humanity, which it claims to see in Jesus Christ, was achieved through the most intimate union of that humanity with God. J. Maritain makes a slightly different distinction from Shinn, dividing humanism into 'theocentric' and 'anthropo-

centric'. Only the former, he claims, is an 'integral' humanism, providing for the fulfilment of the whole human person.

H. J. Blackham, *Humanism*, 1968; John Macquarrie, *In Search of Humanity*, 1982; J. Maritain, *Integral Humanism*, ET 1968; R. L. Shinn, *Man: The New Humanism*, 1968.

JOHN MACQUARRIE

Hypostasis

The Greek word *hypostasis* is formed exactly analogously to the Latin word *substantia*, both literally implying 'something standing under'. The Greek word, however, could carry a more passive sense, something 'set under', and in practice had a wide range of uses and connotations; as a result, the correspondence with Latin proves to be misleading in trinitarian discussion. Many of the meanings attested for *hypostasis* are not directly relevant to its theological use, e.g. the meaning 'sediment'. In the NT two usages are found: 1. assurance or confidence, deriving from its use to signify a prop or stay; and 2. substance or underlying reality (as in Heb. 1.3). The difficulty which appears in trinitarian discussion arose from the fact that metaphysically the word, at first used as the equivalent of *ousia* (Origen uses them interchangeably and Epiphanius indicates that the terms are identical in meaning), could refer either to the underlying substrate of something, or, more often, to its individuality. Thus the *hypostasis* of an idol is described as stone, bronze or wood (*hypostasis* as material substance); but elsewhere the *hypostasis* is said to be destroyed if a statue is melted down (*hypostasis* as individual object or concrete existence). This helps to explain how it was that Dionysius of Alexandria could use the *three hypostases* formula to exclude Sabellianism * (i.e. taking *hypostasis* in the second sense), while Dionysius of Rome, assuming that *hypostasis* was the equivalent of *substantia*, accused him of tritheism. Eventually, with acceptance of the Nicene *homoousion*,* a clear distinction between *ousia* and *hypostasis* was established in the East, *ousia* expressing the common divine substance shared by the individual *hypostases*: thus the 'one substance, three persons' formula of the Latin tradition had as its Greek equivalent one *ousia* and three *hypostases*. Acceptance of this formula may be attributed to the influence of the Cappadocian* Fathers, though credit for its formulation belongs elsewhere, probably to Didymus the Blind.

Clarification in the trinitarian field did not, however, serve to clarify use elsewhere. The assumption that *hypostasis* was no different from *ousia* or *physis* (= nature) persisted and contributed to disagreement in the christological debates of the fifth century. Nestorius insisted on maintaining the distinction of two *hypostases*, manhood and Godhead, in the Christ, while Cyril strove to establish the 'hypostatic union' of the natures, meaning that there was one concrete individual Christ, not 'two Sons'. When spelt out in terms of 'one nature out of two', suspicion that it meant union through mixture and therefore adulteration of distinct substances, was not altogether unjustified.

In recent scholarly literature, *hypostasis* has come to be used in another context, namely with reference to the 'hypostatization' of divine attributes believed to have occurred in the intertestamental period. The personification of Wisdom in Proverbs seems to have developed into the concept of an intermediary divine being in the Hellenistic Wisdom of Solomon, if not earlier in the Wisdom traditions; this concretization of an attribute of God into an individual may be paralleled in Philo's Logos*-concept, in the development of angelology*, angels often bearing the names of divine attributes, and, it is sometimes claimed, in Rabbinic usage of terms like Shekinah, Memra, etc. Such developments suggest precedents for the evolution of christology.*

See also **Trinity, Doctrine of the.**

FRANCES YOUNG

Hypostatic Union

The concept of the substantial union of the divine and human natures* in the one person* (hypostasis*) of Christ – taken up in the formulas of the Council of Chalcedon.

J. Pelikan, *The Christian Tradition* I, 1971.

GEORGE NEWLANDS

Iconoclasm

The policy of breaking, or suppressing the use of, images, either painted or carved, in Christian devotion or worship. It was ardently pursued by several Byzantine emperors in the eighth century, but the use of images was allowed by the Second Ecumenical Council of Nicaea (787), and the veneration of icons has always played a large part in Orthodox devotion.

R. P. C. HANSON

Icons

Although from a very early period the church had made use of images, notably in the catacombs and on sarcophagi, it was not until the long and often bloody controversy over iconoclasm* that it began the systematic formulation of a theology of the icons and their veneration which was ratified in the doctrine proclaimed at the Seventh Ecumenical Council at Nicaea in 787 the last, incidentally, to be accepted by both the Eastern Orthodox and RC Churches. The final triumph of the Iconodules, or 'venerators of icons', in 843 is still celebrated in the Orthodox Church on the first Sunday of Lent as 'the Triumph of Orthodoxy', for the Orthodox have always seen in the controversy more than a quarrel about the propriety of Christian art. The true understanding of the incarnation, the redemption and the Christian attitude to the material world are all involved in the defence of the holy icons. The word itself is one of the Greek words for 'image' and it should not be forgotten that in the Greek Bible man is made 'according to the icon and likeness of God' (Gen. 1.26), Christ is 'the icon of the invisible God' (Col. 1.15; cf. II Cor. 4.4) and the Christian is 'predestined to be formed in the icon of his Son' (Rom. 8.29). The two leading theologians of the Iconodules in the eighth century were St John of Damascus (*c.* 675–749) and St Theodore the Studite (759–826).

The first accusation levelled against the Iconodules was that of idolatry, of violation of the second commandment of the Decalogue. In his *Defence of the Divine Images* St John draws a careful distinction between worship (Greek *latreia*) which is paid to God alone, and reverence or veneration (Greek *proskynēsis*) which may be given to men, places or objects. Later theology tends to use the word *doulia* for the latter and to distinguish the *doulia* given to the angels, saints and their relics from the *hyperdoulia* given to the Mother of God. The Decalogue, St John argues, forbids idolatry, that is, *lat-*

reia given to something which is not God, and not the making of images, since God himself orders the making of graven images such as the cherubim which surmount the ark of the covenant. Moreover, the veneration given to the icon is given not to the wood or the paint but to that which the icon represents. In the words of St Basil the Great, which were frequently invoked during the controversy, 'the honour given to the icon is referred to the prototype' (*On the Holy Spirit* 18.45).

But the conflict was not simply over the propriety of images in general; there was in the view of both sides an important christological* point at issue as well. In the words of the Iconoclast synod of 754, 'whoever, then, makes an image of Christ either depicts the Godhead which cannot be depicted and mingles it with the manhood (like the Monophysites), or he represents the body of Christ as not made divine and separate and as a person apart (like the Nestorians)'. The Iconodules replied that since by his incarnation Christ was circumscribed by the flesh and visible to the senses in his earthly life, it was proper, indeed it was a necessary corollary of the doctrine of the incarnation that the incarnate Word be represented in images.

Finally the Iconoclasts had a view of the relation between the divine and the created which differed fundamentally from that of their opponents. The Iconoclasts would have limited the sphere of the divine to certain well-defined areas, while the Iconodules saw all creation as the sphere of the divine activity (cf. St John of Damascus, *Defence of the Divine Images* 11.13).

The holy icons, then, are more than just sacred art; they express in visual form the central doctrines of the faith and are therefore created as an act of loving religious devotion with prayer and spiritual preparation and in conformity with a strict tradition in their presentation. Moreover, since they are an integral part of Orthodox worship, they can be fully understood only in that context. As the worshipper stands surrounded by the icons of Christ, of the Mother of God and of the saints and the events of the history of man's salvation, he is vividly made aware of the reality of both the communion of saints* and the loving economy* of God. The icons become windows on to the divine, through which his prayers ascend and through which God manifests his power by miracles of healing and answers to prayer.

Anthony Bryer and Judith Herrin (eds), *Iconoclasm*, 1977 (contains a useful collection of original texts); Leonid Ouspensky, *Theology of the Icon*, ET 1977; Paul Evdokimov, *L'Art de l'icône*, 1972; St John of Damascus, *On the Divine Images*, 1980.

SYMEON LASH

Idealism

In philosophy and theology this is a classificatory term (it does not refer to moral ideals). As such, it can only be given a general definition in relative terms, i.e. in contrast to opposed positions. Little, however, can reliably be achieved along these lines beyond what Leibniz did when he introduced the term at the beginning of the eighteenth century, in contrast to materialism. In this respect the best that can be said is that idealism denotes any philosophical position which describes the nature of things in terms not of 'matter' but of 'consciousness' or 'mind' or 'reason' and its contents. Indeed, so few major thinkers have been thoroughgoing materialists that idealism has come to have a wide variety of usages referring to very different thinkers and doctrines. Consequently it is sometimes treated as more or less synonymous with the entire history of philosophy and theology – particularly by those who would stress the formative role of social and economic ('historical-material') conditions in experience. Discussion here will be confined to more specific usages.

Platonic idealism refers to the philosophy of Plato. As traditionally understood, Plato identifies real being not with the changing material world perceived by the senses but with timeless Ideas or Forms, wholly distinct from the material world and corresponding to universal definitions 'beauty itself', 'man himself', etc. These Ideas or Forms are united in the supreme form, the good, and are called Forms because they are the archetypes and dynamic causes of existent particular things. As such they constitute an immaterial, eternal and intelligible world which alone is the object of true knowledge – knowledge that can be achieved only by the recall (*anamnesis*) of the pure Forms originally present to the soul in its premundane existence and which involves withdrawal from the dark world of the senses (the Cave) so that the intellectual 'light' of the world of Forms can illuminate the understanding (*see also* **Platonism**). *Theological idealism* refers to Platonic teaching as incorporated into Christian Platonism and scholastic theism*. Augustine regards the forms as the eternal thoughts of a transcendent creator God and so as the source of all temporal things. Knowledge of the temporal world is furnished not by recall (the soul does not enjoy premundane existence) but by the illumination of the human mind by the divine (*see also* **Augustinianism**). Thomas Aquinas combines this theological idealism with moderate or Aristotelian* realism: the essence of each individual thing pre-exists in God as a divine idea and as such individual things in the sense-world are fully real (*see also* **Thomism**). It must be remembered, however, that as used of Aquinas idealism does not denote his overall position but is rather a convenient way of bracketing him with those thinkers, influenced by Platonic idealism, who belong to the history of philosophy prior to the rise of modern science, which brought the problem of epistemology to the fore. Their general position is sometimes termed *ontological idealism* to indicate that they regard the order of ideas as identical with the order of the world.

Clearly, however, such a classification only arises when the identity in question becomes problematic. And so ontological idealism is contrasted with *epistemological idealism*, a term which usually refers to those thinkers from Descartes on who in the light of scientific developments abandon the doctrine of forms as an explanatory principle of the (natural) world and attempt to re-think the now problematic relation of consciousness to the world in terms of a redefinition of 'ideas' as mental entities. Descartes begins with the idea of God as an innate fact of consciousness; God, being no deceiver, would not mislead us as to the existence of our selves as continuous and unified entities or as to the existence of the external world. Locke denies that there are any such innate ideas and claims that the mind is at birth a *tabula rasa*, its basic building blocks being the 'simple ideas' or wholly discrete perceptions of sensible qualities conveyed into the mind by the senses. Nevertheless, Locke

allows that there are objective correlatives ('substances' or 'real essences') to the contents of consciousness, and he explains the constant and regular connection in which discrete ideas appear to us by reference to the will of God. Berkeley, however, maintains that on Locke's own principles the existence of a realm of real essence is otiose and argues that simple ideas and their connections are wholly attributable to the activity of the divine will. Consequently, there are no material existents; nothing exists except minds (finite spirits), the universal mind (God) and the mental content or ideas by means of which God communicates with the finite spirits he has created. Berkeley named his own position 'immaterialism', but he is commonly called an idealist, and indeed for many English-speaking philosophers idealism is synonymous with Berkeley's philosophy. As a result Hume is rarely referred to as an idealist *simpliciter*, though like his predecessors he too maintains that all our knowledge is derived from simple ideas. However, what Berkeley had done to Locke's real essences, Hume does to Berkeley's God, denying that we can legitimately infer the existence of such a being from simple ideas and claiming that the connection of ideas must be explained psychologically as a matter of habit and custom on our part.

Regarded not in the context of the problem of knowledge but as a theory of reality, Berkeley's position is sometimes referred to as *pluralistic idealism* – the view of reality as a community of immaterial spirits. The same term is also used to refer to the philosophy of Leibniz, which teaches that the phenomenal realm is only explicable as a product of the immaterial and self-active character of real individual or simple substances (monads) that have neither extension nor degree nor divisibility and whose ultimate source is God. Because Leibniz regards logic and not sensation as the basis of our knowledge of the real he is sometimes called a *rationalistic idealist*.

Both epistemological and rationalistic idealism influence the complex and all-important *transcendental idealism* of Kant, who denies that the connectedness of experience can be legitimately regarded either as a matter of psychological belief or as a mysterious product of God's activity. Instead, he maintains that reliable knowledge can be guaranteed only by examining the conditions of possible knowledge, i.e. those conditions without which human experience would be impossible and which therefore must be valid of all phenomena. Such conditions Kant calls 'transcendental'; he regards them as 'ideal' because they are part and parcel of the constructive or synthetic activity of self-consciousness or the ego regarded as a purely logical or functional entity in the constitution of experience. For Kant, only because the objects of knowledge are established as such by and within the transcendental conditions of knowledge (which include space, time and causality) do we have reliable knowledge. And because these conditions furnish us with (or constitute) an external world of objects and events, Kant can make the paradoxical claim that his transcendental idealism alone guarantees 'empirical realism'. Thus Kant's transcendentalism both removes the need for recourse to God as the grounding principle of knowledge and denies that God can be an object of knowledge or an existent being, in that objects or existents belong wholly to the phenomenal realm of spatio-temporal and causal conditions. Nevertheless Kant sees God as a practical implication of moral experience and as such genuinely real. Furthermore, although knowledge is restricted to the phenomenal realm, he regards the teleological characteristics of the physical and biological world as lending support to theism*. And he allows that the phenomenal realm may be used analogically to characterize, not the unknowable nature of God, but our relation to him in the moral experience.

It is Kant's work which popularizes the term idealism, and it is from Kant's work that the various idealistic philosophies of the nineteenth century spring. Indeed, it is with reference to one or other of these that the term idealism is now most commonly used. However, only the main forms can be mentioned here.

The *subjective idealism* of J. G. Fichte holds that the world is a product of the knowing subject. The *objective idealism* of F. W. J. Schelling maintains (against Fichte) that the externally real natural world is identical with the thought or activity of the World Mind or Absolute*. The *absolute idealism* of G. W. F. Hegel regards all nature and history as the dynamic and progressive expression or manifestation of the Absolute (*see* **Hegelianism**). The *voluntaristic idealism* of A. Schopenhauer sees the phenomenal world as a product of the operation of a blind and impetuous 'Will'. *British idealism* includes such figures as T. H. Green, who influenced the theology and politics of a whole generation; the monists, F. H. Bradley and Bernard Bosanquet, who regard all finite things as aspects of an impersonal and immaterial One or Absolute; and *personal idealists* such as A. S. Pringle-Pattison, who affirms the reality of the person and the personal nature of God, and J. McTaggart, who sees the ultimate reality as a community of loving spirits. (For American idealism, *see* **Hegelianism**.)

The relation of Kant and the post-Kantian idealists to theology and religion is a complex and problematic affair. But perhaps one particular respect in which Kant's influence has been profound may be mentioned here. For his identification of religion with moral obligation has since provided a fundamental methodological model in theology and religious studies: some feature or aspect of human experience is identified with 'religion', and theology is regarded as the systematic analysis or articulation of religious experience (or latterly, language) so understood. The acceptance of rejection of this methodology has become a defining feature in theological debate.

A. H. Armstrong and R. A. Markus, *Christian Faith and Greek Philosophy*, 1960; G. Buchdahl, *Metaphysics and the Philosophy of Science*, 1969; E. Cassirer, *Substance and Function*, ET 1923; F. Copleston, *A History of Philosophy*, vols 6, 7, 8, 1964ff.; W. Dilthey, *Dilthey's Philosophy of Existence: Introduction to Weltanschauungslehre*, ET 1957; A. C. Ewing, *Idealism: A Critical Survey*, 1934; G. Lukács, *The Destruction of Reason*, ET 1980; G. Watts Cunningham, *The Idealistic Argument in Recent British and American Philosophy*, 1933.

JAMES BRADLEY

Ideas, Divine

In both ordinary language and in philosophy, the term 'idea' refers most specifically to moments in mental life, whether past, present or potential, wherein we think about something regarding which we possess either reasonable knowledge or acceptable conjecture. To 'have an idea' of justice, for example, is to be thinking momentarily about the general concept of the right, though understanding in that instance aspects of it that will, we believe, be always the same.

Ideas, whether of abstract concepts like justice or of physical objects like the pyramid of Cheops, always intend extra-mental realities and events including just actions and material things and their properties as corollaries. Western theology, beginning from hints in Plato's *Timaeus* (30d–31a), has long envisioned the thoughts or ideas of God during the creation as intermediaries between the changeless divine mind and a physically and temporally contingent world. In the first century AD, the Jewish philosopher Philo introduced this doctrine into the Judaeo-Christian tradition, insisting, however, as a bulwark against polytheism that the ideas were created rather than eternally existent (*De Opificio Mundi* 4). From the second to the fifth century both pagan and Christian Neoplatonism * developed the role of the divine ideas further, though in very different ways. For Plotinus (205–270), the Divine Mind or *nous* originated in or, more properly speaking, emanated from The One *, and with the next succeeding emanation, the World Soul, and a host of other pattern-like ideas gave rise to all that is (*Enneads* 5.1, 7). Christian Neoplatonism during this period enhanced its characterization of Jesus as the divine Logos * or Word *, who had proceeded from the trinitarian Father, coming to picture him theologically and artistically as the Pantocrator or All-Creator. Transformations within later Neoplatonism led eventually to a redirection of interest from the doctrine of the divine ideas to its mediaeval Aristotelian * counterpart, the problem of universals, namely, whether terms of general application like 'justice' have the sort of real existence the divine ideas had enjoyed or whether we learn their meaning only *a posteriori* from experience.

The doctrine of the divine ideas has always been allied with, and in comparative-religious terms, may even have originated in religious speculation on the dual role of the stars as celestial messengers and agents of world governance. The regular movements of the constellations and the dependability of the fixed stars, related to the change of seasons and to the calendar, suggested that the stars both predicted the future and brought it about as well. The Priestly narrative of the creation in Genesis took pains to discourage veneration of the stars as controllers of human destiny (1.14–19), an exhortation that recurs later in the OT (Deut. 4.19; Isa. 47.13) and implicitly in the NT (Matt. 24.29; Mark 13.25). Stars, divine ideas and angels shared alike in the ancient world the distinction of possessing pure, excellent and immortal natures, and a lively debate persisted over whether the stars were living things (Origen, *de Principiis* 1.7; Plotinus, *Enneads* 2.3.3). That beings like these not only guaranteed world order but were themselves hierarchically organized became an integral part of the mediaeval world-view through the highly influential writings of the anonymous Christian Neoplatonist of the early centuries known to history as Dionysius the Areopagite. The intermediary tasks of the divine ideas were eventually assigned by Christian theology to the orders of angels and to the stars, the former ordering the actions of humankind on behalf of the divine and the latter the rest of the material creation (Thomas Aquinas, *Summa Contra Gentiles* 3.77–82).

A. H. Armstrong, *An Introduction to Ancient Philosophy*, 1981; Dionysius the Areopagite, *The Celestial Hierarchy*, ET 1949; Philo Judaeus, 'On the Creation of the World', *The Essential Philo*, 1971; Plotinus, *Enneads* 2.1–5, 5.1–6, 9, ET 1930.

JAMES J. HEANEY

Identity

The term means 'sameness', and the concept arises in Christian theology especially in connection with belief in a life beyond death *, whether conceived as the resurrection * of the body or the immortality * of the soul * (and these two ways of thinking of the matter have been confused in theology since the first century). How is it conceivable that the same person could live on either side of death?

The problem of personal identity is not easily solved even if we confine our attention to our life here on earth. In what sense is an old man the same person who was born seventy years earlier? His body is different – it has grown and then to some extent decayed, and the particles of which it is composed have no doubt been renewed several times in the course of his life. If he were asked, 'Are you the same person?' he might very well reply both yes and no. But that would imply that in at least some respects he is the same. He still says 'I did this fifty years ago,' and in saying 'I' he is recognizing an identity that spans the years. There is an 'I' that is the enduring subject through the flux of experiences. It is true that empiricists from Hume onward have criticized the 'I' as a mere fiction or logical construction and have held that there is only a chain of experiences, and nothing but these experiences are revealed to introspection. But this does not account for the unity of the experiences as 'belonging' to an enduring subject and it falls into the category mistake of looking for a subject among objects. However it may be accounted for, and to whatever extent it may be dependent on the brain, there is in all human experience a subject which identifies itself as 'I' through all changes and which cannot objectify itself as an object among the other objects of experience.

Could this 'I' continue to identify itself beyond death? (The expression 'beyond death' is used deliberately, rather than 'after death', for the temporal pattern of our life on earth may not be the pattern of 'eternal life'.) There would seem to be two main possibilities. 1. The subject is also a substance *, viz., a substantial soul. This is the doctrine of the immortality of the soul. It is a doctrine with severe problems. How can we conceive an immaterial substance? Even granted a substantial persisting soul, would it support *personal* identity, which requires memory and therefore, in all probability, a brain? A mere substantial identity, like, say, the persistence of a table in the dining room, could not amount to personal identity. 2. There is the more biblical alternative of a resurrection of the body. This need not be the same physical particles – we have noted that already in this life the particles change, but personal identity continues. Indeed, Paul seems to have been clear that the resurrection body is not the physical body of earthly existence. Can we then suppose a resurrection body which would maintain the identity of the 'I' and the memory of that 'I's existence, and would also serve as the instrument whereby that 'I' is inserted into a new world of experience? Here one can only speculate, but the possible value of such speculation is that it shows the idea of an identity 'beyond death' is conceivable, and by no means nonsense.

P. Badham, *Christian Beliefs about Life after Death*, 1976; J. Hick, *Death and Eternal Life*, 1976; J. Macquarrie, *Christian Hope*, 1978.

JOHN MACQUARRIE

Ideology

Christians often insist that Christianity is not an ideology. Other people often take it for granted that the beliefs, values and ideals that constitute and inform patterns of Christian consciousness are ideological in character. Behind both the denial and the affirmation there lurks a linkage between the notion of ideology and that of untruth or illusion which can be traced back to the earliest uses of the concept. *'Idéologues'* was the self-description of a group of philosophers whose positivistic theories about the formation of ideas were central to their vision of social transformation achieved through educational change. The concept acquired pejorative connotations through Napoleon's attack on this group as impractical theorists, purveyors of illusion.

For the critic of 'mere ideology', true ideas are realizable ideas. When we bear in mind the tendency, in the nineteenth century, to identify true description with scientific description, it comes as little surprise that the question of the relationship between ideology and error should have become intertwined with that of the relationship between ideology and science.

In Marx's writings, and in much subsequent Marxist theory, three related senses of the concept can be discerned. At the most general level, 'ideology' refers to the process of the production of meanings and ideas in any social formation. As descriptive of the 'climate of belief', the more or less uncritically sustained ideas and ideals of a group, the concept has no necessarily pejorative connotations.

In practice, however, any group tends to overlook the extent to which the ideas by which it lives are social, historical products. The way things seem to be is taken to be the way things have ever been and necessarily are. Hence a second sense of 'ideology', the illusory and illegitimate universalization and absolutization of particular ideas.

In the third place, social formations

embody the warfare of conflicting group interests. The conflict is largely invisible: all parties tend to assume that how things seem to be to the dominant group is how they truly and necessarily are. The Marxist quest for 'scientific' theory is a quest, through socially transformative practice, for what is 'really' going on beneath the ideologically distorted 'appearances'. Ideology is not sheer error or illusion: it is a cognitive grasp on reality unwittingly distorted through the influence of power and particular interest.

Though Marx's post-Hegelian atheism led him to regard Christian belief as *necessarily* ideological, it can be argued that the extent to which Christian thinking is ideological (in Marx's second and third senses) is to be decided by examination of particular instances.

Under the influence of Karl Mannheim, 'ideology' is frequently contrasted with 'utopia'. Both express unattained ideals but, whereas the utopian mentality effectively stimulates hopeful activity in the direction of the envisaged ideal, ideologies serve the interests of the status quo by acknowledging the unrealizability of ideals that continue, nevertheless, to be affirmed *as* ideals. On this account, whether Christian ideals (such as that of 'brotherly love') are ideological or utopian is, once again, a question to be decided by examination of particular instances.

See also **Utopianism.**

N. L. A. Lash, *A Matter of Hope*, 1981, Ch. 11; K. Mannheim, *Ideology and Utopia*, 1936; J. Plamenatz, *Ideology*, 1970; M. Seliger, *The Marxist Conception of Ideology*, 1977.

NICHOLAS LASH

Idolatry

Images representing deities were very widely used in the ancient world: Jewish tradition was virtually unique in rejecting them.

There are two different aspects to the rejection of idolatry: (*a*) the rejection of images even of the one God; (*b*) the prohibition of the worship of gods other than Yahweh. It is debatable how early this double prohibition became part of the Israelite tradition.

The patriarchs are represented as monotheists *, but the variety of names under which they worship the deity has evoked doubt about this. Genesis also preserves information which reflects patriarchal use of images (Gen. 31.19ff.; see especially 31.30. Cf. 35.1–4).

The Decalogue in separate commands forbids the use of images and the worship of other gods (Ex. 20.3,4; Deut. 5.7,8; cf. Ex. 20–23 – Book of the Covenant). This suggests that the prohibitions originated in the wilderness period. However, there is evidence for the subsequent use of images, and such use seems sometimes to have been regarded as acceptable. David, like the patriarchs, made use of teraphim (I Sam. 19.13,16). Hosea threatens the withdrawal of 'ephod and teraphim' as if this would be a religious disaster (Hos. 3.4). (The ephod, though some texts presuppose it to be a garment, could also designate a free-standing figure – I Sam. 21.9 – and in Judg. 8.24–27 it is undeniably an idol.) Moreover, the images made by Jeroboam I (I Kings 12.28f.) were presumably in existence up to the fall of the Northern Kingdom. No one prophesying in the North during that period made any recorded objection. In addition to all these, Num. 21.8–9 seems designed to legitimate the use of a serpent image (but see II Kings 18.4). It is evident that in the period between Moses and the seventh century at least some images were regarded in some quarters as legitimate. It was probably after Josiah's reform that the prohibition of images came to be regarded as absolute. By the Graeco-Roman period the prohibition was held to rule out any artistic representation of animal or human figures in any medium whatever.

Condemnations of idolatry abound in scripture, notably in Deutero-Isaiah (e.g. Isa. 40.18–25; 44.9–20; 46.1–2) and in Wisdom (e.g. 13.10–14.31).

The Maccabaean revolt was prompted by imperial insistence that the Jews should sacrifice to Greek gods (I Macc. 1.14–2.30). Under Rome, Jews were excused the otherwise universal loyalty test of offering sacrifice to the divine Caesar.

Christians carried over from Judaism the rejection of idolatry. In their pagan environment this still raised problems. (See, e.g., I Cor. 8.1–13; 10.14–11.1; cf. Rev. 2.14,20).

In the NT there is a tendency to 'spiritualize' idolatry, referring it not to the literal worship of images of gods but to the giving of priority to interests other than God (Eph. 5.5; Phil. 3.19; Col. 3.5). This line has frequently been followed by Christian expositors, e.g. Luther in his Catechism.

J. Gray, 'Idol' and 'Idolatry', IDB, Vol. 2, 1962; 'Idolatry', in *Encyclopaedia Judaica*, Vol. 8, 1971; J. J. Stamm and M. E. Andrew, *The Ten Commandments in Recent Research*, 1962, pp. 79–89.

H. McKEATING

Imagery, Religious

1. Paul Ricoeur has a celebrated dictum, *Le symbole donne à penser* – the symbol gives us the data, or the stimulus, or both, for thinking. This suggests that the symbol is not a consciously elaborated rhetorical device – something designed to make communication more vivid or successful – but something without which thought would not be possible. The symbol, verbal, visual, ritual or whatever, represents in ordered form certain aspects of the world, but also, by so doing, sets a certain distance between the world and the self: it both organizes the immediacy of experience and 'makes it strange'. It proposes structures for understanding and so too suggests questions to be asked. This is true at the level of social ideology, and at the level of individual psychological development (hence in the psychoanalytic context, the significance of the stage of object-formation and the beginning of object-relationships).

Of course, this does not imply that 'symbols' are mysteriously given: they are *formed*. But the point is that they are not formed by the imagination of individuals who are already quite clear about what they want to say and need only a better way of saying it. Their formation is itself the beginning of a process of understanding, bringing something into language. And – as modern linguists and anthropologists insist – the very structure of various languages already contains symbolic responses to the world, hidden symbolic cosmologies.

If such a view is accepted, the development of symbolism in religious language is not a process of the encrustation of an original, simple idea with distracting and extraneous illustration or ornament. Like all other serious human discourse, religious language requires a symbolic foundation. But equally, we should beware of a naive

evolutionism which sees the development of religious language as a progressive emancipation from myth * and metaphor *; this would imply that there might, in the long run, be a form of consciousness which could bypass symbols of any kind – a very problematic idea, and one which characteristically belongs with a particular view of the mind's absolute freedom from social conditioning.

2. The particular problem which confronts religious language is that what it centrally 'represents' is not simply a configuration of perceptible facts in the world, but the unconditioned agency upon which all facts in the world are believed to depend. How, then, can any symbol or image in religious discourse *truly* or adequately introduce God into language? It might be said (rather along the lines of the early Wittgenstein) that all purportedly systematic talk of God should be abandoned. If this were done, nothing could be claimed about the truth or otherwise of religious symbolism; either we should have to regard it as entirely arbitrary, or else we might offer a 'functional' translation of it, seeing it as a cypher for social structures and authority patterns, or for certain policies and priorities in individual moral life. However, if such a translation is complete, the actual form of the original symbol becomes superfluous: it is doubtful whether we can continue to speak of *religious* language or imagery at all.

It is by no means a new problem. From Hellenistic times onwards, philosophers developed various strategies for dealing with it. Perhaps the commonest is that found in Philo, in some Middle Platonists *, and in many Christian writers from the fourth century onwards: God's 'essence' or definition is wholly unknown to us in the conditions of fleshly finitude, and perhaps absolutely unknowable to us in any imaginable conditions; but we can speak of his 'effects' or his 'activities'. *What* God is can never be stated, but we speak of him obliquely by speaking of those features of the world which bear his mark or point to him. Our speech about God is saved from arbitrariness and emptiness by the fact that he is an active God, 'transcending his transcendence' to interact with what he has made.

In the early fifth-century writings of the Pseudo-Dionysius, God is seen as making himself known in his 'processions' (an idea drawn from later Neoplatonism *), the hierarchical diffusion of his goodness, his life and his intelligence in the created order. All things share, in graded proportion (*analogia*), in this out-pouring of being. There is thus a continuity of sorts between God and what is not God: God can be 'named' from his manifestations, and because all these manifestations rest on the simple fact of his will to share his life, 'goodness' is the highest and most inclusive of the names that can be given him from his creation. All this, however, together with a richly elaborated understanding of the angelic orders, the church hierarchy and the Christian liturgy as mediating knowledge of God, is balanced by an intense emphasis on the fact that none of this provides full conceptual knowledge of God. There is no such knowledge available: we have to continue living in the interplay between the darkness of contemplation (beyond image and concept) and the multiplicity of manifestations and images, from the most crudely concrete (God as 'Rock' and 'Shield' and so on in the poetry of the OT) up to the most abstractly generalized ('goodness'). All these images are provided by God in his creative goodness, and to some measure true; yet all must be 'denied' in their human and limited sense, so as to lead us back to silence and unknowing.

This pattern reappears – purged of its more heavily Platonic elements – in Aquinas. God can be named from his effects in the world in the sense that we can only understand and interpret certain aspects of the world as the fruits of goodness or wisdom or intelligence or power, etc. 'Perfections' in creation, manifestations of order and beauty, point to a source of order and beauty which may improperly but not falsely be itself called orderly and beautiful. And the symbols, the metaphors (Aquinas does not distinguish here), which scriptural language provides for us are God's providential highlighting for us of the meaningful and God-directed aspects of various phenomena in the world – sometimes, and least exactly, in terms of simple transference of properties (where the *mode* of God's possession of the same qualities as creatures must be denied), sometimes in a 'proportional' sense (as *x* produces effect *y*, so God produces effect *z*). Once again, none of this gives any information about God's nature as such: we can never say *what* he is.

3. Aquinas also hints at a further point which can be related to the discussion with which this article began. Theology, he says in *ST* Ia I.2, is a 'science' (a discipline, an ordered way of knowing), despite the fact that it deals with stories of particular people, because its interest in stories is not just anecdotal – it seeks to exhibit the authority of the *people* by whom revelation comes to us. In other words, theology seeks to show how this or that life-story *claims* or *demands* to be interpreted as a wrestling with something more than the contents of the world – as an encounter with God. The 'content' of the encounter utterly eludes definition (and we are not here talking of an isolated moment of mystical experience): what is encountered can only be shown obliquely, by reading the whole story in a certain way and within a certain tradition; and this means locating it in a wider story, social or cultural, a pattern of language and behaviour. The life of Abraham, or Moses, speaks to us of God because it emerges from a community that already understands itself in the light of the myth of a God who calls and acts, and *shows* what it is for a life to be lastingly and radically shaped by such a symbol – so lastingly and radically that it is no use trying to see or understand or narrate such a life without exposing oneself to the question of the reality of what the word 'God' or the expression 'God's call' points to. But this question is not to be answered by a conclusive demonstration and definition in the abstract of what 'God' refers to.

Each believing or faith-directed life is therefore a potential symbol for talking about God. And if there were a story so completely and intimately defined in terms of God and his will that it reshaped our judgments of all other lives in that tradition – and all *possible* lives in that tradition – we might be justified in speaking of an authoritative and 'classical' symbol, a normative communication of the meaning of 'God'. This is what Christians assert about the story of Jesus; what is involved in speaking of him as Word and primary Image of God. His reshaping of a tradition involves the reshaping of language, symbolism, ritual, structures of relation. As the Byzantine theologians often affirmed, it is because grace is manifest in a single focal *eikon* that a system of Christian imagery is possible – a system which, when properly realized, seeks constantly to show the transfiguring effect of God's mystery obliquely, in depicting the human world and the human face in the light of God.

Hence too the unavoidability of doctrinal symbols. To call dogma 'symbolic' is not to suggest that it has a 'deeper meaning' to which the more mature ought to be able to penetrate, but to recognize that reflection and criticism in Christian speech do not get under way without the deposit left by the basic upheaval of language and imagery, the deposit of myth, story, rite and creed; and that reflection feeds and sustains itself not by cutting loose from this deposit, but by a repeated and deepening engagement with it, at the imaginative as well as the analytical level.

Cornelius Ernst, OP, 'Metaphor and Ontology in *Sacra Doctrina*', in *Multiple Echo*, 1979; Nicholas Lash, 'Ideology, Metaphor and Analogy,' in B. Hebblethwaite and S. Sutherland, *The Philosophical Frontiers of Christian Theology*, 1982; Aidan Nichols, OP, *The Art of God Incarnate*, 1980; Paul Ricoeur, *The Symbolism of Evil*, ET 1967.

ROWAN WILLIAMS

Imagination

Any attempt to find a place for imagination in faith or theology encounters major problems at the start. For example, the AV/KJV, which was to set a standard of English usage for some three hundred and fifty years, translated three Hebrew words – *yeṣer* (Gen. 8.21; Deut. 31.21), *sheriruth* (Jer. 3.17; 7.24; 11.8) and *maḥashebeth* (Prov. 6.18; Lam. 3.60f), and three Greek words – *dialogismos* (Rom. 1.21), *dianoia* (Luke 1.51) and *logismos* (II Cor. 10.5) – all by the single English word, *imagination*. In each case the intention is pejorative, so that while none of the modern translations retains AV/KJV usage, centuries of evil association cannot be readily sloughed off. In the Reformed tradition the biblical connotations were reinforced by quotations from Calvin, who wrote, 'God rejects without exception all shapes and pictures, and other symbols by which the superstitious believe they can bring him near to them. These images defile and insult the majesty of God' (*Institutio*, 1:xi.1). The suspicion of images thereby engendered in that tradition expressed itself subsequently in architecture, styles of wor-

ship, and in a highly conceptualized form of articulation which sought to reduce image-type thinking on the part of theologians. Any further probability of associating religion or theology with imagination met its most serious discouragement from such statements as those of Hegel that 'Theism in all its forms is an imaginative distortion of final truth', or Feuerbach that 'What has been called the mythopoeic function of imagination creates the object of religion, which in that act stands revealed as delusion', or latterly of J.-P. Sartre that 'the art of imagination is a magical one. It is an incantation designed to produce the object of one's thought, the thing one desires, in a manner that one can take possession of it. I can stop the existence of the unreal object of imagination at any time.'

In sharp contrast to this negative assessment of imagination, there has existed also a very positive tradition. For example, S. T. Coleridge in *Biographia Literaria* (1817), ch. xiii, 202, distinguished between on the one hand, the *primary* imagination, which plays a central role in perception of the external world (cf. 'productive imagination' in Kant) and which is said to be 'a repetition in the finite mind of the eternal art of creation in the infinite I AM'; and, on the other hand, the *secondary* imagination, which 'dissolves, diffuses, dissipates, in order to re-create', and in so doing heightens and intensifies nature without distorting it, penetrating to the essence of the thing, the situation, or the experience.

The idea contained in Coleridge's account of primary imagination, that it is in this respect that man is made in the image of God, reproducing in miniature the mind of God, is given comprehensive expression in an essay on 'The Imagination' published in *A Dish of Orts* (1905) but written in 1867, by George MacDonald, who was later to be regarded by C. S. Lewis as the inspiration of his romantic sagas. For MacDonald the imagination is the medium by which man enquires into what God has made. It occupies a central place in scientific research, particularly in the construction of hypotheses, as well as in historiography where without its influence 'no process of recording events can develop into a history' (p. 16). The latter is an interesting anticipation of the function of '*a priori* imagination' in historiography as set out by R. G. Collingwood in his *The Idea of History* (1946). Aesthetic creation by man is to be attributed to the inspiration of God, while the devotional spirit in man is disciplined and structured by that same divinely ordered imagination, according to MacDonald.

The same positive emphasis upon the place of imagination in theology was furthered by Richard Kroner, who in his *The Religious Function of Imagination* (1941) summed up his thesis in the following manner: 'Religious imagination is more apt than thought to risk the march into the unknown sphere [of the divine mystery], for thought is only a fragment of the mind, whereas imagination embraces the totality of existence' (p. 15).

In much more recent times, however, there have appeared several accounts of the role of imagination in different disciplines, of great significance for the understanding of its place in theology. In philosophy, Mary Warnock in *Imagination* (1976) has traced the history of the concept through Hume, Kant, Schelling, Coleridge, Wordsworth, Sartre and Wittgenstein; she claims that the imagination is a power in the mind which operates in our everyday perception of the world around us, in our thinking about objects and persons when they are absent from us so that we endow them with a kind of presence; which enables us to perceive significance in the world around us, to interpret it and to communicate that interpretation to others, 'for them to share or reject'; which finds expression in, and enables appreciation of, the work of the creative artist (cf. Iris Murdoch, *Encounter*, xxvii, July 1966, No. 1).

In the philosophy of science, two writers express views very similar to one another. Max Black, *Models and Metaphors* (1962), held that the whole process of model making and archetypal construction calls for the exercise of the imagination. The selection and construction of the model or archetype *precede* the processes of detailed rational deductions and precise mathematical verifications, and is not derived from them by any process of logical argumentation. Ian S. Barbour, in *Myths, Models and Paradigms* (1974), makes the case that models are creative expressions of the imagination equally in the sciences as in the humanities, involving a combination of perceptive analogical comparison and imaginative creation of the

wholly novel. Given the wide use of models in theological writing – biblical, expository, dogmatic and ethical – the place of imagination in that discipline is immediately evident.

In phenomenology the importance of images, as the creation of the religious imagination, has been widely emphasized. An 'analytic' of images in this context would draw attention to the following roles which they play: *epistemological* *, as facilitating or even making possible knowledge of religious subjects; *mediative*, of religious realities, seen most potently in the imagery of the eucharist; *hermeneutical* *; *evocative*, of past experiences and re-activating faith, in the present; *normative*, as providing the criteria by which the validity of religious judgments and experiences may be assessed. In the modern study of the philosophy of theology, as it might be called, imagination has been assigned a place without precedent in the previous history of the discipline. For example, David H. Kelsey, *The Uses of Scripture in Recent Theology* (1975) argues that 'at the root of [any] theological position, there is an imaginative act in which a theologian tries to catch up in a single metaphorical judgment [or model] the full complexity of God's presence in ... the Church's common life, and which in turn provides the *discrimen* to criticise the Church's speech and life' (p. 163). George Tavard, examining the Vatican II documents on Revelation in *Scripture and Tradition* (1976, p. 121) speaks 'of an act of imagination in which the theologian selects from the traditions which form his heritage those structures which are to form the system of his theological presentation, prepared for future understanding and adoption' (p. 121). Finally, David Tracy in *The Analogical Imagination* (1981) explains the role which imagination plays in selecting and deploying the focal meanings, the analogies-in-difference, which integrate a religious tradition, a theological system, a whole culture.

Ray Hart, *Unfinished Man and the Imagination*, 1974; Julian Harte, *Theological Method and Imagination*, 1977; Jean-Paul Sartre, *The Psychology of Imagination*, 1940; David Tracy, *The Analogical Imagination*, 1981; Mary Warnock, *Imagination*, 1976.

JOHN MCINTYRE

Imitation of Christ, The

As a Christian ideal this has played an important role in both Christian ethics and spirituality.

It is possible to trace in the development of the Gospel tradition about Jesus a growth of the idea of the imitation of Christ. The Gospels are allegories in the sense that they are about discipleship at the same time that they are about Christ, and are an important monument to the belief that the pattern of the life of Jesus mattered very greatly to early Christian believers.

But does this belief have a foundation in the thought of Jesus himself? There seems to be reliable evidence that Jesus saw his task as an enactment of the way of Israel which he believed had been outlined in certain key parts of the OT. This outline Jesus took as the God-given model for his own mission: the way of the Son of man in which he believed he had to go was indicated to him by the Father in God's summons to Israel to walk in the way of the Lord.

In the Pauline literature the life of Christ is something which, the apostle believes, can be seen being lived out by the operation of the Spirit in the lives of Christians. This is what he calls the mystery of 'Christ in you' (II Cor. 13.3, 5). The new and better 'way' which is Christ himself is to be discerned in the lives of Christ's followers (I Cor. 13). Paul does not shrink from exhorting his readers to imitate him in so far as he is showing marks of the Lord Christ (such as self-abnegation, obedience, charity): but there is no suggestion in Paul that the imitation of Christ is some kind of endeavour literally to mimic the historical Jesus. It is primarily a work of the Spirit who is seeking to mould Christians into conformity with Christ, the model, the image of God, and the principal thing to be imitated is the self-giving and self-abnegation displayed in the process of incarnation* as such, and in the historical Jesus.

The lack of interest in the historical Jesus in the early church prevented an immediate development of the idea that the imitation of Christ was some kind of literal mimicry. The emphasis in the early period was on self-abnegation as the essence of the *imitatio Christi*, and this was to be expressed in martyrdom or its equivalent.

Developments in the Middle Ages (liturgical mysticism and devotion to the sacred humanity of Jesus) produced a notion of the imitation of Christ as a literal archaeological reproduction of the historical Jesus. Examples of this are to be found in Bernard of Clairvaux's meditations on the 'states' of the sacred life and, of course, in Francis of Assisi, where there is the idea of a literal attempt to reproduce the Christ of the past. The most thorough-going attempt at literal mimicry was probably the point-by-point imitation of the 'stations' in the Lord's life in the liturgy of the Mass, where every movement came to be interpreted as a miming of some phase of the Lord's life.

Luther was greatly influenced by such mystics as Bernard of Clairvaux and writings like the *Theologia Germanica* and Thomas à Kempis. But he soon came to react violently against them, for two main reasons: 1. He was repelled by the puerilities and extravagances of some of the Schwärmerei groups (as, for example, when he found old folk playing hoops in the street because it said in the Gospel 'except you become as little children you cannot enter the Kingdom of Heaven'); 2. He became convinced that the whole idea of the imitation of Christ concealed a doctrine of works*. He believed that it became inevitably some kind of exercise to emulate Christ which a man could set about by his own efforts. Consequently he came to dislike the term *imitatio* and preferred *conformitas*, and his view on the whole subject is epigrammatically expressed in his famous saying (in his *Commentary on Galatians*): *'Non imitatio fecit filios, sed filiatio fecit imitatores.'* In Calvin, remarkably, there is a prominent place given to the ideal of the imitation of Christ, and the Christian's mystical union with Christ is worked out in a way which does full loyalty to the NT material.

Two developments in the modern period are notable: 1. S. Kierkegaard, particularly in a work like *Training in Christianity*. Three aspects of Kierkegaard's treatment of the theme are of special interest: (*a*) the distinction which he makes between 'admiration' of Christ and 'imitation' of Christ; (*b*) the relationship between the idea of the imitation of Christ and the doctrines of atonement and grace; and (*c*) the relationship between the imitation of Christ and mysticism indicated in Kierkegaard's idea of 'contemporaneity with Christ'. 2. Since the work of

Rudolf Bultmann in his *The History of the Synoptic Tradition* (1921) and that of the form critics generally, NT scholars have been sceptical about the possibility of recovering the historical Jesus*, and this had made the older form of the ideal of the imitation of Christ unfashionable. Nevertheless, in these circles the imitation of Christ remains an ideal for the Christian, and in the work of some of the followers of Rudolf Bultmann (particularly G. Ebeling and E. Fuchs) it consists of the Christian saying, like Christ, an affirmative to God. 'What came to expression in Jesus,' says Ebeling, 'was faith', and the Christian act is, in fact, to say, like Jesus, 'Yes' to the Father in a way that involves total commitment.

Among the issues of theological importance in any study of the ideal of the imitation of Christ are the role of the Holy Spirit in conforming Christians to the image of God which is Christ, and the doctrines of the church, the sacraments and grace.

E. Malatesta, SJ, (ed), *Imitating Christ*, 1974; *Jesus in Christian Devotion and Contemplation*, 1974; E. J. Tinsley, *The Imitation of God in Christ*, 1960.

E. J. TINSLEY

Immaculate Conception of the Blessed Virgin Mary

This doctrine refers to the belief that Mary, the mother of Christ, was miraculously preserved from the physical and moral effects of original sin* at the moment of her conception. This belief was declared a doctrine of the RC Church by Pope Pius IX in 1854 in the bull *Ineffabilis Deus*. This doctrine has been generally rejected by Protestants and is not accepted in the RC form by Eastern Orthodox, due to a different way of understanding original sin, although they too affirm Mary's 'purity' and preservation from sin.

General ideas about Mary's sinlessness were current in popular Christian piety by the fourth century, but the definition of this belief as Mary's exemption from original sin remained in doubt throughout the Middle Ages. Bernard, Albert the Great, Bonaventure and Thomas Aquinas, among others, expressed reservations about the doctrine of the grounds that it appears to make Mary an exception to the universal fall* of humanity and thus of the need of all creatures for Christ's redemption. The great schoolmen were willing to accept some notion of Mary's sanctification in the womb prior to birth and her preservation from actual sin by a special application of Christ's redeeming grace, but not her exemption from original sin.

The Augustinian view of the transmission of original sin made this a necessary consequence of the libido of sexual coitus. Since Mary was conceived by a natural sexual act of her parents, there could be no basis for exempting her from original sin. The Franciscan theologians of the fourteenth and fifteenth centuries, however, promoted the doctrine by arguing that, while Mary was conceived in original sin by her parents, a special act of grace prevented the actual effects of original sin from being transmitted to her. They sought to trace this 'cleansing' of Mary in the womb back to the actual moment of conception, so that, in actuality, there was never a moment when Mary existed in original sin.

A complicating factor in this definition was the belief that animation, or the infusion of the soul into the embryo, took place, not at conception, but approximately three months later, in the case of a female. Was Mary cleansed at conception or at animation?

The direction of modern Catholic Marian piety has been to close the gap between these two moments and to define Mary's sanctification from the effects of original sin as taking place at the moment of her conception. This has also tended to suppress earlier Catholic ideas about the later animation of the foetus and to define the infusion of the soul as taking place at the moment of conception, a definition that has important bearings on the theological controversies surrounding the issue of abortion.

The Feast of Mary's Conception was traditionally celebrated on 8 December in the Latin Calendar. This was redefined as the Feast of the Immaculate Conception after 1854. The apparitions of the Virgin to Bernadette Soubirous at Lourdes in 1858 in which the Lady declared that 'I am the Immaculate Conception' were taken as a divine affirmation of the papal doctrine.

G. Miegge, *The Virgin Mary*, ET 1955, pp. 107ff; E. O'Connor (ed), *The Dogma of the Immaculate Conception*, 1958; K. Rahner,

Theological Investigations, I, 1961, ch. 6.

R. R. RUETHER

Immanentism

The term has two related meanings. 1. As a principle of explanation, immanentism is the view that any events or phenomena within the world are explicable in terms of other events within the world. Immanentism, in this sense, was declared by Troeltsch to be a basic principle of historical research, and is accepted by virtually all modern historians, including biblical historians. Obviously such a view does not allow the possibility of miracles *, if these are understood as due to supernatural intervention. Indeed, immanentism excludes any direct agency in the affairs of this world by God or any other alleged supernatural powers. Nature and history are all of a piece and must be studied in the light of inner-worldly forces. The view does not, of course, pronounce about ultimate agencies, though many of its adherents might say that there is no way of raising or answering the question about such agencies. As Strauss already noted in the nineteenth century and as Bultmann has noted more recently, one of the major problems for Christian belief is that whereas the NT writers accepted the possibility and even the normality of divine intervention, the modern mentality excludes it. 2. Immanentism can also be understood as a view of God which stresses his immanence or indwelling in the world at the expense of his transcendence. The biblical God is primarily a transcendent God, but much modern theology has sought to give more emphasis to divine immanence. The symbol of depth rather than height has been applied to God, suggesting that he is the inner principle that expresses itself in the world-process rather than an external power separate and independent from the world.

Schleiermacher, the father of modern liberal * theology, is a good example of an immanentist in both senses of the term. He held, for instance, that a miracle is simply an ordinary event perceived in its religious significance, and that Jesus Christ is the completion of the creation of man (though this immanentist christology was qualified by the acknowledgment that there was a new implanting of the God-consciousness in Jesus). Also, in his early writings which were much influenced by Spinoza, he virtually identified God with the Universe.

While a pure immanentism could end only in pantheism * or atheism *, many contemporary theologians believe that the traditional stress on divine transcendence * needs to be considerably modified in the direction of a greater recognition of immanence and have advocated various forms of panentheism * (Hartshorne, Robinson, Moltmann et al.).

JOHN MACQUARRIE

Immolation

A term used in RC eucharistic theology, roughly synonymous with 'sacrifice' or 'offering' (Trent, Denz. 1740–41). The expression does not imply that Christ's sacrifice on Calvary is repeated or supplemented in the Mass; nor that Christ is in some sense put to death in the Mass, though many post-Tridentine theologians followed this false trail. Thomas Aquinas taught that Christ was immolated in the Mass in two ways: 1. in a 'representative image' of Christ's passion; 2. in the sense that through the Mass the church shares in the fruits of the passion (*ST* III.83.1). But RC theology insists that eucharistic sacrifice also involves a Godward movement: the priest, as president of the assembly, offers to the Father with Christ the sacrifice of Christ; the people themselves are offered to God with him (cf. Augustine, *Civ. Dei*, x.6). Recent RC theology (cf. *Missale Romanum*, 1970, Institutio Generalis n.7) expresses the doctrine of eucharistic immolation in terms of the Lord's word *anamnesis* * (memorial: I Cor. 11.24, 25). The church's *anamnesis* of Christ's saving work in the eucharist makes that work present and fruitful in each age: the eucharist is the sacrament of Christ's sacrifice. The explanation gains greater force if one accepts J. Jeremias's view that Christ's words meant '. . . that God may remember me' (*The Eucharistic Words of Jesus*, 1966, pp. 237–55).

Anglican-Roman Catholic International Commission, *Final Report*, 1982, pp. 12–25; L. Scheffczyk, 'Eucharistic Sacrifice', *Sacramentum Mundi*, vol. 2, ET 1968, pp. 273–6; M. Thurian, *The Eucharistic Memorial*, ET 1960.

E. J. YARNOLD

Immortality *see* **Death, Identity, Life after Death, Soul**

Immutability

One of the most significant attributes of God in patristic thought. Fundamentally it meant that God is not subject to the limitations of all created things: coming into being and going out of being, death, moral change. Most Christian thinkers have affirmed the immutability of God in some form ever since.

Often when the early church asserted that God is immutable, it meant that the Word in the incarnation did not cease to be God in order to become a human being, necessarily subject to mutability and death. The question of how God could have preserved his full identity as immutable God and still come among us, sharing a real humanity with us, was fundamental to the christological debates between Alexandrians* and Antiochenes* in the fifth and sixth centuries.

Within the sphere of the Christian moral life, human mutability was contrasted with divine immutability. That human beings change meant not only that they are subject to corruptibility and death, but also that they have no stability in the good that God unchangeably is. Gregory of Nyssa offered a more positive view of human mutability, distinguishing between that which is destructive and that which is not. The instability in the ever-repeated pattern of desire-satisfaction-desire for such things as food, sleep, sex and material goods is quite different from the mutability expressed in the development of a human being towards the good. Indeed, movement towards the good is part of God's intent for human beings. Paradoxically, it is by the continual movement towards God that human beings may imitate God's own immutability, by being fixed in their progress towards God in virtue and love.

Jean Daniélou, 'Changement', *L'être et le Temps chez Gregoire de Nysse*, 1970.

ROBERTA C. BONDI

Impassibility

Impassibility (Latin *impassibilitas*, corresponding to Greek *apatheia*) has been traditionally ascribed to God in order to affirm that God or the divine nature can experience no pain or suffering. The doctrine of divine impassibility (sometimes misunderstood as asserting that God is indifferent or unconcerned) follows from the doctrine of divine timelessness* (according to which God has no duration) and the doctrine of divine immutability (according to which God undergoes no change in his mode of being). It is also connected with the teaching that God is infinite and incorporeal. Those who have ascribed impassibility to God have been much concerned to avoid the suggestion that God can be acted on or affected in his nature as God by anything created. Belief in divine impassibility can therefore be seen as entailed by the doctrine of creation *ex nihilo* (according to which all change must be understood as originating in God's creative act).

Christian theologians have adopted the doctrine of divine impassibility from earliest times. The doctrine, indeed, was taken as axiomatic for centuries. But Christians have also recognized that it raises problems for belief in Christianity largely because of the Incarnation*. Some Christians have therefore abandoned or heavily qualified the assertion that God is impassible. Thus, for example, Jürgen Moltmann has urged that 'Christian theology must think of God's being in suffering and dying and finally in the death of Jesus, if it is not to surrender and lose its identity' (*The Crucified God*, 1974, p. 214). More traditional Christians have argued, however, that belief in divine impassibity is perfectly compatible with Christian teaching. It has been said, for example, that the Incarnation involves a union of two distinct natures (divine and human) in one subject (the Word, the *Logos*). On this view God can be said to suffer since Christ is divine and since Christ suffered. But, so the argument goes, Christ did not suffer in his divine nature. He suffered as man, not as God. A classical statement of this position can be found in the work of Aquinas, according to whom: 'The union of the human nature with the Divine was effected in the Person . . . yet observing the distinction of natures . . . The Passion is to be attributed to the suppositum of the Divine Nature, not because of the divine nature which is impassible, but by reason of the human nature' (*ST*, Ia, 46, 12). Aquinas is saying here that since the subject of Christ's human acts is divine (since in referring to Christ we refer to what is divine), then God truly suffers when Christ suffers.

But, Aquinas wants to add, this is not because Christ suffers as God. It is because that which is both human and divine (the person, or, in Aquinas' terminology, the *suppositum*) suffers as human.

In the twentieth century belief in God's impassibility has come in for particular criticism in the work of process * theologians, according to whom God, *qua* personal, must be said to suffer as one who sympathizes with human suffering and wrongdoing. A prominent exponent of this view is Charles Hartshorne, whose position has been developed in numerous books and articles.

Charles Hartshorne, *The Divine Relativity: A Social Conception of God*, 1948; J. N. D. Kelly, *Early Christian Doctrines*, ⁵1977; Jürgen Moltmann, *The Crucified God*, 1974; H. P. Owen, *Concepts of Deity*, 1971; G. L. Prestige, *God in Patristic Thought*, 1936.

BRIAN DAVIES

Imputation

A metaphor from accounting used to ascribe the theological credit or debit of one to another. Augustine gave impetus to its use and the Reformation, especially in its later systematic expressions, sought to draw out the meaning and perceived implications of biblical references (Gen. 15.6; Ps. 32.1–2; Rom. 4.3–11, 22–25; Rom. 5.13–17; II Cor. 5.19, 21; Gal. 3.6). The concept functions in anthropology and soteriology: 1. solidarity in sin is such that the guilt and punishment of Adam are ours also; 2. atonement entails the laying of the cost of our sin to Christ's account; 3. justification is the reckoning of the righteousness of Christ and its benefits to the believer.

The imputation of Adam's sin and its consequences to all humanity has evoked considerable theological controversy. An organic view holds that imputation signifies the participation of all humanity in the initial act. A forensic position transfers the consequences of Adam's choice to posterity. A 'mediate imputation' perspective attributes judgment to our continuing depravity. Others reject the notion of imputation itself on the grounds of a belief in human goodness or the individual nature of responsibility.

Major theological discussion on the positive aspects of imputation has focussed on its function in justification. Challenging the received mediaeval understanding of infused grace, Reformation interpreters stressed gratuitous pardon based on the imputation of Christ's righteousness to the believer. Faith appropriates without human merit the benefits of Christ's obedience (active and passive).

Recently the assumption that RC and Protestant views on this subject are antithetical has been challenged. A re-examination of the documents of the Council of Trent * and its historical context suggests that the Protestant emphasis upon the declaring just of the believer by imputation does not preclude the R C emphasis on the making just of the believer by impartation.

H. Heppe, *Reformed Dogmatics*, 1861 (1950, English; 1978, American); A. H. Strong, *Systematic Theology*, 3 vols., 1907.

GABRIEL FACKRE

Incarnation

The idea that God or the gods have made themselves present amongst men in human form is widespread in the history of religions. According to Ninian Smart, it constitutes a third, incarnational, strand alongside the numinous and the mystical strands in the religious experience of mankind. The Christian doctrine of the Incarnation represents this strand in its most highly developed form. This central Christian doctrine states that God *, in one of the modes of his triune being (*see* **Trinity**) and without in any way ceasing to be God, has revealed himself to mankind for their salvation * by coming amongst them as a man. The man Jesus * is held to be the incarnate Word or Son of God. Taken into God's eternity and glorified at the resurrection *, the incarnate one remains for ever the ultimate focus of God-man encounter; for he not only, as God incarnate, mediates * God to man, but also, in his perfect humanity, represents man to God. United with him, on earth in his mystical body, the church *, and in heaven, in the communion * of saints, men and women come to share, by adoption *, his filial relation to the Father.

The divine status of the man Jesus is clearly, if sporadically, recognized in the NT itself, most notably in the Gospel of John (the Prologue, the 'pre-existence' sayings, Thomas' confession, etc.) and in the writings of Paul (the 'cosmic' Christ, the 'in Christ' locutions, and the trinitarian formulae, including the equation of the Spirit of Christ with the Spirit of God). But it is also implicit in the way the synoptic evangelists handle the birth narratives, in the opening verses of the letter to the Hebrews, and in the fact that the Apocalypse attributes equally to God and to Jesus the status of being the Alpha and the Omega.

These unsystematized insights, reflecting the early church's sense of the living presence of the risen Christ and their readiness to pray to him and to worship him, were refined over the first five centuries of the Christian era through hard debate, culminating in the ecumenical councils of Nicaea, Constantinople, Ephesus and Chalcedon (see **Christology**). Indeed two further councils at Constantinople carried the debate on into the sixth and seventh centuries. These councils, in turn, rejected Arianism * (the denial of the Son's eternal divinity), Apollinarianism (the denial of Christ's human spirit), Nestorianism * (the denial that the divine-human Christ could be thought of as a single Person), Eutychianism (the denial of Christ's two natures), and Monotheletism (the denial of two wills, divine and human, in Christ). Against these various deviations, the church affirmed in definitions and creeds the full divinity and humanity of Christ, two natures *, united in one person *.

The development of the doctrine of the Incarnation required at the same time a parallel development in the doctrine of God, namely, the specifically Christian doctrine of the Trinity *. For recognition of the divinity of Christ entailed recognition of the internally differentiated nature of God. This too was implicit already in the NT, especially in the Johannine teaching that the mutual love of Jesus and the Father manifests the eternal love which God is.

The doctrines of the Incarnation and the Trinity have given historical Christianity its characteristic shape, transcending the divisions between West and East and between Catholic and Protestant.

The significance of the doctrine of the Incarnation in Christian theism is very great. The gap between God and man is here held to have been crossed from the side of God, who by making himself known within the human world in a life of dedicated self-sac-

rificial love overcomes the vagueness characteristic of religious awareness generally and makes possible a much more personal and intimate saving knowledge and experience of God for the believer. The readiness of God to subject himself to the conditions of mortal life and to take suffering and evil on to himself to the point of the cross yields a more morally credible God than creationist belief elsewhere affords. The concomitant trinitarian theism * also overcomes the religious inadequacy of a concept of God as being dependent on creation for an object of his love. And the belief that God in Christ takes humanity into himself as the permanent channel of man's relationship to God yields a much more specific eschatological focus for the future of creation. Moreover God's own self involvement in the world of human suffering and sin becomes the pattern and the inspiration for Christian ethical commitment, at every level of individual, social and political involvement.

In modern times, the doctrine of the Incarnation has been challenged, within Christianity itself, from several quarters, by the Unitarians * of the Reformation * period, by the deists * of the Enlightenment *, and by various strands in nineteenth-century Liberal Protestantism *. A particularly powerful philosophical reformulation of the significance of incarnation was that of G. W. F. Hegel, for whom the Christian doctrine expressed the union of humanity and divinity in general. In the twentieth century, liberal and modernist theologians, especially within the Protestant churches, have questioned the intelligibility as well as the centrality and truth of the doctrine of the Incarnation. It has rather been seen as a mythical * expression of the religious significance for the Christian of Jesus as the human vehicle of saving knowledge of God. Concentration on what God did in Christ replaces emphasis on Christ's unique ontological * status as God incarnate. Increasing awareness of other faiths has also added its weight to the sense that the doctrine of the Incarnation is a barrier to acceptance of a pluralistic * religious world, and that a diversity of channels of divine-human encounter should be recognized (see also **Christianity and Other Religions**).

On the other hand, if the peculiar contribution of Christianity lies in the gospel * of the Incarnation, and if this can be interpreted in an inclusivist rather than an exclusivist sense, so that the spirit of Christ is discerned universally in the religious experience of man, then it might seem a mistake to try to reduce Christianity to some common denominator in world religion. The doctrine of the Incarnation, then, might better be allowed to commend itself by its moral and religious significance, by its intelligibility and by its truth. Something has already been said of its significance. Recognition of its intelligibility would require a sufficiently nuanced appreciation of the capacity of infinite spirit to make a particular human life the vehicle of its presence and action in the created world. Recognition of its truth would depend partly on the biblical evidence, partly on acceptance of the providential guidance of essential church teaching down the ages, and partly on experience of Christ as the living and active presence of God in the church and in the world.

G. Parrinder, *Avatar and Incarnation*, 1970; O. C. Quick, *Doctrines of the Creed*, 1938, Part II; T. F. Torrance, *Space, Time and Incarnation*, 1969; W. Kasper, *Jesus the Christ*, ET 1976.

BRIAN HEBBLETHWAITE

Indigenous Theology

1. *Concept*. Theological reflection seeking a responsible reception and rooting of the Christian gospel in a given concrete locality. Fundamental to its discussion is the historical process of the Christian proclamation in the various cultural, religious, economic and ideological contexts of humanity. In fact, this historical process is the time and space for any theological thinking at all. '. . . and you shall be my witnesses in Jerusalem and in all Judea and Samaria and to the end of the earth' (Acts 1.8). This passage, theological ('you shall be my witnesses') and missiological ('to the end of the earth'), provides the primary background for indigenization of theology. The reception and rooting of the gospel in given localities constitutes a historical process. No theology is indigenous to a local situation as pineapple is indigenous to the Hawaiian Islands. The challenge to indigenize theology is ever with us, since the world in which we live is culturally and religiously pluralistic, and it is constantly

changing in both smaller and greater degrees. Indigenous theology is a process concept. There is no finished indigenous theology. Indigenous theology means indigenization of theology which is an essential function of theology itself.

The Conference on Theological Education in South East Asia held in Bangkok, Thailand in 1956 expressed the spirit of indigenization of theology in the following words: 'The teaching of systematic theology must be relevant to the environment. It must, on the one hand, be grounded in the Bible; and, on the other, related to the actual situation. The teacher must therefore have a thorough knowledge of both. The theology of the West should not be transplanted wholesale to the East. The Christian faith should be presented in relation to the totality of questions raised by the local situation, and it should not be assumed that certain questions are relevant to all times and situations.'

(*a*) This paragraph, which has given a challenging orientation to Asian theological thinking demands from those who engage in theology a serious knowledge of the Bible *and* of the actual human situation. Indonesian theological educators have called this the 'double wrestle' of theological students and parish ministers and the fundamental principle for the indigenization of theology. In the double wrestle, theological thinking can maintain its historical character.

(*b*) The sense of responsible theological selfhood is expressed in the words, 'the theology of the West should not be transplanted wholesale to the East'. Indigenous theology is an expression of the struggle for theological selfhood from the domination of Western theologies on the part of Asian, African and Latin American Christians. It reflects, historically speaking, a postcolonial Christian experience. In the Asian context indigenous theology implies criticism of theologies that came to Asia during the 'Vasco da Gama era', to use the phraseology of K. M. Panikkar (*Asia and Western Dominance*, 1965). Asian theologians speak about the 'Teutonic captivity of theology'. Expressions such as 'contextual theology', 'relevant theology', 'theological accommodation', 'Asian theology', 'theology in Africa', 'African theology en route', and 'theology from the underside of history' refer, with varied emphasis in methodology, to indigenous expressions of theology. The theme of 'Christ and culture*' is prominent in indigenization, although 'culture' here must be understood in the sense of 'the totality of questions raised by the local situation'.

(c) The above quotation challenges the assumption that 'certain questions are relevant to all times and situations'. This challenge touches upon fundamental questions related to the local communication of the gospel and even to the determination of the contents of the Christian proclamation (kerygma*) itself. 'In the final analysis,' writes an Asian theologian, 'the Word has to assume Asian flesh and plunge into the agony and conflict of the mission of salvation in Asia.' If so, the thesis that 'certain questions are relevant to all times and situations' must be re-examined. The study on 'The Ecumenical Importance of the Nicene-Constantinopolitan Creed' conducted by the Commission on Faith and Order of the World Council of Churches (1981) has this significant line: 'What had to be said then, might not be emphasized now, even though it is basic to faith both then and now. Contrariwise, other things could then be taken for granted, or were not controversial, but might now need to be explicitly stated.' To say that 'certain questions are relevant to all times and situations' seems to reflect a more ideological than theological mind.

2. *Possibility and Limitation of Indigenous Theology.* We may say that the gospel is indigenous to the human situation of the historical Christ, while outside that specific time and space it is not. Yet, the situation is more complicated than we may think. The fact that Jesus and his disciples spoke Galilean Aramaic and that the NT is written in Koine Greek demonstrates the inter-cultural and inter-religious background of the NT itself. There is no such thing as a pure indigenous theology. It is a question therefore whether or not Paul's Epistle to the Romans is 'indigenous' to the cultural world of Jesus. Even in the NT – and in the whole Bible – we find concrete efforts of theological re-formulation and re-expression. 'We seek neither to Hinduize Christianity nor to Christianize Hinduism,' says an Indian theologian, 'Our goal is not a Christian expression of Hinduism, but an Indian expression of Christianity.' Such possibility of an Indian expression of Christianity is rooted in the inter-cultural and inter-religious hermeneutical structure of the entire Bible itself. African expression of the Christian faith is possible. The gospel can be transmitted and translated into hundreds of African sub-cultures without losing the fundamental character of the gospel. The task is a serious undertaking and not risk-free.

W. A. Visser 't Hooft in his 1966 John R. Mott Lectures titled 'Accommodation – True or False' points out that Paul and John took the risk of using such Greek words as *logos, soter, mysteria, metamorphosis* which carry abundant pre-Christian associations. This risk is inevitable. The Christian concept of God cannot be communicated without making some significant references to the 'native' concept of God. Each concept of God has mythical and symbolical stories. And each in turn lives in the network of a more complex symbol system. The gospel must engage in dialogue, then, with such loaded words as *samsara, nirvana, dharma, karma* when it expresses itself to the Hindu world. Such a dialogue carried out with the intention of achieving 'right' reception and rooting of the gospel in a given locality is the focus of the indigenization of theology. In this intense interpretative process there is a possibility that the use of 'native' concepts may influence the contents of the proclamation itself. One prominent Burmese theologian writes: 'The basic theological problem for Burmese Christian theology is not that which is concerned with "the bottle", but that which concerns the "wine" itself. The gospel must not only be understood in a Burmese way, but the Burmese and Buddhist understanding of Man, Nature, and Ultimate Reality must also become inclusive as a vital component in the overall content of the gospel.'

Those who engage in indigenization of theology must realize the presence of this profound challenge. The realization is concomitant with an awareness of the importance of 'the totality of questions raised by the local situation'. In such theological reflection a certain set of criteria is helpful. W. A. Visser't Hooft suggests that the following four questions be asked: 1. Does this new presentation of the gospel interpret it in the light of the Bible as a whole? 2. Does the new presentation 'tell the great deeds of God'? 3. Does the message in its new form make clear that the gospel is concerned with the personal encounter with the living God and with the formation of a community based on that encounter? 4. Does the message in its new form fill the local or national cultural or religious concepts with biblical substance and so revolutionize them?

As the Asians and Africans have proceeded in the indigenization of the gospel, they have often found that what was given to them as 'wine' happened to be a message strongly interfered with and coloured by Western cultural biases. In this context theological debate on the relationship between the proclamation and culture assumes great importance. Christian proclamation and culture, be it Christian culture or Buddhist culture, are not identical. Yet the proclamation cannot be meaningfully transmitted apart from 'the bottle' of the given culture. A poetic image suggested by the Indian Christian Sadhu Sundar Singh, 'Hinduism has been digging channels. Christ is the water to flow through these channels', is inspiring. Yet the relationship between channels and water presents a more complex situation than this, as is suggested by the four questions of Visser't Hooft.

The gospel remains a 'scandal' to all cultures. No culture is able completely to indigenize the gospel (I Cor. 1.22, 23). Jesus spoke the language of his people and used the imageries of everyday life, yet he had to say, 'He who has ears to hear, let him hear' (Mark 4.9). Indigenization does not mean the elimination of the scandal of Christ. That would be a fundamental distortion of the gospel. In the process of the indigenization of theology, Christians themselves must be judged by the scandal of the crucified Christ. '. . . no one can say "Jesus is Lord" except by the Holy Spirit' (I Cor. 12.3). Here is the possibility and the limitation of indigenous theology.

3. *Indigenous theology and biblical hermeneutics* *. Various spiritual orientations and literary traditions can be identified in the Bible. Because of this multiple richness of the Bible, it is possible to find spiritual and cultural patterns in the Bible which are more readily sympathetic to specific cultural situations. For instance, it would be relatively easier to 'indigenize' the theology of the Wisdom Literature portion of the OT to the Buddhist East than to introduce the

theology of the Book of Deuteronomy or Paul's Letter to the Corinthians. But such a suggestion must be carefully examined 'in the light of the Bible as a whole'. 'The Bible as a whole' does not mean the totality of all the words found in the Bible. It means the whole which is so understood by painstaking biblical hermeneutics. It is a theologically constructed whole which 'tells the great deeds of God'.

The Bible tells of the great deeds of God. In the biblical view of history the past illuminates the great deeds of God in the present, and illuminating the present, eschatologically intimates the future. The word of God maintains its freedom from the confinement of compartmentalized past, present and future because it is eschatological *, that is to say it is *always* involved in the reconstruction of history. In the freedom of this hermeneutical context the indigenizer of theology is engaged. The Book of Proverbs or the Epistles to the Corinthians are studied through the perspective of such a reconstruction of history. It is also within this eschatological perspective that we are compelled to explore the meaning of the theological ('you shall be my witnesses') and missiological ('to the end of the earth') which constitute the two important pillars of the indigenization of theology. Seeing the possibility for a reconstruction of history through these two concepts defines the quality as well as the orientation of indigenous theology.

There are a few subjects which emerge as soon as we contemplate the theological and missiological structure of indigenization. These are questions relating to the understanding of the primordial spiritual needs of humanity, such as, how does the divine relate to the human? What is human religiosity? What is the human experience of the holy? What does the cosmos (nature) mean to the human? The study of great historic religious traditions, including the discussions of the historians of religions (e.g. Mircea Eliade, *The Sacred and the Profane*, 1968) becomes an important part of the indigenization process. This is emphatically so because in indigenization of theology we are deeply engaged in the appreciation and understanding of the symbolic life of humanity.

A few examples to indicate this process of interpretation may be necessary. A learned

Buddhist monk in Thailand writes: 'Interpreted in the Buddhist way, the expression "set your mind on God's Kingdom and his justice before everything else . . ." implies total sacrifice which is in Pali *Patinissagga*, literally "giving up" . . . Again the statement in Matthew 7.12, "Always treat others as you would like them to treat you", is but the law of Karma of Buddhism. If we want to make God love us we must love God first. If we wish to make God do to us what we wish, then we must do first what God likes . . . Whether we believe in it or not, the way we act will determine the fruits we receive.' The Buddhist 'giving up' moves in a symbolic world totally different from that of Christian spirituality. 'Setting your mind on God's Kingdom' is not identical with 'giving up'. Yet the concept of 'sacrifice' may open up a new possibility for 'indigenization dialogue' as it brings us to something so basic to human spirituality and religiosity. The gospel is not identical with 'the Law of Karma of Buddhism'. Indigenous theology must affirm this distinction theologically and missiologically. In this affirmation indigenous theology must endeavour to 'fill the local or national cultural or religious concepts with biblical substance and so revolutionize them'. Indigenization of theology thus results in the enrichment, rather than the impoverishment, of theological experience.

John S. Mbiti, speaking about African culture, tells of the 'living quality of the dead'. The presence of the dead in African culture is so vivid. The Christian, while viewing history through the concept of a living God and the doctrine of the Holy Spirit, must take this prominent indigenous view seriously into consideration both theologically and missiologically.

The Maoris of New Zealand describe the past as '*nga rā o mua*', 'the day in front', and the future as '*keimuri*', 'behind'. 'They move into the future with their eyes on the past' (Joan Metge, *The Maoris of New Zealand*, 1967, p. 70). This concept introduces new elements into the discussion of the understanding of grace in history. These random samples only illustrate the almost limitless possibility for enrichment of theology in the process of indigenization.

4. *Challenges that face indigenous theology.* The process of indigenization of theology is challenged by the massive historical forces which are creating global changes in the world today.

(*a*) *Impacts of modernization.* Modernization as we know it today originated in the West, but its impact is universal. In particular, Asia and Africa have been profoundly influenced by efficiency made possible by science-based technology in the areas of transportation, hospitalization, education, economics and communication. The traditional modes of religious symbolism are being challenged. With what can the people associate the Buddhist symbol of the wheel in a world which has so many wheels of all kinds of technological speeds? As public schools came into being in the East, one of the basic functions of the Buddhist monastery, education, was taken away from it. Now wells are no longer dug under the direction of the monks but by the civil authority and with the technology of drilling machines. 'Slow movement' (patient history) has been replaced by 'fast movement' (impatient history). History no longer flows. It is forced. In its response indigenization of theology must be able to discern the negative and positive aspects of modernization. It must critically suggest a possibility of human meaning under the impact of modernization by indicating a competent understanding of this complex historical phenomenon of modernization.

(*b*) *Tension between North and South.* Economic discrepancy between the North and the South, and also between classes within a society, must affect the process of indigenization of theology. Theological expressions from Latin America in recent years, labelled 'liberation theology' *, are an outstanding example of taking this global situation seriously as an aspect of the local human reality. Latin American liberation theology is a responsible theological effort to indigenize theology within the Latin American political and economic situation and at the same time it carries a relevant message about the global situation of humanity today. Other global issues such as militarism, racism, poverty and hunger are so relevant to every local situation that the indigenizer of theology will inevitably find it necessary to deal with them.

(*c*) *To the West itself.* Indigenization of theology is by no means confined to the world outside of the West. In traditional Western Christendom, the same effort of indigenization of theology must be exerted. No theology can remain meaningful to humanity in the rapidly changing world without a constant Christian effort to speak afresh the message of the gospel. Black theology* in America, for instance, contributes to the indigenization of theology in the American scene by forcing upon the dominant theology the necessity for critical self-examination.

J. Omosade Awolalu, *Yoruba Beliefs and Sacrificial Rites*, 1979; Mircea Eliade, *The Sacred and the Profane*, 1968; Douglas J. Elwood (ed), *Asian Christian Theology*, 1980; Abraham J. Heschel, *God in Search of Man*, 1955; Kosuke Koyama, *Waterbuffalo Theology*, 1974; W. Cantwell Smith, *Towards a World Theology*, 1981; Paul Tillich, *Christianity and the Encounter of the World Religions*, 1963; Sergio Torres and Virginia Fabella (eds), *The Emergent Gospel*, 1978.

KOSUKE KOYAMA

Induction

An inductive argument claims to give *probability*, *likelihood*, to its conclusions. The premises do not logically necessitate the conclusion – as they do in a valid *de*ductive argument. That is to say: if the conclusion of a deductive argument is denied, while the premises are affirmed, the result is illogic, contradiction. In an inductive argument it may be unreasonable or 'against all experience' to deny the conclusion; but it can be done without contradiction. The study of induction in a wide sense of the word has been the study of scientific method, the justification of inferences from observations and experiments to laws of nature. Checks need to be devised for eliminating irrelevant factors in would-be causal explanations; hypotheses must be submitted to stringent testing. In some fields of investigation (though by no means all) techniques can be worked out by which we may calculate the degree of probability that is given to a claim by the evidence adduced for it.

Particularly since Hume, philosophers have energetically disputed the basis (if any) for our confidence in inductive procedures. Any general justificatory principle, such as 'nature's regularity', would seem as much in need of support as the arguments it licenses. The extent of our dependence on induction, i.e. all 'learning from experience', is however so vast that no project of *eliminating* it as non-rational could even be coherently imagined, far less carried through. It is quite indispensable to all language-use, and hence to thought. Attempts have been made, notably by Sir Karl Popper, to construe the scientist's procedures as not, after all, resting on induction, but rather on the strenuous effort to falsify 'conjectures'. Debate over these continues. In philosophy of religion lively discussion goes on over the role of induction in arguments* for the existence of God (see the references to R. Swinburne and K. Ward below).

J. S. Mill's *A System of Logic*, 1843, contains a classical study of inductive method. More recent contributions include R. B. Braithwaite, *Scientific Explanation*, 1953; W. Kneale, *Probability and Induction*, 1949; K. Popper, *The Logic of Scientific Discovery*, 1934, ET 1959; R. Swinburne, *The Coherence of Theism*, 1977, and particularly *The Existence of God*, 1979; G. H. von Wright, *The Logical Problem of Induction*, 1941. Compare K. Ward, *Rational Theology and the Creativity of God*, 1982, ch. 5.

R. W. HEPBURN

Indulgences

These are aids to the process of penance given by the RC Church which cancel the temporal punishment for sins by pledging the church's intercession on behalf of the sinner's rehabilitation. Indulgences have been a centre of theological discussion from their first introduction and of controversy since the beginning of the Reformation.

The origin of indulgences is to be found in the strict understanding of penance in the early church. The consequences of sin were considered so serious that while absolution could remove both guilt and liability to eternal punishment, the sinner was still subject to temporal punishment for sin. This temporal punishment was rooted in the holy will of God, the decree of the church, and the nature of reality.

To aid the sinner in this process, the church often set a prescribed period of time, and also certain actions to be performed, as part of the penitential act. These were set according to the gravity and nature of the sin. The origin of indulgences comes about as the church acts to reduce the time of punishment by pledging herself to intercede on behalf of the sinner.

With the development of the concept of the treasury of merit in the mediaeval period, the basis was set for a practice of granting indulgences from the deposit of grace from the sacrifice of Christ and the righteous lives of the saints, a deposit which the church was permitted to administer as part of the office of the keys.

With the development of the concept of purgatory, the notion of indulgence was open to extension to penalties that might extend past death (and eventually to indulgences for the dead in purgatory, although this is a later development from the fifteenth century). Indulgences were not to be seen as forgiveness *per se*, but as an intercession by the church seeking the remission of punishment for sin, which given the superabundant merit of the church could be sought with full confidence that it would be granted. Both the treasury of merit and the notion of intercession for the dead are rooted in a sense of solidarity as a church community – saints with sinners, the living with the dead.

The actual granting of indulgences seems to have begun in France in the eleventh century. Theologians of the thirteenth century completed the theological explanation for indulgences. Thomas Aquinas taught that they had the power not only to remove church penalty but also God's judgment against sin, but that true contrition was a condition for their effectiveness. He also clarified the relationship between the Pope's power to grant indulgences and the power of bishops to grant them which was derivative from that of the Pope.

While the theological basis for indulgences was carefully articulated, there was potential for misunderstanding and abuse in the very subtle relationship of indulgences to the sacrament of penance. Chaucer and others parodied the cheap grace offered for sale by professional pardoners. And in the late mediaeval period when indulgences were seen as a potential means for generating revenue for the church – especially the sale of indulgences for the souls of dead relatives in purgatory – the separation of indulgences from the fullness of penance was complete.

Luther's *Ninety-Five Theses* (1517) were written against the abuses of selling indulgences by Tetzel and other popular preachers of his time. Luther allows that 'if indulgences were preached according to the spirit and intention of the Pope', then doubts about them would not exist (Thesis 91). But in his attack on the abuses connected with their sale, he raised broader questions about the meaning of penance, the authority of the church, and the gospel as 'the true treasure of the church' (Thesis 62) which generated debate not only about selling indulgences, but also about the notions of punishment for sin, merit and purgatory that they presupposed. Luther expanded his views in his *Explanations of the Ninety-Five Theses* (1518).

Protestant practice after 1517 developed in the direction of rejecting penance as a separate sacrament (although this was debated within the first generation of Lutheranism) and towards public confession and absolution for sin. While provision for private confession and absolution and the spiritual guidance that this permits is formally retained in some of the churches (see *Augsburg Confession* XI), the general rejection of temporal punishment for sin, treasury of merit and purgatory made it impossible for indulgences to survive in any branch of Protestantism.

The Council of Trent *, at its twenty-fifth session (1563), affirmed the value of indulgences as 'most salutary to the Christian people' and provided for their retention in the church. Nevertheless the reality of abuses was admitted and the Council urged that 'moderation be observed, lest by too great facility ecclesiastical discipline be weakened'. Indulgences continued to be a popular and widely used spiritual aid in the RC Church in the modern centuries. *The Raccolta* published in English in 1957 listed 781 prayers and spiritual acts authorized as indulgences by the Holy See, and assigned to each either plenary indulgence or a specific time period for the remission of punishment to those that were partial indulgences.

The Second Vatican Council discussed indulgences at several sessions but did not come to definite conclusions about their use. Contemporary Roman practice is shaped by the Apostolic Constitution of Pope Paul VI, *Indulgentiarum Doctrina* (1967). This decree reaffirms the value of indulgences and ties their significance closely to the doctrine of the communion of saints. But it changes traditional practice in removing the precise time period of remission of punishment that had been traditionally assigned to partial indulgences. It reaffirmed that the person receiving the indulgence cannot thereby be released from responsibility for true contrition and the performing of the assigned work of devotion or charity.

Recent ecumenical discussion of indulgences has been dominated by Karl Rahner. He has worked to reassert the historic setting of indulgences within the larger context of the church's penitential practice, to see them as aids towards perfect love which can effect true and lasting conversion, and to develop a concept of the punishment for sin which is seen less as the arbitrary judgment of God and the church, and more as the inevitable consequence of sin as a distortion of reality.

For all these efforts, this is an issue on which there has been little ecumenical reconciliation at the formal level of theological dialogue. And, as Rahner observes, even within the R C church there is decreasing interest in indulgences either for the living or on behalf of the dead. Nevertheless they continue to be available and at least formally commended by the church.

Thomas Aquinas, *Summa Theologica*, Supplement, Questions 25–7, vol III, 1948; Martin Luther, *Ninety-Five Theses*, in *Works*, vol 31, 1957, pp. 17–33; *Explanation of the Ninety-Five Theses*, in *Works*, vol 31, 1957, pp. 77–252; Richard McBrien, *Catholicism*, 1981; Josef Neuner and Heinrich Roos, *The Teaching of the Catholic Church* (ed Karl Rahner), 1967; Karl Rahner, 'Remarks on the Theology of Indulgences', *Theological Investigations* II, 1963, pp. 174–201; 'A Brief Theological Study on Indulgences', *Theological Investigations* X, 1973, pp. 150–65; 'On the Official Teaching of the Church Today on the Subject of Indulgences', *Theological Investigations* X, 1973, pp. 166–98.

TIMOTHY F. LULL

Infallibility

An expression used in R C theology to denote the preservation from error of the church, a General Council or the Pope. Although it is to the Pope that the term is most usually applied, the definition of the doctrine in 1870 (Vatican I, Denz. 3074) makes it clear that the infallibility of the Pope is only one realization of the more fundamental infallibility of the whole church. General Coun-

cils (in which the Pope plays an essential part) are another organ of the church's infallibility.

Infallibility is often contrasted with indefectibility. Both terms express the belief that the Holy Spirit guides the church. But whereas infallibility implies definite moments when the church's act of teaching can be known to be preserved from error, indefectibility affirms more generally that, despite human weakness, the church will never cease to be the church, witnessing to the truth. Those who accept infallibility argue that without it the church could not remain indefectible.

In the early centuries perfect preservation of the faith was thought to be the charism of the whole church of the city of Rome, a gift which was gradually focussed on the person of its bishop. Consequently the seeds of the doctrine of papal infallibility were present long before the assertion of the irreversibility of papal teaching was made in the False Decretals in the ninth century or the term 'infallibility' first appeared in the fourteenth.

The 1870 definition set precise limits to papal infallibility. It does not extend wider than that of the whole church. The Pope cannot promulgate new revelation, but only clarify the deposit of faith. Infallibility is not inspiration, but only negative preservation from error. It is not a permanent, personal attribute of a Pope, but a guarantee that he will be preserved from error on those occasions (in fact rare) when he speaks *ex cathedra*, i.e. formally defining for the whole church doctrine concerning faith or morals.

The only definitions of recent times to which infallibility is generally ascribed are those of the Immaculate Conception (1854) and the Assumption (1950) of the Blessed Virgin Mary*. The Pope's *magisterium* is far more often exercised in ways which are not *ex cathedra*; and a more typical exercise of his infallible teaching authority occurs when he presides (in person or through a legate) over a General Council.

The doctrine of the infallibility of Popes and general councils has not generally found favour outside the R C Church. The Anglican Article XXI affirms that general councils may err (though not that they always do so). It is commonly suggested that the term 'infallibility' should be predicated only of God. However, the Anglican-Roman Catholic International Commission reached wide agreement concerning the church's preservation from error, preferring however to avoid the use of the word 'infallible', and expressing divergence only over the Marian doctrines and the significance of the reception of a doctrine by the church after it has been defined.

Anglican-Roman Catholic International Commission, *Final Report*, 1982, 'Authority in the Church I, II and Elucidation'; E. C. Butler, *The Vatican Council 1869–70*, 1962; E. J. Yarnold and H. Chadwick, *Truth and Authority*, 1977; E. J. Yarnold, 'The Papacy', *The Way*, Oct. 1979 and Jan. 1980.

E. J. YARNOLD

Infant Baptism
see Initiation, Christian

Infinity

The English word derives from the Latin *infinitas*, which signifies boundlessness or endlessness. The corresponding adjective is 'infinite' (Latin *infinitum*, 'boundless', 'endless'). Infinity has been ascribed with varying degrees of clarity to various things including substance, time, space, the universe, number and classes. The concept can be traced in the work of numerous philosophers and mathematicians, notably Anaximander, Plato, Aristotle, Plotinus, Augustine, Scotus, Bonaventure, Aquinas, Nicholas of Cusa, Descartes, Spinoza, Hegel, Cantor and Dedekind. A thorough study of the notion of infinity would require some treatment of all these thinkers.

Though one cannot really talk about a biblical doctrine of infinity, Christian theologians have ascribed infinity to God since the time of the Latin and Greek Fathers. In Christian theology infinity has been thought of as a mark of God's perfection. It has been urged that God alone is infinite and that to call him such is to say that he owes his existence to nothing (that he is uncreated and uncreatable), that he is not limited in space and time, and that he is immeasurably superior to all his creatures. Omniscience, omnipotence, omnipresence and eternity have therefore been thought of as aspects of divine infinity. It has also been argued, notably by Aquinas and comparable writers, that God's infinity is a matter of his being beyond all classification or determination of the kind exemplified by members of a genus or species (cf. *S T* Ia, 3, 7).

The classical Christian concept of divine infinity raises many philosophical problems. For example: if God is infinite, how can he be known by his creatures? Or again: if God is infinite, how can it be possible for evil to exist? But the main features of the classical Christian concept of divine infinity seem inseparable from the notion of a God who is Creator of all things from nothing (*ex nihilo*). Such a God must have supreme power over all things since they continually depend on him for their very existence. He must also lie outside the process of real change, and, on the assumption that time is the measure of change, he must therefore be timeless. But some philosophers, such as Spinoza (who identified God with Nature), have spoken of God as infinite without wishing totally to distinguish him from individual things. Others, such as Mill, have argued that though God is distinct from material things he is not the Creator of matter.

In the twentieth century there has been considerable explicit or implicit theological criticism of the classical concept of divine infinity. Much of this can be found in the work of process theologians such as Charles Hartshorne (*see* Process Theology). Such theologians argue that God's personal nature entails his changeability and existence in time. Process theologians have also maintained that God somehow develops. According to Hartshorne, for example, God grows in personality through his loving response to his creatures.

A. H. Armstrong and R. A. Markus, 'God's Transcendence and Infinity', *Christian Faith and Greek Philosophy*, 1960; John B. Cobb and David Ray Griffen, *Process Theology: An Introductory Exposition*, 1976; A. M. Farrer, *Finite and Infinite*, 1943; Norman Kretzmann, Anthony Kenny and Jan Pinborg (eds), *The Cambridge History of Later Medieval Philosophy*, 1982; H. P. Owen, *Concepts of Deity*, 1971.

BRIAN DAVIES

Ingeneracy

Ingeneracy (Greek: *agennesia*; Latin: *innascibilitas*) is the term used increasingly from the fourth century to express the differentiating particularity of the Father. The

Arians* regarded this characteristic as the sole authentic mark of deity and therefore rejected the full divinity of the Son and the Spirit. The Cappadocian Fathers* drew a sharp distinction between 'uncreated' and 'unbegotten' (*agenetos, agennetos*), two very similar adjectives often confused in the earlier period. The former was the Universal of Godhead, the latter the characteristic of the Father. While in fourth-century polemical theology the negative term ingeneracy was indispensable, the more positive word paternity was equally widely used. Aquinas, however, classifies the two terms differently. paternity is a relation, ingeneracy (which denotes the absence of relations) is a notion.

See **Generation; Procession(s).**

H. E. W. TURNER

Initiation, Christian

The name used by nineteenth-century German and French liturgical scholars to designate the complex of sacramental rites including baptism, consignation or confirmation, and first holy communion, which comprise the final stages of becoming a fully enfranchised Christian, a member of the church, one of the 'faithful'. Since the liturgical reforms of the Second Vatican Council, Roman Catholics include also the catechumenate and post-baptismal mystagogy within this designation.

1. *History.* NT accounts of early baptismal practice describe the water bath within a context of other acts such as kerygmatic preaching, conversion, the laying on of hands by apostles, and the manifestation of the Holy Spirit in pneumatic gifts. Acts 2.14–47, the fullest such account, specifies the result of baptismal initiation to be Spirit-filled life in common, devoted to apostolic teaching (*didache*), fellowship (*koinonia*), the breaking of bread (*klasei tou artou*), and prayers (*proseuchais*). The account is strongly pentecostal* and seems to make specific the four Gospels' allusions to the superiority of Jesus over John the Baptist in that the former would baptize not merely with water but with Holy Spirit and 'fire'. This perception also seems to constitute the basic criterion for judging the adequacy of all other baptisms, such as that of the Samaritans by Philip, a baptism which had to be 'completed' by Peter and John as representatives of the pentecostal community of Jerusalem before the Samaritans could re-

ceive the Holy Spirit (Acts 8.4–25). The total context of Hebrews 1–6, particularly in light of its author's desire not to repeat Christian fundamentals such as 'instructions about *baptismata*' (6.2), seems to reinforce the possibility that Acts 2.14–47 is somehow paradigmatic for Christian baptism after Pentecost. It is important to realize that no NT accounts of *baptismata* occurring prior to the pentecostal consummation of Jesus' messianic task in his death and resurrection, the 'baptism wherewith I must be baptized', mention any manifestation of the Holy Spirit (except the accounts of Jesus' own baptism by John) or the giving of any pneumatic gifts. The rationale underlying NT reports of initiatory policies seems to be this: preceded by authentic, usually apostolic, proclamation of the risen and exalted *Messiah-Christos* ('anointed one') and by conversion, baptism by water and Holy Spirit initiates one into the full life of a community in which the gospel has already become praxis.*

Four main initiatory traditions emerge in the earliest Christian churches before the end of the fourth century. In East Syria, the *Acts of Thomas, Didascalia Apostolorum* and the earliest strata of the *Armenian Ordo* attest that the water-bath was preceded by a messianic anointing (*rushma*, sign or mark) with olive oil (*meshha*) and followed by the eucharist. Only later was a second anointing with chrism (*hatma*, seal) added between the water-bath and eucharist in order, it seems, to bring Semitic East Syrian practice into some conformity with the more Hellenistic churches of West Syria, which stressed water-bath, anointing with chrism, and eucharist. This second pattern can be seen in the post-baptismal catecheses of Cyril of Jerusalem and appears to have been the usage of the non-Roman churches of Gaul and Spain as well. Thirdly, a hybrid of East and West Syrian usages is apparent in *Apostolic Constitutions* where the sequence is (i) a messianic anointing after the renunciation of Satan and acceptance of Christ, (ii) water-bath, (iii) anointing with chrism, and (iv) eucharist. The fourth tradition is that described in Hippolytus' *Apostolic Tradition*, where the sequence is (i) an exorcistic anointing, (ii) water-bath, (iii) anointing with chrism, (iv) a presentation of the newly baptized to the assembled faithful with hand-laying, prayer for the grace of the

Spirit and a second anointing with chrism, and (v) eucharist. Hippolytus' presentation rite constituted the public affirmation of the initiates' *baptism*, which had occurred in private. It is this presentation rite, later called consignation, which became separated from its baptismal context as the Roman liturgy spread into other Western churches, eventually to be called confirmation and to be given its own rationale by mediaeval scholastic theologians as a separate and distinct sacrament with separate and distinct effects upon the recipient.

That such developments were peculiar to the Roman tradition and, through it, to the other Western churches of the Reformation, but not to the Eastern or to the non-Roman Latin traditions and churches, cannot be sufficiently emphasized. The Eastern churches continue, as a rule, to initiate Christians at whatever age (including infants) by baptism, chrismation and eucharistic communion; there is no confirmation rite in these traditions either in connection with baptism or separate from it. In them pneumatology has remained in a more proximate relationship with a messianology and with baptism than is usually the case in the West, a point of theological importance often overlooked.

The Western tradition of initiation came under serious debate in the sixteenth century: the sacramentality of baptism and confirmation was brought into question, the possibility of validly baptizing infants was denied by Anabaptists, and the nature of confirmation as a separate sacrament or ordinance reserved to bishops was rejected by many. The Council of Trent* reiterated the Roman tradition on all three issues but did little more, and the various positions of the Reformation churches hardened into practices which were little questioned until around the time of the Second World War, when the dechristianization of society and the eroding of a vital sense of Christian identity began to be noted by authors both in England and in Continental Protestantism. A literature focussed on Christian initiation ensued, its main contributors including Emil Brunner (1937), Karl Barth (1943), F. J. Leenhardt (1946), Oscar Cullmann (1948), Joachim Jeremias (1958), and Kurt Aland (1961) on the Continent, and in England Gregory Dix (1946), G. W. H. Lampe (1951) and L. S. Thornton (1954). Roman Catholics entered the question only

later, being constrained by official positions on original sin, infant baptism, the necessity of baptism for salvation and its consequent *quamprimum* administration, and the beginnings of liturgical reform – notably the admission by Pope Pius X in 1905 of young children to holy communion even before confirmation, and the restoration of the paschal vigil by Pope Pius XII in 1950.

These preliminary reforms were given much wider scope by the Second Vatican Council, culminating in new orders for the baptism of infants (1969), confirmation (1971) and the full initiation of adults (1972). The latter restored the catechumenate in the Roman Church, stressed baptism by immersion, and made it possible for presbyters involved in the initiatory process to confirm by law in their own right without recourse to episcopal permission, the reason being to reintegrate confirmation into the baptismal liturgy as closely as might be both for pastoral reasons and in view of a consistent theology of the processions in the Holy Trinity. The scope, nature and detail of these reforms have suggested to many commentators that the rites of adult initiation constitute a restored norm for Roman initiatory policy which must be given priority in subsequent theological discussion of the implications of the rites for such issues as Christian identity, ecclesiology, evangelization, catechesis and infant baptism. The extent and radically restorative nature of these reforms have begun to affect other Western churches as well, notably in the new American Protestant Episcopal Book of Common Prayer (1979) and the American Lutheran Book of Worship (1978). Such a development seems to constitute not only a significant ecumenical fact but an even more significant alteration in the manner of dealing with debates which, left to theological processes alone, remain difficult to divest of their sixteenth century formulation. Restoration of a broader, deeper initiatory tradition in liturgical usage has the effect of changing the equation within which theological debates arise and take place, exemplifying the patristic maxim that 'the norm of worship founds or constitutes the norm of belief' (*lex supplicandi legem statuat credendi*).

2. *Theology*. Concerning baptismal initiation it must be remembered that both scriptural and liturgical texts are crucial keys

which give one access to a living, and therefore constantly modulating, tradition of understanding and praxis, both of which reflect what union with God through Christ in the Holy Spirit is. NT texts make clear in their diversity that 'baptism' was not a univocal term for a univocal event: there were *baptismata* which the author of Heb. 6.1–2 could presume his readers were instructed about – including, no doubt, proselyte baptism, the baptisms performed by the Forerunner, perhaps the ritual washings of both orthodox and sectarian Jews (Qumran) and possibly even baptisms by Jesus' followers before his death and resurrection. From Pentecost onward, however, there is greater concern evident with that baptism with Spirit and 'fire' which marked both the beginning and the consummation of the Anointed One's messianic task, and with how previous *baptismata* were to be perfected in its paschal light. It is not the ritual details of this perfecting, however, with which NT authors are concerned, but the substance and meaning of that unique baptism into the messianic Lord and its implications, both objective and subjective, for individuals as well as for communities of initiates. From a Johannine baptism for the remission of sins the tendency is to move towards a consecratory baptism in the Holy Spirit first poured out upon the Anointed One at his baptism by John and later upon the nascent church at Pentecost following the Lord's *pascha*. The consecratory 'anointing' of Jesus with Holy Spirit as messianic king and priest is, as it were, passed on by him to his church on the first Pentecost, from there to flow out into the world (Acts 2.14–47), even into Samaria (Acts 8.4–25).

Subsequent Christian tradition from the earliest times has specified how this is to be expressed and effected in four basically distinct yet complementary ways, which may be regarded as classic examples of how the one gospel is perceived in different ways according to ethnic, cultural and linguistic circumstances: the East Syrian, the West Syrian, Graeco-Latin (e.g. Jerusalem and Gaul), and Roman (Hippolytus, *Gelasian Sacramentary*, *Ordo Romanus* XI). This quadripartite tradition has in common: (i) a water bath; (ii) an array of anointings both exorcistic and consecratory before and after the water-bath in which the messianic condition for the pouring out of Holy Spirit is

regularly expressed; and (iii) eucharist as the finale of the initiatory process. Only the Roman tradition adds a second chrismation with hand-laying and epicletic prayer for the Holy Spirit after baptism and before eucharist, an addition which calls strong attention to the donation of the Spirit but which later tends to separate this donation from the messianic condition (expressed in the first post-baptismal chrismation) as confirmation is increasingly delayed.

In its original integrity, then, the quadripartite tradition affirms Christian life to begin in conversion to faith in the Glorified One by the grace of the Holy Spirit that manifests him in the world, a conversion reaching its normal consummation in a consecratory baptism by water and Spirit which initiates one fully to the eucharistic table-fellowship of apostolic teaching, apostolic unity and prayer. Here, according to I Peter 2.9, is born 'a chosen race, a royal priesthood, a holy nation, God's own people', whose purpose is evangelically baptismal: 'that you may declare the wonderful deeds of him who called you out of darkness into his marvellous light'. In this perspective, Christians are said to be baptized to priesthood; they are ordained only to exercise that priesthood in the orders of service tradition has called the episcopacy, the presbyterate and the diaconate. Priesthood is thus fundamentally a baptismal phenomenon, and it can never lapse among the baptized even though any or all of the ordained orders of service may and have done so.

The quadripartite tradition also affirms that Christian initiation has nothing *per se* to do with the physical, emotional or spiritual 'age' of the initiate, despite the fact that physical age has been considered a factor in the West for the last millenium, largely for reasons that are fundamentally disciplinary or educational (and thus extrinsic) to the traditional meaning of initiation itself. The presumption in the West for the first thousand years seems to have been, as it remains in the Christian East, that if a person is to be initiated into Christ in his church he or she should be received fully rather than only in part. Partial initiation – such as baptism in infancy, eucharistic communion in childhood, and confirmation at some later time – may recommend itself to those concerned with an educational sequence of distinct learning levels. But grace is no more confined by educational requirements than God is restricted to a sacramental order. Furthermore, initiating piecemeal may often suggest that baptism is something less than confirmation, a perception unsupported by the tradition in its integrity as distinct from conventional assumptions of relatively recent date.

It can only be noted that the classic trinitarian creeds * seem originally to have been doctrinal formulations of basic Christian faith which emerged out of the three-fold interrogations concerning faith in Father, Son and Holy Spirit put to those about to be baptized as they stood in the font – an interrogation which constituted the formula of baptism itself. This fact illustrates in a concrete manner how the norm of worship founds or constitutes the norm of belief, mentioned above.

Finally, while the laying on of hands has always played a diverse role throughout Christian liturgical structures, it receives formal mention in early initiatory structures only in Hippolytus, and then in the context of presenting the already baptized to the church along with a second chrismation and epicletic prayer. It does not receive formal mention in other early texts, where the emphasis is on anointing – something which led the recent Roman reforms to stress anointing along with hand-laying as the central gesture in confirmation. Furthermore, the same reforms require that, when confirmation follows baptism immediately, the anointing of confirmation takes the place of the first post-baptismal anointing with chrism.

K. Aland, *Did the Early Church Baptize Infants?*, ET 1963; K. Barth, *The Teaching of the Church Regarding Baptism*, ET 1948; G. R. Beasley-Murray, *Baptism in the New Testament*, 1962; E. Brunner, *Truth as Encounter*, ET 1964; O. Cullmann, *Baptism in the New Testament*, ET 1950; C. Davis, *Sacraments of Initiation: Baptism and Confirmation* (in England *The Making of a Christian*), 1964; G. Dix, *The Theology of Confirmation in Relation to Baptism*, 1946; J. D. C. Fisher, *Christian Initiation: Baptism in the Mediaeval West*, 1965; *Christian Initiation: The Reformation Period*, 1970; P. Jagger, *Christian Initiation 1552–1969*, 1970; J. Jeremias, *Infant Baptism in the First Four Centuries*, ET 1962; A. Kavanagh, *The Shape of Baptism: The Rite of Christian Initiation*, 1978; J. N. D. Kelly, *Early Christian Creeds*, 1950; G. Kretschmar, 'Die Geschichte des Taufgottesdienstes in der alten Kirche', *Leitourgia. Handbuch des evangelischen Gottesdienstes* 5, 1970, pp. 1–348; G. W. H. Lampe, *The Seal of the Spirit: A Study in the Doctrine of Baptism and Confirmation in the New Testament and the Fathers*, [2] 1967; F.-J. Leenhardt, *Le Baptême chrétien, son origine, sa signification*, 1946; L. Mitchell, *Baptismal Anointing*, 1966; Murphy Center (ed), *Made Not Born*, 1976; B. Neunheuser, *Baptism and Confirmation*, ET 1964; K. Rahner, *The Church and the Sacraments*, ET 1963; H. Riley, *Christian Initiation: A Comparative Study of the Interpretation of the Baptismal Liturgy, etc*, 1974; A. Schmemann, *Of Water and the Spirit*, 1974; R. Schnackenburg, *Baptism in the Thought of St Paul*, ET 1964; A. Stenzel, *Die Taufe: eine genetische Erklärung der Taufliturgie*, 1958; L. S. Thornton, *Confirmation: Its Place in the Baptismal Mystery*, 1954; G. Wainwright, 'The Rites and Ceremonies of Christian Initiation', *Studia Liturgica* 10, 1974, pp. 2–24; G. Winkler, 'The Original Meaning of the Prebaptismal Anointing and Its Implications', *Worship* 52, 1978, pp. 24–45; E. Yarnold, *The Awe-Inspiring Rites of Initiation*, 1971.

AIDAN KAVANAGH

Inner Light

The idea of faith as illumination, enabling the soul to see the truth, is a very ancient one. In more modern times the Cambridge Platonists * identified it with reason. But in the Society of Friends *, to whom the concept of the Inner Light is central, it is neither reason nor (as some imagine) conscience. George Fox, the founder of the Society, taught that 'every man was enlightened by the Divine Light of Christ' and used the term almost interchangeably with that of the Holy Spirit. He seems to have been influenced by the German spiritual reformer Sebastian Franck, by Boehme and by the Arminian * Baptists. But more than any of these, Fox took an optimistic and almost Pelagian * view of human nature, believing that there was an inner unity between God and man, 'that of God in every one'. This Inner Light or Christ Within had two functions. It was 'that which shows a man evil' and 'that in which is unity'. Clearly there were dangers of Ranterism in this approach, but Quakers largely escaped these thanks to their plainness of life and their corporate discipline. The conviction that everyone has a share of this light, no matter what their faith or moral reputation, has made Quakers natural mediators and peace-makers, impatient of religious obsessions with sin and total depravity.

Rachel Hadley King, *George Fox and the Light Within*, 1940.

GERALD PRIESTLAND

Inspiration

It seems to have been the Babylonian defeat that provoked the Jews to put together their scriptures. In earlier days Israel and Judah kept their memories mostly by oral recitations. Ancient writings were scattered: royal chronicles in the archives, oracles of the prophets in shrines, landmark litigation and law codes in the temple(s). It was the convulsion of the sixth century BC, when so many of Judah's institutions perished, that a new anxiety for tradition and national identity possessed the exiles. They formed a network of local assemblies, synagogues, for regular worship. The fragments of their shattered past became most precious then, and some of the scribes trained for the civil service now began to recover, edit and expound the ancient writings for those meetings. When Judah was refounded, those readings continued to be read at synagogue worship, and to be augmented occasionally by other newer writings. As Jewish communities sprang up around the Mediterranean, synagogues where Greek was the tongue of both converse and worship provided themselves with translations of the old texts, and contributed some new ones composed in Greek.

The earliest Christians, after their attempts to explain in synagogue how the scriptures were to be construed in the light of Jesus met with increasing impatience there, regrouped into synagogues where their own understanding of Israel's past could be honoured. The anecdotal memories of Jesus and of the earliest ventures of his disciples, and the epistolary instructions of their roving leaders were received into the library from which they read at worship. As with the Jews, so with the Christians: a community consensus slowly formed about what

writings were to be kept within the canon*, or roster of writings sacred enough to be read out and expounded at public worship. When the communities divided over their understandings of tradition, sects and churches were identified by the canon of books they received as theirs.

Some books were selected for their authoritative authorship, like Jeremiah and Galatians. More often the books were anonymous, like Ruth and Jonah, or published under a pseudonym by writers or editors who saw themselves as spokesmen for more ancient figures, e.g. Genesis, Ecclesiastes, Titus. However authorship was not the only criterion for inclusion in the canon. Some books had no known authorship, and others attributed to charismatic figures were set aside. The believing community was choosing for itself scriptures that made sense to their contemporary faith. Also, both Jews and Christians eventually closed their canons. Instead of incorporating the best of their ongoing writings, the scriptures were to serve as the inaugural for the community's belief.

Whether or not the individual authors were known, the community came to regard them and their books as inspired. Every human was imagined to have his or her lungs inflated by God's breath at birth, and to yield back that life-breath at death. Heroic figures like the judges and prophets were believed to have been inspired with a fuller burst of divine breath to strengthen them for their divine mission. In this sense the authors of the scriptures came to be considered inspired.

Both Jews and Christians have at times felt their faith undermined if not grounded on sacred writings reliably free from error. Theologians of this persuasion, taking the Bible as an authority of last rather than first resort, have supposed that inspiration somehow suppressed the human faculties of the writers and conveyed through them a message of flawless doctrine. Such theories have had less appeal for scripture scholars whose familiarity with the texts persuaded them that they embody all the confusions, conflicts, inconsistencies and regressions through which the Jewish and Christian community faltered its way along. They have seen it as a residual record of the faith's development during the first millenium. It displays the track of faith's early trajectory.

The authority of the inspired scriptures resides, not in an intrusive control of the writing process, nor in an error-free presentation, but in a reliable expression of the faith in the unique period of its earliest gestation.

See also **Biblical Criticism, Scripture.**

Paul J. Achtemeier, *The Inspiration of Scripture*, 1980; James Tunstead Burtchaell, CSC, *Catholic Theories of Biblical Inspiration Since 1810: A Review and Critique*, 1969.

JAMES TUNSTEAD BURTCHAELL, CSC

Insufflation

A blowing or breathing upon a person or thing to symbolize and/or effect the giving of the Holy Spirit (cf. John 20.22) and the expulsion of evil spirits. In the primitive and mediaeval periods insufflation was a feature of exorcism, of the rites of the catechumens and, from thence, of baptism; it also forms part of the blessing of the font and the chrism or holy oil. It remains a feature of RC ritual and is found in some Eastern rites, particularly those that have undergone Latin influence, e.g. the Maronite.

J. G. DAVIES

Intercession see **Prayer, Theology of**

Interiority, Interiorization

From at least the period of the 'Rhineland' mystics (Eckhart, Tauler, Suso), there has been a rhetorical tradition of speaking about the mysteries of Christ's incarnate life as realized, or to-be-realized, in the soul of the individual believer. One of its best-known expressions is the dictum of the eccentric seventeenth-century writer Angelus Silesius: 'If Christ were born a thousand times in Bethlehem and yet were not born within your heart, then for you he died in vain.' The divine Word must come to birth in the soul, purified and refined to virginal simplicity and receptivity: there is a constant dialectical movement between the absolute silence and stillness of the generating contemplative state and the emergence of self-less compassionate action – the Word's image imprinted in the believer.

This has obvious affinities with Origen's interest in biblical history as a coded account of the story of the soul, and with all the long-standing conventions of 'spiritual' interpretation of scripture; and it also relates to a variety of ways of understanding the conformation of the Christian to Christ. What is rather different, however, is the stress on the relative unimportance of what is objectively wrought in Christ as opposed to the subjective appropriation of the Word. The risks of individualism and illuminism, an exclusive reliance on the authority of 'inner testimony', did not go unremarked. Anything which suggested that Christ's life and death were only, so to speak, a dramatized projection of the self's inner history would be hard to reconcile with an orthodoxy concerned to defend the idea that God assumes real and particular human existence in Jesus, and that this is a free act of grace, providing a new image of humanity, a new focus of hope. Jesus 'redefines' the human psyche, it does not define him.

However, the issues are complex and wide-ranging. In the present century, Jung has provided a detailed and sophisticated reading of Christian doctrine as a symbolic representation of the historical processes (and personal processes) leading to individuation and maturity: the era of Christ means, in terms of the stay of the psyche, a move towards a higher and more nuanced self-awareness. Jung thus saw the promulgation in 1950 of the dogma of Our Lady's Assumption*, for instance, as a climacteric moment in this story – the extension of a trinity into the fully-balanced quaternity, the reception into the God-image of the hitherto ambivalent female element. And in his famous *Answer to Job*, Jung treated the incarnation as a representation of God coming to full self-awareness – i.e. as a myth of the kind of integration for which humanity strives.

For Jung, the question of whether God 'existed' independently of the human psyche was unanswerable – perhaps even incapable of intelligent formulation. All we can speak of is the way the image functions in the self. For H. A. Williams, approaching the problem from a Freudian* standpoint in the 1950s and 1960s, this mode of understanding talk about God did not foreclose the question of God's objectivity. But more recently Don Cupitt has argued with passion and trenchancy that to understand the function of 'God' in the psyche is necessarily to abandon any commitment to his objectivity or 'extra-religious reality'.

The problem with interiorization of this drastic kind is that much of the function of the God-image depends on its being integrally connected with the idea of the uncontrollable and unassimilable challenge of a given – not merely an 'interior' – reality. The challenge, the dynamism and the critical edge of the notion of an 'objective' God are what saves the interior life from indulgence, stasis and insensitivity to the possibilities of self-deceit. It *may* be that we can only speak of 'God' as the functioning of an image; yet it remains necessary to acknowledge that the image is more than a replaceable and decorative sign for psychological processes. This is the openness of authentic negative theology; and it allows also for the recognition that we do not inhabit a privileged interior world, but are historical, material and social beings.

Don Cupitt, *Taking Leave of God*, 1980; C. G. Jung, *Psychology and Religion, West and East*, 1958; D. Z. Phillips, *Faith and Philosophical Inquiry*, 1970; H. A. Williams, 'Theology and Self-awareness', in A. R. Vidler (ed), *Soundings*, 1962.

ROWAN WILLIAMS

Interpretation *see* Biblical Criticism, Doctrinal Criticism, Hermeneutics

Invincible Ignorance

Is ignorance sin? The question was discussed in detail by Thomas Aquinas, *S T* I, 2, q. 76. He identified culpable ignorance as ignorance of the faith, of the universal natural law, and of the skills which belong to everyone's particular profession. No one in Christendom could not have knowledge of these, and to be ignorant was to sin by omission. But no one could be said to sin if ignorant of things he could not possibly know; such ignorance was 'invincible'. In nineteenth-century RC apologetics it was argued that 'a Protestant who thinks the Catholic religion idolatrous, and cannot reasonably be expected, considering his education, circumstances, &c., to think otherwise, is guiltless so far in the sight of God' (Addis and Arnold, *A Catholic Dictionary*, revised by T. B. Scannell, 1893). The doctrine of invincible ignorance was applied to the case of the good pagan to lead to the conclusion that, although he could not be saved, because unbaptized, he would be consigned only to 'the first circle' of hell where he would suffer no pain. Dante posed the question most acutely. 'A man is born on the bank of the Indus, and none is there to speak, or read, or write of Christ, and all his desires and doings are good, so far as human reason sees, without sin in life or speech. He dies unbaptized and without faith. Where is this justice that condemns him? Where is his fault if he does not believe?' (*Paradiso*, canto xix).

J. C. O'NEILL

Jansenism

This movement owes its name (originally awarded by its detractors) to Cornelius Otto Jansen (1585–1638), a leading theologian of Louvain, promoted Bishop of Ypres in 1636. His *Augustinus* (posthumously published 1640), with its rigorist presentation of Augustine's theology of grace, provoked immediate and violent hostility from Jesuits and their allies in Paris. The case of Jansen was defended by Antoine Arnauld (1612–94), a disciple of Jean Duvergier de Hauranne, Abbé de Saint-Cyran (1581–1643), Jansen's close associate. Arnauld had several relatives (including two abbesses) at the convent of Port-Royal, originally Cistercian but independent since 1627, which followed Saint-Cyran's spiritual teaching and much more than the theological technicalities of the *Augustinus* came to represent the focus of Jansenism. A community of male solitaries, bound by no vows, had grown up near the original site of Port-Royal (near Versailles) and through schools, retreats and religious writings disseminated Jansenist ideas to a wide public. The principal teachings are that grace is irresistible, that even the righteous may on occasion sin through insufficient grace, that in sacramental discipline strict standards should be observed (e.g. in confession the penitent should never be given the benefit of doubt through casuistry; abstaining from communion may be right or necessary if preparation is inadequate or simply as a means of mortification) and that the moral life of the Christian must make no concessions to self (e.g. the theatre and luxury are condemned, charitable works are demanded). Hostility to man-centred Jesuit theology polarized doctrine, ruthless persecution hardened attitudes. Arnauld was condemned in 1657, briefly rehabilitated, then forced into exile in 1679. At his death, the Oratorian P. Quesnel took over the leadership and was the primary target of the bull *Unigenitus* (1713), which provoked schism in Holland (perpetuated by the Old Catholics). Port-Royal suffered continual persecution until the community was finally dissolved in 1709, and the buildings razed next year. Jansenist self-righteousness and their partisan spirit were ultimately self-defeating, though the movement continued into the nineteenth century, but the issues they defended were fundamental and in no way trivial.

N. J. Abercrombie, *The Origins of Jansenism*, 1936; A. Adam, *Du mysticisme à la révolte*, 1968; L. Cognet, *Le Jansénisme*, 1961.

ALBAN KRAILSHEIMER

Jesus

1. The name Jesus (Greek *Iesous*, a rendering of the Hebrew *yeshua‘*, Joshua) is used in contemporary theology to refer to the person Jesus of Nazareth as known from historical research. From the nineteenth century onwards there was constant mention of 'the Jesus of history' ('historical Jesus'), implicitly contrasted with a Jesus who is not 'of history', the obvious alternative being Jesus as presented in the Christian tradition from the NT onwards. However, this term has now come to seem rather dated. It arose in a situation of controversy to express the conviction that there were elements in the church's picture of Jesus which, when examined critically, would prove to be later embellishments; their removal would reveal a figure different from, perhaps even contradictory to, the main lines of that picture, who could become a more appropriate focal point for a modern version of Christianity. In other words, there was an implicit opposition between 'the Jesus of history' and 'the Christ of faith', between critical study of the story of Jesus of Nazareth and the development of Christian doctrine, specifically christology*. But while it is important to note this opposition in looking at the history of modern scholarship, perpetuation of it is likely to distort an understanding of the subject-matter. We know Jesus of Nazareth only through the

tradition of the church with its varied theological colouring; while it is possible to notice tensions within that tradition between various portrayals of Jesus, some elements in which may be more close to the person who gave rise to Christianity than others, it is now impossible to go back in any substantial detail to an original historical figure and recreate the story all over again in a different way.

As both the understanding of the nature of the evidence for the life and work of Jesus and the understanding of historical criticism* have changed considerably over the past two centuries, the complex factors involved in any portrayal of Jesus at all can best be shown by a survey of developments over that period.

2. *The Sources.* Despite the meagreness of the non-Christian evidence for Jesus (Tacitus, Suetonius, Josephus, the Talmud) and the problem, in some cases, of its authenticity, there is no reason to doubt that he existed. Recent studies seeking to demonstrate that he did not, do not carry conviction. When we add to this evidence the primary material contained in the NT, and note the character of the controversies carried on in the early centuries after Jesus' death (the fact of Jesus' past existence is taken for granted by all sides), coupled with the tensions in that material noted above, we have sufficient ground for rejecting out of hand the possibility of Jesus having been a purely mythical or invented figure. On the other hand, none of the evidence outside the Gospels (and in addition to the non-Christian evidence that also includes the various apocryphal writings either long known or recently discovered at Nag Hammadi in Egypt, *see* **Gnosticism**) tells us much about what Jesus said or did that can claim to have independent historical value. Consequently, while the background to the age in which Jesus lived is being increasingly illuminated by further discovery and research, not least in modern Jewish studies, unless we are given any authentic new material bearing *directly* on the life of Jesus, historical investigation into his career is dependent on the interpretation of the Gospels, which by their very nature present exegetical problems of the utmost complexity. Investigations in the early post-Enlightenment period, and many more popular

modern investigations, prove to have been vitiated by insufficient knowledge of the historical background and a failure to realize the interpretative problems.

3. *The 'Quest of the Historical Jesus'*. The first period of critical study of the figure of Jesus takes its title from Albert Schweitzer's classic account, published in English as *The Quest of the Historical Jesus* (ET 1910; German *Von Reimarus zu Wrede*, 1906). Hermann Samuel Reimarus (1694–1768), who for Schweitzer marked the beginning of the Quest, was a teacher of oriental languages in Hamburg. Seven sections of a long criticism of Christianity which he wrote were published after his death by Gotthold Lessing (1729–1781) as the *Wolfenbüttel Fragments*. In the longest of them, 'On the aims of Jesus and his Disciples', Reimarus claimed to be distinguishing what Jesus really said and taught from the (false) account of the apostolic writings. The substance of his argument was that Jesus was a traditional Jew persuaded that he was the long-foretold Messiah. At first Jesus' disciples believed his claims, but after his death they revised the whole story of his career and made the earthly kingdom of Jesus into a heavenly one. Similarities between Reimarus' theory and that of Schweitzer (see below) led Schweitzer to view Reimarus as a great pioneer. The truth, however, is not so simple nor are the similarities quite as striking in context as Schweitzer made out. The work of Reimarus is hardly yet historical reconstruction. The rest of his writing shows him to have been preoccupied with the conflict between reason and Christianity in all its aspects; in this he was strongly influenced by English Deism *; for the most part, his arguments reflect standpoints developed from the beginning of the eighteenth century. The same thing specifically applies to his study of Jesus; rationalist views show through again and again, and the features of the work which so impressed Schweitzer are not least born of the necessity of reconciling the Gospels with convictions held on other grounds. If, however, Reimarus represents little advance beyond his English predecessors, he is significant in that the form of his work and the way in which it was presented raised in Germany the question of the person of Jesus in a way that was to dominate the nineteenth century.

At this stage, historical investigation is, of course, hardly worthy of the name. Enlightenment * historiography with its recurrent inability to see figures of the past other than as eighteenth-century people in different garb leads readily to quite unhistorical accounts, which explain the unusual in terms of misunderstanding and deception. This perspective persisted through the nineteenth century and even into the twentieth.

In the period immediately following Reimarus we see a heightened interest in the miraculous – the unusual in the extreme – an element in which the Gospels are rich. Some early nineteenth-century lives of Jesus, notably that by H. E. G. Paulus (1761–1851), are no more than a collection of explanations of the miracles without any interconnecting links; here, too, possible individual explanations are heaped up at the expense of general historical probability.

As much was pointed out by David Friedrich Strauss (1808–1874), in his first *Life of Jesus*, published in two volumes in 1835–1836 and translated into English by George Eliot (1846). Strauss, too, lacked a historical sense and did not construct a coherent 'life' of Jesus; like his rationalist predecessors, he was concerned to criticize individual points of the Gospel narratives. He differed from them, however, in his introduction and widespread use of the category of myth. Myth is carefully explained and positive and negative criteria are given; it contradicts natural, historical and psychological laws, being poetic narrative which expresses religious concepts, deriving from Christian experience, the OT and elsewhere. By examining the Gospels in the light of this approach, Strauss was able to play off the earlier rationalist approach against the traditional orthodox approach, and found both wanting. Despite his care in explaining the term myth, Strauss gives the impression of using an imprecise concept too loosely and too enthusiastically; it can be employed as a blunt instrument to suppress almost any unwelcome opposition. Consequently Strauss's results are overwhelmingly negative. However, his use of the concept did introduce a new and important element into the investigation and showed up the inadequacies of previous work – nor was his scepticism entirely unjustified.

It was in fact some time before the contribution of Strauss, like that of his great teacher F. C. Baur (1792–1860), the first theologian seriously to come to grips with the beginnings of Christianity in historical terms, really made itself felt. At first it was neglected, even (paradoxically enough) by Strauss himself in his second *Life of Jesus* (1864). By far the most popular writings about Jesus during the latter half of the nineteenth century were the many 'Lives', which attempted to present a coherent picture of him by removing features regarded as inauthentic and supplying material to fill the many gaps in the Gospel narratives. The opportunities for selectivity and elaboration are considerable, and inevitably numerous Lives were written to further specific ideals; there are also numerous examples of sheerly bad historical writing. Details can be found in Schweitzer's book. Even among the best writing, however, an important trend is to be noted. The early lives which presented a coherent picture of Jesus, e.g. K. F. Bahrdt's *Explanation of the Plans and Aims of Jesus* (1784–1792) and K. H. Venturini's *Nonsupernatural History of the Great Prophet of Nazareth* (1800–1802), were predominantly concerned with criticism and explanation of events in Jesus' life; later work was concerned rather with Jesus as a personality. Reconstruction of Jesus' teaching, his conduct, his inner development and his impact on his contemporaries was a means of arriving at this personality. For side by side with the claim that historical method was neutral and discovered facts ran an idealist view of history for which personality was all-important. Man was seen to be a partner in the movement towards the divine goal of the historical process, and shared in this movement by making himself open to spiritual power. From time to time great individuals appeared, who embodied this power to a supreme degree. Chief among these was Jesus, on whom God brought his fatherly goodness to bear, revealing the infinite value of the human soul.

In theory, the great liberal systematic theologians Albrecht Ritschl and Wilhelm Herrmann, along with the liberal historian Adolf von Harnack, set out to maintain a distinction between fact and value, between history and faith. This was, however, more difficult, particularly for lesser lights, to maintain in practice. As a result the work of reconstructing a historical Jesus became fatally entangled with a second task, the construction of a figure considerable enough to replace the Christ of the church's tradition as an object of faith. Two representative nineteenth-century works to be seen against this background are E. Renan's *Life of Jesus* (1863) and J. R. Seeley's *Ecce Homo* (1865); there are many, many others. Believing that they knew the main lines of what the figure of Jesus would embody when he was 'discovered', historians projected what they were looking for on to the lay-figure of Jesus, whether there was support in the Gospels or not. When Schweitzer came to write his book, it was therefore an easy task for him to demonstrate that the 'liberal' lives of Jesus were no more than mirror-reflections of the views of nineteenth-century man. Nor, towards the end of the twentieth century, has Schweitzer's lesson yet been properly learnt. Long after Schweitzer, 'Lives' of Jesus have been written or portraits of him created which reveal more of the concerns of the writers than the likely character of Jesus himself. The difference is that with the weakening of church structures and the increasing specialization of theology, coupled with a decline in general theological literacy, the new pictures of Jesus range over an even wider spectrum, venturing into areas – like the sexuality of Jesus – which in the previous century would have been tabu.

4. *Jesus in his Time*. Johannes Weiss (1863–1914), pupil and son-in-law of Ritschl, influenced by developments in the study of Judaism in the world of Jesus' time, represents another step forward. In his short monograph *Jesus' Proclamation of the Kingdom of God* (1892), Weiss established on an exegetical basis that Jesus was a prophetic Jewish figure, using the thought-patterns of his own time, proclaiming a kingdom of God which was imminent, but had not yet come. Weiss's view was popularized and developed by Schweitzer later; the result was a figure alien to the modern world, even a figure to whom Schweitzer believed that contemporary Christianity could not subscribe. In this too he resembled Johannes Weiss. Weiss recognized the gulf between the 'eschatological' Jesus and the theology of his master, Ritschl. Having come to this point, however, both Schweitzer and Weiss turned their backs on the question of the significance of the Jesus they had found;

given, in effect, a choice between him and their cherished nineteenth-century ideals, they both unhesitatingly chose the latter.

Study of Jesus against the background of first-century Judaism has increased enormously since the time of Weiss and Schweitzer, and their conclusions now appear crude in the light of our new-found knowledge of the world of his time. The growing gulf between the churches and the academic world has also meant that this study is no longer overshadowed by the pressing demand or desire to go on to indicate immediately the consequences for Christian faith of particular findings. For example, writings by Jewish scholars are content simply to see Jesus as the Jew that he undoubtedly was, against as full a background as possible (the best-known example of this kind of work is Geza Vermes, *Jesus the Jew*, along with the related articles which supplement it). In fact it would now be very widely accepted that Jesus, whatever we may prove to know about him, does belong to his day and its thought world, and that the historical Jesus has only an indirect relationship to contemporary Christian questions.

5. *Source criticism*. As was pointed out above, no amount of investigation of the background of Jesus can replace an understanding of the documents which are the prime record of his life and work, and from the late eighteenth century up to the present, 'Lives' of Jesus and similar works, however thorough their research into historical background, fail if they have misconceptions about the nature of the Gospel record. It is to the specialist study of this that we must now turn, retracing our steps to follow a line of development which ran parallel to the writings of the Lives of Jesus so far considered.

Up to the eighteenth century the four Gospels were harmonized, i.e. dovetailed together to form a single picture of Jesus. A first step beyond this treatment was taken by J. J. Griesbach (1745–1812), who in 1775 first published the text of Matthew, Mark and Luke in parallel, together with the relevant material from John. This procedure alone made it quite clear that there was a special relationship between the first three Gospels ('Synoptic Gospels'), whereas John played a different role. In the early period the question whether John or the

Synoptic Gospels came first was an open one. A number of writers, including Schleiermacher, favoured John because of the lesser degree to which the miraculous appeared in his work; Strauss, on the other hand, argued for the secondary nature of the Fourth Gospel. Griesbach himself had argued that Matthew is the earliest of the Gospels we have, and this position was favoured by F. C. Baur and the Tübingen school. In 1838, however, C. H. Weisse argued that Mark was the first of our Gospels, and after a period during which his work was almost forgotten, the theory was revived in 1863 by H. J. Holtzmann (1832–1910). Taken further by scholars in Germany and, most notably, in England, it won almost universal acceptance and became the foundation stone for the later 'Lives' of Jesus. Mark, it was believed, offered a reliable chronological framework on the basis of which the life of Jesus could be portrayed. A substantial majority of scholars have continued to accept the priority of Mark among the Synoptic Gospels, though in recent years it has again been challenged strongly; furthermore, after a period of neglect the historical value of the Fourth Gospel has again been repeatedly argued for. The geographical information it contains is now rated much more highly, and attempts have been made to play down the differences between the discourses attributed to Jesus in the Fourth Gospel and the sayings in the synoptic tradition. Some would see a tradition behind the Fourth Gospel which rivalled that underlying the Synoptic Gospels, attributing it to a community of followers of Jesus other than the Twelve. This has introduced yet more uncertainties into the discussion. Be this as it may, at any rate the assumption that Mark provides a chronological framework for the life of Jesus has long been shattered in pieces.

6. *The 'Historic' Christ*. As we have seen, it was assumed, whether explicitly or tacitly, by those who used historical criticism to construct a picture of Jesus that this 'Jesus of history' was the 'real' Jesus. That fundamental assumption was vigorously challenged by Martin Kähler (1835–1912) in a lecture, first published in 1892, entitled *The So-called Historical Jesus and the Historic, Biblical Christ*. The subtle distinction between 'historical' and 'historic' indicates the

degree of sophistication now reached in reflection upon history and historical method. Kähler uses the word 'historical' (German *historisch*) in the sense, mentioned above, of 'what is discovered by the method of the historian'; on the other hand, a person or event is 'historic' (*geschichtlich*) by virtue of the effect he, she or it has on the future.

Given the choice between the 'historical Jesus' and the 'historic Christ' it is clear, Kähler argues, which is the 'real' Christ. Even more forcibly than Schweitzer and, of course, before him, Kähler argued that the quest of the 'historical Jesus' was a blind alley; indeed, the historical Jesus only served to conceal the living Christ. Kähler commended the quest as a protest against abstract dogmatism, but now it had immodestly gone too far. He unerringly points to the weaknesses: inadequate sources which appear in two basic forms with substantial differences; no certain eye-witnesses; an 'almost incomprehensible' carefreeness in transmission; the material subservient to the evangelists' purpose. (In much of this Kähler is reminiscent of Strauss, to whom in fact he refers.) It is therefore impossible to write a life of Jesus, let alone to 'psychologize' him. Not that this would be possible anyway, for Jesus is different from us *in kind*. This introduces Kähler's positive argument, which moves between two poles. The Christ of the Bible (not just the earthly career of Jesus, but the Lord risen, ascended and proclaimed) evoked in the past and still evokes the confession 'Christ is Lord'; that Christ is Lord is also confirmed by the present experience of the believer. The way in which each of these aspects confirms the other is sufficient to give the believer his certainty. After all, only a few specialist scholars have the training to carry on the work of historical criticism and their work spans barely a century; what of the countless others who still 'know' Jesus?

Kähler's arguments raise important questions to which they do not provide completely satisfactory answers; in fact, some of them are still being discussed today. In a remarkably prophetic way he points to future developments, even in the realm of detailed criticism, in which he himself was not versed.

7. *Form criticism and its aftermath.* In answer to the objection that the picture of Christ on which he relied would itself also turn out to be an arbitrary figment of the imagination, Kähler pointed to the way in which the Gospels offer a series of 'sketches' – examples of how Jesus customarily acted – each one reflecting the full person of the Lord. These 'sketches' were next to occupy the attention of NT critics. This new study did not spring directly from Kähler's work, but from various hints already offered by NT scholars, and more particularly from work pioneered in the OT field in the 'history of forms', now commonly known as 'form criticism'*. In the NT, as in the OT, form criticism was an attempt to trace the history of the biblical material before it was written down. It is based on the recognition that the traditions of a community are shaped and stylized according to its life and needs – various settings and purposes giving rise to quite specific forms. The critic looked for the *Sitz im Leben*, the setting in the life of the community, for the forms which he studied. The undifferentiated use of the term 'form critic' can, however, be misleading, particularly in the NT field, as the three pioneers, whose work appeared independently and almost simultaneously, differed considerably in their approaches. Karl Ludwig Schmidt (1891–1956), in his *The Framework of the Story of Jesus* (1919), examined the framework of Mark and the other Synoptic Gospels and discovered from the details it contained that, far from being original, it represented an attempt on the part of the evangelists to impose an order on material which reached them with no fixed chronological sequence. Connecting links were given to them only towards the end of the Gospels, in the passion narrative. On the basis of increasing information about the situation of the early church, Rudolf Bultmann (1884–1976) in *The History of the Synoptic Tradition* (1921) and Martin Dibelius (1883–1947) in *From Tradition to Gospel* (1919) examined the individual units (pericopes) of which the Synoptic Gospels are now seen to be made up. Bultmann subjected the Gospel material to a thorough analysis and concentrated his attention on the pericopes themselves; Dibelius made an imaginative attempt to picture the life of the community and to see from that the way in which the Gospels might have arisen. Inevitably, in either case the argument was a circular one, by the very nature of the evidence; furthermore, there

was considerable divergence on points of detail, again because of the sparsity of the sources. Nevertheless, some general conclusions of agreed importance began to emerge. The material available to the evangelists had been preserved and shaped in the worshipping life of the Christian community, with the consequences that entails: a public setting, selection of material to suit the community's ends in its preaching and teaching, and a neglect of the information which the modern historian would most like to have. Moreover, the Gospels, too, made up of this material, are themselves written from faith to faith, to meet specific needs in the churches of their origins. This led to study of the Gospels *as a whole* along these lines, which has come to be given the name 'redaction criticism'; here an attempt is made to elucidate the features which go to make up the theological portraits presented by each of the evangelists. It is impossible to give a detailed account of such theological work here, but from what has been said it will be evident at how early a stage study of Jesus turns into christology*. As to knowledge of Jesus of Nazareth, it is evident (see above) that the framework of Mark, the backbone of the nineteenth-century lives, no longer sustains the weight placed on it; and because of the process through which the Gospel tradition has passed, the historicity of its details can be asserted *confidently* only where their origin cannot be explained from the life of the church. Since one cannot, on the other hand, argue that Jesus was unique in every respect, the would-be biographer has also to assume that in some cases, at any rate, the concerns of Jesus and the interests of the church coincided. Precisely where, however, no one can say. So many are the imponderables that the degree of uncertainty is always likely to be very high indeed, and given the problems it might well seem that to write a 'Life of Jesus' is impossible.

8. *Kerygmatic theology.* Kähler's stress on the 'Christ of faith' was also continued and intensified immediately after the First World War (again, it took time to be assimilated) in the movement, led by Karl Barth, referred to as kerygmatic* or dialectical theology. In reaction to the main trends of nineteenth-century theology, Barth (and Bultmann, whose theology at this period is virtually indistinguishable) turned his back on previous views of the continuity between human personalities and God to emphasize the discontinuity between God and man. This emphatic assertion of the 'otherness' of God brought with it an assertion of the 'otherness' of the Bible and a consequent tension with historical criticism. The all important thing was the *Word** conveyed in the Bible, a Word which could not suffer questioning, but demanded obedience. It carries its own legitimation, and even if there were every chance of success in historical terms, to attempt to legitimize the word by the use of historical criticism would be to deny faith. On this basis, to look for a 'historical' Jesus as the nineteenth century did is not only impossible, but *illegitimate.*

Several factors led to the widespread acceptance of this remarkable assertion. 1. Protestant Germany was still the centre and focal point of theology, and those who called for the rejection of any search for a historical Jesus wielded enormous influence, not only in their own country, but also, through their students, in America. 2. This emphasis accorded very well with the heritage of Lutheran theology and its stress on the *sola fide**. 3. It coincided with the movement in England and America known as 'biblical theology'*, in which interest shifted from historical research to the exploration and systematization of 'biblical' concepts, which were thought to be the most important feature of the Bible. As a result, it was not until well after the Second World War that any substantial advance was made in critical study of the person and work of Jesus (*see also* **Historical Criticism**).

9. *The 'New Quest' of the Historical Jesus.* A generation after Bultmann's pioneering work and the ban pronounced by kerygmatic theology on looking for a 'historical' Jesus, Bultmann's pupils had risen to occupy distinguished academic posts in Germany. They began to express their dissatisfaction at the accepted state of affairs and set out to change it. Two of the most important works to mark the new development were a lecture by Ernst Käsemann, 'The Problem of the Historical Jesus', given in 1953 and published a year later (ET in *Essays on New Testament Themes*, 1964, pp. 15–47) and Günther Bornkamm's book *Jesus of Nazareth*, published in 1956 (ET 1960). In these two

very different studies, two points are agreed and stressed: on the one hand it is quite impossible to write a 'Life' of Jesus, as the necessary material is simply not available. On the other hand, it would be quite fatal if scepticism were to lead to a complete disengagement of interest from the earthly Jesus. The question what can be known about Jesus is an extraordinarily difficult one – but that does not mean that no attempt can be made to answer it. The change is thus one in theological position; it is a reaction to claims that it is illegitimate to go beyond the church's kerygma. The critical position hardly changed: this can easily be seen from a comparison between the factual material about Jesus in Bultmann's own *Jesus and the Word* (1926, ET 1934) and Bornkamm's *Jesus of Nazareth*; in these terms the latter represents virtually no advance over the former. But whereas Bultmann was saying *vis à vis* the nineteenth century, 'We only know this', Bornkamm was saying *vis à vis* Bultmann, 'We know *all* this'. The 'new quest' might not have been discussed so widely but for a personal contribution by its main chronicler to its progress. James M. Robinson argued that it was possible to be more optimistic about having knowledge of Jesus because of a change in the understanding of history brought about by the work of Dilthey, Croce, Collingwood and others. Whereas the historians of the nineteenth century were concerned with facts – names, places, dates, events, sequences – this new view of history is aware of a deeper plane. It sets out to grasp the act of intention, the commitment, the meaning for those involved, behind the external events. It is concerned with the 'selfhood' of those involved, and material about the 'selfhood' of Jesus, he argues, is precisely what we do have in the Gospels. Through this we *can* know Jesus. This optimistic view has not established itself; if it is difficult enough to 'understand' a Luther or a Newman, with all the copious material available – how can this be possible in the case of Jesus? The 'new quest' looks all too much like the old in yet another form.

10. *Conclusion.* There is a good deal that we probably do know about Jesus; the trouble is that we cannot always be sure precisely what it is. Because of the very nature of historical research, discussions about Jesus always contain countless approximations, and one of the most confident recent studies (A. E. Harvey, *Jesus and the Constraints of History*, 1982) concedes that 'it can still be argued that we can have no reliable historical knowledge about Jesus with regard to anything that really matters' (p. 6). This being so, it is remarkable that attempts to restate the significance of Jesus without the doctrine of Incarnation* can be based on what amounts to an interpretation of the character of Jesus which is actually based on very little historical evidence. However christology may be worked out, there is no escaping our considerable ignorance about actual facts.

Günther Bornkamm, *Jesus of Nazareth*, ET 1960; Rudolf Bultmann, *Jesus and the Word*, ET 1934; A. E. Harvey, *Jesus and the Constraints of History*, 1982; John H. Hayes, *Son of God to Superstar*, 1976; Martin Kähler, *The So-called Historical Jesus and the Historic, Biblical Christ*, ET 1964; James Mackey, *Jesus the Man and the Myth*, 1979; D. E. Nineham, 'Epilogue', in *The Myth of God Incarnate*, ed. John Hick, 1977; D. Pals, *The Victorian Lives of Jesus*, 1982; H. S. Reimarus, *Fragments*, ed. Charles H. Talbert, ET 1971; James M. Robinson, *A New Quest of the Historical Jesus*, 1959; Edward Schillebeeckx, *Jesus. An Experiment in Christology*, ET 1979; Albert Schweitzer, *The Quest of the Historical Jesus*, ET 1954; David Friedrich Strauss, *The Life of Jesus Critically Examined*, ET 1846 reissued 1972; Barnes Tatum, *In Search of Jesus*, 1982; Johannes Weiss, *Jesus' Proclamation of the Kingdom of God*, ET 1972; William Wrede, *The Messianic Secret*, ET 1971.

JOHN BOWDEN

Jungian Psychology

Where Freud offers a wholly negative critique of religious belief, Jung offers a critical reconstruction. Theologians remain divided about whether Jung has provided fresh evidence for the *anima naturaliter christiana* thesis or whether he has erected an aesthetically beguiling alternative to Christianity. Some find in him liberating possibilities for renewal of faith. Others fear that, undoubted therapeutic success to one side, Jung is the kind of friend of whom the theologian might well be wary lest theological truths be swallowed up in sympathetic psychological understanding.

Jung found that in the majority of his patients in the second half of life questions of religious meaning, whether acknowledged or not, were of crucial importance in psychological distress and its resolution. A significant portion of his work concerns topics like prophecy, visions, the Christ image, sacraments, the Trinity, the Virgin Mary. Whether polemical or constructive, astute or perverse, his observations are invariably penetrating, often revolutionary. Disagreements arise over his tendency to use psychological data to modify or supplement Christian doctrines. This has been particularly so over the question of God's responsibility for evil, dramatically stated in the *Answer to Job*.

An important thread in Jung's thought is his understanding, or misunderstanding, of the implications of Kant's philosophy. 'The psyche cannot leap beyond itself. It cannot set up any absolute truths, for its own polarity determines the relativity of its statements . . . All comprehension and all that is comprehended is in itself psychic, and to that extent we are hopelessly cooped up in an exclusively psychic world' (*Memories, Dreams, Reflections*, pp. 322–3).

This view sets a limit to any absolute or transcendental claims of a religious or metaphysical kind, though Jung did not consistently observe this limitation himself. Sheer relativism and subjectivism may, however, be avoided if it can be shown that there are cross-cultural regularities in our dispositions, moods and thoughts, fantasies and visions which can be correlated with the more orderly, public and reflective material of religious teachings and religious myths. Further, if these regularities and recurrences are indicative of a generic drive towards meaning in the psyche, pressing individuals towards their unique fulfilment, then something like an empirical correlate of religious claims about reality may have been found.

Jung discovered such regularities in a level of unconscious functioning which was not explicable in terms of actual personal experience or personal desire. This unconscious level which is basically the same in all humans he thus terms 'objective' or 'collective', and the recurrent motifs which it produces 'archetypal'. Jung's usage of the term 'collective' fluctuates between a sense

of a *sine qua non* of human life (like the possession of a brain) and more psychologically controversial ideas of a collective entity (like an *anima mundi* or God) in which as individuals we participate or inhere.

In either case, the hypothesis of a collective unconscious with an inherent drive towards meaningfulness sharply distinguishes Jung's thought from that of Freud. If he is right, then meanings can in no way be reductively related to the vicissitudes of more basic instincts and their adaptation. For Jung it may as well be that a spiritual need manifests itself inappropriately as a sexual or other disturbance as that (Freud) a sexual or other need inappropriately manifests itself in spiritual guise. If there is an innate drive towards symbolization, then symbols are a natural phenomenon. Unlike the conscious mind nature has no intention to deceive. Thus symbols are not, in the first instance, to be examined as substitutes or disguised expressions of disavowed desires for something else. It follows that not only may symbols be important indicators of non-symbolic states of affairs but that the response to and appropriation of symbols may be a necessary and even transformative experience. Resistance to taking symbols seriously may be as destructive of well being as the flight from reality into symbol in classical psychoanalysis.

Freud's theory is fundamentally one of inescapable and ultimately irresolvable conflict between instincts and civilization, the claims of fantasy and desire and those of reality. Jung, too, has sometimes been described as a dualist, but the accent and basic premises are quite different. Psyche and society will conflict, but psyche itself is seen as a system of oppositions with a natural tendency towards self-regulation: a move in one direction will always be met by a countervailing tendency. Such different kinds of opposites as aggression/tenderness, hope/despair, confidence/doubt, engagement/depression, morality/immorality, cannot be resolved in the sense of a permanent triumph of one over the other. The tension of opposites is in Jung's view the definition of energy, and energy is life. It is by painfully living through the conflict of opposites that individuals may come, not to be redeemed from them, but better able to live beyond them. An unresolved theological aspect of Jung's thought is whether God is to be considered as the *coincidentia oppositorum* or a reality beyond all conceivable opposites, as Nicholas of Cusa, to whom Jung refers, thought. It is characteristic of their basic directions that at the breaking point of their collaboration, in 1912, Freud called his book, with its fundamental critique of religious symbolism, *Totem and Taboo*, while Jung called his extraordinary and compelling work, *Symbols of Transformation*.

In Jung's view it is the prime task of adulthood to come to terms with the archetype of the God-image in the quest of the realization of the self, the focussed totality of all psychic contents. For Jung the self symbolizes the totality of man, and he is not whole without God: the symbols of the self coincide with those of the deity. Whether this deity coincides with that of Christian theism has remained a matter open to continued controversy. The Kantian strain in Jung is constant: there are numberless images of God, but the original behind them is inaccessible to us; one can say that God approaches man in the form of symbols but one cannot be sure if the symbol is 'correct' or not.

The obvious affinity between Jung's preoccupations in religion and those of natural theology, his extensive writings on topics like the symbolism of the mass, often lead to the idea that he was primarily addressing himself to and in critical sympathy with the Catholic tradition. Such a picture can sometimes be seriously misleading.

If he were to be assigned a Christian position, he more than once described himself as an old-fashioned radical Protestant and referred to the important influence of Schleiermacher in his family. Certainly his views of Jesus had more in common with his Protestant than his Catholic contemporaries. The number of basic themes common to the works of Schleiermacher and Jung in their responses to Enlightenment* thought indicate that there is a good case for considering Jung as a major figure in the history of Liberal Protestantism*.

James W. Heisig, *Imago Dei, A Study of C. G. Jung's Psychology of Religion*, 1979; C. G. Jung, *Psychology and Religion*, Collected Works, Vol. 11, 1969; Victor White, *God and the Unconscious* (rev. ed.), 1982.

ADRIAN CUNNINGHAM

Justification

The term, as an expression for salvation* through Christ, is rooted in the soteriological* vocabulary of the OT, finds its canonical definition in Paul's letters to the Galatians and the Romans, and has moved to the centre of subsequent Christian thinking whenever the problem of a legalistic or moralistic piety has reappeared.

1. *The NT*. In Paul's letters to the Galatians and the Romans, as in Judaism, righteousness is the condition for salvation. 'Righteousness' (*dikaiosune*), in this context, carried over the forensic connotation of the Hebrew *ṣedeq* or *ṣᵉdāqāh*: it refers not to moral quality but to standing in the eyes of the judge or court. To be 'justified' is to have the verdict of 'just' or 'righteous' passed upon one (in Greek the three words are cognates from the same root *dik*-): that is, to be acquitted, vindicated, *declared* right or innocent. In this sense, even God may be said to be justified (Ps. 51.4, quoted in Rom. 3.4; cf. Luke 7.29), and the contrary of 'justified' is 'condemned' (Rom. 8.33–34; cf. II Cor. 3.9).

In common with Judaism, Paul understands justification eschatologically*. It used to be supposed that he differs from Judaism in that for him the forensic-eschatological righteousness is already imputed* to the believer in the present. But since the discovery of the Dead Sea Scrolls, it is recognized that the eschatological presence of the divine verdict is by no means distinctively Pauline. The difference, rather, is that whereas Paul saw in Judaism a righteousness of the law, he himself taught a righteousness through faith in Christ (Rom. 9.30–31; 10.4–6; cf. Phil. 3.9), apart from law (Rom. 3.21): 'For we hold that a man is justified by faith apart from the works of the law' (Rom. 3.28; cf. Gal. 2.16; 3.11; 5.4). The same thought, that no one is justified by his own works, is expressed also by saying that justification is by grace*, through the redemption* in Christ Jesus (Rom. 3.24), and that the righteousness of faith is the righteousness of God: that is, at least in some passages, it comes from God (Rom. 10.3; cf. Phil. 3.9).

Whether justification is the heart of the Pauline gospel, or only a polemical form of it, the term seldom occurs in Paul's other letters (see II Cor. 4.4; 6.11) or in other books of the NT (in something like the Pauline sense, the verb appears in Matt. 12.37; Luke 10.29; 16.15; 18.14; Acts 13.39; Titus 3.7). In the Letter of James the Pauline terms are used in a different sense and for a different purpose: to deny that a Christian may rest content with mere intellectual belief (James 2.14–26).

2. *Roman Catholic Interpretations*. The first post-canonical theologian to devote major attention to the doctrine of justification was Augustine (354–430), who was provoked by the Pelagian* heresy. The spirit of Paul's teaching shines through Augustine's often passionate assaults on pride or boasting, but it is mixed with some un-Pauline elements. Justification, for Augustine, is a *making* righteous – a healing activity of God in which, by pouring love into the hearts of sinners, he redirects their desires from earthly things to himself as their highest good. A key textual warrant for this conception was found in Rom. 5.5, 'love of God' being taken for an objective genitive: 'love *for* God', which is *caritas*. In consequence of the 'infusion of charity', the Christian is enabled to perform meritorious acts; he makes progress in righteousness, and what is still lacking God forgives: 'Our very righteousness, genuine though it is because directed to the genuine good as its goal, is nevertheless of such measure in this life that it consists more in the remission of sins than in the perfection of virtues' (*De civ. dei*, xix.27).

Much the same view prevailed in Thomas Aquinas' (1224/25–1274) conception of justification as the effect of the operative grace transmitted in the sacraments; but it was jeopardized in late mediaeval theology by Nominalist* (or Occamist) teaching that justifying grace must be earned – even if only by the deficient merit (*de congruo*) of doing the best one can without it. It is disputed whether or not the Council of Trent* (1545–1563) intended to rule out the Nominalist view. However, the subsequent elevation of Thomism in the Roman Church gives special weight to the Thomistic view. Modern RC scholars do not deny the forensic meaning of the Pauline verb 'to justify', but their concern is to stress the efficacy of divine grace in bringing about an actual ('ontological') change in the one who is jus-

tified. Further, they maintain that only a faith 'formed by love' (*caritate formata*) can unite the Christian with Christ, a claim supported from Gal. 5.6 and I Cor. 13.

3. *Protestant Interpretations*. Martin Luther (1483–1546) protested against the Nominalist doctrine of preparation for grace and raised justification by faith alone to the status of 'the chief article' of Christian belief. Curiously, however, there is much dispute about what he meant by his chief article, when and in what way he departed from 'catholic' teaching, and whether, in the interests of the new ecumenical climate, a 'catholic' construction could be put on his famous watchwords 'by faith alone' and 'righteous and sinner at the same time' (*see also* **Sola fide, Simul justus et peccator**). The conceptual problems lie partly in the fact that Luther, like Augustine, thought of Christian righteousness as consisting in two things: both a healing or making righteous and a forgiving or counting righteous.

Luther's fundamental conception of justification is summed up in the formula: 'Faith begins righteousness, imputation perfects it' (*Weimarer Ausgabe*, 40, 1.364.27). One can certainly find in Luther adumbrations of the 'legal fiction' of later Protestantism, according to which God reckons sinners to be what in reality they are not – righteous. But his main thought is that God counts faith as righteousness because that is what it is, even if it is only an incipient righteousness: the man who reposes all his confidence in God through Christ is *right*, and God so pronounces him. His faith is not a human work* prerequisite to justification; it is a work of God, who imparts it by showing himself worthy of confidence through the proclamation of the word. But the principle of 'faith alone' by no means excludes human works after justification: in Luther's view it makes them possible, because it liberates one from the anxious struggle for salvation and so liberates one to attend to the needs of others.

A number of Protestant theologians since Luther have made significant contributions to the development of the doctrine of justification, notably Ritschl, Barth, Reinhold Niebuhr, and Tillich. Much of the twentieth-century discussion has turned around the question whether, for one reason or another, the entire conception of justification no longer speaks to the condition of modern man.

Rudolf Bultmann, *Theology of the New Testament*, Vol. 1, ET 1952; B. A. Gerrish, *The Old Protestantism and the New: Essays on the Reformation Heritage*, 1982; Ernst Käsemann, *Commentary on Romans*, ET 1980; Hans Küng, *Justification: The Doctrine of Karl Barth and a Catholic Reflection*, ET 1964; Albrecht Ritschl, *The Christian Doctrine of Justification and Reconciliation: The Positive Development of the Doctrine*, ET 1900, reissued 1966; Paul Tillich, *The Protestant Era*, 1952.

B. A. GERRISH

Kairos

An important word in the Greek NT, it means 'the appointed time in the purpose of God' (e.g. Mark 1.15, 'the *kairos* is fulfilled'). Paul Tillich gave it prominence in his theology, in which it appears to mean those crises or turning-points in history which demand specific existential decision while the opportunity is still present; the coming of the Christ is the unique example of such *kairoi*.

ALAN RICHARDSON

Kenosis

The concept of the 'self-emptying' of God, based on the Greek of Phil. 2.7 (*kenoō*), 'he emptied himself', and used to indicate the nature of God's condescension in incarnation*. Kenotic love is constitutive of God's being. Expressed through reciprocal divine-human self-giving in Christ, God's love overcomes evil and creates salvation through death and resurrection. Theories of *kenosis*, arising in sixteenth-century Lutheran debate, were revived in the nineteenth century to reinterpret classical doctrines of incarnation. Much criticized, e.g. by W. Temple and D. M. Baillie, they have been explored again, notably by Barth and Rahner.

See also **Christology**.

K. Barth, *CD* IV/1, IV/2, ET 1956; K. Rahner, *Theological Investigations* 4, ET 1966, pp. 114f.; L. J. Richard, *A Kenotic Christology*, 1982.

GEORGE NEWLANDS

Kerygma

A noun from the Greek verb *kēryssein*, referring to the function of the herald (*kēryx*, cf. I Tim. 2.7), important in the ancient world in secular and religious contexts. Hence 'to proclaim', 'to announce', generally an event, especially a victory. The noun means either 'what is proclaimed' or 'the act of proclaiming'. It has played a considerable role in modern theology in two ways.

1. In biblical theology* as a term for what was believed to be recoverable as a single original core of the Christian gospel* within the varied NT writings, which gives them an internal unity. In Continental theology this was identified with the Pauline preaching of the cross, or cross and resurrection (I Cor. 1.23; 15.3ff.); in British theology it was extended to include the pattern of preaching in Acts 2–13, and seen as underlying e.g. Hebrews and I John and the shape of Mark's Gospel. This view of a single original *kērygma* may have to be modified if the 'sermons' in Acts are judged to be 'speeches' supplied by Luke in his overall plan and reflecting a later theology, or if a place is to be found for the expectation of the parousia appearing in the summary of the message in I Thess. 1.10.

2. In theology more widely as emphasizing that the Christian gospel is essentially not general statements of religious truth, but the announcement of salvation* in and through particular events interpreted as decisive acts of God – in the case of Jesus his proclamation of the initiation in his ministry of the final reign of God, calling for repentance and discipleship; in the case of the early church the proclamation of his death and his resurrection to universal lordship as God's inauguration of the final age of eternal life, requiring the response of faith.

This has led to two persistent questions. 1. Since the proclamation of, and about, Jesus, and the gospel narratives that go with it, are 'mythological' in the sense of being a story about God acting on earth, how are actions of God to be conceived and recognized, and what is their relation to observable historical events?

2. Since the 'mythological' language which gave this message its force was that of the eschatological* expectations of first-cen-

tury Judaism (kingdom of God, Son of man, resurrection, victory over heavenly powers, etc.), which presupposes a certain understanding of the world and of God's relation to it, how can it retain that force when the world can no longer be understood in that way? The debate initiated by R. Bultmann's attempt to translate the message into the language of existentialism* continues (*see also* **Demythologizing**). For while that attempt is shown to be proper, inasmuch as the message is addressed to the individual person (what is Christ to and for me?), and so to his self-understanding, it can also be judged that such a translation cannot be made without the omission of external elements vital to the message, and prior to its appropriation by the individual person, e.g. God's relation to Christ, or his relation to the whole world.

H. W. Bartsch (ed), *Kerygma and Myth*, ET Vol. 1, 1954, Vol. II, 1962; C. H. Dodd, *The Apostolic Preaching and its Development*, 1937; John Macquarrie, *The Scope of Demythologizing*, 1960.

C. F. EVANS

Kerygmatic Theology

An alternative name for crisis theology* or dialectical theology*, used to indicate the character of such theology as a proclamation of the revelation and saving acts of God, the *kerygma*.

JOHN BOWDEN

Kingdom of God

The centrality of the idea of the kingdom of God (or in Matthew, 'the kingdom of heaven') in the teaching of Jesus is beyond all question: 'The time is fulfilled, and the kingdom of God is at hand' (Mark 1.15); 'But if it is by the finger of God that I cast out demons, then the kingdom of God has come upon you' (Luke 11.20); '. . . the kingdom of God is in the midst of you' (Luke 17.21); '. . . know that when you see these things taking place, you know that the kingdom of God is near' (Luke 21.31). The kingly rule of God is certainly present in the person of the King-Messiah; but it will be fully manifested only at the end of time.

The tension between the present ('already now') and future ('not yet') aspects of the kingdom has been reflected in almost every period of Christian history. Often the tendency has been to opt for the one *rather than* the other. Often, too, the use of the term 'the kingdom of God' has been a means of speaking of a Christian theology of history.

The early church expected the final manifestation of the kingdom in the very near future (cf. Mark 9.1); but as this original hope waned, the kingdom came to be identified either with the visible church itself, or with the rule of Christ over the individual believer. It was in opposition to the former interpretation that the Reformers stressed that the kingdom is not identical with any organization. To Luther it was synonymous with the realm of divine grace, while Calvin saw it as in part embodied in a theocratic* society, in the establishment of which individuals might play an active part under God. There were the seeds here of later controversy among Protestants.

The point at issue was whether individual Christians might work toward the coming of the kingdom, or whether it remains wholly in God's hands as a gift of grace. Pietists and Evangelicals linked 'the extension of the kingdom' with evangelistic and missionary work (cf. Matt. 24.14), believing every convert to be a new citizen of 'the kingdom of Christ'. A further theological element was introduced by Kant, Schleiermacher and Ritschl, who saw the kingdom as the realm of ideal human relations on earth, and therefore as an ideal Christian society. This opened the way for a secularization* of the kingdom idea in terms of notions of progress, development, evolution and material prosperity. This dominated liberal theology* down to the 1930s. In the USA the 'Social Gospel'* was very largely a practical kingdom theology.

Beginning in about 1900, German Lutheran theologians criticized this 'Anglo-Saxon', 'Calvinist' view of the kingdom bitterly and often. Their reasons were partly political and partly theological. Johannes Weiss, Albert Schweitzer and others emphasized that the 'Anglo-Saxon' view was a fruit of the Enlightenment*, and not of the Bible, and stressed the eschatological aspect of the teaching of Jesus*. At first this was mainly a historical exercise, but the disasters of the later war years (post-1917) for Germany's part gave force to eschatological interpretations over against evolutionary idealism. Between the wars there were repeated confrontations on this issue, beginning at the Stockholm 'Life and Work' conference of 1925. During the 1930s the eschatological interpretation was further strengthened by the progressive collapse of idealism, by economic crisis, by the witness of dialectical and neo-orthodox theologians, and by the findings of 'biblical theology'*. However, the notion of 'bringing in the kingdom' survived in liberal circles, and in popular piety, chiefly in the English-speaking world. But by the later 1950s and 1960s, virtually the only acceptable interpretation of the kingdom of God among Protestant scholars was eschatological in character.

Since the mid-1960s, however, the notion of the kingdom of God as an ideal society, characterized by equality, justice and truth, has once more been gaining ground, partly due to a fresh injection of ideas from the direction of religio-political socialism. This newer form of kingdom theology is closely allied to various theologies of liberation*, though it has deep roots in a tradition of Christian Socialism reaching back at least to the mid-nineteenth century. It has been expressed repeatedly in recent years, not least at the Melbourne 'Your Kingdom Come' conference of 1980. As in earlier phases, this latest wave of socio-ethical kingdom theology has aroused opposition from Conservative Evangelical and (Lutheran) confessional groups.

In evaluating Christian interpretations of the kingdom of God, much depends on what a particular age or school of thought has come to regard as the *antithesis* of the kingdom, since each interpretation has emerged in opposition to a manifest evil, ranging all the way from slavery in the nineteenth century to transnational companies in the late twentieth. Conservatives still tend to regard the kingdom in its individual and future aspects, liberals in its corporate and present aspects. Thus although the *words* 'the kingdom of God' remain constant, their *content* has varied greatly. Often that content has been determined as much by sociological and political as by biblical considerations.

In recent Christian history, the words 'the kingdom of God' have been used repeatedly to provide biblical justification for programmes of social renewal. How far these programmes are related to anything which Jesus may have meant by these words remains a highly controversial issue, on which

there is nothing approaching a consensus. It is perhaps not surprising, therefore, that no historian of theological ideas has yet attempted a comprehensive account of all the varieties of 'kingdom' interpretation in Christian theological writing. Even the best of the existing literature remains as a rule silent on the wider socio-political issues involved.

J. Bright, *The Kingdom of God in Bible and Church*, 1955; C. H. Dodd, *The Parables of the Kingdom*, 1961; G. Lundström, *The Kingdom of God in the Teaching of Jesus*, ET 1963; H. R. Niebuhr, *The Kingdom of God in America*, 1937; N. Perrin, *The Kingdom of God in the Teaching of Jesus*, 1963; H. G. Wood and others, *The Kingdom of God and History*, 1938.

ERIC J. SHARPE

Koinonia

The Greek word for 'fellowship', 'communion': e.g. 'the fellowship of the Holy Spirit' (II Cor. 13.14; Phil. 2.1).

ALAN RICHARDSON

Laity

Most scholars maintain that in the NT there is no clear distinction between clergy and laity. All share one common vocation* to be people of the new creation. They hold one common priesthood* as the *laos* of God, though they have different and complementary gifts and ministries (I Peter 2.9ff.; I Cor. 12). These ideas reflect OT teachings about the vocation of the people Israel. However, by mediaeval times a sharp differentiation had developed which degraded the ministries of lay people and emphasized the special functions of the clergy.

At the Reformation* some Protestants recovered much of the NT teachings, especially Lutherans, Calvinists, Anabaptists and Mennonites. The Evangelical movements of the eighteenth and nineteenth centuries (see particularly the teachings of John Wesley) laid great emphasis on the responsibilities of all committed Christian people. Nevertheless, laity were still normally expected to help clergy in church work rather than to develop their own ministries in their occupations, politics and so on; and they were often considered, and considered themselves, a lower grade of Christian than the ordained ministers.

By 1900 there was some restlessness about these questions, particularly among overseas missions (which gave women laity much responsibility). And in the twentieth century, and particularly since 1945, there has been a determined and world-wide attempt to understand the vocation of the laity. The remarkable recovery of the churches in West Germany included the development of enormous Kirchentags (lay assemblies) and of lay 'academies' and centres. There were similar developments in the Netherlands and indeed all over Europe; and there are now some seventy centres in the Association of Laity Centres in Europe and also considerable networks of both RC and Protestant adult Christian educators. In Britain there was the work of J. H. Oldham and the Christian Frontier Council, of Archbishop William Temple, Miss E. M. Batten and the Iona Community in Scotland. The early assemblies of the World Council of Churches (especially Evanston 1954 and New Delhi 1961) included much consideration of the role of the laity in the modern world. The Christian Councils of Asia and Africa followed this lead. The RC Church, after many hesitations and arguments, strongly endorsed an understanding of one people of God, clergy and laity together, at the Second Vatican Council.

It is important to note that these developments not only emphasized what have been called 'Sunday ministries' – the laity, both men and women, as church councillors, local preachers, readers, charismatic prayer leaders, stewardship organizers and so on, and their 'personal ministries' – friendly and family relationships. There was also much concern about the laity's 'Monday ministries' – their responsibilities in the structures of industrial, commercial and political life, and about questions of *justice*. And in recent years there has been new thinking about their 'Saturday ministries' – the involvement of Christians in the worlds of entertainment, sports, television, leisure and tourism.

However, this development of a strong and committed laity has not been easy. Some churches – RC, Orthodox, 'high' Anglican – have experienced serious tensions about the authority of bishops and priests and the awkward questions raised by lay people; for example, the difficulties of accepting the resolutions of the RC National Pastoral Congress in Liverpool in 1980. Many clergy and laity, both Catholic and Protestant, find it difficult psychologically to work out a fruitful partnership together; and these problems grow when, as in many African churches, laity have sometimes enjoyed more formal education than their clergy. Some theological colleges and seminaries still encourage a certain infuriating paternalism and continually emphasize the laity's churchly rather than their secular responsibilities. At the same time many lay people would 'rather not be called'. They are happy to accept a lower standard of Christian commitment and behaviour than the clergy, and to give them nominal respect while actually considering them rather utopian and feeble people. Some congregations find it very difficult to develop the skills of Christian controversy, and to distinguish between the responsible compromises which many lay people have to live with day by day, and the need to speak out against gross social injustices, e.g. in Latin America.

Again, the active involvement of lay people in liturgy and worship, and the encouragement of suitable styles of lay spirituality, has not proceeded smoothly. Some RCs have made extraordinary progress in making the Mass something in which priests and laity participate together; but surprisingly, in many other churches, Catholic or Protestant, worship is still very much clerically designed and led. Liturgy is not yet the active work of the congregation.

The budgets of many churches still show a very inadequate provision for adult Christian education and development for the laity. This is particularly true for the support of ministries outside church structures and outside the local parish. There is certainly some money and staff time for various crisis issues, such as nuclear disarmament and unemployment; but often there is no careful strategy for the growing of mature, informed laity which can match the provisions for developing the clergy.

So the world position is distinctly patchy. Certain American and European churches are working very energetically on these questions, as are some African and Asian churches (though these, from simple shortage of clergy, sometimes concentrate too much on laity as 'church workers' and assistants to the clergy). Other churches, and unfortunately many British ones, have so disappointed the hopes of many laity that these are more and more giving up effective church membership, though not necessarily their Christian beliefs. The phenomenon of 'churchless Christians' and the development of groups of believers who meet only in informal house groups and house churches is one which demands urgent study.

Nevertheless, in many churches, and particularly in R C ones, the position of the laity today, as compared with 1900 or even 1945, shows extraordinary changes. Most of these give us great hopes for the future.

See also **Basic Communities.**

Walter M. Abbott, SJ (ed), *The Documents of Vatican II* (especially Constitution on the Church, Constitution on the Church in the Modern World, and Decree on the Apostolate of the Laity), 1966; F. O. Ayres, *The Ministry of the Laity: A Biblical Exposition*, 1962; Marvin Brown, *On Time and In Place. The Work of the Evangelical Academies in West Germany*, 1980; Hendrik Kraemer, *A Theology of the Laity*, 1958; Hans Küng, *The Church*, E T 1967 (especially ch. 1); R. J. Mouw, *Called to Holy Wordliness*, 1980; S. C. Neill and H. R. Weber (eds), *The Layman in Christian History*, 1963; Letty M. Russell, *The Future of Partnership*, 1979.

MARK GIBBS

Language, Religious

Language used in belief and worship raises separate issues for theology, comparative religious studies, and the philosophy of religion. Theology asks how humans can speak intelligibly and truthfully about an infinite and eternal God. In moments of worship and awe some have hesitated to use words at all (cf. Eccles. 5.2). Some, like the mystical theologian Pseudo-Dionysius, advocated a negative way of describing God (as incorporeal, immortal, infinite, etc.) so as to avoid anthropomorphism *. In modern times, many have agreed with Rudolf Otto's view of religious awareness as being never fully expressible in words (*The Idea of the Holy*, 1917).

Classic Christian theology, however, presupposes that we are able to speak of God, since God has created us with speech and reason by virtue of which we share in the divine mind. This view (drawn from the Bible and reinforced by Platonism *) underlies the thinking of Augustine, for instance, who found the Trinity * itself represented within the human mind (*see also* **Psychological Analogy**). For Anselm, too, the mind is a mirror able faintly to reflect the image of God. Aquinas taught that although our words are used first in speaking of creaturely things, some of them we may legitimately apply to God by analogy *, in senses appropriate to God's being, because of the relation between creatures and their Creator. Indeed with words like 'goodness' or 'wisdom' it is when used of God that they have their truest meanings. While attempts to construct from this a general theory of analogy to account for human knowledge of God have been widely criticized by philosophers, as a way to explain religious language (rather than to defend or justify it) versions of Aquinas's approach are still adopted by many theologians.

Protestant thinkers, emphasizing the effects of sin on human reason, have preferred to justify theological language by reference to revelation *. Karl Barth carried this view to its limits, replacing the *analogia entis* of the scholastics with the view that it is only God's gracious gift of faith that makes theological knowledge possible. He thus rejected reliance on any natural human capacity for thought or speech about God who is 'Wholly Other'. In theology influenced by thinkers such as Kierkegaard and Heidegger, profoundly concerned with human existence and subjectivity, God is never merely 'thought about' or 'spoken of', but is known only in an authentic personal response of faith and commitment. Thus even where scripture and doctrine have in their mythological form lost plausibility for holders of a modern world-view (so the existentialist * theologian Rudolf Bultmann maintained), their true meaning survives, in the significance they have for personal faith (*see also* **Demythologizing**). Paul Tillich and other recent theologians have similarly sought to explain the language of Christian doctrine using existentialist modes of thought.

In the comparative study of religion, myths and cosmologies, prophecies, eschatologies and doctrines about salvation are gathered from religions world-wide. When Christian language is placed in this wider context it becomes one among many ways of speaking and thinking about ultimate truths. It is insufficient to argue, with Barth, that Christian theology has a unique status *vis à vis* other religions, being purely and simply a response to God's word. For by no means all Christian theology has seen itself in Barth's terms, and in any event it is open to other religions likewise to argue for a unique status for their revelations. Throughout their histories, religions have drawn on and will continue to share much common material, especially in the language and concepts they use to express themselves. Similar methods of historical, literary and textual criticism can thus be applied to the collected writings of most religions. They are open to interpretation by anthropologists, sociologists and psychologists. Their economic and political meanings may be demonstrated, i.e. the classes or groups they support and the interests they serve. Even when the language of a particular faith is approached with care taken to preserve the intentions of those who use it (the so-called 'phenomenological method' as in Ninian Smart's *Phenomenon of Religion*, 1973) the effect may be to show it to have features typical of many belief-systems, rather than to be the unique and distinctive body of scripture or tradition it takes itself to be. At the same time, the phenomenological method can help preserve genuine religious significance, by its recognition that terminology used loosely and generally (e.g. 'myth', 'archetype', or even 'religion') may distort the true sense of words and actions within a particular faith (*see also* **Phenomenology**).

Since mid-century a sustained critique of theology through analysis of religious language-use has formed the main point of contact between philosophy and religion in the English-speaking world. While commonly attributed to the attack on metaphysics by logical positivists popularized in Britain by A. J. Ayer's *Language, Truth and Logic* (1936), the analytical and linguistic developments in post-war philosophy draw from a far wider range of philosophical sources. The critique has commonly been presented as a challenge to defenders of religion to show that their statements, beliefs and doctrines are 'cognitively meaningful'; that they convey factual information and do not merely evoke and express emotions; and that they form a coherent system free from basic inconsistencies. Until some account of what would conclusively verify (or, more pointedly, falsify them) is provided, would-be religious assertions will fail not only to convince, but to make any sense at all. For if no experienceable state of affairs is incompatible with their truth, what real difference, it is asked, can their being true or untrue make so far as humans are concerned? This 'verificationist challenge' has attracted a variety of responses. Some have rejected the demand for verifiability as being itself unverifiable as a condition of meaningfulness. Others hold that the demand can be met, by appealing to experiences (in this life or a future one) capable of conclusively confirming or refuting beliefs which, in the meantime, are meaningfully expressed by parable, metaphor or analogy. Ian Ramsey (*Religious Language*, 1957) suggested that the 'logical oddness' of theological language, with its stretching of words beyond their ordinary usage, is the very means by which religious insight is produced. Alternatively, theological language has been excused from verification on the grounds that it is essentially non-descriptive; that its primary function is to express commitment to certain ideals and ways of life, reinforced by stories or parables which support an appropriate world-view. (Examples of all these positions can be found in *The Philosophy of Religion*, ed. Basil Mitchell, 1971.) Other writers, following ideas in Wittgenstein's later philosophy, have argued that religious language can be understood only within the living context or 'form of life' in which it is typically used. This removes from individual utterances the need for verifiability according to external standards. The approach is carried even further by some theorists who suggest that different communities of language-users live within distinct 'worlds' constructed by and represented in their languages. Attention has thus turned from questions about the factual significance of religious statements, to the wider issue of whether meaning, truth or factuality are themselves notions that can be applied generally. Despite this broadening of the debate, the question of verifiability cannot safely be ignored by any religion that seeks to carry conviction in the modern world. For so long as believers regard their beliefs as worth holding because they are true, and worth preaching because they contain important information, then a demand that their language have empirical 'cash value' (i.e. be open to some genuine tests of experience) is clearly not an unreasonable or narrowly positivistic demand.

There is a further respect in which religious language is challenged by modern philosophy, with its emphasis on logical rigour and its suspicion of informal and analogical argument. A general possibility of meaningfulness may be conceded to religious language without in any way guaranteeing the particular statements of Christian theology. Given current philosophical understanding of such key concepts as 'person', 'substance', or 'nature' it is by no means certain that the reasoning which led to orthodox formulations of doctrines such as the Trinity* or the Incarnation* will be found entirely coherent by today's criteria of logic. Modern doctrinal criticism* is thus provided by philosophy with some sharp analytical tools, as well as high standards of argument and clear thinking.

There remains the wider question of the contemporary significance and power of Christian language in all its forms, preaching, apologetics, liturgy, etc. To that question modern biblical studies and hermeneutics* have vital contributions to make, while linguistics, literary criticism*, and the study of symbols and imagery* (including social and sexual stereotypes) have also become increasingly relevant.

See also **Analogy; Analytical Philosophy; God; Hermeneutics; Revelation; Symbolism.**

G. B. Caird, *The Language and Imagery of the Bible*, 1980; M. Charlesworth, *The Problem of Religious Language*, 1974; P. Donovan, *Religious Language*, 1976; J. Macquarrie, *God-Talk*, 1967; R. Swinburne, *The Coherence of Theism*, 1977.

PETER DONOVAN

Law and Theology

Both in Jewish and in Christian theology God is understood to be a God both of justice and judgment on the one hand, and of mercy and grace on the other. According to rabbinical tradition, he said to himself at creation, 'If I create the world by mercy alone, sin will abound. If I create it by justice alone, how can the world endure? Therefore I will create it by both.' The Psalmist antici-

pated with joy the coming of the Lord 'to judge the world', and the prophets hailed God's judgment and his law as a regeneration of the whole society. Christian theology has been more troubled by these paradoxes than Judaism, partly because Christianity has greatly emphasized the punitive aspect of justice and judgment.

Jesus followed traditional Jewish thought in identifying justice with love. The essence of the Mosaic law, he said, is to love God and neighbour; and he charged the Pharisees with neglecting 'the weightier matters of the law, which are justice, and mercy, and good faith'. Yet Jesus and his followers also placed great stress on two other elements in God's relationship to man, faith and forgiveness, and these were seen as being in a certain tension with law. Paul, in particular, challenged the belief that willing obedience to just laws, including those that implement the commandment to love God and neighbour, is sufficient for salvation.

In Western Christianity, with the emergence of the Church of Rome as a corporate political and legal entity, theology had to deal with the significance not only of the biblical law but also of the canon law* of the church, including the current legislation and decisions of popes and of church councils convened by popes. The canon law became an integrated system of legal concepts, principles, rules, procedures and institutions, covering virtually all branches of law; it regulated almost all aspects of the life of the clergy and many aspects of the life of the laity. It did not purport to be divine law or natural law (though it included many principles drawn from divine law as revealed in scripture and from natural law as understood by reason and conscience); nevertheless, as the law of the 'spiritual arm', it was considered to be on a higher plane than the law of kingdoms, feudal domains, cities and other secular polities. Disobedience to the canon law was a sin, and obedience was, for the faithful Christian, a path to salvation. This doctrine was dramatized in the Western vision of purgatory as a condition of postmortem punishments of faithful Christians proportional to the sins committed by them during their life on earth.

The Protestant Reformation* started with Luther's rejection of the belief that by doing good a person could earn divine forgiveness. This led him and his followers to reject the concept of a spiritual law. The church's 'power of jurisdiction', including its authority to make laws and to hand down judicial decisions, was denied. All law was removed from the 'heavenly realm' of faith and grace.

Luther's belief in justification * solely by faith * did not, however, lead him to antinomianism; indeed he denounced the antinomianism of the Anabaptists and other radical reformers. He believed that law is an essential part of the 'earthly realm' of God's creation. That included not only the civil law of the secular polity but also the Mosaic law, which, though not directly binding on Christians as a matter of divine command, was nevertheless in Luther's view a reflection of natural law discernible by human reason.

Luther attributed to law two 'uses'. The first, which he called its 'civil use', is to deter recalcitrant people from misconduct by threat of penalties. The second, which he called its 'theological use', is to make people conscious of their obligations and hence repentant of their sins. Subsequently a third 'use' of the law was accepted by Lutheran and Calvinist theologians, namely, to guide faithful people in the paths of virtuous living. Calvin in particular emphasized the 'third use of the law', stating that by study of the law the faithful, in whose hearts the spirit of God already reigns, will not only obtain a purer knowledge of the divine will, but in addition 'will be excited to obedience'.

The antinomian position that the resurrection of Christ introduced a new era of grace, in which Christians living at the end of time are freed from all legal and moral bonds, has a parallel in the theory of some contemporary theologians that Christian love is a free gift that must not be restrained by moral or political rules. In this conception law is said to be abstract, objective and impersonal, whereas love is concrete, subjective and personal. Augustine's statement is quoted, 'Love and do as you wish.' The sharp contrast between law and love reflects, however, a very narrow view of each; law is reduced to a set of rules and love is excluded from social situations involving large numbers of people. Although sometimes traced back to Luther's sharp distinction between law and gospel, the separation of law and love was expressly denied by Luther, who treated love, like other works of the law, as an active virtue of a person, whereas faith in his view is a passive virtue, being received as a gift from God.

Most theological writings on law have dealt with it from the viewpoint of its relation to personal salvation and personal morality. Indeed traditional Christian theology in general has been much less concerned with God's action in society than with his action in the mind, heart and soul of the individual person. Law, however, is above all a social process for resolving conflicts and creating channels of co-operation; its main purpose is to help to give society the structure of rights and duties needed to maintain its inner cohesion. Only with the development in the twentieth century of such disciplines as Christian social ethics and the emergence of such movements as those referred to as the social gospel * and liberation theology *, has a start been made towards creating a social as contrasted with a personal theology. Thus far, however, social theology has been more concerned with ends than with means, and consequently has had little that is constructive to say about the processes of law.

On the other hand, a newly emerging body of literature on legal ethics written from a theological perspective is concerned with the religious ministry of the lawyer. Also a much larger body of literature on major social-legal problems, written from a religious though not necessarily theological perspective, has appeared in recent decades. Finally, mention should be made of a number of books published in the 1960s and 1970s, of a historical and philosophical character, on the relation of law to religious belief. These, too, have contributed to an understanding of the significance of law for theology and theology for law.

Harold J. Berman, *The Interaction of Law and Religion*, 1974; *Law and Revolution: The Formation of the Western Legal Tradition*, 1983; F. Edward Cranz, *An Essay on the Development of Luther's Thought on Justice, Law and Society*, 1959; Jacques Ellul, *The Theological Foundation of Law*, 1969; Alfred Jonsen, *Responsibility in Modern Religious Ethics*, 1968; Edward Long, *A Survey of Christian Ethics*, 1967; H. Richard Niebuhr, *The Responsible Self*, 1963; Reinhold Niebuhr, 'Love and Law in Protestantism and

Catholicism', *JRT* 9, 1952; Thomas L. Shaffer, *On Being a Christian and a Lawyer*, 1981.

HAROLD J. BERMAN

Liberalism

In defining liberalism, a distinction needs to be drawn between Liberal Protestantism*, which was a theological movement of the nineteenth and early twentieth century, and the liberal perspective in Christian theology of which there are both contemporary and ancient representatives. The nineteenth-century movement known as Liberal Protestantism is rooted in the thought of Immanuel Kant (1724–1804) and Friedrich Schleiermacher (1768–1834), and is best represented in the writings of Albrecht Ritschl (1822–1889).

The most important proponents of the Ritschlian school in Germany were Wilhelm Herrmann (1846–1922), Julius Kaftan (1848–1926) and Adolf von Harnack (1853–1930). In France, Auguste Sabatier (1839–1901) and Jean Réville (1854–1907) are dominant representatives of liberal theology. William Ellery Channing (1780–1842), Ralph Waldo Emerson (1803–1882) and Horace Bushnell (1802–1876) reflect the liberal movement in America. The movement in England is best represented by H. Scott Holland (1847–1918) and the *Lux Mundi* essays.

Liberalism, broadly defined, is often juxtaposed to conservatism and Fundamentalism* and refers to the attempt to be open to scientific investigation, historical research and the contribution of the arts in one's understanding of religion. H. Richard Niebuhr identifies liberalism under the 'Christ of Culture' label, or Culture-Protestantism type, and sees liberals as accommodating Christianity to the prevailing culture*. In Niebuhr's 'Christ of Culture' model, Christianity and culture are neither in tension, nor radically opposed to each other; rather, Christ's message is compatible with the highest ideals and greatest truths that are promulgated within a given cultural context.

Immanuel Kant's primary contribution to liberalism is stated in his understanding of *Religion within the Limits of Reason Alone* (1793). In that work, Kant reflects the influence of the Enlightenment*: a belief in the power of reason and the freedom of the individual. Friedrich Schleiermacher is often viewed as the 'father' of liberal theology. Heavily influenced by Romanticism*, he stressed the subjective character of religion as 'the feeling of absolute dependence'. In so doing, he addressed the 'cultured despisers' of religion, arguing that religion need not be hostile to self-fulfilment, but indeed parallels the aesthetic* sphere of poetry and art. Theology is a description of experience, not metaphysical categories in the mind of God. God is grasped intuitively, as a feeling and experience of the infinite. Albrecht Ritschl, influenced by Kant, Schleiermacher and also Rudolf Lotze (1817–1881), viewed theology essentially as a 'value-judgment' in which one affirms the good, God as love being the highest expression of the good. For Ritschl, God cannot be known 'in himself', and for this reason the biblical record of Jesus of Nazareth is important. Ritschl opposed both subjectivism and mysticism and grounded Christianity in the New Testament view of the 'kingdom of God'*, a decidedly moral image of the Christian's responsibility.

A number of characteristics of liberalism can be identified, some of which emerge directly from Liberal Protestantism of the nineteenth and early twentieth century, and others of which reflect the spirit of theological liberalism more broadly defined.

1. Liberalism is receptive to contemporary science, the arts and humanities. Liberalism pursues 'the truth' wherever it is found; there is no discontinuity between human truth and the truth of Christianity – hence, liberalism shuns compartmentalization as well as the disjuncture between reason and revelation, God and man, learning about oneself or nature and understanding the nature of God. Truth is to be found in experience, guided by reason, more than it is to be known in tradition or authority. Liberals oppose dogmatism, exclusivism, and appeals to non-verifiable realities. Liberals are open to the truth of other religions. Christianity is not viewed as the only expression of man's search for God or of God's revelation to man. God's revelation of himself is ongoing and present in all places and at all times. Liberals tend to assume a broadly ecumenical attitude. Ernst Troeltsch (1865–1923), from an earlier generation of theologians, or more recently,

Paul Tillich (1886–1965), are both good examples of Christian liberalism.

2. Liberals have been sympathetic to applying the canons of historiography to their interpretations of sacred scripture (*see also* **History**). They have been proponents of both higher and lower biblical criticism*. They have attempted to distinguish the authentic message of the gospel from the cultural accretions that form its narrative context. The Bible is seen by liberals as a human document whose primary validity lies in the fact that it records the experience of persons who are open to God's presence. The Bible is not a revealed text, nor is it God's exclusive revelation* to humankind. The continual task of the liberal Christian is to interpret the Bible in light of a contemporary world-view and the best of historical research, while at the same time interpreting society from the perspective of the gospel story. Rudolf Bultmann (1884–1976) stands as a good example of a liberal biblical scholar.

3. Liberals stress the ethical implications of Christianity. Christianity is not a dogma to be believed; it is a way of life, a moral vision to be enacted. Although personal virtues are deemed important, liberals have often emphasized the systemic and structural character of social evils such as poverty, war and racism. Likewise, liberals have called for collective solutions, emphasizing the need to reform public policy and to restructure society. Liberals have often been optimistic concerning the possibilities of change and have not infrequently seen evil as a product of ignorance rather than the result of man's intrinsically evil nature. Walter Rauschenbusch (1861–1918) is a good example of the liberal social conscience.

Liberalism has not gone unchallenged. Critics have argued that liberalism loses its prophetic edge by accommodating too readily to cultural trends and assumptions. God becomes nothing more than a name for commonly agreed upon civic virtues. The transcendent character of a radically monotheistic God collapses into an immanental deity who is devoid of all transcendence, and therefore of any moral leverage outside human experience. Liberalism, say critics, tends towards self-reliant humanism. Liberal Christianity, in its stress on human reason, finds itself devoid of the uniqueness of a community responding to Christ's command which may offend human reason (e.g., Søren Kierkegaard's rendition of the Abraham story). In its accommodation to cultural values, liberal Christianity runs the risk of becoming a bourgeois community of the intellectual élite, one that is self-satisfied and uncritical in its acquiescence to the 'spirit of the age'. Many of these charges were brought against Liberal Protestantism by Karl Barth (1886–1968), and the neo-orthodox movement which he spawned was comprised largely of disenchanted liberals. Liberalism, however, is often misrepresented and misunderstood when read exclusively through the neo-orthodox spectacles of either Barth or Emil Brunner (1889–1966).

Liberalism in the broad sense of the term is an enduring perspective. It is represented currently in writers as divergent as John A. T. Robinson and David Tracy. Empirical theology at the University of Chicago, rooted in the philosophical perspective of Alfred North Whitehead and Charles Hartshorne, has given rise to a continuing scholarly movement of liberal theological reflection. Bernard Loomer, Daniel Day Williams, Bernard Meland, Schubert Ogden, and John Cobb all stem from the Chicago tradition. Process theology*, drawing its inspiration from Whitehead and Hartshorne, is perhaps the most vital contemporary expression of Christian liberalism.

Karl Barth, *Protestant Theology in the Nineteenth Century*, ET 1972; L. Harold DeWolf, *The Case for Theology in Liberal Perspective*, 1959; H. R. Mackintosh, *Types of Modern Theology*, 1937; Bernard E. Meland, *The Future of Empirical Theology*, 1969; Donald E. Miller, *The Case for Liberal Christianity*, 1981; H. R. Niebuhr, *Christ and Culture*, 1951, ch. 3; B. M. G. Reardon, *Liberal Protestantism*, 1968.

DONALD E. MILLER

Liberal Protestantism

A somewhat vague term descriptive of certain dominating trends in nineteenth- and early twentieth-century theology. Liberal Protestants claimed freedom in two directions: (i) from traditional dogmas and credal formulations; (ii) in the handling of historical texts and sources. They argued that theology must be formulated in the light of advancing knowledge in philosophy, the sciences and other disciplines, and accordingly tried to be astringent critics of what they considered to be theological and ecclesiastical obscurantism. Historically the roots of nineteenth-century liberal Protestantism are to be found in post-Renaissance science and in the critical philosophy of the Enlightenment *, of which that of Immanuel Kant (1724–1804) was both typical and influential. The effects of Kant's thinking on theology were twofold: (i) his attack on metaphysical thinking cast doubt upon the validity of traditional natural theology, of which the classical demonstrations of God's existence and of personal immortality were an integral part; (ii) his attempt to establish man as a thinking and moral creature, transcendent over nature, was immensely influential in nineteenth-century theological circles. Partly as a result of his work, the demonstrative, metaphysical approach to theology was gradually abandoned in favour of one emphasizing man's transcendent status and unique inner awareness.

Nineteenth-century theological liberalism's greatest debt was probably to the thought of the German systematic theologian F. D. E. Schleiermacher (1768–1834), who, having rejected speculative natural theology, sought to base Christian belief upon the universal, trans-subjective awareness of God rooted in man's inner aesthetic and religious response to reality as a whole. Man's 'feeling of absolute dependence *' was for Schleiermacher the essence and basis of religion in general and Christianity in particular. Parallel, in a sense, to Schleiermacher's teaching was the idealistic philosophy of G. W. F. Hegel (1770–1831), stressing the rationality of reality and that process whereby immanent Absolute Spirit attained to self-awareness in human thinking, ideas which were to be immensely influential upon subsequent theological enterprises. The overall effect of the thought of Hegel and Schleiermacher was to give nineteenth-century German Protestant theology a strongly anthropological character and to emphasize a firm continuity between human thinking and feeling on the one hand and Christian revelation on the other.

Within the context of liberal theology the other dominant influence was the system of Albrecht Ritschl (1822–1889) and his school. Reacting sharply against contemporary naturalism, positivism and determinism, and against the influence of all metaphysical thinking upon theology, Ritschl, influenced by neo-Kantian idealism, sought to base Christian theology upon the 'purely factual' historical basis of the NT, in which is portrayed in archetypal form 'man's supremacy over nature'. Jesus *, whose being is threatened by hideously hostile forces, trusts absolutely in God's love and power; in so doing, he reveals man's true response to God, revealed as unqualified love and grace. Jesus is thus considered within Ritschlianism to be Archetypal Man and also the unique revelation of God. Upon this basis, Ritschl erected his theology of 'value-judgments'; contemporary man, understanding himself as threatened by blind, mechanistic, impersonal nature (as portrayed by nineteenth-century naturalism) can be delivered from this situation only by the work of Jesus mediated to him by the Christian church. Man can attain to religious knowledge only through the awareness of the 'value' or 'worth' imparted to his life by God through Jesus. There is no religious knowledge apart from this value-knowledge; there are no valid religious propositions apart from these value-judgments of faith. Those who are delivered from the threat of nature by the work of Jesus form, in community, the kingdom * of God, a social entity destined gradually to redeem and transform ethically the society in which it is set. Ritschl's basic theological ideas were developed in various directions by such theologians as Adolf von Harnack (1851–1930), Wilhelm Herrmann (1846–1922) and Julius Kaftan (1848–1926).

The roots of nineteenth-century liberal Protestantism are also to be sought in the development of the literary and historical criticism of the Bible. Briefly, by this is meant the application to the biblical sources of those techniques which were applied to non-biblical materials, in order that they might be 'objectively' interpreted in the context of the historical circumstances in which they originated. In practice, the tendencies were to isolate the biblical materials from later, especially Greek, philosophical 'accretions'; to regard them as literary and historical creations rather than as the numinous sources of unquestionable sacred doctrine; and frequently to interpret them in the light of fashionable contemporary philosophies, for example, Hegelianism*.

In the light of this analysis of the origins of nineteenth-century liberal Protestantism, it is possible to attempt a characterization of it. 1. Liberal Protestantism exhibited a tendency to regard Christianity as not distinctively and exclusively unique, but rather as one 'religion' among others, and sometimes as one cultural movement among others. This was clearly an implication of Schleiermacher's theological method (adopted by later theologians), which defined first a universal religious awareness and only then dealt with Christianity as the highest but not the only form of this. This tendency found its most extreme expression in the views of the so-called History of Religions School (*Religionsgeschichtliche Schule**), whose leader was Ernst Troeltsch (1865–1923). In its studies this school directed attention to those common features which Christianity shared with other religions; Troeltsch even admitted that it was conceivable that Christianity might be superseded as the highest form of religion.

In trying to deal with, for example, the Gospel narratives 'scientifically' and 'objectively', critics such as H. E. G. Paulus (1761–1851) and D. F. Strauss (1808–1874) tried in a rationalistic manner to make apparently miraculous events accord with the laws of nature, as these were understood by nineteenth-century science. The result was a radical 'desupernaturalization' of these narratives. Linked with this tendency was another; namely, the tendency to distinguish sharply between the 'natural facts' of the Gospel stories and later legendary or 'mythical' accretions. Strauss's *Life of Jesus* (*Das Leben Jesu*) was a classic example of this kind of attempt (*see also* **Jesus**).

3. There was a strong tendency to apply to Christian sources (the Bible, the history of dogma and the church) the presuppositions and categories of contemporary philosophical movements. The influence of Romanticism * on Schleiermacher is marked; the influence of Hegelianism on Strauss and F. C. Baur (1792–1860) is even more obvious; and, as we noted, Ritschl was heavily influenced by anti-naturalistic and anti-positivistic philosophy of a neo-Kantian type. It has been widely maintained by certain twentieth-century theologians that such philosophical influences produced varying degrees of distortion and impoverishment of the theological materials. Such distortion and impoverishment are most clearly seen in the work of Strauss and Baur.

4. In the highly critical atmosphere of nineteenth-century intellectual life, theologians tried to define the perennial 'essence' (German: *Wesen*) of Christian faith. By the end of the century this had hardened into the distinction between the religion of Jesus (often regarded as simple, ethical, practical Galilean) and the religion about Jesus (often regarded as Paulinist, Hellenistic, metaphysical, miraculous, supernaturalistic). Celebrated attempts to isolate and analyse Christianity's timeless essence were Ludwig Feuerbach's *The Essence of Christianity* (1841) and *The Essence of Religion* (1845), and Adolf von Harnack's *What is Christianity?* (ET 1900). Ritschl, through his rejection of all metaphysics in theology, and by his attempt to base Christianity upon 'purely historical' facts to which we attach moral and spiritual values, also contributed strongly to this tendency. In practice, overconcentration upon Christianity's perennial essence led to the well-known liberal distrust of traditional creeds and dogmas. It also contributed to the fundamental lack of awareness in liberal theology of the basically 'kerygmatic*' character of the NT writings, of the insight that they represent an inseparable unity of fact and interpretation.

5. Much liberal theology tended to overlook the 'historic eventfulness' of Christianity as a happening in which God had acted, radically altering the entire human situation. Christianity, as we have noted, was regarded rather as the supreme concrete expression of those religious drives and insights which permeated *all* history as such. Christianity's 'uniqueness' tended to be located, not in its historic eventfulness, but in the uniquely sublime teaching (about God, man and man's relationships with his fellows) and moral example of Jesus, and in the unique effect of these upon the progress and welfare of human society. In this sense it can be said that Christianity's uniqueness consists in the timelessness and unchangeability of its teaching rather than in the unique historicity of its central events.

6. The final characteristic of liberal theology is to be found in its attitudes to sin and salvation. Human sinfulness was not uncommonly regarded as a (merely negative) lack of knowledge or insight, or a dulled

spiritual awareness. Correspondingly salvation tended to be regarded as a filling of this lack by inspiration, information, correction or even education. Typical of this teaching was the Ritschlian conception of sin as a confused misunderstanding based upon man's ignorance of God's true nature. It is therefore not accidental that the typically nineteenth-century liberal doctrine of the atonement * tended to be of the exemplarist, moral-influence type. It is notoriously difficult to judge how far liberal theologians were influenced here by the nineteenth-century faith in human progress, whether linked with contemporary economic utopianism * or with Hegelianism, and how far their well-known participation in schemes for social, political and educational reform was motivated by their theological convictions.

The revolt against nineteenth- and early twentieth-century theology was initiated and carried through by the Swiss theologian Karl Barth (1886–1968), strongly influenced by the Danish religious thinker Søren Kierkegaard (1813–1855), and by the writings of the sixteenth-century Reformers, Calvin particularly. Over against liberalism, Barth denied that Christianity is one religion among others, stressing rather that it concerns only God's unique self-revelation. He vigorously tried to free Christianity from philosophical influences; he stressed the centrality and the kerygmatic character of the biblical writings, the radical discontinuity between God and human nature, and made much of the concepts of crisis, judgment and grace. Above all, against liberalism * he taught God's unqualifiable and indissoluble subjectivity: it is God who acts upon and towards man and not vice versa.

It is rather unfortunate that in the earlier part of the present century there took place what R. R. Niebuhr called a 'Barthian captivity' of the history of modern Christian thought. This was due largely to the immense influence exercised by Barth's *Protestant Theology in the Nineteenth Century* (1947, ET 1972). Consequently too many became acquainted with the nineteenth-century liberal tradition through the rather hypercritical accounts of it given by Barth and Emil Brunner (1889–1966). This was unfortunate because it obscured the positive, apologetically valuable aspects of the liberal tradition.

See also **Liberalism**.

Karl Barth, *Protestant Theology in the Nineteenth Century*, ET 1972; H. R. Mackintosh, *Types of Modern Theology*, 1937; John Macquarrie, *Twentieth-Century Religious Thought*, 1981; B. M. G. Reardon, *Liberal Protestantism*, 1968; *Religious Thought in the Nineteenth Century*, 1966; James Richmond, *Faith and Philosophy*, 1966; A. R. Vidler, *The Church in an Age of Revolution*, 1961.

JAMES RICHMOND

Liberation Theology

Victor Hugo declared that one thing stronger than armies is an idea whose hour has come. In the 1950s the idea of liberation came to colonial Africa and spread throughout the Third World. The idea seemed no sooner formulated than the imperial powers rushed to be rid of their lands for which so many had died. Once the idea of liberation was expressed, its essential rightness could not be ignored and the will to maintain possession of the colonies collapsed. If this had been uniformly true, then of course there would not be such a thing as a theology of liberation. Liberation theology has arisen because liberation has not come about universally: the struggle continues, and insofar as it is a just struggle, some Christians have stated its biblical basis and the basis of their own support for the movement. In the African context the meaning of liberation was uncomplicated. The demand was to be free from colonial rule. Liberation was achieved by decolonization, whether by armed struggle or by non-violent protest or by negotiation. However, liberation movements in other parts of the world have been involved in more complicated situations: theological reflection on these has also been more complex.

The term liberation theology originated in Latin America, and was clearly influenced by the liberation movements in that part of the world. But these countries had long since been decolonized. From what did they need to be liberated? Dependence. The terms of international trade are such that Third-World countries not only are dependent upon the rich but are destined to remain so. With a few notable exceptions their economies are geared to supply primary commodities at low cost to the developed nations. These are then used in the manufacture of expensive goods which are sold to the poor countries. Economic colonialism is continued through international investment agencies. But dependence also takes place within countries. There is an enormous difference between the standard of living of the rich and the mass of the people, whether in the illegal shanty towns around the cities or in the countryside. And finally there is dependence at an individual level. Poverty and hopelessness enter into the mind so that those who are marginal to the main economic and cultural life of the country remain outside.

In Latin America the liberation movements have therefore had to deal with a more complicated situation than old-fashioned colonialism, and have had to face problems apparently more intractible. Liberation theology has also addressed itself to these three areas. 'Liberation movement' suggests groups of bearded men with guns, ambushing government troops, but such struggle is not itself a liberation movement. Che Guevara said that he and his men spoke to the village people about their lives, and *that* was the revolution. Unless the people understand why things are as they are, unless they come to see themselves as capable of initiating and participating in change, then nothing can be achieved. This work is called 'conscientization', and it is the most fundamental level of liberation, the freeing of the mind. As these marginals, these objects within another's world, come to life there is a spiritual birth which has in practice led to a new appropriation of the word of God in the Bible, a new spirituality in the life of prayer. Even religious dependence is dismantled.

As conscientization proceeds, there is a growing appreciation of the inequalities and injustices experienced within the country. It is at this point that confrontation takes place. The marginals ask to be allowed to live as men in their own country, but asking achieves nothing. Those who benefit from existing structures are determined not to allow change, and they also control the forces of 'law and order'. When Oliver Twist asks for something to eat, it is he who is blamed for making trouble. Liberation theology has also developed at this stage, not least because of the responsibility of religion in the past for legitimizing these same structures of injustice, responsibility for

impressing on the poor their duty to remain poor.

The theology of liberation presupposes the liberation of theology. Until theology ceases to identify with the values, interests and goals of those who benefit from structural injustice, then theology can have nothing to contribute to the liberation movement. But a theology which has itself been liberated can contribute at each stage, including the third, that of international relations. In the developed countries theology still legitimizes an unjust world order. For this reason theologians from Latin America have toured the developed world, to lecture and to confer, to attempt to begin in the North the process of conscientization. They believe that until there is change within the North, no change can be effected in world relations.

Theologians in Latin America have now embarked on the revision of all Christian doctrine from the perspective of liberation. Liberation is a constant theme of both OT and NT, but it has become 'spiritualized' as if it referred only to some private, inner life of man. There are other more prophetic dimensions which are to be restored.

Not surprisingly, liberation theologies have arisen in other parts of the world. The contexts are always different, and consequently so are the theologies. Asian theologies of liberation have meditated long on the experience there of persecution. In South Africa the liberation theology is concerned with internal colonialism. But wherever people are prevented from living their own lives Christians are reflecting on liberation. Thus there is black theology* of liberation in the USA and there is also the theology of women's liberation (*see also* **Feminist Theology**). These experiences contribute to the liberation of theology in the recognition of the part that religion has played in the domination of race and of sex.

The main danger for these theologies is that as they are so closely in touch with people who are becoming liberated from one form of oppression that the theologies themselves may escape one master only to become enslaved to another. There is the danger in Latin America that instead of liberating theology, contact with the movement will lead Christians simply to legitimize revolution with a few biblical proof texts. There is the danger in the USA that black theology will in its desperation to show that it is entirely freed from white domination, fall into legitimizing black fascism. And there is a danger that feminist theology will, in escaping from Genesis 2, fail to rediscover Genesis 1. But liberation theology is itself an idea whose hour has come, and while it can be improved, it cannot be denied.

T. Balasuriya, *The Eucharist and Human Liberation*, 1979; J. M. Bonino, *Doing Theology in a Revolutionary Situation*, 1975; E. Dussel, *History and the Theology of Liberation*, ET 1976; J. England, *Living Theology in Asia*, 1981; G. Gutierrez, *A Theology of Liberation*, ET 1974; A. Kee, *A Reader in Political Theology*, 1974; *The Scope of Political Theology*, 1978; J. Segundo, *The Liberation of Theology*, 1977; J. Sobrino, *Christology at the Crossroads*, 1978.

ALISTAIR KEE

Liberty, Religious

The condition in which individuals or groups are permitted to express and, up to some point, act upon beliefs concerning religious matters, free of interference or penalties imposed by outsiders, including the state.

The curtailment of religious liberty by means of coercive and injurious measures intended to alter, discourage, penalize or suppress certain beliefs and practices concerning religious matters is what is meant by religious persecution. Religious discrimination is the curtailment of religious liberty by withholding, selectively and unfairly, the opportunity to express beliefs and perform practices in respect to religious questions. Religious intolerance is the disposition to practise religious discrimination or persecution.

The quest for religious liberty is not culturally specific. Indeed, it is virtually true by definition that since a belief about religious questions (whatever else it may be) is a serious conviction about matters of critical importance, to hold such a belief is to desire the opportunity to express and act upon it without external frustration. Moreover, recent international resolutions in favour of religious liberty have attracted extensive intercultural support. For example, the *Declaration on the Elimination of Intolerance and of Discrimination Based on Religion or Belief* was adopted unanimously by the United Nations General Assembly (25 November 1981).

In its principal emphases, the Declaration provides that, 'Everyone shall have the right to freedom of thought, conscience and religion. This right shall include freedom to have a religion or whatever belief of his choice, and freedom either individually or in community with others and in public or private, to manifest his religion or belief in worship, observance, practice and teaching' (Art. 1.1); 'No one shall be subject to coercion which would impair his freedom to have a religion or belief of his choice' (Art. 1.2); 'No one shall be subject to discrimination by any State, institution, group of persons or person on the grounds of religion or beliefs' (Art. 2.1). The only permissible restriction is 'such limitations as are prescribed by law and are necessary to protect public safety, order, health or morals or the fundamental rights and freedom of others' (Art. 1.3).

Nevertheless, while formulations of this sort resonate, in different ways, in most of the world's cultural and religious traditions, the language bears the unmistakable mark of Western experience. The political strife and conflict caused by contending religious groups in sixteenth-, seventeenth- and eighteenth-century Europe, England and America eventually made a system of religious liberty and toleration attractive from many points of view. Against that historical background there is a special poignancy in the words of the Preamble to the Declaration: 'Considering that the disregard and infringement of human rights and fundamental freedoms, in particular the right to freedom of thought, conscience, or whatever belief, have brought, directly or indirectly, wars and great suffering to mankind . . .'

Out of those agonies arose a variety of experiments in toleration. Henry IV of France issued the Edict of Nantes in 1598, which temporarily extended a large measure of religious liberty to the French Protestants, the Huguenots. In 1689 the Act of Toleration modified, at least, the religious struggles characteristic of seventeenth-century England. In colonial America, tentative but significant attempts at religious liberty were articulated in the Maryland Toleration Act of 1649 and the Rhode Island Charter of 1663, the fruit of Roger Williams' indefatigable efforts. The culmination of the impulse towards institutionalizing religious liberty came in 1785 in the form of the Act Establishing Religious Freedom in Virginia, authored by Thomas Jefferson. These documents all, to varying degrees, provided a model for expressing contemporary prescriptions such as the UN Declaration on Intolerance.

At the same time, this record of the 'travail of religious liberty' in the West is incomprehensible apart from the system of ideas and the attitude towards the organization of church and state embedded in Christianity. The crucial feature was the predilection of primitive Christians to differentiate sharply between the ecclesiastical and the civil order, and thus to place the realm of Christian liberty beyond civil control and coercion. The implication was that the ideal religious life had to be conceived of, chosen, organized and put into practice as the result of voluntary election and commitment, rather than as the result of political affiliation or ethnic or racial identity. If the ideal life was voluntary, then individuals should be free to accept or reject religious teaching without civil penalty or discrimination.

This impulse toward religious liberty, particularly after the Constantinian Settlement in AD 312, competed with a countervailing tendency in Western Christianity towards the civil establishment of religion and uniformity of belief and practice.

See also **Freedom**.

Roland Bainton, *The Travail of Religious Liberty*, 1951; M. Searle Bates, *Religious Liberty: An Inquiry*, 1972; A. F. Carrillo de Albornoz, *The Basis of Religious Liberty*, 1967; Wilbur K. Jordan, *The Developnment of Religious Toleration in England*, 4 vols. 1932–40; Joseph Lecler, *Toleration and the Reformation*, 1960; Anson Phelps Stokes, *Church and State in the United States*, 3 vols. 1950.

                                    DAVID LITTLE

Life after Death

Christianity inherited from Judaism the belief in a life to come and the polarity of heaven and hell. For Jesus apparently sided with the Pharisees in affirming the resurrection of the dead against the Sadducees who denied it. In the previous two centuries the resurrection * belief had emerged and become widespread within Judaism, originally as an expectation of the physical reanimation of the many faithful who lay buried in tombs and graves. This continued as the prevailing popular conception of resurrection well into the Christian era, and is reflected for example in Matt. 27.52–53. But Jewish writings of the first century BC also increasingly reflect a more spiritualized understanding according to which resurrection does not consist in the raising and reanimating of dead bodies, but in renewed life in some kind of 'spiritual' (*pneumatikon*) body. This latter was taught by Paul (I Cor. 15.36–44) and may well have been assumed by Jesus (Mark 12.35; Luke 23.43). But the more physical interpretation also continued, and Christian pictures of the future life became extremely various and sometimes mutually inconsistent.

It has been customary to draw a strong contrast between the Hebraic conception of the resurrection of the embodied self as a psycho-physical unity, and the Greek conception, expressed classically in Plato's *Phaedo*, of the immortality of the soul *. (The contrast was pressed by Oscar Cullmann, *Immortality of the Soul or Resurrection of the Dead?*, 1958.) According to the one idea we perish totally at death, but are resurrected or re-created by a special divine act; according to the other idea the soul is by nature immortal and continues in being after the death of the body. The distinction, whilst valid, can, however, be over-stated. For in a radically theistic context it makes no ultimate difference whether God bestows eternal life upon us by creating us initially as immortal souls or by individually re-creating us immediately after death – in either case our continued existence, like our present existence, is the gift of our Maker.

What is the basis for the Christian belief in a life beyond death? Is it, as some of our Easter hymns and sermons affirm, the resurrection of Jesus? In fact both Jesus and his disciples, as Jews who were in this respect of the Pharisaic tradition, already believed in the resurrection of the dead. Today we believe as Christians in 'the life everlasting' for two basic intertwined reasons. One is that Jesus believed this. Several of his parables depict our present phase of existence as leading to another phase and urge us to take account now of this larger context. The other reason centres upon the Christian understanding of God as our loving heavenly Parent. If God loves each one of us and is seeking to draw us into a perfect relationship both with one another and with the divine Thou, does it not follow that God will hold us in being beyond the end of this short earthly life? Could it be an expression of infinite love to create us with immense spiritual potentialities but with so short a career, and often in such inauspicious circumstances, that those potentialities are normally destined never to be fulfilled?

It has been claimed by some that in addition to these religious considerations there is evidence for a life after death in the findings of parapsychology or psychical research. This evidence consists both in mental interactions between the living, labelled 'telepathy', which do not seem to be physically mediated and which thus suggest that mind is capable of functioning other than through the physical nervous system; and also in supposed communications, through trance mediums, automatic writing, visions, etc., from people who have died. Christian opinion remains strongly divided concerning the value of this evidence; but the obligation to take it seriously becomes increasingly evident. It is impossible to cover the matter adequately here: the best comprehensive account of the evidence itself is in Benjamin Wolman (ed), *Handbook of Parapsychology* (1977) with an application to Christian belief in Paul and Linda Badham, *Immortality or Extinction?* (1982).

These considerations, both religious and empirical, are, however, rejected by a number of contemporary religious thinkers, who reinterpret the language of eternal life either as referring to a moral quality that is possible in (and only in) the present life (e.g. D. Z. Phillips, *Death and Immortality*, 1970), or as claiming that our earthly lives will be eternally remembered by God (e.g. Charles Hartshorne, *The Logic of Perfection*, 1962, ch. 10), or that eternal life consists in this life as seen from the divine perspective (Wolfhart Pannenberg, *What is Man?*, 1962). Such thinkers reject the idea of a continuation of conscious personal existence after death for one or both of two reasons: 1. We have to accept the general assumption among scientifically-minded contemporaries that mental life is absolutely dependent upon – if not identical with – the functioning of the cerebral system. (In response it is insisted by others that this question remains an open one, the subject today of active debate.) 2. The desire for personal survival is self-centred and therefore basically irreligious: we ought not to be concerned about the perpetuation of our little human egos. (To this it is replied that the Christian belief in a life after death is not grounded in human desires but in the nature of God, who has created us in the divine image and whose love will hold us in being beyond the boundaries of this present life.)

What form might a life after death take? Might it be a purely disembodied existence? This possibility has been spelled out by the contemporary philosopher H. H. Price ('Survival and the Idea of "Another World"', *Proc. Soc. for Psychical Research*, Jan. 1953, and reprinted frequently, e.g. in J. R. Smythies, ed., *Brain and Mind*, 1965). Assuming consciousness to continue, but without any sensory input, he suggests that the mind then creates its own world, as in dreams. As experienced, such a world would be as real and solid as our present environment; but its materials would come from memory, selected and formed by desire. The next world will thus be a wish-fulfilment world. It will not, however, necessarily for that reason be wholly pleasant. For as well as conscious desires we also harbour unconscious desires whose fulfilment, and whose conflicts with our conscious thoughts, may sometimes produce 'dreams' that are more hellish than heavenly. Thus far the theory seems to postulate a separate and private 'solipsistic' world for each individual. But Price also suggests that disembodied minds may communicate and interact telepathically, collaborating to form common worlds for communities of relatively like-minded people. (There seems, however, to be a tension in this hypothesis between the shared character of such worlds and their wish-fulfilment character; for the desires of many different persons concerning the details of their environment can hardly be continuously and totally harmonious.)

Price suggests that as our desires are externalized in a thought-world they may either evoke in us new and better desires, so that we gravitate to 'higher' worlds; or alternatively, they may finally expend themselves, thus leading to a final non-existence.

A basic theological question concerning Price's hypothesis is whether worlds formed by desire could serve a divine purpose of person-making. For in the present life it is precisely the objective character of the world, as an environment shared with others, that generates the moral pressures by which we may grow as persons.

This difficulty underlines the value of the alternative idea of resurrection or re-embodiment. Embodiment involves continuity with an objective environment which is common to a community of embodied persons. According to Buddhism and Hinduism, re-embodiment takes the form of rebirth in this world, and occurs many times (*see* **Reincarnation**). According to Christianity, our re-embodiment is in another 'world' and occurs only once. One has a 'spiritual' body, which is an expression of one's inner nature in relation to the new environment and its inhabitants, as the present physical body expresses our nature in relation to our present environment and its co-inhabitants. The development of the idea of the 'spiritual body' (as expressed, e.g. by Paul) out of the earlier notion of the reanimation of the physical corpse has generally led Christians to assume that the resurrection body will have the same shape as the present body, but at an optimal age and somehow glorified (*see* **Resurrection**).

A major division in Christian thought concerns the question whether, after death, life continues in the sense of there being continued person-making through real moral decisions in situations which demand such choices; or whether life in that sense ends definitively at death, to be followed by an eternal heaven and hell. The main Christian tradition, both Catholic and Reformed, has adopted the latter scheme. There is, however, a counter-indication in the thought that human beings, at the time of death, are seldom good or evil enough to come immediately into the presence of God or to be consigned to eternal punishment. And so the idea of purgatory developed as a process of purification through which those judged worthy of heaven are gradually prepared for it. In traditional Catholic theology purgatory does not provide a further opportunity for a fundamental turning to God; it is only for those who have already made their decision for God. On the other hand in some circles of nineteenth-century Protestant thought the idea arose of an 'intermediate state' in which there could be a 'second chance' to respond savingly to God. As a further development of this there is the speculative theory (suggested by Eastern thought) of a series of embodied lives (though perhaps separated by disembodied phases), in other 'worlds', each subject to the creative pressures set up by the boundaries of birth and death, through which we may progress towards our perfected humanity in the divine presence.

The notions of heaven and hell were inherited by Christianity from Judaism. Heaven has been pictured in many different ways – as eternal rest; as the beatific vision * of God; as the heavenly city; as an interminable liturgy in which the saints sing hymns around the throne of God; as an unending movement through the infinite dimensions of God's creativity, enjoying ever new aspects of reality. The basic conception is that of a final (though not necessarily therefore static) state in which those who please God live eternally in God's presence and enjoy the limitless riches of the creative divine love. Hell has likewise been pictured in many ways – as a place of perpetual quasi-physical torture; as an experience of the unending mental torment of remorse and of the awareness of the irrevocable loss of heaven; or, as a milder modern interpretation, as simply passing finally out of existence.

The question of universal salvation has been debated throughout Christian history (*see* **Universalism**). During most of this long period the idea was regarded as heretical, though during the last century or so it has come to be widely accepted. The issue hinges upon the apparent contradiction between divine providence and human freedom. Even though God may desire the salvation of all human beings, must not any genuine creaturely freedom make it impossible for God to ensure this? For if the creature is free, then he or she must be able to reject God. It has been suggested, however, that this way of posing the problem is misleading because it forgets God's original creation of us in the divine image, thus bestowing upon us a nature which is fundamentally directed towards God. 'Thou hast made us for thyself, and our hearts are restless until they find their rest in thee' (Augustine, *Confessions*, Bk. I, ch. 1). Thus our nature may be such that we shall in fact eventually come to God in our own freedom. But in that case has not our human nature been programmed – so that we are no longer free? The answer seems to be: Yes, but no more programmed than would be the case if humanity had been initially formed with some other basic structure, whether by God or by nature; and our human freedom can only be a freedom within the given structure of our nature. But the whole question remains debatable and debated.

See also **Identity.**

Russell Aldwinckle, *Death in the Secular City*, 1972; Paul Badham, *Christian Beliefs about Life after Death*, 1976; John Baillie, *And the Life Everlasting*, 1934; R. H. Charles, *Eschatology*, 1899, new ed. 1963; David Edwards, *The Last Things Now*, 1969; John Hick, *Death and Eternal Life*, 1976; Michael Paternoster, *Thou Art There Also*, 1967; John A. T. Robinson, *In the End, God*, new ed. 1968; Geoffrey Rowell, *Hell and the Victorians*, 1974; D. P. Walker, *The Decline of Hell*, 1974.

JOHN HICK

Limbo

From Latin *limbus*, a hem or edge: the notion that persisted from the early Middle Ages, that there must be some place where after death souls (e.g. those of unbaptized infants) undeserving of condemnation or of the beatitude of heaven could enjoy their natural state of happiness in eternity. There were many different forms of the notion (*see also* **Life After Death**).

ALAN RICHARDSON

Limit Situation

This concept (*Grenzsituation*) is important in the thought of Karl Jaspers. It originated in his early work as a psychiatrist and becomes part of his general philosophy, being fully discussed in *Philosophie* (1932) and later writings. The human being is said to experience certain situations which differ from the ordinary situations of life in that they bring him, as it were, to the end of his resources; this is like colliding with a wall. Such are situations when one confronts death or is overwhelmed by grief or suffering or is tortured by guilt. These situations are taken to be profoundly revelatory of the human condition. They show clearly on the one hand the finitude of human existence. They belong inevitably to our humanity, and show that there comes a point at which we cannot cope or understand. They show, too, the limitations of what can be objectified

and what resources we can derive from the realm of the objectifiable. In such a limit situation there may occur a 'foundering' (*scheitern*), virtually a technical term with Jaspers. It means the break up of the familiar pattern of life, based on one's own subjectivity and the world which, as subject, one has objectified, and initiates a new relation to what Jaspers calls 'transcendence'. This is the name he gives to the all-encompassing reality which lies beyond the distinction of subject and object. Transcendence cannot be simply identified with God, though the personal God is one of the many 'ciphers' which we use to represent the transcendent. Jaspers inclines rather to see transcendence as the nameless absolute reported by mystics of all religious traditions. It was said above that the limit situation *may* lead to encounter with transcendence beyond the limit, but there is nothing automatic in this and Jaspers is careful to say also that it *may not* – indeed, he expresses astonishment that human beings are so often in limit situations without hearing 'the voice of transcendence'. This effectively answers Barth's criticism that millions of people have known limit situations without encountering the 'wholly other' or even becoming a little bit other themselves. A more serious criticism came from Bonhoeffer: the teaching about limit situations reserves faith for the borders of life, but does not address it at its centre. There are obvious similarities between this teaching of Jaspers and that of such theologians as Bultmann and Tillich.

K. Jaspers, *Philosophie*, 3 vols., 1932; *The Perennial Scope of Philosophy*, ET 1950; E. T. Long, *Jaspers and Bultmann*, 1968.

JOHN MACQUARRIE

Literary Criticism

Literary criticism, in the broadest sense, is the attempt to understand works of literature as fully as possible. Depending on the age, nature, and historical and cultural background of the literature, the language in which it is written and the way in which it has come down to us, this attempt to understand will mean the use of a variety of disciplines, which are constantly being extended as interpretation becomes more sophisticated. By the nineteenth century, it had become widely recognized, despite ongoing opposition from some quarters in the churches, that the Bible, too, was to be read like any other literature, and in fact to quite a substantial degree the literary criticism of writings from classical antiquity (e.g. Homer) and biblical criticism went hand in hand, each discipline drawing on the insights of the other.

It is still the case that much of the work that is done under the heading of biblical criticism is in fact literary criticism: problems of e.g. textual criticism, source criticism and translation of the Bible are those which arise in similar fashion in other contexts. However, particularly during the 1970s, 'literary criticism' of theological texts, and primarily the Bible, came to have quite different connotations from 'biblical criticism'. The reason for this was that the nineteenth-century scholars who laid the foundations for modern biblical criticism were excessively preoccupied with the question of historicity, to a degree which prevented them from appreciating the literary characteristics of the Bible. This concern for historicity had led in OT scholarship to a neglect of those parts of the OT which were manifestly not historical (like the wisdom literature, culminating in the book of Job) and had extended so far over the NT that it even came to dominate interpretation of the parables of Jesus, which as practised by e.g. Joachim Jeremias set them in too narrow a perspective. Consequently literary criticism in a theological context tends to be used principally of an approach which seeks to treat texts predominantly from a literary perspective (though that need not rule out historical understanding).

For some of the issues involved in literary criticism in theology, see especially **Hermeneutics, Metaphor, Narrative Theology, Parable, Structuralism**.

Erich Auerbach, *Mimesis*, ET 1953; William A. Beardslee, *Literary Criticism of the New Testament*, 1969; Brevard S. Childs, *Introduction to the Old Testament as Scripture*, 1979; Northrop Frye, *Anatomy of Criticism*, 1957; Frank Kermode, *The Genesis of Secrecy*, 1979; Dan O. Via, *The Parables: Their Literary and Existential Dimension*, 1967.

JOHN BOWDEN

Liturgical Movement

This has three basic theological principles: a true understanding of the Incarnation *, pro-ducing a deeper appreciation of the dignity of human life; a true understanding of the sacrifice of Christ, producing a commitment to sacrificial living; and a true understanding of the church as the body of Christ, creating a deeper sense of community both in life and in worship. The church, as the body of Christ, shares in his redemptive activity and commits itself to the task of bringing all men within its sphere. The Movement is therefore of pastoral, missionary and ecumenical significance; and it has strongly influenced the work of liturgical revision, with its recognition of the need for indigenous forms of worship, the use of the vernacular, and active participation by the laity. It aims at renewal rather than revolution. While recognizing that there are lessons to be rediscovered from the worship of the early church, it seeks to establish not an antique form of worship, but one which is relevant to the life of the contemporary world and recognized as the well-spring of Christian life and mission.

The Movement is commonly regarded as having begun in the Roman Church with Abbot Prosper Guéranger (1805–75) at the French Benedictine Abbey of Solesmes, which became famous for its exact performance of the Roman rite and for the correct chanting of plainsong. Although accused by his critics of antiquarianism and romanticism, Guéranger preached a love of worship for its own sake, and his influence on other Benedictine liturgical centres such as Maria Laach was undoubted. In the early days of the twentieth century the Movement received impetus from Pope Pius X (1835–1914) and from Dom Lambert Beauduin of Mont César, Louvain, with his book *La Piété de l'Eglise* (1914), while the Encyclical of Pope Pius XII *Mediator Dei* (1947) gave it official recognition.

It would be an exaggeration, however, to attribute its origins entirely to the Roman Church. A parallel movement can be detected in the Church of England during the nineteenth century through the activities of the Tractarians, the Cambridge Camden Society, and such individuals as George Howard Wilkinson, Richard Twigg and Robert Dolling. The work has continued in the present century through the work of Gabriel Hebert and others, and through the Parish and People Movement. Furthermore the influence of the Movement in the Anglican Communion as a whole is indicated in the Report on Worship by the Lambeth Conference of 1958. This Report might well be regarded as the Anglican counterpart of *Mediator Dei*.

There have also been movements in other parts of the Christian church. Note, as examples, the work of Eugène Bersier of the French Reformed Church, continued subsequently by Wilfred Monod and Richard Paquier, and by the Taizé Community; or the work of Friedrich Heiler and the High Church Movement in the German Lutheran Church; or of Nikolai Grundtwig in Denmark. In recent times the Church of South India has played an influential role on the ecumenical front with the publication of its eucharistic liturgy in 1950.

J. D. Benoit, *Liturgical Renewal*, ET 1958; L. Bouyer, *Life and Liturgy*, 1956; T. S. Garrett, *Worship in the Church of South India*, 1958; H. G. Hageman, *Pulpit and Table*, 1962; A. G. Hebert, *Liturgy and Society*, 1935; P. L. Jagger, *A History of the Parish and People Movement*, 1978; G. Wainwright, *Doxology*, 1980.

R. C. D. JASPER

Liturgical Theology

The systematic interpretation of the whole economy of Christian liturgy as living worship. Its primary task is, in A. Schmemann's words, 'the elucidation of the meaning of worship'. Such disciplined articulation focusses upon the theological meaning of the church's symbolic action in various rites, including the interrelation of Word and sacramental action, drawing out implications for doctrine and for the faith experience of the church in the world. Liturgical theology may thus be regarded as both a discipline within theological studies and a particular way of doing theology – one which construes belief and doctrine as beginning and ending in worship and prayer.

The idea of liturgy itself as a primary source (*locus theologicus**) for thought about God, creation, redemption and related doctrines is not new. This was a feature of early church and patristic theology, summed up in the phrase *lex orandi lex est credendi*: the rule of praying governs, or more precisely, 'constitutes' (*statuit*) the form and content of believing. In its twentieth-century form, then, liturgical theology seeks to interpret and to articulate the fundamental doctrines of Christianity and of various families within it by explicating the meaning of specific structures, texts and rites of worship, both as historically developed and in current transition of reform and renewal. Liturgical theology may be distinguished, then, from a 'theology of worship' on the one hand; and, on the other, from mere devotional reflection and spiritual interpretation of the church's prayer. Much sacramental theology* in the West has taken the form of interpreting liturgy by applying various metaphysical theories of sign and symbol to the rites, rather than by unfolding the meaning of symbolic action in the living tradition. Until recently 'liturgics' was conceived primarily as a study of the rubrics and canons governing the practical ordering of public worship.

With the impact of both the liturgical and ecumenical movements, and most especially with the advent of widespread liturgical reforms across all major Christian traditions, spearheaded by the Second Vatican Council's 'Constitution on the Sacred Liturgy', liturgical theology has emerged as a distinct discipline. Liturgical studies in general are no longer focussed on Roman and Anglican rites. Rather, the increasing shared historical scholarship and the decidedly ecumenical work of reform now brings Orthodox and Protestant Christianity into the common search for a more adequate understanding of the meaning and point of worship. In this respect, liturgical theology need not be confined merely to the 'liturgical churches', since the concepts and phenomena to be investigated have encouraged a method of studying what lies behind and beneath the received historical structures and forms.

Liturgical studies have traditionally incorporated insights and methodological patterns from biblical studies and comparative historical studies, including textual and linguistic analysis. Increasingly, as attention has been given to contemporary reform and renewal, insights from the social sciences – especially social history, sociology and cultural anthropology – have come to form a significant part of the interdisciplinary matrix for the work of liturgical theology proper. A complex set of relationships exist between liturgy, the living community of faith and theological reflection. This is why, methodologically speaking, liturgical theology is itself interdisciplinary. Beginning with the bedrock of comparative studies of the historical rites in their development, liturgical theologians must interpret the specifically theological meanings embedded in particular forms and types of liturgical events such as the eucharist *, initiation * rites, daily prayer, and the pattern of readings and prayer over cycles of the seasons. Only in the light of these considerations may particular proposals be made concerning God, christology, soteriology, ecclesiology and related matters.

The aims and method of liturgical theology emerge in considering four primary facts:

1. Liturgy both forms and expresses human beings in the Christian faith, whether adequately or inadequately, in any given age or tradition.

2. There is a recognizable 'canon' of fundamental elements comprising the church's worship which undergirds all historical developments – inititation rites, the eucharist, the daily prayer office, and the various cycles of time which pattern the use of scripture and the remembered history of God's acts.

3. The immense array of historical developments in Jewish and Christian liturgy is not of equal value and significance for present theological reflection or liturgical usage.

4. The current cultural and ecumenical situation forces the question of norms and criteria for adequacy and authenticity of the church's worship.

With these factors in mind, liturgical theology must investigate key concepts and develop a coherent methodology. In recent work several concepts occupy centre stage: remembering (*anamnesis*), invocation (*epiclesis*), thanksgiving (*eucharistia*), blessing and praise (*berakah*), offering (*oblatio*) and sacrifice. Liturgical theology discovers and articulates the meaning of these concepts and explores the relationship between them in particular historical rites and the actual celebration of living communities of faith.

Thus the method must serve to establish the patterns and structural elements of liturgical life in light of both history and the current cultural context of the church's experience and self-reflection. A principal aim of such a way of theology is to make explicit what is formed and expressed by the language of worship and prayer concerning all the classical *loci* of dogmatic theology. At the same time this brings the question of new developments in liturgical life into necessary critical dialogue with theological norms which are not immediately 'read off' the surface of liturgical texts. Rather, the depth structures of what it means to praise, to bless, to give thanks, to invoke, to offer sacrifice and to supplicate serve to guide future developments in liturgical renewal.

The future of liturgical theology is promising precisely because it stands both as a disciplined receiving point of the church's ongoing experienced life of worship, and as a normative discipline for liturgy and doctrinal formulation alike. In the final analysis, the work of liturgical theology will be tested by its capacity to understand and to illuminate the whole liturgical life of the church as knowledge of God, and to provide a convincing account and rationale for the mutual interdependence of theology, worship and spirituality.

Peter Brunner, *Worship in the Name of Jesus*, 1968; Louis Bouyer, *Rite and Man: Natural Sacredness and Christian Liturgy*, E T 1963; A. Schmemann, *Introduction to Liturgical Theology*, 1966; Cyprian Vagaggini, *Theological Dimensions of the Liturgy*, E T 1976; J. J. Von Allmen, *Worship: Its Theory and Practice*, 1965; Geoffrey Wainwright, *Doxology*, 1980.

D. E. SALIERS

Loci Theologici

Loci theologici ('theological topics') or *Loci communes* ('common topics') appeared in the titles of numerous works of dogmatics during the Reformation and in the period of Protestant Orthodoxy that followed. The practice originated with Philip Melanchthon's *Loci communes rerum theologicarum* of 1521, the first systematic presentation of Protestant doctrine. Adapting the model of *loci communes* from the Renaissance humanists, especially Rudolf Agricola and Erasmus, Melanchthon produced a simplified Protestant equivalent of Lombard's *Sentences* (the standard textbook of mediaeval theology), and it rapidly achieved a similar significance in Lutheran theology. Stemming originally from the *topoi* of Greek rhetoric and dialectic, the notion of fundamental topics or *loci* became an element of Roman rhetorical tradition (especially in

Cicero), and was later adopted by the humanists in their struggle against the Aristotelian* philosophizing of mediaeval Scholasticism*. Melanchthon, grandnephew of the humanist Reuchlin and an admirer of both Agricola and Erasmus, fell under the spell of Luther soon after coming to Wittenberg in 1518. He summarized the new evangelical faith for his students by describing the 'common topics' of theology, taking as his original model Paul's letter to the Romans. The first edition of 1521, which drew high praise from Luther, grew through subsequent revisions to four times its original size while changing considerably in content. The idea of presenting dogmatics in the form of *Loci communes theologici* became a model for later generations of theologians, culminating in Johann Gerhard's famous work of that name (1610–1622), the high point of Lutheran Orthodoxy. The phrase also appears in the titles of dogmatic writings of Reformed Orthodoxy. With the coming of the European Enlightenment* and the decline of Orthodox dogmatics after the middle of the seventeenth century, the writing of *Loci theologici* fell out of fashion. Karl Barth tried to revive the model in the twentieth century, commending it on methodological grounds as an alternative to theological system-building, because it eschews the goal of dogmatic unity and seeks instead to respond open-endedly to the leading of the Holy Spirit. Barth describes the four basic topics of his *Church Dogmatics* as *loci* rather than first principles of axioms.

In the RC tradition, beginning with the *De locis theologicis* (1563) of Melchior Cano, the expression is used rather for the 'sources' of theology or the places where doctrines can be 'proved'.

K. Barth, *Church Dogmatics*, I/2, ET 1956; P. Joachim, *'Loci communes'*, *Lutherjahrbuch* 8, 1926, pp. 27–97; A. Lang, *Die Loci Theologici des Melchior Cano und die Methode des dogmatischen Beweises*, 1925; P. Melanchthon, *Loci communes theologici*. ET in *Melanchthon and Bucer*, LCC 19, 1969.

GARRETT GREEN

Logic

Logic can claim to be both the most technical, specialized branch of philosophy and the branch that has more general relevance to other disciplines than any other part of philosophy. Its breadth can be seen in its concern with the structure of argument as such. It can be defined as the systematic study of argument, the methods to be used in distinguishing correct from incorrect – valid from invalid – patterns of reasoning. Reasoning is investigated also by psychology, but as a human activity, a process, a series of events. The logician is primarily interested in the reliability or unreliability of inferences.

The degree of development and specialization logic has now attained is a relatively recent phenomenon, our own century having seen an enormous extending of logic as traditionally conceived, and an equally great effort to give all possible rigour to logical systems. The traditional Aristotelian* logic was not able adequately to analyse the logic of propositions – where the elements of the arguments are not 'terms' but complete propositions. Stoic* logicians had in fact worked on the logic of propositions, but traditional logic failed properly to incorporate their researches. Only recently, too, philosophers and mathematicians have elaborated theories about the foundations of mathematical reasoning. The augmented field of elementary logic includes such topics as the nature of definition, types of proposition, the study of forms of argument (among which the syllogism retains a place, although among many other forms), methods of testing deductive arguments for validity, the reducing of a logical system to its formal essentials – displaying its axioms and rules of inference. Again, 'modal' logic investigates arguments which turn upon words like 'must', 'cannot', 'may', arguments about what is possible, impossible or necessary.

Logic is by no means confined to the study of deduction alone. In *inductive* inference no contradiction is produced if the premises of an argument are affirmed and the conclusions denied. Yet, of course, there are good and bad, better and worse, arguments here, too. This is the field of 'reasonable', 'probable' inference, where a claim can be supported by evidence more or less weighty, more or less flimsy (*see* **Induction**). Inductive logic has been developed, historically, as the analysis of scientific canons of reasoning.

'Philosophy of logic' is the study of higher-order questions like 'What are propositions?' 'What do we mean by "truth", "validity", "probability", "logical necessity"?' It includes the study of 'meaning' in general, the problems of how logic and metaphysics are related: what assumptions, if any, the logician makes about the world, and what implications, if any, his studies have for our overall view of the world.

At what points, finally, does the study of logic bear most directly upon the conduct and assessment of theological argument? In so far, of course, as logic deals with the conditions for any consistent discourse and correct argumentation, it bears on it at *every* point. From a contradiction, e.g., any proposition whatever may be deduced, however absurd or palpably false. The theologian needs to develop, therefore, a logic that will give a satisfactory account of any apparent contradictions he finds himself moved to affirm. This is an arduous task: renaming the problem-cases 'paradoxes' will do only as a first move.

Again, the traditional theistic arguments have involved a great deal of complex logic. The dispute over the ontological argument *, for instance, is largely a dispute over the logical nature of the words 'exists', 'existent', 'exists necessarily'. Does 'existence' figure among the perfections – so that to omit existence from the account of God's qualities would count as failure to conceive of God as the 'greatest conceivable being'? Or is 'existent' of an entirely different order from all predicate-words? When the cosmological argument * speaks of God as 'necessary being', does 'necessary' here mean 'logically necessary' (i.e. does the denial of God's existence involve contradiction)? If so, the ontological argument and its difficulties return once more. If 'necessary' is used in some other sense, there needs to be a logical analysis of that sense, and its relation to other senses of the word.

The study of religious language* raises many more logical cruces. If language about God is analogical or symbolical or in some other way 'oblique', we need (as part of a theory of meaning) an account of how this language operates, how it can be kept from extravagance or emptiness, of how the symbols refer to the God they ostensibly are *about*. Claims about God's infinity bring logical problems of their own. Expressions that normally are perfectly comprehensible may become logically perplexing if 'infinite' or 'infinitely' is prefixed to them. How far

are analogies from the mathematics of infinite series illuminating or misleading? The complexity and obscurity of many of the notions a theologian deals with, the way in which they hover on the borderline between sayable and unsayable, in the attempt to characterize an essentially mysterious subject-matter – all this makes the pursuit of logical rigour and precision a most difficult task for the theologian; but, for the very same reasons, a most necessary task also.

On formal logic see, e.g. E. J. Lemmon, *Beginning Logic*, 1965; Benson Mates, *Elementary Logic*, 2, 1979; W. V. O. Quine, *Methods of Logic*, 1952.

R. W. HEPBURN

Logical Positivism
see **Analytical Philosophy**

Logos

Originally the Greek noun derived from *legein*, 'to say', which implies a significant statement; not mere talk (*lalein*), nor prayers, commands, etc. Logos thus means a statement, narrative or discussion at any length; an argument; consideration; a mathematical ratio; or again, man's ability to use such expressions, his reason. For Greek philosophers it implied a rational account of the world and human life, as opposed to mere opinion or story-telling. Heraclitus, who saw the world as perpetually changing, detected a logos (i.e. law) which governed its changes; and the Stoics, who also thought of the universe as evolving, used 'logos' as a term for its controlling principle, which they identified as organizing or constructive 'fire' or warmth, intelligence in man being a small-scale copy of this cosmic logos.

Christian logos-theology was influenced by developments in later Judaism which tended to conceive God as remote and transcendent, communicating with the world by agencies such as his Word (*memra*) or his Wisdom, which came to be separately personified (see e.g. Prov. 8.22ff.; Wisdom 9). In particular Philo of Alexandria, interpreting the Greek OT in terms of Greek philosophy, depicted the Logos as the intelligible element in God's mysterious being; the means of God's self-disclosure to the world; the source of its rational order, understood as Plato's 'Forms', and its controlling principle; occasionally described both as 'Second God' and 'Son of God'.

John's Gospel sees Christ as the incarnate Son of God, who existed with him in glory before the world was made. The title Logos ('the Word') is used in the opening verses of the Gospel, perhaps deliberately linking the OT tradition of the Word as God's revealing utterance with a philosophical tradition akin to that of Philo. Later Christian theology continually returned to these verses.

The description of Christ as both Son and Logos posed a problem for theologians; was he 1., as 'Logos' might suggest, simply an expression of the single divine mind, or 2., as 'Son', a distinct person alongside the Father, or 3. were these two titles interchangeable, pointing to a mystery beyond our comprehension? For Tertullian, the Son's distinct existence begins with the creation; before this God discoursed with himself, and this discourse was his 'word' (*ratio*); but at creation it was uttered as a command or *spoken* word (*sermo*), identified with God's Son, who later took human form.

Early Greek theologians attempted to explain the generation of the Logos as an act by which God produced another form of himself, yet without division. In commending Christianity to sympathetic pagans they tended to represent the Logos as a subordinate power, to whom the Father delegated his less exalted concerns. For Justin, the Logos is God's agent in creation, but also exists in a disseminated form as the principle of man's natural reason; it is by the Logos that men are logical. Clement and Origen also tend to assign the Logos a limited activity compared to the Father, but Origen contends that he exists from all eternity; whereas the doctrine that the Logos is 'younger' than the Father, as well as subordinate, was still held in the early fourth century by Eusebius and Arius (*see also* **Arianism**). After the condemnation of Arianism the titles 'Son' and 'Logos' became virtually interchangeable, and the divine persons were declared to be coeternal and equal in dignity; though traces of older thinking survive even in Athanasius, who regards the Logos as less inaccessible to our understanding than the Father.

James D. G. Dunn, *Christology in the Making*, 1980 (esp. sections 6 and 7); T. E. Pollard, *Johannine Christology and the Early Church*, 1970.

CHRISTOPHER STEAD

Love

The centrality and (consequent?) elusiveness of love in secular discourse apply to its Christian and theological usage. It is, however, possible to discern in both secular and Christian usage the three elements of value recognized or bestowed, intimacy/unity achieved or sought, and care exercised in service combining in various ways and degrees to constitute love as relating two personal poles. Love for non-personal objects (by persons), e.g. for food or truth, is considered secondary to and derived from the inter-personal reality. In much religious and secular discourse the paradigm of inter-personal love is the love of man and woman, sexual and marital. The centrality and elusiveness relate to this paradigm.

In both OT and NT love is central. Any suggestion of opposition between a God or covenant * of fear in the OT and a God or covenant of love in the NT is unfounded. Love (*ahabh, agape*), with the associated themes of loving-kindness (*ḥesed*) and grace (*ḥen*), mercy (*raḥam*) and forgiveness (*salaḥ*), and above all fidelity (*'emeth*), forms a constituent and constant feature of Yahweh's covenant commitment to Israel. Its intimacy, intensity, fidelity and generosity are depicted in terms of a faithful husband's love for his (erring) wife (Hosea; Ezekiel; Isaiah). Yahweh's love calls for love in response, not only for Yahweh but for the neighbour. The story of Yahweh's loving pursuit of humankind and Israel with the triangle of love involved (Yahweh's love for human beings, human beings' love for Yahweh and for one another) manifests the distinctiveness of divine love which reaches a new climax in the story of Jesus. God once again takes the initiative, this time in sending his Son (John 3.16) while human beings were still sinners (e.g. I John 4.19). The fullness of that love is expressed in the most radical of all testimonies, laying down one's life (John 15.13). God's love of humankind transcends all boundaries. It requires and empowers a human response to God and the neighbour which are inextricably bound together. Such response in love is the way to God, the way to know God, for God is love. The history of God's persistent love of Israel and humankind reveals the very reality of God as love.

The force and distinctiveness of love in OT and NT is underlined by the distinctive usage of *agape** (LXX, NT). Unusual in extra-biblical Greek, it predominates for all three dimensions of love to the near-exclusion of *philia* (love of friendship) and the total exclusion of *eros* (love of desire, sexual love).

In the history of Israel and of Jesus God provides the source and standard of loving. Christian human loving derives from his loving and is measured by its standard (I John 4, etc.; Matt. 5.48). The divine initiative in loving takes the original and radical form of creating human beings as loving, inviting and enabling them to love God in return and persisting with this offer and empowerment despite continuing human refusal. In so far as *agape* describes God's love for human beings, it bestows value in bestowing existence, the dignity of being loved by God in face of failure and the capacity to return love. In this respect Nygren is correct in seeing *agape* as entirely free and gracious, bestowing rather than recognizing and desiring goodness and lovableness. So it is completely distinct from *eros* as love characterized by desire, attraction or need. *Agape* is gift- rather than need-love (Lewis). Nygren is mistaken in excluding *agape* as a genuine possibility for human beings in their response to God and neighbour.

The creative, enabling-to-be character of human *agape* obviously cannot match the originating and radical creativity of God. Yet as it operates at least between human beings by the gift and power of God, it gives by its recognition, attention and sensitivity the space, freedom, encouragement and aid to the other to realize his or her potential, overcome obstacles and be healed of injuries. The letting-be of the human other, loving him or her into their own potential and for their own sake is the human reflection of the divine activity of creation, letting-be (Macquarrie). It expresses *amor benevolentiae* (Aquinas) in a way that is genuinely other-regarding (Outka). In this it manifests its divine source and observes the divine standard.

As response to God, *agape* presents greater difficulties. It is easily open to Nygren's criticism of Augustine* for his apparent Neoplatonic* reduction of love for God to satisfaction of human need (*Conf.* 1.1). If loving God is understood as letting God be God in correspondence with the divine claims and prophetic criticisms in OT and NT, a 'creative' element analogous to that in human love of neighbour emerges. This would be loving God for his own sake. Letting God be God for his own people, his elect and the whole human race reveals the fuller depth of what God had to offer in his loving creation of humankind. The mutuality (equality) which Aristotle found an obstacle to divine-human friendship (*Nic. Eth.* 7) is made possible. The intimate and indeed intrinsic unity between love of God and love of neighbour (Rahner), manifest in OT and NT, emphasizes how the letting-be of neighbour is a letting-be of God.

For many people, secular and religious, the critical feature of love is the intimacy and unity achieved or at least sought. Such intimacy and unity imply mutuality. Love is or is to be returned. God's love of his people was always seeking this return: his people, their God. Covenant was the great symbol of unity and reciprocity between God and his people. The intimacy and unity of marriage offered a parable of the mutual love of God and his people. Communication-of-self seeking return, as with husband and wife, indicates the thrust of God's love in history of Israel. With Jesus the divine self-communication achieves a new and critical breakthrough. The unity and community of God and humankind involves the inner trinitarian life of God as human beings are admitted to that inner life. They become sons and daughters of the Father in and through Jesus Christ by the gift of the Spirit. Their new (love) life with God (grace) constitutes them at the same time sisters and brothers of one another, the basis of their gift and call to love one another. Unity with God in love which is both given and to be expressed and achieved, forms the community of love, partially realized in the church and destined for all humankind. In its gift of divine love the church is the sacrament of the unity of all. In its loving unity marriage symbolizes and realizes in the NT as in the OT the divine-human community of love (Eph. 5).

As source of love for, by and between human beings God also provides the standard of practice or behaviour whereby love as creative and unitive is both witnessed and realized. The deeds of love for God and neighbour constitute the Christian life-task. In this context love is spoken of as the root and form of all the virtues (Aquinas). It has been recently invoked as the primary and architectural principle of moral theology (Gillemann). The earlier and stronger version, 'Love and do what you will' (Augustine), was given fresh relevance by Fletcher and others in a 'situation ethics' that is practically antinomian and finally incoherent (McCabe, Ramsey).

The Christian discussion of love in action has been largely confined to one-to-one relationships. Christian love, like so much of Christianity, had been privatized (Metz) and sentimentalized. Attempts to rectify this have invoked justice as more hard-edged and reaching beyond the face-to-face range of love (Reinhold Niebuhr). The use of the term 'social love' (John Paul II) restores the social dimension of the biblical use of *agape* and underlines its close covenant connection with divine righteousness or justice. In seeking to enable all peoples to realize their potential and to establish amicable and supportive links in what must for survival's sake develop into a world community, the name and deeds of (social) love return Christians to the source and standard of *agape*. As coming from God and empowering human beings, *agape* is the very saving presence of God which Jesus also proclaimed in that other great social symbol of divine-human community, the kingdom*. The kingdom is the measure, historically and eschatologically, of love's social significance.

The creative, letting-be dimension of love attends to the other in all his or her fullness even at the cost, the ultimate cost, of the self. Mutuality and unity may not be historically attainable. The only service finally appropriate may be that of dying for the beloved. This may be read from the lesson of history and the example of Jesus. His death takes love and its final cost beyond history with threat of meaninglessness. Love prevails over destruction in the gracious raising by the Father of Jesus to guarantee the ultimate meaning of his love initiative in human creation and election.

J. Burnaby, *Amor Dei*, 1938; M. C. D'Arcy, *The Mind and Heart of Love*, 1945; Gerard Gillemann, *The Primacy of Charity in Moral Theology*, ET 1959; Jean Guitton, *Essay on Human Love*, 1948; C. S. Lewis, *The Four Loves*, 1960; Herbert McCabe, *Law, Love and Language*, 1968; John McIntyre, *On the Love of God*, 1962; Anders Nygren, *Agape and Eros*, ET 1957; Gene Outka, *Agape*, 1972; G. Quell and E. Stauffer, *Love*, ET 1949; C. Spicq, *Agape in the New Testament*, ET 1963; Viktor Warnach, *Agape*, 1951.

ENDA MCDONAGH

Lutheranism, Luther

Martin Luther (1483–1546), educated at the University of Erfurt and in the monastery of Augustinian Hermits there, while young, was familiar with mediaeval theology. As a professor in Wittenberg he struggled through a time of deep anxiety concerning his own salvation. When he fully yielded to the Pauline teaching of justification* by faith he felt as if the gate of heaven had been opened to him. His lectures on Romans (1515–16) bring to expression the elements of this doctrine. The Reformation controversy began at the point where this conviction was brought to bear on the practice of indulgences. As his theology was widened in controversy he still kept the emphasis on justification by faith. With intensity and mounting force, and with constant reference to scripture, he challenged the constituent elements of scholastic theology and ecclesiastical claims to authority. The papacy itself was soon involved, and all the pressure it could employ was insufficient to silence him. From 1517 to 1530, protected at Wittenberg by the Electors of Saxony, Luther and his associates through teaching, preaching and writing, wrought a vast and lasting change in the religious scene. The wide response to his daring course of thought and action was made possible by previous widespread dissatisfaction with the old order. The new invention of the printing press, called by him 'God's latest and best work to spread the true religion', gave to a man of Luther's gifts a protean power to alter the motivating beliefs of millions. He wrote in Latin and German, and translations spread his message beyond the readers of these languages to most parts of Europe. The foundation of his new theology was laid in five brilliant treatises published between May and November, 1520: the *Treatise of Good Works; The Papacy at Rome; Address to the German Nobility; Babylonish Captivity of the Church; Freedom of a Christian Man*. From the Ten Commandments, the stress in good works is laid on wholesome social behaviour and useful tasks. The church is seen not as a hierarchical structure but as a spiritual community. Those in political authority are summoned to aid in reform by means of a series of councils. The sacraments are expounded from the NT, and are to be released from the captivity in which they have been held under the papacy. The doctrine of the priesthood of all believers is strongly presented in the last two treatises mentioned. The most impressive, and the least controversial of the five, is the *Freedom of a Christian Man*, which manifestly reflects his experience of emancipation through faith. The Christian is 'the most free lord of all', in union with Christ partaking of Christ's kingship, and of his priesthood in virtue of which Christians share with each other the things of God. So also the Christian is 'the most dutiful servant of all', helping others without hope of reward and joining in mutual service even to the extent that we become 'Christs one to another'.

These early treatises present simply and powerfully the doctrines most emphasized throughout his later writings. He had already made himself a biblical scholar, and he constantly challenged his opponents to meet him on the ground of scripture. A great deal of his life work had to do with the translation and interpretation of the Bible. He could count on the fact that the authority of scripture was a common presupposition in theology. But among the clergy there had long prevailed a strong sense of peril in placing it in the hands of laymen. To Luther scripture-testimony rather than tradition or scholastic opinions was the sufficient test of all doctrines, and laymen were not only to be instructed in the Bible but also to read and meditate upon it for themselves. If he speaks of the Bible as the Word of God he does not mean that all parts of it are in equal degree divine utterances. Out of proportion to other passages, the words of Jesus in the Gospels, the Epistles, Romans, Galatians, Ephesians, I John and I Peter, with many of the Psalms and certain chapters of Isaiah, contributed to his thoughts, since in them he recognized most readily a revelation of Christ. The OT is a book of law and the NT a proclamation of grace, yet the former is not to be lowly esteemed. The key is in John 5.39. 'Search the scriptures because . . . they . . . bear witness to me.' Accordingly

Genesis is 'almost a gospel book' and in the Psalter the Holy Spirit composed 'a short Bible'. A certain antagonism appears between scripture and reason. In his repudiation of reason as a means of knowing God he thinks of reason as wayward and egocentric and intolerant of the unknowable, in opposition to faith for which God is both known and unknown, *revelatus* and *absconditus*.

Luther's doctrine of the church has negative and positive aspects. He gives habitual expression to his intense dissatisfaction with prevailing conditions and with the whole system of ecclesiastical thought and practice associated with the papal hegemony. Obedience to popes and bishops is not required where they are disobedient to God's Word. The true church is in essence not any visible entity but the invisible society of the true Christians which, however, presses towards visibility in the preaching of the Word and the administration of the sacraments. Among these he gives to penance a place subordinate to the two NT sacraments. The satisfactory works of penance * are worthless by comparison with the spirit of repentance and the renewal of man's life by faith. On the eucharist he abandons transubstantiation * and rejects the Zwinglian conception of a spiritual presence of Christ's spatially absent body. The bodily presence is emphasized, but the miracle does not occur in the hands of the priest; it becomes real to the worshipper through the scripture passages in the rite, such as 'This is my body', 'This is my blood . . . shed for many for the remission of sins'. The sacraments express and enhance that holy communion of saints in which the church consists.

Contrary to Luther's wishes, his followers came to be called and to call themselves 'Lutherans'. The term 'Lutheranism' is used to refer to the doctrines adopted and authoritative in Lutheran churches, and as a general term for these churches in their entire extent. The early expansion of Lutheranism through Sweden, Denmark and Norway left in these lands national churches that have endured in strength. Swedish Lutherans have been particularly active theologically during the present century. German and Scandinavian Lutheranism has accompanied the spread of the peoples of these countries throughout the New World, while modern missions have planted many Lutheran congregations also among the peoples of Asia and Africa.

The standard edition of Luther's works is the *Weimarer Ausgabe* (*WA*): Martin Luther, *Werke. Kritische Gesamtausgabe*, 1883ff.; a translation, *Luther's Works*, ed. J. Pelikan, is in progress, to be completed in 55 vols. *See also* R. L. Bainton, *Here I Stand: A Life of Martin Luther*, 1950; A. G. Dickens, *Martin Luther and the Reformation*, 1967; G. Ebeling, *Luther*, ET 1970; V. H. H. Green, *Luther and the Reformation*, 1964; G. Rupp, *The Righteousness of God: Luther Studies*, 1953; E. G. Schwiebert, *Luther and his Times*, 1950; I. D. K. Siggins, *Martin Luther's Doctrine of Christ*, 1970; J. M. Todd, *Martin Luther*, 1964.

On Lutheranism see W. Elert, *The Structure of Lutheranism*, ET 1962; J. Pelikan, *From Luther to Kierkegaard. A Study in the History of Theology*, ²1963.

J. T. MCNEILL

Magisterium

All baptized believers are anointed and guided by the Spirit (John 14.26; 16.13; Rom. 8.14; I John 2.27), and in some degree have a prophetic responsibility for announcing the good news about Christ. Those who have the authority to proclaim and teach officially share in the church's magisterium. Roman Catholics believe that this magisterial authority belongs to the whole college of bishops (as successors to the college of apostolic witnesses) and to individual bishops united in hierarchical communion with the Bishop of Rome. The bishops generally fulfil this magisterium on a day-to-day basis (various kinds of 'ordinary' magisterium), or – when assembled in a council or represented by the pope – they may teach some revealed truth to be held absolutely and definitively (the 'extraordinary' magisterium).

As a specific service on behalf of the whole community, the magisterium officially recalls Christ's saving truth to clarify and apply it in the face of the new challenges of each age and situation. The office of the magisterium comes from Christ himself, is guided by (and does not supplant) the Holy Spirit, and is exercised within the whole community of the faithful, who were and remain the primary recipients of God's self-revelation.

The inter-subjective nature of truth lends credibility to the existence of such a magisterium. Truth, including revealed truth, is experienced and maintained by human beings in community. This makes it more plausible that the church should be equipped with an institution (the magisterium) which functions to help people experience and abide in the truth of revelation.

In the Middle Ages theologians and, especially, the theological faculties of great universities were also credited with exercising a certain magisterium. Such an authority rested on the quality of their personal gifts, just as apparently there was a similar 'charismatic' basis for the role of 'teachers' in the NT church (I Cor. 12.28; Acts 13.1).

See also **Apostolic Succession, Authority, Bishops, Church, Hierarchy, Infallibility, Pope.**

Avery Dulles, *The Survival of Dogma*, 1971, esp. pp. 79ff.; John Macquarrie, *Principles of Christian Theology*, ²1977, pp. 416–19; Karl Rahner, 'Magisterium', *Sacramentum Mundi* III, pp. 351–58; Vatican II, Dogmatic Constitution on the Church (*Lumen Gentium*), nn. 24–25.

GERALD O'COLLINS

Manichaeism

The term is derived from Manes (styled in Latin, Manichaeus, AD 215–275), a Persian, who founded the religion, which spread rapidly to the West. For nine years before his conversion St Augustine himself was a Manichee, Manichaeism was an extreme variety of Persian dualism* (cf. Zoroastrianism, by which it was regarded as heretical). Because matter itself was held to be evil, an extreme asceticism was practised by its adherents.

F. C. Burkitt, *The Religion of the Manichees*, 1925.

ALAN RICHARDSON

Marcionism

Marcion (d *c.* 160) rejected the OT on the ground that the Demiurge* or Creator-god of the Jewish religion of Law was utterly incompatible with the God of Love revealed in Christ. He found it necessary also to re-edit St Luke's Gospel, which, along with the ten Epistles of St Paul (excluding the Pastorals), constituted his canon of Holy Scripture. In modern theological discourse the term 'Marcionite' is used somewhat loosely to describe interpretations of Christianity which are judged to undervalue or to misunderstand the place of the OT in the elucidation of the Christian revelation.

E. C. Blackman, *Marcion and his Influence*, 1948; J. Knox, *Marcion and the New Testament*, 1942.

ALAN RICHARDSON

Mariology

The NT references to Mary, the mother of Jesus, are few and ambivalent. In some traditions (Mark 3.31–35; Matt, 12.46–50; Luke 8.19–21; John 2.1–11) Mary represents the unbelieving family or the old Israel. The Lukan infancy narrative, by contrast, makes Mary the first believer and the representative of the church. The Gospel of John, but not the synoptics, has Mary present at the crucifixion (19.25–27), and Luke includes Mary among the community of the upper room at Pentecost (Acts 1.14). The infancy narratives of Matthew and Luke imply Mary's virginal conception of Jesus. All four Gospels record brothers and sisters of Jesus (Mark 6.3; Matt. 13.55; John 7.3).

Popular Christian piety in the second and third centuries elaborated the story of Mary. She is portrayed as miraculously conceived in her parents' old age (Anna and Joachim) and vowed as a virgin in the temple at the age of three. These accounts proclaim her virginity, not only in the conception, but also in the birth of Jesus (*The Gospel of the Birth of Mary*; *The Protevangelion of James*). Justin Martyr (*Tryph.* 100); Irenaeus (*Contra Haer.* 3, 22) and Tertullian (*De carne Chr.* 17) develop the theme of Mary as the New Eve who, by her obedience to God's word, reverses the disobedience of the first Eve.

The late fourth-early fifth centuries saw new emphasis on mariological piety. Jerome defended the perpetual virginity of Mary against rival monastic writers (*Ad. Helvid.*). His interpretation of the brothers of Jesus as 'cousins' became standard for traditional RC exegesis. In the struggles between Antiochene * and Alexandrian * theology in this period, the title *Theotokos* (Mother of God) was debated. The Antiochenes, who distinguished the human from the divine natures of Christ, preferred the title Mother

of Christ. The Alexandrians defended the title Mother of God because they regarded the human and divine natures as having merged into one new human-divine nature in the incarnation. The doctrine was proclaimed by Cyril of Alexandria at the Council of Ephesus in AD 431. Although the Council of Chalcedon (AD 451) partially accepted the Antiochene view of the continued distinction of the two natures in the incarnate Christ, they allowed the title *Theotokos* on the ground of the unity of Christ's person. The dispute was primarily christological, but the acceptance of the title Mother of God greatly promoted the veneration of Mary.

In the late fifth century there appeared several apocryphal accounts of Mary's preservation from death (*see* **Assumption**). The legends of Mary's translation to heaven allowed the popular imagination to visualize her as seated on Christ's right hand, mediating to him the prayers of the faithful (*see* **Mediatrix**). By the end of the sixth century a cycle of Marian feasts had developed in the East: the Annunciation (March 25); the Presentation in the Temple (Nov. 21); her Nativity (Sept. 8) and her *Dormition* (Falling Asleep) (Aug. 15). These were gradually adopted into the Western liturgical calendar as well (by AD 1000). The Feast of Mary's Conception (Dec. 9 in the East; Dec. 8 in the West), was adopted in the Eastern churches by about AD 1000, but was not general in the Latin calendar until the fifteenth century.

Mediaeval Latin Christianity produced a fervent cult of Mary. As Christ came to be seen as distant and judgmental, Mary became the representative of mercy and forgiveness to whom the miserable sinner could appeal. Mediaeval typologies of Mary are many. She is the hieratic Queen of Heaven, enthroned with the child Jesus upon her lap. Or she is the mother of sinners of the Mary legends who bends the rules of strict justice for those devoted to her. She is the *Maria Lactans* of mystical piety whose mother's milk symbolizes overflowing mercy, or the virginal Lady of religious courtly love. In the Franciscan piety of the late Middle Ages she becomes the earthy peasant housewife seated barefoot on the ground with her bouncing baby, while Joseph labours in his workshop nearby (M. Warner, *Alone of All Her Sex*, 1976).

The doctrine of the Immaculate Conception remained in dispute in mediaeval theology. The theologians of the twelfth and thirteenth centuries had rejected it, but the Franciscan school of the fourteenth century accepted it. For nominalist * theology, Mary represents *natura pura* or good human nature uncorrupted by sin which the sinner seeks to recover through perfect contrition: H. A. Oberman, *The Harvest of Medieval Theology*, 1963, pp. 304ff. (*see* **Immaculate Conception**).

Nineteenth- and early twentieth-century Roman Catholicism saw a continual escalation of Marian devotion, fuelled both by popular apparitions and official church declarations. The apparitions have been mostly to peasant children and young women: La Salette (1846); Lourdes (1858); Fatima (1917) and Beauraing (1932) are the best known. The Immaculate Conception was declared a doctrine by Pope Pius IX in 1854, and the Assumption by Pope Pius XII in 1950. This promotion of Marian piety represented a cultural counter-attack by Catholicism against what were perceived as the anti-Christian forces of secularism, rationalism, republicanism and communism.

Since the Second Vatican Council (1962–65), there has been a re-evaluation of Marian piety among Catholic theologians and a concern for ecumenical rapprochement with Protestant criticism of it. The emphasis of recent Catholic Marian theology links her with the theology of the church. Mary is the first believer and the archetype of the church. Her privileges, however great, are to be understood as those of the redeemed creature, not those of a quasi-divinity (Hugo Rahner, *Our Lady and the Church*, 1961; O. Semmelroth, *Mary, Archetype of the Church*, 1964; Karl Rahner, *Mary, the Mother of the Lord*, ET 1963; E. Schillebeeckx, *Mary, Mother of the Redemption*, ET 1964).

A new direction in Marian theology may be emerging from Latin American Christianity. In Mexico, the Virgin of Guadalupe represents the Indian people. The declarations of the Third Latin American Bishop's Conference at Puebla (1979) emphasized the Magnificat as the key text for understanding Mary as archetype of the church. Mary represents God's preferential option for the poor. She is the oppressed of the world to whom God brings justice in Christ by 'putting down the mighty from their thrones and lifting up the humble' (Luke 1. 52) (CELAM III, IV, 27; XVIII, 12).

See also **Mediatrix, Virgin Birth.**

For general background, see Donald Attwater, *A Dictionary of Mary*, 1956; Hilda Graef, *Mary. A History of Doctrine and Devotion*, 2 vols., 1963; G. Miegge, *The Virgin Mary*, ET 1955.

R. R. RUETHER

Marriage, Theology of

Marriage in law is the union for life of one man and one woman. It is made by their mutual consent. When it is made, it is not a simple contract to be ended by the mere decision of the parties themselves, but a 'contract conferring status'. Christian theology agrees. The Christian doctrine of marriage is that this 'pairbond', found in various forms in all human societies, belongs to God's creation of people as male and female. Its biological function is the nurturing of children; but its character as *relationship* is part of its proper nature, not a discovery of a contraceptive age. The creation stories (Gen. 1.26–27; 2.20–25) affirm that man and woman are fit companions for one another and belong together. The 'one-flesh' union is more than physical pleasure and more than fertility (cf. I Sam. 1.8).

This positive doctrine, before any negative 'Thou shalt not', is reaffirmed by Jesus when he is questioned about divorce (Mark 10.2–12). The story of his honouring the marriage at Cana (John 2.1–11) is about a human celebration, not a 'Christian marriage' before a Christian priest. The kingdom of heaven is likened to a wedding feast (e.g. Matt. 22.1–14).

The church has always insisted that marriage is good; indeed that it is fit to be an image of the union between Christ and his church (Eph. 5.25–32). Yet in some Christian minds negative views have predominated: fear of our physical nature, legalism, depreciation of women. Much of this can be ascribed to unregenerate humanity: but undeniably some of it comes from 'hard sayings' in the NT. Christ remains unmarried and commends celibacy (Matt. 19.10–12). He likens divorce to adultery. Harder still, he pronounces that in the kingdom they do not marry but are like angels in heaven

(Mark 12.25). Paul lent his authority to the ideas that marriage is a second best (I Cor. 7) and that women are inferior (e.g. I Cor. 14.34–35; but cf. Gal. 3.28 and Rom. 16.1–2).

Without tendentiousness, certain answers suggest themselves. Paul's least liberal sayings appear not so much 'hard sayings' as *easy* sayings, showing him as a child of his age. There is much to balance them in Paul himself and the NT at large.

It is increasingly being recognized that the legalism which besets the understanding of 'indissolubility' is out of keeping with the total picture of the teaching of Christ presented in the Gospels; but that the alternative cannot be a vague permissiveness but, somehow, an enabling mercy.

Hard sayings are not to be ignored, but it is defeatist to take them as harshly ascetic. Rather, they are reminders that neither sex nor family is absolute. The more the spirit of our age emphasizes the goodness of sexuality, the more the church needs to remember that it exists also for the misfits, the awkward, the untypical, the solitary, the distinctively dedicated. The more we commend the family, the more we must acknowledge that no human institution can be translated straight into heaven. Resurrection needs death and rebirth. What we are led to expect is recognizable transformation of all we care about.

Marriage and the Church's Task, The Report of the Church of England General Synod Marriage Commission, 1978; Ronald Fletcher, *The Family and Marriage in Britain*, [3]1973; D. Sherwin Bailey, *The Man-Woman Relation in Christian Thought*, 1959.

HELEN OPPENHEIMER

Martyrs, Martyrdom, Martyrologies

The secular meaning of the Greek word *martys* (martyr) is a witness, one who bears testimony (compare Acts 1.8), and witness formed an essential part of the Christian usage. In late-Judaism, however, witness to the truth of the Law was becoming associated with a readiness to die for that truth. The priest Eleazar was prepared 'to die willingly and nobly a glorious death for the revered and holy laws', when confronted with an order from King Antiochus IV's officials to perform sacrifice (II Macc. 6.24–

28). In the Johannine literature the word *martyria* often has the sense of positive missionary witness to the truth by Jesus and his disciples (e.g. John 5.30ff.; 18.37) and that this witness was sealed in 'water and blood' (John 19.34–35). When Jesus has ascended, the witness would continue through the Spirit. The Spirit bears witness concerning Christ (John 15.26) and would speak through the mouths of Christians in their hour of peril when brought before 'governors and kings' (Mark 13.11). The additional expiatory nature of Christ's death and those of the prophets is prominently expressed in Hebrews (1.3; 9.22; 10.19). Christians had to 'resist unto blood', 'striving against sin' (12.4). In Revelation we find a developed martyr-idea. Christians had gained their victory 'because of the blood of the Lamb', and 'because of the word of their testimony, they loved not their life, even unto death' (12.11). At the Last Judgment martyrs would become the judges, casting the idolators into 'the lake of brimstone which is the second death' (21.8). Thus, by the end of the first century AD, suffering, witness, judgment and ultimate triumph have been welded together in the single concept of martyrdom. Witness to Christ's gospel, imitation of his passion and apocalyptic hopes all formed part of the martyr's aspiration.

The correspondence between Pliny and the emperor Trajan in 112–113 shows that the profession of Christianity was illegal and Christians were liable to summary execution (Pliny, *Letters*, X, 96, 2). While imperial policy was not to seek out Christians, the latter became increasingly hated by the urban mobs in cities where Christian communities had become established. Detailed *Acta Martyrum* in the form of letters of survivors to other churches are preserved by Eusebius in his *Ecclesiastical History* (iv.15 and v.1–2) recording the martyrdoms of Polycarp, Bishop of Smyrna (c. 156 or c. 165–168) and of the Christians at Lyons in 177. The terrible fate of the latter in the amphitheatre and the heroism of the slave Blandina form one of the epics of early Christianity.

At this early stage, it would seem that some churches, including Rome, may already have had their roll of honour for martyrs whose 'birthdays' were celebrated each year. The niche in the Red Wall in the cemetery under St Peter's, Rome, may be the earliest known material evidence for a cult of martyrs.

In 180 the church in North Africa emerges suddenly into history with Acts of the Scillitan martyrs (17 July 180). These show how the apocalyptic element in Christian martyrdom was becoming associated with anti-imperial sentiment. The confessors did not 'recognize the kingdom of this world', but only Christ. The North African church richly merited its title – 'Church of the Martyrs'. In 202/203 the Acts of Perpetua and Felicitas indicate the belief that the confessor had the right to visions of the Beyond, to access to Christ himself, could make successful intercessions on behalf of the dead even if these had been pagan, and on becoming a martyr would achieve rest and serenity in Paradise. Ordinary Christians could associate themselves with martyrs by listening to the reading of their Acts on their anniversaries (*Passio Perpetuae* 1.5–6). For Tertullian martyrdom was 'the baptism of blood', completing baptism of water and redeeming all sins committed after baptism (*Apol.* 50.16).

In the Decian persecution of 250 these ideas were developed further. Cyprian wrote (*Ep.* 12.2) instructing his clergy in Carthage 'to record the days of their (the confessors) death so that we may celebrate their memories among the commemorations (*memorias*) of the martyrs'. Commemorations took the form of a eucharist, and Cyprian was not slow to assert that 'while all the brethren should rejoice in martyrdom, in the common rejoicing the greater part belongs to the bishop' (*Ep.* 13.1). During the Valerianic persecution of 257–259 he explicitly forbade Christians to offer themselves voluntarily for martyrdom (Ep. 81).

The Great Persecution (303–312) resulted in many martyrs, especially after the Fourth Edict in the spring of 304, but also brought out further conflict between the episcopal and popular view of martyrdom in the West. This was one of the factors that lay behind the outbreak of the Donatist * schism in 312. Despite the conversion of Constantine and the gradual establishment of Christianity as the religion of the empire, the Donatists continued to exalt the ideal of martyrdom as the true aim of a Christian life (see Augustine, *Contra Litteras Petiliani* ii.89.196

and *Acta Saturnini* 20 = Pl. 8, col. 703A). The Catholics, whether in Africa or elsewhere in the West, tended to idealize martyrs and martyrdom as aspects of the heroic era of Christianity under the pagan emperors. The steadfastness of the martyrs was held up as an example to Christians, but their ideal was now shorn of any apocalyptic significance. (Thus Prudentius, *Peristephanon*, and Augustine, *Sermo* 273, 274, 280, 282, 302, 326 and *In Psalmum* 120.) The cult of relics in the West was a direct legacy of martyrdoms.

In the East, the cessation of persecution coincided with the emergence of monasticism as the highest form of Christian endeavour. Monks and holy men regarded themselves as successors to the martyrs, 'martyrs in intention' (see *Barlaam and Iosaph* ii.103, ed. Mattingley), aspiring through their abstinences and feats of asceticism to the heavenly reward once accorded to martyrs. As in the West, the cult of martyrs' relics, particularly those attached to shrines and places of pilgrimage such as SS Sergius and Bacchus at Resapha or Mennas outside Alexandria, prospered greatly. The 'military martyrs' such as George, Demetrius and Theodore, played an enormous part in the religious life of the Syriac, Coptic and Nubian churches during the early Middle Ages.

The fourth century saw the beginnings of official registers of martyrs or martyrologies. The earliest were collations of already existing lists of martyrs held in individual churches, such as the calendars of Rome (354) and Carthage (505). More general in scope were the Hieronymian Martyrology, the *Breviarium Syriacum* and the Coptic Synaxarium. Later, there came into being 'historical' martyrologies, such as those of Bede (*c.* 730), Florus of Lyons, Rabanus, Ado and Usuard (all ninth century). By this time the practice had grown up in religious houses in the West of reading in choir at Prime the martyrology for the day.

H. von Campenhausen, *Die Idee des Märtyriums in der alten Kirche*, ET 1936; Y. M. Duval, *Les martyrs de l'Afrique du Nord*, 1982; W. H. C. Frend, *Martyrdom and Persecution in the Early Church*, 1965; G. Lanata, *Gli atti dei martiri come documenti processuali*, 1973; G. Lazzati, *Gli sviluppi della letteratura sui martiri nei primi quattro secoli*, 1956; O. Michel, *Prophet und Märtyr-er*, 1932; H. Musurillo (ed), *The Acts of the Christian Martyrs*, 1972; Y. Saxer, *Morts, martyrs et reliques en Afrique chré-tienne aux premiers siècles*, 1980.

W. H. C. FREND

Marxism

More than a third of the population of the world lives under Marxist political regimes. Marxist ideas have profoundly influenced disciplines as different as economics, political theory, aesthetics, psychology, history, literary criticism, philosophy and theology. So widespread a political force, and the increasingly diverse ideas which inform it, are as resistant of summary definition as is Christianity.

There are at least three ways in which 'Marxism' may be defined. As the doctrine of a mass movement which combined revolutionary fervour with a sense of history and the conviction that it held the key to the explanation of patterns of social change, Marxism (or, rather, what Stalin christened 'Marxism-Leninism': a simplified amalgam of aspects of the thought of Marx, Engels and Lenin) became the 'official teaching' of Soviet Communism and of those political parties which took the USSR as their model. This teaching, complete, self-sufficient and contained in a canon of sacred texts, the masses took on faith. Its exposition was reserved to officially approved interpreters.

In the second place, Marxism has, from Lukàcs onwards, often been taken to mean not a body of doctrine but a *method*: a way of tackling, practically and theoretically, fundamental problems of social existence and transformation. Marxism as 'a way of life'; as 'orthopraxis*' rather than mere 'orthodoxy*'.

Christianity, like Marxism, is sometimes defined as a corpus of beliefs, sometimes as a method or a way of life. The parallel holds good for a third meaning of Marxism: as a historically discernible tradition of thought and action. And if, by now, the Marxist tradition has become so internally diverse as to render all talk of a *single* tradition suspect, the same can perhaps be said of Christianity.

What is often forgotten (by both Christians and Marxists) is that many of the arguments in favour of defining Marxism (or Christianity) in one of these ways rather than another are also arguments in favour of preferring the same definition for Christianity (or Marxism).

Marxism as 'official teaching' has proved as intellectually sterile as it has been disastrous in practice. And if we take the term in the second or third sense, an account of Marxist ideas would have to attend as much to the thought of (for example) Lenin and Lukàcs, Kautsky and Rosa Luxembourg, Trotsky and Mao, Adorno and Althusser, Gramsci and Sartre, as to Marx himself, or even to Marx and Engels. However seminal and enduring Marx's influence, what counts as 'Marxism' cannot be decided by reference to his writings.

Nevertheless, some indication of principal themes in those writings is in order. This is not easy, for two reasons. 1. Marx's restless attempts to integrate a wide variety of topics and disciplines issued in a body of thought the incompleteness and ambiguity of which is too easily dismissed by the hostile as incoherence. 2. The movement which bears his name achieved institutional and theoretical solidity several decades before many of his most creative writings were published in the 1930s and 1950s. There has therefore been much debate about the unity of his thought and, especially, concerning the relationship between the earlier, more 'philosophical', and the later, more 'scientific', writings. Today, the majority of commentators would agree that Marx's thought should be read as a continuous exploration of central themes first treated in about 1844.

Marx was above all concerned to understand the causes and destiny of the social and economic revolutions of his time and, by understanding the process of change, to contribute to it. His central vision was of man's fourfold 'alienation' – from himself, his work, his products, and his fellow-man – in capitalist society, and the possibility of man overcoming that alienation, of controlling his own destiny through communism. Even the theory of 'surplus value', a key feature of his economic analysis, may be seen as the definitive version of the theory of alienated labour. The control of one's own destiny is fundamental to human freedom. In this sense, Marx's thought is a theory of the process of human liberation, of what he himself called 'the total redemption of humanity'.

Marx was unduly optimistic in his conviction that this 'total redemption' was historically attainable. He paid insufficient attention to the insurmountability of the 'barriers' of mortality and egotism. But to claim that he incorrectly predicted the future is misleading. He was not interested in peering into the future, but in understanding what was going on in nineteenth-century capitalist societies. He was convinced, on historical and economic as well as on philosophical grounds (derived from Hegel) that the internal contradictions of capitalism would ensure its eventual abolition, and he came to believe that the 'agent' of this abolition would be that class which contributed most and received least of the material wealth which capitalism has produced: namely, the industrial proletariat.

In societies torn by conflicting interests, social existence takes the form of political struggle, the struggle for power. And the institutional expression of the dominance exercised by one group over another is the state. In a society in which the alienation of man from man, group from group, had been abolished, there would therefore be no place for such an institution. Marx took it for granted that 'God' was and could only be a symbolic expression of man's subservience to 'alien powers': to the work which had become the worker's master, rather than the means of his self-production and self-expression, and to the repressive force of the state. Therefore, in a society in which man's fourfold alienation had been transcended, in which work had been 'humanized' and the state abolished, the question of God simply would not and could not arise. 'The struggle against religion is indirectly the struggle against that world whose spiritual aroma is religion.'

While Marx's chief concern was with understanding the processes which would bring about the overthrowal of nineteenth-century capitalism, the success of the Bolshevik revolution necessitated a shift of attention. The twin problems which now confronted Marxist thinkers were, economically, the construction of a communist society after the revolution and, politically, the relationship of the Party to the working class. In the USSR, the economic problem was tackled, eventually, through massive industrialization, whereas in China the leading role was initially allocated to agricultural development. In the West, the re-

silience of the capitalist system led to a decline of interest in Marxist economics, an interest which has recently revived in the context of renewed crises within capitalism, and of relationships between the West and the 'Third World'.

Politically, both the Soviet Union and China opted for Lenin's idea of a 'vanguard' Party which would embody revolutionary consciousness and instil it into the working class. In practice, the Party has become an élite divorced from the class it purports to represent. In the West, several groups of Marxist thinkers have ceased to believe in the revolutionary potential of the working class; some have come to see education, rather than revolution, as the lever of social transformation.

Especially since the publication of Marx's early writings, philosophical debate has become increasingly lively among Marxists. Central topics have included: the sense in which Marxist theory is to be understood as 'scientific', problems of 'ideology', and the nature of Marx's debt to Hegel. While most forms of 'official' Marxism have remained as hostile to religion as was Marx himself, many major theorists (such as Ernst Bloch, Roger Garaudy, and the founders of the 'Frankfurt School', Adorno and Horkheimer) have treated theological questions with impressive seriousness.

Marxists have usually failed to appreciate the internal diversity of Christianity and, especially, the variety of ways in which Christians relate their religious beliefs and practices to other aspects of their life, thought and activity. Christians, for their part, have usually failed to take the Marxist critique of religion sufficiently seriously. In recent decades, the development of Christian-Marxist 'dialogue' in Europe, and increasing collaboration between Christians and Marxists in the Third World, have called in question the assumption that Christianity and Marxism are inevitably, in all circumstances, simply antithetical.

Some Christians have sought to separate the economic and political aspects of Marxism from its philosophical components, in order to endorse the former while continuing to reject the atheism built into the latter. At least where Marx's own thought is concerned, this project is not feasible. Marx's understanding of the process of history (and hence his 'political economy') was tightly interwoven with his philosophy, his conception of the 'essence' and destiny of man.

Since, as mentioned already, what counts as Marxism is not to be decided by reference to Marx's writings, it is difficult to exclude *a priori* the possibility that there could develop forms of Marxism, and forms of Christianity, which would be such as to render the concept of 'Christian Marxism' coherent. Whether such developments would be recognized, by other Christians and other Marxists, as authentic, is another matter. Nevertheless, in so far as Christians and Marxists are in fact engaged in the work of the liberation of mankind, the work of man's redemption, they may discover, in the future, more scope for collaboration, more common understanding and common hope, than they have achieved in the past.

See also **Ideology, Materialism.**

L. Kolakowski, *Main Currents of Marxism*, 3 vols., 1978; N. L. A. Lash, *A Matter of Hope*, 1981; D. McLellan, *Karl Marx, His Life and Thought*, 1973; *Marxism after Marx*, 1979.

NICHOLAS LASH

Marxist Theology

The phrase appears to be a contradiction in terms, when judged by what are taken to be the fundamental premises of Marxism and Christianity. On the Christian side there is belief in God, the truth which is revealed to man by God, and the purpose of God which directs the affairs of men and nations, and indeed the course of history itself. In stark contrast are the Marxist premises that there is no God, except the God that man creates for himself; that religion brings not truth but a reversal of consciousness about the realities of the world; that history is not directed by powers outside it, but by the desires and interests of men. Marxism culminates in historical materialism, a doctrine which is determinist at least in the sense that while man can freely associate with that process which is governed by successive modes of production, he cannot alter or negate it. Theology teaches that man is made in the image of God, is free to respond to the gracious invitation of God in Christ. The strength of each is perceived by the other as a weakness. Thus to be 'materialist' is the proud boast of Marxists, while it is a dismissive accusation when used by Christians.

Christians claim superiority by affirming the truth of the 'spiritual' world. But for Marxists, the so-called 'spiritual' is but the halo legitimizing oppression. For Christians, life after death is the great prize offered by God to his people, while for Marxists it is an opiate which dulls the mind to the evil of this life, and teaches submission to intolerable conditions. In other words, while Marxism and Christianity are so conceived there can be no accommodation between the two: Marxist theology is in these circumstances a contradiction in terms. When Marxism was identified with the atrocities of Stalinism in the USSR there could be no *Marxist* theology. And when Christianity in its Catholic form was all too ready to sign a concordat with Hitler, and in its Protestant form to affirm the divine right of capitalism, there could be no Marxist *theology*. In the Cold War the theoreticians of Marxism and of Christianity were expected to legitimize their respective political systems. However, in the 1950s and 1960s several important developments changed the relationship between Marxism and Christianity. The changes were both external, concerning the ways in which each side perceived the other, and internal, dealing with the self-understanding of each system.

In the 1950s the writings of the young Marx became available in Europe for the first time, differing in certain important respects from the conventional view of Marxism. The golden thread which runs through these documents is not historical materialism, as Engels claimed, but humanism of a highly idealistic form. Their dynamic is not the seeking of power, but rather the denunciation of everything which dehumanizes man – including several forms of communism. And while the critique of religion forms the premise of these further critiques of social injustice, Marx is equally impatient with those who continue with religion (Feuerbach, Bauer) and also those who continue with strident atheism, as if the attack on religion was an end in itself. The appearance of these documents coincided with the invasion of Hungary by the USSR in 1956. The result was the formation in Western Europe of the New Left, Marxist but not Communist. It was with these new Marxists that a dialogue became possible. Not of course possible for all Christians, because Christians too had to change, to admit that much of what they had previously identified as Christianity was Western political ideology. Significantly, the first centre of the Marxist-Christian dialogue was in Czechoslovakia. The initiative was taken by J. L. Hromadka of the Comenius Faculty of Theology in Prague. Jan Comenius, the seventeenth-century theologian, had actually proposed international disarmament and an international court of peace. Hromadka organized the Christian Peace Conference in the decade from 1958–1968. Many cynically rejected these conferences as a plot, yet they ended with the invasion of Czechoslovakia by the USSR. On the Catholic side the encyclicals of Pope John XXIII ended the official anti-Communist crusade and began a new atmosphere in which dialogue was possible. The dialogue had a marked influence on many of the leading Marxists in Western Europe, but here we should draw attention to the fact that the dialogue became ecumenical, in the sense of involving not only Catholics and Protestants, but also Christians of the Third World. Whatever Marxist theology means, it is ecumenical in a way that very few theologies have ever been, and from this fact alone we might assume that it should be examined seriously.

The emergence of what might be called Marxist theology took place in two phases.

1. *The Marxist–Christian dialogue.* In this, Christians came to terms with the criticism of religion offered by Marx and Marxists. Atheism * was of course a fundamental issue, and if discussion had begun there no progress could have been made. Rather, the dialogue began by examining what the two traditions had in common. This proved to be considerable; not surprisingly, bearing in mind the profoundly religious assumptions which Marx inherited both from his family and from Hegel *. At this stage the dialogue identified common themes. Marxist theology contained no essentially new elements, but rather a change in priorities. Three examples illustrate this phase. (i) For Marxism man is a species-being. This does not mean simply that man happens to live in society, but that it is through social relations that his distinctively human nature is developed. This view of man, found in the Bible from the story of the garden to the vision of a city, has been endangered in Catholic thinking

by Aristotelian * essentialism and Protestant * individualism. The effect of the dialogue was not to lead Christians astray, but to turn them towards home. (ii) The unifying question which guides the work of the young Marx is how man can be emancipated, freed from whatever dehumanizes him. Marxism is fundamentally concerned with identifying the roots of oppression and specifically injustice. Now this, too, is a constant theme of biblical religion linking Jesus to the classical prophets. However, Christian theology has constantly legitimized institutionalized oppression and structural injustice. Once again, the dialogue has not distorted theology, but raised before it a mirror in which to see the failings of its past ways. (iii) Marxism is profoundly concerned with history, for two reasons. One is to find the real basis for historical movements, a basis which is discerned in different modes of production rather than in the realms of idealism. But Marxism is also to be a philosophy of the future, which far from explaining why things must be as they are, points the way to the changing of the social world in the future. These two motifs, of seeing a pattern in history and anticipating a revolutionary change in the future, far from being foreign to biblical religion, are probably taken directly from it. The Bible is full of the rehearsal of the past, as the basis for a hope for the future. And yet theology has often been content to refer to the events of the past in such a way as to produce no hope for this world at all, merely a hope for souls after death. The dialogue recalls theology to Christian responsibility for the future.

2. *Internal dialogue.* In a later stage dialogue became internal in the sense of being pursued solely by Christians, and also in some cases where Christians accepted the basic premises of Marxism and attempted to reinterpret Christian faith from this perspective. This, of course, does not mean replacing Christ with Marx. Marx was a significant thinker of the nineteenth century and his critical social philosophy is now widely used in the social sciences and in other fields. It is necessary to distinguish between this social philosophy and the metaphysical conclusions which Marx and some of his followers have drawn from it. One specific example of this concerns his atheism. Historically his critical philosophy

begins with the criticism of religion, for it is here that he identified the reversal of reality which he went on to uncover in philosophy, the state, civil rights, money, alienated labour and private property. However, it is possible to accept his analysis of the reversal of reality, without accepting atheism. As in the case of Feuerbach, from whom he took the idea, the projection * account of religion deals with what is believed about God, not with the question of the existence of God.

Theology has to formulate the implications of biblical faith for different cultures, at the various stages of their development. What are taken to be the classical statements of Christian theology have been formulated on premises taken from Plato and Aristotle, both of whom were profoundly un-Christian, not least in their social ethics. Marxist theology has at least the advantage of using a critical philosophy which, as indicated, is not only compatible with biblical religion but is actually in large part dependent on it.

See also **Marxism.**

J. Bentley, *Between Marx and Christ: The Dialogue in German-speaking Europe 1870–1970*, 1982: H. Gollwitzer, *The Christian Faith and the Marxist Criticism of Religion*, 1970; A. Kee, *A Reader in Political Theology*, 1974; N. Lash, *A Matter of Hope: A Theologian's Reflections on the Thought of Karl Marx*, 1981; D. McLellan, *Marx Before Marxism*, 1972; J. P. Miranda, *Marx Against the Marxists: The Christian Humanism of Karl Marx*, 1980.

ALISTAIR KEE

Materialism

Materialism has meant many things. Although the term only appeared in the seventeenth century, materialist doctrines are as old as the mind of man. (In the sense of acquisitiveness or carnality, materialism is a practical problem of limited theoretical interest: most morally serious people disapprove of undisciplined self-indulgence.)

Materialist theories concerning the constitution of the world may take the form either of declaring all entities to be material or of affirming matter to be the basic reality which is the source of the non-material.

The first group would include the metaphysical thesis that all there is is stuff, and that whatever is not stuff is nonsense, as well as research strategies based on the success of the physical sciences. Marx's 'historical materialism', with its insistence that it is people, and not 'mind' or ideas, that make history, belongs to the second group (as do many evolutionary theories). Man, for Marx, is part of material reality, and it is in 'working' that reality of which he is part, with his muscles and his mind, that he becomes what he has it in him to be. On the other hand, doctrines of 'dialectical materialism' would seem to be monistic theories of the first type. It is not clear, however, whether Engels' version should be construed as antispeculative scientism or as a full-blown metaphysical doctrine.

It is far from clear that, in order to safeguard Christian convictions concerning human freedom, the hope of resurrection, and the reality of God, it is necessary or desirable to espouse a metaphysical * dualism * according to which the items that constitute the furniture of the world can be exhaustively distributed between two classes of entity: 'mental' and 'physical', 'spiritual' and 'material'. On the contrary, the ascription of man's intellectual and ethical capacities to any 'entity' *other* than the corporeal (and hence material) human person could be objected to on theological, as well as on scientific and philosophical grounds. The rejection of metaphysical dualism seems quite compatible with the acknowledgment that some materialist doctrines are unwarrantedly determinist * or reductionist *. Moreover, the recognition that types of cognitive discourse are irreducibly diverse, that the language of 'spirit' is as indispensable as the language of 'stuff', does not justify the inference that to each type of discourse there corresponds a distinct class of substances.

Those who assume there to be two and only two ultimate classes of entity sometimes suppose God to be an entity of the 'spiritual' type. Not only does this beg important logical questions concerning the propriety of locating God within any class of entities, but it implies that God is either a kind of mental event, a thought rather than a thinker, or that he is of the same order as the entities investigated by students of the paranormal. For the consistent dualist, God is either an idea or a ghost.

No Christian is obliged to engage in ontological enquiry. But, if he does so, he would be advised to forego the imaginative satisfaction of popular dualisms. An ontology * which was 'materialist' at least in the twofold sense of rejecting metaphysical dualism and resisting the temptation to suppose that ideas, rather than people, are the motor of historical change, might better serve attempts to speak of a God who is neither *Geist* nor demiurge *, but creator, redeemer and destiny of the material (including the human) world.

The literature is immense. *See* 'Dialectical Materialism', 'Historical Materialism' and 'Materialism', in *The Encyclopedia of Philosophy*, ed. P. Edwards, 1967. On Christianity and Marxist materialism, see N. L. A. Lash, *A Matter of Hope*, 1981, chs. 8–12.

NICHOLAS LASH

Matter

Throughout Western history ideas of the definition and role of matter have changed and developed continually. Contemporary technical definitions of the physical sciences – biology, chemistry, physics and the anthropological sciences – differ from one another and from ordinary parlance in which 'matter' indicates the concrete material world of visible and tangible bodies and substances. In the history of philosophy the term 'matter' has been important as a designation for the material sustaining ground of life and existence in distinction from its form. Aristotle described matter (*hyle*) as the common ingredient in all things that is never found in experience in isolation from the form of an object or entity. Although matter and form are always found together in experience, Aristotle analytically contrasted the 'pure potency' of matter with the 'act' by which form is given. In Christian theology, the concept of matter has traditionally been distinguished from 'spirit' rather than from form, but several central Christian doctrines affirm the unity of matter and spirit in human experience. The doctrine of the creation * of the world by God *ex nihilo* was formulated to reject the dualism * of the Greek concept of creation from an already-existing material component. Matter is understood to be the good creation of God. The implication of creation *ex nihilo* is that God is the source of all existence and therefore nothing in existence is inherently evil. The doctrine of the Incarnation * of Jesus Christ, in which God as spirit entered the material world in the form of a human embodied being, further reinforces the Christian refusal to construe God and the material world as mutually antagonistic. Sacramental doctrine and the doctrine of the resurrection * of the body complete Christian affirmation of the material world as a permanent and integral participant in the salvation and ultimate transfiguration of creation.

Langdon Gilkey, *Maker of Heaven and Earth*, 1959; Stephen Toulmin and June Goodfield, *The Architecture of Matter*, 1962.

MARGARET MILES

Mediator

The history of religions contains many examples of figures who mediate between the transcendent and the human worlds, whether in respect of revelation or salvation. Depending on how the fundamental needs of the human condition are religiously conceived – whether in terms of ignorance or of sin – the mediator channels divine power, illuminating darkness or dispelling guilt in the name of the divine. Medicine-men, priests, gurus, prophets, sacred kings, avatars and founders of great religions are all, in different ways, believed to effect some, more or less temporary, bridging of the gap between the transcendent, however it is conceived, and ignorant or sinful man.

In the religion of the Hebrew Bible, prophets, priests, judges and kings all mediate, as do the Law and the sacrificial cult themselves, between the holy God of Israel and his wayward chosen people. They make known the will of God, proclaim the judgment and the mercy of God, and represent God to the people and the people to God.

It is a cardinal principle of NT religion that all these mediatorial roles were taken over and exercised with finality and permanence by Jesus Christ. He is the 'one mediator between God and men, Christ Jesus, himself man, who sacrificed himself to win freedom for all mankind' (I Tim. 2.5; see also Heb. 9.15; 12.24). It is through the mediation of Christ alone that, according to Christian preaching, salvation from sin is available to man (*see* **Atonement, Sacrifice, Salvation**).

In this sense, Christian theology, both Catholic and Protestant, has affirmed the sole mediatorship of Jesus Christ. Thomas Aquinas argues (*ST* 3a, 26.1) that, while it is not unreasonable to speak of subordinate mediators who prepare the way for or co-operate in Christ's mediation (ministers of the sacraments, for example), it is the office of Christ alone to reconcile men with God. Protestant theology (especially in the Calvinist tradition) has tended to emphasize Christ's sole mediatorship to the exclusion of talk of subordinate mediators, while Catholic theology has tended to develop the idea of subordinate mediation through priests, saints, angels and the Blessed Virgin Mary. But, fundamentally, there is no disagreement over the unique mediatorship of Christ in effecting our salvation. Karl Rahner has indicated the possibility of ecumenical agreement over this issue by speaking of 'one mediator and many mediations'. His point can be generalized. Without denying the sole salvific mediatorship of Christ, one can recognize that many individuals and institutions, including the language of religion itself, exercise some mediating function between God and man and between man and God.

Thomas Aquinas held that it is as man that Christ is mediator of God and man (*ST* 3a, 26, 2); for only as man is he distinct from God and only as perfect man is he distinct from sinful man, and the office of mediator 'implies being set apart from both extremes'. This may be deemed to be somewhat artificial. For Christian incarnational theology supposes that it is God himself in the person of his Son who breaks down the barriers between God and man by identifying himself with sinful man. It could equally well be argued that far from being set apart from both extremes, Jesus Christ so unites God and man as to do away with the need for a mediator altogether.

E. Brunner, *The Mediator*, ET 1934; G. van der Leeuw, *Religion in Essence and Manifestation*, ET 1938, ch. 106; K. Rahner, *Theological Investigations* IX, ET 1972, ch. 11.

BRIAN HEBBLETHWAITE

Mediatrix

The claim that Mary, the mother of Jesus, is the mediatrix of all graces is central to Marian piety. Mary, assumed into heaven and seated at Christ's right hand, is seen as the one through whom all the graces won by Christ are dispensed to the faithful. Mary's role is still seen as subordinate to that of Christ. If Christ is the 'head' of the church, Mary is the 'neck' through which the grace of Christ flows to the 'body', the church. Prayers to Christ through Mary are seen as especially effective, because Mary intervenes with Christ for sinners who are especially devoted to her. This theme was stressed in theologians such as Alphonsus Liguori and in modern papal encyclicals: Pius X in *Ad diem illum*. Post-Vatican II RC theology has played down the theme of Mary's mediation in favour of a direct relation to Christ. Exaltation of Mary as mediatrix is related to the exaltation of the ecclesiastical hierarchy* as mediator of Christ's grace.

See also **Mariology.**

R. R. RUETHER

Meon

A term used in theodicy* which perceives of evil as not having ultimate reality – evil as meonic. Derived from the Greek *mē on* i.e. not-being. In philosophical discourse the term is used to indicate that physical evil in fact does not exist because the events which are called evil are in fact neutral, ethically speaking. The scriptural foundation for the view of evil as meonic is Gen. 1.31: 'And God saw everything that he had made, and behold it was very good.' In the patristic* tradition the foundational concept that creation is good as created by God prevents evil from being considered an ultimate reality. Gregory the Theologian thus was representative of the patristic view when he taught that evil is neither substance, nor kingdom, nor without cause, nor self-caused, nor created by God. St John of Damascus summarizes the patristic view: 'Virtue was given by God to nature and he is the beginning and cause of every good,' but 'evil is nothing other than the withdrawal of the good, just as darkness is the withdrawal of light,' or in other terms, 'it is not in man's nature to sin, but rather in his choice' (*De Fide Orthodoxa* II, 30). As such, evil is meonic, i.e. not ultimate. However, it is existent. A result of self-determining choice, it is experienced as an empirical reality, since the withdrawal of good is a source of disruption, disharmony and perversity in created reality and more particularly in human life.

See also **Evil, Problem of; Non-Being**.

S. HARAKAS

Mercersburg Theology

Mercersburg Theology arose in the 1840s at the theological seminary of the German Reformed Church in Mercersburg, Pennsylvania. Positively, it was a restatement of classical German Reformed theology, ecclesiology and liturgy, informed by currents of romanticism * and idealism *; negatively, it was a reaction against the revivalism then so strong in American Protestantism. It had two conspicuous leaders: Philip Schaff (1819–1893), Swiss-born, German-educated professor at Mercersburg, 1844–1863, author of *The Principle of Protestantism* (1845); and John Williamson Nevin (1803–1886), graduate of Union College and Princeton Seminary, professor at Mercersburg, 1840–1853, and the author of *The Anxious Bench* (1843), a spirited attack on the system of the revival in favour of the system of the catechism. In articles in the *Mercersburg Review* and in his greatest work, *The Mystical Presence* (1846), Nevin emphasized the objective and organic aspects of the Christian tradition, and stressed the 'spiritual real presence' of Christ in the Lord's Supper. The Mercersburg theology did not make much impression on the church of its time, except in liturgy, but it forshadowed aspects of twentieth-century neo-orthodoxy, ecumenicity, and liturgical renewal.

Jack M. Maxwell, *Worship and Reformed Theology: The Liturgical Lessons of Mercersburg*, 1976; James H. Nichols, *Romanticism in American Theology: Nevin and Schaff at Mercersburg*, 1961; (ed), *The Mercersburg Theology*, 1966.

ROBERT T. HANDY

Mercy

From the OT onwards, there are two related but distinct aspects of mercy, the divine and the human, the theological and the moral. It is a word which traditionally describes both an attitude (even *the* attitude) of God to man and a disposition which should characterize human dealings. On the former side, it is bound up with considerations like God's justice; on the latter, it is a basic moral duty. But the two aspects, though distinct, are related and intertwined. Thus, the mercy (or 'steadfast love' or 'loving kindness' as it is commonly rendered in recent versions of the OT) which should mark human relationships marks, in the first place, God's relationship with human beings. And in so far as human creatures exercise justice on God's behalf, they are confronted with the question of the bounds of mercy. In the Bible, the two aspects are bound together in the deeper setting of the covenant *. As this links not only God and his people but his people among themselves, so the character of the covenant is stamped on them all by virtue of their status within it. In other words, the moral aspect flows from the theological, the human from the divine. And in the OT, the overwhelmingly dominant use relates to the divine side.

This pattern, established in the OT, gives a unity to Christian ideas about mercy. Nevertheless, there are shifts of emphasis related to wider movements of thought and sensibility. The OT roots of the term give it a central and characteristically practical role. It is central in that it is one of the commonest words (Hebrew *hesed*; Greek *eleos*) used to describe the disposition of faithful kindness with which God regards his people (Ps. 138.8; Jer. 33.11) and the obligation of helpfulness they should feel for each other (Micah 6.8; Judg. 1.24); practical in that the attitude is expected to find expression in deeds (Isa. 63.7; Zech. 7.9). The strength which inheres in this quality is highlighted when it is contrasted with the Stoic idea of *eleos*, where it is seen as an emotion of weakness in that it involves a departure from strict equity into partiality.

The NT uses of the word are in line with OT practice, as passages like Matt. 9.13; 18.33; Luke 10.37 make plain. However, while it is not a prominent NT term, it is brought into the Christian scheme of things. Thus, the saving act of God in and through Christ is seen as the crowning expression of his mercy, as resulting in both the establishing of the new Jew-Gentile church (Rom. 9.23; 11.30–32; I Peter 2.10) and in the call of the individual (I Cor. 7.25; II Cor. 4.1). And the expected consummation may also be described in terms of mercy (Matt. 5.7; II Tim. 1.18).

It is thus one of a number of words for the gracious, outgoing and dynamic purpose of God for man's salvation, fulfilled in Christ. Its biblical tone is therefore predominantly personal; yet associations of law and justice, so commonly providing a framework of imagery for man's relations with God, were there from the start, and they came to the fore in so far as Christian life came to be seen in such terms, especially in Latin Christianity. Mercy (Latin *misericordia*) now appeared as the clemency which man must hope to receive from God, in mitigation of the condemnation which was his entitlement and his doom. It thus found a place in the vocabulary of the protracted and tortuous controversies on God's grace and the terms on which justification or salvation are available, in the time of Augustine and Pelagius and onwards, down to the period of the Reformation. 'Mercy' hit off the unmerited character of salvation for fallen man who can have no claims on the just God.

In Christian prayer, the plea for mercy has long been the dominant expression of the suppliant coming before God, seen so commonly under the image of the great lord or king. Its origins go back to the psalter (Ps. 6.2f., LXX; 51.1), and its presence in Gospel stories (Matt. 9.27; 15.22; Mark 10.47f.) may reflect its use as a formula of petition already in the early church. By the end of the fourth century, its liturgical use is attested, as the response of choir or congregation to prayers, and, now without the accompaniment of a litany of such petitions, it retains its place in Western eucharistic liturgies, tending to be associated with the penitential opening of the rite. The traditional reiteration of 'Lord, have mercy', more striking still in the worship of the Eastern churches, testifies vividly to the prominence in Christian faith and feeling over the centuries of the set of religious ideas and emotions in which mercy has so important a place.

J. L. HOULDEN

Merit

Brought from common usage as 'character and conduct worthy of reward' into theological employ, the term connotes the property of an act which justly requires (condign merit) or befits (congruent merit) divine compensation. Traditional R C teaching acknowledges that the divine gratuity makes all good works possible, but declares that these acts of charity (such as prayer, almsgiving, celibacy, and most of all martyrdom) deserve a reward from God. Further, heroic acts done by some in the state of grace accumulate merit that is transferable to others for the reduction of purgatorial disciplines. Traditional Protestant theology, on the basis of the doctrine of justification* by grace through faith, has either rejected the term and concept or has changed the agent to Christ in his human nature whose merits of passive and active obedience redeem. The merits of Christ are also spoken of in RC teaching as those that assure the possibility of reward for our own. Based on a methodical study of the polemical texts and the historical context, recent discussion has questioned the intractable nature of old disagreements.

The formulation of the traditional doctrine of merit has drawn upon biblical passages that state or imply recompense for virtuous human action (Prov. 19.17; Deut. 5.28–33; Ex. 23.20–22; Matt. 5.3–12, 46; 6.1, 18; 7.21; 11.29; 25.34; Luke 12.8; John 4.36; Rom. 2.2, 6; I Cor. 3.8.; II Tim. 4.8; Rev. 2.10; 14.3). In early fragmentary expression in the Apostolic Fathers and the Apologists, good works were urged upon the believer after the grace of baptism as a way of gaining eternal life. Tertullian added a strong juridical quality to the developing idea, and made use of the term itself to describe the way in which divine favour could be secured. Augustine*'s effort to hold together the priority of grace with the reality of its effects in the believer left its mark on all subsequent discussion of subjective soteriology* and thus on the question of merit. His oft-quoted words evidence the dialectic of his thought: 'God does not crown your merits as your merits, but as His own gifts' (*On Grace and Free Will* VI, 15).

Aquinas, seeking to stay within the Augustinian framework, maintained the polarity but sought to identify more precisely the lines of interrelationship, regarding grace as operative in justification but as co-operative in putting in motion the free will that responds to the divine working in us, a secondary causality deserving of reward. The Council of Trent* further refined this tradition and gave dogmatic expression to it in its sixth session (chapter sixteen) under pressure of Protestant criticisms of merit. These Augustinian notes were sounded: the merits of Christ make possible our justification; the state of grace is entered by divine initiative; all our good works are grounded in divine grace; there is no warrant in the doctrine of merit for self-glorification. However, the Tridentine tradition conceives of justification as intrinsic not extrinsic, entailing the ontological transformation of the believer as manifest in good works. Co-operation with the love infused into the justified is catalysed by the same, but when the believer demonstrates responsiveness to its initiatives by acts rising from a right disposition, these good works are judged meritorious. Trent detailed seven conditions for merit and noted these results of it: the increase of grace in this life, the possibility of attaining eternal life, the attainment itself after the divine initiative assures perseverance, and the increase of glory. The text on 'many mansions' (John 14.2), with its suggestion of degrees of eschatological attainment, was cited as proof of the function of merit in the process of salvation.

Popular defence of the traditional doctrine of merit declares that the denial of its results in 1. antinomianism; 2. rejection of the biblical texts that promise reward for obedience; 3. failure to see that the majority of human beings, including Christian believers, require the promise of rewards or chastisements as incentive for good behaviour.

Protestant criticism of Trent's doctrine of merit and its antecedents has been: 1. the acknowledged all-sufficiency of grace and the depth of human sinfulness have been compromised by the intrusion of human capabilities and rewards into the soteriological relationship; 2. where grace brings justifying faith, good works follow either in spontaneous love or in a will to obey the moral law, and thus antinomianism is precluded.

Current attempts to transcend earlier polemic seek to find a place for both R C and Protestant emphases. The Protestant stress on salvation as ultimately from God's grace and the insistence on the removal of all grounds for self-glorification are acknowledged from the Roman Catholic side, and are even read as the intention of Trent. On the other hand, heirs of the Reformation have abandoned Protestant caricatures of the R C view (as salvation by works), and have acknowledged that the accent on justification does not require the denial of grace as power as well as pardon (a theme that appears within Protestant tradition itself in

Wesleyan and Anabaptist correctives to a too exclusively juridical view of justification). Justification is by grace alone and by faith alone, but its authenticity is inseparable from moral and spiritual fruits that witness to an intrinsic change in the believer as well as an extrinsic alteration of the relation between the believer and God. The question remains, however, whether the word and concept merit, associated as they are with the earning of a reward, have the ability to convey a post-polemical consensus on the fecundity of justifying faith.

Hans Küng, *Justification*, 1964; C. S. Sullivan, *Formulation of the Tridentine Doctrine of Merit*, 1959.

GABRIEL FACKRE

Messiah

Anointed One, *Christos* in Greek, *Masiah* in Hebrew. Christ is the favourite title of Christians for Jesus of Nazareth.

The origins of the word are to be found in the O T in the idea of anointing persons for particular tasks: e.g. the king (I Sam. 24.6, 10), the priest (Lev. 4.3ff.), even a foreign king (Isa. 45.1); the verb is used in connection with the commissioning of prophets (I Kings 19.16; Isa. 61.1). The connection of the word with the hoped-for king of Israel can already be found in passages like Ps. 89.38 (R S V). In the O T there are indications of the emergence of a belief that a descendant of David would arise to redeem his people and introduce a period of harmony in creation (Isa. 11), a promise based on the covenant * made between God and David in II Sam. 7.12ff. The belief blossomed in post-biblical times and can be found in its most developed form in the pre-Christian Psalms of Solomon 17.5ff. Belief in the coming of a descendant of David was one component of messianic expectation. O T usage meant that no unified concept of the Messiah emerged, nor was the title confined to the king who was to come. In several works we find the title applied to a priestly figure as well as to the descendant of David (*1QS* 9.11; Test. Levi 7; Test. Judah 21.1ff.). Towards the end of the first century we find that the title Messiah is used with greater consistency to speak of the descendant of David who would act as the eschatological agent of God (e.g. II Esdras 12.32; Syr. Bar. 29.3; 39.7; 40.1; 70.9; 72.2).

Messianic belief was one facet of the eschatological* beliefs of Judaism. The future hope was clear in its essential outlines, but the place and prominence of the Messiah in these hopes varied greatly. Two constant elements in the eschatological hope were the expectation that there would be a period of tribulation before the coming of the new age and the expectation that God's reign would be established on earth. Not every text gives prominence to the Messiah in this process.

In the light of the eschatological character of the early Christian message it will come as no surprise to find that the title Christ was from the very first used to speak of Jesus and his mission (Mark 8.29; Acts 2.36). There has been much debate whether Jesus thought of himself as the Messiah. What we know of the attitude of Jesus makes it difficult to believe that he accepted the title without qualification, particularly in the light of the emerging connection between it and the descendant of David who would purge the land of all defilement and destroy the enemies of God. There are indications from the Gospels which suggest that he may have accepted the title (Mark 11.7ff.; 14.62 par.), albeit with a rather different understanding from the popular one (note Luke 4.18f.). Certainly his proclamation of the imminent reign of God would have led many to suppose that he should be identified with one of the eschatological agents spoken of in the Jewish tradition (Matt. 11.2ff.; Luke 7.16; John 6.14f.). Very quickly the word Christ began to be used as a proper name. This trend is already evident in Paul's letters, though when the title Christ is used on its own in contexts dealing with eschatological salvation accomplished through him it retains its eschatological references (e.g. Rom. 5.8; II Cor. 5.19), as elsewhere in the N T (John 7.27; 7.44; 20.31). As the eschatological emphasis of the Christian message waned, that dimension of the term faded into the background also and the use of the word as a proper name became widespread.

A. E. Harvey, *Jesus and the Constraints of History*, 1982; M. Hengel, 'Christos in Paul', in *Between Jesus and Paul*, 1983; M. de Jonge and A. S. van der Woude, *Christos*, *TDNT* 9, 1974, pp. 483ff.

CHRISTOPHER ROWLAND

Metaphor

Metaphor is distinguished from symbol (something that represents another thing), image (an imitation or representation of something) and analogy (partial resemblance between things), for in metaphor a word or phrase ordinarily and primarily used of one thing is applied to another. The effect of a good metaphor is a shock of recognition for its appropriateness in spite of its unconventionality and inadequacy: 'all the world's a stage', 'a mighty fortress is our God', 'war is a chess game'.

The history of efforts to understand the nature of metaphor begins with Aristotle, whose view constitutes one of the two major perspectives on it. In spite of his appreciation for its importance, his relegation of it to the mark of genius indicates that he saw it principally as a rhetorical device rather than as central to language as such. His view can be called 'substitutable' while the other major view sees metaphor as 'unsubstitutable'. That is, Aristotle's understanding of metaphor and the opinion that prevailed until at least the nineteenth century was that what metaphor said could be said some other and more direct way. But, increasingly, over the last century, that opinion has been reversed and metaphor has been seen not as a trope but as the way language and, more basically, thought works.

The principal contemporary theorists on metaphor as unsubstitutable are I. A. Richards and Max Black. Richards says, 'we all live, and speak, only through an eye for resemblances' (*The Philosophy of Rhetoric*, 1965, p. 89). Richards' definition of metaphor gives the reigning 'interactive' view of it: 'In the simplest formulation, when we use a metaphor we have two thoughts of different things active together and supported by single word, or phrase, whose meaning is a resultant of their interaction' (p. 93). The most important element in this definition is its insistence on *two active thoughts which remain in permanent tension or interaction with each other*. Thus, in an example from Max Black, 'war is a chess game', the vitality of the metaphor depends upon keeping both thoughts and what Black calls their 'systems of associated commonplaces' active in the mind.

The implications of this understanding are several: 1. if the tension is lost, literalism results: e.g., war is identified with chess and the ways in which war is *not* like chess (destruction, death) are forgotten; 2. both partners of the metaphor are affected by being in interaction: e.g., war not only is seen through the grid or screen of chess but vice versa; 3. metaphors have both structural and attitudinal power: e.g., the commonplaces associated with chess help us to speak coherently and systematically about war and these commonplaces also influence how we feel about war.

While metaphor has always been considered important in poetry, its centrality to fields as various as computer science, philosophy, political science, anthropology, psychology, and the biological as well as natural sciences is more recent. Atomic physics is especially dependent on metaphors and models for understanding the behaviour of invisible entities such as protons and neutrons. Constructive and especially creative thought in any area of learning is increasingly seen as a process of moving from the familiar to the unfamiliar by using what is known as a metaphor for the unknown. The 'fit' between the two will be only partial and always inadequate; hence, many metaphors will be needed and caution exercised at all times to avoid collapsing the metaphor and its reference.

Metaphor is also becoming of increasing importance in Christian theology as theologians recognize the centrality of metaphor in scriptural language as well as of models (i.e. dominant metaphors such as God the Father, Son, and Holy Spirit) in the tradition. Many NT scholars now see the parables of Jesus as extended metaphors, as grids or screens which attempt to express through familiar stories the novel and unfamiliar message of Jesus' ministry – the kingdom of God. Metaphorical language is abundant in both Testaments, from the psalmists' metaphors of fortress, mother, creator, father, lover, lion, and rock for God to John's metaphors of the way, the truth, and the light for life with Jesus. Like poetry and atomic physics, theology can deal with the unknown only through the known, as biblical language amply illustrates. While the church has occasionally forgotten this, the great theologians from Origen through Augustine to Thomas, Luther, Calvin and on up to Barth and Tillich have known it and in one way or another have acknow-

ledged both the inadequacy of all language about God and the need for metaphorical language to express our relationship to God. What is new in the last thirty years or so is the deepening recognition that metaphorical and conceptual language are intrinsically related: metaphors need conceptual interpretation while concepts need metaphorical richness (see, for instance, the writings of Paul Ricoeur, Langdon Gilkey, Gordon Kaufman, David Tracy).

As metaphor becomes more central in theology, it raises questions regarding traditional language. One set of questions concerns the literalization of theological language. If religious/theological language is intrinsically metaphorical, then the *tension* in it must always be maintained, or the metaphors and models become idols and literalism results. A metaphor always says something negative as well as positive: God is/is not father. Religious and theological metaphors are especially prone to idolatry and literalism because of their powerful attitudinal potential and because they settle deeply into consciousness through liturgical repetition. As Richard Braithwaite has said, 'The price of the employment of metaphors is eternal vigilance.'

A second set of questions concerns the relevance of traditional theological language, especially those metaphors and models which have achieved hegemony to the exclusion of others. For instance, many women, blacks, and Third World peoples are raising questions about the patriarchal and hierarchical metaphors of the tradition, claiming that such language excludes them. If theological language is seen as truly metaphorical, then it is relative, receptive to revision, and open to complementary metaphors and models from experiences of relating to God of traditionally excluded groups of Christians.

In sum, the study of metaphor has moved from seeing it as a substitutable rhetorical trope, necessary in poetry but reserved for the genius, to understanding it as the unsubstitutable foundation of language and thought from which conceptual formulation emerges and to which it must return for its funding. As John Middleton Murry says: 'Metaphor is as ultimate as speech itself, and speech as ultimate as thought ... metaphor appears as the instinctive and necessary act of the mind exploring reality and ordering experience' (*Countries of the Mind: Essays in Literary Criticism*, second series, 1931, pp. 1–2). It is no surprise, then, that theology which attempts to speak of ultimate reality in some orderly fashion must do so in metaphors at all stages and dimensions of its discourse.

The literature on metaphor is vast and growing rapidly. Ian Barbour, *Myths, Models and Paradigms: A Comparative Study in Science and Religion*, 1974; Max Black, *Models amd Metaphors*, 1962; Robert Funk, *Language, Hermeneutic and Word of God: The Problem of Language in the New Testament and Contemporary Theology*, 1966; Sallie McFague, *Metaphorical Theology: Models of God in Religious Language*, 1982; Andrew Ortony (ed), *Metaphor and Thought*, 1979; I. A. Richards, *The Philosophy of Rhetoric*, 1965; Paul Ricoeur, 'Biblical Hermeneutics', *Semeia* 4, 1975; Sheldon Sacks (ed), *On Metaphor*, 1979; Warren A. Shibles, *Metaphor: An Annotated Bibliography and History*, 1971.

SALLIE MCFAGUE

Metaphysics

Practically everything about metaphysics is subject to vigorous philosophical dispute, including the question of what it is. But the philosophers traditionally regarded as metaphysicians have in common that they attempt to provide and to justify an account of the most basic constituents of reality, and the manner in which these are related to one another. It has been inferred from this that particular forms of human inquiry into the nature of things are all carried out under assumptions which it is the business of metaphysics to make explicit, and either to justify or to amend. The method and scope of metaphysics are often, whether for good or ill, contrasted with the method and scope of the sciences; though it has been pointed out that the thesis that scientific method is the only proper means of finding out the truth about the real world, being for its own part incapable of scientific justification, is itself metaphysical.

'Metaphysics' has been quite largely a term of abuse in modern analytic philosophy, and sometimes perhaps the intensity of the abuse has been a good deal more evident than exactly what it is which is being abused. The logical positivists and linguistic philosophers have, each from their very different points of view, frequently regarded metaphysics as something which ought to be eliminated, a kind of pathological outgrowth from the philosophical and scientific process. This polemic is to a large extent based on the principle that facts are to be discovered by empirical methods, while unaided reason can do nothing but concoct definitions and deduce their consequences. A compromise between the metaphysical and anti-metaphysical point of view is attributable to Kant, whose 'critical philosophy' may be said to set out methodological principles deemed to be common to the sciences, yet which, while they cannot be reduced to logic in any usual sense of the term, make no claim to state facts, even facts of a very general kind. Quite recently, in the wake of the alleged refutation of logical positivism, the claim that linguistic philosophy is not only trivial but covertly dogmatic, and the revival of materialism, more serious attention has been given by philosophers to metaphysical doctrines and questions. According to one recent approach, it is the task of metaphysics to provide an account of the basic nature and structure of the real world as it must be, owing to the fact that we can come to know it in the particular way that we do. Less general types of inquiry, typified by the natural and human sciences, would employ experience to arrive at the more detailed and particular account of the nature of things which cannot be attained in such an *a priori* manner. Metaphysics, then, while renouncing some of its more extravagant traditional pretensions, would remain of importance as supplying the framework into which could be fitted other types of knowledge and inquiry, and which could curb, or conceivably justify, but at least subject to critical appraisal, the imperialist pretensions made more or less explicitly by certain thinkers on behalf of certain sciences (e.g., 'physicalism' for physics). At this rate Hegel would be right in maintaining that while metaphysics is not the whole *of* knowledge, it is the whole *in* knowledge.

A useful distinction has been made by Strawson between 'descriptive' and 'revisionary' metaphysics. Outstanding among descriptive metaphysicians are Aristotle and Kant, who may be held to clarify, articulate and justify our usual basic conception of reality. Revisionary metaphysicians, on the other hand, make it their business to argue that this conception ought to be more or less radically overhauled, as based upon error. Berkeley's attempt to get rid of 'material substance' is a notable example of revisionary metaphysics in this sense, as is Hegel's effect to articulate and defend the view that matter is no more than a product of spirit at a certain stage of its striving towards self-realization.

Metaphysics has traditionally been regarded as closely related to theology, and no wonder; since those who are concerned with the nature of things at the greatest level of generality are *ipso facto* preoccupied with the question of how God is related to other actual or alleged basic constituents of reality, such as matter, mind, space, time and cause; and of whether the existence, nature and interrelation of such entities provide reasons for thinking that God does or does not exist, or clues as to his nature. On the other hand, metaphysics has been attacked by two very different types of religious believer and theologian, those who stress the importance of divine revelation, and those who emphasize the role of religious experience; on the grounds that the theories expounded by the metaphysician, while they may be claimed or appear at first sight to corroborate such revelation or validate and intensify such experience, in the long term are apt to supplant them.

A. J. Ayer, *The Central Questions of Philosophy*, 1973; R. G. Collingwood, *An Essay on Metaphysics*, 1940; E. Coreth, *Metaphysics*, 1968; B. J. F. Lonergan, *Insight. A Study of Human Understanding*, 1970; A. Quinton, *The Nature of Things*, 1973; I. T. Ramsey (ed), *Prospect for Metaphysics*, 1961; P. F. Strawson, *Individuals. An Essay in Descriptive Metaphysics*, 1959; R. Taylor, *Metaphysics*, 1963; W. H. Walsh, *Metaphysics*, 1966.

HUGO MEYNELL

Methodist Theology

The doctrinal teaching of the Methodist Church has from the beginning been closely bound up with the theology of John Wesley, though not limited to it. In the 'Doctrinal Clauses' of the Deed of Union, by which the British Methodist Church was legally constituted in 1932, at the union of the three chief Methodist denominations, Wesley's

Notes on the New Testament and the 'first four volumes of his sermons' are included among the 'doctrinal standards' of the Church, alongside 'the inheritance of the Apostolic Faith' and 'the fundamental principles of the historic creeds and of the Protestant Reformation'. There are similar provisions in the constitutions of the other Methodist Churches across the world.

Wesley's theology has been frequently reinterpreted and sometimes modified in various parts of world Methodism, but it still shows considerable vitality. This may be partly due to the continuing popularity of the hymns of Charles Wesley, deliberately intended by both Wesleys to 'contain all the important truths of our most holy religion, whether speculative or practical'.

The primary sources of this theology are the Bible and the formularies of the Church of England. Wesley was also versed in Orthodox, Roman Catholic, Puritan and Pietist writers over a wide range of themes, especially those relating to the spiritual life, but they did not affect his central allegiance.

Thus he took for granted the teaching of the Church of England on such matters as the Trinity, the Incarnation, the deity of Jesus Christ and the Holy Spirit, the salvation of the world through Jesus Christ, the holiness, unity and catholicity of the church and the supreme authority of scripture. He had the greatest respect for tradition as Anglicans understood it, and gave a high place to reason.

But during his spiritual pilgrimage he had been gradually convinced that the Church of England in his time had come to neglect certain vital elements of the 'Scriptural Christianity' to which it professed allegiance. It was the business of the Methodists to restore these to their proper place. One of them was the doctrine of 'justification by faith'*, which the Articles asserted but contemporary preachers and teachers, even bishops, had replaced by a doctrine of justification by good works. Therefore he insisted on 'prevenient grace' (often identified with conscience) by which God prepared all men for conversion, and on free, sovereign grace by which all those who come to the Father through Christ in faith, with no reliance on their own goodness, are freely pardoned (which is his understanding of 'justified'). Thus we are saved by grace through faith; and the suggestions, put forward by some of his critics, that, according to him, we are saved by feeling, or by works of repentance, are wholly unjustified. The faith of which he speaks is 'the faith of a son, not of a servant'; 'it is a sure trust and confidence that Christ died for *my* sins, that he loved *me* and gave himself for *me*'. The washing away of original sin and 'regeneration' are, indeed, given by the baptism of infants; but the good effects of baptism are afterwards 'sinned away' by all of us, and all of us need to be 'born anew' through grace by faith.

The second missing element in Anglican teaching, for him, was the doctrine of assurance – that the Holy Spirit 'witnesses with our spirit that we are the children of God'. Assurance is not to be confused with certainty, which is not granted to human beings on earth; it is an inward awareness, given to some but not all Christians, that relieves them from the anxiety of wondering whether they are indeed accepted by God (*see* **Assurance**).

The third, and for Wesley the most serious, is the doctrine of Christian perfection *. Wesley can be said to have overreacted against this omission when he claimed at one stage that true believers were free from sin. From his many restatements of this position emerges the teaching that all believers are called and enabled by the Holy Spirit to strive towards a state in which they love God and their neighbours completely, and not only their outward actions but their inward dispositions conform to the will of God. This state is attainable by all, and reached by a few, in this life.

On one great issue that divided the Church of England at the time he took a very decisive stand. He denounced Calvin's doctrine of predestination *, inherited by the Puritans, as a blasphemous fable, and asserted that God's grace is free for all without exception (though not accepted by all). His Arminianism *, however, was not of the semi-humanistic kind common at the time, but very near to the actual teachings of Arminius, who claimed that God foreknows, but does not predetermine our salvation or damnation.

On the eucharist Wesley had no explicit teaching, but his brother's hymns approximated closely to the account of the Real Presence and of the 'application' of the benefits of Christ's sacrifice to the faithful soul in D. Brevint's *Christian Sacrament and*

Sacrifice. On the church, he allowed for the presence of 'the congregation of the holy' within the one church, but regarded schism * as almost the worst sin.

Nineteenth-century Methodist theologians maintained the general pattern of Wesley's teaching, but discounted his doctrine of baptismal regeneration and emphasized the role of individual conversion. They also stressed the value of personal experience much more than Wesley, who had thought of it simply as confirming the truths which the Bible revealed.

Methodists have entered fully into all the biblical and theological debates of the twentieth century, into ecumenical conversation, and more recently into the 'liberation' controversies. In so doing they have re-captured many of the 'catholic elements' in Wesley, without his doctrine of baptismal regeneration, and at the same time have qualified their assent to particular schools of thought by asserting the universal scope of the gospel, the necessity of Christian unity, the significance of personal religion, and the unremitting quest for perfect love. They have, however, played little part in the construction of systematic theologies.

The Standard Sermons of John Wesley, edited and annotated by E. H. Sugden, 2 vols., 1921; W. R. Cannon, *The Theology of John Wesley*, 1946; Rupert Davies and Gordon Rupp (eds), *The History of the Methodist Church in Great Britain* I, 1965, ch. V; Rupert Davies, Raymond George, Gordon Rupp (eds), *The History of the Methodist Church in Great Britain* III, 1983, ch. IV; Harald Lindström, *Wesley and Sanctification*, 1946; Colin W. Williams, *John Wesley's Theology Today*, 1960.

RUPERT DAVIES

Method, Theological

The term has both a narrow and a broad meaning in relation to Christian theology. Used narrowly, it refers to explorations of the conditions under which theological claims may be true. Used broadly, it refers to an array of decisions every Christian theologian must make in the course of doing theology. Here it will be taken in its broader sense, inclusive of the issues to which the narrower use is limited. In neither sense does 'theological method' refer to some one normative method which is followed, at least implicitly, in every genuinely theological investigation (on analogy with the 'scientific method' which, it is sometimes alleged, is employed by every physical or life scientist who has achieved a genuinely scientific advance). If there were such a method, 'theology*' would name a more nearly unified enterprise. However, it is a commonplace that today 'theology' names an unprecedented variety of quite different enterprises. What they have in common may be no more than a set of points at which the theologian must make a decision about what it is to do Christian theology and how to do it best.

There are at least six such points. 1. What is the material subject involved in doing theology? 2. What difference does it make that theology is done in the context of a particular culture? 3. To whom is theological work addressed? 4. From the situation and vantage point of what group is theological work done? 5. What aims for the subject matter are there in doing theology? 6. What are the criteria for theological arguments? And if those criteria are challenged, how will they be defended? These are the major methodological decisions Christian theologians face. The first four tend to fall together in one group, and the last two tend to be a second group. However, the answers any one theologian gives to them all will be interdependent in complex ways. To study theological method, i.e. to examine a theologian's method, is to attempt to map those interconnections.

I. *Interconnections among the first four questions.*

1. *Subject matter.* Theologies currently exhibit three kinds of answer. (*a*) Doctrines of the church or concepts well established in church discourse (orthodox theologies, e.g. pre-Vatican II RC theology, confessional Lutheran and Calvinist theologies). (*b*) Biblical and traditional Christian symbols, images and mythic stories treated as symbols or complexes of symbols (liberal theologies, e.g. R. Bultmann; E. Farley; G. Kaufman; J. Macquarrie; S. Ogden; K. Rahner; P. Tillich; D. Tracy). (*c*) Biblical narratives (narrative theologies, e.g. K. Barth; G. Gutierrez; J. Moltmann). Of course God is the ultimate subject of all these theologies, but only as God is thought in and through one of these more proximate sorts of subject matter. The decision of orthodox theologies is seen as an act of obedience: God has given

these doctrines and concepts as the means God has commanded that we use to think theologically. The decision of liberal theologies rests on the judgment that biblical symbols and myths are the publicly available expressions of an otherwise inaccessibly private presence to God in (i) a religious dimension of every individual person's general experience (J. Macquarrie; P. Tillich; D. Tracy; K. Rahner), or (ii) the structure of a community's common experience (E. Farley), or (iii) the event of transition from an inauthentic to an authentic mode of existence (S. Ogden; R. Bultmann). It can instead rest on the judgment that these symbols are the material out of which Christian concepts of God may be constructed insofar as they give ways in which to take the complexity of our experience as nonetheless *a* world, a whole unified in ways suggested by the symbols, relativized by a transcendent ground to which it is related in modes of relationship also suggested by the symbols (G. Kaufman). The decision of narrative theologies rests on the judgment that God is rendered present publicly, not privately, either through the history of God's mighty acts which the narratives recite (G. E. Wright), or more specifically, in mighty acts of liberation (G. Gutierrez), or in an unsubstitutable identity description given by the narratives (K. Barth).

2. *Contemporary cultural context.* This places high value on open inquiry, autonomous judgment, and critical investigation of all truth-claims in every field of inquiry. Those are secularizing values because they rule out uncritical appeal to traditional religious authorities as a way to adjudicate those truth claims. What difference does that context make to theology? There seem to be three basically different answers. (*a*) The secularizing values central to contemporary culture may be seen as forming a systematic unity that is as a whole fundamentally incompatible with the systematic whole constituted by Christian doctrine. Indeed, part of the task of theology is to exhibit their inadequacy to human fulfilment. Hence dominant values and convictions at the root of modern culture are not to be allowed a role within theology. This is generally characteristic of orthodox theologies. (*b*) It may be held that as a creature of this culture, a Christian (theologian or not) is inescapably committed to these same

values, taken as an interconnected whole, and must give them an inner-theological role. This is the decision characteristic of liberal theologies. These are in two versions. For 'classical' liberals (e.g. F. Schleiermacher; J. Cobb; G. Kaufman) the central theological task is to show the compatibility of the values and beliefs that comprise modern consciousness with the traditional biblical message suitably reinterpreted. 'Neo-orthodox' liberal theologians (e.g. R. Bultmann; S. Ogden; K. Rahner; P. Tillich; D. Tracy; G. Gutierrez) relate the two more dialectically. They agree that the 'modern mind' inescapably requires a reinterpretation of the biblical message; they give the central values of modern culture a role within theology. At the same time, in contrast to the classical liberals, they stress that the biblical message calls modern consciousness into question. In its unself-critical optimism that in our autonomy we have the technological possibilities for endless self-improvement, modern consciousness is blind to the way it generates ways of being human that are inauthentic because they surrender genuine human freedom. Neo-orthodox theologies characteristically try to show that the biblical message calls for a way of being human, a mode of existence that is genuinely modern and hence compatible with modern consciousness, but truly authentic, and hence a decisive transformation of modern consciousness. (c) There may be a denial of any one identifiable, unitary reality to be called 'modern consciousness' or that the values highly esteemed in contemporary culture fall together systematically in a network. On this view (e.g. K. Barth), the theologian cannot adopt any methodological principle, either systematically to exclude modern consciousness from having any role in theology (orthodox theologies), or systematically to incorporate it within the doing of theology (liberal theologies). Instead, the question of the bearing of these values on theology must be settled *ad hoc*, theological topic by theological topic and value by value. Indeed, these decisions are not to be addressed directly and explicitly, but are allowed to be made tacitly and implicitly along with decisions on other methodological questions discussed below.

3 and 4. *Audience and group situation.* Answers here largely turn on the answers given to the previous question about the role

to be assigned to modern consciousness in doing theology. Two issues intersect: (i) Are the human situations of faith and unfaith so dichotomous that those in unfaith cannot understand what is said in faith? (ii) Does one's cultural or social setting determine what one is able to comprehend? (a) One type of theology addresses those in all cultural or social settings who identify themselves with Christian communities, and does so from within the same community of faith. Of these, some ground this answer in the judgment that what is to be communicated consists of doctrines that are timelessly true for people in any and all cultures but for whose intellectual comprehension faith is a necessary condition (some orthodox theologies). Others judge that what is to be communicated is the existential situation of faith itself, which is adequately evoked and expressed in all cultures by traditional Christian symbols or motifs but which can be understood only within the circle of those who already share that condition. Even if it is granted in neo-orthodox fashion that both theologian and audience also participate in modern consciousness marked by non-faith, nonetheless theology is confined to the circle of faith because it is only those who already share that condition that can understand the symbols and motifs expressive of faith (certain neo-orthodox theologies, e.g. G. Aulen). (b) A second type addresses those who identify themselves with the Christian community, but does so from the vantage point of those whose economic and political placement as members of minority groups, as women, or as citizens of third-world nations subjects them to oppression. This is based on the view, whether in its neo-orthodox or narrative theology form, that culturally shaped consciousness inescapably plays a role within theology and, furthermore, on the judgment that the consciousness of the oppressed uniquely empowers them to grasp the distinctive shape of the existence to which the Christian gospel calls us (some narrative theologies, e.g. J. Moltmann; certain neo-orthodox black*, e.g. J. Cone; feminist*, e.g. R. Ruether; and third-world liberation theologies*, e.g. G. Gutierrez). (c) A third type addresses everyone, those who do not identify themselves with the community of faith quite as much as those who do, and does so from the perspective of those who acknowledge that they are at once within the circle of faith and somehow also outside it too, as creatures of a thoroughly secular modern consciousness. This stance is based on the confidence that what is intelligible to persons shaped by the central values of modernity who are within the circle of faith, including the theologian, can be shown to be intelligible to anyone else too. For many theologians this confidence is based on the fact of a shared modern consciousness which must, accordingly, be vigorously affirmed and celebrated (most classical liberal theologies, e.g. F. Schleiermacher; G. Kaufman; and many neo-orthodox liberal theologies, e.g. R. Bultmann; E. Farley; J. Macquarrie, S. Ogden; K. Rahner; P. Tillich; D. Tracy). By contrast, a few theologians root this confidence much more unsystematically in the humanity that those inside and outside the circle of faith share and which by God's grace can be illuminated by the gospel as much despite the shared modern consciousness as by means of it (some narrative theologies, e.g. K. Barth).

II. *Formal matters.* Every theologian must go on to make two decisions (points 5 and 6 above).

5. What is the goal of doing theology, i.e. what does one hope to do to, with or for the subject matter? There seem to be three variously inter-related goals. (*a*) All theologians aim to exhibit the meaningfulness or intelligibility of their subject matter (doctrines, or symbols and myths, or narratives). This is a descriptive enterprise. (*b*) All theologians aim to use their subject matter in some way to show that certain things said and certain things done are or are not adequate in Christian terms. This is a critical or normative enterprise, seeking to assess whether certain patterns of thought and behaviour are truly faithful to Christian commitments. (*c*) In addition, some but not all theologians seek to show the truth of what is said by or on the basis of their subject matter.

6. Undoubtedly the most important debate about method in Christian theology today centres on the question: How should one go about accomplishing these goals? To what should one appeal in order not merely to assert the intelligibility, Christian adequacy and truth of one's theological proposals, but beyond that, to demonstrate it? The opposing positions on this question may be called 'foundationalist' and 'non-foundationalist' theological methods.

Foundationalists adopt the view that it is possible and necessary to ground the entire network of Christian theological proposals in an argument that will show both the intelligibility and perhaps even the truth of Christian claims about the reality of God, and show them in ways that are as persuasive to those outside the circle of faith as to those inside it. There are two main ways in which this is undertaken today. Both assume that as an intellectual enterprise theology is most similar to some type of philosophical undertaking. One way involves a turn to objective reality. It focusses on the way the reality we experience is a whole. It seeks to develop a conceptual scheme that can be used to identify as precisely as possible what are the principles that make it a whole. Prominent among these principles is God. This approach is adopted both by certain kinds of RC and Protestant orthodox theologies and by some kinds of classical liberal theologies (e.g. G. Kaufman and, in the 'process metaphysics' manner, J. Cobb). The other way involves a turn to the subject. It involves an analysis of human consciousness that may uncover those universally shared structures of consciousness which are logically prior to our having any particular experience, and are the very conditions of the possibility of our having experience, including cognition, at all. For if we know the conditions for all knowing, and if we can show that the peculiar cognitive claims made in theology meet those conditions, then we can show that those claims are both intelligible and true. This approach is adopted by many sorts of theological liberalism, both classical (e.g. F. Schleiermacher) and neo-orthodox (e.g. J. Macquarrie; K. Rahner; P. Tillich). It should be noted that among foundationalists the phrase 'theological method' is used to name discussion, not of the entire range of decisions reviewed thus far nor even of the question whether a foundation for theology should be sought, but more narrowly of the question of how best to provide such a foundation.

The foundational conceptual scheme is used in a variety of ways. All foundationalist theologians rely on such a scheme to secure the *intelligibility* of theological remarks. If the subject matter of theology is doctrines, then a metaphysical conceptual scheme which has already been independently shown to be intelligible can be used to re-state the doctrines, guaranteeing their intelligibility (orthodox theologies). If the subject matter of theology is a distinctively Christian set of symbols and myths expressive of a religious dimension of all experience or of an authentic mode of existence, then an analysis of the structures of consciousness can be used to show the possibility of just such experience or existence and how such symbols and myths might function to express and evoke it (classical and neo-orthodox liberal theologies). Further, all foundationalist theologians rely on such a scheme to help show the Christian *adequacy* of their proposals. For all of them the test of Christian adequacy is in some way the congruence of the proposals with the contents of the Bible. If the subject matter of theology is doctrines, then the Bible is construed as a collection of texts teaching doctrine. The foundational conceptual scheme can then be used as a language in which to restate biblical doctrines as well as to state the theologian's contemporary doctrinal proposals, thereby making it easier to show such formal relations as consistency, coherence and entailment between the two sorts of doctrines. When symbols and myths in the Bible are the subject matter of theology, the criterion of Christian adequacy is the distinctive experience or mode of existence expressed and shaped by the symbols and myths. The foundational analysis of the structure of consciousness can then be used to formulate a description of the specifically Christian mode of the religious dimension of experience or of authentic existence. That can then be used to assess the relative adequacy to the Christian centre of various proposals concerning appropriate patterns of thought and action by Christians. Some orthodox theologies and neo-orthodox liberal theologies (e.g. R. Bultmann) rest content with those two uses of foundational conceptual schemes. Others use them also to exhibit the *truth* of theological proposals (orthodox theologies, e.g. pre-Vatican II RC 'natural theology'; classical liberal theologies, e.g. G. Kaufman and, in the 'process' mode, J. Cobb; neo-orthodox liberal theologies, e.g. E. Farley; J. Macquarrie; K. Rahner; P. Tillich). And some rely on an analysis of the structure of consciousness to found the intelligibility and Christian adequacy of theological proposals and on a metaphysical analysis of the structure of reality to found the truth of theological proposals (e.g. S. Ogden; D. Tracy).

Non-foundationalists, by contrast, deny both the necessity and the possibility of grounding the entire network of Christian theological proposals in any argument. This could take the form of fideism, i.e. be based on the view that faith is a matter of uncritical belief of what is taught by an authority and that therefore it is religiously wrong or faithless to entertain sceptical questions, let alone seek to answer them. But this is almost entirely without genuine instance in contemporary theology. Non-foundationalism can take quite another form. It may assume that theology is the self-description of the Christian community, and doing it is far more like a cultural anthropologist giving a 'thick description' of a culture than like a philosopher identifying the structure of either reality or consciousness. On this view, the *intelligibility* of Christian claims is rooted, not in 'meanings' that might be restated more precisely in an ideal language consisting of a technical conceptual scheme, but in the fact that in the Christian community (as in any community) claims are made by using language in ruled ways. The Christian *adequacy* of theological proposals can thus be assessed by identifying the principal rules that govern Christian discourse, to see whether the proposals in question are properly 'grammatical'. The *truth* of theological proposals can be shown by showing that there are good reasons for believing them. But what counts as a 'good' reason is itself a function of how the community's culture shapes one's construal of oneself and of the historical and natural contexts of life. So the very motion of universal and *a priori* canons of intelligibility and truth, on which foundationalism rests, are rejected. Some confessional Lutheran and Calvinist orthodox theologies and some neo-orthodox liberal theologies (e.g. G. Aulén) are of this sort. Narrative theologies are usually non-foundationalist (e.g. K. Barth). To take biblical narratives to be the subject matter of theology is to judge that they give identity descriptions both of God and of human life in nature and history, and that those identity descriptions function in the Christian community to provide norms by which to assess whether patterns of thought and behaviour are faithful to those identities.

L. Gilkey, *Naming the Whirlwind,* 1969, pt I; G. Kaufman, *An Essay on Theological Method,* 1975; D. Kelsey, *The Uses of Scripture in Recent Theology,* 1975; A. Nygren, *Meaning and Method,* 1972; P. Tillich, *Systematic Theology,* vol I, 1951; D. Tracy, *Blessed Rage For Order,* 1975, ch 2.

D. H. KELSEY

Middle Platonism

Throughout its first two centuries of doctrinal and theological development Christianity came at various times under the influence of philosophical systems flourishing during the period. One of the most important of these was Middle Platonism, that portion of the Platonic tradition dating roughly from the fall into scepticism of the Old Academy at Athens towards the end of the second century BC to the rise of Neoplatonism * in the first half of the third century AD in the person of the learned and mystical Plotinus (204–269/70). Although many of the most important themes of Middle Platonism, most notably those describing the inner nature of the Godhead and the multiplicity of sub-divine forces operative in creation, were never taken over wholesale into Christianity, they nonetheless contributed greatly to that transition in language and concept that distinguishes patristic * theology from that of Paul and the Gospels.

Modern scholarship has often viewed Middle Platonism as an eclectic and even idiosyncratic philosophical persuasion rather than a definable school of thought. With later Platonic revivals, however, and in clear distinction from Gnosticism * and the Stoicism * of the period, it shares a pointed interest in the speculative cosmology and theology Plato set forth in the *Timaeus* and, to a lesser degree, in the *Phaedrus* and other works. This fascination with cosmology provided in great measure Middle Platonism's appeal to a Christianity struggling in the early centuries to develop a doctrine of God appropriate to belief in the divinity of a visible Jesus and a doctrine of creation * adequate to replace the waning apocalyptic * eschatology * of the apostolic age. Both Justin Martyr (*c.* 100–*c.* 165) and Clement of Alexandria (*c.* 150–*c.* 215), among others, subscribed to the belief that Plato had learned his cosmology from Moses, one way of legitimizing in religious terms their recasting of semitic doctrines of God and the world in the more cosmopolitan and culture-independent language of popular Platonism (*1 Apology* LX, 6–7; *Stromateis* V, 12:78, 2).

The most important Middle-Platonic contributions to Christian theology include its replacement of the Creator in Gen. 2, a worker in the image of a human potter at the wheel, with the abstract and mythical Maker of *Timaeus* 28c, a figure of far more cosmic scale and scope of intentions. This Maker is also, however, in a measure distant from the creation, a position secured by ancillary intermediate forces of one sort or another. For pagan Middle Platonism these could take the form of the Divine Ideas *, of a lesser race of 'daemons' reminiscent of the 'daimon' of Socrates, or, as suggested in *Timaeus* 40d, of the gods of the Homeric pantheon. Christian Middle Platonism preferred the persons of the Trinity * to have a more exclusive inner life and control over the divinity's external functions (Clement, *Stromateis* V, 14:103, 1; Justin, *1 Apology* L, 6–7), finding in Middle-Platonic speculations on the Good, the Mind and the Soul, however, inspiration for later theorizing on trinitarian inner relations. The presence of demiurgic * entities, whether Ideas or lesser divinities, played counterpoint to increasing emphasis in both pagan and Christian thinkers on the ineffability and unknowability of God, a sentiment introduced by Plato in the *Timaeus,* 'But the father and maker of all this universe is past finding out, and even if we found him, to tell of him to all men would be impossible' (28c), and echoed in Albinus (*Epitome* X, 1; 3; 4), Justin (*1 Apology* IX, 3) and Clement (*Stromateis* V, 12:78, 3).

In ethics and spirituality, Middle Platonism encouraged Christian theology in appropriating a notion already attractive in Gnosticism, the Fall *. Where the biblical Adam had sinned and suffered expulsion from the Garden into a hostile but ethically and eschatologically neutral world, the soul in Christian Middle Platonism has *fallen* into this world like that in *Phaedrus* 246c (cf. Tatian, *Oratio* 20) and must seek to return to that in the image of which it first was made. And, of course, in place of the reawakening and resurrection of the just at the eschaton as envisaged by Paul, there is the ascent of the soul to the 'supra-celestial place' of *Phaedrus* 247c, startlingly like that heaven mediaeval theology would reserve for those who in the afterlife attained the 'beatific vision'.*

Although the fact that Middle Platonism is a period in the history of Western thought rather than a localizable school of philosophy has hampered attempts to evaluate its influence on the development of Christian theology, we can discern in the works of Justin, Athenagoras, Tatian, Clement of Alexandria and Origen, though the latter is arguably more a Neoplatonist, additions to the theological vocabulary that would become permanent fixtures in the Western tradition.

Jean Daniélou, *Gospel Message and Hellenistic Culture*, 1973; John Dillon, *The Middle Platonists 80 BC to AD 220*, 1977; R. E. Witt, *Albinus and the History of Middle Platonism*, 1937.

JAMES J. HEANEY

Millenarianism, Millennianism

A doctrine derived from Jewish apocalyptic speculation (esp. by way of Rev. 20.1–7) and held by certain heretical sects and some orthodox theologians in the early church, according to which there would be a thousand-year (millennium) reign of the saints before the return of Christ. It was revived by Anabaptists and others after the Reformation and has been held tenaciously by Adventists and other evangelical sects until the present day. The rise of modern historical criticism* has, however, made this kind of biblicist speculation impossible for theologians who do not reject its methods and results.

See also **Eschatology.**

ALAN RICHARDSON

Ministry

Christian ministry is a ministry of salvation in the service of the world. It originates in the charge given by Christ to the church to carry on his ministry. All baptized are called to share in this service in accord with their states of life, special gifts and roles within the social structure of stable Christian communities.

All forms of ministry have three basic traits: proclamation of the gospel of Jesus Christ, service of the needs of the neighbour and worship of God. But each type of activity has something proper to it. Preaching provokes the hearer to respond in faith. Loving service of the neighbour leads the other to recognize self as truly other and so to affirm the source of otherness: the Father. Communal worship is realized through the gathering of the baptized in the name of Jesus for the purpose of expressing communion with God and with one another in Christ. All the participants have responsibility for the realization of this communion which takes the form of joyful praise, confidence in faith and thanksgiving.

Christian ministry, however, is never simply a ministry for the Christian community. Christians grow in the life of faith precisely by serving others. Preaching the gospel, which moves others to accept Christ, awakens the preachers to the awareness of the active presence of Christ in their preaching. The loving service of the neighbour occasions a deeper insight into the otherness of the other and so leads to affirm the Father as the source of that otherness. The individual participants of communal worship are carried by the faith of the community beyond the scope of their personal appropriation of the faith to a new level of consciousness of the mystery of salvation.

1. *Ordained Ministry.* The special ministry of leadership of Christian churches is exercised at various levels by the ordained. The tripartite form, bishop*, presbyter and deacon*, found almost everywhere in the post-apostolic age, is retained by the traditional episcopal* churches. Since the sixteenth century in the West, several types of leadership structure have emerged in churches derived from the Reformation movement.

Divergent interpretations of the role of the ordained fall into two main categories: those which stress the dependence of the community on the ordained; those which highlight the mutual dependence of all on one another. The unilateral application of the paternal or partnership models has led in the past either to the assimilation of all ministries to the ordained or to a purely utilitarian interpretation of the function of leadership. Today it is generally conceded that the Pauline doctrine of charisms (I Cor. 12) excludes both extremes. More commonly, an organic, synodal model is favoured, in which the church is viewed as realizing a common life in Christ through the mutual sharing of the gifts possessed by each member. In this view the ordained do not monopolize all ministerial gifts, authority and responsibility, nor do they merely function to preserve the external order of the community.

2. *Theology of Ordination.* Candidates for the ministry of leadership are chosen by some form of election and customarily incorporated into the special service by a rite of ordination*. This rite is normally carried out by one or more ordained ministers and includes a petition that the Spirit be given for effective exercise of the ministry together with an imposition of hands: a gesture which symbolizes the bestowal of the Spirit. Two common theological interpretations of the rite of ordination can be mentioned. The first is typical of some Reformation churches; the second corresponds to the understanding of the RC and Eastern churches. These two approaches converge on the following points: through ordination the community expresses and acknowledges that the candidate is called by God for a special service. Consequently the community affirms that it is God who ultimately empowers. This is expressed by invoking the Spirit to grant the grace of the ministry. Through ordination the candidate is united in a special way to other ministers of the same order in the fellowship of a common mission and to the laity who share the same life of faith. The peculiarity of this special service lies in the sphere of responsibility. Only the ordained are called by God and commissioned by the community as a whole and so responsible for fostering the unity and life of the community as a whole. However, a typical Reformation theology of ordained ministry argues that the institutional structure of special services is not established by divine institution. Therefore it can change with a view to better service of the gospel, and the rite of appointment can take various forms. Correspondingly, the special ministries traditionally exercised by the ordained are not absolutely restricted to them. As the situation demands, and according to their gifts, any baptized person can perform these services. On the other hand, the Eastern and RC churches hold that only the ordained qualify to exercise certain ministries in virtue of the gift of ordination. These include authoritative teaching of

revelation, government of Christian communities, and leadership of essential forms of worship, especially the Lord's Supper. In this theology the special gift of the Spirit is described either as a deepening of the baptismal grace or as a power distinct from it. But the main emphasis falls on the representative function of the ordained. Only the ordained can represent Christ, head of the church, in the types of ministry for which they have been empowered by the Spirit. From this standpoint structures of special services are established in some way by divine institution. Hence the offices of bishop, presbyter and deacon must be maintained and the rites of ordination, related to them, cannot be altered in their essential aspects.

3. *Ecumenical Consensus.* The historical and theological problems associated with the various denominational interpretations of the ordained ministry are based in part on divergent, temporally and culturally conditioned images of the ordained. A resolution of these problems can only be attained, in the ecumenical sphere, by fashioning a new image based on the integration of the theology of ordained ministry into a more general theology of Christian ministry and grounded on a common understanding of church. Among the principles which should govern this synthesis are the following: 1. All ministry exists for the benefit of the church and the world; 2. all baptized have received their gift from the Spirit for the common good; 3. the church is a communion of those who live in Christ, fashioned by the Spirit after the life of the Trinity* in which unity and multiplicity are bound together in a dynamic union of divine love.

Baptism, Eucharist and Ministry, Faith and Order Paper 111, 1982; Hans von Campenhausen, *Ecclesiastical Authority and Spiritual Power in the Church of the First Three Centuries*, 1969; Yves Congar, *Lay People in the Church*, 1967; William H. Lazareth, *Growing Together in Baptism, Eucharist and Ministry*, Faith and Order Paper 114, 1982; David N. Power, *Gifts That Differ: Lay Ministries Established and Unestablished*, 1980.

EDWARD J. KILMARTIN

Miracle

Miracles impinge on central issues of Christian belief, but raise problems to the modern mind. Miraculous happenings are recorded in both OT and NT. They do not differ significantly from accounts of miracles in the ancient world in general and in many different cultures throughout the ages. Properly attested miracles have long been regarded as the essential prerequisite for the canonization of a saint in the Roman Catholic Church. Pentecostalists and other Christians influenced by the charismatic movement* continue to claim miracles. Many Christian groups in Africa retain African traditional belief in miracles.

Since the age of the Enlightenment* it has been customary to define a miracle as 'a violation of a law of nature by a god' (cf. David Hume, *Enquiry concerning Human Understanding* X: 'Of Miracles', 1748). It is a mistake to suppose that earlier ages would have dissented from this definition. Miracles in the ancient world are normally attributed either to a god or to a holy person's capacity to use supernatural powers. Obviously this shades off into magic, and there is no clear division between the concept of divine power and popular ideas of mana. Thus contact with Elisha's bones restores a dead man to life (II Kings 13.20f.). All such events are recognized to be contrary to the regularity of nature. But nature was held to be ordered by divine decree and therefore capable of being set aside by divine power. Nevertheless the ancient world had its sceptics, like Porphyry, who scoffed at claims to the miraculous.

It is thus not surprising that the Gospels and Acts include traditions of miracles by Jesus and the apostles. Paul himself claims to have performed 'signs and wonders' (Rom. 15.19; II Cor. 12.12), which confirm the truth of the gospel. In the Gospels the miracles of Jesus are closely allied to his message of God's kingdom*, but he resists pressure to use his powers to establish a personal claim. This reticence may have exercised restraint on the subsequent growth of the tradition. The death and resurrection of Jesus are accompanied by portents, but the resurrection itself is primarily a theological statement about the status of Jesus, who died as Messiah* and was raised as Messiah (I Cor. 15.3f.). It depends for its validity not on any purported miracle but on the widely held Jewish conviction of the time that the dead are raised up (I Cor. 15.16). Developments in christology* led

to more far-reaching miraculous elements in the portrait of Jesus, especially in John.

The expansion of the church brought the need to emphasize the miraculous effects of the gospel of salvation, e.g. against the cult of Asklepios. The early apologists appealed to the miracles as confirmation of the truth of the Christian faith. But in fact claims to miracles diminish at the same time as they are elaborated in fictitious 'acts' of apostles. Chrysostom (*Hom. in Matt.* 32.11) admits that the age of miracles has passed. They had opened the way to faith, and now the real miracles are the changed lives of believers. The miraculous powers of Jesus attest his divinity, just as his sufferings attest his humanity, but they cohere with the power of God in creation. They transcend nature, but are not contrary to it.

Along these lines a theological understanding of miracle was achieved which persisted throughout the Middle Ages. The biblical miracles came to be regarded as essential proofs of the divine origin of the Christian revelation. Aquinas held that Mohammed's failure to give miraculous signs was proof of the inferiority of Islam to Christianity (*Contra Gentiles* 1.6). After the Reformation the necessity of miracles to establish religious claims was reaffirmed for example by Hooker (*Laws of Eccles. Polity* vii.14), and in the eighteenth century by Butler (*Analogy* 2.1, 7).

The modern discussion begins with the impact of Newtonian physics on the thinkers of the eighteenth century. Though Locke and others accepted the Gospel miracles as credentials of divine revelation, the growing impression of fixed laws of causality left little room for miracles. Hume really takes the line that miracles do not happen. Attempts were made to save the biblical stories by naturalistic explanations, but they were scarcely convincing.

Recent biblical criticism has turned attention to the aims of the evangelists, who used traditions of varying worth to present the permanent truths of the gospel. Bultmann started a lively debate by his contention that all reports of miracles, including the resurrection of Jesus, are 'mythological' expressions relevant to the questions of existence which confront everyone (*see* **Demythologizing**). I. T. Ramsey defined miracle as a 'disclosure situation', i.e. an unusual complex of incidents with which a new insight into truth is inextricably bound up. It can be objected that most reported miracles do not come into this category and many 'disclosure situations' are not miracles. C. S. Lewis claimed the incarnation as the central miracle for Christianity, to which all other miracles are related. This is a variant of the traditional interpretation of miracles as revelation.

Two factors in contemporary thought point the way for future discussion. 1. Quantum physics has questioned the concept of fixed laws of nature and substituted a more fluid view of the random effects of a fundamental indeterminacy. This gives broader (but still limited) scope for naturalistic interpretations of unusual events, but does nothing to prove divine origin. The crucial problem of the intervention of God remains open. 2. The observation of Durkheim that religion belongs to the human sciences points to the social function of belief in miracles. *Miracle stories attributed to a holy person* are testimonies to the impact of that person on society. *Claims to perform miracles* belong to the sphere of manipulation of power and come close to shamanism. *Personal experiences of miracles*, like special providences, have spiritual value only if they are received as free gifts from God, evoking praise and dedication. For the person who receives them they are 'disclosure situations', whereby sensitivity to the hand of God in the *whole* of life is confirmed and enhanced.

R. M. Burns, *The Great Debate on Miracles*, 1981; Mary Hesse, 'Miracles and the Problem of Providence' (forthcoming); Ernst and Marie-Luise Keller, *Miracles in Dispute*, 1969; C. F. D. Moule (ed), *Miracles*, 1965; I. T. Ramsey, *Religious Language*, 1957; C. S. Lewis, *Miracles*, 1947; Alan Richardson, *The Miracle Stories of the Gospels*, 1941; Richard Swinburne, *The Concept of Miracle*, 1970; F. R. Tennant, *Miracle and its Philosophical Presuppositions*, 1925.

BARNABAS LINDARS

Mission, Theology of

Theology of mission, reflection on the purpose and nature of Christian mission, became a recognized branch or dimension of Christian theology in the course of the modern missionary movement which began at the end of the eighteenth century. It has tended to be articulated mainly in the West, the source of the movement, and more recently through Western-influenced conferences and Western-trained theologians. But a new theology of mission and a new exegesis of the Bible are now emerging through the shared life of growing numbers of small, often poor or persecuted groups of Christians, many of them in the heart of hitherto Islamic, Hindu or Buddhist worlds, in Communist China, Russia and its satellites, in the shanty towns and rural areas of Africa, Asia and South America, or in the inner cities of the West.

The members of these groups are close in spirit to the first Christians. Like them they come out of frameworks of faith and culture which have been shaken apart. They have sensed a new breaking-open of a gulf always latent in human experience: a gulf between heaven and earth, ideal and reality, between a spiritual depth on the one hand and on the other the hard inconsequential surface of mundane life. Faiths and ideologies have sought to span this gulf by varied means: by manipulating the world into harmony through ritual cleansing and spirit possession; by moralizing the world, pressing it into conformity with a divinely revealed law; or by attributing to some members of society a special purity, empowering them to spiritualize the world into some ultimate underlying unity.

But now these people have been attracted by the sense of an actual divine presence in this world, in the figure of a wounded man alongside them, and the release, through him, of a new love, bringing together justice and mercy, ideal and real, heaven and earth. They would claim that the Divine Spirit flows out through the life and above all the death of that wounded man, Jesus the Christ, sent forth from God and in turn sending out others (John 20.21). As they apply his cross, in shared repentance, to their corporate life, they sense the movement of the Spirit empowering and equipping them to be channels in the new Love, integrating divine and human, community and social structure, spiritual and material, with a new redemptive energy.

This also happened in NT times. But as the church grew in size, influence and conformity to this world, it tended to lose hold of the central integrating force of the gospel *, and to fall back into the patterns of human culture *. The church also would manipulate the world into harmony, impose an order on the world or seek to spiritualize it into one.

The quest for the original wholeness, hidden and implicit in the central crucified and victorious figure, for a participation in his death and resurrection, became the motive energy of both renewal and of mission: through wandering prophets; martyrs; monks and friars; Anabaptists; Moravians and evangelicals; Tractarians and ultramontanist Roman Catholics; those in the Holiness movement and its offshoots, revivalists worldwide; Pentecostals * and parachurch movements still multiplying. In the Reformation, Luther and Calvin both grasped something of this wholeness of grace, but within the movements that followed, it tended to be lost. The divide in the Christian consciousness remained: a divide between heaven and earth, ideal community and actual structure, spiritual and material. The Enlightenment * of the late seventeenth and eighteenth centuries drastically deepened the rift. As spiritual authority seemed to shift from external, objective institutional sources to internal, subjective personal sources in the human mind or heart, there followed a dissociation of reason and emotion. Rationalism *, powerfully reinforced by scientific success, was countered by a new romanticism * and pietism *. The dissociation spread, in a chain reaction, through the expansion of Western industrial power, into all cultures. Every people either embraced much of the new secular * rationalism or strove to replace it with an alternative, magically controlled, morally imposed or mystically evoked order of their own.

Christendom was no exception. The modern missionary movement sprang partly from this polarization, and was deeply marked by it from the outset. The notion of 'mission' has thus been given a widely contrasting content.

Mission has been regarded at two extremes, either as an attempt to draw human beings out of a sinful world into a totally spiritual transformation within the church, or to absorb the church, its faith and its message into a totally secular transformation of the world. Both these extremes allowed the church to be used by the world, and the gospel to be distorted, in contrasting ways. Proponents of the first view took as their key point a spiritualized interpretation of the traditional basis for mission, the great commission (Matt. 28.19, 20). More recent proponents of the second view have emphasized a secularized interpretation of Jesus' sermon at the synagogue (Luke 4.16–21).

The latter approach to mission has developed gradually from a Victorian and Edwardian view of mission once shared by most of those engaged in it, as the spread of 'civilization'. It ran from 'progress' and the social gospel, on to the 1960s, which was a watershed, a fresh welling-up from Enlightenment springs. Mission then, with a new emphasis on God's own activity in the world ('Missio Dei' as it was called), came to be regarded both in World Council of Churches and Vatican II circles as 'humanization'. More recently, a more drastic economic relativism *, arrived at in the struggle of churches against political and economic injustice, especially in Latin America, locates authentic mission only within the enclosed circle of a Marxist theory of truth. Mission and Christian revelation * itself can be discerned only 'from the underside of history', from within the struggles of the poor and oppressed (liberation theology *), the exploited races (black theology *) or the exploited sex (feminist theology *). A similar relativism confronted with an increasingly pluralist world of many faiths no longer views the Christian gospel as their displacement or fulfilment (two traditional views) nor even the cosmic Christ as the key to the interpretation of all faiths (a more recent view), but tends to adopt a Hindu philosophy, regarding all so-called religions as part of one truth. It may also, influenced by a romantic subjectivism, tend to merge Christ with the Buddha (a fashionable identification), or even to equate Christian faith with a theoretical African or primal religion (see also **Indigenous Theology**). Many practitioners of what is called dialogue have seemed to become hostile to any suggestion of evangelism, regarding it as spiritual colonialism. For all these views of mission, the very place of the church as a separate religious community is called into question.

Over against this absorption of the church into the world around it, the more conservative reaction among both Catholics and Protestant evangelicals has sought to define mission exclusively in terms of evangelism * and the conversion of groups and individuals, of church planting and of church growth. The world has offered, at most, unconscious assumptions, or, recently, models and techniques supplied by sociology and capitalist market research. The 1930s and 1940s saw a swing away from the optimism of the 1920s, an affirmation of the distinctiveness of church and gospel over against a fascist world, which lent itself to the idea of a 'radical discontinuity' (Kraemer) and a sense of insulation within the church and isolation from other faiths and cultures. There are those who would still perpetuate and intensify this distancing from the world in all its aspects, partly as a defence against the relativizing of their own absolutes and of their own culture, as, like those of all other faiths, they confront a widening and swiftly changing world (*see also* **Christianity and Other Religions**).

Obviously many on each side of this divide have long seen their need for each other and for a larger apprehension of the new relationship of heaven and earth in Christ. They would harvest the insights of the 1930s as well as the 1960s, and hold together discontinuity and continuity. At both evangelical and ecumenical mission conferences in the late 1970s and 1980s, there has been a noticable feeling towards a greater wholeness; a recognition that, in the words of Emilio Castro, Secretary of the Council for World Mission and Evangelism of the WCC, 'liberation, development, humanization and evangelization are *all* integral parts of mission . . . and cannot be set apart from one another without becoming simply caricatures of what they really are'. Varying groups, from the Mennonites to the Taizé community, have come to symbolize this integral mission, a kind of third way, attempting to get back behind some of the wrong divides of Christian history. In this quest, the renewal in parts of the Orthodox Churches, Russian, Eastern and Coptic, and the recovery of their insights into the relation between contemplation and theology, worship and evangelism and social witness, are crucial.

But it is from the actual experience of those freshly grasped by the whole gospel today that a clearer sense is coming that the mission of God in Christ, and through his people, is the restoring of a dialectical relationship between God's grace and the world. The absence of the sense of this vital relationship is a symptom of the lack of openness to the Spirit, and thus of agape love, which prevents the church from playing its rightful part in the whole interaction. Once the church participates more fully in the death and risen life of its Head, that whole work of witness, in word, deed and being, which is mission, becomes, as in the NT church, more of a gift exchange, set in a context of friendship and genuine caring. Then it can be seen that Christ on his cross indeed grapples with the issues confronting all human beings and societies and their shifting faiths and cultures now as then. The truest exponents of mission are people in the Spirit committed, with Christ, to this grappling, people profoundly grasped by his divinely sharp yet wounded love, which is fully 'in the world' but yet never 'of it'.

Towards integral mission

Gerald H. Anderson and Thomas F. Stransky (eds), *Mission Trends*, nos. 1–5, 1961; D. J. Bosch, *Witness of the World – The Christian Mission in Theological Perspective*, 1980; Lesslie Newbigin, *The Open Secret: Sketches for a Missionary Theology*, 1978; SEDOS, *Foundation of Mission Theology*, 1972; D. Senior and C. Stuhlmueller, *The Biblical Foundations for Mission*, 1983; J. Verkuyl, *Contemporary Missiology: An Introduction*, 1976; Max Warren, *I Believe in the Great Commission*, 1976.

New perspectives from the Third World

Vincent J. Donovan, *Christianity Rediscovered – An Epistle from the Masai*, 1982; Raymond Fung (ed), *Households of God on China's Soil*, 1982; Joseph Healey, *The Fifth Gospel*, 1981; Marie Louise Martin, *Kimbangu – An African Prophet and his Church*, 1975; Ayako Miura, *The Wind is Howling*, 1976. *Evangelical Theology of Mission*: Orlando E. Costas, *The Church and its Mission – A Shattering Critique from the Third World*, 1974; Donald McGavran, *Understanding Church Growth*, 1970; John Stott, *Christian Mission in the Modern World*, 1975; Peter Wagner, *Church Growth and the Whole Gospel*, 1980.

Christian mission in a world of many faiths
David Brown, *All Their Splendour*, 1982;
Kenneth Cragg, *The Christian and Other
Religion*, 1977; John Hick, *The Second
Christianity*, 1983; Leslie Howard, *The
Expansion of God*, 1981; H. Kraemer, *Re-
ligion and the Christian Faith*, 1956; Ninian
Smart, *Beyond Ideology*, 1982; C. S. Song,
The Compassionate God, 1982.

SIMON BARRINGTON-WARD

Mithraism

Mithras was a Persian sun-god, whose cult
invaded the Greek-speaking world in the
centuries before Christ and eventually
reached Rome a decade or two after Christianity had arrived there. It was popular
with the Roman army, and hence the mem-
orials of Mithraism may still be seen as far
north as Hadrian's Wall. Its sacramental
system had sufficient in common with the
Christian rites and ceremonies for Tertullian to be driven to argue that they were
plagiarized versions of the Christian sacraments, while in more recent times some *religionsgeschichtliche** scholars, actuated by
motives precisely opposite to those of Tertullian, claimed that Mithraism was one of
the oriental mystery-religions* from which
early Catholicism had borrowed several
features of its cultus. According to the cult-
legend of Mithraism Mithras had overcome
and sacrificed the bull from which all living
creatures were descended. The *taurobolium*,
or bath of bull's blood, used in the initiation-
rites of various mystery-religions (especially
Attis and Cybele), can be shown to have any
connection with Christian baptism only by
means of the more eccentric ingenuities of
scholarship.

L. Patterson, *Mithraism and Christianity*,
1921; W. J. Phythian Adams, *Mithraism*,
1915.

ALAN RICHARDSON

Modalism

Modalism is one of the extreme limits of the
doctrine of the Trinity* emphasizing the
unity of the Trinity at the expense of the
plurality. The term is derived from the fact
that the three Persons are assigned the status
of modes or manifestations of the one divine
being: the one God is substantial, the three
differentiations adjectival. Its aim was to
preserve monotheism* and assert the unity of

Father and Son in redemption; its defect was
its undermining of the doctrine of God's
immutability.

Modalism was an Asiatic movement
(Noetus of Smyrna), from there transferred
to Rome where it made a determined
attempt to capture the church (Noetus,
Epigonus, Cleomenes, Callistus). It spread
to Africa where Praxeas was opposed by
Tertullian and to Libya (Sabellius). Basil
still regarded Modalism as theologically
dangerous in the second half of the fourth
century.

It made a strong appeal to the church's
instinctive monotheism and basic religious
concerns. It turned into a theological theory
early religious forms of expressing the unity
of the Father and the Son in the work of
redemption (Ignatius 'the passion of my
God'). It sought to provide within the limits
of a single theory both for the unity of God
and the divinity of Christ, two facts which
the church found it difficult to hold together.
From the inference that the Father suffered
as the Son (Noetus) is derived the nickname
Patripassian*. Early Modalists phrased
their doctrine in a twofold manner (Father
and Son) in line with much contemporary
church thinking (*see* **Binitarianism**), but
on their premises three modes presented
no more difficulty than two. Sabellius introduced this, possibly with other refine-
ments, into the doctrine in the third
century.

Tertullian's charge that modalism offered
'a turncoat Deity' (*Deum esse verspipiellem*)
and Basil's more sophisticated criticism that
the modalist God 'metamorphosed himself
to meet the changing needs to the world'
are both relevant. Modalism offered a
Trinity of manifestation, not even a Trinity of economy, still less a Trinity of
being.

H. E. W. TURNER

Model

The word was introduced into theology
from the language of scientific theory and
given wide circulation by I. T. Ramsey. A
scientific model is more systematized than
an analogy* and less far-reaching in its
scope than a paradigm*. It is an aid to
theorizing about some phenomenon under
investigation in terms of some simpler
system whose properties are already known.
Bohr's model of the atom as a miniature

solar system is a classic example. Like all successful models, it not only allowed the internal structure of the atom to be pictured, but also suggested further hypotheses about its behaviour and the relationship between its parts. A model need not necessarily be concrete or picturable. Mathematical models arc much sought after for their precision and internal coherence, but they may be less fertile than cruder realistic models in providing clues for new hypotheses and, because of their very abstractness and generality, less easy to falsify. In some theories models are indispensable. The genetic code, for example, relies as a concept on the analogy with human codes and languages, and there is in fact no other suitable way of describing how genes are believed to do their work.

The construction of appropriate models is thus an important part of scientific thinking. It generates the risk, though, that successful models may be identified with reality. The so-called 'billiard-ball universe' in which everything was explained in terms of mechanical interactions between particles moving on determined courses, was a typical example of this kind of mistake. Newtonian mechanics had been so successful in its own field that it was treated as the ideal model in all other fields as well, and hence as the ultimate clue to the nature of things.

The theological use of models takes their limitation as descriptions of reality as its starting point. Theological statements about God are necessarily made in terms of models derived from ordinary human experience which then, in Ramsey's terminology, have to be revealed as inadequate by means of 'qualifiers'. God is good, but not merely good as human beings understand goodness; he is 'infinitely good'. The word 'infinitely' qualifies 'good' to the point at which the model of goodness breaks down, leading to what Ramsey referred to as 'a disclosure', in which the mysterious reality of God is glimpsed, even if it cannot be articulated.

It will be seen that this use of the word 'model' is significantly different from its use in a scientific context, though it is possible to discern a faint analogy between Ramsey's process of disclosure and the fertility of a scientific model in disclosing new aspects of a phenomenon. The key resemblance, however, is that both theological and scientific models are distinct from the realities which they attempt, inadequately, to describe. Beyond this, the common use of the word should not be pressed too far.

Christian theology already has a well-developed doctrine of analogy which does essentially the same work as the language of 'models'. Furthermore, recent emphasis on 'stories' as the main content of revelation (see **Narrative Theology**) makes the use of the word 'model' appear slightly strained. There may be a use for it, however, as when different understandings of the same phenomenon, e.g. different 'models' of the church, are compared with one another. The word underlines the exploratory element in doctrinal formulations.

I. G. Barbour, *Myths, Models and Paradigms*, 1974; I. T. Ramsey, *Models and Mystery*, 1964.

JOHN HABGOOD

Modernism

This was the term employed by Pope Pius X and his senior curial advisers in their attempt to identify, describe and condemn certain liberal, anti-scholastic, and historico-critical forms of thought occurring in the Roman Catholic Church between *c.* 1890 and 1910. The term has thus for more than half a century been inescapably bound up with the condemnation of 1907. This circumstance continues to pose problems of definition for scholars anxious to achieve a more detached and comprehensive view of Modernism than that provided by the Roman documents which condemned it.

The Modernists were a heterogeneous and geographically dispersed group of RC scholars who appreciated the need for their church to come to terms with scientific, critical and historical developments in the post-Enlightenment world. Their leading spirits were to be found mainly in France, England, Italy and Germany. Modernism was less a school of thought than a shared liberal and anti-scholastic attitude to philosophy, theology, history and church order. It never possessed the unity and cohesion of purpose attributed to it by its ecclesiastical opponents. The Modernists in fact differed, often sharply, among themselves.

Although biblical criticism, church history and the history of religions all played a significant part in the eventual drama, the most contentious issues were philosophical. All the Modernists expressed radical dissatisfaction with the Neo-scholasticism which provided R C orthodoxy with much of its conceptual structure and apologetical methodology. Furthermore they were aware of the critical damage done to essentialist metaphysics and epistemology (and consequently to fundamental theology) by the Kantian critique.

It was in the sphere of fundamental theology* (then largely identified with apologetics) that the divergence between the Modernists and the Neo-scholastics was most apparent. Maurice Blondel (1861–1949) pioneered the 'method of immanence' which took its point of departure from human experience and ascended thence through 'the philosophy of insufficiency' to the 'insufficiency of philosophy' – a process which, according to Blondel, laid the enquirer open to the claims of Christian revelation. Blondel gave this internal dimension an apologetical prominence which conflicted with the 'extrinsicism' of Neo-scholastic apologetic. Lucien Laberthonnière (1860–1932), developed this Blondelian method of immanence into a theory of 'moral dogmatism', which expounded the moral dimension of religious affirmation.

Although the publication of Blondel's book *L'Action* in 1893 can be taken as initiating the Modernist challenge, Alfred Loisy's *L'Évangile et L'Église* (1902) is usually seen as Modernism's most representative text. Loisy (1857–1940) has been called 'the Father of Catholic Modernism' and was undoubtedly the author principally envisaged in its condemnation. Though primarily a biblical scholar, Loisy in fact operated from a rudimentary philosophical position which regarded truth as essentially contextual and therefore changeable. His dynamic epistemology led him to challenge both the liberal Protestantism of Adolf von Harnack and the scholastic essentialism of Roman theology.

This double antagonism, which puzzled many liberal Protestant and Anglican contemporaries, raises the important question of the relationship between liberal Protestantism and Catholic Modernism. The relationship was a subtle blend of acceptance and rejection. The challenge faced by each was similar, viz., the altered consciousness of educated post-Enlightenment man and the consequent realization that Christian theology must take critical stock of this altered consciousness. Where liberal Protestantism was concerned principally with Christian origins and sources, the Modernists generally addressed themselves to the dynamic process whereby Christianity has developed in history. Loisy took issue with Harnack's conception of a changeless 'essence' of Christianity and depicted the church as the necessary historical extension of the gospel.

Dissatisfaction with both liberal Protestantism and Catholic scholasticism is prominent in the writings of the Anglo-Irish Jesuit, George Tyrrell (1861–1909), who emphasized the experiential character of primary revelation and the symbolic character of subsequent dogmatic statements. Edouard Le Roy (1870–1954), a disciple of Henri Bergson, attacked the prevailing R C view that dogma* is an integral structure of extrinsically imposed and interconnected truths demanding intellectual assent from the believer. Dogmas, according to Le Roy, have a practical meaning: they can be understood only from the inner experience of living them.

Friedrich von Hügel (1852–1925), who was competent in biblical, historical and philosophical scholarship, gave, by his indefatigable letter-writing, some sort of coherence to an otherwise disparate group of liberal Catholic scholars.

Disparity of purpose is particularly evident in Italy, where Modernism merged with the campaign for Christian Democracy in the north of the country, while the Roman radicals, led by Ernesto Buonaiuti (1881–1946), addressed themselves to purely theological, biblical and philosophical matters.

Although several German Catholic scholars can be properly described as Modernists, Germany was not a major theatre in the drama which unfolded and reached its climax during the first decade of the twentieth century. The German Catholic bishops felt able to congratulate themselves on the absence of a German Modernist challenge.

The condemnation of Modernism took the form of a Decree of the Holy Office, *Lamentabili sane exitu* (3 July 1907), and an Encyclical Letter of Pope Pius X, *Pascendi dominici gregis* (8 September 1907). The Encyclical, together with the *Motu Proprio,*

Sacrorum antistitum (1 September 1910), prescribed swingeing measures for the extirpation of Modernism root and branch from the church. Vigilance committees were to be set up in every diocese and a system of draconian censorship operated both regionally and centrally. An Oath against Modernism, prescribed by *Sacrorum antistitum*, had to be taken by office-holders in the church.

Although the severity of these measures was considerably mitigated with the passage of time, 'Modernism' remained a term which could be invoked against liberal or non-scholastic initiatives in the R C Church during the half-century which followed the condemnation of 1907. The Second Vatican Council marked the end of the anti-Modernist period. Much for which the Modernists had campaigned was either incorporated in the conciliar documents or facilitated by the new climate created by the council.

G. Daly, *Transcendence and Immanence: A Study in Catholic Modernism and Integralism*, 1980; R. Haight, 'The Unfolding of Modernism in France: Blondel, Laberthonnière, Le Roy', *Theological Studies*, 35, 1974, pp. 632–66; T. M. Loome, *Liberal Catholicism, Reform Catholicism, Modernism*, 1979; E. Poulat, *Histoire, dogme et critique dans la crise moderniste*, 1979; A. R. Vidler, *A Variety of Catholic Modernists*, 1970.

G. DALY

Modes of Being

The phrase was introduced into theology by Basil (*see* **Cappadocian Fathers**) in contrast to 'modes of revelation' which he used to describe modalism*. It is normally used in connection with the characteristic particularities of the three Persons (*see* **Ingeneracy**; **Generation**; **Procession**) to express the internal relations within the Trinity*. The transition to the meaning 'mode of existence', the characteristic style of being God the Father, the Son and the Spirit was an easy one. It is contrasted with *ousia* by Amphilochius of Iconium and combined with (and therefore not identical with) *hypostasis** by Maximus the Confessor. It is a corollary of but not a substitute for *hypostasis*.

Karl Barth revived the phrase in his definition of Person as mode of being (*Seinswesen*) but with a different emphasis. Both Basil and Barth reject the modalist interpretation but, while Basil stresses the full, objective and independent status of the hypostases, using the phrase to describe their relations, Barth seems anxious to avoid the use of Person as unduly tritheistic and to substitute 'modes of being' as a weaker equivalent.

H. E. W. TURNER

Monarchianism

The term is used to describe two trinitarian heresies of the second and third centuries which took as their starting point the unity of God. The word derives from the Greek word *monarchia*, the sole rule of God or one sole originating principle in God. The formula 'monarchy in triad' is an early expression for unity in Trinity. Outside trinitarian contexts it expressed Christian monotheism against gnostic* or Marcionite* dualism*. Within the doctrine of the Trinity it could refer either to a strong concentration on the unity of God or to the derivation of the whole Godhead from the Father as its origin or as the fount of deity. The former harmonizes with a monist starting point; the latter, as in Origen and the Cappadocians*, is compatible with pluralism.

Its application to the two heresies arises from the assumption that their motivation was a concern to protect the monotheism of the Bible in the face of christological claims. 1. Dynamic monarchianism was held by the two Theodoti, Artemon (or Artemas) and possibly Paul of Samosata. These held that the divine rested upon the man Jesus as a power (*dynamis*), a view referred to as Psilanthropism (*psilos anthropos* = mere man) in the ancient sources, adoptionism* being an alternative modern description. Whether its motivation was initially monarchian is doubtful. Paul of Samosata probably taught a combination of adoptionist and modalist tenets. 2. Modalist monarchianism (Noetus, Praxeas, Sabellius) certainly has a monarchian character. It started from the unity of God and reduced the plurality to the status of modes.

See **Modalism**; **Patripassianism**; **Sabellianism**; **Trinity**.

J. N. D. Kelly, *Early Christian Doctrines*, 1958, pp. 115–23.

H. E. W. TURNER/FRANCES YOUNG

Monastic Theology

A type of Christian ascetic life can be traced in some form in the early church; this took on distinctive monastic forms in the fourth century in Egypt, Syria and Palestine, and spread to the West, most of all by the use of the *Rule of St Benedict*. The theology implicit in this way of life was first articulated by Evagrius Ponticus and John Cassian who related the ascetic * experience of the monks to the fundamental themes of Christianity in terms of the cross and resurrection of Christ. While there is no distinctive 'school' of theology to which all monks adhere, it is a way of life dependent upon a certain theological approach to Christian truth, an approach which is properly called the 'monastic tradition'.

This tradition depends upon the fact that 'God was in Christ reconciling the world unto himself' (II Cor. 2, 5) and the assimilation of this fact to each person. The monk is a baptized Christian who makes his whole life a detailed and specific response to the gospel to the exclusion of all other interests and responsibilities. His aim is to receive Christ in the centre of his being, by the power of the Spirit, to act in him for the redemption of creation. This therefore demands a radical and visible break with the 'world' in order to enter into the eternal moment of the Cross of Christ and to be made thereby into the New Adam. All monastic practices thereafter are directed to this theological end. Basic to this way of baptismal life is continuous meditation on the scriptures, both in solitude and in the corporate worship of the liturgy. Monastic service flows from this central work of the monk, so that his pursuit of the first commandment to love God becomes also his fulfilment of the second, to love the neighbour whether through prayer or service.

The theology of the monastic life follows simple and basic Christian lines as a special form of baptismal commitment. However, monks have also made contributions to the discussion of theology in various ways; this has usually been distinguished from the academic and scholastic style of theology by a concern with *sapientia* rather than *scientia*, with a practical experience of God through prayer and meditation on the scriptures rather than the speculation of the intellect alone.

The dangers of this way of life from the point of view of Christian orthodoxy have often been demonstrated. It can become a way of salvation by works alone; it can become an individual and personal search for salvation which has less than the full rigour of Christian doctrine to support it; above all, it can become a dualistic theology, with a rejection of matter implicit in its renunciations, which leads to a perfectionism, in which the monastic way of life is a higher and more perfect Christian way, restricted to a few. The conversion of the monk is not, however, meant to imply a rejection of the material world; it emphasizes rather the sacramental character of the created order, and its redemption by Christ through those who are in him.

While monastic life is common to most of the major religions, in Christianity it takes its specific form from the basic doctrines of Christian theology and subordinates the ascetic practices of monasticism to the Christian revelation. It is therefore in the light of baptismal and eucharistic theology that the theology of Christian monasticism is most properly understood.

L. Bouyer, *The Meaning of the Monastic Life*, 1955; Columba Marmion, *Christ the Ideal of the Monk*, 1926; Thomas Merton, *The Climate of Monastic Prayer*, 1969; *Contemplation in a World of Action*, 1971; C. J. Peifer, *Monastic Spirituality*, 1966; *Consider your Call, a Theology of the Monastic Life Today*, 1980; *La Théologie de le Vie Monastique: études sur la tradition patristique*, 1961.

BENEDICTA WARD

Monism

This term was introduced by the German philosopher Christian Wolff (1679–1754) to refer to systems of thought emphasizing the unity rather than the diversity of the world and of our experience. It has come since then to be used as well of theories of the human person which insist that it is a single thing rather than a composite of body, soul, spirit or other parts. Monism contrasts with both dualism * and pluralism * because it refuses to surrender its intuitive perception of a common element in things, though monisms differ widely as to whether that element is being, idea, soul, substance or material reality.

Christianity's roots in the theology of the OT were arguably monistic in those aspects of biblical belief that focussed on the immediate historical presence and action of God as a superior though not totally dissimilar being to humankind and where human life was essentially limited to the span between birth and death. There are hints in later OT literature of belief in a transcendent, more metaphysical deity and in personal continuance after death, but only the influences of Hellenistic religion and later Greek philosophy beginning with the NT period would successfully establish as Christian the now familiar distinctions between body and soul, visible and invisible worlds, present life and after life, and contingent and non-contingent being.

Despite the triumph of Neoplatonism*, perhaps through the social agency of late-third-century Egyptian monastic piety, in canonizing both divine transcendence and the distinction between body and soul into Christian orthodoxy, monistic leanings have appeared regularly throughout the history of Christian theology. So-called Modalists* of the early third century, for instance, had preferred a unitary Godhead without personal distinctions to the more difficult trinitarian* doctrine. Christological* controversies of the fourth and fifth centuries concentrated in great measure on whether the divinity and the humanity of Christ should be distinguished from one another (monophysitism*), as also his divine and human wills (monotheletism*). Echoes of disbelief in the dividedness of the ordinary human will are also discernible in the Pelagianism* battled by Augustine. The alleged pantheism* of John Scotus Eriugena (c. 810–877) was an early forerunner to that of Benedict Spinoza (1632–1677), whose phrase *deus sive natura* (God, that is, nature) became the classic expression of monistic pantheism.

The modern world has experienced a resurgence of monism in several forms, ranging from an idealistic variety that reduces the diversity of physical reality to one-dimensional ideal categories of knowledge (Kant) to certain kinds of materialism*. The most important of these latter is that of Ernst Heinrich Haeckel (1834–1919), whose belief in the unity of all things in the evolution of a single universal substance was communicated to the English-speaking world by Paul Carus (1852–1919), the founder of the still active philosophical journal *The Monist*.

Perhaps the most challenging instance of a monist view today is found in contemporary behaviourist psychology, which categorically excludes classic Christian beliefs in a duality of body and soul for a unitary explanation of human behaviour. The latest theological recurrence of monism is thought by some to be seen in process theology*, particularly in Alfred North Whitehead's belief that there is one ultimate reality actualizing itself in all the entities we can know or think, a doctrine characterized by some as panentheism*.

R. Bultmann, *Primitive Christianity in its Contemporary Setting*, ET 1956; John B. Cobb, Jr, *God and the World*, 1969; E. H. Haeckel, *The Riddle of the Universe*, ET 1899; John the Scot, *Periphyseon on the Division of Nature*, ET 1976; Benedict (Baruch) Spinoza, *Ethics*, 1675, pt 1, Props. xiv–xv; A. N. Whitehead, *Science and the Modern World*, 1926.

JAMES J. HEANEY

Monoenergism

A theological position closely tied to the monothelete controversy which was addressed by the Sixth Ecumenical Council (Constantinople: 680–1). An outgrowth of monophysitism*, monotheletism held that the divine and human natures of Christ were so closely bonded, that there was only one will (*thelēsis*) in the person of Jesus Christ. The monoenergistic position is first attributed to Severus, who taught 'one is the agent and one is the activity (*energeia*)'. Often, the terms 'energy' and 'will' (*thelēsis*) are treated as synonyms. In general discussions of monophysitism and Chalcedonian christology a distinction of the terms is not always necessary. But the two terms are distinguishable as to their referent. Both Maximus the Confessor and John of Damascus use the term 'energy' to designate the activity appropriate and fitting to each nature. Thus, the divine nature and the human nature in Christ have their proper and distinct energies. However, the human nature, having been created in accordance to the 'image and likeness of God', incorporated in its own nature the requirement to be in communion and harmony with the divine nature. When the energies (activities) of a given nature are expressed in an uncoerced, harmonious fashion and in a full and appropriate manner, freedom is said to exist. However, each concrete hypostasis (person) also is held to have a self-determining ability known as the 'gnomic will' which may act either in accordance to one's nature or against it. In this sense monothelitism held that Jesus Christ had only one self-determining will in the hypostasis of the person; while monoenergism held that Jesus Christ had only one energy appropriate to the natures. The Sixth Ecumenical Council rejected both positions, holding that there were two energies: a divine energy appropriate to the divine nature and a human energy appropriate to the human nature, which, though acting in full concert, clearly preserved the integrity of the two natures of Christ. This required condemnation of monoenergism as heretical.

See also **Christology.**

John of Damascus, *De Fide Orthodoxa* II, xxiii, xxiv; III, xiii, xiv; John Meyendorff, *Byzantine Theology: Historical Trends and Doctrinal Themes*, 1974, ch. 2.

S. HARAKAS

Monophysitism

The teaching that there was one single nature* in the incarnate Christ. Associated with Eutyches (died *c.* 454) and condemned at Chalcedon, the position was one line of development in Alexandrian* Christianity. As often, political and diplomatic as well as theological considerations determined the course of events.

S. L. Greenslade, *Schism in the Early Church*, ²1964.

GEORGE NEWLANDS

Monotheism

The term that has been used to describe the belief that only one God exists, who is the creator and ground of all that is. It describes the object of faith of Judaism, Christianity and Islam, and represents a foremost feature of the religious ideology presented and presupposed in the Bible. In its essential character the revelation contained in the Bible of the ultimate source and ground of reality has been defined as 'ethical mono-

theism'. Within this framework such an ethical monotheism has conceived of its object as a single personal supreme being, and the ancient Israelite name for God, probably Yahweh, has been broadened since biblical times into the titular description LORD. Following the publication of Hume's *The Natural History of Religion* in 1757, biblical scholars have come to recognize a process of development in the emergence of a monotheistic faith in the Bible, which has sometimes been described as a progressive revelation* of God. This recognizes its movement through a number of stages, primarily consisting of animism* and polytheism*, leading ultimately to monotheism. Various other intermediate stages have at times been suggested, and in particular the earliest Israelite stage of the worship of Yahweh from the time of Moses has sometimes been described as henotheism*.

Recent anthropological studies have increasingly questioned the rightness of this emphasis upon an ideological development in antiquity, with monotheism forming a culminating end-point. Rather, attention has been drawn to the contrasts implicit in the antithesis of polytheism with monotheism, with emphasis on the fact that such terms are essentially definable only in relation to each other. From a historical perspective the religious developments of the ancient Near East show both unifying and diversifying tendencies in the understanding of the divine realm, and this also appears to have been more widely true among the early religions of mankind.

From the biblical standpoint this awareness of the 'One' and the 'Many' in the understanding of deity has proved valuable in explaining the many contrasting features of the Israelite awareness of God, together with its background in the ancient Near East. The contention that the earliest phases of man's religion witness to a primitive monotheism, or monotheistic tendency (animism), has largely been abandoned in recent study. Evidence exists, however, of early monotheistic tendencies, both in ancient Egypt (Akhnaton) and in Mesopotamia. In Babylonian religion the veneration for the deity Marduk as 'King', and in the Canaanite sphere the regard for El as 'Father of the gods', have shown the widespread presence of unifying, monotheistic, tendencies in religion, without attaining to true monotheism in denying the existence of other gods.

Doubts remain as to the extent of the influence of any of these developments upon the Israelite regard for Yahweh as the one supreme deity. The superiority of one deity to all others has led W. F. Albright to trace monotheism back to the time of Abraham, whilst greater plausibility exists for the contention that the work of Moses initiated what H. H. Rowley has described as 'incipient monotheism'. Yet, in the stricter sense in which monotheism denies the reality and existence of other gods, such a faith did not explicitly appear in Israel until the sixth century BC (cf. Isa. 41.21–24; 43.10–13; 44.8, etc.). It was based upon a sense of the superiority of Yahweh to all other gods, which appeared much earlier (C. J. Labuschagne). The movement therefore appears largely to have been one in which the relative unimportance of other deities was pressed into a denial that they possessed any reality at all.

Yet monotheism could be interpreted with a good deal of ambivalence, on the one hand leading to a categorical denial that any truth was to be accorded to the non-Israelite religious traditions. Against this, a more inclusive approach remained possible in which some validity was accorded to these non-biblical traditions, with the claim that God had revealed himself in other ways through them (cf. Mal. 1.11), or was imperfectly understood within them (cf. Acts 17.23–28; Rom. 1.18–23). Furthermore, in Judaism and later in Christianity, the sense of diversity and an awareness of the 'many' in the divine order led to a widespread popularity of the belief in angels and other intermediary beings who were held to be not fully divine. For a period in Judaism the insistence on a very forcefully held monotheism encouraged the concern with a mystical interest in intermediary powers of the divine world. Attempts to reconcile the multiplicity of human religious traditions with the singleness of a pure monotheistic faith were also undertaken by resort to concepts of Spirit and Wisdom (cf. Wisdom 13.1ff. and the writings of Philo). The emergence of the Christian doctrine of the Trinity * was firmly based upon the central affirmations of monotheism, and was in no way an attempt to counter them, save in a few fringe movements.

W. F. Albright, *From the Stone Age to Christianity*, ²1953; O. Keel, *Monotheismus im Alten Israel und seiner Umwelt*, 1980; C. J. Labuschagne, *The Incomparability of Yahweh in the Old Testament*, 1966; H. H. Rowley, *The Faith of Israel*, 1956; 'Moses and Monotheism', in *From Moses to Qumran*, 1963, pp. 35–66.

RONALD CLEMENTS

Monothelitism

The opinion that there was only one will in the incarnate Christ. A development of the Monophysite * position, it was condemned by the Council of Constantinople in 680.

J. N. D. Kelly, *Early Christian Doctrines*, ³1965.

GEORGE NEWLANDS

Montanism

Montanism was a fervent apocalypticist movement of a type which has become familiar in more recent ages of the church. It looked for the immediate fulfilment of the prophecy concerning the pouring out of the Spirit in the last days (Joel 2.28–32; cf. Acts 2.16–21) and it regarded the utterances of its own prophets and prophetesses as the first instalment of this consummation. Its name is derived from Montanus, who began his revivalist preaching in Phrygia in the latter half of the second century. It was condemned by Pope Zephyrinus before the end of that century, but by this time it had spread to various churches, including the African, where it won a notable convert in Tertullian. Ascetic in character, it upbraided the churches for their laxity and lack of zeal.

ALAN RICHARDSON

Moral Theology

A term most used by Roman Catholics and Anglicans for the study of ethics and ethical questions in the light of Christian self-understanding. (The terms Christian Ethics or Christian Social Ethics are common among other contemporary Christians.) From its beginnings, moral theology has normally not been a one-rubric, fideistic approach to moral questions but has employed a variety of approaches, biblical, traditional and philosophical, in its quest for moral truth.

The history of moral theology begins with

the scriptures. The Christian scriptures reveal certain elements of a systematic moral theology. First, they are based on the proclamation of the reign of God in our midst (Mark 1.15) and the revelational vision of a coming 'new heaven and a new earth' (Rev. 21.1–2). This is foundational. The Christian scriptures also give central importance to Jesus as the moral symbol of God. We must love as Jesus loved to fulfil the law (John 13.34–45). Loving as Jesus loved implicates us in justice, prophecy and reconciliation which culminate in joy, hopefulness and *shalom*.

The scriptural moral theology did not eschew specifics of conduct. Some activities befit the reign of God, and others do not. 'Idolatry, sorcery, enmity, strife, jealousy, carousing, and the like' are condemned; the praised virtues are 'love, joy, peace, patience, kindness, goodness, faithfulness, gentleness, and self-control' (Gal. 5.19–24). Extensive lists of virtues and vices can be garnered from the pages of the Christian biblical writings. These writings also adapt freely from non-Christian sources. Since Christians were heirs to the Hebrew theology of the cosmic lordship of Yahweh, they could, with consistency, welcome insights from any source, and they often did.

Moral theology in the Fathers did not attempt to present complete systems of moral teaching. Wholistic tracts would not appear until the thirteenth century. The Fathers, however, did not just repeat scripture. Beginning with the Didache, composed at the end of the first century, we find a charting out of the way of good and the way of evil, foreshadowing again later moral theology's concern with lists of virtues and catalogues of sins. The Fathers often wrote with pastoral concern in a pastoral vein, speaking to particular issues of the day. They did not hesitate to speak on the duties of political leadership, for political power too must serve God's purposes.

The Fathers illustrate, too, that moral theology will take many forms as its seeks to bring its evangelical impetus into culture. Reflecting a sense of the universal relevance of Christianity, they enlisted 'pagan' wisdom and sought out the 'seeds of the Logos *' wherever they could be found. We see this in a notable and remarkably systematized way in the writings of Clement of Alexandria and Origen in the third century.

Ambrose and Augustine also could readily baptize the cardinal virtues of Plato and Aristotle. Indeed, with very little originality, Ambrose could take the *De Officiis* of Cicero and construct his own similarly entitled work. He does not, however, simply take instruction from Cicero, but, with an eye to the Gospel tradition, he excludes certain things from his treatment of justice such as 'revenge' and 'private property'. The patristic dialogue with the surrounding culture maintained a critical edge.

Clearly, Augustine was the moral theologian of greatest impact among the fathers. It can be argued that speculative moral theology was born with him. His authority resonates throughout Christian history on such questions as the notion of God as the sovereign good, the eternal law, the nature of sin, the role of the passions in moral experience, the definitions of virtue and sin, the necessity of faith in Jesus Christ, the efficacy of prayer, etc. On special issues of moral theology, such as lying, war, suicide, and private property, Augustine also became an authority for subsequent generations.

As with any great thinker, not all of Augustine's influence was benign. On the subject of war, Augustine departed too radically from the peace tradition of Christians. While he would still not allow a private citizen to kill in self-defence, he did concede much warring power to Caesar. The Christian soldiers under Julian 'were, for the sake of their everlasting Master, submissive to the temporal master' (*Enarrationes in Psalmos*, cxxiv, 7). Surrender of personal responsibility to government and holy war can be seen to be foreshadowed here.

Augustine also reflected a certain pessimism and negativity towards sexuality and towards women particularly. His personal experiences, recounted in his *Confessions*, did not bequeath him a positive attitude towards human sexuality. Given his massive influence, this negativity is found in much subsequent moral theology of sex.

The period from 600 to 1200 is generally conceded to be the historical nadir of moral theology. The period was dominated by the 'penitential books'. These books, which originated in Ireland then spread across the continent, were casuistry run amok. Interminable species of sin were described for which penances were parcelled out. A passion for hairsplitting and legalistic dissection was common, as when some books distinguished at least twenty forms of homicide, each deserving a distinct kind of penance. Though creativity was largely in abeyance during this period of moral theology, the penitential books did insinuate a new kind of flexibility into the penitential discipline of the church and thus had some benign influence. On the negative side, they reinforced the penchant for juridical bickerings that have marked moral theology, early and late. Since Tertullian, a stern juridical approach to salvation in terms of punishment and debt due to sin was reflected in significant papal teaching in Innocent I, Leo I, Gelasius and Gregory I. In the penitential books, this harsh tradition was entrenched. The books also confirmed a tendency to focus too exclusively on act-analysis. They contributed further to the separation of moral theology from scripture and from what later would be called dogmatic and mystical theology.

In the twelfth century, Peter the Lombard produced the *Liber Sententiarum*, which was to dominate the theological scene for four centuries. The work treated moral theology only incidentally, and so, while the *Sentences* held centre stage, moral theology was slighted. It is to Peter's credit, however, that the assumption of his work was that moral and dogmatic considerations were inextricably linked. The Franciscan school in the thirteenth century expanded the systematic treatment of moral theology, especially in the work of Alexander of Hales, John Duns Scotus, and Bonaventure. It was Thomas Aquinas, however, who gave to theology a sense of the centrality of moral choice. Building upon all that went before, but especially upon the work of Augustine and Aristotle, Aquinas, in the second part of his *Summa*, became the founder of systematic moral theology in the modern sense. Persons come from God and by grace and moral choice, they return to God.

Synthesis of the work of Aquinas is not patient of quick summation. Notable and often neglected in modern references to Thomas, however, are the following teachings: the New Law is not something written but is rather the grace of the Holy Spirit which is poured into the hearts of the faithful. The Gospels and the teachings of church officials and theologians are all 'secondary'

to the 'primary' illumining presence of the Spirit of God (*ST* I, II q. 106 a. 1). The implications of this for claims of infallibility at the 'secondary' level are not slight. Also, Aquinas' realistic ethical epistemology found room for cognitive affect and avoided 'the intellectualistic fallacy'. His treatment of the moral virtues, faith, knowledge by way of connaturality, and delight postulate an affective component in moral knowing. In some parts of his writings, Aquinas acknowledges the contextual aspects of ethical inquiry. 'Human actions are good or bad according to their circumstances' (*ST* I, II, q. 18, a. 3). He taught too that very generic moral principles are exceptionless, but that the many specific and practical moral principles are open to exceptions. The more you descend into the particularities of life, the more likely such exceptions are to appear (*ST* I, II q. 94, a. 4, a. 5). Aquinas also displayed modesty regarding ethical inquiry. Ethics, as a *scientia operativa*, does not enjoy simplicity or great certainty because of the multiplicity of contingencies it must bring into unified consideration (*In XII Libros Metaphysicorum*, I, I, lect. ii). Though he has often been only selectively honoured, his teaching achieved official standing in the R C Church. *The Code of Canon Law* directs that professors of theology should follow the 'method, teaching and principles of the Angelic Doctor, and treat these as sacred' (Canon 1366, no. 2).

The work of Aquinas did not, however, enjoy immediate success. During the fourteenth and fifteenth centuries it was the *Sentences* of Peter Lombard that held sway. Alongside the commentaries on the *Sentences*, there did appear the penitential summas which in some instances became rather systematic. That of St Antonine, which affords a broad picture of moral life in the fifteenth century, is most notable. With the sixteenth century, Aquinas' work began to return to favour and a development of moral theology ensued, particularly in Spain.

The seventeenth century witnessed another separation of moral from the rest of theology, and a concern for the work of the confessional returned. Spurred by the Council of Trent's * insistence on numbered and specified confession of sins, moral theology was consumed with questions of doubtful consciences and the direction of troubled penitents. Happily, however, a major development came out of this narrowed focus in the form of a moral system for dealing with ethical doubt called Probabilism. The long debate over the moral systems was, at root, concerned with the legitimacy of pluralism in matters moral. Probabilism triumphed among the competing systems which bore such names as Mitigated Tutiorism, Absolute Tutiorism, Compensationism, Probabiliorism, Equiprobabilism, and Laxism. The cardinal principle of probabilism was *lex dubia non obligat*: a doubtful law does not oblige as though it were certain. Thus, when a rigorous moral consensus was challenged by a liberal dissenting view, the liberal dissenting position could be followed in good conscience when it became 'solidly probable'. This could come about 'intrinsically' when the individual person discovered 'cogent though not necessarily conclusive' arguments for disagreeing with the reigning consensus. 'Extrinsic probability' was achieved by relying on 'five or six' moral theologians known for their 'prudence and learning', even though all other theologians disagreed and defended the rigorous position. Both intrinsic and extrinsic probability were based on insight, not on permission, and thus Probabilism legitimated dissent from 'official' R C teachings on moral matters. Modern pluralistic Catholicism has renewed its interest in the historical achievement of Probabilism.

It was in the seventeenth century too that the Church of England produced some notable moral theologians, such as Jeremy Taylor, R. Sanderson and J. Hall. The study of moral theology, however, was less emphasized in this tradition, though the work of K. E. Kirk in the twentieth century was to meet with considerable success.

The outstanding figure of the eighteenth century was Alphonsus Liguori, who combined piety, balance, and a prodigiously documented form of scholarship. His *Theologia Moralis* contained no fewer than 80,000 citations from more than 800 authors. The nineteenth century saw the dominance of the 'moral manuals' in the R C Church. These works, casuistic and unimaginative, became the basis for seminary moral theology up until the time of the Second Vatican Council. They embodied a static notion of natural law which became the basis for closely held negative moral absolutes. They were also juridical and individualistic in tone. Their treatment of justice was narrow and fixated upon the rights of the propertied. The Popes did considerably better than the manuals when, starting with Leo XIII, the problems of social and industrial upheavals became a major papal concern. Leo XIII also led in calling for a Thomistic revival.

The character of moral theology has changed radically since the Second Vatican Council. Protestant and Catholic scholars collaborate in what has become a thoroughly ecumenical moral theology. Differences no longer run along denominational lines; common interests now unite. The renewal of biblical studies and attention to social problems are newly prominent today. The rise of bioethics has enlivened moral theology and has led to more study of the linkage between science and formal ethics. Given the limiting analytical preoccupations of much British and American moral philosophy, moral theology, or Christian ethics, has become the major locus of philosophical ethics on a number of methodological issues. Liberation theology* in Latin America is now a font of enrichment in its blending of moral and dogmatic considerations and in its championing of social justice. The cause of justice and peace is assuming hegemonic importance among many contemporary moralists. Significantly, too, moral theology is no longer a clerical preserve. Increasingly, it moves from seminary to university and is now plied, for the first time in history, by women as well as by men. Moral theology is entering a new epoch. It is emerging as post-clerical, post-sectarian, and as newly open to dialogue with the modern world.

Charles Curran, *American Catholic Social Ethics*, 1982; George Wolfgang Forell, *History of Christian Ethics*, 1979; James M. Gustafson, *Protestant and Roman Catholic Ethics*, 1978; Edward LeRoy Long, Jr, *A Survey of Christian Ethics*, 1967; Daniel C. Maguire, *The Moral Choice*, 1979; Richard McCormick, *Notes on Moral Theology: 1965 Through 1980*, 1981; Stephen Charles Mott, *Biblical Ethics and Social Change*, 1982; Warren Reich (ed), *The Encyclopedia of Bioethics*, 1978; John Howard Yoder, *The Politics of Jesus*, 1972.

D A N I E L C. M A G U I R E

Mortal Sin

In Catholic thought a distinction has been made between mortal and venial* sins. A mortal sin is one that separates a person from God so that if one dies with a mortal sin unforgiven he or she receives eternal damnation*. The sacramental grace of the church provides forgiveness for mortal sins. Venial sins are either sins that are in themselves less serious or sins that, although mortal in nature, have been committed in passion or ignorance. Penance by the sinner can remove the guilt of venial sins and even after death such guilt can be removed in purgatory.

This is a point at which Luther and Calvin broke decisively with Catholic thought. They understood sin as basically unbelief and pride, that is, sin is the state in which a person lives separated from God. The problem of sin is the problem of the total orientation of one's life; a person either lives 'in sin' or 'in Christ'. Where sin is so seen, the distinction between greater and lesser sins becomes irrelevant. The cure for such sin can never be found in the sinner's penance but only through God's forgiving love welcoming the prodigals home.

See also **Guilt**.

WILLIAM HORDERN

Mystery

The meanings to be attached to the word depend upon whether one is considering it in its biblical or in its Hellenistic background. In Hellenistic mystery religions, the mystery is a secret rite or ritual, a kind of password, through the knowledge of which a person is initiated into the immortal life of one of the gods. In the biblical literature, however, the word 'mystery' is used in a distinctive way, for two main things. First, for the plan of God, the purpose of God in history, his eternal purpose and sovereignty; and second, for the thing or the situation which is the medium by which the secret plan of God is disclosed. It is with these meanings that the NT speaks of Christ as the mystery of God. By that is meant that he is the perfect, the unique medium by which the plan of God in history has been disclosed: Christ is the open secret of God, the open mystery of God.

In the Hellenistic tradition the mystic is the person who, having got possession of the secret ritual or the secret password, is thereby initiated into a new experience of oneness with the life of the god. In Christian mysticism there is no question of any secret ritual or password. The mystic is one who by his close attention to the mystery-situation, the particular person of Christ, for instance, realizes through this agency his oneness with the Father.

Odo Casel, *The Mystery and Christian Worship*, 1962; M. B. Foster, *Mystery and Philosophy*, 1957; A. Plé and others, *Mystery and Mysticism* (a symposium), 1956; Hugo Rahner, *Greek Myths and Christian Mystery*, 1963; P. Tillich, *Systematic Theology* I, 1953.

E. J. TINSLEY

Mystery religions

A term which relates to that form of religion which is associated particularly with the Hellenistic world from roughly about the time of the conquests of Alexander the Great onwards (latter part of the fourth century BC). These religions were enormously popular at the time of Christ, and it is easy to trace in the NT the influence of the vocabulary of these relgions. One could also point to such early Fathers as Clement of Alexandria and Origen as Christians who were willing to think of their religion as a greater and newer form of mystery religion.

The mystery religions were essentially religions of redemption, offering to those initiated into them release from the tragedies and limitations of human existence. This release was obtained by a process of initiation whereby, after long and arduous purifications, the initiate was taken up into the life of the god of the particular religion and thus attained immortality.

See also **Gnosticism**.

S. Angus, *The Mystery Religions and Christianity*, 1925; H. A. A. Kennedy, *St Paul and the Mystery Religions*, 1913.

E. J. TINSLEY

Mystical Theology

A term used in divergent ways within the Christian community. Its most familiar use is found in pre-Vatican II RC handbooks as a division of practical theology, as seen in the writings of Adolf Alfred Tanquerey. 'Moral theology' dealt with normal and 'minimum' acceptable behaviour for the

Christian life. 'Spiritual theology' dealt primarily with the ascetical way, including such things as prayer, fasting and discipline. It was understood as 'perfection'* in the Christian life. 'Mystical theology' served as a guide for spiritual directors which assisted them in evaluating the special religious experiences of those under their spiritual direction.

Eastern Christianity has also used the term. In the East, however, it tended to be used in a way which closely related the moral life and the experience of God by Christians with doctrinal and theological teaching. Two Eastern writers are particularly important in the development of mystical theology in the patristic tradition, Gregory of Nyssa (c. 335–394) and Pseudo-Dionysius (c. 500). Gregory used Neoplatonic* terms and approaches in explicating the Christian life, but his work is essentially Christian in that the crucial and major doctrinal emphases are solidly based on Christian revelation and Orthodox doctrine (*What is the Christian Name?*, *On Perfection*, *The Life of Moses*, *On the Beatitudes*). Central to his thought are the doctrines of the image of God which permits both a moral imitation of God and a spiritual communion with God. The mystical vision which finally permits the creature to 'step outside' one's self and freely (without coercion and exercise of will) to 'adhere to God' is a mystical ascent which occurs only after one has spiritually struggled (with the leading of divine grace) to overcome the passions present because of sin.

The Pseudo-Dionysian corpus (*Celestial Hierarchy*, *Ecclesiastical Hierarchy*, *The Divine Names* and *Mystical Theology*), though more heavily influenced by Neoplatonism, retains the same Eastern Christian doctrinal foundation which is based on 'image and likeness doctrine' and growth toward deification* (*theosis*). The writings of Gregory Palamas (fifteenth century) form an Eastern Christian summation and refinement of this tradition. Vladimir Lossky defines Eastern Christian mystical theology as 'a spirituality which expresses a doctrinal attitude'.

Recent Western studies in mystical theology tend to adopt the more holistic and doctrinal focus of the Eastern approach, leaving the practical analysis of religious experience to more clinical and psychological approaches.

J. Daniélou, *Platonisme et Théologie Mystique. Essai sur la Doctrine Spirituelle de Saint Grégoire de Nysse*, [2]1954; V. Lossky, *The Mystical Theology of the Eastern Church*, London, 1957; J. Moltmann, *Experiences of God*, ET 1980. pp. 55–80; A. A. Tanquerey, *Synopsis Theologiae Moralis et Pastorialis*, 3 vols, 1902–1904; *Précis de Théologie Ascetique et Mystique*, 1949; M. Viller and K. Rahner, *Aszese und Mystik in der Väterzeit*, 1939.

                                                    S. HARAKAS

Mysticism

Great care is required in defining the meaning of the term. A common tendency, especially in German reformed theology, has been to equate mysticism with Neoplatonism* (or Neoplatonism as popularized by Dionysius the Areopagite) and then to insist on the incompatibility of mysticism with the Bible and the Christian religion. Another common practice is to use the word 'mysticism' in such a way that it covers not only religious experience in general but all kinds of awareness of transcendental reality. The most satisfactory procedure is to examine accounts of mystical experience, and see if there is a common pattern. When this is done the main characteristics of mysticism seem to be: 1. there is a profound, compelling, unforgettable sense of union and unity; 2. the successive character of time is transcended in an awareness of simultaneity; 3. the experience is not felt to be a mere subjectivity; it is rather a disclosure, what Julian of Norwich called a 'showing', or what William James called a 'noetic' experience; 4. there is always a sense of enhancement of joy, exultation, a suffused sense of well-being; and 5. there is also an overwhelming sense of 'presence', of the utter nearness of the transcendent.

The early Christian use of the term 'mystical' suggests that mystical experience was always associated with something concrete and factual, with what was called 'the mystery'; which could be, for example, either the written words of scripture or the action of the liturgy. To see in them not only symbols but the reality symbolized was to have what has been called 'mystery-mindedness'. This is what the early Fathers of the church meant by 'mysticism': the 'sign', the concrete event or situation, or piece of scripture, and thing signified were taken as inseparable. This patristic type of mysticism is a genuine mysticism, and at the same time is completely compatible with Christian belief in a historical incarnation.

As well as this kind of mysticism, which is biblically based, there is a strong current of Neoplatonism* in the early church which interpreted mystical experience along different lines. This type of mysticism stemmed from a metaphysics which was reluctant to ascribe significance to what was finite, material and bodily, and consequently denied the necessary place of the 'mystery' in mysticism. Mysticism thus came to be used, not for the whole complex of sign and thing signified, but for the thing signified only. Hence mysticism now meant a knowledge of reality apart from the symbolic image or sign. Mysticism therefore amounted to an unmediated experience of external verities, a heightened state of awareness and direct experience of God, an ecstatic sense of fusion with ultimate reality (see Ecstasy). The basic structure of 'mystery-mysticism' as seen in the early Fathers and in mystics like Julian of Norwich is very similar to what Paul Tillich describes as the process of revelation. There are two elements in mystical apprehension as described by Tillich: 1. there is first of all the 'sign-event' which is a real historical happening (or a concrete situation, a particular human relationship, an external object); 2. perception of this concrete particular as a sign is the result of 'ecstasy'. This ecstasy is not a mere experience, nor is it a specially vivid anticipatory realization of some truth which could be reached by discursive reason, or scientific analysis. It is a quite special turn of mind, having its own coercive character.

Hostility to mysticism has arisen for a number of reasons. The basic misgivings can perhaps be traced back to Luther, who was, initially, very much influenced by Bernard of Clairvaux and the Theologia Germanica (see Imitation of Christ). The main lines of the indictment against mysticism are: 1. that it really conceals a doctrine of works* and is a system of self-endeavour by which one can effect one's own salvation and enlightenment; 2. that it interprets sin not as moral evil, but as either ignorance or imperfection, and redemption is therefore taken to depend not on a divine act of atonement but on some process of illumination, or progressive enlightenment; 3. that it is thought to have a very loose hold on the historical incarnation and its derivatives, the church and the sacraments; 4. that it is believed to be indifferent to ethics and to hold to a kind of asceticism*, which is a denial of the Christian doctrine of creation; 5. that it is thought to be incompatible with Christian eschatology* because the mystic identifies the beatific* vision-to-come with his own mystical experience.

It would not be difficult to refute each of these charges from the works of accredited mystics themselves. 1. For example, it could not seriously be held that a denial of the doctrine of grace* is necessarily a feature of mysticism in all its forms. An emphasis on grace is the characteristic of such very different mystics as Henry Suso, Julian of Norwich, St John of the Cross or St Teresa. 2. It would not equally be possible to state categorically that mysticism in all its forms is alien to the Christian doctrine of sin, even including the doctrine of original sin, and the insistence on a divine act of atonement in Christ. Again, illustrations of this could be made from Henry Suso and Julian of Norwich. 3. A marked feature of mediaeval mysticism was its attachment to the liturgy, to the doctrine of the church, and to its sacramental actions. 4. It is, if course, true that mysticism in many of its forms does insist upon an ascetical discipline, the whole aim of which is to increase the practitioner's detachment from a created existence. In some cases this attitude is influenced by a dualistic denial of the relevance of material existence; but this is an aberration rather than a necessary characteristic of mysticism. Even such a harshly ascetical writer as St John of the Cross will insist upon a discipline by which detachment is reached, but this, he insists, enables the mystic to appreciate the delights of created existence all the more. 5. With regard to eschatology, it is not at all self-evident that the mystic does identify his own experience with the beatific vision-to-come; on the contrary, the majority-tradition insists that the mystical experience is but a transitory token of what is to come. It could, therefore, more feasibly be argued that the mystic takes his eschatology very seriously indeed; the mystical experience is a particularly acute realization in the present of that which is to come.

There seem to be two main types of mysticism. 1. Introvertive, where the mystic by turning inwards on his own consciousness and experience, and by stressing the necessity for discarding from his mind all visual or concrete images, comes to realize in a peculiarly coercive way his essential oneness with ultimate reality (see **Via Negativa**). 2. The type of mysticism which is closely akin to the experience of the poet and the prophet: this is a mysticism which is closely linked with the objective experience, or circumstance, with what the early Christian Fathers called the 'mystery'. This 'mystery-minded' mysticism is that which is particularly congenial to the Christian tradition.

J. Dalby, *Christian Mysticism and the Natural World*, 1950; F. von Hügel, *The Mystical Element in Religion*, 1927; T. Hywel Hughes, *The Philosophic Basis of Mysticism*, 1937; Ursula King, *Towards a New Mysticism*, 1980; Roy C. Petry (ed), *Late Medieval Mysticism*, 1957; A. Plé and others, *Mystery and Mysticism* (a symposium), 1956; W. T. Stace, *Mysticism and Philosophy*, 1961.

E. J. TINSLEY

Myth

Few terms in contemporary theological discourse are as open to misunderstanding. One reason for this is that in most of its ordinary uses 'myth' continues to mean something purely fictitious or imaginary, whether narrative or explanation, person or event. In fact, as it is commonly used, it carries the further connotation of something false, as, for example, when it refers to a collective belief in racial superiority that is untrue and without foundation and yet is accepted uncritically and used to justify social segregation.

Of course, there is nothing new in this pejorative use of the term. Although in early Greek the word *mythos* from which it is derived seems to have meant simply narrative or story without any connotation of truth or falsity, in Attic Greek *mythos* became a technical term for stories about the gods, and from the Sophists on was regularly opposed to *logos* * as the false to the true. This is also the sense in which, beginning with the NT (I Tim. 1.4; 4.7; II Tim. 4.4; Titus 1.14; II Peter 1.16), the word and its derivatives were consistently used in traditional Christian witness and theology. Even with the Enlightenment *, this negative meaning remained, although there was an important shift from revelation to reason, and more specifically science, as the basis for judging myth to be false.

In its later phases, however, the modern study of myth (sometimes called 'mythology') has given the term a rather more positive meaning. Several disciplines have contributed to this development, but especially through ethnological study of archaic societies there has been a growing appreciation of myth's foundational role in human culture. Also important for the new sense in which myth now tends to be understood is the application to its study of psychological insights, particularly those of psychoanalysis.

Not surprisingly, recent Christian theology, also, has increasingly allowed for a more positive use of the term. No doubt part of the reason for this is that historical-critical study of Christian scripture and tradition has left no question that much even in them can only be classified as myth. But hardly less important has been the ever growing certainty that science alone is an insufficient basis for judging what is true and important about human existence. In any event, for two generations now theologians have widely agreed with the dictum of Reinhold Niebuhr that myth must always be taken 'seriously but not literally'.

If for Niebuhr himself this required one to argue for 'the truth in myths', other theologians have inclined rather to a non-cognitivist understanding of myth as of religious language generally. But even where theologians have agreed, as the majority of them have, that the significance of myth is in its way cognitive, they have still been of different minds about whether myth can and must be interpreted in other non-mythical terms. As a matter of fact, it has been widely supposed, however erroneously, that Rudolf Bultmann's famous project of demythologizing * is by way of rescinding Niebuhr's dictum. And yet even where theologians have accepted Bultmann's project, assured by him that demythologizing is a matter of *interpreting* myth rather than of *eliminating* it, they have by no means concurred that his method of existentialist interpretation, or, at any rate, his own use of this method, is the best way to carry it out.

There are several points of controversy, then, even among theologians for whom the meaning of 'myth' is primarily positive. And this is the other reason why theological uses of the term are easily misunderstood.

Even so, one ought not to exaggerate the difficulty of defining 'myth' theologically. Granted that any definition will be arbitrary, not every definition need be equally so; and there are gains to be had from any serious attempt to define the term as it is properly used at the present stage of discussion both in theology and in the other disciplines that help to define it. With this in mind, we may define 'myth' here by means of three closely related statements:

1. Myth is a particular way of thinking and speaking that, like other such ways, represents (i.e., re-presents, presents *again*) the reality presented in one basic mode of human experience.

2. The reality that myth represents is the ultimate reality presented in our original, internal, non-sensuous experience of ourselves, others, and the whole.

3. The particular way in which myth thinks and speaks of this ultimate reality is as a narrative or story determined, on the one hand, by its intention to answer the existential question of the meaning of this reality for us and, on the other hand, by its use of concepts and terms proper to the other basic mode of human experience, namely, our derived, external, sense experience of others and ourselves.

It will be noted that on this definition myth is understood, not, as it often has been, simply as story about the gods or God, but, rather, as story about the ultimate reality for which 'gods' or 'God' is the constitutive concept and term in theistic religions. In this way, justice is done to the observation that not every narrative that otherwise appears to function as a myth has the being and action of God or the gods as its subject matter. Contrariwise, the definition explains equally well why there can be stories even about God or the gods that are not properly myths – insofar, namely, as they have some other intention in thinking and speaking of the divine than to address the existential question of the meaning of ultimate reality for us. By the same token, one can account for the differences between myth and such other types of narrative as fable or folk-tale, saga and legend.

Distinctive of the definition, however, is its claim about the particular way in which myth realizes its intention to answer the existential question by making use of concepts and terms drawn from our sense-perception of ourselves and the world. Thus myth is represented as committing by its very structure the kind of 'category mistake' that Gilbert Ryle takes to be committed whenever there is 'the presentation of facts belonging to one category in the idioms appropriate to another' (*The Concept of Mind*, 1949, p. 8). On the other hand, by representing this mistake as precisely as it does, the definition avoids the familiar difficulties of defining 'myth' too loosely as thinking and speaking about the divine in concepts and terms that properly apply to the non-divine. What makes myth myth is not simply that it thinks and speaks about the ultimate whole of reality non-literally in concepts and terms that literally apply to ourselves and others, but that it presents facts belonging to the category of our existence as such in the idioms appropriate to the very different category of the reality presented by our senses.

So defined, myth can be distinguished from other forms of religious thinking and speaking, even other non-literal forms, and the history of religion conceived accordingly as allowing for post-mythical as well as properly mythical phases. Similarly, this definition of 'myth' enables one to understand both the relation and the difference between myth and science as well as between myth, on the one hand, and metaphysics and morality, on the other. Because the concepts and terms of myth are taken from our external sense-perception, there is reason for thinking of it as a primitive form of science, which thinks and speaks in the same kind of concepts and terms. At the same time, myth appears in its difference from science insofar as its intention is not to provide a picture of the world disclosed by our senses but to represent the ultimate reality of our own existence in its meaning for us. But this also explains why myth is different from metaphysics, which thinks and speaks of the same ultimate reality, only not in its meaning for us but in its structure in itself. In somewhat the same way, myth is also seen to be both related to and different from morality in that, in thinking and speaking of the meaning of ultimate reality for us, it directly addresses our self-understanding, as distinct from being concerned with the ways of acting and the specific actions arising from our self-understanding, with which morality properly has to do.

Finally, this definition allows one to take myth seriously even while insisting that demythologizing is both possible and necessary – possible, because myth's own intention to answer the existential question is only imperfectly realized by the narrative form in which it itself thinks and speaks; and necessary, because it is only insofar as one overcomes the 'category mistake' that myth involves by interpreting its meaning in other more appropriate concepts and terms that one can make good on the claim that its answer to this question is at least capable of being true. In this way, the project of demythologizing, far from denying the truth in myths, is shown to be the one means of vindicating it.

H. W. Bartsch (ed), *Kerygma and Myth*, 1953; M. Eliade, 'Myth', *EB*; R. Niebuhr, 'The Truth in Myths', in *The Nature of Religious Experience*, ed. E. G. Bewkes, 1937, pp. 117–135; T. A. Sebeok (ed), *Myth: A Symposium*, 1958.

SCHUBERT M. OGDEN

Narrative Theology

Recognition of the many problems arising from a view which sees divine revelation* conveyed by propositional statements, in the form of uniquely authoritative scripture*, creeds* or dogmas*, together with an appreciation of the insights into human nature to be found in classical literature up to and including the modern novel have caused increasing importance to be attached to the contribution made to theological reflection and understanding by narrative or story. Narrative theology, still inevitably an imprecise discipline, is concerned to relate the impressions made by narratives and the insights arising out of them to theological questions, and in particular to give substance to these insights and to suggest criteria by which they, and the stories which prompt them, may be judged to be true or false.

Because the Bible contains a good deal of narrative of one kind or another, narrative theology is not least concerned with a new evaluation of the biblical stories. For a long period, from the seventeenth century onwards, attention was concentrated on whether or not the Bible was historically accurate and the question asked was whether or not narratives were 'historical' (*see also* **Historical Criticism**). In the context of narrative theology it is now thought more appropriate to say that the biblical story is 'history-like' (Hans Frei), i.e. that 'it is not a simple reportage of history, but it is also not a fictional story having no contact with history' (James Barr).

This approach leads to other possibilities of assessing the 'truth' of a story than arguing that it is true as a record of historical events. It may also, or indeed instead, be 'true to life', i.e. because it awakens in the reader or hearer a response rising out of a perception that authentic human experience has been deepened by the story. Or the story may contain teaching about life or a vision of the future which inspires a particular reaction or life-style in the present as well as communicating information about the past. Thus an interpretation of the Bible in terms of narrative theology would be concerned with its truth in all these dimensions rather than just in terms of 'Did it really happen?'

Of course narrative theology is not focussed only on biblical narrative; its raw material includes the stories told in other religions and works of secular literature. Not that a dividing line between the two can be drawn all that clearly once it is accepted, as has been the case at least since the nineteenth century, that the Bible is a book which can be read like any other book. And Erich Auerbach and Northrop Frye have both shown the extent to which Western literature has been influenced by the Bible, so that there is a reciprocal relationship involved.

Much literature is, of course, irrelevant to narrative theology. What is of special interest to it is the examination of certain texts, events, images, myths, rituals, symbols (and here it is evident how loose a term 'narrative' can be) which are generally recognized to be 'classic', in which 'we recognize nothing less than the disclosure of a reality we cannot but name truth' (Tracy).

The relationship of narrative theology to other forms of theology has yet to be defined clearly. On the one hand there are those, more conservative in approach, who would see narrative theology as being a useful tool of modern apologetic and an enrichment in the interpretation of a tradition which is not in need of radical reconstruction. A more radical view would see narrative theology as a departure in the direction of a completely new way of doing theology, leading to a relativizing of religious traditions (*see also* **Cultural Relativism**) and a privatizing of religious claims, in the context of which many of the dogmatic statements advanced in the past by Christians (including, for example, the doctrine of the incarnation*) are no longer defensible in any strict form.

For any form of narrative theology, however, the crucial issue is that of criteria for the truth of the stories and interpretations of them which it commends. Because the criterion most often used in theology generally is that of scripture, it would seem very difficult indeed to avoid an almost impossibly circular argument, since it is precisely the authority and self-sufficiency of scripture and the way in which it is the foundation for theology that is being put in question. And why should one 'classic' be preferred to another; is not judgment in this sphere simply a matter of taste?

These are important and problematical questions, but the difficulty in answering them should not detract from the importance of the contribution made by narrative theology, particularly against the background of a modern pluralistic world society. *See also* **Literary Criticism.**

Erich Auerbach, *Mimesis*, ET 1953; Northrop Frye, *Anatomy of Criticism*, 1957; A. E. Harvey (ed), *God Incarnate: Story and Belief*, 1981; Frank Kermode, *The Genesis of Secrecy*, 1979; Sallie McFague, *Metaphorical Theology*, 1983; Gerd Theissen, *On Having a Critical Faith*, 1979; David Tracy, *The Analogical Imagination*, 1981.

JOHN BOWDEN

Naturalism

A term more frequently met with fifty years ago than today, meaning those types of philosophy which assert that the world can best be accounted for by means of the categories of natural science (including biology and psychology) without recourse to the supernatural or transcendent as a means of explanation. It is thus wider than positivism*,

which regards physico-chemical explanation as the valid type of philosophical reasoning. Nor is it restricted to empiricism, for Spinoza was essentially a naturalist. In fact, it covers a wide variety of philosophies, including that of Samuel Alexander (1859–1938), cf. his *Space, Time and Deity* (1920). The title of C. D. Broad's *The Mind and its Place in Nature* (1925) illustrates the inversion of the Hegelian* idealistic standpoint of the earlier generation, which would have spoken rather of 'nature and its place in Mind'. While the older naturalisms were often close to materialism, some theologians now speak of a broader naturalism, such as the philosophy of Whitehead. Though this abandons the dualism of the natural and the supernatural, its concept of the natural is sufficiently rich to make room for spirit and even for God.

R. G. Collingwood, *The Idea of Nature*, 1945; J. B. Pratt, *Naturalism*, 1939; C. A. Strong, *Origin of Consciousness*, 1918; J. Ward, *Naturalism and Agnosticism*, 1898; D. D. Williams, 'Christianity and Naturalism', *Union Seminary Quarterly Review* 12, 1957.

ALAN RICHARDSON/
JOHN MACQUARRIE

Natural Law

Along with his concept of natural theology, Aquinas developed the concept of natural law. Human beings, by their own reason, can gain knowledge of the ethically good without any reference to God's revelation*. This knowledge forms the natural law or law of human nature. Natural law is distinguished by Catholics from the theological virtues of faith*, hope* and love*, which are known only through revelation and which can be performed only by one who receives grace*. Natural law is the area in which Christian and non-Christian can find a basis for agreement and co-operation in ethical action.

The concept of natural law has gained wide, but not universal, support in secular thought in general and in legal thought in particular. Protestants never have put as much emphasis upon natural law as has Catholicism, and many Protestants have denied the concept. A major problem is that on many important issues, such as birth control, there is no agreement upon what the natural law teaches.

A major difficulty with the concept of natural law has been its tendency to see morality fixed in the nature of reality. As a result morality cannot change or develop. This, however, is in contradiction to the history of morality which differs in different societies and has changed drastically even in the same society. Furthermore, natural law theorists have tended to defend the status quo since it presumably is based on the nature of things.

John Courtney Murray and others have attempted to find ways of relating natural law to human historicity. Natural law is no longer seen as being based upon the ultimate metaphysical nature of reality. Rather it is based upon the human's experience of the world and other persons in it. Because the human experience undergoes historical change, natural law can change and it can be critical of any status quo.

Thomas Aquinas, *Summa Theologiae*, 2.1. 1.90ff.; Anthony Battaglia, *Toward A Reformulation of Natural Law*, 1981.

WILLIAM HORDERN

Natural Theology

Natural theology is traditionally that knowledge about God * and the divine order which man's reason can acquire without the aid of revelation *. Thomas Aquinas formulated the distinction between natural and revealed theology clearly and authoritatively, as over against the older Augustinian * view that there is no 'unaided' knowledge of God. On the Thomist * view reason can assure us that God is and can infer by analogy * certain truths about him; but only divine revelation could acquaint us with the truths of revealed theology, e.g. the doctrines of the Trinity *, the Incarnation *, the Atonement *, etc. The word 'natural' in this connection reflects the ancient Stoic * and Platonic * conceptions of the natural as the rational; natural theology is rational reflection on the question of divine existence.

From the eighteenth century onward, natural theology, especially the traditional proofs of the divine existence, has been subjected to severe criticism (*see* **Arguments for the Existence of God**). First Hume and then Kant showed that there are serious flaws in these proofs, while at a later time the theory of evolution *, with its doctrine of a natural

selection, further undermined the argument from design, often regarded as the most persuasive of the theistic proofs. In the face of this criticism, the arguments of natural theology have been increasingly refined to meet objections, and though most theologians would nowadays hesitate to speak of 'proofs' of God's existence, many would claim that natural theology provides a cumulative argument in support of theism *.

Natural theology has long been criticized from the other side by theologians who believe that it is incompatible with a doctrine of revelation. Karl Barth, in particular, has criticized natural theology as an illegitimate attempt on the part of man to grasp the knowledge of God. This is said to turn God into an object, and such an object is an idol rather than the true God, who can be known only as he has revealed himself through Jesus Christ. Theologians who would not go so far as Barth in restricting the knowledge of God to the Christian revelation alone might nevertheless hold that *some* revelation is implied in the knowledge of God, just as we could hardly know another human being unless he had made himself known or opened himself to us. They would not deny a genuine knowledge of God apart from the specific Christian revelation, but they would question whether any knowledge of God could be 'unaided'. On this view the boundary between natural and revealed theology becomes blurred.

F. H. Cleobury, *A Return to Natural Theology*, 1967; B. S. Mitchell, *The Justification of Religious Belief*, 1973. The series of Gifford Lectures on Natural Theology, given at the Scottish universities since 1888, contains many notable volumes on the subject by, among others, William James, Edward Caird, Bernard Bosanquet, A. N. Whitehead, Sir Arthur Eddington and C. von Weizsäcker.

ALAN RICHARDSON/
JOHN MACQUARRIE

Nature

This term (Greek *physis*, Latin *natura*): became crucial in the christological debates of the fifth century, even though it had never acquired any technical metaphysical sense. Just as the English equivalent can refer to 'the natural world' (creation with its order and natural laws), or 'the essence of some person or thing' (sc. divine nature, angelic nature, human nature, animal nature), or 'the character of some person or thing' (e.g. bestial nature), so could the Greek word, and with equal lack of precision. The reference of the term was supplied by the context in which it was used. In the christological debates it was assumed without any attempt at definition to be equivalent to *hypostasis* and/or *ousia* (Latin *substantia* – see Leo's *Tome*), and these terms were themselves used without the careful distinctions by now made in the trinitarian formula. The Antiochenes* objected to Cyril's insistence on a natural or hypostatic* union on the grounds that it not only involved a 'mixture' of the divine and human, but also implied a 'physical' union which therefore happened 'by necessity', not by divine will and grace. On the other hand, Cyril of Alexandria, and later the Monophysites*, objected to the two-natures formula eventually adopted at Chalcedon* on the assumption that it implied two separate entities subsisting and persisting in the Christ so as effectively to divide him into 'two Sons'. Yet they did admit that Christ was one 'out of' two natures. In fact the terminology was too vague to carry the weight required of it. There were real issues at stake in the debate, but this is so obscured by confusion over the sense of this ill-defined term that it appears as a squabble over a preposition: 'in' two natures (Chalcedonian) or 'out of' two natures (Monophysite).

FRANCES YOUNG

Nature, Theology and

In the narrow sense, the realm of nature is made up of all that happens or exists without human contrivance. In a wider, it includes everything that happens in space-time, or all that is accessible to scientific inquiry, or all that exists in dependence on the divine Creator (*natura naturata*). 'Nature' may also signify the force or principle that sustains the aggregate of natural things (*natura naturans*): whether this is God himself or some lesser, created powers (including rebel angels).

1. One trend in Christian thought has been to secularize nature, to see what happens naturally as merely the framework for human activity: the powers that engender natural change exist only to serve human beings, and Christian missionaries have set themselves to free the heathen of 'irrational' fears or taboos which prevent a full use of what is 'given'. Nothing in nature is sacred. This doctrine has been held responsible for a uniquely exploitative attitude to the world, but there is good reason to think that other human societies have done as badly. Another trend has been to see nature as the expression of God's glory, and to care for her as stewards. A still more radical view has been that humankind has no unique place in God's creation, and need not expect to manage everything, even with good intentions.

2. Those who look on nature merely as the field of human endeavour have supported themselves by appeal to the sort of mathematical or mechanistic explanations given by Western science, which have largely replaced older explanations in terms of the will of personal beings. When only persons really matter, and nature has become the realm where personalistic explanation is out of place, nature cannot really matter. The barrier between impersonal nature and personal humanity is ill-defended: more and more of our own behaviour seems likely to end on the wrong side of the line. On the other hand, speculative physicists sometimes suggest that supposedly elementary laws and particles exist as they do because of our decisions and observations. The 'modern concept of nature' is no longer of a realm of demonic and angelic powers, but an ill-coordinated mixture of mechanicism and subjective idealism. Genuine realism about nature, that there is a truth independent of our wills which we can hope to discover, is not a promising option of we are the sort of beings that Western science supposes, namely the by-product of the 'selfish gene's' proliferation on a minor satellite of a minor star.

3. Theists* have also differed in their theodicies*: some have held that nature is perfect just as it is, and our revulsion at some of its manifestations merely sentimental; others have held that nature as it is cannot be the product of a perfectly just and compassionate being, but must be counted as fallen, perverted by the fall of humankind or of prehuman powers. Some have abandoned traditional theism (where the supremely worshipful is reckoned also to be the maker of all things), and so lost any convincing standard against which to judge

that nature is indeed corrupt. The view that whatever is is right can be used to justify either quietism or the most radical-imaginable interference with what goes on (since human activity is also part of nature). The view that nature is fallen has tempted people to remake her in accordance with human ideas of what is valuable, and also encouraged them to grieve with our fellow-sufferers.

4. The natural has figured as a standard of morality, and as its enemy. That what is and what ought to be are logically distinct has sometimes been used to suggest that what ought to be can owe nothing to what is, and that talk of what is 'natural' (i.e. common) is irrelevant to moral decision. On the other hand, any attempt to deny that there are ethical truisms which all rational beings can be expected to feel in their bones, and which owe their force not to logic but to 'nature', leads to a picture of morality as the rationalization of personal taste or will to power. Ethical decency rests upon a belief in God as *natura naturans* within a world of many opposing powers.

Robin Attfield, *The Ethics of Environmentalism*, 1982; J. N. Black, *The Dominion of Man*, 1970; R. W. Hepburn, 'Nature', *Encyclopedia of Philosophy*, ed. P. Edwards, 1967, Vol. 5, pp. 454–8; C. S. Lewis, *The Abolition of Man*, 1943; M. Midgley, *Beast and Man*, 1978; D. S. Wallace-Hadrill, *The Greek Patristic View of Nature*, 1968.

STEPHEN R. L. CLARK

Neo-Orthodoxy

This term refers to the deplorable imposition of an out-dated synthesis of theology and secular thought in an altered contemporary situation. It is also used of theologians of the schools of Karl Barth and Emil Brunner in the sense of their reassertion of the principles of the Reformation in a post-liberal form.

JAMES RICHMOND

Neoplatonism

Neoplatonism is a generic term covering the revival of Platonist* tendencies in philosophy from the third to sixth centuries AD. The two predominant personalities involved were Plotinus (c. 205–270) and Proclus (411–485). Some regard Plotinus as the real founder of the doctrine; others ascribe the honour to his teacher, Ammonius Saccas (c. 175–242). Another pupil of Ammonius was a certain Origen, who may or may not have been the Christian Alexandrian. Plotinus' immediate disciple, biographer and literary executor was Porphyry (c. 232–303), whose contributions were more scholastic than original. He was the teacher of Iamblichus (c. 250–c. 330), a Syrian who developed the specifically religious elements in the Neoplatonist tradition. In the fourth century Marius Victorinus translated some of Porphyry's and Plotinus' works, and re-established their influence in Rome, so becoming an important mediator in the transmission of Plotinian philosophy to Augustine. Proclus was the last master of the Academy in Athens. On the one hand he was much more scholastic than Plotinus, and on the other hand much more devoted to the quasi-magical practices of theurgy and respectful of the 'inspired' authority of the Chaldean oracles. Certain elements of his synthesis, notably his doctrine of evil, were adopted by Pseudo-Dionysius the Areopagite. Practice varies as to the extension of the term 'Neoplatonism'; there is already so much breadth in it, if both Plotinus and Proclus are accommodated, as to make it reasonable to speak also of Christian Neoplatonists. In any case, unless one restricts the term to the philosophy of Plotinus alone, it is necessary to be extremely diffident in presenting any doctrine as characteristic of Neoplatonism.

The common ground among Neoplatonists is a respect for the text of Plato. Ammonius and Plotinus are said to have attempted to harmonize his philosophy with that of Aristotle, but Proclus is less sympathetic towards that project. Plotinus was opposed to Gnosticism*, which he regarded as a confusion introduced in the name of religion into philosophical contemplation. He was to some extent influenced by the 'agnostic' tendencies of Indian wisdom, which he knew from researches during an expedition to Persia. The rather purist Hellenism of Plotinus was much modified by Iamblichus and Proclus in their attempts to ally Platonism with pagan mystery religions, whether of Greek, Mesopotamian, or Egyptian origin. Manichaeism* was generally regarded as an arch-enemy, its dualist principles being in outright contrariety to the supremacy of the One*. The priority of the

One over the many can fairly be called the keystone of Neoplatonism. Based on a particular exegesis of Plato's dialogue the *Parmenides*, the doctrine determines both the ontology and the epistemology, and therefore also the soteriology of the Neoplatonists. The One or the Good, being perfect, begets in his own image the *Nous*; the *Nous* in turn begets as the fruit of its contemplation of the One, the *Psyche*, or world-soul. The soul is the efficient cause of the rest of the universe: of other lesser souls, of the heavenly bodies, and of matter. The final cause of all is the One, to which all things return by their conversion in knowledge and desire back through the *Psyche* and the *Nous*. Thus the universe is constituted by the twofold ecstasis in which creatures proceed or emanate from the One, and return to it by conversion. Such is the basic framework of the Plotinian system. Other Neoplatonists elaborate various parts of it more or less extravagantly. Proclus fits in a whole pantheon of mediating deities in groups of threes and nines. Some lesser writers of the school tend to associate evil with the emanation of matter, but Proclus explicitly rejects such a solution to the problem of evil. His doctrine that evil is always a particular parasitic defect in a particular good entity was to be adopted by Thomas Aquinas, through the mediation of the pseudo-Denis. Neoplatonism cannot be called pantheistic without qualification. It insists that all beings participate in the being of the One, who is thus universally present even in matter, but it also maintains firmly the multiplicity of beings at various levels of existence, and the union with the Good which is aimed at is a union of knowledge and love rather than ontological annihilation. The doctrine of the emanation* of creatures from the One usually preserves the distinction between the divine nature which does not proceed, and the divine 'workings' or 'energies' which do. Correlative with this is a positive programme of contemplation – more intellectual in Plotinus, more magical in Proclus – culminating in a 'negative' ecstasis in which the transcendence of the One is recognized. Plotinus speaks of a super-intellectual faculty for this last experience; Proclus equates it with the 'flower of the mind', which is one of the sources of the mediaeval theory of the *apex mentis*.

The assertion that the idea of a divine incarnation is incompatible with Neoplatonism is somewhat gratuitous. The apparent pantheism involved in Erigena's theology is not a necessary consequence of Neoplatonist views. Augustine and Pseudo-Dionysius were both strongly influenced by Neoplatonism, and the traces of the system in mediaeval scholasticism were seriously underestimated until recently. Particularly the mediaeval theories of participation and analogical predication are due to Neoplatonic as much as to 'purely' Aristotelian* sources. In the humanist renaissance, Gerson, Ficino and Nicholas of Cusa were among many who drew heavily on Neoplatonism.

Proclus, *The Elements of Theology*, ed. E. R. Dodds, 1963; A. H. Armstrong, *Introduction to Ancient Philosophy*, ²1949, chs. XVI–XIX; (ed), *The Cambridge History of Late Greek and Early Mediaeval Philosophy*, 1967, Parts III–VI; E. R. Dodds, *Select Passages Illustrating Neoplatonism*, text, 1924, translations 1923; W. R. Inge, *The Philosophy of Plotinus*, 1918; R. T. Wallis, *Neo-Platonism*, 1972; T. Whittaker, *The Neo-Platonists*, ²1928.

PLACID SPEARRITT

Neoscholasticism

The term is used interchangeably with Neo-Thomism to describe a philosophical movement among Roman Catholics in the nineteenth and twentieth centuries that made the thought of Thomas Aquinas the norm against which all other philosophy and theology was judged.

Aquinas had long been a leading authority among Catholic thinkers since the first revival of his thought in the fifteenth and sixteenth centuries, when he was championed both by Dominicans and Jesuits. Then, in the nineteenth century, as a way of counteracting Positivism* and Modernism*, Aquinas was revived, particularly through the efforts of Sanseverino, Kleutgen, Stockl and de San, leading to the founding of the Accademia di San Tommaso in Rome in 1874. In 1879 Thomas was made the leading 'Doctor of the Church' by Pope Leo XIII in his encyclical *Aeterni patris*. Within a few years, chairs of mediaeval philosophy were established at several European and American universities. Similarly, journals were established to provide vehicles for the growing literature on Thomas and scholastic thought: *Divus Thomas, Revue thomiste, Revue néo-scolastique, Rivista di filosofia neoscholastica,* and in the twentieth century: *Bulletin thomiste, New Scholasticism* and *The Thomist.* The Institut de Philosophie was founded in 1891 by Mgr Mercier.

Perhaps the principal moving force behind Neo-Thomism and Neoscholasticism at the turn of the century was Maurice De Wulf, professor of mediaeval philosophy at Louvain. In many of his works he argued for a common scholastic teaching, a synthesis of Aristotelian* philosophy and Christian doctrine that was achieved in the thirteenth century, primarily by Aquinas. This *philosophia perennis* was broader than Aquinas' thought, since it was, for De Wulf, a common achievement of the great doctors of the thirteenth century, including Bonaventure and Scotus, and excluding some aspects of Greek and mediaeval thought, particularly regarding celestial bodies, that had been disproved by modern, scientific thought. Yet Aquinas was the principal component in Neoscholasticism as understood by De Wulf.

Neoscholasticism gradually became less influential in the twentieth century. Some Catholics felt it to be reactionary and too isolated from modern intellectual currents. Moreover, through the work of P. Mandonnet, E. Gilson, M. Grabmann and F. Van Steenberghen, despite differences, the thought of Aquinas was gradually separated from Neo-Thomism, and thirteenth-century scholasticism was shown to have been far more complex and less synthetic than once supposed. Finally, both in terms of mediaeval philosophy and in modern Catholic thought, Thomism has receded from its premier position and is now seen as an important but not exclusive approach in Catholic philosophy and theology.

M. D. Chenu, *Towards an Understanding of St Thomas,* 1964; E. Gilson, *The Christian Philosophy of St Thomas Aquinas,* 1961; M. Perrier, *The Revival of Scholastic Philosophy in the Nineteenth Century,* 1909; M. de Wulf, *Introduction à la Philosophie Néoscolastique,* 1904.

WILLIAM J. COURTENAY

Nestorianism

The teaching that there were two distinct persons* in the incarnate Christ, one human and one divine. Nestorius (died *c.* 451), working in the Antiochene* tradition, stressed the two natures* of Christ, fearing Monophysitism*. His opponents accused him, inaccurately, of denying the oneness of Christ's person and teaching 'a duality of sons'.

A. Grillmeier, *Christ in Christian Tradition* I, ²1975.

GEORGE NEWLANDS

New England Theology

The most conspicuous theological movement in American Calvinism in the last half of the eighteenth and the first half of the nineteenth centuries. Centred in Congregationalism and known also as the 'New Divinity', it was founded by Jonathan Edwards and continued after his death in 1758 to debate issues he had discussed, such as native depravity, the divine permission of sin, the nature of regeneration, human freedom and responsibility, the nature of virtue, and the relationship of both regenerate and unregenerate to the church. As leaders of the New England theology continued the Edwardsean tradition they felt free to make adaptations, but failed fully to catch the poetical and imaginative power of the founder. Joseph Bellamy wrote *True Religion Delineated* (1750), which served for about a century as a practical guide in American Calvinism. Samuel Hopkins, Edwards' literary executor and author of a two-volume *System of Doctrines* (1793), made certain 'improvements' in the New Divinity which in its strictest form became known as 'Hopkinseanism'. Jonathan Edwards Jr advocated the 'governmental' or 'benevolence' theory of the atonement, while Nathaniel Emmons compiled his sermons into a late expression of New England theology in the two-volume *System of Divinity* (1842).

The New Divinity was a shaping force in the wider circle of New England theologians, including Timothy Dwight, Leonard Woods, Nathaniel W. Taylor, Bennet Tyler and Edwards A. Park. New England theology was involved in the founding of three theological seminaries: Andover, Yale and Hartford. Especially in the encouragement it gave to revivalism* and missions, it influenced American Protestantism far beyond its own circles, with particular impact on Presbyterianism.

Sydney E. Ahlstrom (ed), *Theology in America*, 1967; Frank H. Foster, *A Genetic History of the New England Theology*, 1899.
ROBERT T. HANDY

New Testament Theology

The term can be used for the theological position of the NT or of its parts, and so for a strictly descriptive account of this. It can further be used to mean a theology that is derived from the NT but is also authoritative for Christians today. How far these are identical, and how far one influences the other, have been crucial questions for two centuries.

1. *The descriptive task*. It is now commonly agreed that the thought of the NT must first be described in its own terms, though it must never be forgotten that the person doing the describing lives in the twentieth and not the first century, nor that this involves great differences in outlook and mental furniture. The basic problems of such description are:

(a) Although all the NT writers had their own theological and especially christological positions, and although as a consequence all NT books are strongly theological, none of them was written to provide a comprehensive theology. The Gospels tell a story, a story that is theologically slanted, but still a story (so also the Acts). The letters (and also the book of Revelation) aim to deal with concrete and often local issues in the early church, and though all are written out of strong theological convictions none presents theology for its own sake. They are strictly occasional writings. The total theology of every NT book has thus to be inferred from material that is not straightforwardly theological.

(b) This means that the space given to a subject is no sure indication of its importance to the writer. For example in I Corinthians, because of particular local problems, the question of food offered to idols is given extended treatment while justification by faith is barely mentioned, yet the latter is central to Paul's thought and the former peripheral and a derivative matter. Moreover, some things are seldom made explicit not because they are unimportant but because they are entirely taken for granted. An example of this is monotheism *, a basic presupposition everywhere in the NT but explicitly stated somewhat infrequently. The NT also has a background in the OT and Judaism, seeing Jesus as the culmination of God's activity in the past, and the church as the renewed people of God, and taking it for granted that the God and Father of Jesus is also the God of Israel. This background is often explicit but is everywhere implicit. The NT theologian must set what is said against the background of what is presupposed in order to elucidate meaning.

(c) Careful attention has to be given to the individuality of different writers, to different works by the same writer, and even to different parts of the same writing. This is true in the use of important words. For example, 'flesh' (Greek *sarx*) can sometimes mean the physical stuff of which we are made, sometimes our human relationships, but especially in Paul it can sometimes refer to the orientation of life as a whole away from God. It would be highly misleading to suppose the same meaning were present everywhere. Much more fundamental is the recognition that each NT writer makes his own peculiar response to Jesus and that this shows in everything he touches. Any attempt to describe the theology of the NT without first grappling with the theologies of the NT is bound to lead to serious distortion. Premature and unjustifiable harmonization which does not allow to the various writings their individuality is the enemy of good NT theology, which can exist in the singular only after the writings have been interrogated on their own terms. They are not all concerned with the same things: Paul is greatly exercised about the relation of Christians to the Law, though not equally in all his letters, and yet hardly at all about their relation to the cult (contrast Hebrews); Matthew is much exercised to show that the church is the true Israel, Luke hardly at all. Different answers are given to the same problem, for instance Paul, Matthew, and James on the Law. In different circumstances Paul can take different stances, for example on circumcision, which is unimportant in I Cor. 7 but is emphatically not to be submitted to in Galatians. Many of these differences can be accounted for, but not by harmonizing in advance. Very few NT theologies now try to treat a topic across the board. Rather, as a first step the various theologies are treated one by one (contrast A. Richardson's *An Introduction to the Theology of the New Tes-*

tament, 1958, and even E. Stauffer's *New Testament Theology*, German 1941, ET 1955). Even the practice of taking the Synoptic Gospels as a block has now been abandoned, and much NT research since the 1950s has been concentrated on the distinctive theologies of Matthew, Mark and Luke. This is the fruit 1. of form criticism *, which revealed the extent to which the gospels met the needs, including the theological needs, of the communities out of which and for which they were written, and 2. of redaction criticism, which has revealed the contributions of the evangelists themselves (*see also* **Jesus; Biblical Criticism**). These contributions are commonly identified in the total architecture of each Gospel, in the explicitly editorial seams, in selection and omission from sources, and in minor alterations to sources. The search for origins, for the Jesus of history obscured by the theological interpretations of the evangelists, has been replaced by a preoccupation precisely with those interpretations which the liberals had attempted to strip away. Indeed it is now commonly thought that access to Jesus is better gained through the varying interpretative responses to him than by trying to remove them, and in any case that the traditions about Jesus were theologically coloured from the very beginning. The Synoptics are therefore now treated as John has long been treated, as sources for the theologies of their writers or communities and not least for their christologies. Of course they share basic assumptions like the centrality of Jesus as revealing God's purposes and activity, but their emphases and interests are not identical.

(*d*) In probing the intentions of NT writers, it is essential to know the background of thought and culture against which they wrote. This is true where word meanings are concerned: for instance in the case of 'flesh' (*sarx*) already mentioned, an understanding of Paul's usage requires an examination of the OT (especially the Septuagint, the Greek version), the Qumran Scrolls, contemporary Greek usage, the circumstances of the Galatian church, and so on. As in this case, it is often vital to know what battle a writer is fighting at any given point. Another instance is the lordship of Jesus: is the model for this the lordship of the Roman emperor, or that of a cult figure in a mystery religion *, or that of Yahweh?

Is there a move from one model to another as time goes on? Detailed historical work must be done before we know in any given text what it means to call Jesus 'Lord'. It is not enough to know the general cultural, religious, and intellectual background of NT times. We need to know the background of each writing. The fact that our main evidence comes from the writing itself, so that there is a circular element in the enquiry, makes it the more delicate.

(*e*) There is always the danger that the interpreter's or historian's own idiosyncratic or confessional or cultural spectacles will so thoroughly condition his observation that not only Jesus but the whole NT is modernized. The role of the interpreter must be an active one simply because of the character of the NT writings as occasional and non-systematic (see *a* above). However unobtrusively the interpreter tries to exercise that role and however serious is the attempt to let the NT speak in its own terms, the very provision of a coherent account can be made only by someone who belongs to another time and another culture and who stands at the end of two-thousand years of Christian tradition. The interpreter will try to minimize this conditioning, by immersion in the world of the NT, in contemporary Judaism and Hellenism, not to mention the OT, and also by rigorous attention to lexical and historical questions and by not taking anything for granted. To be aware of the danger is partly to disarm it. Interpreters and historians go to great lengths to enable them to think as far as possible like first-century men or women in Corinth or Antioch or Jerusalem. Even so, in what is selected as significant, and in the way significant things are put together to give a coherent account of the theology of Mark or Paul or John, the role of the historian can never be entirely passive. We shall see below that some think this to be no bad thing, that the task of the interpreter ought not to be merely descriptive. At all events, the element of subjectivity is so clear that all description must be regarded as provisional.

(*f*) Granted all that has been said, the problem of the unity of the NT cannot be ignored, if only because all these writings exist as a single collection in the canon * of the NT. The question inevitably arises about what unites these varying responses to the life, death and resurrection of Jesus. If the writing of NT theology cannot consist of taking material from here and there and arranging it in a pattern provided by the conceptions and interests of the interpreter, nor of seeking a lowest common denominator of the varieties of NT witness, where does it find a unity? On many issues a diversity of opinion was permissible within the early church, a diversity that is reflected in the NT not to mention extra-canonical materials. Yet clearly there were limits to the permissible diversity: for instance it was not acceptable to hold that Jesus was not a real human being, or to suppose that John the Baptist was the definitive revelation of God. The several writers and their churches belonged to recognizably the same movement and centred on the same figure. Can we do any more than simply reassert the fact of the canon, so that all these theologies belong together somehow or other? Some theologies of the NT that were written to serve as theology for the modern church have of course sought to identify a centre: Cullmann's in terms of the story of the saving acts of God in history (*see also* **Heilsgeschichte**), Bultmann's in terms of liberation to new and authentic existence (*see also* **Demythologizing**). Attempts are also made, however, by those whose intention is strictly descriptive, of which notable recent examples include Kümmel, Ladd and Dunn. W. G. Kümmel (*The Theology of the New Testament*, German 1972, ET 1974) gives weight to the distinctive concerns and methods of presentation of the Synoptics and Paul and John and concludes that their unity in multiplicity consists in their common witness to God's saving action in Jesus Christ, to his establishment of the church by the Holy Spirit, to his freeing men and women from the world and for active love, and to the future consummation of that Christ-centred saving action. From the conservative side, G. E. Ladd's position is similar (*A Theology of the New Testament*, 1974). Like Kümmel he takes the Synoptics together, but otherwise treats the NT writers separately and sees them all as centred on the. one great saving event in Jesus Christ, his person and his work. Essentially both Kümmel and Ladd do NT theology by studying NT theologies. Dunn's work is particularly interesting (*Unity and Diversity in the New Testament*, 1977) for he deliberately sets out to explore theological diversity

within the early church and the limits that were set to the diversity that was acceptable. On many issues he finds those limits to have been very wide, but he concludes that what was not allowable was any fracture of the identity of the historical Jesus with the exalted Christ. To deny that identity was to step outside the limits, and only then did the terms 'heresy' and 'orthodoxy' become appropriate.

In current NT scholarship there is therefore little interest in writing NT theology in a synthesizing way. Where a unifying centre is looked for it is usually found, not surprisingly, in the broad area of christology*. This is not to say that the NT writers are held to have the same christology, for they do not (Paul is not much interested in Jesus as Messiah, unlike Matthew, or as High Priest, unlike Hebrews, but characteristically presents him as Lord and as Last Adam; the examples could be multiplied). Nevertheless in some way Christ is the central point of all NT writings, and all (with perhaps the exception of James) made it clear that whatever they have to say derives from him. It must be added immediately that the death and resurrection, the presence of the Spirit, the relation of Christ to his people, the relation of all these to Israel and its history, hopes, institutions, and its Torah, are all placed a hair's breadth from that centre.

Finally it does not seem to matter much whether we call the descriptive task the delineation of NT theology or of NT religion, through some prefer the latter as avoiding confusion with NT theology regarded as authoritative and normative for the modern church.

2. *NT theology as normative for the church.* For two hundred years there has been a view that the business of the NT scholar as such is solely with the descriptive task, but since the very beginning there has also been a desire to use NT theology as divine revelation and so as normative for the contemporary church. This is still so. In the Middle Ages the NT together with the OT was used as a quarry for the extraction of statements that would support the church's dogma. The Reformation self-consciously returned to the Bible as the primary rather than as the supportive source of doctrine, and in the case of Luther it was especially Paul and his theme of justification* by faith that constituted the theological arbiter. Theology

became the systematic setting out of biblical teaching around that as the centre. Later a new scholasticism set in, and once again the Bible was used as a quarry for supports to dogma, though now Protestant dogma. The Enlightenment* introduced critical historical study to the NT and led both to the attempt to be strictly descriptive and also to the question whether in its theology the church could use all the NT material equally and without discrimination. The nineteenth century saw the great liberal flowering which was preoccupied with the attempt to reach behind the early church's theologizing in order to recover the historical Jesus* who would, it was hoped and believed, speak directly and simply to its own day. Probably the greatest figure was F. C. Baur of Tübingen, whose researches led him to argue that the original teaching of Jesus was not theological but a straightforward expression of religious consciousness. Theology began with Paul and with the debate over the relation of Christians to the Jewish Law. The outcome was the institutionalizing of Christianity in the later books of the NT and in the second century generally. His rigorous historical work was accompanied by a belief that the unfolding of history is itself the movement of the Holy Spirit and that in following the course of development we encounter that Spirit afresh. In general the liberal enterprise (which reached its peak in Harnack) believed that it could discover the true and original heart of the teaching of Jesus in such things as the Fatherhood of God, the Golden Rule, and the supreme value of the individual, things of permanent relevance, once the theology of the writings was stripped away. Liberals shared with conservatives the belief that the NT could speak directly to their own day, differing, however, in their view of the amount of material that could do so. Both sides believed that to answer the question of meaning *then* was to answer the question of meaning *now*.

At the end of the nineteenth century and the beginning of the twentieth this confidence began to break down. On the one hand William Wrede argued for NT theology as a strictly historical and descriptive discipline which could not be limited to the canon but must take account of the whole spread of early Christianity, and must apply the critical-historical methods of 'the history of religions'. He rejected any interest in making the NT speak to the present time as liable to pervert the historical enterprise. On the other hand, out of the mainstream of scholarship of his own day but later very influential, Adolf Schlatter maintained that the business of NT scholarship was both to ask 'What did it mean (then)?' using the methods of historical enquiry, and also to ask 'What does it mean (now, for us)?' It was above all Albert Schweitzer (in *The Quest of the Historical Jesus*, German 1906, ET 1910) who showed the enormous difficulty of reading off the answer to the second question from the answer to the first. He showed how again and again the liberal scholars found their own theological reflections because they had discarded from the NT what did not answer to their own interests, needs, and preconceptions. A rigorous attention to 'What did it mean (then)?' resulted in the discovery of a thought-world alien to ours both in the case of Jesus and in the case of Paul (see *The Mysticism of Paul the Apostle*, German 1930, ET 1931, much of the work for which was done a great deal earlier). In both cases he found Jewish eschatological thought to be a basis and not a husk that could be discarded. Jesus was the disappointed herald of the divine consummation, the End, and Paul too saw him as the beginning of that End, an End that did not come. A thorough understanding of the NT on its own terms thus made it not easier but harder to let it speak to twentieth-century men and women who did not share its basic eschatological presuppositions. Although many of the details of Schweitzer's case have not withstood criticism, the dilemma he posed has remained. Moreover, about the same time that he was showing the profound Jewishness of Jesus and Paul others were stressing the Hellenistic background and structure of much NT thought, including Paul's, and thus were raising the same problem from another angle.

The three most notable twentieth-century attempts, despite all this, to write NT theology as theology for today are those of Karl Barth, Rudolf Bultmann, and the 'biblical theology'* movement exemplified most eminently by Oscar Cullmann.

(*a*) Barth in his commentary on Romans (German 1918, but extensively and repeatedly revised, ET 1933) believed that God could speak through his ancient witnesses to make his word contemporary when those witnesses were interpreted in preaching. He did not despise the historical task but took it for granted that the fundamental situations of Paul's readers and his own were sufficiently close to enable the word of God still to be heard. Whether fairly or not, most scholars have considered that his commentary tells us more about Barth's theology than about Paul's.

(b) Bultmann's *Theology of the New Testament* (two volumes, German 1948–1953, ET 1952–1955) spent little time on the original message of Jesus. Insofar as it can be recovered at all (not very far) it was existential, a call for decision. We ought to be concerned with external history only where it can speak to our personal histories. Eschatology is only apparently about what happens in the external cosmos. It is mythology, an externalizing of personal existential truth and needs to be reinterpreted for its real and timeless message to be heard. That message concerns the end of my old world, my old existence with its false securities and goals, and the beginning of my true and authentic existence. It is not only that modern men and women are alienated by eschatology as by much of NT mythology, though that is true and a serious barrier to the gospel. It is even more that until the mythology is reinterpreted the real offence and challenge of the message, the kerygma*, cannot be heard and responded to. And that kerygma is a call to our own authentic existence. John and above all Paul understood this and presented the kerygma accordingly; as a result Bultmann's *Theology* is essentially a study of Paul and John. Bultmann was not in the liberal tradition: he tried not to jettison what was difficult or uncongenial but to reinterpret it. In effect theology became anthropology, concerned not primarily with the study of God or of Christ but with who I am and what I may become. The desire to find solid historical ground for faith to rest upon he regarded as the way of unfaith. In short, his whole demythologizing* programme was designed to show that beneath the mythology (eschatology, angels, heaven and hell, and so on), what the NT meant *then* does still speak directly to modern hearers and readers because of its existential character. Few now follow his line in its entirety partly because few share his extreme historical scepticism, partly because he did

not find a satisfactory place for the biblical and modern concern for the world and for external as well as personal history, and partly because existential categories are not now widely held to be philosophically adequate. Nonetheless his was the most striking and within its limits most successful attempt that we have yet seen to write a NT theology that fulfilled the demands of historical criticism*, and that also spoke authoritatively and intelligibly to the twentieth century. The kerygma was in effect timeless and in order to hear it modern men and women did not need to turn themselves into people of the first century.

(c) Cullmann is the best-known representative in the NT field of the movement that flourished in the fifties and sixties of this century known as 'biblical theology' (a confusing term because much biblical theology did not and does not belong to the 'biblical theology' movement). The Bible was seen not as a system of beliefs but as primarily a story, an account of the mighty acts of God in history, an account which is in itself revelatory. This approach assumed that interpretation of the acts was needed for revelation* to occur: 'Jesus died' is history but not revelation until we make the interpretative addition 'for us'. The movement was diametrically opposed to Bultmann's programme, for instead of seeing external historical events as dispensable it saw them as central. To some extent it built on work by C. H. Dodd (*The Apostolic Preaching and its Developments*, 1936) who attempted to recover the primitive Christian preaching which he saw as having been a recital of God's saving action in Christ, his death, resurrection, the coming of the Spirit, and the promise of future consummation. At the same time the movement also often claimed that Hebraic, biblical thinking was uniquely concerned with history, with time and functions and activities rather than with abstract truth and essences, with things as wholes rather than with analysis, as opposed to the alleged character of Greek thought. It was usually agreed with the Bultmann school that Luke's theology was of this 'salvation-history' (*Heilsgeschichte*) character, that he saw Christ as the centre of time prepared for by God's acts towards Israel and followed by the age of the church and the Spirit, though still looking towards a final consummation. The difference was that the Bultmannians regarded Lukan theology as a NT aberration, a decline from the true (when interpreted existentially) kerygma, while 'biblical theology' saw it as conveying the central message of the NT both then and now. Most of the exponents of 'biblical theology' saw no great difficulty in moving from 'What it meant (then)' to 'What it means (now)'. The classic statement of this salvation-history approach is to be found in Cullmann's *Salvation in History* (German 1965, ET 1967).

The opponents of this position see its weaknesses to include the fact that it never successfully clarified the relation of saving history to ordinary history; that it did not really tackle the hermeneutical problem (*why* should the exodus or the return from exile be a message of liberation for modern men and women – and why select those events and not, say, the killing of Goliath?); that its assumption of fundamental difference between a biblical and a Greek and modern way of thinking has failed to be sustained (see especially James Barr in *The Semantics of Biblical Language*, 1961; *Biblical Words for Time*, 1962; and many subsequent publications); and that it required modern readers to archaize themselves, to turn themselves into first-century Semitic readers, an impossible demand. In any case it is not the case that the whole Bible is strongly orientated towards strictly historical thinking.

Attempts to write a theology of the NT that can serve as a theology for the present have thus not been notably successful. Two problems obtrude: the variety of theologies in the NT itself, and the strangeness of the biblical thought-world with the consequent danger that the contingent and culturally conditioned be made absolute. It is not surprising that increasingly a division is made between the task of description, and the task of interpretation or hermeneutics *.

3. *The interpretation of the NT*. No modern theology can be simply identical with NT theology. The NT belongs to a different world and a different conceptual framework and answers questions that are sometimes ours but sometimes not. Few modern Christians hold to the biblical eschatology as it stands. Few are as concerned with the relation of Christianity to the Law as Paul was. Much of the ethical material in the NT is to be seen against a background alien to us: we

do not accept slavery, nor the subservience of women to men, as entirely right and normal. Even justification by faith does not mean quite the same to us as to an audience in close contact with pious Judaism. We have different cultures, histories and circumstances, and therefore different ears. When the same thing is said the same thing is not heard (though the extent to which this is a problem is variously assessed). Nevertheless the existence of the canon and its own history mean that the church cannot ignore the NT. A threefold task therefore remains:

1. To examine critically and historically what was written.
2. To determine the intention of the writers in their own terms and culture.
3. To ask what this says to us in our terms, concepts, and culture.

There may be occasions on which it says little or nothing. Always we must be ready to work not directly, applying something from the NT straight to the modern situation, but indirectly, listening in the light of our culture and conceptions to what the NT says from within its culture and conceptions, and then making our theological or ethical response. At least it is now clear that in the process we must not confuse 3. with 1. and 2.

In addition to works cited above in the text: H. Conzelmann, *An Outline of the Theology of the New Testament*, 1969; W. J. Harrington OP, *The Path of Biblical Theology*, 1973; E. Käsemann, 'The Problem of a New Testament Theology,' *NTS* XIX 3, 1973, pp. 235–45; W. G. Kümmel, *The New Testament: the History of the Investigation of its Problems*, 1973; R. Morgan, *The Nature of New Testament Theology*, 1973; P. Stuhlmacher, *Historical Criticism and Theological Interpretation of Scripture*, 1979.

J. A. ZIESLER

Nicaea *see* **Christology, Trinity**

Nihilism

The basic meaning of nihilism, a rather vague and wide term which means literally 'belief in nothing', is probably the rejection of all moral and religious principles, and historically it became current in nineteenth-century Russia, where in revolutionary circles it was almost indistinguishable in meaning from 'anarchy'. Occasionally, especially in Eastern philosophy, it means the denial that anything at all is real. But, especially in more modern and contemporary philosophy, it can refer to a philosophical trend which directs our attention to the cognitive value of affective states such as boredom, cynicism, lack of concern, emptiness, or a trend which warns of the spiritual dangers attendant upon such states and attitudes.

JAMES RICHMOND

Nominalism

Primarily a term used to describe a position on the philosophical problem of universals, namely that individuals are the primary reality and that universal concepts are mental descriptions for features that are similar among individuals.

Nominalism has its roots in the Aristotelian * critique of Platonic * idealism and was first espoused by Roscelin of Compiègne (c. 1050–1125) and in a milder form by Peter Abelard (1079–1142), to be revived in the early fourteenth century by William of Ockham (c. 1290–1349). Ockham was among the first to reject the idea of a common nature inhering in things of the same species that make them similar. The universal is our mental composite of those qualities that are similar in individuals of the same species. Ockham's solution to this problem became widely accepted in the late Middle Ages and has been revived at various times in the modern period.

Theological nominalism describes a particular body of theological views that are compatible with (but not derived from) philosophical nominalism and were adopted by a number of thinkers in the late mediaeval period. The fundamental notion lies in the idea of covenant *, through which is viewed both the relationship of God and creation and the operation of the orders of nature and grace. God is free and could have (and theoretically still can) establish other physical and moral laws than those that are now operative. If one views divine power absolutely (de potentia absoluta), God can do anything that does not involve an inherent contradiction. God has, however, bound himself to act in specific ways and has chosen a particular physical and moral order, which he will uphold. Thus when one views divine power from the standpoint of

creation and revelation (de potentia ordinata), the present order is reliable and operates unfailingly.

Although there are many areas of nominalistic theology in which this perception functions, the two principal ones are in the doctrines of justification * and sacramental causality. Both doctrines were modified by the notion of ascribed value, developed in the thirteenth century by the Dominican theologians Richard Fishacre and Robert Kilwardby, and further elaborated by the Franciscans Bonaventure and John Duns Scotus. Causal efficacy results not from forces or inherent virtues placed within created things but rather from a value which God ascribes to things and which he rewards on the basis of a covenant or agreement with creation and the church. In the doctrine of justification * the meritorious quality of good acts is not inherent in them but is accorded them by God when he accepts them (acceptatio divina) as being worthy of grace and eventually of eternal life. Similarly, the sacraments, apart from the eucharist, operate, ex opere operato *, on the basis of a covenant by which, when properly performed, God will give grace to the recipients.

This view of justification has been viewed as semi-Pelagian *, since the system operates semi-automatically and because God has bound himself to reward with grace and eventually with eternal life those who try their best, to do what is in them.

P. Boehner, Collected Articles on Ockham, 1958; H. A. Oberman, The Harvest of Medieval Theology, 1963; M. M. Tweedale, Abailard on Universals, 1976; Vignaux, Nominalisme au XIVe siècle, 1948.

WILLIAM J. COURTENAY

Non-Being

In classical Christian theology the ancient Greek doctrine of degrees of being (or perfection) was universally accepted. God (ens realissimum) alone possessed the fullness of being; all created things possessed only partial being (or perfection). The absolutely evil was the absolutely non-existent. In modern existentialist * theology, however, non-being takes over a positively threatening character. Man (referred to as Dasein, German for 'being there'), aware of his 'being there' in the world and aware too that one day he will no longer be there, is anxiously (*see* **Angst**) aware of non-being, because his existence is threatened by it. It is, of course, logically impossible to think of non-being, for how can we think of that which does not exist? Nevertheless, according to Heidegger, although non-being cannot be thought, it can be apprehended through anxiety as a kind of indescribable, ultimate dread. Our lives are bounded by this ever-present threat of non-being. Tillich affirmed that God is 'the power of being' which overcomes the threat of non-being. There is thus an interesting parallel between the classical Christian-mediaeval conception of evil * as non-being and the modern existentialist teaching about the sinister or dreadful character of non-being. But whereas the former is mainly philosophical and intellectual, the latter strictly defies conceptualization and comes to us through 'apprehension' (in both senses of the word).

See also **Meon**.

M. Heidegger, *Being and Time* (1927), ET 1962; P. Tillich, *The Courage to Be*, 1952.

ALAN RICHARDSON

Novatianism

A rigorist schism arising out of the Decian persecution (249–250). Its author, Novatian, was a leading Roman presbyter and an accomplished theologian whose *de Trinitate* represents the Roman orthodoxy of his day. At first prepared to accept tolerant views on the reconciliation of the lapsed, he swung over to rigorism partly owing to disappointment at the election of Cornelius as Pope. Consecrated rival Bishop of Rome, he soon became the focus of conservative disciplinary forces throughout the church. Apart from Dionysius of Alexandria, who as an Origenist was not in sympathy with Novatian's starting point in trinitarianism, no serious charge was raised against the orthodoxy of the schism. Indeed, Constantine summoned the Novatianist bishop of Constantinople to Nicaea where he assented without difficulty to the anti-Arian decisions of the Council. It was their boast that their churches were completely free of Arian influence. Nicenes and Novatianists suffered together during the Arian controversy and at times seemed on the verge of reconciliation. Socrates, the church historian, was well informed on Novatianist

affairs and might even have been an adherent. Some of its leaders were highly regarded within the Great Church. At least in the larger centres of Christianity the movement seems to have died out by the end of the fifth century. It had made its disciplinary point (however unsuccessfully) and after the achievement of trinitarian orthodoxy had nothing further to offer.

A. d'Alès, *Novatien*, 1924; E. Amann, *DTC*, XI, cols. 826–49.

H. E. W. TURNER

Numinous

A term particularly associated with the work of Rudolf Otto, notably in his book *Das Heilige* (1917; ET, *The Idea of the Holy*, 1923). In this book Otto used 'numinous' as a category for distinguishing the particular features of religion. Otto saw the origin of religion in what he called the *mysterium tremendum et fascinans*. By this, Otto meant that particular experience, usually for primitive people some confrontation with natural forces, but for the more sophisticated some depth of personal relationship, where simultaneously one is both attracted and repelled by a sense of awe.

Criticism of Otto's discussion of the numinous has called in question his thesis that this is an experience which is characteristic only of religion, and it has questioned further whether the numinous is as isolated from the moral sense as Otto maintained. It has been argued, perhaps rightly, that the undifferentiated sense of the holy, what Otto called the numinous, is in essence indistinguishable from the root of the aesthetic sense or the moral sense.

See **Ecstasy**.

R. Jones, *The Concept of Holiness*, 1961; Rudolf Otto, *The Idea of the Holy*, 1923.

E. J. TINSLEY

Objectification

In general terms, objectification is the process or the result of the process whereby a thing or person expresses itself in the form of objects or things external to it. In Hegel, the terms objectification and alienation * are barely distinguished, but for Marx, all human creativity involves objectification, and so objectification can be regarded as a permanent feature of human existence.

Alienation for Marx has to be sharply distinguished from objectification because alienation is the historical form which the universally necessary processes of objectification take practically within capitalist society. In capitalist society, human wage labour 'objectifies' itself in the form of capital, and so by his labour the labourer creates the class which is its opposite.

Objectification is therefore linked with the processes whereby the activities of human wealth-creation impoverish the very creators of wealth, and therefore with the processes whereby the makers of human objects become imprisoned by the objects they make. In a phrase of Sartre's, men become 'the products of their own product'.

DENYS TURNER

Occasionalism

The term describes a variety of epistemological, metaphysical and theological opinions that deny causality * between things on the basis of inherent, necessary virtues or powers. God is the principal and sole active cause; created things are the occasion for, not the causes of, the observed effects. Occasionalism can be, but need not be, related to material and/or temporal atomism. In examining occasionalism one must be careful to distinguish metaphysical occasionalism (the belief that there are no direct causal connections between things) and epistemological occasionalism (the belief that we cannot know or prove causal connections, which may nevertheless exist). One should also distinguish between those who argue that God *could have* created a world in which there was only direct, divine intervention, and those who maintain that he in fact did so.

Most forms of occasionalism have been religiously motivated, attributing direct causal activity to God and thus reducing the causal role of created things. Al-Ghazali, the eleventh-century Islamic theologian, attempted to undermine Greek necessitarianism by affirming epistemological occasionalism, particularly as applied to the doctrines of creation * and various forms of causality. In the West, William of Ockham in the early fourteenth century used similar arguments to attack the idea of necessary, inherent causes in things. For Ockham, causal connections between created things are not demonstrable; yet one may legitimately infer that in the order of physical nature things do have causal power placed within them by God. In the order of grace and salvation, however, God has established a system whereby things, be they good acts properly motivated or sacramental signs, such as the baptismal water or the oil of consecration, are *sine qua non* causes whose efficacy * depends on the system God has established, not on any inherent virtue. When certain conditions are met, a certain result will take place by reason of the ordained will of God.

The views of Al-Ghazali and Ockham were revived, often independently, in the following centuries. Towards the middle of the fourteenth century Nicholas of Autrecourt at Paris reaffirmed epistemological occasionalism, as did Nicholas Malebranche and David Hume in the seventeenth and eighteenth centuries. A version closer to Ockham's was put forward by Gabriel Biel at the end of the fifteenth century, which was very influential in the early sixteenth century.

W. J. Courtenay, 'The Critique of Natural Causality in the Mutakallimum and Nominalism', *HTR* 66, 1973, pp. 77–94; M. Fakhry, *Islamic Occasionalism and its Critique by Averroes and Aquinas*, 1958; N. Malebranche, *Recherche de la Vérité*, 1674.

WILLIAM J. COURTENAY

Old Testament Theology

The theology of the OT is one of the most controversial branches of the study of the OT today, not so much because there are so many points of detail, more or less important, about which there is disagreement among experts, but because there is fundamental difference of opinion about the actual nature of the discipline itself. In a short article such as this it is obviously impossible to offer even a summary of the subject-matter with which OT theology, on any view of its nature, is concerned. That would have to be so superficial as to be of little value. What is possible and might prove helpful is to consider the nature of the problem associated with the idea of a theology of the OT and certain of the solutions which have been offered, in the hope that the issues may to some extent be clarified, even though no way beyond the present impasse can be found.

Almost all discussions of the problem

with which we are concerned refer to the famous distinction drawn by J. P. Gabler in 1787 between biblical and dogmatic theology, according to which the former should confine itself to a description of the religion of the Bible and refrain from passing any normative judgments which would involve trespassing into the domain of dogmatic theology. On this view OT theology would restrict itself to the OT evidence and would resist any temptation to criticize the material with which it dealt even from the point of view of the NT.

Gabler's distinction was a useful one, since it did much to break the stranglehold of dogmatic theology upon the study of the OT and so left scholars free to look at it without preconceived ideas as to what they should find. The result was an increase of interest in OT history and religion and a growing appreciation of the extraordinary variety of points of view to be found in the OT. More and more, however, was interest directed to the history of the development of OT thought, in conjunction with a rearrangement of the literary material. This did not indeed lead to the disappearance of attempts to treat the religion of Israel systematically – the books of G. F. Oehler, H. Schultz and others are proof of the contrary – but, as time went on, the truly theological interest in the OT lessened. The emphasis came to be on religious experience and religious psychology. In particular the Hebrew prophets acquired a new significance and were treated primarily as men of religious genius with a message directed to their own time and only in a secondary way to the future. Concurrent with the interest in religious experience was the intensive study of the literature of the OT, which concerned itself in the first instance with the presumed sources of the existing documents and their relation to each other and later with the even more fruitful form-critical * study of the various literary types in the situations which determined their character.

Apart from A. B. Davidson's *The Theology of the Old Testament* which appeared in 1904 and showed genuine theological characteristics and so was prophetic of what was to come, the period of a revived interest in OT theology was inaugurated in 1922 by E. König's *Theologie des Alten Testaments*. There followed a number of articles by prominent OT scholars who concerned themselves with the question of the nature of the discipline, in particular by O. Eissfeldt in 1926 who distinguished sharply between the history of OT religion and OT theology, confining the latter to a study of timeless truths as they were revealed to the men of the OT on the basis of faith, and by W. Eichrodt who adumbrated the views which he subsequently developed on a grand scale in his well known *Theology of the Old Testament*, which began to appear in 1933 (ET 1961, 1967). Of less importance, though deserving of mention, were works by E. Sellin (1933) and L. Köhler (1936). In 1924 and 1942 were published the controversial volumes of W. Vischer, entitled *Das Christuszeugnis des Alten Testaments* (The Witness of the OT to Christ), which, inspired as they were by dialectical * theology, placed the OT on the same level as the NT by employing the methods of typology and allegory * to justify the claim that the OT is from beginning to end direct witness to Jesus Christ and his atoning work. Though undoubtedly a passing fashion of interpretation, this type of theological handling of the OT had its historical importance during the church struggle in Germany and it did something to conserve a truth about the Bible which should not be overlooked, even though the method by which this was done must be rejected. It represented a gallant, if misdirected, effort to maintain the relevance for Christianity of the OT at a time when the latter was the main target of the attack of paganism on the Christian faith. In 1949 two more OT theologies appeared, the posthumous one of O. Procksch and the original Dutch edition of that of T. C. Vriezen which subsequently in its German and English editions played a notable part in the debate, alongside the work, above mentioned, of W. Eichrodt and the highly original *Old Testament Theology* of G. von Rad published in German in 1957 and 1960 (ET 1962, 1965). A smaller but admirable *OT Theology* by a French scholar, E. Jacob, was published in French in 1955 (ET 1958). Though traditional in its arrangement, unlike the works of Eichrodt, Vriezen and von Rad – it adopts like Köhler's book a dogmatic scheme – it is distinguished by a full treatment of the action of God in history which makes the book relevant to the modern debate.

There is, of course, an extensive literature of monographs and articles (for the latter see, for example, the volume *Essays on Old Testament Interpretation*, ed. C. Westermann, 1963, and *The Old Testament and Christian Faith*, ed. B. W. Anderson, 1964) dealing with the nature of OT theology and the various conflicting views which have to be taken into account in any thorough discussion of the subject. The names of some of these scholars will be mentioned below, but this article cannot do more than clarify a few of the more important issues involved. It should perhaps be mentioned here that one of the most useful and balanced discussions of the various issues is given by Vriezen in the first part of his book; he is deeply concerned about the questions of the relevance of the OT to the Christian and of the relation between the Testaments.

What is involved in all this discussion can best be appreciated by looking at the works of Eichrodt and von Rad and at the criticisms of von Rad by a scholar who has not yet been mentioned, F. Baumgärtel, whose book entitled *Verheissung* (Promise) was published in 1952 and who may be said to have kept up a running fight with von Rad on certain fundamental issues of biblical interpretation. F. Hesse, *Das Alte Testament als Buch der Kirche* (1966), will be found very helpful for an understanding of Baumgärtel's rather involved thought.

It would be a mistake to regard these scholars as being at variance all along the line. Eichrodt, for example, is full of admiration for von Rad's skill in delineating the main features of the various OT 'theologies', those of the Yahwist, the Deuteronomist, the Chronicler and so forth. Similarly Baumgärtel pays generous tribute to the brilliance of von Rad's traditio-historical work. It can be safely asserted that no one can read von Rad's *Old Testament Theology* without being immensely stimulated by his flashes of insight and his original handling and combining of evidence. The very brilliance of his achievement, however, should not blind the reader to certain defects in his thought which are all the more difficult to detect as one is carried away by the beauty of his style.

Eichrodt and von Rad contrast sharply in their methodology. The former, as is well known, lays the emphasis on the underlying unity of the OT. This he demonstrates by the method of the cross-section which brings to light the fundamental and enduring features of OT religion and religious institutions. The central thought is alleged to be that of the covenant* between Yahweh and Israel which eventually broadens into Yahweh's willingness for fellowship with all men. Within this systematic scheme Eichrodt makes full allowance for historical development. There are many who think that Eichrodt has come nearest to producing a theology of the OT which does justice to the nature of the material and to the unity in variety and movement.

Von Rad's main contention, on the other hand, is that the correct way in which to write a theology of the OT is that of reportage, retelling the story of Israel's salvation-history (*Heilsgeschichte* *) as it was 'confessed' at the ancient Israelite sanctuaries in credos like those in Deut. 26 and Josh. 24 and subsequently expanded in various ways (cf. G. E. Wright, *God Who Acts*, 1952, and, as a contrast, the penetrating criticism of the idea of revelation through history by James Barr, *Old and New in Interpretation*, 1966). This method results in an elaborate study of Israel's historical traditions which record the varied interpretations of God's dealings throughout the centuries with the people of Israel as put forward by the Hebrew writers. At this point it is important to quote what von Rad actually says about this variety: 'Unlike the revelation in Christ, the revelation of Jahweh in the Old Testament is divided up over a long series of separate acts of revelation which are very different in content. It seems to be without a centre which determines everything and which could give to the various separate acts both an interpretation and their proper theological connection with one another. We can only describe the Old Testament's revelation as a number of distinct and heterogeneous revelatory acts.' One is left wondering how in these circumstances one can speak of revelation* at all.

What is perhaps even more serious than this denial of a fundamental unity in the OT is von Rad's apparent lack of concern at the violent separation he makes between Israel's salvation history and the actual course of history as it is approximately determined by modern scientific methods of historical investigation. The contrast is pressed by von Rad to such an extreme that it becomes clear that, if he is right, there is simply no historical basis for some of the most important elements in Israelite belief. His extreme scepticism about the role of Moses, which he shares with M. Noth, is a case in point. It is perfectly true, of course, that the modern historian does not, in the character of historian, permit himself expressions of faith regarding the events he is describing. Moreover the biblical evidence for events is to a very large extent cast in the form of witness to God's activity in history. That, however, does not entitle us to conclude that, from the theological point of view, what actually happened is a matter of indifference. For one thing the salvation history itself, as soon as it was recited, became a part of the actual history of Israel and influential in determining the subsequent course of events in that history. This failure on von Rad's part to realize the importance of actual history is one of the points specially singled out for criticism by Eichrodt, who connects it with von Rad's existentialist * approach to the OT (see the excursus at the end of Eichrodt, *Theology of the OT*, Vol. 1). That Eichrodt should do so – probably quite correctly – is nevertheless a little odd, since Baumgärtel, in his criticism of von Rad's use of typology in passing beyond mere description, seems to think that he is lacking in the existential point of view, contenting himself with pointing out analogies between events (or supposed events) in the OT and the NT and failing to ask the fundamental question of relevance which interests Baumgärtel. Von Rad, he feels, lays himself open to the charge of not really passing beyond mere description and an aesthetic interest in correspondences.

Eichrodt follows a similar line and criticizes von Rad for a typological procedure which compares a NT act of faith with a supposed OT type, the detection of the correspondence being left to the arbitrary choice of the expositor disguised as the expositor's *charisma*. (Baumgärtel declares that what von Rad is really talking about is 'pneumatic exegesis'.) Eichrodt does indeed recognize that there are parallels of structure between the Testaments which lend some justification to the typological procedure and are valuable for elucidating the meaning of religious terms and the significance of religious institutions. Nothing, however, should be allowed to divert us from the recognition that in the OT we have the record of how God worked out the salvation of

Israel in the concrete events of history, and how what he accomplished in his dealings with the men of the OT eventually found its fulfilment in Christ. What God was doing in OT times was no mere shadow-play with no ultimate significance for the actors in the events. Nor have we just a succession of hypotheses without any ultimate ground in history. Rather in all the undoubted variety of the OT we have as centre and focus the purpose of God working itself out in the movement of history.

Part of the trouble with von Rad's thought is that he lays himself open to the charge of inconsistency. When he ostensibly confines OT theology to reportage of the salvation history of the OT and contrasts it sharply with the actual history in which the modern critical historian is interested, he seems to forget that he himself is employing critical methods in his assessment of the documents and so does not confine himself to reportage. For example he does not accept Deuteronomy at its face value as an address of Moses, but chooses to take up a highly criticial position as he determines its place and time of origin. Moreover, when he insists that attention should be confined to the saving acts of God in history and that the history of Israel's faith and piety is irrelevant for an OT theology, he seems to overlook the fact that the very salvation history of which he speaks is itself an expression of Israelite faith. The divine act and the human response in faith in fact belong together. Von Rad would probably agree that this is so. But then he must recognize the consequences for his theory. Eichrodt and Baumgärtel are at one in criticizing von Rad's over-emphasis on the supposed external facts as if they were not inseparable from the internal facts of faith. By cutting off the 'facts' of the salvation history both from the actual facts of history on the one hand and from the accompanying faith of those who proclaim them on the other, von Rad is in danger of condemning his salvation history to the status of myth. Eichrodt's words may be quoted: 'It seems necessary to us to emphasize that the withdrawal from all "conceptualism" with regard to the activity of God in history ought never to involve isolating this activity in such a way as to ignore the testimony of faith evoked in response to it from the Old Testament community. It is rather that the latter affords the only legitimate commentary on that activity. It is the interior overmastering of the human spirit by God's personal invasion which in the first place brings to life the Old Testament understanding of history. Here is to be found the decisive inward event, without which all external facts must become myth.' Eichrodt goes on to insist that the divine activity and the human response must be held together in thought.

There is still another feature of his thought in which von Rad lays himself open to criticism, namely, his view that there were actual breaks in the salvation history when it came to an end and that there was a pause until God intervened with a new creative act. This is really to forget that the salvation-history consists not only in God's positive saving acts towards Israel but also in his negative acts of judgment. In fact the judgments are all part of the one continuous saving act of God. Von Rad indeed is inconsistent in the way in which he writes of the prophetic work of reinterpretation. Sometimes the language he uses seems to imply a complete break with the past – Yahweh's original appointments in election, covenant, law, conquest and monarchy – whereas in another place he admits that there is continuity in the reinterpretation. He cannot have it both ways. After all, the grandiose movement of interpretation and reinterpretation of Israel's tradition, with God's promise always pointing towards the future and ever more complete fulfilments, would seem to imply continuity of purpose amid all the variety. At the same time it may be admitted that there is a relative truth in von Rad's division of the salvation history into stages.

Whether or not von Rad is correct in his contention that the events of Israel's history clearly point forward to the future fulfilments within the OT period itself and beyond it in Christianity, is a question on which there are strong differences of opinion. It should not be forgotten that to the Jews the OT with its continuation in early Judaism is not a torso requiring the completion given by Christianity. It is only from the point of view of NT faith that the incompleteness of the OT is apparent and Christians should be humbly aware that their faith is challenged by the adherents of a faith which claims the OT as its own rightful property, drawing out its implications in rabbinic thought.

In the last resort, if we leave on one side von Rad's highly original and controversial theory, there are two main views of the nature of OT theology, first that it must restrict itself to being purely descriptive, second that it must include a normative element. In his earliest discussion of the matter Eichrodt inclined to the former view, maintaining that the OT theologian must confine himself to historical description, though he went so far as to admit that, for the correct performance of this task, there must be a relation of 'congeniality' between the scholar and his subject matter. It is probable that Eichrodt, while still regarding it as his primary task to demonstrate the unity of the OT system of faith, moved some way towards the view that it does make a difference to one's assessment of the OT whether one views it in a Christian or a Jewish perspective. The names of R. C. Dentan (*Preface to Old Testament Theology*, rev. ed., 1963) and K. Stendahl (*IDB*, 1, pp. 432ff.) may be cited as examples of scholars who consider that a rigid insistence on the descriptive character of OT theology is more than a phenomenology of Israelite faith. But then, as we have seen, he seems to find in typology a satisfactory way of indicating the normative relation of the NT to the OT. Baumgärtel regards this as much too vague and arbitrary a procedure for the purpose of making OT theology serviceable to dogmatics. There must, he thinks, be a much more scientific procedure if OT theology is to be taken seriously.

Though Baumgärtel would not agree with R. Bultmann in the latter's depreciation of the OT history which he dismisses as a history of failure or miscarriage, the two men have this in common, that they draw a very sharp line between Israel's religion and Christianity. The OT, they maintain, is not directly relevant to the Christian. Baumgärtel works out his position as follows. The keyword for the understanding of the Bible, OT and NT alike, is *epangelia*, promise. God's basic promise, which is undoubtedly historical, even though there may be some doubt as to where it is to be pinpointed in history, consisted in his choice of a people for himself. It is expressed in the proclamation of Yahweh as the God of Israel and Israel as the people of Yahweh, and again in the preface to the Decalogue. 'I am Yahweh your God who brought you out of the land of Egypt'. Throughout the OT period this promise is represented by promises, the partial fulfilment of which maintains the life of Israel, so that they are relevant to Israel, but must be kept distinct from the original basic promise which is always valid and does not require fulfilment in the material ways on which Israel ever and again set its heart. This basic promise was confirmed and sealed in Christ, and we are pointed forward to the eschatological fulfilment, when it will become finally manifest that God's purpose in choosing Israel was the salvation of all mankind. As we look back over history we must frankly recognize that there is no possible rational proof that God did make such a basic promise as the inner meaning of history. That has to be accepted by faith. Apart from faith history remains opaque. We can only believe that God is active 'in, with and under' the historical process. But that God did so act in real history and that his promise is still valid is quite essential for Christian faith. This is what we should mean by salvation history.

What then is our relation to the OT as Christians? Baumgärtel maintains that, as we are not Israel, the partial fulfilments of the promise, which meant so much to Israel, are not directly relevant to us. The OT, however, retains its validity for us by its witness to the basic promise and further by the ambiguous nature of its witness to God's dealings with Israel throughout its chequered history. For the OT possibility of partial appropriations of the promise is still a possibility for us as Christians. The partial witness has a positive side which can help us on our way of faith and a negative side which can warn us of the many possibilities of misunderstanding and error.

It will be clear that this view of Baumgärtel's implies that the OT witness to the promise of God is to be judged by the norm of Christianity, the application of which makes clear the limited and ambiguous character of the OT and enables it to reflect the ambiguous quality in ourselves. The difficulty may be raised that the NT witness to Christ is varied and even contradictory, so that we do not have the unambiguous norm that seems to be required. It may also be objected that a truer view of the relation between the testaments would recognize that they have a reciprocal influence upon each other, the OT being required to throw light

on the NT, just as the latter is required to throw light on the former. It may be suggested, however, that the difficulty is made greater by the tendency to look at it too exclusively from the intellectual point of view as a puzzle to be solved. Christianity is first and foremost a way of life and our Christian judgment is gradually formed by the experience of living it. We learn through our relations with other people, not only with those within the Christian fellowship but also with those outside it, by our ventures of faith, by our failures and betrayals as well as by the times when the Spirit moves us to acts of true brotherhood and loyalty. Perhaps the most helpful way of looking at the whole matter is to remember that the God who made the promise to Israel which was confirmed in Christ is the living God who gives life to his people. The OT with all its limitations bears witness to that communication of life, and we know from our own experience as Christians, both in the Christian fellowship and in our contacts with the world outside, that Christ does indeed communicate the life which is more abundant. With that experience we can enter the world of the OT through its varied literature and, recognizing our kinship with these men of old, of whose faith ours is the fulfilment, discover that their witness, for all its limitations, can guide us into the presence of the living God. Theology is theology and not life, but unless the theologian, and that includes the biblical theologian, keeps close to the source of life and allows his thinking to be enriched by the wisdom which only life can impart, his theology will be defective for the discharge of its critical function.

James Barr in his challenging book, *Old and New in Interpretation* (1966), doubts if there requires to be a discipline called OT theology, but recognizes that there has to be 'criticism of the aspects of theological currents which lie close to relevance for the Old Testament and . . . the pointing out of ways in which these currents might have to be altered if they are really to do justice to the Old Testament texts' (p. 170). He may be right. Certainly it should be clear from what has been said that the theological task, whatever form its end product should take, can be carried out properly only if thought and life act upon each other. Such thought need not be arbitrary or irresponsible, but unless the biblical theologian is prepared to take some risks he may fail in his task of mediation.

In the manner in which the subject of OT theology has developed since the death of G. von Rad in 1971 a quite striking diversity of views has emerged. Two volumes have appeared which demonstrate a relatively established and conventional approach to the subject, but with markedly different emphases. The first by W. Zimmerli (*Grundriss der alttestamentlichen Theologie*, 1972; ET *Old Testament Theology in Outline*, 1978) seeks to deal with the ideological aspects of the main institutions of Israel's life: the Law, the kingship, the levitical priesthood, the land of Canaan. It views them all as manifestations of God's love towards Israel. In this regard Zimmerli sees the 'theology' as primarily the conceptual framework which surrounded the more concrete features of Israelite religion. A comparable volume, published in the same year, by G. Fohrer (*Theologische Grundstrukturen des Alten Testaments*, 1972) follows a fairly similar path, but introduces fuller discussion of the social and intellectual environment of Israel. So Israel's theology is seen to contrast markedly with the practices of magic and to demand a given range of assumptions concerning the whole structure of the social and moral order. In this way OT theology comes very close to representing the Israelite 'world-view'.

The volume by G. F. Hasel entitled *Old Testament Theology. Basic Issues in the Current Debate*, 1972, is, as its title indicates, a kind of prefatory introduction to major problems of a methodological kind. However, its main thrust is along relatively conventional lines, arguing for a presentation of the main concepts to be found in the OT arranged about a 'centre', rather in the fashion advocated by W. Eichrodt.

Not surprisingly, in view of its many-sided approach to a number of fundamental issues, the work of G. von Rad has stimulated some dramatically new approaches to the question of an OT theology. Most striking, and perhaps consequentially most controversial in this regard, has been the work of H. Gese. In his essay entitled 'Erwägungen zur Einheit der biblischen Theologie', *Vom Sinai zum Zion*, 1974, pp. 11–30; cf. his essay 'Tradition and Biblical Theology', in

Tradition and Theology in the Old Testament, ed. D. A. Knight, 1977, pp. 301–26, he argues for a thoroughgoing acceptance of the category of 'tradition' as the formative subject-matter of theology. Hence the formulation, development and progressive reformulation of such 'tradition' constitutes the basic datum of biblical theology*. He then proceeds to argue from this that we can, by means of the traditio-historical method of enquiry so ably used by G. von Rad, follow through the stages through which the biblical tradition passed. We can re-examine its form in OT times, but, more pertinently, see that NT writers present a thoroughgoing recasting of the OT form of the tradition. Each new stage in the growth of the tradition effectively subsumes the earlier stages within itself. As a result a truly biblical theology must look at the latest (NT) formulation of the tradition in which the earlier stages are taken up. The most unsatisfactory feature in this approach by Gese is that it leads to a kind of obliteration of the earlier forms of the tradition as they become overlaid by its later forms. It also elevates the traditio-historical method of examination into an over-dominant position, effectively overturning the canonical form of the scriptures. However, it has succeeded in re-invigorating the notion of a biblical theology which would be more than simply a juxtaposing of separate OT and NT theologies. Furthermore Gese has succeeded in re-affirming the importance for a Christian understanding of the OT to be found in the ways in which the NT writers make use of its ideas and images.

To a noteworthy extent this openness to the way in which the NT looks at the OT is also to be seen in the stimulating volume by A. H. J. Gunneweg, *Vom Verstehen des Alten Testaments. Eine Hermeneutik* (1977; ET *Understanding the Old Testament*, 1978). This takes various aspects of the overall way in which the OT has been interpreted in Jewish and Christian tradition and uses these to provide key insights into the modern understanding and use of it. Particular attention is given to the use of typological and allegorical patterns of exegesis*, and their general unsatisfactoriness on account of their undisciplined arbitrariness. Most of all, however, Gunneweg is concerned with the way in which the OT has appeared as a book of 'Law' in both Jewish and Christian interpretations of it. He sees the relationship of the Christian church to the OT consequently as broken and indirect, much more so than has been the case with most authors of OT theologies in the nineteenth and twentieth centuries. Overall Gunneweg is concerned not to write another OT theology, but rather to ask questions about how the OT has come to us, and imposes itself upon us in a theological manner. It provides an instructive illustration of the recognition that the attempt to present a formal, and internally coherent, 'OT theology' may not be the best, nor the most effective, way of drawing out the theological implications of the OT for the Christian. It has the advantage of recognizing the role of the OT in Judaism, a feature which has been strikingly lacking in most Christian OT theologies, which have displayed too many hidden assumptions drawn from within a distinctively Christian hermeneutical tradition. Hence it opens up fresh possibilities of meaningful dialogue between Jews and Christians over the OT.

A similar concern with the relationship of the OT to the continuing life of the church is to be seen in C. Westermann's work, *Theologie des Alten Testaments in Grundzügen*, 1978. Some aspects of this were anticipated in his earlier study entitled *Der Segen in der Bibel und im Handeln der Kirche*, 1978. In his OT theology Westermann fully recognizes the 'living' character of the biblical view of God, who is not an isolated object of reflection, but a presence and power evident in human life and human history. So God's salvation and judgment are not abstract concepts, but rather living experiences in Israel's history, and his mercy and blessing are similarly made concrete through positive acts of redemption and restoration within a moral social order. This divine activity is to be viewed as continuous with his action in Jesus Christ and in the life of the Christian church.

It must appear in reflection on the work of the past two decades that the expectations of providing a single unified and coherent OT theology have foundered through lack of any agreed methodology that is to be employed. Instead, the impetus generated by the subject has extended further in the direction of using the OT as a theological subject by relating it more directly to the fundamental categories of interpretation which have been applied to it throughout

Jewish and Christian history. This calls for a recognition that a purely historical and descriptive OT theology of the kind once thought necessary and desirable now appears scarcely attainable at all. Against whatever loss this implies must be set the gain that it does not render the OT theologically valueless, but instead relates it more closely to a number of central issues of a theological nature. Questions of theological definition and hermeneutics are too closely intertwined for them to be dealt with in wholly separate studies.

J. Barr, *The Bible and the Modern World*, 1973; 'Biblical Theology', *IDB, Supplement*, pp. 104a–111b; F. F. Bruce, 'Theology and Interpretation of the Old Testament', *Tradition and Interpretation*, ed. G. W. Anderson, 1979, pp. 385–416; R. E. Clements, *Old Testament Theology. A Fresh Approach*, 1978; H. Graf Reventlow, *Hauptprobleme der alttestamentlichen Theologie im 20. Jahrhundert*, 1982; 'Basic Problems in Old Testament Theology', *JSOT* 11, 1979, 2–22; Werner H. Schmidt, 'Theologie des Alten Testaments "vor und nach von Rad"', *VuF* 17, 1972, pp. 1–25, *The Faith of the Old Testament: A History*, 1983; W. Zimmerli, 'Biblische Theologie 1. Altes Testament', *TRE* VI, pp. 426–55.

NORMAN W. PORTEOUS/
RONALD CLEMENTS

Omnipotence

The word means being all-powerful. In every monotheistic * faith, God is held to be omnipotent. In its religious use, the attribute sums up the sovereignty of God over all things. All other powers depend on God for whatever power they possess, and no other power can ultimately thwart him. The existence of evil * and suffering * have often seemed inconsistent with God's omnipotence, when God is also conceived to be wholly good. Evil and suffering can only be explained if a morally sufficient reason can be given why a good, omnipotent God permits their existence in the world. Such a reason might be the logical impossibility of creating a world of persons without setting them in a regularly ordered environment and giving them the gift of freedom. If there are necessary conditions of a world of creaturely persons, then not even omnipotence can avoid the risk of evil. Philosophical theologians have also considered certain other paradoxes of omnipotence which arise when omnipotence is taken as the power to do all things. Thomas Aquinas recognized that the scope of such a definition must be restricted. It makes no sense to say that God can do the logically impossible. But further restrictions are necessary; for surely God cannot do evil. A more satisfactory definition has been provided by A. Kenny: omnipotence is 'the possession of all logically possible powers which it is logically possible for a being with the attributes of God to possess'. On this understanding, God cannot contradict himself, nor can he do evil of any kind. But neither can he destroy himself, nor – to cite a favourite philosopher's example – can he make a being whom he cannot control. An omnipotent God can, however, exercise *self*-limitation. It is of the essence of Christian theism to hold that God exercises his omnipotence by limiting himself in creation, providence and grace, and especially in incarnation. The characteristic mode of God's action, in John Oman's words, is not 'omnipotence directed in a straight line by omniscience' but 'gracious personal relation'. But it is more accurate to see God's acts of grace as themselves acts of omnipotent self-restraint. It is God's power that is made known in weakness. On a Christian understanding of omnipotence, God's almighty power is discerned most profoundly in the cross of Christ and in what he achieves thereby.

See also **Theodicy.**

P. T. Geach, *Providence and Evil*, 1977, chs. 1 and 2; A. Kenny, *The God of the Philosophers*, 1979, chs. 7, 8 and 9.

BRIAN HEBBLETHWAITE

One, The

A preferred name among the Neoplatonists* from the third to the sixth centuries AD for God, the first principle and source of all reality. (Their other preferred name is 'the Good', from Plato's *Republic* VI 506D–511E, esp 509B, 8–10, which was of central importance for the Neoplatonists. They find their Platonic justification for their use of 'One' in the *Parmenides*.) The origin of this use of 'One' as a name for the first principle seems to be Neo-Pythagorean. In the revived Pythagoreanism of the last centuries BC and first

centuries AD the numbers which are, or symbolize, the primary and essential realities are thought to derive from the original Monad: and Plotinus and his successors took over and developed this view of reality as a structured plurality springing from a primal unity. But their understanding of what the name 'One' indicates or points to went far beyond anything which can safely be attributed to the Neo-Pythagoreans or earlier Platonists. From Plotinus onwards 'One' was interpreted in terms of the negative or apophatic* theology, as pointing towards a divine unity and simplicity so absolutely without internal divisions or external limits that our thought (which must divide to conceptualize and define) cannot grasp it or our language (which is incurably disjunctive) express it. God, for the Neoplatonists, does not hide himself. Nor is he just too great for our limited minds to grasp. We cannot think him because there is nothing there to think. Yet in the direct vision or union which is possible at the end of the long moral and intellectual ascent, we can be aware of him, though rarely, as supreme creative power and generosity, the source of all the many beauties and goods which he is not because he is above them, and as such the ultimate goal of all desire, the Good. When the name 'The One' is understood in this way, it can be seen that the influence on Christian thought of the side of Neoplatonism which it represents has been much wider than can be appreciated if the doctrine of the One is conceived as no more than a kind of Pythagorean thinking about God and the world in terms of one and many rather than being and beings or maker and made. It extends not only to a long line of Christian mystics but to thinkers who are not usually classed as mystical, to Eriugena and Nicholas of Cusa and to some extent to Thomas Aquinas. (It should be noted that even Christians strongly influenced by this way of thinking seldom use 'The One' as a preferred name for God.) Since the Reformation the negative theology of the One has not played a prominent part in either Catholic or Protestant theological thinking. But in our own time it is coming to be better understood and is sometimes seen to have considerable value in an age when we are less inclined than our fathers to assert that we know a great deal about God.

A. H. Armstrong (ed), *The Cambridge History of Later Greek and Early Mediaeval Philosophy*, 1970; R. T. Wallis, *Neoplatonism*, 1972.

A. H. ARMSTRONG

Ontological Argument

This was framed by Anselm of Bec (1033–1109), in his *Proslogion*. His first book, the *Monologion*, a meditation on the Divine Being, contained 'a chain of arguments', he said, and he wanted to find a single argument (*unum argumentum*) which would, by itself, suffice to show that God exists and everything we believe about the divine nature. The argument came to him in a moment of intuition after a long period of preoccupation and distraction from his duties. It gave him intense pleasure, as he believed it would others.

Anselm addresses himself to the Fool of the Psalms, who said in his heart that there is no God. He argues that it is possible for everyone to conceive of 'that than which nothing greater can be thought'. This must, therefore, exist at least in the mind. But if it exists only in the mind, he says, it is inferior to that which exists in the mind and also in reality. It must therefore be the case that that than which nothing greater can be thought exists both in the mind and in reality (*Proslogion*, Chapter II). Anselm goes on to develop a second form of the argument. This 'that than which nothing greater can be thought' so truly is that it is impossible to think of it as not existing. What we cannot conceive of as not existing must be greater than what we can conceive of as not existing. If that than which a greater cannot be conceived could be thought not to be, there would be something greater which we can conceive, and that would lead us into an absurdity.

Anselm sets this argument and its second form or second argument in a context of prayer, and he goes on as he promises in succeeding chapters to show how it can be used to demonstrate the attributes of the Divine Being: mercy, justice and so on.

The argument attracted interest from the first, however, not for its usefulness in these areas, but for the proof it seemed to afford of the very existence of God. Gaunilo, a monk of Marmoutiers, attacked it in Anselm's lifetime, on the grounds that it could equally well be used to prove the existence of an imaginary island which is the most beautiful that can be thought of. Anselm was pleased to have evoked so intelligent a response and he replied to Gaunilo with the view that the argument would work only for the case of God, because God's existence is uniquely a necessary existence. Gaunilo's reply and Anselm's answer were copied with the *Proslogion* itself for circulation, on Anselm's instructions.

The ontological argument stands alone among the arguments which have been advanced for the existence of God because it rests upon the very definition of the idea of God and works, if it works at all, solely within the mind. All other 'proofs' depend upon external evidences, signs of God's work as creator or cause or Prime Mover. Thomas Aquinas perceived that it was an argument of a different kind. He did not include it among his five proofs for the existence of God in the *Summa Theologiae*. Instead, he placed it among the unconvincing arguments in his discussion of the question: 'Is the existence of God self-evident?' The fact that the Fool of the Psalms can say in his heart that there is no God is ample proof for Aquinas that it cannot be self-evidently true that God exists – for self-evident truths are, by definiton, obvious to everyone.

The ontological argument has been the subject of discussion in every century. Descartes was a thinker with some natural sympathy with Anselm's first principles; Hegel *, like other Idealists *, believed that to think rationally amounts in itself to affirming the existence of God: the ontological argument simply sets out for us explicitly this necessary entailment of our thinking at all. Kant, like Hume, takes the opposite view, Kant arguing that existence is not a real predicate, so that the predicate of existence can be rejected without contradiction, Hume putting the view that 'there is no being . . . whose nonexistence implies a contradiction'. In this century, Bertrand Russell re-examined the status of existence as a property, and came to the conclusion that it is a property only of propositional functions. Karl Barth has pointed out the difference between the arguments or forms of the argument in *Proslogion*, Chapters II and III. Charles Hartshorne and N. Malcolm find the second form valid but not the first.

See also **Arguments for the Existence of God; God**.

J. Hopkins, *A Companion to the Study of St Anselm*, 1973, has a complete bibliography up to 1972. See, too, *The Many-Faced Argument: Recent Studies on the Ontological Argument for the Existence of God*, ed. J. Hick and A. C. M. McGill, 1967. There is a translation facing the Latin text, with commentary, by M. Charlesworth, 1965; ET in B. Ward, *The Prayers and Meditations of St Anselm*, 1973.

G. R. EVANS

Ontologism

A philosophy developed chiefly by V. Gioberti (1801–1852), according to which the human mind has direct, innate knowledge of being as such. This was an attempt to overcome the epistemological problem which has been a principal concern of modern philosophy since Descartes, and especially since the empiricists and Kant, who argued that we know only the way things appear to our minds, not how they are in themselves. Gioberti considered his view necessary to avoid scepticism. He maintained further that being as such is identical with God, and therefore the mind has innate, direct knowledge of God; not, however, with clarity, as he is in himself, as perceived in the beatific vision, but confusedly. The first in being is also the first in knowledge. From this direct knowledge of being all necessary truths about the essences of things can be deduced. For knowledge of particular things, however, it must be combined with sense experience. The ontological argument is not a logical proof, but an explication of the knowledge we already possess of God's existence.

Ontologism was widely accepted in Belgium (G. C. Ubagh, A. Tits, N.-J. Laforet, M. Boucquillon), France (L. Brancherau, J. Favre d'Envieu, F. Hugonin, M. Baudry, H. L. Maret) and Italy (T. Mamiani della Rovere, V. Miceli), as a philosophy which overcame the threat of scepticism, and was capable of providing a secure foundation for Catholic theology.

Prominent church thinkers such as Augustine, Bonaventure, Malebranche, Bossuet and Fénélon, and even Justin, Clement of Alexandria and Origen, were claimed to have held some form of it. In 1891, however, it was condemned by Rome as 'unsafe to teach' because of its doctrine of the immediate vision of God in this life.

T. PATRICK BURKE

Ontology

Literally 'the doctrine of being'. A term used differently by different philosophers.

1. For Christian Wolff (1679–1754), who made the term current, ontology is a body of necessary truths about being, known *a priori*. Together with psychology, the doctrine about living things, and cosmology, the doctrine of the inanimate world, it makes up metaphysics. These terms are still used in these senses by scholastic philosophers.

According to Hume and Kant, however, there can be no necessary truths which would give us any information about being, because existence is not a property. Truths can be necessary only in a very different sense, that they are entailed by the relationships between our ideas, and so tell us only about such relationships. This view is accepted by most modern philosophers.

2. For Heidegger an ontology is the most fundamental set of categories we use to interpret existence and the world. Thus in *Being and Time* he sets out to 'destroy' the traditional ontology of the West, derived from Plato and Aristotle, in favour of his own existential analysis.

3. For W. V. O. Quine a person's ontology is the set of things he believes there are. In Quine's view different ontologies can be equally true, i.e. adequate, so long as they are self-consistent. In practice, however, we commit ourselves by the terms we use to accept the existence of certain kinds of things. Thus the English language functions with terms, i.e. variables, for physical objects, and so when we speak English we commit ourselves to the existence of physical objects. For 'to be is to be a value of a variable'. Quine terms this 'ontological commitment'.

T. PATRICK BURKE

Opera ad Extra

The distinction between *opera ad intra* and *ad extra* is applied by the scholastic theologians both to finite agents and to God. The former relates to actions considered from the standpoint of the agent himself, the latter with reference to their external effects.

With God all his operations can be considered as internal to himself since they depend unilaterally upon his will and character. Some, however, can also be considered as external in relation to their effects. From this point of view we can refer creation to the Father, redemption to the Son and sanctification to the Spirit, provided that we remember that the external operations of the Trinity are indivisible (*opera sacrosanctae Trinitatis ad extra sunt indivisa*) since behind them lies their dependence upon the interior will and character of the One God. While then we can speak of one Person as eminently involved in a given operation, all three Persons are involved in the operation of each.

See also **Trinity.**

H. E. W. TURNER

Orders, Holy

The term refers to the several offices or ranks of ministry within the Eastern Orthodox, RC, Anglican and certain other churches. The three named recognize episcopacy, presbyterate and diaconate as distinct orders; there are also lesser offices which historically have been regarded as clerical orders, those of subdeacon, acolyte, exorcist, lector, cantor and porter. Some of these are still retained by the RC and Orthodox churches. The term also refers to the sacrament which is conferred by the rite of ordination*.

Since its inception, ministry in the Christian church has admitted a certain degree of diversity. The NT speaks of emissaries (*apostoloi*), elders (*presbyteroi*), overseers (*episkopoi*), servers (*diakonoi*), proclaimers (*prophetas*), teachers (*didaskaloi*), pastors (*poimenoi*) and others who had sometimes differing and sometimes overlapping functions within the earliest Christian communities (cf. Acts 6.1–7; 13.1–3; 15.22–24; Rom. 12.4–8; I Cor. 12.28–30; I Tim. 3.1–13; I Peter 5.1–5). It seems impossible to determine on the basis of scriptural evidence alone, however, whether some or all of these were offices or orders as they later came to be understood; which ones, if any, were always conferred by a ritual imposition of hands; and whether the non-inclusion of women in some of them was considered to be a *de facto* or *de jure* situation.

During the second and third centuries, the need for increased organization in a growing church led to the emergence of a hierarchical structuring of ministries, and the ever-present possibilities of apostasy and heresy led to an increased concern to distinguish legitimate ministers from others. The universally recognized church order at the end of the fourth century included the offices of bishop (*episkopos*), priest (*presbyteros*) and deacon (*diakonos*), and many tasks which had been originally lay functions in the community were assigned to clerics of various ranks. Ordination by laying-on of hands or other ritual gestures became a *sine qua non* for valid ministry, and women were excluded from clerical orders although they continued to exercise ministries (e.g. service to the poor, organization of monasteries) which did not require ordination.

This hierarchical ordering of ecclesiastical ministries continued into the Middle Ages, but there were also some notable developments of lasting significance. Quite early, the bishop of Rome assumed a pre-eminence over other European bishops, and although the papacy* was never considered a distinct order, it became regarded as the highest office in the Catholic church. In the twelfth century, the practice of clerical continence (the willing renunciation of marriage rights) became a rule of celibacy in canon law, mandated by the First and Second Lateran Councils. And by the thirteenth century, scholastic sacramental theology acknowledged the existence of a permanent priestly character* which was received in the soul of all those who were validly ordained.

The Reformers rejected the mediaeval ordering and conception of ministry, preferring to return to what they considered to be more scriptural models of the pastorate and presbytery. The Anglican church retained the sacramental priesthood and the episcopal* form of church government, but the validity of these orders was rejected by the Roman church. Catholics and Orthodox, on the other hand, recognize the validity of each other's orders, even though the churches themselves are separated by schism. In the Roman church marriage is still regarded as a bar to priesthood, while in the Eastern churches only bishops must be celibate. Thus far, only the Anglican church has admitted women to major orders in the traditional sense of that term, although female ministers are to be found in other Christian denominations.

B. Cooke, *Ministry to Word and Sacraments*, 1976; N. Mitchell, *Mission and Ministry*, 1982; J. Mohler, *The Origin and Evolution of the Priesthood*, 1969; E. Schillebeeckx, *Ministry*, ET 1981.

J. MARTOS

Orders, Religious

These are societies living under a rule; they originated in the monastic movement in the early church. The ideal of a mortified life has never been absent from Christianity since its beginnings, and in the second and third centuries many congregations had inner groups of virgins and ascetics. In the second half of the third century a number of men adopted a form of anchorite life, chief among whom was Antony (*c.* 251–356), who is usually regarded as the founder of monasticism. This is an oversimplification, since factors were at work other than his influence, e.g. the apparent compromise of the church with the world following the conversion of Constantine and the economic situation that led many to forsake the world that cost so much. At first monasticism was outside the organized community life of the church. It was a protest of individuals seeking their own salvation. Its primitive eremitical character was changed by the labours of Pachomius (*c.* 296–346), who provided a pattern of ascetical life within a community under a rule. His example inspired Basil of Caesarea (*c.* 330–379) and later, among the pioneers in the West, John Cassian (*c.* 360–435), who was followed by Benedict of Nursia (*c.* 480–*c.* 550). There can be little doubt that these men and women, living under vows of poverty, chastity and obedience, preserved Christian learning and moral values throughout the centuries of chaos that followed the collapse of the Roman empire.

Later religious orders were in effect groups living under rules reformed in accordance with the ideals of their founders. So the Cistercians or White Monks were reformed Benedictines, while the Cluniac reform, issuing in the Black Monks, was also Benedictine in character. The Carthusians, on the other hand, were a contemplative order, founded by Bruno in 1084, while the Franciscans and Dominicans of the thirteenth century were mendicant friars, being religious orders devoted to service and preaching. The Jesuits were a product of the Counter-Reformation* and were concerned to support the papacy and catholic teaching and to undertake missionary work among the heathen. Suppressed in England at the Reformation, religious orders were refounded in the nineteenth century, while within the Reformed Churches a community was created at Taizé in France in 1940.

In the second half of the twentieth century religious orders are experiencing something of a crisis as ideas and society rapidly change. The more positive understanding of sexual relations has led to a questioning of the intrinsic value of celibacy*; the Western promotion of democracy led to a stress on participation rather than on obedience to a superior; the desire to foster community led to a reduction in the size of houses and a multiplication of smaller units linked with other groups outside the orders. An increase in political awareness has resulted in an attempt to become more socially oriented and to be present in the world to accompany modern men and women in their quest for meaning. The religious still wish to live a consecrated life, but one that is more open and less under the limitations imposed by the traditional rules.

See also **Monastic Theology.**

P. Anson, *The Call of the Cloister*, 1955; P. Huizing and W. Bassett (eds), *The Future of the Religious Life, Concilium*, New Series 7.10, 1975.

J. G. DAVIES

Ordination

A liturgical action of the church by which some of its members are designated, commissioned and consecrated to public pastoral ministry*. The word itself relates to the concept of church order, and refers to the public organization of the church community. People are ordained to, and thereby established in, ministries of service and leadership in the community. In churches that have preserved episcopacy*, the major orders of deacon*, presbyter and bishop* are customarily conferred through the presidency of the bishop, with varying degrees of participation by others in the assembly. This signifies that these orders pertain to the communion of churches, or universal church, and are not exclusively to a particular local church. Other orders or ministries which are established for the local church are more usually assigned through the local pastor or governing body.

1. *Scripture*. The Hebrew scriptures offer several paradigms which have shaped the tradition of Christian ordination: the council of elders formed to assist Moses in leading and guiding the people (Num. 11.16–17); the anointing of David as God's elected king (II Sam. 2.4); Melchizedek the priest (Gen. 14.18), though little is known as to how he became priest of God. A late influence is the cultic priesthood of Aaron, which originally was set in contrast to the priesthood of Jesus Christ.

In the NT Christ is designated priest, prophet and king by the consecrating act of God, and it is the church as a whole, formed at the resurrection by the Spirit's coming, that is seen to be the embodied continuance of Christ's saving work. The newly formed communities of the church adapted various structures of leadership and ministry to serve this common mission.

The probable operative gesture in the assignment of these leadership and prophetic ministries, though the evidence is scant, is the laying on of hands, implicitly or explicitly invoking God's Spirit upon those ordained. A well-known exception to the rule is found in Hippolytus (*c.* AD 215), who specifies that a confessor of the faith, by the very act of confession and without the laying on of hands, be considered among the ranks of the presbyters.

2. *History*. Ordination in the early church must be seen as an evolving action with an evolving understanding. As is frequent with liturgical realities, there is usually a first-level development that is practical and functional, which is only later embellished with religious meaning. What seems to be constant throughout the history of ordination is this: (*a*) that the action by which an office or ministry is assigned changes to express the community's understanding of that office or ministry; (*b*) that the assignment ritual becomes more formal as the charismatic nature of the community yields to more formal structuring.

While there are bits and pieces of this evolution available prior to the third century, the first major witness to public rituals of ordination is the *Apostolic Constitutions* of Hippolytus, where the term begins to be restricted to the ministries of deacon, pres-

byter and bishop. Placement in other orders of the church assembly, such as penitents, catechumens and widows, goes by other names. While there is some evidence of the ordination of deaconesses* in the fourth and fifth centuries, the dominant tradition of both East and West has focussed on these three major orders.

Yet the understanding of these ministries themselves changed radically in the fourth century with an inevitable effect on the practice of ordination. The third-century deacon was the administrative assistant to the bishop, while the presbyterium constituted a collegial reality more ceremonial than functional. Presbyters did at times preside over 'lesser' eucharists, but this only at the designation of the bishop and in his place. It was the bishop alone who was high priest and public embodiment of the priestly church.

In contrast, and as a result of a despute which was largely one of protocol, the fourth century saw the emergence of the presbyter-priest, and a shift to more cultic paradigms for his ordination and ministry. The priest became the regular presider at the eucharist, and his ordination, as indeed all ordinations, began to be viewed in terms of empowerment rather than designation and commissioning. Moreover, other ministries, including that of deacon, became subsumed under the priesthood. As a result, the practice developed in the Middle Ages of four minor orders (exorcist, porter, acolyte, lector) and three major orders (sub-deacon, deacon, priest) being administered in succession, and only to those who were to be priests (*see also* **Orders, Holy**).

In the sixteenth century, the Reformation communities adapted a different understanding of church, church order and ministry, and hence of ordination. The Catholic response was firmly to adhere to the *status quo*. Since Vatican II, however, this latter has begun to shift its own understanding and practice by recognizing a variety of proper lay ministries, by establishing again the diaconate as an office in its own right, and by restoring the collegial nature of the presbyterium and its proper relationship to the bishop.

3. *Theology*. For those who view ordination as a functional assignment, there is little room for a theology that goes beyond that of baptism and ordinary Christian mission. Such is in fact the position of some Christian

communities. For others who hold the sacramental nature of ordination, the key questions are: (*a*) Sacrament of what? (*b*) Sacrament to whom?

The ordained serve a symbolic as well as a functional ministry for the church. There is the symbolic link to the apostolic church expressed in the ministry of the ordaining bishop and the traditional laying on of hands. There is also the symbolic manifestation of Christ made present in the ministries of proclamation, healing and leadership of prayer. There is finally the symbolic embodiment of the church itself made present in *sacrament** so that the church can see in visible form its own nature and destiny. It is for the church primarily that the ministry of the ordained is established. It remains the mission of the whole church to be the embodied continuance of the saving work of Jesus Christ. The sacramental ministry of the ordained is to manifest in life and action the ways of Jesus Christ, not simply for the church to be passive recipient of God's grace, but more that the church be led by its ministers to become what is made visible, and to activate in their own lives what their ministers display in their midst. It is in function of this awesome commission of the church to some of its members that the church deems it proper, and indeed essential, to lay on hands and to entrust the minister and the ministry to the power of God's Spirit.

N. Mitchell, *Mission and Ministry*, 1982; J. Mohler, *The Origin and Evolution of the Priesthood*, 1970; D. Power, *Gifts that Differ: Lay Ministries Established and Unestablished*, 1980; J. Provost (ed), *Official Ministry in a New Age*, 1981; E. Schillebeeckx, *Ministry*, ET 1981.

PETER E. FINK

Original Righteousness

The term used to describe the state in which humanity was created and remained until it fell. Through the early centuries of Christianity this was believed to refer to a historical time in history. Mediaeval and Reformation theologies give extensive descriptions of the perfections possessed by human beings at this period.

With the rise of evolutionary* theory the concept of original righteousness was thrown into doubt. Liberal theology* in the nineteenth century tended to abandon it along with the doctrine of original sin*. The first humans, liberalism thought, were primitives. Nevertheless, with J.-J. Rousseau, some liberals thought that primitives did dwell in a state of idyllic innocence that was spoiled by the later development of civilization.

In the twentieth century many theologians have restored the concept of original righteousness without identifying it with a historical past. They find the concept necessary to describe the paradoxical aspects of human nature. The sinner is never content to be simply a sinner. He or she rationalizes his or her conduct and tries to interpret it in a better light. Humanity cannot accept its sinful state as normal. Thus the concept of original righteousness is used to refer to humanity's essential nature which is dimly apparent even in the existential state of sin. Reinhold Niebuhr locates original righteousness in the 'perfection before the act'. That is, the self looks out on its world from the perspective of its values and ideals and has a righteousness that is lost when it tries to put its ideals into practice.

Martin Luther, *Lectures on Genesis*, see especially commentary on Gen. 2.9, 11, 15, 16, 17, 25; Reinhold Niebuhr, *The Nature and Destiny of Man*, 1, 1941, ch. 10.

WILLIAM HORDERN

Original Sin

The doctrine which holds that, by the very fact of birth into the human race, a person inherits a 'tainted' nature in need of regeneration* and with a proclivity to sinful conduct. The biblical bases for this belief are generally found in Gen. 3; Ps. 51.5: 'I was brought forth in iniquity, and in sin did my mother conceive me'), and Rom. 5.12–21. The first and last of these passages, as traditionally interpreted, explain why the existential situation of human sinfulness was described as 'original' (*see* **Fall, The**).

Whether this condition of human sinfulness implied personal guilt on the part of each individual or merely the sharing of a defectible and deprived human nature was a matter for debate in early patristic theology. Similarly, later theology has been divided over the issue of the extent to which original sin has affected human nature. Augustine, followed generally by the early Reformers, taught that the essence of original sin lay in concupiscence*; in its extreme forms, this view led to a concept of a wholly corrupt human nature bereft of free will. Catholic theology eventually levelled off to the teaching of Thomas Aquinas: original sin had reduced mankind to the state of pure nature, leaving mind and will intact, but depriving him of the praeternatural gifts without which he cannot attain the supernatural destiny intended for him by God. In this view, too, personal sinfulness is inevitable, not from a lack of free will but from the lack of divine grace.

At least as an existential fact of the human condition, and however it may be called or explained, original sin remains a doctrine of traditional Christianity, Catholic and Protestant. Against a purely naturalistic assessment of human destiny, it affirms man's inability to attain his purpose in life without confessing his native inadequacy and seeking his salvation as God's gift through faith.

BRUCE VAWTER

Orthodoxy

The root meaning is belief in, or assent to, the fundamental truths of the faith. But how are these truths to be defined? In the NT there are no creeds, but brief confessional formulae such as 'Jesus is Messiah' (Mark 8.29; John 11.27), 'Jesus is Lord' (Rom. 10.9; Phil. 2.11; Col. 2.6) or 'Jesus is the Son of God' (Acts 8.37; Matt. 14.33). There is also frequently expressed a concern for sound doctrine and right belief (e.g. I Tim. 6.3–4; II Tim. 1.13–14). The brief formulae grew into lengthier and more detailed statements of Christian belief which drew a frontier between orthodoxy and heresy* in terms of the acceptance or rejection of a creed*. They were brief proclamations of the faith of the church as well as tests of the conformity of individual believers to that faith. The Apostles' Creed, the Nicene Creed, and the so-called 'Athanasian' Creed or *Quicumque Vult* (probably fifth century) are the best known and most commonly used ancient creeds. Other criteria of orthodoxy were more comprehensive, and much vaguer: for instance an appeal to the consensus of the Fathers, or Vincent of Lerins' formulation: 'that which has been believed everywhere (*quod ubique*) always (*quod semper*) and by all (*quod ab omnibus*)'.

With the Reformation there came a further wave of confessional statements. Church after church felt the need to define and declare its distinctive beliefs, partly as a claim to orthodoxy and partly as a way of defining its boundaries and justifying its separate existence. Reformation confessions such as the Anglican Thirty-Nine Articles*, the Scots Confession (1560) or the Westminster Confession (1647) define the churches which adopted them over against Rome and the mediaeval church in particular, claiming orthodoxy for themselves and denouncing the opposition to right and left as heretical. Such confessions make no claim to be propounding any *new* doctrine or belief; they are to be tested against scripture: 'Protesting if any man will note in our Confession any chapter or sentence contrary to God's Holy Word,' runs the preface to the Scots Confession, 'that it would please him of his gentleness and for Christian charity's sake to inform us of it in writing.' Orthodoxy was seen primarily as conformity of belief with scripture and the primitive church.

The Roman Catholic Church, on the other hand, has recognized that dogma* develops (*see also* **Development, Doctrinal**) and therefore there may be definitions of orthodox belief made by the Pope speaking *ex cathedra* which require the assent of the faithful and are extensions or clarifications (depending on your point of view) of the substance of orthodoxy. In modern times the three such definitions have been the Immaculate Conception* (1854), Papal Infallibility* (1870) and the Assumption* of the Blessed Virgin Mary (1950). Protestants have been less productive of confessional statements or definitions in recent times. The most notable exception was the Barmen Declaration (1934), in which the German Confessing Church declared 'the truths of the gospel' in such a way as to deny the claims of Nazism and show that the 'German Christians' had fallen into heresy. Modern ecumenical discussions, whether sponsored by the World Council of Churches' Faith and Order Department, or bi-lateral conversations between two 'confessional' families (such as the Anglican-Roman Catholic International Commission), or negotiations for a specific union of churches, have tended to concentrate on ecclesiological issues, particularly ministry, authority, baptism and the eucharist. While this narrowing of interest is clearly related to hopes for the reunion of the church, the increasing consensus on such matters should not obscure the fact that there is vigorous debate about other clauses of the ancient creeds and Reformation confessions, and some theologians are antagonistic to any credal criterion of orthodoxy.

The word 'orthodoxy' is ambiguous. It can mean 'right worship' or 'right belief'. The 'Athanasian' Creed affirms that, 'We *worship* one God in Trinity and the Trinity in Unity.' Orthodoxy is not a matter of purely intellectual assent to propositions; it involves giving glory to God. This emphasis on worship shows clearly that right belief, assent or opinion, correct dogma, was not understood in abstraction from praxis*. Hence we see that the contemporary concern with *orthopraxis** is not something entirely new but is the development and recovery of something that has been recognized as an essential component of orthodoxy from early times. A recent case in point is the decision of the Lutheran churches and the World Alliance of Reformed Churches to regard the practice or support of *apartheid* as an issue of *status confessionis*, i.e. to declare those who practice or support apartheid as being in a state of heresy.

J. N. D. Kelly, *Early Christian Creeds*, 1972; Hans Küng, *On Being a Christian*, 1977; The Doctrine Commission of the Church of England, *Christian Believing*, 1976.

DUNCAN FORRESTER

Orthopraxis

A term introduced into theological discussion in the early 1960s by Nikos Nissiotis and J. B. Metz, which quickly became a central concept in political theology* and in much ecumenical thought flowing from the Uppsala Assembly of the World Council of Churches (1968). The idea, however, is much older. The praxis* of Jesus is seen as the model of orthopraxis. Since Jesus' praxis culminated in the cross, we are reminded that orthopraxis encompasses suffering and feeling, passion as well as action. The NT emphasis that doing the will of God is the condition for coming to the light or knowing the truth is developed by many contemporary political theologians (such as Sobrino or Boff) into the assertion that we can only know Jesus as we follow him. Christian truth

is not accessible to detached contemplation, but only to those whose praxis is that of the kingdom. Knowing and doing are thus dialectically related to one another, as are belief and practice, so that Visser t'Hooft could assert that Christians who neglect their responsibility for the needs of the world 'are just as much guilty of heresy as those who deny this or that article of faith'. Thus praxis becomes a criterion of theology and of faith. This is not to suggest a pragmatic test of theology: 'does it work?' Nor is it an affirmation of activism, let alone a revival of justification by works. Christians should expect their accustomed patterns of praxis to be challenged by the grace of God and converted into the praxis of the kingdom*. And *that* orthopraxis is world-transforming. All this line of thinking is influenced both by the Bible and by Marxism*. Christianity is an orthopraxis of a gracious rather than legalistic sort, and theology's role (reflecting Marx's eleventh *Thesis on Feuerbach*) is not so much to explain, legitimate or justify the world as to change and convert it.

L. Boff, *Jesus Christ Liberator*, 1980; Charles Davis, *Theology and Political Society*, 1980; Jon Sobrino, *Christology at the Crossroads*, 1978.

DUNCAN FORRESTER

Oxford Movement

The usual name for the first stage, from 1833 to 1845, of a movement in the Church of England which is now known as Anglo-Catholicism*. The original, largely clerical, group was led by John Keble (1792–1866), John Henry Newman (1801–1890) and Edward Pusey (1800–1882), all of them members of Oxford colleges. Alarmed at the widening gulf between Christianity and the modern state, they tried in *Tracts for the Times* (1833–1841) to revive faith in the Anglican Church as a divine institution, maintained in truth by the episcopal succession; from the High Church tradition, and from Romanticism*, they drew a fresh enthusiasm for sacramental worship, for the ascetic tradition, and for a not very well understood mediaeval culture. The movement survived the loss of Newman to the Roman Catholic Church in 1845, and has lived ever since in tension with Anglican Evangelicalism. (There is no connection with the so-called 'Oxford Group' of the 1930s.)

R. W. Church, *The Oxford Movement*, 1891, provides a glamourizing account, too much focussed on Newman; for a more critical view see K. A. Thompson, *Bureaucracy and Church Reform 1800–1965*, 1970.

JOHN KENT

Palingenesis

From Greek *palin*, again, and *genesis*, birth, origin: hence the word is the equivalent of Latin *regeneration*. In secular usage it may mean a transformation or metamorphosis, as of insects.

ALAN RICHARDSON

Panentheism

The doctrine that all is in God. It is distinguished from pantheism*, which identifies God with the totality or as the unity of the totality, for it holds that God's inclusion of the world does not exhaust the reality of God. Panentheism understands itself as a form of theism*, but it criticizes traditional theism for depicting the world as external to God.

Charles Hartshorne has been the leading twentieth-century advocate of panentheism. He juxtaposes this 'di-polar' theism with the 'mono-polar' theism of much of the tradition. Monopolar theism affirms that the perfection of God consists in the divine absoluteness, immutability, eternality and complete independence. Panentheism, or di-polar theism, affirms that true perfection involves absoluteness, immutability, eternality and independence but also perfect relationality, perfect mutability or responsiveness, perfect temporality and perfect dependence. Since God includes the world, God's experience is related to the world, altered by changes in the world, involved in time, and dependent on what happens in the world. Nevertheless, God's character or essence is absolute, immutable, eternal and independent. Hartshorne argues that this conforms better than traditional theism or pantheism to the biblical understanding of the living God who loves and knows the world, acts within it, and shares the joys and sorrows of the creatures. He believes that the monopolar view was based on a Greek prejudice against time and change. Modern thought is freeing itself from that prejudice, and it allows recovery of the biblical understanding of divine-creaturely interaction.

Panentheists suggest the mind-body or mind-brain analogy for conceiving of God's relation to the world. If we think of the brain as composed of numerous cells or, better, cellular and sub-cellular events, then the mind, or unified human experience, cannot be simply the totality of these. It is not enough to say that it is the unity of this totality, for it has many characteristics, such as consciousness, that are lacking in the entities or events it unifies. Nevertheless it includes all, or at least many, of these brain events. What happens in the brain is clearly important for the content of human experience and, on the other hand, human decisions have great importance for what happens in the brain. Similarly, what happens in the world contributes to the divine experience which in its unity transcends qualitatively and quantitatively the contribution of the world. And God's decisions in their turn profoundly influence, but do not completely determine, what happens in the world.

See also **Process Theology.**

Charles Hartshorne, *Man's Vision of God*, 1941; Charles Hartshorne and William Reese, *Philosophers Speak of God*, 1953.

JOHN COBB

Pantheism

The word is derived from the Greek *pan*, 'all', and *theos*, 'God' and denotes the doctrine that everything is the mode or appearance of one single reality, and accordingly that nature* and God are identical. The word itself is of comparatively recent origin, having been first used, apparently, in 1709 by a critic of the deist* John Toland , who had coined the word 'pantheist'. The idea, however, has a long history, going back to the Greeks Xenophanes, Parmenides and Anaxagoras. It also characterizes much of Eastern religious thought, notably Hinduism and certain schools of Buddhism. Pantheism has been developed in a variety of ways, the two extremes being, on the one hand, that view which sees God as the total reality, the world being appearance and ultimately unreal (acosmic pantheism) and, on the other hand, the view which sees God as part of the world, immanent within it (immanentist pantheism). For Spinoza (1632-1677), there could only be one unlimited substance with an infinite number of attributes: hence *Deus sive natura* ('God or nature'). In Christian thought, pantheistic tendencies have been evident among the mystics who have wanted to stress union with God or individual participation in the divine (e.g. Meister Eckhart, Jakob Boehme), and among those theologians who have wanted to expound Christianity in monist (e.g. Hegelian) terms. Christian theists, however, have opposed pantheism on two grounds: 1. it obliterates the desirable distinction between Creator and creature; 2. if carried to extremes it could obliterate the distinction between theism* and atheism*. A middle position between pantheism and theism has been sought in panentheism*.

D. W. D. SHAW

Papacy

The title 'pope' (papa – father) was in the early Western Church given to any important or outstanding bishop (e.g. Cyprian) and in the Eastern Church it was applied to the bishop of Alexandria. But it gradually became restricted to the bishop of Rome. During the second and third centuries the bishop of Rome exercised considerable moral authority, based partly on the political pre-eminence of his see but more on the fact that both Peter and Paul had been martyred and were commemorated in Rome. He must also by the third century have exerted some executive authority over a large area round the city of Rome itself, for Cornelius in 251 was able to depose the rural bishops who had consecrated his rival Novatian. The jurisdiction of the bishop of Rome over the Western Church, in the sense of his right to hear appeals, as contrasted with his merely occupying a position in which he could be appealed to (which he had long enjoyed), was recognized by the Council of Sardica (343). Thereafter the history of papal authority in the West is one of increasing claims and increasing power, marked by various milestones represented by Leo (440–461), Gregory VII (1073–1085) and Innocent III (1198–1216). The climax was perhaps reached with Boniface VIII (1294–1303), who in his bull *Unam Sanctam* (1302) declared that both the temporal and the spiritual power were in the power of the church and the former was subject to the latter, and concluded that it is altogether necessary for the salvation of every human creature to be subject to the Roman pontiff.

Boniface VIII was not able to maintain in practice his extensive claims (as Innocent III had been able) and from his reign dates the origin of the gradual erosion and finally the virtual extinction of the Pope's temporal power. But the papacy still maintains its claim to universal spiritual authority and jurisdiction.

The Eastern Orthodox Church has usually allowed the pope primacy and indeed authority over the Western Church. On occasions of extreme pressure (e.g. the Council of Lyons, 1274–1289, and the Council of Ferrara-Florence, 1438–1445) its representatives professed themselves ready to admit all the claims of the pope of the period, but these admissions were never consistently endorsed by the Orthodox Church as a whole. The churches of the Reformation began by rejecting the jurisdiction of the pope (for the Reformation was essentially a crisis of authority) but quickly found that his temporal power and all his other claims were bound up with this. The identification of the pope with anti-Christ was first made by the defeated minority movement within the Franciscans in the fourteenth century, but was ardently taken up by most of the Reformed traditions. Though it has appealed in some forms to a few modern theologians (e.g. Reinhold Niebuhr) it is now virtually restricted to extreme and fanatical minority groups. The controversy about the papacy today usually turns on the interpretation of the scriptural evidence about the position of Peter, the relation of Peter to his successors (if any), the subject of authority and the question of infallibility. Most non-RC Christians today would find the historical claims of the papacy uncongenial not only on the ground that they cannot find satisfactory support in scripture and tradition but also because many of them appear to betray a repulsive spirit of self-aggrandisement masquerading under religious pretexts, difficult to reconcile with a proper Christian humility. But two recent developments have tended to modify this attitude. One is the great increase of esteem for the pope simply as a leader of Christian opinion shown since the pontificate of John XXIII (1958–1963) by the leaders of non-RC communions in the last few years, and especially displayed in the new practice of their paying visits of courtesy to the pope. This is to be distinguished from one not inconsiderable section of Anglican opinion which has always shown itself ready to accord to the pope a primacy of honour (but not jurisdiction) as head of the Western Church, much as the archbishop of Canterbury is accorded a primacy of honour in the Anglican community. The other recent development is the tendency showed in the Second Vatican Council to limit the authority of the pope by emphasizing the relationship of 'collegiality' which all bishops enjoy towards him as a fellow-bishop, without ostensibly affecting his historic claims to be bishop of bishops and to exercise a plenitude of power over all bishops.

This tendency was nevertheless checked under Paul VI (1963–1978), who in the encyclical *Humanae Vitae* (1968) went against collegiate advice by deploring artificial birth control; and it showed signs of being reversed under John Paul II (elected in 1978 and, as a Pole, the first non-Italian pope since 1523), who held a conservative line not merely on family morality but also against changes in the priesthood and against free theological enquiry. Both men were assiduous travellers, further developing the papacy as a repository of worldwide Christian leadership, and paying special attention to the great concentrations of Roman Catholics in Latin America. At theologian level, ecumenical discussion between the Vatican and other Christian communions advanced at a less spectacular pace.

H. Burn-Murdoch, *The Development of the Papacy*, 1954; Owen Chadwick, *The Popes and European Revolution*, 1981; J. Chapman, *Studies on the Early Papacy*, 1928; Patrick Granfield, *The Papacy in Transition*, 1981; J. Derek Holmes, *The Papacy in the Modern World*, 1981; T. G. Jalland, *The Church and the Papacy*, 1944; B. J. Kidd, *The Roman Primacy to AD 461*, 1936.

R. P. C. HANSON/JOHN WHALE

Parable

The Hebrew is *mashal*, to set side by side; Greek *parabolē*, a placing beside, a comparison. While parables, like fables, allegories and myths, are stories with hidden significance, they are clearly distinguished from these other kinds of stories because of their peculiar characteristics. These characteristics have been identified only during the last hundred years, when, beginning with the work of A. Jülicher, parables were rescued from the centuries-old tradition of interpreting them as allegories or, alternatively, as moral tales. The parable form is rare; a careful classification limits them to a few in the OT, those of Jesus and of Franz Kafka, and perhaps some from Eastern religious writings.

A now classic definition of the parables of Jesus by C. H. Dodd suggests their characteristics: 'At its simplest the parable is a metaphor or simile drawn from nature or common life, arresting the hearer by its vividness or strangeness and leaving the mind in sufficient doubt about its precise application to tease it into active thought' (*The Parables of the Kingdom*, 1934, p. 16). In this definition, a parable emerges as a *metaphor* which implies its significance by *mundanity*, *extravagance* and *indirection*. As a metaphor – and many NT exegetes would say an 'extended metaphor' to stress the *narrative* quality – a parable is or exemplifies what it signifies rather than standing for or pointing to what it signifies. That is, as metaphor, a parable is unsubstitutable; it does not illustrate an idea, but embodies it. In order to interpret Jesus' parables, one must add two other widely-accepted points, namely, that the principal mode of Jesus' teaching was in parables and that the content of this teaching is the kingdom of God *. Thus, the conclusion emerges that Jesus taught about the kingdom of God through metaphorical stories which are mundane, extravagant and indirect.

As *mundane*, the parables imply that the rule of God applies to secular, ordinary and, in many instances, relational life, both personal and public. While some of the parables are naturalistic and only minimally narrational, such as the ones dealing with the mustard seed, the lost coin, and so on, most of them are personal and relational, concerned with conventional versus radical ways of dealing with other people: the Unjust Judge, the Prodigal Son, the Wicked Husbandman, the Great Feast, the Labourers in the Vineyard, the Good Samaritan. The identification of the kingdom of God with mundane decisions that people make in their relations with one another implies that whatever 'the rule of God' may be said to mean, it is intimately related to secular existence.

As *extravagant* or extreme, the parables imply – through tensions in their plot – that the ways of the conventional world are not the ways of God (what Robert Funk calls the tension between a 'logic of merit' and a 'logic of grace'). The heart of a NT parable is its *plot*. As Paul Ricoeur has said perceptively, the interactive partners in permanent tension in a parable are two ways of being in the world, one of which is the conventional way and the other, the way of the kingdom. The plot of a parable forms one partner of the interactive metaphor while the conventional context against which it is set is the other partner. Reality is redescribed through the tension generated by these two perspectives. Thus, in the parable of the Great Feast (Luke 14.16–24), the guests who by convention should be invited to such a feast – the 'worthy' – are usurped in the plot of the parable by the unconventional guests – the 'unworthy'. We *know* the worthy guests because of conventional standards of worth, but it is only through the plot of the parable that we glean a dim sense of how the unworthy guests might be considered worthy according to a new standard. That sense depends upon the tension between the two standards, a tension that redescribes reality as conventionally understood. The *action* in a parable is indicative of the kerygmatic* quality of parables, for they are paradigms of persons encountering the kingdom, not abstractly, but concretely and existentially. A parable says: if you want a suggestion of what the kingdom is, listen to this story of a man who invited worthy guests to dinner, and when the guests declined claiming business and family obligations, the man invited social outcasts to his feast. The extravagance of the action is essential in a parable, for as Flannery O'Connor has said, 'to the hard of hearing you shout, and for the almost-blind you draw large and startling pictures' (*Mystery and Manners*, 1969, p. 34).

Finally, as *indirect*, the parables imply that their significance must be grasped in a 'shock of recognition' as listeners apply the stories to themselves. In the parable of the Great Feast the whole story is the extended metaphor and what it models is the kingdom: the structure of human relationships which it suggests; its inversion of expectations; its intimation of a new, radical set of priorities; its existential, ordinary and secular quality – all of this is the grid or screen which allows us to see what life in the rule of God is like. It is obvious in this example that one cannot get the point of the story except by keeping the tension between the two descriptions of reality (of how life is to be lived in the world), for the 'point' of a parable is not a moral, concept, or resolution, but the play of the interactive partners, which as C. H. Dodd says, 'teases the imagination into participatory thinking'. What it causes us to think about is life under the reign of God, and the parables, while giving no definitions of that life, provide – by the indirection of their plots – exemplars or models of it.

For some NT exegetes, these characteristics of parables are epitomized in seeing Jesus as 'parable' of God. In the life and especially the death of Jesus – at one level a mundane, secular story – the listener sees an 'enacted parable' of extravagant action which upsets the conventions of life as suffering love sides with the oppressed, the outcast, the sinner. As an illustration of Jesus' life as enacted parable, see Matt. 11.19: his practice of eating with 'sinners and tax collectors', the outcasts of society.

Parables are powerful teaching devices because as stories they stay in the memory in a way that concepts and precepts do not. In addition, these stories persuade listeners to 'teach themselves' as they apply them to their own situations. Jesus' parables are also *disorienting* teaching devices, embodying the reversal of expectations which is at the heart of the gospel – the scandal of Jesus' identification in his table-fellowship as on the cross with outcasts and sinners.

See also **Allegory and Typology.**

John Dominic Crossan, *In Parable: The Challenge of the Historical Jesus*, 1973; Robert Funk, *Language, Hermeneutic, and the Word of God*, 1966; Joachim Jeremias, *The Parables of Jesus*, ET 1954, rev. ed. 1972; Paul Ricoeur, 'Biblical Hermeneutics', *Semeia* 4, 1975; Mary Ann Tolbert, *Perspectives on the Parables: An Approach to Multiple Interpretations*, 1979; Amos Wilder, *The Language of the Gospel: Early Christian Rhetoric*, 1964.

SALLIE MCFAGUE

Paraclete

Paraclete is a Greek word meaning 'defending counsel' (in a lawsuit). It is used as a title of the Holy Spirit in the Fourth Gospel (John 14.16, 26; 15.26; 16.7;). The older English versions translated it by 'comforter' (i.e., strengthener, helper), but Vulgate and NEB 'advocate' is the better. The spirit defends the Christian against the accusations of his adversary (i.e. Satan). The idea behind 'comforter' was drawn from the context of the word in the Fourth Gospel: the Spirit would 'console' the disciples after Christ had 'gone away'.

ALAN RICHARDSON

Paradigm

The word attained its present popularity through its use in T. S. Kuhn's *The Structure of Scientific Revolutions*. This was a direct and largely successful challenge to received ideas about the development of science as a logical progression through trial and error. According to Kuhn 'normal science' is a routine puzzle-solving activity which takes place within the context of a network of assumptions, insights and techniques which set the terms of the puzzles and specify what counts as a solution. This network or disciplinary matrix Kuhn called a 'paradigm', and for him the main creative moments in science occur when the anomalies built up within a particular paradigm result in a scientific revolution, or 'paradigm shift'. Thereafter the work of normal science continues within the new paradigm, until that too succumbs to internal crises. A major paradigm shift, e.g the transition from Ptolemaic to Copernican astronomy, entails far more than an adjustment of existing theory. The change is so radical and fundamental that the two paradigms are 'incommensurable', and the switch from one to the other has to take place by a non-logical process akin to conversion*. It is this latter claim which has given Kuhn's ideas a particular attraction for religious apologists, and which has been most hotly contested by his critics.

Kuhn's concept of 'paradigm' is complex and diffuse, and can easily be misrepresented. One commentator listed no less than twenty-one different senses in which he used the word, but these are not necessarily incompatible. In part it has a sociological content, referring to a set of scientific habits, intellectual, verbal, behavioural and technological, which provide the context for scientific activity in a particular time and place. The existence of paradigms in this sense answers the question, a very difficult one in Popper's philosophy, about how science can be done prior to the conscious formation of theory.

A second layer of meaning in the word moves it a step closer to the ordinary concept of 'theory'. A paradigm is a fundamental insight applicable within a particular field, around which theory can subsequently be organized. To begin to think of heat, not as an invisible weightless fluid, but as a form of energy, is to hold the key to a whole new branch of science. But it is only in the subsequent puzzle-solving activities of generations of scientists that the theory becomes fully articulated.

A third layer of meaning approximates to the word 'model'. A key insight, set within a particular scientific milieu, needs to acquire a concrete form if it is to work as a fruitful basis for puzzle-solving. It is in this sense that a classic experiment can define a science; it becomes a paradigm for subsequent research.

The success and popularity of Kuhn's ideas has inevitably diluted them. Any fundamental set of ideas can now be called a paradigm. In its transference to theology the word might be used to draw attention to the corporate, and often unexpressed, background to individual beliefs. More usually it simply means 'standard example'.

Ian G. Barbour, *Myths, Models and Paradigms*, 1976; T. S. Kuhn, *The Structure of Scientific Revolutions*, 1962; M. Masterman, 'The Nature of a Paradigm', in *Criticism and the Growth of Knowledge*, ed. I. Latakos and A. Musgrave, 1970.

JOHN HABGOOD

Paradise *see* **Life after Death**

Parousia

In classical Greek the word usually means 'presence' or 'arrival'; in Hellenistic Greek, it can mean an official visit by a monarch. It is used of the Ptolemies in the papyri. In the NT there are five distinct usages: 1. Christ's expected appearance at the consummation of the age (often); 2. the appearance of the Antichrist just before the end (II Thess. 2.9); 3. the impression made by Christ at the transfiguration (II Peter 1.16); 4. Paul's outward appearance (II Cor. 10.10); 5. the presence of Paul or his colleagues among the churches he founded (several times). There is no phrase in the NT corresponding to 'the second coming', but cf. Heb. 9.28: 'so Christ will appear a second time'. The NT writers do not seem to think *parousia* a suitable word to apply to Christ's life on earth, perhaps because he came then in humility, not in glory. The phrase 'the second coming (*parousia*)' occurs in Justin's *Apology* (c. AD 150).

ANTHONY TYRRELL HANSON

Passion

In a Christian context, this word applies exclusively to Christ's redemptive suffering, particularly to the last days culminating in his crucifixion. It derives etymologically from the Latin *passio* (suffering), not from the Greek *pascha* (Passover). Christians have grown accustomed to think of Christ's passion and suffering, but that should not blind us to the fact of its utter inappropriateness and incongruity to a Greek of the first century on first hearing the gospel*, for the Greek mind could never allow suffering and sympathy and feeling to be associated with God. The very adoption of the word begs the entire work of God's costly redemption* of man, and carries the whole connotation of atonement*.

JAMES ATKINSON

Pastoral Theology

1. *Definition.* The term pastoral derives from the Latin word for shepherd; hence pastoral theology is the theology of shepherding or the work of ministry. Historically the term has had varied, often imprecise meanings, but principally: (i) The theory of ordained ministry in general, including a definition of its functions and duties (or offices), underlying theological principles, moral and spiritual requirements, methods of actual practice, and related disciplines of training and education. (ii) The theory of the cure or care of souls (pastoral care and counselling), distinguished ambiguously from other pastoral functions by its primary focus on individual need and the personal character of the pastor's involvement with the parishioner. (iii) A form of theological understanding arising within the context and practice of the church's ministry and mission, thus a certain perspective on the whole of theology. (iv) The theology of the whole life and work of the church in its contemporary, empirical context, including the specialized work of ordained ministry only as a special instance.

The first definition, in terms of the pastor's total work, is the traditional concept of pastoral theology that generally prevailed through the nineteenth century in both Catholic and Protestant traditions (though Protestant theory usually treated homiletics separately). The focus on the theory of individual care (definition ii) has emerged strongly in twentieth-century Protestantism, often mingled with the older view and with the concept of the discipline as a mode of theological reflection distinguished by its particular context (definition iii). This third meaning is also closely related to the fourth, the contemporary Catholic understanding, distinguished by its emphasis on ministry as the work of the whole church, not the clergy alone.

2. *Relation to Other Disciplines.* Pastoral theology is distinguished from biblical, dogmatic and moral theology by its primary concern for discovering how theological understandings can find appropriate practical expression in the concrete, empirical situation of the church and the world. Its content and method cannot, therefore, be derived exclusively from those disciplines but require also an understanding of the human situation in its historical particularity and contingency and the experimental development of fitting and effective practical methods. Traditionally, its method was said to entail an 'application' of abstract principles to specific situations (with certain auxiliary skills and virtues). Contemporary thinking, however, tends to embrace more dynamic and dialectical conceptions of method in which context and practice help to shape theory and deepen or critically revise theological understanding, even as theology guides practice and calls it into question.

Historically, pastoral theology has had an especially close relation to moral theology and casuistry, reflecting the considerable extent to which shepherding has taken the form of moral guidance and penitential discipline through much of the church's history (McNeill). In the twentieth century, however, pastoral practice has become strongly oriented towards essentially therapeutic concerns, especially in Protestantism but increasingly also in Catholicism. This shift has tended to broaden and reorient pastoral theology from ethical questions of guidance and discipline to more theologically conceived issues in anthropology* and soteriology* (Protestantism) as well as ecclesiology and liturgical theology (Catholicism). A major issue in current Protestant pastoral theology in fact concerns the recovery or clarification of its ethical character and purpose after several decades of increasingly psychotherapeutic orientation, while in Catholicism these new emphases have challenged and expanded the historic understanding of the sacramental system as the fundamental and comprehensive expression of the church's care.

The distinction between pastoral and practical theology is traditionally troublesome in view of the ambiguous meaning of both terms. Since its appearance in the mid-nineteenth century, practical theology has generally functioned as a collective term for the various arts and disciplines of ministry including homiletics, liturgics, pastoral care, etc. This scheme has tended, on one hand, to leave unanswered the question of its coherence as a discipline, while on the other hand segregating practical studies from the rest of theology (and compartmentalizing the practical sub-disciplines). In any case, the term practical theology has been gaining new and more significant meaning in recent years, both as a (sometimes preferred) synonym for the new Catholic understanding of pastoral theology (definition iv) and as a concept in liberation theology* involving the Marxist notion of *praxis**. In this view all theology is practical in the sense that the aim of all thinking as such, including theology, is not to interpret the world but to change it. How such conceptions of theology will relate to established definitions and methods of pastoral theology is yet to be fully discerned.

Another ambiguous distinction involves pastoral psychology, a term ordinarily referring to the application of psychological theories and methods to pastoral problems, usually without explicit theological interpretation or critique. Pastoral psychology has never achieved much coherence or identity as a discipline, despite hopes held for it earlier in this century when it was viewed by some as an empirical science by which pas-

tors would discover the 'laws of the soul'. Instead of supplementing pastoral theology it has tended to replace it by appropriating secular psychologies without adequate theological critique. Though the term may still have some constructive value, a concept of pastoral theology that includes the critical appropriation of secular psychologies would appear to make pastoral psychology, as a distinct discipline or subject-matter, unnecessary.

3. *History and Emerging Issues.* Literature on shepherding and the cure of souls is as old as the Christian church and constitutes a rich and varied corpus, with antecedents deep in Jewish and Hellenic culture. As a systematic discipline, however, pastoral theology did not emerge until the Tridentine reforms of the sixteenth century (Catholicism) and then not as a major disciplinary enterprise until the mid- to late-eighteenth century in both Catholicism and Protestantism, occasioned by the increasing need for practical education and guidance of clergy. By the end of the nineteenth century in Europe and America a considerable literature had evolved, some admittedly anecdotal and inspirational, but also including voluminous, systematic treatises that attempted to incorporate the best science and philosophy of the day (including 'mental philosophy' and psychology) along with the accumulated wisdom of pastoral experience. Systematic writing in the field declined sharply after the turn of the century, however, when the 'new psychology' of James, Freud and others swept aside the faculty psychology and naive practical methods on which the old discipline had largely depended and opened new vistas on the soul with theories of the dynamic unconscious and the relation of religion to neurosis. In this situation the pastoral theologians were not entirely overwhelmed, but they were confronted with an array of complex and intriguing new problems that made confident systematic formulations of the field increasingly problematic.

Especially important was the emergence of the pastoral care movement in America under the leadership of Anton Boisen, Richard Cabot and others in the 1920s and 1930s. The movement developed methods of training pastors in clinical settings and ultimately reoriented American pastoral care strongly in psychiatric and psychotherapeutic directions (though that was not its original intent). This development profoundly influenced Protestant pastoral theology in America, which has been especially concerned to interpret psychotherapeutic process and experience, and its impact is now widely felt in Europe and other parts of the world. The movement's clinical emphasis has undeniably had the virtue of engaging pastoral theology concretely, and in depth, with the complexity and interrelatedness of human need, both intrapsychically and interpersonally, and has equipped ministry with a greatly enhanced range of practical methods and a greatly enriched sense of the meaning and value of personal care. Yet its explicit development as a theological discipline has lagged behind. Though there have been a number of attempts to think theologically in the new situation the discipline as a whole has not generated a notable theological tradition. The prevailing influence of neo-orthodoxy during the formative decades of the movement, with its rejection of or reservations about natural theology*, posed difficult methodological problems that doubtless discouraged theological development. The dominant theological orientation of the field has instead been liberal, turning most often to Tillich and to process theology*.

Undoubtedly the major task for contemporary pastoral theology in all of its traditions and locations is to develop a significant theological self-understanding and methodology capable of critically engaging the empirical and practical complexities of ministry in modern society. New understandings of the church and its mission in modernity, the sophisticated development of hermeneutical theory, and basic reconceptualizations of the theory-praxis relationship in recent theology are among the developments offering significant challenges and resources for the future of pastoral theology as a serious theological discipline. Involved in the task also is the need to reassess and clarify the role of non-theological disciplines, especially the social sciences, in pastoral theological method, a problem rendered especially difficult and confusing by the heightened consciousness today of their historical and social relativity and uncertain authority. A particular problem in this regard concerns the nature and role of psychology, which has acquired some of the functions of religion in Western societies and is a major vehicle of moral consciousness and direction for many people, and therefore needs to be carefully and critically understood as a cultural phenomenon within the larger task of pastoral theological method. An even further set of issues is raised by the advent of Eastern religious or spiritual psychologies in the West, which not only offer alternative spiritualities but perhaps more importantly cast the whole Western psychological tradition into a new light, from psychoanalysis to behaviourism, and may stimulate pastoral theology to develop a deeper understanding of Christian spirituality than its psychological theories have envisioned thus far. Presumably this will entail further exploration of the mystical tradition and the practices of spiritual direction in pastoral theology. At the same time the discipline is powerfully confronted by the prophetic criticism of political* and liberation* theologies and faces the need to develop methods and theories of pastoral ministry that are at once consonant with the church's larger social mission and faithful to the tender and respectful care of persons that lies at the heart of the pastoral task of the church. Such questions could well be addressed ecumenically and cross-culturally also, and will need to be so addressed if pastoral theology is to develop as a discipline adequate to the range of tasks before it.

H. Ammer, J. Henkys, G. Holtz, H.- H. Jenssen, G. Kehnscherper, E.- R. Kiesow, G. Kretzschmar, W. Nagel, E. Schmidt, H. Wagner, E. Winkler, F. Winter, *Handbuch der Praktischen Theologie*, vol. 1, 1975; F. Arnold, K. Rahner, V. Schurr, L. Weber, *Handbuch der Pastoraltheologie* (5 vols), 1970–72; D. Browning, *The Moral Context of Pastoral Care*, 1976; S. Hiltner, *Preface to Pastoral Theology*, 1958; E. B. Holifield, *A History of Pastoral Care in America*, 1983; J. Lapsley, *Salvation and Health*, 1972; J. T. McNeill, *A History of the Cure of Souls*, 1951; K. Rahner, *Mission and Grace* (3 vols), 1963–66; M. Thornton, *The Function of Theology*, 1968; E. Thurneysen, *A Theology of Pastoral Care*, ET 1962; Frank Wright, *The Pastoral Nature of the Ministry*, 1980; *Pastoral Care for Lay People*, 1982.

R. J. HUNTER

Patripassianism

Patripassianism is a nickname applied to modalism* by its opponents taken from a corollary of the doctrine. 'If Christ is God, he must be identical with the Father, and, if he is identical with the Father, then, since Christ suffered, the Father suffered' (Noetus). According to Tertullian, Praxeas maintained that 'the Father was born and the Father suffered'. The term is drawn from Tertullian's charge that Praxeas 'banished the Paraclete (through his opposition to Montanism) and crucified the Father (through his modalist views)'. An improved variant of these modalist statements is also cited by Tertullian, 'the Son suffered, the Father co-suffered' (*patitur, compatitur*); but this is either a mere verbal amendment or shipwrecks the modalist position, since 'What else is compassion but "suffering with"?' (Tertullian). At least at this stage of its development modalism regarded the modes as successive and not simultaneous. The compassion of the Father with the Son (purged of any modalist associations) became orthodox teaching on the subject.

H. E. W. TURNER

Patristics

The study of the large body of literature stemming from those known as the Fathers (Lat. *patres*). Most of these were bishops or scholars of the church in the early centuries, and those principally studied wrote in Greek or Latin. Some important and influential figures wrote in one or other of the ancient languages, like Syriac, Coptic or Armenian, as for example the Syrian hymn-writer Ephraem; and some originally Greek or Latin works survive only in ancient translations, especially those of writers later branded as heretics. There is some disagreement about how long the patristic period may be considered to have lasted. Some would use the term of the whole period up to the time when the mediaeval Schoolmen took over (*see* **Scholasticism**), others would limit it to the earliest centuries: thus, the Orthodox Church honours as Fathers writers like Gregory Palamas (1296–1359), whereas the Protestant tradition tends to accept the date of the Council of Chalcedon (451) as an approximate *terminus*.

This literature may be classified in various ways. One would be genre:

1. *Epistles*, beginning with the writings of the early Apostolic Fathers, and culminating in the published correspondence of major ecclesiastical figures like Basil of Caesarea or Ambrose of Milan;

2. *Homiletic works*, from the dramatic *Paschal Homily* of Melito from the second century to the extended exegetical collections of preachers like John Chrysostom and sermons on topical or theological themes from many of the famous bishops;

3. *Apologetic works* directed to the outsider or opponent, ranging from the fairly short explanatory essays of the early apologists to Origen's extensive debate with Celsus and the massive proofs of Eusebius' *Praeparatio Evangelica*;

4. *Controversial literature*, describing, condemning and arguing against teachers and heretics, once our only source of information and heavy with bias, now happily supplemented by the rediscovery of some proscribed literature, like Nestorius' apology known as *The Bazaar of Heraclides*, or the Gnostic* works of the Nag Hammadi library;

5. *Biblical commentaries* (sometimes in the form of collections of exegetical homilies), from scholars like Origen, or from many of the leading bishops of the later period;

6. *Catechetical lectures*, instructing new converts in the faith during Lent and preparing them for baptism at Easter;

7. Personal works, like Gregory Nazianzen's *Poems* or Augustine's *Confessions*;

8. Works modelled on classical literature, like *histories*, *philosophical treatises* on themes, etc.;

9. *Hagiographical works*, *Lives* of saints and martyrs, or panegyrical homilies delivered on saints' days;

10. Collections of official papers from the later Oecumenical Councils (i.e. not Nicaea), known as *Conciliar Acts*.

Many of these different genres, for example, the apologetic or exegetical, built up standard arguments, or traditional methods and approaches, sometimes one 'school' being clearly distinguishable from another.

Another way of classifying the literature is according to period or place:

1. *The Apostolic Fathers* include the earliest, non-scriptural Christian writings, often overlapping in date with the later NT documents, and some regarded as scriptural in

certain quarters before the final definition of the canon. An epistle from Clement, a late first-century secretary (bishop?) of the Roman church to the church at Corinth, and epistles from the bishop of Antioch, Ignatius, written on his final journey across Asia Minor to martyrdom in Rome, together with a visionary work known as the *Shepherd of Hermas* and the rediscovered church manual the *Didache*, or *Teaching of the Twelve Apostles*, are the main items included in this class of material.

2. *The Early Apologists* include Justin Martyr, Aristides, Tatian, Athenagoras, Theophilus, Minucius Felix and Tertullian. These were active around AD 120–220.

3. Irenaeus (late second century), Tertullian, Hippolytus and Cyprian (third century) are the important figures of *early Western theology*. Irenaeus originated in Asia Minor but became bishop of Lyons (Gaul), and wrote extensively against the Gnostic heretics, originally in Greek, the language of the commercial classes and at first of the church, even in Western cities. Hippolytus followed in the same task, and although 'anti-pope', was an important literary figure, Greek still being the language of the church in the capital city. Tertullian was the first to write in Latin, and he coined the theological vocabulary which became standard for the Latin-speaking church. He and Cyprian in the next generation represent the rather rigorist theological traditions of North Africa.

4. Roughly contemporary, but very different in temper, were *the Alexandrians*, who developed a particular tradition of philosophical theology, the most important representatives being Clement (*c.* 150–220) and Origen (*c.* 185–255). Origen was later branded as a heretic, whereas Clement was sainted, a strange outcome since in many respects Origen was more ecclesiastical than Clement in his intentions. Clement was explicitly philosophical in his approach and regarded the sophisticated Christian as the 'true gnostic'. Origen was more systematic, more scholarly and more biblical; he composed the *Hexapla*, a massive compendium for establishing the biblical text, setting out the Hebrew and several Greek versions in parallel columns, and he commented or preached on nearly every book of the Bible. The Alexandrians developed allegory to a fine art and gave it a theo-

retical basis (*see also* **Alexandrian Theology**).

5. *The period of Nicaea.* Origen's scholarly mantle was eventually taken up by Eusebius of Caesarea, the first historian of the church, who also wrote massive apologetic works and things like a biblical encyclopaedia. In the West, the apologetic task was embraced by Lactantius. The early fourth century was dominated by three developments: (i) the conversion of Constantine, the Christianizing of the empire and the politicizing of the church; (ii) the reaction against accommodation with the world evidenced in the flowering of the monastic movement, which was to inspire a hagiographical literature of its own; and (iii) the Arian * controversy, which occasioned the First Oecumenical Council at Nicaea and determined the course of ecclesiastical politics and theology for half a century and more. The greatest figure produced by these events was Athanasius. Many of his writings are anti-Arian treatises, but he also produced a little book of perennial influence, the *De Incarnatione*, and probably the classic *Life of Antony*, who was said to be the first monk.

6. *The Cappadocians* * were a trio with close ties, Basil of Caesarea being the student friend of Gregory Nazianzen and the brother of Gregory of Nyssa. The 'Three Great Hierarchs' of Eastern Orthodoxy include Basil and Gregory of Nazianzus, together with John Chrysostom. Letters, sermons, treatises, poems, commentaries – a vast literature survives from their pens. They were responsible for the triumph of Nicene orthodoxy in the later fourth century, gave lasting shape to Eastern trinitarianism, and effected the cultural marriage between Christianity and Hellenism which was to shape the Byzantine world. Basil laid the foundations for the liturgical and monastic forms characteristic of Greek Orthodoxy, and Gregory of Nyssa minted the language and symbols of mediaeval mysticism.

7. The *golden age* of patristic literature *in the East* included not only the major fourth-century writers mentioned, but also John Chrysostom and Cyril of Alexandria. The former was the greatest preacher the Greek church produced, and although not particularly important in the formation of doctrine, his homilies have remained one of the principal influences in the thinking and practice of Eastern Orthodoxy. Cyril's name

is particularly associated with the fifth-century christological controversies, and some of his letters were given canonical status at the Council of Chalcedon, but his interests were not solely confined to dogmatic issues. As in the case of most of the Fathers, scriptural exegesis was an important element in his work. (Significant later writers of the East include Pseudo-Dionysius the Areopagite, whose mystical writings were profoundly influential in the Middle Ages, East and West; Severus of Antioch, the Monophysite theologian, and Leontius of Byzantium, the Chalcedonian, both of the sixth century; Maximus Confessor, seventh century and John of Damascus, the eighth-century defender of images).

8. Meanwhile, *in the West*, the great figures of Jerome (342–420), Ambrose (339–397) and Augustine (354–430) had brought Latin theology to its peak. Together with Gregory the Great (540–604), they are the Doctors of the Latin church. Jerome was responsible for the Vulgate, the authoritative Latin translation of the Bible. Ambrose, amongst many other things, introduced Greek exegetical methods to the West. Although Latin theology tended to be more practical and less philosophical and speculative than the Greek tradition, a little earlier the Neoplatonist* Marius Victorinus, and Hilary, the principal anti-Arian theologian of the West, had given it an intellectual turn and prepared the way for the Augustinian* teaching, a stupendous intellectual achievement which deeply influenced the future of Western theology. Important lines were laid down in trinitarianism (*see also* **Trinity**), the doctrine of the church*, the doctrine of grace* and free will*, etc.; but Augustine is even better known for his monumental essay in the philosophy of history*, the *City of God* and his pioneering autobiographical work, the *Confessions*.

This literature may be studied:

1. *For historical reasons*. It is the primary source material for reconstructing the history of the church during the period with which we are concerned. There is other relevant material of course: references to Christ, Christians or the church in secular literature of one kind and another, archaeological evidence, etc. But the patristic literature is the largest body of extant evidence, and secular historians of the late

Roman empire and early Byzantine worlds have to use it for information as much as historians of the church.

2. *For doctrinal reasons*. It is the primary source material for reconstructing the early history of dogma*, though the doctrinal study of the Fathers has often gone beyond mere historical interest. For the Orthodox Church, the Fathers are a major source and authority alongside scripture and venerated as such; all truth will be found somewhere in the literature, and the theological task is essentially an exegetical one. Catholics would invest authority in the church and not confine it to the patristic period; yet the establishment of the orthodox* tradition was very much the work of the Fathers, and their pronouncements enshrined in the creeds* and decisions of Councils are accorded the utmost respect. The creeds and the doctrinal debates which went into their composition have remained important for classical Protestantism*, and for Anglicanism particularly: thus Nicaea and Chalcedon are still treated as 'tests of orthodoxy' in many theological debates (*see also* **Christology**). Attitudes have changed a good deal as evolutionary models of the history of doctrine have replaced the previous confidence in a primordial orthodoxy always known or latent and constantly distorted or threatened by devilish heresy. Interest in the Fathers' teachings now is inevitably less dogmatic and more strictly historical: i.e. the reconstruction of why the leaders of the church thought as they did in the early centuries and how they reached the doctrinal conclusions which have become enshrined in the classic pronouncements and creeds*.

3. *For liturgical reasons*. It is the primary source material for reconstructing the early history of the liturgy. Texts of liturgies begin to be available from about the fifth century, but prior to that, and even after that, the patristic literature is an indispensable source of information: e.g. for descriptions of practices which help to date their emergence or explain their intention, quotations of early prayers, hymns, ritual formulae, etc. The recent liturgical movement which has led to revision of liturgies in most mainstream churches has been deeply influenced by the rediscoveries of historians of the liturgy who have mostly made those discoveries by studying the patristic material.

4. *For biographical reasons*. Some of the

writers were outstanding personalities worth studying in their own right. The development of modern biographical interests has on the whole succeeded the older hagiographical approach. Augustine, Jerome and many others have been the subjects of serious studies, and increasingly those tarred with the heresy brush have attracted the sympathetic attention of scholars, notably Origen and Nestorius.

5. *For spiritual reasons,* and *philosophical or theological reasons.* Particularly in the Orthodox and Catholic traditions, the spiritual, mystical and ascetical aspects of the Fathers' teachings have had a continuing influence; and there has been more confidence than in Protestant (especially the more radical) theological streams that the Fathers still have important philosophical and theological truths to convey. Reaction to this tends to depend upon whether a degree of Platonic idealism * remains intellectually acceptable or not.

Generally speaking, it may be said that there is a lively international community of patristic specialists and a tremendous industry producing better critical texts and monographs, centred especially in Europe and Catholic America; but that for theological studies in general, patristics has a declining influence. The traditional authorities, scriptures, creeds, church, have been subjected to intense critical fire in modern theological thinking, and the emergence of the *historical* approach to scripture and other once authoritative literature, has tended to distance the material from modern interests and concerns, with a resultant slackening in interest among systematicians (*see also* **Doctrinal Criticism**). How could someone in the third, fourth or fifth century say anything relevant to the theological and philosophical puzzles of the twentieth century? If biblical study has suffered from the 'hermeneutical gap', how much more has patristic study; for the gap is most seriously felt precisely in those theological streams which have honoured scripture above ecclesiastical tradition. Radicals who have found scripture difficult to accommodate have not hesitated to be quite cavalier in their attitudes to the Fathers: Nicaea and Chalcedon can hardly continue to be binding as Christian theology is adapted to the modern world. Critical reference to patristic formulations and some major heretical

movements may still figure in systematic discussions, but there is an enormous gap between serious study of the patristic material, largely conducted in historical terms, and modern theological interests.

On the whole this gap is to be regarded as unfortunate. In spite of all the differences in terms of culture, methods of reasoning, presuppositions, etc., the Fathers did belong to an important intellectual tradition, and they did wrestle far more openly than is often realized, with many of the same issues as now face Christian theologians and apologists. Questions about God and his relationship with the world, his activity in the world, his essential nature; questions about other religions (Christianity then being a powerless and derided 'new superstition'); questions about faith and knowledge, science and revelation; questions about meaning and interpretation; questions about the nature of prayer and providence – all these, quite apart from the more obvious matters like the doctrine of the Trinity and christology, are issues with which the Fathers wrestled. To see these questions debated in a quite different intellectual setting is important, for it enables us to step outside our own culturally-conditioned presuppositions and see the issues in a different way. All too often the contribution of the Fathers has just been dismissed for one reason or another: e.g. regarded as a sellout to Hellenic ways of thinking without proper attention to the Bible; criticized for over-allegorization and failure to take history seriously; condemned for being prescientific and tied to outdated 'substance' categories. Now it is true that the Fathers may try the twentieth-century patience – their style and approach is not ours. Yet they were intelligent and perceptive men and they often saw things to which we have become blind. Critical distance is necessary, but sympathetic insight may discover treasure. As the historic-critical method of biblical interpretation comes under attack, the value of psychological and spiritual ways of reading the Bible is being recognized: what was allegory if it were not a serious attempt to devise a coherent and imaginative method of bridging the hermeneutical gap? As religious language becomes a major issue in theological discussion, the respectability of metaphorical and imaginative ways of speech is being reasserted; the personal

Deity is being refined as the a-personal aspect of God is being admitted; these and many other theological developments are anticipated in the highly sophisticated work of the major Fathers. And it may be that we have something to learn from them in the epistemological sphere. It is increasingly claimed that the Western scientific mind has allowed the logical and analytical half of the brain to over-dominate the intuitive and imaginative and that the balance needs redressing: in the Greek intellectual tradition the balance was right – the critical and analytical process was given full weight as the method of refining concepts and eliminating falsity, but ultimately truth was grasped by the purified mind through intuition. This is sometimes dismissed as 'mystical', but it was a serious epistemological view about the functioning of the mind and about knowledge of true reality. The Greek Fathers laid claim to this tradition. To rediscover it could help the modern theologian to renewed confidence in the ability *to know God*, as distinct from regarding God as merely an imaginative figment or projection.

Introductory books

H. von Campenhausen, *The Fathers of the Greek Church*, 1963; *The Fathers of the Latin Church*, 1964; G. L. Prestige, *Fathers and Heretics*, 1940; M. F. Wiles, *The Christian Fathers*, 1966.

Selected and translated texts

H. Bettenson, *The Early Christian Fathers*, 1956; *The Later Christian Fathers*, 1972; M. F. Wiles and M. Santer, *Documents in Early Christian Thought*, 1975.

Textbooks
A. Grillmeier, *Christ in Christian Tradition*, [2]1975; J. N. D. Kelly, *Early Christian Doctrines*, 1960; J. Quasten, *Patrology*, 3 vols., 1963; F. M. Young, *From Nicaea to Chalcedon*, 1983.

                                   FRANCES YOUNG

Patrology

Patrology is the science of studying the writings of the early Fathers of the church, whose number is generally reckoned to have ceased with John of Damascus (*c*. 675–749).
                                   R. P. C. HANSON

Pelagianism

The name given to the belief that human beings are able to achieve their salvation by their own powers. This was the teaching of Pelagius, a British lay theologian and exegete (his *Expositions on the Epistles of St Paul* have come down to us), who at the end of the fourth and the beginning of the fifth centuries was influential among the Roman aristocracy, and later in N. Africa and Palestine. Pelagius aimed to establish a perfect church of the élite as an example to the sinful world. He praised free will* as the highest human endowment, understanding it as *utriusque partis possibilitas* (the possibility of either side), in particular the power to choose between good and evil. He was outraged by Augustine's teaching that all depended on grace: *da quod iubes et iube quod vis* (give what you command and command what you will: *Confessions* X.29). By means of free will, Pelagius thought, even atheists could become virtuous. Christians, however, had the added help of grace, which Pelagius understood in his own way as the example and motivation provided by Christ. Original sin was no more than Adam's bad example, not an inherited defect which impaired the freedom of the will. Adult baptism seems to have been important for Pelagius as providing a psychological break with the past, not as the means of remitting inherited guilt; infant baptism did not fit easily into the Pelagian system.

Through the determined opposition of Augustine the heresy was condemned by councils at Milevis and Carthage (416 and 418), by Popes Innocent I and Zosimus, and by the Emperor Honorius. Thenceforth Pelagius' disciples Caelestius and Julian of Eclanum took the lead in defending and refining their master's doctrine. The last twenty years of Augustine's life were dominated by his controversies against the Pelagians.

See **Semi-Pelagianism**.

P. Brown, *Augustine of Hippo*, 1967; *Religion and Society in the Age of St Augustine*, 1973; R. Evans, *Pelagius: Inquiries and Reappraisals*, 1968.

                                   E. J. YARNOLD

Penance

The word derives from the Latin *paenitentia*, meaning penitence or repentance. In Christian history it has variously designated an inner turning to God or a public returning to the church, any of a series of ecclesiastical disciplines designed to facilitate such inward or outward reconversion, and the various works that had to be performed as part of such disciplines. In the Middle Ages the standard *sacramentum paenitentiae* was private confession, which in English came to be known as the sacrament of penance. Today in the R C church it is also called the sacrament of reconciliation.

There is scriptural evidence that early Christians continued the Jewish practice of 'binding and loosing', i.e. restricting recalcitrant members from full participation in the community, and then later releasing them from such restrictions when they mended their ways (cf. I Cor. 5.1–13; II Cor. 2.5–11; Matt. 18.15–18). All Christians, of course, had been enjoined by Jesus to forgive one another, but it was not until the second century that their leaders began publicly to readmit to the church those who had once renounced their faith (cf. *The Shepherd of Hermas*, Mandate 4).

From this simple beginning, the practice of public repentance and reconciliation with the church, not only for apostasy and heresy but also in cases of serious sin such as murder and adultery, grew during the early patristic period into a fully-fledged penitential discipline. The penances imposed sometimes lasted for years, and they culminated in a ritual of reconciliation with the church, represented by the bishop. The length and severity of the discipline, however, combined with the fact that canon law* allowed such ecclesiastical reconciliation to be received only once in a lifetime, eventually led to a practice of deathbed repentance. It must be remembered, however, that during these centuries the vast majority of Christians were never directly involved in public penitence.

During the sixth century Irish missionaries introduced the monastic practice of private, repeated confession, made to a priest rather than a bishop, to the European mainland. After some initial resistance from the hierarchy, the new penitential practice grew in popularity and eventually replaced the older form, and during the course of the centuries the harsh penances originally imposed by the monks were supplanted by prayers and other such spiritual works. Also, by the twelfth century, the priest's prayer for the forgiveness of the penitent

had evolved into a pronouncement of absolution for sins, and it was in this form that the ritual became one of the seven ecclesiastical sacraments of mediaeval Christendom.

Most of the scholastic theories of penance were concerned to explain how the forgiveness* of God came to individuals through the ministry of the priest, but Luther and other Reformers in the sixteenth century insisted that God's grace was immediately available to Christians. This, combined with the conclusion that justification* is not dependent on the performance of good works, led them to repudiate the mediaeval practice and its theological rationale. Some allowed, however, that confession could be beneficial in certain circumstances (cf. Luther, *Large Catechism*, 'A Short Exhortation to Confession'; Calvin, *Institutes of the Christian Religion* III, 4, 12–14). Nevertheless, confession as a general practice eventually disappeared from most churches of the Reformation, including the Anglican, which retains it as one of the five, non-dominical sacraments.

Both the R C and Orthodox churches retain the sacrament and regard it as instituted by Christ, although the rites and the theologies behind them are somewhat different in each case. The official Roman rite was revised in 1973, and both before and since that revision the Catholic understanding of the meaning and nature of ecclesiastical reconciliation has been shifting away from the scholastic and somewhat legalistic interpretation of the late mediaeval period, and towards a more biblical and pastoral interpretation of the sacrament.

M. Hebbelthwaite and K. Donovan, *The Theology of Penance*, 1979; M. Hellwig, *Sign of Reconciliation and Conversion*, 1982; B. Poschmann, *Penance and Anointing of the Sick*, E T 1964; O. Watkins, *A History of Penance*, 1920.

J. MARTOS

Penitence *see* **Penance, Repentance**

Pentecost

The term derives from *pentēcostē*, the Greek name for the Jewish Feast of Weeks at the close of the grain harvest fifty days after Passover and Unleavened Bread (Tob. 2.1). In the early church Pentecost at first designated the whole period of fifty days from Easter; only later did it refer particularly to the fiftieth day, which became a feast in its own right.

The fifty days celebrating Christ's resurrection*, the firstfruits of the end, were one 'great Sunday' (Athanasius), the 'most joyful season' (*laetissimum spatium*: Tertullian, *On Baptism* 19). There was no kneeling for prayer, but only standing (to mark the heavenly location of believers in Christ, in anticipation of the general resurrection); and there was no fasting (a foretaste of the heavenly banquet with the messianic bridegroom). The 'Alleluia' was a hopeful sign of the time when 'we shall become a perpetual praise' (Augustine, *Sermo* 254). With geographical variants, the Fourth Gospel, Acts and Revelation emerge as the favourite sources for lections.

In the fourth century the fiftieth day was regarded as the seal of the period, with the Ascension* of Christ and the Descent of the Holy Spirit* as its twin themes (as seems to be still the case at Jerusalem in Egeria's *Travel Diary*). By the end of that century and into the fifth (from Chrysostom and the Gregories in the East to Augustine in Africa and Leo at Rome), two distinct feasts of Ascension (forty days after Easter; cf. Acts 1.1–11) and Pentecost (cf. Acts 2.1ff.) had emerged, doubtless as part of a growing post-Constantinian tendency towards historical commemoration, but also motivated by a post-Arian* dogmatic recognition of the full divinity of Christ and the Holy Spirit. The unity of the fifty days eventually became further disrupted by octaves, rogations and the post-Ascension fast.

First in sectarian Judaism in the intertestamental period, and then in rabbinic Judaism by the second and third centuries, the Feast of Weeks had become associated with the lawgiving and covenant* of Sinai. Sermons at the feast of Pentecost by Christian preachers of the fifth century relate the new covenant of the Spirit to the old covenant of the Law. Further, the gift of speech for apostolic preaching is considered as a reversal of Babel, bringing unity and catholicity* to the church and its mission. The vigil of Pentecost became a baptismal occasion, and the white robes of the baptized account for the English 'Whitsunday'.

In the twentieth century the feast has lent its name to a 'Pentecostal*' movement which enjoys the more spectacular gifts of the Spirit such as glossolalia*, prophecy* and healing. Ecumenically, the Eastern Orthodox also see themselves as bringing a pneumatological ecclesiology, typified in the event of Pentecost, to correct the greater institutionalism of the Western church.

R. Cabié, *La Pentecôte: l'évolution de la cinquantaine pascale au cours des cinq premiers siècles*, 1965; J. Gunstone, *The Feast of Pentecost: The Great Fifty Days in the Liturgy*, 1967; W. J. Hollenweger, *The Pentecostals*, 1972.

GEOFFREY WAINWRIGHT

Pentecostalism

A movement of Christian renewal typified by the first Christian Pentecost, when the Holy Spirit, descending upon the fearful apostles, transformed them into bold, ardent and convincing evangelists. It is characterized by the reappearance of the charisms* of glossolalia*, healing, miracles, etc. whence it is also known as the Charismatic*Renewal. The movement arose in mid-Western America in the very first year of the twentieth century, although it had nineteenth-century antecedents in England (Irvingites) and Armenia (cf. D. Shakarian), as well as in American revivalism*. The Welsh revival led by Ervan Roberts (1904ff.) also stimulated the American development.

This began in a non-denominational Bible school in Topeka, Kansas, on 1 January 1901, when a Sunday school teacher, Agnes Ozman, after being prayed with for the 'baptism in the Spirit', experienced a powerful interior renewal and began to praise God in an unknown tongue, later identified as Bohemian. As others shared this experience, especially, from 1905 on in Los Angeles, an enthusiastic movement took form. Rejected by the Holiness, Baptist and Methodist churches from which most of its early participants came, this movement engendered many new churches, commonly known as 'Pentecostal', which today embrace over twenty-two million adherents, making them the fifth largest Protestant group in the world.

From about 1960 on, Episcopalians, Lutherans, Presbyterians and members of other established Protestant churches, after receiving the Pentecostal experience, insisted on remaining in their denomination; they are known as 'neo-Pentecostals'. From 1967 onwards, Roman Catholics, and a little later some Greek Orthodox, embraced Pentecostalism, while tending more and more to prefer the term Charismatic Renewal.

This renewal is based on belief in the Holy Spirit* as a real gift imparted by the glorified Lord Jesus to his disciples. Without limiting the working of the Spirit to the supernatural charisms listed in I Cor. 12.8–10, it holds to the reality and value of these charisms as manifestations of the Spirit's activity (I Cor. 12.7). The earliest Pentecostals regarded glossolalia* as the necessary sign of having received the Holy Spirit. A more sober view that is tending more and more to be adopted, especially among Roman Catholics, regards it as only one among many gifts of the Spirit, none of which are given to everyone. In any case, it is by far the most widespread of the charisms, and has become in a sense the banner of the Pentecostal movement. It is not the miraculous power to speak a foreign language; normally, the tongues-speaker does not understand the meaning of his own utterance (cf. I Cor. 14.14). If he receives a message for the community, what he utters in tongues will need to be declared by someone endowed with the charism of interpretation (I Cor. 14.27–28). Usually, however, this gift is employed, not to communicate a message, but as a vehicle for praising God, as was the case at the great Pentecost (Acts 2.11).

There is much argument about whether the 'tongue' spoken is a genuine language. Most Pentecostals seem to believe that this is so, and there are abundant instances reported in which the language has been identified. It is difficult, however, to obtain any scientifically controlled data. Others, mostly theoreticians, regard glossolalia as a non-conceptual mode of expression. In any case, it is not ecstatic or trance-like as often supposed. The tongues-speaker can use his gift at will, and calmly; only he does not determine what he is going to utter.

The gift of healing is the most impressive charism; however, it is by no means peculiar to Pentecostals. Miraculous healings have been a part of Roman Catholic experience from NT times onwards. After having been rejected vehemently by the Reformers, they reappeared in the Protestant world through the instrumentality of the German, Joseph Blumhardt (1805–1880). Nevertheless, it is predominantly among Pentecostals (of whatever denomination) that 'faith healings' are most often reported today. They are not just spiritual or psychic; many involve deliverance from physical conditions such as deformed limbs, blindness, deafness and paralysis. Here, too, there have been few rigorous scientific investigations; but the impressive number of people who have discarded crutches, wheel chairs, etc. after the intervention of this charism has convinced thousands, perhaps millions, that the Spirit of God has really been at work.

While these and other such charisms have drawn attention to the Charismatic Renewal, they are not its chief strength. The latter derives rather from an inner peace and joy, a vivid awareness of the presence of the living God and his love, a strong sense of loving communion with one's fellows, and a new courage and power in witnessing to Christ, that flow from the 'baptism in the Spirit'. These 'fruits of the Spirit' have made Pentecostal communities milieux of loving communion, and sources of effective evangelism (see also **Spiritual Gifts**). For Pentecostalism is not primarily a doctrine, method or strategy, but an experience – a personal experience of the inner working of the Holy Spirit. The movement did not arise out of any plan devised to bring about Christian renewal. It is true that in 1897 Pope Leo XIII wrote an encyclical letter urging renewed devotion to 'the forgotten person of the Blessed Trinity'; and in 1961 John XXIII invited all Christians to pray God to 'renew (his) wonders in our time as though for a new Pentecost'. But neither in its beginnings in 1901, nor in its further developments during the 1960s, was the Pentecostal movement conceived as a response to these papal pleas. It simply happened – to the astonishment of those who found themselves caught up in it.

Whatever be its future as a distinct movement, it has already made a large number of Christians today more aware and convinced of the reality of the Holy Spirit and his work. In an age when the exploits of technology seem to impress people more than the Word of God; when Bultmann says it is impossible to believe in miracles; when embarrassed exegetes explain supernatural events as mythical expressions for the unutterable;

Pentecostalism may be seen as the Holy Spirit's effective rejoinder that God is still leading his people towards the Promised Land 'with outstretched hand and a mighty arm'.

N. Bloch-Hoell, *The Pentecostal Movement: Its Origin, Development and Character*, 1964; W. J. Hollenweger, *The Pentecostals*, ET 1972; K. McDonnell, 'The ecumenical significance of the Pentecostal Movement', *Worship*, 1966, pp. 608–33; *Presence, Power, Praise. Documents on the Charismatic Renewal*, 3 vols., 1980; E. O'Connor, *The Pentecostal Movement in the Catholic Church*, [2]1974; V. Synan, *The Holiness-Pentecostal Movement in the United States*, 1971.

EDWARD D. O'CONNOR

Perennial Philosophy

A translation of *philosophia perennis*. This is a modern thesis about the central strand of human spirituality, both Western and Eastern. It is the title of a book by Aldous Huxley published in 1946, in which he set forth evidence to show that the great religious traditions all contain a strand of ancient wisdom pointing to a single divine Reality. Huxley was influenced by Vedanta, and his position was in part a reflection of the theme of the unity of all religions which had become so prominent in modern expositions of Hinduism from the latter half of the nineteenth century onwards. The theme of unity was illustrated by the writings of many of the contemplatives of different traditions. Thus the perennial philosophy has its most obvious examples (according to its exponents) in the life and thought of such figures as Plotinus, Pseudo-Dionysius, Eckhart, Boehme, the Jewish Kabbalists, the Sufis, Shankara, Sri Ramakrishna, Tibetan, Zen and some other types of Buddhists. Three main strands of thought can be picked out in Huxley's account: (i) that there is one divine Reality; (ii) that this is an impersonal Absolute – not the anthropomorphic God of much theism (as he saw it); (iii) that the way back to this divine Source is through contemplative practice. Later he took up the possibility that one could gain the fruits of contemplation by the use of such drugs as mescalin, and he thus came to be influential upon the drug scene of the 1960s in America, with his *The Doors of Perception* (1954).

Behind Huxley was the tradition of neo-Vedanta, which had its most important roots in the life and writings of Ramakrishna (1834–1886) and Vivekananda (1863–1902), but more widely reflected much modern Hindu thinking among English-speaking Indian writers. It is a theme in the widely read works of S. Radhakrishnan (1888–1975), who was Professor of Eastern Religions and Ethics in Oxford before World War II and later President of the Republic of India. Though the Theosophical movement never had great influence in the West, it was a factor in the development of Hindu thinking and higher education, primarily through the vigour of Annie Besant (1847–1933), who also espoused the theme of an ancient wisdom which can be found in the different religions of the world. For these writers the attraction of Hinduism lay in its very diversity as well as its inner unity. Thus it could be seen as long having taught the idea that different paths lead to the same Goal, and that it is possible to see religions as existing at differing levels, of which the highest is realization of unity with the One Reality. This was seen as the essence of the Upanishadic teaching. Generally it was the interpretation of Shankara's Non-Dualistic Vedanta which was taken as authoritative. But there have been writers who have approached the perennial philosophy from out of other religious traditions – such as Edward Conze (1905–1978), and the Islamic Westerners Frithjof Schuon and René Guénon.

The most vigorous opponent of the ideas of the Perennial Philosophy was R. C. Zaehner, a successor of Radhakrishnan in the Spalding Chair of Eastern Religions and Ethics in Oxford. He himself experimented with hallucinogenic drugs in order to have a first-hand basis for disposing of Huxley's psychedelism. More importantly, he sought to show in a number of major works, notably *Mysticism Sacred and Profane* (1957) and *At Sundry Times* (1958), that it is not the case that mysticism is essentially the same the whole world over. So there was not strictly speaking a perennial philosophy but rather different strands of mysticism *, and of other kinds of religion, such as prophecy *. He in particular distinguished between monistic and theistic * mysticism – the latter being characteristic of Christianity and of Islam and theistic Hinduism, the former being especially evident in Hindu yoga and Buddhism. In a later, rather strange, work, *Our Savage God* (1974), he ascribed some of the antinomianism of the 1960s typified in the Manson case to elements of neo-Vedanta thinking.

There is much debate as to whether Zaehner's analysis of mysticism is right, and this debate continues among both contemporary historians and philosophers of religion. Even if there is essentially only one sort of mysticism, it does not show that the perennial philosophy thesis is true, because of the importance of other elements of religious experience *. But there can be little doubt that the thesis is a popular one among many who find the divisions between the great religions uncomfortable. The Ramakrishna Vedanta movement among others continues to give institutional expression to this appeal to the transcendental unity of all religions. A more recent expression of a similar viewpoint, but using rather different vocabulary, is found in the writings of the American religion scholar Huston Smith, who writes: 'I am not unhappy with that phrase (sc. perennial philosophy), but to bring out the fact that this philosophy nowhere originated, nor has it succeeded in maintaining itself operatively, save in a cultic context . . . I prefer . . . the designation "the primordial tradition".'

Aldous Huxley, *The Perennial Philosophy*, 1946; *The Doors of Perception*, 1954; S. Katz (ed), *Mysticism and Philosophical Analysis*, 1979; S. Radhakrishnan, *Eastern Religions and Western Thought*, 1940; F. Schuon, *Transcendent Unity of Religions*, 1953; R. C. Zaehner, *Mysticism Sacred and Profane*, 1957; *At Sundry Times*, 1958.

NINIAN SMART

Perfection

That men should perfectly love God and worthily magnify his holy name is the goal of the Christian life. Christian perfection is defined in terms of the Great Commandment (Matt. 22.37–39) – of love of God and man. Absolute perfection lies beyond this life, in the vision of God, when faith and hope have passed away, but the love of God endures (Aquinas).

Thus for Christians all other virtues are subsumed in love. But this is no abstraction. The perfect human life has been shown to men in Jesus, whose Sermon on the Mount

(Matt. 5.48; Luke 6.4) illustrates committed discipleship. NT writers express their teaching about perfection in differing ways. Paul describes its absolute quality in his hymn to love (I Cor. 13), while confessing his own imperfection and that of his fellow Christians and exhorting them to 'press on' (Phil. 3). The writer to the Hebrews sets perfection against his austere call to Christians to persevere in a dark and dangerous hour. The Johannine literature is orientated around the doctrine of love and the divine indwelling in our souls.

The ideal of perfection was constantly reaffirmed as the end of the Christian life in the early centuries, though there was Stoic influence upon the picture of Christian character, as appears in the attractive picture of the Christian Gnostic in the writings of Clement of Alexandria, and there is Neoplatonic * influence evident in the spirituality of Augustine *, and still more in the writings of Pseudo-Dionysius, who was greatly influential in the next centuries. The Desert Fathers and their monastic successors called Christians to seek evangelical perfection in renunciation of the world. Though it was admitted that Christians might reach perfection in the world and in any state of life, stress came to be laid on the importance of the 'counsels of perfection', poverty, chastity and obedience. At the Reformation the Reformers denied this distinction and any similar 'double standard' among Christians. But they affirmed that in this life men are always sinners, though they affirmed the true end of man to be his perfection, and thought that sanctification might be completed *in articulo mortis*.

That perfection might be attained in this life had been the teaching of various sects, of the Gnostic Cathari in the Middle Ages, some Anabaptist radical groups of the sixteenth and among some Puritan sectaries of the seventeenth centuries. In the seventeenth century there was a reaction against Protestant Orthodoxy, and in 1583 Coornheert had affirmed against the Dutch Calvinists that men may in this life perfectly fulfil the law of Christ. The Pietist Spener also stressed the importance of seeking Christian perfection. The mystic tradition in the church had always stressed the progress of the soul towards union with God, and in the seventeenth century the Quietists raised the question whether there could or should be a disinterested love towards God. In England William Law's *Treatise of Christian Perfection* affirmed that all Christians face the absolute demands of Christ, which he expressed in an austere pattern of devotion and renunciation. While accepting this ethical pattern, Wesley sought to put 'Christian Perfection' within a view of salvation, seeing it as the divine gift of perfect love. This teaching he regarded as the 'grand depositum' of his movement and it brought him into sharp conflict with the Calvinists. He taught that perfection was a complete commitment of the soul in love to God, but that such perfection was capable of infinite growth. He believed that the Christian, though always subject to infirmities of body and soul, might have victory over sin, defined as 'voluntary transgression of a known law'. He believed that mature Christians should seek and expect to enter into perfect love in an experience which might be instantaneously given. The teaching of some nineteenth-century 'Holiness' cults appears to be a simplistic version of part of Wesley's teaching. R. W. Dale thought that Christians generally had insufficiently considered the corporate aspect of Christian perfection and its relation not only to individual souls but to communities. The lives of the saints have always been for Christians the reminder that in this life men and women of all kinds, temperaments and cultures have touched the heights of Christian experience and have committed themselves utterly to the service of their fellows.

R. N. Flew, *The Idea of Perfection in Christian Theology*, 1934; W. Law, *Practical Treatise of Christian Perfection*, 1726; J. Wesley, *Plain Account of Christian Perfection*, Works, Vol. XI, 1856.

E. G. RUPP

Perichoresis *see* Coinherence

Perseverance

This term, Latin *donum perseverantiae, perseverantia sanctorum*, denotes the gift of persistence in faith and the preservation of believers to the end in temptation and persecution. The doctrine of perseverance is the other side of the doctrine of election * (predestination *). Thus just as the doctrine of election does not base the event of faith on human chance or arbitrariness, but on the free, prevenient grace of God, so the doctrine of perseverance directs the believer to God's reliable faithfulness and does not leave his future open to uncertainty: God remains faithful to his election, his covenant * and his creation *. Therefore the elect, the people of the covenant and the created world will not be lost either. There are emphatic expressions of this assurance in the OT psalms and in Paul (Rom. 8.31–39). In the Gospel of John, faith and abiding are brought so close together as to be virtually identical. In Hebrews abiding in faith is depicted as the patience of hope. The theological doctrine of perseverance gives expression to the assured hope of believers, just as the theological doctrine of election depicts the assured faith of those who hope.

In his controversy with the Pelagians *, Augustine * had deepened his doctrine of grace so that it became a doctrine of predestination *. If grace is really grace and the gift of God, then it is grounded only in the will of God and not in human desires or achievements. Even faith itself is God's grace. Therefore men and women come to faith not through their own will, but through the will of God. The grace of faith is rooted in God's gracious election. On the other hand, as a result it becomes impossible for human beings to lose true faith. The 'gift of perseverance' (*donum perseverantiae*) is bound up with the gift of grace. Therefore those who truly believe remain believers to the end. This assurance is not based on their own strength but on God's faithfulness, which cannot deny itself or his choice. Augustine also presents his view of the *donum perseverantiae* in his doctrine of freedom: the first human being had the freedom not to sin. The sinner loses this original freedom. He becomes the slave of sin and therefore can no longer not sin. Man under grace is man liberated for freedom. However, his new freedom consists in no longer being able to sin, but being able spontaneously to do what is good. This freedom is therefore inalienable. It is already an anticipation in history of freedom in the realm of glory.

In the mediaeval scholastic tradition Augustine's statements about predestination and perseverance were thought to be 'exaggerated'. People agreed on a mild semi-Pelagianism *. This meant that Augustine's doctrine of freedom was also forced into the background. The only argument was whether a state of grace could or could not be forfeited. The thoroughgoing doctrine of the inalienability of grace seemed to restrict human responsibility and therefore human morality. In the twelfth century this led to an agreement that in principle it was possible to forfeit the state of grace, for example through mortal sin*. Exceptions from this state of uncertainty were the mother of God, the apostles and the saints who had received special revelations. The Council of Trent* argued against the Reformers' assurance of salvation through faith that in principle the believer could not be certain of election and therefore of his or her perseverance to the end (Denz. 806, 826). To last out, there was need for 'the special help of God', which went beyond his universal grace.

The Reformation doctrine of the gospel from grace alone which brought justification* through faith alone necessarily led to the doctrine of the assurance* of salvation in faith. Therefore the Reformers once again took up Augustine's doctrine of predestination and accentuated its anti-Pelagian elements in the face of scholastic theology. However, they did not agree over the doctrine of the assurance of perseverance in faith. Whereas Luther, Melanchthon and the Lutheran tradition held that it was possible to lose faith, in that moral sins could drive out the Holy Spirit, Bucer, Calvin and the Reformed tradition held that it was impossible to lose true faith. However, they avoided objectifying it so that it became donum perseverantiae and described it in personal and relational terms as perseverantia sanctorum: persevering and abiding in faith to the end is grounded in election and preservation through God's faithfulness, in Christ's sacrifice and intercession and in the constant indwelling of the Holy Spirit in the hearts of believers.

The Reformed doctrine of perseverance could certainly also lead to the endorsement of Calvinist self-righteousness (Max Weber), but it was tested in practice in the trials, persecutions and martyrdoms of the Huguenots. Formulated in terms of 'holding out to the end', the doctrine of perseverance is a polemical doctrine of Christian hope* and not an expression of irresponsible self-assurance. It proves illuminating in situations where the existential question is whether to run away or to stand fast (H. E.

Richter). In such situations, the assurance of salvation necessarily becomes the certainty of perseverance. In general it follows from the experience and recognition of these situations that Christian faith is to be understood neither as a habitual state (as in the Middle Ages) nor as decision (as in modern times), but essentially as faithfulness to God on the basis of his own faithfulness. Continuity understood in historical terms must be understood as faithfulness.

See also **Final Perseverance.**

Augustine, De dono perseverantiae; G. C. Berkouwer, Geloof en Volharding, 1958; H. Jonas, Augustin und das paulinische Freiheitsproblem, ²1965; J. Moltmann, Prädestination und Perseveranz, 1961; Theology of Hope, ET 1967; H. E. Richter, Flüchten oder Standhalten, 1976; O. Weber, Die Treue Gottes und die Kontinuität der menschlichen Existenz, 1967.

JÜRGEN MOLTMANN

Person

The term is derived from the Latin persona, which originally referred to an actor's mask and hence to a role or part (whether on stage or in society) and to the individual who sustains such a role. By the first Christian century it was in normal use to mean simply an individual human being. Persona was the natural Latin equivalent of the Greek prosōpon, which itself could bear the sense of 'human individual' but whose most persistent connotation was that of 'face' or 'countenance'.

Persona was introduced into the theological vocabulary in consequence of its use to render prosōpon. Following a custom of classical rhetoric, Philo of Alexandria had employed prosōpon to refer to the source or speaker of a scriptural saying; Christian adoption of this practice led, in Latin writers like Tertullian, to the appearance of such phrases as 'the person of the Father', 'the person of the Christ'. This use to denote divine figures as individuals may have been encouraged by Valentinian gnostic* employment of expressions like 'personal substances' and 'person' with regard to the aeons of the divine realm in their distinctness. It is no surprise, then, to find Hippolytus of Rome using prosōpon to stand for the individual identities of Father and Logos*; but it was Tertullian who gave to the word 'person' its technical status in trinitarian and christological discourse. He opposes 'person' (by which he seems to mean an individuating quality which gives concrete reality to a general kind of being) to 'substance' (by which he means roughly a general kind or way of being). Thus God is, for him, one substance (defined as 'spirit') which actually exists concretely in three persons through the derivation of Word and Spirit from the Father. In the incarnate Christ, on the other hand, he sees one 'thing' or person which concretizes two distinct ways of being: i.e., the divine and human substances *.

In view of the trinitarian formula which emerged in the East between the councils of Nicaea (325) and Constantinople (381), the theological sense of 'person' was adapted to that of the Greek *hypostasis* *. In the terminology of the Cappadocian * Fathers, this denoted a concrete and objective reality and was defined as a way or mode in which God is (*tropos hyparxeōs*). Augustine of Hippo, strongly conscious of the inadequacy of *persona* for its theological task, took over the Cappadocian suggestion that the three divine hypostases were distinguished from each other, and thus constituted, solely by their mutual relations. In this way he laid the foundation for the later definition of the divine persons as 'subsistent relations'. Since, however, his analogates for the divine persons were the modes – memory, understanding, and will – in which the human self ('mind') is present for itself, this doctrine of the persons as relations embodied, in Augustine's formulation of it, a strong theological monism (*see also* **Psychological Analogy**). It therefore became difficult to reconcile with the equally influential definition of Boethius, according to whom 'person' meant 'an individual substance of rational nature'. It was no doubt the tension occasioned by these different uses which led Richard of St Victor to redefine 'person' in more general terms as 'an incommunicable and singular existence' and to treat Boethius' definition as applying only to created persons.

In modern thought, 'person', if one thinks in Augustinian terms, has shifted its denotation. Instead of referring to the distinct ways in which the self is present for itself, it is rather taken, in line with Boethius' definition, to denote the very subject of self-awareness and so of freedom. In the critical philosophy of Kant, this subject is the 'transcendental ego', whose cognitive activities constitute the object-world of nature and which, for just that reason, cannot be grasped as part of the object-world but only in moral experience as the subject of freedom and as a moral 'end-in-itself'. In one direction from Kant lie the Absolute Ego of Fichte and the Absolute Spirit of Hegel (*see also* **Idealism**); in another lie various personalist philosophies which conceive persons not in relation to nature but as existing in and constituted by relations to other self-aware subjects: e.g. the 'I–Thou' philosophy of Martin Buber.

In theology these developments have produced two distinct tendencies. 1. There have been those who sought to interpret the classical trinitarian *persona* along modern lines as the unique subject of consciousness and self-consciousness, and so to explain the unity of God as a quasi-social unity. 2. The established habit of referring to God (in the singular) as 'person' or 'personal' has, in the eyes of some thinkers, rendered the language of 'three persons' confusing at best. Hence Barth has argued that the proper theological use of 'person' in contemporary speech is to denote the one God, who would then be modelled as 'an I existing in and for Itself with a thought and will proper to It': in effect a plea for a return to the substance, though not the terminology, of the Augustinian position.

See also **Christology, Trinity**.

E. J. Fortmann, *The Triune God*, 1972; A. Grillmeier, *Christ in Christian Tradition*, [2]1975; G. L. Prestige, *Fathers and Heretics*, 1952; C. Welch, *The Trinity in Contemporary Theology*, 1953.

                                    R. A. NORRIS

Personalism

A philosophical standpoint which takes as its starting-point human personality, or which finds in such personality the main key to central metaphysical problems. Many personalities have posited a personal God as our key to understanding the ultimate nature of the world. While thinkers like M. Buber (1878–1965) and N. Berdyaev (1874–1948) have sometimes been described as 'personalists', the term is best reserved for members and adherents of the Boston

(Mass.) school of philosophical personalism, such as B. P. Bowne (1847–1910) and E. S. Brightman (1884–1953).

JAMES RICHMOND

Phenomenology

Both a philosophical movement, with its roots in the thought of Edmund Husserl (1859–1938), and a group of methods of studying and understanding religion, to which the label 'the phenomenology of religion' is attached. The main thrust of Husserl's thinking was that philosophy should be put upon a descriptive and scientific basis. The way to do this was by concentrating upon the actual contents of human consciousness and setting on one side the presuppositions and interpretations of reality which surround and affect our experience. Thus we may get to the pure structures of consciousness. One main reason why students of religion have taken up this descriptive aim is in order to delineate the experiences and practices of religion without bringing external theological presuppositions to bear upon them. Phenomenology of religion, then, is often seen as a neutral way of understanding and describing religious phenomena. Theology takes a stand from within the beliefs of a faith; but the comparative study of religion (history of religions, science of religion – various terms are used) aims at describing religions and religious themes as they appear in the life and consciousness of those who participate in religion.

Husserl follows the general tradition of Descartes, and emphasizes the importance of consciousness as something with its own structures, over against the objects of the outer world which are the subject of scientific investigation in the manner of the natural sciences. The mode of exploring consciousness is by suspending or holding back from the array of judgments which we make about outer reality. This 'holding back' Husserl called (using the relevant Greek expression) *epochē*, and also 'bracketing' – that is, putting in brackets all those elements in experience which do not belong to consciousness itself. These terms, *epochē* and bracketing, have gained a wide currency in modern methodological discussions of the study of religion. For Husserl, the method of phenomenological reduction of experience to pure forms of consciousness removes from it all particularities, so that the essences which the methodology reveals are unlocated and timeless. Thus one can by introspection see that consciousness is intentional; that is, it has an object (e.g. one is aware of a book in front of one): but such intentionality is a pervasive feature of consciousness and does not need any *particular* object. Again, seeing something coloured is seeing something extended. These structural features of consciousness are pure essences, and it is the job of philosophy to describe them.

Others took Husserl's programme in various directions. Thus Max Scheler (1874–1928) applied his method to the realm of feelings and values (the object or correlative of feelings). He saw values as belonging to a hierarchy (and in this was going beyond a merely descriptive account), at the summit of which were the religious values – the holy and the unholy. Scheler thought of the permanent possibility of religious experience as being the eternal in man: through it the human being participates in the divine love. Scheler, in moving the phenomenological enterprise onwards to an explicit exploration of the emotions, has affinities with Kierkegaard and with later existentialists *, also influenced by the phenomenological movement. Thus Heidegger and Sartre claimed to present phenomenological themes, but they were embedded in more speculative structures than Husserl would have wanted. Closer in some ways to Husserl's programme is Paul Ricoeur's exploration of the phenomenology of action (in his *La philosophie de la volonté*, 1950–1960).

When Rudolf Otto's *The Idea of the Holy* appeared in 1917, Husserl saw in it a masterly analysis of religious consciousness, and the phenomenological method was taken up by other comparativists, notably by Gerardus van der Leeuw (1890–1950). What appealed to them, apart from the eschewing of theological judgments, was Husserl's idea of essences, revealed to the investigator's eidetic vision (Husserl had used the adjective 'eidetic' which derived from the Greek *eidos* or form). What van der Leeuw and others set out to do, then, was to delineate the forms or essences of religion. At one level what they were doing was a typology of religious elements – for instance, differing types of religious experience (prophetic, mystical, shamanistic, etc.), rituals (sacrifice, worship, etc.), divinities (one God, High God, gods, etc.). Thus sometimes the term 'phenomenology of religion' is used to mean a descriptive typology. A notable example is van der Leeuw's *Religion in Essence and Manifestation* (1933, ET 1938). The typological investigation was conceived very much in the tradition of Husserl, and yet at the same time within the context of philological and historical scholarship. Thus van der Leeuw in a famous appendix to the above volume sees the method as (i) assigning names to what 'appears' (e.g., 'sacrifice', 'prophecy'); (ii) the interpolation of the phenomenon into our lives, sympathetically; (iii) the application of *epochē*; (iv) the clarification of what is observed, by structural comparison and contrast with other phenomena; (v) the achievement through the foregoing of understanding; (vi) the checking of the results by philology, history, archaeology, etc.; (vii) the realization of a kind of objectivity – letting the facts speak for themselves.

It will be seen that element (ii) above introduces the idea that the phenomenologist has somehow to enter into the experience of others. This notion lies behind a rather different use of *phenomenology* from that used either by Husserl or by typological theorists. In this usage a *phenomenological* approach means looking at a religious phenomenon from the standpoint of the believer. This view of the task was especially emphasized by Brede Kristensen (1867–1953), for whom in a certain sense 'the believer is always right'. It is clear that this involves bracketing my beliefs if I am trying to delineate the experiences, actions and beliefs of another; but it does not of itself involve typology, for it is involved in using imagination and empathy upon concrete and particular elements and episodes of religious life. It is indeed a general requirement of doing history, and echoes the dictum of R. G. Collingwood (1889–1943) that the historian's main task 'is to think himself into the action, to discern the thought of its agent'.

There has been great debate as to whether or how far such neutral empathy can be realized in practice, and some of the religious phenomenologists, notably van der Leeuw and Joachim Wach (1898–1955), the father of the post-World War II Chicago School of historians of religion, have in fact looked at the material from a particular religious point of view. The project of trying to let religions speak for themselves, through the practice of a kind of informed or structured empathy, is sometimes referred to, within the context of religious education, as 'the phenomenological approach'. Generally speaking, then, there are two main uses of phenomenology in the history of religions: one attempts to create a typology of religious phenomena, while the other stresses the need to bracket one's own beliefs in trying to enter imaginatively into the beliefs of others.

Sometimes, however, phenomenology rests on a theory of religion and human nature, and so goes beyond either of these two enterprises. Thus the work of the leading figure in the Chicago School, Mircea Eliade (1907–), involves a perspective on life in part influenced by Jung's* theory of archetypes and in part derived from a view of history drawn from Eliade's own experience and reflection. His wide-ranging analysis of archaic religious forms, in shamanism, Indian yoga and small-scale societies and in some major religious traditions, suggests a mythic ontology* which such societies and traditions share. Reality shows itself through manifestations of divinity and power in which humans encounter the eternal. Their rituals celebrate the recurring or cyclical nature of life, which is threatened by the sense of history, i.e., of an unrepeatable and open sequence of events, which has been brought into being by the Jewish and Christian faiths and emphasized by the terrors of modern secular history.

One effect of the phenomenological movement has been to put much emphasis on experience*; since Husserl's programme pointed towards structures of consciousness it was natural for religious writers influenced by phenomenology to look to the structures of religious experience. This in turn has generated an interest in the actual relationship between experience and the interpretations which colour and overlay it. Thus there has more recently been a convergence between analytic philosophy* and phenomenology in the discussion of mysticism*, itself a controversial area in the history of religions.

Mircea Eliade, *The Quest*, 1969; John Macquarrie, *Twentieth-Century Religious Thought*, rev. ed. 1980; Eric J. Sharpe, *Comparative Religion – A History*; Ninian Smart,

The Phenomenon of Religion, 1978; G. van der Leeuw, *Religion in Essence and Manifestation*, 1964; 'Phenomenology', *Encyclopedia Britannica*, Macropaedia, 1974.

NINIAN SMART

Philosophy of Religion

This topic falls out according to four main issues. 1. *The general relationship between philosophy and religion as areas of concern.* This issue is frequently cast in terms of the encounter between reason and faith. There are those who maintain that philosophy and religion have essentially *nothing* to do with one another. This position has its historical roots in the likes of Tertullian, Pascal, Hume, Kant and Kierkegaard. It is interesting to note that this posture has been used both as a defence and as a criticism of theistic belief! At the opposite end of the continuum are those who affirm some form of *synthesis* between philosophy and religion, and whose heritage includes such thinkers as Augustine, Anselm, Descartes, Spinoza, Hegel and Hartshorne. In between stand those thinkers who seek to construct some sort of *functional* relationship wherein the two concerns are distinct yet interrelated; Aquinas, Locke, William James, F. R. Tennant and Tillich.

2. *The reasons that can be given for and against religious and/or theistic belief.* Here, too, the field is divided amongst a variety of approaches. There are those who would focus on *rational analysis*, either to argue in favour of belief or to argue against it. In addition, there have always been thinkers who have appealed to various aspects of *human experience* – psychological, sociological, historical – in order to establish the reasonableness or the unreasonableness of religious belief. Finally, there are those who maintain that any form of reasoning about religion is a waste of time – either because religion lies beyond reason or because it lies beneath it!

3. *The structure or meaning of the religious use of language.* This is an issue which has recently come to the centre of the stage. The 'God-talk' debate arose out of the general concern of contemporary analytic philosophy with language and meaning, powerfully focussed in the work of Ludwig Wittgenstein. Traditionally there have been thinkers who assume that talk of God is essentially the same as *scientific* discourse,

only on a grander scale (metaphysics *). Over against these have stood thinkers who argue that although religious language seeks to function in this way, it fails in this effort and can only be regarded as *unintelligible* (positivism *). In between these extremes stand thinkers who affirm that while God-talk is not to be understood as some sort of 'super' scientific language, it by no means follows that it must be regarded as nonsensical. Those taking this approach range between R. M. Hare and R. B. Braithwaite (God-talk as the expression of moral commitment) and John Hick and Frederick Ferré (God-talk as empirical discourse with provisos).

Currently the most fruitful work would seem to be that which follows the pioneering efforts of Ian Ramsey, Austin Farrer and John Wisdom to explore the analogical * and metaphorical * character of religious discourse. This approach has received a great deal of impetus from the recent revival of interest in metaphorical expression on the part of both analytical (e.g. Max Black) and phenomenological (e.g. Paul Ricoeur) movements. Three helpful exponents are David Burrell, David Tracy and Sallie McFague.

4. *A fresh approach to the traditional question of the relation between world religions.* A good deal of effort is being focussed on ways of understanding and evaluating different religious faiths while avoiding the usual pitfalls of ethnocentrism and bland syncretism *. H. D. Lewis, John Hick and Maurice Wiles exemplify this effort in Britain, while W. C. Smith, Peter Slater and R. Panikkar do so in North America (*see also* **Christianity and Other Religions**). Here again, the central issue seems to be whether to follow a traditional, rationalistic course (comparing and contrasting belief systems, etc.) or to explore a more phenomenological posture (examining the metaphorical and mythological bases of religious belief).

A. Flew and A. MacIntyre (eds), *New Essays in Philosophical Theology*, 1955; John Hick, *Philosophy of Religion*, 1973; Sallie McFague, *Speaking in Parables*, 1975; W. C. Smith, *Towards a World Theology*, 1981; David Tracy, *The Analogical Imagination*, 1981.

JERRY H. GILL

Pietism

The movement among seventeenth- and eighteenth-century Protestants which sought in a personal and practical 'heart religion' a living alternative to the system-bound scholasticism of Lutheran (and to a lesser extent Reformed) orthodoxy. Prefigured in the works of Lutheran mystical writers, the movement was founded by Philipp Jakob Spener (1635–1705), Lutheran pastor at Frankfurt, who in 1670 initiated twice-weekly meetings of devout lay-people for Bible study and mutual edification; these *Collegia Pietatis* gave the movement its name. In his *Pia Desideria* (1675) he urged intensified devotional study of the Bible, fuller realization of the doctrine of the priesthood of all believers, emphasis on the charitable aspects of Christianity, and the transformation of university theological studies to serve devotion rather than science.

Spener's influence spread, but Pietism aroused considerable opposition. This might have driven it into separation and obscurity but for the crisis confronting beleaguered Protestantism in central and eastern Europe, where the persecuting advance of the Counter Reformation* produced waves of Protestant refugees, among whom the intense personalism of the pietist movement and its millennarian hope for the downfall of the papacy and the achievement of the kingdom encouraged a series of 'revival movements'. The lay piety and field preachers characteristic of these movements reappear in early Methodism. At the same time, the Prussian monarchy found in Pietism a way of short-circuiting the confessional differences of its hostile Lutheran and Reformed subjects and a means of over-riding the patronage of the gentry within Lutheranism. Under Spener's disciple A. H. Francke (1663–1727), the new University of Halle, and Francke's Orphan House there (housing 3000) founded in 1695 became a focal point for mission and education, including a publishing house. Halle became the pattern for similar Protestant ventures all over Europe and America, not least Herrnhut, founded by Count Ludwig von Zinzendorf (1700–1760).

Ironically the pietist movement was a major factor in the emergence of heterodox elements within the Enlightenment*. Hostile to confessional emphasis on doctrine, stressing experience and practicality, committed to educational reform, loosely yoked to ecclesiastical structures and control, the movement from the beginning had rationalist sympathizers and fellow-travellers, and among its unorthodox products were Gottfried Arnold, Johann Semler and Friedrich Schleiermacher.

M. Schmidt, *Pietismus*, 1972; F. E. Stoeffler, *The Rise of Evangelical Pietism*, 1965; Johannes Wallman, *Philipp Jakob Spener und die Anfänge des Pietismus*, 1970.

EAMON DUFFY

Platonism

Plato (427–347 BC) was a brilliant and versatile philosopher who profoundly influenced Christian theology over many centuries. He interpreted and developed the thought of Socrates, who asked searching questions about the meanings of important words such as justice and goodness. Plato suggested that these stood for Ideas or Forms; e.g. the Form of justice was a single objective reality embracing all just acts, and was itself eternally and perfectly just. He thus associated goodness with unity, and saw perfection culminating in a Form of the Good. This doctrine also suggested an impressive defence of the immortality of the soul (in the *Phaedo*, which portrays Socrates' discourse before his execution); and was fully developed in the *Republic*, which explored the prospects for goodness in an ideal state and made proposals for education. These included a censorship of poems and religious mythology; corrupt religion misleads, purified religion can suggest elements of truth. His later dialogues (*Theaetetus, Sophist* and others) made important contributions to logic and the theory of knowledge, and the *Parmenides* suggested some unease about the theory of Forms itself. Plato was feeling after the notion of a universal term, but associated this with ideal perfection. On the first account, there should be as many Forms as there are general classes, and Plato had spoken of a Form of disease as well as health; but clearly there can be no *ideal* of bad health.

A dialogue of especial interest to Christians was the *Timaeus*, an imaginative account of the world's creation by a craftsman who modelled his work upon the Forms.

Modern critics question how seriously this was intended, and in any case the Craftsman appears to imitate, not initiate, goodness; but Christians accepted the dialogue as a valuable confirmation of Genesis.

Plato's most distinguished pupil was Aristotle, who broke away by rejecting the notion of transcendent Forms and founded his own school. Platonists of the second century BC were predominantly sceptical; but Carneades, rejecting Stoic theories of determinism, developed an acute and influential defence of the freedom of the will. A 'dogmatic' revival that soon followed emphasized the moral and religious aspects of Plato's thought, making it firmly theistic and interpreting the Forms as thoughts in the Creator's mind, or as created, intelligent beings.

The 'Middle Platonists' * of the first and second centuries AD revived a theory of knowledge based on discovering the interrelations between the Forms, which was adopted by the Christian Clement of Alexandria. Holding that unity is God's supreme characteristic, they formulated a distinction between the absolute and the relative One which influenced Christian teaching on God and his Logos *. The most original Platonist of the Christian era was Plotinus (c. 205–270), regarded as the first 'Neoplatonist' *, who taught a triadic scheme of reality. At the summit is the One *, the absolutely simple Goodness; from him proceeds Mind (Nous), a unity which comprehends the system of Forms; and from Mind, the World Soul which embodies these Forms in matter. Plotinus' writings were too difficult and too original to be quickly accepted; more immediately influential was his editor Porphyry, who took the important step of adopting Aristotle's logic. Porphyry was violently anti-Christian, as were most of his successors; this ultimately provoked a reaction under Justinian, who closed the schools at Athens in AD 529, though the later Neoplatonists included a few Christians.

NT writers were little influenced by philosophy; but from the second century onward Christians appealed to Plato for evidence of God and also his Logos; of the heavenly world (Plato's 'intelligible world' reinterpreted, with the Forms as angels); of creation, free will and future judgment, and of the soul's immortality. Clement and Origen added an intellectualist spirituality, in which control of the body and its passions was to be gained by cultivation of the mind, ascending from little-regarded secular studies to philosophy and study of the Bible, which was expounded so as to encourage Platonic meditation on moral and spiritual ideals. Methodius wrote a work in imitation of Plato's Symposium (The Banquet) in praise of virginity and asceticism. Eusebius, though no philosopher himself, collected numerous, mostly Platonic, philosophical texts in support of Christian doctrine; and Gregory of Nyssa won especial regard for his allegorical or 'mystical' interpretation of scripture, developing Origen's tradition in a more imaginative and poetic style and with greater caution in matters of doctrine.

Plotinus' influence on Christians is first clearly seen in Marius Victorinus, and through him in Augustine. It was 'Platonic books' which convinced Augustine that there could be reality which was non-spatial and eternal. He adopted the view (already found in Irenaeus) that God is a uniquely simple unity whose attributes are identical with each other and with himself. He identified reality with goodness, holding that evil is lack of reality; to God everything is in some degree good. He criticized the Platonists, however, for ignoring the incarnation and rejecting any resurrection of the body, and for their doctrine of reincarnation, which Origen had already been blamed for accepting.

Among later Greek theologians Dionysius 'the Areopagite' is remarkable for his mystical teaching and for a close imitation of the elaborate triadic theology of the later Neoplatonists.

In the West Plato's writings were lost in the so-called Dark Ages, apart from a Latin version of the Timaeus, and ability to read the original Greek, even when available, was hardly recovered before the Renaissance; though the influence of Augustine and Dionysius remained strong. Direct influence reappears with Nicolas of Cusa and especially Marsilio Ficino. Platonic scholarship was important in England in the sixteenth century (e.g. with Sir Thomas More, whose Utopia recalls Plato's Republic), with the seventeenth-century Cambridge Platonists *, and from c. 1870 onwards; though many features of Platonism, for instance the static view of the universe implied by the theory of Forms, have been discredited by modern science. Plato has moreover been attacked as advocating authoritarian government; but also applauded as upholding the objective reality of goodness.

The literature is enormous; see J. B. Skemp, *Plato*, 1976, for detailed survey. As first introductions, try Adam Fox, *Plato and the Christians*, 1957 (parallel passages); R. W. Livingstone, *Plato, Selected Passages*, 1940; J. E. Raven, *Plato's Thought in the Making*, 1965. More advanced are I. M. Crombie, *An Examination of Plato's Doctrines*, 1962–1963; R. C. Cross and A. D. Woozley, *Plato's Republic*, 1964; A. E. Taylor, *Plato, the Man and his Work*, ⁴1937. For later Platonism see A. H. Armstrong (ed), *The Cambridge History of Later Greek and Early Medieval Philosophy*, 1967; John Dillon, *The Middle Platonists*, 1977 (both with good bibliography); E. von Ivanka, *Plato Christianus*, 1964; R. Klibanski, *The Platonic Tradition during the Middle Ages*, 1930; E. Cassirer, *The Platonic Renaissance in England*, 1953.

CHRISTOPHER STEAD

Pluralism

The word seems to have been first used for the system or practice of one person's holding more than one ecclesiastical benefice or living at the same time (whence its use more generally for the holding at once of two or more offices of any kind). But it has since come to have two other meanings that are of much greater importance for Christian theology.

The first is the use of the word in philosophy since the end of the nineteenth century to designate a metaphysical theory or system according to which there is more than one ultimate subject of predication or more than one kind of such ultimate subject. Thus, as this meaning of the term is usually defined, a distinction is made between *substantival* pluralism, according to which there are many substances rather than merely one substance (as asserted by substantival monism), and *attributive* pluralism, according to which there are many kinds of substance, not simply one or two kinds (as asserted by attributive monism or dualism). Of course, with the advent of philosophies of process (*see* **Process Theology**), the usual distinction between 'substance' and 'attribute' is relativized by the claim that events

rather than substances are the ultimate subjects of statements capable of being true or false. But if any adequate definition today must accordingly allow for a metaphysics of 'event pluralism' as well as for a traditional metaphysics of 'substance pluralism', it must still distinguish between pluralisms asserting more than one ultimate subject of discourse and pluralisms asserting more than one or two kinds of such ultimate subject. In fact, one must insist on this distinction because failure to observe it makes it impossible to account for some of the metaphysical theories or systems that philosophers have actually developed. Spinoza, for instance, while a monist in asserting only the one ultimate substance, 'God or nature', is also a pluralist in asserting a plurality, indeed, infinity, of attributes. On the contrary, if Whitehead is a monist in developing 'a one-substance cosmology' for which 'all final individual actualities have the metaphysical character of occasions of experience', he is nevertheless a pluralist in asserting a plurality of 'actual entities'.

There seems little question that Christian faith and witness and, therefore, Christian theology as well have a stake in the metaphysical issues between pluralism and monism in both senses of the terms. As Schleiermacher puts it, there are certain distinctions, such as between God and the world or good and evil, that are 'the original presuppositions of the religious self-consciousness' (*The Christian Faith* § 28). Therefore, even if one clearly distinguishes Christian faith from its metaphysical presuppositions, one can deny that it necessarily makes such presuppositions only by divesting the Christian witness of all cognitive significance. Once allow that the statements of Christian witness are capable of being true or false, and it appears to follow that the metaphysical implications of such statements are pluralistic rather than monistic with respect to the number of ultimate subjects. Metaphysical pluralism in this first sense seems implied not only by the foundational distinction between the one Creator and the many creatures but also by the further distinction, essential to the concepts of sin and redemption, between creatures generally and the particular creatures who, being specially endowed with self-understanding and self-direction, are morally free and responsible. Clearly, the division of responsibility presupposed by any coherent solution to the problem of evil * implies that God cannot be the only ultimate agent and hence is anti-monistic in this first sense of the word.

On the other hand, it is arguable that the metaphysical theism implied by Christian faith in God is anti-pluralistic in the second sense of the word insofar as it implicitly denies more than one kind of ultimate subject. If God, as classical theology has contended, is not only *a* being but in some sense being itself (*esse ipsum*), then any so much as possible ultimate subject of predication is so only insofar as it participates in the being of God and, therefore, is of ultimately the same kind as every other. To be of some irreducibly different kind from any other ultimate subject would be to be utterly different also from God, and hence no ultimate subject at all but simply nothing. Because this is so, theologies accepting an ultimate dualism between mind and matter even while conceiving God to be supreme mind are implicitly self-contradictory. For if mind and matter are accepted as mutually irreducible kinds of ultimate subject, then any assertion of subjects that are merely material must imply the radical incoherence of the concept of supreme mind even as any assertion of God as supreme mind must imply that the concept of mere matter is similarly incoherent.

It is significant, however, that Schleiermacher's point in the passage cited is not only that the presuppositions of the religious self-consciousness impose limits on the philosophical systems whose language is fit for use by Christian theology. He also stresses that, even within these limits, 'the great diversity of views and of their expressions' in all realms of philosophy such as psychology, ethics, and metaphysics 'makes the suitable management of language in dogmatic presentation a most difficult problem'. Thus already over a century-and-a-half ago we have a clear reference to the phenomenon that has only quite recently come to be designated 'pluralism' in yet a second meaning of the word.

More exactly, Schleiermacher refers to what we today would distinguish as '*theological* pluralism', as well as, of course, to the philosophical pluralism that he takes to lie behind it. This distinction is necessary because one sense of 'pluralism' as now used is to refer more generally to the state or condition of a larger social group in which members of a number of sub-groups – ethnic, racial, cultural, religious – maintain their many sub-group traditions and identities within the common culture of the larger group. So, for example, historians and social scientists now commonly speak of the religious pluralism typical of contemporary society in the Western world, with its plurality of denominations comprehended in the three larger communions of Protestantism, Catholicism and Judaism. If we also keep in mind that for most Westerners this plurality of religious groups has long since come to seem desirable, it can further serve to illustrate the other closely related sense of 'pluralism' when it is used to refer not to a state or condition of such plurality but to a doctrine or policy advocating this state or condition.

Of the greatest importance for Christian theology is the religious and cultural pluralism that now exists or is deemed desirable within an emerging global society and culture. If the advocacy of such pluralism obviously challenges the exclusivist claims of much traditional Christian witness and theology, the sheer existence of so many different communities and traditions immeasurably complicates the theological task. In fact, the plurality of data that theological reflection must take into account in order to make good the truth-claim of the Christian witness is practically limitless. It comprises not only all the classic expressions of Christian faith in both religion and culture generally, but also all the more or less radical revisions of these expressions, including the modern secularistic humanisms both evolutionary and revolutionary, as well as all the other religions and ideologies, theistic and nontheistic, that are now known to belong to our common human legacy. To try to take account of so extensive a pluralism of both religions and cultures is to realize at once why any claim theology may make for the truth of the Christian witness is bound to be problematic (*see also* **Cultural Relativism**).

Only slightly less problematic, however, is any theological claim that a given witness is appropriately Christian. One reason for this is the kind of theological pluralism that Schleiermacher already recognized to be a difficult problem. But as certain as it is that the plurality of philosophies makes for a corresponding plurality of theologies, it is clearly not the only source of the difficulty. The writings of the NT remove any doubt that even when the language of faith was myth* rather than philosophy, the one Christian witness was never present except in the many Christian witnesses. Moreover, there appears to be an irreducible pluralism even in locating the Christian canon, with Protestants traditionally appealing to 'scripture alone' against the classical RC principle of 'scripture and tradition', even while revisionary theologians in both communions have increasingly looked to 'the historical Jesus' as the real Christian norm. Yet if frankly recognizing such pluralism, to say nothing of advocating it, raises the profoundest questions about Christian unity, any alternative position now seems to belong to the past of Christian theology rather than to its future.

J. Hick, 'Pluralism and the Reality of the Transcendent', *Theologians in Transition*, ed. J. M. Wall, 1981, pp. 60–6; A. M. Quinton, 'Pluralism and Monism', *EB*; K. Rahner, 'Pluralism in Theology and the Oneness of the Church's Profession of Faith', *The Development of Fundamental Theology*, ed. J. B. Metz, 1969, pp. 103–23.
SCHUBERT M. OGDEN

Pneumatology

Pneumatology is derived from Greek *pneuma*, spirit: the branch of theology which deals with the doctrine of the (Holy) Spirit *.
ALAN RICHARDSON

Political Theology

The term has become extensively used since the 1960s. Those who hear it for the first time may be puzzled as to its meaning, not because it describes a phenomenon with which they are unfamiliar, but because it seems to attempt to bring together two things which they regard as incompatible. Adapting Dr Johnson's comment, they will be less interested in whether the two have been accommodated well, than in whether they have been accommodated at all. In an increasingly pluralistic culture there would still be widespread agreement that politics and religion should be kept apart. To do something called political theology by mistake would be one thing, but to claim to do it or even aspire to do it would seem to many not just mischievous but anti-social and dangerous.

Such suspicion concerning political theology is understandable. It would be difficult to argue against the view that the combination of religion and politics has been the single greatest cause of suffering in human history. In an increasingly secular Western culture there is incomprehension as well as anger at the intrusion of religion in political life. This is witnessed in the outsider's view of the strife in Northern Ireland. In such circumstances something called 'political theology' would appear to be mistaking the poison for the cure.

But suspicion of political theology also comes from within the Christian church. Many conservative Protestants seem to assume that somewhere, either at Mount Sinai or in the Sermon on the Mount, it is specifically enjoined on Christians that they must avoid any mixing of politics and religion. The reasons for this view are twofold. On the one hand it comes from a rejection of the kind of institutional involvement they associate with the RC Church. They see too close a parallel between the Vatican State and other states. The interests of the church are too easily identified in terms of property, wealth, privilege and prestige. Protestants lay great stress on freedom of conscience and they see church/state relations in Catholic countries leading to the enforcement of religious beliefs through civil legislation. On the other hand the stress on personal decision as the basis of Protestant Christianity has strengthened a view that religion is essentially private and is concerned with the inner spiritual life of man. If the world is evil, then Christians, on this view, have a duty not to become involved in politics. This privatized religion can be maintained and developed better when it is divorced from the political sphere.

There would seem to be a widespread suspicion of political theology as bringing together two things which always mean trouble. As we have seen, there are those who even believe that it is a matter of principle that the two should be kept apart. And finally there are those who are less concerned about religion entering politics than politics entering religion. There is the example of National Socialism in Germany in the 1930s, acting against Judaism and against Christianity, to eliminate one and make the other merely an arm of its own long-term strategies.

What all of these examples have in common is this, that they do *not* represent a bringing together of politics and religion. What they have in common is that the two are joined in battle, each seeking to overcome, dominate and use the other. Political theology is not an example of the age-old conflict between politics and religion. It is not the advocacy of such struggle nor its pursuit as if it were a moral goal. On the contrary, political theology is the attempt to overcome the conflict which has brought distortion to religion and untold suffering to humanity. Political theology is not the old, not the best of the old, but the death of the old – to bring to life something new.

The starting-point of political theology is the examination of the ways in which politics and religion have been falsely brought together in the past. There are, first of all, examples of how political objectives have been deliberately presented in religious terms. This is seen in the Imperial Cult of ancient Rome. Different oaths were required of the various strata of society, but all had to make a formal sacrifice to the Genius of Caesar. This was not a real religion, but a device by which to test political loyalty. This requirement brought the early church into conflict with the state. It was for religious reasons that, through loyalty to the Lord Jesus, they would not sacrifice to the Lord Caesar. But the Romans assumed that the refusal must be based on political grounds, since they themselves saw the cult as political and not religious. Again, in the fourth century Christianity was made the state religion, under Constantine. This was not done for evangelical reasons, but rather because the emperor required something to unite his deeply divided empire. This political policy of unification was presented as if it were the will of God. Finally, in the twentieth century we have seen even more blatant examples of political movements entering the religious sphere. The Nazi leaders systematically presented Hitler not simply as a political figure, but as a messianic religious figure. Prayers in school were not *for* Hitler, but addressed *to* Hitler. Thus the devotion which is appropriate within religion was required in support of political policies.

These are examples of a false relationship between politics and religion. It is one in which politics dominates religion, indeed takes over the role and trappings of religion. Religion is used and pushed aside, religious values and goals eliminated. They do not provide any basis for political theology, but they do warn of the dangers which stem from politics blatantly entering the religious sphere. However, there are other dangers to which political theology must be alert, when religion enters the political arena, or, at least, religious leaders and spokesmen enter. Returning again to the Roman Empire, we might reflect on the passages by which Paul legitimizes the powers that be, as if they were appointed by God. Paul urges Christians to see its laws as in accordance with God's truth, yet the empire was founded on war and the enslavement of millions of innocent people. Its duly appointed representative in Judaea ordered Jesus to be crucified. Religion is the most powerful instrument of legitimation, because it presents the things of this world as if they were the things of God. Similarly, in the fourth century, Eusebius is at pains to describe the Emperor Constantine as if he were in all things the representative of God on earth. Thus the imperial policies, laws, institutions and values are legitimized and placed beyond discussion. In the twentieth century the Vatican signed a concordat with National Socialism in Germany, thereby giving it legitimation at least for millions of Catholics. A more recent example is found in that broad movement in the USA which is referred to as the New Religious/Political Right. While this looks like an ultra-Protestant religious movement, it is better understood as an ultra-conservative political coalition which is enlisting religion to legitimate its values and goals. The 'Congressional Report Card' drawn up by Christian Voice presents the voting record of members of the Senate and House on a selected number of topics of right-wing interest.

Political theology is therefore primarily theology conscious of the false ways in which politics and religion have been related in the past, and indeed still are in the present. Attention is paid to political movements which use religion for their own ends, and religious movements which simply legitimize political interests. The examples given have been of influences from the political right.

But in the modern world there is a new danger, namely that religion might be used to legitimize the goals and values of groups on the political left.

In face of the complexities already indicated, it would be tempting to conclude that it would be safer if religion did indeed stay out of politics. There are two reasons why this is no solution.

1. In practice to withdraw from the political sphere simply provides a legitimation by default. If there is no religious protest against certain policies or injustices, then there seems to be a tacit approval of them. One motive for declaring that religion should stay out of politics is to silence such criticism.

2. Political theology is opposed to the privatization of religion, to the narrowing down of religion merely to the inner life, the private sphere. Religion must always be personal, but not private; it must always be the religion of a particular person, but far from being restricted to the private sphere, this means that religion is immediately involved in a variety of social relationships and responsibilities.

Political theology therefore attempts to regain the biblical perspective of social responsibility. But it is not simply a social theology, because social responsibility leads quickly into the political sphere. 'Political theology' is a generic name, which includes many examples of theology which has become politically conscious. Black theology* is a specific form of political theology, as is feminist theology*. In both cases theology brings biblical perspectives to bear on social ills. But discrimination on the basis of race or sex is not simply a social matter, and when it is institutionalized, it can only be countered by political action. In both of these cases we see political theology first of all bringing to light ways in which religion has been used to legitimize discrimination in the past. It then goes on to indicate how biblical perspectives lead to a new understanding of race and sex. As already noted, political theology must now guard against being used by new groups to legitimize equally extreme views.

A. A. Boesak, *A Farewell to Innocence*, 1978; J. H. Cone, *Black Theology and Black Power*, 1969; A. Fierro, *The Militant Gospel*, ET 1977; S. S. Hill and D. E. Owen, *The New Religious/Political Right in America*, 1982; A. Kee, *A Reader in Political Theology*, 1974; *The Scope of Political Theology*, 1978; J. Metz, *Theology of the World*, ET 1969; J. Moltmann, *The Crucified God*, ET 1974.

ALISTAIR KEE

Polytheism

The belief in many gods and the implied opposite of monotheism*, the belief in a single all-powerful God who transcends the universe. It is commonly assumed that virtually all religions are polytheistic except for Judaism, Christianity and Islam, in which the unity and uniqueness of God* are central dogmas. Philosophy tends to verify monotheistic belief and to demonstrate the inconsistency of polytheism. The notion of God as self-subsisting being or pure act cannot admit of multiplicity. On philosophical grounds, therefore, a strict equality or equilibrium among gods is an absurdity, while the exaltation of one among many gods (henotheism*) and the practical veneration of one god while believing in the existence of other gods (monolatry) raise the question of whether, or in what sense, these other divinities are 'God'. Human beings, however, do not arrive at their beliefs through abstract reasoning but through the interpretation of experience within a cultural tradition. The monotheism of ancient Israel in the midst of neighbouring polytheistic religions derived from an experience of divine reality as personal and as a free autonomous power at work in human history.

Evolutionary thinkers have suggested either that polytheism was a stage in the religious development of mankind which culminated in monotheism, or that it was a decline from primitive monotheism that resulted in the 'withdrawal' of God who effectively became a *deus otiosus* ('lazy' or 'inactive' God) in a henotheistic system. There is little evidence for a spontaneous evolution from polytheism to monotheism, and the notion of a high god who no longer cares about his creation is difficult to maintain in theory, let alone verify in practice. Nevertheless it would appear that polytheism typifies the religion of societies in the early stages of conspicuous cultural or technological development, such as those of ancient Egypt, ancient Greece and Rome, the metropolitan kingdom-cultures of West Africa or the civilizations of the Far East; and that monotheism itself denotes a change of theological scale, moving from an objectified view of God to a more spiritual view, as happened in ancient Israel.

Religion * offers a unifying dimension to the human mind grappling with the diversity of actual experience. It is not surprising, therefore, that the philosophical concept of polytheism is almost impossible to identify in the actual religions of the world, which in various ways present reality as a single underlying or paramount whole. For this reason the high god is almost universal in the characteristically theistic traditions of so-called primitive religion. In Hinduism, not only are there accepted ways of systematizing the gods, but the gods themselves are subordinated to the ultimate ground of all being and to the principle of the non-duality of the real; while in Buddhism the gods are secondary to the higher goal of illumination or to the Buddha himself venerated theistically at the popular level.

It appears that polytheism is a term which covers a number of distinct phenomena. One of these is fundamentally a semantic problem – the scandal of the philosophically trained scholar of religion when confronted by the unsystematic plural approaches of mythological language. Another phenomenon is the tendency of certain cultures to personalize experience without necessarily treating the personalizations as objects of unconditional divine worship. Yet another is the phenomenon of arrested theological development in which there are competing images of divine reality. Finally, there is the ambivalent role of mediators * who can be placed on a theological spectrum going from hypostases * or 'refractions' of God at one end to plenipotentiaries of God at the other.

Having said this, it must be admitted that there are explicitly pluralistic * concepts of divine reality which are more deserving of the name polytheism. In these instances the gods do not represent the diverse experience of nature so much as specialization and departmentalism in an increasingly sophisticated human life. Polytheism reflects socio-political realities and offers a theological 'federalism' that parallels the body politic. It also celebrates human achievement by deifying political rulers or tracing their descent from divine ancestors. But

ultimately polytheistic religion lays greater stress on the trans-personal than on the personal in its understanding of divine reality. Even in the Judaeo-Christian tradition it is admitted by theologians that there are limits to the usefulness of the analogy of 'person' * when applied to a unique and transcendent God. In polytheistic religions personal deities are subordinated to a trans-personal concept and the rivalry of the gods is less significant than their dialectical interplay. The concept (proposed by E. Bolaji Idowu) of the 'diffused monotheism' of the high god reveals a Judaeo-Christian or a Eurocentric concern which is probably misplaced when applied to a polytheistic religion such as that of the Yoruba of Nigeria. Ultimately, polytheism represents a more pessimistic and a more terrestrial concern than monotheism in the religious interpretation of reality which is always a unity-in-diversity. It is a mood rather than a categorical alternative to monotheistic belief.

John Bowker, *The Religious Imagination and the Sense of God*, 1978; Richard F. Gombrich, *Precept and Practice*, 1971; E. Bolaji, Idowu, *Olodumare: God in Yoruba Belief*, 1962; R. G. Lienhardt, *Divinity and Experience*, 1961; Raimundo Panikkar, *The Trinity and the Religious Experience of Mankind*, 1973; S. Radakrishnan, *East and West in Religion*, 1933; John A. T. Robinson, *Truth is Two-Eyed*, 1979; Hans Schwarz, *The Search for God*, 1975.

AYLWARD SHORTER

Pope see Papacy

Positivism

A philosophical position belonging to the empirical tradition, according to which man can have no knowledge of anything but phenomena, that is, of whatever is directly apprehended by the senses, or one of them. 'Positive' knowledge is here associated with the various fields of science; there must be no question of going beyond the limits of what is given in observation: inevitably, both theology and metaphysics * are regarded as speculation. The term 'positivism' was introduced by the French socialist thinker, Saint-Simon (1760–1825), but was popularized by his pupil, Auguste Comte (1798–1857). Both men rejected both Christianity and the existing social system.

For all his positivism, however, Comte, like some other nineteenth-century thinkers, easily persuaded himself of the value of a speculative view of history*, which in his case proposed three stages of human thought: the theological, when explanation of the natural invoked the supernatural; the metaphysical, when philosophical, but abstract, concepts, replaced theology; and the positive stage, which was to be characterized by the ability of science, on the basis of its study of phenomena, to predict. Both Saint-Simon and Comte were convinced that the resulting scientific study of man and society would provide the basis for a rational reorganization of society, and some of this nineteenth-century optimism still clings to sociology in the twentieth century. Both also thought, however, that the new community would still need a religion to enforce its morality (an idea which they borrowed from Rousseau). In Victorian Positivist Societies, such as that run in London by Frederick Harrison (1832–1923), the worship of Humanity was to replace the worship of God, and one was to find one's immortality in the happiness of future generations: attempts were made to find liturgical expression for such ideas. There have been less generous ideals and more destructive societies: some of the abler administrators of British India were inspired by positivism. As a socially radical humanism, however, the movement was rapidly outpaced from the Left and declined. The effect of positivism on late nineteenth-century theology can be seen in the Liberal Protestant tendency to eschew metaphysics* altogether (and so dogma*), to emphasize the idea of divine immanence*, and to assert that theologians should apply 'scientific method' to their own objective field, which consisted of the data of the religious consciousness, and the documents which that consciousness produced. The approach was subtle in the case of Auguste Sabatier (1839–1901; *Outlines of a Philosophy of Religion*, 1897), vulgarly optimistic in *Liberal Christianity* (1903) by Jean Réville (1854–1907). One detects the same tradition in the Catholic Modernist* protest, circa 1900, against the official revival of Thomist* metaphysics. In Protestantism, however, by 1900, the dominant philosophical influence was idealism*, which dismissed positivism. From 1920, a new philosophical school, often called 'Logical Positivism', extended the older empiricist hostility to metaphysics and argued that metaphysical claims were literally meaningless, because they did not admit of verification or falsification by experience. In Britain, this movement was associated with the publication of A. J. Ayer's *Language, Truth and Logic* in 1936 (second, modified version, 1946. *See also* **Analytical Philosophy**). For Ayer, theological statements were at most emotive utterances. It has been said that the value of Ayer's critique of ethics and theology lay principally in its showing that the statements of ethics and theology were of different kinds from the statements of science and everyday experience (John Macquarrie). Since 1945, the appeal of positivism, as an appeal to science and commonsense, has weakened. The philosophy of science has become much less dogmatic about the status of scientific statements, and scientific advance has seemed to threaten humanity's survival, quite as much as to offer it social salvation. The common-sense attack on metaphysics seems less persuasive now that the stability and surface rationality of High Victorianism have disappeared. Although some theologians, alarmed by the positivist critique of language, have fallen back on the argument that Christianity is based solely on revelation*, it now seems unnecessary to rest the case for Christianity on an alleged once-for-all divine act which has no ground in either reason or experience. Other theologians no longer feel that they have to abandon metaphysics altogether, but have sought instead to reconstruct a natural theology on the basis of the analysis of religious and theological language.

R. B. Braithwaite, *An Empiricist's View of the Nature of Religious Belief*, 1955; D. Cupitt, *Taking Leave of God*, 1980.

JOHN KENT

Practical Theology

The theological discipline which is primarily concerned with the interaction of belief and behaviour. In the past its exclusive concern was with matters of ministerial formation, as its traditional component studies – homiletics, liturgiology, catechetics or Christian education, and pastoral theology – suggest. Sometimes it became little more than 'hints and tips' for budding parsons, taking existing patterns of church life and ministry as axiomatic and teaching students how to communicate and apply in a parochial setting the truths learned in their systematic and biblical studies. More recently there have been two significant developments. First, ministerial formation has been understood as a form of practice which is more than the application of truths independently arrived at, but must be in critical dialogue with theory, and much has been learned in this connection from the formation experience of other professions. Secondly, the scope of the discipline of practical theology has been extended so that its traditional concerns are now pursued in the context of critical theological reflection on Christian practice and indeed on practice as such. It is accordingly closely related to Christian ethics and to the behavioural and social sciences, particularly sociology and psychology.

A. V. Campbell, 'Is Practical Theology Possible?', *SJT* 25, 1972, pp. 217–27; D. B. Forrester, 'Divinity in Use and Practice', *SJT* 33, 1980, pp. 1–11; W. Pannenberg, *Theology and the Philosophy of Science*, 1976, pp. 231–41 and 423–40.

DUNCAN FORRESTER

Pragmatism

Often considered to be America's most important contribution to philosophy, this made its greatest impact on philosophical and theological thought in the first forty years of the twentieth century. Pragmatism drew heavily on empirical, scientific and evolutionary thought in its reaction to idealism *. The thought of Charles Sanders Peirce (1839–1914) laid the foundation of the position when he affirmed that beliefs are really rules for actions which establish habits; to determine a thought's meaning it is necessary only to determine what conduct it is fitted to produce.

William James (1842–1910), Harvard professor of philosophy, who had been educated there in science and medicine, developed this principle of pragmatism as a test of truth. In his definitional work *Pragmatism* (1907) he declared that true ideas are those that can be corroborated and verified, while false ones are those that cannot. Truth is what happens to an idea; an idea is made true by events. Thus the meaning and value of all assumptions and ideas must be evaluated in a radical way by attention to their practical consequences in use. In *A Pluralistic Universe* (1909), James rejected any fixed or static interpretations of the universe to insist on the changing and evolutionary character of reality. He was fascinated by religious questions; in his famous Gifford lectures, *The Varieties of Religious Experience* (1902), he explained that there are certain observable justifications for religious experiences in the way they enrich life and shape conduct. His was an open, seeking, non-traditional attitude towards religion; his study led him to suggest that the God of the pluralistic universe was finite.

The other great exponent of pragmatism, John Dewey (1859–1952), was much less interested in theological matters. As a religious humanist he argued for the separation of religious values from organized religion in *A Common Faith* (1934). Much of his philosophical work centred on the epistemological problem. In *The Quest for Certainty* (1929) and other writings he rejected any association of ideas about value with Antecedent Being, insisting that they should be associated always with practical activity. His version of pragmatism was often called 'instrumentalism' or 'experimentalism'. Through his writings in many fields he exerted a wide influence on the thought of his time.

Pragmatism had a considerable impact on liberal Protestant theological and ethical thought. The religious education movement drew heavily on pragmatically-based ideas. The rise of realistic and neo-orthodox trends in the 1930s tended to check the influence of pragmatism on Protestantism. The leading exponent of pragmatic philosophy outside the United States was F. C. S. Schiller (1864–1937) in England, though he preferred the term 'humanism'. Pragmatism also had some influence on the Catholic Modernist * movement in Europe.

John J. McDermott (ed), *The Writings of William James: A Comprehensive Edition*, 1967, 1977; John E. Smith, *Purpose and Thought: The Meaning of Pragmatism*, 1978; H. S. Thayer, *Meaning and Action: A Critical History of Pragmatism*, 1968.

ROBERT T. HANDY

Praxis

Praxis, or practice, is a pattern of activity or behaviour such as the exercise of a profession, occupation or skill. When it is spelt 'praxis' the emphasis is usually on social and political activity which is innovative and directed towards a transformation of the socio-economic system. The term has been a central concept in Marxist thought, and passed from Marxism either directly or by way of the Frankfurt School (*see* **Critical Theory**) into modern political theology. It is, of course, true that Christianity has taken praxis very seriously from the beginning, and many theologians recognize an affinity between Christian and Marxist uses of the concept. In as far as Christianity is about discipleship, the following or imitation of Christ, it is clearly centrally concerned with praxis. At the heart of Christian praxis is worship, the encounter with God which illumines, signifies and sustains the whole pattern of Christian praxis. Only those who follow may know Jesus, and the praxis of loving God necessarily encompasses, and issues in, loving one's fellows, and being concerned for the conditions of their life. Theology, as reflection on, and response to, Christian praxis and the praxis of the church, has often been recognized as a 'practical science'; it cannot survive as Christian theology in isolation from that praxis. Theology is not an apolitical and detached approach to reality which 'leaves things as they were before' (Wittgenstein); it is involved constantly in the dialectic of theory and practice. Praxis is not the application of an independently arrived at theory, nor does theory emerge spontaneously out of a praxis which it does no more than reflect and justify; they interact with one another dialectically. Truth is encountered and demonstrated in praxis, and it is praxis which validates theology.

Charles Davis, *Theology and Political Society*, 1980; Alfredo Fierro, *The Militant Gospel*, 1977; Rosino Gibellini (ed), *Frontiers of Theology in Latin America*, 1980.

DUNCAN FORRESTER

Prayer, Theology of

Since the earliest days of Israelite religion, prayer to Israel's God was spontaneous, natural and unaffected, however formalized it may have become in later Judaism. The God to whom Israel prayed was the saving, protecting and judging God of prophetic religion. The Psalms exemplify the direct approach of Israel to God: the Israelite, whether individually or corporately, poured out all his concern to God – for his safety, his harvest, his sins and failures, his joys and sorrows, his thanksgiving and praise. Such spontaneous address was possible only because God was essentially 'Thou', the one who called forth the response of those who knew his name.

Jesus and his disciples inherited this long and rich tradition of personal approach to God. But Jesus added a new intimacy to the prayer of his followers. The OT is certainly familiar with the idea of God as Father of Israel, his 'son' (cf. Hos. 11.1), but the prayer of Jesus introduces a distinctively personal relationship, as is instanced by his use of an intimate family-address, *Abba*, 'daddy'. The seven petitions included in the prayer which he taught to his disciples ('the Lord's Prayer') indicate what he considered to be the seven most important things about which Christians should pray. The first three of the petitions concern God's name, God's will and God's reign. Among the other petitions the prayer for God's forgiveness is characteristically made conditional upon the supplicant's own willingness to forgive.

The NT requires and indeed assumes that Christians will pray without ceasing. It also teaches that prayer should be made 'in the name of Jesus', as indeed it is only 'through Jesus Christ our Lord' that Christians have access to God at all. Christian prayer thus contains only those petitions which can be genuinely offered in the name (character, spirit) of Christ, the same Christ who 'at the right hand of God' makes intercession for us. This rules out all selfish requests and every suggestion that prayer is a kind of magic by which God's attention can be caught or his will influenced. The essence of prayer is not asking but offering, not self-seeking but self-dedication: 'not my will but thine be done'.

It is often objected that, if God is a loving father who knows that his children have need of all sorts of things, there is no purpose in intercessory prayer. Yet Jesus himself says 'Ask ... knock ... seek' (Matt. 7.7f.), shortly after saying 'Your heavenly Father knows that you need all these things'

(Matt. 6.32). This implies that intercession is not begging for necessities which might otherwise be withheld; in fact, we are not to worry about our own food and clothing. Our prayer should be concerned with God's kingdom of righteousness: with those who suffer from injustice, deprivation, disease, violence. A father expects his children to be concerned, as he is, for other members of his family in distress. He also expects them not merely to speak to him and then leave him to do everything; he desires their active co-operation. If our communion with God is even a faltering reflection of Jesus' own intimate sonship, we shall not be able to prevent ourselves from bringing to our heavenly Father all the concerns which press upon us. If we have the Spirit of Jesus in us, these concerns will be for others rather than for ourselves; but our own personal griefs and problems will, quite naturally, not be excluded from our speaking with God. The Christian will turn spontaneously to God, the Father of Jesus Christ, as the one who is always 'there'.

But can we expect God to interfere with the laws of nature for our or others' benefit when we pray to him (e.g.) for the rain in time of drought? Much depends upon the way in which this question is formulated. The question as posed above implies a deistic conception of God (see **Deism**) and is an unreal one for Christians today. We must first clarify our conception of the God to whom we pray. Christian prayer is possible only if we believe in the God whom Jesus called Father, not the clockmaker God of the deists, or the Absolute in whom all differences are reconciled, or the 'problem-solver' or Aladdin's Lamp of popular misconception. If our belief in God is the childlike (not childish) trust in one to whom we can always turn quite spontaneously, there is nothing that can be asked 'in the name of Jesus' about which we cannot pray to God. But will our prayers be answered? Yes, though not necessarily in the way we would have chosen; there is much to be learned from the so-called unanswered prayers of Jesus (e.g. Mark 14.35f.). Of course, we will pray for deliverance from danger or for rain: the child cries to his father for help, even though he knows that his father is doing the best that can be done in the situation. Christian prayer is possible only where Jesus' own utter trust in the loving Father is

present. In this it differs from all other prayer: other relgions have developed well-tested methods of contemplation * and of mystical identification with what Tillich would call 'the power of being', and these might indeed be valuable accessories to the prayer-life of the Christian. But they do not approach the distinctively Christian continuous intercourse (not merely on formal occasions, whether individual or corporate) with the Father of Jesus, and our Father.

Three other things remain to be said about the theology of Christian prayer. First, Christian prayer is always corporate in character, even when we enter into our private chamber to pray. Even then it is the church, in heaven and on earth, praying through us. We cannot enter alone into the presence of 'our' Father; God is 'my' God only because he is the God of my fellow-men, and therefore my concerns are his concerns and vice-versa. Secondly, the state of our feelings, when we pray, is unimportant. If we are thinking about what we feel, or are concerned with our own religious satisfaction or enjoyment, we shall not be praying in the Christian sense. If we are preoccupied with psychological problems, such as whether there is anyone there at the other end of the line, we shall not be praying. Prayer is utter dedication and self-forgetting; it should lead to action, not to introspection. Questions about the psychology of prayer are legitimate matters for discussion at the right time and place, but they should not obtrude upon our personal prayer life. Lastly, all men in every age, including our own, at least at certain moments in their lives, spontaneously and yet inevitably experience an urgent desire to pray. This universal compulsion is given its true expression and fulfilment in Christian prayer, in which divine grace perfects the essential nature of man as such. In the last resort men pray because they must, because the need of their hearts will not be repressed without violence to their human nature.

See also **Contemplation; Worship.**

P. Baelz, *Prayer and Providence*, 1968; F. Heiler, *Prayer*, ET 1932; J. Jeremias, *The Prayers of Jesus*, ET 1967.

ALAN RICHARDSON

Preaching

By derivation the word means proclamation. The first English form of the word 'preach' was *prechen*, which came through the Old French *prechier* from the Latin *praedicare* to proclaim, to announce, to declare. This word in *Novum Testamentum Latine* is a translation of the Greek *kerussein*, used in the New Testament in a similar sense. The noun from the same stem, *kerux*, means 'herald'. The NT also uses the verb *euaggelizesthai* of preaching, usually coming into the Latin as *euangelizare* and into the English as evangelize. The meaning of *euaggelizesthai* includes a reference to the content of what is being proclaimed: it is glad tidings, good news, gospel. The nature of the good news is indicated in the NT with both verbs: it is, in the case of the preaching of Jesus, the gospel of God, the good news of the kingdom and in the case of the first Christian preachers, the good news concerning Jesus, crucified and risen, the Christ. Such good news contains facts as well as interpretation and attempts by scholars to distinguish sharply between *didache* (teaching) and *kerygma** (preaching) in the NT have not been fully successful.

Christian preaching is still rooted in the biblical revelation, where it has a three-fold responsibility. It has first to elucidate for the hearers the meaning of the biblical text for those who first wrote it and first heard or read it: the work of exegesis; it has to translate that meaning into the terms and understanding of twentieth-century culture: the work of interpretation; it has to relate the meaning of the text to the contemporary situations, personal and corporate, with which the hearers are confronted: the task of application (*see also* **Hermeneutics; Demythologizing**). The church believes that this three-fold operation is sustained and used by God the Holy Spirit. Preaching so defined normally takes place within a liturgical context, in church, but in a less structured form it can be addressed to those other than Christians in secular situations. The aim is to deepen, or to initiate, Christian faith.

Preaching in church is usually embodied in a sermon, an ordered discourse which is expected to have a progression of thought with points clearly made in intelligible language, illustrative material and an attempt to evoke a response from the members of the congregation. Though the sermon has its roots in the biblical revelation, it may use material gathered from the tradition and experience, past and present, of the church and from the preacher's own experience. Some recent work on the sermon has advocated a move from the form of the ordered discourse to that of the story (*see also* **Narrative Theology**).

During the twentieth century large claims for preaching have been made by some theologians: it has been seen as part of God's eternal action in Christ (P. T. Forsyth), as the means of God speaking and acting in an almost totalitarian fashion so that there is nothing more momentous and decisive than preaching (Karl Barth), as setting forth the cross and resurrection of Jesus so that through the preaching (and only through the preaching) those who believe can be saved (Rudolf Bultmann); as the essential action of the church, renewing its life as it proclaims the kingdom (C. H. Dodd).

Whether such claims can be substantiated on the evidence of the church's experience is at least arguable. The latter half of the twentieth century has seen the demise of the great preachers whom crowds flocked to hear. In the life of the church the increased emphasis upon laity and clergy together, and in that order, as the people of God has tended to diminish the significance of authority figures of which the preacher was one. Here theological belief has been supported by sociological factors. Furthermore, the uninterrupted discourse of the preacher has been challenged, if not overtaken, by other methods of communication. As for preaching to the unconverted, the church has passed through a period in which listening in empathy to non-Christians and entering into dialogue with them seemed more appropriate stances than those of announcement and proclamation. It is thus contended that the large claims do not correspond with what has in fact happened.

Be that as it may, the 1980s have shown signs of a fresh interest in preaching and a renewed belief that preaching which expounds the biblical revelation and relates that revelation to the daily lives of its hearers is in fact offering Christ as Lord, by which offer and the response of faith the church lives and the world can believe.

See **Homiletics**.

Ernest Best, *From Text to Sermon*, 1978; R. E. C. Browne, *The Ministry of the Word*,

1958; Reginald H. Fuller, *The Use of the Bible in Preaching*, 1981; Richard A. Jensen, *Telling the Story: Variety and Imagination in Preaching*, 1980; Ian Pitt-Watson, *A Kind of Folly*, 1976; John Stacey, *Preaching Reassessed*, 1980.

JOHN STACEY

Precious Blood

The allusions of Christ at the Last Supper to the blood of the New Covenant (Mark 14.24; Matt. 26.28) and to the Paschal Lamb (John 19.36; see also 1.29; 1.36), added to the fact that the apostles associate the blood with the passion and death of Christ (I John 1.7; Rev. 1.5; I Peter 1.2, 19; Rom. 3.25; Eph. 1.7; Heb. 9.12), gave rise to the idea that the precious blood is a part of the sacred humanity and is hypostatically * united with the second Person of the Trinity *. It is argued that this view goes back to Ignatius of Antioch. This idea grew in the Middle Ages into a cult of veneration. There was a fruitless debate in the fifteenth century between the Franciscans and the Dominicans on whether the Blood shed remained united to the Word, the Dominicans arguing for, the Franciscans against. Since the Council of Trent * referred to the body and blood of Christ as *partes Christi Domini*, it was subsequently argued that the blood shed during the passion was united with the body at the resurrection, save for those few particles which were now holy relics (i.e. the blood that adhered to the spear, the scourging pillar, etc.). The RC church long had feasts of the Most Precious Blood, but these were abolished with the reform of the calendar and liturgical books in 1912. The object of the feast was not, though, the alleged relics of the Blood of Christ (which Aquinas refused to accept as authentic) but the love of the redeeming Christ of which the Blood was and is the sign.

See also **Blood of Christ.**

JAMES ATKINSON

Predestination

This is the doctrine that God foreknows, and ordains, from all eternity, who will be saved. The doctrine has been interpreted in many ways, and has been the source of endless disputes. We shall briefly review the chief historical phases of these disputes before considering some general comments.

The original ground for the doctrine is to be found in the Bible; 1. through the teaching of a divine providence in nature, man and history, that pervades both Testaments; 2. more particularly, through the teaching of St Paul. Of special importance is Rom. 8.29: 'those whom he foreknew he also predestined (*proorise*) to be conformed to the image of his son . . .' The controversy over the interpretation of this, and other passages that mention the election of God, came to a head in Augustine's * battle with the Pelagians *, who were alleged to claim that man could bring about his salvation through his own efforts, and with the semi-Pelagians * (among whom may have been Pelagius himself), who, while admitting that man needed grace for salvation, also insisted that this grace was given in response to man's free choice of the good. According to Augustine, however, it is not human merit that is the ground of election *, but the inscrutable will of God. Holiness is the *result* of election, not its source. There were two essential elements in predestination: 1. foreknowledge, whereby God infallibly knows who will be saved; 2. an act of will by which God decrees to save those who are to be saved.

At a series of councils at Carthage, from 416 to 419, and at a number of later councils, Augustine's position on predestination became official Catholic teaching, but it continued to be expounded in different ways. Aquinas taught that meritorious acts are the effects, not the cause, of predestination, but he tried to combine this with a more liberal account of free will * than can be found in Augustine. Among later Catholic interpreters three schools of thought are of special importance, each of which tries to deal with the problem of the apparent injustice of God in ordaining only some men to glory. The Jesuit, Molina, and his followers, claimed that God had freely chosen one set of possibilities over against others. God infallibly knows all possible events, and out of these he chooses one in which he has seen, in his prevision, that men will make the best use of the grace that would be granted to them. In this way Molina sought to deny 'predeterminism', which he thought would destroy free will, while at the same time denying that merit was itself the cause of man's election. The cause was rather God's choice of this set of possibilities instead of another. The Dominican, Banez, and his followers, strongly opposed the Molinist view, insisting that predestination to glory is decreed before any prevision of merit whatsoever. Between these two schools there have been various attempts at compromise, including those of the 'Congruists', such as Suarez.

However, it is within Protestantism that we find the most familiar and the most outspoken defenders of predestination. Luther revived the full Augustinian doctrine, together with a new stress on the total depravity of fallen man. Since, in Adam, all are guilty before God, all deserve eternal damnation, and therefore it is no injustice in God if some are lost; rather, it is a sign of infinite love that some are saved. In Calvin we find a still more uncompromising statement of the position, including the famous theory of 'double predestination', according to which some are eternally ordained to glory, through the sheer will of God, and the rest are ordained to eternal torment.

While Calvin has often been singled out for attack on behalf of this doctrine, its assessment must be made in the context of Calvin's overall position. In his actual teaching Calvin tended to stress predestination to life, and with it the doctrine of assurance *, with which it is closely linked. Further, whatever may be the logic of his theory of predestination, he in fact used it to emphasize human responsibility among the elect, rather than a passive acceptance of privilege. This was one reason for the activism of many of his followers, and for the famous 'Protestant ethic', which, even if sometimes exaggerated, had enormous social consequences. It must also be remembered that a theory of double predestination is implicit in many other formulations, Catholic and Protestant. If God has ordained only some to glory, and has chosen whom these are going to be from all eternity, then except in so far as some theologians made allowance for a limbo *, this effectively consigned all the others to hell. Mistaken as Calvin may well have been on this matter, he was at least more consistent than many of his detractors. Having started with a doctrine of sovereignty which (mistakenly) saw an absolute will as the essential attribute of God, Calvin drew the inevitable consequences.

More liberal Protestant views can be found in Arminius, who rejected Calvin's doctrine of irresistible grace. Although opposed by most of the Reformed churches, Arminian * views became extremely influential through Wesley and the Methodist movement, who accepted Arminius' account of free will. Among more recent writers, special mention should be made of the important, though complex, account of predestination found in Barth, who sought a christological presentation of the doctrine that avoided the errors of the past. In this theory Christ is both the electing God and the elected man, in communion with whom man can discover his own election. In some sense all men are elected in Christ, and this has led to a debate as to whether Barth's position commits him to universalism * (the doctrine that all men will eventually be saved).

It is tempting for contemporary liberal Christians to reject the doctrine of predestination altogether as an unfortunate relic from the past. However, despite the undeniable errors that can be found in most, or perhaps all presentations of the doctrine, it does stand for at least one extraordinarily important element in Christian teaching, without which Christianity would scarcely be recognizable. This is the realization by the Christian that he depends on the grace of God. 'By the grace of God I am what I am' (I Cor. 15. 10). If I depend on my own performance, then I am eventually led to despair, unless I am blind to the truth of my state. One of the continuing tasks of Christian theology is to combine this insight with an adequate account of that human freedom without which man ceases to be a creature made in the image of God, and becomes a complex puppet or machine. At the heart of this issue is the need for a proper understanding of the relationship of the will of God to his essential goodness. An alternative to Calvin's view can be found within the Platonic * and Thomist * traditions. Here the stress is on an absolute goodness or love as the essential attribute of God, and a will that cannot be understood except in the context of this goodness. Thus God's will can never be seen as arbitrary, and indeed, as Aquinas pointed out, even God works in accordance with a kind of law. This is the 'eternal law' which Hooker, following Aquinas, brought into Anglican theology (*Eccl. Pol.* I, II, 2). When God's will is understood in this context the excesses of positions like those of Calvin become clear.

See also **Foreknowledge, Providence.**

Aquinas, *ST* la, q. 23; Augustine, *De prae-destinatione sanctorum*; Calvin, *De aeterna praedestinatione Dei*; C. H. Dodd, *The Epistle of Paul to the Romans*, 1922 (on Rom. 8); M. J. Farrelly, *Predestination, Grace, and Free Will*, 1964.

M. J. LANGFORD

Pre-existence

The belief that Jesus Christ did not originate at his birth in history but in some sense existed beforehand as an eternal being or hypostasis* within the Godhead is first found in Paul. It is definitely stated in the 'song of the incarnation' in Phil. 2.1–11, and is implied in such passages as I Cor. 8.6; II Cor. 8.9 (*pace* J. D. G. Dunn, *Christology in the Making*, 1980). The doctrine is extended by the author of Colossians (taken here not to be Paul but a disciple of his); Col. 1.15–20 elaborates what is a fully-fledged Logos* doctrine in all but name. The same belief in pre-existence is found in Hebrews, which opens with a bold assertion that he who appeared in the period of the incarnation* as Son has always existed as the *apaugasma* ('reflection') and *charaktēr* ('facsimile') of God's very nature. But whereas Paul has no hesitation in using the name *Iēsous* and *Christos* of the pre-existent being, Hebrews appears to hold that he should be thought of as *kyrios* ('Lord') or even *theos* ('God'). He did not become Son till the incarnation. The doctrine of pre-existence reaches its apogee in the NT in the Fourth Gospel, where the pre-existent being is identified with the Word (Logos) of God, who has always existed with the Father. John also uses 'Son' freely of the pre-existent Word.

The doctrine arose probably among those who, like Paul, the author of Hebrews and John, were fully conversant with the Wisdom tradition of Judaism. In Wisdom 10, for example, Wisdom is represented as supervising all the history of the patriarchs and the people of Israel up to the entry into Canaan. It was not difficult to substitute Christ or the Word for the divine Wisdom. The motivation to do so probably lay in the perfectly reasonable desire to safeguard the faithfulness of God, to show that the incarnation was not an isolated incident, or a divine intrusion, but was part of an on-going history of salvation. It is also possible that the experience which the earliest Christians had of the risen Christ in the Spirit contributed to make the doctrine of pre-existence seem to be a theological necessity.

The NT writers are not content to claim that the Son or Word always existed with the Father; they also attempt to trace the activity of the pre-existent one in Israel's history. Thus Paul sees him as present with Israel in the wilderness (I Cor. 10.1–11). John represents him as having been seen by Abraham (John 8.52–58); even the Epistle of Jude probably attributes the exodus from Egypt to the pre-existent Jesus (see Jude 5, where the best mss. read *Iēsous*).

This doctrine of pre-existent activity was very popular with the early Fathers up till the outbreak of the Arian* controversy. Arians welcomed the idea, since a pre-existent being in history relieved the Father of the odium of acting in the world, something which they regarded as unworthy of true God (the Son was not true God). We therefore find most orthodox writers abandoning the attempt to trace the activity of the pre-existent Christ in OT history, though not of course the doctrine of the Logos, which was a keystone of their christology*.

As far as modern theology is concerned, some sort of a Logos-doctrine has been very widely accepted (e.g. by Tillich and Pannenberg), and is by no means incompatible with the modern approach to the incarnation, though the way in which the divine Word is described as related to Jesus of Nazareth is a point on which there is wide divergence. The activity of the pre-existent Christ in OT history is almost impossible to defend in the terms in which the NT writers express it, not least because so much of what they regarded as history we must describe as legend. What we can say, however, is that, in as far as God was known by anyone in OT times, he must have been the same God who is now known to Christians as the God revealed in Jesus Christ.

O. Cullmann, *The Christology of the NT*, ET 1959; J. D. G. Dunn, *Christology in the Making*, 1980; R. G. Hammerton-Kelly, *Pre-Existent Wisdom and the Son of Man*, 1973; A. T. Hanson, *The Image of the Invisible God*, 1982.

ANTHONY TYRRELL HANSON

Presbyter *see* **Elder, Ministry, Priest**

Presbyterian Theology

The term 'presbyterial government' or 'presbytery government' was used towards the end of the reign of Queen Elizabeth I of England to designate a form of church government by which lay elders were united with ministers in enforcing spiritual discipline in the church; presbyterial government opposed the exercise of spiritual discipline by bishops, ecclesiastical courts, or civil magistrates. The term derived from one element in the system, the presbytery, a body made up of ministers and elected elders from each of the congregations in one area. By the time of the Civil War in England, this form of church government was being called 'Presbyterian discipline' and its advocates 'presbyterians'. In 1645 the Assembly of Divines at Westminster with the assistance of Commissioners from the Church of Scotland published *The Form of Presbyterial Church-Government and of Ordination of Ministers*, which became the nominal directory (although little enforced) for the Church of England until 1660. The Church of Scotland had adopted presbyterian government with the *Second Book of Discipline* (1578), which was recognized by the Act of 1592 'ratifying the liberty of the church, recognizing a legal jurisdiction in its courts . . . and providing that presentations by patrons should henceforth be directed, not to the bishops, but to the presbyteries within whose bounds the vacant benefices lay'. Presbyterian church government was restored in Scotland by an Act of 1690. At the same time in Ireland the General Synod of Ulster, which originated in a presbytery of the chaplains and elders of the Scottish army, 1642, started to meet again.

Whole churches came to be called Presbyterian in the eighteenth century. In Scotland the popularly named Cameronians (after Richard Cameron, died 1680), members of the 'United Societies', organized themselves as the Reformed Presbytery in 1743, and became known as the Reformed Presbyterian Church. In Ireland a union of Secession synods called itself 'The Presbyterian Synod of Ireland distinguished by the name of Seceders' in 1818. In the United States of America and Canada, and later in Australia, New Zealand and South Africa, Scottish and Irish immigrants founded various presbyterian churches. The Presbyterian

or Calvinistic Methodist Church of Wales was formed as the result of the evangelical revival.

The theology behind all Presbyterianism is predominantly Calvinism. Presbyterians held that the form of church government was laid down in scripture. God the Father through Jesus Christ had committed the spiritual government of the church to governors: those who deal in the Word and sacraments (pastors or ministers, and teachers or 'doctors') and those who do not deal in the Word and sacraments (elders and deacons). Elders * sat with ministers in presbytery and helped 'to see good orders kept and manners reformed and godliness increased throughout the whole church' (Thomas Cartwright, 1535–1603). Consequently, lay people and ministers were constantly consulting together about the proper interpretation and application of the Bible.

Although there has never been a single presbyterian theology, it was always possible to discuss the theology of presbyterians. Theology was often a matter of intense debate inside presbyterian churches, and those outside these churches were from time to time in a position to point to the presbyterian theology of their day.

In England from the 1730s onwards, more and more leading presbyterian ministers became Arians, and by the end of the century presbyterian theology was predominantly Unitarian *, except in Northumberland. The evangelical revival and the coming in of Scots to England in the nineteenth century led to the revival of orthodox Presbyterian churches.

In Scotland and the New World, presbyterian theology was greatly influenced by the eighteenth- and nineteenth-century revivals. The austere intellectual system of Calvinism, with its doctrine of double predestination * whereby God is held to choose the elect and the damned from all eternity, was combined with an inward burning love for Christ. The combination was potent, as in the theology of Jonathan Edwards (1703–1758), the defender of predestination, who could also write, 'I very often think with sweetness, and longings, and pantings of soul, of being a little child, taking hold of Christ, to be led by him through the wilderness of this world.' Nevertheless, these two strands were often represented by two opposing parties in the presbyterian churches.

In the late nineteenth century the doctrines of predestination and penal substitutionary atonement* were challenged in presbyterian churches, and various devices found for easing the consciences of ministers on these parts of the Westminster Confession, to which they had to subscribe. At the same time biblical criticism*, after some notable heresy trials, like that of William Robertson Smith (1846–1894), was gradually domesticated in presbyterian theological colleges and seminaries.

In the twentieth century, presbyterian theology was deeply influenced by the social gospel*, and by the new interest in the theology of the Reformation. Reinhold Niebuhr, although not a presbyterian, influenced presbyterian theology, and paved the way for the wide acceptance of the theology of Karl Barth. A notable product of these forces was the Confession of 1967 of the United Presbyterian Church in the USA.

Presbyterian churches in the eighteenth and nineteenth centuries seemed inherently to be subject to schism. In Scotland the eighteenth century produced the Secession of 1740 (leading to Burghers and Anti-burghers, Old Lights and New Lights), and the Relief Church of 1761. In the nineteenth century the Church of Scotland was divided by the Disruption of 1843 which produced the Free Church of Scotland. Nevertheless, many of the eighteenth century divided Scottish churches reunited to form the United Presbyterian Church in 1847, and they in turn united with the Free Church in 1900 to form the United Free Church, leaving the Wee Frees. In 1929 the United Free Church and the Church of Scotland reunited as the Church of Scotland. In Ireland the Secession Synod united with the General Synod of Ulster to form the Presbyterian Church in Ireland in 1840. In the United States the 1741 schism between the Old Side 'churchly' party and the New Side revivalists was healed in 1758, and the schism between the Old School philosophical realists and conservatives and the New School philosophical idealists and anti-slave-traders of 1837 was healed in 1869, although only after the loss of the large Old School southern constituency at the Civil War. The Presbyterian Church together with the United Presbyterian Church in the USA are voting on a plan for union which calls for the writing of a new brief statement of faith (1982). Pres-byterians have entered united churches in Canada, South India, England and Australia, leaving strong conservative presbyterian churches behind in Canada and Australia.

Contemporary presbyterian theology has largely abandoned strict Calvinism, without abandoning the attempt to derive doctrine, church order, and social order from the Bible. Presbyterian theology is concerned with ways to express the sovereignty of God in corporate legal and institutional forms.

G. D. Henderson, *Presbyterianism*, 1954; Lefferts A. Loetscher, *The Broadening Church: A Study of Theological Issues in the Presbyterian Church since 1869*, 1954.

J. C. O'NEILL

Priesthood

1. *Scripture*. Priesthood in the Hebrew scriptures is principally embodied in the professional class of Levites and Zadokites, and develops more as a function of lineage than of office or vocation. While the early priestly task consisted mainly in consulting the 'lots' to determine God's will, a function later absorbed by the prophets, priesthood gradually shifted towards the functions of worship, and especially cult sacrifice. In contrast to this dominant Aaronic priesthood, the obscure figure of Melchizedek represents another kind of priesthood, namely the priest-king, who is independent of Levitical lineage. It is this 'royal' priesthood, rather than the cultic, that shaped the Christian imagination in speaking of the priesthood of Jesus Christ (Heb. 7.26).

In the NT, it is only in Hebrews that the term priest is applied in detail to Jesus. His is a unique priesthood deeply in sympathy with the human condition and ordered to it. In so far as priesthood is associated with sacrificial activity, Jesus is named priest in his own definitive, once-for-all sacrifice which has rendered the sacrifices of Israel, and presumably its cultic priesthood, obsolete. In the new era inaugurated by Christ, believers may enact *his* sacrifice in the mode of remembrance (*anamnesis/zikkaron*), and may manifest its effect in their lives, but they have no need of any other sacrifice (I Cor. 5.7f.).

Also in the NT, the term priesthood is given to the community of the church (I Peter 1.9–10). The theological principle operative here is the union of all the baptized with Christ, the naming of the corporate reality of the baptized as Christ's body, and in particular the participation of all in the mystery of Christ (I Cor. 10). Nowhere does the NT identify any individual in the church as priest. Christ alone is high priest, and the church, in so far as it embodies and manifests Christ in its corporate life, is the prime manifestation of his one priesthood.

2. *History*. It is not until the beginning of the third century that the term priest appears attributed to a member of the church. In the *Apostolic Tradition* of Hippolytus (*c*. AD 215) the ordination prayer for a bishop explicitly names him high priest, and invokes on him the 'spirit of the high priesthood'. This stands in contrast to the presbyteral ordination which employs images of Moses and the seventy elders to identify the presbyterium. Certainly one step towards this naming of bishop as priest is the gradual localizing of the church reality in the office of bishop that began in the previous century, a localizing which was representative in nature. Ignatius of Antioch illustrates this early trend: 'Wherever the bishop is, the whole congregation is present, just as wherever Jesus Christ is, there is the whole church' (*To the Smyrnaeans* 8).

In the third and fourth centuries, as temple imagery replaced synagogue imagery for the church's self-understanding, the term priesthood was extended to include both bishops and presbyters. Presbyters joined bishops as regular, and not simply delegated, presiders at the eucharist, and the cult language of the levitical priesthood helped solidify a permanent relationship between priest and eucharist. The priesthood of the church was lost sight of, along with the mediatorial role of the church in the act of ordination. It was no longer the priesthood of the church which was invested in a representative way in its bishops and presbyters. The priesthood of Christ was directly conferred upon the ordained.

The loss of the church's priesthood as the necessary link between the priesthood of Christ and that of ministerial priests was but the first in a series of shifts which altered and distorted the subsequent development of priesthood. Several others during the Middle Ages need to be noted.

The image of Christ at the Father's right hand replaced that of Christ in the midst of the church creating the need for mediators upon the earth to represent this now absent Christ. Thus the priest came to be seen as speaking to God for the people and acting on their behalf. The eucharist, more and more the preserve of the priest, moved from sacred action to sacred drama, with the priest its principal actor. Intense concentration on the 'sacred species' as yet another graphic representation of Christ on earth brought forth the cult of adoration, and highlighted the priest as consecrator and transformer of the elements. Finally, the allegorical representation of the mass as enactment of the passion along with the theology of merit as it evolved around Christ's sacrifice forged the image of priest as offerer of sacrifice for the people and dispenser of God's grace to them.

This theological combination, of mediator priest offering sacrifice for the sins of the people, and consecrating the host to bring Christ to them, inevitably fed the pastoral abuses which caused Luther and the Reformation traditions to reject both priesthood and sacrifice together. While the Catholic response did clear up many abuses, and preserved both priesthood and sacrifice in its canons, it did not resolve the issues which the Reformation raised, nor restore the priesthood of the church to its proper place. It may be said of the Reformation aftermath that Catholics simply preserved the mediaeval understanding of priesthood, while Protestants introduced a radically new concept, namely, the priesthood of the individual baptized. The truth of the original priesthood of the church was thus split into two opposing traditions, each preserving what the other lost and losing what the other preserved.

3. *Theology*. The heart of a theology of priesthood must be to understand the four realities of priesthood, namely, Christ, church, minister, individual Christian, in relation to each other, and not in opposition. It cannot begin with either the ministerial priesthood of the ordained or with the classic priesthood of all believers. It must begin with Jesus Christ, who possesses the only Christian priesthood, and see the others as manifestations of this one priesthood of Christ. To advance beyond the polemic of the sixteenth century, it must likewise regain the theological 'missing link', and recover the corporate body of the church in its corporate manifestations as the primary human

reality which embodies Christ's priesthood and priestly activity. Both the priesthood of the baptized and that of the ordained can only be understood if their proper relation to the corporate church is secure. Baptism and ordination 'order' one to a relationship with the assembled church; neither makes sense apart from the corporate priesthood of the church.

The church is priest in the act of worship, and Christian worship is always the faith act of an ordered assembly. The baptized stand in relation to Christ before Abba, and by the Father's gift of Spirit stand in relation to each other. This relationship constitutes the priesthood of the baptized. Within the assembly, the ministerial priest, however he or she be named, is symbol of the Christ who gathers, who leads, and who prays. This symbolizing is the ministry of acting *in persona Christi*, and is a ministry of incarnating Christ for the priesthood of the church. Ministerial priesthood exists in order to activate the priesthood of the entire church.

A critical issue in the theology of priesthood concerns the empowerment that is associated with it. Western theology, whether one accepts or rejects the mediaeval understanding of priesthood, has viewed ordination as the conferral of power by Christ, specifically, the power to consecrate, to offer sacrifice and to forgive sin. What needs to be recovered is the fact that Christ's own priesthood is given him by the Father through the consecration of the Spirit. So it is also with all manifestations of Christ's priesthood. The power of priesthood, whether of the church, of the baptized, or of the ministerial priesthood, is not possessed, but trusted. The invocations of both baptism and ordination are acts of entrustment whereby individuals are placed at the disposal of God's Spirit, and their lives and ministries entrusted to the Spirit's care. Any image of either baptism or ordination which sees the power of priesthood possessed by individuals, or even by the church, seriously distorts the reality of the Holy Spirit who is the source of all Christian priesthood.

A second issue, which is highly disputed among the churches, is the admission of women to the ministerial priesthood. Those who stress the priesthood of the baptized are inclined to favour it more than those whose position derives from the mediaeval Catholic view. Where *in persona Christi* is understood in a literal sense, the pressure is strong to retain an exclusively male priesthood. More than a question of mere practical decision, this issue urges the recovery of the priesthood of the corporate church, and of the ministerial priesthood as representative embodiment of that corporate church, where the Christ whose body is both male and female may find sacramental expression in both.

B. Cooke, *Ministry to Word and Sacrament*, 1976; N. Mitchell, *Mission and Ministry*, 1982; J. Mohler, *The Origin and Evolution of the Priesthood*, 1969; J. Provost (ed), *Official Ministry in a New Age*, 1981; E. Schillebeeckx, *Ministry*, ET 1981.

PETER E. FINK

Procession(s)

The term is used in Cappadocian theology as the characteristic particularly of the Spirit. In arguing for the full deity of the Spirit, the charge had to be met that if the Spirit and the Son were both *homoousios** with the Father, the Father had two sons; in establishing the unity of the Godhead and the distinctions of the hypostases, a term was needed to describe the peculiar mode of being of the Spirit parallel to the accepted characteristics of the Father (ingeneracy*) and the Son (generation*). The term was drawn from John 15.26, and its precise content is hard to define; it was intended to signify a different mode of derivative being from sonship without using the suspect language of emanation. Prior to the Cappadocians, no specific term had won currency; most often it was assumed that the Spirit was *genētos*. Subsequently in Eastern theology a clear distinction was drawn between the eternal procession of the Spirit within the Godhead, and his procession (= mission) in the 'economy' of salvation. Eastern theologians maintained that the Western doctrine of Double Procession* confused the two.

In Thomist theology the word was applied both to the Son and the Spirit in their relation to the Father. Processions are immanent operations since they issue in Persons of the Trinity and remain within the divine Essence. Aquinas relies on John 8.42 for the Procession of the Son and John 15.26 for the Procession of the Spirit. The distinction between the two Processions corresponds to that between intelligence and will. The Procession of the Word is an operation of the divine Intelligence by way of similitude (the Son is the image of the Father) and is called Generation because 'like begets like'. The procession of the Spirit is an act of the divine will by way of impulse and movement. This is implied by the very name Spirit and confirmed by the special relationship of the Spirit to Love which depends upon will and issues in the movement between the Lover and the Loved.

Two corollaries are drawn from this principle: 1. Since Will also implies Intelligence, the Word is involved with the Father in the Procession of the Spirit. 2. Since Will and Intelligence exhaust the possible modes of divine operation, there must be two and can only be two divine Processions from the Father.

Thus Aquinas uses the term procession in a double sense, more widely to include both the Son and the Spirit and more narrowly to cover the specific relation of the Spirit to the Father and the Son (*see* **Spiration**). Patristic and most modern theology prefers the narrower usage.

See also **Trinity, Doctrine of the.**

H. E. W. TURNER/FRANCES YOUNG

Process Theology

In a broad sense the description can be held to apply to any theology which emphasizes event, becoming and relatedness as basic categories for its understanding rather than those of substance* and being*. Although this way of understanding can claim antecedents in such ancient sources as Heraclitus' observation that all things are in flux and Buddhist teaching that there are no static substances behind the flow of experiences, the general background to its modern expressions is to be found in Hegelian views on the dynamic nature of reality as history, in developments in scientific thought (particularly evolutionary notions and the collapse of Democritan views about the atom in modern physics) and in the experiential and empirical pragmatism* of such American philosophers as Charles Sanders Peirce (1839–1914), William James (1842–1910) and John Dewey (1859–1952). In this broad sense 'process theology' embraces such varied views as those expounded by Henri Bergson (1859–1941) and Pierre Teilhard de Chardin (1881–1955) in France, by Samuel Alexander (1859–1938), Conwy Lloyd Morgan (1852–1936), William Temple (1881–1944) and Lionel Spencer Thornton (1884–1947) in Britain, as well as by Alfred North Whitehead (1861–1947) and Charles Hartshorne (1897–   ), together with those influenced by them (including Henry Nelson Wieman, Daniel Day Williams, Schubert M. Ogden, John B. Cobb, W. Norman Pittenger, Lewis S. Ford and David Ray Griffin), in the USA. A narrower use of the designation 'process theology' is to refer to the theological movement which developed in the Chicago Divinity School during and since the 1930s as the socio-historical approach in theology, whose major exponent there was Shailer Mathews (1863–1941), was modified in different ways in response to Whitehead's thought by Wieman and Hartshorne and their pupils. Most commonly of all, however, 'process theology' is used to indicate the kind of theological understanding which is based on the philosophical and religious insights of Whitehead and Hartshorne and employs the conceptual structures which they developed to express their insights. It is in this sense that the topic of 'process theology' will be treated in the remainder of this article.

Although it is easy to exaggerate their significance, there are differences between Whitehead and Hartshorne, as well as between those influenced by them, which should not be ignored. Whitehead, for instance, employs an empirical methodology. His metaphysical understanding is reached through seeking to identify by empirical analysis those elements which are necessary to all experience whatsoever and therefore are stable and universally recurring, taking as the primary point of insight not a universalized physics but what we find in our experience as human bodies. His ideas, furthermore, have at times the provocative fruitfulness of concepts with fuzzy edges rather than the precision of components of a fully finished system. Hartshorne, in comparison, is much more committed to using *a priori* reasoning to reach his conclusions, on the grounds that metaphysical truths are *a priori* truths which apply to any possible state of affairs. In consequence he sees a version of the ontological argument* as an appropriate way to investigate the reality of God. His views, furthermore, tend to be more precisely and rigorously worked out. As for their respective treatments of the notion of God, Hartshorne's is by far the more fully developed and, in terms of its stress on the temporality of God, much more akin to the agential God of biblical theism than Whitehead's God who, somewhat puzzlingly, is envisaged as being a single actual entity rather than as a living person. It should be noted, furthermore, that their conceptualities are not the same. Whitehead's dipolar distinction between the primordial and consequent natures of God is not the same as Hartshorne's dipolar distinction between the necessary existence and contingent actuality of God. Much confusion and error, especially in British comments on process theology, have arisen from the failure to observe these differences.

For all their differences, however, the various forms of process theology generally share a common understanding of reality. Basically this maintains that what is real is essentially in process. To be unchanging in all respects is to be dead, past or abstract. To be actual, that is, is not to be a static substance but to be a momentary event in a series of events in which each successive 'actual occasion' creatively determines itself within limits as it responds to its grasp of the previous state to which it is the successor and of its environment, including in the latter the lures of what it is possible for it to become. What are commonly observed as objects are societies of such actual occasions, each of which constitutes an 'enduring individual' by massively inheriting the characteristics of its preceding actual occasion. From this analysis of reality it follows that what is actual is temporal: it has a past to which it responds and it is pointed towards future occasions to whose aesthetic satisfaction it can contribute. The real is also essentially social. There are no absolutely independent individuals. Each actual occasion not only massively inherits the characteristics of the previous occasions of which it is the successor in constituting an enduring object; it is also, with degrees of 'importance' varying from the massive to the infinitesimally trivial, related to all other actual occasions. The universe is therefore not merely bound together by universally applying rules. As such it constitutes a social process where the state of any actuality in principle influences all future ones. In this universe, though, the ultimate power is held to be exercised through that lure of love, or persuasiveness of attraction, which draws rather than coerces actual entities into producing what is creatively novel and aesthetically satisfying. Finally, in order to find a model * for its understanding of reality, in most expressions process thought adopt some form of panpsychism. This is a difficult notion to understand. It is not obvious that a process view requires its acceptance, although it does provide a fruitful model for describing the non-coercive interaction between God and the world and the autonomy of each entity. Those who do adopt it describe the process of concretion by such psychical terms as 'feeling', 'enjoyment', 'experience' and 'satisfaction'. What these notions refer to in relation to the basic constituents of nature is not easy to fathom, especially since those who use them are also concerned to point out that such mental operations need not be – and in most cases are not – conscious processes. Consciousness, rather, is a quality of high-grade mental activity.

According to Whitehead, 'God is not to be treated as an exception to all metaphysical principles, invoked to save their collapse. He is their chief exemplification.' In his cosmological understanding God may be seen as that reality who ensures the continuation and orderliness of the processes of actualization and who is the basis of the appearance of novelty through those processes. In order to expound this understanding Whitehead distinguishes between the 'consequent' and the 'primordial' natures of God. The former refers to God's conscious receptivity of all that is actualized in the world, preserving it without loss in the immediacy of his own life. The latter refers to God's eternal envisagement of 'the absolute wealth of potentiality', presenting thereby to each concretizing actuality the whole range of possibility as it is purposively lured towards intensity of experience rather than mere preservation. On the basis of this cosmological understanding Whitehead sees God not as 'an imperial ruler' nor as 'a personification of moral energy' but as working 'slowly and quietly by love'. He is affected by as well as affecting all that happens in the world. Thus Whitehead describes him as 'the great companion – the fellow-sufferer who understands' and as 'the eternal urge of desire' who interacts with the world in 'the creative advance into novelty'.

Hartshorne's understanding of God may be described as a sustained attempt to solve the problem of how to conceive coherently of God as loving – i.e., to conceive of God both as ultimate and divine (and so as absolute, necessary and unchanging) and as genuinely loving (and so as having the relative, contingent and changing experiences involved in a loving relationship with the members of his creation). Following the principle of non-contradiction, theologians have generally considered that if God is to be described as absolute, necessary and unchanging (and a being who is not so described seems to be other than what is meant by 'God'), he cannot without incoherence be also described as relative, contingent and changing (and so, without inconsistency, be describable as loving, compassionate and purposive). At the heart of theistic understanding, therefore, there seems to be fatal incoherency. Hartshorne, however, suggests that such apparent contradictions are due to inadequate analysis of the notions involved. In the case of God both sets of formal qualities are to be seen as required by different aspects of his dipolar nature. Whereas, for example, all but God has a relative, contingent and changeable mode of existence, God's existence is uniquely to be understood as absolute, necessary and unchanging. God exists whatever else happens to be the case. There is no possible state which is not dependent upon him. At the same time the character of God's actuality is determined partly by his own choices and partly by the actual states of the creation to which he is related as its God – and so is relative, contingent and changing according to those choices and states. Again God's love is absolute, necessary and unchanging in the abstract sense that God's relationship to his creatures is always one of pure love: in actual practice, though, the concrete expressions of that love must be appropriate to (and so relative to, contingent upon and changing with) the actual states of those creatures and what in the circumstances is the most fruitful relationship to them.

It is this analysis which leads Hartshorne sometimes to describe his concept of God as 'dipolar'. He also speaks of it as panentheistic*, holding that whereas theism* so divorces God and creation that it has

difficulties in relating them significantly, and pantheism* so identifies them that it is difficult to distinguish them, the most satisfactory understanding is achieved by seeing everything as 'in' God. What this means is that all that occurs in the world is immediately experienced by God, and yet God is not merely a cipher for the sum of these experiences. He responds to and so affects the world as well as being affected by it.

The adoption of the dipolar panentheistic concept of God in process theology leads to – or at least makes possible – revision in how various attributes of God are understood. God is seen, for example, not as being outside time (whatever that could coherently mean) but as being 'eminently temporal' – 'temporal' in that God knows the past as determined and chooses concerning a future that is as yet indeterminate but 'eminently' so in that there never was and never will be a moment to which he is not present. God's knowledge is similarly understood as an omniscience which knows all that is to be known (i.e. what has been and is now actual and the present range of possibilities) but which does not know what is unknowable (such as the logically impossible, the factually untrue and the future as the not yet determined). God's power is seen as an unremitting influence which acts persuasively as a lure, respecting the integrity of the creatures, rather than as a coercive force. From this it follows that God is to be seen as supremely passible and supremely active – he is affected by all that happens in the world, suffering both its pains and its joys, and seeks to affect it by evoking in it the greatest enrichments possible. As for God's perfection, it is understood as a state of 'dual transcendence', where God is unsurpassable by everything other than himself but in which his later states will exceed in incremental value his earlier states – e.g. in terms of the perfection of God's awareness: at time t_1 God as perfect will be aware of all that has been and is then the case, but at a later time, t_2, his awareness will embrace more since it will then additionally include all that has come to be the case between t_1 and t_2. At no time, though, will God's awareness be in any way deficient.

Although process thought has particularly been used in relation to the doctrine of God*, its insights and conceptual structures have also been fruitfully – and, in the judgment of some, provocatively – applied to the doctrines of man, nature, the incarnation, soteriology, the church, death and eschatology as well as to the problems of evil and ecology and to Christian political responsibility. Underlying all these applications is the view that God is lovingly and ceaselessly active in the created order, respecting the integrity of his creatures, cherishing the values which they have produced, and motivated by the desire creatively to transform it so that it may actualize further and greater aesthetic riches.

Delwin Brown, Ralph E. James and Gene Reeves (eds), *Process Philosophy and Christian Thought*, 1971; John B. Cobb, Jr, *A Christian Natural Theology*, 1965; *Christ in a Pluralistic Age*, 1975; *Process Theology as Political Theology*, 1982; John B. Cobb, Jr and David Ray Griffin, *Process Theology, An Introductory Exposition*, 1976; Ewert H. Cousins (ed), *Process Theology, Basic Writings*, 1971; Charles Hartshorne, *The Divine Relativity, A Social Conception of God*, 1948; *A Natural Theology for Our Time*, 1967; *Creative Synthesis and Philosophic Method*, 1970; Schubert M. Ogden, *The Reality of God*, 1967; Alfred North Whitehead, *Religion in the Making*, 1926; *Process and Reality*, 1929 ('corrected edition', ed. David Ray Griffin and Donald W. Sherburne, 1978); *Adventures of Ideas*, 1933.

DAVID A. PAILIN

Proclamation

Proclamation often translates *kerygma**. It also represents such words as *an-angello, ap-angello* (both frequent in the Septuagint), *ex-angello, kat-angello*; behind the biblical Greek stands the Hebrew *higgid* (from *ngd*), which is used for a solemn declaration, a recitation of faith before God (Deut. 26.3–10), a publication of God's name and deeds among the nations (Ps. 9.11; 40.5; etc.). In the NT *katangello* is used for proclaiming Christ (Acts 17.3; Phil. 1.17f.; Col. 1.28), the gospel (I Cor. 9.14), the word (Acts 13.5; 15.36; 17.13). At I Cor. 11.26 it refers to the eucharistic proclamation of the Lord's death until he come. *Exangello* occurs at I Peter 2.9: 'that you may proclaim the excellencies of him who called you out of darkness into his marvellous light.' Closely related in meaning is *(ex)homologeo(mai)*, which is usually rendered 'confess' (the name and

deeds of God or of Christ), the context often making clear the attitude of praise and thanksgiving (often in the Psalms and in I and II Chronicles; Rom. 15.9; Phil. 2.11; Heb. 13.15; etc.).

The good news (*eu-angelion*) is proclaimed in many ways. For example: 1. Evangelistic preaching, in different circumstances and by various methods, to invite outsiders to faith. 2. The liturgical reading of the scriptures and their exposition in homily or sermon. 3. The recitation of the creeds in the course of worship ('Denys the Areopagite', *Ecclesiastical Hierarchy*, III.3.7, calls the creed a *eucharistia*). 4. The eucharistic 'preface', a term which J. A. Jungmann derives from *prae-fari*, to 'speak before' an audience; other significant names for it have included *praedicatio, contestatio, exomologesis* (J. A. Jungmann, *The Mass of the Roman Rite*, Vol. II, 1955, pp. 102, 107, 115). 5. The Easter proclamation (*praeconium pascale*), that is, the *Exsultet* with its praise of the night of redemption ('*Haec nox est*'); since Jerome (*Letter to Praesidius*) we know that the basic theme of the blessing of the Easter light was the proclamation of the 'mysteries of the church' and the 'Passover in which the Lamb was slain'. 6. Authoritative pronouncements from the various instances of the church's teaching office.

Christian proclamation bears at least four aspects.

1. It is doxological. It is done before God and for God's glory. The message comes from God, and it leads people to call on the name of the Lord (Rom. 10.8–17). As believers speak out the faith, grace extends to more and more people, and the thanksgiving increases (II Cor. 4.13–15).

2. It is anamnetic (*see* **Anamnesis**). It 're-calls' to God and men the saving work of Christ (cf. I Cor. 11.25f.). It puts us in touch with Christ and asks God to extend and complete our redemption (see J. Jeremias, *The Eucharistic Words of Jesus*, 1966, pp. 249–55; cf. pp. 106f.). The content of Christian proclamation is bound to Jesus Christ, the Word made flesh, to whom the scriptures bear normative witness.

3. It is epicletic (*see* **Epiclesis**). The announcement of the gospel and response to it take place in the power of the Holy Spirit (I Thess. 1.5; I Cor. 12.3). That is why the Holy Spirit is 'invoked' before evangelism, worship and doctrinal definitions. God is

free to give or to withhold ('where and when God pleases' is the phrase of the Augsburg Confession, 5); on the other hand, in Christ the promises of God are sure (II Cor. 1.18–22).

4. It is eschatological*. In the midst of the present world the church as royal priesthood proclaims the mighty deeds of the God who brings from darkness to light (I Peter 2.9f.). The preaching of the gospel of God's kingdom throughout the world is a prelude to the end (Matt. 24.14); it gives all nations an opportunity freely to bow the knee and confess that Jesus Christ is Lord, to the glory of God the Father (cf. Phil. 2.10f.).

J.-J. von Allmen, *Preaching and Congregation*, 1962; J. A. Jungmann, *Announcing the Word of God*, 1967; P. Milner (ed), *The Ministry of the Word*, 1967; O. Semmelroth, *The Preaching Word: On the Theology of Proclamation*, 1965.

GEOFFREY WAINWRIGHT

Projection Theory

This claim that gods are no more than objectifications of human needs and desires forms a varied class of reductionistic accounts of theistic belief. However great the differences in detail, most projection theories exhibit a reflexive pattern: some subjective need or desire is projected outward upon some other object, but then acts reflexively upon the original subject as if it were an external agent. Such accounts, which occur both in antiquity and in modern times, may be proffered either as general theories or as theories which apply to only a limited set of theistic beliefs. Some ancient Greek philosophers held that, unlike their own rationally purified concept of the One*, the gods of popular religions were created in man's image. Within early Christian theology, Augustine intimated in his *Confessions* that, in contrast to the one true God, pagan gods were merely projections of human sexual desires and were used to legitimate lascivious behaviour on earth. A general theory of projection, encompassing every sort of deity, seems to be lacking in Western antiquity, but may be found in some varieties of Buddhism. The Tibetan *Book of the Dead*, for instance, instructs the dying that gods and devils alike are 'dream images' to which one should form no

attachment since they are but projections of inner karmic forces. General theories of projection in modern Western thought stem either from Feuerbach and Marx or from Freud and the psychoanalytic school (*see also* **Freudian Psychology**). Social psychologists such as Eric Fromm are indebted to both Marx and Freud for their understanding of projection. Ludwig Feuerbach argued that what in religion is worshipped as God is nothing more than the objectification of human nature, purified and freed from the limits of the individual self. God is self-alienated humanity. Properties traditionally predicated of him belong properly to humankind. Man can become fully human only by reclaiming those attributes for himself, by translating theology without remainder into anthropology. Karl Marx agreed that God is the self-alienated projection of human nature, but developed his case in more sociological terms than had Feuerbach. Human nature is social and historical. Religion is regarded as the product of particular social conditions; change those conditions, and religion will wither away. The influence of Feuerbach and Marx on theories of projection within recent sociology has been firmly felt, not least in the work of Peter Berger. Projection theory within psychoanalysis attempts to explain the workings of that defence mechanism discovered by Sigmund Freud whereby painful feelings or unacceptable impulses are rejected by the individual and projected upon some other person, real or imaginary, who may then become a threat to the individual. Projection is said to be a common way of dealing with anxiety and with unconscious feelings of inadequacy or insecurity. Hallucinations constitute a complex and particularly severe form of projection. Belief in gods originated, according to Freud, from the wish to be able to experience in adulthood the security of fatherly protection against external threats remembered from childhood. Gods are psychological wishes projected onto a cosmic screen. These wishes are satisfied most fully in monotheism*, in which alone is preserved the intimacy and intensity of the child's relationship to his father. Religion persists because those wishes are strong.

Robert Banks, 'Religion as Projection: A Re-Appraisal of Freud's Theory', *Religious*

Studies, IX, 1973, pp. 401–26; Peter Berger, *The Social Reality of Religion*, 1973; Van A. Harvey, 'Ludwig Feuerbach and Karl Marx', *Nineteenth-Century Religious Thought in the West*, Vol. I, ed. N. Smart, J. Clayton, S. Katz and P. Sherry, 1983; Hans Vaihinger, *The Philosophy of 'As If'*, ET 1924.

J. P. CLAYTON

Prolepsis

The principle of 'prolepsis' or real anticipation goes back *both* to the OT history of divine promise and human hope *and* to the apocalyptic eschatology of the NT. The risen Christ as 'the first fruits of those who have fallen asleep' actually anticipates that final state when God will be 'everything to everyone' (I Cor. 15.20, 28). Baptism (Rom. 6.3–8) and the eucharist (I Cor. 11.26) enact or represent now in advance what will be experienced in the ultimate and universal future.

The last line of Thomas Aquinas' antiphon for the vespers of Corpus Christi (*et futurae gloriae nobis pignus datur*) enshrines a key principle of his theology of the sacraments and grace. The sacraments, especially the eucharist, already provide believers with a real pledge of future glory (see John 6.54). The life of grace has initiated now the life of glory to come.

In recent years Wolfhart Pannenberg has stood out for his systematic appeal to the principle of prolepsis. It was there as a keynote in his theology of revelation (*Revelation as History*, 1961, ET 1969), his christology (*Jesus, God and Man*, ET 1968) and his interpretation of dogmatic statements (*Basic Questions in Theology*, ET 1970ff.). It was no surprise to find the same principle of prolepsis turning up repeatedly in Pannenberg's masterly *Theology and the Philosophy of Science* (ET 1976), when he discussed philosophical models for interpreting reality (pp. 69ff., 100ff.), hermeneutics (e.g. p. 284), religious experience (e.g. 333) and the doctrine of God (e.g. p. 310; see also 'The Question of God' (1965), in *Basic Questions in Theology*, II, 1971, pp. 201–33, especially pp. 222ff.).

Jürgen Moltmann, as well as various other exponents of the theology of hope*, political theology*, and the theology of liberation*, also uses the language of prolepsis to speak, for example, of the Christ-event* as 'a real *anticipation* of the future of history

in the midst of history' (*Religion, Revolution and the Future*, ET 1969, p. 212). Nevertheless, Moltmann's appeal to the principle of prolepsis differs from Pannenberg's not only because he insists much more on a real anticipation of the new kingdom* of God which is coming to us (as opposed to some extrapolation out of or projection from the present), but also because such an anticipation takes place in a history of divine promise* and human hope (the earlier Moltmann of *Theology of Hope*) or in the history of divine and human suffering (the later Moltmann of *The Crucified God* and subsequent works). Pannenberg characteristically has thought in terms of universal history and has had relatively little to say so far about evil and suffering.

See also **Eschatology; Hope**.

GERALD O'COLLINS

Promise and Fulfilment

These are themes of prophecy* and interpretation, especially in the Christian tradition. 'Promise' can equally be called a covenant* theme, while 'fulfilment' is correlative not only to promise and predictive prophecy but also to 'types', i.e. OT persons, events or institutions viewed as foreshadowing symbols and believed to be intended as such by God (*see* **Allegory and Typology**). The patriarchal traditions in Genesis are organized in function of covenant promise, progressively fulfilled or 'established' (*heqym*) in the rest of the Pentateuch. The Davidic kings claimed establishment by a covenant promise. The earlier prophets concentrate on moral judgment in God's name, but oracles of promise come to be added to those of judgment. The conflict between prophets of judgment and those promising prosperity (*shalom*) in divinely-protected Jerusalem are not resolved by the Deuteronomic criterion of fulfilment. The prophets of judgment came to be seen as justified, but oracles of promise were preserved, perhaps because they still awaited fulfilment. If prophecy wins recognition yet is not verified by fulfilment, it gets reinterpreted, as is often illustrated by the Targums. Themes of promise concerning the indefinite future ('in the last days') increase in late prophecy and the apocalypses*, though the messianic element can be exaggerated, and slipshod confusion of 'apocalyptic' with 'eschatology*' needs to be guarded against. Both the Qumran sect and Christianity claimed to represent the fulfilment of God's promises and symbolic hints: the former especially by interpretation (*pesher*) of OT passages with reference to their founder, the latter by similar reference to Jesus and his work ('All the promises of God find their Yes in him', II Cor. 1.20). Jesus himself preached fulfilment especially of God's promised kingdom (*basileia*, Aramaic *malkutha*), which must be understood differentially, now as God's *kingship* (proclaimed in Jesus' preaching), now as God's active *reign* (to which Jesus calls people to submit) and now as God's *realm* (initiated on earth by Jesus and his disciples, but still awaiting final fulfilment). Thereafter Christianity recognizes fulfilment of God's promises as essentially begun in the church but not yet complete, since the struggle between grace and sin continues in every age (see e.g. Augustine on Ps. 109[110]).

Christian history reveals two besetting dangers: on the one hand over-excited expectation of final fulfilment, fostered by misguided identification of details in Daniel, Revelation and subsequent 'prophecies'; on the other, an excessive identification of the kingdom with the church, its structure and liturgy, which leads to mistaking cultural fixity for the revelation of God's eternity and immutability, and to the ecclesiastical attitude described at Vatican II as 'triumphalism'. Both extremes, most dangerous respectively for fundamentalist* sects and for churches in the Orthodox and Catholic traditions, fail to maintain the necessary tension of 'already' and 'not yet' in understanding the fulfilment of God's promises in Christianity. The 1960s brought a renewal of theological thinking about the as yet unfulfilled future. The belated publication of Teilhard de Chardin's essays in evolutionary theology began to make its impact. Vatican Council II, turning decisively from a static to a more biblical and historical understanding of Christian teaching, emphasized the church's 'pilgrim' stage on the way to fulfilment (*Lumen Gentium*, chs. I, VII). Jürgen Moltmann's *Theology of Hope*, developing a model borrowed from the Marxist Ernst Bloch, re-emphasized the pivotal place of the resurrection* and viewed the future as 'the future of Christ'. The resultant theological renewal has led to a deeper awareness of the church's involvement in the world, especially through the work of J. B.

Metz and the Latin American 'liberation theology*' movement.

R. P. Carroll, *When Prophecy Failed*, 1979; J. Moltmann, *Theology of Hope*, ET 1967; G. Gutierrez, *A Theology of Liberation*, ET 1974.

R. P. R. MURRAY

Prophecy

Prophecy can be defined as human utterance believed to be inspired by a divine or transcendent source. (Prior to utterance we may speak of experience of God but not of prophecy.) Its expressions may be words, signs, actions, way of life or sacrifice of life. Utterance recognized as prophetic has played a determining part in Zoroastrianism, Israelite religion, Christianity and Islam. If the biblical data are taken as normative, the prophetic function may be exercised by men, women or children, individuals or groups, lay persons or religious ministers; it cannot, however, be exercised *ex officio* or authenticated in advance, but requires evaluation and eventual recognition by the community it addresses. Especially since Max Weber's *Sociology of Religion* it has become common to set prophet against priest, and likewise the kinds of religious community, charismatic* or institutional, which each represents and fosters. The biblical tradition with its heirs, Jewish and Christian, represents God both as commanding people to found religious institutions and as calling individuals to criticize and challenge these. The prophet claims autonomous divine authority; the institution with its counterclaim may try to silence the prophet, but if the latter wins recognition, the institution will incorporate his message within its system and will come to represent itself as embodying the prophetic function. Historically much prophecy has taken the form of poetry, and the process from conception through utterance to recognition is analogous in both. The subject matter of prophecy is as varied as its possible agents. Typically, it communicates a deeper awareness of God, of fundamental values or of the responsibility of human existence; it challenges conventional beliefs by its interpretation of the world, of past history and present events and trends, and consequently it frequently describes the future and calls for a change in attitudes and behaviour. Prediction has come to dominate the common understanding of prophecy; in reaction, Bible teachers often emphasize 'forthtelling, not foretelling', but this can underplay the importance of forward-looking and warning notes.

In ancient Israel prophecy emerges from a Semitic background of divination and ecstatic utterance, coming to prominence as a critical reaction to kingship and the royal cult, and declining with the transformation of religion after the exile. Some prophetic texts (including some psalms) point to activity within the cult, but the eighth-century prophets and Jeremiah all stress God's call for justice and mercy rather than cultic service. The Deuteronomic movement reflects an interpretation of this tendency; this led to a revision of Israelite tradition which ascribed all the essentials of religion to Moses, who combines the king's roles as legislator and cultic leader with the moral role of the prophets. The problem of the criteria for true prophecy reached its crisis with Jeremiah, but those who canonized him never formulated coherent or adequate criteria. Consequently the principles on which the other prophets were canonized remain obscure; what is clear is that the scribal establishment eventually found it possible to interpret them within its religious synthesis.

After the exile the personal claim to autonomous * authority is frequently replaced by an anonymous claim to deliver revelation * communicated by patriarchs or angels. (In perspective of the prophetic function, a distinction between prophecy and 'apocalyptic *' has little significance; too sweeping use of the latter category obscures the fundamental differences in the visionary literature which are determined by favourable or hostile attitudes to the Jewish establishment).

The autonomous voice sounds again in Jesus, though his followers soon needed other categories besides 'prophet' to evaluate his significance. The church claimed prophetic authority by its interpretation of the scriptures and by according the same status to new writings. However, the chief monument of early Christian prophecy, the book of Revelation, took about two centuries to win universal recognition, while the *Shepherd* of Hermas, early accorded almost scriptural status, later lost its appeal. The Montanist movement, in the later second century, may mark the crisis and defeat of prophecy in the early church. By the fourth century the church had developed the means of institutionalizing autonomous charismata, especially through the organization of monasticism; movements which resisted control (e.g. Messalianism and Priscillianism) were denigrated and persecuted. In the seventh century the rise of Islam could not be viewed but as false prophecy, though John Damascene's evaluation is much fairer than the later universal execration. Within the church prophecy became a charism of 'saints', but interpretation and prediction in an 'apocalyptic' style continued unbroken, on levels from theological sophistication to popular demagogy, and with intentions varying from influencing power in church and empire to helping the disorientated and oppressed to interpret the evils around them. Prophecy in the service of the church flowered in the great women Hildegard of Bingen (twelfth century), Brigitta of Sweden (thirteenth century) and Catherine of Siena (fourteenth century), who all won recognition as authentic prophets. The systematic prophetic interpretation of history by Joachim of Fiore (twelfth century) influenced, for good and even more for ill, both the Franciscan movement and many others, including Dante, whose work has a markedly prophetic dimension, and Girolamo Savonarola, whose character and work have never reached agreed evaluation. At the other end of the spectrum prophecy tended to become sectarian *, especially after the Reformation. Though the increasing institutionalization of canonization allowed no category of 'prophets' subsequent to biblical times, in the eighteenth century Prospero Lambertini (later Pope Benedict XIV) discussed the prophetic function in the most illuminating treatment till recent years. The nineteenth century brought notable resurgences of 'prophetic' activity, e.g. those which gave birth to the Catholic Apostolic Church and to the Mormons. As Russia advanced towards revolution, powerful prophetic voices arose in Fyodor Dostoyevsky and Vladimir Soloviev, followed by others down to Alexander Solzhenitsyn. Opposition to Nazism likewise produced figures of prophetic stature such as Dietrich Bonhoeffer.

Since Weber's analysis, 'charisma' and 'prophetic' have become debased to clichés through loose journalistic use. Meanwhile the systematic theology of the church has taken up again the patristic trio of Christ's functions as prophet, priest and king (used by Calvin and developed by Newman), till Vatican II could represent all the church's witness, preaching and teaching as exercise of the prophetic function. Such a view urgently needs complementing so as to respect the tension of charisma and institution which, as J.-L. Leuba argued, is constitutive of the church. The danger of exaggerating the institution's claims is moderated by a renewed emphasis on the church's historical and eschatological character (*see* **Promise and Fulfilment**), but conflict between autonomous utterance and institutional control continues, e.g. as regards the place of women in the church, the 'theology of liberation' and the nuclear disarmament and ecological movements, which claim consideration as potentially prophetic in perspectives wider than that of Christianity alone. The church as a whole cannot be prophetic in the full sense, and its official ministry as such, only rarely; but all stand under the command to evaluate potential prophecy patiently: 'do not quench the spirit, do not despise prophesying, but test everything' (I Thess. 5. 19–21). The criteria for evaluation cannot be enumerated or applied as simple rules; the recognition of the true charism of prophecy is a task for 'discernment of spirits' on the part of the whole church. Though in some instances the charism has been acclaimed almost at once and never thereafter denied (e.g. in Francis of Assisi), recognition may take so long that the prophet must be thought of as 'sent' to later times. Small groups may find that they can recognize prophecy regularly and guide their lives by it, but those who have won recognition must always be subject to the exercise of discernment. The criteria must include compatibility with the essentials of the gospel and of basic ethics, indications that the 'prophet' speaks from personal intimacy with God (stressed by Jeremiah), personal moral character, stated or apparent intentions in relation to the church and the foreseeable fruits of the 'prophet's' utterances or actions. Where the criteria seem to be met yet conflict remains, the 'prophet' must face the further test of suffering, which has often been his/her lot in history. Between the need to counter the perpetually endemic superstitions of popular pseudo-prophecy and the reasonable sense that church government cannot always wait for prophetic messages to win responsible recognition, it is understandable if Paul's injunctions have often been neglected; but the church does so at its grave peril.

J. Blenkinsopp, *Prophecy and Canon*, 1977; M. Buber, *The Prophetic Faith,* ET 1949; N. Cohn, *The Pursuit of the Millennium*, 1957, [2]1970; J. L. Crenshaw, *Prophetic Conflict*, 1971; G. Dautzenberg, *Urchristliche Prophetie*, 1975; J. D. G. Dunn, 'Prophetic "I"-Sayings and the Jesus Tradition', *NTS* 24, 1977–78, pp. 175–98; E. S. Fiorenza, 'Feminist Theology as a Critical Theology of Liberation', *TS* 36, 1975, pp. 605–26; R. Gill, *Prophecy and Praxis*, 1981; A. Heschel, *The Prophets*, 1962; D. Hill, *New Testament Prophecy*, 1979; P. Lambertini, *De Beatificatione Servorum Dei et de Canonizatione Beatorum* (1734–8) = *Heroic Virtue*, 1850–53, Vol. III, pp. 135–211; J.-L. Leuba, *New Testament Pattern*, ET 1953: J. Lindblom, *Prophecy in Ancient Israel*, ET 1962; B. McGinn, *Visions of the End, Apocalyptic Traditions in the Middle Ages*, 1979; N. I. Ndiokwere, *Prophecy and Revolution*, 1981; W. H. Oliver, *Prophets and Millennialists*, 1978; M. Reeves, *Joachim of Fiore and the Prophetic Future*, 1976; C. Rowland, *The Open Heaven*, 1982; F. A. Sullivan, *Charisms and Charismatic Renewal*, 1982, ch. 7; P. Synave and P. Benoit, *Prophecy and Inspiration. A Commentary on the Summa Theologica* II, 171–8, ET 1961; Vatican Council II: *Lumen Gentium*, ch. II; *Gaudium et Spes*, ET ed. A. Flannery, 1975; M. Weber, *The Sociology of Religion*, ET 1963; N. Zernov, *Three Russian Prophets*, 1944; *Prophecy, Concilium* 7.4, 1968.

R. P. R. MURRAY

Propitiation *see* **Atonement**

Proselytism

Proselyte was originally the Jewish word for convert, and in the Septuagint could be used to translate *ger*, the sojourner of the Pentateuch. In NT times these converts to Judaism attended the synagogue, without being circumcised, as 'godfearers'. But Palestinian Jews tried to press them into accepting the whole ritual law, including circumcision, and into renouncing both

Gentile heirs and Gentile friends. Hence perhaps Jesus' criticism of those who 'traverse sea and land' to make proselytes, only to drag them under the full weight of the law (Matt. 23.4; cf. Gal. 5.3).

In spite of this, the word proselyte remained an innocent term for convert in Christian usage. 'This is a creature,/Would she begin a sect, might quench the zeal/ Of all professors else, make proselytes/ Of who but she would follow' (*The Winter's Tale*, V, I, 108). Here the word implies a willing captivity to Perdita's intense attraction!

The OED shows the first negative use of the term in the eighteenth century, where its usage begins to reflect a typical Enlightenment* – and 'modern' – distaste for enthusiastic conviction. But the Enlightenment at least offered a stringent critique of such conviction, and that astringency can clarify and test the nature of true conviction, and indeed of conversion. Today proselytism is used in a negative sense to characterize evangelism*, both by those Christians who are dubious as to whether it is any longer necessary or justifiable, and by critics from within other faiths, who would define such evangelism as 'inducement to convert either by force or bribe', as in some recent legislation in Israel and India. The charge is hard to prove, and Christians naturally rise in protest at exaggerated allegations about the recruiting of 'rice Christians', or about Christian use and abuse of hospitals and schools to bring pressure to bear on people at a disadvantage. Christians can regard this as the seemingly distorted polemic of opponents of other faiths.

But when, as a first step to genuine evangelism, Christians start to try to see themselves as others see them, they realize just how much in the worlds of other faiths Christian mission has been associated with the traumatic effects of Western power and dominance. Christian evangelism can appear to be the extension of Western values and goals by Western methods. Both the World Council of Churches since the 1960s and the Vatican more recently have accepted the term proselytism to describe any kind of manipulation of another or encroachment upon their personal freedom to choose. Christians are beginning to see how much they have talked and how little they have listened, how they too can become prisoners within the vicious circle of polemic. Evangelists need to recognize how easy it is for them, like the Pharisees, to seek to justify themselves by making others like themselves. Proselytism in this sense of the term is the mark of spiritual immaturity. If the cross is indeed the crucial part of the Christian message for those of all faiths or none, Christians have to seek, like Paul, to commend it most by bearing the marks of it on their own bodies, their very selves. They need a 'crucified mind' (Koyama). In many areas today it may be that 'the role of scapegoat may be the creative expression of evangelism' (David Kerr). There are some Third-World evangelists who can teach Western Christians how to enter more deeply into the death and risen life of the one who sent them, to arrive at gift exchange, in a context of simple friendship. The language of humble love speaks across all barriers to attract all men freely to its source.

B. Bamberger, *Proselytism in the Talmudic Period*, 1968; Vincent J. Donovan, *Christianity Rediscovered*, 1978; W. G. Braude, *Jewish Proselytising in the First Five Centuries of the Common Era*, 1940; A. D. Nock, *Conversion*, 1933; Don Richardson, *The Peace Child*, 3 1974; Samuel Sandmel, *Judaism and Christian Beginnings*, 1978; Bilquis Sheikh, *I Dared to Call Him Father*, 1979; Philip Van Akkeren, *Sri and Christ –A Study of the Indigenous Church in East Java*, 1970.

SIMON BARRINGTON-WARD

Prosopon

A term used as an alternative to *hypostasis* * to express the plurality of the Godhead. In secular Greek usage it could mean an actor's role or mask but rarely a concrete individual. In wider theological usage it could express the Hebrew conception of the face of God, his form or manifestation, and in exegetical contexts it could pin-point the application of an OT passage to the richer subject-matter of the Christian revelation. In trinitarian usage it enjoyed a vogue among Western writers who wrote in Greek. Here it secured a greater firmness of application possibly as a result of the influence of the Latin *persona*. Early modalists* seem to have used the word for the One God and not for his temporary manifestations, though it is possible that at a later stage the word acquired Sabellian undertones. Seldom used at Alexandria (Athanasius uses it only in anti-Sabellian passages), it failed to maintain itself in Eastern theological terminology. The existence of the more adequate alternative *hypostasis* and its lack of metaphysical background militated against its adoption.

The term played its part in the terminological misunderstandings which were resolved by the Council of Alexandria (362). Its use as a translation of the Latin *persona* was suspected (together with the generally monist approach of the West) of Sabellian influence.

In christology it is used by Antiochene theologians (Theodore of Mopsuestia and particularly by Nestorius) in an attempt to provide a satisfactory alternative theory of the unity of the Person of Christ to the Cyrilline use of *hypostasis*.

See also **Person**.

H. E. W. TURNER/FRANCES YOUNG

Protestantism

The word 'Protestants' was applied in political circles to the Lutheran signatories of the Protest made at the Diet of Speyer, 19 April 1529, against the annulment of that decision of the Diet of 1526 by which, until a church council should meet, the governments of individual states were to regulate religious affairs. The term was soon applied to Lutherans in general and finally to all adherents of the Reformation* including Anglicans and left-wing groups. Few of the many branches of Protestantism have adopted the designation 'Protestant' in their titles. In many minds it beats connotations of controversy and of contrast with 'Catholicism', where this term is made equivalent to Roman Catholicism. In this sense the word becomes a convenience for statisticians. Protestantism has always shown great variety and rapid change. Sharp internal controversies and numerous secessions on points of theology or conscience were long characteristic; but this individualistic trend was indirectly conducive to the liberal recognition of variety. Early in the twentieth century scholars drew a clear distinction between the Old and the New Protestantism. The latter is marked by adoption of the principle of disengagement of the church from the state together with that of toleration, thus showing the influence or imitation of the opinions of earlier spiritual humanists, Baptists and Independents. These con-

cepts were most effectively written into political theory by John Locke. The New Protestantism has also been profoundly affected by two movements that gained headway in the nineteenth century and are still rapidly advancing, critical biblical scholarship and the physical and biological sciences. Protestant foreign missions were instituted largely on the initiative of individuals, but their vigorous activities led to the enlistment of entire denominations with the growth of a vast network of organization. This century is strongly marked by a movement away from Protestant individualism. The disadvantages of a competing denominational approach to missions became painfully apparent and various plans of co-operation were put into effect, many of which have already resulted in acts of union. The Ecumenical* Movement has felt a strong impulse from missions and missionary organization; but it is also a revival of the largely frustrated unitive projects and efforts of the Reformers and their seventeenth-century followers, and has been shared by Eastern Orthodoxy. Ecumenical Protestantism and Orthodoxy are now in friendly contact with Roman Catholicism. This new development is thought of by some as prelude to a veritable transformation of Christianity in its structures, worship forms, and functions in relation to the world society and non-Christian religions.

Karl Barth, *Protestant Theology in the Nineteenth Century*, ET 1972; J. C. Brauer, *Protestantism in America*, 1965; J. Dillenberger and C. Welch, *Protestant Christianity*, 1954; G. W. Forell, *The Protestant Spirit*, 1960; A. Heron, *A Century of Protestant Theology*, 1980; P. Tillich, *The Protestant Era*, 1951; J. S. Whale, *The Protestant Tradition*, 1955.

J. T. MCNEILL

Protestant Principle

A phrase sometimes used by Protestant theologians to denote what is considered to be the central affirmation of Protestantism, namely, the doctrine of justification* by faith*, *sola fide*, *sola gratia*. The phrase has been used in a more specialized sense by Tillich. He contrasted the Protestant principle with the Catholic substance (i.e. the dogmatic tradition), and held that the latter needs to be constantly corrected and reformed by the former, understood as implying critical questioning in the light of the sources.

ALAN RICHARDSON/
JOHN MACQUARRIE

Providence

In its strict sense divine providence refers to God's prior knowledge of and provision for the world, being derived from the Latin *providentia*. In practice, however, the term is usually used to refer both to this foreknowledge and to God's *government* of nature, man, and history. Christian writers have distinguished different aspects of this government as it is displayed in the Bible. There is God's creative activity, especially as recounted in Genesis. There is the sustaining activity of God as he upholds man and the world (e.g. Isa. 41.10). There is the activity that came to be called 'general providence', which refers to God working in and through the natural order, as when he makes the rain fall on the just and on the unjust (Matt. 5.45). There is what some writers would later call 'special providence', as when God speaks through a prophet, or works through some other *specific* action. Finally, there is what came to be called miracle*, that is, when a specific action is one that defies any purely natural explanation. Although all five of these activities relate to providence in a broad sense, most theologians restrict the term to the categories of general and special providence, sometimes using both these expressions, and sometimes, like Aquinas, assuming both under the term 'providence'.

The most controversial aspect of these distinctions concerns miracle. The distinction here is not a biblical one, since it only arises when nature is seen as an *order*, with its own laws and autonomy. In Aquinas, because of his overall philosophy of nature, we find a sharp distinction between providence, wherein God works 'interiorily in all things' (*ST* 1a, q.105, a.5), and miracle, which is 'something that happens outside the whole realm of nature' (*ST* 1a, q.114, a.4). Many recent theologians have rejected this distinction, sometimes because of a nervousness as to whether God can or does intervene in nature, sometimes because of uncertainty about the maning of being 'beyond' nature. Others maintain that some distinction along the lines of Aquinas' position is essential: for example, in order to make the resurrection significant.

A closely related issue concerns the notion of 'universal providence', as implied in the Bible, and taught explicitly by Calvin. According to this, God is in direct control of every event, including every human thought and action. But in this case what sense can be made of human responsibility and free will*? Aquinas and his followers, while sometimes using language that suggests a universal providence, especially when discussing grace, tend to describe nature and man in a way that leaves room for some real autonomy. The doctrine of primary and secondary causality is the chief element in this approach, which Aquinas contrasted with the absolutist account of God's rule taught by contemporary Islamic philosophers. While God is 'first cause' of all things, the immediate or secondary cause of events in nature ought to be sought in nature itself. To deny this, Aquinas claimed, was to detract from the power of God in creation.

Recent thinkers have found other ways of trying to preserve a significant doctrine of providence while rejecting universal providence. Christian existentialists*, such as Bultmann, restrict God's providence to the human order, where they see it as personal rather than mechanical or coercive. There is some support for this view in the NT, where the emphasis is on man's interior change, through forgiveness and redemption, rather than exterior change, through the manipulation of nature or other persons. However, although the actual word for providence, *pronoia*, is used only once, and then to refer to human forethought (Acts 24.2), there is no doubt that God's providential activity is seen as pervasive, and not as limited to the human order. Another important approach can be found in the process philosophers, following the lead of Whitehead (*see also* **Process Theology**). Although this school of thought does not limit God's influence to the human order, as do many of the existentialists, it sees God's influence everywhere as being persuasive rather than coercive, and in the working out of this view some thinkers are prepared seriously to modify traditional accounts of God's omnipotence* and omniscience. This they regard as essential if we are to preserve meaning in the notion of human freedom, and of God's loving relationship with man. Within their view of providence, since God works by a continuous persuasion that respects the freedom and dignity of man, there can be a sort of inevitability in the long run, and thus a significance in the idea of providence, but there has also to be a radical contingency in the short run, with a consequent stress on human responsibility.

The doctrine of providence, while much neglected in recent times, is crucial for theological reflection. Without it the idea of God is largely irrelevant to what is going on in the world. Moreover, the view that one holds as to the nature of providence affects the Christian approach to prayer and action. For example, is a nuclear war necessarily going to occur, or to be avoided, by divine providence, or has providence left this as contingent on our prayers and actions, with the terrifying responsibility that this entails? *See also* **Foreknowledge, Free Will, Predestination.**

Aquinas, S T 1a, qs. 19–25, 103–5; M. J. Langford, *Providence*, 1981; W. G. Pollard, *Chance and Providence*, 1958; M. Wiles (ed), *Providence*, 1969.

M. J. LANGFORD

Psychological Analogy

This is an attempt to cast light on the mystery of the Trinity by investigating triadic structures in the working of the human mind. The first to develop the analogy in depth was Augustine. He was influenced by the Neoplatonic* tradition, which envisaged a triad of the One* (who is above being) giving rise to Mind (*nous*) and the World-Soul. Augustine adapted this conception to the Christian doctrine of the Trinity in the second half of his work of that title. Starting from the presuppositions that man is the image of God, and that that image will be found above all in the highest part of man, namely his mind (*animus*), Augustine examined the workings of the mind for traces of the trinitarian pattern. He first considered the triadic pattern of human love (the lover, the beloved and the love); when the analogy is applied to the Trinity, the Spirit, corresponding to human love, is the bond between the first and second Persons. Augustine then pointed to a number of similar patterns in the workings of the mind: most important, the mind, knowing and loving itself (love is the bond

between mind and knowledge); memory (i.e. self-consciousness), understanding and will (which again is the bond between the first two members of the triad); and, at the highest level, the mind remembering, knowing and loving God.

K. Rahner criticized Augustine's use of the analogy in that it is based on a questionable analysis of human knowledge and love which assumes that knowledge involves the production of a mental image of the thing known. But, like K. Barth (*CD* I/1, p. 389), he allows that the analogy has a value in illustrating a doctrine which has already been accepted on other grounds.

See also **Analogy, Trinity, Vestigia Trinitatis.**

Augustine, *The Trinity*, in *Augustine: Later Works*, ed. J. Burnaby, LCC, 1955; K. Rahner, *The Trinity*, ET 1970, pp. 115–20.

E. J. YARNOLD

Psychology of Religion

The psychology of religion in the twentieth century has had as varied and chequered a history as that of theology. Failure to recognize the diversity of psychological approaches to religion and the diversity of theological views of psychology has been one of the main stumbling blocks in attempts at better correlations of the two.

At several points in the century relations between psychology and theology have been little better than those between the village atheist and the village preacher – and with the covert interdependence that the allusion may suggest. Psychologists' concern with establishing a professional identity as scientists led them to be wary of terms like soul* and spirit, the autonomy of belief or the question of whether specifically, even exclusively, religious phenomena could be found. On the other side, theology was wary of what it saw as determinism* or reductionism* in psychological thought and was hesitant, if not fearful, about new and powerful relations between body, emotions and psyche to which parts of the new sciences addressed themselves. Both theology and psychology tended to operate on different sides of a shared dualistic view of human beings.

An important ingredient in recent rethinking of the standard positions has come from clearer understandings that at least three partners, each comprising many variants, are involved in dialogue and not just two: psychologies, theologies and religions. Recognition of this pluriform situation avoids the errors of thinking of psychology as a single monolithic method and the highly contested question of whether there is or is not an 'essence' of religion apart from or inherent in the various religious traditions.

The diversity of studies embraced by psychology and its derivation from specifically modern Western assumptions can be seen if one asks what kind of science it is and what its objects are. If, on one definition, it is taken as the science of the mind and of mental phenomena, then it shares with modern Western thought in general barely compatible ideas of what the mind is.

Thus psychology may span the study of areas as diverse as brain processes and bodily states in humans and animals; the development of personality, the perceptions, values and feelings of individuals; interpersonal relations of friendship, sexuality, hostility, the interactions of family groups, the processes of aging, dying and mourning; the social and collective behaviour of groups from football crowds to nations. Some parts of psychology belong in subject matter and method with the natural sciences; other parts are more relevantly to be grouped with the social sciences of anthropology, sociology and politics. It is obvious that in the end mind and matter are, for both theologian and psychologist, in some way connected. What is certain is that no single line of approach can characterize psychology *per se*. Methods suitable for the investigation of brain and chemistry are no more appropriate for the study of the psychology of religious vegetarianism, say, than vice versa. Behaviourism in psychology was a response to this troublesome imprecision. Rejecting all discussion of intention and subjectivity it restricted itself to the study of observable behaviour in relation to environment.

Such considerations are relevant to the question of whether a psychology of religion is reductionistic. Certainly there has been *a priori* anti-religious animus in much psychology of religion. Whether the approach be that of psychoanalysis, experimental or social psychology there has been a desire to reduce religion to infantile or historical origins or to see it as merely a confused variant of other than religious factors. This was part and parcel of the crusading zeal of a new science keen to demonstrate its credentials. The simplistic elements in this have started to abate as the resistance of religious and other phenomena to exhaustive explanation has persisted and as the confidence of psychology as an ordinary ingredient in intelligent reflection upon life has increased. What can still cause confusion on both sides is inadequate recognition of the correct limits of a science of human behaviour and experience. Insofar as it is a science, psychology will tend in terms of its methods to be agnostic about the reference point of non-ordinary or transcendent experiences, and it will favour parsimony of explanation. Ideological reductionism as an anti-religious bias and scientific reductionism as the attempt to establish unarguable essentials need careful clarification if a fruitful dialogue of psychology and theology is to continue.

The founding period of the psychology of religion lay in the first two decades of this century. William James's *The Varieties of Religious Experience* (Gifford Lectures 1901–1902) remains as an impressively thought-provoking example of these early inquiries. There is always a tendency for the psychologist of religion implicitly to define religious phenomena in terms of the assumptions about psychology he has or the psychological tenets he wishes to exemplify. In James's case the emphasis is functional and adaptive: religious experience is seen as a given and religious reality is seen as a power or force experienced as outside or beyond a person's normal awareness. The effects of this experience of power are studied in terms of their facilitating personal and social adaptation and adjustment. This line of interest made experiences of conversion a focal point for early researchers. The movement from initial sudden experiences of isolation and guilt through to their resolution and readjustment of personality are carefully described and discussed. The appeal of conversion* experiences was obvious: psychological and specifically religious factors seemed to combine in a single experience which was open to investigation. This focus was important, if ultimately limiting, for the psychology of religious life is not exhausted by study of conversion experiences and such experiences are not necessarily crucial to the definition of religion. But these early classic works were overtaken more by changes in the general culture than by their inherent limitations. Psychology of religion, after this very promising start, failed to develop in any systematic way that could command the continuing attention of psychologists, theologians and students of religion.

In psychology, growing professionalism and the desire for an identifiable scientific method led to a renewed stress upon highly detailed experimental or clinical work; the emphasis was upon controlled observations and replication – a development at odds with the experiential and biographical emphasis of James. Further, there was a drastic simplification of the hodge-podge of concerns inherited as 'psychology' in terms of a behaviourist norm; all non-observable and not readily testable phenomena were excluded from, or at least bracketted in, psychological investigation. The new science was to restrict itself to observable and measurable overt behaviour, whether of persons or their bodies. Behaviourism as an intelligible research strategy also became an ideology. Because psychology as a science restricted itself to overt behaviour, it came mistakenly to be assumed that everything other than overt behaviour was epiphenomenal. Theologians were not alone in resisting this ideology; much important work in the sciences of religion between the wars was carried out by the less hidebound anthropologists and sociologists.

The period 1900–1920 also saw the flourishing of psychoanalysis, which, at this early period, seemed radically to undercut the Jamesian approach to religion as well as contribute, by reaction, to the narrowing of professional psychology, though in its Freudian* form it shared the standard psychological stance of excluding religion as a part of normal experience.

There were also changes in the religious world which made the Jamesian approach seem dated. Not only had theologians to adjust to the new situation of a polarization between psychoanalysis and professional psychology; the rise of Barthianism and other later 'existentialist' theology denied key points in the assumed common ground upon which James and his contemporaries had worked. In the reaction to liberal* Protestantism the very term 'religion' became questionable as one of other than Christian opprobrium. Emphasis fell upon 'theological existence' rather than religious experience*, and suspicion of scientific reductionism made for hostility rather than collaboration in any psychology of religion. With the rise of psychological behaviourism on the one hand and theological existentialism on the other, both psychologists and theologians tended to agree that there could be no such thing as a psychology of religion.

The subject languished, and it is only in recent times that there has been a significant quickening of interest as both theology and psychology have in their seperate ways been forced to move beyond the securities of living within the now ossified limits of the bold departures of half a century ago.

Since there is not a single clear-cut science called psychology, psychology of religion will always be at most a useful umbrella term for a variety of psychological approaches to religions. Modern academic and professional psychology no longer tends to define itself in terms of the rivalry of major schools like behaviourism and psychoanalysis, but rather in terms of areas of inquiry. Thus experimental psychology has three main branches: developmental, concerned with the mental process and maturation of the child; cognitive, concerned with perception and learning in adults; and social psychology, which now includes the study of attitudes, motivation and personality. Findings in these areas relate to the various branches of applied psychology: clinical, educational, industrial, occupational, etc. Whilst this taxonomy is neutral with regard to different schools of thought, in practice the old conflicts remain. Psychological work relevant to religion does not readily fit in with this taxonomy, and it is perhaps simplest to think of five major strands or lines of approach.

1. Phenomenological psychology has drawn on the James tradition and also on phenomenological and existentialist philosophy. It focusses upon the structure of consciousness and immediate experience of the individual in relation to social roles and situations. Its forté has tended to be descriptive and philosophical. The work of R. D. Laing and his associates has advanced this approach to incorporate ideas from psychoanalysis and Marxism* to give a group or social explanation of conditions

like schizophrenia. In phenomenological accounts of such borderline conditions of personal identity religious issues can arise and be sensitively handled, as, for instance, in Aaron Esterson's *The Leaves of Spring*.

2. Psychoanalysis has demonstrated that basic preoccupations of human beings with food, God, sex, life and death are more fundamentally linked for good as well as ill than some people have affected to believe. With its distinctive emphasis upon the role of fantasy as a causal factor in human behaviour (largely negative in the case of Freud, far less so in Jung), psychoanalysis has made important, if often questionable, changes in the understanding of religious behaviour and religious symbolism. The Freudian tendency has been largely anti-religious, reducing myths and symbols to illusory representations of the past, whether that of the individual or a group, in order to clear the way for a rational decision in the present. However, from the outset, with Freud's colleague the Protestant pastor Oskar Pfister, there have been significant attempts to draw on psychoanalytic theory within Christian thinking. Often this is seen as a way of purifying religious belief of illusory or distorted features such as neurotic guilt, God as a projected father-figure, the denial or deflection of the role of sexuality. The psychoanalytic account is taken as prophylactic to proper religious understanding, not as an alternative to it.

Psychoanalytic theories are usually at their most persuasive in terms of individual cases, and there have been important biographical studies of religious figures from this perspective – Erikson's *Young Man Luther* being the most obvious example. There are also a small number of psychoanalytically informed studies of a more generally historical kind like Erich Fromm's *The Dogma of Christ*. Despite major efforts by some Jungians*, psychoanalysis has produced little on non-Western traditions to match its work on Judaism and Christianity. In recent decades psychoanalytic ideas, both intelligently selective and merely eclectic, have become far more taken for granted as part of the acceptable intellectual equipment and therapeutic repertoire of secular and religiously minded Westerners alike. Though rarely remarked, it remains true that psychoanalysis was and is the only systematic attempt in this century to give an account of the origin and nature of personality, what the Western tradition terms the soul, other than a religious one. In so far as Christian apologetic has taken the soul as its bedrock, psychoanalysis remains among the most potent of its rivals.

3. Developmental psychology, drawing primarily on Gestalt theory and the work of Piaget, is concerned at its most ambitious with establishing invariant stages of cognitive, moral and psychological development in human beings. It thus by definition has the advantage of being cross-cultural, but it also tends to make no distinction between traditional and modern societies or between religious and non-religious factors. Nonetheless it has led to the development of a large body of work on the religious development of the child and the implications of this for religious education. There have also been studies of the variations in religious feelings and affiliations at different stages of life.

4. Those branches of psychology concerned with physiology and brain functioning have had little relevant bearing on religious issues. A major change, however, may have been initiated in the last fifteen years or so with research into hallucinogens, altered states of consciousness, and related claims for distinctive functions (rational, intuitive, etc.) for the two hemispheres of the brain. It is too early to be sure, but apart from revival of interest in the psychology of mysticism in this wholly unexpected context a major change in the fundamental orientations of mainstream psychology may follow from the confluence of this work and that arising from the increasingly widespread varieties of psychotherapy and counselling.

5. Social psychology includes a very large body of research on personality types, attitudes, values and motivations investigating correlations between, say, authoritarianism and teetotalism or church schooling and incidence of religious practice or differing attitudes to work among Catholics and Quakers. Research of this kind is increasingly drawn upon by church bodies themselves. In psychological studies of religion from this perspective certain basic strategies of inquiry can be observed. The key issues are whether the correlations proposed are taken as simply descriptive or whether one (usually the non-religious one) is given preference or even explanatory power, and

whether there are any specifically religious variables – i.e. whether there are elements which are only intelligible on religious grounds. In general, work here has tended to use religious data as exemplifications of religiously neutral theories, e.g. churches as a genus of the species 'institutions'. There are at least four major possibilities here. The first could be called neutral: parallel features of sociability may be found in the reasons people give for belonging to a church and belonging to a club. Sociability is tested without any necessary implication for membership of one or the other. Or, such correlations may be studied because certain ordinary variables are especially prominent in religious data: for instance, are church-goers more likely to be politically conservative or radical than a sample of non-churchgoers? In both these cases the religious data are basically an extra resource for testing psychological hypotheses rather than an investigation into religion as such.

There is a significant change when enquiry is directed by a search for a specifically religious factor. It may be argued that in religion there is a unique *constellation* of variables also found separately elsewhere, so that religion is distinctive, but distinctive as a particular combination of factors in standard psychological study. Alternatively, the stronger claim can be made for a not only distinctive but uniquely separate variable, e.g. 'the religious factor', a 'religious sentiment', or the impact of a numinous experience.

If we turn to theological responses to psychology, several general strategies can be observed, regardless of the school of psychological thought addressed. (i) A suspicion of psychological approaches to experience and religious experience in particular. Here there tends to be a retreat to biblical or other justifications for rejecting scientific investigation of human personality on the grounds of alleged reductionism, materialism or general secularity. In consequence there is often the assertion that traditional Christianity has within itself sufficient or superior means of responding to the mysteries of experience, its peaks and its troughs, and that recourse to secular theories and techniques would be to admit a deficiency or limitation in the religious view of life. (ii) A more positive response recognizes the separate resources of both the bib-

lical and later Christian tradition and those of psychology as legitimate and complementary. (iii) There can be a radical acceptance of psychological truth as part of God's truth (Paul Tillich would be an obvious example). This position can be particularly attractive to Christians with a strongly incarnational belief, seeing psychological discoveries as a twentieth-century correlate of incarnational thinking.

These latter two responses are most attuned to the growth of various schools of pastoral counselling, but over the last twenty years few branches of the Christian church have not developed some form of counselling training. Pastoral counselling can range from pragmatic response to specific personal problems to the adoption of particular theological or thereapeutic positions. This development is partly a consequence of the increasing taken-for-grantedness of psychological and especially psychotherapeutic notions in contemporary culture, and partly a response to what are experienced as intolerable crises of family relationships, child development and religious vocation in the latter half of the century. What is at issue here is the profound and painful tensions of traditional assumptions and practices under strain. This is particularly so with the transformation of attitudes towards sexuality, its centrality and its mysterious and occasionally frightening variations, and the increasing if very uneven reassessment of relations between men and women, a struggle to discover to redefine equality and difference here which runs against the greater part of religious and secular history.

This multiple crisis in such fundamental areas as sexual identity, authority, the family, the religious life, focusses upon the questions: What is it to be a person? What is it to be the person I am and the person I could or should be? Such questions are perennially religious ones, but they occur at present in an urgently pervasive and public form to which the existing psychological and religious resources are not seen as generally adequate. There are signs of greater humility both among psychologists and theologians as they face the necessarily ambiguous powerful demands for self-assertion and personal quest, involving selfishness as well as self-realization.

Like theologians, psychologists have had to reassess their understanding of humanity's place in nature and arrive at a better balance between the claims of groups and the claims of individuals. The increasing attention given to death and the processes of dying and mourning is one instance of novel kinds of work generated in this context. Research on hallucinogenic drugs like LSD from the 1960s onwards has produced a body of writings on 'altered states of consciousness', whether these are artificially induced or arise from meditational or yogic practice. This has put psychological studies of mysticism and religious experience back upon the agenda after a very long period of neglect. Another sign of change is in the psychotherapeutic area with the development of 'transpersonal psychology', which respects the spiritual aspect of experience and draws upon Eastern and Western spiritual traditions, symbols and myths as well as Western psychological and scientific theories in trying to elucidate the unique nature of the individual's quest for meaning. In any such development there is scope for naive eclecticism and innocent or not-so-innocent quackery, but the basic impulse is a positive and inspiring one.

As stressed at the outset, future fruitful work will not arise from seeking a comprehensive psychological theory of an essence of religion, but from multiple small initiatives in the critical context in which psychologists and theologians are now operating.

Michael Argyle and Benjamin Beit-Hallahmi, *The Social Psychology of Religion*, 1975; L. B. Brown, *Psychology and Religion*, 1973; Heije Faber, *Psychology of Religion*, 1976; H. N. Maloney (ed), *Current Perspectives in the Psychology of Religion*, 1977.

ADRIAN CUNNINGHAM

Purgatory *see* Life after Death

Puritanism

Many distinct and mutually discordant movements reflecting the influence of their personal founders are embraced within historic Puritanism. Tendencies analogous to Puritanism are easily identified in the teaching and discipline of Stoics, Pharisees, monastic reformers and mediaeval biblical sects. In Tudor England the influence of the continental Protestant refugees Martin Bucer, Peter Martyr Vermigli, John à Dasco

and others, and of the writings of Heinrich Bullinger and John Calvin, and the associations formed by the Marian Exiles, contributed notably to the shaping of the Puritan spirit. In the reign of Elizabeth I those who on narrowly scriptural grounds objected to ceremonies and vestments prescribed in the *Book of Common Prayer* were called 'precisians' or 'puritans', and the word was also applied to opponents of the Anglican episcopate, many of whom shared the same scruples on ceremonial. Many classed as Puritans sought the recognition of their principles within the establishment; others readily formed separatist groups. Theologically Puritanism was far from homogeneous, but the larger segments, Presbyterians, Independents and Baptists, were prevailingly Calvinist. On predestination, a number of outstanding Puritans, such as John Goodwin and Richard Baxter, were nearer to the Arminian* position. William Perkins (d. 1602) and in the seventeenth century William Ames, John Preston, John Milton, John Bunyan, Richard Baxter and John Owen were among representative Puritan writers on theology and ethics. Puritan piety rested upon scripture and was in only a few instances mystical. It tended to emphasize the experience of conversion, daily self-examination, and a firm and demanding moral code for social and economic life, for which numerous treatises on casuistry were written. Puritan teaching on austerity and industrious pursuit of one's calling as service to God and man has been associated with the rise of capitalism, but can be largely duplicated from typical Anglican writers. The Mayflower Pilgrims were separatists who had been in exile in the Netherlands, while the Massachusetts Bay colony consisted of Puritans who had never broken from the Church of England and refused to be classed as separatists. American Puritanism produced much serious theological writing, culminating in the brilliant and original Jonathan Edwards (d. 1758).

P. Collinson, *The Elizabethan Puritan Movement*, 1967; C. H. George and K. George, *The Protestant Mind of the English Reformation*, 1961; W. Haller, *The Rise of Puritanism*, 1938; M. M. Knappen, *Tudor Puritanism*, 1939; J. T. McNeill, *Modern Christian Movements*, 1954; 1968.

J. T. MCNEILL

Quakers *see* **Friends, Society of**

Rapture

In salvation history the rapture is the expected event when the Lord Jesus will return to raise the blessed dead, and believers who are still alive will, 'changed' (I Cor. 15.51f.), be 'caught up' with them (*harpagēsometha*; *rapiemur*) in the clouds to meet the Lord in the air, 'and so we shall always be with the Lord' (I Thess. 4.13–18). Dispensationalists * distinguish between a first and secret return of the Lord for the rapture and his final manifest return in glory after a seven-year period of tribulation upon earth to establish his millennial kingdom (J. F. Walvoord, *The Rapture Question,* 1957; *The Blessed Hope and the Tribulation,* 1976); but the biblical evidence for this is not compelling (see G. E. Ladd, *A Theology of the New Testament,* 1974, pp. 550–68).

An anticipation of the rapture may come to the individual in mystical experience, and the NT basis for this is found in Paul's description of 'a man in Christ' who was 'caught up' (*harpagenta*; *raptum*) to the third heaven or paradise (II Cor. 12.1–4). To the being 'rapt out of the senses' Richard Rolle, in *The Fire of Love*, prefers the rapture of the self-possessed lifting of the mind to God in loving contemplation, which is a 'foretaste of everlasting sweetness'. Sexual imagery often accompanies mystical experience (cf. the church as bride, II Cor. 11.2; Eph. 5.25–27; Rev. 21.2, 9), and 'to know' is used biblically of human intercourse and of knowing God. Our knowing God is eschatological (I Cor. 13.12).

The grace may be irresistible, but the element of willing consent is expressed by P. Tillich's notion of 'ecstatic reason' (*Systematic Theology* I, 1952, pp. 124–30; III, 1964, pp. 121–27). Mystical experience sometimes issues in poetry, and the selection of Wesleyan hymns by H. A. Hodges and A. M. Allchin is aptly entitled *A Rapture of Praise* (1966).

GEOFFREY WAINWRIGHT

Rationalism

This term is used in at least three different senses in philosophical and theological contexts.

1. It is often used to designate the epistemological posture taken by such thinkers as Descartes, Spinoza and Leibniz in the seventeenth and eighteenth centuries on the Continent of Europe. The *goal* of this approach to knowledge was that of objective certainty. The *method* for achieving this goal was deductive or demonstrative reasoning from a *basis* of self-evident truths ('I think, therefore I am') or innate ideas ('The cause must be at least as great as the effect'). These thinkers believed that one can formulate these indubitable truths into definitions and axioms from which it is possible to deduce yet further purely rational knowledge, all without the aid of any experiential verification. This posture was and is contrasted to empiricism, the approach of such British thinkers as Locke and Hume, which maintained that knowledge and ideas derive from sense-experience alone.

2. In theological contexts the term is frequently used to designate a tradition, from Aquinas to the deists *, that held that there are certain things that can be known about God by the use of human reason alone, without the aid of revelation or the activity of the Holy Spirit. It was held by many to be possible to demonstrate the existence, power and wisdom of God by the use of rational arguments based on the implications of certain concepts, such as 'necessary being' (thus the ontological * proof of God's existence), or certain aspects of experience, such as motion and causation (thus the first cause proof), contingency (the cosmological proof), design (the teleological proof), and morality (the moral value proof. *See also* **Arguments for the Existence of God**).

3. In the nineteenth century the term became equated with secularism *, or atheism *, or agnosticism *, terms designating positions which base their rejection of religious belief on the use of human reason. In recent years thinkers who take these positions generally refer to themselves as humanists rather than as rationalists (*see also* **Humanism**). However, there is also an increasing tendency for the term to take on a negative connotation in religious circles, especially with respect to the claims of science. 'Scientific rationalism' is now often seen as an enemy of religion because it refuses to acknowledge the possibility of truth which is extra-scientific.

JERRY H. GILL

Realism *see* **Nominalism**

Real Presence
see **Eucharistic Theology**

Reason

In theological and religious circles the axis of the discussion revolving around this concept has to do with its relation to the notion of revelation* and/or faith*.

1. There have been those, and there are many today, who define this relation as one of antagonism or at least dichotomization. Some of these thinkers maintain that human reason, along with other aspects of the image of God, has become completely unreliable as a source of knowledge about God. Tertullian went so far as to say, 'I believe *because* it's absurd.' In modern times such thinkers as Hume, Kant, and Kierkegaard all agreed that reason must be set aside in order to allow for faith.

2. There have been and still are those thinkers who contend that the relation between reason and faith is one of harmony, if not identification. For some this means that faith flows from or is based upon the reasoning process. Certain mediaeval Islamic thinkers, such as Averroes and Avicenna (*see* **Averroism**), took this approach, while in the West modern deists* argued for what Locke termed 'the reasonableness of Christianity'. There are, of course, those who maintain that a reliance on human reason necessitates giving up on the notion of faith altogether.

3. A view which also has both traditional and contemporary advocates is that which asserts that reason can only operate on the basis of certain faith commitments or within certain revelatory frameworks. The idea here is that once the basic truth about God and/or Christ has been given and received we can and must use reason to comprehend its meaning and implications. This was the view of Augustine, who said 'I believe in order to understand', and of Pascal, who said, 'The heart has reasons that reason knows not of.' Karl Barth might be taken as a twentieth-century exponent of this approach.

4. There is the point of view that sees the relation between reason and faith as one of separation without inequality. It is possible to view reason as providing an important, even though limited knowledge of God based on the nature of the universe and human moral experience (frequently termed 'general revelation'), while at the same allowing faith to serve as the proper response to God's self-disclosure (termed 'special revelation'). Aquinas, for instance, claimed that all people can know *that* God exists, as well as something about God's power, wisdom, and goodness, by reason alone, but that we only know *who* God is by means of revelation received through faith. William Temple, Austin Farrer, John Smith and Bernard Lonergan are all modern-day proponents of this posture, though they all see reason and faith as related more functionally and less separably than Aquinas.

JERRY H. GILL

Recapitulation

The word is the Latin equivalent of the Greek *anacephalaiosis*, a summing up, or summary. The term occurs in Eph. 1.10, where it is stated that God summed up all things in Christ. Irenaeus (*c.* 130–*c.* 200) made it especially his own, interpreting the term both as the restoration* of fallen humanity to communion with God by the incarnation* and as the summing up and completion of the entire *Heilsgeschichte** in the incarnation. This idea was taken up by the Fathers, and its importance in a theology of the atonement will be readily appreciated. The recapitulation in Christ connotes the total work of God for man's redemption. In Christ are summed up the 'sure word of prophecy', which had always looked for a new Messiah, a new redemption*, a new exodus, a new covenant*, a new inheritance, a new eternal hope*. More is being said in this doctrine than that Christ sums up all the prophecies, aspirations, hopes and promises associated with the OT. It means also that none of these ideas of the OT can be appreciated unless they be interpreted 'backwards from Christ'. Recapitulation means the summing up in Christ of God's long and sure purpose of redemption, a dimension meant to include not only the present aeon of incarnation but the eternal aeon of ascension.

JAMES ATKINSON

Reconciliation
see **Atonement, Forgiveness**

Redemption

The concept is derived from one of the most basic features of human life in society: the urge to exchange something in one's own possession for something possessed by another. All kinds of objects have been exchanged, normally with the conviction that what was received was equal to or even more valuable than what was given.

Redemption, meaning *buying back*, implies that a situation has existed in which an individual or a society has been brought into some kind of bondage. This may have been of an earthly kind, e.g. an individual may have become a slave, or a tribe may have been subjugated by a stronger nation. Alternatively the bondage may have been of a superhuman kind, e.g. an individual may believe himself to have been paralysed by a spell or a taboo or by some demonic agent; a society may be deemed to lie under a ban or a sentence of condemnation. It is because of the manifold ways in which humans have felt themselves to be confined, oppressed, threatened, doomed that the prospect of *redemption* has captured the human imagination.

This was particularly the case in the historic experience of Israel. The terms redemption, redeem, redeemer occur frequently in the OT (AV/KJV). From its basic meaning to buy back by paying a ransom, the term was extended to cover major deliverances of any kind, whether or not a payment was involved. Above all, redemption was regarded as the appropriate word to describe the grand liberation of the Hebrew tribes from the bondage of their Egyptian oppressors.

The fact that this supreme deliverance could not have been achieved by the tribes themselves meant that the Deuteronomist in particular exhorted his people to remember that it was Yahweh, their God, who had redeemed them from the house of bondage (7.8; 13.5; 24.18). Further, when disaster came, resulting in the Exile in Babylon, the great message of hope centred upon the proclamation that Yahweh is the Redeemer (Isa. 41.14; 43.14; 44.24): 'In a little wrath I hid my face from thee for a moment; but with everlasting kindness will I have mercy on thee, saith the Lord, thy Redeemer' (Isa. 54.8).

In the Greek NT two words underlie the translations redeem and ransom. These two words have as their background the common scene of a market-place with eager buyers and sellers completing transactions. It was one of the most familiar scenes within the Hellenistic world, and frequently amongst the commodities for sale were human slaves. It is no wonder that New Testament writers fastened upon the purchase of goods and the releasing of slaves as apt symbolic forms to represent what Christ had done for mankind.

Yet redemption remains a fairly general term: there is no working out of detailed correspondences in an effort to construct a comprehensive theory of atonement. We are left in no doubt that the great deliverance has been achieved; that it was a costly process involving the precious blood of Christ (I Peter 1.18–19); that its benefits (freedom from bondage to sin, the law, demonic powers) could now be appropriated by faith (Rom. 3.24), and that what could now be enjoyed in part by the redeemed would receive its fulfilment in the age to come (Rom. 8.23).

The exchange of goods through buying and selling has remained, through the centuries, one of the fundamental institutions of mankind. It has consequently provided a vivid model by which the human imagination has tried to envisage God's activity in and through Christ. Did God 'buy back' that which had somehow been lost? Did he redeem that which had fallen into the possession of evil forces? Did he indeed make the supreme payment – the entrance of the beloved Son into the human situation of bondage and evil, an entrance which resulted in the death on the cross?

In the ancient world, and even in certain areas of the modern world, the institution of enslaving fellow-humans has given the imagery still greater emotional intensity. The emancipation of a slave signals the beginning of a wholly new life. Did the Son of God somehow pay the price to set free those enslaved by evil tyrants, however those tyrants might be named?

The experiences of buying and selling, slavery and emancipation, imprisonment and release are so familiar to all peoples that they have proved to be amongst the most popular of imaginative aids for those seeking to interpret the meaning of the work of Christ. Sometimes this has resulted in what seems to have been bizarre dramatic stories, especially in relation to transactions with the Devil* in order to secure man's release. But serious difficulties have arisen only when attempts have been made to press details and to insist on crude literal correspondences. The central theme represented by such words as redemption, deliverance, liberation is that of divine compassion leading to active succour on behalf of those oppressed and unable to help themselves. The danger in redemption theology has been a tendency to compare the divine action with that of victorious warriors or of champions using physical force. The writers of the NT insist that the divine redemption involved identification with the human lot, refusal to use physical instruments of compulsion, submission to man's last enemy, death. By identifying himself with humans in their temptations, trials, hopelessness, suffering and death he paid an immeasurably costly price and brought into being a new humanity, bearing his own image and committed to following his example.

The most eloquent celebration of Christian redemption is found in the Epistle to the Ephesians (1.7, 14; 4.30). Here the cost, the immediate effects and the final goal of redemption are vividly portrayed. All earthly deliverances are but types and models of the *eternal redemption* (Heb. 9.14) which Christ has obtained for us.

See also **Atonement, Salvation.**

H. Wheeler Robinson, *Redemption and Revelation*, 1960.

F. W. DILLISTONE

Reductionism

An analysis aimed at simplifying a complex idea or phenomenon into its component parts, reductionism can easily become the belief that complex data can be *explained* in terms of something simpler. The idea of diminishment has become firmly attached to reductionism: in modern theological writing to describe someone as a 'reductionist' is often to imply that he attempts to dilute or explain away traditional dogmas, or that he reduces the hard core of essential beliefs in the hope of making what remains more palatable, or that he consents to the 'reduction' of religious phenomena and ideas to some 'simpler' psychological, sociological or linguistic explanation. These pejorative uses of 'reductionism' do not settle the argument, which has to be concerned with the cogency of the claims that reductionism has actually taken place. Here it is convenient to distinguish between religion and Christian theology. Broadly, the attempt to reduce religion to either psychological or socio-economic factors has been unconvincing, not because the various factors suggested have nothing to do with religion, but because they seem to account for religious ideas and behaviour only in part. Much religious behaviour is neurotic, but that is not to say that religion is no more than an illness; religious institutions may identify themselves so completely with an existing social order that they seem to have no other identity, but such social statements are generalizations which fail to account for all the ideas and behaviour of the individual members of the institutions. And one can apply the method to the method: when Durkheim, the French sociologist, attempted to 'reduce' the idea of God to society's sense of its own oneness, he did so, the historian may say, because he was a frightened moralist anxious to detect social forces which might be relied on to unite what he saw as a disintegrating French society in the early twentieth century. It is also true that religious writers, not least ecclesiastical historians, have often produced very simplistic accounts of religious institutions, underplaying economic factors and taking apparently religious motivation very much at face value. Nevertheless, religion has for the moment survived reductionism, as a basic individual human response to the problems of existence. In terms of Christian theology, reductionism has perhaps been less obvious but more effective. Of course, for orthodox theologians who assert the divine inspiration* of scripture, however defined, reductionism has always been either irrelevant or mistaken. Nevertheless, the attempt to reduce Christian theology to a variant of older theologies was made: the most famous example is still *The Golden Bough* (15 vols, 1890–1915), by the anthropologist, Sir James Frazer, who assimilated the dying and rising Christian redeemer to a primitive archetype of a god who dies and is reborn. As for reductionism as a demand for the reduction of the dogmatic content of Christianity, this has been a characteristic of 'liberal' theology since the later eighteenth century. Officially, the mainstream churches have not reduced the dogmatic structure of orthodoxy*, and the Roman Catholic Church formally added the dogma* of the Assumption* to what is 'necessary to salvation' in the present century. It is important to note, however, that pleas for the dropping of specific tenets were not made on strictly 'reductionist' grounds, but on the ground that a particular dogma was not credible as traditionally understood.

J. Bowker, *The Sense of God*, 1973; E. Durkheim, *The Elementary Forms of the Religious Life*, 1912.

JOHN KENT

Reformation, Reformation Theology

The sixteenth-century Reformation in Western Christianity was the culmination of countless movements in which discontent was registered, usually with an appeal to scripture, against beliefs and practices of the mediaeval church. None of these antecedent movements explicitly generated the Reformation. It was made possible by the peculiar social and educational conditions of the age, the commanding leadership of Martin Luther*, and the dedicated services of many other gifted and competent scholars, preachers and organizers. Amid general deterioration in the church, the abuses connected with penance and indulgences offered the point of departure in 1517. Luther was no cynical satirist but a sensitive Christian whose assurance in controversy came from a personal religious experience. John Calvin*, Huldreich Zwingli, Heinrich Bullinger and other eminent Reformers were likewise men who had passed through an inward struggle to an earnest and undoubting assurance of a biblical and evangelical faith. The Reformers were also a company of singularly able men, thoroughly versed in the Bible and the Church Fathers and familiar with the writers of pagan antiquity. A sometimes forgotten factor in the advance of the Reformation is the fact that its opponents themselves accepted the authority of scripture. When they invoked tradition and papal decisions they could always be embarrassed by an argument to the contrary drawn from scripture. John Eck confessed at Augsburg that the Roman cause could not be defended

from scripture alone. The Bible had been much utilized in mediaeval theology, but in general had been so interpreted as to avoid calling in question prevailing ecclesiastical practice. The Reformation presented the holy writings as the exclusive norm of belief and worship, often utilizing, with critical appreciation, the patristic interpreters in rejection of the scholastics. It is safe to say that the canonical scriptures had never before been so intensively studied and so exclusively employed as the basis of Christian thought and action, and as presenting a divine challenge to church reform.

The Reformation gained its successes essentially by persuasion rather than force. The power of certain states was, indeed, used in its behalf. But the great powers of Europe, under Hapsburg and Valois rulers, and many of the smaller principalities did what they could to crush it. In England the preaching of the Cambridge evangelicals led by Bilney and the circulation of Tyndale's N T antedated Henry VIII's abolition of the papal jurisdiction and ambiguous course of legislative reform. These early witnesses were in large degree the inceptors of that scriptural and truly religious phase of the English Reformation later represented by Hooper, Latimer, Cranmer, Ridley and Jewel. The view that the Reformation was either a product or a cause of nationalism runs counter to some weighty facts. The formation of territorial and national churches in the sixteenth century may be thought of as culmination of a process already far advanced under the system of papal concordats and through the frequent intervention in church affairs by princes and local governments. International intercourse among the Reformers was constant and none of them wished to circumscribe his religious fellowship to a national church. The works of many early Protestant theologians passed without hindrance from nation to nation in Latin, and not a few of them were promptly rendered into various vernaculars. Flight from repressive governments caused much fruitful dispersion of scholars and teachers and promoted a mutual acquaintance of churches distantly separated. Sixteenth-century Protestantism largely shared a common stock of ideas and beliefs and was disturbed by the same theological discords. National borders did not halt the intercourse of thought. The radical sects with their emphasis on local group authority were nevertheless constantly stirred by visiting teachers from other political areas and made aware of the struggles of their fellow-radicals everywhere. A great mass of correspondence among religious leaders of the era gives evidence that they felt free to advise and consult as Europeans, or, on matters of high moment, as members of the one holy catholic church.

The social and economic impact of the Reformation has been tendentiously interpreted. A substantial development of capitalism took place in the previous era, and the mediaeval church was deeply involved with the bankers, notably in connection with the indulgence traffic. Economic habits were of course considerably affected by the stress laid upon the lay vocations as a means of a holy service to God and of usefulness to one's fellow, as well as by the abolition of many economically unproductive holy-days. In the Reformed churches especially, thrift became a Christian virtue, but it was approved not as a means of amassing wealth but as a means of helping others. A strict accountability in the use of one's time, as of one's worldly possessions, was enjoined and idlers and spendthrifts were disciplined. To relieve unemployment in Geneva Calvin initiated the establishment of new industries. But nowhere was there in the trail of the Reformation an outburst of capitalistic enterprise. The notion of the individualistic accumulation of wealth was habitually rebuked from the pulpit.

With the affirmation of biblical authority there were differences with regard to its application in the field of worship. Lutheranism and Anglicanism admitted a large element of traditional ceremonial not specifically drawn from scripture. Lutheranism was disturbed at the middle of the sixteenth century by the controversy over adiaphora *. What was the range of these things neither enjoined nor forbidden, and how far was it permitted to use them in accommodation to Roman Catholic ceremonial? In England the debate between Anglicanism and Puritanism turned in part on the same issue. The vestments John Hooper was required to wear were admittedly 'things indifferent'. 'Why insist upon them?' he asked; 'Why make a point of rejecting things indifferent?' was in effect Cranmer's reply. Hooper had been trained in Zurich, where all un-scriptural features had been rigidly eliminated from worship. The order of worship used by Bucer in Strasbourg, based upon a drastically altered version of the Mass, was imitated by Calvin, who opposed Melanchthon's wide range of acceptable adiaphora, and essentially observed, with less rigour than Zwinglians and Puritans, the negative scripture rule. With regard to the ministry, a similar issue can be discerned. But none of the major Reformers adopted either the high presbyterian or the high episcopalian view.

While the entire Bible was their arsenal in assailing the mediaeval system, it was from the Pauline letters that the Reformers drew their most effective arguments. The doctrine of justification * by faith is rooted in Paul's thought, as is also that of the priesthood of all Christians. A new stress was laid by all Reformers upon exegetical preaching, and this was received with keen attention by hearers who were themselves devout readers of the text. The lay folk also participated heartily in singing, whether using the spontaneous hymnody of Lutheranism or the versified vernacular Psalms characteristic of Calvinism. In these ways the Reformation brought a new dimension to the religion of the common people. By spreading the Bible to the people, it made every man a potential participant in its Bible-centred theology.

R. L. Bainton, *The Reformation of the Sixteenth Century*, 1952; O. Chadwick, *The Reformation*, 1964; A. G. Dickens, *The English Reformation*, 1964; *Reformation and Society in Sixteenth-Century Europe*, 1966; G. R. Elton, *Reformation Europe, 1517–1559*, 1963; H. J. Grimm, *The Reformation Era*, 1954; H. J. Hillerbrand, *The Reformation in its Own Words*, 1964 (with extensive source material); K. Holl, *The Cultural Significance of the Reformation*, 1959; T. M. Parker, *The English Reformation to 1558*, 1950; W. Pauck, *The Heritage of the Reformation*, 1961; B. M. G. Reardon, *Religious Thought in the Reformation*, 1981; J. M. Todd, *Reformation*, 1972.

J. T. MCNEILL

Regeneration

Rebirth or second birth. The key NT texts are Titus 3.5, 'he saved us . . . by the washing of regeneration and renewal in the Holy Spirit', linked with John 3.5 (Latin, *re*born); and Matt. 19.28, where 'the regeneration' is the general resurrection for judgment. From this arose a problem: If the Christian is regenerate as a result of the work of the Holy Spirit in baptism, why the need to pray, 'Forgive us our trespasses'? Augustine's solution was, 'Baptism washes away indeed all sins ... but it does not take away the infirmity which the regenerate man resists when he fights the good fight ...' Another solution was, 'Baptism is not the new birth ...; the one is an external, the other an internal, work; the new birth ... does not always accompany baptism' (John Wesley).

J. C. O'NEILL

Reincarnation

This is the idea that we live many lives on earth, being reborn as babies after interim periods of disembodied existence. In varying forms this is believed by hundreds of millions within the Hindu and Buddhist worlds, as well as within various other smaller groups. In its more popular forms in which the belief also has a certain currency in the West, it is claimed that the same self that is now living has lived before and will live again, with continuity of character traits and occasionally with flashes of memory of a previous life. It is claimed that regression under hypnosis can sometimes recover such memories. There are also a number of cases on record – mostly in societies in which reincarnation is an accepted idea – of children apparently remembering a recent life and providing information about it which has been able to be verified.

As it occurs in Hindu philosophy the idea has a more subtle and complex character. It is not the present conscious self that is reborn. On the contrary, in each incarnation there is a new empirical self, which comes into existence at conception and ceases at death. But underlying this series of selves, through which it lives, is an eternal spiritual reality, the *jiva*. This is enclosed in various 'bodies' or modes of expression, including the physical body which perishes at death, and the 'subtle body' (*linga sharira*) which persists beyond death and is later re-embodied by attaching itself to a developing embryo. It is this 'subtle body' that bears the individual karma, which is the basic dispositional character that both selects the kind of birth appropriate to it and is in turn modified by the actions of the living indivi-

dual in whom this karmic state is currently being expressed. A complete memory of the whole series of lives exists in the *jiva* and occasionally, by a kind of leakage, living individuals become conscious of fragments of this memory. When at last, at the end of the series of incarnations, the embodied *jiva* attains to enlightenment (*moksha*) the enlightened person has access to this memory. But this is his/her last earthly life; for in the movement towards enlightenment, or liberation, such a one has transcended self-centredness and become consciously one with the universal *atman*, or self, which is ultimately identical with Brahman, the eternal absolute Reality.

The Buddhist understanding is essentially similar, except that that which is successively reborn is not a continuing entity, the karma-bearing 'subtle body', but the stream of karma itself.

The compatibility or incompatibility of reincarnation with Christian belief has been discussed from time to time. Resurrection and reincarnation both constitute re-embodiment; heavenly resurrection is a kind of reincarnation in another world, whilst reincarnation is a kind of resurrection in this world. But whether we have lived on earth before should presumably be regarded as a question of fact. If and when the fact can be definitively ascertained, any belief system should then include or exclude reincarnation in response to the evidence.

See also **Life after Death.**

John Hick, *Death and Eternal Life*, 1976, chs. 16–19; Geddes MacGregor, *Reincarnation as a Christian Hope*, 1982; Ian Stevenson, *Twenty Cases Suggestive of Reincarnation*, 1966; id., *Cases of the Reincarnation Type*, 3 vols, 1974–1979.

JOHN HICK

Relativism, Cultural

Relativism as a philosophical thesis states that truth is not absolute but relative to particular societies or cognitive systems or to the historical epochs in which different societies function. The relativist holds not that there is no absolute truth (a thesis more properly to be termed scepticism) but that each society has its own values and canons of truth and that such values may be different for each society or historical epoch. Cultural relativism in particular would hold that each society has its own value system, the meaning of which can be sought only within that system. Comparison of one system with another is therefore illegitimate.

The origins of cultural relativism are complex but may be traced back to the spirit of the Enlightenment *, which led eventually to the destruction of the concept of a classical culture * valid for all time. Kant's discovery that knowledge depends as much on the conditions imposed by the knowing subject as on the object known led in its turn to the realization that meaning and truth are relative to the society or historical perspective in which they are formulated. Thus the rise of the social and historical sciences drew attention to the context in which ideas and beliefs develop. The new science of social anthropology recognized the danger of reading into other cultures the thought-patterns of one's own. Other societies have sometimes very different religious values and moral codes, and the Western observer has no right to impose his own set of values on another society or to expect what are purely European modes of thought to be normative for all societies. At worst this is cultural imperialism; at best a form of projection. Thus a 'monolithic' concept of the human condition or of human culture is challenged by our modern historical, scientific and sociological consciousness which insists that every view of man and the world is conditioned by the historical and cultural presuppositions accepted by a particular community.

The relativist attitude in general affects all aspects of contemporary culture. As a theological and hermeneutical * problem it springs originally from the application of critical historical methods to the NT (see Biblical Criticism), but has been made particularly acute by the pluralism * of modern religious culture. Modern historicism has made theologians only too well aware of the cultural gap which exists between one age and another and of the difficulty of discovering an adequate hermeneutic * which will mediate between twentieth-century culture and the first-century world of the NT. But the issues which divide one religious culture from another are in principle no different. The historian recognizes that all philosophies, ideologies * and religious movements are conditioned by the cultural roots out of which they grow. He does not deal with a mass of material which can immediately be translated from one particular context to another, but with individual facts and occurrences which only make sense when related to their proper background. Theologians too have to recognize that they, as much as historians and anthropologists, are conditioned by their cultures. No longer is it obvious that they can 'get inside the skin' of a first-century Christian, still less inside that of a first-century – or even twentieth-century – Buddhist.

1. The problem raised by cultural relativism is one of communication and continuity *, for if the thesis is taken to its extreme it makes all transcultural and transhistorical contact impossible. But 2. what happens to the absolute claims of the Christian theologian? If a religious tradition can only be understood within its own historical and cultural context, does it not follow that it is only true within that context? How does the theologian reconcile his affirmation of the eternal significance of the truth disclosed in Jesus Christ with an acceptance of the contingency of all historical and cultural manifestations of truth?

It makes sense to consider the two dimensions of the problem together if only because it was the History of Religions school (see **Religionsgeschichtliche Schule**), and particularly Troeltsch, which brought it to the forefront of theological thinking. Troeltsch's account of religious traditions as a series of separate complexes and more particularly of Christianity as a historical phenomenon which must be set in its own context and not treated as a unique supernatural entity which owes nothing to the culture out of which it has been formed has had a lasting influence on both historians and biblical exegetes. At the same time, Troeltsch the theologian was concerned to seek out elements of transcendent value in the multiformity of religious culture and thus avoid the danger of simply sinking into a total relativism. The result is a semi-Hegelian identification of Christianity as the highest spiritual attainment among the historical religions. But while Christianity is in practice normative within European culture, it is not necessarily *the* absolute religion. Troeltsch himself clearly stands within the whole tradition of nineteenth-century liberal * theology, and it is not surprising that, while his historical work has been generally accepted, especially by form criticism *, his theological solution to methodological cultural relativism has proved much more problematic.

The difficulty with the term cultural relativism is that it covers a wide variety of theories which, at any rate in the theological world, are rather ill-defined. Troeltsch's legacy is implicit in much of the theology of *The Myth of God Incarnate* but has been taken up most notably by Dennis Nineham. Historical relativism raises serious problems of interpretation and method in theology – issues which arise from what Nineham calls the wider 'cultural revolution'. Nineham discusses various attempts to deal with the problem – among them the nineteenth-century liberal, the Barthian and Bultmann's existentialist * – all of which have in common the conviction that the essential content or basis of Christianity is to be found in the pages of the Bible. But therein lies the problem, for the Bible is the product of a culture very different from our own and different from that of any of its historical interpreters. The Jesus * of history remains for our time, in Schweitzer's words, 'a stranger and an enigma' – a projection of the liberal * theologian's imagination. We cannot just assume that an interpretation which was meaningful at a particular period of history will continue to bear that meaning for a later cultural totality.

Nineham is right that the Troeltschian problematic will not just go away by turning theology into a defence against the reductionism * of historians and social scientists. But, if the merit of his work is that he underlines a problem which has bedevilled biblical scholarship for a century and a half, the weakness is that he never analyses what cultural relativism means. It is one thing to say that cultures are very different and that meaning depends on context; it is another to insist that different perspectives are so discontinuous as to be quite unintelligible. The plausibility of relativism derives from the rich diversity of human culture and from the feeling that it is not obvious that there is only one conceptual scheme or set of translateable concepts which enable us to make sense of a plurality of practices and beliefs. But cultural pluralism does not imply cultural relativism. The observation that what one society believes to be true may not be what another society believes is no doubt correct. Clearly we are faced at one level with a multitude of beliefs and practices which are, strictly, non-equivalent. But it does not follow that they are non-comparable. This is the crux of the matter, for some theologians speak as if they are faced by so many mutually exclusive contexts of meaning which prevent any discussion of the absolute truth of any one, or indeed of all, religion. The most we can do is several 'language games' – such as Christianity, Buddhism, etc. – which are *per se* fundamentally irreconcilable. But this is agnosticism * rather than relativism. In fact, some philosophers object that any form of relativism is self-refuting since it is impossible to hold simultaneously that all doctrines, religions and conceptual schemes are relative *and* that a doctrine of relativism is itself true in an absolute way. The 'anthropologists' heresy' stresses that 'right' can only mean 'right for a given society', and that it is therefore wrong for one society to criticize or interfere with another. But the introduction of an absolute in the second proposition makes the argument inconsistent.

It is therefore essential to distinguish between relativism as method – the sort of 'tool' advocated by, for instance, Ninian Smart as appropriate for the scientific study of religions – and an epistemological relativism which asserts that truth is somehow inherent in and formed by a particular cultural context. It is not obvious that the former leads to the latter, nor that the latter is a straightforward univocal concept. The statement that 'truth is relative to culture' can mean a number of different things, from the uncontroversial observation that societies decide what is ultimately meaningful within their own cultural framework, to the total scepticism of saying that truth is *determined* by cultural context. As philosophers have discovered, relativism is a curiously ambiguous term and the questions of truth and meaning which it has raised are ultimately insoluble in purely theological terms. Nevertheless various attempts to counter the problem can be distinguished.

1. The radical supernaturalism of dialectical theology. This more or less rejected Troeltsch's relativism out of hand. Barth's distinction between religion and the revelation of God in Jesus Christ was intended as a critique of all human religiosity. Faith cannot be made to depend on the contingent

facts provided by historical research, nor can God's miraculous intervention be seen as simply one more facet of the pluralism of modern religious culture. But a Barthian theory of inspiration cannot obscure the fact that the meaning of words is essentially related to their cultural context. The historical question remains: why are some events uniquely revelatory and not others? There must be some criterion of choice other than the unassailable assurance of faith. On the other hand, the strength of the Barthian position is the insistence that faith is not dependent on any one culture. The words in which the gospel is expressed are relative, but the Word of God is the incarnate Word *for and of* all mankind. The problem is then shifted to that of inculturation or adaptation to local culture, with results like that of Panikkar's *Unknown Christ of Hinduism*, which seeks to find the *mysterium Christi* at the heart of non-Christian religions.

2. The main Catholic response has been based on theories of 'doctrinal development *'* – what Schillebeeckx calls the Catholic counterpart of the 'hermeneutical problem'. A renewed historical consciousness in Catholic circles can conveniently be dated from the promulgation of the encyclical *Divino Afflante Spiritu* in 1943 which freed scripture scholars to use the historico-critical method and thus brought to an end the period of ultra-conservatism caused by the modernist crisis. An excessive dependence on 'logical' theories of development has given way to a deeper understanding of the *consensus fidelium*, the idea that the *whole* church in its belief and practice expresses and carries forward the truth of the tradition. Both Rahner and Schillebeeckx owe much of their inspiration to a return to the biblical sources. Faith is the work of the Spirit responding to a revelation * which is a continuing and developing process in the life of the church. The task of the theologian is to show how contemporary belief is faithful to the original message. Rahner's fulfilment theology springs from the fundamental conviction of Catholic humanism that all good comes from the Holy Spirit *. All human life is set in a supernatural perspective and is already orientated towards its fulfilment in God.

3. In the 'perspectivism' described by Bernard Lonergan, based on the two phases of theology – the 'mediated' and the 'mediat-

ing' – theological method is seen as leading to an accumulation of insights which brings an ever-deepening appreciation of the fundamental truths of the tradition. History, therefore, is progress, not in the sense that more evidence becomes available, for the historian is finite and his information incomplete, but in that a certain continuity is achieved between successive historical perspectives by recognizing that standpoints are different yet complementary. Lonergan's hermeneutic depends on his theory of the fundamental invariance of human cognitional structure, but his view of history is similar to that of H.–G. Gadamer, who develops the idea of the expansion and fusion of different cultural horizons – a position taken up in his own way by Pannenberg.

4. Nineham himself, convinced that the idea of a unique divine intervention of the sort recorded in the Bible is totally alien today, prefers to invoke Maurice Wiles's distinction between 'history' and 'story' and recommends that the theologian use the method of the psychoanalyst and the literary critic as well as that of the historian. This is a move towards imaginative dialogue (*see also* **Narrative Theology**). The interpretation of the text will thus depend on our ability to distance ourselves from the text and to enter imaginatively into the life of the community which gave rise to the original stories. Such a programme finds support both in systematic form, as in David Tracy's concept of the analogical imagination as a tool for the appropriation of the religious 'classic', and in the remythologizing of John Dunne, who has developed the idea of 'passing over' imaginatively from one culture to another, thereby participating in the life of other groups and recreating in some way what is dormant in one's own.

5. Finally, to turn from the problem of continuity within the Christian tradition to the theology of religions, the experience of dialogue between religions has led to a deepening awareness not just of what religions hold in common but of those elements which are most expressive of their particularity. The encounter of religions, in other words, makes the participants more aware of their own traditions. This is in marked contrast to the vision of W. Cantwell Smith, who has long advocated a dialogic meeting of religions. Instead of thinking in terms of so many rival ideological

systems associated with particular cultures, Smith sees the religious life of mankind as a dynamic continuum, part of the wider history of human culture. As communication increases and a more open-ended dialogue between religions takes place, Smith expects religious thinking to transcend cultural boundaries and questions of truth and meaning to be decided by a response to the whole religious tradition of the world (see also **Christianity and Other Religions**).

This, of course, is to ignore the theologian's problem, for each religion in ordering its own apprehension of the Divine within a particular cultural context implicitly sets itself off from and passes judgment on all other religious traditions. Phenomenologically* the different religions of the world are just that: different configurations of basic religious beliefs and values. But theologically they do claim to be true – and not just for their own tradition but, in some sense, for all traditions. The more positive attitude to the great religious traditions which emerged from the Second Vatican Council has also set up a tension between the claims of dialogue and evangelization – between, that is, respect for the genuine spiritual values in non-Christian religions and the claims of Christ – which is the most crucial of contemporary theological problems.

These and so many other questions are part of the complexity of what is rather vaguely called cultural relativism. That there are plenty of fruitful lines of enquiry emerging is clear. What is now needed, both in hermeneutics and in the theology of religions, is more precise philosophical analysis, so that questions of meaning and truth associated with cultural relativism can be adjudicated in theological circles.

See also **Historical Criticism, Pluralism.**

James Barr, *The Bible in the Modern World*, 1973; Van A. Harvey, *The Historian and the Believer*, 1967; N. L. A. Lash, *Change in Focus*, 1973; *Theology on Dover Beach*, 1979; B. J. F. Lonergan, *Method in Theology*, 1972; Jack W. Meiland and Michael Krausz [eds], *Relativism, Cognitive and Moral*, 1982; Dennis Nineham, *The Use and Abuse of the Bible*, 1976; W. Pannenberg, *Basic Questions in Theology*, ET Vol. I, 1970; Vol. III, 1973; E. Schillebeeckx, *God the Future of Man*, ET 1969; E. Troeltsch, *The Absoluteness of Christianity*, ET 1972.

MICHAEL BARNES

Relics, Theology of

Although many religions, including Buddhism and Islam, have a cult of relics, there are particular theological reasons for it in Christianity, stemming from the belief that the body of the Christian is the dwelling of the Holy Spirit, that it has been sanctified by baptism and the other mysteries of the church and that it too, together with the soul, will be transfigured in glory at the final resurrection. This means that Christians have always treated the bodies of those 'who sleep in Christ' with great reverence. Since the sub-apostolic age at least, special veneration has been given to the bodies of those who have either given their lives for Christ or who have been recognized as men and women of outstanding sanctity.

Together with the veneration of the bodies of the saints must be included that given to clothing and to other objects and places associated with the saint during his life. The most important of such relics are those connected with the life and passion of the Lord: the Cross, the Nails, the Tomb, the Manger, etc. In the NT we read of miracles worked through handkerchiefs and cloths which had been in contact with St Paul's body (Acts 19.11–12), and similar customs grew up around the relics of the saints. By the middle of the second century there is clear evidence of the cult of the relics of the martyrs and of the theological principles behind it in the account of the martyrdom of St Polycarp, and the bones of the saint are described as 'more valuable than precious stones and finer than pure gold'. The account also makes it clear that the Christians were already accused of idolatry because of this cult and so the defence of the cult of relics has much in common with the defence of the Icons*. The Fathers of both East and West insist strongly on the fact that the honour given to relics is only relative and that the only object of worship is God, whose servants the saints are. St John Chrysostom, who defends the custom of dividing and distributing relics in language very reminiscent of that used in connection with the Holy Eucharist, stresses that one of the main purposes of the cult of relics is to rouse the Christian to imitate the virtues of the saint whose relics he contemplates, and the church has always held that God frequently uses the relics of the saints as channels of grace and instruments of healing, and St John of Damascus compares them to the rock in the desert which gushed forth water for the Israelites, though he may also be alluding to the widely attested phenomenon of the sweet-smelling liquid or the sweet fragrance produced by the relics of some saints, even many centuries after their deaths.

SYMEON LASH

Religion

As a concept this has undergone considerable debate in modern times. How to define it obviously affects the scope of the study of religion, while the comparative study of religion has posed problems for traditional Western ideas of religion. Thus the West has typically thought of religion as involving belief in, and response to, God * or the gods, while for some Eastern religions, notably Buddhism and Jainism, the gods are not important and there is no Creator God – the emphasis rather is upon liberation. A parallel issue is about the definition of *a* religion: it can be argued that modern Western notions of such entities as Hinduism, Buddhism and so on, are imposing foreign concepts upon the human facts – thus there is a strong contemporary critique of the concepts of religion and religions by Wilfred Cantwell Smith, the noted North American scholar. Another question concerns whether religion is simply to be regarded as a human phenomenon and a human construction, or whether it has some kind of transcendent origin and reference-point. Since the first part of the nineteenth-century, there has been a growing tradition of projection * theories of religion, i.e. theories which see religion as resulting from the projection of human feelings and ideals on to outer reality, and which have an economic (Marx), psychological (Freud), sociological (Durkheim) or theological (Barth) basis (*see also* **Freudian Psychology, Marxism, Sociology of Religion).**

1. *Problems of definition.* It may be that the quest for a simple definition of religion is misguided, since religious traditions and ideas are so varied. Durkheim (1858–1917), as one especially interested in small-scale societies, and influenced also by his Jewish

background, saw religion very much in social terms: thus 'a religion is a unified system of beliefs and practices relative to sacred things, that is to say things set apart and forbidden – beliefs and practices which unite into one single community . . . all those who adhere to them'. With some changes related to the delineation of sacred things here, Durkheim's definition would still command a fair amount of assent among social scientists. But this leaves out a sense of the Transcendent, which is important for drawing a line between religions and secular ideologies *. An influential modern formulation of the sense of the Transcendent is Paul Tillich's (1886–1965) description of religion as relating to what concerns man ultimately. Yet the tenor of his writing was on the whole Western, and did not easily accommodate Buddhism, where the ultimate is not being, but nirvana, or by another formulation, Emptiness. Tillich used his account to draw a line between genuine religion and secular ideologies by referring to the latter (Marxism, Fascism, etc.) as quasi-religions. It is perhaps best to think of differing systems of belief and practice as world-views, some of which are traditional religions and have some concept of the Transcendent and some of which are secular ideologies which while having many of the features of traditional religions nevertheless do not point to 'another world'. This does not mean that traditional religious and secular world-views cannot borrow from one another or indeed form syncretisms *. Thus sometimes religion combines with nationalism (itself an array of relatively modern ideologies) to form religious nationalism – as in Iran, Poland and elsewhere.

This way of defining religion makes use of the concept of the Transcendent – a wider notion than God because it includes the state of nirvana (for instance), in which there is liberation 'beyond' the empirical world, that is, the world of spatio-temporal interconnections. But it also needs to characterize religion in terms of its typical form, for the notion that religion relates to the Transcendent is highly abstract. One way of doing this is to make use of a six-dimensional analysis, i.e. to see religion typically as involving six aspects or dimensions – doctrine*, myth * (here used in the technical sense to mean sacred narrative * including historical narrative of transcendental significance), ethics, ritual, experience and social institutions. Thus Christianity has doctrine (e.g., the Trinity*), myth (e.g., the story of creation*), ethics (the two great commandments), ritual (the sacraments), experience (the conversion of Paul, the sense of the numinous, etc.) and social institution (the church). These dimensions require to be understood in mutual relationship: thus the doctrine of the Trinity has to be linked to worship (ritual); the story of Easter (myth) relates again to ritual (the Easter liturgy), and to experience (being 'born again' and raised from the dead with Christ) – and so on. Different religions emphasize different dimensions. Buddhism is stronger on doctrine and experience, weaker on ritual and myth; Hinduism is strong on ritual and social institutions; and varieties of each religion differ too – Quakers stress ethics and experience (*see* **Society of Friends**), while Eastern Orthodoxy* stresses ritual. But these are just differences of emphasis. We can see also that secular ideologies also possess the dimensions. Soviet Marxism has doctrine (Marxism–Leninism), myth (the story of the Revolution), ethics (being a good Soviet citizen), ritual (May Day parades, pilgrimage to Lenin's tomb), social institutions (the Party) and, in a limited degree, experience – the sentiments which are supposed to animate the loyal Marxist. But all this is expressed in this-worldly terms, with a mundane eschatology.

An alternative way of looking at religion is more personally. Thus Wilfred Cantwell Smith sees religion centrally as the faith relationship, and in this regard a person can be regarded as more or less Christian, according to the intensity of his relationship to Christ, or more or less Muslim. This indeed can vary from morning to afternoon. So for him religion must be seen as a matter of the quality of life and faith of concrete individuals. As for religions – they are so many cumulative traditions which have grown out of and through the faith of individuals over the centuries. At the same time Cantwell Smith has been very critical of abstractions such as 'Hinduism', seeing these as modern Western conceptual impositions.

Cantwell Smith's personalistic approach has the merit of dealing, as Tillich's 'ultimate concern' also does, with individual religiousness which may lie outside formal institutions. Especially today there are many people who, while not practising religion in a formal and institutional way, regard themselves as having some kind of faith*. This may include adherence to some kind of secular world-view, such as humanism*.

The definition affects the scope of the study of religion. It has become increasingly accepted that religious studies, which covers religions in the plural and so includes the comparative study of religion as well as philosophical, theological and social-scientific debate about religion, should include in its scope the study of secular world-views, though looking at these from an appropriate 'religious' perspective. That is, it may use the methods evolved for the study of traditional religions to illuminate the study of secular world-views. Thus also religious education is often taken to include 'implicit religion' – that is, those features of life which have religious meaning or raise religious questions, while not being necessarily given an explicitly religious interpretation.

2. *Theories of religion.* The nineteenth and twentieth centuries have seen a number of influential theories to account for the origin of religion, whether through some kind of cultural evolution, or genetically in society and in the individual. From Feuerbach (1804–1872) these theories have typically involved seeing religion as a human projection (*see* **Projection Theory**). Though there are criticisms that can be made, from the standpoint of the scientific study of religion, to parts or all of these various theories (from Marx to Berger and from Freud to Fromm) – for one thing few Western theorists grasp the implications of Eastern religious phenomena – they have areas of considerable plausibility. Moreover, the projectionist notion has had Christian-theological importance in modern thinking about 'religionless' Christianity. The most important idea in this connection is contained in the thought of Karl Barth (1872–1968); for him, religion is a human construct, and this includes the Christian religion. He thus accepted the projection theory, but with a difference – namely that he also affirmed the revelation of God in Christ. God as wholly Other reveals himself, and is not dependent on anything human for this self-revelation. Thus at best religion is a response

to revelation, but it is a human one. From this it was a step to Bonhoeffer's (1906–1942) view that there can be a 'religionless Christianity' now that man has 'come of age'. Christ works, so to speak, at the heart of the secular world.

However, it is doubtful whether in any empirical sense either Barth or Bonhoeffer could be said to avoid being essentially religious: it is only that they wanted to put the Transcendent outside the definition of man-made religion. They affirmed in their differing ways a view about the origin of faith, and thus in principle were after all in opposition to reductionist accounts of faith. In so far, therefore, as faith is part of the definition of religion, the notion of 'religionless Christianity' is contradictory, though as an affirmation of the faith to involve itself directly in the very marrow of human secular concerns it represents an important drive within modern Christianity.

3. *Alternative concepts*. Since Cantwell Smith has criticized modern Western notions of religion, it is worth noting that other cultures have alternative concepts, such as *dharma* (teaching, law), *mārga* (way), and *darśana* (world-view) in Sanskrit, and *chiao* (teaching) and *Tao* (way) in Chinese. But these concepts, though different, look both to the idea of a transcendent principle and to the idea of a pattern of conduct and custom. They thus correspond to the patterns both of the Cantwell Smith and dimensional approaches.

Ninian Smart, *The Phenomenon of Religion*, 1978; *The Religious Experience of Mankind*, ³1983; W. Cantwell Smith, *The Meaning and End of Religion*, 1963; J. Waardenburg, *Classical Approaches to the Study of Religion*, Vol. 1, 1978.

NINIAN SMART

Religionsgeschichtliche Schule

Literally, the 'History of Religions School'. This was a German theological school of thought, active in the closing decades of the nineteenth century and in the opening decades of the twentieth, which studied and laid theological stress upon parallel developments and common doctrines within Christianity and Judaism, and later, within Christianity and other, mainly Near Eastern, religious traditions. The school, whose viewpoint orginated partly in reaction

against the christocentric and bibliocentric emphasis of the Ritschlians, counted among its members H. Gunkel (1862–1932), W. Bousset (1865–1920) and W. Heitmüller (1869–1925).

See also **Liberal Protestantism**.

C. Colpe, *Die Religionsgeschichtliche Schule*, 1961.

JAMES RICHMOND

Religious a Priori

This notion is used, especially by philosophers of religion, to express the view that the sense of the divine is due to a special form of awareness which exists alongside the cognitive, moral and aesthetic forms of awareness and is not explicable by reference to them. The concept of religion, as concerned with the awareness of and response to the divine, is accordingly a simple notion which cannot be defined by reference to anything other than itself. Even though the forms by which religion is expressed are culturally conditioned, religion itself is *sui generis*, essentially irreducible to and underivable from the non-religious. Friedrich D. E. Schleiermacher (1768–1834) makes such a view of religion the basis of his defence of it in his *Speeches on Religion* (1799) when he distinguishes it from thought and morality. In *The Christian Faith* (1821–2, ²1830) he further elucidates this position, maintaining that religion is not primarily a matter of knowing or of doing but that it finds its essence in the 'feeling of absolute dependence'. Ernst Troeltsch (1865–1923) also took up the notion of the religious a priori. He called for a science of religion which recognizes that religion must be analysed, at least provisionally, in its own terms as 'a completely independent phenomenon' and as a 'qualitatively distinct aspect' of human consciousness. Rudolf Otto (1869–1937) located this a priori * basis of religion in the experience of the 'holy' or 'numinous' which combines both rational and non-rational elements and of which we become aware through 'an original and underivable capacity of the mind'.

R. Otto, *The Idea of the Holy*, ET 1923, ²1950; F. D. E. Schleiermacher, *On Religion, Speeches to Its Cultured Despisers*, ET 1893.

DAVID A. PAILIN

Reparation

The reparatory satisfaction * for our sin that we by ourselves were incapable of making, made by Christ in his passion, when he accomplished the reconciliatory sacrifice, and finally redeemed us from the slavery in which we were set by our sin (cf. *ST* 3a, q. 48, a. 1–4). In RC devotion the word signifies those prayers, good works, acts of self-denial and the like offered to God and the saints to make good the evil or sacrilege committed by men.

JAMES ATKINSON

Repentance

In ordinary use, the word refers to a person's regret of a past action or thought deemed unacceptable. In scripture, however, repentance (*metanoia*) implies acceptance of the challenge to human beings to respond to God's call in Jesus Christ that they 'repent, for the kingdom of God is at hand'. This response consists of a turning away from a life of rebellion, inertia or perversity, and a turning to God in Christ with faith. In this context, repentance is not a single act, but an ongoing responsiveness to the will of God, a continuous experience made possible through the gift of grace. The gospel enables the person to be gracious when confronted with the reality of his or her failures and with the magnitude of the gulf between the individual and the perfect will of God. But concrete steps are necessary for the renewal of life in Jesus Christ to occur. The genuineness of one's repentance is demonstrated by actual changes in actions, thoughts and feelings: through one's evaluation of their life in the light of scripture, through honesty in confession, and through receptivity to forgiveness. Thus does repentance enable a person to grow ever closer to God in Christ.

LEWIS R. RAMBO

Representative

According to the dogmatic tradition, Christ intercedes for us sinners before God by taking on himself 1. our guilt and 2. the punishment which necessarily follows from it. Both notions are rooted in magical thought, and there is evidence for them in countless parallels in the history of religions (cf. the scapegoat, Lev. 16). The NT makes use of magical categories like defilement, purification, sacrifice and punishment, but these are interchangeable images to express the significance of Christ's dying for us. They break apart because the NT has an anthropology which goes against them. Men and women are seen as persons, with a responsibility for the world which they cannot surrender, directed completely towards others. Directed towards the forgiveness, help, comfort and truth of others, and responsible for the success of their lives, I gain my life only from others. Their wholeness heals me, their destruction destroys me in a way which cannot be contained within the magical understanding of guilt. No one can remove my guilt like a thing, but they can bring me out of it and open up a new future for me. It is not just that I have committed sins; I *am* a sinner, i.e. I have never shown enough love to change the world. The conditions in my world accuse me. The punishment is not inflicted on Christ the representative, as is supposed in magical and religious thought; rather, in the specific consequences of my sin it affects those who suffer innocently without my doing anything to change things, and who are exploited with my help or to my advantage. If representativeness is used to avoid or suppress the radical and personal awareness of sin that is being referred to here, it destroys the substance of faith. Personality is the end of all magic. Forgiveness is not understood where it has to be preceded by the sublime need for vengeance embodied in an 'expiatory offering' and projected on to God. God means to resocialize us in Christ, not to punish us.

A new understanding of representation which does not confuse Christ with the scapegoat has as its christological basis the principle that Christ is humanity as God meant us to be, no 'more' and not otherwise. As this 'firstborn among many brethen' (Rom. 8.29), he represents us before God. That means that he represents humanity. As representative he expresses the truth of our life caught up as it is in resignation and deceit; he reminds us of what we are meant to be. In him we can see what it means to live a human life. The humanity of Jesus is unsurpassable. The fact that he represents us 'before God' makes his claim absolute: all men and women have a right to real life, which he called eternal life. For us that involves the demand that we should be responsible for life on our earth, for creating conditions in which people should have the possibility, largely denied them today, of entering upon the way of Christ. That Christ represents us before God means that Christ represents to all social powers, including the churches, every person's chance to become human, i.e. to learn to love.

Thus Christ as representative presents us with a demand, and also with a promise. Christ represents God among us. He makes God 'event', even where he is not known, that is, where the misuse of God prevails. In Christ we can see what 'God' means between human beings, how God can live in us. He invites us here and now to be in God by neither postponing eternal life to a later stage nor making it dependent on religious and moral demands. He gives us love – for no other reason than because we need it. The person to whom Christ promises God is caught up into the infinite movement of love in which he or she, while still being a sinner (*simul peccator*), can accept themselves and be able to change the world (*simul justus*). For such a person Christ plays the role of God by pointing to this infinite movement even when the individual despairs of him or herself or the world, and no longer believes in a God who intervenes directly and works miracles. Christ represents God precisely to those who despair of meaning and value in their lives, and assures them of the truth of their lives.

It is necessary to interpret 'Christ' if we are not to be deceived by religious magic all over again. Not, that is, Christ in his historical form, the humanity of which poses a representative claim to all and for people, but rather in his risen form, which is what we are. This Christ has made himself dependent on us. He does not live except in us; again and again he has died to no purpose, as we do. We represent the absent God for one another in the fact that 'one becomes a Christ to another' (Martin Luther).

Dorothee Sölle, *Christ the Representative*, 1967.

DOROTHEE SÖLLE

Reserve

Reserve in the communication of doctrine means the practice of withholding profounder and more difficult doctrines from simple believers and divulging them only to the educated or more advanced spiritually. It was first recommended and employed by the Christian Platonists of Alexandria in the third century.

R. P. C. HANSON

Restoration of All Things

The phrase has biblical roots. In the prophetic coin that carried on its obverse denunciations of doom, the reverse spoke of restoration. This expectation was attached to the reappearance of ancient worthies, i.e. Elijah (Mark 9.12; Matt. 17.11). It seems to have been present in some disciples after the resurrection in the form of an expectation of the 'restoration of the kingdom to Israel' (Acts 1.6). But other disciples understood that the 'restoration of all things' could not take place immediately after the resurrection* (Acts 3.21). Restoration implies a return to a previous state of well being. In Israel's messianic vision the kingdom of David provided the measure for evaluating the present and the future. But the apocalyptic*vision of the end of all things in a total conflagration saw 'a new heaven and a new earth' rather than the restoration of a former condition.

The identification of Jesus with Elijah in order to link Jesus with the restoration of the kingdom was supported by Malachi's prophecy of the appearance of Elijah before the great and terrible Day of the Lord. But Malachi had spoken of the restorer of *hearts* (Mal. 3.23 LXX). Working with OT traditions, but with Stoic rather than messianic or apocalyptic interests, Philo of Alexandria wrote of the wanderings of the Israelites as the process for the restoration of the *soul* from a state of fluidity, before good and evil, to the arrival to wisdom and virtue (*Heres*, 293–9). Thus at the time of the beginnings of Christian theology there were available visions of the restoration of all things both in terms of a universal dénouement of history, and in terms of the reintegration of the life of humans to life with God. These views had their roots in the Jewish prophetic tradition that spoke of the rule of kings over nations and the Hellenistic philosophical tradition that spoke of the rule of reason in the soul.

Origen's use of the phrase gave it theological importance. Views of salvation were in real tension. Not only was there tension between individualistic and universalistic views, but also between salvation conceived as a radical change for the better, totally discontinuous from the accidents of present life, and salvation conceived as a process guided by God's providence which in gradual stages lifts souls upwards towards integration into the divine life itself. Origen's genius was to attempt to incorporate the two perspectives by affirming both that the present conditions of existence are to be removed, and that the life of the soul establishes continuity in history. For him bodily existence was what placed human existence at a rather low level in the chain of being, and the restoration of all things meant the ultimate removal of the chain of being brought about by the Fall. Final release from the chain of being allows the soul to have a diaphanous vision of God 'without words, symbols and types' (*Martyrdom*, 13). In his doctrine of the restoration of all things, Origen integrated the Christian teaching of the parousia * to a view of history as a spiral ascent from creation and fall to the restoration through successive universes.

This vision of a departure from and a return to the One* was, to say the least, congenial to a Neoplatonic* scheme of things and became a major intellectual pattern in Western Christianity thanks to the good offices of Augustine. Thus Christian theologians who have their roots in this tradition are likely to work on the basis of a spiral return to the restoration of all things, and to see salvation primarily as the divinization of human beings. They are, therefore, vulnerable to the charge that they place in jeopardy the *newness* of eschatological existence.

Augustine, *On True Religion*; Origen, *Exhortation to Martyrdom*; G. W. F. Hegel, *Phenomenology of Spirit*, 1977 (German 1807); P. Teilhard de Chardin, *The Divine Milieu*, ET 1957.

HEROLD WEISS

Resurrection

Resurrection was central and constitutive in Christianity from the first – cf. the early gospel formula in I Cor. 15.3f., and that in Rom. 10.9, where salvation depends on confession of the lordship of Jesus, which itself depends on his resurrection. All but a few of the smaller NT writings testify to this

faith, and resurrection can underlie statements about the purpose of God for life (I Peter 1.3ff.), possession of the Spirit and true life (Rom. 8.9ff.) and ethics (Rom. 6.5ff.; 7.4ff.). It was not a neutral concept, simply one expression for life beyond death, but carried with it a positive theological interpretation. It was absent from the OT, which was content with the traditional idea of Sheol as the permanent abode of the shades of all departed, until the late apocalyptic book of Daniel (12.2). There it is an answer to the crisis for faith in the Maccabaean struggle, in the form of a double resurrection – to life for those who had been loyal under persecution even to death, and to condemnation for those who had not. The surviving literature of the inter-testamental period shows the emergence of resurrection belief in diverse forms: resurrection of righteous Israelites only, of righteous and unrighteous Israelites, of all men to judgment; to earth, to a transformed earth, to paradise; in a body, in a transformed body, without body. Sometimes (Wisdom; IV Macc.) the individualistic Greek concept of the immortality of the soul was incorporated. By the first century AD it was probably widespread in Judaism, being a tenet of the Pharisees, but not universal there (cf. Mark 9.10), being rejected by the Sadducees as unscriptural; and it is not certainly attested at Qumran. Common to most versions is that resurrection belongs within the eschatological action of God whereby, in consummation of his creation, he would resolve the contradictions of human life, would finally discriminate between good and evil in judgment, would destroy evil and permanently establish a righteous elect. In face of death, thought of either as a sleep or as an evil intruder in creation (Wisdom 2.24; Rom. 5.12) this involved resurrection – both verbs used, *egeirein* and *anistanai*, can mean either 'to awaken' or 'to make stand upright'. God is always the subject of the verbs, or they are in the passive, 'was raised', *sc.* by God (it is exceptional when in John Jesus is said to raise himself).

The concept plays little part in Jesus' teaching, though he asserts it emphatically against the Sadducees on the ground that a relationship once set up between God and mortal men cannot be temporary. Since, however, that teaching is so frequently given in the form of a connection and contrast between present human action and what God will make of it (beatitudes, parables, warnings, promises, kingdom of God, Son of man, etc.), it is congruous with resurrection. That 'Jesus was raised' thus means basically that the final things, including the future general resurrection of men, have begun to take place in advance in a single person. This constitutes his uniqueness as messiah or ruler in God's kingdom* (Acts 2.36), as the righteous one exercising the divine function of judge with respect to good and evil (Acts 10.42), and as the lord (a title closely connected with his resurrection) of the elect and of the world and its future (Rom. 14.9). (The same can be said by 'exaltation' e.g. Phil. 2.5–11; Heb. – but resurrection identifies the exalted Lord more precisely with the earthly and crucified Jesus.) This identification brings about a dislocation of the established eschatological pattern which is creative for Christian thought. Since the end has not come, the resurrection of Jesus remains still anticipatory of his parousia, or presence with full effect, while the non-arrival of this parousia gives rise to new things in the present having the quality of resurrection – a universal mission (Acts, Paul, the Gospels), a relationship with God (righteousness) available to all by faith (Rom. 4), in a community of the elect entered by baptism which is a present union with Christ's death to sin and a future union with his risen life (Rom. 6.1ff. – a present union, Col. 3.1), in possession of the Spirit which is an earnest of final glory (Rom. 8) and of a life which has passed through judgment and is eternal in quality (John).

It is the presence of some of these spiritual truths in the resurrection narratives of the Gospels which makes them at once powerful as expressions of resurrection faith, and also difficult to assess as evidence for the event which had given rise to that faith. They hardly tally at all with the list of witnesses in I Cor. 15.5–7, and are too diverse in respect of locale, manner and purpose to be harmonized with one another or combined into a single story, and to some extent reflect the theological outlook of the gospel to which they form a climax. In Mark this is not a resurrection appearance, but the angelic message at the tomb that the now risen Lord will precede (go ahead of? lead?) the disciples to Galilee. In Matthew the already exalted and omnipotent Lord is the author in Galilee of a universal mission of conversion, baptism in the threefold name, and instruction in his teaching, and guarantees his abiding presence to the end. In Luke the risen but not yet exalted Lord is with disciples over a period of forty days, promises the Spirit as the agent of a universal mission, interprets his passion and glorification as the burden of the OT, and ascends. In John the risen Lord on the way to ascension* gives Mary a message for the disciples, commands them to a mission (which is successful when he directs it), and inbreathes them with the Spirit of new creation for the exercise of forgiveness and judgment.

Complexities further arise from the application of the necessarily symbolic language of eschatology* to a particular historical figure. As the divine act of new creation the resurrection itself is unobservable and indescribable (Matt. 28.2ff. comes nearest to it). What is narrated is the outcome of its having taken place. The empty tomb, the four accounts of which have significant variations, does not prove it, but when interpreted by supernatural agencies is a pointer to it and to the element of continuity in discontinuity. The appearances of the risen Lord, as self-manifestations from eternity to disciples in space and time, are the result of its having taken place and the means of establishing that it has taken place (albeit temporary means, for they cease, and are not the mode of the permanent relationship of the Lord with his own). This is conveyed less by depicting a plainly 'supernatural' figure – the form of the risen Lord is not described, though he can be said to appear and disappear at will – than by the speaker's assertion of identity beyond death ('It is I'), and by what he then proceeds to say. This identity indicates not survival of death but the overcoming of it, and not the leaving behind of the past but its taking up into life. It can, however, be asserted in a factual and physical manner (e.g. Luke 24.39; John 20.27) which could obscure this, and which is very different from the visionary form of heavenly voice and light in the 'appearance' to Paul, at least as described in Acts.

A similar complexity attaches to the use of the word *sōma* ('body', perhaps 'person' or 'personal form') with reference to the resurrection of the elect, which is involved in the resurrection of the Lord as the 'firstborn from the dead' (Col. 1.18). In the earliest form of this (I Thess. 4.13–17) those alive at the parousia will undergo apocalyptic rapture * to meet the heavenly Lord in the air along with Christian dead who have undergone a metamorphosis through resurrection. In the exposition in I Cor. 15 of a resurrection which, despite present experience of it, still lies in the future, the natural body is to be replaced by a 'spiritual body', which is both continuous and discontinuous with it, and is modelled on the Lord's body of 'glory' (cf. also Phil. 3.10–11, 21). The ultimate outreach of this is the divine transformation of mankind (Rom. 8.19ff.; Phil. 3.21). In the second century the resurrection was at the centre of doctrinal controversy, but chiefly with reference to the future life of the individual, and in the form of 'the resurrection of the flesh', and frequent recourse was had to the text 'With God all things are possible' to argue that God was able to reassemble the physical body for resurrection however dispersed.

The core of resurrection faith is that already within the temporal order of existence a new beginning of life from God, and a living of life under God, are possible, and are anticipatory of what human life has it in it to be as divine creation; and that this has been made apprehensible and available in the life and death of Christ regarded both as divine illumination of human life and as effective power for overcoming whatever obstructs it. This is cosmic in its scope and also reaches to the depths of the human person. The doctrinal question is how far, and in what way, this faith is to be held and stated when it is of necessity divorced from the matrix of eschatological thought in which it was produced. Since the lordship (control) of the risen Jesus over the world and its future through the Spirit was what emerged as the specifically Christian form of resurrection faith, subsequent experience of that lordship in the church, as well as further understanding of the world and of the human person in the world, will have their contributions to make to any statement of the significance of resurrection.

C. F. Evans, *Resurrection and the New Testament*, 1970; Lloyd Geering, *Resurrection: A Symbol of Hope*, 1971; W. Künneth, *The Theology of the Resurrection*, ET 1965; X. Léon-Dufour, *Resurrection and the Mes-*

sage of Easter, ET 1974; W. Marxsen, *The Resurrection of Jesus of Nazareth*, ET 1968; C. F. D. Moule (ed), *The Significance of the Message of the Resurrection for Faith in Jesus Christ*, 1968; A. M. Ramsey, *The Resurrection of Christ*, 1945; P. Selby, *Look for the Living*, 1976.

C. F. EVANS

Revelation

By 'revelation' is generally meant the disclosure of what was previously unknown or only uncertainly apprehended. In theology such disclosure is normally regarded as caused by the agency of God (and so to be distinguished from other occasions of discovery which are part of the secular experience of coming to understanding – as when we say of a problem that after puzzling over it 'the light dawned and I suddenly saw the solution') and as making known hidden aspects of the character and purposes of God, of humanity in its relationship with God and of what is to occur in the future through the providence of God. This unveiling of what was concealed may be either through some means of communicating information on these topics or in the form of what is taken to be a self-manifesting encounter with God. In either case God is the agent who reveals and human persons are the subjects who receive the revelation. God's revelatory activity need not be considered wholly in terms of causing certain disclosive events to occur. It can also take the form of bringing persons to perceive theological insights in and through situations which can also be interpreted non-theologically as parts of the ordinary course of nature and history.

Although in the OT there are some references to revelation through nature (cf. Pss. 19.1; 18.13; 29.3; but cf. I Kings 19.11ff.) and in visions (cf. Ex. 33.22; Num. 24.4; Isa. 6.1ff.) and dreams (cf. Gen. 28.11ff.; I Sam. 28.6), revelation is mainly understood directly as the hearing of God's Word (cf. Isa. 5.9; Jer. 23.18,22) and indirectly as the perception of God's activity in the history of individuals (cf. Pss. 3.1ff.; 118.13f.) and of the nation (cf. Ex. 15.1ff.; Ps. 98.2f.; Jer. 33.16). It is also regarded eschatologically in terms of the complete manifestation of God and the culmination of his purposes in 'the day of the Lord' (cf. Hos. 2.19ff.; Jer. 31.31ff.). In the NT, while 'revelation' occasionally refers to the miraculous reception of supernatural knowledge (cf. Matt. 11.27; 16.17; Gal. 2.2; I Peter 1.12), the dominant use of the concept is to refer to that future event in which God finally discloses himself (cf. I Cor. 13.12; I John 3.2) or his Messiah * (cf. Luke 17.30; I Cor. 1.7; Rev. 1.7) in judgment and salvation (cf. Rom. 8.18f.; I Cor. 3.13; I Peter 1.5). It is an event which those who have faith perceive to have been effected already in the event of Jesus (cf. John 3.17ff.; 9.39; Rom. 1.17; Heb. 9.26; I Peter 1.20).

The dominant influence on the treatment of revelation in Christian theology, however, is the distinction between natural and revealed theology. Although there are earlier suggestions of this distinction, it was brought into prominence by Thomas Aquinas (c. 1225–1274). Basically it distinguishes between those truths about God which can be determined by unaided human reasoning and other truths which cannot be apprehended, or cannot be apprehended without doubt and the risk of distortion, unless they are disclosed by God. The former ('natural theology' *) are usually held to contain such truths as that God exists and that he is eternal, while the latter ('revealed theology') include such matters as God's triune nature and the manner of his redemptive activity. According to the prevalent view in Christian theology, it is only when the former are augmented by the latter that humanity has the saving knowledge of God which it seeks.

Theologians have defended the need for revelation in various ways. 1. Some, as has already been indicated, maintain that revelation is necessary to augment natural understanding since certain crucial truths about God and human destiny are beyond the competence of human reason. Thus Thomas Halyburton wrote to show *Natural Religion Insufficient, and Revealed Necessary to Man's Happiness in His Present State* (1714), while Karl Rahner speaks of 'the real revelation' as disclosing 'something which is still unknown for man from the world: the inner reality of God and his personal and free relationship to spiritual creatures'. 2. It is maintained that revelation is needed to give humanity an immediate and accurate grasp of essential truths which in principle could be discovered by natural reason and to provide a standard for testing the con-

clusions reached by such reasoning. Thomas Aquinas, for instance, holds that even in the case of those truths about God which human reason is capable of reaching, it is 'necessary' that God should reveal them, since otherwise they 'would only be known by a few, and that after a long time, and with the admixture of many errors'. 3. Revelation is seen as providing the theologian with key ideas from which his understanding can develop. It is possible, for example, to interpret Anselm's grasp of the definition of God which his *Proslogion* rationally explicates and Ian Ramsey's notion of 'cosmic disclosures' as describing such revelatory experiences. 4. Revelation is required if humanity is to be able to enter into relationship with God as personal since the personal can only be adequately known through acts of self-manifestation. Thus Gordon Kaufman has interpreted revelation in terms of 'our knowledge of other persons, when profound and true'. Such knowledge is accessible to us only when and to the extent that other persons are willing to unveil their selfhood to us. 5. Some form of revelation can be held to be required to make known the active and material qualities of God as agential. According to this view, it is proper to infer from the formal definition of God as ultimate, perfect and personal, that God will be totally aware of each situation and respond to it in the most value-enhancing manner possible. To live by faith appropriately, however, requires some understanding of the material character of God's responses. This cannot be ascertained by *a priori* reflection. It is perceivable only by means of some revelatory manifestations of it. 6. Some theologians reject any kind of natural theology and hence argue that no genuine knowledge of God is available apart from God's revelation of it. Karl Barth maintains that God is 'not the one man thinks out for himself and describes as God'. God, rather, is only 'thought and known when in His own freedom God makes Himself apprehensible', not only giving the revelation but also giving to individuals the capacity to apprehend it. According to this doctrine of the '*analogia fidei*' or '*analogia gratiae*', it is 'God himself who opens our eyes and ears for himself'.

Unless, though, both the initial perception and the subsequent communications of revelatory insights are held to involve miraculous events which provide individuals with superhuman modes of understanding, revelations cannot provide us with communicable knowledge of matters which are totally unlike the contents of our natural experience and understanding. In order to ease such limitations, some theologians have suggested that what is provided in revelation may, in part at least, be symbolic or parabolic indications of the divine nature which permit people to make a valid practical response to God. Others have suggested that revelation gives insight into the nature of humanity as it exists before God rather than knowledge of God himself. In no way, though, can revelation provide direct information about that which is 'wholly other'.

Traditionally revelation has been understood in terms of verbal or quasi-verbal communications by God to recipients who then pass on what they have heard – 'Thus says the Lord ...' Revelation is thus understood to have a propositional form and faith is seen as assent to the revealed propositions. Thomas Aquinas accordingly describes 'sacred doctrine' as 'established on principles revealed by God'.

The primary location of these revealed propositions, furthermore, is commonly held to be the Bible. Although authority may also be ascribed to the unwritten tradition of the church and to the works of the Fathers, the Bible has been seen for most of the history of Christian thought as the work in which the divinely conveyed propositions are expressed. It is thus describable as 'the Word of God'. Thomas Aquinas states that God is 'its author' and John Calvin speaks of it as 'the only records in which God has been pleased to consign his truth to perpetual remembrance' and its contents therefore as having as 'full authority' as if 'God had been heard giving utterance to them'. Nevertheless, even if the revealed truths are held to have been given in some verbal form, they still have to be understood and applied. The story of Christian theology provides numerous examples of how differences of understanding can arise concerning the meaning of the supposedly revealed statements.

Since the Enlightenment *, however, and to an important extent as a result of critical study of the Bible, the propositional view of revelation has widely (though by no means

universally) given way to the view that divine revelation is through events and that the Bible, so far as it is authoritative for theological understanding, is so as the record of these events and of faith's perception of their revelatory significance. According to the so-called *Heilsgeschichte* *(salvation history) school, God reveals himself by means of certain events in history. G. Ernest Wright, for example, describes history as 'the chief medium of revelation' and theology as 'the confessional recital of the redemptive acts of God in a particular history'. For Christian theology this history consists of the events which are reported in the Bible. A different emphasis in the understanding of events as the locus of revelatory insights finds the disclosure not in the apprehension of some events as mighty acts of the redeeming God so much as in the way that certain events are found to be interpretable in a way that illuminates the rest and in particular our lives. William Temple writes of revelation as arising from the 'intercourse of mind and event' whereby the world-process is grasped for 'what it truly is', while H. Richard Niebuhr describes revelation as 'that special occasion which provides us with an image by means of which all the occasions of personal and common life become intelligible' as having 'rationality and wholeness' and 'order'. A third type of the non-propositional understanding of revelation stresses that it is not a matter of the imparting of information but one of immediate encounter with the divine. Thus Paul Tillich states that 'revelation is not communication concerning a being, even concerning a transcendental being' but 'the self-giving of the absolutely hidden, which by the very fact of its self-giving emerges from its concealment' in a total manner.

A crucial problem for claims to revelation is their justification. Some theologians have denied that any kind of rational justification is legitimate, either because in revelation the believer is given supernatural insights which natural reason is incompetent to judge or because the revelation provides the norms of judgment or because God's Word * is its own authentication. Others, though, recognize that in a world containing competing claims to revelatory truth, it is necessary for any claimed revelation to be authenticated. For propositional views of revelation this has generally been attempted by such means as alleging that the persons bringing the revelation have shown themselves to be divinely authorized by their power to perform miracles and to foretell the future and by their unblemished character, while their messages are shown to be divine by their quality and their effectiveness in winning converts. All such arguments, though, are much disputed. As for the view that revelation is given through historical events, there arises here the fundamental difficulty of showing that God is significantly disclosed in any particular series of events. As G. E. Lessing points out, there seems to be a logical type-jump between historical judgments and claims about the divine. It is not yet clear either how God is to be identified as an agent in historical events or how theistic ways of understanding are to be justified by reference to historical events (*see also* **History**).

Finally it is arguable that the distinction between 'natural' and 'revealed' theology ought to be abandoned. Those who maintain that all genuine knowledge of God is fundamentally revelatory prefer to distinguish between a general revelation given to all humanity and the special revelation, recorded in the biblical story, which gives a fuller knowledge of God. Alternatively it can be held that all theological understanding is a matter of gaining insights into the ultimate nature of reality and that the only significant difference between supposedly 'natural' and supposedly 'revealed' insights is that the former are derived from considering an apparently broader (though still selected) range of situations than the latter. In both cases, though, the ultimate justification is by showing that the resulting understanding is a coherent, comprehensive, fruitful and convincing view of the fundamental character of all reality.

John Baillie, *The Idea of Revelation in Recent Thought*, 1956; Karl Barth, 'The Christian Understanding of Revelation', in *Against the Stream, Shorter Post-War Writings 1946–52*, ed. R. Gregor Smith, 1954; Emil Brunner, *Revelation and Reason*, ET 1947; Van A. Harvey, *The Historian and the Believer*, 1966; Gordon D. Kaufman, *Systematic Theology: A Historicist Perspective*, [2]1978; H. Richard Niebuhr, *The Meaning of Revelation*, 1941; Wolfhart Pannenberg (ed), *Revelation as History*, 1969; James M. Robinson and John B. Cobb, Jr, (eds), *Theology as History*, 1967; Paul Tillich, *Systematic Theology*, I, 1953.

DAVID A. PAILIN

Revivalism

Revivalism in America began with five 'harvests' in the Congregational Church at Northampton, Massachusetts, during the ministry of Solomon Stoddard (1643–1729). It spread through the colonies in the period of the 'Great Awakening', beginning in the middle colonies in the 1720s, reaching its peak in New England in the 1740s, and continuing in the South, especially among Baptists and Methodists, into the 1770s. Outstanding leaders were Gilbert Tennant, a Presbyterian; the Anglican itinerant, George Whitefield; and Stoddard's grandson and successor, Jonathan Edwards. Edwards' work became known in England through John Wesley's abridgment of five of his writings on revival.

At the dawn of the nineteenth century came the so-called 'Second Great Awakening'. In both its more orderly eastern forms and in its extremer western 'frontier' ways, revivalism eroded traditional patterns of theology and practice for more pietistic, freer styles. Methods of promoting revivals were carefully studied and consciously employed; classical Protestant theologies were modified in the effort to secure converts. Such eastern revivalists as Lyman Beecher and Nathaniel W. Taylor showed this tendency, but the most conspicuous exponent of modern revivalism was Charles Grandison Finney (1792–1875). Converted in 1821, he soon set out on revivalist tours, and despite lack of formal university or theological training was ordained as Presbyterian (later Congregationalist) evangelist. He systematically developed techniques of 'stirring up' revivals by such 'new measures' as services at unusual hours, gatherings 'protracted' for many days, inquiry meetings, and 'the anxious bench'. In many writings, especially *Lectures on Revivals of Religion* (1834–5) and *Lectures on Systematic Theology* (1846–7), Finney articulated a theology designed to get revivalistic results out of biblical, Calvinist, Methodist, Pelagian and pietistic elements. Revivalism became widely popular; denominations which employed revivalistic patterns most extensively – Methodist, Baptists, Disciples of Christ – grew rapidly. The nation-wide, seemingly 'spontaneous' prayer-meeting revival of 1857–8 illustrated how deeply revivalist theology and practice had shaped American Protestantism.

Though more on the periphery of British than of American religious life, revivalism played a role in Britain, especially in the Free churches. Some of the prominent American revivalists, such as Finney, travelled round the British Isles. So did the leading exponent of urban mass evangelism of the later nineteenth century, the Congregational layman, Dwight L. Moody (1837–1899). Early in the twentieth century, the American Presbyterian William A. ('Billy') Sunday brought modern revivalism to a peak of mechanical efficiency, but his fundamentalistic and vulgarian overtones contributed to its marked decline. At mid-century, the more theologically perceptive William F. ('Billy') Graham gave chastened revivalism a new lease on life.

Richard Carwardine, *Transatlantic Revivalism*, 1978; Alan Heimert and Perry Miller (eds), *The Great Awakening*, 1967; William G. McLoughlin, *Modern Revivalism*, 1959.

ROBERT T. HANDY

Righteousness

Among the Greeks and Romans righteousness (Greek *dikaiosunē*, Latin *iustitia*) had meanings which included both the strict justice with which states ought to be governed and laws administered, and more generally the correct behaviour of people within the various relationships of family, neighbourhood, society and state. In the second sense it was often synonymous with virtue itself.

Christian theology has continued to use the word in both these senses, though there is a tendency for Catholic tradition to prefer 'justice' for both meanings while Protestants call the first 'justice' and the second 'righteousness'. Luther's revolution in theology began when he realized that in Rom. 1.17 God's righteousness was not his strict justice, punishing the wicked and rewarding the upright, but rather his deliverance of the wicked from their guilt and sin. Few exegetes now dispute that something like this is what the term means in that verse. The Lutheran

view is further that in justification * God's righteousness is given to the sinner, who is thus enabled to stand before God acquitted, with the status of righteous. Whether the sinner is given a new character in the process, or whether the righteousness is merely imputed, has been much debated, as has the question how far the Lutheran understanding of the relation between divine and human righteousness accurately reflects Paul's thought. Very broadly, Protestants have tended to speak of imputed righteousness, perhaps a confusing term, introduced into the discussion because Paul in Rom. 4.3 and Gal. 3.6 quotes Gen. 15.6 which uses the term; he does not use it otherwise when he is writing freely. To speak straightforwardly of justification is preferable. Catholics have not disputed the new status given in justification, but have added that the sinner really does become righteous in character and life. The argument has both exegetical and confessional sides.

In the OT God's righteousness (*ṣedeq/ ṣedāqāh*) is his treatment of his covenant * people which, though it takes different forms in different circumstances, is always informed by an underlying consistency which means that he can be completely relied upon in his government of the world, his judging, his vindication of Israel when oppressed, and his assurance of salvation. Indeed so constant was Israel's need of deliverance in the later OT period and after, that God's righteousness and his salvation became virtually synonymous, though righteousness also retained its wider range of meaning.

On the human side, righteousness meant life and behaviour appropriate to the covenant and embraced all aspects of an Israelite's relations with God and his fellows. Its meaning thus ranged from right worship to care for the poor. Right government and justice in the narrow sense were included, but were not the main elements of it. In the later OT period and beyond, 'the righteous' (*ṣaddīqīm*) were increasingly those who were faithful to Yahweh and the Torah in the face of oppression from without and compromise from within.

In the NT 'righteousness' and its cognates are particularly important in Matthew and Paul and in both cases there is debate about the meaning. In the case of Matthew the issues are: 1. whether righteousness is simply

God's demand, or his gift as well as his demand (see Matt. 5.6, 20), and 2. whether a rigorous keeping of the Torah is intended by the term. In the case of Paul the chief issues are the two closely connected ones of the relation between righteousness and justification (*dikaiōsis*) and the meaning of the phrase 'the righteousness of God'. The Lutheran view (see above) is that God's righteousness, at least in justification contexts, means his granting his own righteousness to sinners, who appropriate it by faith * and so are acquitted. Righteousness and justification (e.g. in Rom. 3.22) thus become virtually indistinguishable. However, it is usually agreed that at least sometimes Paul uses righteousness for human uprightness of life and behaviour (e.g. II Cor. 9.9, 10), and it is possible that it always has such connotations. In that case, if God's righteousness is consistently gracious activity towards men and women, both rescuing them from their guilt and delivering them from the power of sin, human righteousness is the new life (not just new status) that becomes possible to those who respond to the divine initiative in Christ. Such righteousness never becomes a person's possession, but rests entirely on God's power and grace and the continuing human response of faith *. It is thus by no means certain that Paul does use 'righteousness' simply for a status before God. Paul is more concerned with the means (faith) by which righteousness is received than with the precise attitudes and behaviour it involves. However, it is not a matter of following the Torah (Rom. 9.30f.; Phil. 3.9), but part of the new life in Christ (I Cor. 1.30).

E. Käsemann, ' "The Righteousness of God" in Paul', *New Testament Questions of Today*, ET 1969, ch. 7; G. Klein, 'Righteousness in the NT' in *IDB*, Supplement; B. Przybylski, *Righteousness in Matthew and his World of Thought*, 1980; E. G. Rupp, *The Righteousness of God*, 1953; J. A. Ziesler, *The Meaning of Righteousness in Paul*, 1972.

J. A. ZIESLER

Rigorism

This has a precise technical meaning in Christian moral theology, but it is also a term used in a wider sense. In technical moral theology rigorism is used of that tradition in ethics which forbids the Christian to take the benefit of the doubt no matter how probable the doubt may be. In the wider sense, rigorism is opposed to laxity, to all those attitudes which seem to compromise Christian ethics with the standards of secularism.

K. E. Kirk, *The Vision of God*, 1931.

E. J. TINSLEY

Risen Christ, The

Though the writers in the NT are unanimous in their assertion that Jesus Christ rose from the dead on the third day after his crucifixion, the actual accounts which we find in the NT of the nature of his appearances after his resurrection are conflicting, confusing and vague (*see also* **Resurrection**). Paul, in his very valuable list of resurrection appearances in I Cor. 15.4–8, does not appear to make any distinction in mode between the appearances to the disciples and the appearance to himself on the Damascus road. In other accounts (e.g. Luke 24.36–43) there seems to be some tendency to rebut the suggestion that what appeared was a ghost or a phantom. It would be very rash to draw any firm conclusions about the nature of the risen body. Paul writes in Phil. 3.21 of Christ's glorious body, which will be made known to us at the parousia.*

The church has always found it difficult to answer satisfactorily the question: what happened to Christ's risen body after the ascension*? In general two incompatible schools of thought emerged. The Eastern Fathers (and a few Westerners such as Hilary) followed the lead of Origen in regarding the body as having been so spiritualized as to have escaped from virtually all the conditions of finitude. The Western tradition, deeply influenced as usual by Augustine, held firmly to the continuing reality of the humanity of the Word, and was therefore left with the problem of explaining where the glorified body was to be found. Thomas Aquinas with remarkable boldness says that the humanity of the Son is not generally available to the faithful, as it is finite by its very nature. They can only know the divinity of the second person of the Trinity*. The great exception to this is the eucharist*, wherein by the miracle of transubstantiation* the faithful can receive the true body and blood of Christ.

The question of the location of the Lord's body was a burning one for the Reformers. They all repudiated transubstantiation, but they had therefore to give their own explanation of the availability or non-availability of the Lord's body. Luther, following a suggestion originally made by John Scotus Erigena, held that the risen body was ubiquitous. So difficult a concept has appealed to few but Lutherans. Calvin and, for example, the Anglican *Book of Common Prayer* (rubric at the end of the Communion Service) firmly maintained that the Lord's body is in heaven and therefore cannot be available for the faithful in the eucharist. This view implies the existence of a spatial heaven, just tolerable perhaps in the sixteenth century, but incredible today.

The important point for Christians to defend today is that God the Word is known to us in Jesus Christ. This does not necessarily (indeed probably should not) imply that believers can know the human personality of Jesus in the same way that he was known when on earth – though this is a claim unthinkingly made by many Christians still. We can only hope to know the humanity of Christ in the hereafter. We do, however, now know God in Christ in the sense that God is known by us in the image and character of Jesus Christ. God the Word (or Son) has made himself known to us in the life, teaching, death and resurrection of Jesus Christ, so that the Word now bears for us the image of Christ.

J. G. Davies, *He Ascended Into Heaven*, 1958; A. T. Hanson, *The Image of the Invisible God*, 1982; H. B. Swete, *The Ascended Christ*, 1910; A. J. Tait, *The Heavenly Session of Our Lord*, 1912.

ANTHONY TYRRELL HANSON

Ritual

Rituals are regular, repetitive, rule-determined patterns of symbolic behaviour, performed by one or more people, that utilize any or all of the following components: language, action, visual imagery, personification and characterization, specific objects imbued with meaning, and music. Rituals common to most cultures mark universally shared experiences – the new year, for example, occasions rituals in all cultures – or significant stages in the life-cycle, such as birth, puberty, marriage and death. Familiar

religious rites comprise offerings of thanksgiving, petitions, sacrifices and adoration. In society, secular rituals apparently serve to regularize communal human life and make it manageable and predictable. In religious contexts rituals are generally agreed to serve as a bridge between the profane and sacred realms or, on a more individual level, between a believer and the deity.

Rituals are perhaps somewhat more accessible to study in the religious realm, though the meaning of specific religious rites might be debated as heatedly as that of secular ritual actions. To the religiously committed person, the performance of prescribed rituals is a solemn duty and a means of achieving communion with the deity. The specific details of given rituals are important because they are tested means of achieving the believer's desired goal: to enhance his or her relationship with the deity, thus bringing satisfaction to the deity that in turn results in the believer's receipt of blessings, forgiveness and favour. Further, ritual behaviour can be nurturing to the believer, binding anxiety and releasing emotions that renew and console the individual both by confirming belief and bringing the person's life into focus within the reality of the deity.

Interestingly, though the primary goal of religious ritual is to express belief and acknowledge the believer's relationship with the deity, in practice believers actually learn about their faith and intensify their belief by performing the prescribed patterns of behaviour. Thus, from this point of view ritual is a means of educating potential believers and receiving them into the faith. Some might argue that social rituals, if their purpose is to teach and confirm the society's belief system to individual citizens, function in the same way.

The form of rituals varies considerably. Some rituals are imitations of real life, some are re-enactments of myths, and others are designed to compensate those who perform them for a loss sustained in life or to console them in their grief for a loved one. Rituals can be either positive or negative – that is, behaviour patterns which express thanks or hope for a desired or appreciated phenomenon and those which express dread and evasion of a phenomenon considered evil or destructive or even awesomely powerful. Furthermore, ritual behaviour is by no means restricted to formal cultural or religious contexts, but is often performed by individuals as an aid in meditation or to alter consciousness. Whatever its form, ritual is apparently a fundamental mode of human communication, though the meaning it expresses is open to diverse interpretations.

LEWIS R. RAMBO

Roman Catholic Theology

1. *General.* (i) R C theology has undergone substantial changes in its history (from patristic and scholastic theology, through the theology of the post-Reformation controversies, baroque and Neoscholastic theology down to the various forms of contemporary theology). Today it embraces a multitude of disciplines with different methods (biblical, historical, systematic and practical theology, along with canon law). Thus it is an extremely complex phenomenon, combining unity and multiplicity, obligation and freedom, charisma and institution, mystery and rationality.

(ii) R C theology has three essential characteristics: (a) it is not more general religious or philosophical discourse about God or the divine, but discourse about God on the basis of his revelation of himself in the O T and the N T, discourse about the God of Jesus Christ. Thus R C theology is *theology of revelation*, which is concerned with the interpretation and spiritual influence of the Gospel of Jesus Christ which has been revealed once for all. (b) Because revelation can be grasped and understood only in faith, R C theology is a discipline of faith, i.e. a discipline which not only has faith as its object but is also practised from faith with a view to new faith. To this degree it is not just theoretical; it is always at the same time a practical discipline which stems from the proclamation* and praxis* of faith and is aimed at proclamation and living faith. (c) The primary subject of faith and the confession of faith is not the individual believer but the church as a community of believers, with a tradition of faith to which individuals with their own personal faith attach themselves. To this degree R C theology is a church discipline, which cannot be detached from the life and above all the liturgy of the church.

(iii) Since the development of the ecumenical attitude inaugurated by Vatican II, ecumenical collaboration has become an obligation for R C theology; in the meantime it has followed virtually as a matter of course. The R C church recognizes that 'many elements of sanctification and truth are found outside its visible confines. Since these are gifts belonging to the church of Christ, they are forces impelling towards Catholic unity' (*Lumen gentium*, cf. *Unitatis redintegratio* 3f.) Emphasis today lies more on those elements common to all churches and theologies than on what divides them. The specific features of R C theology which above all distinguish it from the theologies of other churches are the particular way in which it is rooted in the church and the way in which it is practised as a discipline.

2. *R C theology in the church.* (i) As a community of believers, the church stands under the word of God. It is first a listening church and only then a preaching and teaching church (*Dei Verbum* 7–10). This subordination to the word of God takes the form of being bound to Holy Scripture and tradition. Holy Scripture contains all the truths of faith necessary to salvation; exposition of it must be the very soul of all theology (*Dei Verbum* 24). Tradition is not an external addition to scripture; it bears witness to the one gospel which is written by the Holy Spirit, not just on parchment, but also in the hearts of the faithful (cf. II Cor. 3.2f.). It is the word of God living in the hearts of the faithful, which expresses itself through various witnesses in the tradition (confessions, liturgy, church fathers and church teachers, the witness of saints, church art and so on). All these testimonies are *loci theologici** (sources of theology).

(ii) The interpretation of scripture and tradition is a matter for the whole church, i.e. for all believers along with the ministry in the church (*Lumen Gentium* 12). Authentic interpretation can of course be carried out only by the teaching ministry of the church endowed with a special charisma, i.e. the totality of the episcopate together with the Pope (*Lumen Gentium* 15). This ministry can pronounce in an ordinary or an extraordinary way. The latter happens either through a General Council or an *ex cathedra* decision by the Pope as the head of the College of Bishops. If such a judgment is made in a definitive way which binds the whole church in matters of belief or conduct, then (and only then) it is infallible, i.e. the truth of the pronouncement is attested by the church as being ultimately binding (Denz. 3074). This does not exclude a historical perspective and the possibility of and need for such definitions being interpreted (*Gaudium et spes* 62; *Mysterium ecclesiae* 5).

(iii) R C theology has relative independence within the church. Not only is there considerable room for free discussion and free expression of views in addition to dogma, but there is also considerable latitude in the interpretation and systematization of dogma itself. Thus there have always been different schools within R C theology (Thomists, Scotists, Suarezians and so on) and today many indigenous theologies (Asian, African and Latin American) are coming into being. R C theology does not simply derive from the teaching ministry; it also has an effect on that ministry through the training of future clergy, through inquiries made of the teaching ministry and through the influencing of public opinion in the church. Thus Pope John Paul II in particular has supplemented what was previously a one-sided model of dependence and delegation by defining the relationship of teaching ministry and theology by the model of co-operation and dialogue. Of course it is impossible to think of any definition of this relationship which in principle would be free from conflict. All life is bound up in polar tensions; it is where these fruitful tensions become absolutized oppositions that there is rigidity and ossification, which in extreme cases destroys the communion of the church (heresy and schism).

3. R C *theology as a discipline*. (i) Theology has to give an account of hope to all men (I Peter 3.15). Therefore its dimensions are not restricted to the church; they are universal. Theology is *fides quaerens intellectum*, faith in search of understanding (Anselm of Canterbury). This is intrinsically possible because faith has specific existence only in human hearing, understanding, speech and action. Therefore faith always involves a human element of belief which has usually not been thought through, and which theology develops and deepens in a methodical and systematic way.

Thomas Aquinas in particular has become a norm for the practice of R C theology as a discipline, on the one hand through his distinction between faith and knowledge (theology and philosophy) and on the other through the utilization of human knowledge

for theological exploration of the faith. Thus R C theology differs on the one hand from theological rationalism, which either reduces faith to knowledge (philosophy, anthropology, sociology and so on) or takes it up into what is claimed to be a higher knowledge (Gnosticism), and on the other from traditionalism and fideism, which understand faith purely in positivistic and supernatural (fundamentalist) terms, either as a sheerly authoritarian standpoint or as mere feeling, intuition and the like. Over against such positions R C theology maintains that by virtue of its self-transcendence human reason can in principle be addressed by God and his revelation (*potentia oboedientialis*) and indeed that by nature it already possesses the fundamental possibility of knowledge of God (Denz. 3004), so that while faith is not a purely rational act, it is nevertheless in accord with reason (Denz. 3008–10). Acknowledgment of God and his revelation does not contradict human value, but lays a foundation for it and perfects it, since only God is the complete answer to the question which human beings pose by their very existence (*Gaudium et Spes* 21). Of course what any human statement about God cannot say is more than what it can say (Denz. 806).

This doctrine of the analogy between faith and knowledge distinguishes R C theology from the renewal in Reformation theology represented above all by Karl Barth and, though not so fundamentally, from the Orthodox tradition, which has more the character of a wisdom stamped by liturgy and doxology. Of course the universality with which Catholicity is concerned also has to be regained within R C theology through critical discussion with many forms of constriction and isolation, as a result of dialogue with the religions, modern science, modern art and culture, modern philosophies, ideologies, utopias and especially with modern atheism.

(ii) To the degree that R C theology has been concerned with the questions of modern men and women, since Vatican II its classical form, largely shaped by Thomas Aquinas, has been in crisis; in the meantime it has largely given place to a bewildering theological pluralism. Classical R C theology began from an essentially homogeneous culture and accordingly from a view of reason which was generally accepted. Historical criticism and, even more, dialogue with the modern world have brought with them awareness of the various ways in which men and women are socially and economically conditioned and the forms in which this is expressed. The question is whether in the light of this historicity there can still be one theology, or whether the classical form of theology must not be replaced by a new paradigm of theology in which theology is understood as the process of translating the original message into the various different situations of individuals and societies.

The *théologie nouvelle* of the 1940s and 1950s and the salvation–historical theology of Vatican II already pointed in this direction. In principle the problem was posed on the one hand by hermeneutical * theology (H. G. Gadamer, B. Lonergan) and on the other hand by political * theology, which is less oriented on an idealistic hermeneutic of meaning than on the problem of the relation of theory to praxis. However, today in particular it is important to stress that despite all the differences there is a common human nature which gives the same human value to all men and women and unites them in solidarity with one another. This presupposes a common rationality and calls for a theology which for all its different expressions is in principle capable of being communicated. Today, above all, God who embraces everyone and everything and in whose truth all have a share must be the one unifying theme of theology (thus Thomas Aquinas, *S T* I q.1 a.7).

The most fruitful beginnings towards such a new form of Catholic and therefore universal theology lie in the various kinds of transcendental theology which, in their concern with specific historical phenomena, enquire into the ultimate grounds of these phenomena. This theology has a more subjective and *a priori* character in K. Rahner and B. Lonergan, more of a historical orientation in the developments represented by the Catholic Tübingen school. Of course, there are basic problems of more recent R C theology here which are as yet unsolved. R C theology is anything but a completed system; rather, it is on the way towards an open future along with the theologies of other churches.

W. Kasper, *Der Gott Jesu Christi*, 1982; B. Lonergan, *Method in Theology*, 1972; K.

Rahner, *Foundations of Christian Faith*, ET 1978; *Mysterium Salutis. Grundriss heilsgeschichtlicher Dogmatik*, Vol. 1, 1965.

WALTER KASPER

Romanticism

The adjective 'romantic' designates a historical *period* (1760/80–1830/40), *traits* of character, and a *typology* for literature, painting and music. Each definition has its ramifications for the interpretation of theology. The major figures, their family resemblances, and some continuing effects of the romantic temper in theological questions are as follows.

1. *Period*. Late eighteenth- and early nineteenth-century figures searched for an appropriate mode of personal autonomy * in a constantly expanding and increasingly diverse social world. The Reformation *, the internecine religious wars of the seventeenth century, and the consequent pleas for civil tolerance and rational beliefs in the eighteenth century indicated that confessional allegiance had become a matter of choice. Travelogues described alternative, sometimes exotic societies for mercantile export where human beings existed unaffected by Christian education. The English colonial (1776–1783) and then French national (1789) revolutions made it plausible to opt for civil organizations other than the ones under which generations had lived. The qualitative increase in data about peoples, languages, societies and religions made it clear that history was at least partially under human control.

It is significant that early nineteenth-century theological writers in Europe and the United States were also literary figures of some stature. Friedrich Schleiermacher (1768–1834) belonged to cultural circles at Berlin which included Friedrich Schlegel (1772–1829), philologist; Ludwig Tieck (1773–1853), critic and novelist; and the scientist Johann Wilhelm Ritter (1776–1810). The Tübingen theologians Johann Sebastian Drey (1777–1853) and Johann Adam Möhler (1796–1838) were heavily influenced by Schleiermacher and Friedrich W. J. Schelling (1775–1854) the philosopher. Samuel Taylor Coleridge (1772–1834) was always better known as poet than as a theologian. Ralph Waldo Emerson (1803–1882), Unitarian minister, poet and essayist, recast religious thought by borrowing from oriental and Western cultures. Horace Bushnell (1802–1876) saw his own origins in Coleridge's *Aids to Reflection* (1829), introduced and published by James Marsh (1794–1842), philosopher and president of the University of Vermont (1826–1833). René Chateaubriand (1768–1848) was the author of novels (*Atala*, 1801) as well as *La Génie du Christianisme* (1802). They hoped to establish a Christian rhetoric, credible within an often unbelieving public world of science, art and politics.

These nineteenth-century debates on religious identity were framed by Immanuel Kant (1724–1804) in his *Critiques* of speculative reason (1781), practical reason (1788) and aesthetic judgment (1790). Certain knowledge of objects could only be attained through sensibility and understanding. Some topics (God, freedom and human identity) could be both proved and disproved by purely rational discourse. One must act only *as if* they existed, since that is the risk of freedom. Kant believed this limit on pure reason left room for the faith of practical reason as a moral and religious duty. Aesthetic appreciation verified this, since it was subjective intention which attributed to artistic creations a value which could not be known as having originated in the object-in-itself.

Many found Kant's refusal to grant rational meaning to religion successful, though they believed his location of belief solely in moral duty to be excessively narrow. They proceeded to justify religion through art and aesthetic* values. Thus Schleiermacher, in his *Speeches on Religion* (1799), maintained that religion has its origin, not in scientific thought, nor in morality, but in the feeling of absolute dependence* upon God. Schelling, early in his career, identified religion and art. Georg W. F. Hegel (1770–1831) described Christianity as a religion of images whose content could not be superseded, but whose proper form was the evolving philosophical idea. Drey and Möhler, and others of the Catholic theological faculty at Tübingen, argued that Christian tradition developed historically through various creative, doctrinal and institutional forms. Coleridge stated that all religion was symbolic and required the existential engagement of the perceiver to be grasped. Chateaubriand began his apologetic with an appeal to the mysterious and

spoke of Christianity as poetry and passion. Emerson reformulated Christian experience into an American religion of nature, a sense of the supreme beauty which ravishes the soul. If Emerson could see sermons not only in stones, but also in 'mud puddles on Boston Common', Horace Bushnell viewed religious nurture as a way to evoke innate Christian goodness through a process of maturation. He believed that the appropriate mode of religious education was in symbolic, organic and literary language.

2. *Traits.* The family of characteristics which linked disparate countries and individuals surrounds history, subjectivity and praxis. Thinkers hoped to reinsert their own religious traditions within the public and political quest for human freedom. To do so, they often looked back to older historical unities (such as the Gothic Middle Ages), but always with an eye to the future. The criterion for determining a truthful faith was the authentic human subject. Religious experience*, the self-transcendence of the individual especially through feeling and art, preceded doctrines and the biblical word as the foundation upon which Christian life was based.

These attempts to recover Christianity followed two paths which sometimes diverged. One emphasized disclosures of transcendence* within the sublime (occasionally extraordinary or bizarre) aspects of natural landscapes; the other sought to interpret confessional history through the beautiful artifacts of human creativity. Imagination* was the tool to translate this dual book of revelation. The language of religion was metaphoric, visual and densely symbolic. Janus-like, it could encounter the particular (history) as universally applicable and see multiplicities (nature) in a single figure. As William Blake (1757–1827) said: 'The eternal Body of Man is Imagination. That is God Himself, the Divine Body, Jesus.'

But creative vision also disclosed a religious transcendence ambiguously unacquainted with Christianity. So the early William Wordsworth (1770–1850) of the *Prelude* (1805) and *Tintern Abbey* (1798) experienced divine presence simply within nature, a beauty fostering holiness. Percy Bysshe Shelley (1792–1822) in the *Hymn to Intellectual Beauty* (1816) declared that beauty alone gives 'grace and truth to life's unquiet dream', echoing John Keats' (1795–1821) belief that 'Beauty is Truth', and truth beauty. Christianity might prove to be appealing and beautiful; but beauty could easily become religion. There was only a brief journey from the apostle to the aesthete.

Where specific Christian doctrines were operative, they were reformulated through the newly-won subjective religious awareness. Church structures were defined in organic terms, stressing the interdependence of congregations and offices. Christ became symbol of the best human aspirations, a non-exclusive presence of divine care for the universe. Natural utopias, and the achievement of social reforms (praxis), were a medium for grasping the finality of heaven. Ethical responsibilities were filtered through the questions projected by interested desire.

3. *Typology*. Romanticism was contrasted with classicism as imagination opposed to reason, subjectivity versus objectivity, and private mystical, lyrical introspection against prosaic, social institution. Romantic thinkers struggled for the public credibility of religion by thinking the latter values through the former ones. Traces of this project are operative in twentieth-century thought because the developing rational analysis and historical criticism of eighteenth-century religionists have not yet been integrated individually, politically or ecclesially with the quest for the transcendent. The methods of early nineteenth-century theology were sporadically applied and often flawed by their lack of subtlety. The fundamental goal of a religious praxis which is credible in terms of head, heart and society remains incomplete.

Meyer Abrams, *Natural Supernaturalism*, 1971; Karl Barth, *Protestant Theology in the Nineteenth Century*, ET 1972; James C. Livingston, *Modern Christian Thought from the Enlightenment to Vatican II*, 1971; Thomas O'Meara, *Romantic Idealism and Roman Catholicism*, 1982; H. G. Schenk, *The Mind of the European Romantics*, 1969; René Wellek, 'The Concept of "Romanticism" in Literary History', *Comparative Literature* 1, 1949, pp. 1–23; 147–172.

STEPHEN HAPPEL

Rule of Faith
see **Creed**

Sabellianism

Sabellianism is an alternative description of modalism*, derived from Sabellius (early third century) who gave the doctrine its most sophisticated form. He was a native of Libya (though some think of Rome) where his movement gained firm hold. Though the evidence for his opinions may reflect the opinions of later heretics (e.g. Marcellus of Ancyra), the following points seem well established. 1. He extended modalism into a threefold form in line with rising interest in the doctrine of the Spirit. He could still, however, describe God as a Son-Father, probably reflecting earlier trends. 2. God is by nature a monad, one *hypostasis*＊ with three names. Yet he gives a more objective character to the modes as modes of revelation (*see* **Modes of Being**). He did not, it seems, regard them as simultaneous, but only as successive. The term 'expansion' which might suggest the contrary probably arises from confusion in the sources with Marcellus. 3. He may have used the term *prosopon*＊ to describe the modalities of the Godhead. This is disputed (Kelly, Prestige) on the ground that this was not the accepted usage of the word. But trinitarian terminology remained fluid for a century after Sabellius and one secular meaning of *prosopon* could support him. The word drops out of Eastern trinitarian vocabulary in the late fourth century when Basil in particular feared its Sabellian implications.

See also **Trinity**.

H. E. W. TURNER

Sacrament

In ancient Roman times, *sacramentum* referred to a sacred pledge of sincerity or fidelity, publicly symbolized by a visible sign such as a deposit of money or an oath of allegiance. The Latin word was also used to translate the Greek *mysterion*, referring broadly to hidden realities or specifically to sacred rites such as those found in the Eastern mystery religions*. The apologist Tertullian (d. *c.* 220) is the first known Christian to have referred to the ritual of baptism, through which initiates pledged fidelity to Christ, as a *sacramentum*.

During the patristic era, *sacramentum* still had a generic meaning, and could be applied to anything that signified a Christian mystery. Augustine defined sacrament as 'a sign of something sacred' (*Letters*, 138, 1), and saw both baptism and marriage as sacramental in nature (cf. *On Baptism against the Donatists* and *On the Good of Marriage*). Likewise Innocent I (d. 417) referred to both the eucharistic bread and wine and consecrated oil as sacraments (*Letters* 25), but the term could also be used to designate any ecclesiastical rituals or the symbolic elements within them.

It was not until the Middle Ages that scholastic* theologians came to distinguish between 'sacraments' and 'sacramentals*', the former referring to those liturgical rituals which were deemed to have spiritual effects in virtue of their proper performance (*ex opere operato**), the latter referring to those religious actions and objects (e.g. blessings, holy water) which mediated grace in less specific ways. Partly because of the symbolic significance of the number seven, partly because of apparent scriptural grounds for them, and partly because of the widespread adoption of Peter Lombard's (d. 1160) *Sentences* as a theological source book, scholastics and ecclesiastics alike enumerated Lombard's seven as the sacraments of the Catholic church by the thirteenth century: baptism, confirmation, penance, eucharist, holy orders, matrimony and extreme unction (cf. Second Council of Lyons, 1274).

Protestant Reformers in the sixteenth century, reacting to abuses such as superstition and simony, rejecting scholastic explanations of the mediation of grace through ecclesiastical rituals, and applying more stringent scriptural criteria to the claim of dominical institution, eliminated all but baptism and eucharist (also called the Lord's supper, or communion) from their listing of the Christian sacraments. The Council of Trent* (1545–1563) reasserted the R C doctrine of seven sacraments, but recognized the need for practical reforms in administering them.

Today most Protestant bodies acknowledge two sacraments, though Baptists refer to them as ordinances, and some (e.g. the Society of Friends* and the Salvation Army) do not even admit these as important Christian rituals. Both the Roman and Orthodox churches have retained seven sacraments, as does the Church of England, which, however, distinguishes between baptism and eucharist as instituted by Christ, and the remaining five as 'sacraments of the church'.

D. Baillie, *The Theology of the Sacraments*, 1957; B. Leeming, *Principles of Sacramental Theology*, 1956; J. Martos, *Doors to the Sacred: A Historical Introduction to Sacraments in the Christian Church*, 1981; E. James, *Sacrifice and Sacrament*, 1962; O. C. Quick, *The Christian Sacraments*, 1927.

J. MARTOS

Sacramentals

'Sacramentals are sacred signs, resembling the sacraments; they signify certain effects, particularly spiritual ones, which are obtained through the intercession of the Church. By them men are prepared to receive the chief effect of the sacraments, and the various circumstances of life are sanctified.' Thus the *Constitution on the Liturgy* (60) of 1963. Sacramentals, then, are visible signs, like those of the sacraments, having certain effects when received worthily. But unlike the sacraments, which engage the redeeming action of Christ, they have their effect through the intercession of the church, seen as the body of Christ which is always united with him.

Sacramentals can be divided into two classes: 1. those closely associated with the sacraments (e.g. the blessing of water in baptism, the blessing of the ring in marriage); 2. those connected with various human activities (e.g. the solemn profession of a monk, the prayers for the harvest and the blessing of fields). The former are clearly extensions of the sacraments, preparing people for their reception or unfolding their meaning (e.g. the preliminary rites of adult baptism; the clothing with the white garment and handing of the candle after baptism). Those in the second category can cover almost every circumstance of human life and are adaptable to different ages and cultures.

The term 'sacramentals' appears for the first time in the writings of the theologians and canonists of the twelfth century, but they existed from a very early time: e.g. the washing of the feet in the baptismal rite which for St Ambrose had a spiritual effect.

New Catholic Encyclopedia XII, 1967, pp. 790–2; *Sacramentum Mundi*, E T 1970, 5, pp.

375–8, the most extensive treatment is *DTC* XIV, 1939, I, pp. 465–82, s.v. 'Sacramentaux', now a little out of date.

J. D. CRICHTON

Sacramental Theology

If a sacrament is a rite in which created things become vehicles of God's blessing, man can be defined as a sacramental being. Recent anthropological studies have suggested that rites are necessary for defining a person's place in society, and enable one to set aside part of one's life for God in the hope that the whole of life will in this way become sacred. The sacramental potential of all nature is realized through the consecration of some elements of it in an explicitly sacramental rite.

For Christians a sacrament is an effectual sign of grace performed at Christ's behest. In recent theology Christ himself has been seen as the fundamental sacrament: his human nature is the sign of contact between God and humanity. Under Christ the church is also the fundamental sacrament: man has saving contact with Christ and therefore with God through Christ's body the church in its visible, sociological, hierarchical reality. In this sense the church can be described as the 'continuation' of the incarnation. The church fulfils this function by word and sacrament.

Word and sacrament must not be dissociated. The proclamation of the word is itself a sign by which Christ bestows grace *. A sacrament not only includes the oral proclamation of the word, but is itself an acted proclamation.

The R C and Orthodox Churches administer seven sacraments, by means of which Christ's sacramental action through his church is applied to a Christian's daily existence and to key moments in his life (cf. the anthropological understanding of 'rites of passage'). The seven are: baptism, confirmation, eucharist, penance (confession, reconciliation), matrimony, holy order and the anointing of the sick. Anglican tradition, on the other hand, distinguishes between the 'two sacraments ordained of Christ our Lord in the Gospel', i.e. baptism and eucharist, and the other 'five commonly called sacraments', which 'have not any visible sign or ceremony ordained of God' (Article XXV, see **Thirty-Nine Articles**). The difference between the two positions is less than it

might seem, for though it is R C doctrine that all seven sacraments were founded by Christ (Trent, Denz. 1601), more recent theology is content with a 'generic' foundation implied in the foundation of the church.

Developing the teaching of Augustine, theologians have taught that the final effect (*res*) of a sacrament, namely grace, is conferred through an intermediate effect (*res et sacramentum*), which is a new or deeper incorporation within the church. In the case of the three unrepeatable sacraments (baptism, confirmation and holy order) the *res et sacramentum* is permanent and is commonly called a character*.

The efficacy* of a sacrament is not due to the holiness of the minister or the faith of the recipient but to the working of the Holy Spirit. The Zwinglian position that would restrict sacraments to signs which express or stimulate faith has not found general acceptance even among the churches of the Reformation, though it contains some truth. The psychological power of the sacramental symbolism is a means by which the Holy Spirit works; and he can work only to the extent allowed by the recipient's faith and charity. The baptism of babies, who are incapable of faith, therefore presents a problem. Augustine proposed that the faith of the church supplied for the lack in the baby; baptism, as the 'sacrament of faith' makes up for the child's lack of actual faith (*Ep.* 98).

See also **Ex opere operato**, **Sacrament**, **Validity**.

M. Douglas, *Natural Symbols*, 1973; M. Eliade, *The Sacred and the Profane*, 1961; B. Leeming, *The Principles of Sacramental Theology*, 1957; J. Martos, *Doors to the Sacred*, 1981; O. Quick, *The Christian Sacraments*, 1927; K. Rahner, *The Church and the Sacraments*, ET 1963; E. Schillebeeckx, *Christ the Sacrament of Encounter with God*, ET 1963; A. Schmemann, *The World as Sacrament*, ET 1966.

E. J. YARNOLD

Sacrifice

In Christian theology, the term has principally been applied to the death of Christ, 'the full, perfect and sufficient oblation for the sins of the whole world', and its commemoration in the eucharist. Whether the mass was in fact a sacrifice became a bone of contention at the Reformation, but the sacrificial character of Christ's death, being scriptural teaching, was not questioned before nineteenth-century liberals began their reassessment of the doctrine of the atonement *. By the time of these debates it was assumed that sacrifice could be defined as 'propitiatory offering', an assumption which imposed serious limitations upon the discussion. In fact, sacrifice is a practice which seems to have been universally characteristic of religion, and no simple definition is possible. Pioneering anthropological studies and the work of Frazer in *The Golden Bough* stimulated an interest in the origins of sacrifice which has affected OT study, but no general theory of sacrifice has proved satisfactory, and the complexity and cultural variety of sacrificial practices has to be recognized. The OT itself contains a great wealth of vocabulary for sacrifice and provides a vast compendium of different sacrificial rites for different occasions.

To understand the meaning of the sacrificial language engrained in the Christian tradition, it is essential to appreciate why it is there and what assumptions led to its use. At first Christians were accused of atheism because they refused to perform sacrifice, for religion without sacrifice was unthinkable in the ancient world. In defence of their position, Christians claimed 1. that they offered 'rational sacrifices', putting into practice the teaching of philosophers who had long criticized sacrifice on moral and theological grounds and recommended more spiritual ways of worship; 2. that the prophets had denounced sacrifice and demanded justice, mercy, repentance, fasting, charity, etc., instead; 3. that interpreting the scriptures not according to the letter but the spirit, they offered the spiritual sacrifices which had been foreshadowed in Jewish ritual practices; 4. that in Christ the whole Law, ritual as well as moral, had been fulfilled and made obsolete. Thus sacrifice was repudiated, but sacrificial language was lavishly used to describe Christian worship, Christian life and the central tenets of the faith. If the meaning of this language is to be discerned, the implicit instinctual understanding of sacrifice which converts carried over from their pre-Christian past, as well as the implications of sacrifice in the scriptures, must be uncovered.

1. The primitive assumption that God/the gods needed food or sustenance (see e.g. Ps.50.12ff.) was generally superseded by the idea that the fragrance of sacrifice gave pleasure to the divine recipient (a notion lying behind II Cor. 2.14, 16; Eph. 5.2; Phil. 4.18), on the grounds that no real God could be dependent upon men for anything; yet this assumption was sufficiently near the surface in the pagan world to be used by satirists like Lucian to ridicule religious practices, and also by Christian preachers who warned that sacrificing to pagan gods was in fact to provide sustenance for evil daemons.

2. That sacrifice established communion between God/a god and his worshippers was a common assumption. Sacrifices consumed by the worshippers in a state of ritual purity were originally regarded as celebratory feasts in which God/the god shared. Though largely obsolete in Judaism (the centralization of the cult in Jerusalem had long since removed sacrifice from the daily lives of the people and led to concentration on other aspects of it), Paul still assumes this notion in I Cor. 10.18–22. That this was an early understanding of the eucharistic sacrifice is clear from the fact that ritual purity was required of the participants.

3. That sacrifice was a gift offered to reinforce prayers of petition and intercession and influence God/the gods in one's favour was characteristic of pagan assumptions, could find some support in scripture, and in spite of its threat to the doctrine of God's immutability, passed over into patristic material which speaks of spiritual exercises, and even the eucharist (see Cyril of Jerusalem), in these terms.

4. That divine anger could be appeased through sacrifice was an assumption common to Greek myths, and some OT stories (e.g. II Sam. 24). Some of the Fathers (e.g. Chrysostom) felt no embarrassment in suggesting that the sacrifice of Christ turned aside the Father's wrath.

5. That evil spirits could be kept off by sacrifices was also a deeply rooted instinct, reflected in parts of the OT as well as pagan material. Such rites are often referred to as 'apotropaeic'. The idea that the blood of Christ averted the devil, or paid him off, is frequently found in early Christian literature and was encouraged by the traditional typological parallel drawn between Christian salvation and the Exodus: as the blood

of the Passover lambs kept away the angel of death, so the blood of Christ protected the Christian from Satan. Such ideas were applied to the eucharist and the sign of the cross; more fundamentally they shaped the 'ransom theory' of the atonement.

6. That sacrificial blood cleansed pollution is particularly characteristic of the scriptures, for after the exile, increasing stress upon the blood rites and their expiatory significance tended to submerge other interpretations of sacrifice. Both the NT and the Fathers assume without question the efficacy of the blood of Christ to cleanse sin (e.g. Heb. 9.22).

7. That sacrifice was the appropriate ritual to seal a compact or covenant * was reinforced by biblical stories of God's covenant with Abraham and with Moses. The association, already present in the NT, of cross and eucharist with 'new covenant' gave this kind of meaning to both in the Christian tradition.

8. That sacrifice was offered in homage or praise, or as a thank-offering, was universally accepted. It was the earliest understanding of the offertory in the eucharist (Irenaeus); it was the natural view of the Christian's self-oblation in worship and service; it was one way of understanding the obedience of Christ (e.g. Heb. 10.5–10).

'True sacrifice,' said Augustine, 'is every act which is designed to unite us to God in holy fellowship' (De Civ. Dei x.6). No definition of sacrifice is found prior to this, for none was needed as long as sacrifice remained a living reality in everyday experience; but Augustine's definition should have kept alive the fact which is also clear in Rom. 12.1, that sacrifice was essentially *the means of worshipping*, and that it was capable of bearing whatever meaning the worshipper(s) wished to invest in it, whether praise or repentance, petition or thanksgiving. At the Reformation some were sufficiently aware to suggest that the eucharist was a sacrifice of thanksgiving, even if it was not a propitiatory offering; but generally sacrificial language was impoverished by dissociation from the basic culture of the people using it. There are some signs that renewed interest in sacrifice and a richer understanding of its place and meaning in the Christian tradition will issue from African theologians, for whom sacrifice has a continuing reality in

the immediate cultural background, as it had for the early church.

M. F. C. Bourdillon and M. Cortes, *Sacrifice*, 1980; R. J. Daly, *The Origins of the Christian Doctrine of Sacrifice*, 1978; P. E. J. Thompson, 'The Anatomy of Sacrifice', in *New Testament Christianity for Africa and the World. Essays in Honour of Harry Sawyer*, ed. M. E. Glasswell and E. W. Fasholé-Luke, 1974, pp. 19–35; R. de Vaux, *Studies in Old Testament Sacrifice*, 1964; R. K. Yerkes, *Sacrifice in Greek and Roman Religion and in Early Judaism*, 1953; F. M. Young, *Sacrifice and the Death of Christ*, 1974.

FRANCES YOUNG

Saints, Cult of the

A cult is the veneration of persons or objects in a religious setting, and in the case of the Christian church it is a veneration of those Christians who through death are believed to be most closely united with Christ. Since God is the basis of Christian veneration and worship, the cult of the saints is based upon the worship of God. The holiness of the saints is the restored image of God in them which is so established that it is possible to say that after death they are in Christ in heaven and can therefore continue in communion with men through Christ. Veneration for the saints began as the spontaneous respect of the early Christians for those most closely associated with Christ in his earthly life, i.e. the apostles and the Mother of God. It continued in reverence for the martyrs and in particular took the form of prayer at their places of burial. After the peace of the church this respect was extended to other Christians who were felt to have shown Christ-likeness during their lives, whether as bishops, religious, or while engaged in secular life.

The saints are venerated for their participation in the life of Christ; their lives are imitated as true images of that life; and it is also the custom of Christians to offer prayers to the saints requesting them to continue to pray for their fellow Christians still on earth. The intercession of the saints depends as a concept on the idea of the church as a family united in heaven and on earth as one body, in which all members are 'alive unto God' who is their life. Communication is therefore not interrupted but only changed by death. 'All the members form the same body of Christ in the unity of the Spirit and all must communicate to one another the goodness of divine grace' (Basil, *De Spiritu Sancto*, xxvi, 61, *PG*, xxxii, col. 180).

In the Middle Ages the cult of the saints in the West took the form of pilgrimage to shrines, in addition to the liturgical veneration accorded to the saints by the whole church. The veneration of the bodies of the saints became the cult of relics and was open to the abuses later denounced by the Reformers. In the eleventh and twelfth centuries a system was evolved for determining whether a local and spontaneous cult of a saint should be approved or not and the official procedure of papal canonization was established. Inquiry is made into the virtues of the saint during his life and also into the miracles performed by his prayer both during his life and after death, as signs of the power of God working through him. The procedure was laid down by Benedict XVI in his *De Servorum Dei beatificatione et beatorum canonizatione* (1734–1738).

Texts of saints' lives are found in the *Acta Sanctorum*, 64 vols, 1943–   , ET of some in Butler's *Lives of the Saints*, revised by H. Thurston and R. A. B. Mynors, 4 vols, 1953–1954; *The Oxford Dictionary of the Saints*, ed. D. H. Farmer, 1978, for the English saints. The work of the Bollandists in their periodical *Analecta Bollandiana* (1882–   ) brought the study of the cult of the saints to a fine level of critical scholarship. In English, there is the *Legends of the Saints* by H. Delehaye, 1971, and more recently P. Brown, *The Cult of the Saints*, 1980.

BENEDICTA WARD

Salvation

The language of salvation plays an important part in Christian theology, liturgy and spirituality. The phrase 'for our salvation' in the Nicene creed points to the purpose of the incarnation; and the standard form for referring to the central figure of Christianity is 'our Lord and Saviour Jesus Christ' (II Peter only in NT). Nevertheless, study of the history of the doctrine shows that there have been considerable shifts of emphasis from time to time, and that the terms have been understood in diverse ways at different periods of the church's history.

In the earliest documents for which we have direct evidence, namely the genuine letters of Paul, 'salvation' is used to refer to the future event in which God will judge the world, destroy the wicked and establish his final kingdom on the earth; so Paul can say to the Romans, without any need for further explanation, 'salvation is nearer to us now than when we first believed' (Rom. 13.11), implying, as the context shows, that the parousia of Christ and the last judgment were expected to take place before he and his readers had died; otherwise it would have been more appropriate to have used the language of the uncertainty of life and the sudden and unexpected coming of death (as e.g. in Luke 12.20). The future reference of salvation is also clear in the distinctions Paul makes between justification * and reconciliation in the present and salvation in the future in Rom. 5.9ff. (and note 'the hope of salvation' in I Thess. 5.8). Paul himself, in these surviving authentic letters, only once refers to Jesus as Saviour, and this too is in respect of his future work: 'We await a Saviour, the Lord Jesus Christ, who will change our lowly body to be like his glorious body, by the power which enables him even to subject all things to himself' (Phil. 3.20f.); Jesus is called saviour because of what he will do, not because of what he has already done.

Paul's use of the words in the 'save'-group seems to be a continuation of Jewish intertestamental usage, though it is not easy to quote passages in which it is clearly evident that by salvation the writer meant the new heaven and the new earth of Jewish apocalyptic * expectation. But the use of the words in the later chapters of Isaiah, for example, could readily have been understood in this sense whatever their original meaning, e.g. 'Behold, your salvation comes' (62.11); 'There is no other god besides me, a righteous God and a Saviour' (45.21).

The future sense is also found in the Synoptic Gospels, where to be saved is identical in meaning with entry into the kingdom * of God (see, e.g. Mark 10.23–26).

A shift of emphasis from the future to the past can be seen in the Deutero-Pauline writings; e.g. the helmet is now not 'the hope of salvation' as in I Thess., but simply 'the helmet of salvation' (Eph. 6.17), and the same writer can say, without qualification, 'by grace you have been saved' (2.5, 8; cf. I Cor. 15.2, but note the conditional clause 'if you hold it fast'; similarly 'in this hope we were saved', Rom. 8.24).

An inevitable consequence of this change from future to past is that the conception of what is to be saved has to be altered. In Paul the salvation that is the object of hope involves the release of the whole creation from its bondage to decay and the redemption of our bodies through resurrection (Rom. 8.18f.; Phil. 3.20f.): i.e. the participation of all things in the glory of God. But when salvation is spoken of as present, all that can be saved in this sense is human beings, believers (I Tim. 4.10), or even only 'souls' (I Peter 1.9).

Together with this move, there also appears a greater freedom than in Paul to give Jesus and God the Father the title Saviour (Pastoral Epistles, II Peter, Jude); perhaps the earlier reluctance to do this had been due to its use in the emperor-cult, or in connection with nationalist leaders.

Although the title 'Saviour' is applied to Jesus only twice in the four Gospels (Luke 2.11; John 4.42), the idea is far more frequent. E.g. Matthew explains the name Jesus as the one who saves his people from their sins (1.21); and in many of the healing miracles restoration to health is taken to be a sign of salvation – an ambiguity that was possible through the two-fold meaning of the Greek word 'save': to restore to physical health and to deliver from the final divine wrath. Hence 'your faith has saved you' invites the reader of the Gospels to adopt a theological interpretation of the miracles of Jesus; the healing stories are symbols or images of salvation, which the believer hopes for, or rather, believes that he has received.

The old idea lingered on in some of the later writings of the NT, e.g. the author of I Peter speaks of 'a salvation ready to be revealed in the last time' (1.5) and in the Letter to the Hebrews Christ who is said to have been offered once to bear the sins of many, will appear a second time to save those who are eagerly waiting for him (9.28).

The belief that Jesus is the Saviour of the world has enabled Christianity to express itself in different forms, according to the needs that were uppermost at the time. The content given to the title Saviour depended on what it was thought most necessary to be delivered from. At the time of Paul and in his churches this seems to have been destruction by the wrath of God in the last judgment (I Thess. 1.10). At a later date, in a less Jewish milieu, that from which salvation was most wanted was the power of world-rulers, astral deities, and all the malign forces that were believed to control the world. An associated idea is that salvation is from ignorance through enlightenment; then Jesus is seen as the revealer who saves by disclosing who he is, i.e. that he is the Saviour (so the Fourth Gospel). Yet another way of seeing salvation is that it is from sin, guilt and death; and then the idea of sacrifice* is frequently used to explain how Jesus saves (e.g. Hebrews). In the patristic* period, one way of expressing salvation was in terms of deliverance from mortality through participation in the divine nature.

For the notion of salvation to make sense at all and to act as an interpretative category it is necessary first of all to recognize that the situation is such that something needs to be done in order to put it right; if all is well there is no room for a Saviour nor any need. The situation may be either that of the individual (*qua* sinner; *qua* mortal) or that of the whole creation of which he is a part and without which so far as we know he cannot exist.

Secondly, it must be possible in some way to relate what is said about the Saviour and his saving work to the situation that needs deliverance. It is at this point that most of the theories of the atonement* seem inadequate; they involve mythological conceptions that no longer answer the old question, How can this man save us? (I Sam. 10.27).

It is possible to detect a difference of emphasis between two ways of stating a doctrine of salvation, at the present time. The more traditional type of doctrine continues to apply the term Saviour to Christ as the agent of the Father and to maintain the distinction between the Father and the Son. The other type of doctrine regards the death and resurrection of Jesus as parabolic of the love of God for his world and of his intimate involvement in it; according to this way of thinking, the title 'Saviour' is appropriately applied to God the Father (as in Luke 1.47; I Tim. 1.1, etc.).

A final point that needs to be borne in mind is this: Christian faith from its beginning has never asserted its hope for salvation in such a way as to justify an easy-going optimism. It has always seen salvation as on the other side of destruction, even of total cosmic collapse (e.g. Mark 13, Revelation). The faith that God will save the world does not exclude the possibility that humanity will first destroy it.

J. C. FENTON

Salvation History see Heilsgeschichte

Sanctification

Making holy or being made holy*. In the primary sense, only God is holy. It is practically a tautology when the company of heaven and earth sing 'Sanctus, sanctus, sanctus'. Yet we are commanded and taught to pray 'Hallowed be thy name': let God be God! Since God's love has overflowed in creation and the desire for our salvation, God is best God when we requite his love. God's elect people is told: 'Be holy as I am holy' (Lev. 11.41f.; I Peter 1.15f.; cf. 2.4–10). Christians are called to be saints (Rom. 1.7; etc.). The being, character and action of God determine holiness. Creatures become holy when they reflect or participate in God.

It is clear that sanctification is God's gift before it is our goal. Using the passive verbs of divine agency (signified in baptism), Paul writes: 'You were washed, you were sanctified, you were justified in the name of the Lord Jesus Christ and in the Spirit of our God' (I Cor. 6.11). Yet further purification seems to be needed on account of the post-baptismal sin which so perplexed the apostle and the early church; and the final verdict appears to await a future judgment (e.g. II Cor. 5.10). In Western theology, sanctification is the name usually given to the process which is begun in the baptismal washing and the associated coming to faith and which will be irreversibly completed at the final judgment (cf. Eph. 4.30). It is the process of becoming holy, of being made saints.

The Holy Spirit has been shed abroad in the hearts of believers (Rom. 5.5), and Christian lives may be expected to produce the fruit of the Spirit (Gal. 5.22–25). To show the transformative power of God's work in us – which is appropriately ascribed to the Holy Spirit* – the mediaeval West spoke of the real change thus wrought in the human person as 'created grace'. Lutherans have preferred to keep grace for the favour of God into which we are received at initial justification and have hesitated to speak of a 'growth in grace' for fear of works-righteousness (but see Luther's own writing Against Latomus for a more nuanced view). The Council of Trent*, with appeal to the then collect of Pentecost XIII, taught an increase in justification which amounts to a growth in sanctification: 'Increase in us, O Lord, faith, hope and love' (Denz. 1535). Calvinists have been ready to speak of sanctification and a new life in obedience according to the 'third use of the law'. John Wesley, with predecessors in the Catholic tradition, preached a carefully defined 'entire sanctification' or perfect love of God and neighbour as a gift to be prayed and striven for in this life.

Eastern Orthodoxy's characteristic term in this connection is *theosis* or *theopoiesis*, dependent on II Peter 1.4 ('partakers of the divine nature'). It designates that attainment to the likeness of God for which humanity was created in God's image (Col. 3.10); the transformation of believers from glory into glory has already begun (II Cor. 3.18). Rightly understood, such 'divinization' no more abolishes the distinction between Creator and creature than the best Western teaching pictures a merely extrinsic relation between them.

In liturgical usage, places and objects may be sanctified. This is usually connected with the part they play as 'means of grace' in human salvation; but the cosmic dimension of God's purpose should not be reduced by anthropocentrism.

T. Hopko, *The Spirit of God*, 1976; H. Lindström, *Wesley and Sanctification*, 1950; J. Meyendorff and J. McLelland (eds), *The New Man: An Orthodox and Reformed Dialogue*, 1973; A. M. Ramsey, *Holy Spirit*, 1977.

GEOFFREY WAINWRIGHT

Satan

In Hebrew the word 'satan' simply means 'adversary' (esp. in law-suits). In the older OT conception 'the Satan' is a member of the heavenly court, whose function is to identify evil persons and to accuse them before God (Job 1f.). By NT times, however, his character has degenerated and he has become the lord and leader of the evil spirits who oppose God and oppress men. In the Fourth Gospel he retains his role of accuser, and the Holy Spirit appears as counsel for the defence (*see* **Paraclete**). Until the age of Enlightenment* belief in an objectivized personal Devil* and his minions was all but universal among theologians. Today, however, it is generally recognized that belief in Satan, the leader of the fallen angels, etc. is not a satisfactory answer to the problem of evil*: it still leaves us asking the question how evil got into the world which God created and saw was 'very good'. But as a pictorial way of representing the existence of superhuman evil forces in the universe Satan and his hosts call our attention to a very important question for theology.

See also **Demonic, Devil.**

ALAN RICHARDSON

Satisfaction

Amends for a wrong done (*see* Dan. 4.27 NEB). Tertullian *On Repentance* argued that repentance was open to those who sinned after baptism; this repentance, which consisted of fasting, public mourning, kneeling to the presbyters, and asking for prayers from all, made satisfaction to God for that sin. The *Sentences* of Lombard summarized Augustine in teaching that repentance consisted of three parts: contrition or compunction of the heart, confession of the lips, and satisfaction by works. Absolution was attached to confession, and satisfaction thus became the subsequent chastisement. This teaching made room for the giving of indulgences. Calvin argued that all penalties are removed by Christ; any subsequent chastisement, as of David (II Sam. 12.13, 14), is not for punishment but for correction. This distinction, perhaps a quibble, goes back to Augustine.

The term satisfaction was made into a prominent part of the doctrine of the atonement* by Anselm, who drew on remarks in the teaching of Athanasius and Augustine that God had just claims against sinful mankind. Anselm argued that, as a result of sin, God's honour had to be satisfied; sin had either to be punished or atoned for. To the objection that we are commanded to forgive without either of these requirements, Anselm replied that we had to leave vengeance to God or his agents; we were in no position to ask satisfaction. God the Father could only be satisfied by the freely willed death of God the Son, God become man. Only thus could human nature be restored. No one unless he were man *ought* to repay

what man owed to God for sin; no one unless he were God *could* pay it. What the Son did could not be done in vain; it must be given to those for whom he made himself man, 'his kindred and brethren, whom he sees burdened with so many and so great debts'.

Hooker neatly combined the teaching of Tertullian and Anselm on satisfaction by arguing that Christ's satisfaction for sins made God content with the little satisfaction we could make.

Tertullian, *On Repentance*; Anselm, *Cur Deus Homo?*; J. McIntyre, *St Anselm and his Critics: A Re-interpretation of the Cur Deus Homo*, 1954; A. Ritschl, *The Christian Doctrine of Justification and Reconciliation*, ET 1872, 1900.

J. C. O'NEILL

Scepticism

In the extreme sense, scepticism is the view that human reason cannot attain sure knowledge of how things really are. Historically, extreme sceptics have often been called 'Pyrrhonists', after Pyrrho of Elis (*c.* 360–270 BC), who advocated suspension of judgment on all issues, moral or epistemological, as the way to attain calmness of mind, or ataraxia. The revival of sceptical views by Montaigne (1535–1592) and Pierre Bayle (1647–1706) contributed to the growth of intellectual and religious toleration as an ideal of the eighteenth-century Enlightenment*. By the nineteenth century the term 'sceptic' was used to suggest a person who doubted the truth of religion in general and of Christianity in particular. It was to combat such a position, which he associated with the philosophy of David Hume, that the Anglican theologian, Richard Whately (1787–1863), wrote his ironical *Historic Doubts Relative to Napoleon Buonaparte* (1819), intended as a *reductio ad absurdum* of the sceptical approach by showing how it could be used to cast doubt on Napoleon's ever having existed. Nevertheless, throughout the nineteenth century it was regarded as reasonable in many quarters to doubt the truth of theological claims, because no adequate evidence or proof could be offered in support of them. By 1900, however, William James (1843–1910), for example, was saying that 'the whole defence of faith hinges upon action', that one must be free to act on 'the religious hypothesis', that a passive scepticism was not inherently more respectable intellectually than committed belief, a position which may be compared with that of the Catholic philosopher, Maurice Blondel (1861–1949), whose influential *L'Action* appeared in 1893. James's religious pragmatism was quite different from the orthodox theologian's appeal to revelation* or to the church as sources of absolute authority. Indeed, the Roman Catholic dogma* of papal infallibility*, as defined by the First Vatican Council in 1870, completely dismissed the sceptical view that uncertainty must be man's final position in matters of religious faith and morals. Although in the twentieth century scepticism has ceased to be the name of a distinct philosophical position, the approach has remained powerfully present in the naturalistic and materialist traditions, as well as in some forms of positivism* and analytical philosophy*, all of which are sceptical of any metaphysical move which tries to transcend experience in any radical way. Theologians, on the other hand, stimulated by new interests in myth*, symbol and the nature of religious language*, now speculate more confidently. Compare, for example, the Catholic theologian Karl Rahner's pancosmic view of immortality, that at death the termination of the soul's* relationship to an individual body enables it to enter into relations with the entire material cosmos (see his *On The Theology of Death*, 1961), with the Protestant theologian Paul Tillich's theory that man's immortality is the eternal presence of his earthly life in the memory of God (see his *Systematic Theology*, 3, 1964. *See also* **Life after Death**). Modern theologians are much clearer than some of their predecessors about the limits of this kind of speculative thought.

William James, *The Will to Believe*, 1897; R. Popkin, *The History of Scepticism from Erasmus to Descartes*, 1960.

JOHN KENT

Schism

The Greek word, of which the English is a transliteration, means a tear or rent, e.g. in a piece of cloth (Mark 2.21), and so a division between two groups of people (John 7.43). It is now generally applied to the church to refer to a breach in its unity, to the division of the church into separated and mutually hostile organizations.

Paul used the term of the rival factions at Corinth (I Cor. 1.10). But his question on that occasion – Is Christ divided? – was answered by a universal negative in the period of the early church. The patristic writers were convinced of two things: first, of the blasphemy and sinful character of schism – hence, according to John Chrysostom, 'nothing angers God so much as the division of the Church; even if we have done ten thousand good deeds, those of us who cut up the fullness of the church will be punished no less than those who cut his body' (*Homily on Ephesians* xi. 5) – and second, that schism is always outside the church, i.e. of any two bodies at odds with each other and each asserting itself to be the church, only one of them had the right to the claim.

There was not, however, always a clear distinction between schism and heresy, but the former ultimately came to mean, in the words of Optatus, that which 'breaks peace, goes out from the root of mother Church, but retains the faith and the sacraments which they acquired within the Church' (*Against Parmenian*, 1.10–12). Hence Augustine had little to object against the Donatists* on the grounds of belief, but argued that they were outside the church since their breach of unity proved their lack of love and therefore of their possession of the Holy Spirit who is its source.

In the light of nine hundred years of experience of a state of schism between the Eastern and the Western churches, and four hundred years of schism between Western Catholics and Protestants, we ought to be able to acknowledge by now that some of the patristic conclusions were mistaken: schism is not outside the church. On the contrary, the only conclusion that makes sense of the present divided condition of the Christian church is that our schisms are internal, not external. Despite our strenuous efforts, we have not succeeded in dividing the church into two or more churches. There is only one church, and that church does not coincide with any one of the existing 'denominations'. It includes them all. This conclusion is virtually, though not formally, admitted by the Second Vatican Council.

This does not mean that schism does not matter, or that we can ignore it. It is a sin, and a serious one. It is still possible to perpetuate, and even compound, the internal schism of the church, and we can point to some examples of very modern schisms (e.g. the 'Paisleyites' in Ulster). Those who are responsible for initiating arbitrary and self-willed schism are to be condemned, not condoned. And we are all to some extent guilty of schism as long as we are content to continue in a state of internal schism without taking any steps to end it.

This view of schism does not mean that any body of people claiming the name of 'Christians' must automatically be regarded as part of the one church. External schism is only another name for apostasy, and is better called apostasy*. There are some forms of alleged Christianity which are so far from the NT and so alien to Christian tradition that they must be regarded as groups of apostates rather than as schismatics within the church. Thus in ancient times the spread of Islam in formerly Christian lands was not the emergence of a heretical form of Christianity but represented a vast movement out of the Christian church. In modern times Christian Scientists and Mormons must be regarded as adherents of two non-Christian religious sects rather than as schismatic Christians. The difficulty of deciding where to draw the line between schismatics and apostates is real but inevitable. It is no more difficult than was the problem of deciding in the case of historical schisms which body was the 'real' church.

S. L. Greenslade, *Schism in the Early Church*, 1953; A. T. Hanson, *Church, Sacraments, and Ministry*, 1975; T. A. Lacey, *Unity and Schism*, 1917; K. Rahner, *Theological Investigations*, Vol. 12, ET 1974, pp. 98–115.

J. G. DAVIES/A. T. HANSON

Scholasticism

The approach to inquiry into God and the world called 'scholasticism' distinguished itself from its predecessors by an ostensibly more rigorous method, much as Descartes intended to set himself off from his scholastic training by an innovative and more powerful method. The period from Anselm of Canterbury to Descartes, however, covers six centuries, and many diverse movements paraded as 'schoolmen' during that time.

The distinguishing mark of the method was a fascination with logic, and a resolute application of it wherever one could succeed in making its clarifying powers felt. Anselm (1033–1109) learned logic from his teacher Lanfranc, and employed it to respond to his brothers' request to develop a single argument for making plausible the existence of God (*see* **Ontological Argument**). It was, of course, the logical works of Aristotle, the first ones to reach the West, which provided the syllabus and the impetus for this new mode of inquiry.

As a result, exposition of questions in natural philosophy as well as in theology, which had previously arisen in the context of extended biblical commentary, could now be posed in a more architectonic fashion, and afforded a more systematic treatment. The result was the books of *sententiae* (assertions), most notably those of Peter Lombard (*c.* 1095–1160), followed by the *summae* (summaries). The shift in style corresponded roughly to one of location, as the seat of learning moved from monastery and cathedral school to the universities, in the twelfth to thirteenth centuries. The commentary was not lost, as the same individual (notably Aquinas) would compose *summae*, commentaries on Aristotle and on specific biblical books, as well as 'disputed questions'. But the new mode – a specific question introduced by a dialectical opposition of objection and response, and followed by a logically elaborated *expositio* – established the celebrated scholastic method.

Peter Abelard (d. 1142) is generally credited with initiating the method in his *Sic et Non*, where apparently contradictory statements of the church fathers are juxtaposed, with rules for reconciling them. Yet a similar approach had been adopted before him by those working with canon (church) law*, notably Bernold of Constance (d. 1100) and Ivo of Chartres (d. 1116). Moreover, it is difficult to call so external an opposition a 'method'. It seems more plausible to recognize the influence of Aristotle's logical works, especially on the structure of the *disputatio*, which vied with lecture (*lectio*) and sermon (*praedicatio*) for a distinct form of teaching by the time of John of Salisbury (d. 1180). Moreover, there is recent evidence of direct influence from Muslim religious law, where 'the *sic-et-non* method was part of the Islamic orthodox process for determining orthodoxy' (Makdisi, p. 649). A fruitful comparison can also be made, in style and temper, between Ibn 'Aqil (1040–1119) and Aquinas (1225–1274), especially in the ways they sought to use reason in untangling religious questions (ibid., pp. 650–57).

The scholastics are justifiably best known for their various elaborations of the relations between reason and faith. In fact, their treatments of the reasonableness of faith could never be identified as a form of 'rationalism', so interior did they regard the relations between the two. It is this finely synthetic character of the work of the best of them which merits the special place of this movement in shaping Western philosophy and theology. Aquinas' teacher, Albert the Great (c. 1195–1280), directed his attention more to questions of natural philosophy, while the Franciscan Bonaventure (1221–1274) was more resolutely concerned with the individual's relation to God – as were the Victorine theologians Hugh (d. 1141) and Richard (d. 1173). Yet the goal implicit in the efforts of all, and epitomized in Aquinas, was to lay out an understanding of the world of nature (creation) so as to display the power of its creator, revealed also to be its redeemer. Or, as Chesterton described Aquinas' avowed task: to show the independence of dependent things.

If logic was the mind of movement, faith its soul and prayer at its heart – for the houses of study were also religious houses with common prayer each day – its subsequent course might be traced by noting the relative weight of each factor. In the measure that the university began to take an autonomous course, logic would become the dominant guide. And as one becomes preoccupied with arguments themselves, a certain scepticism regarding their real import may well emerge. The fourteenth century saw the production of *summae logicales*, following that of Peter of Spain (1210/20–1277). Moreover, substantive theological works came to display an abundance of close reasoning and fine distinctions. The *disputatio* format, so integrally connected with teaching and intellectual formation, gave way to extended exposition. A comparison of John Duns Scotus (1265–1308) or his later contemporary William of Ockham (1280–1349) illustrates this shift. The tendency of these thinkers to a form of nominalism * is well-known, yet a movement as diverse as scholasticism would expressly tolerate such overt philosophical differences. What proved more telling for the life of the form of inquiry was this shift in style, audience and temper. Although it would enjoy another century of vitality in Spain, the judgment of Descartes that philosophy needed new life and method was so quickly adopted because it responded to a general impression.

Yet it is fair to say that philosophical movements are eclipsed not so much because they fail as because they had succeeded. So subsequent generations within the movement are content to comment on the acknowledged masters. Such may be taken as a fair description of 'late scholasticism'. Mention must be made, however, of the 'scholastic revival', identified principally with the first half of the twentieth century. Inspired in part by the nineteenth-century romantic recovery of the Middle Ages, it was given specific impetus in 1879 by the encyclical of Pope Leo XIII: *Aeterne Patris*. Students in Catholic colleges and universities, especially those preparing for priesthood, were to receive specific training in the 'principles and methods of the Angelic Doctor' (Thomas Aquinas). And to prepare a cadre of teachers for such a task, higher institutes of study were directed to prepare programmes of research into the thought of Aquinas.

While it is fair to say that an intellectual movement cannot be legislated (or resuscitated), it would be unjust as well not to note the benefits of this act of ecclesial leadership. In the measure that it generated a doctrinal recapitulation of Aquinas called 'Thomism *', it proved short-lived; but to the extent that it fostered critical research into the scholastic period in an effort to understand the elements germane to the peculiar synthesis of faith and reason operative there, one can speak of a genuine recovery of the thought of Aquinas. Scholasticism, then, can be considered as an intellectual movement which endured nearly six hundred years, peaking in the thirteenth century. It can also be regarded for its lasting contribution in relating human understanding to the convictions of religious faith. In this respect, the scholastic movement can be credited with employing philosophical notions in the service of understanding faith, and hence giving theology the status of a systematic inquiry. This achievement is the more notable in that it appears to be a uniquely Western and Christian endeavour. The adage 'distinguish in order to unite' allowed one to distinguish philosophical from theological inquiry, nature from grace, yet without opposing one to the other. Similarly, human freedom and the contingent order proper to creation were regarded as themselves reflections of the power unique to the creator as universal (or analogous) cause. These fundamental positions, explicated variously in different phases of the scholastic movement, represent nonetheless commonly shared attainments in relating faith to reason.

M.-D. Chenu, *Nature, Man and Society in the Twelfth Century*, 1968; E. Gilson, *La Philosophie au Moyen Age*, 1947; M. Grabmann, *Die Geschichte der scholastischen Methode*, 1957; B. J. F. Lonergan, *Verbum: Word and Idea in Aquinas*, 1967; G. Makdisi, 'Scholastic Method in Medieval Education: An Inquiry into its Origins in Law and Theology', *Speculum* 49, 1974.

DAVID BURRELL

Science and Religion

Much of the history of Western civilization for the past 350 years might be included under this heading. Science and science-based technologies have grown during the period into a position of cultural dominance, with profound consequences for religion. The relative failure of most faiths to come to terms with them at sufficient depth has been one of the factors responsible for the marginalization of religion in the modern world. Popular discussion of the subject is still in large measure influenced by stereotypes derived from ancient conflicts, and many religious believers remain unnecessarily defensive about it. There are, of course, many exceptions to these sweeping generalizations. They are made, however, to draw attention to the wide scope of the subject, and to its practical importance.

The word 'science' is used in a number of different senses. It can mean a body of more or less reliable knowledge, divided into individual 'sciences', which together cohere in a potentially comprehensive world view. It can also mean a method of investigating experience through critical study and ex-

periment, and by the formation of testable hypotheses. It is also used loosely to describe a practical source of power for good or ill, as when people talk about 'science' producing the hydrogen bomb. These meanings are clearly inter-related, but there is value in distinguishing them, not least because in recent years the focus of interest has tended to move away from conceptual questions, e.g. how can the scientific and religious world views be reconciled?, towards ethical and political questions of the kind, how can human beings avoid being dehumanized by scientific and technological developments which leave no place for specifically human concerns? 'Religion' likewise has a wide range of meanings which need to be clarified if confusion is to be avoided. Theology, faith and religious practice all relate in their different ways to scientific counterparts.

The classic controversies between science and religion were mainly conceptual, though they had methodological and practical overtones. Galileo's concepts were resisted by the church, not because churchmen were blind to the evidence, but because, if accepted as true in some absolute sense, they would undermine the Aristotelian* framework of mediaeval Christendom with enormous practical consequences. The issue thus became focussed on ecclesiastical authority versus free investigation, and in that guise has become part of the mythology of science. The same forces were at work in the Darwinian controversy where genuine arguments for and against evolution* were confused with the issue of biblical literalism, the authority of the Christian revelation, and far-reaching questions about the nature and dignity of man. Other controversies have arisen when belief in God has, unwisely, been united too closely with some phenomenon hitherto regarded as inexplicable (*see* **God of the Gaps**) or when scientists have made illegitimate and sweeping claims about the religious and philosophical implications of their discoveries.

For scientists the key issue in these controversies has been that of autonomy*. Science cannot be itself as long as some external authority can dictate what has to be believed, or insist on an explanatory concept, e.g. God, which cannot be subjected to normal scientific scrutiny.

This autonomy has now for the most part been conceded, and there have been various attempts to express it in terms of rigid separation between the scientific and religious spheres. The danger this poses for religion has already been mentioned. A religion cut off from the common ground of empirical understanding loses its relevance to the major part of life. Furthermore a religion which is wholly inward, or existential, or which is content to use its own technical language ('play its own language-game') without finding points of contact with other experiences and languages, is in the long run difficult to distinguish from fantasy.

The problem is how to relate autonomous disciplines, without sacrificing their proper autonomy, and to find what I. T. Ramsey used to call an appropriate 'empirical fit'. Much has been done in this field, and there are some encouraging signs of scientists and theologians beginning to find fruitful ground for dialogue.

A notable example of the change in attitude is the retreat from dogmatic scientific positivism*, according to which scientific knowledge is the only kind of knowledge accessible to us. As a definition of knowledge this has proved in practice to be far too narrow. Our knowledge of persons, for instance, is no less real than our knowledge of physical processes, but it is not amenable to the same kind of analysis, nor can it be reduced to the same kind of concepts. To use a familiar metaphor, the scientific net catches those phenomena which present scientific techniques are best fitted to study, but this does not give scientists the right to make pronouncements about the whole contents of the ocean of reality. A consciousness of their limitations has made both science and religion more humble in their approach to one another, and imperialistic claims, whether scientific or religious, are less frequently heard.

Much attention has been given in recent years to the element of commitment within the process of scientific discovery. The work of Polanyi and Kuhn (see **Paradigm**) has encouraged theologians to explore analogies between scientific and theological methods, both of which in their different ways entail 'faith seeking understanding'. Torrance, starting from a different point, has pushed the methodological analogy to its limit, and in a long series of books has claimed that 'theological science' is just as objective and intellectually rigorous in relation to its sub-

ject matter as the new physics inaugurated by what he calls 'the Einsteinian revolution'. He also makes much of the theological context within which modern science had its origin, and seeks to prove the necessity for science of a view of the world as both intelligible and contingent, in accordance with the classic Christian doctrine of creation*.

The growth of studies in the history and sociology of science has revealed the extent to which, like any other activity, science is conditioned by its environment. Some have stressed this to the point at which all claims to objective knowledge of the way things are have been dropped, and science is regarded as purely instrumental, a means of successful prediction and no more. At first sight this might seem to leave the field open for a religious metaphysic, but it follows that if science is conditioned, so too is religion. For religion the consequences of such relativism would have to be agnosticism*. For science the abandonment of all truth-claims would leave it vulnerable to external influence in a way which could in the end destroy its character. Faced with these unwelcome results, both might find a common interest in asserting that, beyond all the conditioning factors, there is some fundamental, albeit largely unknown, objective reality towards which together they aspire.

Religious experience* has been brought under scientific scrutiny by the Religious Experience Research Unit at Oxford under Sir Alister Hardy, with some surprising results. It is claimed that such experiences are much more widespread than was previously supposed, and bear no relationship to the kind of infantile regression once asserted to be their basis. A different kind of approach to religious experience, through sociology, anthropology and psychology, has been made by John Bowker in a profound study which explores the extent to which human religious behaviour points to and is grounded in some external object of encounter. His theme links in significant ways with that of the previous paragraph, and he concludes that it is not illegitimate, even within the terms of a scientific study, to find the origin of the sense of God in God himself.

These are only a few examples of the kind of dialogue now taking place. A common assumption is that science and religion share a concern with the same reality, while approaching it from different viewpoints and with different questions in mind. One of the motives for persisting with such dialogue is a consciousness of the fragmentation of modern knowledge, coupled with a sense that the sharp distinction made in the early days of science between the world of fact and the world of value has somehow been humanly disastrous. Science makes progress by breaking up the continuum of experience into manageable sections which can then be studied in isolation. It is less successful in relating the parts to the whole and retaining a grip on those human, and ultimately religious, values without which it could not itself have come into being.

Mention was made earlier of another trend, the perception of science not so much as knowledge, but as power. Questions on this level, often with a precise practical content, are increasingly directed towards the scientific community in ways which cause resentment and alarm. The motives are partly political, but they are also one of the consequences of an instrumentalist view of science. If science is to be judged by results, not just making theoretical predictions, but as an actual force for good or evil in the world, then willy-nilly it is brought firmly into the political and religious arena. Discussions of the subject within, say, the World Council of Churches, tend to have this character, one of the reasons being the presence of many whose countries or groups have not yet received much direct benefit from scientific advance. From the perspective of the 'have nots' it is not hard to question the claim of the whole scientific enterprise to be objective and value-free. For them, science is what it does.

Such comments may seem strange in societies where science has long held a respected place. It is likely, however, that within a world perspective, future dialogue between science and religion will be conducted most keenly by those who seek to use science in pursuit of their religious and political values, rather than by those who are striving for some theoretical synthesis.

I. G. Barbour, *Issues in Science and Religion*, 1966; J. Bowker, *The Sense of God*, 1973; A. C. Hardy, *The Biology of God*, 1975; W. Pannenberg, *Theology and the Philosophy of Science*, 1976; A. R. Peacocke, *Creation and the World of Science*, 1979; M. Polanyi, *Personal Knowledge*, 1958; T. F. Torrance, *The Ground and Grammar of Theology*, 1980; World Council of Churches, *Faith and Science in an Unjust World*, 1980; J. Ziman, *Reliable Knowledge*, 1978.

JOHN HABGOOD

Scripture, Doctrine of

Christian practice in worship, preaching, personal and social morality, pastoral care and teaching always inescapably involves judgments about the nature and functions of the writings comprising the Christian Bible (Bible: Latin *biblia*, fem. sing., from the Greek *biblia*, neut. plur., 'books'). These judgments are, or imply, some doctrine of holy scripture. Thus e.g. the ancient church had, by the early third century, adopted a collection of writings received from Judaism, concerning God's covenant* with Israel, and added a collection of texts concerning God's covenant in Jesus Christ. That they were characterized precisely as *holy scripture* expressed the church's judgment about its nature and functions: that the collection is a coherent whole because in various ways every part witnesses to some moment in the 'economy' or administration of God's saving work throughout history; as such, it must function in the life of the church to give shape and content to worship, to give comfort and encouragement in Christian living, to guide the resolution of moral quandaries, to shape Christians' affections and beliefs, to guide resolution of doctrinal disputes. To call this collection 'holy scripture' is to judge that it is not merely an anthology of texts, but that it ought to fill an indispensable and decisive function at the very centre of the church's life with the holy God. What is the relation of the 'ought' to the 'functions'? That is the question that generates the agenda of issues which a doctrine of holy scripture must address. In some respects these issues are perennial in Christian theology; in other respects intellectual developments since the eighteenth century have made them radically new.

I. The classical view of the relation between the functions scripture fills in the life of faith and the claim that it ought so to function has been grounded, not in a pragmatic argument that experience has shown that if it is allowed so to function desirable results follow, but in the strictly theological claim that God is uniquely related at once to the origins of these texts in the past and to their uses now. Since in regard both to its writing and to its use God intends it to function in these ways, it would be faithless not to employ it.

God's relation to the origin of scripture has traditionally been explicated in a doctrine of the inspiration* of its authors by the Holy Spirit. To assert scripture's inspiration has been to stress two major themes.

1. Scripture is grace, conveying a message given at God's free initiative prior to our response to it in faith, and given to be that which shapes and rules faith. Where the texts are recitals of historical events, it has been stressed that the authors were eye-witnesses, or scribes for eye-witnesses, whose inspiration consists in divine guidance accurately to report what transpired. Where the texts are of other sorts (psalms, proverbs, prophecies, etc.), their authors' inspiration consists in divine guidance both as to what to say and as to how to say it. Detailed explanations of the dynamics of inspiration vary in the ways they hold together God the Holy Spirit's control of the writing, on one side, and the authors' human freedom to express themselves in their own styles, on the other, ranging from views that make the authors virtual dictating machines to views that assign the Holy Spirit only the most general oversight of the writing. What they all express, however, is the judgment that scripture is a witness *to* faith. This involves a claim about a property of the text: It is ordered to a particular end. It is not merely a reflection of extant faith. Rather, it is given to call faith into being, to give it its peculiar shape and, if necessary, to correct it.

2. Emphasizing scripture's inspiration is to stress that it is unqualifiedly trustworthy as the norm of both right action and right belief. This involves a claim about another property of the text: It is true. Although there have been disagreements concerning the range of topics of which this is claimed, varying from the view that the trustworthiness of texts is limited to religious matters to the view that they are inerrant regarding every subject matter on which they touch, all are agreed that at the very least scripture is unqualifiedly true in its expression of the message that is the basis of faith. Here too there have been disagreements, whether given texts express only one message or whether by God's inspiration they might

perhaps simultaneously convey one message at the straightforward literal level and another encoded at an allegorical* or typological level. Nonetheless, it was part of the classical view to insist that the literal meaning of the text was its message for faith and that, if there are other levels of meaning, they are based on and somehow controlled by the literal meaning. To stress its inspiration is to assert emphatically that scripture is characterized by a certain property: its literal meaning is true, and hence reliable as the basis of faith.

God's relation to contemporary uses of scripture has traditionally been explicated in a doctrine of the Holy Spirit's illumination of the members of the church now. To assert the church's illumination has been to stress that the context in which the purposes for which God the Holy Spirit ordered and structured scripture are fulfilled is the on-going life of the church as it handed on the gospel from person to person and generation to generation. It is in the context of that process that people's minds are illumined to grasp the meaning of the biblical message and their wills and affections empowered to appropriate it so that it gives rise to faith and shapes their very lives to be more holy. This provides the setting for classical theology's understanding of the relation of scripture, respectively, to tradition* and reason. 'Tradition' meant, in the first instance, not so much a body of content perhaps (in oral form) deposited in the church by the Holy Spirit in addition to and other than scripture, but rather the church's activity of handing on the gospel (*actus tradendi*). Hence, it could be insisted both that scripture is the ultimate norm for right belief and action in the church, including right 'traditioning', and that scripture's normative status is actualized only through 'traditioning' and as 'traditioned'. So, too, since the gospel is always being handed on into new and, in varying degrees, unprecedented circumstances, its traditioning inescapably involves reasoned elaboration, yet 'reason' is always in the service of the scriptural message, aiming to exhibit as powerfully as possible its capacity to illumine life in (relatively) novel situations. Thus in the classical view scripture's present functions and the claim that it ought so to function were held together in the theological claim that the inspiration of its writing in the past as witness to faith and our illumination in our use of it now are but two moments in one continuous work of the Holy Spirit.

II. Intellectual developments from the eighteenth century on have raised questions that the classical doctrine of scripture never contemplated. In some ways the traditional agenda of issues remains: How are the functions that scripture fills related to the claim that it ought to fill them? Does explication of the 'ought' involve ascribing certain properties to biblical texts? How is the relation of scripture to tradition to be understood? To what extent is reason autonomous in relation to scripture? However, the two central claims of the classical position came under novel critique and turned out to be ambiguous: that scripture is witness to faith, and that faith rests on the literal meaning of scripture. What makes modern doctrines of scripture modern, whether conservative or liberal, is their effort to address the traditional agenda of issues in the light of exposés of the ambiguity of these two claims.

1. The first notable development was the rise of historical science. To begin with, its methods were taken to provide new and peculiarly appropriate ways to determine the literal meaning of scripture, i.e. its meaning as a narrative of God's acts in history which is the basis of faith. However, historians' methods aimed at the reconstruction of the history of what 'really happened'. They required that scripture's inspiration be disregarded and that the text be examined by the same methods by which any other ancient texts would be studied to uncover the evidence they provide, explicitly or implicitly, regarding what 'really happened'. That had two consequences. It drove a wedge between scripture's religious meaning (i.e. its 'natural' or 'obvious' meaning when used within the church's common life as the basis of faith) and its historical sense (i.e. its sense as witness to the historical circumstances in which it was written) which had classically been identified. And it brought into question classical claims about properties of scripture. It showed that the texts themselves had histories, that they were the work of series of editors often centuries removed from the events reported, and not of the allegedly eyewitness authors to whom they were traditionally ascribed, that they were not theologically consistent with one another, and that

they were not inerrant.

2. The second notable development was a change in understanding of what is involved in interpreting scriptural texts which challenged the classical meaning of the slogan 'scripture is a witness to faith'. In the classical view, this slogan meant that scripture is a witness by faith to its 'object', viz. God's saving acts in history. This brought with it the view that interpretation of biblical texts involves, first, ascertaining how the text would have been understood by its original readers and then, second, explaining that subject matter in contemporary terms. Early in the nineteenth century Friedrich Schleiermacher formulated a contrasting and enormously influential view of interpretation. In this view a text is the expression of a process of thinking within the writer. Interpretation involves a reversal of this movement, moving from the text understood on its own terms in its historical setting back, by an intuitive act, into the creative process in the author so that the interpreter actually relives the author's thought process. On this view, the scriptural text which is being interpreted is a witness, not to faith's object, but to faith itself as a subjective state in the author which has come to expression in the text (*see also* **Hermeneutics**).

In which sense does 'faith rest on history'? and in what sense is 'scripture a witness to faith' and how are the religious and historical senses of scripture to be held together? Reflection on these questions has generated five types of doctrines of scripture in modern theology.

Two are conservative. 1. This type affirms that the classical view that scripture is inspired means that it is inappropriate to use modern historiographical methods to ellucidate scripture. 'Scripture is a witness to faith' means that scripture is an inerrant witness of faith's object, God's saving acts in history. However, while part of world history, these acts are beyond the grasp of historian's methods because they are a sort of reality knowable only in faith. Hence, while rational capacities must be employed in interpreting it, scripture cannot be made subject to reason in the sense of historically critical assessment. 'Faith rests on history' means that faith stands or falls with the accuracy of scripture's reports of this sequence of events. What are inerrant are not the extant texts, but the originals of which they are copies. Thus understood, scripture is other than and norm of tradition, coherent and self-explanatory, and so not needing interpretation by tradition or the mind of the church.

2. This also affirms classical claims about scripture's inerrancy, coherence and perspicuity. It differs from 1. in taking 'scripture is a witness to faith' to mean that scripture expresses, not so much the object of faith, as the feelings and experiences of the person of faith. And 'faith rests on history' refers to the history of miraculous transformations of persons' subjectivities. It means that faith depends on the accuracy of that report, but that the events reported are inaccessible to historians' methods because they are known only to faith. In both of these views the religious and historical senses of scripture are held together by keeping both separate from the historians' interpretation of scripture. For them both what is important in scripture is what it teaches, i.e. doctrine.

Two are liberal. 3. 'Scripture is a witness to faith' can be taken to mean that scripture is a witness to faith's object, Jesus * of Nazareth as he 'actually lived'. 'Faith rests on history' means that faith rests on the historian's reconstruction of the life of Jesus and the sort of faith he had, which we are to emulate. Here the religious and historical meanings of scripture are identical in that they both refer to the historian's Jesus. This view is free to abandon all the classical claims about both the properties and the divinely intended functions of scripture, for what is important in scripture is solely the evidence it can provide for a reconstruction of the life of Jesus in its setting in the history of Israel.

4. For this type 'scripture is a witness to faith' means that it expresses faith as an existential state or mode of subjectivity. What is important in scripture is the kerygma, the proclamation of this new and authentic mode of subjectivity as a genuine possibility for our existence today. 'Faith rests on history' means that faith is a response to the proclamation of the news that this mode of existence was instantiated once in the life of Jesus and is a possibility we can actualize in our own histories. Here religious and historical senses are held together in that they both refer to the same mode of subjectivity. This type can join 3. in abandoning classical claims about the properties of scripture. But it retains classical claims that what makes biblical texts 'scripture' is their function in the life of the church as the basis of its proclamation. Indeed, here what makes the texts scripture is no property at all, neither inerrancy nor evidentiality, but solely their function in the common life of the church.

5. This holds a curiously middle position among the preceding four. What is important in scripture are its narratives. 'Scripture is witness to faith' means that its narratives give an identity-description of both the object of faith, i.e. God as known in Jesus Christ, and the existential state of faith, i.e. the covenant * relationship between God and human-kind. 'Faith rests on history' means that faith is called into being by these narratives. On this view the meaning of the texts lies in the narratives themselves and not in events somehow 'behind' the texts, so it rejects the stress in 3. on historical reconstruction. By the same token it rejects the stress in 1. and 2. on a 'history' inaccessible to historians' methods. So it can join 3. and 4. in affirming the appropriateness of historians' methods in explicating scripture and in saying that what makes the texts 'scripture' is their functions in the life of the church and not such properties as inerrancy and coherence. On the other hand, it rejects the view of 3. and 4. types that what is important for faith in scripture is some sub-set of texts (viz., whatever is reliable evidence for the life of Jesus; whatever is kerygmatic) and (as do 1. and 2) insists that the entire canon of scripture is a unity constituted, not by doctrinal consistency (as in 1. and 2.) but precisely by the coherence of its one extended narrative.

See also **Biblical Criticism, Exegesis, Historical Criticism.**

J. Barr, *The Bible in the Modern World*, 1973; S. L. Greenslade (ed), *Cambridge History of the Bible: The West From the Reformation*, 1963; C. Henry, *God, Revelation, and Authority*, Vol. IV, 1979; D. Kelsey, *The Uses of Scripture in Recent Theology*, 1975; W. Marxsen, *The New Testament as the Church's Book*, 1972; D. Nineham, *The Use and Abuse of the Bible*, 1976; C. Wood, *The Formation of Christian Understanding*, 1981.

DAVID KELSEY

Sect

Within the Christian tradition, the sect constitutes a distinctive, persisting, and separately organized group of believers who reject the established religious authorities, but who claim to adhere to the authentic elements of faith. A sect may be distinguished, on somewhat different criteria, from both a church and a denomination. Whereas the church is inclusive of a population, a sect is exclusive; whereas church members may be 'inborn', sect allegiance is always voluntary. Dual memberships are not tolerated. Theoretically, allegiance is total and equal, and sects usually reject (especially at the time of their origin) ordained ministry, encouraging lay, and sometimes purely informal, leadership. Sects have frequently begun with an ideal of creating a new basis of Christian unity, often on explicitly scriptural premises; this was the early expectation of the Disciples, the Brethren, Christian Science and the Unification Church. Sects begin in various ways: by schism from other religious bodies (e.g. such schisms have occurred widely among Baptists in the USA; Pentecostalists; Brethren; and Mormons); by the mutual discovery of seekers (Brethren, Holiness movements); through revivalism (some Pentecostal groups such as the Elim Church, and the first Methodists and Bible Christians); around a special exegesis of scripture (Christadelphians; Seventh-Day Adventists; Jehovah's Witnesses); or in support of additional teachings which augment traditional Christianity (Christian Science; Mormonism; Unification Church). Sometimes more than one of these items, or response to a charismatic leader, is involved. Schism is less common as the original cause of major sects than as a cause of secondary divisions. Over time, sectarian practice tends to become routinized, and leadership, initially sometimes volatile or uncertain, tends to become institutionalized, sometimes leading to the development of a full-time, paid class of officials. But sects do not, contrary to the opinion of H. R. Niebuhr, always evolve into denominations. This development might be indicated for several conspicuous American movements, including Methodists, Disciples, the Church of Nazarene and Seventh-Day Adventists, even though some of these bodies retain sectarian characteristics. Prominent examples of sects that have not been denominationalized are Christadelphians, Jehovah's Witnesses, Plymouth Brethren, Exclusive Brethren, Hutterites and some groups of Mennonites. The emergence of a second generation is often a crucial element in promoting denominational tendencies. Sects generally protest against either the church or, more significantly in modern times, against the secular culture. Their votaries usually adopt a more rigorous moral position than other people, and sect allegiance becomes the primary social attribute of the individual's identity. Since sects reject the liturgical and ecclesiological traditions of the church, they are often able to adopt contemporary techniques in administration and witness, thus combining the appeal of scriptural premises and rational procedures. The general image of the sect is of a relatively small community, and there are many such sects in existence in Christendom, but a number of large-scale movements maintain an international presence. Jehovah's Witnesses, Seventh-Day Adventists and Mormons each claim millions of members worldwide, and among Pentecostal * movements, of which the most prominent is the Assemblies of God, numbers are even higher. These sects often combine the sense of sustained, close, communal relationships of local congregations with a proud claim to international fellowship. Sects are of very diverse character, and various attempts have been made to provide a basis of either classification or typification. Sects may be typified according to certain dominant orientations to the world and the provision of salvation. *Conversionist* sects emphasize the need for men to experience a change of heart: Pentecostalists and Salvationists are of this type, which is close to the evangelical tradition. *Revolutionist* sects emphasize God's part in overcoming evil by the second advent and subsequent millennium: Jehovah's Witnesses and Christadelphians are examples. *Introversionist* sects stress withdrawal from the world as the way of salvation, and the cultivation of in-group purity, as among the Hutterites and the Exclusive Brethren. *Manipulationist* or gnostic sects canvass knowledge of special doctrine by which experience may be reinterpreted to produce harmony and happiness, as in Christian Science and various New Thought movements. *Thaumaturgical* sects encourage the idea that by miraculous dispensations from the normal operation of cause and effect, the individual may transcend worldly evils, as in Spiritualism. *Reformist* sects promote piecemeal amelioration of social conditions as the means of salvation – a position adopted by modern-day Quakers. The *Utopian* sect believes that evil will be overcome only if men seek to reconstruct society according to God's blueprints, and here the nineteenth-century Oneida Community, the Shakers and the Bruderhof movement provide examples.

Bryan Wilson, *Sects and Society*, 1961; (ed), *Patterns and Sectarianism*, 1967; *Religious Sects*, 1970.

BRYAN WILSON

Secular Christianity

An influential current in the theology of the decade 1960–1970. It sought to reconcile Christianity with the modern secular mentality, urging theologians to come to terms with human autonomy*, the achievements of science and technology, the withdrawal of many aspects of life, including morality, from ecclesiastical control, and so on. Some of the inspiration came from D. Bonhoeffer, with his call for involvement in the affairs of the world and his plea to respect the maturity of the modern person. Among the principal exponents of secular Christianity were F. Gogarten, H. Cox, P. van Buren and Ronald Gregor Smith. But just to mention these names is to indicate the variety of views, some of them conflicting, embraced by the general description 'secular Christianity'. Gogarten, appealing to Galatians, stressed the notion of 'man come of age' and portrayed Jesus as the one who liberates from heteronomy. Cox claimed that modern science and technology are implicates of the biblical doctrine of creation* and perhaps tended to glorify uncritically the achievements of technology. P. van Buren is sometimes counted one of the 'death of God'* theologians and advocated the reduction of Christian theology to the history of Jesus as the exemplary free man and to the ethics derived from him. R. G. Smith understood secularization to mean the radical historicizing of thought, and tried to apply this idea to Christian theology. He was sharply critical of those secular theologians who advocated the elimination of God, and equally of those who were optimistic about

the prospects of a technologically based civilization. In spite of some exaggerations, these writers had the salutary effect of encouraging more serious dialogue between Christian theology and contemporary thought and of promoting Christian involvement in the affairs of secular society.

P. van Buren, *The Secular Meaning of the Gospel*, 1963; H. Cox, *The Secular City*, 1965; F. Gogarten, *Verhängnis und Hoffnung der Neuzeit*, 1953; J. Macquarrie, *God and Secularity*, 1967; E. L. Mascall, *The Secularization of Christianity*, 1965; R. G. Smith, *Secular Christianity*, 1966.

JOHN MACQUARRIE

Secularism

Confusion often persists in the use of the terms secularism and secularization*. The latter is a neutral concept relating to broad processes occurring within society, while secularism is an ideology advocating the elimination of religious influence in the state and social institutions, particularly in education. The early secularists were essentially an anti-clerical party, but more generally secularism came to imply opposition to all religion, and a demand that secular criteria should determine social policy and education. The term was first used in 1851 by G. J. Holyoake, founder of the first secular societies, which came to number well over a hundred in nineteenth-century Britain. The secularist tradition owed much to Tom Paine and Robert Owen, and was thus associated with the rise of socialism. Holyoake held that science was the sole providence of mankind; that morals were independent of Christianity; that reason was the criterion of truth; that man's proper concern was the elimination of inequalities in this world rather than the possible compensation for such inequalities in another life. He held, and so did the later International Society of Freethinkers, that the state should be neutral in religious matters, and that equal tolerance should extend to all religious and philosophical positions. He was less extreme than Charles Bradlaugh, who campaigned more vigorously against religion as such, and who for thirty years until 1890 presided over the National Secular Society. Secularism is often taken as a synonym for humanism* and rationalism*, but today self-styled secularists are usually the most extreme of the various movements that oppose religion.

Susan Budd, *Varieties of Unbelief*, 1977; Colin Campbell, *Towards a Sociology of Irreligion*, 1971.

BRYAN WILSON

Secularization

The process by which property, power and prestige passed from religious to lay control is referred to as secularization. The term was first used in reference to the laicization of church lands by the Treaty of Westphalia in 1648, but the concept has since been extended in its application to refer to the general process by which religious agencies have been divested of their economic, political and social influence. The word is used to allude to diverse aspects of social and religious change, including such items as the following: sequestration by political powers of the property and facilities of the church; the transfer to secular control of activities formerly undertaken by religious agents and of social functions which religion previously fulfilled; the decline in the proportion of their time, energy and resources which men allot to religious concerns; the decay of religious institutions – churches, Sunday schools, uniformed organizations and ancillary organizations; the supplanting in matters of behaviour of religious precepts by demands that accord with purely technical criteria; the suppression of specifically religious consciousness by empirical, rational, instrumental and matter-of-fact attitudes; the increased separation of evaluative and emotional dispositions from cognitive orientations; decline in religious observance and the dimunition of such practices as rites of passage, genuflexion, saying grace, church attendance and membership. The term secularization is variously employed to embrace all these – and perhaps other – social phenomena, and in its width of application the concept sometimes loses cogency, but the many-sided nature of this broad process of change does not warrant the abandonment of a concept which denotes, albeit loosely, the way in which religious institutions, actions and consciousness lose their social significance.

The process of secularization has been documented at many levels, principally by sociologists, and particularly with respect to the social functions of religion. Whereas the church, in time past, fulfilled a variety of functions vital to society, these have steadily been taken over in very large part by more consciously instituted and rationally specialized agencies. Thus, in traditional society, religion served to sustain and, according to Émile Durkheim, even to forge a sense of cohesion within the community; it conferred a sense of identity both on the individual and the group; through its teachings concerning afterlife rewards and punishments and by the canvass of a divine command morality it instituted a system of social control which induced good behaviour in individuals and established a regulated pattern of social order. Christianity also supplied an intellectual conspectus, purporting to explain and justify not only the supernatural and the moral, but also the nature and purpose of the cosmos. The church served regularly to legitimize both political authority (conspicuously from the time of Charlemagne) and the actual content of political and social policy. It justified a nation's wars; enjoined the rich and powerful to be merciful and charitable; and urged upon the poor both forbearance and contentment with their lot, providing theological rationale – a theodicy – for social inequalities of wealth, power and status, and the injustices that occur in nature. It provided the means of comforting the afflicted, particularly in the face of illness and death. Almost all of these functions have now been lost to the church, and hence have been secularized. Religion is not now central enough to supply society with a sense of cohesion, and men conspicuously diverge widely with respect to their social and religious values: modern society depends less on cohesion, as manifested in shared consciousness among men, than on contrived and planned systems of social integration effected through bureaucratic, fiscal and technical arrangements. Individual identity is today no longer a product of religious initiation (confirmation is the pale vestige of that once important social rite) or of religious commitment. Group identity is expressed more typically in political, class or ethnic terms than in religious terms (the cases of some conspicuous minorities and politically oppressed nations notwithstanding). Modern society relies on increasingly technical arrangements for the maintenance of social control: neither supernatural afterlife sanctions nor the pronouncements of moral theology are much invoked as ways of preserving social order. Explanation of natural and social phenomena no longer take God as their departure point, but rely on tested propositions of science. The church no longer seeks to justify social structure, and politicians invoke religion less and less in justification of their policies. In the matter of providing emotional support for the afflicted, religion still fulfils an extensive function for individuals, but even here secular agencies, from social work to psychotherapy, challenge the role of the clergy. A different way of documenting these associated processes of secularization might be to indicate the growth of a variety of specialist professions – teachers, civil servants, social workers and even entertainers – at least part of whose functions were once among the activities of the clergy. The process is one in which the erstwhile latent social functions of religion have been increasingly rationally planned and undertaken by more specialized departments.

Commensurate with these broad secularizing processes in society, there is a range of empirical evidences of the attendant loss of religious influence over the lives of individuals. Such are the statistics of church attendance; the decline in the proportion of live births that are followed by baptism; the diminishing proportion of those baptized who get confirmed; the decline in the numbers of the clergy; the ageing profile of that profession, and the diminution of the social reward (both in stipend and status) which the profession now commands.

Secularization is a neutral and not a normative term indicating a factual process of social change. It does not postulate the disappearance of religion nor conflict with the fact that in secularized societies, in which religion has ceased to be of much importance to the operation of the social system, religion manifestly persists and continues to command the convinced support of a minority. Some commentators have suggested that (from the time of pre-Christian Judaism) the rationalization of religious dispositions has been a necessary part of the development of great religions, and that in eliminating 'extraneous' functions the modern practice of religion is more authentic and purposeful, but these are value judgments about secularization on which commentators may differ.

Karel Dobbelaere, 'Secularization: A Multi-Dimensional Concept', *Current Sociology* 29, 1981; Richard K. Fenn, *Towards a Theory of Secularization*, 1978; David Martin, *A General Theory of Secularization*, 1978; Bryan Wilson, *Religion in Sociological Perspective*, 1982.

BRYAN WILSON

Self-Understanding

Self-understanding is a term introduced into contemporary theology by R. Bultmann from the existentialist * analysis of M. Heidegger. It is an integral element in the existentialist programme of demythologizing* representing in a form which it is claimed is intelligible to the modern man what was formerly understood by such terms as 'salvation'. Acceptance of the kerygma * brings a change in man's understanding of himself, releasing him from the fear of nothingness, insignificance and death. Bultmann insists that a change in a man's understanding of himself involves a change in the man himself (conversion). He thereafter lives authentically, whereas formerly his existence was inauthentic.

See **Existentialism.**

ALAN RICHARDSON

Semantics

Semantics means the study of meaning in language. It is possible to distinguish between semantics as a department of logic and semantics as a department of linguistics. A primarily logical question, for instance, would be that of the relation of the linguistic sign to that which is signified by it (e.g. between the word *horse* and the entity horse, its 'referent' to which it refers). Statements about this relation are connected with other logical questions, such as the differentiation of different kinds or strata of language (scientific language, ordinary language), the status of signs (like *unicorn*) for which no real referent exists, the relation of individuals to classes (this horse to the class *horse*, this God to the class *gods*), questions of truth and falsehood, and methods of argument, verification and proof. Logic is not primarily concerned with the description of the different natural languages, such as Hebrew, Greek or English.

As a part of linguistics, on the other hand, semantics deals with the identification and description of meaning in the natural human languages. Two approaches can be distinguished. A synchronic approach attempts to describe the meanings with which words (and other linguistic elements) function in a language at one time. In a diachronic approach the linguist tries to state the ways in which meanings have changed and developed in the history of one or more languages.

Both the logical and the linguistic kinds of semantics are relevant for theology, and perhaps some of the major problems of theology lie in questions of meaning in the logical sense. Nevertheless it is rather in the linguistic sense that the term 'semantics' has been most used in recent theological discussion. It has appeared mainly in questions of the interpretation of Hebrew and Greek linguistic phenomena and their use in the structure of theological argument. The following circumstances are relevant:

1. The massive philological scholarship of the nineteenth century, though rich in the gathering of material and the classification of forms, was often weak and naive in its approach to questions of meaning. The rise of the newer general linguistics in the mid-twentieth century, with its greater emphasis on synchronic description, favoured a closer attention to semantic study.

2. The Judaeo-Christian tradition includes a long history of fascination with etymology as a means of clarifying obscure expressions and adapting them to use in theological argument. Nineteenth-century comparative philology, by setting etymology on a historical basis, accidentally strengthened this tendency, and it was further supported by the use of etymologies (usually fictitious) in philosophies such as that of Heidegger, which exercised some influence upon theology. The recent semantic discussion involves, among other elements, the reassertion of function against etymology.

3. The relation between OT and NT language has been a particular centre of concern. Early in the present century many words of biblical Greek, which had previously been supposed to be unique, were identified in the Hellenistic papyri. In reaction against an apparent Hellenizing interpretation of the NT, some argued that the words came from the Greek world but their meanings from the Hebrew background. In turn it has been argued that evidence was distorted in order to fit it into this picture. The matter is part of a larger question, namely, that of the use of the contrast of two ways of thought, the Hebrew and the Greek, to which some currents of theology have assigned positive and negative values respectively.

4. An important issue raised has been the contrast between word-meanings and sentence-meanings. Many attempts to state theological meanings took the form of dictionary articles on words, and gave the impression that characteristics of the Judaeo-Christian revelation were intrinsic to each of the biblical words. Against this it has been argued that theological distinctiveness belongs not to the meanings of words (even biblical words) but to sentences and larger complexes, and that this fact makes possible the translation of theological ideas into other languages, in which all individual words are different.

5. In general, much new analysis is needed in order to penetrate the process by which the modern scholar apprehends and evaluates the indications furnished by an ancient text in Hebrew or Greek. Even the reader of the Bible who does not consider himself a scholar gives only an extremely superficial impression if he says he makes up his mind by looking at a translation, consulting a commentary or using a dictionary. Among scholars, it may be suspected that the dryness and dullness of many commentaries and exegetical discussions arise from the simplification of a very complex series of semantic indications, and that a greater consciousness of semantics as a discipline may do something to improve the level of exegesis generally.

For modern semantics in general, S. Ullmann, *Semantics, An Introduction to the Science of Meaning*, 1962; J. Lyons, *Semantics*, 1977. For application to biblical problems, J. Barr, *Biblical Words for Time*, 1962; *The Semantics of Biblical Language*, 1961; 'Hebrew Psychology', in *The Encyclopedic Dictionary of Psychology*, 1983.

JAMES BARR

Semi-pelagian

A term which has been used to describe several theories which were thought to imply that the first movement towards God is made by human efforts unaided by grace*.

The term seems first to have been used at the end of the sixteenth century in the controversy within the R C Church concerning grace and free will. In modern writing the description is applied to writers of the fifth and sixth centuries (esp. J. Cassian, Vincent of Lérins and Faustus of Riez) who taught that one must take for oneself the first step towards salvation. None of these writers had any connection with Pelagius. The Semipelagian teachings were condemned at the second council of Orange in 529; Pope Boniface II endorsed the verdict in 531.

See **Pelagianism.**

O. Chadwick, *John Cassian*, ²1968, ch. 4; H. Rondet, *The Grace of Christ*, E T 1967, ch. 9.
E. J. YARNOLD

Senses of Scripture

Until comparatively recent times the question uppermost in the minds of those who studied the Bible was 'What does the text mean?' The educated man of the early Christian centuries had been trained in grammar and rhetoric and philosophy, and he had a sophisticated technical understanding of the nature and functioning of language. He was also familiar with the use of examples and illustrations and analogies in poetry and oratory to aid understanding or to heighten appreciation. It was natural to such readers of the Bible to look not only at the obvious meaning of the words but also at the possibility that they might stand for something other than at first appeared. To find that they did was to discover in the human authors of scripture a rhetorical skill and an elegance altogether admirable. Augustine of Hippo (354–430) devoted the fourth book of his *De Doctrina Christiana* to a search for examples of such devices because he wanted to convince his educated contemporaries that the Bible was to be respected as fine writing.

Augustine had, too, an explanation to put forward which made it clear why it was necessary for God to proceed in this way, not speaking to his people directly in scripture, but addressing them in stories and images. The effect of Adam's sin upon the minds of his progeny was to make them unable any longer to see God clearly when he spoke to them, and so God had to adapt what he said so that they could understand it. By giving scripture figurative meanings

he made it possible for everyone, even the simple and those new to the faith, to understand something of what it was saying. This view takes it as fundamental that scripture is directly and verbally inspired by the Holy Spirit.

The general notion that there might be figurative as well as literal senses of scripture early gave rise to the possibility that there might be not one but several non-literal meanings. These came to be commonly identified as three: allegorical, anagogical and tropological. The early history of this fourfold division (with the literal sense making the fourth) is by no means clear-cut, but Origen and Augustine were perhaps the principal sources of its diffusion in the West and it was the work of mediaeval exegetes to clarify the differences between the three figurative senses.

By the twelfth century the allegorical sense was taken to involve some form of *translatio*, or transference of meaning from the literal, as when Christ is called the Lion of Judah. We see in a real lion certain qualities or attributes which by analogy we may see as 'Christlike'. (The difficulty raised by Aquinas and others before him about the possibility of any created thing being 'like' God disappears if we take Augustine's view that God himself placed these comparisons in the world as aids to human understanding of the divine.)

The anagogical sense looked prophetically forward into history or beyond time to eternity. It became customary to regard the O T as prefiguring the N T in this way, in such detail that each O T figure had a counterpart in the N T. Joachim of Fiore worked out a scheme in which the prophetic pattern was continued into the period beyond the N T and served as a means of recognizing the imminence of the end of the world. This sense also provided hints of heaven.

The tropological sense was the moral one. Lessons were drawn from the Bible for the living of a good Christian life. Or, to be more precise, the text was 'turned' or 'bent' (*trope*) so as to make such points.

The view that scripture has several senses was not universally held from the beginning. The Antiochene* scholars of the patristic period had no time for such interpretations. The Alexandrians* (notably Origen) followed the pioneering footsteps of the Jew

Philo of Alexandria in developing their elaborate system of higher senses. The keynote of their explanations is that these are indeed higher or more profound meanings; it is not a matter of resorting to a figurative interpretation where the text is puzzling if we take it literally, but of searching it for layer upon layer of meaning, trying to extract from it the last holy secret, the last divine mystery which God had placed there for man's edification.

See also **Allegory and Typology, Sensus Plenior.**

H. de Lubac, *Exégèse médiévale*, 4 vols., 1959, is a full general study of the history of the four senses. On the study of the Bible from patristic times to the full development of this system in the high Middle Ages, see B. Smalley, *The Study of the Bible in the Middle Ages*, ²1952.

G. R. EVANS

Sensus Plenior

In recent decades there has been a revival of the patristic and mediaeval view that scripture is to be understood not only in the literal sense, but as having other, deeper meanings (*see* **Senses of Scripture**). Aquinas, adopting an ancient division which had been clarified in the twelfth century, distinguished between the 'literal' meaning of the words of the text and the 'spiritual' meaning of the 'things' described in scripture (*Quodlibet* VII. q. 6. a. 14). It is with this meaning of the *res* or 'things' of scripture that the *plenior sensus* is concerned.

The return to interpretation of this sort raises a number of questions. Was the human author conscious of the *sensus plenior* as he wrote? If not, can he still be said to be an author? How many kinds of 'fuller sense' are there? Are they reducible to the allegorical, anagogical and tropological types of standard mediaeval exegesis? What is the evidence that God intended a particular *plenior sensus* to be understood in a given passage? Will the *plenior sensus* always be found to be in harmony with the literal sense?

See also **Allegory and Typology.**

Full bibliography and survey of the question in R. E. Brown, 'The *Sensus Plenior* in the Last Ten Years', *CBQ* xxv, 1963, pp. 262–85; see id., 'The History and Development of the Theory of a *Sensus Plenior*', *CBQ* xv, 1953, pp. 141–62.

G. R. EVANS

Similitudo Dei

The term means likeness of God. Gen. 1.26 reads 'Let us make man in our image, after our likeness'. Modern scholars are confident that 'image' and 'likeness' (Hebrew: *ṣelem* and *demuth*) in this verse are used synonymously in a typical example of Hebraic parallelism. Some theologians, however, interpreted these terms as two different concepts. For example, Irenaeus contrasted the image of God with the likeness of God (Latin: *similitude*), arguing that the image of God is humanity's endowment with reason, etc. while the *similitude* represents the relationship to God for which humanity was created. Thus in the Fall * the latter was lost, while the former was retained.

WILLIAM HORDERN

Simul iustus et peccator

This Latin tag means 'at the same time a righteous person and a sinner'. It comes from Luther's lectures on the Epistle to the Romans delivered at the University of Wittenberg in the three semesters 1515–1516. The lectures were not fully published until 1908. The church historian Karl Holl seized on these lectures as showing a heroic Luther whose thought was later cramped by the necessity of taking account of mediocrities like Melanchthon. Holl quoted a long passage from Luther's commentary on Rom. 4.7. Luther had just argued that we are sinners in ourselves and yet righteous in God's eyes, through faith. It is like the case of a sick man who believes his physician when he assures him that he will recover. 'Can one say that this sick man is healthy? No; but he is at the same time both sick and healthy. He is actually sick, but he is healthy by virtue of the sure prediction of the physician whom he believes. For the physician reckons him already healthy because he is certain that he can cure him, indeed, because he has already begun to cure him, and does not reckon him his sickness as death.' The passage continues later, 'Now can we say that the patient is perfectly righteous? No; but he is *at the same time both a sinner and righteous*; a sinner in fact, but righteous by virtue of the reckoning and certain promise of God that he will redeem him from sin in order, in the end, to make him perfectly whole and sound. And, therefore, he is perfectly whole in hope, while he is in fact a sinner . . .' Holl argued that this early view of Luther placed the sole emphasis on God's activity; and that the later teaching, when Luther became a reformer, made faith a merit by which one could gain election *. Holl interpreted Luther's early teaching to mean that 'the believer must learn constantly to think of the two contradictory judgments of God as applying to himself at the same time, the utter rejection and the equally unconditional grace and acceptance . . . He should go down in penitence to the point of nothingness, to the feeling of the worthlessness of his whole person, and yet he should overcome this feeling (which he still keeps hold on) by irrevocable faith in God's promise.'

As a result of the propaganda of Holl and O. Scheel, the slogan became very common in German theology. Barth, for example, quoted Luther's words in the original order, *simul peccator et iustus*, and said: 'but no half sinner and consequently no half righteous one, but both, completely'. A long dispute about the adequacy of the phrase as an interpretation of Paul was initiated by Adolf Schlatter.

Luther's lectures on Romans were opened up to English readers by E. Gordon Rupp, *The Righteousness of God: Luther Studies*, 1953, and translated partially in 1954, and fairly fully in 1961.

Muras Saarinvaara and others have disputed that Luther in his lectures on Romans had yet discovered the gospel he was to preach as a reformer. Whatever value or meaning we attach to the slogan, it seems unwise to use it as a key to Luther's thought from 1517 onwards.

Wilhelm Pauck, *Luther: Lectures on Romans*, *LCC*, 1961; Karl Holl, 'Die Rechtfertigungslehre in Luthers Vorlesung über den Römerbrief mit besonderer Rücksicht auf die Frage der Heilsgewissheit' (1910), reprinted in *Gesammelte Aufsätze zur Kirchengeschichte, I, Luther*, [4, 5] 1927, pp. 111–54; O. Scheel, 'Rechtfertigung II Dogmengeschichtlich', *RGG²*, Vol. 4, cols. 1749–58.

J. C. O'NEILL

Sin

'Sin is any word or deed or thought against the eternal law' (Augustine). All people are supposed to know the commandments of the moral law (summed up in the Ten Commandments), although Israel, because of God's love for his people, has clearer knowledge (Amos 1.3–2.8; 3.2; Rom. 2). Every transgression of the law deserves punishment; although sin often produces suffering in the innocent, it is wrong that the innocent should suffer: 'The soul that sinneth, it shall die' (Ezek. 18.4). Transgressors often escape punishment, and righteous men and women in the Bible like Abraham, Moses and the prophets and Paul used this opportunity to preach repentance to sinners, and offered in prayer to accept the punishment due to sinners so that sinners might have greater opportunity to repent. God also provided animal sacrifices * for men to offer to him, partly to deal with the effect of sin. The heart (the seat of thought and action) is assumed to be wicked and constantly producing evil (Gen. 6.5; cf. 8.21; Jer. 17.9; Matt. 15.19). Man was therefore vulnerable to the forces of chaos and evil (sometimes pictured as Leviathan), and to temptation by the devil and other fallen angels. The corruption of mankind and the importance of the guilty inclination and of 'the first sin' (original sin) was particularly emphasized in the centuries before Christ (see Qumran, e.g. 1QH i.21–23; ix.13; xvii.15). The theme was also found in contemporary Roman literature (e.g. Horace, *Odes* iii.6, cited by Kant; Virgil).

Christian theology states that 'Christ died for our sins' (I Cor. 15.3). How his death achieved salvation for sinners is much disputed.

The early church assumed that baptism cleansed the wicked heart (Jer. 4.14), and in general denied that there was any chance of repentance for those who sinned after baptism, although eventually the possibility of a second repentance was agreed. This debate assumed a distinction between sins unto death and sins not unto death (I John 5.16f.). Augustine fixed the main lines of the Western church's teaching about sin by saying that baptism washed away all sins, whether inherited original sin * or added sin, but did not take away the infirmity which the regenerate man could not always resist. He distinguished between the *peccata* of the baptized which did not lose them salvation and their *crimina* or crimes. The practice of private confession in Celtic monasteries spread to the whole church and ousted public penance. The Reformers rejected the distinction between mortal* and venial* sins; none of the sins of the elect are imputed to them by God, because of their faith; while true believers still sinned, and they must fight against sin all their lives, the sin is not 'counted' or imputed (see **Imputation**).

The depravity* of man after the Fall* was denied to be complete by the Council of Trent*, and the Arminians* raised similar questions from within Calvinism. In the eighteenth century traditional teaching about sin and punishment was sharply questioned; it was argued that 'the wrong sense or false imagination of right and wrong ... can proceed only from the Force of Custom and Education in opposition to Nature' (Shaftesbury), and that 'the people is never corrupted, but it is often deceived' (Rousseau; cf. Marx). The debate continued: Kant and Schopenhauer taught that 'man is by nature evil'; but Nietzsche and Freud saw consciousness of sin as a weakness. Recent Christian theology has tended to be fascinated by the figure of the 'holy sinner' (Dostoevsky).

William Telfer, *The Forgiveness of Sins: An Essay in the History of Christian Doctrine and Practice*, 1959.

J. C. O'NEILL

Sobornost *see* Conciliarity

Social Analogy

The use of a group of human beings as an analogy of the Trinity* was first advanced by the Cappadocians*. Basil cites Peter, James and John in this connection. Its further development as a full-scale analogy belongs, however, to the nineteenth and twentieth centuries in England and America (Illingworth, Thornton, Lowry and Hodgson) under the influence of recent views of personality. While older views had stressed impermeability as its leading characteristic, the modern view emphasized capacity for fellowship as equally important. The tripersonality of God could, therefore, be interpreted on the analogy of human selves in society. Thus Thornton, arguing against Idealist* attempts to find in the universe the

necessary counterpart as object to God as subject finds on the basis of this analogy the subject-object relation adequately embodied within the Godhead itself. Applying this analogy C. C. J. Webb claimed that Christian orthodoxy spoke of personality *in* God rather than the personality *of* God as the psychological analogy implies. The motive of the analogy is pluralist, its target a Trinity in Unity and its inherent weakness (without proper qualification) a tendency to tritheism.

See **Psychological Analogy.**

L. Hodgson, *The Doctrine of the Trinity*, 1943; L. S. Thornton, *The Incarnate Lord*, 1928; C. C. J. Webb, *God and Personality*, 1918; C. Welch, *The Trinity in Contemporary Theology*, 1953, pp. 133–52.

H. E. W. TURNER

Social Gospel

The term does not permit of precise definition. It was, however, a type of activist Protestantism which arose in the late nineteenth and early twentieth centuries in industrial, urban North America. Its best-known theorist was a German-American theologian, Walter Rauschenbusch (1861–1918), author of *A Theology for the Social Gospel* (1917) and other books.

The Social Gospel criticized the Protestantism of its day for being too individualistic and too little concerned with practical social service. It claimed to be 'the old message of salvation, but enlarged and intensified', believing the institutions of human society, as well as individuals, to be redeemable. It sought to bring about repentance for collective sins, and to create a middle path between 'an unsocial system of theology and an irreligious system of social salvation'. It did not reject the notion of individual salvation, but stressed that the fruits of that salvation must be seen in the social sphere.

Its chief theological focus was 'the kingdom of God',* which it understood as being the heart of the ethical system of Jesus, a collective notion and the only alternative to 'the greedy ethics of capitalism and militarism'. Against the kingdom of God are ranged the manifestations of 'the kingdom of evil'. Purely individual notions of sin are inadequate to explain the universal yoke of evil and suffering in human experience. The Social Gospel therefore sought to identify social, collective evil, and to foster a spirit of solidarity among Christians over against those manifestations. This involved the possibility of collective repentance and collective conversion for nations, organizations, companies and other social units.

Followers of the Social Gospel were often severely critical of the churches. Christianity must be shaped and corrected by the ethical standards of the kingdom of God. In the absence of such correction the churches are powerless for anything save self-preservation. The kingdom of God provides the prophetic element in the churches' life; without that element, they can breed only priests and theologians, and easily become lost in tradition and dogma. The church must not see itself apart from the kingdom, for it has power to save only to the extent to which the kingdom is active within it.

Although the Social Gospel contained a millennial element, its language was chiefly that of evolution and development. It believed that the change 'from catastrophe to development' was essential if modern man was to be able to understand the Christian hope. But catastrophe was not ruled out: Rauschenbusch wrote that: 'The coming of the Kingdom of God will not be by peaceful development only, but by conflict with the Kingdom of Evil.'

Neo-Orthodoxy* criticized the Social Gospel on many points. At its best, though, it was by no means as naive as has often been supposed, and many of its characteristic concerns have been revived since the 1970s.

R. T. Handy (ed), *The Social Gospel in America, 1870–1920*, 1966; C. H. Hopkins, *The Rise of the Social Gospel in American Protestantism, 1865–1915*, 1940; H. R. Niebuhr, *The Kingdom of God in America*, 1937; W. Rauschenbusch, *A Theology for the Social Gospel*, 1918; W. A. Visser 't Hooft, *The Background of the Social Gospel in America*, 1928.

ERIC J. SHARPE

Socinianism

The name Socinianism was given in recognition of the influence of Faustus Socinus (1538–1604) of Siena. Having felt the influence of Italian humanism and of his liberal-minded uncle, Laelius Socinus, he made contacts in Lyons and Geneva but returned to Italy, remaining uneasily within the Roman communion. In 1574 he went to Basle and in 1578 removed to Poland where his later life was spent in active effort to organize a church of his persuasion. His principal treatises, *De sacrae scripturae auctoritate* (1571), *De statu primo hominis ante lapsu* (1577) and *De Christo Servatore* (1578) show a complete disregard of Nicene-Chalcedonian orthodoxy, especially on the person and work of Christ. Christ is true God only in the sense that the Father shared his power with him at the Ascension. His *De baptismo aquae disputatio* (1580), written to refute a Czech treatise against paedobaptism, condemns the rebaptism of those baptized in childhood. Socinus strove to unify the discordant elements in the Minor Reformed Church of Poland, and the Racovian Catechism of 1605 was compiled from writings left by him. This church was crushed in 1638, but the dispersal of a remnant of Polish Socinians to Transylvania, East Prussia and the Netherlands resulted in the spread of Socinian doctrines in Western Europe. In seventeenth- and eighteenth-century England Socinian influence may be traced in the opinions of Latitudinarians and liberal philosophers and of the so-called Arians of the Church of England.

A. J. McLachlan, *Socinianism in Seventeenth Century England*, 1951; E. M. Wilbur, *A History of Unitarianism: Socinianism and its Antecedents*, 1945; *A History of Unitarianism in Transylvania, England and America*, 1952; G. H. Williams, *The Radical Reformation*, 1962.

J. T. MCNEILL

Sociology of Religion

This discipline is concerned with analysing religion in so far as it is a social phenomenon. As a modern social scientific discipline it has flourished only in the last twenty years. The 1930s and 1940s were characterized by a significant neglect of religion as a variable in modern Western society worthy of sociological attention. In contrast a number of the pioneers in sociology, Emile Durkheim, Max Weber, the church historian Ernst Troeltsch and even Karl Marx at times, gave considerable attention to religion as a social phenomenon. All have firm roots in eighteenth- and nineteenth-century rational empiricism, but it is primarily to them that most recent sociologists turn.

The French scholar Emile Durkheim presented one of the most complete attempts to provide a social explanation of the origins, meaning and continuing function of religion. His seminal study *Suicide* (1897) found that religion was a significant social factor in determining who is most likely to commit suicide (Protestants being considerably more suicide-prone than Catholics or Jews). His classic study of aboriginal religion, *The Elementary Forms of the Religious Life* (1912), concluded that religion is a key factor in the stability and integration of a society. His theory is contained succinctly in his definition which combines substantive and functional aspects of religion: 'Religion is a unified system of beliefs and practices relative to sacred things, that is to say, things set apart and forbidden – beliefs and practices which unite into a single moral community called a church all those who adhere to them.' Despite the unsatisfactory evolutionary assumptions involved in using the Australian aborigines as exemplars of 'primitive' religion, Durkheim's definition and functional analysis of religion in society has continued to influence present-day sociologists. Some, like Yinger, have sought a more general functional basis for religion, using Tillich's concept of 'ultimate concern' as a means of defining religion, Others, like Robertson, have argued for substantive types of definition, extending Durkheim's sacred/profane distinction into a more general distinction between empirical and non-empirical modes of explanation and regarding the latter as the subject matter of religion.

Recent discussion of the overall social function of religion has been dominated by theories and counter-theories of secularization*. Thoroughgoing secularization theories have been forwarded by Wilson and Berger, particularly in their earlier writings. For Wilson, secularization is the process by which religious thinking, practices and institutions have been gradually marginalized in Western society. For Berger secularization is a more diffuse cultural/social process, which he traces back to the transcendent monotheism of Judaism, whereby religious thinking and now institutions become increasingly remote from and deviant in the modern world. Other theorists, like Martin

and Greeley, have questioned whether any such overall process is discernible in Western societies. They have pointed instead to the persistence of private forms of religion, even in situations of considerable institutional decline, to the comparative resilience of some religious institutions, and to the large variations in religious practice in Europe and North America. These criticisms have helped to generate a growing interest in 'folk' or 'implicit' religion and in the patterns of belief and practice of those not represented by main-stream churches – an interest which owes much of its inspiration to Thomas Luckmann's innovative *The Invisible Religion* (1967). In America there has been particular interest, largely due to the work of Robert Bellah, in the generalized theistic language of presidential addresses and the rituals of public occasions, often termed 'civil religion'.

The German scholar Max Weber has proved to be perhaps the most important influence on present-day sociology of religion. His seminal study, *The Protestant Ethic and the Spirit of Capitalism* (1905), has generated very considerable interest in the Catholic/Protestant variable in modern society. Less functional in outlook than Durkheim, he took seriously the possibility that specifically theological ideas – notably those of election*, predestination* and sanctification* in popular Calvinism* – were formative in the initial stages of capitalism. This thesis has generated considerable research into continuing Protestant/Catholic differences of attitude to work and education and more recently has been a fruitful source of dialogue between sociologists, historians and theologians. Whereas Durkheim tended to see Protestant/Catholic differences as more the result of social structures than differing understandings of theology (the relative social integration of Catholicism and Judaism countering tendencies to individual suicide), Weber was always anxious to explore differing theological nuances. His overall sociological approach is characterized by a stress on both the importance of social structures and on the social analyst understanding in depth the meanings subjects attached to these structures (i.e. his stress on *Verstehen* or understanding).

Weber sought to extend his Protestant Ethic thesis to a wide variety of societies, including those of India and China. His work, of which his unfinished *Sociology of Religion* (1922) is only a small part, shows that he was also well aware that the sociology of religion ought to be applied to all the major world religions. Only recently have his ideas on Islam been explored by sociologists, and the discipline is only slowly attempting to make its criteria applicable to religions other than Christianity. However, this attempt, which most sociologists support in theory, in practice has brought enormous difficulties to the discipline. For example, it has proved very difficult to find a definition of religion, substantive or functional, which applies equally to Western monotheism, atheistic Theravada Buddhism and the varied forms of religion in Africa and Papua New Guinea. The lack of any such definition raises very considerable problems, not least for theories of secularization or religious decline.

One of Weber's most enduring contributions has been in the area of social typologies. He always insisted that social types are ideal types: they are heuristic* devices abstracted from reality to aid analysis and are not necessarily to be found in their pure forms in reality. On this basis he sought to distinguish differing types of bureaucracy and patterns of leadership in both secular and religious institutions. In the latter he distinguished, for example, the church from the sect and the prophet from the priest. The church is an inclusive institution, both doctrinally and in terms of its membership, whereas the sect is typically exclusive both in its claims about salvation and in its acceptance of individuals as members. The priest typically belongs to a church and is a conservative figure concerned with maintaining a given rite and orthodoxy* and endowed by his church with authority to do this. The prophet is typically a lay and iconoclastic figure, endowed with personal charisma rather than external authority, who gathers only committed believers around himself. The charismatic prophet can be an agent of profound social change. Whereas Durkheim tended to ascribe only a conservative and integrationist function to religion, Weber insisted that religious movements and religious leaders could on occasions have very radical social effects. However, one of the key difficulties for a radical religious movement, particularly one

focussed upon an individual charismatic prophet, lies in the transition it must make to survive once this prophet dies. This transition Weber characterized by his notion of the routinization of charisma: the process by which purely individual charismatic authority is transferred to an established priesthood. This process has been explored by a number of recent sociologists, particularly Roy Wallis, investigating patterns of leadership and authority in Scientology, the Unification Church and the Jehovah's Witness Movement.

The pioneer scholar who developed church/sect typology furthest was the German church historian Ernst Troeltsch in his *The Social Teaching of the Christian Churches* (1919). For him the church emphasizes grace, attempts to cater for the masses, adjusts itself to the world and is characterized by objective sacramentalism. The sect, on the other hand, is a voluntary society consisting of strict and definite believers who have experienced new birth and who are living apart from the world in small groups, are eschatologically inclined, and emphasize law rather than grace. The sect is typically a movement of the working-classes and dispossessed. A third type is constituted by mysticism, consisting of informal groups based only on personal and inward experience and lacking strict structures of worship, doctrine and organization. As a theologian Troeltsch insisted that all three types are implicit in and essential to the gospel. And as social historian he saw all three types present in the history of Christianity.

Recent sociologists of religion have found Troeltsch's analysis particularly useful. Tending to disregard Troeltsch's theological motivation, and indeed often seeing his mixture of theological and non-theological criteria as limiting church/sect typology too narrowly to Christianity, they have sought to identify further types and types within types. Yinger has produced a six-fold typology: the universal church (as in thirteenth century Catholicism), the ecclesia or national church (as in the Church of England or the Church of Scotland), the denomination (as in English Methodism), the established sect (as in the Jehovah's Witness Movement), the sect and the cult. Wilson, who tends to see sectarianism as the only institutional form of religion that will survive secularization, has concentrated instead upon differentiating between various types of sect. Originally advancing a four-fold typology of sects, he now proposes a seven-fold differentiation based upon the sect's deviant response to the world: conversionist (e.g. assemblies of God), revolutionary (e.g. Jehovah's Witness Movement), introversionist (e.g. Exclusive Brethren), manipulationist (e.g. Christian Science and Scientology), thaumaturgical (e.g. Spiritualism), reformist (e.g. current Quakerism) and utopian (e.g. communal sects in colonial North America). He argues that these types can also be applied to non-Christian religions.

In addition to typology there has also been considerable interest in church/sect dynamics. Richard Niebuhr's *The Social Sources of Denominationalism* (1929) argued that sects are necessarily short-lived phenomena: second-generation sectarians tend to be upwardly socially mobile, losing their working-class and socially dispossessed sectarian basis, and becoming less susceptible to the deviant doctrines of their parents. As a result, sects either die out altogether in the second generation or they become more denominational and less exclusive. Wilson's *Sects and Society* (1955) disputed this thesis, showing that some sects, like Christian Science, are in origin primarily middle-class institutions, and that in any case successful sects develop complex social mechanisms for maintaining intact the orthodoxy of the second generation. Detailed studies of a number of sects, including that of Scientology in Roy Wallis' *The Road to Total Freedom* (1976) and the Jehovah's Witness Movement in James Beckford's *The Trumpet Call of Prophecy* (1975) have supported Wilson. Wallis argues that some sects even become more exclusive in time: a loosely organized cult focussed upon a single charismatic figure became in the early 1950s the highly exclusive sect that is Scientology today. Further, Martin has suggested that denominations in the English context have been denominations from their outset and did not initiate as sects. Although the sociology of religion has again tended to focus upon sectarianism within Western, predominantly Christian, society, there is a growing recognition that anthropological accounts of millenarian sects and 'nerms' (new religious movements) merit sociological attention. Wilson's *Magic and the Mil-*

lenium (1973) makes a major contribution to this study.

An interesting feature of recent sociology of religion has been its attempt to extend into a number of areas largely uncharted by the pioneers. A number of sociologists, including Wilson, Berger and Lee, have offered sociological explanations of the ecumenical movement. Towler and Coxon in *The Fate of the Anglican Clergy* (1979) have studied ordinands from the perspective of sociology. And there is a growing interest in the sociology of liturgy and religious experience.* In addition, a number of churches have attempted to use sociological analysis to clarify the social context of mission – notably the Roman Catholic Church, starting with the pioneer work in religious sociology by le Bras and Boulard. Mady Thung's *The Precarious Organization* (1976) even uses sociology to produce a blueprint of the future church. Whilst not all sociologists are sympathetic to such use of the discipline and are critical of some of the theological assumptions of le Bras and Boulard, an increasing co-operation between some sociologists, theologians and churchmen is evident.

Finally, a continuing Marxist tradition of sociology, particularly in France and the Soviet Union, remains interested in religion but critical of the Western empirical tradition. Within this Marxist tradition, religion is typically analysed as alienating ideology. In Karl Marx and Frederick Engels' *The German Ideology* (1845), religion and theology are identified as ideology, reflecting a spurious division between mental and material behaviour and expressing the position of the privileged, ruling classes against the ruled. Although Marx and Engels were not wholly unsympathetic to all exemplars of religion, Marxist sociologists have generally continued to see religion as a form of alienation and as a tool of the bourgeoisie. Within this tradition the millenarian movements and cargo cults of Papua New Guinea have sometimes been seen by scholars like Worsley as precursors of genuine political protest. The combination of concern for the oppressed and overt value-orientation of the Marxist tradition has proved particularly attractive to recent liberation theologians and is usefully summarized in Gregory Baum's *Religion and Alienation* (1975).

See also **Liberation Theology; Marxist Theology.**

Introductions
Michael Hill, *A Sociology of Religion*, 1973;
Roland Robertson (ed), *Sociology of Religion: Readings*, 1969; Betty R. Scharf, *The Sociological Study of Religion*, 1970; Robert Towler, *Homo Religiosus*, 1974; Bryan Wilson, *Religion in Sociological Perspective*, 1982; J. Milton Yinger, *The Scientific Study of Religion*, 1970.

Subject areas
Peter L. Berger, *The Social Reality of Religion*, 1973; Robin Gill, *The Social Context of Theology*, 1975; *Theology and Social Structure*, 1977; David Martin, *A Sociology of English Religion*, 1967; *The Religious and the Secular*, 1969; *A General Theory of Secularization*, 1978; Roland Robertson, *The Sociological Interpretation of Religion*, 1970; Bryan Wilson, *Religion in Secular Society*, 1966; *Religious Sects*, 1970; *Contemporary Transformations of Religion*, 1976.

ROBIN GILL

Sola fide

'By faith alone' – the phrase denotes the theological nerve-centre of the Protestant Reformation initiated by Martin Luther. Wrestling with his deeply personal question of how one could become righteous before a holy God, Luther focussed on Paul's quotation from Habakkuk in Rom. 1.17: 'The righteous shall live by faith.' To the Latin *fide* Luther added his gloss *sola*, thereby underscoring the apostle's argument that it is not by keeping the law that man can be made righteous ('justified') before God, but only by acceptance of Christ and *his* righteousness. Luther was thus able to turn Paul's polemic against salvation by works of the law into an attack on the late mediaeval system of acquiring merit sufficient for salvation through pious deeds, works of penance and mortification, and purchase of indulgences.

Certain points are crucial for a true interpretation of *sola fide*. The faith by which a person is justified is not merely intellectual or credal acquiescence, but 'a living, daring confidence in God's grace, so sure and certain that a man would stake his life on it a thousand times' (Luther). But neither is it an independent possession or activity of the believer, which would make it yet another 'work' of merit. It is the obverse of *sola gratia*. Further, *sola fide* does not

denigrate the true place of good works in the Christian life. Rather, he who rests in faith upon Christ and his righteousness is made one with Christ, the loving actions flow naturally from this union with the living Christ.

See also **Faith**.

M. Luther, *Preface to the Epistle to the Romans* (1522).

KEITH CLEMENTS

Sola gratia

'By grace alone' expresses the absolute initiative and sufficiency of God for salvation, of which *sola fide** is the human experiential side, in the thought of Martin Luther and the tradition following him. It may not initially appear to convey anything very different from a general view of God turning in succour to man. But there is a vital difference between a view of grace which, for example, sees God's love as primarily imparting strength to enable man to live more acceptably before God, and a view which sees God as turning to man and accepting him – however unacceptable his condition. To Luther, much mediaeval theology and spirituality presupposed the former view: grace as a divine infusion into the soul, raising it to a level of virtue compatible with communion with God. There could be no final assurance thereby, since in face of the utterly holy God the soul's standing would always be in question. And the human heart, incorrigibly 'turned in upon itself', can never truly love God. But in grace, God reaches man in the very depths of his sinfulness, offering the forgiveness of sins as the beginning, not the end, of his ways with man.

Sola gratia has implications covering the totality of the life of the Christian, the church and theology. The Christian always relies on grace for his sanctification through the Holy Spirit, and in fact always remains a sinner dependent on the righteousness of Christ with whom he is united by faith. Theology itself operates *sola gratia*. Unaided human reason cannot uncover the divine majesty; but faith beholds the condescension of God in the humanity of the incarnate and crucified Christ. Here, as always, *sola gratia* is grounded in a Pauline theology of the cross.

See also **Grace**.

M. Luther, *Commentary on the Epistle to the Galatians* (1531).

KEITH CLEMENTS

Sola scriptura

'By scripture alone' is the Reformation principle, originating with Martin Luther, that scripture is the sole source of authority for the Christian and the church. Luther's explicit adoption of this principle was somewhat later than his conviction of *sola fide** and *sola gratia** as central truths, and emerged in his struggle to defend these. The claims to inerrancy made for the papacy (which sanctioned indulgences) and general councils (one of which had condemned John Huss with whom Luther was in substantial agreement) successively sank before his eyes. Scripture alone remained for adoption by him and subsequent Protestantism.

Sola scriptura must be understood in relation to what it originally opposed in the polemics of the sixteenth century. It rejects the idea of revelation given to the church apart from scripture, and of the church being the supreme and always correct interpretor of scripture. Because the literal accuracy of the Bible was not an issue either for Luther or his opponents, to see a 'fundamentalism*' in *sola scriptura* is anachronistic. Further, as always with Luther, *sola scriptura* is christocentric* in intent. Scripture is the Word of God because in it *the* Word, Christ, is revealed; it is 'the crib wherein Christ lieth'. The Bible is therefore to be read in order to find Christ, using reason and prayer for the Holy Spirit's guidance. In this sense the Bible will be its own interpreter and will direct the church (not *vice versa*). This also allows room for degrees of significance to be attached to different parts of scripture, as with Luther's famous comment that in comparison with the Gospels and Pauline and Petrine epistles 'the epistle of James is an epistle full of straw, because it contains nothing evangelical'.

See also **Scripture.**

M. Luther, *Preface to the New Testament* (1522).

KEITH CLEMENTS

Soteriology

The Christian tradition has long held that we can understand who Jesus was only by looking at his whole life and activity. Recent theology has stressed this inseparability of the person and work of Christ. Here we come to the other side of christology*, to the work of salvation* through Christ, in the NT and in the history of the church.

There has never been an 'authorized' version of soteriology. The understanding of salvation has been, and probably always will be, as diverse as the humanity to which it comes. People have thought of salvation as rescue and restoration, as revelation and reconciliation, as representation and substitution, judgment and making righteous, liberation and the establishment of specific forms of social and political orders. Salvation is from God himself, and it comes through Christ.

Sometimes the work of Christ is seen primarily in the rescue of mankind from some great evil, corresponding to a generally pessimistic doctrine of man, in the tradition of Paul, Augustine and Luther. Sometimes the imagery centres on the positive fulfilment of the goal to which man is naturally inclined by his creator, in the tradition of Irenaeus, Origen and the Renaissance. Modern theology usually attempts to take account of the advantages of each line, stressing on the one hand the reality of human freedom and the dignity of man, and on the other side the reality of the gulf between human frailty and the goodness of the transcendent God, and the assurance of grace to all men.

Soteriology has sometimes been seen as Christ's cosmic victory over an evil force, sometimes as the healing of a disease. However, just as it is not necessary for the caseworker to become completely identified with his or her charge, it is not necessary to argue that God had to come into our world and take human flesh in order to redeem us. A transcendent God does not need to add to his experience in order to be able to act. Yet Christians still want to affirm that God is always involved with us in the constancy of his love.

On the other hand, salvation may be seen as the goal to which men have been directed from the beginning of creation. Jesus of Nazareth brings God's message to his fellow men, transforming the law of Israel and inviting us to live as free men and women. The problem here is that the will to action is sometimes precisely what we lack in times of disaster. Still, we may hope for grace in creation and redemption to lead us on, however hesitantly.

We can see again perhaps how the understanding of soteriology depends on our understanding of the nature of God as the author of salvation. Many Christians would affirm that to be God is to be able among other things to give oneself in such a way as to enable mankind to give itself without restraint, to destroy alienation from within. The God of the NT narratives freely chooses to involve himself in human life and death, and overcomes death in the raising of Jesus. God is involved in creation and providence, and in salvation through the life, death and resurrection of Jesus.

The work of Christ is, then, a work of God's love from beginning to end. It is also a work of man, of the man Jesus, a person sustained in thought and action by devotion to God. Soteriology depends on Jesus' humanity, and on God as the source of his unique freedom as a human being. Here the lasting value of 'exemplarist' theories of the work of Christ can be appreciated. Atonement * must evidently include both subjective and objective elements. Simply because men may not always be in a position to respond to a moral example does not take away from its intrinsic value as a deed done. The human cost of soteriology in the struggle of Jesus through love with evil can hardly be over-estimated.

Soteriology in the early church developed along the two main lines indicated above, in parallel with christology. The dictum that what is unassumed is unredeemed had a powerful effect on doctrines of Christ's person. The mediaeval christologies of the West, following Augustine, stressed the gulf between God and man, and tended to be interested not so much in the nature and person of Christ, the fact of incarnation, as in the salvation he brought. The forgiveness of sins, the ransom paid on the cross, coupled with the development of a theory of penance, was the main theme. Atonement dominated the discussion. So Anselm's brilliant *Cur Deus Homo* centred on the satisfaction * made by Christ for the sins of men. The mediaeval emphasis on the penalty paid by Christ in his death – the wages of sin – to atone for man's treason against God was continued at the Reformation.

Since the time of Calvin, doctrine in the churches of the Reformation has tradi-tionally represented the work of Christ in terms of his three offices (*triplex munus*) of prophet, priest and king. This has the advantage of bringing together three important strands of the biblical tradition. It does, however, tend to break up the unity of soteriology, choosing three categories at the expense of others (e.g. shepherd, saviour and servant), and scarcely takes adequate account of the extent to which the OT categories are transformed through Christ – their fulfilment is also in an important respect their abolition.

Soteriology examines the means by which, Christians believe, God wills to bring the created order into a perfected relationship with himself in the eschatological future. It includes a personal relationship to the creator for all human beings, of any faith or none. Somehow, this relationship has been worked out in God's involvement with the created order, in his engagement with a single human life through Jesus. God is involved, in a way which remains largely mysterious to us, in Jesus' life. Jesus lives a completely human life in devotion to God and man. He dies, an example of integrity and a witness to a particular understanding of God, exposing the contrast between the divine love and lesser loves.

But when the creator becomes directly involved in creation more takes place. The resurrection, however partial our understanding of it, indicates the significance of the life and death which have preceded it. A new way has opened up for a renewed humanity. We can see here that the traditional imagery of soteriology was not unperceptive. There is a great gap between God's love and ours. God's personal involvement in human life and death has bridged the gap and has done what we could not do for ourselves. How can we see soteriology as effective? It is because Jesus was involved with God that he is involved with us, and because God was related in a particular way to Jesus that he is related to us in a new way. He has related himself decisively to contingent historical experience within his own created order. This historical order is in turn taken up into God's being, providing the eschatological dimension of soteriology. Death will not separate us from the constancy of God's love. For this love is effective not through sentimental benevolence but through agonizing decision and infinite cost.

P. Baelz, *The Forgotten Dream*, 1975; D. Cupitt, *The Debate about Christ*, 1979; F. W. Dillistone, *The Christian Understanding of Atonement*, 1968; A. O. Dyson, *Who is Jesus Christ?* 1969; J. Hick, *God and the Universe of Faiths*, 1973; J. McIntyre, *St Anselm and his Critics*, 1954; D. M. MacKinnon, *Borderlands of Theology*, 1968; E. L. Mascall, *Theology and the Gospel of Christ*, 1977; M. Machovec, *A Marxist looks at Jesus*, 1976; S. Ogden, *The Point of Christology*, 1982; T. F. Torrance, *Theology in Reconciliation*, 1975; M. F. Wiles, *The Remaking of Christian Doctrine*, 1975.

GEORGE NEWLANDS

Soul

In primitive religions, talk of the soul expresses a convinction that after bodily death life continues in some shadowy mode of being. Traces of this view survive in some OT allusions to *sheol*, but it is more characteristic of ancient Judaism to identify *sheol* with the grave, to presuppose the psychosomatic unity of the human person, and to discount a future life. However, during the Maccabean period belief in a future resurrection* entered Jewish thought, and in the first century BC a Platonic* concept of the soul as a metaphysical entity created by God for immortality is found in the Book of Wisdom. The NT lays principal stress on the resurrection of the dead and states that God 'alone has immortality' (I Tim, 6.16). However, its authors are not entirely consistent and traces of dualistic* thought may also be found.

The early Fathers all assume belief in the immortality of the soul, but see resurrection of the body as the distinctive Christian claim. This view is endorsed by Thomas Aquinas, who sees the soul's survival as the guarantee of personal continuity, yet who thinks that the soul exists in an unnatural and diminished state until its body is returned to it. Belief that the soul is immortal was defined as an article of faith by the Fifth Lateran Council, while the First Vatican Council endorsed the view that souls are directly created by God and infused into the developing embryo.

In traditional forms of prayer prescribed for use in the contexts of dying, burial and memorial, the soul is constantly referred to. Likewise the duty of safeguarding the spiritual well-being of the soul receives much pastoral attention.

However, during the present century advances in evolutionary biology, genetics and neurophysiology along with philosophical analysis of the concept of a person have led many to question the validity of soul language. Within Christian theology this questioning has been encouraged by the realization that the concept owes more to Greek philosophy than to biblical revelation.

On the other hand, the soul is not without its supporters, who claim that a form of dualism* which accepts that soul and body continually interact does full justice to the factual concomitance of mental experiences and brain processes while leaving open the possibility of their separation at death.

Some even argue that reports from people who have been resuscitated from the point of death suggest that they temporarily experienced just such a separation. However, more research is needed before these reports are treated as evidential. For Christian theology such discussion is no side issue. Without belief in life after death, Christianity would be a very different religion. But few today interpret resurrection in terms of reconstituting cremated corpses, and any other view of resurrection depends upon supposing that personal identity can be guaranteed from one life to the next by continuity of mental characteristics and emotional life. This is precisely what the concept of the soul affirms, and hence belief in the soul would appear to remain essential.

See also **Body, Identity, Life after Death, Reincarnation.**

Paul Badham, *Christian Beliefs about Life after Death*, 1976; John Hick, *Death and Eternal Life*, 1976.

PAUL BADHAM

Spiration

A Scholastic term used in relation to the Spirit. According to Aquinas there are four immanent relations in the Godhead: Paternity, Sonship, and active and passive spiration. The first two concern the Father and the Son, the last two relate to the Spirit. Active spiration describes the activity of the Father and the Son in the procession of the Spirit, passive spiration to the Spirit as the result of their common operation. Spiration is not a property either of the Father or of the Son but a characteristic of both since both are concerned. Aquinas offers an analogy from human love where the act of attachment by the lover and the response of the beloved are both necessary to lead to a union of the two.

H. E. W. TURNER

Spiritual Gifts

Influenced by Isa. 11.2 (in the Septuagint version) Christian tradition has developed the theology of the seven gifts of the Holy Spirit, given to all Christians with sanctifying grace, although to different degrees. Much more important is the Pauline teaching on those gifts of the Spirit called 'charisms' (from the Greek *charisma*, meaning 'grace'), a teaching developed over the centuries and especially in recent times. A charism is a grace, a freely bestowed gift of the Spirit, given to some persons but not to all, for some useful purpose, and as a special way of being in relationship with God. The Pauline letters contain several lists of charisms (Rom. 12.6–8; Eph. 4.11; I Cor. 12.8–10, 28–30; 13.1–3; 14.6, 26). There is no complete list, nor do all the lists together seem to be complete. Some charisms the letters name are: prophecy, teaching, leading, governing, evangelizing, miracles, healings, tongues, almsgiving, helping, serving, doing works of mercy, and administering material goods. A charism is always a gift of the Spirit, even if some charisms have natural gifts as correlates (e.g. teaching, leading) and may be built upon natural inclinations. In the charisms the Holy Spirit is almost, we might say, visible, audible, tangible; all the charisms manifest the one Spirit whose gifts they are. Charisms have always been a part of Christian tradition. Every age has had its teachers, its religious leaders, its miracle workers. The founding and rapid spread of the Franciscans marked a great outpouring of the charism of evangelical poverty. There have always been many with the charism of missionary work, and with the charism of consecrated celibacy (see I Cor. 7.7). Charisms are referred to fourteen times by the Second Vatican Council; the most important passage (*Dogmatic Constitution on the Church*, no. 12) states that 'charismatic gifts, whether they be the most outstanding or the more simple and widely diffused, are to be received with thanksgiving and consolation,

for they are exceedingly suitable and useful for the Church's needs'.

See **Charismatic.**

Francis A. Sullivan, *Charisms and Charismatic Renewal*, 1982.

ROBERT FARICY

Spirituality

This is a word which has come much into vogue to describe those attitudes, beliefs and practices which animate people's lives and help them to reach out towards super-sensible realities. It has not always had this meaning in English. In the fifteenth and sixteenth centuries, it stood for the clergy as a distinct order of society, and sometimes for ecclesiastical property or revenue. Later, it distinguished the spiritual from the material or bodily. Its modern meaning was covered by 'piety' or Jeremy Taylor's 'the rule and exercise of holy living'. 'Spiritualité' was used in seventeenth-century French, though in a pejorative sense at first. 'La nouvelle spiritualité' of Madame Guyon was a type of mysticism* to be condemned because *inter alia* it was too refined, rarefied, insufficiently related to earthly life. But it was no large step from this for spirituality to become an irreproachable term defining the life of prayer and discipline with perhaps a hint of 'higher levels' and mystical elements. The Abbé Pourrat divided theology into three branches – dogmatic, moral, and – 'above them but based on them' – spiritual. In this last, R. Newton Flew's *The Idea of Perfection in Christian Theology* (1934) claims to be an essay. He would, however, disagree with Pourrat's statement that spiritual theology is founded on the rational formulations of the other two. 'I would rather say that the *Theologia Dogmatica* of the future which may be different from previous structures must be built on the *Theologia Spiritualis* of the past' (p. xi).

What is not always recognized is that 'spirituality' need not necessarily be Christian, i.e. derived from and inspired by the revelation of God in Christ. All religions have their spiritualities. And 'spirituality' is not always good. Adolf Hitler was a spiritual being, a man, more than most, 'possessed'; yet his spirit was surely evil (*see also* **Values, Religious**).

People may be deceived about the real sources of their spirituality. Consciously and outwardly they may be committed to Christ, convinced that he is the power of their lives and the motive of their actions, whereas they are merely the children of their times – or of their parents' times, if not indeed governed by self-interest and evil desires, which masquerade as Christian. Voices may deceive, which is why the great spiritual directors have taken so seriously the Johannine injunction, 'try the spirits whether they be of God'.

Christian spirituality is itself a synthesis, and has undergone many developments from its Jewish and NT origins. It was profoundly influenced by Neoplatonist* philosophy and monastic rule in the first millennium, and in our own time many Christians feel the lure of Eastern religions, though this is not new, and there are clear affinities between Buddhism and St John of the Cross.

There have been attempts to maintain that 'spirituality' is more Catholic than Protestant, and that the latter has kept pure a biblical and Pauline understanding in contrast to the former's syncretism. But sharp dichotomies are out of place. Not only do evangelical Christians now use the term 'spirituality'; modern research has shown that, although there are distinctions to be drawn, there is often a striking unanimity in the understanding of the soul's relation to God. St John of the Cross is not only a Christian who sometimes writes like a Buddhist. He is a Spanish Catholic who may sound remarkably like Luther or Kierkegaard.

L. Bouyer et al., *A History of Christian Spirituality* (three vols), 1968, 1982; Peter Brooks (ed), *Christian Spirituality,* 1975; V. A. Demant, *A Two-Way Religion,* 1957; F. Heiler, *Prayer,* 1932; P. Pourrat, *Christian Spirituality* (three vols), 1922–7; Rowan Williams, *The Wound of Knowledge,* 1979.

GORDON S. WAKEFIELD

Stoicism

The name is derived from the Greek *stoa* or 'porch', in which Zeno (335–263 BC), the founder of the movement, taught in Athens, Stoicism, a leading religious philosophy in the NT period (cf. Acts 17.18), influenced the language and perhaps the thought of St Paul (cf. his use of the terms 'nature' and 'conscience') and exercised a continuing influence upon the development of Christian thought, which eventually incorporated Stoic ideas and language into its system. Two Stoic ideas are especially significant in this connection. The first is that of the *Logos** ('word', 'reason'), or world-soul in which every man coming into the world participates (the so-called 'divine spark' in every man). Was the Fourth Evangelist deliberately using Stoic language so that educated Greeks could understand the significance of Christ in their own thought-forms (cf. John 1.1–14; there is nothing in this passage which could not be derived from the language and thought of the OT)? The Logos-conception undoubtedly played the large part which it did in early Christian theology because of the prevalence of Stoic modes of thought. The second important teaching of the Stoics concerns the identification of nature with reason; the natural is the rational: therefore live according to nature. Man's highest good is to obey the law of his own nature, or reason, thus disregarding ('being Stoical about') the pleasures or sufferings of the moment (and being indifferent to the misfortunes of others as well as to one's own). Stoicism developed a genuinely cosmopolitan attitude; race and nationality were mere accidents which could be disregarded: to be human was the property of no one group or class. Seneca was a slave; Cicero a Roman consul, and Marcus Aurelius the Roman Emperor. Cicero's *De Officiis* (a handbook for his son on moral conduct), centuries after his death (43 BC), was the model for St Ambrose of Milan's (AD 339–397) most notable work. *De Officiis Ministrorum*, which transmitted the ethic of reason to the Christian Middle Ages. The whole mediaeval conception of natural law (and hence in its turn the possibility of the rise of modern science) would hardly have been developed had it not been for the broad stream of Stoic thought which had flowed into it.

See **Natural Law.**

Cicero, Seneca, Epictetus and Marcus Aurelius in LCL; E. V. Arnold, *Roman Stoicism,* 1911; E. R. Bevan, *Stoics and Sceptics,* 1913; R. D. Hicks, *Stoic and Epicurean,* 1911; R. W. Livingstone, *The Mission of Greece,* 1928; P. E. More, *Hellenistic Philosophies,* 1923; R. M. Wenley, *Stoicism and its Influence,* 1924.

ALAN RICHARDSON

Story *see* **Narrative Theology**

Structuralism

The term designates a variety of methods which seek to understand the meaning conveyed by a (biblical) text to those who read it rather than the meaning which the author intended to convey in the composition of the text. These methods are characterized by an interdisciplinary approach and the application of some principles developed in the field of linguistics to the understanding of the biblical texts.

To some degree the structuralist methods share Paul Ricoeur's notion of the semantic* autonomy* of a text, i.e. that a text is meaningful in itself somewhat independently of the process by which it was composed and the intention of the author who composed it. Thus the structuralists opt for a synchronic approach to the text, rather than a diachronic approach. The latter is that of the historical-critical method which seeks to understand the genesis of a text; it concentrates on the history of the text. The former takes the text as a given reality in the present; it concentrates on the text's present ability to convey meaning. Because of this approach a structural analysis of the text does not claim to arrive at the meaning of the text; what it attempts to do is to clarify the meaning of the text, its 'meaning effect'. From this perspective a text does not have a meaning; it is meaningful in that it conveys meaning – indeed, a gamut of meanings – to those who read it.

The Swiss linguist, Ferdinand de Saussure, is often regarded as the father of structuralism. At the heart of his system is the notion that the human brain functions according to certain patterns, called structures. These structures are expressed in the products of the human brain, notably its written compositions. In structural analysis the human brain is 'the uninvited guest' (Robert Spivey). An appreciation of how it works is essential to the structuralist approach to texts. Thus structuralists seek to understand both the superficial structures of a text and its deep structures. In structuralist terminology, structure does not refer to the outline of a text as it does in most literary analysis. Rather, structure has to do with the interrelationship among the various elements within the text (the superficial structure) and the interrelationship among the deeper anthropological realities to which these textual elements make reference (the deep structure).

Among the notions of linguistics which are particularly important in structural analysis is the distinction, maintained by Saussure and others, between language and discourse. Language (*langue*) is a timeless system of signs (sounds, or written signs) which is the possibility of discourse. Discourse (*parole*) is a unique expression of meaning, created by a specific interrelationship of signs. Also taken from the field of linguistics and particularly significant for the structuralists is the notion that language is both informational and symbolic. While a more classic approach to exegesis would emphasize the informational function of language, the structuralist approach highlights the symbolic function of language.

Within the field of biblical studies, the use of structuralism is a reaction both to the historicism of the historical-critical method (text, source, form and redaction criticism) and the subjectivism of an existential* analysis of the biblical text (R. Bultmann and the post-Bultmannians). Interest in the structural analysis of the biblical text has developed principally in France, Germany and the United States. In France, the principal centres of interest are the École des Hautes Études in Paris and the University of Lyons, where much theoretical study has been devoted to the structure of narrative*, by the so-called French narratologists. In Germany, the principal centre is Bonn, where Erhardt Güttgemanns has developed his theory of generative poetics, which is concerned with the production of meaning by a text. In the United States, structuralism is reflected in the work of the American school of parable* interpretation (John Dominic Crossan, Dan O. Via, etc.), and in the work of Vanderbilt University's interdisciplinary colloquium (Daniel Patte et al.).

Among the various methods which collectively are called structuralism, and whose praxis is generally called structural analysis, a dominant strain follows a Propprian model of syntagmatic analysis. The approach is particularly useful in the analysis of a narrative, the units of which manifest a linear development. The method is based on the analysis of the Russian folk-tale developed by Valdimir Propp, who identified thirty-one functions in the unfolding of the narrative. Schematically presented by A. J. Greimas by means of an 'actantial model' which features a power axis, a communication axis and a volitional axis, the method highlights the underlying structure of a narrative at a more fundamental level than that of the plot and its dénouement.

A paradigmatic model of structure analysis is based on the seminal essay, 'The Structural Study of Myth', by Claude Lévi-Strauss. Lévi-Strauss noted the persistence of fundamental binary oppositions (supernatural/natural, male/female, good/evil) in all myth and observed that the function of myth is to mediate the opposition. In his analysis the mythic structure is basic to the operation of all minds. Thus myth, characterized by timelessness, is in fact relatable to all times. The myth functions as a basic metaphor which provides for the ordering of discontinuous events and experiences.

A semantic model of structural analysis analyses narrative from the standpoint of the essential relationships of its functions, rather than from the standpoint of their sequence. For A. J. Greimas, whose initial studies were devoted to the Lithuanian folk-tale, the notion of a contract is essential to a narrative, since the narrative is set in motion by the breaking of the contract. Between the acceptance of a contract and its resolution is a struggle in which the hero must pass a series of tests (the qualifying, principal and glorifying tests). Essentially the model professes that there is a deep structured layer of narrativity to which any individual narrative corresponds.

An interrelational or eclectic model of structural analysis admits that a text can be understood only within its context, i.e. within an even larger series of contexts. Thus it would be attentive not only to mythic structures but also to narrative structures, and would relate a given (partial) text to the entire text and that text in turn to a culture's entire literary output. The whole serves as a symbol of the society's mythic structure, just as a text serves as a symbol of an individual's mythic structure.

The eclectic method clearly draws attention to the fact that all narrative is meaningful at a variety of levels. This is the phenomenon of polysemy, to which struc-

turalists hold deeply. The structuralist conviction that narratives are meaningful because of their deep and surface structures points to the importance of form in the understanding of a text. A parable *, for example, conveys a direct confrontation with the deep structure of one's rational expectations. Because of their narrative character and their clear use of symbolic language * the parables have proven to be a fertile field for structural analysis, a variety of methods that has thus far been principally employed in the understanding of the narrative sections of the Bible.

In evaluating structuralism, some exegetes deem the method to be a useful complement to the classic methods of biblical exegesis; others, however, judge that the method at its worst leads to a merely formal interpretation of texts which thereafter seem to have little relevance to historical persons and events.

See also **Exegesis, Hermeneutics.**

R. Barthes et al., *Structural Analysis and Biblical Exegesis: Interpretational Essays,* 1974; Daniel and Aline Patte, *Structural Exegesis: From Theory to Practice. Exegesis of Mark 15 and 16. Hermeneutical Implications,* 1978; Robert M. Polzin, *Biblical Structuralism: Method and Subjectivity in the Study of Ancient Texts,* 1977.

RAYMOND F. COLLINS

Subjectivism

At one time the term meant what belonged to things as they were in themselves, independent of our knowledge of them, but in the seventeenth century the use of the terminology changed. For Descartes, for example, the only thing whose existence seemed directly certain was man's consciousness, or mind, and so 'subject' came to designate the conscious mind, and 'subjective' what belonged to it. If our own mental activity is the only unquestionable fact of our experience, all our knowledge may be called 'subjective', and views which start from this position may be called 'subjectivist'. In ethics, for example, extreme subjectivism means the view that all moral judgments are simply matters of personal feeling, as distinct from 'objectivism', the belief that some moral judgments would remain true whether any one thought or desired them to be so, the view to which traditional Christian theology is committed, since its ethics are held to depend ultimately on revelation*. In modern theology subjectivism became an issue in the Romantic period. Schleiermacher (1768–1834) appealed from the rational piety of the Deists* to an inner religious experience of dependence, and so to the specifically Christian consciousness of God, which takes the form of inclusion in the God-consciousness of the risen Christ; while Kierkegaard (1813–1855), appalled by Hegel's reduction of the individual to a mere event in the history of the World-Spirit, asserted that religion was a one-to-one relationship between man and God, and that in this sense 'subjectivity was truth'. Both Schleiermacher and Kierkegaard thought of the consciousness as the scene of an 'objective' encounter between God and the self, and so would have denied a charge of 'subjectivism'. But this did not satisfy those Protestant theologians in the nineteenth and twentieth centuries who thought that Christian dogma* must be objectively established in history and scriptural revelation. Catholic Modernism*, officially condemned in 1907, may similarly be interpreted as a shift from the traditional Roman stress on the objective authority of church, scripture and tradition*, to the 'subjective' authority of an immanent experience of the divine; Von Hügel (1852–1925) tried to mediate between the two positions in *The Mystical Element of Religion* (1908), a study of Catholic mysticism. This may be compared with *Varieties of Religious Experience* (1902), by William James (1843–1910), the Protestant philosopher of religion, who concluded that the study of religious experience* suggested the possibility of a life-enhancing relationship between the individual and an 'objective' over-soul, to whose theological description James attached little importance. Von Hügel and James represented the high point of the appeal to the religious consciousness; after World War I Protestant writers like Karl Barth rejected the tradition running back to Schleiermacher as anthropocentric, i.e. they condemned its religious position as essentially subjectivist and sought a solution in a renewed 'biblical realism'. The pressure was increased by the work of psychologists like S. Freud*, whose book, *The Future of an Illusion* (1927), identified religion with illness, not health; and by the rise of sociology,

which offered ways of interpreting allegedly objective religious experience in terms of society (*see also* **Sociology of Religion**). The study of religions has weakened the appeal to inner experience in the case of any single religion, like Christianity. As subjectivism has become more effective in its criticism of religious feeling, modern theologians have become more cautious in appealing to a 'religious consciousness'.

———

T. R. Miles, *Religious Experience*, 1972; K. Ward, *The Concept of God*, 1974.

JOHN KENT

Subordinationism

This refers to any christological position which subordinates the Son to the Father in such a way as potentially to endanger his essential divinity. The classic example of subordinationist teaching is Arianism*, and the confuting of Arianism ensured its repudiation in principle. Recent reassessment of the teaching of Arius himself does not alter the fact that Arianism was understood to have defined God as ingenerate, i.e. as the uncaused cause, and by attributing this characteristic to the Father alone on the basis of the Son's generation from the Father, to have excluded the Son from fully divine status: a derived divinity could not be of the same essential nature as true divinity. Subordinationism of a less extreme kind was in fact characteristic of pre-Nicene christology. Origen, for example, had thought in terms of a hierarchy of being in which God the Father was the ultimate one and the Logos* was the mediating link between the ultimate and created essences. The Logos had ontological* links with both the higher and lower orders of being, so being describable both as creature and as second God. Such teaching was very influential in the East, and it explains the immediate attractiveness of Arianism and the protracted nature of the struggle over subordinationism in the fourth century. Although not Arian, the thinking of Eusebius of Caesarea was subordinationist, and like many of his contemporaries, he was deeply suspicious of the *homoousion**, not only because of its Sabellian* leanings, but also because it seemed to undermine the essentially mediating role of the Logos.

Another form of subordinationism was the parallel refusal to accord fully divine status to the Spirit. This emerged in an explicit form in the years after Nicaea, and its adherents are often referred to as Macedonians or Pneumatomachians. The Cappadocians * were instrumental in confuting this doctrine, and it was excluded in 381 by the Creed of Constantinople (popularly known as the Nicene Creed). Even apart from the Origenist tradition, some degree of subordinationism is generally characteristic of trinitarianism before Nicaea. There was a tendency to assume that God meant the Father, in spite of claims about Christ's divinity. In the so-called 'economic trinitarianism' of Irenaeus and Tertullian, the Word and Spirit of God, eternally part of his make-up and yet projected forth in creation, revelation and redemption, were subordinate to God (= Father) and acted as his agents. The roots of this subordinationism lay in the Logos theology of the Apologists; and indeed by the standards of Nicene orthodoxy, the NT itself is subordinationist in tendency.

The affirmation of the *homoousion* in relation to both Son and Spirit excluded subordinationism in the sense that the divinity of the Son and of the Spirit also was equated with that of the Father; neither could again be described as a lesser or secondary divine being or agent, and a fully trinitarian concept of the one God was worked out. However, an orthodox subordinationism survived in the doctrine that within the Trinity the Father was the fount, origin or cause of the Son and the Spirit.

See also **Trinity.**

FRANCES YOUNG

Substance

Like the Latin *substantia*, this represents a group of philosophical notions which have been repeatedly used by Christian thinkers to formulate their ideas of God and especially of the Trinity *. *Substantia* translates the Greek word *ousia*, the abstract noun of the verb 'to be'; and its technical use begins with Plato. Plato represents Socrates asking 'What *is* justice, courage, etc.', requesting not examples thereof, but a definition. The definition, he thought, represents an eternal prototype or 'Form' of justice, etc., of which human acts of justice were only imperfect copies. Plato, moreover, deduced that mathematical expressions and natural species have such Forms, and used the term *ousia* to refer to them; though it could also denote the imperfect and changeable beings of this world.

Aristotle rejected Plato's theory of a separate world of Forms, but explained natural objects as combinations of formless matter with a Form characteristic of each species; *ousia* could mean either the matter or the Form or their combination. He also gave *ousia* the more specific sense of 'substance', something which can exist independently, whereas qualities, relations, etc, exist only in connection with substances. In his *Categories* he calls the individual person or thing a 'primary substance', while 'secondary substance' means the species or genus to which it belongs. This was confusing, because elsewhere he suggests that the species is primary; for only the species can have a definition. The definition expresses what the species really is; this is sometimes called its 'essence', though 'essence' could also have the same broad range of meanings as 'substance'.

Plato's successors came to regard the Forms, not simply as intelligible, but as intelligent beings; and this doctrine was adapted by Christian writers to confirm their belief in transcendent realities: God and his angels were, or had, 'intelligible substance'. At Nicaea the divine Word was declared to be 'of one substance with the Father', the true expression of his being, involving no change or diminution; though the new phrases of the Nicene Creed were imprecise until defined by the Cappadocian Fathers * some fifty years later. They explained the relationship of the three persons to the one substance on the analogy of three members of a single species (cf. Aristotle's 'secondary substance'), while also affirming that the Godhead is an indivisible unity. By this time interest in Aristotle's philosophy was reviving. Augustine considered 'essence' a more appropriate term for God's being than 'substance', since an essence must be immaterial, while a substance need not be. However, Aristotle's doctrine of categories kept the term 'substance' in use; it was axiomatic that God must be a substance, as preeminently endowed with independent existence.

In mediaeval times 'essence' was possibly the more significant word; but both were involved in the lengthy debate about universals *, 'realism' * versus 'nominalism' *: were universals, like Plato's Forms, objective realities or were they mere names? 'Substance' is still a significant word for, e.g. Locke and Kant; but many modern empiricists hold that it brings together a number of problems that are better handled separately: persistence and change, individuals and universals, referring and predicating. To many modern theologians 'substance' seems too impersonal a term for God's being; it fails to emphasize his holiness and love. Some, especially process theologians, would also wish to modify the suggestion of immutability in favour of a doctrine of constant divine purpose perpetually finding new expressions (*see* **Process Theology**).

See also **Essence, God, Trinity, Platonism.**

C. Stead, *Divine Substance*, 1977; E. Gilson, *Being and Some Philosophers*, ET 1952; A. Quinton, *The Nature of Things*, 1973, cover the early, mediaeval and modern periods respectively.

CHRISTOPHER STEAD

Suffering

Confronted with a man blind from birth, Jesus' disciples are reported to have asked, 'Rabbi, who sinned, this man or his parents . . .?' (John 9.2). That suffering is some kind of punishment is a persistent popular notion, and in the biblical tradition, it was reinforced by a number of factors: e.g. 1. the wisdom teaching that wickedness led to disaster, righteousness to prosperity; 2. the strongly monistic teaching of Deuteronomy (32.39ff.) and Isaiah (45.5–7), which had its roots in 3. older 'demonic' conceptions of Yahweh's dangerous power (e.g. II Sam. 6.6ff.), as well as 4. the pre-exilic prophetic warnings that national disaster would be the outcome of God's judgment upon the nation's faithlessness. Jesus appears to have repudiated the suggestion that suffering necessarily implies guilt, though not in every case: see e.g. the Healing of the Paralytic, where healing is closely related to forgiveness of sins. For the most part Jesus seems to have acted upon another popular assumption, namely that the source of suffering was the activity of malignant supernatural powers opposed to God: exorcism was a sign of the kingdom* (Matt. 12.28/Luke 11.20). Inevitably from this material the question arises: is suffering

God's will or not? Two diverse attitudes to suffering have arisen in the Christian tradition as a result of this dilemma: 1. the acceptance of suffering, either as a disciplinary measure on God's part, or as the highest way of following and imitating Christ; and 2. a sense of outrage that there should be suffering at all and efforts to eliminate it on the grounds that its removal is God's redeeming purpose.

Outrage at the existence of suffering has been an important factor in the modern debate with atheism*: with some justification, the proportion of evil and suffering in the world has come to be regarded as the most telling argument against the very existence of a good Creator God, and with the loss of general belief in an evil agent like Satan, the question 'Why suffering?' has become a serious problem at the popular, pastoral level. Justifying the ways of God (theodicy*) is not a new problem for Christian believers, but it has become an urgent one. One influential approach to this problem has been to treat pain and suffering as essentially positive. Suffering, it is said, ennobles: there could be no courage without suffering or the risk of it. Pain is a good thing, since its fundamental purpose is to act as a warning sign so that preventative action can be taken before damage is done (e.g. removing the hand from the hot plate). Both pain and suffering have an important role in the overall purpose of life, which is to produce free, mature persons: overcoming obstacles is the only way to foster moral qualities of the highest order. Suffering stimulates love and compassion of a deeper quality. These arguments may be reinforced by appeal to scripture and the vision of a loving Father obliged to chastize for the good of his children (see e.g. Heb. 12.5–11). They can find plenty of precedent in patristic preaching and traditional pastoral counselling: Basil, for example, distinguished between moral and physical evils, arguing that physical evils only appear evil to us and have a positive purpose; Gregory Nazianzen took the opportunity of a desperately destructive hailstorm to urge self-examination and amendment of life; John Chrysostom in comforting a parishioner, not only appealed to the value of imitating Christ, but argued that God is not the source of evil, yet permits suffering as a factor in the learning process, for discipline and judgment – the only real evil is sin. There is a good deal of wisdom in much of this, and deep within the Christian tradition is a sense that suffering is redemptive, both for oneself and for others: the uncelebrated everyday saints are those who live with suffering in a spirit of joy and thankfulness. But there are also serious objections: (i) such an approach cannot explain 'irrational pain', e.g. the extremes of nerve pain with no obvious purpose; (ii) nor can it explain mass suffering as distinct from individual suffering; (iii) it cannot cope with innocent suffering – it is one thing to feel that someone has 'got his deserts', another to watch the severe suffering of innocent victims; (iv) much suffering is haphazard – earthquakes, epidemics, birth defects, etc. – and disastrous in the sense that no good outcome is possible, certainly not good enough to counterbalance the evil effects; (v) the outcome of suffering is in fact entirely ambiguous and unpredictable – it may ennoble but it often embitters; it may stimulate love and compassion, but it can equally well cause impatience, cruelty and rejection; (vi) perhaps most serious for the Christian tradition, this kind of explanation, if taken as the whole answer, cannot do justice to the central focus of the faith – the suffering of Jesus Christ upon the cross. To do justice to that it is necessary to admit that suffering is a real and not an imaginary problem, that there is something radically wrong with the world, of which sin and suffering are both indications; and it is necessary to admit that God's saving action involves confrontation with all the 'gonewrongness' of his world, without attempting a sharp dichotomy between moral and physical evils, which are so often in practice intimately related.

There is no satisfactory simple answer to the fundamental question of theodicy which is now so urgently pressing. But one characteristic of Christianity is a devotional response to the suffering of Christ which can effect the transformation or transcending of suffering. The doctrine of incarnation* permits the believer to see in the cross God's very presence in the midst of the suffering as well as the sin of the world, his redemptive entering into and bearing of the consequences of the existence of evil in his creation. Response to the love of God thus displayed, the sense thus mediated of God's presence in spite of everything, the realiza-

tion that God has taken all upon himself and the cross has power to release humanity from its chains, can make a genuine difference to the situation, and in some cases produce actual healing. For many Christians, the book of Job voices their own protest, mystification, even blasphemy, in the face of innocent suffering; yet foreshadows the cross in that it points to the only acceptable response – that in God's presence all hurt and pain, all protests and questions cease, and worship begins.

See also **Evil, Problem of; Theodicy.**

John Bowker, *The Problem of Suffering in the Religions of the World,* 1975.

FRANCES YOUNG

Summa

Devised in the twelfth and thirteenth centuries as a textbook of systematic theology. During the course of the twelfth century the number of masters teaching in the schools of northern Europe increased markedly, and the schools began to develop into universities with growing syllabuses and a corresponding pressure of time acting as a constraint upon teaching. Lectures on the Bible, as on all set books, followed the sequence of the text, explaining difficult words and obscure passages. The students raised questions, which the masters tended at first to answer as they went along. By the second half of the century the questions were so numerous and such an interruption to the sequence of exposition that it became customary to set them aside to be dealt with in a separate session. They were gradually put into order so that they could be treated systematically, by such theologians as Peter of Poitiers and Alan of Lille. Peter Lombard's *Sentences* of the 1150s were designed to serve a not dissimilar purpose, providing extracts from the Fathers arranged under topic headings.

Thomas Aquinas found the teaching available in his day still in urgent need of reduction to order. Trivial questions crowded in, and there was a good deal of repetitiveness and overlapping of areas of the syllabus. He wrote two *summas.* The *Summa Contra Gentiles* contains arguments against all the heresies known to Aquinas, old and new, arranged not by heresy but according to a topical order. The second, the *Summa Theologiae,* helped to establish what was already becoming the standard pattern for such collections, dealing first with the nature of theology as a discipline, then with the existence and nature of God, the Trinity, the created world, man, the Fall of man and its consequences, the sacraments and the Last Things.

W. Farrell, *A Companion to the Summa*, 4 vols., 1974; M.-D. Chenu, *Toward Understanding St Thomas*, ET 1964.

G. R. EVANS

Summum bonum
see **Beatific Vision, Vision of God**

Supernatural, The

That reality which lies beyond the natural world. Its existence is denied by pantheists*, who include God within the realm of nature and so have no need to postulate that there is anything beyond it, and by those who exclude the existence of God or any being or substance other than that which can be observed and accounted for within the frame of reference of the observable natural world.

Those who hold that it exists have regarded it as meta-physical, that is, higher and greater and larger than the physical world, as the source of the physical and natural world, although not itself material in the sense in which the term may be used of the natural world. Although it is beyond space it may be said in some sense to contain the natural world. It has also been thought of as a realm where spiritual beings such as angels and their fallen brothers the demons have their home, together with the minor spirits, fairies or other good and mischievous beings which intervene in human lives. Spiritualists hold that the souls of those who have died can be communicated with in their new life in the supernatural world. It has traditionally been thought that it is there that heaven and hell lie and God dwells.

Its character has proved difficult to define, precisely because it lies beyond the world to which familiar natural laws apply, and because the use of such terms as 'place', 'dwell', 'lie' are strictly inappropriate. The Deists* of the eighteenth century admitted that God is distinct from the world he created but regarded him as subject to the same laws. Thinkers who have not wanted to limit God in this way have nevertheless

often believed that it was possible to understand something of him and of the supernatural world by analogy, by reasoning from the existence of his world to his own existence, as Aquinas does in more than one of his five proofs of the existence of God; or by reasoning from the qualities displayed in the created world to the attributes of the Creator, as William Paley and a number of eighteenth and nineteenth century contemporaries attempted to do.

B. Kaye, *The Supernatural in the New Testament*, 1977; M. T. Kelsey, *The Christian and the Supernatural*, 1977; J. Rogerson, *The Supernatural in the Old Testament*, 1976.

G. R. EVANS

Symbolics

This discipline is that branch of theology which studies the formal creeds* and confessions (symbols) of the various churches. While symbolics might have been considered dying out in this century, the task – under whatever name – holds new interest because of the success of the ecumenical movement (*see* **Ecumenism**).

The development of the earliest creeds of the church took place in the context of the baptismal liturgy. Pressures of self-definition against heresy* forced expansion of creeds and composition of formal statements by councils such as those of Nicaea (325) and Constantinople (381). Slowly the creeds came to have a place in the eucharistic liturgy as well.

But theology in the mediaeval period was not symbolic in the sense that it was basically concerned to comment on these symbols of the church. While councils continued to make theological decisions, much of the formal theology was dominated by apologetic or mystical concerns.

The Reformation* represented a crisis in the traditional method for doing theology and an opportunity to open new approaches. The Reformers' insistence on the centrality of scripture* led to a re-examination of certain traditional formulae and a search for the biblical basis of the faith of the church.

Yet the Reformation was not anti-credal in any simple sense. There was in the Lutheran, Reformed and Anglican churches a conserving streak that valued the creeds and affirmed them. Attitudes towards tradition were more diverse, but even here some of the traditional material (decisions of early ecumenical councils of the church, for example) was affirmed and studied with new intensity.

The various strands of the Reformation each made it own distinctive confessions with authority within that emerging tradition. The status of the *Augsburg Confession* (1530, Lutheran), the *Second Helvetic Confession* (1566, Reformed) and the *Thirty-Nine Articles* * (1563, Anglican) was not precisely the same within each community. Yet the various new confessions influenced each other and created a situation in which the churches were defining themselves both over against Rome and against one another. There were also Anabaptist confessions (see, for example, the *Schleitheim Confession* of 1527), but a strong streak of anti-credalism ran through the more radical wing of the Reformation.

Over against the Reformation the RC Church defined its own position in the decrees and in the creed and catechism of the Council of Trent * (1545–1563). A great many positions attributed to the Reformers – especially Luther – were specifically condemned. Recent studies have questioned how well the theology of Luther was understood by those at the Council. Another problem for symbolics is that the official teachings of the various Protestant churches have to be distinguished from the private theological comments of the various theologians, which may or may not be representative of the communions.

In this situation the discipline of symbolics developed. On the RC side it came to be known as controversial theology, some forms of which were more polemical while others were more eirenic. RC theology continued to develop during this period and reached a point of even greater theological distance from the Protestant churches in the decrees of Vatican I (1870).

On the Protestant side there was a need to answer the new Catholic certainty and to systematize the Protestant position. Among Lutherans a key figure in this enterprise was Martin Chemnitz, author of the *Examination of the Council of Trent* (1565–1573) and a framer of the *Formula of Concord* (1577), a Lutheran confession written to re-establish unity among the Lutherans. In this same period the Lutheran confessional writings were gathered into an official collection, the *Book of Concord* (1580), a collection of documents including not only those from Luther and Melanchthon, but also the three ecumenical creeds.

With the compiling of the *Book of Concord*, the confession-making process came to an end for Lutherans. The Reformed churches continued to write confessions into the next century (*Westminster*, 1646), and never settled the issue of which of these were authoritative within the Reformed family. The Anglicans gave a certain stress to the *Thirty-Nine Articles*, but tended to balance their authority with that of the *Book of Common Prayer*, the *Homilies* and the authority of bishops.

In such a situation Lutherans took the lead in the development of symbolic theology, beginning with Leonhard Rechtenbach in 1612. Most of these works were polemical against RC and Reformed theology, although some figures occasionally showed an eirenic spirit reminiscent more of Melanchthon than of Luther; a prominent example was George Calixtus (1586–1656), who argued for reconciliation on the basis of the *Apostles' Creed* and the unified faith of the church of the first five centuries. Eventually works of symbolics could be found from the Lutheran, Reformed and RC points of view. The discipline of symbolics in its broader definition of giving a description of the comparative life and teachings of the churches became known in Germany as *Konfessionskunde*.

The Enlightenment's * critique of Christian theology challenged the adequacy of strong confessional positions, Schleiermacher raised the question whether one could deal honestly and fairly with the confessions of churches other than one's own. His own *The Christian Faith* (1821–1822) represented an attempt to produce a theology from the confessional standpoint of the newly created Union Church of Prussia. F. D. Maurice engaged in a notable attempt to give an overview of the various Christian churches in *The Kingdom of Christ* (1838).

In the twentieth century the dogmatic certainties of the older confessional symbolics often seemed theologically inadequate. Yet Neo-orthodoxy * gave a certain impetus to taking the church confessions seriously, even if their content was to be reconsidered in the light of the Word of God.

Barth wrote several expositions of the creeds and of Reformation confessions. The *Barmen Declaration* (1934) comes out of the German Church Struggle and raises the question of the connection between all credal and confessional statements and their political/social context.

But it is the ecumenical movement of the twentieth century which has been especially responsible for the modern revival of interest in symbolics. The Faith and Order Movement studied the traditional positions of the churches and tried to find ways around the old separations. Modern biblical and historical studies opened up new ways of looking at historical documents and raised some restlessness within each of the churches with the adequacy of traditional formulations.

It was the influence of Vatican II (1962–1965) that opened up a new climate for ecumenical theological work based on the official teachings of the divided churches. The *Decree on Priestly Formation* (*Optatam Totius*) specifically called for priests to be trained in a theology that included a 'more adequate understanding of the Churches and ecclesial Communities separated from the Roman, Apostolic See'. This led not only to many individual theological projects but also to formal theological dialogues between representatives of the R C Church and those of other Christian churches.

These bi-lateral dialogues have generated much new material for the construction of a revised symbolics or comparative dogmatics. Traditional issues of division have in some cases found resolution, in others restatement towards convergence. The status of the creeds, baptism, eucharist, teaching authority, papal primacy and infallibility have been among the topics considered. Dialogues with Roman Catholics have led divided Protestants to a new round of bilateral dialogues among themselves, and some notable agreements have been achieved here as well.

One problem for this kind of theology is scepticism about the degree to which churches are actually bound by the formal, confessional teachings. The several churches vary in their self-understanding in this matter, and all are shaped by non-theological factors to a degree that may escape their notice. In some cases formal agreement may be achieved while it is at the same time

doubtful that the theological representatives have actually spoken for their constituents. Empirical research about the churches can be an important tool for symbolics at this point.

An important attempt to move beyond the bilateral dialogues is found in the World Council of Churches' Faith and Order Report 111, *Baptism, Eucharist and Ministry* (1982). In this statement theologians from Orthodox, Protestant and R C groups have tried to state a common position on these topics which have been especially troublesome in the history of the relations among the churches. It remains to be seen to what extent member churches of the Council will receive these statements and what further progress might follow from their acceptance.

The field of theological inquiry which was traditionally known as symbolics is being recast as ecumenical theology in a changed church situation. Yet in that very process, the traditional techniques of symbolics (historical and theological examination of formally held positions of the churches) still play a helpful role. So great have been the changes in recent decades that the major modern works of symbolics remain to be written at this time.

Paul Empie and Austin Murphy, *Lutherans and Catholics in Dialogue*, vols. I–III, 1967; H. E. Jacobs, *Outline of Symbolics* (E T and revision of G. B. Winer's book of 1837), 1929; J. N. D. Kelly, *Early Christian Creeds*, 1972; John Leith, *The Creeds of the Churches*, 1963; Josef Neuner and Heinrich Roos, *The Teaching of the Catholic Church* (ed. Karl Rahner), E T 1967; Wilhelm Niesel, *The Gospel and the Churches*, 1962; Alan Richardson, *Creeds in the Making*, 1935; Theodore Tappert (ed), *The Book of Concord*, 1959; Barry Till, *The Churches Search for Unity*, 1972; World Council of Churches, *Baptism, Eucharist and Ministry* (Faith and Order Paper 111), 1982.

TIMOTHY F. LULL

Symbolism   *see* Imagery, Religious

Syncretism

The term *synkretismos* was explained by Plutarch as meaning coming together to oppose an external foe, as frequently squabbling Cretans were supposed to do. Erasmus used the term *synkretizein* to mean a prudent alliance, and Melanchthon and other Reformers also used the term in this sense. Thereafter it took on the negative nuance of an inadmissible mixture of religious belief or practice, and came to be applied as a term of abuse in theological circles. Modern studies with a history-of-religions perspective (see **Religionsgeschichtliche Schule**) emphasized the syncretistic nature of some phases of Israelite religion and of early Christianity (Gunkel, Bultmann), while Wach and Van der Leeuw saw syncretism as an aspect of all religions. Syncretism has now become a technical term in the systematic study of religion, although its precise application is still a subject of discussion (surveyed by Rudolph, see bibliography).

The common elements in modern usage of the term syncretism are as follows: 1. it refers to a coexistence of socio-cultural and/or religious elements which are also known to have existed independently; 2. the coexistence of these elements appears to be more or less satisfactory to the religious believers concerned, who may be conscious or unconscious of it; 3. but latent tensions may eventually surface, leading to the drawing apart of competing belief-patterns or the repression of one by another. With these features in view, syncretism is considered to be a universal aspect of religion, and moreoever one which is to be understood dynamically, that is, as an aspect of religious growth and interaction, decay and revival.

Well-known examples of syncretism include the adoption by Israelite religion of some features of Canaanite agricultural religion, the accommodation with Hellenistic thought-forms in Christianity, the relation of Buddhism and Jainism to the tantric style of religious practice and art, the reverence paid to the black stone at Mecca, and the emergence of the Sikh faith at the crossroads between Indian religion and Islam. It may also be documented in many different cultures in the interaction between major religious traditions and localized belief systems. Needless to say, the believers of the religions mentioned may not perceive their own faith descriptively or analytically in terms of syncretism. However, objections to its use frequently reflect an outdated understanding of it as implying a merely static mixture of beliefs or practices where deeper religious values are lost. The claims of revelation or of mysticism are neither affirmed

nor denied in the recognition that the socio-cultural expressions of belief and practice are drawn from diverse sources. Indeed it may be said that any fundamental religious idea or value requires for its statement and communication a more generally comprehensible symbolic language. Thus a tension between admixture and purification is usually to be expected, or, as J. Kamstra put it, 'To be human is to be syncretist'.

S. Hartmann (ed), *Syncretism*, 1969; K. Rudolph, 'Synkretismus – vom theologischen Scheltwort zum religionswissenschaftlichen Begriff', in L. Neulande et al., *Humanitas Religiosa, Festschrift für Haralds Biezais*, 1979.

MICHAEL PYE

Synergism

Greek, 'working together with': the doctrine, such as that of Melanchthon that the human will has a part to play along with the Holy Spirit (or the grace of God) in the process of conversion.

ALAN RICHARDSON

Systematic theology

One of the series of disciplines (others, for example, would be biblical studies or church history), which together constitute the study of theology*. Systematic theology is, in general, that form of specialism which seeks to give a rational and orderly account of the content of Christian belief, sometimes held to include (and certainly very closely connected to) Christian ethical beliefs.

One may distinguish three senses in which the term 'system' may be used in connection with this discipline. 1. Order in systematic theology may simply mean the use of a series of separations or distinctions in the assembly of the elements of Christian doctrine. Thus one might distinguish between the doctrine of the triune God, the doctrine of the person and work of Christ, the doctrine of the church, the doctrine of the Holy Spirit, the doctrine of the Last Things, and so forth. This procedure was followed by Calvin in his *Institutes* (see also **Calvinism**), where he set himself the task of expressing in a certain order the material which is otherwise elaborated in his commentaries on the Bible. For Calvin the *Institutes* and the commentaries are complementary. In both cases the biblical language is the primary datum.

2. By systematic theology may be meant the attempt to express the substance of Christian theology in a consistent terminology. Since the language of the Bible is not itself consistent, the misunderstanding of meanings in different contexts is always possible, and a determined effort can be made by a systematic theologian to express the content of Christian faith in a carefully controlled vocabulary. An example of such an endeavour is to be found in the work of Friedrich Schleiermacher (1768–1834), who distinguished three kinds of speech; poetic (the language of original inspiration), rhetorical (the language of preaching) and what he called 'descriptively didactic' speech, that is, language in which the highest degree of definite and concise meaning is the explicit aim. The writing of his own systematic theology, *The Christian Faith* (1821, ET 1928), is an example of this last mode of discourse.

3. A more ambitious way in which order can be given to the expression of Christian doctrine is rooted in an explicit attempt to relate the content of Christian faith to a theory of human rationality. The fundamental premise of such an endeavour is the conviction that there is one divine source of truth, and that there is an inner consistency between the diverse truths which persons may know. In this sense a systematic theology would be obliged to include a theory of how human beings perceive (cognitional theory) and the criteria for human knowledge (epistemology). Thomas Aquinas (1226–1274) provided a classic example of such an enterprise (*see* **Thomism**), by deploying Aristotle's notion of abstraction as the source of all human knowledge.

Modern examples of this latter method may be seen in the works of the Protestant theologian Paul Tillich (1886–1965) and the Roman Catholic Bernard Lonergan (b. 1903). Crucial for Tillich is his account of sin as the estrangement of existence from essence resulting in anxiety and loneliness, and the human quest for reconciliation in the 'New Being', that is, in the Christ. Tillich's systematic theology (*see also* **Correlation, Ultimate Concern**) entails an exploration of the function in human understanding of the symbol which is held to be the source of all human meaning and rationality. Lonergan, on the other hand, has attempted to demonstrate the human necessity of intellectual, moral and spiritual 'conversion', and to relate all theological enquiry to a pattern of interacting operations by which all human knowledge is attained.

The project of systematic theology is not without its critics, but it is obviously important to be clear what precise meaning of the term 'system' is being employed. Karl Barth (1886–1968) is the most notable modern example of a theologian drawing a sharp distinction between dogmatic theology * (compare his own *Church Dogmatics*) and systematics. His complaint against systematics is two-fold. 1. A system usually entails the use of an arbitrarily chosen methodology derived from a source outside theology (especially from philosophical epistemology). This theory then becomes the implicit criterion of meaning in theological utterances. Theologically this involves the exaltation of a merely human standpoint, and a refusal to let the subject matter of theology, that is God himself, stand in judgment on human intellectual pride. 2. Systems by their very nature ignore the rupture between God and humanity, what he calls 'the necessary brokenness of all theological utterance'. This is usually apparent, he claims, in their account of evil and sin. On the contrary, according to Barth, the human situation is such as to require theologians to speak about God even in acutely paradoxical ways (e.g. in their accounts of the existence and power of evil).

Despite these criticisms Barth has plainly organized his theology according to a pattern, and explicitly approves of Calvin's theological method. Some critics of Barth have claimed to detect even more signs of systematic construction than Barth himself would have allowed.

A further criticism of systematic theology derives from the modern perception of the plurality of intellectual disciplines to which theology is supposed to be connected. Whereas in earlier times a learned person of very great diligence might be expected to master the basic procedures of enquiry in the entire range of human knowledge, such is the degree of specialization and complexity in differing fields relevant to the study of human culture and personality that a systematic interrelation of knowledge has now, it is said, become impossible. All that theology can attempt to do is to provide either special studies of one or other aspect of this interrelationship, or a more or less popularized version of the basic picture of the human situation arising out of the other disciplines. Systematic theology, confronted by an irreducible plurality of methods for interpreting life, is forced to abandon its earlier claims for a comprehensive rendering of the interrelation of all forms of knowledge. But at the same time it seems to be a human necessity that a unified perspective on Christian truth should be available, even in the form of inherently disputable theses, in order to focus the mind on individual problems.

G. W. Bromiley, *Introduction to the Theology of Karl Barth*, 1979; B. Lonergan, *Method in Theology*, 1971; J. Macquarrie, *Principles of Christian Theology*, 1966; K. Rahner, *Foundations of Christian Faith*, 1978; P. Tillich, *Systematic Theology*, Vols. 1–3, 1953–1964.

S. W. SYKES

Teleological argument
see **Arguments for the Existence of God**

Temptation

In general, allurement or enticement to do evil; temptation is like a trap into which the unwary can fall (I Tim. 6.9). Temptation is also the state of being tempted to do evil, as in the phrase 'the hour of temptation' (Luke 8.13). Any test of moral virtue is a temptation to the one being tested, but the one who tests may or may not desire the one being tested to fall. In contemporary English we distinguish between God or an assayist who can test but not tempt, and someone like Potiphar's wife who tempts. Hebrew and Greek used the one set of words for both testing and tempting. (James 1.2f., AV/ KJV: count it all joy when ye fall into divers temptations; RSV: . . . when you meet various trials.) The Devil is called the tempter (Matt. 4.3) because his testing is designed to destroy. Human beings are inherently likely to succumb to temptation because of their own strong desires (James 1.14).

The petition 'And lead us not into temptation' has always raised difficulties. The first solution was to read 'trials' for temptation. But if God wishes us to be tested, as he tested Abraham, it is perhaps false modesty to ask not to be tested. The more recent suggestion, that the temptation referred to the period of tribulation before the end of the world (Rev. 3.10), is little better. This period must be assumed to be a necessary stage of history, and the prayer can hardly be asking for its postponement. The true difficulty probably lies not in the noun but in the verb 'to lead', which disguises a Semitic idiom: 'And let us not yield to temptation' (C. C. Torrey).

J. C. O'NEILL

Theandric Acts

More properly 'theandric action', i.e. divine-human action, a phrase coined by Dionysius 'the Areopagite', *c*. AD 500. to describe the events of Christ's incarnate life. It was agreed that Christ performed miracles *, yet also shared our human condition, e.g. by eating and sleeping. Some theologians had given the impression that he simply alternated between displays of divine power and human subservience; so perhaps Leo of Rome, 449. Others emphasized the interplay of both factors; thus Athanasius, commenting on John 9.6: 'They occurred, not separately, but in conjunction; for he spat indeed in human fashion, but his spittle was charged with divinity' (Letter 4 to Serapion, 14); and Cyril, commenting on a similar passage, speaks of 'a single activity'. Dionysius follows this tradition. The phrase was later criticized, as suggesting a monophysite * view of Christ as 'one nature', so that in effect his human condition would be overruled by the divine power; but it was also defended as consistent with the 'two natures' doctrine expounded at Chalcedon; although Christ performs both divine and human acts, they are in a sense one as he is one.

CHRISTOPHER STEAD

Theism

The doctrine that there exists a God, in the sense of a being who is personal, without a body, omnipresent, perfectly free, perfectly good, omnipotent, omniscient, creator and sustainer of the universe, the proper object of human worship and obedience, eternal and necessary. Christians, Jews and Muslims are all theists, though each group holds further beliefs about God's nature and activity, in which they differ from each other. To say that God is personal is to say that, likc humans, he acts intentionally (i.e. to bring about purposes) and that he has knowledge. Humans, however, have to act and derive knowledge through one chunk of matter, their body* – they can only bring about effects by moving parts of their bodies or acquire knowledge of other things through their effects on their sense organs. God is omnipresent in that he can bring about effects and acquire knowledge everywhere without needing to act through a body. He is perfectly free in that nothing makes him do as he does, but he is perfectly good in that he does only what is good. On one view, expressed by William of Ockham and many classical Protestants, actions are made good or bad by God's free choice (God could, if he so chose, make murder a good act); on the other view, expressed by Aquinas, some actions at least are good or bad in their nature – God sees them to be so, and so does them and commands others to do them. He is omnipotent in that he can do anything; 'anything' is normally construed as 'anything which does not involve a self-contradiction', but some have held that God can even break the rules of logic. He created the universe at a time (if it had a beginning, as theists have normally supposed); and sustains it in existence for as long as it exists. As creator of men and all else, he is entitled to their worship and obedience. He is omniscient in that he knows all things, past and future (though a few theologians have put some qualification on his knowledge of the future free actions of humans). Theists differ about the sense in which God is eternal. On the view held by the great philosophical theologians from Augustine to Aquinas, he is eternal in being outside time; but for many other theistic philosophers, before and since, he is eternal simply in existing at all times, past, present and future (*see also* **Time and Timelessness**). These attributes, described above, belong to God necessarily (he cannot lose them or destroy them); and he himself exists necessarily. For some the necessity of God's existence is logical necessity (i.e. he exists, because it would be self-contradictory to say that he does not); for others it is factual necessity (i.e. his existence is the ultimate brute fact).

Richard Swinburne, *The Coherence of Theism*, 1977, especially Parts II and III.

R. G. SWINBURNE

Theocentricity

In the context of the theology of religions, theocentricity is the view that the great world faiths constitute different perceptions of and response to the one ultimate divine Reality which Christians call God. In the past each religious tradition has generally seen its own gospel as uniquely final* and salvific, thus creating an obligation to try to convert others to the one true faith. In Christian terms this was expressed as both the Catholic dogma *Extra ecclesiam nulla salus* (outside the church, no salvation) and the nineteenth-century Protestant missionary conviction that outside Christianity there is no salvation*. Since World War II a widespread acceptance has developed (reflected in the pronouncements of Vatican II and the publications of the World Council of Churches) that salvation is in fact taking place not only among Christians but also among Jews, Muslims, Hindus, Buddhists, Sikhs, etc., this salvation being, however, made possible only by the sacrificial death of a Christ (*see also* **Christianity and Other Religions**). Karl Rahner expressed this by saying that devout people of other faiths may be regarded as 'anonymous* Christians'. Whether or not this particular term is used, it probably expresses a majority view among churchmen today.

However, from a theocentric standpoint this is an arbitrary position which falls short of a fully realistic interpretation of the wider religious life of mankind. Each tradition is of course at liberty to define other traditions as inferior to and salvifically dependent upon itself. Thus Christians can see devout Muslims, etc., as anonymous Christians, and Muslims can see devout Christians, etc., as anonymous Muslims. But such definitional victories fail to do justice to the spiritual depth, power and integrity of each tradition. If Christians, Muslims, Hindus, Jews, etc. are saved, this must be because their traditions constitute valid contexts within which the transformation of human existence from self-centredness to Reality-centredness is effectively taking place. More broadly, the world faiths embody different perceptions and conceptions of, and correspondingly different responses to, the Divine from within the major variant cultural ways of being human. The great religious traditions are accordingly to be regarded as alternative soteriological* 'spaces' within which, or 'ways' along which, men and women can find salvation/liberation/fulfilment.

The term 'theocentricity', although often used, is ultimately inadequate to describe this pluralist position; for the divine Reality is known not only as personal but also (within Buddhism and certain streams of Hinduism) as non-personal (see also **Pluralism**). The relation between these two very different ways of experiencing and conceiving the divine Reality is perhaps analogous to the complementarity in physics between the wave-like and particle-like descriptions of light. When we experiment upon it in one way light is found to behave in a wave-like manner, and when in another way, in a particle-like manner. Analogously, when human beings approach the divine through one kind of religious mind-set and spiritual practice they experience the divine as the personal Yahweh, or Holy Trinity, or Allah, or Shiva, etc.; and when through another kind of religious mind-set and spiritual practice, as the non-personal Brahman, Nirvana, Dharmakaya, Sunyata, etc.

John Hick, *God and the Universe of Faiths*, 1973; *God Has Many Names*, 1980; Wilfred Cantwell Smith, *Towards a World Theology*, 1982.

JOHN HICK

Theocracy

Just as 'democracy' signifies government by the mass of the people in any society or by their duly elected representatives, so 'theocracy' signifies government by God or by his representatives. Ancient Israel provides the most notable example of a theocracy. Since, however, the will of God is not an empirical reality as is the will of the people or of any other constitutional group, a theocracy is always more of an ideal than a fact and belongs primarily to the sphere of profession and faith rather than to that of plain practice.

N. H. G. ROBINSON

Theodicy

1. The term (from the Greek for 'justification of God') goes back to G. W. F. von Leibniz, *Essais de Théodicée sur la bonté de Dieu, la liberté de l'homme et l'origine du mal*

(1710). However, Boethius had already given classical expression to the question of theodicy: *Si Deus justus – unde malum?* (If God is righteous, why evil?). He gave the answer as follows. Either God wishes to prevent evil but cannot, in which case he is just but not omnipotent. Or he can prevent evil but does not want to, in which case he is omnipotent but not just. I. Kant put the question of theodicy in more general terms as the question of the 'defence of the supreme wisdom of the author of the world against the accusation raised against it by reason, as a result of what thwarts his purposes in the world'. Of course the problem is not limited to the area of the Jewish–Christian tradition, but is as old as mankind's faith in a supreme power which orders the world. For faith in divine justice makes experiences of suffering* and guilt* a problem, and conversely these experiences necessarily raise the question of divine justice. In all theistic* religions, before the attempt at a rational solution to the problem of theodicy we find questions, lamentations and reproaches to the deity for evils that are experienced. In the history of religion and philosophy we keep finding two different solutions. (i) *The dualistic* conception*. A good principle and an evil principle are in conflict in the world. People have to make a decision about the side they want to take in this conflict. Only good comes from God; evil comes from an anti-God, the power of darkness. This conception is to be found in Parseeism, Manichaeism, Jewish, Christian and modern apocalypticism. (ii) *The monistic conception*. Only the good has existence; evil does not, or is that which does not exist. It has no quality of being, but only the quality of the negation of being. Therefore in history it serves the good in one way or another, and the good shows its greater power in the negation of negation. This conception is to be found in Platonism and Jewish and Christian creation* faith.

2. In the biblical traditions, especially in the Psalms, Job, Lamentations and the passion narratives, the question of theodicy emerges in such an elemental form that it seems impossible either to abandon or to answer. If God is just, why must the faithful suffer and why do the godless fare well? If God is faithful, why is Israel handed over to the power of the Gentile nations? If God is 'the Father', why did he 'abandon' Jesus 'the

Son' on the cross (Mark 15.34)? Faith in God takes up these questions and points them in particular directions. (i) There is a kind of evil which people bring on themselves. Evil actions already carry within themselves a punishment in the form of evil consequences. This complex of action and outcome is part of the divine justice. To this degree God is responsible for the existence of disaster, but not for causing it. The 'wrath * of God' is manifested in the fact that God 'gives over' sinners to a course of temporal and eternal destruction which they themselves have chosen (Rom. 1.18ff.). This view can be found in the Yahwistic, Deuteronomistic and Chronistic histories, the prophecy of judgment, the Gospel of Matthew and the Letters of Paul. (ii) But there is a kind of suffering which is undergone by the righteous, and not by the wicked. The complex of action and outcome is not applicable to the suffering of the righteous. Here trust in God can only be maintained as an accusation against God (Job). God's action is unfathomable. Man has no right to accuse him (Rom. 9.20). His only role is tacit humility. (iii) Finally, there is a kind of suffering undergone by God himself. Through his covenant * with Israel and the indwelling of the name in this people, God himself takes part in the persecutions, sufferings and captivities of Israel. He is the companion of the righteous in suffering. When Israel is redeemed, the God who suffers with it redeems himself and glorifies not only Israel but also himself. This Israelite conception of the fellow-suffering of God (theopathy) is the basis for the NT account of the passion of Jesus, the Son of God. He is the merciful servant of God who suffers with us, does 'for us' and in this way frees us. His suffering is divine suffering, redemptive and in solidarity with us.

3. The Church Fathers, above all Irenaeus and Augustine, attempted to solve the problem of theodicy with the help of Middle Platonism *: evil has no existence and is a lack of good. Therefore the creator God is not the cause of it. Moral evil is the result of mankind's free choice and therefore sin. Physical ills are a divine means of punishment and education, aimed at purifying and cleansing mankind. Even metaphysical evil – the devil – must serve the plans of God. The Reformers played down these ways of justifying God from creation and from salvation history (see **Heilsgeschichte**), because for them the justification * of man 'before God' was the focal point of theology. By justifying the sinner through grace *, God shows his righteousness to be creative, justifying righteousness. In his justifying righteousness God sets himself at rights and to that degree also justifies himself. The doctrine of justification is the Reformers' answer to the question of theodicy. Only in Protestant orthodoxy is evil again described within the framework of God's universal rule of the world: God allows evil without endorsing it; he directs evil so that it brings about good; he sets limits to evil and will overcome it in the end. It is understandable that the Lutheran philosopher Leibniz formed his optimistic conception of the 'best of all possible worlds' from this approach: God permits moral evil for the sake of the freedom of human will and uses physical ills to punish and educate. The optimistic conception of the world held by the thinkers of the Enlightenment * collapsed in the experience of the Lisbon earthquake of 1755: where tens of thousands die a senseless death, all theodicy turns to lies.

4. In the eighteenth century, with the Lisbon earthquake confidence in the harmony of the world and a gracious ruler of it was shattered. Human self-confidence was shattered in the twentieth century in the unspeakable crime and horror of the holocaust of Auschwitz and Hiroshima. The symbols of the 'death of God *' and the 'death of man' express the end of any theodicy and any anthropodicy. How can one speak of 'God' after Auschwitz? How can one even speak of humankind after Auschwitz? Three points have become important in Christian discussion of a theology after Auschwitz. (i) The question of the justification of God cannot be answered, but it can never be abandoned. The question of God lives on in an irresistible hunger for righteousness. (ii) There cannot be a theology *after* Auschwitz which does not take up the theology *in* Auschwitz: the prayers of the victims. God himself was present in their prayers; as their companion in suffering he gives up hope where no more can be hoped for. (iii) The question of theodicy remains open until a new creation, in which God's righteousness dwells, gives the answer.

See also **Evil, Problem of**.

A. Herschel, *The Prophets*, 1955; J. Hick, *Evil and the God of Love*, 1966; J. Moltmann, *The Crucified God*, London 1974; W. Philipp, *Das Werden der Aufklärung*, 1957; R. Rubinstein, *After Auschwitz. Radical Theology and Contemporary Judaism*, 1966.

JÜRGEN MOLTMANN

Theologia Crucis: Theologia Gloriae

'Theology of the Cross' is Luther's name for the doctrine that our knowledge of God must be drawn from the suffering Christ in his humiliation. He contrasted this with the view of mediaeval scholasticism* which maintained that a 'natural' knowledge of God could be obtained by the unaided human reason. He called this view a 'theology of glory'.

ALAN RICHARDSON

Theology

A term which has had a number of meanings at different times in history. In the English-speaking world today, it would now widely be taken to refer to the rational account given of Christian faith, as furnished by a series of sub-disciplines such as biblical studies, church history, systematic theology*, theological ethics, and practical* or pastoral* theology. The preparatory study for giving such an account would be largely determined by syllabuses of instruction in institutions of higher or further education, such as faculties of theology, seminaries or theological colleges. Here theology is studied either according to conventions of rationality deriving from the theory and practice of modern universities, where specialized disciplines deal with different departments of knowledge, or according to the requirements of a modern understanding of the ordained ministry of the church, frequently with a close resemblance to the development of professional expertise. In both cases theology would be regarded as appropriate to a minority of Christians, usually seen as an intellectual élite. Theological study would be broken down into sub-disciplines, the study of the scriptures (entailing knowledge of the original languages), the study of the history of the church (including its authoritative declarations and decisions in their original languages), and the study of the intellectual and

practical tasks of the contemporary church in relation to any discipline of special assistance or relevance (for example, philosophy, sociology or psychology). Needless to say, such a study makes formidable demands on students, and its conception and practice is integrally related to the dominant models of education prevalent in the Western world.

It is necessary to distinguish, however, between the long-standing Christian tradition of respect for learning, and the contempory Western understanding of 'theology'. Interest in painstaking scholarly activity is already evident in the activities of Origen (*c.* 185–254, *see also* **Biblical Criticism**). As head of the Catechetical School of Alexandria from 202–231, he was the author of a remarkable variety of works including biblical criticism, commentaries, ascetical theology, speculative theology and apologetics. Some of these works are specifically designed to appeal to educated non-Christians; others are presented as of relevance to a minority of spiritually advanced Christians.

Acknowledgment of, and respect for learning is, however, an even older phenomenon. Paul was 'as to the Law a Pharisee' (Phil. 3.5), and had probably studied for the Rabbinate in Jerusalem, perhaps under Gamaliel. Jesus himself was at least called Rabbi, or teacher. At the same time Jesus plainly appealed to those without formal education ('children'), and Paul strongly denied that the 'word of the cross' could appropriately be likened to human wisdom (I Cor. 1.18–25). Christianity is a religion with respect for learning rather than a learned religion.

The development of learning as one of the activities of the church has its basis in three characteristics of Christianity. 1. The adoption of certain writings as a norm or canon* for the content of the faith necessitated the study of texts. Even before the canon of scriptures was practically fixed, Christian authors widely used collections of 'testimonies' from the OT, interpreted according to the 'key' provided by Jesus Christ. Christians were ready to 'prove' from the scriptures that Jesus was the promised Messiah (cf. Luke 24.27). Once the church determined the boundaries of its own canon, and had come to attribute divine inspiration* to the writings, it was bound to study these writings with close attention, and according to established methods (*see* **Hermeneutics**).

2. The expansion of the Christian movement into cultures lacking any familiarity with the concepts and vocabulary of the OT required a creative process of interpretation of the original message. The OT and NT gave rise to disputes about meaning, which in turn required patient elucidation. Thus with the expansion of Christianity, a tradition of learning was required in order to solve problems in the communication of the gospel and its practical application in new cultural contexts.

3. Disputes as to meanings quickly gave rise to separations and schisms within the Christian community. This is already apparent in the books of the NT, especially the epistles, in which theological argumentation is deployed in order to distinguish between truth and error (see **Heresy**). The practical necessity for such skills has much to do with the fact that theology has been, and still is, an important weapon in controversy, highly developed where controversies are much in evidence and part of both the undergirding and undermining of traditional authorities.

Theologia as a Greek term is not found in the NT; on the other hand, *gnosis* (knowledge) is a frequent enough, and perhaps controversial term (I Cor. 8, and see **Gnosticism**), used to refer to the status of spiritual and intellectual enlightenment into which Christians have been inducted. Perhaps because of the problem of Gnostic heresy, Christian writers from the time of Origen onwards adopted the term *theologia* to refer to the gift of insight into the divine being. In the Arian* controversy, 'theology' in this sense was contrasted with 'economy', that is, the plan of salvation through Christ. 'Theology' thus had a mystical connotation, and in the Greek tradition is closely connected to contemplation, and to the negative (or apophatic*) way.

The Western fathers scarcely used the word *theologia*, and the first to apply the term to a methodical investigation of Christian teaching was Peter Abailard (1079–1142). In the twelfth century the long-standing tradition of learning began to acquire an increasingly self-conscious method, and the terms of the relationship between 'natural' and 'revealed' knowledge became a discussion of central and lasting importance (*see* **Systematic Theology**).

Inherent in theology, regarded as a specialized discipline, requiring high intellectual qualities and prolonged training, is the perennial problem of faith and knowledge. Repeated attempts have been made to challenge the élitist pretensions of theologians from the side of spiritual humility, mysticism*, religious experience (Luther), or (most recently) social practice. The most effective challenge, however, is the comparatively recent discovery that there is a diversity of forms of rational argument in different disciplines, each of which have a close relation to the interests of a particular culture or group. The application of this insight to the procedures of theological argument forces the theologian to attend to the fact that Christianity exists in liturgies, rituals, art forms and other forms of cultural expression. Without the necessity of denying or undervaluing the tradition of learning characteristic of Christianity from the first, that tradition has carried out its own internal self-criticism.

S. W. SYKES

Theonomy

An interpretation of man's moral life is theonomous if it finds the ultimate ethical authority in the divine will, as the principle of autonomy* finds it in a law which is self-imposed and that of heteronomy* in a law which comes from without. According to Paul Tillich, theonomy is the law or principle which unites the law of one's own being with the ground and source of all being. For others, elements of autonomy and theonomy might well be regarded as immanent and transcendent elements respectively in the ethical side of theism.

N. H. G. ROBINSON/D. W. D. SHAW

Theophany *see* **Epiphany**

Theotokos *see* **Christology, Mariology**

Thirty-nine Articles

These were adopted as a doctrinal standard by the Convocation of the Church of England in 1571 and enforced by the Canons of 1604. They deal with such subjects as the doctrines of God, of salvation, of the church and sacraments, and the sources of and norms of Christian belief. In the modern Canons of the Church of England, the Articles are said to be 'agreeable to the Word of God' and 'may be assented unto with a good conscience by all members of the Church of England' (Canon A2; following the terms of both 1571 and 1604). Furthermore, together with the Book of Common Prayer and the Ordinal, they are a place where the doctrine of the Church of England is to be found (Canon A5).

The Thirty-nine Articles do not occupy the same authoritative position in all provinces of the Anglican Communion, many of which make no reference to them in their Constitutions or Canons. The 1968 Lambeth Conference (the assembly of all diocesan bishops in the Anglican Communion) adopted a resolution suggesting that the printing of the Articles in the prayer books of the churches and the practice of requiring assent of them from ordinands be discontinued (Resolution 43). The argument lying behind these recommendations was based on the view that Anglicanism, in assigning a role to reason (not least historical and philosophical inquiry), must present the Articles as a monument in a continuous process of a developing tradition, rather than as a final statement of its confessional standpoint.

The Articles are similar in intention, and in much of their content, to the studiously moderate doctrinal statements contained in the Lutheran *Confessio Augustana* (1530), largely the work of Melanchthon. Their theological character, like that of the *Confessio Augustana*, is formed by the desire both to affirm the faith of the catholic and ecumenical creeds, and at the same time to adopt a position as irenical as possible on matters on which it was believed that the Roman Church had erred.

A number of the Articles repudiate doctrines held by 'Anabaptists' or radical reformers. Most of the Articles dealing with the evangelical doctrines do so in a form in which both Lutherans and Calvinists could agree, consciously avoiding partisan terminology. The eucharistic teaching of Articles 28 and 29 stands somewhat closer to Reformed than to the stricter Lutheran version of the doctrine.

The interpretation of the Articles has varied quite widely in the course of their use in the Church of England. Frequently held to be not in the strict sense a confession, but rather 'pious opinions fitted for the preservation of unity' (John Bramhall, 1658), they were roundly attacked as illiberal in the eighteenth century (Feathers Tavern

Petition, 1772), and given an interpretation congruous with the decrees of the Council of Trent (by the tractarian, John Henry Newman, in 1841). Though they were mainly used in the past to regulate clerical opinion, since 1975 the Church of England has abandoned the practice of requiring specific assent to them from its ordinands. The new Preface and Declaration of Assent treats them as, in effect, an outstanding monument of the Anglican tradition.

S. W. SYKES

Thomism

This name is given both to the doctrine of the Dominican Friar, Thomas Aquinas (1226–74), and to various later schools of thought claiming descent from him. What follows is intended as an exposition of the former.

Aquinas' view of the autonomy* of the created determines his thinking on the place of human reason in theology, on the relationship of human freedom to divine omnipotence and grace, and on political society. Creatures are autonomous not by being independent of God but because their dependence on God is *total*, so that the activity of the creator is not an interference in their lives which sets a limit to their own activity; rather it is by God's activity that they are and behave as themselves. We are free not in spite of God's power but because of it. God brings it about both that the acts of unfree creatures are causally determined by other creatures and that the acts of free creatures are not so determined. Unfree acts are, at one level, the result of natural causes, at another level, of God. Free acts are the acts of creatures that are simply brought about by God. Thus, freedom is not a manifestation of distance from God but (like a miracle) a manifestation of the power of God alone without intervening natural causes.

This view depends on Aquinas' notion of God as creative sustainer of everything actual in the universe and thus as not himself a member of the universe. God does not belong in any class with his creatures, so it is not possible to add God and creature to make two. God does not compete with any creature such that some things it does are due to the creature alone and others to God. All creatures act as instruments of God.

To recognize the existence of God is to

recognize that which altogether transcends the universe and all distinctions within it. God is thus not the 'Necessary Being' as distinct from 'contingent beings'; creation itself contains both necessary and contingent beings. The latter are perishable, being the actualization (by a form) of (material) potentiality. The materiality of contingent things is their liability to be destroyed as some agent replaces their form by another. Also, since matter is that factor in things which is not formal (intelligible, actual), it is the principle of individuation in virtue of which there may be many individuals of the same form, the same intelligibility. Individuals, because of their materiality, are not in themselves intelligible to us – thus no individual thing could be the meaning of a word. We know individuals as such only by sense knowledge. Subsistent forms which do not actualize matter (angels) are necessary beings, neither individual nor perishable. Intelligible in themselves, they are nevertheless unintelligible to us because of the limitation of our mode of understanding which can only work through the creation and understanding of the meanings of material symbols in the imagination. All we can understand in this way are the forms of material things. The act of understanding is, for us, the act of raising the forms of individual things to. intelligibility. The mind is where such forms exist intelligibly (intentionally). This is what Aquinas means primarily by abstraction: the act by which the forms of individuals, hitherto sunk in matter, become the meanings of symbols. We grasp truth by using such meanings to make judgments, expressed in statements.

Since even a major part of creation (the angelic world) is beyond our understanding, *a fortiori* God is wholly unintelligible to us. We have no idea what God is. In his arguments* for the existence of God Aquinas tries to prove that questions posed by the world of experience inevitably lead us to some form of the most radical question concerning the existence, *esse*, of things: why does anything exist instead of there not being anything? Simultaneously we recognize that the answer to this question (which we label 'God') is unknowable to us. It is not anything we know of God but what we know of the radical questionableness of creatures that gives us our meaning and use for the word 'God'. Concerning God we

know only that he exists (there is an answer) and that he is the cause of all that is (for this is the question to which it is the answer). Apart from this we can know only what God *could not be* if he is to be such an answer.

Thus in God there could be no distinction of matter and form (he is not contingent, nor an individual, nor a member of any class); but this is true even of the created angels. They cannot perish, but nonetheless there is a sense in which they might not exist – for their existence is received from God who might not have created them. Even the essence of an angel is in this sense potential with respect to its existence. In God this could not be so. Not only the distinction of matter and form but also the distinction of essence and existence must belong solely to the created world and have no place in God, the sheer actuality in which there can be no potentiality of any kind. Aquinas' creator God is outside the scope of Aristotelian* categories. In creation it is as though God did in terms of *esse* itself what Aristotelian natural causes do in terms of the form by which a thing has *esse*. Aquinas invokes the same difficult notion in his doctrine that God can understand individual material things as such, as well as in his equally un-Aristotelian eucharistic theory of transubstantiation*, according to which the *esse* of the elements becomes the *esse* of the individual, Christ.

God cannot exist in any place or at any time, though he is present, as sustaining its existence, to anything in any place, and the proposition that God exists will be true at any time that it is uttered or conceived. Thus eternity, which properly belongs to God alone, does not mean interminable duration. There is no sequence in God's life. He does not do or know one thing after another, though the objects of his doing and knowing may succeed each other in time.

God's omnipotence means that he can bring about any thing you could mention (such as, for example, a universe without beginning or end in time). Square circles and the changing of the past are excluded not by any limitation of God's power but because a self-contradicting expression like 'square circle' or 'past event that did not happen' cannot be used to name what God might make because it cannot function as a name at all. God cannot make evil*, because 'evil' signifies not a being but an absence or failure of being, a deprivation of what might be expected to belong to a thing of a particular nature.

Given his view of the absolute transcendence (and, for that reason, immanence) of God, Aquinas needs an account of how our language can apply to him. He distinguishes between metaphorical language (e.g. 'The Lord is my shepherd') and literal usage (e.g. 'God is good'). The former is compatible with its denial, the latter is not. Within literal usage, however, he recognizes terms used analogically, i.e. when their use is non-univocal but not by mere punning. Analogical use of language is systematically ambiguous: as when we say we love our friends, good wine and our country, where the meanings of 'love' are distinct but not unrelated. Thus when we apply the word 'good' to God we extend its meaning so that it simply points towards a mystery and we do not even know what the goodness of God means. Nevertheless the word is not used equivocally (by a pun), for its meaning remains related to that of its use in familiar contexts. Analogy, for Aquinas, is a theory of language usage; to say that a word is used analogically of God is a warning not to treat it as though we knew what it meant and could make simple inferences from the predication. (Some modern Thomists have spoken of the 'analogy of being', but this is an extension or distortion of Aquinas' teaching.)

Aquinas rejects a dualistic view of man as consisting of two substances: a body and a soul. In any material thing the substantial form is the principle in virtue of which it *is*, and *acts* and is *what* it is, while matter is the principle of vulnerability, of possibly not being and not being what it now is. In a living thing its life (or soul) is its form and its living is its being. Thus a dead cat is not a kind of cat nor is it a cat's body minus its soul; it is a different substance altogether. In any animal, all its own vital acts are acts of its soul; in irrational animals, bodily acts of the soul. In man, however, some of his acts, thinking and choosing, for example, are acts of the soul (*his* acts) but not in themselves processes in his body – although they are not naturally possible without certain concomitant bodily acts of imagination, sensation, etc. Thus the human soul has more than the job of making this body a human body with human bodily operations;

it is also the principle of some acts which transcend the body. For this reason, when the body ceases to be by turning into a corpse, it does not follow that the soul ceases to be. What it can be like for a soul to be without fulfilling its role as animator of a human body Aquinas has some difficulty in explaining, but he is clear that such a 'separated soul' is not itself a human person and that human persons could not be said to survive death were it not for the revealed doctrine of the resurrection.

Irrational things tend towards their ends and their own fulfilment because of the natural causes which brought them into existence and determined their nature; human beings, which can act in virtue not only of the forms they have by nature but also the forms they have intentionally in the mind, can choose not only how to attain their purposes (as higher animals can) but also what these aims will be. The nature of man as a political, rational animal determines that certain goods he might aim at are more important to his flourishing than others, but it is possible for us to set our minds and hearts on lesser goods at the expense of greater. In this way we fail to reach fulfilment and happiness. The moral virtues are dispositions (basically, justice in the will, courage and self-control in the emotions) acquired through education, which incline us to aim at what will in fact lead to and constitute our flourishing, dispositions to behave in a truly human way. Their exercise depends on a similarly acquired practical intellectual virtue of good sense, *prudentia*, which disposes us to determine what is to be done, given these aims. In all this, Aquinas follows a broadly Aristotelian line, but for him, man as political animal, part of the life of society, is merely a two-dimensional map of the solid reality of men as called to share the life of God, by grace in this world and glory in the next.

Grace is primarily a matter of the nature we have; not an alternative to but a deepening of our political nature by which we participate in the divine nature. Just as the acquired moral and other virtues correspond to the social nature of man, so there are virtues, not acquired by education but simply given by God (infused), to correspond to our graced-nature. These are primarily faith, hope and charity. Faith, a willing intellectual acceptance of God's

Word, is presupposed to hope and charity a sharing into the love which is the Holy Spirit. Because of the corruption of sin it is not in practice possible for us to live a flourishing human social life without being taken beyond it to a share in divine life. Thus there is no lasting authentic social virtue without charity, and no charity without faith in God's love for us.

After his death, Aquinas' teachings were condemned by the church both in Paris and Oxford. Later he was rehabilitated, and canonized in 1323, and by the time of the Council of Trent* (1545–63) was being treated as a touchstone of Roman orthodoxy. He was then largely neglected until the rise of twentieth-century 'Thomism' which, however, because of its curiously conservative bent, became unpopular in the Roman Church at the time of Vatican II. There are signs of a revival of interest, but Aquinas' reputation is still, perhaps, higher amongst secular philosophers than amongst his co-religionists.

Aquinas' greatest theological work is the *Summa Theologiae*; others include the *Summa contra Gentes* and the early *Scriptum super Libros Sententiarum*. Outstanding amongst the commentaries on Aristotle is the *De Anima*.

Modern introductions include: M. D. Chenu, *Introduction à l'étude de saint Thomas d'Aquin*, 1950; F. C. Copleston, *Aquinas*, 1955; P. T. Geach, in G. E. M. Anscombe and P. T. Geach, *Three Philosophers*, 1961; E. Gilson, *The Christian Philosophy of St Thomas Aquinas*, 1957; A. C. Kenny, *Aquinas*; (ed), *Aquinas: A Collection of Critical Essays*, 1969; *The Five Ways*, 1969; J. Pieper, *The Silence of St Thomas*, 1957; J. A. Weisheipl, *Friar Thomas D'Aquino*, 1975.

HERBERT MCCABE

Time and Timelessness

The Bible consistently speaks of God* as eternal: he is not an idol with a temporal beginning and subject to possible destruction, he does not become weary or grow old, his years have no end. God is the God of the living; his name is Y H W H, interpreted often as 'I Am' or 'He who is'. On the basis of lexical studies, Oscar Cullmann and others have argued that 'eternal' in the Bible

should be taken to mean 'endless duration' rather than timelessness, such that when we say that God is eternal this is equivalent to saying that God endures throughout all time. However James Barr, in his study of biblical time-words, has pointed out that philosophical and theological conclusions cannot legitimately be read directly off simple lexical data. The fact that a time word has a temporal sense when applied to an earthly situation (e.g. perpetual slave) is no guarantee that the same word must bear a temporal rather than a timeless sense when it is applied to God: the subject must be allowed to qualify the meaning of the adjective.

The philosophical framework in which the Fathers formulated the doctrine of eternity was one which favoured its interpretation as timelessness. Plato in the *Timaeus* defined time as 'the moving image of eternity' and taught that true Being could not be temporal. Plotinus carried this forward by speaking of the One* as true Being to whom tensed expressions cannot apply because it is utterly immutable and has life 'all together and full, completely without extension or interval' (*En.* III.7.3). Sometimes the One is spoken of in mathematical terms, leading to a negative conception involving timelessness and changlessness. At other times, however, Plotinus describes the One as the giver of form, beauty and goodness, as Father and Maker. When those two ways of thinking about the One are held together and given a Christian baptism, one result is a doctrine of divine eternity modelled on the timeless character of a mathematical entity. This leads directly to Boethius' classical definition of God's eternity as 'the total, complete, simultaneous possession of eternal life' (*Cons.* V.6). This theme is taken up repeatedly by mediaeval theologians, who sometimes speak of God as the 'eternal Now' and at others as utterly outside time – not strictly compatible notions.

Given the Platonic conception of eternity as timelessness, Christian philosophers of the Middle Ages found it congenial to contrast the eternity of God with the temporal spread of the universe, and invoked spatial metaphors to try to clarify their meaning. One of the most important of these metaphors was direction. Space is three-dimensional, and hence has three pairs of directions; time can then be thought of as one-dimensional, having the directions of past and future. Both time and space can be specified in terms of their relationship to some standardized point of reference: for spatial location one can refer to one's position relative to the equator or the North Star; for temporal location to an event like the birth of Christ. However, there are also puzzling asymmetries between the notions of space and time; one of the most striking is that one can travel in any spatial direction, but one cannot 'move about in time' in any analogous way, travelling at will into the future or the past.

This disanalogy contributed to a new series of metaphors of time as a great ocean upon which we sail, or alternatively as a stream which flows over us, who are always in the present, in its relentless transition from future to past. These ideas of the flow of time have been labelled 'the myth of passage' because they rest on a confusion. Movement, change or flow is itself temporal; motion and time are not separable. But if one were to speak of *time* flowing, then this movement of time would have to take place relative to some 'hypertime'. It makes no sense to ask how fast time flies, since any answer would have to be given in terms of time and would thus beg the question. The conclusion to which this drives us is that time itself does not change. Things change, and their changes can be temporally measured and located, but it makes no sense to speak of a temporal movement or location of time itself.

Included in this is the further conclusion that anything that changes must be temporal, not timeless. Conversely, if God is timeless he must be absolutely immutable. This, however, raises the problem of how a timeless world could relate to a spatial and temporal world. Aristotle, who put the problem in the frame of reference it would subsequently assume, thought that reflection on the nature of time showed that any doctrine of creation* was impossible. His argument was that it is inconceivable that time should have a beginning, because for any postulated beginning we can always ask what occurred before it – thus seemingly referring to a time before the beginning of time. Augustine tried to solve the problem by insisting that time itself is a part of creation: God is timeless and the maker of time, and therefore although it seems to make

sense to ask what God was doing before he created the world, in reality this is a senseless question. Thus Augustine held that although Aristotle was right to say that the idea of a beginning of time is inconceivable, this inconceivability is psychological, not logical.

Thomas Aquinas recognized, however, that ascribing the inconceivability of the beginning of time to our human weakness is inadequate. The logic of the concept of an event requires that there must have been a 'before' and an 'after' – this is not just a function of our psychology. Aquinas accordingly suggested a distinction between real time – the time of the world – and imaginary time, which is the time we can conceive of. Although we can conceive of time before the creation of the world, this time would be only imaginary. Real time began with the beginning of motion of created things. This view, however, has the insuperable difficulty that no further account can be given of this postulated imaginary time. By definition it has nothing to do with change or motion, since that is the prerogative of real time: but then why should it be called time at all? Furthermore, we would still have to account for how God is related to this imaginary time. If, for example, he created it too, the problem begins all over again.

A new era in science dawned when Newton called into question Aristotle's premise that time and motion are essentially linked. Newton distinguished between relative space and time, which we measure by means of the motion of bodies, and absolute space and time, which are infinite and not essentially related to motion. Time for Newton is thus the infinite 'place' of the succession of things. God, omnipresent in space and time, 'constitutes duration in space' – time and space are aspects of God, at least in the sense that God wholly permeates the infinite containers, time and space, which are substantial entities. Thus although creation took place at a moment of time, time itself existed, occupied only by God, infinitely. On Newton's view, God's eternity could not be interpreted as timelessness but as omnitemporality. Leibniz criticized Newton's ideas of absolute space and time, arguing that there can be no such thing as empty time. Although we can conceive of something happening before the creation of the world, strictly this means only that we can conceive of a possible world which existed before this actual world, and which contained the imagined event. Leibniz considered that this was the only way to resolve Augustine's puzzle of why God did not create the world sooner: on this view time began with the creation of things.

Kant, however, provided an alternative approach. Given a Newtonian view (which Kant accepted), it seems difficult to escape the view that if God constitutes time then he is in some sense the container of the universe and all its events. But he would then be neither timeless nor immutable, for every change in the universe would be a change in God. Kant overcame this by distinguishing between the world as we perceive it and the world as it really is. The world as we perceive it is indeed characterized by infinite time; contrary to Leibniz even empty time is conceivable, only timelessness is not. The reason for this, however, is not to be sought in the objective structure of the world. Rather, time, like space, is a sort of grid which we place upon all our perceptions, the framework we impose on the world. Whether the real world is temporal or not we have no way of knowing, though we need not suppose it to be temporal from the mere fact that we perceive it as such, because this is our inevitable contribution to perception rather than a fact about the world. Since God is not part of the world of appearances, it is possible to affirm Newtonian physics for this world and still maintain that God is timeless. The theological problem with this view is that it banishes God from the world of experience; he cannot be a personal and active being, and we can know literally nothing about him or about the 'real' world.

In 1887 A. A. Michelson and E. W. Morley devised and conducted an experiment intended to confirm Newton's ideas of absolute space and time – and it failed. This led to a radical rethinking of fundamental Newtonian notions, especially the idea of simultaneity. On the basis of this, Einstein argued that there could be no way of establishing that two events which are spatially separate are temporally simultaneous unless we can first establish that two spatially separate clocks are synchronized. But because there is an upper limit on the velocities of the signals we can use to coor-

dinate these clocks (namely the speed of light), this is impossible. Therefore we could never have recourse to absolute space or absolute time; space and time are relative to one another and cannot properly be treated separately. Nevertheless, time is more basic than space. Anything spatial must be temporal, but it might be the case that there are temporal things which are not spatial – conscious processes of disembodied persons, for example, are not ruled out solely by the theory of relativity. If God is incorporeal, it does not follow that he is timeless.

However, it remains to ask whether the concept of a timeless living being is coherent. Mathematical entities, in whatever sense they exist, are not temporal; they have no history. But they could not serve as a model for divine timelessness, since they are static, not active, and God is a living being who created the world and acts within it. Nelson Pike has argued that if God were timeless, this would be impossible, since creation and actions are events and thus are inescapably connected with temporality, and this as part of the logic of the terms, not merely our conceptual finitude. Life involves change – succession – and if that life is causally related to this world, the causality as much as the life itself demands the applicability of temporal predicates.

Crucially connected with the doctrine of divine timelessness is that of immutability, the doctrine that God cannot change. The argument thus far is that a living God cannot be static: life implies change and hence temporality. This means that the doctrine of immutability cannot be interpreted as absolute changelessness, which would preclude divine reponsiveness, and must rather be taken as steadfastness of character. These two are not equivalent: a person with an unchanging character and purpose may change his methods to fit varying contingencies as they arise, may respond to requests and attitudes, and have real internal relations with other persons and things, whereas an absolutely immutable being could do none of these things. The former, clearly, is nearer to a biblical conception of God, though many theologians have propounded on the latter.

One of the ways in which it has been attempted to preserve the doctrines of immutability and timelessness is by drawing a distinction between willing a change and changing the will: God would have eternally and changelessly willed that changes occur at specific times. Built into this could be a system of response to contingent human actions, such that God willed from all eternity that if humankind acted in one way, A would occur, but if they acted in another way B would occur. However, this will not save the day for a doctrine of timelessness, since theologians normally wish to say that it is not merely God's intention (which could perhaps extend through all eternity) but his action which brings about A or B, and action is itself a temporal notion. And even if it could be plausibly maintained that these events are somehow built into the system so that from the fact that they occur now it does not follow that God does them now, this could not be true for that set of God's acts which is most significant to us: his personal response to our ongoing situation and attitudes. A God who could not respond to us and indeed could not be in any way affected by us would be far removed from the God of Jesus of Nazareth. A timeless and immutable God could not be personal, because he could not create or respond, perceive or act, think, remember, or do any of the other things persons do which require time. Thus within the framework of a theology of a personal God, the doctrines of divine timelessness and immutability cannot be retained.

James Barr, *Biblical Words for Time*, 1962; Anthony Kenny, *The God of the Philosophers*, 1979; William Kneale, 'Time and Eternity in Theology', in *Proceedings of the Aristotelian Society*, 1960–61; Nelson Pike, *God and Timelessness*, 1970; Richard Swinburne, *The Coherence of Theism*, 1977; Bas C. Van Fraassen, *An Introduction to the Philosophy of Space and Time*, 1970; Keith Ward, *Rational Theology and the Creativity of God*, 1982.

GRACE JANTZEN

Tradition

In ecclesiastical usage the word can have a number of different meanings. It can stand for the whole of Christianity considered as a complex of doctrines, practices, norms of behaviour, cult and religious experience, handed down from the beginning. It can be used to mean a particular strand of doctrine or of practice (as in 'the tradition of teaching

about the atonement', or 'the tradition of celebrating the eucharist', or 'Lutheran tradition of preaching'); it can denote a piece or fund of information, whether historical or legendary, about a person or thing (as in 'the tradition that Peter was crucified upside down', or 'the tradition that Christ wrote a letter to Abgar king of Edessa'). But its proper and most widely accepted meaning is the teaching and practice of the church, formally distinct from the words of scripture, as this teaching and practice has been carried on continuously from the beginning. In this sense tradition is a necessary part of historical Christianity, and no Christian denomination or communion has existed, or could have existed, without tradition, because all have taught and lived the Christian faith. Even those who have attempted to exist without tradition have only succeeded in establishing a tradition of dispensing with tradition.

The important question is not, whether tradition exists, but what its relation is to other parts of the Christian faith. This question has usually been posed in the form of a decision about the relation of scripture to tradition. It is impossible to avoid the conclusion that the tradition about Jesus existed in an oral form before the NT was written, and that oral tradition about Jesus continued to circulate in the church for some time after the NT had been written, side by side with written tradition. Several early church Fathers during the second half of the second century and the first half of the third appeal to something which they call the *rule of faith** or 'the rule of truth' or some similar name, and there is no doubt that this 'rule of faith' is formally distinct from scripture. Irenaeus, Clement of Alexandria, Tertullian, Hippolytus, Origen and Novatian, and a few others, give it considerable prominence, and Irenaeus and Tertullian appear sometimes to regard it as in some circumstances a substitute for scripture. Again, the Creed is another example of very early tradition whose origins were undoubtedly independent of the NT, that is the original, interrogatory, baptismal creed, one example of which ultimately became our 'Apostles' Creed'. The later conciliar creeds (such as our Nicene Creed), composed in the fourth and later centuries, are also, of course, examples of tradition, but not of tradition independent of scripture, for they all profess to be interpretations of scripture (*see also* **Creed**). Some have professed to find in the sacraments of baptism and of the eucharist, and some even in the Christian ministry, examples of tradition independent of scripture, inasmuch as they all derive from a period prior to the writing of the N T. Some very ancient customs and practices in the church have also been claimed to constitute original tradition independent of scripture, such as the custom of turning to the East to pray, the practice of Christians crossing themselves, and the threefold interrogation in baptism.

The R C account of tradition has since the formulation of the decrees of the Council of Trent * (1545–63) usually taken the form of claiming that unwritten traditions formed a second, independent, original, authentic source of information and doctrine alongside of scripture, capable of supplementing it, though never contradictory of it. The words used by the relevant part of the decree of Trent appeared to support this view (Session IV, April 1946), 'this truth and this discipline are contained in written books and in unwritten tradition'. Some confirmation of this opinion can be found in the words of some of the Fathers, and notably in the *De Spiritu Sancto* of Basil of Caesarea. But in recent years many theologians in the Roman communion have rejected this account of tradition, and have given a different interpretation both of the doctrine and of the words of the Council of Trent, claiming that the R C view of this subject is that scripture and tradition are identical in content though different in form and that therefore tradition is only formally, but not materially, independent of scripture, a view which allows much more room for ecumenical discussion of the subject. The question may be said to be an open one in the R C Church, because the Dogmatic Constitution on Divine Revelation of the Second Vatican Council (§§ 8 and 9) appears deliberately to have left it so. The concept of tradition is of capital importance to the Eastern Orthodox * Church. For the Orthodox, tradition means in effect the life of the Holy Spirit in the church, sustaining, quickening and directing all the church's thought, prayer and activity. Tradition in this view cannot either conflict with or supplement scripture, but must interpret it, and any doctrine or practice once securely established by tradition is virtually immut-

able. The Anglican attitude to tradition has from an early period in the history of the Church of England been clear and consistent, and can be identified both in the characteristic Anglican practice of expressing doctrine by means of liturgy and in Articles VI, VIII, XIX-XXI and XXXIV of the Thirty-nine Articles*: tradition is to be accepted as a necessary part of the Christian faith, but tradition judged by and found agreeable to scripture. Tradition is, in this view, the church's interpretation of scripture, and therefore cannot be independent of scripture. Almost all the churches of the Reformation have in fact accepted this view of tradition, though not all have been as explicit in stating this as has the Church of England. For instance, the Westminster Confession of Faith (1646) professes to reject all traditions of men in preference to scripture but reproduces with approval the words of the Nicene Creed and the Chalcedonian Formula. Again, the Lutheran Augsburg Confession (1530) is most emphatic in endorsing the traditional dogmas of the undivided church. On the subject of traditional practice and custom, however, where scripture for the most part provides little or no light, different churches have differed very widely.

Closely associated with the subject of tradition is that of doctrinal *development* *. This subject was brought into prominence by J. H. Newman (*Essay on the Development of Christian Doctrine*, 1845), who first realized its importance. He realized that the dogmatic definitions of the church of the fourth and fifth centuries represented, not merely a logical unfolding of what was there already, but in some sense an addition of something new. He asked, what was to be the criterion of true development? His answer was, the development which took place within that church which could be shown to be the only true one, the Church of Rome. Any development thus guaranteed should be regarded as legitimate, and any such developments must be held to be consistent with scripture and previous tradition because the Church of Rome said that it was. In this sense tradition could certainly be said to supplement scripture and only just to fall short of constituting new revelation. Though many R C theologians have been attracted by Newman's doctrine and have shown his influence in handling the subject of tradition, his view has never been offically adopted by the Roman Church. Other churches have repudiated Newman's doctrine, but no theologian of a Reformed tradition has yet produced a satisfactory or generally acceptable explanation of the development of doctrine.

In fact, much of what is claimed to be original tradition independent of scripture can be shown not to be so. Significant, authentic oral tradition had virtually died out by about 250, unable to withstand the influence of the written tradition of the N T. The 'rule of faith' was a summary, in the form of articles, of the Christian faith as preached and taught in the church of the writer who referred to it, in substance the same everywhere but varying a little according to local differences. All the Fathers agree that its contents is identical with that of scripture and all (even Irenaeus and Tertullian) appeal to scriptural texts to confirm it. The baptismal creed * in the early centuries is so meagre and bare in its substance as to constitute no serious rival to or supplement of scripture. Baptism, the eucharist and the ministry antedate the N T, but without the N T our knowledge of them would be so uncertain and indefinite as to render them useless as vehicles of tradition. As a source of original information independent of scripture, tradition is useless.

But as a necessary part of living, historical, developing Christianity, tradition is essential and deserves the considerable attention which it is now commanding from theologians of many denominations. In particular, the role of tradition in the interpretation of scripture is of capital importance for both Catholics and Protestants. That which creates a sense of unity among different churches today in spite of their divisions, and has made possible the Ecumenical Movement, is not the awareness of a common allegiance to scripture, but the sense of sharing a common tradition deriving from the period of the undivided church. An appreciation of the necessity, the limits, and proper function of tradition is essential for all parties in the ecumenical debate.

F. F. Bruce, *Tradition Old and New*, 1970; Y. Congar, *Tradition and Traditions*, 1966; R. P. C. Hanson, *Tradition in the Early Church*, 1962; N. Lash, *Change in Focus*, 1973; J. H. Newman, *Essay on the Development of Christian Doctrine*, 1845; J. Pelikan, *Historical Theology: Continuity and Change in Christian Doctrine*, 1971.

R. P. C. HANSON

Traditionalism

A nineteenth-century, largely French, fideistic reaction to Enlightenment * rationalism and the influence of Descartes. Its principal proponents were Joseph de Maistre (1753–1821), Louis de Bonald (1754–1840), and Félicité de Lamennais (1782–1854). The Traditionalists denied that religious, moral, or metaphysical knowledge can be derived from individual human reason. Certainty in these matters rests upon faith in a general divine revelation communicated to man at the dawn of history and thence transmitted to succeeding generations by tradition. Society, not the individual, is the repository of religious and moral truths, which are infallibly guaranteed by the fact that all men agree upon them. De Bonald held that language is prior to thought and was communicated to man together with the primal revelation. Lamennais contributed the doctrine of *Sensus Communis*: 'Authority, or the general reason, or what all men are agreed upon, is the rule for governing the judgments of the individual man.'

Louis Bautain (1796–1867) refined some of the cruder elements in Traditionalism and fertilized it with ideas borrowed from German philosophy, notably the distinction between discursive reason and intuitive intelligence.

The First Vatican Council (1869–1870) effectively excluded Traditionalism from Roman Catholic orthodoxy by its teaching on the role of reason in the steps preparatory to the act of faith.

G. A. McCool, *Catholic Theology in the Nineteenth Century*, 1977; B. Reardon, *Liberalism and Tradition: Aspects of Catholic Thought in Nineteenth-Century France*, 1975.

G. DALY

Transcendence

The concept came to have a place of prime importance in the Christian doctrine of God because of the dual nature of its origin. On the one hand O T teaching had a great deal to say about the many ways in which God's nature and form of being differed from the existence of men and women (e.g. Isa. 45.15; 55.8f.). On the other hand, deriving from Plato's reference in *The Republic*, VI 509b, to the Form of the Good 'as beyond being and knowledge', followed by Aristotle's account of the 'unmoved mover of the spheres' and much later by the Neoplatonic* doctrine of the One*, there had grown up in Greek philosophical circles the idea of a supreme entity of a totally other form of existence from that of mankind.

So the theme runs consistently through the history of Christian thought, appearing in patristic* theology, as in Athanasius, who speaks of God as 'incomprehensible Being', or in RC theology, as it defines God in Vatican I, as 'eternal, immense, incomprehensible, infinite in his intellect and will and in all perfection . . . distinct from the world in existence and essence', or in scholastic Protestant theology, which speaks of God as *spiritus independens, ens spirituale, a se subsistens*. Precise definition of transcendence may be arrived at by analysing the different forms which in the history of its use it has been thought to take, thus: 1. The *ontological* form of transcendence is the otherness of God's existence which makes it discontinuous with our own, setting it in a different order, and which is most clearly expressed in God's role as Creator of the universe and mankind. Kierkegaard expressed this form of transcendence most influentially for modern theology in his reference to 'the infinite qualitative difference between God and ourselves'. 2. In the *linguistic* form, transcendence is reflected in the ineffability or rather the unnameability of God, which springs from the OT view that to name a person is to gain power over him (Gen. 2.19). 3. The *moral* form which transcendence takes is that of the holiness of God, which in Judaeo-Christian thought is much more significant than metaphysical otherness. 'God is perfectly just, good and the overflowing fountain of goodness.' 4. The *epistemological* form of transcendence is God's incomprehensibility, which sometimes seems to be equivalent to total unknowability in some types of mysticism, but may, less extremely, be combined with a doctrine of revelation, which holds that it is the believer in Christ who is truly aware of how incomprehensible God is. 5. The *logical* form of God's transcendence has been expressed variously in the history of language

about God, in the *via negativa** originally most forcefully formulated by Dionysius the Areopagite, the *via analogica* which endeavoured to take account of the similarity-in-difference in the ways we speak of God and of his creatures (*see also* **Analogy**), and the language of *paradox* which endeavours to combine the insights of the other two.

The classic form of the concept of transcendence which emphasized the otherness, the aseity*, of God and which seems to commit theology to an ultimate dualism*, has been considerably modified and reinterpreted in recent theology. For example, there is the development of Bonhoeffer's views by R. Gregor Smith, *Secular Christianity* (1965), which departs from the metaphysical postulating of two substances or two heterogeneous entities and substitutes the notion that transcendence is the way in which we express the historical reality of encounter with others, a venture of mutual existence (p. 122). Again, C. Hartshorne, *Creative Synthesis and Philosophical Method* (1970), departs from the transcendent as *ens realissimum*, describing it as a pseudo-concept, and seeks to correct what he calls 'an oversight . . . occurring through millennia' that the difference between ordinary things and the transcendent consists in their being, on the one hand, selective or non-universal forms, and on the other, universal forms, of dependence *and* independence (p. 230). He calls it 'the principle of dual transcendence', which we reach not by negating dependence but limiting the scope of both dependence and independence. Finally, the plea is made (notably by Hendrikus Berkhof, *The Christian Faith*, ET 1981) that transcendence be seen to realize itself in condescendence, as described by Karl Barth who says that God's transcendence actualizes itself in love; his being expresses itself in the event of his action in Jesus Christ, crucified and risen – (CD II/1, pp. vi, 28–31).

Karl Barth, *Church Dogmatics*, II/1, 1957; Hendrikus Berkhof, *Christian Faith*, ET 1981; E. L. Mascall, *The Secularization of Christianity*, 1965; Wolfhart Pannenberg, *Basic Questions in Theology* II, ET 1971.

JOHN MCINTYRE

Transcendentals

Aristotle* taught the world how to use language as a philosophical resource, showing how to find reflected therein the shape of our world. His treatise on the *Categories* distinguishes *substance* from nine *accidents* by identifying these latter as the characteristic ways we have of speaking *about* things. That which is spoken about is *substance*, taking the subject place in a declarative sentence, while what we attribute to it takes the predicate place. Yet certain predicates do not attribute features to an object, and so cannot be located in one or another of these ten categories. The most pervasive such predicates, 'one', 'being', 'good', and 'true', are called *transcendentals*, as their use transcends the limits of the categories ('beautiful' is sometimes added to the list as well, for analogous reasons.)

It was Plato * who observed the odd behaviour of these indispensable terms (variously in the *Republic*, *Gorgias* and *Sophist*), and his treatment supplied Aristotle with abundant indicators of their peculiar logical status. Yet it is Aristotle's categorial scheme which shows their transcendental status most succinctly. A corollary of that status is their inherently analogical character: they can be used properly in quite diverse contexts. Thus anything at all, insofar as it be made an object of consideration, is by that fact *one* (in the transcendental sense). This 'formal fact' clearly generates unities quite diverse one from another; hence Aristotle's specific concern to distinguish the transcendental use of 'one' from its numerical sense. Similar observations about 'being' led to his insistence that 'to be' can be said (properly) in many ways, though all with reference to one exemplary sense: the celebrated 'analogy of being'. A modern corollary of this treatment would be Kant's insistence that 'existence is not a predicate', for it does not express a feature of things.

'Good' and 'true' offer perhaps the most interesting examples for us, after the recent (and now 'classical') treatments of G. E. Moore and G. Frege respectively. Moore treated 'good' as a special sort of predicate, a 'non-natural predicate'; while Frege set 'the True' (and 'the False') apart from predicates, making them the objects true (false) sentences name. Another way of understanding this logical pecularity is to reflect how transcendentals function at once within a language, and (as it were) outside it. That is, they assess a situation reported, and do so in a way indispensable to human con-

cerns. Although they do not succeed in expressing a feature of things, they intend to assay whether one's expression of a feature is accurate. In this respect, it is humanly unthinkable to propose a language for actual use without such terms. So their use may be said to *show* something of the actual features of language as we use it.

The mediaevals were fascinated with transcendentals, both as logically unique and hence peculiarly apt for use *in divinis*. Aquinas' central treatment of the formal features which display the uniqueness of God culminates in 'God is one' (*ST* 1, 11).

See also **Analogy; Attributes, Divine.**

Aquinas, *Summa Theologiae*: Vol. II: *Existence and Nature of God*, ET 1964; G. Frege, 'Function and Concept', in *Translations from the Philosophical Writings of Gottlob Frege*, ed. Peter Geach and Max Black, 1967; G. E. Moore, *Ethics*, 1925; I. Kant, *Critique of Pure Reason*, ET 1929.

DAVID BURRELL

Transfiguration

The term is used to refer to the event in the life of Jesus Christ and three of his disciples (Peter, James and John) described in the Synoptic Gospels (Matt. 17.1–9; Mark 9.2–10; Luke 9.28–36) and referred to in II Peter 1.16–21. However, only the verb form of the word (*metamorphousthai*) 'to be transformed', appears in the Matthean and Markan accounts, and not at all in the Lukan account. In these descriptions Jesus is seen by his disciples as appearing in an unusual radiance which permeates him. He is accompanied by Moses and Elijah * and a divine voice, coming from a cloud, is heard by the disciples proclaiming that 'This is my (beloved) Son' and that they should 'hear him'. These elements are frequently present in OT theophanies as well (Moses – Ex. 24; 33; 34; Elijah – I Kings 19; Dan. 10). In the narratives the event takes place, significantly, about a week following Peter's declaration that Jesus was the Christ and the clear forecast by Jesus that he was to suffer, die, be resurrected, that his disciples were to share in the cross, and of the eschatological coming of the Son of man (Matthew) and the kingdom (Mark and Luke). Universal ancient tradition holds that the event took place on Mount Tabor. Some modern scholarship places the event on Mount Horeb.

Depending on theological presuppositions, the evaluation of the transfiguration varies. Some biblical scholars hold that it is a misplaced resurrection* appearance narrative, or that it is a symbolic literary form devised to express the disciples' faith in the messiahship* of Jesus. Others see it as an idealized description of an otherwise normal event, embellished with mythological elements, while other interpretations describe it as a strictly historical event in a literal fashion, which would have been physically observable to any onlooker. Among the Latin Fathers, the event was seen chiefly as a revelation of the Holy Trinity*. Augustine interpreted it in purely allegorical terms and Pope Leo viewed it christologically, focussing on the human nature of Christ. In the East, where its liturgical observance came very early, the transfiguration took on very important significance. The date of its observance is exactly forty days before the feast of the elevation of the cross. The Greek Fathers gave the transfiguration much attention. The first to interpret it, Irenaeus, using the typological method, set the pattern for all subsequent Greek patristic exegesis by seeing it eschatologically and soteriologically including not only the objective event in Christ, but the spiritual involvement of the two prophets and the three disciples. Thus, Moses is at last permitted to see the face of God on Tabor, having been denied this experience on Sinai. Clement of Alexandria describes the light of the transfiguration as a spiritual light, which was manifested to the disciples according to their ability to receive it. Uncharacteristically, in his *Commentary on Matthew*, Origen does not interpret the event only allegorically, but in the light of eschatology where the vision of the divine light of the transfigured Christ is accessible only to those who live beyond the 'six days' of this world, and in the 'new sabbath', requiring thereby an inner spiritual discernment. The Greek Fathers in general see the transfiguration as a revelation of Christ's divine nature and as a pointer to his Parousia* and the fulfilment of the kingdom. As a revelatory experience there is a correspondence between the transfiguration of Christ and the transfiguration of human nature. The Pauline connection of 'beholding the glory of the Lord' and 'being changed in his likeness' (II Cor. 3.18) becomes an hermeneutical paradigm of the transfiguration for the later Greek fathers, such as Patriarch Proclus, St Athanasius the Sinaite, St Maximus the Confessor, St Andrew of Crete, and especially St Gregory Palamas and his Hesychast monastic supporters. For these latter theologians, the light seen on Tabor is in fact, God himself in the divine energies, which are perceived as physical light only because the disciples themselves are open, by faith and spiritual illumination, to receive it. The transfiguration is thus both a physical as well as a spiritual event. This interpretation is embodied as well in the hymnology of the Feast of the Transfiguration of the Orthodox Church.

Peter A. Chamberas, 'The Transfiguration of Christ: A Study in the Patristic Exegesis of Scripture', *St Vladimir's Theological Quarterly* V. 14, 1970, Nos. 1–2, pp. 48–65; A. M. Ramsey, *The Glory of God and the Transfiguration of Christ*, 1949.

S. HARAKAS

Transubstantiation

A word used in RC eucharistic doctrine to describe the process by which the 'substances*' (i.e. the deepest reality or subjects of the bread and wine) are changed into those of the body and blood of Christ, while the 'appearances' (properties, accidents*) of the bread and wine remain intact. The doctrine, therefore, excludes the 'Capernaite' belief that Christ's body is physically present and literally masticated; for it is the accidents of bread and not the substance of Christ's body with which the senses make physical contact.

Although the term 'transubstantiation' is a late invention, the idea was often expressed equivalently, though perhaps less precisely, by the Fathers, who referred to the eucharist such words as (in Greek) *metabolē* (change), *metarruthmizō* (rearrange) and *metastoicheiō* (transelement), and (in Latin) *convertere* and *mutare* (change), *fieri* (become) and *transfigurare* (transfigure). The expression *metousiōsis* (change of essence) was adopted by the Eastern Orthodox at the Synod of Jerusalem of 1672. In the official declarations of the West, the verb 'transubstantiate' first occurs in a decree of the Fourth Lateran Council (1215). When the term (in the form of a noun) finally entered into a definition of faith at Trent* in 1551 (Denz., 1652; cf. 1642), a distinction was drawn between the doctrine and its verbal expression. The doctrine of the total conversion of the substances is affirmed as a matter of faith, but the articulation of that doctrine in terms of transubstantiation only as 'appropriate' or 'most apt'. (Although in describing what remains of the bread and wine after the consecration the Council chose the untechnical word 'appearances' [*species*], it would be going too far to say that the Council had rejected Aristotelian* concepts altogether.)

The doctrine has been criticized on many grounds. The Anglican Article XXVIII judges that it 'overthroweth the nature of a sacrament' as well as being unscriptural; it has been alleged to imply a crude materialistic presence; to commit the RC Church to Aristotelian metaphysics or to a Lockean concept of substance as a formless substratum, or to an unscientific view of substance; its doctrine of properties without a subject has been thought meaningless. Many of these objections, however, are not applicable to the doctrine as understood at Trent; Christ was not understood to be present in the same material sense in which the bread and wine were present; the presence is sacramental, not physical.

Several recent RC theologians have sought ways of expressing the doctrine without recourse to the concepts of substance and accident, e.g. by use of such terms as transfinalization or transignification. These expressions imply that the fundamental transformation in the eucharist is not that of the physical entities of bread and wine, but of their deeper reality, which is their relationship to God and man. The power of bread and wine to nourish the body and to symbolize natural table-fellowship is transformed into the symbol and the means by which Christ gives himself to his disciples, forming them into his people of the New Covenant and offering them with himself to his Father. Pope Paul VI, without rejecting this new approach, insisted on the ontological nature of the eucharistic change. It has been urged in reply that the transformation of purpose and symbolic meaning at so deep a level does indeed involve a new ontological status.

See also **Eucharistic Theology.**

E. Gutwenger, 'Transubstantiation', in *Sacramentum Mundi* 6, ET 1970, pp. 292–5;

J. Halliburton, 'The Patristic Theology of the Eucharist', in *The Study of Liturgy*, ed. C. Jones et al., 1978, pp. 201–8; E. Schillebeeckx, *The Eucharist*, ET 1968; H. E. Symonds, *The Council of Trent and Anglican Formularies*, 1933, ch. 6; Anglican–Roman Catholic International Commission, *Final Report*, 1982: 'Eucharistic Doctrine and Elucidation'.

E. J. YARNOLD

Trent, Council of

The Council was assembled by Pope Paul III and met under the presidency of papal legates. Sessions i to viii were held at Trent from 13 December 1545 to 11 March 1547. Against the Emperor's wish it was then removed to Bologna where sessions ix and x took place from 21 April 1547 to 23 January 1548. It was resumed at Trent on 1 May 1551 in the pontificate of Julius III and to 28 April 1552 held sessions xi to xvi. Its final period, under Pius IV, was from 18 January 1562 to 4 December 1563. Procedures were slowed by disagreements, particularly between prelates representing the papal and the imperial interests. Protestant states sent delegates in 1551, but their demand that the Council, following that of Constance, have superiority to the pope, was dismissed. The chief theological decisions set forth in the Council's Canons and Decrees were specifically framed to combat Protestant statements. The Apocryphal Books, Tobit, Judith, Wisdom, Ecclesiasticus, I and II Maccabees, were included in Holy Scripture, while an equal veneration is professed for 'the unwritten traditions' received by the apostles from Christ or from the Holy Spirit which have been preserved in the church; and the Vulgate, Latin version of scripture, alone is held authoritative. The merit of good works, which are the fruit of justification, is strongly affirmed. The seven sacraments are expounded in detail. In the decree on the eucharist it is taught that 'as much is contained under each species as under both'. Transubstantiation* is asserted in Thomist* terms and both veneration and reservation of the host are approved. To each of the twenty-five decrees is added a series of canons in which those holding opposing doctrines are anathematized. The decree on Holy Orders, a field of keen debate, makes bishops successors of the apostles, but they are not said to derive their authority from Christ.

Denzinger-Schönmetzer, *Enchiridion Symbolorum*, [36]1976, pp. 363–427; J. H. Leith, *Creeds of the Churches*, [3]1982, pp. 400–41; H. Jedin, *History of the Council of Trent*, E T I, 1957; II, 1961.

J. T. MCNEILL

Trinity, Doctrine of the

The doctrine of the Trinity is primarily a christological doctrine and its most widely accepted form is a product mainly of the fourth century A D. It was the christological concerns of the early Christian centuries which persistently motivated and which finally fashioned most of classical trinitarian doctrine, and in modern times the declared purpose of that doctrine still is to point to the presence and action of God in this world in Jesus the Christ (economic Trinity). Although trinitarian doctrine as we know it was prefigured in some authors before the fourth century and underwent some minor developments since then, its basic form owes more to the controversial needs of that century and to the religious imagery accepted by Christians and non-Christians alike at that time than to any other influence either before or since.

Scriptural authority for the development of trinitarian doctrine has become a much-debated topic, but in view of the supreme normative role which all Christian traditions in one way or another accord to scripture, it is a topic that is likely to be debated for some time to come. Views on this topic range from the conviction that trinitarian doctrine is little more than a summary of explicit data otherwise scattered across O T and N T, to the assertion that it is an important aid in worship but without any real foundation in the Bible (Richardson). In between these extremes Emil Brunner, for instance, argues that a trinitarian doctrine which respects the strict 'economic' order of salvation and revelation, the order in which Father, Son and Spirit come 'after one another', is biblical, whereas 'essential' Trinities which place the 'persons' 'alongside one another' in a transcendent relationship represent no more than an aberration of theological thought which, however, has dominated church preaching and worship from the fifth century onward.

The debate on this topic is at present complicated by a number of factors. 1. The great variety of material which surrounds in the Bible each of the key terms of trinitarian theology: Father, Son (or Word) and Spirit. As special cases of this variety one might mention the fact that a full reading of scripture reveals no one order in which these three stand, but rather a variety of possible orders (Moltmann), or the fact that amongst the acknowledged variety of christologies in the N T there are spirit-christologies, that is to say, christologies in which spirit, and not word, is the key symbol for what came to be called the divinity of Jesus (Lampe). 2. The biblical term 'spirit' in particular refuses to be restricted to a third, or indeed to any distinguishable element within divinity, or even in God's outreach to the world: it can stand for God transcendent and immanent, for Jesus as risen Lord (in the spirit-christologies mentioned), for that of God and Jesus ever operative in the world. 3. The status of pre-existence language, particularly in connection with the Son or Word, is, once again, the subject of continuing debate. Anticipated in canonical and extra-canonical Wisdom literature concerning Word/Spirit and in some messianic speculation, even those N T texts where pre-existence* imagery is undoubtedly present no longer yield unquestioned assurance that they themselves offer any insight into the inner being of God which was not already accessible to those who used that language before Jesus the Christ. The genuine pre-existence texts of the N T may be little more than ways of claiming that God's Word or Spirit, of which the Wisdom literature made so much, was in Jesus of Nazareth more than, or rather than, in the Torah (the Law) for example. Thus, while pointing to self-differentiation in God, as did their textual predecessors, they may have been intended to point to Jesus as God's revealer rather than to give any additional information about such pre-existing divine self-differentiation.

The safest assumption at this time would seem to be the very general assumption that developing trinitarian doctrine selected rather stringently from this rich variety of biblical material on Father, Son (Word) and Spirit, with a view to meeting the missionary and the polemical needs of the first Christian centuries. The extent to which such selective exegesis is either normative or useful today will depend on the account that can be given of the missionary and polemical endeavours of a time so very long ago.

The missionary requirements of the task of the early Christian theologians were dictated, naturally, by the kind of theology then emerging from the dominant religious vision of the culture with which emerging Christianity then had to grapple. This was the theology of Middle Platonism* and, from the third century onwards, of Neoplatonism*. Middle Platonism provided a scholastic period in the development of early Graeco-Roman theology, as ways of approaching the major questions concerning God and the world were gradually standardized and, simultaneously, major elements of Stoic*, Aristotelian* (and others such as Pythagorean) philosophy were fused with a still dominant Platonism* (Dillon). This provided for the missionary endeavours of the first Christian theologians not only a standardized theological terminology in which to present their message, but a powerful religious vision the very attractiveness of which could thwart their efforts to re-mould it in recognizably Christian form. Building upon that basic Platonic theme of the aching desire (eros) at the heart of human existence for release from the evils of this world and for the unitive vision of the Good, a desire at once supported by and seeking the conviction that God first loved the world, at the very least in the sense that the very existence of this world came out from God's overflowing goodness, Middle-Platonist theology can be described as emanationist*, predominantly binitarian, and possibly subordinationist*.

Not much needs to be said about the Middle-Platonist preference for emanation* imagery in its theology of origins, partly because such imagery remains just as much at home in Christian binitarian and trinitarian theology, partly because, if creatio ex nihilo is taken to mean that things take origin from no other than God, emanation language can express this as well as any other, and some Middle Platonists (and, later, Arius) did hold to it. Hence a simple preference for one of these images over the other cannot be in any degree decisive in testing the truth or adequacy of binitarian or trinitarian theologies. The real force of saying that this Greek theology is emanationist, therefore, can be translated into Christian language by saying that it is in-

escapably 'economic'. Next, although triadic structures are quite frequent in Middle-Platonist theology, as far as properly divine being or substance* (ousia) is concerned one generally gets the impression that there are two, rather than three, distinguishable levels, or grades, or perhaps entities of some kind within it. Finally, and this will be even more true of Neoplatonism, partly because of the Greek theory of analogy* (the dominant analogy being, of course, the emanationist analogy of sun, rays and illumined objects or root, trunk and fruit) and the concomitant theories of the way of ascent and the way of negation (Albinus, Didaskalikos), it is frequently difficult to know if Greek theologians take the names for the two or three to be names for really distinct levels or entities in the divine being, or whether they take these to be simply terms, accommodated to the weakness of the human mind in this world, by which we seek to talk about the One*, ineffable divine being, in its salvific outreach to our world.

The manner in which the Jewish theologian, Philo of Alexandria, part contemporary of Paul, appropriated this Middle-Platonic theology in order to present his distinctive faith is extremely instructive for Christian historians, if only because Philo's procedure proved influential on later Christian thinkers. Philo's Jewish faith in a God who could not be apprehended by human vision seemed eminently translatable into the Greek theology of the One* or Monad, indeed one 'beyond Monad', for whom no creaturely language whatever availed. Yet Philo's God gave origin to the world and was active within it. So God could be known at least through his powers (dynameis) and their works or effects (energeiai). The two major dynameis Philo named as Creator (ktistes, demiourgos) and Lord. And the term which denotes that (level) of divinity which is apprehensible to us, which is manifest as these dynameis in their energeiai, is Word (logos*). This Word Philo describes as the first-begotten Son of the uncreated Father, the 'second God', the mediator of creation, the 'man of God', and in his Life of Moses he conveys the impression that this Word was incarnate (or at least empsychos) in Moses par excellence.

It could be said that Philo was doing no more than making a more expansive use of Greek theological models than some

Wisdom literature had already done, and so the really distinct status of these apparently intermediary levels of divinity was no more an issue for him than it was for Hellenized Jewish literature in general. But Christian theologians appeared to operate, inevitably, from the outset, what Lampe called the 'double projection'. For to them Jesus, the incarnate Word of the Fourth Gospel, was certainly a distinct individual. Hence in their inevitable speculations about pre-existence, they projected the distinct individuality of Jesus back on to the pre-existent Word, thus increasing whatever impressions of real distinctions were already conveyed by some uses of the Greek model, and this distinct and pre-existent divine individual was then projected onto Jesus of Nazareth – often, as must shortly appear, to the over-shadowing of his historic life. Now the appropriation of the Greek theological model, together with the by now indelible impressions of really distinct levels or 'individuals' of some kind within the divinity, yields sub-ordinationism. Since the Greek model is unalterably 'economic', designed strictly and solely to describe the salvific and re-velatory outreach of the essentially un-known God, those who appropriate it to describe really distinct levels or grades or 'persons' within the divinity cannot avoid the implication that these are successively 'lower than', subordinate to the One God, unoriginate Source of all. The only way to avoid this implication would be to replace the model.

The final recreation of this predominantly Platonic, but by now also quite syncretistic * theology was achieved by Plotinus in the third century A D and has since become known as Neoplatonism (Wallis). This theology is now quite definitely trinitarian. In fact, in addition to the trinity of One, Mind and Soul in the writings of Plotinus, in which the term *hypostaseis* * is actually used for these three, there is also a trinity of Being, Life and Intelligence, to take just one other alternative, and this factor allowed for much variety of structure and interpretation in the trinitarian theologies of the successive teachers of a Plotinian system which natur-ally influenced Greek Christian theology and reached the most important trinitarian theologian of the West, Augustine of Hippo, mainly through Marius Victorinus and Ambrose of Milan.

Those who are aware of no more than the mere presence of spirit-christologies in the N T, and who understand the coincidence of triadic patterns with basically binitarian theologies in the pagan milieu to which the earliest Christian theologians addressed themselves, will not be at all surprised to find binitarian theology, noticeable mainly in the interchangeability of Word and Spirit, side-by-side with triadic patterns in pre-Nicene theology. In much early theology of the eucharist, for instance, it seems a matter of indifference whether one invokes the Word or the Spirit to come upon people and elements and make the body of Christ present in on-going history; and the triadic formula in baptism merely echoes the struc-ture of the baptismal confession of faith which did little or nothing to distinguish specifically the Spirit of its final part from the One God, the Father, or even the Lord Jesus, of its previous two parts.

Subordinationism, too, despite the efforts of post-Nicene historians to discount it as careless or incidental, seems to have been a natural and generally accepted result of Christian appropriation of a Greek model which was quintessentially emanationist or 'economic', designed specifically, that is to say, to find names for God (Word, Spirit) which related to the creation of the world and to God's action within it. Little wonder, then, if the origin of Word or Son is so often in pre-Nicene theology related to creation * or even incarnation *.

In describing the polemical requirements of the task of early Christian theology little help really derives from the labels created by later historians. 'Modalism' * as a term could as well describe Barth's theology of God's three modes of being (*Seinsweise*) as anything that went on in the early church. And 'Monarchian' * in its obvious reference to God as supreme monarch of all he surveyed points to the commonest convic-tion of all. It seems best to say, then, that some Christian theologians refashioned the Greek emanationist model to their purposes and differed from each other often as to how the refashioning should be accom-plished, while yet others seem to have entirely rejected all implication of this re-fashioning of Greek models to the effect that there was in any sense of the word 'another' in God beside the One called Father. In the course of this many-sided polemics the main lines of orthodoxy* and heterodoxy* were laid down, at least for the early church.

It is not at all easy at this point in time to be fair to those who were finally deemed heretical; so much of their literary remains was destroyed, leaving only fragments, if even that, or scattered quotations in texts composed by hostile witnesses, and their very names have lived on as ciphers for theological positions which, in such obviously questionable forms, they may never actually have held.

Amongst those who, as a result of deeply monotheistic conviction, refused any 'other' in God beside the One called Father were men like Noetus of Smyrna and one Praxeas. The latter insisted that it was the Father who entered the Virgin's womb and suffered on Calvary, though he seems to have advanced in subtlety on the former by talking of the Father's co-suffering with the human Jesus. Later in the third century one Paul of Samosata seems to have reached a similar conclusion while starting more from considerations concerning the person of Jesus rather than convictions about monotheism. It is not possible now to know just how inadequate were Paul's speculations about God as Spirit coming upon a 'mere' man, Jesus, or how better he could have appropriated scriptural spirit-christologies in order to deal, as they did, with the divinity of Jesus. In that same third century a theologian emerged who seemed to want to go some small distance at least with the Greek pagan model towards recognition of 'another' one or two in divinity. His name, Sabellius, quickly came to stand for one option which one reading of the Greek schema did indeed allow, viz., the emanation from the divinity entailed a kind of expansion (*platusmos*) by which the divine Monad or Father projected himself as Son and then Spirit, to retract again once creation-redemption was complete, as the Greek imagery of emanation and return could suggest. In this form, Sabellianism* was rejected by the mainstream tradition and other ways of appropriating the Greek model were sought.

As a characteristic response to the first Christian plea for an undifferentiated monotheism Tertullian's *Against Praxeas* proved quite influential, at least terminologically. God's *monarchia*, he claims, is not in the least compromised by what he calls the 'economy', just as the emperor's power is quite undiminished when exercised by one of his plenipotentiaries. Tertullian fully accepts the emanationist-economic features of the Greek model (indeed his understanding of the divine substance is decidedly materialist in the Stoic sense); he is apologetic about using the word 'another' for the Son but feels it is justified by the distinguishable 'grades' in which the divine substance and power is deployed. He uses the word *persona* for these second and third 'grades' in divinity (though not nearly as frequently as some English translations of his text would imply): but it is certainly not the formula 'one substance, three persons' which secures distinctions between a first, second and third in the divinity; rather, it is the emanation-economy of 'grades' in divinity which gives the formula its meaning and support. And any doubt about Tertullian's easy acceptance of the subordinationism endemic to Christian appropriation of the Greek model would disappear on reading his work *Against Hermogenes*. Read together with Hippolytus' work *Against Noetus*, it gives the unavoidable impression that the Word was not perfect (expressed) Word 'before' creation and perhaps not perfect Son before incarnation: yet, full status once achieved, it does not seem ever destined to recede. Origen in this same third century is credited with insistence on eternal generation of the Son, but it must be remembered that Origen equally insisted on the eternal creation of everything, at least in 'noetic' form, so that God could not be thought to have changed. Thus this insistence, as Origen's own thought proves, does not qualify in the least the successive subordination of Son and Spirit in such 'orthodox' Christian appropriations of a Greek emanationist-economic binity or trinity as the first three centuries witness.

The first decades of the fourth century brought this fluctuating debate to an unprecedented climax, with the advent of Arius, a presbyter of Alexandria. Arius, with his early supporters Eusebius of Nicomedia and Asterius, was motivated by an interest in soteriology* and directed by what he believed to be a major thrust of the Bible. The dominant biblical model for relationship of Father to Son was, in their view, the will and good-pleasure of the Father and the salvific obedience of the Son (Gregg and

Groh). This model the early Arians projected into pre-existence; nowhere do they suggest that Son or Word became such only at creation or incarnation, so the Son's obedience characterizes his role as the one through whom was made all that was made. The use of substance-language for the relation of Son to Father the early Arians continued to reject, as unbiblical and basically unsuitable. Now the combination of such scriptural imagery as the early Arians, with every apparent right, preferred with the Greek emanationist-economic model which was by this time the common inheritance of all did indeed so highlight the subordinate status of the Son or Word, who Arians still insisted was divine, that it all seemed to threaten the Christian conviction that in Jesus the one, true God, and not a much lesser deity, was reconciling the world to himself. In one sense the Arians were merely showing up some of the inherent dangers involved in Christian appropriation of pagan Greek theology (*see also* **Arianism**).

The negative side of the response to Arius is somewhat less than edifying; the positive side came to centre more and more on the definition of the Council of Nicaea (AD 325) that the Son or Word was one in being or substance (*homoousios* *) with the Father. The great variety of meaning of which the term *homoousios* is capable, its shady pre-Nicene history, the political, indeed imperial machinations behind its adoption at Nicaea, the almost universal embarrassment it caused immediately afterwards, the many alternatives sought, its eventual adoption by Athanasius of Alexandria as the standard of orthodoxy for all subsequent trinitarian theology, all this makes difficult reading. Suffice it to say that Marcellus of Ancyra, one of its stoutest defenders in the fourth century, managed to combine the *homoousios* with emanationist-economic features quite reminiscent of Tertullian, Hippolytus or Theophilus (*Ad Autolycum*), and although he explicitly rejected the term *hypostaseis* adopted later in the century by the Cappadocian Fathers * (Gregory of Nyssa, Gregory of Nazianzus and Basil) for the three, on the grounds that it introduced too great a degree of 'otherness', he seems to have saved himself from Sabellian charges by suggesting that the flesh rather than the Word in the saviour would have no relevant permanence.

Athanasius linked the term *homoousios* with the image of generation in order to justify it and give it meaning. However, when faced with reports of people nick-named Tropici who accepted the Nicene definition but thought the Holy Spirit a superior angel, Athanasius (*Letters to Serapion*) extended the *homoousios* to the Spirit. Basil (*On the Holy Spirit*), on the other hand, faced with genuine Arian 'Spirit-fighters' who logically placed the divine Spirit even lower than the Son, contented himself with asserting the equality of the Spirit in terms of equal worship and glory. All assumed by now that the only way to defend the divinity of the Spirit was to make it a third co-equal one in the Godhead. And persistent Arian pressure for admissions of subordination and consequent difference between the three gradually forced the conclusion that *homoousios* meant one identical substance of the three. Successive victories over the Arian case for the Son, and then for the Spirit, were costly. The very extension of the *homoousios* to the Spirit broke its explanatory link with the image of generation *, thus opening the door again to other images of origin (for the Spirit could not be said to be generated); at the same time the rejection of every last vestige of subordination in the economic 'order' of divine being and act simultaneously removed the very means of distinguishing two or three within divinity which the older emanationist-economic appropriation had offered. In spite of Marcellus, the Cappadocian Fathers did introduce the term *hypostaseis* for the three but, apart from the problems caused (notwithstanding Gregory of Nyssa's brave little *Answer To Ablabius: That There Are Not Three Gods*) by their relating *ousia* to *hypostasis* as general to particular on the analogy of three men sharing the same nature, the point must be repeated that it is not a formula which secures inner divine distinctions. On the contrary it is the successful securing of inner divine distinctions which gives to any such formula whatever meaning-content it may possess.

In general the Cappadocian Fathers attempt to secure these distinctions in two ways: by the properties or distinguishing characteristics of each of the three, and by the 'works' of each. One gets the impression, however, from Gregory of Nyssa's *Against Eunomius*, for example, that the properties are names still for relations of origin or non-origin, and his auxiliary means of distinguishing the three according to order (*kata taxin*) both requires the older subordinationist model for support and is vulnerable to the Arian insistence that what takes origin of any kind *must* be less divine than that which is source of all. Success in distinguishing *hypostaseis* by means of their works is compromised, particularly in the case of the Spirit, by the need to use their 'works' to prove their full divinity, i.e. the presence in action of the one divine *ousia*. Hence the insistence that each is always involved with the others (*perichoresis* *) moves towards the principle *opera ad extra* * *sunt indivisa*, and the suspicion grows that the only way of differentiating their contributions in this co-operative activity towards the world is to reintroduce the 'order' (*from* the Father, *through* the Son, *in* the Spirit) which again seems to call for the older economic-subordinationist model.

Augustine of Hippo, by far the most influential trinitarian theologian of the West, if only through his so-called psychological analogy* (*see also* **Vestigia Trinitatis**), took the argument to its next logical step in the fifth century. His starting point in his *De Trinitate* is the Nicene dogma of the *homoousios* of the three (and his commitment to the term 'persons' for the three comes down to the need to say something rather than stay silent!); to this his elaborate exegetical exercises and his considerable powers of perception and analysis are entirely devoted.

It is Augustine who promotes the concept of relations within the divinity as a means of securing distinctions, while making little or nothing of the fact that these are relations of origin. Instead, emphasis now lies on the relativity or co-relativity of the terms used to describe the three; or what Aquinas, who did little more in the thirteenth century than systematize Augustinian thought on this matter, called oppositeness of relations. So Father and Son are obviously co-relative terms, 'opposites' in relational language. But even in this schema the great difficulty of finding any distinguishing term for Spirit in homoousiite theology, a difficulty already only too familiar from the work of the Cappadocians, increases. With brave, if desperate, exegesis Augustine tries to define the Spirit as Gift (relative to Giver?), or

uniquely as Love. And Aquinas uses for purposes of 'distinguishing' a third, the Spirit, for purposes of arriving at three, and only three divine persons, the famous or infamous '*filioque* * (origin of the Spirit from the Father *and the Son*). The disreputable side of the *filioque* story, its introduction into a creed in the West, its role in political manoeuvring and unchristian polemics, must be told in another place. In this context it must be seen simply as yet another attempt to secure some distinguishing characteristic for the Spirit on the assumption that Christian theology simply must be trinitarian. As such it simply takes its place with other terms and phrases tried out for this purpose – phrases parallel to the *filioque* are found in the East in Epiphanius and Cyril of Alexandria, just as phrases such as 'from the Father through the Son' are found, for instance, at home in Aquinas – and as such it is no more successful than any of the others (this at least the bitter polemics go to prove). With no more biblical support than any of the other ways of attempting to 'distinguish' a Holy Spirit, and with a theological and patristic base in a so-called psychological analogy which Augustine himself dismembered before he closed his work, the *filioque* is not worth fighting over. For fighting merely hides from view the fact that since the *homoousios* found its justificatory and explanatory support in its link with the image of generation of a Son, homoousiite theology never really succeeded in doing any justice to Holy Spirit.

Relations *of origin* recede even further – and with them the last vestige of the old emanationist-economic model – in Augustine's treatment of the divine missions. Since divine 'substance' * which is identical in all three already implies omnipresence, Augustine asks how divine 'persons' can be sent to where they already are. He answers that they appear in *external* manifestations in new ways, but the principle, by now sacrosanct, that *opera ad extra sunt indivisa* makes him imply that the *external* creations – the sound of a voice, tongues of flame, the human nature of Jesus – are produced by the one God and appropriated to one or other of the 'persons'. Apart from the rather obvious artificiality of this explanation when applied to biblical material, its most distressing feature is the further contribution it makes to the growing impression conveyed in developing trinitarian theology that the actions and passions of the human Jesus have little intrinsic relationship to the Word. Arian preference for texts of scripture which described the Son as ignorant, suffering, abandoned even, had already driven their opponents to erect almost to a principle the contention that all such actions and passions are attributed to the 'flesh', the humanity of Jesus, and not to the Word, the divinity. Hence the impression grows that trinitarian doctrine has to do primarily with inner divine processions, emanations, relationships, and little or nothing to do essentially with, in Augustine's own phrase, 'all those things which the Word made flesh did and suffered for us in space and time'. The latter may be necessary to inform us about the former or somehow to heal the blindness of sin so that we can again 'see' the former, but trinitarian theology does have to do with the former and the latter is at most epistemological precondition or soteriological appendage. This impression is strengthened by Augustine's treatment of the *Vestigia Trinitatis**, and it yields in Aquinas' treatment of real inner-divine relationships the thesis: 'there is no real relation in God to the creature.' Only in some such way as this, it seems, can one understand the recession of the older economic Trinity, its gradual replacement by an immanent or 'essential' Trinity*, and the persistent appeals in contemporary trinitarian theology for the reunion of the two (Rahner, Moltmann).

There were, apart from Marcellus of Ancyra, other attempts at Christian appropriation of the Greek theological model in its trinitarian or Neoplatonic forms, and some had worthwhile features. These, however, though they were not rejected with neo-Arian or 'quaternian' forms which did emerge in later centuries, did not succeed in influencing in any significant way the mainstream development of the doctrine as outlined above. Marius Victorinus, for instance, provided an important link between Neoplatonism and Augustine. Conscious of the danger of tritheistic impressions in the formula 'one divine *ousia*, three *hypostaseis*', he suggests that from God comes one Son, who is, however, as he says, *geminus*, that is, both life and understanding. As life it reaches us in the form of Jesus of Nazareth who died that we should live; and it reaches us also as understanding in the twinned form of Spirit which enables us to see our way to God through Jesus. Hence it would make as much sense to say, as early Syriac theology did, that the Spirit is 'mother' of the Saviour, as to say that the Son is source of the Spirit.

As another example of alternative appropriation, this time from mystical theology*, one might take the writings of the mediaeval mystic, John of Ruysbroek. Though he frequently uses the terms of the mainstream trinitarian theology, many of his most personal passages create the impression that Spirit is the name for God's innermost essence or being driven outward in love, in need almost, through its incarnate Word, Jesus, to struggle for and with the often recalcitrant spirit of the creature. In these two examples, one might suggest, prospects for binitarian thought are kept alive, binitarian models which offer much more expansive theologies of Holy Spirit than either the earlier economic Trinities or the mainstream development ever seemed able to provide.

As a final example of alternative appropriation, there is a persistent impression conveyed, again at the more mystical, or at least apophatic* reaches of the theological tradition that stretches down the ages from the Pseudo-Denys through the great Irish theologian of the ninth century, John Scotus Eriugena, the impression that trinity, after all, belongs at a second or lower level of the divine being (as some Neoplatonic trinities of Being, Life and Intelligence certainly did). The inner being or essence of God, where God is most truly God, is still hidden from us while *in via*, and our trinities of Fatherhood, Sonship and Spirit name the salvific outreach of God to us, enabling us to do little more than express recognition, give praise, and worship, but truly enabling us to do all that. Familiar echoes of some forms of economic trinitarianism can sometimes be heard in such systems and, although one must repeat that none of these alternatives seriously influenced mainstream development, it is significant that the wish to reunite features of the older economic model with those of the newer essentialist model never altogether ceases to be expressed.

The Reformers of the sixteenth century did little to advance the mainstream development of trinitarian theology. Luther's theology of the Crucified God had to await its full trinitarian development by Molt-mann; but it is interesting to note how Calvin distrusts the ability of relational models to distinguish the 'persons'. He opts for a safer, if uninformative notion of 'in-communicable qualities' to accomplish this task. But, more significantly, he insists on fully reinstating what he calls 'a reasoned order' of the 'persons' which is strongly reminiscent of the older economic models of trinitarian thought. Calvin even concludes that, when we mention Father and Son to-gether, or Spirit with them, the very word God applies then particularly to the Father, whereas when the word 'God' is used with-out particular reference to any of the 'per-sons', it designates indistinguishably the three. Calvin's strong insistence that the one who wishes to talk about the one, true God must at all times talk about the triune God, since all else is vanity and idolatry, is thus qualified in the reader's mind by the impres-sion that features of the older economic Trinity must be recovered in order to make the essentialist or immanent Trinity intel-ligible, and indeed, one may repeat, that is a common claim in contemporary trini-tarian theology.

Karl Barth could be said to have attemp-ted this reunion of economic and immanent, because of his opening view that revelation is the ground or 'root' of the classical doc-trine of the Trinity; and not any general idea of revelation, but the actual salvific revela-tion of the sovereignly free Lord in the flesh of Jesus and in the Spirit thence breathed into this world. But if the structure of God's free self-revelatory act authorizes trinitarian theology, it is very much the immanent, essential Trinity (*see* **Essential Trinity** par-ticularly at this point) of the developed mainstream tradition that one finally reads in Barth.

It is difficult to avoid the conclusion of Moltmann's recent work – and it is im-possible to avoid the fact that this is a con-clusion – that the mainstream development of trinitarian doctrine has failed to secure a genuine Trinity. Considering two main forms of mainstream doctrine, viz., Supreme Substance with its differentiation into 'persons' of questionable definition and status, or the Absolute Person whose self-differentiation can be described only in the fragile terms of 'modes', Moltmann con-cludes that undifferentiated monotheism has

triumphed in both cases behind all the verbal fanfare, and an adequate theological case for a 'real' trinity still requires to be made, or to be recovered from scripture and tradition.

Moltmann opts for a brash and un-compromising social doctrine of the Trinity, as it is called, and this is no mere illustratory analogy, but the conviction, with which one must begin as well as end, that there are really three distinct though inseparable divine personal beings. The unity of the divine being, arguably the Achilles' heel of this social model, can be adequately secured, Moltmann believes, on the analogy of the way in which any human society fashions individual persons in function of exactly the same process by which individual persons form any society, and by more central use of the patristic concept of *emperichoresis* (*circumincessio*).

There is no gainsaying the claim that this social model yields a very real Trinity, and it has the added advantage of being able to accommodate the variety of orders in which in scripture Spirit, Father and Son stand to one another in different contexts, rather than attempt to force all of these into the strict order of Father, Word, Spirit of an essentially Greek schema. Yet it must be said that its case for the 'reality' of three distinct pre-existent divine persons is constructed on very shaky exegetical foundations, and its case for the unity of the Godhead involves the very risky manoeuvre of making central to trinitarian argument a concept (*peri-choresis*) which in patristic theology is more derivative and therefore peripheral, while ignoring the persistent, if often implicit criticism of this social model which virtually all forms of the theological tradition have in common (continual redefinitions of the term 'person' * are relevant here, as are mediaeval condemnations of the artistic representation of the Trinity as three men).

The development of that theology which became so firmly established in trinitarian form was inspired in its most formative years by christological concerns. Whatever judg-ment one may responsibly form about the obsolescence or otherwise of its many types and variations, one may presume that the same christological concerns must underlie all suggestions for retention or replacement. Arius, the greatest by far of the heretics whose influence fashioned the most familiar forms of trinitarian doctrine, was found wanting, after all, because thoughtful-Christian leaders suspected that in the end he could not really say that in Jesus the one, true God was reconciling the world to himself, and not some lesser divinity, and in Jesus, the Lord of history, through whom and for whom the very world is being created, the one and only Spirit (of) God is still to be experienced. It is perhaps important to recognize that this can be said well enough *without* the use of any of the extant forms of trinitarian or binitarian doctrine, and can be said at all only by ignoring some of the very questionable features of some of these. No doubt the intellectual 'unpacking' of this central Christian credal conviction will always require some tentative account of what much contemporary trinitarian theology calls God's self-differentiation, and as long as the demonstrative nature of doctrine is acknowledged in whatever is retained or emerges – its ability, that is to say, to point out and to point to the life, death and Lordship of Jesus as the *locus* of encounter with God and of such dark knowledge of God as we may here possess – all will be well.

See also **Christology, God, Holy Spirit.**

E. Brunner, *The Christian Doctrine of God*, 1950; John Dillon, *The Middle Platonists*, 1977; R. C. Gregg, D. E. Groh, *Early Arianism*, 1981; J. N. D. Kelly, *Early Christian Doctrines*, 1958; G. Lampe, *God as Spirit*, 1977; J. P. Mackey, *The Christian Experience of God as Trinity*, 1983; Jürgen Moltmann, *The Trinity and the Kingdom of God*, 1981; K. Rahner, *The Trinity*, 1970; Cyril Richardson, *The Doctrine of the Trinity*, 1958; R. T. Wallis, *Neo-Platonism*, 1972.

J. P. MACKEY

Typology *see* **Allegory and Typology**

Ubiquity

This signifies the same as 'omnipresence', and in theological contexts is traditionally ascribable to the God of theism*. Since the theistic God is not a body (is incorporeal), theologians and philosophers have tried to give some account of how he can be present everywhere without being physically locatable. The usual theistic solution has been to say that God is present everywhere as the creative source of the existence of all things. Thus, for example, Aquinas observes: 'God

exists in everything . . . as an agent is present to that in which its action is taking place . . . He it must be who properly causes existence in creatures . . . During the whole period of a thing's existence, therefore, God must be present to it . . . So God must exist and exist intimately in everything' (*ST*, Ia, 8, 1; cf. Ia, 8, 2–4). This view seems to be directly entailed by the doctrine of creation according to which a thing is caused to exist by God as long as it exists. The view is not presupposed in any systematic way in the Bible; but it seems to be at least pointed to in the numerous biblical references to God's power and presence (cf. Ps. 139.7–12; Acts 17.24–28).

In Lutheran contexts, in the theory known as *ubiquitarianism*, ubiquity has been ascribed to Christ in order to defend the doctrine of Christ's real presence in the eucharist against the charge that the body of Christ is only in one place, i.e. in heaven. According to ubiquitarianism Christ can be present in many consecrated hosts because his human nature shares the divine omnipresence. The theory can be traced in the work of Luther himself, and its popularity among Lutherans owed much to its defence by Johann Brenz (1499–1570).

Francis Clarke SJ, *Eucharistic Sacrifice and the Reformation*, 1960; R. E. Clements, *God and Temple: The Idea of the Divine Presence in Ancient Israel*, 1965; H. P. Owen, *Concepts of Deity*, 1971.

BRIAN DAVIES

Ultimate Concern

A central problem in Tillich's early work was the meaning of religion. His earliest publication, the famous lecture 'on the idea of a theology of culture', is in a sense nothing other than an attempt to answer this question in a radically new way. It distinguishes two senses of religion – (*a*) the sphere of social or cultural life commonly so called, (*b*) experience of the unconditioned which is a dimension of the various forms of cultural existence. Religion is not itself properly seen as either a mental faculty or a sphere of culture; but the religious principle is a dimension of the whole of human existence. By the time he wrote *Systematic Theology* (1951–64) Tillich had learned how to exploit the ambiguities of the English language and was talking of religion as 'ultimate concern'.

This phrase was particularly useful, for it enabled him to encompass both the subjective and the objective. Consequently he refers to God too as 'ultimate concern'. Moreover he was able equally to speak of ultimate concern as his philosophical translation of the first commandment. Also his phenomenological* account of 'the existential question' to which ultimate concern was 'the theological answer' exemplified his method of correlation*.

J. HEYWOOD THOMAS

Una Sancta

Una Sancta is a Latin phrase describing the church when regarded as indivisibly one and holy, in contrast to any theory of the possibility of its being divided.

R. P. C. HANSON

Unction

From the Latin, *unctus*, anointment, the word broadly designates any rite of anointing* with oil. Specifically it refers to the sacramental rite of anointing those who are ill or approaching death. In the Church of England it is called the sacrament of unction; in the RC Church the recently revised rite has been officially designated as anointing of the sick.

There is scriptural evidence (Mark 6.13; James 5.14f.) that anointing the sick was practised in at least some early Christian communities, and there is scattered patristic evidence (e.g. the *Apostolic Tradition* of Hippolytus, 5.1f; the *Prayer Book* of Serapion, 29) that oil was blessed for this purpose in various regions of Christendom. Unblessed oil could also be used, and it could be applied externally or taken internally, usually with an accompanying prayer for healing.

Through early mediaeval times in Europe, such anointing could be performed by lay persons or clerics, but the Carolingian reforms of the ninth century introduced an ecclesiastical rite of unction and restricted its administration to the clergy. In this form the rite eventually made its way into the Roman sacramentary. The elaborateness of the ritual and the lack of the modern medicine led to its being performed mainly for persons who died soon afterwards, and the words accompanying it were appropriately changed from petitions for recovery to requests for divine clemency. In this form the rite came to be known as *extrema unctio*, the last anointing or extreme unction, and it was included among the seven ecclesiastical sacraments of the Catholic church by the late twelfth century.

Most churches of the Reformation* rejected the claim of unction to sacramental status, because even though attested to in James there was no scriptural proof of its institution by Christ. The Roman and Orthodox churches have retained it, although under differing forms. Though it is acknowledged by the Church of England as one of the five 'commonly called sacraments' which were not of divine institution, the Book of Common Prayer contained no complete rite of unction between 1552 and 1928.

Currently in both the Roman and Anglican Catholic communions, the practice and theology of anointing the sick reflect the more ancient notion that through this liturgical ritual Christians can seek and receive spiritual and even physical strength from God, instead of the late mediaeval notion that through it they are prepared for the afterlife.

J. Empereur, *Prophetic Anointing*, 1982; C. Orteman, *Le Sacrement des Malades*, 1971; F. Puller, *Anointing of the Sick in Scripture and Tradition*, 1904; H. Vorgrimler, *Büsse und Krankensalbung*, 1978.

J. MARTOS

Unitarianism

Modern Unitarianism emerged in the sixteenth century in England and Hungary as an anti-trinitarian form of Christianity, more especially associated with the name of Socinus (Fausto Sozzini of Siena, 1539–1604), and with the Polish Racovian Catechism of 1605, which he did not write but strongly influenced. Socinus denied that the One God could properly be spoken of as three Persons*, and he therefore rejected the doctrine of the Trinity*; he asserted that God forgave sins as freely under the New Covenant as he had forgiven them under the Old Covenant, and therefore that the death of the divine-human Jesus Christ was not a necessary sacrifice for sin; instead, he emphasized the resurrection and ascension of Jesus, who had been subject to death in his earthly existence, but whom God raised to divine power, as an effective proclamation of God's loving-kindness towards his creatures. This seventeenth-century Unitarianism, which combined a strong attachment to the figure of the biblical Jesus with an optimistic attitude to man which was foreign to the mainstream Reformation* tradition, survived orthodox persecution and adapted successfully to the rationalism* of the Enlightenment*. The first separate Unitarian congregation in England was Essex Chapel, opened in London in 1774 by the former Anglican priest Theophilus Lindsey (1723–1808), and English Unitarianism was recognized by English law in 1813; in the United States, the most fruitful field for Unitarianism, the first congregation was formed at King's Chapel, Boston, in 1785. The most prominent Unitarian of the period, Joseph Priestley (1733–1804), although determinist* and materialist* as a scientist, still centred his religious imagination on Jesus, whom he saw as a man commissioned by God to make clear the truths about creation and ethics which unaided human reason and conscience could glimpse, but never know with certainty without divine revelation*. Many Unitarians, like Priestley, were radical in politics, and they suffered from the religious and political conservative reaction in England after the French Revolution. As a result, the rational theism of the eighteenth century declined, and James Martineau (1805–1900) in England, and W. E. Channing (1780–1842) and R. E. Emerson (1802–1882) in the United States, encouraged a shift, influenced by Romanticism*, to a more intuitive piety which could come close to pantheism*. As the nineteenth century progressed, however, a new school of Unitarianism developed, which was anti-supernaturalist, which interpreted German biblical criticism* as throwing doubt on the authority of the Gospels, which rejected the uniqueness of Christianity (a position which the older schools of Unitarianism had maintained) and increasingly stressed the religiousness of man rather than the existence of God. Present-day Unitarianism sees itself as a movement with no set creed, which believes in the goodness of man and the plurality of divine revelation. Unitarian writing has not noticeably affected the growth of criticism of the doctrine of the divinity of Christ in modern Protestant theological work; that criticism has developed from distinct roots in the philosophy of history and of language.

C. G. Bolam et al., *The English Presbyterians: From Elizabethan Puritanism to Modern Unitarianism*, 1968; E. M. Wilbur, *A History of Unitarianism*, 2 vols., 1945–1952.

JOHN KENT

Universalism

The belief that ultimately all people will be saved. Orthodox Christian doctrine teaches the finality of heaven and hell. Some Christians think this contradicts the revealed character of God as Love, who would not create people knowing they were destined for eternal punishment. Many Christians today agree that God's will is for all to be saved, but argue that universalism denies human free will. Universalists say God does not coerce, but in his forgiving love never finally abandons anyone. Further, if the cross is really a 'full, perfect and sufficient sacrifice for the sins of the whole world', then universal salvation *must* be a real possibility. Equally, the joy of heaven will not be complete whilst anyone is excluded.

Texts can be cited for and against this view (cf. I Cor. 15.22 with Matt. 25.41, 46). Is teaching about eternal punishment part of the authentic message of Jesus? Did he stress the necessity and importance of decision rather than make future predictions? Some early Fathers, such as Clement of Alexandria, Origen and Gregory of Nyssa, taught a universal restoration* (Greek *apocatastasis*) but this view was condemned at Constantinople in AD 543 as heretical, although some mediaeval mystics and others believed it. It re-emerged in the USA in the late eighteenth century. George de Benneville, a French mystic, and his disciple Elhanan Winchester taught it, also the former English Methodist John Murray who founded the first Universalist Church in 1779. In the early nineteenth century the teaching had some popular success, challenging the hellfire preaching of orthodox revivalism. Universalist churches were founded in several states and in Scotland and Japan. Elhanan Winchester had already founded a Universalist church in London in 1793.

In the Church of England, controversy was sparked in 1846 by the publication of an essay by F. D. Maurice on *Eternal Life and Eternal Death.* He argued that 'eternal' in the NT did not mean 'of endless duration'. Eternal life meant knowledge of God and of his Son, and eternal death, separation from God. Both are present realities. His view seemed to contemporaries to remove a powerful sanction for moral behaviour. There was a storm of protest and Maurice was dismissed from his chair at King's College, London. Nearly a century later, *The Doctrine in The Church of England Report* (1938) recognized that there must be room in the church 'for those who hold that the love of God will at last win penitence and answering love from every soul that it has created' (1957 ed, p. 219). It is probably still a minority position (*see also* **Damnation**).

In the USA many Universalists were also Unitarian * in their belief. In the nineteenth century the two groups were critical of each other. In this century the two churches gradually moved together and a merger took place in 1961 to establish the American Unitarian Universalist Association.

Unitarians have usually recognized the inspiration of other religious teachers besides Jesus, so universalism is also used of the belief that God's salvation is not confined to the church but is available to all people. In traditional churches there is growing recognition that God's love is offered to all and some RC theologians speak of world religions as the 'ordinary' means of salvation (*see also* **Christianity and Other Religions**).

The term is also sometimes used of those OT prophets who held that God's purposes were not to be limited to the people of Israel but embraced other (or all) nations.

John Hick, *Death and Eternal Life*, 1976, ch. 13.

MARCUS BRAYBROOKE

Universals

The main philosophical problem about universals is, whether there is something in the nature of things corresponding to our use of universal terms. At one extreme is the 'realist' * account exemplified by Plato's doctrine of 'Forms' * (*see* **Platonism**); each individual is of the kind that it is by relation to an individual of a different type, one of the Forms. This doctrine gives rise to notorious difficulties. If all horses are horses only by virtue of relation to the subsistent Form

horsehood, is not yet another Form required for both horses and horsehood to be related to, and so *ad infinitum*? At the other extreme is the 'nominalist' * account, which asserts that only individuals are real, and that universal terms are merely conveniences for human thought and speech. But it would surely be just as odd for there to be individuals which fell under no universal description, as for there to be real descriptions which did not apply to anything. 'Realism' * has a theological and ethical twist; if 'Forms' are exemplars in the divine mind, man's duty may be inferred to be conformity with some ideal of humanity implicit in his creation as man. Theologians of nominalist sympathies object to this as an aspersion on the sovereignty of God, who can command what he wills, and is not bound by any prior ideal of 'man' to give men this command or that.

M. J. Loux (ed), *Universals and Particulars*, 1970; H. Staniland, *Universals*, 1972.

HUGO MEYNELL

Utopianism

With the publication in 1516 of his political fantasy *Utopia* Sir Thomas More introduced a new word, but not a new idea. The word means 'no place', or 'nowhere', and utopia has come to mean an ideal or longed-for life or society which, sadly, does not exist. Of all man's capacities which might be said to distinguish him from the natural world, perhaps the most striking is the capacity of man to reflect on himself and his situation, in particular to reflect on how things are and how they could be, or ought to be. It is this capacity of man to dream that leads to utopian visions. It is not a capacity peculiar to any race, culture, society or epoch, and has been present in all cultures in history of which we have knowledge. At one level it is the expression of that weakness in human nature summed up in the expression that the grass is always greener on the other side of the fence. So in cold and inhospitable barren lands, men sit by the fire and dream of a land in which they would be warmed by the sun, in which food would be in abundance without hard work. Alternatively, in a hot and arid land, men dream of cool water, deep shade, lush grass for cattle. Modern man no sooner installs central heating to eliminate the disadvantages, inconveniences and inefficiencies of burning coal than he insists on a fireplace for burning logs.

But there are more profound expressions of utopian thinking, stirred not by such considerations as creature comforts, but by a deep-seated ethical desire to establish society on a new basis and thereby transform man himself. In ancient literature the most famous blueprint for social change and personal enlightenment is found in Plato, *The Republic*, in which we see one of the most ominous and distasteful elements in utopianism, namely, the control and coercion of the lives of the majority, without their consent – 'for their own good'.

The higher religions are necessarily utopian, since once evil is identified in this world, an alternative order is conceived of, either in this world, or more often, in a life to come. Utopianism in the Bible is sometimes of the greener grass variety, where God blesses patriarchs with long life and many comforts. But even this is an ethical utopianism, since it is a reward for faithfulness. Although it seems to refer to a primordial past, the opening chapter of Genesis is in fact utopian since it is declaring something about God's intention in creating the world, an intention which has yet to be realized. The Bible ends with the utopian vision of a heavenly city, which reflects a certain resignation about the reformability of this world.

The most dramatic element in biblical utopianism is the figure of the Messiah, who will come to judge the earth with righteousness and put down evil. The world will then be transformed in accordance with God's will. The messianic faith sometimes thought of the destruction of this world followed by a new creation. For the early church the messianic faith was developed to refer to the Second Advent, the return of Christ as judge and king.

Utopianism, which was a central theme of early Christianity, soon died out. The immediate reason was that the Second Advent did not take place as anticipated. The long-term reason was that when Christianity became the state religion in the fourth century the church no longer looked for the destruction of the empire. However, the utopian faith was never lost. It is to be seen in the founders of monastic movements who conceived of a new form of Christian community which could be found nowhere in existing society. It is to be seen in the attempt of Thomas Müntzer to set up a self-contained Christian city state. One answer to the problem of utopia is to go to a new land and make a fresh beginning. Behind the Constitution of the USA lies the utopianism of the Puritans.

Utopianism has recently reappeared in Christian theology, not from reflection on monasticism or Puritanism, but under the influence of Marxism*. The Christian church at large had lost faith in utopia, had placed it beyond death for the individual and at the end of the world some millennia in the future. It is therefore ironic that Marx should have taken up the utopian vision found in the Bible, of a new society founded on justice and peace. The church had narrowed down Christian hope to mean hope for the world to come. Marx took up the prophetic hope for this world. Perhaps more ironic still, Marx himself used the term 'utopian' in a dismissive way to describe contemporary socialists such as Bakunin because he believed that they were deficient in their critical philosophy of how to move from the present to the future. Their utopianism was merely a dream.

During World War II Ernst Bloch wrote *Das Prinzip Hoffnung* (The Principle of Hope), in which he analysed the fundamental position of this principle in human existence. Just as the Marxist/Christian dialogue in general saw Christians rediscover forgotten or underestimated elements in the biblical faith, so the effect of Bloch's thinking has been to lead theologians to reintroduce the utopian element into present-day theology. In the work of Jürgen Moltmann this has been a dynamic process. It has been unfortunate that More's work on utopia suggested that the ideal either exists or does not. The possibility, even probability, of failing to right all wrongs did not prevent the prophets from laying their vision before the people. Christian hope can be hope for this world without detracting from its fulfilment in the life to come.

R. A. Alves, *A Theology of Human Hope*, 1970; E. Bloch, *A Philosophy of the Future*, 1970; J. W. Johnson (ed), *Utopian Literature: a Selection*, 1968; K. Mannheim, *Ideology and Utopia*, 1936; J. Moltmann, *Theology of Hope*, 1967; E. Schillebeeckx, *Christ*.

The Christian Experience in the Modern World, 1980.

ALISTAIR KEE

Validity

Validity is a term applied to a sacrament of which the divinely appointed sign has been duly performed and to which therefore is necessarily attached the divinely promised gift. Hence the notion of validity arises from the belief that sacramental reality is present when there is a particular outward sign specially appointed by divine authority to be the instrument and expression of some inward and spiritual good. This means that when the sign is performed the spiritual good is conveyed through it, although it has to be acknowledged that it can only be effective for salvation to those who are spiritually fitted to receive it. This concept, which is common to Roman Catholics and many Anglicans, plays an important part in discussion about the sacraments, in so far as for a sacrament to be a sacrament it has to be valid, i.e. the divinely appointed sign must be duly performed. So, e.g. if one holds that the only proper minister at the eucharist is one who has been ordained by a bishop * in the apostolic succession *, one would also maintain that a eucharist celebrated by any other person not so ordained would be invalid. It is important to note further that this concept of validity is to be distinguished from that of efficacy.* The spiritual gift is present in every valid sacrament, but the valid sacrament may not be efficacious for good if the recipient is unworthy. Conversely, the gift which is present in the valid sacrament may be conveyed efficaciously apart from it in certain conditions. So, to apply the term, a Roman Catholic would contend that a Methodist eucharist was invalid, since the minister was not episcopally ordained, but he would not thereby be arguing that it was inefficacious, since the spiritual good conveyed by the sacrament is not always restricted by its validity.

J. G. DAVIES

Values, Religious

The term 'values' in ethics is recent and usually covers what were in the past called 'goods' or 'virtues'. The term is sometimes used subjectively (and descriptively) to designate what a person holds as worthwhile, whether or not anyone would agree. Thus, one might speak of the values of Adolf Hitler. The term 'values' is also used prescriptively, with an effort to be objective and normative. In this sense we speak of Judaeo-Christian values, Hindu values, etc.

The association of religion with values is complex. First of all the term 'religion' is a term of reference to some transcendent reality beyond the apparent and the palpable. This reality might be personalized, assigned gender, and described in terms of a special moral persuasion. Thus the Yahweh God of the Jews and the 'Father' God of Jesus have a quite specific moral character and relationship with humankind. However, the term religion is also applied to more abstract conceptualizations of ultimate authentic reality. Thus, religious grounds for conscientious objection in the United States do not require adherence to the personal God of the classical religions.

Historically, religions and moral values are not always linked. 'The Babylonian woman who was required, once in her lifetime, to serve as a hierodule in the state temple, may have done so in revolt against every moral dictate of her conscience. But such was religion' (Bruce Vawter). Similarly, the ancient Egyptian who took to his tomb elaborate formulae for deceiving Anubis, the god of judgment, did not assume that good morals and religion coincided. On the contrary, ancient Israel believed that persons must be holy and good as their God is holy and good. Christianity is heir to this connatural linkage of religion and values.

In general, there are four ways in which religion and moral values are associated.

1. Religion is often the perceived source of moral value knowledge. Thus, Muslims believe God revealed his will to his prophet Mohammed. This revelation is recorded in a sacred text known as the Koran. Such revelation may be seen as the source of ritualistic as well as ethical obligation. Thus the Muslim believer is required to express faith by praying facing Mecca five times daily, to fast during the Arabic month of Ramadan, and to make a pilgrimage to Mecca once in a lifetime. He/she is also required, however, to practise alms-giving and do other good works. The basic Hebrew Torah is also presented as divinely given, and it too is enshrined in a sacred scripture.

Religion as a perceived source of moral knowledge may be magicalized and thus fulfil the yearning for an oracle which would bypass the normal perils and labours of moral inquiry. In a more religiously genuine way, however, revelation may be seen as knowledge which is not the product of magicalized divine forays into epistemology, but as precious knowledge which is perceived as gift and privilege and as a manifestation of divine largesse. Such knowledge, then, scripturally stored, becomes an ongoing stimulus to the doing of ethics within a credal community. It does not become a substitute for ethics.

2. Religion may also be a sanction for moral obligation. Thus, the Hindu *karma* gives major incentives for doing good and avoiding evil since, according to this doctrine, one's actions determine the quality of life one will have in a subsequent existence. For Jesus, the principal motive for following his moral teaching is the reign of God. Hell, perceived as unending *post-mortem* punishment, was for long periods in Christian history a major moral sanction. Christian theology and faith have moved away from this harsh and ultimately dualistic conception of after-life (*see* **Life after Death**), but resurrection * faith and immortality still are generally seen as foundational motives for rising above enlightened self-interest to agapic * love.

3. Religion also functions as a rationalization of moral value choices. It may simply serve to justify class privileges in what Max Weber called 'a theodicy of good fortune'. 'Other things being equal, classes with high social and economic privilege will . . . assign to religion the primary function of legitimizing their own life pattern and situation in the world' (*The Sociology of Religion*, ET 1963, p. 107). In this usage of religion, wealth becomes a sacrament of God's favour. This tendency is often too exclusively attributed to Calvinist teaching, but, as Weber notes, it is a more universal ploy than that. Religion tends to be corrupted by class interests. A comparative study of Christian and Muslim Lebanese villagers led to the conclusion that: 'Differences in religion, insofar as they affect orientations and philosophies towards life in general, tend to be overridden and rendered insignificant by the wider impact of Arab culture generally and the historical-economic-geographical concomitants of rural Lebanese life in particular' (George

Fetter, *JSSR* 4, 1964, pp. 48–59). This tendency is notable in other cultures as well.

4. Finally, religion functions as prophetic critique in the cause of social justice. Stephen Charles Mott writes of the Judaeo-Christian Bible: 'The biblical message of justice creates a basic loyalty to the poor and weak and a commitment to their defence.' Such a commitment does not proceed only from 'resentment' among the deprived but is inspired in the Judaeo-Christian traditions by a profound sense of social-distributive justice as a primary religious value. It arises out of a conviction that the religious message is 'good news to the poor' (Luke 4.18). Holiness, in this view, essentially involves active concern for the dispossessed and helpless in society.

Bruce C. Birch and Larry L. Rasmussen, *Bible and Ethics in the Christian Life*, 1976; Stephen Charles Mott, *Biblical Ethics and Social Change*, 1982; J. Milton Yinger, *The Scientific Study of Religion*, 1970.

D A N I E L C. M A G U I R E

Venial Sin

The N T, while not using the terminology of 'venial' as opposed to 'mortal' sin, does indicate some difference between sins which 'exclude from the kingdom of God' (I Cor. 6.9–10; Gal. 5.19–21; Eph. 5.5) and those which do not do so (James 3.2; I John 1.8; 5.16). Augustine's reflections, and various penitential practices of the early church, prepared the way for Thomas Aquinas' elaborated distinction between mortal sins which, in his analogy, bring spiritual death to the soul, and venial sins which cause a kind of sickness and disorder but do not break the basic union of charity and life with God. In its sixth and fourteenth sessions (1547 and 1551) the Council of Trent * formally adopted the distinction. Whereas for mortal sin baptized Christians need forgiveness through the sacrament of reconciliation or penance, venial sin does not bring the loss of sanctifying grace and may be forgiven without recourse to the sacrament.

Recent moral theology * has struggled with criteria for distinguishing venial and mortal sin, recognizing normally that they are not two species of some one genus but that 'sin' is extended only by analogy to cover the case of venial sin. Some authors have contrasted mortal sin (as a truly fundamental option against God) with serious sin (which involves objectively grave 'matter' but not the actual sinner's radical choice against God) and venial sin. Many authors have tried to get away from post-Reformation casuistry which often took a 'reified' view of venial sin, as if it were merely some kind of minor offence of an individual against certain objective rules. In general, venial sin is understood not to entail *both* a fully malicious and freely intended fundamental decision against God *and* an action which in itself is gravely wrong. Nevertheless, theologians like Karl Rahner note ways in which venial sins mean some alienation from oneself, from others and from God. Rather than being minor refusals to obey the divine law (interpreted as a set of rules 'out there'), such sins offend against one's basic calling as a creature and a baptized member of Christ's community. In their own (minor) way venial sins also express a refusal to love.

See also **Mortal Sin, Sin.**

GERALD O'COLLINS

Vestigia Trinitatis

The material which this term denotes is often treated in a diffuse, if not confused manner, partly because, particularly in studies on Augustine, to whom it is frequently traced, it seems to have so many alternative names: as well as 'traces of the Trinity', 'psychological analogy'*, and 'likeness' or 'image of God' in humans or in the creation generally. What seems certain, especially from Augustine, is that the material originates in a conflation of the Christian doctrine of the image of God in the Word through whom all was created, and subsequently in humans, with the Greek theological conception of each lower level in divine creative-emanation as image of the one above, and each successively less perfect. The imagery of sun, rays, illumined objects, or root, branch, fruit is an *analogy** for the manner in which the divine is with successive imperfection imaged forth: taken as an *image* this would belong with other physical images (three-leaved shamrocks) as the most imperfect and dispensable illustrations of the divine. According to the Neoplatonists* the least imperfect image of God is in *nous*, for this, like the Christian Word, is the first emanation of God; hence it is to the inner

human *nous* that Augustine repairs for his least imperfect image of the inner being of God. Augustine makes it perfectly clear that it is only because of God's previous revelatory-salvific outgoing to the human *nous* that humans can find there an image of God; hence Barth's critique of the *vestigia*, born of his phobia about largely non-existent natural (as opposed to revealed) theology*, is simply not appropriate; indeed Barth's opposing suggestion that *scripture* gives us sets of appropriated terms from God's creative-salvific outreach which enable us to trace the inner-divine distinctions (creator, reconciler, redeemer, or holiness, mercy, goodness) is scarcely less vulnerable than Augustine's. What does need more sustained criticism, however, is the manner in which Augustine's preference for inner *nous* as image of the triune God, since this belonged to wisdom (*sapientia*), over the mere knowledge (*scientia*) of all that Jesus did and suffered, contributed substantially to that second-rating of the incarnation which is a growing feature of developing trinitarian theology, and left people of small expertise in the logic of relations with little more than the crude psychological analogy of knowledge and love which Augustine himself went to such lengths to dismantle.

See **Trinity, Doctrine of the.**

J. P. MACKEY

Via eminentiae *see* Analogy

Via Negativa

Historically, this refers to a method of speculative theology associated particularly with the Neoplatonists*, in the first instance Proclus (AD 410–485), and developed in a way most important for its influence on Christian theology by Pseudo-Dionysius (*c.* 500) in his *Mystical Theology*. In essence the *via negativa* is a way of using language about God which keeps constantly before the attention of its user the fact that human language is hopelessly inadequate to use of the ineffable God. The method begins by trying to reduce, as far as possible, the effects of the necessarily anthropomorphic* character of human theological language. The stripping away process begins by removing from consideration those human creaturely qualities which are inappropriate when applied to God. The *via negativa* is therefore a method of theological speech which is a constant reminder that speech originated and developed to deal with human relationships and is not equipped to deal adequately with the divine-human encounter.

The *via negativa* has been regarded as a necessary first exercise for the theologian in both Western and Eastern traditions. Thomas Aquinas regards it as a necessary preliminary to the *via positiva**. In the tradition of the Eastern Orthodox* Church the *via negativa* is specially stressed and is known as the apophatic way.

The *via negativa* was criticized by W. R. Inge because he believed that it led necessarily to a Buddhistic self-annihilating cult of *apatheia*. Other theologians have felt that it inevitably involves a turning of one's back on finite existence and a despising of it. Here it needs to be remembered that the *via negativa* is a way of theological speech which is determined by a profound sense of the utter transcendence of God. It has a right place, therefore, as a religious ascesis, but it is inadequate as a theological method if used in isolation. It needs to be balanced, as it is balanced in the theology of Thomas Aquinas, by a use of the *via positiva*. The relation of the two methods has perhaps never been better described than by Charles Williams when he wrote: 'Both methods, the affirmative way and the negative way, were to co-exist, one might almost say to coinhere, since each was to be the key to the other' (*The Descent of the Dove*, 1939, 57).

V. Lossky, *The Mystical Theology of the Eastern Church*, 1957; John Meyendorff, *Byzantine Theology*, 1974.

E. J. TINSLEY

Via Positiva

Like the *via negativa*, this is a theological method taken over into the Christian tradition from Pseudo-Dionysius. He explains what he means by the *via positiva* in his book *The Divine Names*. The *via positiva* is a method which theologically relies on the doctrine of creation*, with its implication that marks of the Creator are necessarily discernible to a greater or lesser extent in his work of creation, and more particularly on the doctrine of man as made in the image* of God. The highest human qualities are pointers which can be confidently taken as signs of the perfection of God. But the method emphasizes that while it is possible to take certain human qualities as pointers to God, and therefore to use them of God, it is necessary to emphasize that these things are true of God only in a pre-eminent way. This is the reason why the *via positiva* is sometimes referred to as the *via eminentiae*.

E. J. TINSLEY

Virginal Conception of Jesus

Although 'Virgin Birth' is a more familiar designation, the only NT evidence (Matt. 1.18–25; Luke 1.26–38) pertains to the *conception* of Jesus in the womb of Mary, 'from the holy Spirit' and not by male agency. (In the second-century *Protevangelium of James* 19–20 Mary is described as giving *birth* miraculously and with sexual organs intact.) Very dubious are the attempts to find implicit references to a virginal conception in Gal. 4.4 and Rom. 1.3, where Paul does *not* use 'begotten' of Jesus (*gennētheis, gegennētai*) as he does of Ishmael or Isaac; or in Mark 6.3, where Jesus is called 'son of Mary' instead of 'son of Joseph'; or in the poorly attested variant reading of John 1.13 ('he who was begotten . . . not of the will of man but of God'). Some would challenge whether Luke 1.35 excludes male agency (alongside the Holy Spirit), since the conception is future; more often it is suggested that this verse was added to a hypothetical pre-Lucan narrative of natural conception. However, the Lucan parallelism of lesser to greater between the infancy of the Baptist and that of Jesus demands that a miraculous conception of John be followed by a more miraculous conception of Jesus, specifically, a virginal conception.

The Matthean and Lucan accounts of the virginal conception are independent of each other, so that a pre-Gospel tradition antedating either is plausible. Although the primary interest of each account is christological (the conception of Emmanuel or of the Son of God) and not biological, both evangelists apparently accepted the facticity of the event. That the two infancy narratives, which agree on little else, agree on the virginal conception is a factor favouring historicity. Also, it is hard to think of a Christian inventing the story in Matt. 1.18 which raises a suspicion of sinful behaviour by Jesus' mother, making him illegitimate. Yet, if one posits historicity, the silence (and apparent ignorance) about a virginal conception in the rest of the NT and even in the rest of Matthew and Luke, and the affirmation of a natural birth by some second-century Jewish and Gnostic Christians, are hard to explain. Mary, who remained alive into the early church period (Acts 1.14), should have been available to inform all about it; but rumour about the child's illegitimacy (implication of John 8.41?) might have been a complicating factor.

Difficulties also face the modern nonfactual explanations of the virginal conception tradition: 1. That it arose through imaginative reflection on OT expectation is implausible, for there is no evidence of a pre-Christian expectation of virginal origins for the Messiah. (The Hebrew of Isa. 7.14 does not stress virginity; and the LXX of 7.14 speaks of future conception by the woman who is now a virgin and does not exclude natural union.) Seemingly the Isaian passage was employed in Matt. 1.22–23 to illustrate an *existing* Christian belief. 2. That the tradition arose through theological reflection on Jesus as God's son and is a pure theologoumenon is also dubious. Many NT authors designate Jesus as Son of God without any inference that he had no human father; indeed, the adjacent designations 'son of Joseph' and 'Son of God' are not seen as incompatible in John 1.45, 49. 3. That the tradition was shaped by Graeco-Roman legends of the gods begetting children of earth-women is unlikely; for the NT imagines an asexual generation, and the Holy Spirit does not function as a male agent in the conception but as a creative force. Moreover, the thought-context of the two NT infancy narratives is Jewish rather than Graeco-Roman. Behind such nonfactual explanations lurks a distrust of the miraculous, but historicity cannot be decided on the basis of either modern incredulity or ancient credulity. In fact, the arguments drawn from biblical criticism *are not overwhelmingly persuasive for or against historicity; and so most make their decision on other bases, e.g. inspiration of scripture, church teaching, or philosophical attitude towards divine intervention.

The virginal conception has played various roles in subsequent theology. The credal 'born of the virgin Mary' shifted the emphasis to birth, signalling that *part* of the interest was now on the reality of Jesus' humanity against a docetic* heresy: the proof of his humanity is that we know the agents of his birth (Mary) and death (Pontius Pilate). According to Ambrose and Augustine, the transmission of original sin * is bound up with the sexual nature of propagation and the carnal desires aroused by procreation. That Jesus was asexually conceived explains how he was free of original sin – a connection made even in our times in a more sophisticated manner by Karl Barth. For some conservative Christians, belief in the virginal conception is a bellwether of belief in the divinity of Jesus. Consequently, denial of the one (or even that Isa. 7.14 prophesied it) is a denial of the other, even though in classical trinitarian theology the position of the Son as the only-begotten of the Father antedates the virginal conception. Recognizing that the theme of virginal conception in Matthew and Luke and the theme of pre-existence in John were alternative ways of explaining the divinity of Jesus, W. Pannenberg has taken the paradoxical stance of denying the former in order to stress the latter! In much RC thought the virginal conception is primarily a mariological* statement. It constitutes the first part of a threefold statement generally deemed to be infallibly defined doctrine: Mary was a virgin before birth (*ante partum*), in birth (*in partu*, often implying that the hymen remained unbroken), and after birth (*post partum*: she never had marital relations with Joseph). The last affirmation, not found in scripture, was hinted at in the *Protevangelium of James'* explanation that the 'brothers of Jesus' were children of Joseph by a previous marriage. It became enshrined in the ancient formula 'ever-virgin', a formula *not* rejected by the sixteenth-century Reformers but maintained by few Protestants today.

T. Boslooper, *The Virgin Birth*, 1962; R.E. Brown, *The Virginal Conception and Bodily Resurrection of Jesus*, 1973; *The Birth of the Messiah*, 1977, pp. 517–33; H. von Campenhausen, *The Virgin Birth in the Theology of the Ancient Church*, 1964; J. G. Machen, *The Virgin Birth of Christ*, 1930.

RAYMOND E. BROWN

Virginity

Virginity (*partheneia*) and virgin (*parthenos*, common gender) appear to have undergone an important change in meaning in secular and early Christian literature about the third century. Initially *parthenos* denoted the age rather than the marital status of a person and was akin to *bethulah* (Hebrew for virgin), which was defined as a girl under 12½ years and 1 day, even though she were married. Virgin also denoted a young married person or a person who had been married as a virgin and remained in monogamous marriage. Tombstone inscriptions in both Hebrew and Greek witness to these 'married virgins'.

In paganism one finds virgin deities usually associated with fertility. They were regarded as saviours (*sōteirai*) and protectors in time of distress. For the Greek, virginity symbolized *autarkeia* (self-sufficiency). In Rome the institution of the Vestal Virgins goes back to 716–673 BC. Numa Pompilius placed distinguished women in its sacred hierarchy. A virgin-priestess was supposed to live in conjugal relationship with her god.

The conception of Jesus by a virgin is reported by Matthew and Luke. In early literature Mary is called 'all virgin' and 'ever virgin'. Jesus and Mary are both portrayed as virgins. Otherwise, fidelity to one spouse, even after death, seems to have been the aspiration of the more fervent Christian rather than virginity. Many modern exegetes interpret Jesus' teaching about eunuchs for the kingdom as referring to abstinence from second marriage. Paul's teaching in I Cor. 7 remains an enigma; at least five different interpretations have been offered, but it is unlikely that he was advocating celibacy.

Virginity, however, became highly prized as martyrdoms diminished, and it was seen as another form of martyrdom, a special aspect of ascetic consecration. The practice seems to have flourished particularly from the mid-third century onwards, but was hindered in some respects from being accepted in the universal church because of heretical teaching on marriage and women especially among the Gnostics* and Encratites (*see* **Chastity**). Notable in this respect are the apocryphal* writings, e.g. *Acts of Paul and Thecla* and the *Gospel of Thomas*. Heterodoxical* tendencies about virginity are also found in the 'recently' discovered literature from Nag Hammadi, e.g. in *Thomas the Contender*, 144: 'Woe to you who loved intimacy with womankind and polluted intercourse with it!'

One must also mention the extremes which were reached in Syriac Christianity. Here the concept of virginity was almost identified with the proclamation of the gospel, e.g. see the *Odes of Solomon* and the *Acts of Thomas*. Here one finds arresting statements against marriage and also against begetting children, who might lower the ethical standards of their parents. This is contrasted with the freedom and felicity which virginity brings. Some taught that Christ is bridegroom only to virgins. These tenets obviously arise from Encratic principles. There appear to have been not infrequent cases where baptism meant embracing virginity or renouncing marriage.

Yet there was also a moderate and fruitful view of virginity. By the fourth century Christ and his mother were held up as models of virginity (*see also* **Mariology**, **Virginal Conception**). Embracing virginity was almost the only way for a woman to win independence from family, husband and state. The church's promotion of the virginal life helped women to realize their equality with men which they had acquired in baptism. The virginal life offered more than spiritual freedom.

It is very difficult to know when a vow of virginity became a custom. At first virgins remained in their own homes, and later 'monasteries' were formed. Eventually ecclesiastical legislation about virgins was introduced. This dealt with such subjects as required age and the assurance that the candidates had chosen this state of life of their own volition. Virgins were never ordained, and appear to have remained inferior to widows and deaconesses for a considerable time. They were under the bishop's jurisdiction (*C. Chal.*, canon 16) and were given their own places in church assemblies (*Const. Ap.* 2.57, 12).

An informative way to see the various opinions (and especially laudatory ones) of the virginal life is to peruse Methodius of Olympus' *Banquet*. In this treatise there are eleven speeches by virgins and a hymn. The speeches form a summary of much of the theology of virginity which is found in other orthodox Christian writings. All the speeches are give by women and therefore no mysogyny is present.

Orthodox Christian writers show that their praise of virginity must be carefully distinguished from condemnation of marriage. See, for example, the treatises on virginity by Basilius of Ancyra, Gregory of Nyssa, John Chrysostom and Ambrose. One principle frequently annunciated was that God provided the begetting of children to compensate for the immortality which Adam and Eve lost. Now, however, the world is sufficiently populated and marriage and begetting of children are superfluous. For the above authors virginity enabled one to be totally orientated towards God and one's neighbour. It is not physical virginity but the pure state of the soul which makes one a virgin. It is a foretaste of the angelic and celestial state.

J. Massyngbaerde Ford, *A Trilogy on Wisdom and Celibacy*, 1967; A. Vööbus, *Syriac and Arabic Documents regarding legislation relative to Syrian Asceticism*, 1960.

J. M. FORD

Virtue

This is not a NT 'keyword', though it is significant that *aretē*, the word traditionally translated as 'virtue', appears in the RSV twice as 'virtue' (both in II Peter 1.5) and twice as 'excellence' (Phil. 4.8 and II Peter 1.3). Christian discussion of virtue goes back to Aristotle's *Ethics*, where the virtue of man is defined as 'the dispositon which makes a man good and causes him to do his own work well' (Book II C2). The upshot of such good activity is to be *eudaimonia*, another word hard to translate but approximately 'happiness' or 'blessedness'.

For Aristotle, virtue can be characterized as a disposition to choose the mean between two extremes. For instance, courage is the mean between cowardice and rashness, liberality between prodigality and meanness, pride or rather 'greatness of soul' between 'empty vanity' and 'grovelling humility' (*Ethics* II, c 3).

In the Christian tradition, the three theological virtues of faith, hope and charity (cf. I Cor. 13) have been superimposed upon the four cardinal virtues, prudence, justice, temperance and fortitude, of the ancient pagan world to make a more or less tidy scheme of seven. There has been much discussion of the difference between virtue 'acquired' by man or 'infused' by God so that we may be fit to inherit eternal life (cf. Mortimer, *The Elements of Moral Theology*, 1947, pp. 105ff.). It has been debated whether the

virtues are a unity; whether a good man must be good 'right through', so to speak; whether the undoubted bravery of a burglar or a terrorist is the virtue of courage or not: a question which must surely be resolved by care in the use of words. It is also a temptation to become enmeshed in problems about the sense in which the virtues are beneficial not only for mankind but for their individual possessors. Somehow we have to keep the balance between recognizing that virtue may *not* pay and is to be prized for its own sake; and affirming with Bishop Butler that virtue after all is in everyone's truest interest (e.g. Sermon III para. 10). As P. Geach put it, 'Men need virtues as bees need stings' (*The Virtues*, p. 17).

When these discussions are conducted in too scholastic a manner they defeat themselves. Meanwhile 'virtue' shrinks its meaning: to conscientiousness, or sexual propriety, or even to priggishness. Yet recently there has been a revival of interest in the Aristotelian understanding of virtue as what people need if they are to attain the ends proper to a human being. Without asking naively, 'What is a human being for?', as we might ask, 'What is a knife for?', we can take into ethical account 'the built-in teleologies of human nature' (Geach, p. vii). It can become respectable again, with care, to get an 'ought' from an 'is'.

For Aristotle, in the last resort *eudaimonia* is the contemplative life; but lately there has been more emphasis, from different points of view, upon the virtues people need as beings who characteristically live in *community*. Such an emphasis seems more comprehensive and hardly less Aristotelian. Christians should be able to enter into such discussion hopefully.

Aristotle, *Ethics*; Peter Geach, *The Virtues*, 1977; Alasdair MacIntyre, *After Virtue: A Study in Moral Theory*, 1981, esp. ch. 14 and p. 245; James D. Wallace, *Virtues and Vices*, 1978.

HELEN OPPENHEIMER

Vision of God

To be aware of God in the perfection of his being, in Christian tradition, has always been closely associated with the beatitude of Christ: 'Blessed are the pure in heart, for they shall see God.' In the biblical tradition, the vision of God is an eschatological * reality only possible to man in the life beyond death. In general, the OT uses the metaphor of the vision of God reluctantly as far as human experience in this life is concerned. 'No man shall see God and live' is an OT refrain. The only people who see God in the OT are exceptional persons like Moses, for example, and even he is spoken of as being granted a vision only of the 'back parts' of God. Nevertheless, it would not be true to say that in the OT the human experience of God is described exclusively in terms of the hearing of God. Frequently enough the prophet sees the word of God as well as hears it (*see* **Mysticism**).

In the NT also the vision of God is an eschatological reality. But again significantly in the records of the mission of Christ the imagery of seeing is very frequent indeed in relation to the responsibility which is laid upon disciples for the way they interpret Jesus ('Having eyes do you not yet see?', 'Blessed are the eyes that see the things that you see').

In mysticism the vision of God is regarded as the apex of the whole process of ascetical discipline (*see* **Asceticism**; **Ascetical Theology**). Similarly in the Christian monastic tradition the vision of God was awaited as the crown of monks' discipline. And there are instances where Christian mystics speak of the vision of God in an extravagant way which, strictly speaking, would make it incompatible with Christian eschatology. That is to say, they identify their experience of ecstasy* with the beatific vision. It is for this reason that the Protestant tradition of Christianity has been hesitant about the whole notion of the vision of God. In it there inevitably lies concealed, Protestants have insisted, the idea of a ladder which a man is able to scale by his own endeavour and achieve the beatific vision, independent of the work of grace. Inevitably, it was believed to involve a sidetracking of the central place of the humanity of Christ and the historical incarnation and atonement.

But if the vision of God is seen to be an inadequate metaphor for the profoundly personal reciprocal character of the human communion with God in its perfection, the inadequacy of the metaphor of hearing God must be realized also. Both are required for expressing the transcendental and immanental aspects of religious experience.

To isolate one metaphor and concentrate on audition, word, speech, often leads to a denigration of art and aesthetic experience which a close hold on the necessity of retaining the metaphor of vision would have avoided (*see also* **Beatific Vision**).

John Baillie, *Our Knowledge of God*, 1939; John Burnaby, *Amor Dei*, 1938; K. E. Kirk, *The Vision of God*, 1931; Ray Petry (ed), *Late Mediaeval Mysticism*, 1957.

E. J. TINSLEY

Vocation

In the NT the 'calling' or 'vocation' of a man or woman is invariably to the acceptance of salvation* and new life in Christ, or, by a natural extension of usage, to the apostolate which is charged with witnessing to that salvation (*see* **Calling**). There is no suggestion that God calls anyone to enter a particular profession or occupation; all those who are called are expected to show in daily life and work that they are so called.

But because of, or perhaps simply in line with, the development of the 'double standard' in Christian ethics, according to which some Christians obey the 'counsels of perfection' and others only the 'evangelical precepts', the divine calling came to be emphasized in relation to those who obeyed the 'counsels' and devalued in relation to those who simply lived by the 'precepts'. In the Middle Ages only those who entered monastic orders were said to have a divine vocation, and their vocation included the taking of the vows of poverty, chastity and obedience (or, in the case of the Benedictines, stability of residence, obedience and monastic zeal – poverty and chastity being taken for granted).

Luther rejected both the double standard and the monastic vows, the latter on the ground that the vows imply salvation by the monastic life, and give to those who take them a false security based on the community of the order, whereas true faith is in God alone, to be worked out in the difficult circumstances of marriage and ordinary life. Relying on what is now held to be a false interpretation of I Cor. 7.17–24, he maintained that all stations in life in which it is possible to live honestly are divine vocations (*Berufe*). They include those which are to be found in the family – to be husband, father, wife, mother – those which belong to economic and commercial life – to be cobbler, shopkeeper, milkmaid or slave – and those which are part of political life – to be king, governor or subject. They include the vocation of a soldier. All these vocations are 'masks' of God, by which the work of God in human life is both revealed and concealed. Through those whom he calls, God rules the family, governs the state and milks the cows. There are callings both in the kingdom of this world and in the kingdom of God, and a calling to the ordained ministry is one among many. Each Christian in his calling is to look for God's 'right time' (*Stündelein*) for doing his Christian task.

Calvin interpreted 'vocation' in a way very similar to Luther's. God, he says, has appointed duties and a way of living for everyone, and these ways of living are 'vocations', to be compared with the sentry posts which mark the boundaries of a soldier's activities. This is God's provision for the stability of the common life and to counter rebellion. A man of humble station, as well as a magistrate, will discharge his functions the more willingly because he knows that they have been given to him by God, aware that 'no task will be so sordid or base, provided you obey your calling in it, that it will not shine and be reckoned very precious in God's sight' (*Institutes* X, 6).

Max Weber and R. H. Tawney have noted a connection between Calvin's teaching at this point and the development of capitalism, but other scholars (e.g. J. T. McNeill) hold that they have overstated the closeness of the connection, since for Calvin vocation is essentially to be seen in its religious context.

Since the Reformation*, and not only in Calvinistic countries, the religious element has been drained out of the concept, and everyone regards himself as entitled to speak of his calling without any reference to God.

J. T. McNeill, *The History and Character of Calvinism*, Part II, 1957; G. Wingren, *The Christian's Calling*, 1958.

RUPERT DAVIES

Voluntarism

Voluntarism (from the Latin word *voluntas* = will) covers any theory that stresses the temporal or ontological primacy of the will over the intellect, or reason. It can be divided into two types, often but not necessarily related: divine and human.

Throughout Christian theology there has been a tension between moral absolutes (things are good in and of themselves) and divine freedom (God did not create things because they were already good; they are good because God created them so). This tension was already present in pre-Christian thought between Platonic* idealism, which acknowledged absolute goods, and Protagorean voluntarism. Christian theologians wished to affirm the freedom of God and yet protect the inherent rationality of the moral and physical universe. Consequently we find voluntarism to be a matter of emphasis, and theologians to be voluntarists on some issues, rationalist on others.

For example, Augustine understood God primarily as reason or intellect, and his debt to Neoplatonism* made it difficult for him to view the metaphysical and moral orders other than in terms of absolutes that reason seeks to know. And yet, largely as a result of his re-evaluations of the doctrines of creation and justification, Augustine came to view both as grounded in the inscrutable will of God. Creation* *ex nihilo* means that nothing but God precedes his creative act, which was not made out of previous matter nor any pre-determined plan that God was forced to adopt. Moreover, God predestines to eternal life by reason of his will; he does not do so on the basis of human actions or foreseen merits.

It is largely on the basis of his stress on the freedom and omnipotence of God, on the primacy of the divine will, and on predestination before foreseen merits (*ante praevisa merita*) that John Duns Scotus has been called both an Augustinian and a voluntarist. Over against Thomas' stress on divine reason, Scotus understood God primarily as will. This was expanded to include the ethical norms, which are good solely because they were chosen and established by God, who did not choose them because they were already good. William of Ockham shared with Scotus this stress on the freedom and will of God, with two important reservations. Ockham believed that predestination was based on foreseen merits (*post praevisa merita*) and, more fundamental, that there is no distinction in God between reason and will. Voluntarism in this sense found many supporters in the late mediaeval and more modern periods. It can be found in the thought of Pierre d'Ailly, Gabriel Biel, Martin Luther, John Calvin, Blaise Pascal and Søren Kierkegaard.

Human voluntarism, the belief that in human action the will is superior to and the force behind reason, was rarely adopted in the patristic or mediaeval periods, other than in the Augustinian sense that God initially endowed man with free will, the ability to sin or not to sin. Whatever the ultimate source of the rational and moral orders, all mediaeval theologians believed that the will followed, or should follow, the dictates of right reason.

Several thinkers in the modern period have affirmed that man acts primarily from his will, not his reason. Thus Thomas Hobbes, David Hume, Arthur Schopenhauer, J. G. Fichte and William James.

WILLIAM J. COURTENAY

Witness of the Spirit

The Holy Spirit, the Spirit of truth, gives witness to Jesus Christ (John 15.26; 16.13–15) and to the truth, guiding the followers of Jesus into all truth (John 16.13), for Christ is truth (John 14.6). In fact, the Spirit witnesses to the truth of Christ because the Spirit too is truth (I John 5.7). Since Christian truth is truth-to-be-done, the Spirit's witness takes place not only in words but in action, in the words and actions of Jesus' followers who with the Spirit bear joint witness to Christ (John 15.26–27). The one Spirit manifests himself in various ways for useful purposes according to the gifts of the Spirit given to each disciple of Jesus (I Cor. 12.4–7). Filled with the Holy Spirit, Jesus' disciples speak the word of God with boldness (Acts 4.31), and through them God works healings, signs, and wonders (Acts 4.30). The Spirit testifies not only to Jesus but to the righteousness of God in raising up Jesus, to the judgment of God because the prince of this world stands already judged, and to both God's righteousness and his judgment by convicting the world of sin (John 16.8–11). Finally, the Spirit bears witness to us that we are God's children (Rom. 8.16), for it is by means of the Spirit that we cry 'Abba, Father' (Rom. 8.15) together with the Spirit praying in us and for us (Rom. 8.26).

The same Holy Spirit touches our hearts and reveals to us the significance of God's word when we read or hear, or hear preached the scriptures. This doctrine, although expressed and explained differently in different Christian churches, is a commonly held teaching. John Calvin writes of 'the inner witness of the Spirit'; the Holy Spirit witnesses to God's words by penetrating our hearts to convince us of their meaning and their truth' (*Institutes*, i.7.4–5). Thomas Aquinas writes that 'the letter kills and the Spirit gives life; . . . and so even the letter of the gospel kills unless the healing grace of faith is present interiorly' (*ST* Ia–IIae, q. 106, a. 3, *responsio*). The beginning of the *Westminster Confessions* (1643) speaks of 'the inward word of the Holy Spirit bearing witness by and with the word in our hearts'. John Wesley expressed the experience of his conversion of heart (1738) in terms of the interior witness of the Spirit. The Second Vatican Council, in its *Dogmatic Constitution on Divine Revelation*, speaks of the Holy Spirit who continues to speak to our hearts and so to speak to the church, especially through those who have the role of teaching: 'Thus God, who spoke in the past, continues to converse with the spouse of his beloved Son; and the Holy Spirit, through whom the living voice of the gospel rings out in the Church – and through her in the world – leads believers to the full truth, and makes the word of Christ dwell in them in all its richness' (n. 8).

See also **Holy Spirit, Spiritual Gifts.**

ROBERT FARICY

Word of God

A term used constantly (with a capital W) in dialectical * or kerygmatic * theology, as represented by e.g. Karl Barth and Emil Brunner, to stress the autonomy * and sovereign character of the subject of their theology. Because the Word is God's Word, theology takes the form of a response to it, and in responding to that Word does not have to conform to any philosophical or scientific criteria. The Word is to be distinguished from any human words, even the words of the Bible. The Word has its centre in Christ, and is attested to by the Bible, but is known only through the grace of God. Barth and Brunner differed over whether there was a point of contact for the Word on the human side (*see* **Crisis Theology**), but both are virtually unanimous that there is a total disjunction between the Word of God and human thought. For the more traditional background to the concept *see* **Logos**. *See also* **Dialectical Theology**.

JOHN BOWDEN

Work

The 'Biblical Theology* Movement' of the 1940s and 1950s reminded people of central biblical emphases: God is a God who acts, who works, in creation, redemption and sanctification; Christians participate in the work of God through their furtherance of the gospel; and daily work is a necessary part of Christian living, although the fallenness of things ensures that human work does not offer the fulfilment or creativity that it should. Luther, and other theologians in his tradition, saw daily work as a matter of calling* or vocation*. God calls us to particular roles in society, and in our due fulfilment of our callings we participate in the work of God and show his love and justice. This positive understanding of daily work as having spiritual significance went alongside an emphatic denial of jusification by works: no human works are such as to earn or merit salvation. But among the Calvinists and other associated groups there developed the belief that although works* are useless as a means of earning salvation, hard and successful work is a sign of salvation and brings assurance of election. This strong affirmation of the religious significance of an ethic of hard daily work was seen by the sociologist, Max Weber (*The Protestant Ethic and the Spirit of Capitalism*, 1904–5, ET 1930) and R. H. Tawney (*Religion and the Rise of Capitalism*, 1926) as providing the attitudinal base on which modern capitalism developed.

Any theology of work must now take into account the thought of Karl Marx (*see* **Marxism, Marxist Theology**). Work he sees as man's productive, creative activity which he engages in within a network of relations of production appropriate to the methods of production being used. In capitalist society work is flawed or alienated; man has a wrong relationship to the product of his labour, is deprived of the proper enjoyment of the fruits of his toil, can only express a small part of his creative potentiality, and experiences a tension between the co-operative relationships necessary for production and the competitive and oppressive relationships of ownership, control and the en-

joyment of the fruits of work. In a communist society alienation will be overcome and work will be a free expression of man's creativity and sociability: the utopian* vision sees the very division of labour as becoming obsolete: 'It is possible for me to do one thing today and another tomorrow, to hunt in the morning, fish in the afternoon, rear cattle in the evening, criticize after dinner, just as I have a mind, without ever becoming hunter, fisherman, shepherd or critic' (Marx and Engels, *The German Ideology*). Work and the way it is organized both shapes society and people and reflects the social structure.

An adequate theology of work must hold together insights from scripture and the tradition of the church, together with the results of modern sociological and psychological studies. Among issues which are attracting particular contemporary attention from theologians and Christian ethicists are the adequacy of the Protestant work ethic, and the social and psychological implications of unemployment.

Gregory Baum (ed), *Work and Religion*, *Concilium* 131, 1980; Roger Clarke, *Work in Crisis*, 1982; Alan Richardson, *The Biblical Doctrine of Work*, 1952.

DUNCAN FORRESTER

Works

The Bible assumes throughout that God rewards everyone according to his works (Prov. 24.12; Ps. 62.12; Matt. 16.27; Rom. 2.6; Rev. 2.23, etc.). However, it also assumes that all have sinned, for 'surely there is not a righteous man on earth who does good and never sins' (Eccles. 7.20; Ps. 143.2; Rom. 3.23, etc.). Consequently, the sinner has to find how to become righteous by some other way than by works alone; he needs God's mercy and forgiveness. Various descriptions were given of how this mercy was to be sought. It is generally assumed that sins cannot be forgiven by God unless the sinner repents and offers God a sacrifice*. The prophets insisted that sacrifice without repentance and mercy was useless. Much-discussed passages about the works to be done by sinners in order to be forgiven were the account of David's repentance and forgiveness after he had killed Uriah (II Sam. 12), and Daniel's advice to Nebuchadnezzar, 'redeem your sins by charity and your iniquities by generosity to the wretched' (Dan. 4.27 NEB; Protestant translations usually give, 'break off your sins . . .').

In the OT the issue had already been raised whether faith or trust was not the primary requirement for sinners to be justified before God. The key passages were Gen. 15.6, 'And [Abraham] believed the Lord; and he reckoned it to him as righteousness'; Isa. 28.16; and Hab. 2.4, 'the righteous man shall live by his faith' ('by being faithful', NEB). The roll call of faith in Heb. 11 is thoroughly Jewish. It is conceivable that the polemic against faith without works in James 2.14–26 reflects an old Jewish dispute.

Faith and works seem to be mutually excluded in the epistles of Paul, and he seems to condemn outright 'the works of the Law': 'for no human being will be justified in [God's] sight by works of the law, since through the law comes knowledge of sin' (Rom. 3.20; cf. 3.28; Gal. 2.16; 3.2, 5, 10; Eph. 2.8–10; Phil. 3.9, etc.). Perhaps faith could have its own works ('faith working through love', Gal. 5.6).

Taking the NT as a whole, Christians were required to do good works (Matt. 5.16) which were prepared by God beforehand for them to walk in (Eph. 2.10), but which did not earn salvation (Rom. 4.4f.), since this had been decided before they were born, or had done anything either good or bad (Rom. 9.11, 18).

Theology has struggled ever since with the moral difficulty that such teaching would seem to encourage us to 'continue in sin, that grace may abound' (Rom. 6.1; 3.8). Augustine put forward the two classical solutions: that God not only imputes righteousness to sinners so that they are counted righteous (*see* **Imputation**), but that God also imparts righteousness to sinners so that they are enabled to work righteousness because he gives the increase from within. Luther insisted on the imputation of righteousness and wanted to root out the term 'good works' from the language. He translated Rom. 3.28, 'by faith *alone*'. Nevertheless, he taught that 'as the sun necessarily shines since it is the sun . . . so the righteous man, being a new creature, does works by an unchangeable necessity (Eph. 2.18)'. The Council of Trent* chose the second of Augustine's two points and taught that 'Jesus Christ himself continually infuses his

virtue into the justified' and that the justified are accounted to have satisfied the divine law by these works, which have been done in God.

See **Good Works.**

J. C. O'NEILL

Worship

The word is derived from Anglo-Saxon *weorthscipe*, honour. In older English usage worship can be rendered to men of excellence (cf. in England, 'the Worshipful the Mayor'): so AV/KJV, Matt. 8.2, not necessarily implying divinity. Except in archaic forms (e.g., the *Book of Common Prayer*, 1662, Solemnization of Matrimony: 'with my body I thee worship') or in extravagant speech, the word is nowadays used only in religious language. In the Bible God alone is supremely the object of worship and adoration; no one and nothing is to be worshipped beside him.

The word 'worship' is very useful in the English religious vocabulary, and other languages (e.g. German) which have no precise equivalent are the poorer for their lack of it. Though God is to be worshipped in life as well as in word, 'worship' in its normal usage refers to the expression in corporate gatherings of adoration, praise and thanksgiving to God through Christ. From the earliest times and down all the Christian centuries Christians have gathered, whether in churches specially built for the purpose or in improvised surroundings, to worship God in this way, for this is their spontaneous (though it may become formalized and conventional) response to God's revelation of his saving acts. Worship is thus essentially thanksgiving (cf. Greek *eucharistia*) and praise. It may be offered formally according to fixed rites: *ritual* is the fixed form of words ordered by authority for specified days or times (though the word is commonly misused to denote ceremonial). Or it may be offered in 'free' worship, i.e., without fixed forms, and perhaps with *extempore* prayer, in which individuals in the congregation may participate. It may be offered with full and rich *ceremonial*, i.e. accompanying actions, processions, vestments, genuflexions, etc., and with choirs and music, as in a High Mass or Sung Eucharist. Or it may be offered with a minimum of ceremonial, or in corporate silence as in a Quaker meeting. But the purpose of all worship is the same: to offer praise to God for his grace and glory.

In most corporate acts of Christian worship certain elements are usually found: a preparation, consisting of a general confession of sin, followed perhaps by a declaration of absolution by an authorized minister; the ministry of the word – the reading of scriptural 'lessons' and the sermon which expounds the truth and relevance of the scriptures; the singing of psalms or hymns; and the prayers or intercessions (*see* **Prayer, Theology of**). In many Christian Confessions these acts of devotion are followed by the celebration of the Lord's Supper (by whatever name it is called – Holy Communion, Mass, Eucharist, etc.). The intention of all such acts of worship is to declare the saving power of God and to make this power a reality in the hearts and lives of those who participate in them. However diverse may be the forms which Christian worship may take, there is a common intention underlying them all. This truth is perceived in our own ecumenical age, as it has not always been perceived in previous times. The *Directory of Public Worship*, compiled by the Westminster Assembly (1645), abolished the *Book of Common Prayer*, and indeed there are significant differences between the two works; yet the basic elements of Christian worship may be seen to be present in both.

Forms of worship designed for special occasions (e.g. baptism, marriage, sickness, burial) are to be found in almost all Christian denominations. It is appropriate that special occasions in the lives of Christian families or congregations should thus be solemnized in an act of worship. In comparatively recent times it has become common to compile special services or acts of worship for specific occasions (e.g. Harvest Festivals) or for specific vocational groups or interests (e.g. Hospital Services). Whatever defects these improvised occasional services may have, they are a means of witnessing to the relevance of the Christian faith in particular areas of life and reminding people of their duty of Christian worship, if they profess the name of Christ.

A matter of great theological importance is the recognition of the priority of worship over doctrinal formulation. The normal order of things is that worship precedes credal formulation and theology. The earliest Christians fond themselves worshipping Christ before they had reached any formal theological definitions of his person and nature. To make the point in another way: the earliest Christian confessions of faith would seem to have had their origin in worship, as (e.g.) in the Christ-hymn in Phil. 2.5–11, which in the opinion of many scholars was not composed by St Paul but was quoted by him from a familiar act of Christian worship. It was only long after Christ had been worshipped as the divine Lord and Saviour that the church's theologians began to work out an intellectual *rationale* of Christ's nature as the God-man. Hence the saying, *lex orandi, lex credendi:* we believe according as we worship. Worship is primary; theology is secondary – a point frequently overlooked in academic circles. Theology is often incredible because worship is neglected. On the other hand, it should be emphasized that theology has a most important function to fulfil in relation to worship. Theology must prune worship of all that is foreign to Christian truth, constantly bring it under the critique of rational judgment, and articulate its essential meaning so that those who worship with their hearts may worship with their understanding also. But the truth remains that worship is the *raison d'être* of theology, not vice-versa.

See also **Prayer, Theology of; Liturgical Worship.**

W. K. Lowther Clarke (ed), *Liturgy and Worship*, 1932, and subsequent editions; P. Dearmer, *The Art of Public Worship*, 1919; J. O. Dobson, *Worship*, 1941; L. Duchesne, *Christian Worship: its Origin and Evolution,* ET 1903; Cheslyn Jones, Geoffrey Wainwright, Edward Yarnold, *The Study of Liturgy*, 1978; R. Otto, *The Idea of the Holy*, ET 1923; Evelyn Underhill, *Worship*, 1936; G. Wainwright, *Doxology,* 1980.

ALAN RICHARDSON

Wrath of God

The nouns wrath, anger, the verb to be angry and even the verb to hate are used in the Bible with God as the doer of the action expressed or implied (e.g. Deut. 11.17; Ex. 4.14; Ps. 85.4f.; Hos. 9.15). God is also said to be 'jealous', that is, displeased with people for what they do (Ex. 20.5). The wrath of

God is directed both to sinners and their sin. These ideas are found in the NT as well as in the OT. It is true that the phrase 'the wrath of God' in the NT usually refers to the wrath to come at the day of judgment when sinners will receive punishment, but at least once it refers to present retribution (Rom. 1.18). Nevertheless, the idea that present sin in the individual has been punished by God with sickness is present (Matt. 9.1–8), as well as the idea that individual suffering can be undeserved (John 9.3). The sufferings of the people as a whole are also seen as the effect of God's wrath on their sin: the eschatological discourse of Jesus warns of deserved punishment in history and at the end, unless people repent (Matt. 23.37–38; 24; see also the cleansing of the Temple). The 'fear of the Lord' is the proper human reaction to God's wrath in both the OT and the NT (Ps. 2.11; Luke 7.16; II Cor. 7.1).

As soon as Jews preached to Gentiles in the Hellenistic world, questions were raised about how God could have wrath; a God who was angry would seem to be a God who changed from being something else. Philo explained that Gen. 6.7, where it is said that God was sorry he had made man, was to correct people who could not be corrected otherwise; in truth God is inaccessible to 'passions'. This seems to be a fair point; when the Psalmist prays, 'O Lord, rebuke me not in thy anger, nor chasten me in thy wrath!' he means that he has now repented from the sin which deserved that wrath (Ps.

38); *he* has changed, for God cannot change (Mal. 3.6).

The idea that God loves but cannot condemn seems to have come into Christian theology from the teaching of the Stoics* (e.g., Marcus Aurelius, *Meditations*). It was systematically worked out by Marcion, who distinguished between the OT God who was angry and judged, and the 'higher' God who loved and was merciful.

In the eighteenth century the idea that sin deserved punishment was attacked as immoral, on the grounds that the good man would not be truly good if he acted from self-interest to avoid punishment. This argument, as well as being untrue (Joseph Butler), is practical atheism, for a God who does not reward good and punish evil need not exist. Nevertheless the argument deeply influenced theology. Schleiermacher rejected the idea of retributive punishment and with it the wrath of God. A. Ritschl said the wrath of God was wholly eschatological in the NT and therefore of no religious interest. C. H. Dodd argued that the wrath of God was wholly impersonal in the NT and in the long run inconsistent with God as personal.

Lactantius, *A Treatise on the Anger of God addressed to Donatus*; A. T. Hanson, *The Wrath of the Lamb*, 1957; A. Ritschl, *De ira Dei*, 1859; *The Christian Doctrine of Justification and Reconciliation*, ET 1872, 1900; R. V. G. Tasker, *The Biblical Doctrine of the Wrath of God*, 1951.

J. C. O'NEILL

INDEX OF NAMES

INDEX OF NAMES